UPGRADING AND REPAIRING NETWORKS

THIRD EDITION

Terry William Ogletree

201 West 103rd Street,
Indianapolis, Indiana 46290

Contents at a Glance

Upgrading and Repairing Networks, Third Edition

International Standard Book Number: 0-7897-2557-6

Library of Congress Catalog Card Number: 2001090369

Printed in the United States of America

First Printing: September 2001

04   03   02   01   4   3   2   1

Trademarks

Warning and Disclaimer

Executive Editor
Rick Kughen

Acquisitions Editor
Jenny L. Watson

Development Editors
Mark Reddin
Todd Brakke

Managing Editor
Thomas F. Hayes

Project Editor
Tonya Simpson

Copy Editor
Linda Seifert

Indexer
Larry Sweazy

Proofreader
Plan-It Publishing

Technical Editor
Jim Cooper

Team Coordinator
Sharry Gregory

Media Developer
Michael Hunter

Interior Designer
Anne Jones

Cover Designer
Karen Ruggles

Page Layout
Mark Walchle

Contents

IV Network Operating Systems, Protocols, and Services 319

Dedication

To my parents, Charles and Billie Jean Ogletree.

About the Authors

Terry William Ogletree is a consultant currently working in New Jersey. He has worked with networked computer systems since 1980, starting out on Digital Equipment PDP computers and OpenVMS-based VAX systems. He has worked with Unix and TCP/IP since 1985 and has been involved with Windows NT and Windows 2000 since they first appeared, as well as the newest addition to the family, Windows XP. Besides being the lead author of the second edition of this book, he is the author of *Practical Firewalls* and has contributed chapters to many other books published by Que, including *Microsoft Windows 2000 Security Handbook* and *Special Edition Using UNIX, Third Edition*. When not writing for Que he has on occasion contributed articles to *PC Magazine*.

You can e-mail him at two@twoinc.com, or visit his home page at http://www.twoinc.com. When between jobs and writing for Que, he can often be found on street corners holding a sign that reads "Will work for hundreds of thousands of dollars."

Thomas Crayner (Chapter 1) currently is the Director of Applications and Infrastructure Services at a leading pharmaceutical company, where his department keeps 300 servers running in support of R&D operations. Starting with UNIX and TCP/IP in the mid-80s as an applications developer, he slowly worked his way into infrastructure development. During the course of his career, Tom has designed and implemented systems and networks of all shapes and sizes. On the weekends, he can still be found enjoying his original hobby: system and application development.

Dwight Tolay, Jr. (Chapter 5) started out as a computer test technician in the 1970s. Branching out into the electrical construction industry, he became familiar with data and fiber-optic cabling, has worked with coax Ethernet and IBM Token Ring and followed the evolution up to today's Category 6 and Gigabyte cabling methods. Currently, he is a general supervisor for Ortlip Electric Co. He is a graduate EE, ISA certified Level III control systems technician, licensed electrical contractor, and a certified high-voltage test technician. In addition to being a certified fiber-optic and teledata instructor at a local trade school for the past 13 years, he has contributed as technical editor on various books and currently is involved in a book on Home Data and Electrical Systems Integration.

Scott and Kalinda Reeves (Chapters 26 and 27) live in the scenic Cabinet Mountains in Heron, Montana. They are married and have five children. Together, they have written several networking exam books.

Scott has had a passion for computers since the early 1980s and, over the years, has accrued his certifications as a Master Certified Novell Engineer (MCNE), Microsoft Certified Professional (MCP) in Windows NT, and Compaq Accredited Systems Engineer (ASE), Comptia Network+ professional, and Comptia A+ certified technician. He has more than 15 years in the computer industry, the last five of which have been focused on customer support in a reseller environment, and has worked in the networking field for more than 11 years. Currently, he is a networking and computer consultant to small businesses in northern Idaho and western Montana. When Scott turns the computer off, his main hobbies are amateur radio and star-gazing in the clear Montana sky.

Kalinda has more than 16 years experience writing research, business, technical, and engineering documentation for government, military, and civilian customers. The topics include system- and circuit-level hardware; uniquely developed, hardware-specific programs; and programs that are implemented across government and military communications systems. Kalinda currently works as a freelance writer. When she is not writing, Kalinda home schools her children and has a diversity of hobbies, which include amateur radio, gardening, and all manners of crafts.

Acknowledgments

Most of the credit for getting this book done must be given not to the author, but to Jenny Watson, Que's senior acquisition editor, and Todd Brakke and Mark Reddin, the development editors of this book. There is no way I could ever have gotten this book finished (almost on time!) without their consistent, persistent, wonderful help. Jenny is a great taskmaster, always reminding me that the book has to be out on time, and she has been able to find several contributing authors for this edition that I think added some excellent information. Todd Brakke has worked with me on three other books, and I think both he and Mark Reddin deserve a lot of credit for the material you'll find inside. Along with Rick Kughen, the executive editor of this book, they have contributed both questions and ideas about the new material that we've included. Tonya Simpson expended a lot of effort coordinating a lot of the people involved in this project. As I am not the best writer in the world, I must also give credit to Linda Seifert, the copy editor, for correcting my grammatical errors and for making helpful suggestions about better ways to write this book's text. Writing for Que is a team effort!

During the initial development phase of this book, the outline that was proposed was submitted to many highly technical persons for review. The input from these reviews was a great help toward deciding what to include and how to organize the material. I would especially like to thank Chad Zook, whose review was very insightful and contributed a lot to the decision-making process during the development of the table of contents for this book. Without a doubt, Chad knows his stuff when it comes to networking, and I expect you might hear from him someday should he decide to get into the writing business! I also would like to acknowledge Sharon Terdeman, the Solutions Editor of *PC Magazine*. Several of the articles she assisted me with spurred further research that resulted in more coverage of those topics in this book.

During the actual writing of this book I have been working at Bristol-Myers Squibb in New Jersey. Without the patience of Robert G. Venard and Tom Crayner I would not have been able to complete this book in a timely fashion. Robert also was a great source for information about the early days of ethernet and local area networks. Tom is a top-notch network engineer, and also is the author of the first chapter of this book.

Most of my contracting jobs during the past five years have been the result of the efforts of John Rogue and Angelo Simeo of The Computer Merchant firm in Norwell, Massachusetts. The jobs they have been able to find for me not only pay the bills, but also have enabled me to greatly further my knowledge of computers and networking. I can recommend this firm to anyone who is looking for highly skilled employees or consultants in the computer and networking fields.

A special thanks to Carl and Nanette Chiappetta for helping me stay focused on work and enjoy life to its fullest. Thanks again to Jo and Jeff Johnson for being such good friends, and the same for Jordan Scoggins, Andy Jones, James Garrett, Vicki Harding, Steve McGuire, Gina Stone, Sari Gurney, Rodney Foster, Neelima Raval, and Rick Clayton.

It goes without saying that, without the help of Michael D. Parrott and Associates (and Michael's lovely and incredibly brilliant wife, Brenda), I never would have been able to find time to write. MDP&A is the ultimate super-accounting firm that goes more than the extra mile to take care of matters I just don't have time for.

As always, I would like to acknowledge my family. My brother, Gordon Ogletree, is a Solaris Wizard and my sister a fantastic organizer. And, of course, I wouldn't be here if it were not for my parents. This book should be arriving at your local bookstore at about the same time they celebrate their 51st wedding anniversary. I hope we have 50 more reasons to celebrate!

Tell Us What You Think!

As the reader of this book, *you* are our most important critic and commentator. We value your opinion and want to know what we're doing right, what we could do better, what areas you'd like to see us publish in, and any other words of wisdom you're willing to pass our way.

As an associate publisher for Que, I welcome your comments. You can fax, email, or write me directly to let me know what you did or didn't like about this book—as well as what we can do to make our books stronger.

Please note that I cannot help you with technical problems related to the topic of this book, and that due to the high volume of mail I receive, I might not be able to reply to every message.

When you write, please be sure to include this book's title and author as well as your name and phone or fax number. I will carefully review your comments and share them with the author and editors who worked on the book.

Fax: 317-581-4666

Email: feedback@quepublishing.com

Mail: Dean Miller
Que
201 West 103rd Street
Indianapolis, IN 46290 USA

Introduction

Writing the third edition of *Upgrading and Repairing Networks* was not the easy task that I thought it would be. So much has changed in such a short time that you'll find the content of this book useful for both traditional network technologies, such as ethernet and token-ring networks, as well as leading-edge technologies, such as wireless networking and 3G wireless products. This book contains more than 1,000 pages of information, which has been organized into chapters that target specific topics, with cross-references to other related information. I think that the organization of the material enables you to quickly find the information you need without having to wade through nonessential reading. Yet, if you are new to the field of networking, this book can serve as a textbook to help you learn a heck of a lot in a very short time.

Who Should Use This Book?

This book is geared toward the experienced network administrator or technician. Given the rapid pace at which new technologies are being deployed, this book can prove an invaluable reference for both planning and troubleshooting as you incorporate new components or software into your network. Although you might already be knowledgeable in some of the areas discussed in this book, you might find that it can help you relate your current knowledge to other topics that you want to learn. I don't mean to exclude those who are new to the field of networking. Indeed, you also might find this book an invaluable learning and reference tool as you become acquainted with computer networks.

What You'll Find Inside

Part I, "Up Front: Network Planning and Design," starts off with a chapter on network topologies. Today you need careful preplanning to create a large, complex network. This part also contains information that will help you put together a network design or upgrade strategy, as well as some ideas about preventive maintenance that can be used to keep problems from happening in the first place.

Part II, "The Physical Network," covers the physical components that make up your network, from the network cables and network adapter cards to the devices that are used to connect these components. Chapter 7 discusses legacy technology such as repeaters, bridges, and hubs, while Chapter 8 gives you a quick lesson in network switches, an integral component in a medium to large networks today. Chapter 9 discusses virtual LANs (VLANs), which make managing a large network easier, and Chapter 10 discusses routers—those devices that connect most networks to the Internet.

Part III, "Choosing a Network Solution," is where you'll find information about the many different kinds of technologies you can use to create a network. This section starts with the oldest networking technology, ARCnet, which is still around today, and then covers ethernet and token-ring networks. In this section you'll also find expanded coverage of wireless networking, which is about the hottest topic in the networking field today. Chapters 18 and 19 cover dial-up and dedicated connections, and the material here ranges from a simple dial-up modem to broadband cable and DSL connections, and also includes helpful information about ATM, Frame Relay, and the T-carrier system.

Part IV, "Network Operating Systems, Protocols, and Services," takes you one step further. After you've decided on the underlying technology that will get your bits and bytes from one place to another, you must decide on higher-level protocols. Although TCP/IP is the *de facto* standard on the Internet today, you'll also find coverage in this section of Novell NetWare, NetBIOS, and NetBEUI, as well as routing protocols. Two chapters are set aside to give you detailed information about Novell Directory Services (NDS) and Microsoft's Active Directory. In addition to extensive coverage of the mechanics of TCP/IP connections and IP addressing, there are separate chapters devoted to other protocols and services related to TCP/IP. These chapters cover topics such as DHCP and name resolution, as well as an entire chapter devoted to troubleshooting tools you can use for TCP/IP based networks.

Part V, "Managing Users and Resources," contains information about how user accounts, rights, and permissions are managed under different operating systems, such as Windows 2000, NetWare, and Unix/Linux. In a multiprotocol network, it is important to have a good grasp of exactly what you are doing when you create user accounts and set up resource permissions. You'll also find chapters about protocols used for network printing and a chapter devoted to print servers. Chapter 33, "File Server Protocols," can help explain some of the complexities in setting up and supervising file servers on the network. If you are upgrading your network from one operating system to another, this section can be very helpful when planning your migration and your network resources, and it can help you decide the best way to manage users.

Part VI, "Network Security," covers many timely topics, including basic security measures of which you need to be aware, both in the LAN and in the area of wide area networking. If you are connecting to the Internet, then Chapter 40, "Firewalls," is required reading! Encryption and virtual private networks (VPNs) are also covered in this section. Although most of the trade magazines are giving a lot of coverage to wireless networking as the current hot topic, you can't forget that security is an ongoing issue, and a network administrator must keep up to date with the most recent developments in this field.

Part VII, "Basics of Network Troubleshooting Techniques," starts out by giving you some tips on strategies that you can use to troubleshoot problems on the network. Chapter 44 discusses some of the basic tools, such as those used to verify the integrity of the physical components of the network, as well as more complex tools, such as LAN analyzers, that can be used to troubleshoot protocol and application problems. You'll also find a good introduction to the Simple Network Management Protocol (SNMP) and RMON in this section. For those of you who manage a small office or work from home, there's a chapter devoted specifically to troubleshooting problems in the SOHO environment.

Part VIII, "Upgrading Hardware," contains chapters that you can use to plan a migration from one network technology to another. We start here again with a chapter on upgrading ARCnet to ethernet, and then proceed to chapters discussing upgrades from token ring to ethernet. Next, you'll find chapters that can help you upgrade your network from one version of Ethernet to another, starting with 10BASE-2 and ending up with the new Gigabit Ethernet. Also in this section you'll find out how you can go about replacing bridges with routers or switches to take advantage of newer technology or to help you expand the limited scope of your current LAN. The final chapter in this section discusses strategies you can use to add wireless networking to your LAN. This is something that most network administrators will have to deal with soon, as the workforce becomes more mobile.

Part IX, "Migration and Integration," contains chapters that cover migrating from one operating system to another and chapters on creating networks that integrate multiple operating systems. You'll find information here on NetWare, Windows NT, and Windows 2000, as well as Unix and Linux. In addition to the standard operating system features that can be used for a migration or integration plan, you'll also find information about special applications, such as Microsoft's Services for Unix, which can help ease the integration process.

This section closes out with a chapter appropriately titled "On the Horizon," in which some of the newer technologies are discussed. It will be interesting to find out during the next few years which of these technologies succeed and which ones fall by the wayside. If you are trying to plan ahead, this chapter can give you some idea of where networking is heading and who the major players are.

Finally, the appendixes contain information that can be used as a quick reference. You can get an overview of the OSI network reference model, TCP and UDP ports, and commands used for NetWare login scripts. Also included is an explanation of how directory services work, specifically the Lightweight Directory Access Protocol (LDAP), and an introduction to the Simple Mail Transfer Protocol (SMTP).

What's New in This Edition

Upgrading and Repairing Networks, Third Edition contains a lot of updated content and has been reorganized to make it easier to find the information you need. Entirely new topics have been added based on feedback to the Second Edition and on many new technologies that have become important since the previous publication, especially Windows 2000, wireless networking, and directory services. To assist in this, several contributing authors were brought on board to help, each a veteran in the computer book publishing field, as well as experts in their areas of networking. I'm sure you'll like what you find inside, and I'm sure you'll find that what you are looking for is easier to find in this edition. Also, don't forget to check out the CD that accompanies this book. You'll find a large collection of useful programs—from freeware to shareware and some demo programs—that can help you administer your network.

Finally, this edition contains a glossary of terms that can itself serve as a quick reference. So much new technology has been introduced in such a short time that even experienced network administrators often have trouble remembering exactly what a particular word or phrase means. The glossary at the back of this book will help you quickly find concise, accurate definitions of a wide range of computer and networking terms.

Up Front: Network Planning and Design

SOME OF THE MAIN TOPICS FOR THIS PART ARE

Overview of Network Topologies

Network Design Strategies

Upgrading Strategies and Project Management

Preventive Maintenance

PART I

Overview of Network Topologies

CHAPTER 1

Before you can begin to upgrade and repair your network, you need to understand how it's laid out, how it functions, and how the various parts are related to one another. Knowing how your network components are related will make the extension, expansion, and troubleshooting of your environment more focused and productive. Because network uptime is related directly to productivity, a solid grasp of network concepts is a necessity when facing a troubled LAN.

In this chapter, you will review the topologies in use today and learn the strengths and weaknesses of each.

LAN Topologies

Several unique network technologies have been developed over the past three decades. Different types of networks have different design criteria and, thus, various topologies have come into use. One important distinction needs to be made before entering into a serious discussion on topology: physical topology versus logical topology. The *physical topology* describes the layout of a network media (such as copper and fiber optic cables) and the devices that connect to it. The *logical topology* is not concerned with the actual physical connections but with the logical path through the network that data can take from one place to another. The differences will be more evident as the different topologies are discussed.

The basic topologies you will find in most LANs today include

- Bus
- Star
- Ring
- Mesh
- Hybrids

Using a Bus Topology

The simple bus topology structure was the first type used in ethernet networks. The typical bus physical topology consists of a coaxial cabling common to all computer systems connected to the LAN. This coax is tapped in multiple places along its length, with each tap being used as a point of connection for a computing system. Taps can be physical cores cut into the coax, or BNC-style "T-connectors" that join several individual pieces of coax together to form the common bus (see Figures 1.1 and 1.2 for a comparison of the two methods).

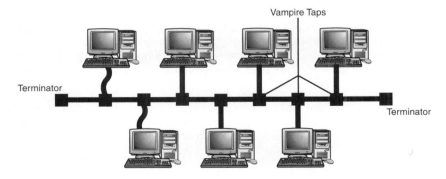

Figure 1.1   Computers can connect to coaxial cables on a bus by tapping directly through the core of the cable. The vampire taps pierce the thicknet cable but not the BNC.

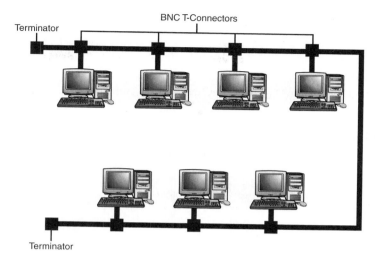

Figure 1.2 BNC style T-Connectors make attaching computers to a bus a simpler operation.

▶▶ You can learn more about how 10BASE-2 and 10BASE-5 Ethernet networks are created using coaxial cables and the bus topology in Chapter 12, "Ethernet."

A bus is also a logical topology. From a device's viewpoint, all other systems are communicating through the same shared path. Because it is a shared media technology, mechanisms must be put into place to arbitrate network traffic over the cable. Typically, collision detection (CD) or collision avoidance (CA) algorithms are used in bus topologies to arbitrate network access along with concepts such as "broadcasts" to reach every device on the cable. This subject is covered in detail in Chapter 12.

The bus topology is very simple and inexpensive to implement due to its low cost requirements for cable installation (there's only one main trunk). But some serious deficiencies make bus topology LANs unattractive to deploy:

- Bus topologies require proper terminations on both ends of the bus to effectively dampen the network signal and to avoid a "reflection" or reoccurrence of a previous transmission. Without the proper terminations in place, expect a very slow or inoperable network.

- The cable itself is a single point of failure. One break, cut, or poor connection negatively impacts the entire LAN.

- Because all workstations or devices share a common cable, troubleshooting can be difficult when problems occur. You must temporarily break the terminations in the network to isolate a device. After you think you've resolved the network problem, you must impact LAN service again to reattach the device to the network. This makes for a cumbersome and disruptive process.

Due to these limitations, the bus topology is typically found only in the smallest or most austere of installations. Some proprietary manufacturing process control systems use a bus topology, but these won't be covered in this book. Bus topologies are discussed a bit more in the chapter covering ethernet LANs.

Using a Star Topology

The concept behind the star topology is simple. Every node on the LAN has a dedicated cable that is pulled back to a centralized point, typically a wiring closet. All cables are terminated in a network component within the closet, such as a hub or switch, which handles the repeating or switching of traffic out to the other nodes on the network (see Figure 1.3).

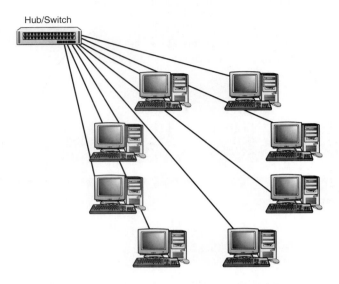

Figure 1.3   The star topology enables you to centralize wiring for a network.

The shortcomings of a star topology network are obvious: The network component is a single point of failure, and a great deal of wiring is involved to implement the star.

However, there are tremendous benefits to a star topology:

- Management of the network is centralized around the hub and switch components. Most of these components have features that allow an administrator to spot congestion and network errors at the port level, which makes troubleshooting problems quick and simple.

- "Smart hubs" can automatically disable ports that exceed use or error thresholds, providing additional stability to the LAN. They are also a central point for watching bandwidth use and overall network health.

- Wiring installation is less obtrusive and therefore does not disrupt LAN service with the addition or deletion of nodes.

- A cable cut or bad connector does not take down the entire LAN segment. No terminators are required as in the bus topology model.

You should note that nearly every popular network technology today uses a star topology for its physical implementation.

When repairing a star topology network, be sure to check error counters and status indicators on your network components. These can provide valuable information in helping you find what is at fault.

Using a Ring Topology

Ring topologies are more complex than the bus and star topologies discussed in previous sections, but they offer some attractive features. Nodes logically communicate in a ring formation, with each node communicating only directly with its upstream and downstream neighbors (see Figure 1.4).

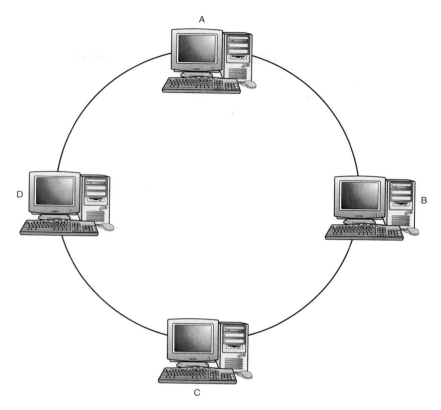

Figure 1.4 The ring topology links each node on the network to two other nodes on the network.

You can probably picture what a mess the wiring would be in an office with hundreds of computer systems, so ring topologies are typically implemented in a physical star topology (see Figure 1.5).

In a ring topology, access to the network is controlled through a token that is passed from node to node as the arbitration mechanism. Each node takes its turn at claiming the token as the token passes from neighbor to neighbor, and when a node possesses the token, it takes its turn to transmit onto the ring. A data packet is transferred from one node to the next until it reaches its destination node. After the destination node has received the packet, it modifies the packet to acknowledge receipt and passes it on. Eventually, the packet makes it completely around the ring and the transmitting node receives it and notes that the receipt has been acknowledged. When the transmitting node is finished, it releases the token to its neighbor, and the process repeats.

▶▶ Token-ring networks are the primary LAN technology that uses a ring topology. You can learn more about this networking technology by reading Chapter 13, "Token-Ring Networks."

The benefits can be readily observed:

- Token-controlled access provides greater overall bandwidth use, because there are no collision avoidance and collision detection algorithms to throttle transmissions on the media.

- Data packet transmission happens within a determinable time interval. Because each node gets a chance to claim the token and ring for itself, it's easy to determine the amount of time before the next transmission can occur (it's based on the number of nodes on the ring). This quality of ring topologies has made it a staple in manufacturing environments in which timing is essential.

■ Because each node knows its upstream and downstream neighbors, this information can be used to determine where problems have occurred on the ring.

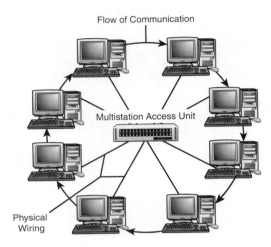

Figure 1.5   The ring topology is usually implemented as a physical star to simplify wiring management.

Another ring topology called Fiber Distributed Data Interface (FDDI) uses dual fault-tolerant rings. This technology requires that the two rings have tokens passing in opposite directions of one another. A breakdown in one ring causes the nodes to shift over to the secondary ring to continue communications.

▶▶   FDDI is another networking technology that uses the ring topology and token-passing for media access. Chapter 17, "Fiber Distributed Data Interface (FDDI)," covers this topic in detail.

The down side of a ring topology is simple: The firmware required to manage the ring is somewhat complicated and must be on every network card that participates in the ring. As a result, other technologies, such as ethernet, have transitioned rapidly to higher networking speeds while ring topologies have never quite jumped the speed gap. The ring topologies that exist today have changed little in the last 10–15 years.

Using a Mesh Topology

A *mesh* topology is an interlacing of multiple connections between several nodes. Typically, a mesh is done for one purpose: redundancy. Any serious campus network must incorporate a mesh to achieve the level of redundancy and fault tolerance that businesses demand from their data networks. There are two types of mesh: full and partial.

A full mesh is not very practical, but is mentioned here for completeness. Full mesh means that every node contained in a network has a connection to every other node contained in the network. It should be fairly obvious at this point why full meshes are not very practical (see Figure 1.6). The cost for such infrastructure would be exorbitant, and 90% of it would never be put to use.

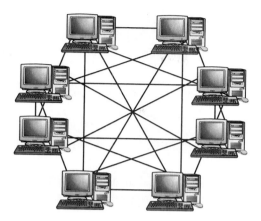

Figure 1.6 A full mesh topology is not a very practical way to wire a network.

Partial meshes are designed to provide redundancy where it is needed. By using a little forethought in design, a network architect could place some additional connectivity where it can provide needed bandwidth and fault tolerance to the network. Suppose for a moment that an important resource were attached to node A (see Figure 1.7).

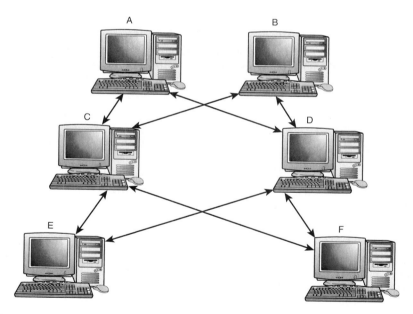

Figure 1.7 A partial mesh topology can be used to provide redundancy for the network.

You can spot several paths that could fail, yet all the nodes of your network would still be able to reach node A as a destination. The true merits of partial mesh are realized when you look at WAN and campus topologies.

Hybrid Topologies

Hubs or switches can be attached to one another to create larger LANs capable of supporting more devices. After this happens, you start getting some interesting hybrid topologies. Three popular hybrids are tree, hierarchical star, and star-wireless.

▶▶   Hubs, along with other devices used to connect LAN segments, are discussed fully in Chapter 7, "Repeaters, Bridges, and Hubs."

Tree

Figure 1.8 shows a combination topology that groups workstations together in a star and joins the stars along a linear bus. The majority of the problems of the bus are eliminated because a single workstation cannot bring the entire LAN to a halt. You still can add or change workstations by plugging them into a different port on the same hub, or on another hub. If one hub malfunctions, it disables only the workstations that are attached to it from communicating on the network. The remaining workstations on the other hubs can continue to function normally.

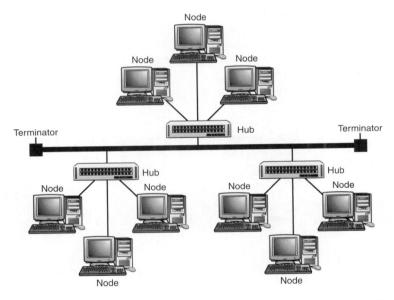

Figure 1.8   A combination of the bus and star topologies groups workstations in a star and joins them along a linear bus.

This is an inexpensive method that can be used to join different work departments in a building. Each local workgroup can have an administrative person who is responsible for managing the connections on the local hub. The network administrator can regulate when and where new hubs are attached to the network. This also can be used to help extend the distance of a LAN. For example, you can use 10BASE-2 cabling to connect two 10BASE-T networks that are in separate buildings. However, today that connection would most likely be accomplished using more modern techniques, such as fiber optic cabling.

The major problem with this type of hybrid topology, however, is that if there is a problem with the backbone bus cable, the network becomes segmented into individual hubs. Workstations on each hub can communicate with each other, but data transfers through the network to workstations on other hubs will be disrupted until the cable problem is diagnosed and corrected.

Hierarchical Star

Another method that can be used to connect hubs is a hierarchical star. This method, shown in Figure 1.9, uses a central hub to link together several hubs that have workstations attached.

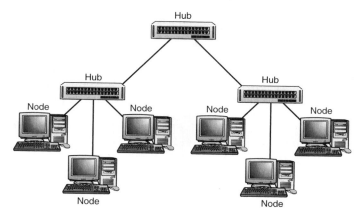

Figure 1.9 The hierarchical star topology is made up of cascading hubs.

This method can be used to build very large LANs; however, there are restrictions on the size of the LAN. Timing issues as well as address space will be driving factors in how many hubs you will be able to attach in the hierarchical star topology without the introduction of routing technology. The various restrictions of different network technologies are discussed in later chapters.

Using a Star-Wireless Topology

A new hybrid topology has arrived with the advent of wireless technology. Wireless LAN technology in its current implementation requires a user to be in the vicinity of an access point attached to the wired data network. A configuration such as this gives you an amorphous hybrid topology of star combined with wireless (see Figure 1.10).

The star topology is necessary to combine the many access points spread across a building to ensure wireless coverage. All the access points collapse back into the main star hub where server resources would reside on the network. As wireless technologies continue to evolve, so will the topologies that support them.

▶▶ For more information about using wireless technology in your network, see Chapter 14, "Wireless Networking: IEEE 802.11b (Wi-Fi) and Home RF," and Chapter 15, "What Is Bluetooth?"

Shared and Nonshared Network Media Topologies

As mentioned earlier, you must abide by some constraints when constructing very large LAN environments. One item that often is overlooked is the size of the broadcast domain for a LAN segment.

Hubs take inbound traffic and pass it outbound on all their other ports. This means that each time a node makes a network request, the request is flooded to all other nodes. The more nodes you have on your LAN, the more traffic you have being flooded throughout the LAN segment. If you are running an ethernet network, all this chatter can keep your LAN segment sufficiently busy enough to keep other nodes from finding an opportunity to transmit.

▶▶ Switches have generally replaced hubs as the wiring concentrator of choice in most LANs. You can learn more about switches and how they work by reading Chapter 8, "Network Switches."

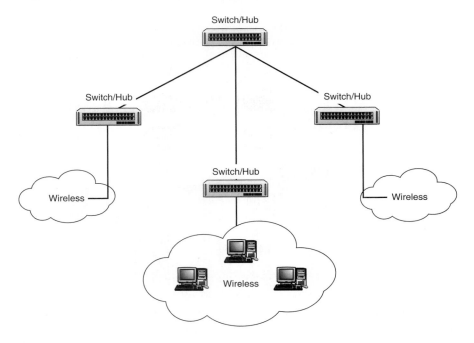

Figure 1.10   Wireless technology adds a new dimension to network topologies.

A solution for this problem is the introduction of a switch into the network environment. By deploying a switch in place of a hub, you dramatically reduce the number of flooded packets. Switches don't just blindly repeat network traffic, they make intelligent port-forward decisions based on the addresses that they recognize within the packets. The net effect of introducing switches into your environment in place of hubs is that your nodes see very little flooded traffic (unless it is addressed to them) and the contention problem is greatly reduced (see Figure 1.11).

Don't forget that you still have the network broadcasts to contend with. Broadcasts get flooded to all ports within a network segment, regardless of whether you use hubs or switches. So always consider the amount of broadcast traffic added to your environment when expanding your LAN.

Full Duplex Versus Half Duplex

The discussion of shared and nonshared media would not be complete without the mention of full-duplex technologies. Everything that has been covered so far has assumed a half-duplex environment, which means that a node can either receive or transmit but cannot do both at the same time. In a full-duplex environment, a node can transmit and receive at the same time using separate receive and transmit pairs. If you realize that separate pairs for transmit and receive mean that there is no chance for packet collisions, you are absolutely correct! If you can afford full-duplex hubs, switches, and NIC cards for your environment, you should strongly consider them because they remove a major impediment in LAN design and performance.

You might ask yourself why a network topology would ever use half-duplex to begin with. The answer is simple: It's historical. Recall that at the time ethernet was invented it was a bus topology with a two-conductor coax cable; there was no opportunity for a dedicated transmit and receive pair.

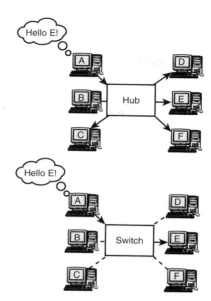

Figure 1.11   Switches can centralize wiring and also provide a greater available bandwidth to the network.

Bridged Versus Routed Topologies

This section reviews bridged and routed topologies to give you a sense of how each technology can be used. Refer to Chapter 7 for in-depth overview of these technologies. Details about routers can be found in Chapter 10, "Routers," and still more information about connectivity devices can be found in Chapter 8.

Bridging

Bridges are intelligent network devices that monitor the MAC level (layer 2) addresses within a packet. A bridge creates a table in its memory and stores the MAC address and port address of each network resource that it sees as a source of network traffic, in effect "learning" on which ports it can find a particular node.

When a bridge fails to recognize the destination MAC address of a packet that it has received, it floods the packet to all its ports. When a bridge knows the destination port, it just forwards the packet to that one port.

Using this methodology, the bridge quickly accumulates an understanding of where all devices reside from its viewpoint and intelligently forwards traffic. Sounds a lot like the switch that was used earlier to replace the hub technology, doesn't it? Indeed, switches are basically just high-speed bridges with a high port density.

Routing

Routers are intelligent network devices that monitor at the network level (layer 3). It is at this level that protocols such as TCP/IP, IPX/SPX, and AppleTalk are defined. Routers understand the routing topology; that is, they have an idea where all LAN segments reside. They perform routing tasks by using special "routing protocols" to communicate with other routers within a network.

▶▶ The topic of routing is covered in two other chapters. Chapter 10, "Routers," discusses how the actual router devices work, and Chapter 29, "Routing Protocols," describes how routers exchange information and maintain the routing tables that make connecting different networks possible.

Routers intelligently forward packets based on the destination segment information contained in the network protocol within a packet.

A nice feature of routing is that routers do not propagate broadcasts. Broadcasts stay within a network segment, and routers are the devices that segment the network.

VLANs

When manufacturers first came out with hubs, these devices could support only one network segment. But what if you needed to support multiple network segments out of the same wiring closet? The answer was simple: You needed more hubs! Virtual local area networks (VLANs) solved this problem by providing trunking protocols that allowed the traffic of multiple LAN segments to be multiplexed across the same fiber-optic riser cable. After the traffic was received, the switch or hub device demultiplexed the traffic and forwarded it to the appropriate ports. In this manner, many subnets could be supported out of a single network component, and collision-domain size could be controlled by carving a large LAN into several small VLANs. A side benefit of VLANs is the security gained by being able to partition workgroups with sensitive security needs off onto their own VLAN for an extra measure of protection.

▶▶ Virtual LANs (VLANS) have become popular in large environments. They simplify subnet and client management and help to centralize wiring. Chapter 9, "Virtual LANs," gives you more information about this technology.

Layer-3 Switching

Layer-3 switching is a hybrid technology that combines the speed of a switch with the LAN segment analysis of a router to make packet forwarding decisions. Layer-3 switching is the best of both worlds because you get the broadcast isolation and segmenting capabilities of a router, yet you have the lightning-fast forward decisions of a wire-speed switching device. A layer-3 switch can typically forward a packet 10–20 times faster than a router! This is covered in greater detail in Chapter 8.

Building Topology

Constructing a LAN within the confines of a building or campus immediately focuses you on the physical topology of your LAN environment. Let's take a look at how you can apply the topologies we've discussed to a physical implementation.

Connecting Network Segments Within a Building: The Backbone

You can think of a backbone as the spine of your network. The backbone integrates all the other LAN segments in one cohesive structure and it facilitates the communication between these different segments. Take a look at Figure 1.12. You can see how a star topology–based backbone has been used to tie together three separate segments in this fictitious three-story building.

Backbones can be implemented with copper wiring, but fiber-optic cables are far more popular for a few reasons:

■ The distance up through the risers of a building can be too long for copper wiring. Fiber-optic cables can usually handle a signal for far greater distances and therefore are a more popular medium for backbones.

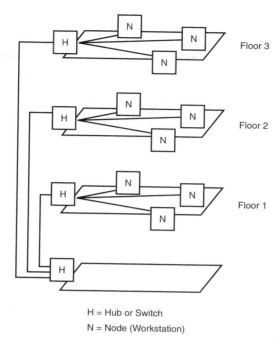

H = Hub or Switch
N = Node (Workstation)

Figure 1.12   A network backbone connects other LAN segments to create a larger network.

- Usually, electrical trunks servicing power for the building are inside the risers. Noisy electrical subsystems can wreak havoc with high-speed data communications, and copper wiring is sensitive to this electrical interference. Fiber optic, on the other hand, uses LEDs or lasers for its signaling and is not prone to electrical interference.

- Because fiber optic does not succumb to electrical interference, it can support far higher network speeds, making it the perfect medium for a backbone. With backbones, you might want to jump to higher-speed LAN technologies as they become available. Higher-speed LAN technologies are not always readily supported on old copper wiring standards and can force you to perform costly wiring upgrades.

Note

After you've decided on a topology for your network, you'll need to determine which types of cables, connectors, and other devices to use. Chapter 5, "Wiring the Network—Cables and Other Components," is a useful reference.

Backbones can also span buildings. Once again, an important point to keep in mind is the distances with which you are working. If you design beyond the specifications of the network technology you are using, be prepared for a poor performing or inoperable LAN environment.

Design Considerations in a Campus LAN Environment

Integrating the LANs of several buildings creates a campus network. As a LAN grows to this scale, you face a few more design challenges: scalability, redundancy, and fault tolerance. Now give some thought to just some of the design considerations you have to keep in mind when designing a campus LAN environment (see Figure 1.13).

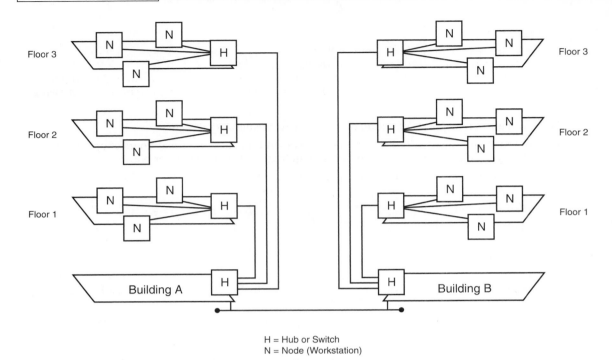

Floor 3

Floor 2

Floor 1

Building A

Floor 3

Floor 2

Floor 1

Building B

H = Hub or Switch
N = Node (Workstation)

Figure 1.13   The topology for a campus network is more complex than a simple bus or star.

You will notice two buildings that are three stories tall as you look at Figure 1.13. Suppose that each "node" represents 100 computer workstations. If this were the case, you would have 300 computer workstations per floor, 900 per building, and 1,800 for the entire campus.

Scalability

Scalability is the capability of the design to meet all the network traffic requirements and to continue to accommodate them as the company grows. The scalability question enters into several areas in your network design. Let's consider just a few of them:

- Where will you place critical server resources that your computer workstations will be using?
- Will the network technology used in your risers be capable of supporting the 300 workstations you have placed on each floor?
- Will the backbone that ties your campus together be capable of supporting cross-building traffic between the 1,800 workstations?
- Will the hubs or switches have enough bandwidth capacity to process the traffic between the three floors and two buildings?
- Will the network protocols allow you to properly address every workstation in this environment?
- Will the LAN environment be capable of accommodating the volume of broadcasts?
- Will the overall distance between the two furthest nodes on the network be outside the bounds of the network technology you have chosen?
- Are there workgroups that have particularly high network demands? How will you accommodate them?

Redundancy

Redundancy is the capability of the network to fail-over to secondary paths when your primary paths are cut or experience some other type of hardware failure. How much redundancy to deploy is often a cost issue. The more redundancy in a network, the greater the cost in implementation. Referring to Figure 1.13, consider the design from a redundancy standpoint, giving some thought to the following questions:

- How many single points of failure do you have in the network design?
- Can the environment afford to accommodate down time during normal hours of operation? Should you consider redundancy between buildings, within buildings, or both?
- Where can you place critical resources so clients could still work even if you lose an entire floor of the building?
- Where will you place resources on the LAN that are critical to the entire campus?
- What if a backhoe were to cut through your cross-building backbone?

Fault Tolerance

Fault tolerance is the aspect of your network that defines how resilient it is to the various problems that will inevitably crop up. Keeping the fault tolerance of the design in mind, consider just a few questions on this topic:

- Could a problem with a single workstation negatively impact the entire campus LAN?
- How would the LAN environment react to a broadcast storm?
- Do you have any isolation features to keep problems from propagating throughout the campus environment?

Whew! And you thought designing a campus LAN would be easy! But don't worry, everything you need to know is discussed in detail in the following chapters.

A Multi-Tiered Network Topology

By combining what you have learned so far about network topologies, you can develop a design that can meet most of the objectives mentioned in the previous section concerning the campus network design. Several powerful features of the new campus design appear in Figure 1.14.

Note that the design is a partial mesh star topology. In the next few sections we'll look at how this topology can be used to provide for scalability, redundancy, and fault tolerance for your network.

Scalability

With the advent of a distribution layer, you have the ability to offload some of the network capacity requirements at a lower level of the network. For example, if you placed your file servers at the distribution layer, the backbone layer would be freed of significant burden and could focus its resources on cross-building and data-center level traffic requirements. The distribution layer would turn around about 80 percent of all the network traffic and respond directly to the client layer, speeding network access. By offloading file and print servers at a lower level in the network, you would have a great deal of scalability.

Note the mesh between the distribution layer and the backbone layer. You could use a high-speed network technology such as gigabit ethernet to deliver the aggregate bandwidth you needed at the top layers of the network to process whatever requests were coming out of the client layers. Having separated this mesh from the client layer switches means, you could slip higher-speed technologies into the mesh as they came along without costly down time to your clients and expensive rewiring of your buildings.

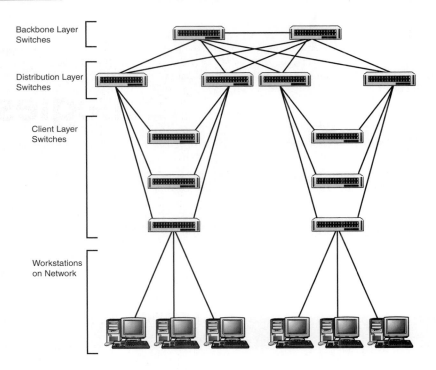

Backbone Layer
Switches

Distribution Layer
Switches

Client Layer
Switches

Workstations
on Network

Figure 1.14   The partial mesh topology can be used to provide scalability, fault tolerance, and redundancy.

Finally, by using VLANs from the distribution layer down into the client layer, you can ensure smaller broadcast domains to further drive down network use.

Redundancy

Significant gains in redundancy have been added by inserting a distribution layer of switching technology between client layer switches and backbone layer switches. This design would not have been possible with hub technology because the redundant connectivity would cause loops in the network, something a switch controls with a process called the *Spanning Tree Protocol*.

A failure at the distribution layer causes the client layer switches to fail-over to a secondary distribution switch. Likewise, if a failure occurs at the backbone layer, the traffic reroutes to the secondary backbone switch. Another nice feature is that because the distribution and backbone have a primary and secondary switch device, you can dual-home your most critical servers at these layers and still have network connectivity if you have a NIC card failure on your server.

Fault Tolerance

By using VLAN technologies, you can control the spread of broadcast, which provides an extra layer of control and fault tolerance to your network. Also, by incorporating some layer-3 switching technology, you can provide further isolation for robustness. Recall that routing does not forward segment broadcasts, so by using layer-3 switching, you also provide a means of isolating problems to a particular segment.

As you can see, a combination of old and new topologies and technologies have provided a solid foundation that can be scaled to great size and yet it offers stability and performance.

Network Design Strategies

SOME OF THE MAIN TOPICS IN THIS CHAPTER ARE

Planning a Logical Network Design

Planning and Design Components

The Physical Network

Other Planning Resources

In the previous chapter, you learned about the various topologies that can be employed when creating a LAN, and also looked at some scenarios in which several separate networks were connected to form a WAN. In this chapter, we will look at another aspect of creating a network: the network's logical and physical design. The physical aspects of your LAN will depend on the underlying physical transport technology—ethernet or token-ring, for example, or possibly ATM, which is now supported in products such as Windows 2000 as a LAN protocol. Depending on which technology you use, there will be one or more LAN topologies from which to choose.

Before you can begin to design a physical network, however, you first must determine your needs. What services must you provide to your user community? What are the resources you'll need? If you have to compromise, what will it take to satisfy the most users or to provide the more important services? You then will have to take into account network protocols, applications, network speed, and, most importantly, network security issues. Each of these figure into a network's logical design. Another important factor you'll probably be forced to consider by your management is cost—you can't forget the budget.

Planning a Logical Network Design

When you plan a logical network design, you can start from one of two places. You can design and install a new network from scratch, or you can upgrade an existing network. Either way, you should gather information about several important factors before you begin the logical design. For example, depending on the services that will be provided to clients, you might need to analyze the possible traffic patterns that might result from your plan. Locate potential bottlenecks and, where possible, alleviate them by providing multiple paths to resources or by putting up servers that provide replicas of important data so that load balancing can be provided. The following are other factors to consider:

- Who are the clients? What are their actual needs? How have you determined these needs, from user complaints or from help desk statistics? Is this data reliable?

- What kinds of services will you provide on the network? Are they limited in scope? Will any involve configuring a firewall between company LANs, much less using a firewall to connect the network to the Internet?

- Can your users tolerate a little down time now and then due to network problems, or is it necessary to provide a high-availability network? Will you need clustered servers to provide for a high amount of uptime, or do your user's applications not suffer from a temporary loss of use of a server?

- In an existing network, will you keep the current protocol or upgrade to a different protocol standard? If you create a network from scratch, what factors should affect your network protocol decision? Ethernet is the most popular LAN technology in the world today. TCP/IP is the most popular protocol suite that runs on ethernet. Yet, there are cases where other technologies have their niches. Consider the implications (such as support costs) to maintain older, proprietary protocols.

Who Are Your Clients?

This seems like a very simple question. However, I'm not saying, "What are your client's names and how well do you know their children?" I am referring instead to what are the job descriptions of the users on the network. You need to assess work patterns for various departments so that you can appropriately place servers, high-bandwidth links, and other such things, in the appropriate physical location of the network. If most of the network traffic you expect to see will come from the engineering department, then you'll need to provide that department with a large data pipe. In Chapter 3, "Upgrading Strategies and Project Management," you'll find more information about surveying the user community to come up with a plan that places resources where they are needed.

What Kind of Services Will You Offer on the Network?

Of course, everyone knows that the most important function of a network today is multiuser gaming. Seriously, though, you need to make a list of the kinds of applications currently in use, as well as a list of those requested by users. Each application should have a written risk assessment document that points out potential security problems, if any. Typical network applications today include FTP, telnet, and, of course, browsing the Net. There are "secure" versions of these applications and there are versions that leave a door wide open into your network. Whatever list of applications you chose to support over the network, keep in mind two things:

- Is the application safe? Most applications today come in secure versions or can be used with a proxy server to help minimize the possibility of abuse. Yet, as we all have seen, even the largest corporations are targets at times, and those companies have the staff that should be able to prevent these things from happening. Because proxy servers are an important component of firewalls, this subject is covered in greater detail in Chapter 40, "Firewalls," and, if you want a secure network, this is recommended reading!

- Does one application overlap another? Every user has his or her favorite application. Some like one word processor, while others prefer a different one. When dealing with applications or application suites (such as Microsoft Office), you'll find it better to make a decision and stick with a single product if it can satisfy the needs of your users. They might not like it, and training might be necessary, but supporting multiple applications that do the same thing wastes money and leads to confusion.

Network Reliability

Just how much down time is acceptable? For most users, the answer would be zero. Important components of your network, such as file servers, should have fault tolerance built in from the bottom up. In large servers, you'll find dual-redundant power supplies (each connected to a separate UPS), and disk arrays set up using RAID techniques to provide for data integrity in the event that a disk goes south. If a link between two offices needs to be up 100% of the time, you should plan for multiple links between the two sites to provide a backup capability. In this case, you also can justify the cost of the extra link by using load balancing so that network response time is improved.

▶▶ The terms RAID and UPS are important in today's networks, as is the concept of load balancing and dual-redundant power supplies in large networks. You can find out more about RAID (redundant array of independent disks) and UPSs (uninterruptible power supplies) by reading Chapter 4, "Preventive Maintenance."

The old saying "If it ain't broke, don't fix it" doesn't apply to networks. You should always be proactively looking for potential single points of failure and doing something to fix them. By building redundancy into the network design at the start, you'll save yourself a lot of grief in the future.

Chapter 4 can give you more suggestions about using clustering, backups, uninterruptible power supplies, and other techniques that can keep the network up and running.

Choosing a Network Protocol

Today the de facto protocol of choice has to be TCP/IP. However, other protocols have their place in some vertical markets. In this book, we talk about NetWare and ARCnet. ARCnet fills a special niche, especially in the factory automation environment. NetWare has been around so long that you might find you have no choice when designing an upgrade to keep using IPX/SPX. However, even NetWare now is moving quickly to using TCP/IP as the underlying protocol. If you will be connecting the network to the Internet, then TCP/IP will be a necessity. Even if you don't expect to have an Internet connection, you'll find that choosing TCP/IP is a more practical choice today because most applications work with it and there is a large market of trained professionals that can be hired to manage a network built on TCP/IP.

In addition to transport protocols such as TCP/IP and IPX/SPX, you must consider application protocols that can be used on the network. For example, to simplify administering configuration information for a large number of computers, you might want to use the Dynamic Host Configuration Protocol (DHCP), which is discussed in Chapter 23, "BOOTP and the Dynamic Host Configuration Protocol (DHCP)." If you want to provide a central name resolution service, you might choose the Domain Name Service (DNS), which is covered in Chapter 24, "Name Resolution." If you are going to operate a Windows network that has pre-Windows 2000 clients, you might need to use the Windows Internet Naming Service (WINS) for backward compatibility.

So, when thinking about a network protocol, remember that it's not just one protocol you need to worry about. After you've decided which protocols are necessary, research the security implications of each.

Planning and Design Components

When it is time to create a plan, what should the product of this effort be? Depending on the scope of the project, the end result might be a simple short document with a step-by-step checklist for adding a few network devices to the network to segment traffic. As the scope grows larger, so do the receivables that should be prepared for upper management as part of the plan. Some of the things you might want to consider including are

- **Documentation**—What kind of documents will be required to implement the plan? This can be in the form of checklists for both simple and complex upgrades, sign-off sheets, informational documents provided to end users, and so on. Don't forget training documentation that will be needed in a major upgrade. Training documentation should be prepared for both administrators and the highly skilled end users (power users) of new technology. Of course, you should have a document that shows the physical layout of the network that is being implemented or upgraded. This sort of document can be very useful when something goes wrong and you are trying to think through a problem. You might find, for example, that the physical network you've designed can't handle the load at certain points.

- **Overall project plan**—Any large project must operate in an orderly manner to be sure that the goals set for the plan are met, or possibly adjusted if necessary. Creating a project plan with a liberal timeline can be very helpful for keeping the project on track by setting milestones to be met. By making the schedule a liberal one, you automatically build in extra time to be used when things don't go quite as you expected they would. If everything works perfectly, then you get gold stars from management for bringing a project in under time!

- **Policies and procedures**—As with any technology, you should plan to develop documents that detail policies and procedures to follow when the new network begins operating. Policies dictate how the network is to be used. For example, you might not allow employees to use e-mail for personal use or the Web browser to view pages not related to your business. Procedures are detailed instructions on how to perform certain actions. With new technology, both policy and procedure should be considered important factors.

Document Everything

Documentation is everything. People have very short memories of things that appear to have only a limited lifetime, such as work projects. It is important that a good project contain several important documents, listed here, but not limited to

- **An executive overview**—You must have some overall plan to present to upper management that explains, without too many technical details, the reasons the upgrade (or new network) is needed, and what benefits the business will obtain from the upgrade. In this sort of document, less is more. Bulleted items make a better point than long, prose-filled paragraphs. Point out the need for the network or the upgrade, and be sure to list the benefits for each point you make. If a benefit can be measured in dollars, be sure to include that.

- **A technical project plan**—This is a difficult document to create. After you've identified the parts of the network to upgrade, you need to create lists of steps detailing the replacement of old equipment with the new, with little disruption to the user community. If you are building a network from scratch, or planning a major upgrade where most of the existing equipment will be replaced, this kind of document works best when done in sections. A three-ring binder can be used and individual sections can be assigned to technologically proficient team members for the initial writing of, and any possible updates to, sections of this document.

- **Detailed checklists**—For each task that must be performed, a detailed checklist can help ensure that an important step is not left out. This is a simple process, but it's a lot easier to get it right the first time if you use a checklist.

Policies and Procedures

Policies, mentioned earlier, are statements about how something should or should not be used. Policy documents are important for several reasons. First, you can't very well discipline an employee for abusing a network resource if you haven't created a usage policy that prohibits the particular abuse. If you don't want your network users to spend their lunch hours shopping for bargains on ebay.com, you should spell this out in an acceptable usage policy.

Policies are important in the design phase of the network because they detail how some resources are to be used. Using the example from the previous paragraph, if you select an Internet connection after calculating what you expect your bandwidth requirements to be, you might find your network under-performing as users begin to use the connection for nonbusiness needs. Another place where policies come into play—to the point of being a necessity—is when you use a firewall. In Chapter 40, "Firewalls," you'll learn more about how important it is to first create a security policy and *then* implement that security policy using firewall technology. If you don't know what kind of network traffic you want to allow through the firewall, setting one up is going to be difficult! For example, most secure sites prohibit users from the Internet to use the standard telnet application to gain access to computers inside the local network from computers located elsewhere on the Internet. Yet, you might have users that work from home.

▶▶ In addition to Chapter 40, you can learn more about network security in Part VI of this book. You'll find chapters on basic security measures, both in the local LAN and in a wide area network (WAN), as well as chapters on encryption and virtual private networks (VPNs).

You can still keep your no-incoming-telnet policy and provide your users with a remote access server that can authenticate dial-in users. By finding out what your users need in advance, you can include the necessary technology up front in the network design and not have to make exceptions to policies at a later date.

Procedures help prevent mistakes from happening in the first place. They are proactive measures that assist technical and nontechnical people when it comes to performing functions on the network. For example, in your network design you might have a team trained to set up several hundred desktop computers and attach them to the network. Although plugging the network card into the wall socket is simple, configuring the desktop machine can be a little more difficult. You'll need to either config-ure the desktop machine with valid addressing configuration information or set it up to use DHCP. Even though you might be doing this on a lot of computers, it's very easy to make a mistake when performing repetitive tasks. By using a checklist for each computer, you can improve your odds of get-ting it right the first time. Don't wait until you've created the network and then start looking for fires to put out. Instead, create procedure documents for commonly performed tasks. This includes tasks involved in the initial setup of the network as well as procedures for performing daily tasks after the network is up and running—such as backups, connecting network drives, and so on.

Training for Technical Personnel

Technical users who will be responsible for helping manage the network should be trained in the procedures for which they will be responsible. Again, this means you should provide training for those who will help you set up the network as well as those who will manage it after it is functioning. Training classes can be conducted by in-house personnel already familiar with the technology, or by one of the many hundreds of consulting services that make their living doing just this sort of thing.

Remember that the technical staff that supports the network are the persons your users must depend on when a problem occurs. Perhaps the most expensive thing that can happen in most networks is *down time*. If you have hundreds (or even thousands) of idle workers getting paid to sit around while someone is reading a technical manual trying to determine the cause for a network problem, you might want to get your resume in order. Up-front training is not inexpensive, but down time can be far more expensive than training the technical staff in the first place.

You Can't Forget the Budget

When planning a network or an upgrade to a network, it is always tempting to use the latest, greatest gizmos. Sometimes, however, you can accomplish the same thing using a much less expensive gizmo. For example, if you have a small home office, you don't need a $2,000–$3,000 router and a T1 line to connect to the Internet. A simple cable or DSL modem and the appropriate broadband service should suffice in most instances.

Plan the budget liberally. Don't include items that really aren't necessary. When you present a list of items to upper management that shows them what the new network will do for the company, the benefits better not outweigh the costs you've come up with. Although this might not be such an issue in a growing company, it's better to manage your network project responsibly so that you will maintain a good rapport with management. When you find that something you have planned and implemented isn't working as you expected, and you need to make changes, management will probably be more responsive if you've been frugal with the initial expenses incurred building the network.

The Physical Network

After you've decided on the network protocols and the services you need to offer on the network, identified potential bottlenecks, and evaluated the security problems associated with your network needs, you can then design the physical aspects of the network.

The previous chapter discussed different physical network topologies. There are tools you can use, such as Visio, to draw a physical network diagram. Tools such as these are expensive but make a much better presentation to management than hand-drawn network layouts. Whichever tool you decide to use to create the actual network drawings, just be sure that the drawings are clear and concise. Looking back at your network application requirements, bandwidth requirements, and the like, you can then start designing the physical network, deciding where to place important servers and redundant devices.

Other Planning Resources

Finally, keep in mind that technology changes rapidly in the computer and networking fields. Although a hub might have been sufficient a few years ago, today most larger networks use switches. Although Bill Gates might have thought (way back when) that no one would ever need more than 640KB of memory, that prediction proved false almost as soon as it left his mouth.

If you are about to set yourself on a course of designing a network, become familiar with all the latest technologies and don't depend solely on past experience. The best way to keep up with new technologies is to read about them. You can use books, such as this one, and you can also talk to knowledgeable consultants who are experts in their field.

Finally, Appendix E, "Other Resources for Network Management," can point you to some interesting books and Web sites that contain helpful information. You'll find links in the appendix to sites that specialize in security, network protocols, and so on. You'll also find sites that maintain copies of Internet Request For Comments (RFCs) documents, which spell out standards that are used on the Internet.

Upgrading Strategies and Project Management

SOME OF THE MAIN TOPICS IN THIS CHAPTER ARE

Determining When an Upgrade Is Necessary—The Evaluation Process

What Resources Are Needed for the Upgrade?

Planning an Upgrade

Testing the Plan

Deployment

User Training

Closing the Book—Documenting What Has Changed and Why

Other Considerations for Upgrading

CHAPTER 3

This chapter discusses some things you should consider when deciding whether an upgrade is needed for the network, and some of the steps that should be taken to accomplish the task.

The first place to start is to determine the need for an upgrade, and then set goals. Next, create a plan to guide the process. After this has been done, carefully investigate to ensure that the upgrade plan will succeed. The following steps are covered in this chapter:

- **Evaluation**—Understanding the current environment.
- **Determining needs**—Why are you upgrading?
- **Setting goals**—What will the upgrade accomplish?
- **Budgeting**—Determining what financial resources are available and set a budget.
- **Planning**—Creating a detailed plan for the upgrade.
- **Testing**—Evaluating components of the upgrade in a laboratory or pilot project environment.
- **Training**—Will users need to be trained on any new applications or features?
- **Backing-out and recovering**—Coping with the unexpected. No matter how well you plan, something can always go awry.
- **Deployment**—Implementing the upgrade plan.
- **Post implementation review**—Did the plan work as expected? Are the results what was expected, possibly more?

Determining When an Upgrade Is Necessary— The Evaluation Process

A data network in a business is much like a nervous system in a living organism. Usually, when the business grows, the network also must grow to keep up with new users and newer functions. When a business suffers and shrinks, the costs associated with a larger network must be reevaluated to determine whether they are still feasible under a smaller business organization. A network rarely goes unchanged year after year.

Before you begin to write an upgrade plan for part or all of a network, you first must determine that there is a need for an upgrade. There are several reasons to upgrade a network:

- **User complaints**—When top-performing users complain, their managers usually do their best to make them happy. Keep in mind also that there are always going to be people who complain about the network. Investigate user complaints to determine whether they are valid.
- **New technology has been adopted**—Sometimes the upgrade can be application driven. A new kind of hardware or software needed by a business unit demands a network with higher performance capabilities or different features.
- **Business mergers and expansions**—After figuring out a way to join two networks when companies merge, a long-range plan must be developed to make the network work best for the new business entity. This can include performance enhancements, adoption of standards, and elimination of duplicated components. This also can result in a major headache if you have to find a way to combine user authorization data from different operating systems.
- **Business is good, let's spend money**—This is not an uncommon motive for making a new system or network purchase. Sometimes when economic times are going well for a business it's also a good time to make long-range plans and upgrade part of the infrastructure.

The first of these reasons, user complaints, probably will never go away. No matter how fast the network or how powerful the machine, there will always be someone who wants more. Usually a network administrator has a good overview of the people or departments that are major consumers of network resources and can filter out realistic complaints. So, when deciding when and if you need to perform some kind of overhauling of the network, you should carefully research your current network's capacity and compare it to the business needs currently loading the network.

Sometimes a simple overview of the network can reveal that all you must do to satisfy one or two small bottlenecks is reconfigure part of the network. Usually a reconfiguration is cheaper and easier to implement than a major upgrade. It's much easier to upgrade a single, growing department to a faster switch than it is to overhaul the entire network.

When reconfiguring the network will not solve capacity problems, it might be time to look at other media to handle the network traffic. Chapter 5, "Wiring the Network—Cables and Other Components," gives a good overview of the specifications and capabilities of this most basic part of the network. Whether you are planning an upgrade or simply extending your network into a larger geographic space, it's not necessarily a good idea to shop around and settle for the cheapest solution. Installing cabling in ceilings, walls, and floors is a labor-intensive, expensive item in an upgrade budget. Yet, if you spend the money up front to install good quality cables, connectors and the like, you will probably quickly recoup the cost in a few years when upgrading to even faster networking technologies. The best example of this is Category 5 cabling. If you have a 10Mbps network and used Category 5 cabling, upgrading to Fast Ethernet or even Gigabit Ethernet won't require that you rewire the entire network.

There are other chapters you might want to consult when planning an upgrade. Chapter 6, "Network Adapter Cards," covers the basics of this topic. You also can find information there about some of the newest functionality being incorporated into NICs, such as Wake on LAN and server NIC load balancing. Once you've got the wiring and NIC issues settled, Chapter 8, "Network Switches," will guide you in the process of replacing overload department hubs with switches to improve performance and connect dissimilar LAN segments.

Adopting new technology usually entails additional tasks such as training users and administrative personnel in the use or management of new products. For example, a major paradigm shift, such as migrating an all-Novell network to Windows 2000 (or vice versa), would have to include months of training for network administrative personnel. For all practical purposes, TCP/IP is now the de facto networking standard for LANs. If you are still running an AppleTalk or IPX/SPX network, you might want to think about future support for these products. Novell already offers TCP/IP support, and there are products that allow interaction between Novell Directory Services (NDS) and Windows Active Directory. Although NDS still might be a useful tool, IPX/SPX LANs are good candidates for upgrading to TCP/IP, especially if your business connects to the Internet.

Another technology that might be ready for a change is the token-ring LAN. Although token-ring technology is a great LAN solution, it's not likely to keep up with the speeds being achieved by newer versions of ethernet. And when it comes to the budget, the number of manufacturers of ethernet equipment dwarfs those who make token-ring hardware. Because of the economics of scale, and competition, ethernet is a far cheaper solution in most cases.

For newcomers, Chapter 12, "Ethernet," and Chapter 20, "Overview of the TCP/IP Protocol Suite," will get you started on the planning process. Other chapters can fill in the details of some aspects typical of TCP/IP based networks. For example, Chapter 21, "TCP/IP Services and Applications," will help you determine which of the basic TCP/IP-based applications will be useful in your network. Chapter 23, "BOOTP and the Dynamic Host Configuration Protocol (DHCP)," and Chapter 24, "Name Resolution," cover the basics of automating network addressing and name resolution.

Finally, one "upgrade" that every network administrator should plan for, if it has not happened yet, is to provide a firewall between the company network and any outside network connection. Chapter 40, "Firewalls," covers this area. The chapters immediately preceding cover other aspects of network and systems security.

Determining User Requirements and Expectations

One of the simplest methods of finding out what is needed on the network is to ask the users. Although this technique might not give you the most accurate results, it will at least give you an idea of what the user community expects from the network. Conducting a simple written survey can bring light to factors that administrative and support personnel might not be aware of.

Similar to surveying end users is soliciting suggestions from support staff who encounter user problems on a daily basis. Logs of support calls can be a valuable source of information. If users are making the same mistakes over and over again, then training, not upgrading, usually can solve the problem. When examining help desk logs, don't limit your scope to the problems. Carefully examine what was done to solve the problem. Maybe your help desk personnel aren't giving out the best advice.

However, the most basic way to determine overall capacity needs is to establish baseline data for your network components and then make comparisons on a regular basis with the production network. By keeping data that reflects the baseline mode of operation, you will have empirical data that can be used to make projections about future use. By regularly benchmarking your systems and keeping track of the data, you also can become aware of capacity problems that begin to creep up before your projections or expectations. Most operating systems provide for monitoring of a sort. Windows 2000 Performance Monitor, for example, can give you very detailed statistics on a server's performance, including network performance. Chapter 4, "Preventive Maintenance," gives an overview of this tool. In larger networks, using a management console that understands SNMP and RMON can help you baseline and monitor many different components in the network. Analysis software can help prepare reports that can be used to justify network changes. Both SNMP and RMON are examined in Chapter 44, "Network Testing and Analysis Tools."

Other factors that can be reviewed to determine whether changes are merited include the following:

- **Maintenance costs**—The network might be functioning nicely with equipment that is several years old. However, the maintenance costs associated with older equipment might be justification for upgrading to newer, more reliable equipment.

- **Existing contracts**—Leased equipment can usually be purchased or returned to the lessor at the end of the lease period. Contracts that are about to expire should be examined and taken into consideration when deciding whether to keep the existing equipment or upgrade. Keep in mind the costs associated with migrating to newer hardware. For example, software licensing might be more expensive on higher-capacity servers, whether or not you need or use that capacity.

- **Network traffic**—Regular monitoring of network traffic to locate bottlenecks or congested areas can be helpful. Is it possible that user work habits or procedures can be changed so that problems that occur only at peak hours or on specific days do not lead you to spending too much on a small problem that can be better solved by other methods?

Maintaining Support for Legacy Applications

There comes a time in every application's life when it really should just die and go away. However, when you consider the costs associated with replacing a legacy software application with one that is state-of-the-art, sometimes what you find might lead you to listen to users who like their software and keep the application around a little longer.

The following are some hidden costs that you might overlook at first glance:

- Ongoing maintenance or support costs
- Employee support costs
- Infrastructure overhead costs

Maintenance and support costs can be hidden in part of the budget for the department that an application or hardware platform supports. When multiple suppliers are involved, you will usually find multiple contracts, some of which even overlap each other. Another problem with ongoing support costs is that manufacturers raise these costs when products become outdated to help encourage users to adopt newer ones.

The number of employees you dedicate to a particular part of the network is an important cost. If you have a large staff that is used for mostly maintaining an old application, consider the costs associated with them, from salary to overhead, and decide if it might be better spent training them on newer technology and replacing the legacy system.

Legacy applications are usually either loved or hated by their users. Some people think with the mindset "But we've always done it that way" and do not want to change for fear of the unknown and love of the familiar. Other users who are used to better technology might hate a legacy application. The point to remember here is that it does not always matter what the user thinks about the application. What is most important to the business's bottom line is the costs associated with it compared with the benefits the company receives.

What Resources Are Needed for the Upgrade?

If you already have a good inventory of the network, you are ahead of the game. Keeping an up-to-date listing of network components, including hardware and software, along with other pertinent information such as network addresses, serial numbers, manufacturer's help line numbers, and so on, is a task that, when done on a regular basis, will yield great results down the line.

Without a good network map document, you won't necessarily be sure that you're not violating some of the topology rules for your network. Before beginning to plan an expansion or the addition of new equipment, review documentation for that which you already possess. You might have some devices that do not need to be replaced. For example, if you already have network adapter cards that are 10Mbps/100Mbps, you would not need to add the cost of new cards to an upgrade plan when going from a 10Base-T network to a 100Base-T network.

Items that you should be sure to inventory include the following:

- Workstations and servers
- Network adapters
- Hubs, routers, and switches
- Test equipment
- Workgroup and end-user software applications
- Mechanisms used to exchange data with contacts outside the company
- Management and control applications, such as SNMP, DHCP, DNS, NIS, and so on

Looking at your inventory, determine how the existing pieces can be used in an upgraded network. For example, it won't do a lot of good to install a faster switch and hook a server to a faster port if the server is not capable of supporting the bandwidth. In such a case, upgrades to the server (or a replacement) would have to be considered as part of the plan. Although installing switches can dramatically improve performance in a departmental LAN, an older hub might be sufficient for a few more years in an office where network utilization is not high. Test equipment and management applications are not generally inexpensive items. Be sure to include the costs of upgrading these when calculating the cost of the upgrade.

When determining your resources, don't forget people. A major project of any kind should always have an identified set of team players that will be responsible for the project. A clearly defined project team will identify the person responsible for each aspect, such as purchasing, infrastructure, systems, documentation, and so on. This will greatly improve communication during the length of the project, because a point of contact is identified for specific areas.

A project leader should be designated to be the focal point for both the project team and for others in the company who need to get information about the project or its progress. Each project team member should have a clearly defined role and area of responsibility. The area of responsibility is a very important one. As in any social interaction, overlapping duties can generate personal resentment between people working on the same project. When a clear, defined set of job responsibilities and duties is spelled out in writing, you have a better chance of achieving harmony among the team members.

A project team will work best when it is dedicated to the project. Giving users multiple roles to fill in their jobs can lead to confusion, unexpected priorities, and degradation in the progress of the overall project. Although the current support staff might be knowledgeable in the network and its quirks, bringing in additional help, by using experienced contact workers, for example, might keep the project focused on its goals and the time frame associated with them.

Planning an Upgrade

Planning is the process of deciding what actions are needed to accomplish a goal. This necessarily implies that the plan will describe the specific goals to be achieved and the benefits that will come from them. However, the steps that are required in a plan are dictated not only by the goals that are to be accomplished, but you also must take into consideration

- How a network upgrade affects users (downtime)
- What established corporate standards must be followed (or possibly reexamined)
- What criteria can be used to measure the progress or success of the plan

Planning for an upgrade should include input from both technical staff members and the user community. After reviewing user requests (and complaints!) and deciding what issues will be addressed, measurable goals can then be established and written documentation can be produced that details the plan, its goals, and how they are to be achieved.

Document the Plan

Planning is essential in a complex environment to ensure that a project will be successful. Planning can encompass more than one document. For example, there can be a detailed plan that contains checklists for tasks that need to be accomplished, along with time-frame assumptions and resource requirements. For top-level department heads, an executive overview can serve to garner support for the project without forcing management to get bogged down in details they do not understand.

Whatever planning you undertake must be put into the form of a written document. Persons representative of the areas that will be affected should carefully review any plans in order to solicit their feedback and ensure their cooperation. However, as with most things in life, even a good plan is likely to undergo changes during its execution. It is important to create a process that can be used to evaluate changes and incorporate them into the plan in an orderly manner. Put the process in writing along with the other details of the plan. If you have it in writing, it becomes much more difficult for a disagreeable person to protest when deadlines must be met and resources are limited. An orderly change process can always include a method for recording potential change ideas so that a decision can be postponed to a later date.

Reminding those who are working on the plan about recent accomplishments and upcoming deadlines can help facilitate cooperation. For example, a short meeting on Monday morning that quickly reviews the previous week's work along with a discussion about goals for the upcoming week might be helpful.

Evaluate the Plan As It Applies to Corporate Policies and Procedures

Before beginning to write any kind of plan that will be used for a major upgrade project, be sure to review the current corporate standards. A company should have one standard word processor that is used throughout the company, or at least throughout any major division of the business.

Most applications today that perform ordinary tasks, such as spreadsheets, or word processing and database functions, also come with tools that enable you to interchange data with other vendor's products. Although this might seem to alleviate the problem of using multiple products for the same purpose, there is another factor to consider: end-user support. Even if data can be easily exchanged, the extra expense of having to support more than one application for a single function is an ongoing cost that doesn't go away.

When developing the plan, first examine the current standards. Then, taking into consideration the future expansion of the network, capabilities of products currently in use, and the direction certain technologies seem to be taking, develop a revised list of standards, and sell it to the organization.

Of course, there will always be exceptions. For example, the corporate standard might require that the Oracle database application be used throughout the company. However, a specific vertical market application used in a research lab might work only with another database product. In cases where there aren't a variety of vendors from which to choose, you might be forced to accept a deviation from the standard here and there.

Setting Goals

Any good plan will have a clearly defined set of goals to provide some kind of benefit to the business. Although an overall view of the project's goals can be used to help sell the idea to upper-level management, the goals that should be included in a detailed project plan must be more specific. The following are two important reasons why you should have a defined set of goals:

- If defined with enough detail, goals can give you something to gauge progress of the upgrade project.
- Goals can keep you on track, preventing you from getting sidetracked by other ideas that will inevitably come up during the project.

After you come up with a written list of the goals that will serve to guide the project, prioritize the list. When initially developing a list of project objectives, your staff might be over-enthusiastic, and you can find yourself with a large shopping list that attempts to solve every problem and please every department. Set realistic priorities based on the benefit each goal is expected to provide, and then remove items from the list that provide little benefit or do not address an immediate need.

Scheduling Downtime

Users should not be expected to understand what goes on behind the scenes in the complicated area of networked computer systems. They might only know that they can or cannot get their job functions performed in a timely manner because "the network is down." By planning ahead and letting everyone know when resources will be unavailable, you will find that users are more likely to cooperate.

Milestones and Criteria

Based on the goals that the project is expected to achieve, build into your plan the procedures that will be used to measure success. Select items from your list of objectives that represent major changes to the network and define the metrics that will be used to determine whether the goal has been met.

For example, a goal can consist of achieving a reduction in network utilization for overloaded segments. Monitoring utilization with a LAN analyzer can be done before and after the upgrade to obtain factual information that can be used to establish the success of this upgrade. Other metrics might include items such as network response times, user satisfaction, or new functionality. The last item is a little more abstract than the others are. How do you measure the impact of new functionality offered by a new application or network configuration? Look at the business function that it provides and find aspects that you can measure. For example, if the turnaround time for a monthly billing cycle is usually 48 hours, and new faster servers or software cuts that time to only 12 hours, then this achievement should be measured and reported to management to justify the upgrade costs.

If you find that you are having trouble deciding what benefits you will gain from the upgrade and cannot devise a list of metrics, it is possible that you haven't fully thought through what you are trying to accomplish. In that case, take time to reexamine your thought process that led you to decide on an upgrade. Once you identify specific goals, rewrite your plan.

Back-Out Procedures

Nobody is perfect, and no plan can ever be precise enough that you can bet your life that everything will go as expected. Whenever possible, for any major modification that you intend to make to the network, you should also have a plan that can be used to restore the network to its previous state. Having good up-to-date documentation about the network can be useful for troubleshooting. When you have scheduled downtime with users and are under a deadline to finish a task or a project, it is more useful to have a definite set of procedures to follow if problems arise that prevent the execution of a task or tasks in the project plan.

A back-out plan does not have to include abandoning the entire plan. Most network upgrades do not occur all at once, but are instead done in stages. At each major step in the plan, have a procedure that can be used to undo the change.

Testing the Plan

The complexity of networking technology today makes it important that you test new equipment and software before committing it to production use. You might find that devices do not function as you expected when deployed using your planned configuration. Management software might be cumbersome and difficult for users to understand. In the end, if users are not satisfied and cannot perform their jobs efficiently using the tools you provide, it is likely they will find someone else who can. During the testing phase is when you'll probably find the most changes to the plan. When tests show that performance doesn't meet your expectations, the plan will be changed and performance measured again. When testing, the laboratory environment should closely mimic the proposed production network.

Evaluating Competing Products

Careful selection of new equipment or software up front can save time and money after the upgrade is finished. Evaluate competing products carefully so that you can select those that best meet the goals of your upgrade plan. When looking at different vendors' products, try before you buy. For a large hardware purchase, many vendors will loan equipment for a trial period so that you can make a better determination as to its suitability to satisfy your needs. Almost all major software applications can now be obtained from a vendor in a "demo" or "evaluation" copy so that you can test its features.

Another very important factor to consider is the vendor itself. You might find a great product that looks like it will work miracles for your network. However, if the vendor is not reliable, what will you do when you encounter problems later on? Things to think about when choosing vendors include

- **Responsiveness**—Do you get through to the help you need when you call the vendor, or do you have to play telephone-tag to get answers?

- **Availability**—Does the vendor have a good stock of products, or will you be subjected to back orders that can take days or weeks? When you have to replace a part due to malfunction, can your network wait until the part arrives?

- **Service**—Does the vendor provide service for the product? Is on-site service available or do you have to return the item to the vendor for repair?

- **Training**—Does the vendor provide training for the product? Is the training of good quality?

- **Price**—Price usually comes into play when a product is a commodity item. For specialized products or applications, price might not be as important as the other items listed here.

The Pilot Project

Every good plan should include a pilot project. This involves taking a small part of the network, such as a network-friendly department, and implementing part or all the project modifications in that localized area. Not only will it help you determine whether you have made the right choices for new hardware or software, it also will help you further refine your installation procedures that will be used to execute the rest of the plan.

If it is not possible to do this in a "live" environment, create a test lab where you can simulate the production environment or network. Use script files to automate processing and perform stress testing on the new components or applications to see if they really perform as you expect.

The results of a pilot project or a test lab setup can be used to refine and modify the plan and make it more likely to succeed.

Deployment

After you have evaluated and reevaluated, tested, and retested, and are sure that your plan is a sound one, implement the plan to upgrade the network. Depending on the scope of the upgrade, the deployment stage can be done all at once, or it can be done in a migration process over time. Adding additional segments to a network for new offices or replacing older cables can be a simple matter accomplished over a weekend. Migrating a large network to a faster topology might require that you deploy only small segments at a time to ensure that disruptions for users are minimized. The success of a software application upgrade can take longer to implement because of such factors as data conversion and user training.

Team Personnel

The personnel that are employed to perform upgrade functions should be well trained far in advance of the actual deployment stage. Each person should be knowledgeable in the area of expertise for the functions they will perform. To aid the upgrade team, it is a good idea to have specific written task lists that describe what is to be done. For example, a recent network upgrade in which I participated required that network adapter cards be replaced in a large number of workstations. The process involved the physical action to remove the old card and replace it with a new one.

After the card replacement, however, there were still additional chores to do. For example, each card had to be configured with the correct drivers so that the operating system would be capable of using of it. Each workstation had to be tested for connectivity to ensure that the card was correctly configured to work with the network. The task list for this was written in detail describing each step the team member needed to perform, and included a check-off box for each step. Why a check-off box? Well, if you have to take the time to check off each step, you are less likely to forget one. When a person is performing the same actions over and over, moving from workstation to workstation, the odds are likely that mistakes will be made.

It is also a good idea to designate one or more persons to be a resource focal point that team members can use when problems arise. If one person is aware of the problems that are occurring, it is easy to implement a fix throughout the project so the same problem doesn't have to be solved over and over.

Keeping Users Informed

Network users should be kept current about the progress of the upgrade. At the beginning of the deployment stage, present the users with an overview of what will be happening and how it will affect their work. As specific tasks are ready to be done, let the users who will be immediately affected know shortly before you begin. For example, if you plan to replace workstations throughout the enterprise, create a list of replacement candidates each week and notify the affected users via a memo or an e-mail so that they will be reminded. For an extended project, it is easy for users to forget what you told them weeks or months earlier.

Along this same line, it is a good idea to get some kind of response from a user when you have made changes to his workstation. For example, having a user test the system for a day or so and then "sign off" on the work lets him know that (for him at least) the process is complete; this is known as user-acceptance testing.

Tracking Progress

Use the metrics that you designed to measure the progress you make as you implement the plan. It is important to keep track of the progress so that you can coordinate your people, resources, and the delivery of additional equipment or outside services. If you find that you are falling behind in one area, it can cause you to reschedule tasks in other related areas. A close watch on progress is necessary so that you can quickly detect when something is not going as expected and begin to come up with an alternative method for getting things done.

The mechanisms you can use to track implementation of the plan might include a spreadsheet, a diary-like text file, checklists, and so on. To present information to upper-level management, you might find that weekly or monthly summary reports help to keep their support. If you find yourself in a position where you need to report on progress to high-level managers, graphical displays, such as graphs or charts, can help get your point across.

User Training

The topic of training can cover a large territory. Users should be trained to acquire the necessary skills needed for new applications or new ways of doing ordinary tasks when the network changes. In-house personnel who have the skills and the time to devote to the process can do training. For large projects it might be more economical to employ outside resources for training users. Additionally, there are a variety of training resources you can make available to your users for most popular applications. These include training videos, computer-based training (CBT) applications, programs presented by user groups, and so on.

Make users aware of the resources at their disposal from the beginning and begin training before major changes are made so that the users will be better able to cope with the new environment. Users who are trained in advance for a new application or procedure are less likely to cause a strain on the upgrade team's resources while the upgrade is proceeding.

Closing the Book—Documenting What Has Changed and Why

When a major project comes to a close, it is a good idea to compile a short report that details the project, from the evaluation and planning stages all the way through to the deployment and user-acceptance stage. This historical document can serve in the future when it comes time again to take on another project of a similar scope. It also can be presented to management to make them aware of the scope of what has been accomplished. This visibility can be very beneficial to a network administrator's career!

Other Considerations for Upgrading

Undertaking a major upgrade to a network is not a task to be taken lightly. As with any large undertaking it is best to try to accomplish your main goals with the least amount of excess baggage. With a large number of users, it is easy to become overwhelmed with a large number of suggestions or requests when the user community finds out that major changes are being planned. However, *for each additional task you add to your plan, you also add to the probability that something will go wrong.* So, after deciding on the basic goals, try to stick to only the tasks that will be needed for them and do not get sidetracked by unimportant issues that can be best settled at a later date.

However, you should consider this time to be an opportunity that can be used to incorporate new technologies or functionality into the network that otherwise would require additional downtime for the network. For example, if you are about to begin upgrading user workstations throughout a department or enterprise and you have been considering adopting DHCP, what better time to do so than now? If you are already going to put the user out of work for a short amount of time, and the workstation is off the network, this kind of situation is ideal for bringing in a new administrative tool such as DHCP.

Housekeeping is another function that can fit nicely into an upgrade plan: Out with the old and in with the new, so to speak. Old programs that never quite went away can be removed during an upgrade process. An upgrade can be a good time to set a deadline for users who have not yet abandoned older applications that can be better performed by newer applications.

Preventive Maintenance

SOME OF THE MAIN TOPICS IN THIS CHAPTER ARE

Power Conditioning and Uninterruptible Power Supplies (UPSs)

Network Monitoring

Server and Workstation Backups

Routine Maintenance

Build Redundancy into the Network

Disaster-Recovery Planning

Justify Preventive Maintenance

CHAPTER 4

Just as you go to your dentist a few times each year to get a check-up, you should build into a network procedures and mechanisms that work to prevent trouble from occurring in the first place, or that at least catch problems before they become too serious and impact users or affect the integrity of the data stored on the network. Preventive maintenance can range from something as simple as using an uninterruptible power supply (UPS) to something more time- and cost-intensive, such as completely replacing older equipment that is more prone to failure.

This chapter looks at some important preventive maintenance ideas to consider employing in your network. The size and composition of your network will determine which of the ideas in this chapter you should use. Not all are appropriate for every network. Some are prohibitively expensive for smaller networks. Yet, it is important to be aware of the possibilities so that as your network grows and you plan for upgrades, you also can make plans for additional procedures and devices that can protect the growing network from downtime and preserve your valuable data.

Power Conditioning and Uninterruptible Power Supplies (UPSs)

Without electricity, you have no network at all, and computers require a well-conditioned electrical source to function properly. The power supply in a computer can't handle an incoming spike of electricity caused by a lightning strike, for example. Similarly, a brownout, in which the voltage level drops for a short period of time, can cause a computer to crash.

Large-scale computer systems used in corporate environments, such as minicomputers or mainframes, also need a good source of power. To ensure this, most large computer rooms use a heavy-duty UPS to interface between the outside source of electricity and the computers and other devices in a computer room.

In most large computer rooms, for example, you'll find that computers—whether they're PC servers or larger systems—are rack-mounted in cabinets, along with tape drives, disk drives, and other peripheral equipment. The cabinet usually contains one or more power distribution units that are used to supply power to components mounted in the cabinet (see Figure 4.1).

As you can see from this figure, several computer systems and the tape drives they use are housed in a single cabinet. Two power distribution units located at the bottom of the cabinet supply power to all devices in the cabinet. These two power distribution units are configured in a dual-redundant manner so that if one fails the other continues to supply power to the cabinet. Each of these power distribution units is connected to a separate UPS in the computer room. This is important for several reasons. First, not all power failures are due to outside problems, such as a downed power line. Sometimes, UPSs themselves fail. An electrician might disconnect the wrong cable during routine maintenance or installation tasks. Sometimes, things just happen! You need to prepare for the unexpected.

To carry the concept further, each UPS in the computer room that the system uses is connected to a separate outside source of power. Thus, if a tree falls and knocks down a power line, an alternative power line is still feeding electricity into the computer room to redundant UPS systems. Because of this second source of power, computers and other devices on the network stay up and running.

Power Is Money

There is an old saying that "money is power." The opposite also is true.

The setup described in the previous section might seem extreme to a network administrator running a small network of PCs where some down time can be tolerated. However, in a high-availability computer environment—such as in a large corporation—the cost of down time can be prohibitively expensive for several reasons:

■ Hundreds or maybe thousands of employees remain idle while the computers they use are down. Employees are still being paid even though they can't work. Add up the dollars and you'll see that each minute of down time is expensive.

■ Customers might be unable to place orders or check on the status of existing orders. Fickle customers might just call someone else. No one likes to hear, "Our computer is down right now, please call back later." After your customer talks to another supplier, you might never hear from that customer again. So, you lose the current order, and possibly future business.

■ An unexpected system crash due to a power failure can cause corruption to data. After the power is restored, it can sometimes take hours (or even days) to determine which files are corrupted and then to restore them to a known state from backup tapes. This additional down time can potentially be more costly than the original power outage that caused it.

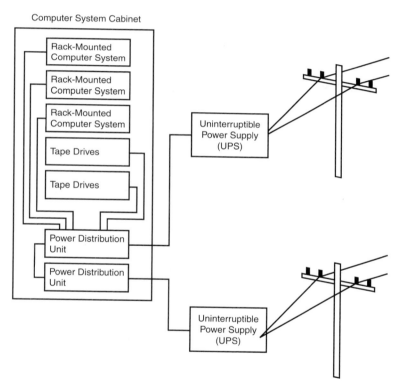

Figure 4.1 Several points in the power supply can be constructed to prevent a single point of failure for powering the network.

If you operate in a large-scale environment like this, you are probably already aware of how important it is to keep computer systems up and running. If you don't provide a steady, secure source of power up front, all your other preventive maintenance measures might prove of little value the next time the power goes out.

A UPS is not an eternal source of power. It is a conduit through which your external power source is routed before it makes it to your computer systems. UPSs operate by storing electricity in one or more batteries so that when the outside source of electricity is unexpectedly lost, the batteries can be switched into use in a few milliseconds. However, batteries can be used only for a limited amount of time. If you are using only a single UPS connected to a single power source, the UPS buys you the time needed to notify users to log off the systems affected and gracefully shut down the computers so that no data is compromised. Although you'll still have idle employees, you won't have to recover data after power has been restored.

Advanced Configuration and Power Interface (ACPI) and Standalone UPS Systems

For PCs and small servers, you can buy inexpensive UPS systems for a few hundred dollars that can be used in an environment in which down time can be tolerated but data corruption cannot. A typical UPS, such as one from American Power Conversion Corp. (APC), can be installed in just a few minutes. Depending on the model, it can provide both a battery backup and some power conditioning.

Be aware that power strips, even those that claim to be able to prevent power spikes from getting through, don't always work as claimed by the manufacturer. The inexpensive models you buy at local discount stores are notorious for not providing the protection they claim to provide. If you depend on the simple mechanics of a fuse or breaker in a cheap power strip to protect your computer, also plan on buying a new computer the next time lightning strikes. For true protection, you really need to spend the extra hundred dollars to get a small UPS for your server or other network devices if you don't use a large-scale UPS.

To allow you to gracefully shut down the operating system when the power goes out and the batteries take over, an industry initiative (involving major players such as Intel, Microsoft, and others) developed the Advanced Configuration and Power Interface (ACPI). ACPI covers a lot of territory, including power management for laptops and other computers. However, ACPI also allows a standard way for a standalone UPS to communicate with a computer and instruct it to shut down when the UPS battery supply takes over from the outside source of electricity.

This communication is accomplished by connecting not just the power cable from the computer to the power UPS, but also attaching a small cable (usually a serial cable) to the UPS and the computer system, and then enabling the UPS service in the operating system. Windows 2000 has a UPS service that you can run in conjunction with an attached UPS that supports APCI. The UPS communicates with the service and instructs the system to perform an orderly shutdown when the loss of power is detected and the batteries take over.

Things to look for in a small UPS include

- **Audible alarms**—I remember waking up to an alarm from my UPS several years ago to find out I was sleeping through a hurricane. Glad I had that UPS hooked up. Saved the computer; saved me!

- **Multiple outlets**—Most small UPSs allow you to connect two to four devices to the unit so you don't have to buy one for your computer, one for your printer, one for your router, and so on.

- **Battery indicators**—Be sure the UPS provides some mechanism (usually an indicator light) for notifying you when the battery is fully charged or is charging. Batteries (and UPSs) don't last forever. Additionally, an indicator light should let you know whether the unit is powering your system by battery power or the outside source.

- **Overload indicator**—Even though multiple outlets are available on a UPS, it might not be capable of supplying sufficient power to the devices you plug into it. A good UPS will indicate (again, usually with a light) that you are straining the UPS to its limit. In such a case, you'll need more than one UPS.

■ **Circuit Breaker**—If you choose to ignore an overload indicator, the UPS should be equipped with a circuit breaker, usually a small button that can be reset, to disconnect itself from the outside power source if you continue to attempt to pull more power through the unit than it can tolerate. When the UPS finds itself at risk, it can trip the breaker, use the battery for a power source, and then instruct your computer to shut down.

Although a large number of vendors manufacture and sell small UPS systems of this type, the Web site for American Power Conversion Corp. (http://www.apcc.com) has information (including documentation) for products that scale from the desktop to full-fledged computer room UPS systems.

As with power strips, when making a purchasing decision about a UPS system, you generally get what you pay for. Balance the cost of the unit with what it would cost you to replace the devices you are going to use it to protect, as well as the cost of down time, data corruption, and so on.

Network Devices

UPS systems aren't just for computers. After all, this book is about networking. Don't forget the routers, switches, and other devices in your network. Although it might be okay to let a printer be offline for a while during a power problem, it won't matter if your computers are up and running if users can't access them through the network. In a large computer room, routers and other such devices should be connected to plugs that terminate in the UPS. In a small office or home office environment, don't forget to connect your broadband switch/router to the UPS just like you do your computer.

Network Monitoring

The Simple Network Management Protocol (SNMP) and Remote Monitoring (RMON) protocol are powerful tools that can be used to manage a medium to large network. In a small LAN, such as in a home office, these capabilities are not needed. However, when a network is spread out over a large geographical area, or when a large number of network devices and computers are on the network, these two protocols can be used with management consoles to help you diagnose problems remotely and gather statistical information about your network. SNMP and RMON also can help you spot trouble before it becomes a real problem.

SNMP basically collects data about computers and other devices on the network, and is used with a management console application to provide a central reporting station. RMON is similar to SNMP but supports additional features, especially on the remote devices. By choosing a good management station application, you can set up thresholds for certain events (such as network traffic, errors, and other statistical information) so that automatic alerts are issued to warn you when something is amiss.

Note

SNMP and RMON are covered more fully in Chapter 44, "Network Testing and Analysis Tools."

Server and Workstation Backups

Ever lose your address book? Did you have another copy? I guess I'm showing my age again, because most people who have computers don't use an address book, but instead store that information on their laptop or possibly a personal digital assistant (PDA). So let me rephrase the question. Ever lose the data on your PC? Did you have a backup? Trivial as it might seem, this is about the most important point to be made in this chapter.

Nothing will save your neck more often than a good backup of all computer systems in your network. It doesn't matter whether you've spent hundreds of thousands of dollars (or even millions) getting state-of-the art RAID (Redundant Array of Independent Disk) disk arrays that have multiple copies of data stored on separate disks. Many financial institutions even have online mirroring of data between distant geographical sites to prevent a natural disaster from causing loss of data. However, no matter how well you prepare your online storage to be fully redundant, there are other reasons you should establish a good schedule of regular backups of all important data on the computer systems in your network.

It's a RAID!

Actually, when the concepts were first developed, RAID stood for Redundant Array of *Inexpensive* Disks. Obviously, the name has been changed because most disks used in large-scale RAID systems are anything but inexpensive! If you want to know more about RAID techniques, from simple disk mirroring to disk striping, and combinations of the two, visit the Web site at `http://www.raid-advisory.com/`. This is the home Web page for the RAID Advisory Board, a group whose members include manufacturers, testing organizations, universities, and others. You'll find excellent documentation here for the various flavors of RAID technology that have been developed.

Also, when purchasing RAID solutions from a vendor, keep in mind that the buzzword "RAID" doesn't have to imply that the solution offered will protect your data. RAID is an overall encompassing term for several different disk technologies, some of which are concerned with preserving multiple copies of data, such as disk mirroring, whereas others are concerned with fast read or write access, such as disk striping. Combinations of the two are usually employed in an environment that requires fast access to online storage with provisions for data protection.

For example, even if you use disk mirroring and other RAID techniques, what are you going to do if a meteor falls out of the sky and lands on your computer room? Boom! There goes all your computers, your data, and, of course, a few operators. You can replace the computers and the operators (with a little training, of course), but can you replace the data?

For a more practical reason to perform frequent, regular backups, just think of your users. When's the last time a user deleted a file (or worse yet, a directory of files) and asked you to restore them? Backups can protect you not only from computer failures and natural (or unnatural disasters), but also from the users on your system.

Nothing can substitute for a good backup, short of a new job (job security tends to drop some if you lose months of corporate data).

Backup Media—Tape, Optical Storage, and CD-R

The standard mechanism used by most sites to create backups of computer data is magnetic tape. You'll find all sorts of tape backup devices, ranging from QIC (quarter-inch tape) cartridges to the more modern high-capacity Digital Linear Tape (DLT) cartridges. You might even still see the old-fashioned, reel-to-reel nine-track tape laying around a computer. However, you should choose the backup media based on several things:

- Is the backup needed for the short or long term?
- If a restore is necessary, can the backup media perform up to your expectations?
- How expensive is the backup media?
- Do you need to exchange data with other sites, such as companies that provide a disaster recovery hot site?

If you have data that is transient and you only need to recover your systems to a known state that doesn't go far back in time, you can use many kinds of backup media. Most likely, your choice will depend on the speed at which you want to create backups and the speed at which the data can be restored. In this case, tape is probably your best choice. High-speed magnetic tape solutions are available that can back up and restore many gigabytes per hour. Magnetic tape also is good for short-term to long-term storage, provided it is cared for properly as specified by its manufacturer. However, for long-term storage, be sure to pick media that can be used in standard devices. For example, nine-track tapes were used for a long time as the standard in the industry for computer backups. However, if you are required to keep backups for several years due to regulatory requirements, for example, be sure you also keep around tape drives that can be used to read back the data stored on those tapes!

Note

At one of my jobs I recently watched the company spend a large sum of money to transfer a large stock of old nine-track tapes to more modern DLT media. Occasionally, a tape was found that was unreadable; however, most of the data was recovered and is now sitting in storage awaiting the next expensive conversion.

For long-term storage, you really don't have much choice because technology is changing so fast. However, be sure to look for a backup technology that is from a reliable manufacturer, who you expect to be in business for a few years to come.

In an emergency, the amount of time required to restore data from a backup can be more important than the amount of time it takes to create the backup in the first place.

For example, it might be possible to break a mirror set cleanly, use one of the mirrored disks to create a backup, and then re-create the mirror set using the software provided by your RAID subsystem. This allows your users to continue using the system with minimal interference from the backup process. If you use a disk-mirroring setup that uses three or more mirrored disks for each mirror set, you can still provide for fault-tolerance while the backup is being produced because multiple disks in the system contain copies of the current data.

Restoring data to a RAID subsystem might take longer than the backup, or it might proceed along at the same rapid pace, depending on the disk controllers, device firmware, and other factors. When choosing a backup solution, don't forget that you need to consider the opposite of the backup: the restore. You might purchase a high-tech, whiz-bang disk subsystem that supports many different levels of RAID techniques, including online backup. However, if the time needed to restore data to multiple disks takes significantly longer than it does to restore to a single disk, you might want to consider an alternative solution.

When the absolute worst thing that can happen happens—your site is down, not just the computers, due to some disaster such as a fire, for example—you must be sure that the backup media you have is compatible with the equipment you will use in a disaster-recovery scenario. This is easy to overlook when shopping around for an off-site, hot-site provider. In this kind of situation, don't take the vendor's word for it. Test it. Take your backup tapes to the hot site and perform a restore. Time the restore. Be sure the media you are using is compatible with the hot site, and be sure the tape drives (or other media drives) are fast enough to get you back up and running in a short amount of time.

Magnetic tape is not the only backup method available today. You'll find a wide assortment of media, from magnetic-optical discs to ordinary CD-R and CD-RW discs being used. The problem with the latter is that CD-R (and RW) discs are still extremely slow (by magnitudes) when compared to the speed at which magnetic tape can be used, for both the backup and the restore process. However, recordable CD technology offers a rather inexpensive method for backing up a computer system if you only need to back up a selected set of files. Because discs are now measured in units of gigabytes, and CD-R discs in megabytes, you should consider this technology only for situations such as a small office or home office where you just need to put a small amount of data in offline storage for backup purposes.

For example, by using CD-RW discs, which can be added to, erased, and reused, it's possible when using the appropriate software to copy important files to the disc occasionally and then store it away. You can do this with many of the popular CD-burner software packages on the market today. Microsoft Windows XP also includes CD-burning technology built-in to the operating system. Using Windows XP, you can use Windows Explorer to drag and drop files to a CD-RW drive at will. For earlier versions of Windows, you'll need to buy third-party software for this.

Backup Rotation Schedules

When you create backups, first determine what data needs to be backed up and how long it must be accessible for restore purposes. If you have a volatile environment in which data older than a few weeks or months is no longer of use, you won't need to keep tapes or other media in long-term storage. However, for most companies, it's important to be able to produce data from months if not years ago to meet financial or regulatory requirements. In this case, you should create a backup rotation schedule that is appropriate for your needs.

For example, you might perform a full backup of all the data on your systems each night. Or, you might want to produce a full backup once a week, and then produce incremental backups during the week—that is, to back up only the files that have changed since the full backup. Using the combination of the full backup and the incremental backup media, you can restore the system to the state it was in at any of the backup points.

In this kind of situation, when the next full backup is performed, the incremental backups might no longer be needed. If that is the case, you can reuse these tapes. The rate at which tapes or other media can be reused is called the *rotation schedule*. A good generic policy (depending on your environment, of course) is to create a weekly backup of all data, and perform incremental backups during the week. This allows you to schedule the full backup for a time (such as the weekend) when it won't impact your users. The weekly incremental backup media can be reused during the next week if the next full backup is successful.

The full backups done on a weekly basis can be stored for a month and then reused. Additionally, you might want to keep one of the end-of-month full backups for long-term storage, depending on the nature of your applications.

Whatever rotation schedule you decide to use for your backup media, be sure that it meets the needs of your users and the applications they use.

Off-Site Storage

The backup media is only helpful if it's safely stored as well. If you only need to restore a file because a user has made a mistake and deleted it, having a tape stored in the computer room makes this a quick and easy job. Pop the tape in the tape drive, restore the file, and then call the user. However, storing backup tapes in the same place that you house your computers is not always such a good idea. For example, this might not help you in the event of some kind of disaster, such as a fire. Not only are your computers lost, but your backups are gone as well.

For important data, the backup media should be sent to an off-site storage location as soon as practical after the backup has finished. In this scenario, if a disaster strikes your site, your tapes are safely stored away at another site and you can use them to recover when you move to a hot site or when you replace the destroyed equipment.

That said, what constitutes off-site storage? You can use several different places for off-site storage, depending on your needs. Consider first how safe the storage site is. Second, consider the amount of time it takes to retrieve the backup media. Third, consider the expense involved. Some sites to consider:

- A company whose business is to pick up, store, and deliver backup media. There are a large number of companies in this business. Be sure to visit their storage site to be sure that the storage conditions are conducive to long-term storage of sensitive backup media. Test the promised restore time window by requesting the retrieval of tapes now and then. Be sure that the site offers 24-hour access to your data.

- If you employ the service of a hot site that can be used to re-create your computer system or network during a disaster, the hot site vendor often can provide services for off-site storage of backup media. In this case, you can save time during an emergency because you won't have to retrieve the tapes from a third party when you activate the hot site.

- If you are a large company, it might be practical to store your backup media at another company site. The odds of a disaster striking multiple sites at the same time should be taken into consideration, as well as the storage conditions at the other site. For example, if both sites are within close proximity of each other, this might not be a good idea. Something as simple as a hurricane or flood might cause a disaster at both places. Consider also the expense in having to regularly send tapes to your other company site. It might be less expensive to pay a professional service to store your tapes than to have employees transferring tapes from one site to another.

- Take the tapes home and stick them under your bed. This is no joke. I once worked at a small company in which the system manager would take the monthly backup home and store it under his bed until the next month. Along the same lines, if you operate a small office at home, you might consider taking your weekly or monthly backup tape to a safety deposit box at your local bank for off-site storage. The point is to make sure that the data is stored away from the computer system so that you can reduce the odds of a disaster from destroying both your systems and your backups.

Routine Maintenance

Although the title of this chapter is "Preventive Maintenance," routine maintenance for computers and network devices needs to be performed on a regular basis. Routine maintenance helps prevent hardware failures due to fatigued or old equipment that breaks down. For example, although all computers, from the small desktop to the large rack-mounted systems, use fans to ensure the smooth flow of air through the system to keep components from overheating, you should periodically be sure dust and other contaminants are not being sucked into the system where electrical charges can cause them to adhere to system components.

Opening the system box and using canned air to get rid of this kind of contamination can be a good preventive technique to use once or twice a year. If you have a home office, this is easily overlooked. If you have a smoker at home, for example, you'll find that cigarette smoke can produce a fine layer of dust on computer components over time. This can also happen, as I know from experience, with cat hair. Don't leave the box closed forever. Open it up and look inside now and then to clean things up.

Tape drives need to be cleaned periodically because the magnetic tape comes in contact with the tape heads inside the unit. A cleaning tape should be run on a schedule recommended by the manufacturer. DLT tape drives usually have an indicator light that comes on when a sufficient amount of contamination has accumulated on the tape head so that parity errors are occurring. If the cleaning tape light comes on more frequently than the cleaning schedule recommended by the manufacturer, you might want to consider looking at which backup tapes were used just before this happened. You might have an old tape that needs to be discarded.

Build Redundancy into the Network

It doesn't matter what kind of support maintenance contract you have with your vendor if it takes them hours or days to get the parts necessary to replace a failed system. For this reason, it's a good idea to build redundant paths in your network from the design phase, so that, for example, if a router goes down, another path through the network will allow users to keep accessing the data they need. Providing for fault-tolerant servers using clustering technology also can be used to ensure maximum uptime for critical systems.

If the time needed to get replacements is excessive (when compared to the cost of paying idle users, the overhead involved in office space, and so on), it might be wise to keep a duplicate device on-site so you can swap it into service to replace a failed device in an emergency. In the case of a router or switch, it's easy to replace the failed device, follow a carefully written plan to reconfigure it, and put the network path back in service.

Disaster-Recovery Planning

Nothing (other than a backup) is more helpful during an emergency than a well thought out disaster-recovery plan. Actually, this is an overall term because you should plan for a variety of disasters, from the loss of a single disk drive, to the loss of a single computer system, to the loss of your entire network. Chapter 2, "Network Design Strategies," stressed that you should always document the network and its components. Disaster-recovery procedures should be part of this documentation.

The problem with disasters is that you can't schedule them. They don't always occur during normal business hours when you are wide awake and functioning well. In the middle of the night after a long day at work, you might get called in to restore a system without having the advantage of a good night's sleep. A good disaster-recovery plan can be helpful if only to keep you from making a mistake during the recovery process.

A good disaster recovery plan includes several items:

- Contact information for key personnel that need to be involved in the recovery effort, as well as personnel who need to be informed of the event, such as application client representatives.

- Contact information for vendors of both the hardware and software components of the system or network. This should include both technical support telephone numbers as well as contact information for local field personnel who might need to come in and assist you with setting up or repairing the damage.

- Step-by-step procedures for remedying the situation. This can involve such things as how to completely rebuild a particular computer system from scratch by reinstalling the operating system and applying the backup tapes. Configuration information for routers and other devices should be documented in the recovery plan.

- After the disaster has been remedied according to your plan, there needs to be a set of tests you can perform on the operating system, the hardware, and the applications to ensure that the recovery effort has been successful.

Justify Preventive Maintenance

Some of the things that have been discussed in this chapter are expensive. Because of this, you might experience problems obtaining funding from upper management for these items. You can do several things to help yourself out in these situations.

First, document all the down time you experience for each system in the network, and try to associate a cost with it. Although you might not be able to get data that allows you to show the impact on your customers, you usually can determine the number of users who are impacted. Assuming that these users can perform only a certain percentage of their daily work without access to the computer or network, try to assign the number of hours lost due to the down time and multiply it by an average hourly rate for the employees affected by the down time. Most likely, you won't have access to accurate pay rates for other employees. However, a way to get around this is to multiply the hours times the minimum hourly wage and show this to upper management if it results in a significant amount. Point out that you've based your costing on the minimum wage. Because upper management is more likely to know the average salaries of experienced computer users, this figure still gives them a good idea of what down time costs. In other words, if you come up with a large figure during your calculations based on the minimum wage, they'll quickly determine that the actual figure is magnitudes larger than that and you just might get support for your preventive maintenance efforts.

The Physical Network

PART II

Wiring the Network—Cables and Other Components

CHAPTER 5

Bridging the gap between the stated standards and the actual implementation of bringing a network to a user's desktop workstation is not the simple task that you might expect. Connecting tens, hundreds, or even thousands of small computers together can become an exercise in futility if proper planning is not done. Planning and installing your cable plant carefully is vital for ease of future upgrading and expanding your network.

◄◄ For more information about the planning necessary for a successful network implementation, see Chapter 1, "Overview of Network Topologies," and Chapter 2, "Network Design Strategies."

This chapter covers quite a few technical details that relate to the network cables that make up your network. Although the definitions and other material that you'll find in this chapter might seem overwhelming at first, this chapter is a good reference when you encounter some of these terms later in the book.

Structured Wiring

In the 1980s, the Telecommunications Industry Association (TIA) and the Electronics Industries Association (EIA) formed a task force to establish a set of standards for installing network wiring in buildings. The first draft was completed in 1991 and became known as EIA/TIA-568. The current version is 568B, which includes the documents for standards covering structured wiring, cables, the network topology, connectors and hardware, electrical performance specifications, physical termination, and support mechanisms.

The 568B standard describes the physical layout and specifications for the physical plant as it relates to the various topological standards.

The equivalent document in Canada is CSAT 529. The International Organization for Standardization (ISO) currently is working on cabling standards for international use. This document is ISO/IDC 11801 (generic cabling for customer premises wiring). Even if you are very familiar with computers, you might never have heard of EIA/TIA-568, but the resulting efforts of the standards affect you every time you use your network.

Before we begin looking at the standard, it is important that you understand a few of the terms which are used in the standard.

The Work Area

The work area specification of the standard includes the telecommunications outlet (that is, the faceplate into which you plug your computer's network cable at your desk), which serves as the work area interface to the cabling system. Work area equipment includes cables used to connect to the telecommunications outlet. These cables now are included within the scope of 568B.1 and 11801. The following are the work area cabling specifications:

- Equipment cords are assumed to have the same performance as patch cords in the same typing category.

- When used, adapters are assumed to be compatible with the transmission capabilities of the equipment to which they connect.

- Horizontal cable links are specified with the assumption that a maximum cable length of 5 meters (16 feet) is used for equipment cords in the work area. This can depend on the actual length of cabling used to connect the work area back to the wiring closet. The important factor to remember is that there is a maximum distance that all cables can add up to, depending on your topology.

The Backbone Cabling System Structure

The backbone cabling system of the standard provides interconnections between telecommunication rooms, equipment rooms, and entrance facilities (see Figure 5.1).

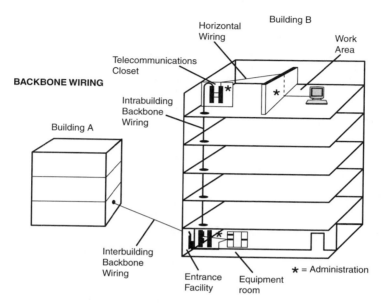

Figure 5.1   The backbone of the network includes the cables that connect different areas of the network.

This cabling system includes backbone cables, intermediate and main cross connects, mechanical terminations, and patch cords or jumpers used for backbone-to-backbone cross connections. The backbone also extends between buildings in a campus environment.

There are some points specified for the backbone of the cabling system:

- Equipment connections to the backbone cabling should be made with cable lengths of 30 meters or less.

- The backbone of cabling should be configured as a star topology.

- The backbone is limited to no more than two hierarchical levels of cross connects—main and intermediate. No more than one cross connect can exist between a main and a horizontal cross connect, and no more than three cross connects can exist between any two horizontal cross connects.

- A total coax backbone distance of 90 meters is specified for high-bandwidth capability over copper. This distance is for uninterrupted backbone runs.

- The distance between terminations in the entrance facility and main cross connect should be documented and made available to a service provider.

- Recognized media can be used individually or in a combination, as required by the installation.

- Multipair cable is allowed, as long as it satisfies the requirement of a minimum of cross-talk.

- The proximity of cabling to sources of electromagnetic interference should be taken into account.

- Cross connects for different cable types must be located in the same facility.

Note that in the specification, bridge taps and splitters are not allowed.

Tip

A *bridge tap* is an extraneous piece of cabling that is left over from a previous connection to a communications line. If not removed, a bridge tap acts similarly to an antenna, and causes impedance mismatches and other problems with the signal that travels down the copper wire. Bridge taps are one of the reasons why it can be difficult to obtain DSL service from your local phone company. As phones are added to your local loop and then disconnected, many dangling wires can be left behind because it's simply too costly to remove them. In a properly cabled network, bridge taps should not exist at all.

Splitters are devices that are used to separate higher frequencies from lower frequencies on a copper wire. Again, splitters serve no purpose on a properly cabled LAN. However, on the public switched telephone network (PSTN), splitters can be installed to make it possible to obtain voice-grade telephone service and DSL service using the same copper wire pair.

For more about DSL, see Chapter 19, "Dedicated Connections."

Horizontal Cabling System Structure

The horizontal cabling system (shown in Figure 5.2) extends from the telecommunications outlet in the work area and terminates in a horizontal cross connect in the telecommunications room. It includes the telecommunications outlet.

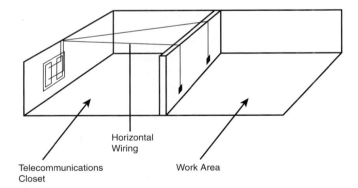

Horizontal Wiring

Telecommunications Closet

Work Area

Figure 5.2   The horizontal cabling extends from the telecommunications closet to the user's work area.

The distance covered by the horizontal cabling is limited by the network topology chosen for your network. For example, in most ethernet networks, this distance is 90 meters.

Telecommunications Room

Telecommunications rooms generally are considered to be floor-serving facilities for horizontal cable distribution. They also are used for intermediate and main cross connects. The telecommunications room is where you place patch panels, as well as hubs or switches that are used to connect individual workstations or servers to the network backbone.

Star Topology

A hierarchical topology is used to connect the various telecommunications closets and equipment rooms. Between the horizontal cross connect there can be only one additional cross connect before reaching the main cross connect.

◀◀   Chapter 1 discusses the hierarchical nature of a modern network topology, including the star topology.

Physical Cable Types

Much attention is given to the specifications used for ethernet and token-ring networks. Most of these specifications deal with the physical makeup of the cabling involved in connecting the individual components of the network. Understanding the cable types; the number of wires in a cable, both shielded or unshielded varieties; and several other electrical factors is critical to successfully upgrading or maintaining your network system. The type of cable you use depends on the type of LAN you are creating. The connectors, terminations, and distances that can be covered by particular cable types will be a determining factor in the kind of LAN you can create. For example, an ethernet network card and a token-ring card can use different connectors and cables.

Important Definitions

When discussing network cables and troubleshooting wiring problems, there are several important terms and concepts to understand.

Attenuation to Cross Talk Ratio (ACR)

ACR is a critical factor in determining the capability of an unshielded twisted-pair cable or screened twisted-pair cable. Attenuation to cross-talk ratio (ACR) is the value of the attenuation less the cross-talk value, both expressed in decibels (db) at a particular frequency. This is a quality factor for cabling. Before you can understand this ratio, you need to understand what the term attenuation means.

Attenuation

Attenuation is the decrease in magnitude of the signal as it travels through any transmitting medium, such as wire or glass. Attenuation is measured as a logarithm of the ratio between the input and output power or between the input or output voltage of the system. It's expressed in db. All good things must come to an end, and this is the case with electricity. As the signal travels down the copper wire (or the fiber-optic cable), some of the signal is lost. This is why it is necessary in a network topology to impose specific limits on the lengths of cable that you can use. After you get past certain limits imposed by a particular topology, the signal becomes so degraded that it cannot be reliably interpreted at the destination.

Figure 5.3 shows that attenuation occurs as the signal travels down the wire. The amplitude of the electrical signal decreases the farther it travels from the transmitting side of the communications channel.

Bandwidth

Bandwidth is the range of frequencies required for proper transmission of a signal. This is expressed in hertz (Hz) as a difference of frequencies.

Characteristic Impedance

Characteristic impedance is the value of impedance (a combination of resistance and reactance) of a transmission line measured over a specific frequency range. Impedance is expressed in units of Z, because it is a calculation based on both resistance and reactance of the network media. Whereas resistance is the capability of a medium to resist the transmission of electrons, reactance is another thing altogether. Reactance, for alternating current (AC), is the medium's tendency to store and then release the current as it flows through the medium.

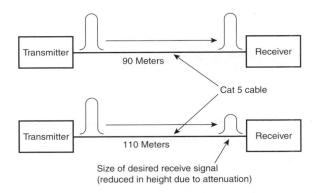

Figure 5.3 An electrical signal degrades as it travels through a copper cable (attenuation).

Cross-Talk

Cables are made up of two or more copper wires that are bundled together with an outer cover so that it's easier to route them through the conduits that form the path your physical network takes. The coupling of signals from one pair of wires in a cable to another pair of wires in the same cable actually can interfere with each other. The electrical signal in a copper wire not only travels down that particular wire, but also *radiates out* and can interfere with other copper wires in the same cable or bundle. This is called cross-talk. This coupling also can occur between wires of different cables that are close to one another. In Figure 5.4, you can see that some of the signal has radiated from one wire and produced noise on another.

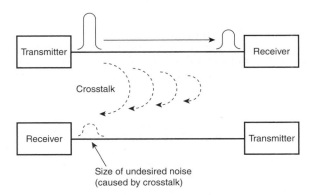

Figure 5.4 A portion of an electrical signal radiates from an adjacent wire, producing interference (cross-talk).

Dialectic

To keep the individual copper wires separated from each other within a cable, an insulating material called *dialectic material* is used. It can be a simple plastic nonconducting material, or a more complex formulation in some high-capacity wire bundles.

Electromagnetic Field

As electrons move through a medium, two fields associated with this movement exist. These are electric fields and magnetic fields. These fields exist at varying distances from the conductors (the wires) as they are brought closer together.

Electromagnetic Interference

Electromagnetic interference (EMI) refers to the interference electromagnetic signals produce by frequent changes of electrons moving through certain media. Network wiring and equipment can be very susceptible to EMI, and they also emit EMI.

Far-End Cross-Talk (FEXT)

Far-end cross-talk occurs between two twisted pairs of the cable at the far end of the cable from the measuring source. The transmitting end of a cable pair produces the stronger electrical signal (because the signal attenuates, or becomes weaker, as it passes through the copper wire), so FEXT can be a more difficult problem to tackle. However, you need to be sure that connectors are properly created at the far end of a connection to prevent interference between copper wires at that point. The signal might be weaker at the end point of a connection, yet it still exists. This is why the specifications allow only a very small amount of exposed copper wire when connecting a cable to an actual connector (such as an RJ-45 jack).

Frequency

Frequency is a measurement of the number of times a periodic action occurs in a measure of time. In terms of alternating current, this is the number of cycles per second and is usually expressed in hertz.

Full-Duplex and Half-Duplex Communication

Full-duplex communications means that communications between two network nodes can occur in both directions simultaneously. Obviously, this is a communications method in which both transmitted and received signals are not simultaneously present. They alternate in time on the transmission medium. In *half-duplex communications*, only one side of the communications line can transmit at any point in time.

Impedance

Impedance is the total resistance and reactance offered by a circuit component. The units are expressed in ohms. The common symbol for impedance is Z. This is a complex numerical value, mathematically expressed as either a complex number or as the polar coordinate number.

Impedance Match

Impedance match is a condition in which the impedance of a device or wiring system is matched to another wiring system or device.

Leakage

Leakage is the undesirable passage of current through an insulator or over the surface of a conductor. This can occur in older cable bundles where the insulating material has become degraded over time and signals from one wire in the bundle interfere with signals in other wires in the same bundle.

Near-End Cross-Talk (NEXT)

Near-end cross-talk is cross-talk that occurs between two twisted pairs measured at the same location, and it usually occurs between wires in a twisted-pair cable. One of the conditions that can introduce this interference is a crushed cable, so care must be used when pulling network cabling and attaching connectors.

Nominal Velocity of Propagation

Nominal velocity of propagation is the speed at which a signal travels through a medium expressed as a decimal fraction of the speed of light in a vacuum.

Power SUM

Power SUM is a measured parameter that includes the sum of the contributions of power from all pairs of a cable system, excluding the pair under test. This is done with all the other pairs of the cable having signals present.

Radio Frequency

Radio frequencies are frequencies in the electromagnetic spectrum that are used for radio communications. These generally occur above 300 KHz.

Radio Frequency Interference (RFI)

Radio frequency interference is electromagnetic interference at radio frequencies.

Shield

A *shield* is a metallic foil or wire screen-mesh that encircles a cable or wires in a cable to prevent electromagnetic or radio frequency fields from entering or leaving a cable. This prevents interference with other cables in the same cable bundle or cables that are in close proximity to the shielded cable. You've probably heard the term STP used in connection with network cables. This is an abbreviation for shielded twisted-pair cabling, typically found in Token Ring networks.

Signal to Noise Ratio

This is the ratio of received signal level to received noise level in a system. It is expressed in decibels and is abbreviated as S/N. The higher S/N ratio, the better B-channel performance.

Time Domain Reflectometry (TDR)

Time domain reflectometry is a method of measuring cable length or faults by timing the period between a test pulse and its reflection from an impedance discontinuity on the cable.

Waveform

Waveform is the amplitude of the signal over time.

Wavelength

Wavelength is the distance between successive identical peaks of a waveform in a transmission medium.

Physical Cable Types

The most basic and common wire type used for LAN wiring is twisted-pair wiring. This wire type also is referred to as unshielded twisted-pair, or UTP. This wire is a derivative of the more common cable that was used in telephone installations in most commercial facilities for years. This type is versatile, easy to install, and has favorable performance characteristics. It comes in a variety of colors, wire gauges, insulation materials, twisting methods, and outer jacket materials.

The basic cable assembly for UTP cable can contain a large number of conductors (or copper wires). Most conductors are grouped into pairs that are twisted around each other. Telephone cables are available in 2, 4, 6, 25, 100, and even larger groupings of conductors. Most of the cable that is used for LAN wiring comes as cable consisting of four pairs of wires.

The four-pair cable has become a standard and is referenced in the EIA/TIA-568B cabling standards. This is the cable around which most of the cable standards and performance tests are based. Several of the LAN topology configurations use only two of the four-wire pairs; however, several use all four pairs. Another common cable type that is found in twisted-pair installations is a 25-pair jumper cable. This cable type is primarily used between patch panels and connector type punch down blocks.

The main difference between typical telephone wiring and LAN wiring is the grading of the assembly of the twisted pairs within the cable. The primary factor that differentiates one cable type from another is the amount of twists per foot that each individual pair of conductors has within the cable. The twisting of the individual pairs to the cable is significant. The twisting of the two wires has a twofold effect electrically on the cable assembly. First, it causes the interline capacitance to be reduced. This is a good thing because the reduction of capacitance reduces any signal shorting between the conductors at high frequencies. Second, twisting the wire couples the electromagnetic fields equally, thus canceling out any interfering signals. This operation is referred to as a balanced transmission. One effect of achieving a balanced transmission is that the high frequencies of a LAN signal do not interfere with the other devices. Some radiation of the signal does occur, but the transmitted signal is kept to a low amplitude, so random emissions remain within acceptable limits.

Typically, wire sizes for UTP cable range between 18 AWG and 32 AWG. AWG is the abbreviation for American wire gauge. This wire gauge is the standard for sizing wires in American manufacturing. Wire size is based primarily on the current carrying capacity of the wire set by the National Electrical Code. As the wire gauge increases, the physical diameter of the wire decreases. So, a number 10 AWG wire is physically smaller than a number 8 AWG wire. Number 10 AWG wire is approximately 0.1 inch in diameter and usually can carry approximately 30 amps of current.

So, for telephone wiring or LAN wiring, the number 18 AWG wire is much larger than the 32 AWG wire. Common sizes for LAN wiring are typically 22 to 24 AWG. This wire is typically solid, not stranded, for ease in termination on insulation displacement connectors (IDCs).

As mentioned previously, the twisting of the wire pairs of conductors that make up cables is important—so important that the cable used for LAN wiring is graded into categories. Category 1 was used for POTS (or plain old telephone service). Category 2 was used in early networking wiring schemes, such as ARCnet, and for connecting terminals to multiuser computer networks. Category 3 uses four twists per foot and is still graded for operating as a LAN wiring system. Category 3 is rated for speeds up to 16MHz and is still used as a cable in token-ring systems. Category 4 is rated up to 20 MHz. Category 5, which was until recently the de facto standard for LAN wiring, has now been replaced by a new category.

Category 5 is rated for up to 100 MHz operation. The new Gigabyte Ethernet standard can use existing Category 5 installations as long as the cables, links, and components are tested to 100 MHz and additional parameters of equal level far-end cross-talk (ELFEXT) loss and return loss. To ensure additional cross-talk headroom for robust application support, 568B also specifies power sum cross-talk. This is because the Fast Ethernet topology actually only requires fundamental bandwidths to 33 MHz because of the complex encoding of the signals used, and all four pair are used to keep the frequency requirements very low.

A new transmission characteristics standard is designated as Category 5E. This is referenced to 568B.1 and B.2 and additional Class D requirements of the ISO/IEC 11801. These requirements are a specified tunable frequency limit of 100 MHz and are a superset of Category 5 and Class D.

During the first quarter of 2001, Category 6 cabling was certified for use as a standard. Transmission characteristics are specified up to 250 MHz. Also classified as Class E according to ISO/IEC, this cable probably will represent the last generation of unshielded twisted-pair cabling that is used in LAN wiring. This cable is different from the standard UTP cable because it contains filler material to separate the twisted pairs from each other, and thereby reduces cross-talk between wire pairs. One of the biggest problems with imposing higher frequencies through the pairs of the cables is that adjacent conductor capacitance is reduced and cross-talk increases. Separating these conductors reduces this capacitance and cross-talk. This also is a consideration when installing cables because if cables are bundled too tightly there can be resulting chance of interference of data signals between individual cables. Hence, modern standard practice dictates that when cables are installed, they are to be installed with either loose cable ties or Velcro straps.

A new category, Category 7 UTP cabling, offers a different approach to twisted-pair cabling architecture. The cable is assembled with an overall shield and individually shielded pairs. The most significant improvement with this type of cable will be in the higher performance bandwidth achieved. Cable rating will be up to 600 MHz. There likely will be a new interface design—jack and plug. There also will be a requirement that this new category be backward-compatible with lower-performance categories and classes. It is interesting to note that TIA is not actively developing a standard for Category 7. This organization probably will try to assimilate a standard with class F standards put forth by the ISO.

Performance Comparison

The choice of cabling insulation material is important. Requirements set forth in the National Electrical Code (NEC) specifically and stringently place requirements on the type of cable insulation allowed in certain portions of buildings. There's an increasing use of large amounts of cable for LAN wiring, and the place where these are usually installed is above drop ceilings and below computer room floors. Unfortunately, these areas are most often used to handle cooling and environmental air. Conventional wire installations installed in these locations were found to be flammable at the very least, and at their worst, would produce toxic gases that would be carried with the cooling or environmental air, thus placing people in the other parts of the building at risk. Additionally, fire can actually be spread through the plenum.

Manufacturers soon developed cable installations that were less flammable and could be used in plenum-rated areas. The National Electrical Code differentiates cable types by voltage, power classifications, and insulation types. It should be noted that there is a definite difference between plenum- and riser-rated cable. It would seem that riser-rated cable would be higher classified than plenum-rated cable, because riser-rated cable is intended for use in vertical shafts that run between floors. The shafts are not normally used to handle environmental or cooling air except in ductwork. Thus, the cable installed in risers does not have to have insulation rated as stringently as that for cabling installed in plenum-rated areas.

The special requirements for cabling insulation and power ratings are covered in detail in the NFPA National Electrical Code Sections 770 and 800, for those who want to pursue these details further.

Color Coding and Marking

Each pair of wires in a twisted-pair cable assembly is color coded so that each wire can be identified at each end of the cable assembly and terminated properly. This color code is shown in Figure 5.5.

Figure 5.5 Wire pairs in a cable are color coded.

As you can see, each pair of the cable is color coded in a complementary fashion. Pair one wires are color coded white-blue and blue-white. The blue-white wire has as its base color blue insulation with a white stripe molded at intervals along its length. The stripe is sometimes called a tracer. The white-blue wire is color coded in reverse, with a white wire that has a blue tracer. The color code is unique for each pair and is repetitive.

The color coding is important in LAN wiring because the system signals are polarity-sensitive. If pairs on the cable are reversed, the signals are reversed and this causes a failure in the receiving equipment. The terms *tip* and *ring*, used to designate the polarity of each pair of wires, stem from the days of the old telephone patch panels. The equipment used consisted of quarter-inch phone plugs, which fit into corresponding jacks on a patch board or switchboard. The switchboard plug consisted of two parts. The tip of the plug was wired through the sleeve or ring of the plug. The plug used on audio equipment and musical instruments is the same plug. The primary color was wired to the ring and the secondary color was wired to the tip.

As mentioned before, there is also a use for 25-pair jumper cable. This color code, broken down by pair, is shown in Table 5.1.

Table 5.1   Color Coding for a 25-Pair Jumper Cable As Specified By the ICEA

Tip Color	Pair	Ring
white/blue	pair 1	blue/white
white/orange	pair 2	orange/white
white/green	pair 3	green/white
white/brown	pair 4	brown/white
white/slate	pair 5	slate/white
red/blue	pair 6	blue/red
red/orange	pair 7	orange/red
red/green	pair 8	green/red
red/brown	pair 9	brown/red
red/slate	pair 10	slate/red
black/blue	pair 11	blue/black
black/orange	pair 12	orange/black
black/green	pair 13	green/black
black/brown	pair 14	brown/black
black/slate	pair 15	slate/black
yellow/blue	pair 16	blue/yellow
yellow/orange	pair 17	orange/yellow

Table 5.1   continued

Tip Color	Pair	Ring
yellow/green	pair 18	green/yellow
yellow/brown	pair 19	brown/yellow
yellow/slate	pair 20	slate/yellow
violet/blue	pair 21	blue/violet
violet/orange	pair 22	orange/violet
violet/green	pair 23	green/violet
violet/brown	pair 24	brown/violet
violet/slate	pair 25	slate/violet

This cable must be rated for the category for which it's to be used. Physically, it mostly is used between patch panels and punch down blocks, or between patch panels to patch panel installations. Cable sizes above 25 pairs are usually in groups of 25-pair cables. Each of these groups of cables is marked within the larger bundle with a wrapped colored leader that, by design, is color coded with the same color code that is used on the twisted-pair cabling scheme. Thus, on a 50-pair cable, which would have two 25-pair cables, the 25-pair bundle has an outer spiral wrap of a blue plastic streamer, while the second group of 25 has a group wrapped with an orange streamer. This color code can be repeated ad infinitum for a very large group of 25-pair cables.

Coaxial Cables

Coaxial cables are the original LAN cable. This cable was first used in ethernet networks, IBM PC net broadband networks, and ARCnet networks, besides being used for video and television applications. It still is in use in many older locations, even though newer installations have converted to twisted-pair. Coaxial cable has been around long enough that it has a mature construction technology and is relatively inexpensive. The primary advantages of coaxial cable are its self-shielding properties, low attenuation at high frequencies, and its moderate installation expense.

Coaxial cables consist of the conductor centrally positioned in a cable surrounded by an insulating medium, which then is enclosed by a shield (see Figure 5.6). The shield can consist of a foil wrapping within an integral drain wire or a wire braid. The coax that is used for thicknet or thick Ethernet might have a double-shield layer.

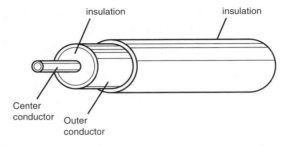

Figure 5.6   Coaxial cable consists of a shielded copper wire.

Placing the center conductor in an insulating medium surrounded by a shielding material theoretically traps all the electromagnetic fields inside the cable assembly. Because this shield has to be grounded, the mode of propagation of the signals in the cable is analogous to that of a mechanical pipeline. The grounded shield helps prevent interfering signals outside the cable from impinging on the center conductor. Conversely, the grounded shield also prevents signals from leaking out of the cable structure. Grounding is very important in this cabling system. A cable installation without proper grounding is susceptible to outside EMI and RFI interference.

Two types of coax cabling are used in wiring local area networks. One type is called thicknet and the other is referred to as thinnet. Thicknet is the original ethernet coax trunk distribution cable now known as 10BASE-5. The cable has a large center diameter conductor of number 12 AWG and has an overall diameter of approximately 0.4 inch. This cable typically is run close to a workstation either in the ceiling or in the walls. A connection is made to the cable by running tap or each half tap, and then the connection is directly made to the computer terminal. The term thicknet was introduced because this coaxial cable is almost half-inch in diameter and when newer, smaller diameter coaxial cable was introduced it looked very large.

The newer standard cable, which is approximately a quarter-inch diameter and is much more flexible, was named thinnet. This type of cable uses BNC connectors with T adapters. It is less expensive, but the distances for a thinnet ethernet segment are limited as compared to thicknet.

ARCnet is another LAN topology that uses coaxial cable. In this topology, the workstations are connected directly to the coax in a star arrangement. Each leg terminates in an active or passive hub.

▶▶ ARCnet is one of the oldest networking technologies still in use today, although you're more likely to find it used in point-of-sale mechanisms, linking electronic cash registers, for example. You can learn more about how ARCnet works by reading Chapter 11, "Heard Anything About ARCnet Lately?"

Typically, the sizes for coaxial cables are designated by an RGB number or manufacturer's numbering system. A summary of cable types follows:

- **Cable RG 59/U-1 (105 482 624)** is a 75 ohm coaxial cable with a 22 AWG (7x30) center conductor, a foamed polyethylene dielectric, a bare copper braid (mm. 95% coverage) outer conductor, and a PVC jacket. (Similar to RG 59/U type.) UL style 1354.

- **Cable RG 59/U-1A (105 521 561)** is a 75 ohm coaxial cable with a 22 AWU (7x30) center conductor, a foamed polyethylene dielectric, a bare copper braid (mm. 95% coverage) outer conductor, and a PVC jacket. (Similar to RU 59/U type.) UL style 1354, UL Listed Type CL2.

- **Cable RG 59/U-2 (105 482 632)** is a 75 ohm coaxial cable with a 22 AWG copper covered steel center conductor, a polyethylene dielectric, a bare copper braid (mm. 80% coverage) outer conductor, and a PVC jacket. (Similar to RU 59/U type commercial.) UL style 1354.

- **Cable RG 59/U-2A (105 521 579)** is a 75 ohm coaxial cable with a 22 AWG copper covered steel center conductor, a polyethylene dielectric, a bare copper braid (mm. 80% coverage) outer conductor, and a PVC jacket. (Similar to RU 59/U type commercial.) UL style 1354. UL Listed Type CL2 per 1987 NEC.

- **Cable RG 59/U-5 (105 482 665)** is a 75 ohm plenum coaxial cable with a 22 AWG copper covered steel center conductor, an FEP dielectric, a bare copper braid (mm. 95% coverage) outer conductor, and an FEP jacket. (Similar to RU-59/U type.) UL Listed Type CL2P per 1987 NEC.

- **Cable RG 62 A/U-1 (105 482 723)** is a 93 ohm coaxial cable with a 22 AWG copper covered steel center conductor, an air dielectric polyethylene dielectric, a bare copper braid (mm. 95% coverage) outer conductor, and a PVC jacket. (Similar to RU 62 A/U type.)

- **Cable RG 62 A/U-1A (105 521 660)** is a 93 ohm coaxial cable with a 22 AWU copper covered steel center conductor, an air dielectric polyethylene dielectric, a bare copper braid (mm. 95% coverage) outer conductor, and a PVC jacket. (Similar to RU 62 A/U type.) UL Listed Type CL2 per 1987 NEC.

- **Cable Ethernet (105 482 798)** is a 50 ohm coaxial cable with a 0.0855 AWU solid tinned copper center conductor, a foamed polyethylene dielectric, a foil shield bonded to dielectric, a tinned copper braid (mm. 92% coverage) a foil shield, a tinned copper braid (mm. 92% coverage), and a PVC jacket. (Similar to Ethernet Type.) UL style 1478 DEC approved. "DEC NET." Xerox specifications/IEEE 803.

- **Cable Ethernet-1A (105 538 037)** is a 50 ohm coaxial cable with a 0.0855 AWU solid tinned copper center conductor, a foamed polyethylene dielectric, a foil shield bonded to dielectric, a tinned copper braid (mm. 93% coverage) a foil shield, a tinned copper braid (mm. 90% coverage), and a yellow PVC jacket. (Similar to Ethernet Type.) UL style 1478. UL Listed Type CL2 per 1987 NEC. DEC approved. "DECnet" Xerox specifications/IEEE 803.

- **Cable Ethernet-2 (105** 482 806) is a 50 ohm plenum coaxial cable with a 0.0855 AWU solid tinned copper center conductor, a foamed FEP dielectric, a foil shield, a tinned copper braid (mm. 93% coverage), a foil shield, a tinned copper braid (mm 90% coverage), and an FEP jacket. (Similar to Ethernet.) UL Listed Type CL2P per 1987 NEC. DEC approved. Xerox specifications/IEEE 803.

Characteristic Impedance

As you can see from the previous list, the characteristic impedance is the first electrical consideration mentioned. This is because this cable was first used for the needs of RF signal propagation, and the coax impedances were specified so that proper load matching could be made at the head end of the RF equipment. Standard impedances for coaxial cable are 50 ohms, 75 ohms, and 92 ohms. The diameter of the center conductor, the dialectic material, and the mechanical properties of the shield contribute and also help define the coaxial cable's characteristic impedance. This impedance value is the value of the impedance at the maximum frequency for which the cable is designed.

For example, if you were using coaxial cable for video service, you would expect to see 75-ohm impedance exhibited at the maximum operating frequency of 900MHz. For cable, there's always a trade-off between frequency headroom and attenuation per cable length. Typically for most coax cable, the attenuation is less than 1.5 decibels per hundred feet at 10MHz. At 100 MHz, the attenuation is up around 5 decibels per hundred feet; consequently, as you increase your cable run, your attenuation goes up. When installing coax, there's always a trade-off between signal strength versus cable length versus frequency bandwidth.

A 10Mbps ethernet segment can be up to 500 meters or approximately 1,640 feet in length using thicknet cable. For thinnet cable, the length can be up to 185 meters or 607 feet. Attenuation and frequency based signal distortion limit segment lengths in ethernet systems, while network lengths are limited by timing constraints that will be seen as bit-rate errors. Of course, at 100MB per second the maximum length is again reduced.

▶▶ The network topology and distances that can be covered in a typical ethernet network are discussed more fully in Chapter 12, "Ethernet."

Wherever possible, when purchasing coaxial cable you should be sure that the connectors are preattached. In many cases this will not be possible. In several instances you will find that where the drops are located and where the connections are made to the equipment, you need the cable adapters and the adapters must be installed by a wiring technician.

The two most common types of connectors are the BNC and the TNC. These are both named after their designers. The BNC connector has been around since World War II. It is a bayonet type and can be installed either as a crimp type, a three-piece type, or as a screw-on connector. TheTNC connector usually is configured as a screw-on type and has been specifically developed for ease of installation with video-type cable. If you have run your own video cable for cable TV, satellite TV, or an antenna system, you should be familiar with the F type connector. In every instance there are several male and female adapters that can be used to connect to almost any type of equipment.

The advantages of coaxial cables are

- Low susceptibility to EMI and RFI pickup
- High frequency bandwidth
- Longer segment lengths than with twisted-pair cables
- Can be matched with fiber-optic and twisted-pair cables
- Lower signal distortion
- Less cross-talk between cables
- Better information security than with twisted-pair cable

The disadvantages of coaxial cable are

- More difficult to install than twisted-pair cable
- Heavier than twisted-pair or fiber-optic cables
- Usually must be daisy chained or home run to workstations
- Does not have the adaptability of twisted-pair cable
- Is more expensive and takes more time to install

Fiber-Optic Cables

Fiber-optic technology is significantly different from copper and uses light transmitted through hair-thin fibers. Fiber-optic cable offers higher bandwidth and lower signal losses. It also allows higher data rates over longer distances.

The advantages of using fiber-optic cables are

- **Information carrying capacity**—Fiber-optic bandwidth capacities are well in excess of that required by today's network applications. The 62.5/125 Micrometer fiber recommended for building use has as its minimum bandwidth a capacity of over 160MHz per kilometer. The bandwidth at over 100 meters is well over 1.5Gbps. If the wavelength is different, the actual bandwidth can rise to 5Gbps.

- **Low signal loss**—Optical fibers offer low signal loss. This low signal loss permits longer transmission distances. In comparison with copper, the longest recommended copper horizontal link is 100 meters; when using fiber it is 2,000 meters or more.

The biggest drawback in using copper cable is that signal loss *increases* with signal frequency. Attenuation or signal loss is higher at 100 MHz than at 10 MHz. Consequently, high data rates increase power loss and decrease practical transmission distances. Loss does not change with signal frequency in fiber-optic systems. Attenuation does change with frequency of the light transmitted through the fiber, but the data rate does not. So, if you have a 10 MHz and a 100 MHz signal in the fiber they both are attenuated alike.

Electromagnetic Immunity

The basic transmission medium in a fiber-optic cable consists of either plastic or glass material. Both of these are considered to be insulators or dielectrics, so these materials are immune to electromagnetic interference. The transmitted signals consist mainly of modulated light signals that are tunneled through the fiber medium and do not escape. No signals emanate outside the cable, so it does not cause cross-talk, which is the main limitation in twisted-pair cable. It can be run in electrically noisy environments such as high-density computer room installations, factory floors, and other electrically dense environments without concern because the cables are immune to outside noise sources.

Size and Weight

Fiber-optic cable weighs considerably less than copper cable. It is typically 22% to 50% lighter than comparable 4-pair Category 5 cable. Less weight makes fiber-optic cable easier to install depending on its durability, which has improved over time. Typical weights for 1,000 feet are as follows:

- Two-fiber cable: 11 lbs.
- 12-fiber cable: 33 lbs.
- 4-pair Category 5 UTP: 25 lbs.
- 25-pair backbone UTP: 93 lbs.
- 10BASE-2 coax: 24 lbs.

Fiber-optic cable is smaller than copper cable. Typically, it's about 15% less in volume than Category 5 twisted-pair cable.

Safety

As stated before, the glass and plastic that comprise the transmission medium of fiber-optic cable are dielectrics, or insulators, and thus do not conduct electricity. Fiber-optic cable therefore does not present a spark hazard and can be used in explosive environments. It also does not attract lightning. Fiber-optic cable has jacket ratings that are comparable to the copper cable jackets and has the same flammability ratings that meet code requirements in buildings.

Security

It wasn't until just recently that the capability to physically tap fiber-optic cables was developed. This requires extremely expensive equipment and a skilled operator. Typically, because fiber-optic cables do not emanate electromagnetic radiation, they are fairly secure against tapping. When compared to other methods of transmission, fiber-optic cable is the most secure medium for carrying sensitive data.

Fiber Construction and Operation

Fiber optics is a technology in which signals are converted from electrical into light signals. The signals then are sent or transmitted through a thin glass or plastic fiber and reconverted to electrical signals. The fiber-optic cable consists of three concentric layers differing in optical parities. As shown in Figure 5.7, a fiber-optic cable consists of

- **The core**—The inner, light-carrying portion of the cable.
- **The cladding**—The middle layer, which confines the light in the core.
- **Buffer**—The outer layer, which serves as a shock absorber to protect the core and the cladding from damage.
- **Outer jacket**—Protects the cable.

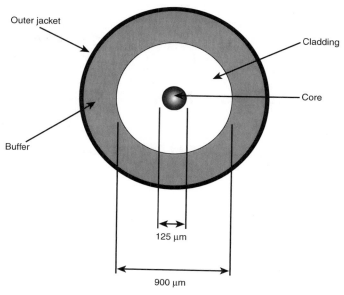

Figure 5.7 Components of a fiber-optic cable.

Total Internal Reflection

Seeing how light travels through optical fiber will give you an understanding of many of the properties of fiber transmission capabilities. Light injected into the core that strikes the core cladding surface interface at an angle greater than the critical angle will be reflected back to the core. Because optically the angles of incidence and reflection are equal, the light is reflected back down the length of the fiber. The light signal is trapped within the core of the fiber. Light striking the interface at less than critical angle passes into the cladding and is lost.

Figure 5.8 shows light traveling through the fiber by total internal reflection.

How Light Travels Through a Fiber-Optic Cable

Light transmission is not random. It is channeled into *modes*, which are possible paths for light rays to travel. There can be as few as one mode or there can be several thousand modes in the design of the fiber. Although the number of modes is significant, it actually relates to determining the fiber's bandwidth. More modes mean lower bandwidth. The cause of this is dispersion. As a pulse of light travels through the fiber, it spreads out over distance. Although there are several reasons for such dispersion, the two principal concerns are modal dispersion and material dispersion. Different path lengths followed by light rays as they bounce down the fiber cause modal dispersion. Material dispersion is caused by different light wavelengths traveling at different speeds. To limit material dispersion, you limit the wavelengths of light transmitted.

Fiber-optic cable can be modified in several ways to achieve different signal transmission characteristics. Modifications can be made to affect bandwidth and attenuation, and to facilitate coupling the light in and out of the fiber.

The stepped index multimode fiber has a large core with uniform optical properties. This fiber supports thousands of modes of operation and offers the highest dispersion and, hence, the lowest bandwidth.

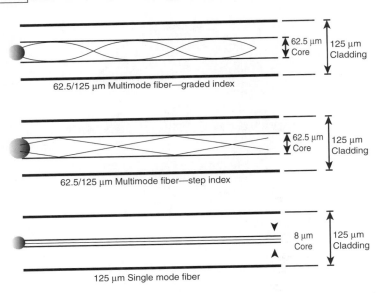

Figure 5.8 Light can reflect off the internal cladding as it travels through the fiber option cable.

The graded index multimode fiber has different optical properties in the core. This type reduces dispersion and increases bandwidth. The graded index makes light following longer paths travel slightly faster than light following shorter paths. The net result is that the light does not spread out as much. Nearly all multimode fiber that is used in networking and data communications has a graded index score.

The single-mode fiber has the highest bandwidth and the lowest loss of performance. The core of single mode fiber is smaller than that of multimode fiber. The bandwidth that this fiber exhibits is much greater than the capacities of today's electronics. This fiber can support speeds in excess of gigabytes per second. It also can carry many channels of information simultaneously. This is done by having each channel carry a differ wavelength of light.

The most common fiber for networking is the 62\125 micron fiber. The two numbers designate the core diameter and the cladding diameter, respectively. In this case the core diameter is 62.5 microns and the cladding diameter is 125 microns. Other common sizes are 50/125-micron and the 100/140 Micron cable.

To summarize:

- Graded index multimode fibers are the preferred fibers for horizontal cable and most backbone applications.
- Single-mode fibers, by virtue of their immense bandwidth and long transmission capabilities, are best for applications requiring additional performance.

Numerical Aperture

The numerical aperture (NA) of the fiber defines which light will be propagated and which will not. As shown in Figure 5.9, the NA defines the light-gathering capability of the fiber.

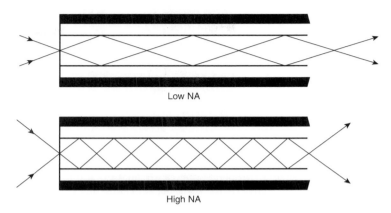

Low NA

High NA

Figure 5.9   The numerical aperture defines which light will be propagated through the cable.

The numerical aperture defines a mathematically defined cone coming from the core. Light entering the core from within this cone will be propagated by the total internal reflection of the fiber. Light entering from outside this mathematical cone will not be propagated.

The higher the numerical aperture and core diameter, the lower the bandwidth of the fiber. The lower the numerical aperture and core diameter, the higher the bandwidth.

Attenuation in Fiber-Optic Cables

Attenuation is a loss of power. During transmission, light pulses lose some of their energy, which shows up as a loss in signal strength. Attenuation is specified for fiber in decibels per kilometer. Attenuation ranges from under one decibel per kilometer for single-mode fibers and up to 2000 decibels per kilometer for large-core plastic fibers.

Attenuation varies with the wavelength of light. There are three prime low-loss windows of wavelengths that are used today. These are

- 850 nanometers
- 1300 nanometers
- 1550 nanometers

The 850 nanometer wavelength is the most widely used because it was developed first, and optical devices such as LEDs (light emitting diodes) operating at 850 nanometers are inexpensive and plentiful. The 1300 nanometer wavelength offers low loss with a slight increase in cost for LEDs. The 1550 nanometers wavelength is mainly used in long-distance telecommunications applications.

Terminations and Connections

For copper cabling, the main criterion is to provide an intimate, gas-tight joint between the connector contacts and the cable conductor. In reality, this seldom exists and there are two approaches to terminations in premise cabling: crimping the center conductor and using an insulation displacement contact (IDC).

When doing either type of connection, it is important to use the correct size and type of wire and also the correct tool. A contact might be rated for a 24-gauge solid conductor. Using a stranded or smaller wire, such as a 28-gauge wire, results in a connection that could become loose or could fail.

Crimping

When a conductor is crimped, the contact is crushed around the center conductor. This cold welds the contact to the center conductor. A myriad of crimping tools are available today for almost any type of connection and cable type. You must use the proper tool and the correct die for a successful crimp. Crimping tools are designed to provide the correct pressure by closing the dies a fixed amount. Using the wrong tool or die can result in either an under-crimp or an over-crimp. Under-crimping results in either a high resistance or loose connection. Over-crimping can crush the wire or the connector so badly that it will be damaged and fail.

Insulation Displacement Contact (IDC)

Insulation displacement contact uses a slotted beam. The wire is driven between the slotted beams. The beams are under spring tension and pierce the wire insulation and provide contact to the conductor inside. The IDC contact can be either a flat form bar or a slotted barrel. IDC terminations are the most common in premise cabling applications.

Modular Jacks and Plugs

Modular jacks and plugs have been around a long time and are familiar to everyone as the connectors that plug into telephone handsets, bases, and wall outlets. The connectors and jacks that are used in premise wiring are different. Residential wiring and equipment uses four-position plugs and jacks. The ones used for premise wiring are eight-position and terminate all four pairs of the cable. In typical nomenclature, the plug is the male end and the jack is the female end.

Modular jacks and plugs often are referred to as RJ connectors. The RJ comes from the term registered jack, and is specified in the USOC specification. USOC stands for Universal Service Order Code. This is a Bell Telephone specification and was developed for specific wiring connections, patterns, and applications within the telephone system.

An RJ-11 is a six-position connector and an RJ-45 is commonly referred to as an eight-position connector. Each of these basic jack styles can be wired for different RJ configurations. For example, the six-position jack can be wired as an RJ-11 C, which is a one-pair jack. It can also be wired as an RJ-14 C, which is a two-pair, or an RJ-25 C, which is a three-point configuration. An eight-position jack can be wired for configurations such as RJ-61 C, 4-pair, and RJ-48 C. The key eight-position jack can be wired for RG-45 RAS, RJ-46 S, and RJ-47 S. The fourth modular jack style is a modified version of the six-position jack, commonly called an MMJ. It was designed by Digital Equipment Corporation, along with the modified modular plug to eliminate the possibility of connecting DEC data equipment to voice lines and vice versa. See Figure 5.10 for an example of these types of jacks.

8-position

8-position keyed

6-position

6-position modified

Figure 5.10   Several types of modular jacks can be used for network cabling.

Modular Plug Pair Configurations

It is important that the pairing of wires in the modular plug match the pairs in the modular jack as well as the horizontal and backbone wiring. If they do not, the data being transmitted might be paired with incompatible signals. Modular cords wired to the T 568A color scheme on both ends are compatible with the 568B systems and vice versa. See Figure 5.11 for a breakdown of jack types and how they are wired.

MODULAR JACK PLUG PAIR CONFIGURATIONS

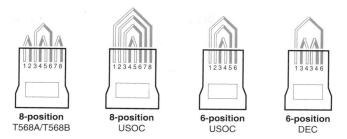

8-position
T568A/T568B

8-position
USOC

6-position
USOC

6-position
DEC

Figure 5.11 A color scheme is used to match up wires at each end of a cable when joining the cable to a modular jack.

Common Outlet Configurations

Several outlet configurations were shown in Figure 5.11; however, it should be noted that the T 568A and T 568B have been adopted by the 568B.1 and 11801 standards. They are nearly identical except that pairs two and one are reversed. T 568A is the preferred scheme because it is compatible with one- or two-pair USOC schemes. Either configuration can be used for an ISDN service or high-speed data applications. Transmission categories 3, 5, 5 E, and 6 are only applicable to this type of pair of grouping.

As shown in Figure 5.12, USOC wiring is available for one-, two-, three-, or four-pair systems. Pair one occupies the center conductors; pair two occupies the next two contacts out; and so forth. One advantage to this scheme is that a six-position plug configured with one, two, or three pairs can be inserted into an eight-position jack and still maintain pair continuity. The disadvantage is the poor transmission performance associated with this type of pair sequence. None of these pair schemes is cabling-standard compliant.

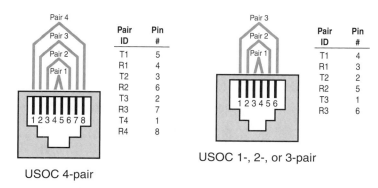

Pair ID	Pin #
T1	5
R1	4
T2	3
R2	6
T3	2
R3	7
T4	1
R4	8

USOC 4-pair

Pair ID	Pin #
T1	4
R1	3
T2	2
R2	5
T3	1
R3	6

USOC 1-, 2-, or 3-pair

Figure 5.12 USOC wiring is available for one, two-, three-, or four-pair systems.

Various other standard schemes appear in Figure 5.13.

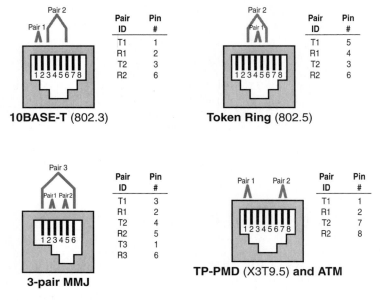

Figure 5.13 Different network cables require different wire connections to standard jacks.

There are a few guidelines you should follow when using the modular jacks and plugs:

- For each category application you must use plugs and jacks for that category.

- You must be sure that you're using the correct plug or jack for your conductor type.

- You must follow termination procedures carefully. With the higher category cables in particular, proper installation procedures are essential to meet performance specifications.

- ANSI TIA/EIA-568B standards specify that all pairs be terminated at the outlet.

- The length of exposed wire (untwisted) shall not exceed 13 mm for Category 5 or higher cables.

- The length of exposed wire (untwisted) for Category 3 shall be within 75mm from the point of termination.

Patch Panels

Patch panels provide a means of rearranging circuits so that adding, subtracting, and changing workstations is made easier. Patch panels are where the circuits are connected and reconnected. Several patch panels use a feed-through connector set into which a cable can be plugged on both sides. Some configurations can have the horizontal cables going to the work areas plugged into one side of the panel.

Typically, feed-through patch panels are not suited for high-speed operation. Category 5 and higher panels feature IDC contacts on the back and modular jacks on the front. Modular jacks are usually 110-style or barrel style. This configuration offers a better electrical performance to reduce NEXT. Fiber-optic patch panels often offer a transition between different connectors. Transition among SC, FDDI, and S T are common.

There are also other ways of connecting and terminating cabling. Two of these use IDC connections. The first is the Type 66 cross connect block. This type of block has 50 rows of IDC contacts to accommodate the 50 conductors of 25-pair cable. Each row contains four contacts. Type 66 blocks represent an older style designed originally for voice circuits. Some of the newer designs meet Category 5 requirements. You should check to be sure that it is rated for the category you're installing, because older block designs have high cross-talk, which makes them unsuitable for high data rate designs.

A 110 cross connect consists of three parts: the mounting legs, wiring block, and connecting block. The legs provide cable routing management and also hold the wire block. The wire block is composed of small plastic blocks that position the cable with index strips. Conductors are placed in the slot of the index strip. The strip usually has 50 slots to accommodate a 25-pair cable. It is marked every five pairs to help visually simplify the installation and reduce errors. This is also color-coded using the standard blue/orange/green/brown/slate color code. Wires used are punched into place with the 110-installation tool. This however, does not terminate the conductors; it simply positions them. The device that does the termination is the connecting block. The IDC connecting block has contacts at both ends. One set of contacts terminates the contacts of the wiring block, the other set on the outside is used for performing the cross connect.

This wiring system can accommodate as many as 300 pairs. Each horizontal strip can handle 25 pairs. A one-hundred pair cross connect requires four index strips. A 200-pair cable requires eight index strips, and so forth.

The system can be used as a prewired assembly for specific applications. One variation uses a 25-pair connector. In this situation, the block is prewired to the connector to allow a 25-pair cable from a hub or PBX to simply plug into the cross connect.

There are pros and cons to using cross-connect blocks. They offer higher densities and require less space than patch panels, and also are less expensive. On the other hand, they are the least friendly for making moves, adds, and changes. Skill is involved in removing and rearranging cables. When using patch panels, almost anyone can rearrange the system. In both situations security, ease of attachment, expense, and physical space are all considerations.

Terminating Fiber

What used to be a challenging task in the past, and is still an important task today, is terminating fiber-optic cable. There is a big difference between terminating electrical wiring and terminating a glass fiber that is only 62.5 microns in diameter. For one, electrical connections require a low resistance connection; the fiber requires a tight tolerance alignment. Misalignment in fiber connections will cause energy to be lost as light crosses a junction of the connector.

There are three functions of the termination process:

- To prepare a smooth, flat, or rounded and service capable of accepting as much transmitted light as possible.

- To provide a precise alignment of the clad fiber within the connector or splice to allow maximum coupling effectiveness.

- To provide a secure physical attachment of the connector or spliced unit to the buffer cable.

Several varieties of common connectors are used in fiber-optics. The following list does not include all connectors but does include those most commonly used for communication applications:

- St
- SC
- Biconic
- SMA

- Mini BNC
- Data Link
- Dual fixed-Shroud (FDDI)

You can see examples of these in Figure 5.14.

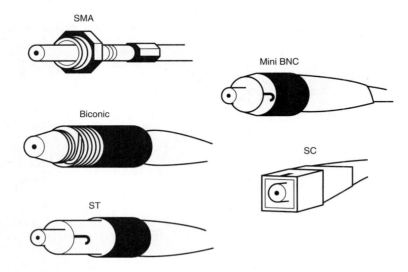

Figure 5.14   Several kinds of connectors are used with fiber-optic cables.

Several techniques are used for installing fiber-optic connectors, but five tasks are common to any termination process.

1. The outer jacket, strength members, buffer tube, and coating must be removed.

2. The fiber must be threaded through the connector housing.

3. Fiber must be secured inside the connector.

4. The connector must be securely attached to the outside of the fiber.

5. The end of the clad fiber extending through the tip of the connector must be cut in preparation to accept the light signal.

The correct installation of fiber-optic connectors requires training, specific equipment, and consumable materials. Thankfully, manufacturers are constantly reducing the amount of time and training required to install the fiber-optic equipment they produce.

Epoxy terminations have long been used to ensure that the fiber is properly held in the connection ferrule. It does have its drawbacks, however. It is an extra step in the process, it's potentially messy, and it requires curing the epoxy. Curing time can be shortened by utilizing an oven. This requires having another piece of equipment. There is also a possibility of spilling the epoxy on carpets and furniture in the finished building.

The epoxy-less connectors require only a crimping tool and eliminate the need for epoxy. The simplest connectors use an internal insert that is forced snugly around the fiber during crimping. Inserts clamp and position the fiber while the crimp secures the cable strength members.

Another variation uses a short piece of fiber, which is factory-assembled and polished and inserted into the end of the connector ferrule. The inserted cable fiber butts up against this internal fiber, which is enclosed by an index-graded gel, and then the cable is crimped in place.

There also is a connector that uses a hot melt adhesive that is preloaded into the connector. This eliminates external mixing and loose components. Next, the connector is placed into an oven for a minute or so to soften the adhesive. The prepared fiber then is inserted in the assembly and is left to dry. Finally, the prepared connector is lightly polished.

The main benefit of epoxy-less connectors is that they take less time and hence increase productivity.

Fiber-Optic Splicing

The splicing techniques were only used for extending the distance of the cable segment by adding another segment to it, or for repairing cut or otherwise damaged fibers. Now, splicing techniques and products have become user-friendly and often are considered a fast, low-loss alternative to traditional connector terminations.

There are two main types of fiber-optic splicing: fusion and mechanical.

Fusion Splicing

This is a process in which two sections of fiber are heated and, in effect, welded together. Fuse splices typically are good connections with attenuation losses as low as 0.1 db. Mechanical strength exhibited by this splice is often as strong as the original fiber.

The steps of a fusion splice include the following:

1. The ends of both fiber sections are prepared.
2. Both fibers are inserted into the splicing unit and precisely aligned.
3. Heat is applied at the interface of both fiber surfaces and they are fused.
4. This place is tested for light loss.

Mechanical Splicing

Mechanical splicing is the process in which two sections of fiber are aligned and either glued or crimped in place within a permanent hood or shell. Mechanical splices are less labor-intensive than fuse splices. In some cases the splices can be installed in less than one minute per unit. Until recently, mechanical splices were relatively high-loss connections and were used for very limited applications. In the past several years, manufacturing processes have developed very low-loss mechanical splice units.

The low-loss connection attributes of today's mechanical splice units created a new technique for terminating fiber. After cleaning and polishing each installed fiber, installers have the option of purchasing fiber jumpers or tails with connectors on one end and quickly splicing these tails to the installed fiber.

Fiber-Optic Patch Panels

Fiber-optic panels are termination units, which are designed to provide a secure, organized chamber for housing connectors and splice units. The typical termination unit consists of the following components:

- **Enclosed chamber**—This can be a mountable wall or equipment rack.
- **Coupler panels**—These hold the connector couplers.

- **The connector couplers**
- **Splice tray**—Organizes and secures splice modules.

Tip

It usually is a good practice to design termination units and jumper cables into fiber-optic installation because such units provide for growth and flexibility. The termination unit can use a patch panel in respect to making changes or additions to a system. It also can be a test point for troubleshooting the system.

Fiber Distributed Data Interface (FDDI)

The fiber distributed data interface (FDDI) was the first local area network designed from the ground up to use fiber optics. Compared to its copper-based counterparts, its performance is quite impressive. The data rate is over 100 megabits per second over a 100 km distance with up to 1000 attached stations.

The FDDI standard recommends 62.5/125 micrometer fiber for multimode applications. It also allows for 50/125, 85/125, and 100/140 micron fibers. The only exception is that the various other sizes do not exceed the power budget of the system, which would distort the signal beyond limits allowed by the specification. The power does not include optical loss at the interface between the source in the connector. This specification also calls for a minimum power to be launched into the fiber.

▶▶   FDDI is covered in greater detail in Chapter 17, "Fiber Distributed Data Interface (FDDI)."

FDDI is usually arranged as a dual-ring token-ring passing topology. The program ring carries information around in one direction, while the secondary ring carries information in the other direction. The reason for two rings is redundancy. If one ring fails, the other one is still available. Redundancy also lessens the likelihood of network failure. There's an inherent protection in the system in the fact that each station is attached only to the adjacent stations in the ring. If a stations fails or a single point-to-point link fails, the network still functions. If the cable breaks between two stations, the stations can accept data on the primary link and transmit on the secondary link. The secondary ring is not needed for redundant operation, but the primary and secondary rings can be used for data transmission to effectively double the network transmission speed to 200 megabits per second.

FDDI uses the optional key system to prevent a cable from being connected to the wrong station port. Most connectors, both electrical and optical, are polarized to prevent mating upside down. The FDDI connector system is keyed even further.

▶▶   For information on FDDI, see Chapter 17, "Fiber-Distributed Data Interface (FDDI)."

There are three main types of cabling errors in FDDI:

- Cabling for dual attached station is reversed. Keying one connector as A and the other as B prevents this error.
- The single attack station is connected on the trunk ring causing a break in the backbone.
- The M port of the hub is connected to the trunk ring, also causing a break in the backbone.

Single-mode fibers use a similar keying system with an S prefix. Single-mode fiber has an additional key to allow only single mode plugs and receptacles to mate. You cannot plug a multimode MIC connector into a single mode receptacle.

General Considerations for Fiber-Optic Cabling

For the insulation of optical fiber connecting hardware, the following recommendation should apply. Connectors should be protected from physical damage and moisture. Optical fiber cable connecting hardware should incorporate high-density termination to conserve space, provide for ease of optical fiber cable, and patch cord management on installation. Optical fiber cable connecting hardware should be designed to provide flexibility for mounting on walls, racks, or other types and distribution frames, and standard and mounting hardware.

You should insist that a minimum of 1 meter of two-fiber cable be accessible for termination purposes. Testing is recommended to ensure correct polarity and acceptable link performance. Clause 2 of 568B.1 provides recommended optical fiber link performance testing criteria.

Connections

Telecommunication outlet and connector boxes should be securely mounted at planned locations. The telecommunications outlet box or connector box should provide cable management means to assure a minimum bend radius of 25 mm and should have slack storage capability.

The fiber types should be identified:

- Multimode connectors or visible portions of it and adapters are to be identified with the color beige.

- Single-mode connectors or visible portions of it and adapters shall be identified with the color blue.

- The two positions in a duplex connector are referred to as position A and position B.

Small Form Factor Connectors (SFF)

Figure 5.15 shows a connector that is relatively new on the market today.

Figure 5.15   Newer small form factor (SFF) fiber-optic connectors are available today.

Some advantages of SFF connectors include compact size, modular compatibility with the eight-position modular copper interface, and adaptability to high-density eight-network electronics. Qualified SFF duplex and multifiber connector designs can be used in the main cross connect, intermediate cross connect, horizontal cross connect, and consolidation points and work areas. A TIA fiber-optic connected inter-mateability standard shall describe each SFF design. This design should satisfy the requirements specified in Annex A of the 568 B-B.3 standard.

Centralized optical fiber cabling provides users with flexibility in designing optical fiber cabling systems for centralized electronics typically in single tenant buildings. It contains information guidelines for design and installation requirements. There are salient points specified in B.1 for a centralized fiber-optic cabling system.

Telecommunications Rooms

There have been some major changes from the EIA/TIA 568A to the EIA/TIA 568B standards transition. One of the major changes is that the telecommunication closet has now evolved into the telecommunications room. These rooms are generally considered to be floor-serving facilities for horizontal cable distribution, and they also can be used for intermediate and main cross connects.

The telecommunications room, or TR, is now defined for design and equipment according to ANSI/TIA/EIA 569A. Some of the specifications include specifications for wire management, relieving stress from tight bends, cable ties, staples, and so on. Horizontal cable terminations cannot be used to administer cabling system changes. Jumpers, patch cords, or equipment cords are required for reconfiguring cabling connections. There's also a further restriction that application-specific electrical components cannot be installed as part of the horizontal cabling.

Open Office Cabling

Additional specifications for horizontal cabling in areas with movable furniture and partitions have been included in TIA/EIA 568B.1. Horizontal cabling methodologies are specified for open office environments by a means of multiuser telecommunications outlet assemblies, or MUTOA. It is preferable to use MUTOAs only when the entire length of the work area cord is accessible to facilitate tracing and to prevent erroneous disconnection. Up to 22 meters or 71 feet of work area cable are allowed.

Consolidation Points

Consolidation points or transition point connectors are interfaces between the patch panels and MUTOAs.

General Horizontal Cabling Subsystem Specifications

Note the ISO/IEC 11801 allows 120 and unshielded twisted pair horizontal cabling. Grounding must conform to applicable building codes as well as ANSI/EIA/TIA 607. You must have a minimum of two telecommunications outlets in the work area. The first outlet must have a 100-ohm twisted-pair category 5E, and the next outlet must also have one outlet with twisted-pair Category 5E. Two-fiber multimode optical fiber must also be installed.

Additional outlets can be provided. These outlets are in addition to and cannot be replaced by the minimum requirements of the standard. Bridged taps and splices are not allowed for copper-based horizontal cabling. Additional specific components cannot be installed as part of the horizontal cabling. When needed, they must be placed external to the telecommunications outlet or horizontal cross connects.

Finally, the proximity of horizontal cabling to sources of electromagnetic interference should be taken into account.

Documenting and the Administration of the Installation

The wiring plant once in place is not a static, immobile structure. It is a dynamic and evolving part of your network. If the plant is not maintained with an up-to-date documented record, then any additions, changes, moves, and upgrading are out of the question.

The TIA/EIA-606 standard provides a guide to documenting a cabling system to make its administration efficient and effective. This provides the administrator with several benefits:

- Allows better asset management
- Increases network reliability and up time

- Speeds and simplifies troubleshooting
- Facilitates movement, additions, and changes
- Allows for disaster recovery plans
- Allows for capacity planning, upgrading, and acceptance of new emerging applications
- Allows the generation of management reports

Documentation should include equipment and component labels, electronic or real records, drawings, work orders, and reports. Realistically, every piece of the physical plant should be labeled. This includes cables, termination hardware, cross connects, patch panels, closets, and anything else that will assist you in developing a meaningful overall view of your system.

Good labeling requires a unique coding scheme that makes sense to you. The label can include a location scheme, a component scheme, or a combination of both. You must realize that a label cannot have all the required information for a specific component, so it should contain enough information to uniquely define the component and point to a specific record. These pointers, or as sometimes referred to, linkages, will point to other records.

Records

The TIA/EIA 606 standard divides a record into four types of information:

- **Required information**—The essential information about the component.
- **Required linkages**—Links to other records.
- **Optional information**—Additional information that makes the record understandable and comprehensive.
- **Optional linkages**—This points to additional records that might be helpful to include. For example, if you are connecting a new PC in a new work area, you might want to include a linkage from the PC record to the record for the new workstation.

Drawings

Drawings are an essential part of your physical plant. They are necessary to locate components within a building. Drawings, especially "as built" drawings, will show the locations of conduits, pull boxes, and other components hidden from view behind walls and ceilings and under floors. These enable you, your installers, and network administrators to define and control space requirements, estimate cable densities, and keep track of equipment.

Work Orders

Work orders should record all equipment and cabling moves, adds, and changes. This should form a history of the cabling system's life or evolution. The records of the pertinent equipment involved should be updated every time the work order is performed.

Reports

A *report* is a group of records organized in a specific manner. This can be in the form of a database that can be selected to show a selected part of a record. For example, a report might show the number of hard drives on a specific server, or it can show the cables running to the device. You can include the hard drive identifiers or, in the case of the cables, the cable numbers.

Several types of cable management software are available that can be used to maintain records and generate reports. There are also specific programs aimed at managing a cabling system. These programs are compatible with structured cabling systems and conform to the TIA/EIA standards.

Network Interface Cards

SOME OF THE MAIN TOPICS IN THIS CHAPTER ARE

Choosing a Hardware Bus Type: PCI, ISA or EISA, or PCMCIA?

The Wired for Management (WfM) Initiative and Wake On LAN (WOL) Technology

Multi-Homed Systems

Load Balancing and Dual-Redundant Network Controllers

Software Drivers

IRQs and I/O Ports

Troubleshooting Network Cards

CHAPTER 6

The *network interface card* (NIC) is the piece of hardware that links a computer or workstation to the network media. The standard ethernet NIC resides at the physical level of the OSI Seven Layer reference model and is the device that is responsible for translating data into zeros and ones for transmission on the network media for the network using electricity or light. The driver software for the card interfaces with the hardware elements of the card and with the protocol stack that runs on the computer to send data to and from other computers.

Note

This chapter focuses on the typical network adapter cards predominately used in most LANs today. These cards use either electricity or light to transmit data on the network. Although wireless networking is still in its infancy, it is likely to become a very important player in the networking field during the next few years. Information about network adapter cards used for wireless networking can be found in Chapter 14, "Wireless Networking—IEEE 802.11 (Wi-Fi) and HomeRF." In addition, for small office, home office (SOHO) solutions, check out Chapter 16, "The Wireless Application Protocol (WAP)," for the adapter cards used for this small network solution.

Although this chapter concentrates mainly on network adapters that are used on ethernet networks, be aware that there are other cards that function differently. For example, cards made for ARCnet do more than provide the functions of the physical layer of the OSI model. They also provide the data link functionality. Token-ring cards also work differently than standard ethernet cards. However, the general troubleshooting methods discussed in this chapter can usually be applied to all these card types.

Most cards manufactured today support Plug and Play (PnP), but not all operating systems do—if life were just so simple! So, although you might find that installing a new workstation or upgrading an old one with a new network adapter card is an easy task, this might not always be the case if you are working on older equipment. In this chapter, we'll look at the differences between card types and the items that are typically configurable for NICs. After that, we'll list some of the methods you can use to troubleshoot network problems when you suspect that the NIC might be the problem.

Choosing a Hardware Bus Type: PCI, ISA or EISA, or PCMCIA?

When you install a card in a workstation or server, whether it is a network adapter card or a SCSI disk adapter card, you insert the card into a slot that connects the card to a *bus*. A bus is nothing more than a communications channel that devices can use to exchange information as the computer performs its functions. Different kinds of cards can be inserted into slots to connect them to the bus in the computer. Before you make a decision on what kind of network card to purchase, you need to know what kinds of bus slots are available on the computer.

The ISA (Industry Standard Architecture) bus was created in the 1980s and was the bus used by the first IBM personal computer architecture. Manufacturers adopted the term ISA as the IBM computer became a standard and vendors began to create many different kinds of cards to expand the capabilities of the PC.

The first version of this bus provided for an 8-bit data channel. The IBM AT computer architecture used an enhanced version of the original ISA bus, allowing for data transfers at a rate of 8MHz, using a 16-bit data channel. This architecture was later expanded on, and the Extended ISA (EISA) bus was created. Although the EISA bus still operates at only 8MHz, it allows for a 32-bit path, allowing more data to be channeled through the bus. When you open up a modern computer and look at the available slots, the EISA slots are the longer ones. The shorter ones are PCI (Peripheral Component

Interconnect) slots. Figure 6.1 shows a picture of both EISA and PCI network adapter cards. The shorter footprint of the PCI card makes it easier to create PCs that have a much smaller design than in the past.

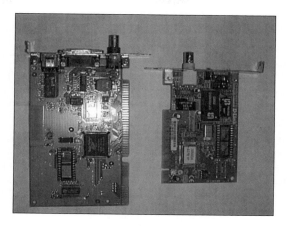

Figure 6.1   The network interface card on the left has an EISA interface, while the one on the right is designed for use in a PCI slot.

Note

Another slot you might find in your computer is the Accelerated Graphics Port (AGP). This slot isn't a multipurpose slot that can be used for a variety of card types such as EISA or PCI slots. Instead, just like the name says, it's a graphics card adapter slot. You can usually distinguish this slot from other types of slots by its pin-out—only an AGP card fits into the slot—and its color, which is usually a beige or light reddish-brown color.

The PCI bus specifications have many advantages over previous standards, including dramatically faster data transfer rates (33MHz) and 32-or 64-bit wide data paths. Devices on the PCI bus can also use a feature called *bus mastering*, whereby a card can take control of the bus and directly transfer large amounts of data to system memory without involving the CPU. Most PCs made during the past few years contain a mix of both PCI and EISA slots. However, several PC vendors are ending support for older ISA and EISA products, a trend that likely will increase over the next few years.

Besides its performance advantage over the EISA bus, the PCI bus also allows for auto-configuration. A PCI card contains internal registers that hold information used for configuration when the system is booted. The kind of information that is stored in these registers includes a 3-byte class code, which indicates the card's base class. For network cards, the value found in this register is 02h. Other possible classes include mass storage controllers (value = 01h), display controllers (value = 03h), the memory controller (value = 05h) and so on. There's even a class represented by the value 00h, which is used for cards that were created before the definitions of class codes was finished, and a class using the value FFh, which indicates that the device doesn't belong to any of the defined classes.

Other information contained in the PCI card's registers tells the system-specific configuration information about the PCI card, such as IRQ and memory information. Usually the PCI card is configured to use an available IRQ when the system detects it. If an unused IRQ isn't found, then the card can, under some circumstances, share an IRQ with another card. In that case, the system interrogates each card that shares the IRQ when the CPU receives the interrupt request. The card making the request can then communicate with the CPU to satisfy the request. Sharing IRQs should usually be done among similar devices.

Note

In addition to the bus types discussed in this chapter, you might occasionally hear about the MCA bus. MCA stands for Micro Channel Architecture. This bus was a proprietary standard that IBM created in 1987. Although MCA was, in most respects, superior to the other bus specifications at that time, it is not compatible with any of them. Because incorporating MCA technology required licensing it from IBM, card manufacturers never widely adopted MCA. Instead, the EISA specification was developed partly in response to the proprietary nature of MCA.

Although EISA and PCI slots typically are used in standard computers for holding adapter cards, smaller computers, such as laptops, are another matter altogether. Indeed, because of their size, it's not possible to include a similar setup of expansion slots that conform to the EISA or PCI specifications.

PCMCIA cards are small, credit card–size cards that can be used in laptops and other small computers. The acronym does *not* stand for "People Can't Memorize Computer Industry Acronyms," which is a popular renaming of the acronym. Instead, PCMCIA is the Personal Computer Memory Card International Association, which is a nonprofit organization responsible for promoting standards for making cards for smaller computers, such as laptops. Although the first cards that were produced according to specifications by this organization were memory cards, you can now find all sorts of add-in cards for laptop computers, including network adapter cards. The term PCMCIA has been used in the past to describe these cards, but most products now use the name *PC Card* instead. Several varieties of cards currently are on the market, but most use a standard 68-pin connector. If you have to connect a laptop to the local LAN, you'll need to evaluate this card to find one that works with your operating system. In Figure 6.2, you can see an example of an Intel PC Card network adapter.

Figure 6.2   PC Cards are much smaller than standard network adapter cards.

Note

To find out more about the Personal Computer Memory Card International Association, and current and proposed specifications, you can visit their Web site at

```
http://www.pc-card.com
```

So, which kind of card should you choose for your networking needs? That can depend on many different factors. For example, you might be limited on the kind of card by how many slots are available in the computers, and of what type. If you have a workstation that already has filled all its PCI slots, you might be forced to use an EISA card if you can't sacrifice one of the existing PCI cards to free a slot. Or, you might be in a situation where you've recently purchased new computers and have older EISA network cards you've salvaged from the computers you are replacing. In that case, if the older cards still work and provide a data transfer rate that meets your needs, why not recycle them instead of buying new cards?

Note

If you want to get a greater understanding of how the different types of buses discussed in this chapter work, I recommend that you check out *Upgrading and Repairing PCs, 13th Edition*, by Scott Mueller, which also is published by Que.

However, if you are in the process of creating a new network or adding to an existing network, the obvious choice is to purchase newer PCI-based cards. The price difference between a low-end PCI NIC and an EISA card is almost negligible now. Even a small cost difference can be overlooked considering that the PCI card provides you with a longer-term solution.

Network Speed

Another factor to consider when making a network card purchase is the speed of your network. Standard 10Base-T networks operate at 10Mbps. Because most newer applications, especially those that involve large data files or graphics-intensive functions, can operate slowly at this speed, it's more likely that you'll be using or upgrading to at least a 100Mbps network. If you are creating a new network, then simply choose 100Mbps cards. If you are upgrading an existing network, and if the cabling infrastructure supports 100Mbps, you can slowly migrate users to 100Mbps by purchasing cards that operate at both speeds. Most 10/100Mbps cards also support *autosensing*, which means that they can detect the speed of the network connection and adjust accordingly. When you swap out hubs or switches to upgrade to a faster network, you won't have to worry about reconfiguring or buying new adapter cards for end-user workstations. Therefore, if you are currently operating in a 10Mbps environment but know that you will have to upgrade to 100Mbps in the next year or two, spend the extra few dollars to buy cards that operate at both speeds.

▶▶ Besides making purchasing choices for network adapter cards, plan ahead for other equipment you might need to buy, such as a new hub or switch. If necessary, get one that supports both speeds and autosensing, and preferably one that works in dual 10/100 mode. For more information about hubs and switches, and these features, see Chapter 7, "Repeaters, Bridges, and Hubs," and Chapter 8, "Network Switches."

Network Cable Connectors and Terminators

In Chapter 5, "Wiring the Network—Cables and Other Components," the various kinds of network cables and connectors that can be used to create a LAN were examined. While most older 10Base-2 networks have already been upgraded to 10Base-T (or greater) networks, there are still a few around that use thinnet coaxial cable with BNC connectors and terminators. If you are operating a LAN of this kind, be sure that any new network card purchases are "combo cards," as shown in Figure 6.3. These cards let you connect either a BNC T-connector to the card or use an RJ-45 jack for the newer 10Base-T networks. In all probability, you will have a difficult time finding network cards that support only BNC connectors. Purchasing combo cards means that you can still use the adapter when you upgrade to 10Base-T.

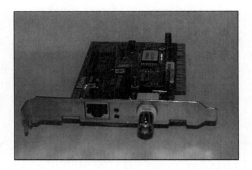

Figure 6.3   A combo card contains both a BNC and an RJ-45 receptacle and can be used on both types of networks.

The Wired for Management (WfM) Initiative and Wake On LAN (WOL) Technology

So far, this chapter has discussed some of the more typical factors to consider when choosing a network card for an upgrade or for retaining existing network cards for use in new computer acquisitions. However, depending on the size of your network, there is another factor to consider—the total cost of managing the computers on your network. The Wired for Management (WfM) initiative is a framework that most of the industry's major players, from IBM to Compaq and Dell, are adopting. You'll find most of the information about WfM at Intel's developer's Web site (http://developer.intel.com/ial/WfM/whatsnew.htm), including one particular key component: Wake on LAN (WOL) technology for network adapter cards.

To understand how WOL fits into this scheme, it's best to start with a simple understanding of the key components of WfM. These are

- Universal Network Boot
- Asset Management
- Power Management
- Remote Wake-Up (Wake on LAN and Wake on Ring)

Universal Network Boot

The Universal Network Boot component is based on technology that allows a network to boot over a network and download an operating system, or other software, from a management server. The Preboot Execution Environment (PXE) technology is the key part of this component. PXE allows a computer to be remotely booted after the remote wakeup function is invoked. By using industry standard techniques, such as DHCP, TFTP, and TCP/IP, adopting PXE technology does not require extensive changes to incorporate it into new PCs. It also allows for older systems, which do not understand the extended uses of these standard protocols, to continue to function because they can simply ignore the extensions.

▶▶   For more information about the specifics of how PXE uses DHCP, TFTP, and TCP/IP and other protocols, see Chapter 23, "BOOTP and the Dynamic Host Configuration Protocol (DHCP)."

Asset and Power Management

The Asset Management component includes a database that keeps an inventory of software and hardware for systems on the network, and allows polling computers to get this information.

The Power Management component is included to provide support for the Advanced Configuration and Power Management Interface (ACPI) and for Advanced Power Management (APM), which helps reduce costs by reducing power consumption that PCs and assorted peripherals use. ACPI is a newer technology that is expected to replace APM. By placing a computer and its peripherals into a lower power state after a predefined time has passed with no user interaction, the computer's electricity use is greatly reduced. This results in money saved and, in some cases, less stress on the computer's components.

Remote Wake-Up

The Remote Wake-Up component is the component that is most relevant to this chapter. The WfM initiative supports two kinds of remote wake ups for computers: by the LAN to which the system is connected, or through a telephone line connected to a modem (Wake on Ring). This second component is considered optional, but the capability to power up a computer by sending a specialized datagram to the computer is a key component that makes other components possible.

For example, taking inventory of existing software, or installing new software on a user's computer, usually must be done during normal working hours. This can result in lost productivity because the user is not able to use his workstation. Performing this same function during off-hours, such as in the middle of the night, removes this expensive obstacle. One alternative is to tell users to leave their computers up and running so that you can use an automated software package to perform the inventory or software installation functions. Yet, there will always be someone who forgets. And there's the fact that while that computer is up and running, waiting to be inventoried or upgraded, electricity is being consumed. When you're talking about hundreds of computers, that also can be an important cost factor.

To wake up a computer from a low-power state or to boot the system if it has been powered off, the network adapter must be capable of sensing a "magic packet" that is directed to it, or to use the newer "packet filtering" method.

The WOL Network Adapter Card

The network adapter that is used in a WOL situation can be a PCI card that you install in a computer just like any other network card. There is also a new LAN on Motherboard (LOM) that places the network card function directly on the motherboard, eliminating the need for a separate card that uses up an expansion slot. The most common method at this time is to use a network card that you have to install, however.

Because the adapter card must be capable of listening to the network, awaiting a signal telling it that it's time to wake up the computer, the card must have a power source. In Figure 6.4 you can see an example of this kind of card. The small cable is used to connect the adapter card to the motherboard to supply a power source so that the card is always listening for wake-up packets.

You don't have to do anything for motherboard solutions. The network adapter circuitry on the motherboard is already connected to the computer's power source. However, the majority of PCI cards available today require that you make a connection between the PCI card and the motherboard, using a small power cable supplied with the card just for this purpose. Read the documentation if you decide to use WOL cards on your network. Note that not only must the LAN card be WOL compliant, but the motherboard must also support this connection. Check the documentation!

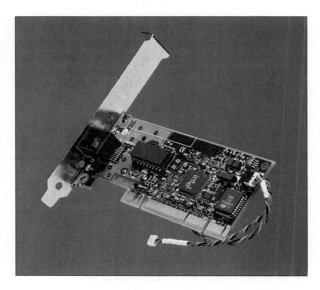

Figure 6.4   A small cable is used on some WOL cards to connect the card to the motherboard so that power can be supplied to the card.

The Alarm Clock: Magic Packets and Packet Filtering

There are two recommendations for signaling the LAN card that it's time to wake up the computer. The first method uses a "magic packet," which is a special packet designed just for this purpose. When a specialized circuit in the network adapter card sees this packet on the network, it initiates the system wake-up.

A second method, which is the preferred method in version 2.0 of the WfM specifications, is that the card recognizes ordinary network packets addressed to it, instead of a specialized magic packet. This second method is referred to in the specifications as *packet filtering* and is not to be confused with the same term when applied to firewall technology.

Whichever method is used, the computer can either be booted when the LAN card receives a wake-up call, or it can simply resume normal operations if the computer has been put into a suspended low-power state without performing a complete shutdown. The preferred method is that the computer be placed in a suspended low-power state, but this is not an absolute requirement.

The "magic packet" method uses a special datagram that contains a source and destination address. The destination address can be a particular workstation's address, or it can be a broadcast address used to wake up multiple systems. The data portion of the packet contains synchronization bytes and the workstation's address repeated 16 times. Optional fields are also present in this datagram, but the point is that, by using this special kind of packet, the WOL network adapter to which it is addressed can begin the wake-up sequence of events. This allows it to either boot the computer or revive it from its low-power suspended state.

Should You Use WOL-Compliant Network Cards?

Whether this new technology is suitable for your LAN depends on how you manage your network. If you have frequent software updates or must be able to remotely manage workstations without having a technician sitting at the keyboard entering commands, you should consider using WOL and other

WfM technologies. To do so you'll also have to use management software capable of formulating and sending out WOL packets, if the network adapter requires it. Using the newer specifications, you might want to purchase cards that can wake the dead, so to speak, by detecting any network traffic directed to them.

If you don't foresee a need for these capabilities in the near future, then save the cash and just purchase ordinary, cheaper network adapter cards. If you manage a small network and have only infrequent changes that you need to make, or if all of your computer systems are located in close proximity to each other, you might find it cheaper to do things the old-fashioned way, by visiting each computer when an upgrade is needed or a problem arises.

As vendors more widely adopt WOL and WfM, the prices for all components, network cards and management software, will most likely drop, making an upgrade in a few years a more cost-effective solution. Because most desktop computers are practically out of date within three to five years, don't feel you need to adopt new technology just because it's available. Evaluate your needs, balance these with the expenses involved, and make a decision based on those factors.

Multi-Homed Systems

Some computers need more than one network card. For example, if you have two subnets in your LAN that both need to connect to the same server, the server computer needs more than one network adapter. Although you can use a router to connect different subnets, it is probably cheaper to simply multi-home a server for a small network than to bother with the administrative overhead of configuring and maintaining a router.

In this case, the server can function both as a file or print server to both subnets and act as a router. It is also possible, depending on the type of computer, to attach more than one network card to the same subnet. In any case, each network card must be set up with its own network address and host name. For example, a high-performance server might be used on an intranet to provide a WWW service and an FTP service to clients. If the server is capable of processing the requests at the required rate but the network adapter card is a limiting factor, you can install multiple cards and assign an address and host name for each service.

One popular reason for multi-homing a server today is to provide a hardware platform that can function as a *proxy server* for a network firewall. In this configuration, the proxy server application intercepts all traffic that passes between the two subnets to which it is connected, and acts as a go-between to enhance security on the network. The proxy server accepts service requests from one adapter and interacts with the service provider through the other adapter. The proxy server examines responses from the service and, if allowed, returns them to the requesting computer using the first network adapter.

▶▶ For more information about proxy servers, see Chapter 40, "Firewalls."

Load Balancing and Dual-Redundant Network Controllers

For important servers, a single network card that is used to interface with the network is a single point of failure. If the card goes bad, the costs involved can be quite large if a large number of users access the server. For many years computer manufacturers have come up with solutions to minimize down time for important systems. The two most basic techniques that come to mind are *clustering* and *redundancy*. Clustering technology allows two or more computers to operate in a manner such that one or more computers in the cluster can service user requests at the same time, as in Compaq's OpenVMS clusters. Another clustering technique, which is used in Windows NT and Windows 2000 clusters, uses a failover technique. One or more computers in the cluster are on standby and ready to take over if another member of the cluster fails.

This second technique is also an example of redundancy. For many years it has been possible to buy disk controllers that operate in a redundant fashion. Redundant node clusters, disk controllers, multiple CPUs, and other mechanisms have made the task of providing maximum uptime for computers an easy task. However, the network card remains a single point of failure.

That problem has been remedied. You can now purchase network adapter cards that work in a dual-redundant manner. That is, one card services network requests while the other waits in standby mode, checking periodically to be sure the other adapter is functioning properly. There are even versions of dual-redundant network adapters that both operate at the same time, providing a load-balancing capability as well as a failover mechanism.

For example, 3Com manufacturers NICs that use a technique where each NIC has its own MAC address, yet all cards that the administrator places in a "group" share the same IP address. Each group can contain from two to eight network cards, which should provide enough redundancy for almost any server. The added benefit of load-balancing to maximize network traffic throughput makes this an ideal solution for a high-end enterprise server that is used by a large client base.

Different methods can be used when load-balancing is implemented with network adapter cards. For example, one scheme is to use a round-robin technique for each packet sent out on the network. Another is to use the client's MAC address and assign traffic for those packets to a specific controller. This technique might not be a good solution if most of the traffic is coming from a router because all the packets from the router share the router's MAC address.

3Com's Dynamic*Access* technology uses a hashing algorithm, taking into account the MAC address and the IP address of the client, and assigns traffic for each connection a client makes to a particular network adapter. If the client establishes multiple connections, then it's possible for the network traffic to be assigned to different adapters for each connection.

Although dual network adapters are not a factor in the desktop environment, they can provide security at that vital link in the network between an important enterprise server and the network. The cost of redundant network adapters, when compared to the expensive server hardware, makes this a cheap solution to a big problem. Because this technology has been around for only a few years, I suggest you check out several vendors, inquiring about the methods used for load-balancing and redundancy. Take into consideration also the management software, if any, that you will need to use to configure or troubleshoot the adapters.

Software Drivers

When networks were composed of mainly proprietary solutions for a particular vendor's systems, the vendor could write a simple software driver that could handle all the functions for the protocols that the vendor chose to implement. In networks today, it is usually necessary to use more than one type of protocol on a network, so now software drivers must be capable of handling more than one protocol.

In the case of servers or routers, another factor to be considered is a system that has multiple network cards installed. The driver software must be capable of distinguishing the different NICs, as well as the protocols supported on each.

The two main types of NIC software drivers that you can find today are ODI and NDIS. Predating both of these, however, is a driver called a Packet Driver, which FTP Software developed in 1986. Because different operating systems or networking software might work only with a specific kind of driver, you must be aware of the kinds of drivers that a network card can be used with if you are planning to upgrade NICs or, perhaps, undergo a more complex change, such as migrating to a new operating system. For example, if you are thinking of migrating to a Novell network, you should concentrate on devices that support ODI drivers. In a Microsoft networking environment, you would need to look for devices that support NDIS.

Packet Drivers

In the early days of PC networking, one of the main problems with network cards and protocol stacks was that they were too closely interrelated; that is, purchasing a network protocol software package meant you had to be sure that it supported the network card you were using. The operating system did not provide the code to interface with the card, but rather the specific protocol package. This, of course, meant that developers of protocol stacks had to spend lots of time developing code to support the many different types of network cards that were on the market.

FTP Software developed the Packet Driver to create an interface that protocols could use to access functions the network card provides. Protocol stacks that use the Packet Driver can exist on the computer and use the network card at the same time. Previously, network drivers were tightly bound to the network card at boot time, and you had to make changes to configuration files and reboot the computer each time you wanted to use a different network protocol.

The Open Data-Link Interface (ODI)

Novell and Apple Computer developed ODI in 1989 with a goal of providing a seamless interface at the network, transport, and data-link levels, as shown in the OSI reference model. The ODI specification can be divided into three components:

- **Multi-Link Interface Driver (MLID)**—This component controls communication between the network card and the link support layer. It consists of a section of code written by Novell called the Media Support Module (MSM) and the Hardware-Specific Module (HSM), written by the card vendor. The MSM provides the functions that implement standard network functions for the media types that are supported by ODI. The vendor writes the HSM code to handle the details of their particular card; the HSM code communicates with the MSM.

- **Link Support Layer (LSL)**—This layer enables multiple protocols to exist on a single network card. The LSL is a gateway that determines to which protocol stack a network packet belongs and sends it on its way.

- **Protocol Stack**—This component gets packets from the LSL and then sends the packet to another higher-level protocol or application.

Because ODI is modular, it makes writing protocol stacks or software drivers easier for third-party vendors. The code developer who works on the software to implement a protocol needs only to write to the specifications of the ODI interface, without regard to the underlying network card or the network media. The network card vendor only has to worry about writing code that can communicate with the MSM to implement the functions that are implemented by the card's hardware.

The Network Driver Interface Specification (NDIS)

Microsoft and 3Com Corporation initially developed NDIS, with Microsoft continuing that development with more recent versions. NDIS serves the same purpose, more or less, that ODI does in that it allows for the development of software for multiple protocol stacks to exist on multiple network adapters in a single computer. The actual implementation details, however, are quite different.

In Windows NT and Windows 2000, transport protocols span a portion of the transport layer, the network layer, and a portion of the data link layer. Transport protocols, such as NetBEUI Frame (NBF) and TCP, are implemented by calling services in the NDIS interface. NDIS doesn't completely hide the underlying network media from the protocol stack the way that ODI does. This limits most drivers to using Ethernet 802.3 or Token Ring 802.5. Most drivers for ARCnet, for example, are written to take this into account and make the media look like ethernet or token ring to the software layers above.

Both ODI and NDIS provide support for each other. ODI provides a program called ODINSUP to support NDIS drivers. Windows NT and Windows 2000 come with NWLink, which is Microsoft's implementation of the IPX/SPX protocols. Windows NT also comes with Client Services for NetWare, which allows Windows NT clients to access resources on NetWare servers. Gateway Services for NetWare perform similar functions using a single Windows NT computer as a gateway to the NetWare services. A separate product called File and Print Services for NetWare is available from Microsoft, and can be used on a NetWare client to give it access to resources in a Windows NT network.

In Part IV of this book, you will find more details about the various networking protocols that are available.

IRQs and I/O Ports

Although many new network adapter cards support plug-and-play capabilities, which means the operating system can automatically detect and configure them, this capability is not implemented in all operating systems, such as many Unix variants. Because of this, you might find yourself having to configure a card manually when upgrading a system with a new card, or when adding other devices that might conflict with the NIC. The two main items you will commonly have to modify are the values for the IRQ (Interrupt ReQuest Line) and the base I/O port.

IRQs

When a device on the computer's bus needs to get the attention of the CPU, it uses a hardware mechanism called the *Interrupt ReQuest Line* (*IRQ*). Hardware interrupts are executed by signaling the CPU through a set of wires that are connected to the pins that attach the CPU to the motherboard. It is a direct connection. Because a variety of devices might need to get the CPU's attention at any particular time, one IRQ is not sufficient. Instead, in most cases each device has its own interrupt line. When a device signals the CPU using an interrupt, it is telling the CPU that it has a processing request that needs to be satisfied as quickly as possible.

When the CPU receives an interrupt, it grants the device its attention for a short period of time—as long as it is not currently servicing another interrupt that is of a higher priority. It is also possible that the CPU is performing some task that is too critical to allow for an interrupt. When that is the case, the CPU does not allow a hardware interrupt to distract it. For that reason, this type of interrupt is called a *maskable interrupt*. This means that the CPU can be put into a mode in which it masks out these interrupts while it is busy on an ultra important task, and then reenables the interrupts when it is again capable of processing them.

The number of IRQs that are available on the system depends on the system bus type. Early PCs that were based on the ISA bus type had only eight hardware interrupts, numbered from 0–7, as shown in Table 6.1.

Table 6.1   ISA Bus Hardware Interrupts

IRQ	Function
0	System Timer
1	Keyboard Controller
2	Available

Table 6.1   continued

IRQ	Function
3	Serial Port 2 and 4 (COM2:, COM4:)
4	Serial Port 1 and 3 (COM1:, COM3:)
5	Hard Disk Drive Controller
6	Floppy Disk Drive Controller
7	Parallel Port 1 (LPT1:)

This small set of IRQs was sufficient for a small system with few devices. As you can see, only one IRQ—2—is available for an additional device in this layout. When the EISA bus was developed, the number of interrupts doubled to 16. However, to do this, two interrupt controllers were needed on the system; one of them funnels its interrupts through IRQ2. This means that there are actually only 15 interrupts available for use by other devices on the system. Table 6.2 shows the devices that usually use these IRQs.

Table 6.2   EISA Bus Hardware Interrupts

IRQ	Function
0	System Timer
1	Keyboard Controller
2	Second Interrupt Controller
8	Real-time clock
9	Network Card
10	Available
11	SCSI card
12	Motherboard mouse port
13	Math coprocessor
14	Primary IDE (Hard Disk Drive) controller
15	Secondary IDE (Hard Disk Drive) controller
3	Serial Port 2 and 4 (COM2:, COM4:)
4	Serial Port 1 and 3 (COM1:, COM3:)
5	Sound card or parallel port 2 (LPT2:)
6	Floppy Disk Drive Controller
7	Parallel Port 1 (LPT1:)

Notice that the IRQ numbers in Table 6.2 are not in numerical order. Instead, they are listed in order of *priority*, with those at the top of the table having a higher priority than those at the bottom. Because the additional eight IRQs were added by a mechanism that uses the original IRQ2, those IRQs all have a higher priority than IRQs 3–7. On some systems, IRQ9 is used to perform the same functions that were done by IRQ2 in the earlier design. For this reason, you might see this IRQ on a card labeled as 2, 9, or possibly IRQ 2/9.

If your computer is a plug-and-play system, you might find that you do not need to make any changes to the card or the system software to select the IRQ. If you do, however, be sure to consult the documentation that comes with the card to determine which interrupts it can use and how they are set. IRQs in non–plug-and-play cards are usually set by jumpers on the card. A jumper consists of a set of pins that can be connected to form a complete circuit by placing a connector between them.

Base I/O Ports

Again, if you find yourself in a situation where your computer's operating system does not provide plug-and-play capabilities, you might have to manually configure the value of the memory address that the network card uses to transfer data to and from the system. After the network card signals to the CPU that processing needs to be done, it uses a memory address called the *base I/O port address* for this purpose. Because many devices in the system might use memory port addresses, it is important to configure each device to use a different address so that any data transfers that are performed do not conflict with each other.

On most systems, 64KB of memory is set up to be used for I/O ports, so they do not represent a limited resource like the IRQ does. Consult your operating system documentation to determine how to display the current memory assignments for this area of memory.

For example, in Microsoft Windows, a utility called Microsoft Diagnostics can be used to display a variety of hardware and software configurations. In Figure 6.5 you can see the utility, displaying the I/O ports on a Windows NT 4.0 Server computer. Note that at the bottom of the display, there are buttons you can use to view other device-related information, such as IRQs and memory allocations.

To run the diagnostic utility on a Windows NT 4.0 Server system, click Start, Programs, Administrative Tools, Windows NT Diagnostics. When the utility appears, select the Resources tab. Click the I/O Port button at the bottom of the utility and your screen should look similar to that shown in Figure 6.5.

Figure 6.5 The NT Diagnostics utility can show you how I/O ports are assigned.

Windows 2000 uses the Microsoft Management Console interface for most system administration utilities. To view hardware resources on a Windows 2000 server computer, use the following steps:

1. Click Start, Programs, Accessories, System Tools, System Information.

2. When the System Information window pops up, expand the Hardware Resources folder you see in Tree section of the MMC.

3. Select the hardware component you want to view from the list that appears under Hardware Resources.

As you can see in Figure 6.6, the hardware resources you can view using this utility include the base I/O port (I/O), IRQs (IRQ), and Direct Memory Access (DMA). In this figure the IRQ item has been selected and you can see a list of each IRQ and the device with which it is associated.

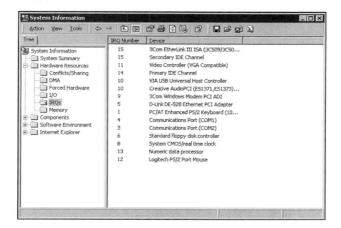

Figure 6.6   Windows 2000 uses the Microsoft Management Console (MMC) application to display system information.

Notice that the first item listed is Conflicts/Sharing. Using this item you can determine whether more than one device on this system is sharing an interrupt.

In addition to the base I/O port, some devices use a section of memory to buffer data temporarily. For this, they require a *base memory address*, which points to the start of the buffer. Your network card might or might not use the computer's RAM, so check the documentation carefully if a conflict arises.

Troubleshooting Network Cards

When you install or replace a network adapter card and find that it does not function, there are several things you can examine to attempt to diagnose the problem. The cause might be due to a hardware problem with the card itself or with the computer. Or, it might be the cable that links the card to the hub or switch, or the hub or the switch. It might be a simple problem of changing the configuration for the device. If you're having a bad day, it might even be a combination of these things!

If you are using Windows NT or Windows 2000, check the system error log using the Event Viewer to see if any errors are being logged when the computer boots and is in the process of checking devices. Using the Event Viewer, you might find that you have a software configuration problem.

When adding a new network card to a workstation, you want to first review the documentation that comes with the card to determine what values you can use for the IRQ, base I/O port address, and so on. You might also need to look at documentation for other devices on the system because resolving a conflict might require you to change some other device instead of the network card.

The good news is that, if all the cards in your system are plug-and-play compatible, you can be sure that an IRQ or memory address conflict is not causing the problem. In that case, begin troubleshooting efforts by checking the cable, hub, switch, and other hardware components that connect the computer to the network.

Check the LEDs—Activity and Link Lights

All network interface cards have some combination of status LEDs (light emitting diode) located on them. To determine the actual meaning of any LEDs, be sure to review the documentation for your specific brand and model of card. For example, some 3Com cards have an LED that is used to indicate the link status. If the light is on, the link is okay. If the light is flashing, there is a problem with the transmit/receive wires in the cable used (reversed polarity). It uses a second LED to indicate network activity (when the network card is sending or receiving data).

Network cards usually have at least one LED, which you can see on the outside of the computer—one for link status and one for network activity. Generally, if the card has only one LED (link) it should be lit if the card is capable of communicating with the hub. Most hubs and switches also have an LED status light for each port, so it is a good idea to check that also. The problem might be in the hub, switch, or the network card. It might even be the cable that connects them.

If it appears that there is a problem with the link, localize the problem and determine where the fault is by trying the following:

- Check all connectors to be sure that they are firmly plugged into their sockets.

- Be sure that the card and the hub/switch port are set for the same type of link; that is, the switch might be set to full duplex, while the card is not, or one end might be set to 10Mbps while the other is set to 100Mbps.

- If your card supports auto-negotiation, try to enable or disable this feature on the switch or hub. If the card's documentation indicates that it does support auto-negotiation, it might not be functioning properly. You might have to manually set the hub or switch port to the proper setting.

- Try another port on the hub or switch.

- Try a different cable, preferably one that you know is in good working condition.

- Try to reseat the card in the slot.

- Try to move the network adapter to a different slot in the computer.

- Check the BIOS settings for the computer. Check the manual for your computer to determine whether you need to reserve certain IRQs for older adapters to keep PCI cards from trying to use the same values. In some computers it is possible to enable or disable a PCI slot by using the BIOS setup program. Be sure the slot is enabled if your BIOS supports this feature.

- Substitute a card that you know is good to see if the problem still presents itself.

If none of the preceding seems to work, try the card in another computer where no problem exists. If it works there, then the problem obviously does not lie in the NIC, and you might have a software or hardware configuration problem on the computer in question.

Run the Adapter's Diagnostic Program

Almost all cards, even those labeled as plug and play, come with a floppy disk that contains software drivers and a diagnostic program. Usually you will find that it is necessary to boot the computer into MS-DOS to run the diagnostic program, and indeed some cards come with a floppy disk that is also MS-DOS bootable. When using a diagnostic program like this you should be careful that no other drivers or memory managers are loaded when you perform the test to help eliminate conflicts that can result in inaccurate results. Note that "MS-DOS" does not mean a command prompt window in Windows 98 or Windows NT/2000. It means booting the computer into the actual MS-DOS operating system.

The kinds of tests that can be run vary, but you will probably get a menu that allows you to run one or all of the tests that the program is capable of executing. This can include simple hardware-specific checks and loopback tests. Some cards provide for an echo test, in which two cards from the same manufacturer can send and receive packets from each other for a diagnostic test. If the card cannot pass all the diagnostic tests that the vendor supplies, and if you are sure there are no other problems (such as a bad slot in the computer's system bus), then you probably have a bad card and need to replace it.

Configuration Conflicts

If the card passes the vendor's diagnostic tests and you can find nothing wrong with the physical components of the card, computer system, or the hub/switch, then it is time to check the configuration of the card. Earlier in this chapter (in the section "Base I/O Ports") you saw how the Microsoft Diagnostics utility under Windows NT (or the MMC System Information utility in Windows 2000) can be used to determine which memory address a device has been configured to use. You can also use these utilities to determine the IRQ and other configuration information for the devices installed in the computer. In Figure 6.7 you can see the Windows 2000 System Information window with the Conflicts/Sharing item selected.

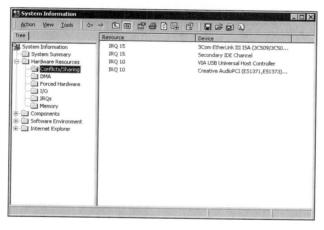

Figure 6.7 You can use the System Information MMC utility to check for device conflicts.

If you are working with a Windows 98 or Windows NT 4.0 computer, you can use the Resources tab in the Microsoft Diagnostics utility to compare device settings. Check the Conflicting Device List field. If you find that other devices appear here, you can take appropriate action and reassign the IRQs or memory addresses as needed until all devices are functioning correctly. Reassigning these values will likely involve using software that comes with the particular adapter card.

Note

Remember that the PCI bus allows for the capability to share IRQs. Thus, if you notice that more than one device is using the same IRQ number, it might not really be the source of your problem. In general, only similar devices should be sharing the same IRQ. When the IRQ line signals the CPU for a shared IRQ, the system interrogates each device that shares the IRQ to determine which device is actually requesting attention from the CPU.

If you are using an older ISA card, you will probably have to use a jumper or a small switch on the card to change configuration information. If you're using an EISA card, the ECU program can usually be used to help adjust configuration information.

For Unix users the situation is more complicated. In many cases, adding new hardware requires that you recompile the kernel and reboot. Many newer systems support plug and play and can recognize well-known hardware components and configure them automatically, but this is not always the case. Depending on the version of Unix, you might be able to examine configuration files to determine the interrupts and memory addresses a particular device uses. Check your system's documentation for further information.

Because there are many different releases of both Unix and Linux, your best bet when troubleshooting NIC problems is to start with the card manufacturer's resources. Some cards can be configured by running a program that comes with the adapter, while others must be installed and configured using utilities the operating system vendor supplies.

Check the Computer's Network Configuration

If none of the previous troubleshooting steps have uncovered the source of your problem, the problem just might lie farther up the protocol stack and might not be a problem with the hardware components. For example, if you are using a DHCP server to allocate IP addresses on the network, the computer might not have been able to successfully obtain configuration information from a DHCP server. Or, if you have configured the IP information manually and have a statically assigned address for the computer, check to be sure you didn't mistakenly use the same address for more than one computer. Be sure that the address you assigned to the computer (and the subnet mask) is the correct one for the subnet to which the computer is attached.

After you've eliminated the hardware components as the problem source, there are other tools you can use to diagnose protocol and routing issues. Chapter 22, "Troubleshooting Tools for TCP/IP Networks," covers the standard utilities that come with most TCP/IP implementations. In addition, that chapter also covers the tcpdump and WinDump programs that can be found on the CD-ROM that accompanies this book. These programs allow you to look at the actual datagrams flowing through the network, giving you a detailed look at what is actually going on. While everything else might check out okay, such as the link LEDs, your network adapter card might be sending out corrupted datagrams. In that case, toss it and buy a new card.

Preventative Steps to Take

Keeping track of system information for the computers in your network can make troubleshooting tasks a lot easier. For example, a spreadsheet that lists all the nodes on your network, along with configuration information, is very useful when you need to upgrade or replace a particular component. If you have this information already available before a problem arises, you will be able to devote more of your time to solving the problem.

This kind of information also can be used to help you make purchasing decisions. For example, if you know the number of ISA and PCI slots that are built into a workstation, and if you know which of these have already been populated, you won't make the mistake of buying an ISA card when there are no slots left in which you can use it.

Repeaters, Bridges, and Hubs

SOME OF THE MAIN TOPICS IN THIS CHAPTER ARE

Simple Network Repeaters

Using Bridges to Connect Network Segments

Using Hubs to Centralize LAN Wiring and Minimize Cable
Problems

Hub Ports

Troubleshooting Hub Problems

Chapter 1, "Overview of Network Topologies," covered the different kinds of network topologies used to join the computers that make up a network. The simplest topology available is the *bus*, which consists of a single segment of cable to which all computers are attached. This topology was the first used for ethernet networks and worked quite well when only a small number of computers were to participate in the network. When minicomputers came into the picture, and most especially when PCs made their appearance during the 1980s, it became obvious that a computer network would have to be able to handle a much larger traffic load and connect many more computers than the simple bus topology would allow. Taking ethernet as an example, there comes a point at which the number of frame collisions becomes excessive and network throughput becomes unacceptable.

This chapter discusses some of the devices that you can use to create larger local area networks. Some of these devices, such as repeaters and bridges, simply allow you to extend the length of the network and add additional computers. Others, such as a bridge, can help to limit the broadcast domain, in addition to allow for a larger LAN. Finally, hubs will be looked at as a solution that allows for all the preceding with the added benefit of centralizing the wiring that connects the network. In the next chapter, we discuss switches, which take the concept of the hub and add to it by creating a broadcast domain consisting of only two nodes on the network—the switch and a single computer.

Note

Because ethernet is based on multiple computers all using the same network media for transmissions, each computer must contend for access to the media, as explained in Chapter 12, "Ethernet." Because it is possible for more than one computer to begin transmitting at the same time, the signals sometimes interfere with each other in what is termed a *collision*. The term *collision domain* is used to specify a portion of the network that is shared by several computers, all of which can possibly transmit packets that could cause a collision.

Simple Network Repeaters

A *simple repeater* joins two physical segments, and functions by amplifying the signal it receives on one port before it transmits it out the other port to the next network segment. Because a repeater only amplifies the electrical signal, and does not perform any actions on the information represented by the signal, it is totally ignorant of any addressing or routing information that might be encapsulated in the frame. This results in the repeater amplifying and sending out not only valid network frames that are transmitted on the network, but also fragmented frames resulting from collisions and background noise.

In a small network, this kind of device can be used advantageously to increase the size of a network based on a bus topology. For example, a thinnet network (10BASE-2) is limited to cable segment lengths of only 185 meters, or about 607 feet. The specification 10BASE-2 allows you to join as many as five cable segments, using four repeaters, which gives an overall length to the network of about 3,000 feet, as shown in Figure 7.1. Remember also that in this kind of network you can attach workstations to only three of the five segments. The other two segments can be used to extend the length of the LAN. In this drawing one segment is used to extend the LAN between floors in the building and another is used on the first floor to add extra distance to get to the location of the users.

Advantages to using simple repeaters include price and simplicity. They are relatively inexpensive devices when compared to bridges or switches and require no management console or intervention by the administrator for configuration. A repeater can be used as a quick remedy when your small LAN segment needs to be extended beyond its normal range and it's too soon to explore further upgrade options.

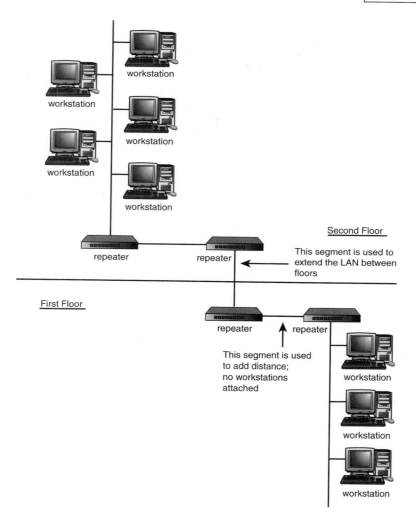

Figure 7.1   Repeaters can extend the network beyond the length allowed for one cable segment.

In Figure 7.1 you can see that each repeater joins only two cable segments. Passive hubs, which are discussed shortly, work much in the same manner, but allow you to connect multiple cable segments to a single repeater. The simple repeater, while allowing you to extend the length of the bus topology, repeats *all* network traffic; thus it does nothing to limit the broadcast domain. You can extend the length of the network and you can add more computers or other devices, such as networked printers, but the more devices you add to the network, the more traffic that is generated on all segments that make it up. The more traffic on a single shared media Ethernet network, the greater the chance of collisions. Therefore, after a certain point, network throughput will suffer because of excessive collisions.

Note

What is a hub? In the examples we've just looked at, you probably can determine that it is a device that centralizes the cabling of your network. Don't worry; we'll get to hubs later in this chapter and explain the different types and how they work.

A repeater that contains more than two ports, called a *multiport repeater*, also can be used to connect many LAN cable segments. Most of these devices provide for the ability to block a port that is causing problems so that they do not affect the other network segments. Using a multiport repeater, you can attach a single computer to each port or create LAN cable segments that contain multiple computers connected to the cable that connects to the repeater port. The problem with the latter method is easy to see. Each segment that contains more than one computer is essentially an independent bus. If the cable is broken or malfunctions anywhere along the line, more than one computer will be unable to communicate on the network.

Although multiport repeaters served their purpose well, for the most part they have been replaced by more modern devices, such as bridges, intelligent hubs, and switches.

Using Bridges to Connect Network Segments

Simple repeaters operate at the *physical layer* of the OSI layered networking reference model. They just connect the cables and amplify the electrical signal before retransmitting it. Another device, called a bridge, also can be useful when joining cable segments. A *bridge* operates at the data link layer and does a little more than just amplify the incoming signal and send it out to the remaining ports.

A bridge is basically a repeater with a little intelligence. At the data link layer the *Media Access Control address* (often referred to as the MAC address or the hardware address) is used to sort out which computers are connected to each cable segment. When a bridge is used to connect cable segments it actually examines header information contained in the frame and finds the source and destination MAC addresses of the frame. The bridge keeps a table in memory storing these hardware addresses and, over time, learns the location of each device on the network. Because a bridge becomes aware of which devices are attached to each of its ports, it can make decisions when it comes to transmitting an incoming frame on the other ports so that the frame is sent out only over the port that will get it to its destination.

In Figure 7.2 you can see a simple network consisting of two cable segments separated by a bridge. On each of these segments there are multiple hubs to which workstations are attached. On one of these segments, a server that is used to service print requests for the network is attached.

When a bridge is first powered up it has no knowledge of the layout of the network. There is no information in its internal tables telling it what devices are on the network, much less to which cable segment they are attached. This information is built up over a period time as the bridge learns the network topology. Consider the following scenario:

- Workstation A sends out a packet that it wants delivered to workstation C.

- The hub to which workstation A is attached repeats the frame on its other ports, one of which is connected to the cable that attaches the hub to the bridge. Because this is the first time that the bridge has received a frame from workstation A, it stores this information as an entry in its internal table, recording the MAC address for workstation A and noting from which port it came.

- At this time, the bridge does not yet know to which segment workstation C is attached. So, to deliver the frame it is necessary for the bridge to repeat the frame on its other port. Workstation C recognizes the frame is addressed to it and communication between it and workstation A can then take place. However, when workstation C then sends a frame back to workstation A, the bridge does not repeat the frame on the other ports. The bridge knows that workstation A is on the same segment as workstation C. At this time the bridge creates an entry in its table for workstation C so that future communications on this segment from A to C are not repeated on the other port.

■ Next workstation B sends a packet destined for workstation F. Again, the bridge notes the port and MAC address for workstation B since it had not heard of it before, and makes an entry into its table. The frame is repeated onto the segment attached to the other port.

■ When workstation F receives the frame it responds and sends back a frame to workstation B. When the bridge sees the destination MAC address for workstation B in the frame, it recognizes it as one stored in its table and repeats the frame on the port that has workstation B attached.

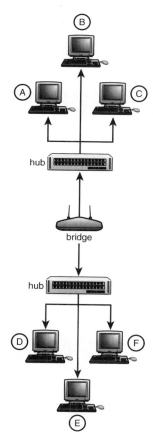

Figure 7.2   A bridge can be used to connect network segments.

As you can see from this example, *once a bridge learns the location of a computer* it does not have to repeat the signal on every segment like a simple repeater does. After the network has been up and running for a short period of time, depending on which workstations are active, the bridge knows the layout of the network and only transmits frames to another segment when it receives a frame with an address that is not in its table.

Note

Because this type of bridge forwards frames without having to interact with the source or destination nodes, the computers attached to the network are not aware of the fact that a bridge exists between them. For this reason, this type of bridge is usually referred to as a *transparent bridge*.

The benefits of a bridge over a simple repeater are obvious. The bridge cuts down on unnecessary broadcasts because it will not forward a frame after it learns the port to which a MAC address is attached, unless it is necessary to get the frame delivered to its destination. For this reason, a bridge limits the broadcast domain. When properly used, you can create a network using bridges that distributes the network traffic so that no single segment becomes overwhelmed with traffic.

For example, you probably wouldn't want to put all file and print servers on one segment and all your user's computers on another segment. In a typical client/server network, the user's computers are interacting with the servers and the network traffic has to flow through the bridge most of the time.

Instead, it makes better sense to place clients on the same segment with the server or servers that they most often use. Thus, the network traffic generated will be localized on that segment. In Figure 7.3, you can see a simple LAN that uses a bridge to join network segments that span two floors in a building.

In this example, you can see that the hub on the second floor has both user workstations and file and print servers attached to it. As long as users only need to communicate among themselves or these servers, the traffic is localized to the hub and does not pass through the bridge. A similar situation exists on the first floor, but two hubs are used instead. In this scenario, the two workstations on the second hub are used for training purposes and are located in a different room. By using a separate hub for these training workstations, it is easy for the administrator to add or remove workstations in the training room without having to run new cables through the ceiling every time an additional computer is needed. Instead, all that is required is that the cable be plugged into the existing hub.

Segmenting a LAN

As Figure 7.3 depicts, bridges can be used to take a simple network and divide it into segments to help isolate broadcast traffic. A rule that is called the 80/20 rule states that you should segment a LAN with bridges so that 80 percent of the traffic will be destined for devices attached to the local segment, while 20 percent might need to pass through a bridge to reach its destination.

By taking a single LAN and placing a bridge between nodes that do very little communication, you effectively increase the available bandwidth because the entire LAN does not have to hear broadcast traffic for every other node. If you have one set of users who make heavy use of a particular server, and another set of users who rarely use the server but send a lot of print jobs to a print server, then separating these two groups with a bridge cuts down on the overall network traffic. Yet, because the LAN is connected by a bridge, any workstation can communicate with any other computer or device on the network if it needs to.

◄◄   There are many ways you can use connectivity devices—such as hubs, switches, routers, and bridges—to segment a network and reduce network congestion. Chapter 1, "Overview of Network Topologies," is recommended reading if you're new to the physical layout of a network.

In a typical business environment most communications take place between users who work in a particular department of the business. For example, most of the network traffic generated in the accounting department is most likely targeted at servers or other workstations in the accounting department. Occasionally it will be necessary to communicate with computers in other departments—e-mail is a good example of this—but for the most part workers in the accounting department are busy interacting with a file server that stores the data (and in many cases the application software) that is used for the accounts receivable/accounts payable and general ledger. Putting these users on the same LAN segment as users in the engineering department would make little sense. The intense amount of traffic generated by CAD software and other applications used by the engineers could result in complaints from users about the "slow network" that they are on.

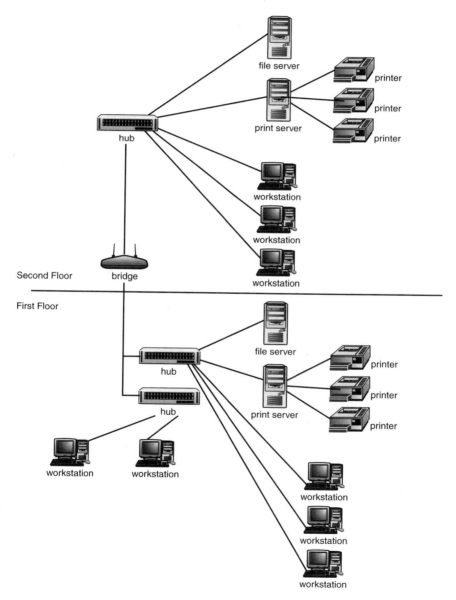

Figure 7.3 A bridge can be used to connect departmental LANs.

So far, only the connection of two LAN segments has been discussed. Although you can see three hubs in Figure 7.3, keep in mind that two of these hubs are on the same LAN segment (on the first floor), so all traffic is repeated to all other computers attached to both of these hubs. Hubs, unlike bridges, do not limit the broadcast domain.

The network is more complicated in most situations. You can use multiple bridges to break up a LAN into more than two broadcast domains. In Figure 7.4, users in Segment A make heavy use of the file and print servers located on their segment. Occasionally, however, they need to access the file server that resides on the other side of a bridge in Segment B. Users in Segment C make the most demand on the print server on their segment, but sometimes need to access the file server located on Segment B also.

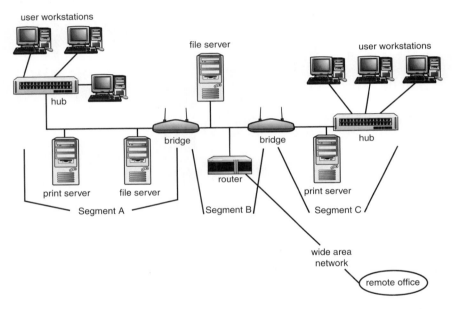

Figure 7.4   You can use multiple bridges to break up a LAN into smaller broadcast domains.

Still, both groups of users need to exchange data with a remote office on a periodic basis. In Figure 7.4, the wide area network is accessible through a router connected to segment B. By placing the router on this segment you keep down the level of traffic the router must process because it will not be seeing every packet that contends for network bandwidth on segments A and C. Because the file server on segment B is used by both groups of users, but not on a frequent basis, the traffic to and from it is not likely to place a strain on the router's capabilities to process packets.

Note

In this chapter, we use bridges and hubs as a means to isolate traffic in small LANs. In a much larger corporation where the number of computers significantly increases, bridges can only connect a limited number of cable segments, depending on the physical layer technology and the topology chosen for the network. In Chapter 10, "Routers," you can find out how it is possible to use routers to connect many smaller LAN segments into a larger network and still limit the broadcast domain.

The Spanning Tree Algorithm

It also is possible to connect two network segments with more than a single bridge. This can be done to provide for fault tolerance. If one bridge ceases to function properly, another path exists between the segments so that users are unaffected, as you can see in Figure 7.5.

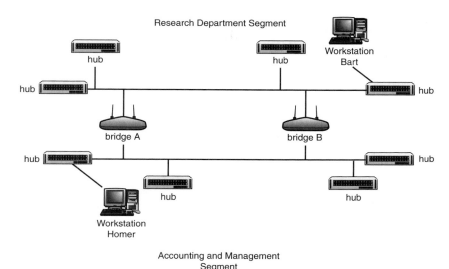

Figure 7.5   You can use more than one bridge to connect the same segments.

However, using multiple bridges could result in a lot of confusion if bridges were not configured to cooperate. For example, consider the following situation:

- If the workstation named Homer sends out a frame that has the workstation Bart as its destination, both bridges A and B see the frame on the segment used by the accounting and management divisions. They both retransmit the frame onto the segment used by the research department.

- Both bridges then add an entry into their internal tables to remember that Homer is connected to the accounting and management segment.

- When bridge B sees the frame that bridge A transmitted onto the research segment it will not understand that this frame is a duplicate of the one that it also transmitted. Instead, because the bridge only looks at the MAC address, it will see it as if the frame were just broadcast by Homer on this segment.

- Bridge B then will decide that Homer must have been moved and will change its internal table so that Homer now is attached to the research segment. Bridge A suffers the same fate, based on the frame that was originally retransmitted by bridge B.

Depending on timing issues, it also is possible that Bart will try to send a frame to Homer. If it is detected by either bridge while they still have Homer listed incorrectly in their internal tables, then Homer will never get the frame because the bridges will assume that workstation Homer is on the same cable segment as workstation Bart. If this is the case, the bridges assume that there is no need to send a copy of the frame over to the segment on which Homer is actually located.

But it could still get worse. After both bridges have retransmitted the other's retransmitted frame back to the first segment, they will again see the other bridge's newly retransmitted packet and once again make changes to their internal tables and once again forward the duplicate frames back to the research department's LAN segment!

This infinite looping would make it impractical to use more than one bridge to connect two segments. In a large environment, chaos could result if an administrator accidentally connected two segments with a second router without realizing the problem.

Note

A bridge does not maintain an entry for a node in its internal table forever. In actuality each bridge has a Time-To-Live (TTL) value that it uses. When an entry has been in the table longer than this value without being refreshed by the bridge again seeing it in a source address, the entry is removed.

To prevent this specific type of situation, the IEEE 802.1D specification defines the *spanning tree algorithm*. This specification allows bridges to interact with each other to initially create and then maintain a loop-free network. Although there can exist many routes that a frame can take through a multiple bridged network, the spanning tree algorithm establishes only one route that a frame can take between any two points. When a new bridge is added or a bridge is removed from the network, the bridges recalculate the paths, and nodes are still able to communicate, provided that more than one bridge can be used to forward the frame.

Several values are used to provide the information needed by the algorithm to calculate the paths that will make up the tree. The administrator of the network can assign these values. They are

- **Bridge ID**—A unique identifier for each bridge.
- **Port ID**—A unique identifier for each port on each bridge.
- **Port priority**—A relative value designating a port's priority.
- **Port cost**—A value that designates a "cost" for a port. The higher the bandwidth of the link, the lower the cost should be for the port.

When a bridge is added to the network it multicasts a message called a *Bridge Protocol Data Unit (BPDU)*, which contains information about it, including its ID and cost information. The bridges in the network evaluate these messages to calculate the correct paths that make up the tree of bridges.

The *root bridge* is selected based on the bridge ID value. The bridge that has the lowest bridge ID value becomes the root bridge. If two bridges both have been assigned the same ID, the one that has the lowest hardware (MAC) address becomes the root bridge.

Every other bridge then must calculate the lowest cost path that connects it to the root bridge. The port that provides the lowest cost path to the root bridge is designated the root port for that bridge. In the case where two ports have an equal cost path to the root bridge, the one with the lowest priority to the root bridge is designated to be the root port.

A designated bridge must be specified for each LAN. If only one bridge is connected to the LAN, then it obviously becomes the designate bridge. If more than one bridge is connected, then the bridge that has the lowest cost path to the root bridge becomes the designated bridge for that LAN.

For bridges that are not a designated bridge for a LAN, each port that is not a root port on the bridge is set to a blocked state so that it does not transmit any data. These blocked ports still listen for BDPU messages, however, so when the network topology changes they can be used to begin the tree calculating process again. Bridges continue to exchange BDPU messages on a periodic basis. When bridges detect that a designated bridge has failed because they do not receive a BDPU message from it within the specified time limit, they begin to recalculate the tree topology.

When to Bridge

As this chapter has discussed, bridges do more than just join segments. They are an inexpensive device that can be used to help grow a network until you reach the point where a switch or router would make more sense. By limiting the area in which a network frame can travel you can use bridges for

- **Reducing network congestion**—Grouping workstations, servers, and other devices that most frequently interact with each other reduces the total number of frames broadcast throughout the entire network.

- **Extending the length of the network**—Bridges allow you to connect multiple segments until you reach the limit for the network topology in use.

- **Minimal security purposes**—Place all workstations that exchange confidential data on a single network segment and use a bridge to connect them to the rest of the LAN. This way only those workstations on that local segment are able to intercept the packets exchanged. A network sniffer on another segment, for example, would be unable to intercept these packets because they never get to that segment. Although this does provide some security, keep in mind that until a bridge learns the hardware addresses of the computers connected to the secure segment, it still passes them on to all other segments! A better solution is to use a firewall, which is discussed in Chapter 40, "Firewalls."

- **Fault containment**—One malfunctioning device on the LAN is less likely to cause a problem beyond the segment to which it is connected.

However, in many cases a bridge makes sense only when used in a moderately sized network unless it is used in conjunction with other devices, such as switches or routers, and is used to limit traffic on a few segments. When the network outgrows the distances imposed by the topology limitations you must use other means as an upgrade path.

Using Hubs to Centralize LAN Wiring and Minimize Cable Problems

So far we have discussed using repeaters and bridges to connect LAN segments to create a larger network and to help relieve network traffic congestion problems. However, another problem with LANs that use a bus topology is that a break or other problem in the cable can cause all computers on a particular segment to lose their connection to the network. As discussed in Chapter 1, in a simple ethernet bus topology a T-connector attaches to a BNC connector at each workstation. The coaxial cable that makes up the network connects to both sides of the T-connector. At each end of the bus (that is, the computers at the far ends of the network), a terminator is used to prevent signals from reflecting back and causing the signal to become garbled. Removing this terminator—as any network administrator knows, users will try anything—can cause the entire segment to fail or experience a dramatic slowdown in communications. In Figure 7.6 you can see the T-connector and a terminator. This figure also shows you the coaxial thinnet cable, with two twisted-pair cables for comparison.

Using a multiport repeater to join segments that each had only one computer eliminated this major limitation of the bus topology. For example, if any cable becomes faulty or a terminator is removed from the end of the segment, only the computers on that segment are disconnected from the network. Other segments connected to a multiport repeater will continue to operate as usual.

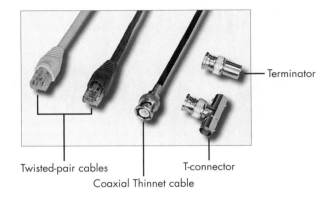

Twisted-pair cables   Terminator   T-connector

Coaxial Thinnet cable

Figure 7.6   Twisted-pair cables simply plug into the card or hub port. Thinnet coaxial cables require a BNC T-connector and a terminator at each end of the network segment.

Another nice feature of a multiport repeater is the fact that it allows you to concentrate LAN connections using a single device. The hubs that have been shown in diagrams in this chapter are essentially nothing more than multiport repeaters, with one major exception. Just like a multiport repeater, a hub concentrates LAN connections at a single point. Unlike a multiport repeater, however, hubs were developed to use twisted-pair wiring instead of the original 10BASE-2 and 10BASE-T coaxial cable. When using a hub, each computer is attached to a separate port. This means that if one cable is defective or broken, the remaining computers on the LAN can still communicate. Because only one computer is attached to each hub port, there is no need for a terminator. Instead, a plug similar to a phone jack plugs into the hub port at one end and to the computer's network adapter card at the other end.

Hubs can be connected, however, so there still does remain a single point of failure if a cable that connects a hub to the network backbone becomes a problem. However, because a hub is usually placed in a secure location, such as the wiring closet, it is unlikely that a user will accidentally disconnect a cable or do anything else that will cause problems for other users on the hub.

A simple passive hub operates at the Physical layer of the OSI reference model. It does no addressing or framing; instead, it just receives data signals from one port and sends them out to all other ports. Because incoming signals are retransmitted on all the other ports, every computer in the broadcast domain can receive the data. This kind of hub is ideal for a very small LAN. However, today's more advanced hubs provide functions above and beyond the simple repeater.

In Figure 7.7, you can see that the hub creates a network based on a star topology from the physical point of view. That is, all the computers are connected by cables that are routed back to the hub, which acts as a wiring concentrator. However, from a logical view, the network still resembles the bus topology because each workstation in the LAN can intercept every packet that is broadcast on the network.

Although the network is still a logical bus (every node can hear every other node), the hub has several features that make it superior to the single-cable bus topology:

- Only a single workstation suffers if a cable problem develops.

- A hub makes it easy to move computers because the entire network does not have to be disrupted when a computer is moved. When using a 10BAase-2 cable type, you must "break" the cable and install a T-connector to add a computer at a new point in the network. Using a hub you just plug the new computer into any available port on the hub.

■ The hub centralizes wiring. Instead of having a single coaxial cable snaking throughout the office or building, each workstation is connected by an easy-to-install twisted-pair cable. Just plug the cables in at each end and you're ready to go.

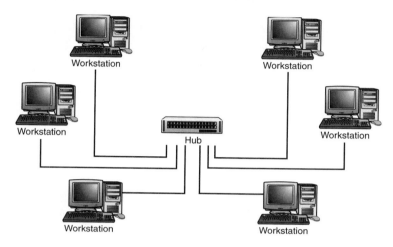

Figure 7.7   The simple hub creates a LAN with a physical star topology.

What Kind of Hub Do You Need?

In general, hubs can be classified by their function or by their construction. By physical construction, you can classify hubs as follows:

■ Standalone

■ Stackable

■ Modular

Standalone hubs are small units that can be used to build a very small workgroup LAN. These are the most inexpensive hubs and can be purchased as a commodity item at most computer stores. These devices usually have a small number of ports (2–10). You can pick up a small hub of this sort for less than $50, and often find them packaged with two network adapter cards for a simple home office networking solution. Figure 7.8 shows an example of a small eight-port workgroup hub. Notice also that you can see a BNC connector sticking out of the back of this hub. Although this hub uses twisted-pair cables to connect user workstations, it allows for a thinnet 10BASE-2 connection to other hubs or to the network backbone.

For a large LAN, stackable hubs provide for easy expansion as the network grows. This is because stackable hubs, as the name implies, can be linked so that they operate much like a single, larger hub. In addition, stackable hubs can be managed as a single unit when using SNMP- or RMON-based management console applications. As you can see in Figure 7.9, creating additional ports is a simple matter of connecting another stackable hub unit to the existing units.

▶▶   The Simple Network Management Protocol (SNMP) and RMON are discussed in detail in Chapter 44, "Network Testing and Analysis Tools."

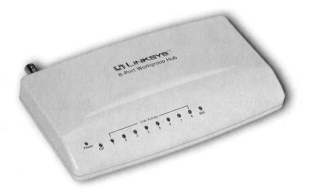

Figure 7.8   A small workgroup hub can connect users to a larger network.

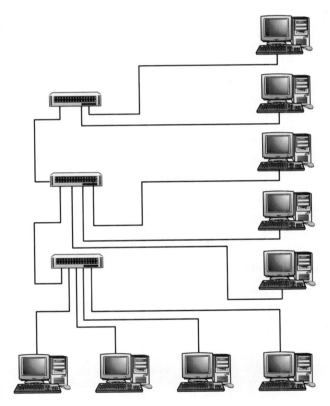

Figure 7.9   Stackable hubs make it easy to expand the network one hub at a time.

In Figure 7.10 you can see an example of a rack-mounted stackable hub. Although it's a simple matter to locate a small workgroup hub on the desktop or on a shelf, using rack-mounted stackable hubs allows you to conserve space by placing a large number of hubs in a single cabinet. Notice that in addition to the 24 user ports available on this hub, there is a single port off to the right side used to link the hub to the next hub in the stack.

Links to other hub

Figure 7.10   Stackable hubs are usually available as rack-mounted equipment that can be stored in a cabinet in the wiring closet.

If you have a network that uses different technologies at the physical and data-link layers, such as a mixed ethernet/token-ring network, then a modular hub can be used to connect computers to the network. In a sense, a modular hub is one step above the stackable hub.

The advantage is that instead of separate units that need to be linked together by short lengths of cable, the modular hub consists of a *cage* or *chassis* with a *backplane* or *motherboard*. Hubs are implemented as cards, with ports that can be inserted into the backplane. This type of hub can be quite sophisticated, incorporating ethernet ports, token-ring ports (MAUs), management modules, and other devices (see Figure 7.11). Whereas stackable hubs each have a separate power supply and therefore require a separate electrical plug in the wiring closet, a modular chassis unit provides a common power supply for all the cards it holds.

Some modular hubs use a standard *backplane*, which consists of a single bus that is shared by all the cards that are inserted into the chassis. Some modular hubs house multiple buses, with each bus being specific to a particular network segment or LAN. A *segment bus* is similar to the multiple bus design, but the administrator can configure ports to be part of different LANs (virtual LANs, which are discussed in Chapter 9, "Virtual LANs"). Finally, a *multiplexed bus* allows for a multiple bus design using a single bus, with each separate LAN multiplexed on a separate channel. These last two types make it easier to move a workstation from one LAN to another. The administrator needs only to use the hub's management software to reconfigure the port to be on a different virtual LAN. This is much simpler than having to physically move a cable from one port to another or from one hub to another.

In spite of the advanced features of a modular hub, you might find that stackable hubs are better suited to your situation. Considering the fact that all cards in the modular hub share a common power supply, you can potentially lose more clients when a power supply malfunctions. Although an easy solution to this problem is to purchase a modular hub that has dual-redundant power supplies, you cannot plan for all possible disasters when using one piece of equipment to house so many things.

Another thing you should think about when considering modular hubs is whether LED indicators are present for each port. Like a network adapter card, most hubs have activity LEDs that can be used to diagnose problems with the port. Because the cards that make up a modular hub can be quite compact, it is often the case that there is no room to put in an LED for each port. Of course, the management application that is used to monitor and configure this kind of hub can make up for this, but when the monitoring console is in one room and the actual physical hardware is a room away (or perhaps miles away), the actual LEDs can be a big help.

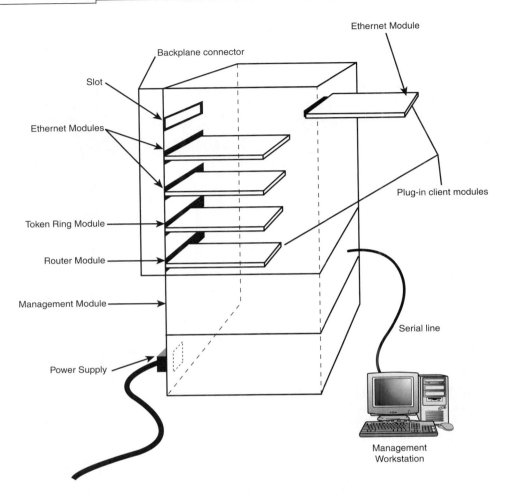

Figure 7.11 A modular hub can house cards for different network types.

With stackable hubs, you can patch around a malfunctioning hub and keep your most important clients connected. Also, modular hubs are meant to be space-savers. Some of the features you expect on a hub, such as the LEDs that indicate the status or error condition, might not exist on individual cards that make up a modular hub.

By function, hubs can be classified into three major types:

- Passive
- Active
- Intelligent

Passive Hubs

A passive hub is the simplest kind of hub. It acts like a multiport repeater and simply repeats incoming frames on all other ports. No signal processing is done when using this type of hub, so you need to be sure to stick with the cable lengths specified by the standard (such as 10BASE-T/100BASE-T) used for your network.

In a small business office that has no need to connect to a larger network, the standalone passive hub is an excellent choice. If you only need to connect 2–10 workstations, you can use this type of hub. For home networking, most computer stores sell these hubs in a kit format ("network in a box") that includes the hub, two network cards, and the cables you need to connect the computers to the hub. For $30–$100, you can set up a network at home or in a small office in less than an hour.

Active Hubs

Attenuation and other factors cause the signal to degrade as it passes through the wire. An active hub has electronic components that can amplify or clean up the signal it receives from a port before sending the data out on the remaining ports; this process is called *signal regeneration*. Some active hubs also have a capability called *store and forward*, in which individual packets can be examined and some simple corrections can be made to packets that have become corrupted during their journey.

Active hubs also can help compensate for ports that are connected to cables or workstations that are more likely to produce timing errors. Packet loss can be compensated for on these slower links because the active hub can retime their delivery. This might at first seem like a bad idea because it effectively slows down communications when faster nodes communicate with the slower one. However, an advantage can be gained because the error-prone computer does not have to make repeated attempts to rebroadcast packets, which itself can cause network slowdowns in an already heavily loaded LAN.

Note

One thing to check for when looking at the specs for an active hub is the type of signal regeneration that is performed. For example, simply amplifying the signal can be a good thing for LANs that cover a long distance. Signal regeneration can be a bad thing when the active hub also amplifies any noise that occurs on the line. Simple things such as fluorescent lights can cause problems on copper wires, and this noise can be passed on by an active hub.

Intelligent Hubs

The signal regeneration function of an active hub is included in an intelligent hub. Network management functions, which enable the administrator to gather information about the hub or each port on the hub, are also included. Statistical data about network traffic and error detection can make a big difference when you are troubleshooting. Some vendors provide their own proprietary management software. If you work in an environment in which the network is expected to keep growing, look to a vendor that supports industry standards such as the Simple Network Management Protocol (SNMP) or RMON, an extension of SNMP. As you add other devices at a later date, they can be incorporated easily into any management console application that supports industry standard protocols.

Note

The Simple Network Management Protocol is a standard protocol that enables management software to manage and monitor devices throughout the network. SNMP provides a communication path between management stations and management agents that reside on the network device. RMON was created to enhance the capabilities of SNMP and allow for additional capabilities on the remote system. You can find more information about both of these standard monitoring protocols in Chapter 44.

Intelligent hubs often include not only monitoring features, but also management features that enable you to do things such as shut down an individual port connected to a computer that is causing problems on the network. For example, if a device on the network is malfunctioning and sending out a storm of broadcast packets, you can detect which port is causing the problem, and then selectively disconnect it from the network until the problem (cable, network card, or perhaps the hub port itself) is fixed.

Hub Ports

The most typical hub has a row of sockets for RJ-45 connectors, which are currently the most widely used connectors for cables connecting workstations and network devices to a hub. When linking hubs to create a larger network, twisted-pair wiring might not be the cabling of choice if you need to span a distance longer than UTP can support. For this reason, you will find additional sockets on most hubs that can be used to connect the hub to a backbone. The RJ-45 connector ports are usually used to connect the cables that connect to a termination point at the user's location. This is typically a faceplate with another socket that can be used to connect the network card to the faceplate with a short patch cable. For more information about the EIA/TIA 568 structured wiring standard for using twisted-pair wiring and how the cables make their way from a hub to the user's environment, see Chapter 5, "Wiring the Network—Cables and Other Components."

For connections to other hubs, switches, or network devices that span a greater distance, you'll typically find that hubs intended for larger networks (that is, not a local home network), use ports that allow for connection to coaxial cables or fiber optic cables.

Note

Smaller hubs, such as the kind that were mentioned for a home or small office network, usually also use an RJ-45 port as an "uplink" connector to another hub. Note, however, that if your small hub has an uplink port, the cable it uses often is not the same as the one that is used to connect to a user workstation. Instead, the send and receive wires in the cable are usually reversed.

UTP, AUI, and BNC Ports

UTP ports are used with RJ-45 jacks to connect twisted-pair wiring to the hub. For connecting a hub to a network backbone, some hubs come with an AUI port, which can connect an ethernet transceiver to 10BASE-5, thicknet cabling. More common is the BNC port, which can be used to connect the hub to a 10BASE-2 thinnet cable. For a high-speed connection you will find a variety of different connector ports that can be used to connect the hub to a fiber optic cable. Indeed, there are hubs used for fiber optic networks that use mirrors to split signals (instead of electronics, as is done with a standard hub).

For management purposes, you might find a port for a DB9 connector that is used to attach a management terminal to the hub. This type of asynchronous serial port is used either for the exchange of simple ASCII characters between the hub and a terminal when performing monitoring or management functions, or to connect the hub to a central unit that manages multiple hubs.

Note

A hub doesn't have to have a serial port that can be used to attach a management console. In fact, most of today's advanced hubs can be configured with an IP address like any other network device, so management applications can use Telnet and other protocols and utilities to perform management and monitoring functions.

Cross-Over Ports

Cross-over ports can be used to connect one hub to another to expand the LAN broadcast area. Sometimes referred to as an Uplink port, this port is wired differently than the others so that the send and receive lines match up when communicating between hubs. Some hubs have a switch next to the cross-over port so that you can toggle it to work as a regular port. This feature can be used to connect an additional workstation to the hub if you don't need to attach it to another hub. When it comes time to expand the network, toggle the switch, link the hubs using a twisted-pair cable with RJ-45 connectors, and use the next hub to connect additional clients.

Autosensing Ports

If you are in the process of expanding an existing network and want to take advantage of faster network speeds, then be sure to check the specifications for any hub you purchase to be sure it supports both 10Mbps and 100Mbps. You also can simply buy separate hubs to accommodate these two speeds, but it's much simpler to have a single hub that can be used for both. As you begin to replace the network adapters in user workstations with faster cards, you won't have to transfer the cable at the hub end to another hub if you have purchased a hub that supports both speeds. Another feature that is pretty much standard for these kinds of hubs is that the ports (and the network cards) can be either manually set to a particular speed (using application software that comes with the hub), or they can sense the network speed. An autosensing port just makes your job easier. Plug in the new network card, reboot, and users are back to work and can work faster!

Troubleshooting Hub Problems

Sometimes, it can be difficult to troubleshoot problems with simple hubs that lack management software capabilities. You can be reduced to having to check the LEDs to ensure the port is actively working or switching the particular computer to another port to determine what is causing the problem. For example, suppose a workstation suddenly stops working on the network. What has happened recently that might have caused the problem? Has new software been configured on the workstation or on the network? Has someone damaged the cable (it's easy to damage twisted-pair cabling if it's lying around the user's area and his chair rolls over it a few times). It's probably best to start your troubleshooting efforts with the network configuration on the workstation, and then check the physical components, from the network adapter card to the cabling.

The following are some of the things you can easily check if you suspect problems with a hub:

- LEDs on the hub
- Whether a new connection or change has been made recently
- Whether a configuration change using management software has been done recently
- Whether the hub itself, or just one port, is totally dead

Check Those LEDs!

After ensuring that no changes have been made to the workstation's network configuration (which you can easily discern if you have a spreadsheet that is used to track this information), check the LEDs on the network adapter. If the link LED is lit, that simply means that you are connected to the hub and data can be exchanged. Next check the LEDs on the hub itself, if the hub provides this function. If the hub LED is not lit, try switching the user's cable to another port and try again. Of course, you should do this using a port you know is in good working order, which usually means disconnecting another user for a short period of time.

If you find that the problem is with the hub port, you have several choices. If it's a cheap hub, connect the user to a free port, if one is available, or toss the hub and replace it. If it's an expensive hub, be glad you signed that maintenance contract (if you don't have one and you're operating a large network, you'll probably be looking for another job sometime soon), and have it fixed or the hub replaced. In a large LAN environment, where downtime is intolerable and you can't wait for a repair person to arrive, having a spare hub stored away for just this kind of problem can be a lifesaver (or, better put, a job saver).

Check for New Connections

If you are having problems connecting a new workstation to the hub, perform the LED check at both ends as just described and try another hub port. One of the most common problems encountered with new connections results from excessive cable length or sources of electrical interference somewhere along the path that the cable takes on its way to the faceplate at the user environment. Remember that the maximum distance a cable can be extended from a hub to the faceplate is about 90 meters, with another 10-meter cable running from the faceplate to the workstation. Of course, this depends on the technology you are using and will differ from 10Mbps ethernet to gigabit ethernet. Check the specs! Also, don't forget that Category 5 twisted-pair cables are the preferred wiring for 10Base-T and faster technologies. If you are still using Category 3 cables and are having problems, use a shorter cable length or, better yet, upgrade to Category 5.

▶▶ You can find out more about the restrictions imposed by ethernet topologies in Chapter 12, "Ethernet" and those imposed on token-ring networks in Chapter 13, "Token-Ring Networks."

Remember also that many environmental conditions can affect twisted-pair wiring. When first used in a token-ring environment, shielded twisted-pair cables were used because it was thought that the shielding would help prevent sources outside the cable from interfering with the signal that the cables carry. Ordinary Category 5 twisted-pair cables aren't shielded and depend on the number of twists-per-inch to help cancel out cross-talk and other factors that can cause problems. Trace the path that the cable takes and move it away from sources that generate electrical fields, such as fluorescent lights, electrical distribution points, and other similar things. You might solve a problem by simply moving the cable a few feet away from such a source of interference.

Check the Hub or Port Configuration

Sometimes the problems you find in a hub are not due to failure of the hardware components. Instead, they can result from an improper configuration. Check the speed and the full- or half-duplex settings at both ends of the cable. In a large organization it might be that one group is responsible for installing and maintaining users' computers, while another group is responsible for hub management. In this case, make sure the communication lines are open (between the people involved!) and that the proper settings are established for both sides of the connection.

Finally, although most modern network adapter cards and hubs support "autosensing" the speed and other settings involved in the connection, they might not work well together. That is, although the hub and the network card might both say they support autosensing, they might use different methods. In such a situation, manually fix the method you want to use at each end.

Check the Hub's Management Software

If you are using (expensive) hub application software to manage your hubs, don't overlook the information that you can obtain from this application. Use the features of this application to assist you in troubleshooting efforts. If you don't use a central management console application, then connect a laptop or character-cell terminal to the serial port on the hub and use the commands available to try to determine what the cause of failure is. If the hub has a good software layer that you can use, there will be tests that can be performed for each port and the hub in general. Make use of these.

Some vendors adhere to standards, such as SNMP, and others use proprietary software solutions. Whichever your vendor uses, be sure to check the documentation and try to use the tests or probes that are available to track down problem ports or hubs. It goes almost without saying that it is best to use hubs that conform to industry standards. This way you can use a central management console application to manage all your hubs, switches, routers, and other network devices from a single place, making troubleshooting efforts much easier in a network that is geographically dispersed. If you do run into a problem, you're more likely to find information that will be helpful for troubleshooting purposes if you are using equipment that adheres to the standards.

General Hub Failure

Many problems you encounter with hubs involve only the failure of a single port. However, occasionally the entire hub could cease to function, disconnecting all its users from the LAN. All electronic equipment has a maximum temperature (and a minimum temperature) beyond which it will not operate properly. If you suspect that this is the problem, try leaving the unit powered off for a half-hour or so to give it time to cool off and then try powering it up again. If this solves the problem, try reorganizing the equipment that is installed in and around the device to make sure that temperature is not the problem.

There are all sorts of factors you can check to ensure ventilation isn't being obstructed. Have you recently added new rack-mounted devices in the same cabinet? Have you checked to see that the ventilation fans inside a particular cabinet are functioning? Has someone inadvertently placed documentation on top of a ventilation area? Is there enough space between each device in a rack-mounted configuration for air to circulate freely? Finally, has the air conditioning equipment in the computer room been checked recently? As a network administrator, these are the kinds of possibilities you must consider in troubleshooting seemingly obscure problems on your network.

Finally, if a hub appears outwardly to be functioning—LEDs are lit, for example, but in reality nothing is working—power-cycle the hub. When powering up, most modern hubs run through a self-check power-on sequence and report problems, either through management software or by a certain sequence of how the LEDs light up or flash. Examine your documentation. If the hub passes its power-on self tests (POST) and still does not respond, check the power supply. Although you can't do this easily for a small hub that has an internal power supply, you can check external sources such as an external UPS. Try troubleshooting or replacing any external power sources. If this does not work, call your vendor and get the darn thing replaced.

Network Switches

8

SOME OF THE MAIN TOPICS IN THIS CHAPTER ARE

How Switches Work

Switch Hardware Types

Switch Troubleshooting and Management

The previous chapter gave a quick overview of network devices that have enabled creating larger LANs, extending the distance of the network, and cutting down unnecessary traffic. This chapter explains network switches. In a small home office, a hub might be sufficient to provide LAN connectivity for a few computers. However, in a large, modern network, a more powerful device is needed. It isn't enough to extend the distance of a LAN, which a simple repeater can do. It isn't enough to centralize wiring, which a hub can do. And, as you can probably guess, it isn't enough to use a traditional multiport repeater, or a bridge, to help eliminate broadcasting packets on ports that don't lead to the packet's eventual destination.

Today's large networks need to provide far more to client and server computers alike, and the next evolution in network connectivity devices for the LAN is the switch. In this chapter, you'll learn that a switch is nothing more than a combination of previously described technologies, with improvements. Without switches, ethernet networks would have been maxed out a few years ago with 100BASE-T (Fast Ethernet) solutions.

NOTE

Routers can be used to extend a network. However, the difference between a network router and a LAN switch is significant. *Routers* are used to direct network frames to the correct network or subnet on which the destination host resides. This is a WAN concept, not a LAN concept. *Switches*, in the form most used today, are used to get past the limitations imposed by traditional LAN technologies. However, at the end of this chapter, you'll see how switching is moving up into the WAN market.

How Switches Work

In a traditional ethernet LAN, you are limited to the number of workstations you can attach to any particular LAN segment or hub. You are limited by the total available bandwidth, which usually is 10Mbps or 100Mbps using older hub technology. The group of network devices—including workstations, servers, and hubs—that are all capable of broadcasting a packet to any other device on the network makes up a broadcast domain. Even if you follow the topological rules for creating a traditional ethernet LAN, it won't matter how many computers you are able to connect to the LAN if network traffic becomes a problem. This can happen when you have several high-end servers or workstations that make heavy demands on the network.

NOTE

For a more detailed discussion about broadcast domains on ethernet LANs, see Chapter 12, "Ethernet." Because the concept of a broadcast domain is central to the CSMA/CD (Carrier Sense Multiple Access/Collision Detect) media access mechanism used in ethernet networks, you might want to review why the broadcast domains, and the topologies used to create them, are important. You'll come away with a greater knowledge of why switches are so necessary in today's high-bandwidth networks.

The solution to this problem is to limit the broadcast domain. In the last chapter, bridges were discussed for this purpose. However, legacy bridges just aren't sufficient for the high-speed networks that are required by today's applications, such as streaming audio and video, alongside more traditional network traffic such as file and print services.

A switch is a cross between a bridge and a hub. You can think of a switch as several bridges, centralized in a single device like a hub, with added monitoring and management capabilities. Switches centralize wiring and cut down on unnecessary broadcasts on the LAN by *switching* network packets from the incoming port only to the outgoing port that will get the packet to its destination. This eliminates the need for other workstations attached to the switch to examine each packet broadcast on the network. The other workstations never see the packet to begin with.

Switches and bridges aren't that different. They perform just about the same function. However, early bridges usually had only two ports to connect two LAN segments and, thus, divide the broadcast domain in half. As silicon technology developed rapidly in the 1990s, it became possible to create multiport bridges (sometimes called multiport repeaters), which you could use to attach multiple LAN segments. Switches today can be used to connect multiple LAN segments or to connect individual workstations or servers to the network. The difference between a switch and a bridge is that it's easier to sell a switch than a bridge. Just using the term "bridge" *sounds* like old technology. Tell the customer that you're going to put a switch in his network and it just sounds a lot more modern.

So, although the term "switch" sounds new, it's just an evolutionary update of an older technique—bridging. You can use switches to perform the same functions that were performed earlier using bridges.

Segmenting the Collision Domain

In Chapter 12, you'll learn more about the limitations imposed for configuring a network based on the technology used. Each type of ethernet, from 10BASE-2 to 100BASE-T, has its own rules about the number of computers that can be connected, the length of cables, and so on. After you reach the maximum allowed length or number of computers imposed by the particular topological rules, you have to create a new LAN and, usually, connect them with a router.

The switch can eliminate these limitations. In Figure 8.1, a switch is used to segment a LAN into multiple broadcast domains. This is the same function that a multiport bridge used to perform.

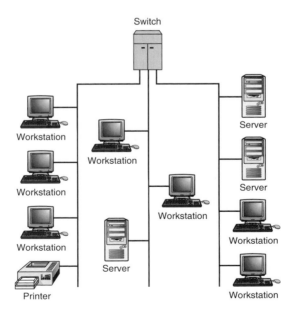

Figure 8.1 The switch can be used to segment a traditional LAN.

Used in this manner, a larger LAN can be created because each segment attached to the switch is its own broadcast domain. The topological rules apply only to each segment connected to the switch, not to the entire LAN that is joined together by the switch.

Other Reasons to Switch

If a switch could segment the broadcast domain and nothing more, it probably would still be called a bridge. However, you can take limiting the broadcast domain a step further using a switch, and effectively create a LAN as large as you need. In Figure 8.2, a switch is used to connect individual workstations, servers, and other network devices. In the previous example shown in Figure 8.1, each LAN segment is a broadcast domain and any devices attached to that segment still have to contend for access to that part of the shared media for the network. The switch was used to provide more broadcast domains and limit traffic that passes between them.

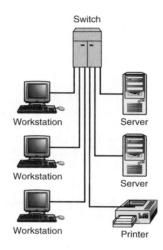

Figure 8.2 You can connect individual computers to a switch port.

The benefits of using a switch in this manner should quickly become apparent. The broadcast domain, when using the standard half-duplex ethernet CSMA/CD technology, is limited to just two devices: the switch port and the computer attached to it. That means you have increased the bandwidth on the LAN to the point that each computer attached to the switch has the full bandwidth available to it. In this standard half-duplex mode, however, collisions still can occur if the switch and the computer attached to it sense that the network media is silent and both attempt to transmit at the same time. This is exactly what happens in a traditional ethernet LAN and the CSMA/CD mechanism described in Chapter 12 is used. However, with only two devices competing for network access, bandwidth is greatly improved.

If you were to substitute a hub for the switch in Figure 8.2, the network traffic from all the workstations attached to the hub would have to compete for access to the network media. This means that using a hub, the actual bandwidth available to each workstation would be less than when a switch is used. As more and more workstations on a hub begin to generate large amounts of network traffic, the effective use of the network media begins to lessen as more and more collisions occur. Using a switch solves this problem.

Full-Duplex Ethernet Switches

The switch makes another new concept in ethernet technology possible: full-duplex communication. As discussed in the last section, in a standard ethernet implementation, each device must contend with all others that want to use the transmission medium. The CSMA/CD mechanism is used so that only one device successfully ends up talking on the wire at any particular time. The more stations that are added to the collision domain, the lower the total throughput because collisions increase and retransmissions become more frequent.

When a single workstation is connected to a switch, you want to further increase bandwidth by eliminating the collision domain altogether. This is exactly what happens when you use a switch that supports full-duplex communication. In this type of switch, separate wires in the network cable are used for transmitting and receiving. Thus, the switch port can be transmitting frames to the workstation on one wire, while the workstation is transmitting frames to the switch port on another wire.

Because there are no competing devices, the switch and the workstation can send and receive from each other at the same time, the result of which is a full-duplex operation. No collisions occur because there is no contention for the wire. Not only can you achieve the actual 10Mbps or 100Mbps throughput capabilities of the wire for each port attached to a full-duplex switch, you can double those speeds.

To achieve these speeds, you must incur some extra expense, however. Ordinary ethernet cards are not fashioned to operate in this mode, so if you want to upgrade to a switch and allow for full-duplex operation, you also might have to purchase new network adapter cards. This might make sense in some situations, but not for all devices on your network. For example, you upgrade and replace a hub with a switch that is capable of full-duplex operation. Most of the workstations are for ordinary users, none of which individually generates a lot of network traffic. Also note that most network cards available today, even inexpensive ones, are autosensing 10/100Mbps cards and can operate in full-duplex mode when running at 100Mbps.

NOTE

Full-duplex communications are the key to faster ethernet technologies. After you pass the 100BASE-T speed of 100Mbps, the packet size and round-trip timing required for ethernet networks just doesn't scale very well. Newer technologies, such as Gigabit Ethernet and 10 Gigabit Ethernet, depend on this full-duplex capability and the removal of the CSMA/CD media access control mechanism.

On this same network, you have a high-end server that is capable of processing many end-user requests rapidly. The bottleneck is the network adapter card, which is a standard ethernet card capable of sending or receiving, but not both at the same time.

You can increase the availability of the server to its clients, and incur only the expense of a new network card for the server, by replacing the network card on the server with a full-duplex card and plugging it into a port on the switch that supports full-duplex operations.

To make upgrading to a 100Mbps switch easier, most vendors provide the capability of dual-speed ports. This is similar to the dual-speed 10/100Mpbs network cards. In addition, many switches can autosense the network speed of the workstation attached to the port. However, some require that you manually set the speed, using management software. The best switches support both autosensing and a good management program that can be used to configure ports.

Using Switches to Create a Collapsed Backbone

Because switches can effectively eliminate the broadcast domain, you also can use them to eliminate the traditional backbone used to connect multiple hubs or other devices. For example, it's easy to set up a hub or switch in a wiring closet on each floor of a building, and then run a single cable through the floors to connect each hub (as shown in Figure 8.3). This cable is the *backbone* for the network. However, this does nothing to eliminate the collision domain for all the traffic it receives from the switches or hubs.

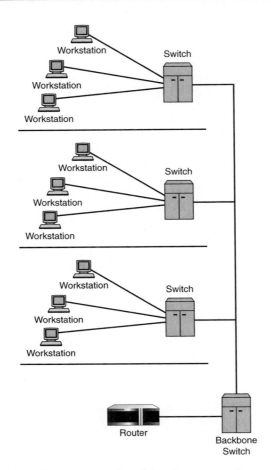

Figure 8.3   A single backbone becomes a bottleneck in a large network.

In Figure 8.3, each workstation that is attached to the switch on its floor easily can exchange data with other workstations that are attached to the same switch. However, if a workstation needs to communicate with a server or other resource that is not directly connected to that switch, then the network traffic flows over the backbone that connects the other departmental switches. Again, this isn't a problem if you have a network in which you can locate important servers closer to the actual clients that use them and prevent traffic from entering the backbone at all.

In today's environment, however, it's common to find many business functions centralized in large servers or possibly clustered servers that manage huge databases. In this type of scenario, it isn't always easy to move a server closer to the client. And, with the advent of e-mail and other Web-based applications, it's more likely that the old 80/20 rule—80% of network traffic stays within the local LAN, whereas only 20% is destined for other locations—has been turned around. Now most clients need to exchange only a small amount of data with local computers, sending the 80% figure to the larger network. With the centralization of larger servers, most likely you'll see this paradigm in all but the smallest networks in the future.

In Figure 8.4, switches are cascaded so that the switch can become a network backbone-in-a-box. Each switch in the building is connected to a central switch that serves as the backbone, once again limiting or eliminating the collision domain, depending on whether full- or half-duplex switch ports are used.

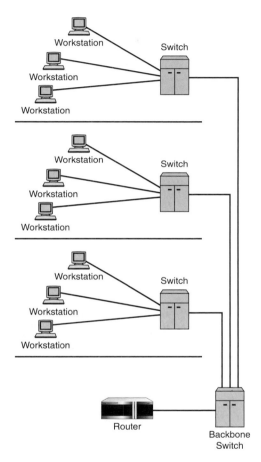

Figure 8.4 A hub can serve as a collapsed backbone to concentrate departmental switches.

Of course, in this example, the switches appear on each floor, but you could just as easily attach hubs at the department level or use a mixture of both hubs and switches. No need to throw out a hub if it provides the bandwidth you need for a specific situation. However, if you are planning on upgrading to a newer hub—from older 10Mbps to Fast Ethernet, for example—it's time to switch to switching! At this time, the cost difference between switches and sophisticated hubs is not that great. As manufacturing capacity ramps up to produce more switches, you can expect that ordinary hubs will quickly become ancient relics in the realm of network devices.

In Figure 8.4, it's important to note that, instead of sharing a single backbone network cable, each departmental switch has its own cable to the switch, so the full bandwidth of the network media is available to each switch. The backbone no longer becomes a bottleneck.

Switch Hardware Types

Many architectures are used for switching. Because switching is a hot technology, many approaches are being tried. Some involve software that makes decisions much like a router and sends frames on their merry way. Others are hardware-based and can perform much better because no single component, such as a CPU, can be bogged down when too much traffic passes through the switch. Two modes of operation can be used by a switch when it forwards a packet out of a selected port: cut-through mode and store-and-forward mode.

Cut-Through Switches

A cut-through switch begins transmitting the incoming frame on the outgoing port after it receives the header information, or about 20 or 30 bytes. All the switch needs to determine on which port to output the frame is the *destination address* (hardware address), which is contained in the frame header. The switch continues to receive information and transmit it until the frame has been "switched" from one port to another. The advantage to this mode of operation is speed. As long as nothing else goes wrong, the packet continues on to its destination at a fast pace with little time involved in the switch. The switch is said to be switching at wire speed. That is, the delay introduced by the switching function is so insignificant that to the end workstations, the full bandwidth is available for use.

This method has several disadvantages, however. The switch begins to send the packet out before it knows whether the frame is damaged in any way. If the frame has corrupted data, the switch won't be able to detect it unless it first receives the entire frame and then computes the CRC (cyclic redundancy code, sometimes called cyclic redundancy check) value stored in the frame check sequence field. If a frame is badly malformed, as when an NIC sends out a frame that is too long, a cut-through switch might think it is a broadcast packet and send it out of all ports, causing unnecessary traffic congestion.

Store-and-Forward Switches

In the store-and-forward switch mode, the switch buffers the frame in its own memory before beginning to send it out the appropriate port. This technique boasts two main advantages:

- The switch can connect two different topologies, such as 10Mbps and 100Mbps networks, without having to worry about the different speeds.
- The switch can operate like a bridge and check the integrity of the frame, allowing it to discard damaged frames and not propagate them onto other network segments.

Although the store-and-forward technology increases the latency factor, this delay usually is not a big concern when you consider the increased throughput you can achieve with a switch. And the fact that the switch can drop damaged frames can help to localize errors so that the destination workstation doesn't have to deal with these kinds of errors.

Layer 3 Switches

Just as switches are on an evolutionary upgrade path from hubs and bridges, a new breed of networking device is becoming increasingly popular in large networks. Layer 3 of the OSI model is the network layer, on which higher-level protocol addresses are introduced into the network. Generally, switches are deployed in a LAN, whereas routers, which use layer 3 addresses, are used to connect LANs that are separated by some distance, such as in a campus LAN, or to connect Wide area networks. The main difference here is that the switch must examine only a small amount of the frame header to determine the hardware address of a frame and then send the frame out the correct port. Routers, however, need to dig further into the packet to find the higher-level protocol address, such as an IP address. Routers also must modify the frame header, substituting the router's MAC address as the source address of the frame, examining and modifying the TTL field in the packet and performing checksum calculations to ensure the integrity of the packet. Because of the extra processing involved, routers generally operate at a lower speed than do switches.

Standard routers operating at slower speeds than switches tend to become bottlenecks in a network. To solve this problem, layer 3 switching devices usually take a different approach to the functions a router performs. Routers are like computers (indeed, sometimes a computer with multiple network adapters is used for routing in a small network), and a processor must examine each packet and perform all the functions just mentioned. Layer 3 switches usually implement these functions in application-specific integrated circuits (ASICs). By implementing these functions in hardware, some layer 3 switches can operate at just about wire speed, which ordinary routers cannot do.

Some layer 3 switches use proprietary technologies, because standards are not complete for this type of device at this time. Whatever method they use, the idea is to identify streams of traffic that are all traveling to the same destination, and output them on the appropriate port as fast as possible.

Most products that advertise themselves as layer 3 switches also function as routers. Layer 3 switching is employed for traffic streams that are easily identifiable. For small traffic loads, the device operates much like a router. In the next few years, you can expect to see layer 3 switching come down in price, making it feasible in smaller networks. For now, however, the cost might not justify the increase in speed you will achieve. For example, if a router is a bottleneck in your network that sits between client computers and servers, consider moving servers closer to the clients so that the network traffic flow doesn't have to pass through the router.

Another interesting development in routing technologies, called Multi-Label Protocol Switching, is discussed in Chapter 29, "Routing Protocols." This method of wire-speed switching, generally found in high-end Internet core routers, is defined by RFC documents.

Put a Switch in Your Home Office

Switches, similar to hubs, come in all sizes and shapes. You can find them in a local computer store for only a small increase in the cost of buying an identical hub. Although most home offices can easily get by with a 10Mbps or 100Mbps hub, if you work a lot with large files, multimedia applications, or the like, then a switch just might be a good idea for a home office.

Installing a switch of this sort requires very little effort. You basically plug it in and start switching. If you expect your network to grow during the next year or two, be sure to find out whether the smaller switch supports an uplink port so that you can add additional capacity as needed. However, because the price of a small switch is now minimal, the cost of replacing a smaller switch with one that has a greater port density shouldn't be too much of a factor.

Be sure, however, that you purchase a switch that will work with the network adapter cards you have in your home network. Or, plan on purchasing newer cards. Because 10/100Mbps cards are so inexpensive, you might as well replace the hub with a switch and upgrade your network cards at the same time!

Stackable and Chassis Switches

For larger networks, you'll find that switches also come in stackable and chassis models, similar to those discussed in the previous chapter. Stackable switches have an interconnect port that you can use to link them together so you can add capacity as your network grows. Chassis switches fit a lot of switching capacity into a very small space, providing a large number of ports. These kinds of switches also provide other functions, such as better management capabilities, support for the Simple Network Monitoring Protocol (SNMP) and Remote Monitoring (RMON), and the capability to create virtual LANs, which is the subject of the next chapter.

Switch Troubleshooting and Management

You troubleshoot a switch just like you troubleshoot a hub. If the switch has a link light (or LED), be sure it's on, indicating that the port is operating as it should and receiving a signal from the network adapter attached to the client computer (or another switch, as the case might be). Management software for the switch can be based on the SNMP or RMON specifications, or it might be proprietary in nature. In either case, all but the low-end home office switches provide the capability to examine, test, and set parameters for each port on the switch.

For example, if you have a client computer connected to the switch, and the client's network adapter is autosensing, meaning that it can determine the network speed, it might not be compatible with the autosensing functionality of the switch. In that case, you might have to manually configure the switch port to match the higher speed that the network adapter can support.

For more information about troubleshooting switches using SNMP and RMON, see Chapter 44, "Network Testing and Analysis Tools."

Virtual LANs

CHAPTER 9

Chapter 8, "Network Switches," discussed switches that can be used to reduce the broadcast domain limit imposed by earlier networking technologies, such as hubs and bridges. Modern switches can be used to solve more problems than just reducing network traffic, however. This chapter discusses a new application for switches: virtual LANs, or VLANs. Besides reducing the broadcast domain, switches configured for use in a VLAN can be used to solve many other problems:

- The changing physical topology of the LAN
- Security on the LAN
- Centralized management of multiple LANs
- Impose limitations on multicast traffic

Whereas a router also can be used to reduce a broadcast domain and create separate subnets in a network, switching technology works at a much faster pace. Thus, using VLANs in your network probably can enable you to get rid of a few slow routers that currently are being used to segment a LAN.

Virtual LANs and Network Topologies

When discussing local area networks, most network administrators think of the physical topology of the LAN; that is, the hubs, switches, and the servers and workstations, and how they connect to form the LAN. The physical topology, as you learned in Chapter 1, "Overview of Network Topologies," doesn't have to match the logical *topology* of the LAN. As an early example, the token-bus network topology (IEEE 802.4 standard) uses a single coaxial cable to connect computers into a LAN. However, the method in which individual computers gain access to this shared cable is not the order in which they exist on the cable. In Figure 9.1, you can see that six computers are connected to a single cable. In this example, you can assume that the computers are numbered in a manner that represents their actual network address (token-bus addresses actually can range in size from 2–5 bytes). For this figure, the numbers 1–6 are used instead of the network address. In a token-passing network, a token frame is passed from one computer to another, and it is this token frame that gives a computer the right to transmit data on the network.

Terminator   Terminator

Computer 1   Computer 6   Computer 3   Computer 2   Computer 4   Computer 5

Figure 9.1   An early token-bus network uses a token frame to determine which computer can transmit data on the cable.

Although in this figure it might seem logical that the token frame would be passed from Computer 1 to Computer 6, and then to Computer 3, that is not how token-bus networks function. The physical topology is a linear bus, in which a message broadcast on the cable by Computer 1 would travel down the wire until it reaches the terminator that is placed after Computer 5 at the end of the segment.

The logical topology of a token-bus network, however, is that of a ring. Although all computers on the same cable segment can "hear" the broadcast that every other computer makes, communications take place in an orderly manner. The token frame is "passed" in numerical address order from Computer 1 to Computer 2, then to Computer 3, and so on. This example is intended to show you the difference between a logical and a physical topology. The physical layout of the network is a linear bus. The logical topology of this network is a ring.

So, what does this have to do with virtual LANs? A lot. Early LAN technologies, such as ethernet, were limited in their size and distance by the physical topology of the LAN. You can read about this in Chapter 12, "Ethernet." Even token-ring networks, which are described in Chapter 13, "Token-Ring Networks," are limited in size based on the physical topology of the network. Switches, as you learned in the previous chapter, enable you to greatly expand the number of computers you can place on a LAN, and you can use high-speed communication links between switches to greatly expand the distance of a LAN.

However, using switches to create a huge LAN just solves the problem of distance and the number of devices that can be attached to the network. In today's networking environment, there are other factors to be considered, such as security. Perhaps you don't want all your computers connected to the same LAN. The more computers you have on a single LAN, the greater the odds are that a security breach will occur—giving an intruder to access to other computers on the LAN.

Virtual LANs, which can be created using switches, enable you to *separate* the *physical topology* from the *logical topology*. That is, although you might have all your computers interconnected using a switch or several switches, appropriately configured switches make it possible to configure individual virtual LANs that are independent of the physical topology. Remember that hubs and repeaters allow all computers on the LAN to see every message that gets transmitted by every other computer in the same broadcast domain. Switches make connections only between the transmitting computer and the switch port that will get the network frame to its eventual destination. By limiting the network frame to just the sending and receiving stations, and the switches that stand between them, you take a big step toward preventing eavesdropping on the LAN.

Switching Based on Network Frames

Using a variety of techniques, then, it should be obvious that it is possible to physically connect a large number of computers using switches, but use software to program the switches to limit which computers can transmit frames to other computers. In other words, you can define LANs using software inside the switch, instead of creating LANs based on the actual physical cabling (see Figure 9.2). This single switch connects several computers, printers, and a server. However, the switch separates these devices into three separate virtual LANs.

Of course, this is a very simplistic example. If you have such a small number of computers, one of the only reasons you would want to create virtual LANs would be for security reasons. This example is meant to show you that you can connect multiple network devices (computers, printers, print servers, file servers, routers, and so on) to the same switch, or a set of switches, and then use software that comes with the switch(es) to assign each computer to a separate virtual LAN. Computers on the same virtual LAN can communicate with each other just as if they were joined in an old-fashioned hub-based broadcast domain. However, just because all these networked devices are connected to the same switch, it doesn't mean that they can send or receive data with devices that are configured on a different virtual LAN. In essence, it appears that you are partitioning the ports on the switch as though they were separate switches. That doesn't have to be the case, but was the first step in creating VLAN switches.

Port-Based VLANs

The earliest switches that were used to create VLANs made assignments based on the switch's ports. That is, the administrator could simply designate what VLAN each port would be a member of. This is a fast way to switch frames in a VLAN because no processing needs to be done on the frame itself.

Instead, the switch merely outputs the frame on all ports that are in the same VLAN as the incoming port. To place a particular workstation or other network device into a VLAN, you simply have to connect it to a port that is a member of that particular VLAN.

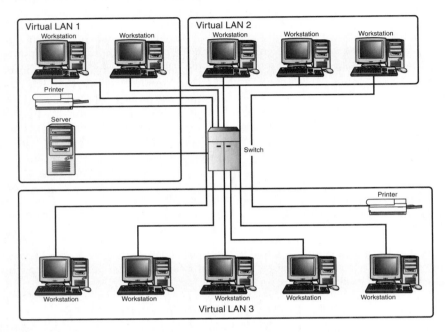

Figure 9.2   Virtual LANs can be created so that separate LANs exist on the same switch.

For the most part, the ports are configurable through software, so you can assign an identifier to each port to tell it which VLAN it is a member of. Using software management tools to configure a VLAN in this way means that when a user is moved to another VLAN but their physical location doesn't change, you don't have to make any cabling changes or plug them into a different port. You just use the management software that comes with the switch to reassign the port to the new VLAN.

Port-based VLANs are the easiest type of VLAN to implement because the switch must do less work. The switch doesn't have to look up an IP address, a hardware address, or anything else to make a forwarding decision. It just looks up the port on which the frame arrives and outputs it on all other ports configured for that particular VLAN. This can be a security issue, though, if you do not physically secure connections to the switch. If the switch is not locked away securely, it's quite possible for someone to plug in a computer to a port and become a member of that VLAN. Of course, you'd probably configure the ports so that any unused ports are not part of *any* VLAN. However, what's to prevent some informed intruder, such as an unhappy employee, from unplugging one cable and plugging in another? Keep important network devices such as switches and routers locked away!

Implicit and Explicit Tagging

In more modern VLAN switches, the individual network devices or ports are not used to define the VLAN; the network frames—each handled on a case-by-case basis that the switch receives—are used.

A modern VLAN, then, is based on frames, not on the computers that generate them or those to which they are addressed, or the ports to which either is attached.

In VLAN terminology, the term *tagging* is used to indicate what data is used to associate a frame with a particular VLAN. There are two kinds of tagging: implicit and explicit.

Implicit Tagging

Implicit tagging means that the decision is based on data that is already present in the existing frame format, such as an ethernet frame. The data is already there, and nothing has been added, so the switch simply must examine data in the frame header and implicitly decide to which VLAN it belongs. When using this type of tagging, no additional data needs to be added to the frame by the sending computer, so the devices on the network are considered to be VLAN-unaware. That is, they operate just as they normally would and have no idea that they are on one or another VLAN. You might as well just call this "non-tagging," but the writers of the specifications have to have something to do, so they call this implicit tagging.

When implicit tagging is used, the frame data that typically is used to create VLAN association rules is generally one of the following:

- **Protocol**—The network protocol, such as IP or AppleTalk.

- **Data Link Source Address**—The hardware address of the source of the frame. Remember that hardware addresses, also known as MAC addresses, are unique addresses burned into the card at the factory when the card is manufactured. They provide a flat address space, but should be unique from any other such address through the world.

- **Upper-level protocol identifiers**—In addition to a protocol type, such as IP, a subnet address identifier may be used to identify with which VLAN a frame is associated.

Another method that can be used for implicit tagging involves upper-level applications. However, because this can create literally hundreds of rules, it often is not used.

Explicit Tagging

Explicit tagging refers to actually attaching an extra few bits of data to a network frame to specify its VLAN association. For this to work, however, the sending station must be aware that VLANs exist. The switch itself also must understand explicit tagging and know where in the frame to look for the tagging data. For example, in a VLAN-aware network adapter, it is common to place a few bytes after the source address in the ethernet frame. These additional bytes provide the explicit VLAN tag that the switch can examine to determine which VLAN the frame belongs to. Instead of having to apply a set of rules, the VLAN-aware switch can simply examine this value and quickly switch the frame to the correct output port. Because the tag is placed inside the ethernet frame after the source and destination address, however, a switch that is not VLAN-aware (that is, it does not use explicit tagging) cannot make decisions based on protocol type or other fields. This is because additional fields will be offset a number of bytes, depending on the length of the explicit tag. This can lead to non-aware switches or computers misinterpreting the tagging data and produce unpredictable behavior.

The solution to this is to use "edge switches" that receive explicitly tagged frames from VLAN-aware devices, and remove the tags when they forward the frame to a port connected to another switch or device that is not equipped to handle explicitly tagged frames.

Explicit tagging does have some advantages over implicit tagging, however. Because the switch only has to look at the tag, and it's always in the same place (for a given protocol), it's easy to implement in hardware a quick switching fabric that can handle a large number of frames in a short period of time. Implicit tagging must check the rule set to determine what VLAN a frame belongs to, and this can involve more processing time. Although the amount of time might be just a few milliseconds, which seems like a short amount of time to you or me, that's a lot of time when you're switching hundreds of thousands of packets in a short period of time. As you'll find out in the next chapter, a similar situation occurs with routers. A switch forwards a network frame quicker than many routers because the router must spend time digging into the frame to find the protocol address, and then perform a lookup in a routing table to determine how to deal with the frame and recalculate the frame check sequence (FCS).

On the downside, when a switch that uses explicit tagging has to forward a frame to a switch or device that does not, it must remove the tag. When this happens, it's necessary to recalculate the frame check sequence (FCS) value because part of the frame bits have been removed. Another drawback is that attaching an explicit tag to a large frame can cause the frame to exceed the maximum size allowed by the transport protocol, and the frame will be dropped.

MAC Address VLANS

If you have a lot of mobile users, creating a VLAN that bases its membership on a list of MAC addresses can be a good idea. Because these addresses are unique, when you plug into any switch port, a quick lookup is all that's necessary for the switch to determine to which VLAN your computer's MAC address belongs. And, because MAC addresses are typically the way traditional switches work, there's not much more circuitry or software that has to be tweaked to create this kind of VLAN-capable switch. The downside is that the administrator must manually assign each hardware address to the correct VLAN in the first place. However, that's not a difficult chore when you are simply adding a few new computers to a VLAN. When implementing a set of VLANS that involve hundreds or thousands of computers, you can get tired fingers!

If you decide to use this type of switch there is one thing you should check before purchasing the switch. What happens when a computer is connected to a port and the computer's address is not a member of any of your configured VLANs? Some switch manufacturers will implement a mechanism that further looks into the frame and then forwards the frame based on a higher-level protocol address. This allows anyone to connect to your switch, provided you've not taken the necessary physical security precautions and locked your switching equipment away in a secure computer room. Check to be sure that frames which have no VLAN mapping for a MAC address are dropped before using this type of switch.

Protocol Rule-Based VLANs

In a virtual LAN, the decision a switch makes when deciding whether to output a frame on a particular port can be based on a set of *association rules* that are based on the network protocols used on the network. Each frame received on a switch port is examined and, based on a set of rules, is output on one or more other ports. The set of rules can be based on many things, such as the IP subnet addresses. However, it's quite possible to create VLANs that subdivide event a subnet.

▶▶ For more information about IP subnets and how they can be used to segment the IP address space into smaller units, see Chapter 20, "Overview of the TCP/IP Protocol Suite."

Other protocol-based VLANs can be created so that AppleTalk- or NetWare-based networks all can exist on the same switch—each on its own virtual LAN. In this kind of protocol-based VLAN switch, you usually can further subdivide each major protocol into smaller VLANs based on identifiers used in the protocol headers.

One factor to consider about protocol-based VLANs is that if the computer is running multiple protocol stacks (such as TCP/IP and IPX/SPX), the switch can be configured to allow the device to participate in separate VLANs based on these protocols. Because this kind of switch enables you to join diverse kinds of networks, it still is quite popular, and you'll find that it is possible to buy this type of switch for an inexpensive price. Decision trees that are used to map different protocols into separate VLANs have been implemented in hardware, which is faster than having to use software and a processor to examine frames, extract the protocol information, and then make the forwarding decisions.

For the standard IP-based network, using a switch that bases VLANs on IP subnets has another advantage. If you don't choose to divide the subnet itself into further VLANS, the switch can, after you've associated an IP address to the LAN adapter card, extract the MAC address from the frame, and from then on use the hardware MAC address to make decisions. Thus, when you move a computer from one location to another on the switch (or a series of interconnected cooperating switches), you won't have to change the IP address of the computer. The new port simply looks at the IP subnet address, creates an entry in its table for the MAC address, and it's basically plug-and-play (or I guess that should be, plug-and-work!).

Using Explicit Tagging on the Network Backbone

It should be obvious by now that most of the network adapter cards that exist in the world today were not created with explicit tagging in mind. In the near future, by which I mean one or two years, this might be an important factor to look for when purchasing network cards and switches. However, LAN switches have evolved to the point that for most small LANs, a VLAN-unaware switch will serve just fine in a small network of a few hundred computers.

However, when you connect a large number of these VLAN-unaware LANs to the network backbone in a larger network, as in a college campus or a large business, the core switches that connect these LANs must handle a much larger amount of network traffic. Because of this, it's typical to use explicit tagging for large, high-capacity network switches than it is in smaller LAN environments (see Figure 9.3).

Here, the core switches that use explicit tagging are able to forward packets they receive within their switched network that understands the tags applied by the edge switches. The edge switches, however, add tags to frames they receive from the VLAN-unaware workstations, based on implicit tagging rules the administrator has set up. They remove the tags when they output frames to the individual workstations that are VLAN-unaware. Of course, these edge switches could just as easily have other switches attached to them, cascaded until you reach the end workstation or other network device. In this illustration, separate workstations are used to simplify the example. The edge switches could be connected to other switches that further subdivide the network and could use implicit tagging to forward the frames they receive from the edge switches.

▶▶ A technique known as Multi-Protocol Label Switching (MPLS) uses a similar tagging technique and is rapidly being deployed in the core routers (or I guess you can now call them switches) that form the heart of the Internet. You can read more about MPLS in Chapter 29, "Routing Protocols."

Within the core of switches that do understand tagging, switching is done at a fast pace.

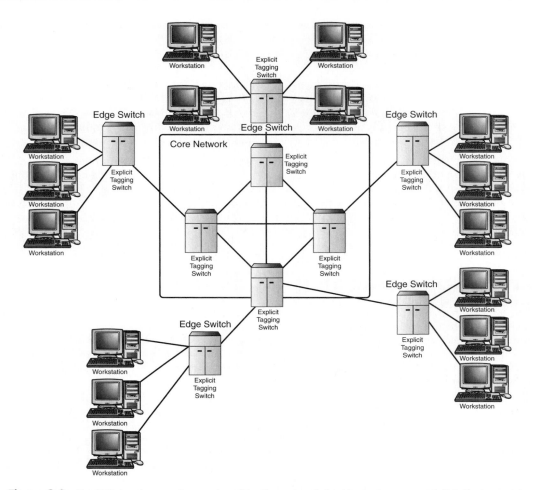

Figure 9.3   Explicit tagging can be employed in the network backbone to connect LANs that are not capable of using explicit tagging.

Switch Standards—The IEEE Standards

There are two standards, at this time, on which many VLANS are based. The first is called IEEE 802.1D, and the second is called IEEE 802.1Q. For the most part, the newer standard builds on and extends the IEEE 802.1D standard. The basic difference is the IEEE802.1D standard defines switches that are VLAN-unaware, whereas the newer IEEE 802.1Q standard provides for VLAN-aware switches.

The actual details of these standards is beyond the scope of this book, much less this chapter. However, there are a few details that should be talked about so that you'll be more VLAN-aware when you make purchasing decisions.

- IEEE 802.1Q includes backward compatibility with switches that were based on the IEEE802.1D standard.

- The default behavior of a switch that is IEEE 802.1Q compliant—*in the absence of any association rules*—is to function as though VLANs were based on ports. This does not mean that IEEE 802.1Q provides for simply port-based VLANs. It just means that it is the default if the vendor doesn't implement any other techniques for using a set of rules to create VLANs.

- The IEEE 802.1Q standard talks about how association rules should be processed, but it does not require any particular kind of rule be implemented on a switch. It's more a guideline to be used if a vendor decides to use one or more rule-based mechanisms for creating VLANs.

- The IEEE 802.1Q standard applies only to switches, not to the creation of network adapter cards that are VLAN-aware. That means if you do purchase adapter cards that support explicit tagging, you should be sure that it's the same method used by your switch!

The IEEE 802.1Q standard adds a filtering database that can be used to map devices to certain ports, and it describes algorithms that can be used with this filtering database to determine which VLAN a frame is a member of. The earlier standard provided for a filtering database, but the newer standard expands on its functionality. Perhaps more important to an administrator in a large network, the standard defines a MIB (management information database) that can be used to manage switches.

▶▶ For more information about SNMP, RMON, and the MIBs they use, see Chapter 44, "Network Testing and Analysis Tools."

For explicit tagging, the IEEE 802.1Q standard defines standard tag formats so that you don't have to worry about different tagging schemes used by proprietary solutions implemented in earlier switches by different vendors.

It also defines a priority mechanism, which is not really necessary for VLAN operation, but was added because some protocols, such as ethernet, don't have a mechanism for this. Although not specifically related to the concept of a VLAN, it was decided during the standards process to include this simply to avoid having to go back later and create another standard for prioritizing ethernet frames. Strange, but true.

Another important concept is that the newer standard sets forth the methods used when a switch is used to connect dissimilar network types—such as ethernet and token ring (and FDDI, though that technology is slowly becoming a dinosaur in today's market). This might not seem important, but there are many differences between the frame types used by these different network protocols (such as the big- or little-endian method of encoding bits—in other words, which bit that is transmitted for a byte is the most significant and which is the least significant?) The newer standard defines the mechanisms for encapsulating dissimilar frames types within the frame type used on the network. For example, it tells which method to use for sending token-ring frames through an ethernet network, and vice versa. Personally, I think that token ring has seen its better days, though there are legacy systems out there which still use it. Using a switch that is IEEE 802.1Q compliant enables you to connect token-ring networks across a link that supports a faster technology, such as Gigabit Ethernet.

The final topic I'll touch on is the fact that IEEE 802.1Q also sets forth a protocol (called GVRP) that can be used by switches to exchange information about VLAN membership. This is perhaps one of its more important concepts. This means that you won't have to configure each switch in the network when VLAN membership is changed.

The IEEE standards cover a lot more territory than I can go into in this chapter. There are entire books on this subject, and if you are seriously considering implementing VLANs in a large network, you should pursue further reading, specifically purchasing the standards from the IEEE and using them to evaluate products to determine whether they meet the standards. However, for most networks today, as long as you use switches from the same manufacturer or from those who state that their products will interoperate with other vendors, you should not encounter many difficulties in setting up VLANs on your network.

What Kind of Switch Should You Buy?

Now that we've covered the basic idea of creating VLANs, let's look at some of the ways that this is done. There are standards, and then there are proprietary solutions. When upgrading a network, you should consider several things when it comes to implementing VLANs in your network:

- Does the switch support VLANs? Small switches you buy at the local computer store for home or small office don't. Medium to high-end switches used in a large network usually do.

- What is the port density of the switch? In a small computer room you might not have space for a large number of interconnected switches. Instead, switches with a larger number of ports can be a better choice.

- If you are using a chassis switch, how many cards can you plug into the chassis? Can you start out with just a few cards for your current needs, and then add additional port cards as your network expands?

- Do ports on the switch have LED indicator lights you can use to check for link connectivity and use, or do you have to rely on software to track down bad or misconfigured ports?

- Does the switch limit broadcast traffic to specific VLANs or does it broadcast this traffic to all the virtual LANs on the switch? This might be desirable, or it might not, depending on your circumstances.

- Does the switch support multiple network speeds (that is, 10/100Mbps or even Gigabit Ethernet speeds for high-end servers)? Does the switch support high-speed connections to other switches and routers?

- Although TCP/IP is quickly overtaking other LAN protocols, such as AppleTalk and IPX/SPX, as the network protocol of choice, does the switch support multiple protocols? If you have a multiprotocol environment, will the switch support creation of VLANs to separate these distinct protocols into separate virtual LANs?

- Is your equipment purchase going to be used for a short period of time (say, a year or two) or is it going to be used longer? If you're in this for the long haul and won't be able to replace expensive VLAN switches for a while, choose a vendor that's known for providing an easy upgrade path (such as a firmware or software upgrade for the switch), or choose one that adheres to a known standard so that you can simply add additional switches as your capacity needs grow.

- What management software is available for the switch? If you want to move a user from one VLAN to another, do you have to physically unplug the user from one switch port and reconnect them to another port? Or, as is more often the case, can you simply use the switch management software to reconfigure that user's port to become a member of another VLAN?

Another concept that might be important in the selection of a VLAN switch needs to be mentioned. Although not as important as those listed previously, some VLAN-aware switches enable you to associate a port with more than one VLAN. For example, in Figure 9.2 we created three distinct VLANs. However, VLAN 1 has a server and a printer as well as workstations configured within its boundaries. In some situations, it might be desirable for a server to be able to participate in more than one VLAN. In that case, you want to be able to specify that the switch port to which the server is connected be part of more than one VLAN. This would not give other computers in the separate VLANs access to other VLANs, but instead it would work in reverse, allowing members of different VLANs to establish sessions with a server, or perhaps a printer or other networked device, that is a member of more than one VLAN.

Routers

10

SOME OF THE MAIN TOPICS IN THIS CHAPTER ARE

What Routers Do

Routable Protocols and Routing Protocols

When to Use a Router

Router Ports and Connections

Router Configuration

Big Routers and Little Routers

Do You Really Need a Router?

CHAPTER 10

Routers are perhaps one of the most misunderstood devices found in a network. After you create a local LAN using simple devices such as hubs, repeaters, bridges, and switches—all of which require little or no configuration—managing a router can be very intimidating. The main reasons for this is that many people do not understand the difference between connectivity devices, such as hubs and switches, versus routers. Another reason is that, unless you use sophisticated network console management software, the management and configuration interface for most routers is not always a simple matter.

Another issue that can make routers seem difficult is the fact that they come in all sizes and shapes. You can find a small, inexpensive router that can be used to connect a small office LAN to a broadband connection (such as DSL or a cable modem). Still larger standalone and rack-mounted units can be used for large-scale networks. At the high end of this market are powerful machines used as Internet core routers.

After you understand the functions that a router performs, however, and after you become familiar with the particular command set for the routers you use, everything starts to fall into place.

What Routers Do

Bridges and repeaters can be used to add to the number of computers and extend the distance covered by an ethernet or token-ring LAN. Bridges, intelligent hubs, and most switches operate at level 2 in the OSI network model, making decisions by hardwired MAC addresses of the installed network card for each system on the LAN. Remember that the hardware addressing scheme produces a flat address space. If you want to create a switch that communicates easily with all the computers hooked up to the Internet, it would need to store millions upon millions of these unorganized addresses in memory—an impossible task indeed!

Note

Although it is convenient to think of switches, routers, and hubs as separate devices, in reality you often find network devices that perform multiple functions. For example, although routers generally are used to connect different LAN segments or networks, you also will find routers that contain built-in hubs, as well as support for bridging and other tasks. In this chapter, the focus is on routing. Don't be surprised if the equipment you purchase offers other capabilities.

Routers operate one step further up the OSI model at the third layer, the network layer. The network layer offers logical addressing, which makes it easier to organize networks and route traffic between networks, overcoming the flat address space provided by lower-level devices. Each router contains two or more network interfaces. One or more of these interfaces can be used to connect the router to a wide-area network, while other interfaces can be used to connect to local network segments. Routers receive input from one network interface, and then make routing decisions based on which interface can best get the packet to its eventual destination. The port on which the packet is retransmitted can lead to another router or another LAN segment directly connected to the router.

◄◄ Read more about repeaters, bridges, and hubs in Chapter 7, "Repeaters, Bridges, and Hubs."

Switches are covered in Chapter 8, "Network Switches," and in Chapter 9, "Virtual LANs."

If you're interested, the OSI network reference model is covered in Appendix A, "The OSI Seven-Layer Networking Model."

Hierarchical Network Organization

The important difference between MAC addresses and logical network addresses (such as TCP/IP and IPX/SPX) is that the logical network addresses allow for the organization of a collection of networks into a hierarchy. This logical distribution of network addresses can be modeled after the logical organization of your business, as in a collection of departmental LANs based on an organizational chart. Or, it can represent a geographical model of a business, with individual LANs located in branch offices. Or, as is usually the case, it can be a combination of both of these.

The router is the device that can connect all these different LAN segments so larger networks can be created that go beyond the limits imposed by LAN topology standards, such as ethernet and token-ring. The Internet is the prime example of a large collection of separate networks, all managed in a decentralized manner. Routers connect these many thousands of networks and make decisions on how best to deliver network information from one client to another on a different network, all based on constantly changing, constantly updating, routing information. They do this by storing information about how to deliver packets to different networks on the Internet. A routing table keeps track of these routes, which can include multiple routing hops on the way to the eventual destination. A router does not always know the entire route that a packet will take to get to its destination. If the destination is on another LAN segment attached to the router, it does know the immediate network destination. However, on the Internet, a packet usually passes through many routers to reach its destination. In this case, a router simply keeps in its routing table the "next hop" that the packet needs to be set to in order to reach its destination. Each router on the way to the destination knows the next hop in the path.

Routers are not limited to using the TCP/IP protocols, though perhaps most of the routers in the world today—on the Internet—are used for IP routing. Most routers can be configured to route many other protocols, such as IPX/SPX and AppleTalk, in addition to TCP/IP, and do it all at once.

Note

Although most of us tend to think of routers as just another kind of network device, computers—from PCs all the way up to mainframes—also can perform routing functions. All that is needed is for the computer to be equipped with more than one network adapter, connections to more than one network, and routing functionality in the protocol stack. For example, you can set up Windows NT/2000 or Unix systems to perform routing for your network. Windows 2000 even allows for a feature called *Internet Sharing*, which allows a single Windows 2000 Server to connect a small LAN to the Internet. Windows 2000 Servers can provide routing, DNS, and DHCP for the LAN.

Similarly, both Unix and Linux systems can be outfitted with multiple network adapters and configured to route network traffic. Indeed, many network administrators use Linux systems as part of a firewall. A lot of existing software, both free and commercial, can be used on these systems for this purpose.

Providing Security

When you think about how a router functions—it examines the header information of the network protocol portion of a packet so that it can make routing decisions—it also should become obvious that it is at the router that you can create a "chokepoint" for your network. That is, you can use router configuration rules to allow or deny network traffic based on information found in the network protocol header. For example, when using a router as a first defense mechanism in a firewall, you can enable or disable any TCP or UDP ports, to deny access to network traffic for selected applications. This is how you prevent someone from using Telnet to log in to a computer on your network. You block this function at a router.

A firewall usually is composed of more than just a simple router, and includes things such as stateful-inspection techniques and application proxies. However, routers were the first devices used to create a "firewall" when it became obvious that the ever-expanding Internet no longer was the safe, academic environment that it once was.

▶▶ You can learn more about routers and how they function in a firewall environment in Chapter 40, "Firewalls."

Routers also provide logging facilities. You can use this data when trying to determine whether your network has been infiltrated. Although most serious hackers today are more sophisticated and would spoof IP addresses in a packet, newcomers who simply download the many free hacker utilities off the Internet can be found easily by checking log files on a router. To provide extra safety, some routers allow you to send log file information to the syslog daemon on another host so that if the router itself is infiltrated, the log file data will still be available.

Routable Protocols and Routing Protocols

So far we've discussed routers and what they do, but we have not discussed the protocols involved. There are basic kinds of protocols that you need to understand when it comes to routers: *routable* protocols and *routing* protocols. For a protocol to be routable, it must make some provision for identifying a network as well as the host that's on a network. If a router had to keep track of every host on the Internet, it would be impossible to build a machine large enough to store all the routing table information. Instead, routable protocols specify network addresses as well as addresses of computers on those networks. Thus, routers only need to store a much smaller routing table that tells them where to forward packets based on the network address. After the packet reaches its destination network, it is delivered to the intended host using the host portion of the address field. TCP/IP (overviewed in Chapter 20), for example, sets aside a portion of the IP address to use as a network ID. Other routable protocols include NetWare's IPX/SPX, DECnet, and AppleTalk. Each of these protocols can be used to create diverse network segments that can be tied together using a router. Many routers also support multiprotocol stacks and can route more than just TCP/IP. Examples of nonroutable protocols include Digital's Local Area Transport (LAT) and NetBIOS (although NetBIOS over TCP/IP, or NBT, can overcome this limitation).

A *routing protocol*, on the other hand, is a protocol that routers use to communicate routing information among themselves. These protocols involve exchanging information about new routes, or old routes that no longer work, as well as other metrics that describe the route (that is, the speed and hop count of the route). *Routes* are the path that a packet takes on its journey to its final network destination. At the local network, the host portion of the protocol address will be used to determine which computer on the local network the packet is destined for.

Routing protocols exchange information between routers so that routers gradually build up a view of the networks that can be reached. This information is dynamic because systems and routers can always experience downtime. When this happens, routers exchange information and, if a new route exists that can still reach the destination, the router may change its routing entries. When multiple routes to a destination exist, depending on the protocol, certain metrics, such as the number of hops between the source and destination, are used to determine what route a packet should take.

Many kinds of routing protocols are in use today, each of which has its merits and shortcomings. Some are used for small internetworks, while others function on the Internet core routers. The most popular of these routing protocols is discussed in further detail in Chapter 29, "Routing Protocols."

When to Use a Router

Not every network needs a router. If you operate a small office LAN, a simple hub or switch-based LAN can provide all the file and print sharing your business needs. However, if you have remote locations, or if you connect to the Internet, it's likely you'll want a router for both management purposes and security features. There are several situations in which a router can be an appropriate solution:

- The size of your local LAN has grown rapidly and you are having problems with network congestion.

- The size of your local LAN has grown rapidly and you would like to delegate authority for groups of users to individual departments, each on its own separate network segment.

- You want to connect to branch offices or other wide-area networks, such as the Internet.

- You want to be able to filter the network traffic that passes between one LAN and the next, or between your network and the Internet. This use of a router generally is found as part of a firewall solution.

▶▶ For more detailed information on using packet filtering techniques with a router as part of a firewall, see Chapter 40, "Firewalls."

Growing LAN Sizes

As a business in today's market grows, so do the computing requirements. A company starting out with only a few computers, or even a few hundred, can easily get by using a LAN constructed with switches and hubs. However, there comes a point when you reach the limits of either the traffic capacity of your LAN or the topological restrictions imposed by the type of LAN you create. When this happens, you can segment the network, using a router, thus preventing congestion or topology problems.

The IP address space (as discussed in Chapter 20, "Overview of the TCP/IP Protocol Suite") provides a hierarchical addressing structure. Basically, there are different classes of IP addresses, and for each type a certain number of bits are set aside to record a network address, while the remaining bits are used to specify the host on that network. By using the hierarchical nature of IP addressing, you can configure your IP subnets using routers, in a manner that reflects your business organization.

▶▶ For more information about the different address classes and other techniques, such as classless interdomain routing (CIDR), see Chapter 20, "Overview of the TCP/IP Protocol Suite."

Using TCP/IP, each local network generally makes up both a physical and logical subnet. The physical subnet consists of all the devices that are attached to the same broadcast domain, which includes all devices attached to the same hub and all hubs connected to that hub. Unless you've configured Virtual LANs (VLANs), the same goes for most switches, although the broadcast domain concept is limited when using a switch. For all nodes that exist on a particular physical subnet, it is a good idea to assign IP addresses that fall into the same network address or subnetwork address. Again, Chapter 20 explains how the network portion and subnet portion of the IP address work. The thing to remember here is that each separate physical subnet generally uses a separate IP network or subnetwork ID to identify all computers on that LAN segment. A separate host ID is used for each computer on each subnet.

VLANs allow you to configure the subnet that a port belongs to on a port-by-port basis. This is covered in Chapter 9, "Virtual LANs."

In this situation, each computer on each segment is a peer to all other computers on the same segment. Communications take place on the local segments at the ethernet frame level using hardware (MAC) addresses. In Figure 10.1, for example, workstation A and workstation B can send data frames back and forth, and the traffic they generate between them never passes through the router. The local hardware addresses are resolved using ARP (see Chapter 20 for more about ARP), and both nodes can talk directly to each other using ethernet frames.

If workstation A needs to exchange data with workstation D or E, network traffic travels between the different subnets through routers 1 and 2. To carry the concept a step further, workstation A would have to send a data packet through three routers to exchange data with workstations G through L. As you can see, a router works much like a bridge in that it segregates traffic and passes it on to other segments only when the destination address of the packet isn't on the local segment. However, bridges work at layer 2 of the OSI model and use hardware MAC addresses. Routers switch traffic based on layer 3 addresses, such as IP.

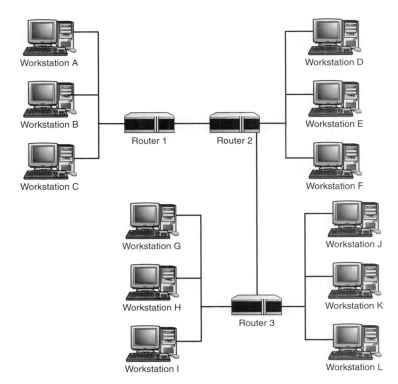

Figure 10.1   Routers are used to link different network segments to create a larger internetwork.

A router is needed only when a packet needs to travel to a different logical IP subnet or network. Routers come in all sizes and combinations. Some have serial-line ports, ethernet ports, twisted-pair, and fiber-optic ports. If you have reached the limit on your LAN and don't want to add more workstations, consider installing a new LAN segment and connecting both your old and new LANs using a router.

Tip

Besides making it easy to organize your network layout by matching IP network and subnet addresses to your business organizational chart, you also can organize your Domain Name System (DNS) names to reflect the business organization. Remember that the host and domain names you assign to a particular network device or computer can, but do not have to, relate directly to the underlying IP address. Instead, these are assigned by the network administrator (or by using DHCP with certain scopes of addresses reserved for selected subnets). Thus, it is possible to use both IP addressing and DNS names to add some organization to the madness that typically makes up a large network. For more about using DNS and how fully qualified domain names are translated to IP and other network addresses, see Chapter 24, "Name Resolution."

Using this method, each subnet has its own unique subnet portion of the IP address space. The router is like all other devices on a traditional ethernet network—it can see all traffic on the segments attached to it. The router, however, has connections to more than one network segment and can transfer packets of information from one segment to another, based on their network address.

Figure 10.1 showed only a simplistic overview of how routers can connect different network segments. In practice, you'll most likely have switches or hubs separating your client computers and servers from the hub. Figure 10.2 shows this view. The router is used to connect several LAN segments, each of which may have a switch (with attached workstations) or a powerful server. Additionally, a WAN port on the router is used to connect to the wide-area network, such as the Internet.

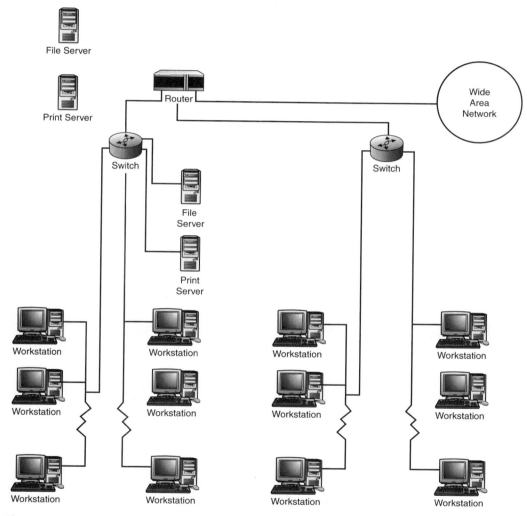

Figure 10.2 In a typical large network, switches or hubs separate individual workstations from the wide-area router connection.

When you configure a client computer to use TCP/IP, you generally specify a *default gateway* (or this value can be supplied by DHCP when the client boots). The default gateway is the address of the router that attaches the local subnet to the larger network structure. Thus, when a client computer wants to send a packet, or series of packets, to a computer that is on a different logical IP subnet, it sends the packets instead to the default gateway—the router. The client computer can tell from its own address what subnet it is connected to. The client software knows to direct a packet to the default gateway when the network or subnet address of the packet differs from the sender's own network address.

A router makes decisions on where next to send the packet based on routing tables. Routing tables can be configured manually (static routing) by the network administrator, or they can be configured dynamically using a variety of routing protocols. Routing protocols are discussed in detail in Chapter 29. Simple routing protocols are useful for small internetworks, and complicated routing protocols are used by Internet core and border routers. However, the principle of routing is basically the same for all these protocols. Routers make decisions based on the network access layer of the OSI model using logical IP addresses. Your local area network uses the ARP protocol to determine the actual hardware address (a flat address space) for communications within the local LAN segment.

When a client computer sends a packet to the default gateway router, it uses the source address in the frame header for the address of the router, even though that is not the eventual destination of the frame. The router is just the next hop for the frame. When the router notices a frame on a port that is addressed to it, it unpacks the frame to expose the IP header portion. Using the IP address, the router then decides on the next hop for the packet and reconstructs a frame to transmit the packet to the next hop. This might be another router or a host on another segment attached to the router. As you can see, routers actually change the packet (or frame) as it travels through an internetwork. For example, the Ethernet frame destination address is changed to indicate the next hop for the frame. Inside the IP header, the router changes the TTL (Time to Live) value. When this value reaches zero, the packet has traveled the maximum hops allowed and a router discards it. Because a router must change fields in the IP header, as well as the Ethernet frame header information, it also must recalculate any error-checking fields for these headers.

At each hop, a router also can be configured with a set of rules that filters out the packet. This capability provides for some security for your network, because you can prevent certain IP addresses or services from passing between your network and the Internet.

Delegating Responsibility for Local Area Networks

Because routers can be used to separate one group of users from another, it makes delegation of administration at the local level much easier. Responsibility implies security. Routers can be programmed using a technique called Access Control Lists (ACLs), which are nothing more than rules that specify

- What direction packets can travel—inbound to the LAN or outbound to another LAN.
- Which IP addresses (both network and host addresses) can pass through the router. Addresses also can usually be specified as wildcards.
- Which IP ports can be allowed to pass through the router.

This packet filtering capability lets a local administrator, who understands the router control, access the local LAN. For security reasons, this can be very important. Most people think of a firewall as a device that sits at the edge of a network and makes the connection to the Internet. That is one use of a firewall. A second use is to isolate departments within a particular network. For example, it's probably a good idea to isolate the accounting department from other sections of your company. You don't want employees probing around trying to break into your payroll records! With a router, you can configure rules that allow only selected users on other LANs (such as the one that services the executive suite), to pass through your router, while keeping others out.

By using controls within your network as well as at the edge, you also can help prevent the spread of any attack or infiltration that does occur.

Another important feature that many routers provide is logging. You usually can log both successes and failures to keep track of how your network is being used. If you find a particular workstation trying to Telnet or FTP to a prohibited LAN, you can use this evidence to discipline the employee. Many routers allow you to designate another system as the location for logging files. Typically, this is done using the Unix `syslog` daemon. This type of feature improves on security. If the router itself is compromised, you will have a record of the events leading up to it. If you regularly review your log files, you can take preventive measures if you even suspect suspicious activity is going on.

Connecting Branch Offices

Many companies have offices in multiple locations. In the early days of computing, when 300 baud modems were the norm, sending data between two sites usually consisted of dial-up access. Today, you can lease lines between central headquarters and multiple branch offices. Additionally, other long-haul services, such as those provided by Frame Relay and Asynchronous Transfer Mode (ATM), can be used to enable you to connect securely to remote branch offices.

▶▶ For more information about using Frame Relay or ATM, as well as other high-speed network connections, see Chapter 19, "Dedicated Connections."

Routers come in all sizes and offer a variety of features. You can use a router to connect branch offices easily. All you need to do is to provide a separate network ID—or more likely subnet ID—for each location and choose an appropriately sized router for each location. Some routers even allow you to use a dial-up line for a remote connection that is used only infrequently. This situation is ideal when all you need to do is poll remote computers after hours to get sales totals and other information of that sort. Still other routers, usually at the low end of the line, allow you to connect to a cable modem or a digital subscriber line (DSL) modem and share that single IP address connection with several other computers. This kind of router/switch combination is ideal for a home office or a branch office that has only a few computers that need to be networked. For more information about using DSL and small hybrid router/switches built for just such a purpose, see Chapter 19.

Using a Router to Protect Your Network—NAT and Packet Filtering

Chapter 40 demonstrates how routers fit into a well-designed firewall solution. However, this topic is important enough to deserve a brief mention here. When the Internet was first being commercialized, there were lots of IP addresses to go around. It was easy back then to get an ISP to assign you a group of IP addresses that were valid on the Internet. As the Internet has expanded year by year at a phenomenal rate, the IP address space has begun to run out.

Most routers provide a function called Network Address Translation (NAT), which is more fully explained in Chapter 40. Briefly, NAT allows your network to use one, or a few, valid IP addresses on the Internet connection side of the router, and a private address space on your local network side of the router. When communications take place between a client on your network and a server on the Internet, the traffic passes through the router, which uses its own valid IP address to make contact with the outside server. Responses received back from the server are repackaged and returned to the original client. Besides using IP address substitution, another version of NAT employs a technique of manipulating port addresses to keep track of multiple connections.

NAT helps keep your network secure because it helps prevent anyone outside your network from finding out any addressing information about servers or workstations inside your network. One of the most important security goals you can accomplish in network security is preventing outsiders from gaining any knowledge about your network, be it network addresses, hardware platforms, or operating systems and applications. The capability for a router to also block certain ports, as well as addresses, makes your local network even more secure. For example, although you might want to allow your users to browse the Web and possibly establish an FTP session with a remote server to download a new driver or software update, you might not want the reverse to be possible. By appropriately configuring your gateway router, you can pretty much block all but the most persistent hacker from getting into your network.

Router Ports and Connections

In a central headquarters, where network segments converge, a larger router with a greater capacity to handle large volumes of network is used. A typical router found in many corporate environments, for example, is the Cisco 2500 series. This router comes in several models—to accommodate different network interfaces—and can provide for both ethernet and token-ring support. The Cisco 2505 appears in Figure 10.3, from the rear, so that you can see the physical connections.

Figure 10.3 A router usually contains multiple interface connections to join different network segments.

In this figure, you can see that the 2505 model provides for eight ethernet 10Base-T connections on the left side that can be used to connect either individual computers or hubs (using crossover cables that swap the transmit and receive wires).

Tip

When configuring a router, you need to supply information about each port, or network interface, that is used. Typically, each port is named to indicate its use. For example, the Cisco IOS (Internetworking Operating System) software uses E0 to represent the first ethernet port, E1 the second, and so on. Serial ports are denoted using an "S" (S0, S1, and so on).

Other local area network interfaces you will find on other models in this series of routers include token-ring connectors (usually a DB-9 connector) and Attachment Unit Interface (AUI, usually a DB-15 connector) used to connect an Ethernet transceiver to the router.

Near the middle of Figure 10.3 are two 60-pin serial connections (DB-60 connectors) that can be used to connect to wide-area networks. These connections usually are made to either a modem or a CSU/DSU that interfaces with the high-speed link. Like LAN ports, different models allow for other kinds of WAN connections. For example, the 2500 series includes support for Basic Rate ISDN to connect your office to a WAN.

In Figure 10.4, you can see a close-up of the serial ports, along with two RJ-45 ports.

Next to the WAN serial connections are two RJ-45 ports labeled CONSOLE and AUX. The console port is used to connect a terminal to the router for configuration and management purposes. In most cases, the cable for this is provided with the router, but check your order to be sure. The terminal you use can be either a dumb terminal (such as a VT-series terminal) or a terminal emulation program running on a PC. Either way, you'll probably also have to obtain an adapter to convert the RJ-45 connector to the type of serial port used on your terminal or PC serial port. Standard serial port converters might or might not be included with the router, so be sure to check the accessories list.

Figure 10.4   Serial connections allow you to connect a router to wide-area connections while the console port allows you to configure and manage the router.

The AUX port can be used to connect a modem to the router. This can be handy for "dial-on-demand" routing, for infrequent connections to remote sites that don't need a full-time dedicated connection. Although you can connect a modem to the console port, this is not always a good idea. Some routers, such as the Cisco 2500 series we're discussing here, don't support RS232 modem controls. This means that when a user using this port logs out, the modem connection is not automatically dropped. If another call comes in shortly afterward, it's possible to access the router without knowing the administrative password, because the session is still in effect.

Router Configuration

Most routers are similar to computers in that they run an "operating system." You can think of the router as a small computer that has only one basic function: Sort out where incoming packets need to go. To preserve your investment, most manufacturers store the router's operating system in non-volatile memory that can be reprogrammed when updates or fixes are released. When the router is first powered up, it runs a small bootstrap program that is used to locate and load the operating system. Most routers also allow you to load the router OS using a trivial FTP server (tftp). This type of FTP server doesn't require a password and shouldn't be used in an insecure environment. However, within a LAN, using a tftp server to download router OS data can make it easier to keep track of different versions of the OS and the routers that are configured to use them.

Cisco's OS for its main router line is called IOS, and it has been updated many, many times over the years and adapted to the newest equipment. Cisco's Web site can tell you which versions are available for the different routers they manufacture. If you deal heavily in Cisco equipment, a good Web site for you to bookmark is the Cisco documentation Web site. Although Cisco routers do ship with a CD that contains most of this documentation, you'll find up-to-date copies at this Web site:

http://www.cisco.com/univercd/home/home.htm

Configuring a router usually begins after you take it out of the box and plug in everything. For each interface (that is, network connection) you need to configure the appropriate information. For example, for a 10Base-T or Fast Ethernet port connecting to a LAN that uses TCP/IP, you must specify an IP address and subnet mask for the port.

There are also tasks you need to perform to configure the routing protocols that the router uses. The information you need for this depends, of course, on the routing protocols you plan to use.

Other configuration issues you need to address include access and security. If the router is being used as part of a firewall, or if there is a need within your network, you might have to set up access control lists to permit or deny network traffic from passing through any of the network interfaces.

One important thing to keep in mind is that the router's OS and the configuration information you enter are separate entities. Both the OS and the configuration file can be stored in nonvolatile memory (NVRAM), and both usually can be downloaded from a tftp server. However, the configuration file that is created when you initially set up a router should be saved in more than one place for backup purposes. Indeed, keeping a printed copy of the information contained in the configuration file can be a helpful troubleshooting tool.

Big Routers and Little Routers

Cisco manufactures a wide range of router products that spans the small home office to Internet core routers. After you get beyond a small basic router that would be useful in a small home office, routers tend to become more configurable—from a hardware perspective. That is, they are modular, and different models can be adapted to different environments by installing interface cards to match your needs. Additionally, all but the smallest routers come in rack-mounted versions so that you don't have to dedicate a large amount of valuable office space to them. No matter what size your LAN or network is, it's a bet that Cisco has a router solution for you.

At the high end of the market are routers capable of serving as Internet core routers. These are the high-bandwidth routers that your local ISP or other large-scale provider uses to connect to the Internet backbone. Such routers allow for line cards that allow them to connect to high-speed fiber optic links, as well as cards that allow for connections to more typical 100Base-T networks.

In addition to Cisco, other router vendors also offer a full range of products. At the high end of the market, however, the competition isn't so great. One vendor, Juniper Networks, markets only high-end routers. This company makes routers that are intended for very large networks and network backbone uses. For example, Juniper's M5 and M10 routers can route and forward network packets at 5 and 10 Gbps (gigabits per second!). Juniper's routers can be configured with various physical interface cards (PICs), each of which contain different network interfaces, ranging from simple 10Base-T ethernet connections up to OC-192c/STM-64 optical fiber link connections. The high-end M160 router (shown in Figure 10.5) is intended to serve as either an Internet core router or as a very flexible, configurable high-end router for a large network backbone.

In Figure 10.6, you can see one of the PIC modules that you can use with the M160. This figure shows a simple Gigabit Ethernet module.

By carefully choosing the modules you configure into a high-end router, it is possible to aggregate smaller links, such as those provided by ISDN or T-carrier lines, into high-speed connections to the Internet. The fact that you can always change out modules to accommodate a changing network infrastructure helps justify the cost of these high-end routers.

Figure 10.5   The Juniper M160 is a high-end Internet backbone router.

Cisco and other manufacturers produce similar high-end routers. However, most users of this book will be dealing with low-end to medium-sized networks, and will find that they don't have to spend a lot of time configuring or managing a router if you set it up correctly in the first place.

For small offices, a multitude of vendors make router/switch/hub combinations that can be used to connect using dial-up or broadband (cable/DSL) to the Internet and other remote networks. Because these devices are basically hybrids and are specifically used for technologies such as DSL or cable modems, they are discussed in greater detail in Chapter 19, "Dedicated Connections."

Figure 10.6 This PIC module enables the Juniper M160 router to connect to a Gigabit Ethernet link.

Using Routers Over Wide-Area Networks (WANs)

You can create a wide-area network (WAN) by purchasing your own set of leased lines—an expensive proposition for many smaller companies—or you can connect your network to the Internet and take your chances there. Using a good router that provides for packet filtering and virtual private networks (VPNs), you can effectively tunnel your network traffic through the Internet in encrypted form. Connecting each branch office, you might find that using DSL technologies is much cheaper than using a more expensive ISDN dial-up or T1 dedicated line. Instead, because you'll have a larger amount of traffic bound to and from the company's headquarters, you can install a large pipe at that point and use cheaper methods out in the field, spending the money for a large data pipe only where it is needed: at the central headquarters.

If you choose to connect a business network to the Internet, you must be familiar with firewall technology. This means you must be familiar with the specific model of router used in your organization. Cisco is perhaps the most widely known brand of routers, but for small offices there exists many viable and inexpensive choices. Besides packet filtering and NAT that are generally supported by most routers, you also should investigate using proxy servers, described in Chapter 40, to further isolate your network from the rest of the world.

Routers Make the Internet Possible

It should be obvious that without routers it would be almost impossible to consider the connection of millions of computers such as the Internet. In the first place, the topological restrictions placed on ethernet, token-ring, and other transport protocols would limit the size to which the network could grow. Second, if routing were not done using a logical addressing scheme, then any device that connects a network to another network would have to keep a table in memory that consists of all nodes on all networks to which it is connected! Although computing power has been increasing at extremely fast rates in the past few years, it's doubtful that anyone could devise a machine that could keep track of all the computers in the world and efficiently route a large number of packets to their correct destinations. The routing table would be so large that it would take forever to route packets.

Instead, all a router must do is know the address of a network, or the address of another router that knows how to deliver packets to the destination network. If you use the tracert command in

Windows (or traceroute in Unix and Linux) to trace the route a packet takes to a particular Web site, you'll most likely see that it goes through many routers before it reaches its destination. As you can see in Listing 10.1, getting from my work PC to a favorite Web site of mine can take a quite a few hops.

Listing 10.1   Using the tracert **or** traceroute **Command to Determine the Routers Between Two Points**

```
G:\>tracert www.bd-studios.com

Tracing route to www.bd-studios.com [207.213.224.83]
over a maximum of 30 hops:

  1    140 ms    150 ms    150 ms  envlnjewsap01.bellatlantic.net
     ➥[192.168.125.173]

  2      *       140 ms      *     192.168.125.158
  3    140 ms    150 ms    151 ms  206.125.199.71
  4    140 ms    150 ms    150 ms  205.171.37.13
  5    140 ms    151 ms    150 ms  jfk-core-01.inet.qwest.net [205.171.30.85]
  6    150 ms      *       150 ms  wdc-core-02.inet.qwest.net [205.171.5.235]
  7    150 ms    160 ms    160 ms  wdc-core-03.inet.qwest.net [205.171.24.6]
  8    180 ms    180 ms    180 ms  hou-core-01.inet.qwest.net [205.171.5.187]
  9    180 ms    190 ms    191 ms  dal-core-02.inet.qwest.net [205.171.5.172]
 10    180 ms    191 ms    190 ms  dal-brdr-02.inet.qwest.net [205.171.25.50]
 11    180 ms    190 ms    190 ms  39.ATM1-0.BR1.DFW9.ALTER.NET [137.39.23.217]
 12    180 ms    191 ms    190 ms  140.at-6-0-0.XR1.DFW9.ALTER.NET [152.63.98.126]

 13    181 ms      *       180 ms  185.at-1-0-0.TR1.DFW9.ALTER.NET [152.63.98.26]
 14    220 ms    231 ms    230 ms  128.at-5-1-0.TR1.LAX9.ALTER.NET [152.63.3.162]
 15    221 ms    230 ms    220 ms  297.ATM7-0.XR1.LAX4.ALTER.NET [152.63.112.181]
 16    220 ms    230 ms    231 ms  193.ATM6-0.GW4.LAX4.ALTER.NET [152.63.113.89]
 17      *       220 ms    230 ms  savvis-lax2.customer.alter.net
     ➥[157.130.236.150]

 18    390 ms    381 ms      *     affinity-2.uslsan.savvis.net [209.144.96.86]
 19    431 ms    460 ms    501 ms  web33.ahnet.net [207.213.224.83]

Trace complete.
```

Clearly, connecting to another computer on the Internet isn't always such a simple thing! High-speed lines and fast, efficient core routers can make it seem (if you are using a fast, digital connection) as if all the servers you access are just around the corner from you. Instead, they could be on the opposite side of the world. Another interesting thing to note about routers is that packets that are part of the same original communication can take different routes to get to the eventual destination. Routing tables change constantly, and what might be a good route at one moment might not be the next. For this reason, higher level protocols, such as TCP, take care of the mechanics involved in determining whether packets are received and reassembled into the correct order.

Do You Really Need a Router?

If you have a small network that doesn't require a lot of security—such as a home network—you probably don't need a router. If you have a network that serves several departments, the advantages of putting each department on a separate subnet outweigh the management tasks of trying to keep track of where each computer is located and also the task of controlling network congestion. Inside your

LAN, use routers to isolate and secure important departments and to localize traffic between specific servers and their clients.

If you are a home office user and use only one computer or use a slow dial-up connection, you probably won't benefit from a router. If you do want to allow more than one computer to use a single Internet connection, you can purchase an inexpensive router/switch for use with a cable or DSL modem. These devices (discussed in Chapter 19) act as a router, in that they use a single valid IP address from your ISP, and as a switch to allocate (through DHCP) addresses from a private address space to other computers on the network. The switch components allow for extremely fast communications on the local home network, while the router functions allow clients to communicate on the Internet.

Choosing a Network Solution

SOME OF THE MAIN TOPICS FOR THIS PART ARE

Heard Anything About ARCnet Lately?

Ethernet

Token-Ring Networks

Wireless Networking: IEEE 802.11 (Wi-Fi) and HomeRF

What Is Bluetooth?

The Wireless Application Protocol (WAP)

Fiber Distributed Data Interface (FDDI)

Dial-Up Connections

Dedicated Connections

PART III

Heard Anything About ARCnet Lately?

11

SOME OF THE MAIN TOPICS IN THIS CHAPTER ARE

Overview of ARCnet

Troubleshooting ARCnet

Of the networking technologies still widely in use today, ARCnet is the oldest. It was created at Datapoint Corporation in the 1970s and is a token-passing system similar in many ways to token ring. For small networks, ARCnet is a reliable technology that is easy to configure. However, also like token ring, ARCnet equipment is produced by only a small number of manufacturers when compared to the huge number of manufacturers making ethernet equipment. Along with its slow network speed (usually between 2.5Mbs to 10Mbps) this makes ARCnet a prime candidate for an upgrade to newer technology for networking desktop systems. Although it was originally developed for the purpose of connecting minicomputers to create a local area network, you would be hard-pressed to find it used that way today.

However, ARCnet is still widely used for other purposes. For example, you can find this technology embedded in a variety of controllers used for industrial automation on factory floors. The basic ARCnet standard is defined as ANSI/ATA 878.1, but extensions and other changes to the original standard have been developed over the years. This chapter gives you a good overview of the details of ARCnet operations and the hardware components involved. However, many vendors offer variations on the original standard, allowing for greater distances between nodes, for example. For those interested, the ARCnet Trade Association keeps a Web page that contains links to many manufacturers of ARCnet hardware. You can visit their Web site at www.arcnet.com.

As a matter of fact, you've probably encountered ARCnet at some point in your life and just didn't know it. For example, the next time you're waiting on your order at McDonald's or White Castle Hamburgers, the cash register (oh, I mean point-of-sale terminal) is probably linked to other similar systems through ARCnet. When you turn up the thermostat at work, there's a good chance that it's connected to a central computer for the building using ARCnet. You'll even find ARCnet used to connect medical devices, such as X-ray machines, at your doctor's office!

So, although ARCnet is the oldest networking technology around today, its stability, simplicity, and low overhead make it a perfect solution for many different kinds of applications. Sometimes newer isn't always better! After all, would you want someone who says "Do you want fries with that?" to be in charge of configuring a TCP/IP network at your favorite drive-through?

Overview of ARCnet

ARCnet stands for Attached Resource Computer Network. Because it is a token-passing system, ARCnet is a deterministic network technology that is useful in situations where a predictable throughput is required. It was a very popular technology during the early 1980s when ethernet was still quite expensive and most local area networks were small. Its speed of 2.5Mbps was more than sufficient for implementing ARCnet in a small office network, given the relative power of PCs and minicomputers at that time. Now, it is most likely to be found in older departmental LANs (though I've never seen one) or in an industrial manufacturing plant or another similar setting. The basic ARCnet operates at a rate of 2.5Mbps and can be used to create a LAN of as many as 255 computers. Some network hardware vendors produce network adapters and hubs that allow for speeds up to 10Mbps.

Although ARCnet is no longer marketed primarily as a PC LAN solution, it does have many features that make it well suited for industrial applications. Factory floor automation requires that controllers and other devices have a communications network in place that allows for reliable, predictable throughput. The following are some of the reasons why ARCnet is still in use today, in environments such as this:

- It's deterministic. That is, because it uses a token-passing mechanism, it is possible to calculate the worst-case amount of time it takes to get a frame from one node to another. Using basic ethernet, nodes on the network must contend for access to the shared network medium, and performance can suffer as network traffic increases.

■ It's simplistic. Other than assigning an address to each ARCnet node, little software configuration or management tasks are needed. This makes ARCnet practically "invisible" to workers using devices that have embedded ARCnet adapters.

■ Although ARCnet is similar to token-ring technology in that it uses a token frame to grant access to the network, no central computer or device is responsible for monitoring or managing the network. All nodes in the network are equal peers. Adding and removing devices from the network is a simple task.

■ ARCnet can be wired using a variety of cables—from coax to fiber optic. This makes connecting devices or adapters from multiple vendors easy.

■ While adapter cards for use in PCs and other computer are generally more expensive than ethernet alternatives, chips used in embedded controllers are usually quite inexpensive.

In an environment such as factory automation, the fact that ARCnet requires little configuration and management makes it a good solution.

Although development was started before the OSI reference model was defined, ARCnet provides functions along the same lines as those defined in the physical and data link layers of the reference model. The ARCnet network adapter card, or the embedded chip in a factory device, takes care of the successful, reliable transmission of a message, relieving the software protocol of these functions.

▶▶ See Appendix A, "The OSI Seven-Layer Networking Model."

Although Datapoint (www.datapoint.com) originally manufactured the chips used to create ARCnet network adapters, the primary manufacturer of chips used today is Standard Microsystems Corporation (SMSC). You can reach their Web site at www.smsc.com. This site contains specific technical documentation for the chips found in most ARCnet products today.

ARCnet Addressing and Message Transmission

The logical topology of the ARCnet network is always a token bus, although it can be physically arranged as a bus, star or a hierarchical star topology, which is a combination of the two (see "Bus and Star Topologies" later in this chapter). ARCnet is a *logical* token bus because no matter which physical topology is used, the *token frame*, which grants permission to a node to transmit data, is passed around in a sequential manner based on a numerical address from one node to the next. Thus, all nodes get an equal chance to access the network media within a maximum set time limit.

◀◀ See Chapter 1, "Overview of Network Topologies."

Note

ARCnet isn't restricted to the factory floor. For Linux users there is even a Linux How-to document, maintained by Avery Pennarun, that can guide you in choosing a card and a network driver so you can link your Linux computers using ARCnet. You can find this How-To at http://www.worldvisions.ca/~apenwarr/arcnet/howto/index.html.

Each node on the LAN is configured with an address from within the range of 1–255. This is because the address fields in ARCnet frames are only 8 bits in length (one byte). Because the largest number you can store in a single byte is 255, this limits ARCnet LANs to small implementations. Of course, back in the 1970s, linking 255 computers was considered exceptional.

The token frame, called an Invitation to Transmit (ITT), is sequentially passed from one node to another based on the addresses assigned to devices in the network. When a node receives the ITT token, it can then transmit a message on the network, or it can pass the frame to the node that has the next highest numerical address in the network. The next node doesn't have to be the node that is located physically closest to the sending node; it can be anywhere on the network. The hierarchy of numerical addressing determines the order in which a node is granted permission to transmit on the network.

ARCnet Symbols and Frames Formats

Two different frame formats are used on an ARCnet LAN. The basic frame format consists of five different types, each of which is used for a specific messaging purpose. The second frame format is the Reconfiguration Burst frame, which is used in configuring the network. All frames, however, are made up using a set of basic symbols (see Figure 11.1):

- **Start Delimiter (SD)**—This symbol consists of six 1's. All the basic frames use this symbol to indicate the beginning of a frame.

- **Reconfiguration Symbol Unit (RSU)**—This symbol is made up of eight 1's followed by a zero. This symbol is used in a special frame, described later in this chapter. It is used to reconfigure the network when a node joins the network.

Besides these two symbols, a set of Information Symbol Units (ISU) are used. Each ISU consists of a bit pattern of 110 followed by an 8-bit value for each ISU. Thus, all ISUs are 11 bits in length. ISUs can serve to indicate the kind of frame that is being transmitted, network addresses, and the actual data that is transmitted inside a data packet frame. Most of the frames you will see on an ARCnet LAN consist of the SD symbol followed by one or more of the following ISUs:

- **Start of Header (SOH)**—This value indicates the beginning of a data packet. Note that the SOH should not be confused with the SD symbol, which precedes the SOH symbol. The SD symbol indicates the start of the frame, while the SOH symbol indicates that the frame contains a data packet. The value for this symbol is 0x01.

- **Enquiry (ENQ)**—This symbol is used in a frame that is sent to determine whether the destination node has enough buffer space in memory to receive a message. The value for this symbol is 0x85.

- **Acknowledgment (ACK)**—This symbol is used to send an acknowledgment. The value for this symbol is 0x86.

- **Negative Acknowledgment (NAK)**—This symbol is used as the opposite of an ACK. It is used in a frame to tell the sender that the destination node does not have free buffer space at this time. The value for this symbol is 0x15.

- **End of Transmission (EOT)**—This symbol is used in the token frame. The node that receives a frame containing this symbol can then begin to transmit a message on the network medium. The value for this symbol is 0x04.

- **Next Node Identification (NID)**—This symbol contains the address of the next logical node in the network and also is used in the token frame. This address is the node to which the token frame will be passed when the current holder releases it. The values of this symbol can range from 0x01 to 0xFF (1–255 decimal).

- **Source Node Identification (SID)**—This symbol contains the address of the sender of a data message packet. Like the NID, this symbol can have a value ranging from 0x01 to 0xFF.

- **Destination Node Identification (DID)**—This symbol contains the address of the node to which a request to send frame or a data packet frame is being sent. Like the NID and SID, this value can range from 0x01 to 0xFF.

- **Continuation Pointer (CP)**—This symbol indicates the length of the data packet. The value of this symbol can range from 0x03 to 0xFF. As explained later in this chapter, data packets come in two types: short and long. Short packets contain one CP symbol, while long packets contain two CP symbols.

- **System Code (SC)**—This symbol is assigned by the ARCnet Trade Association, mentioned earlier in this chapter, and is used to indicate a higher-level protocol. SC symbols are used in data packets. The value for this symbol can range from 0x00 to 0xFF. Using a symbol to specify the protocol allows more than one network protocol to be used on the same network. Note that the value of 0x80 is a reserved code and is used for diagnostic purposes only.

- **Frame Check Sequence (FCS)**—This symbol contains the value of the calculated cyclic redundancy check (CRC-16) used to verify that the contents of the data packet arrived intact and was not corrupted during transit. The value for this symbol can range from 0x00 to 0xFFFF. Because the value of 0xFFFF requires more than 8 bits in binary, two ISU symbols are used to create the FCS in a data packet.

- **Data**—The actual user data contained in a packet is composed of multiple ISUs, each 11 bits in length. Although you need only 8 bits to create a byte, remember that each ISU contains the 3-bit preamble of 110, so each byte of user data is actually represented by 11 bits inside the data portion of a data packet.

Using these basic symbols, it is now possible to define the kinds of frames that can be constructed so that nodes can communicate on the ARCnet LAN. The five basic frame types are

- **ITT**—Invitation to Transmit. This is the token frame that is passed around the logical network, giving the node that possesses the frame permission to send a data message on the network medium.

- **FBE**—Free Buffer Enquiry. This frame type is used by a node to determine whether the destination node has sufficient buffer space in memory to receive a message before it is sent.

- **ACK**—Acknowledgment. This frame is sent in response to the FBE frame if the destination is willing to receive the message.

- **NAK**—Negative Acknowledgment. This frame is sent in response to the FBE if the destination is not willing to receive the message at this time.

- **PAC**—Packet. This frame carries the actual message data. ARCnet uses two different kinds of PAC frames: short and long. Obviously, the long version is meant for sending messages of a larger size.

Figure 11.1 shows the layout of the symbols used to construct the different frame types.

Note that in Figure 11.1 each frame type begins with the start delimiter (SD) symbol. Only the actual data packet frames (PAC) contain the frame check sequence that is used to verify the integrity of the data in the packet. Another interesting thing to note is that a short packet can contain as many as 2772 bits in the data section, while the long packet type has a minimum of 2816 bits for the data section. This is because data ISUs with values of 253, 254, or 255 are not allowed. If a message falls within these bounds, then the message is sent in a long packet, with null padding (a string of zero bytes) added to adjust the length of the packet.

Note also that the number of bits includes the 3-bit preamble for each byte of data in the data portion of the packet. That is, while the data section in a short packet can be up to 2772 bits long, that doesn't mean you can place 346.5 (2772/8) bytes of actual data in the data section. Instead, you can place only a maximum of 252 bytes of data (2772/11) bytes of data. Each byte effectively is represented by 11 bits, with the first three bits being the constant value of 110. Likewise, the maximum number of bits in the data portion of a long data packet is 5577, which means that the maximum amount of bytes that a long packet can carry is 507 bytes (5577/11).

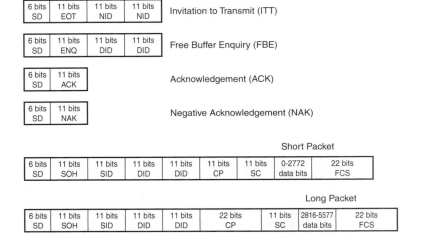

Figure 11.1   Frame types used on ARCnet LANs.

The following basic steps are involved in sending a message in an ARCnet network:

1. A node that has a message to send receives the token frame.

2. Before sending the message, the source node first sends a Free Buffer Enquiry (FBE) frame to the node to which it wants to communicate. Looking back at Figure 11.1, you can see that this is a simple frame and doesn't even contain the source address of the computer or device that is making the request. Only the destination address is contained in the frame, and it is stored in the frame twice.

3. If the destination node has available buffer space to receive a message, it transmits an acknowledgement frame. If it does not have sufficient space in its memory to receive the message, it sends a negative acknowledgment. Again, this frame does not contain the source address of the device that originated the request.

4. When the sender sees the acknowledgment frame, it sends the message to the destination node. The message is sent in a packet that can range to as many as 507 bytes of data. As with most network technologies, the message packet contains a header. Both the source and destination addresses are included in this frame. This frame uses a CRC (Cyclical redundancy Check) value that the receiving node can use to ensure the accuracy of the message received.

5. When the receiving node checks the CRC value against the data and determines that the message was accurately received, it sends another acknowledgment frame around the network. If the message data fails the CRC test, the receiving node transmits nothing. A timer on the sending node eventually expires, so the sender knows that its message was not delivered correctly.

6. After a successful transmission (acknowledgment received) or unsuccessful transmission (timer expires), the sending node relinquishes the token by passing it to the network node that has the next higher address on the network.

In this sequence of events, the node that gains control of the token frame can make only one attempt at transmitting a data packet. If the data does not reach its intended destination—the timer expires before an acknowledgement is received—the sending node does not immediately try to resend the data packet. Instead, it passes the token frame (ITT) to the next logical member of the ring, and waits until the token frame returns to it again before it attempts to send the data packet.

If the message that the sender wants to transmit is longer than 507 bytes, then the sender divides the message into smaller units and must wait until it receives the token again to send each fragment. The receiving node reassembles the fragments to get the full message.

Note

ARCnet also supports a broadcast message, using zero as the destination address. When this type of message is sent, the acknowledgment procedure is not used. Additionally, only nodes that have been configured to respond to broadcast messages will process them.

This simple scheme shows that it is possible to calculate the minimum amount of time it can take to send a message from one node to another. It also shows that the worst-case scenario can be calculated, by taking into account the number of nodes on the network, cable lengths, timer values, and other similar factors. Thus, for real-time applications where network transmit time needs to be predictable, ARCnet can be a good solution.

Network Configuration

ARCnet does not require that the network administrator assign addresses sequentially beginning with 1 and continuing through 255. In fact, as long as each node has a unique address assigned to it, it doesn't matter whether there are gaps in the address space. The ARCnet LAN uses a process that automatically lets each node discover its logical neighbor (the node with the next highest numerical address). When adding or removing nodes from the network, the network undergoes an automatic reconfiguration process.

The method by which a node joins the network uses the second frame format used by ARCnet—the Reconfiguration Burst frame format. This frame contains 765 RSU symbols (eight 1's followed by a zero). When a node determines that it is not part of the logical LAN (that is, it doesn't receive the token within a short period of time) it uses the Reconfiguration Burst frame to effectively disrupt any current transmission or token passing that is in progress at the time. Other nodes on the network then begin a process of reconfiguration.

Each node backs off for a timeout period based on its numerical address. The node that has the highest address will be the first node to timeout. It then will attempt to locate its logical neighbor by incrementing its own address by one and transmitting a token frame. If a node with that address does not respond, the node increments the address again and continues to send a token frame until its neighbor is found. The remaining nodes on the network use this process so that, within a very short period of time, each node in the network knows its neighbor and normal communications can resume.

A node leaving the network is detected easily, and the network again undergoes a reconfiguration process. After a node sends a token frame to its neighbor, it continues to listen on the network to be sure that the neighbor will in turn pass on the token, or perhaps start the process of sending a message to another node. Remember that, although the ARCnet LAN can be laid out in bus and star formations, the address space (1–255) makes the network a logical ring, so that a node can be sure that it will hear something on the network within certain time limits. In the original standard, the maximum time allowed for a frame to make the trip from one node to another is 32 microseconds. In actual applications, it is possible to extend this value by adjusting timers to allow for greater distances between nodes.

Thus, when a node determines that something has gone wrong with its current logical neighbor it then starts to search for a new neighbor. It does this by taking the address of the neighbor that was removed from the network (or failed in some way) and incrementing it by one. It sends out a token based on this new address. This continues until some response is detected (that is, the token successfully passes around the net).

Hubs and Network Wiring

The network can be wired using twisted-pair cables, coaxial cables, or fiber-optic cables. For UTP, Category 3 cables or above should be used. Coaxial cables should be RG11U or RG-59U or RG-62. The distance between network nodes depends on the type of wiring used and what type of hubs are used as wiring concentrators.

Two types of hubs can be used when creating an ARCnet network:

- **Active hubs**—Active hubs provide the longest distance capabilities for the ARCnet LAN. The active hub acts much like an ethernet hub, and is usually manufactured in 8- to 16-port units. The active hub takes the incoming signal and amplifies it before sending it back out on the other ports. Some active hubs perform other tasks, such as segmenting or blocking off a port that exhibits errors so that other segments are unaffected.

- **Passive hubs**—Passive hubs usually have only four ports and do no signal amplification. Instead, a passive hub acts as a simple signal-splitter, taking the incoming signal and dividing it among other three ports. A passive hub can be used to create a very small LAN—that is, one with four nodes or less. The primary function of a passive hub in a larger LAN is to join individual workstations to an active hub. Unused ports on a passive hub usually should be terminated. Unused ports on active hubs, depending on the manufacturer, might or might not need to be terminated.

Bus and Star Topologies

Even though ARCnet is a token-passing technology, like a token-ring network, it can be wired in using several different methods. Unlike token-ring networks, no computer on the ARCnet LAN acts as a monitor to check for errors or otherwise manage the network. The reconfiguration process that ARCnet uses to form a logical ring is not directly related to the physical layout of the network.

Bus Topology

The simplest network topology that can be used for ARCnet is a bus using coaxial cables with BNC T-connectors. Up to eight nodes can be connected to any bus segment in a daisy-chain made up using the T-connectors. The total length of the segment is limited to 300 meters (1,000 feet). For such a small network, no hub would be necessary. However, as you can see in Figure 11.2, an active hub can be used to join multiple segments to create a larger LAN than can be created by using a single cable segment. A passive hub cannot be used to connect individual segments based on a bus topology; only active hubs can do this. Passive hubs can be used only to connect individual workstations.

You also can create a bus topology using UTP cables. The UTP ARCnet adapter has two connectors, usually RJ11 or RJ45. Stations are daisy-chained from one node to the next using both connectors. In some cases, the last node on each end of the bus will need to have a terminator inserted into the last connector. Some cards provide an auto-termination feature. When using UTP you can have as many as 10 nodes on one segment, with any repeater counting toward that limit. Each node on the bus must be separated by a *minimum* of about six feet. The total segment length can be as much as 400 feet (120 meters).

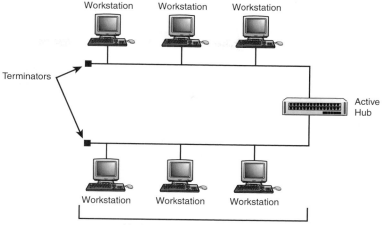

Maximum 1,000 ft. per segment

Figure 11.2 An active hub can be used to join multiple coaxial segments, and might need terminators.

Star Topology

You can create a physical star topology by using hubs. You can create a tree structure of multiple stars by cascading hubs. Figure 11.3 shows a small network that uses both active and passive hubs, and also has workstations that connect directly to an active hub.

The major difference you will notice in Figure 11.3 is that, when a station connects to an active hub, the distance can be as great as 2,000 feet (500 meters). When connecting a station to a passive hub, the distance shrinks to only 100 feet (30 meters). These same rules apply when connecting hubs. The passive hub connected to an active hub cannot be farther away than 100 feet. Two active hubs can be separated by as much as 2,000 feet. The capability of the active hub to regenerate the signal accounts for the longer distances achieved. The overall size of the network should never exceed 20,000 feet (6,000 meters).

Note

You can use active hubs to reach the maximum distance of 6,000 meters. When a large LAN is constructed in this manner, remember that no loops can exist in the physical topology and the total number of network nodes is limited to 255 because of the 8-bit address used.

Many vendors sell hubs, cables, and other network devices that can be used to create ARCnet networks that vary from these topologies and their limitations. The best source for information about vendors who supply ARCnet hardware is the ARCnet trade association.

ARCnet Network Adapter Cards

Because ARCnet has been around for so long, a lot of different network cards are still in use today. ARCnet cards are not interchangeable with ethernet cards. During an upgrade, you will have to incur the cost of new NICs for each node on the network. Two main categories of cards are used in ARCnet networks: Bus NIC (high-impedance driver) and Star NIC (low-impedance driver). As their names imply, they are different in that the Bus NIC should be used on a bus topology and the Star NIC should be used on a star topology. Some newer cards can provide both options.

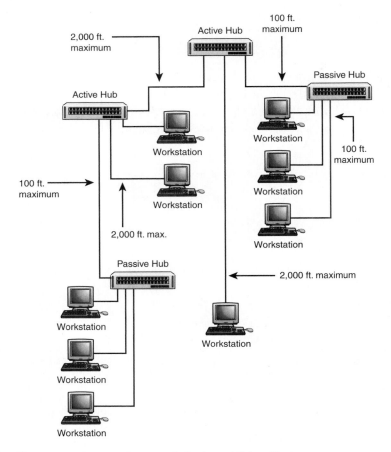

Figure 11.3 The star topology can be extended using additional hubs.

Connecting ARCnet LANs to Ethernet LANs

Because of the different signaling methods used and the different network access techniques, it should be obvious that you can't mix ethernet and ARCnet nodes on the same cable. However, one of the advantages of ARCnet is that there are vendors who manufacture hubs and other devices that allow you to connect dissimilar cabled networks. For example, there are active hubs that allow for coaxial cable, twisted-pair, and fiber-optic cabling. Conversion boxes are also available to bridge between an ethernet network and an ARCnet LAN. Upper-level protocols, such as TCP/IP, can then be used to pass traffic between the two networks.

Troubleshooting ARCnet

Following are some items that you should keep in mind when troubleshooting ARCnet:

- ARCnet active hubs will usually partition off a segment that exhibits problems that might interrupt other network activity. Thus, if a node fails, you should examine all the components between the hub and the network card.

- Network analyzers, including small, handheld models, can be used to check cable problems.

- If a port on the hub is suspected to be the problem, terminate the port and insert the cable in another port.

- As with all network adapters, you can try inserting the card in a different slot in the computer or device, or swap out the card with one known to work, to determine whether the problem lies in the network card.

- When using a bus technology with coaxial cable, be sure that both ends of the segment are terminated properly, either by a terminator or by being plugged into a hub port.

- All BNC T-connectors on a coaxial cable should be examined to be sure that they are connected tightly to the network adapter, as well as to the two cable segments they connect.

- If using twisted-pair wiring, check the vendor's specifications to ensure you are using the correct pin-out for the adapter or hub.

- Standard ethernet twisted-pair cables will most likely not work, so be sure you're using the correct cable when installing a new node.

- As with any LAN networking technology, check to be sure that you've observed the distance and number of node limits imposed by the topology you choose. For example, when adding an additional hub to an existing network, be sure that the cables attached will not exceed the total network diameter and that the nodes attached to the hub will not exceed the 255 node limit for the LAN.

Ethernet

12

SOME OF THE MAIN TOPICS IN THIS CHAPTER ARE

If you sit down at almost any PC or desktop workstation today, it is very likely that the computer will be linked to the local network by one form of ethernet or another. Although other local area networking technologies, such as token ring, are still around, ethernet-connected computers outnumber all other types by at least ten to one. You'll also find that, most likely, ethernet is the underlying networking technology that connects servers, printers, and other devices on your network. Ethernet has become so pervasive that every major manufacturer of networking equipment sells equipment that is designed to work with or provide interconnectivity with ethernet LANs.

So, before we start talking about network transport protocols, services, and applications, it is important that you get a good understanding of what ethernet is and how it functions. It's also important that you understand that there is more than one kind of ethernet. What started out as a simple local area networking technology has evolved to the point that it is now seriously considered a wide-area networking technology. From the first commercial versions that operated at 10 Mbps to the newest 10 Gigabit ethernet, you'll find that there's an ethernet solution to most network problems you encounter. It's on the desktop. It's in the wiring closet. It's the backbone of your network. And it is very possible that, if not today, then tomorrow it will be transporting your data across high-speed wide-area links on the Internet.

In this chapter, we'll first look at how ethernet got its start, and then describe the different versions that were standardized and marketed. After giving you a thorough lesson in ethernet technology, we'll look at techniques that can be used to troubleshoot ethernet networks.

A Short History of Ethernet

Ethernet was originally developed at Xerox PARC (Palo Alto Research Center) Laboratories in the 1970s. Robert Metcalfe was charged with the responsibility of networking a group of computers that could all use a new laser printer that Xerox had developed. Xerox also had just developed what was probably the first personal workstation, and had a need to network more than the usual two or three computers that you would find in a single building during that time.

The original ethernet standard was developed over the next few years, and this resulted in a paper, "Ethernet: Distributed Packet-Switching For Local Computer Networks," written by Metcalfe and David Boggs (*Communications of the ACM*, Vol. 19, No. 5, July 1976 pp. 395–404). This paper gives credit to the ALOHA project that had been done in Hawaii with packet radio transmissions into the "ether," noting that scientists once thought that electromagnetic radio signals traveled through a substance known as "ether." In this first ethernet experimental network described in the paper, the network covered a distance of 1 kilometer, ran at 3mbps, and had 256 stations connected to it. For its time, this was an accomplishment.

Note

The Metcalfe and Boggs paper anticipated many other innovations that would appear in the next few years in the area of networking. They recognized the limits of a local area network using a shared medium. They also anticipated the use of bridges (repeaters with packet filters) and of higher-level protocols that would have an expanded address space that would allow for additional fields that could be used for routing purposes. Another interesting thing to note is that, similar to IBM when it created the now famous personal computer that has become a standard, Metcalfe and Boggs also chose to use "off-the-shelf" parts for the network transmission medium: ordinary CATV coaxial cables and the taps and connectors used with them. This made it even cheaper to think about creating a commercial version of ethernet. An online copy of this paper can be found at `http://users.neca.com/seshipma/cst220/ethernet/`.

Later, a consortium of three companies: Digital Equipment Corporation, Intel, and Xerox further developed the Ethernet II standard, sometimes referred to in older literature as the DIX standard, based on the initials of the participating corporations. These companies used the technology to add networking capabilities to their product lines. For example, at one time Digital Equipment Corporation had the largest commercial network in the world, using DECnet protocols connecting ethernet LANs. Today the dominant protocols used with ethernet are TCP/IP and to a smaller extent, IPX/SPX.

The idea of networking hundreds, and thousands, of PCs into a business LAN would have sounded pretty optimistic back when ethernet was first developed. Yet, in part because of its simplicity and widespread support among manufacturers, ethernet has adapted over the years to survive, running on newer devices and network media. You can now run an ethernet network on coaxial cable, twisted-pair wiring (shielded and unshielded), and fiber-optic cabling.

Variations on a Theme: How Many Kinds of Ethernet Are There?

In 1985, the IEEE standard "802.3 Carrier Sense Multiple Access with Collision Detection (CSMA/CD) Access Method and Physical Layer Specifications" was published. These specifications made it easy for vendors to create hardware, from cabling to LAN cards, which could interoperate. The many different ethernet standards that you will need to know about are all identified by a name that includes "IEEE 802.", followed by a number and possibly a letter or two.

The IEEE 802 LAN/MAN Standards Committee is responsible for creating standards for local and wide area networking. This committee was formed in 1980 and was originally called the Local Network Standards Committee. The name has been changed to reflect the evolutionary development of some of the committee's standards to MAN speeds. The following is a list of the most relevant IEEE 802 standards:

- **802**—This standards document gives an overview of the LAN/MAN standards, describing in general terms the architecture of the protocols that are encompassed by the IEEE 802 LAN/MAN committee.

- **802.1**—This set of standards deals with bridges (covered in more detail in Chapter 7, "Repeaters, Bridges, and Hubs") and their management.

- **802.2**—This standard describes Logical Link Control (LLC).

- **802.3**—This standard sets forth the CSMA/CD method that is used by early versions of ethernet to control access to the shared network media.

- **802.5**—Token-ring network media access is described in this standard.

- **802.7**—This set of standards describes broadband LAN networking.

- **802.8**—This standards document sets forth recommended techniques for using fiber-optic cabling in networks.

- **802.10**—Security is the topic of this set of standards documents.

- **802.11**—Wireless networking is described by this set of standards and is covered in greater detail in Chapter 14, "Wireless Networking—The Wireless Application Protocol."

- **802.14**—This standard discusses techniques that can be used for digital communications over a cable TV network.

- **802.15**—Wireless Personal Area Network (WPAN) is set forth by this set of standards. That is, low-power communications within a "personal operating space (POS)."

Note

Anyone who knows anything about networking knows that LAN stands for *local area network*. Another popular acronym, WAN, stands for wide area network. So what, then, is a MAN? It's a metropolitan area network. Although ethernet was originally deployed in the LAN environment, it has been adapted to newer technologies and much faster network speeds so that it can now compete in the MAN arena, alongside other protocols, such as SONET (Synchronous Optical Networking).

Note

You can learn more about the activities of the IEEE 802 LAN/MAN Standards Committee and the different working groups that concentrate on specific network standards by visiting the Web site at `http://ieee802.org/`.

The committee is made up of various working groups and technical advisory groups. For example, IEEE 802.3 is the working group for standard ethernet CSMA/CD technology, while IEEE 802.3z is the standard for Gigabit Ethernet, which is a faster version of the original 802.3. In Chapter 13, "Token Ring Networks," you'll read about token-ring networking, which is defined in standards documents produced by the IEEE 802.5 Token Ring Working Group.

Different forms of ethernet are also referred to using a naming scheme that links the network speed, the word "BASE" (for baseband signaling), and an alpha or numeric suffix that specifies the network media used. An example of this is 10BASE-T, which is broken down as follows:

- 10 = Ethernet, running at a speed of 10Mbps
- BASE = baseband signaling
- T = over twisted-pair (T) wiring

Today there is a wide assortment of ethernet solutions from which to choose. Originally, ethernet used coaxial cable (10BASE-5) that was "tapped" into when a new workstation was added to the bus network. Later, Thinnet (10BASE-2) was developed and allowed a smaller, more flexible cable to be used to connect the network. With Thinnet, BNC connectors were introduced, making it unnecessary to "tap" into the coaxial cable. The most recent versions of ethernet use twisted-pair wiring and fiber-optic cables and centralized wiring concentrators, such as hubs and switches.

The original Ethernet II network operated at a blazingly fast speed of 10Mbps. The most recent standard that is coming to market fast is Gigabit Ethernet, now that it has been standardized. And as if that weren't enough, almost through the standardization process stage is 10 Gigabit Ethernet, with some vendors already making products for this soon-to-be new ethernet standard.

The most common standards-based ethernet solutions from the past to the present are

- **10BASE-5**—This standard uses thick coaxial cable. The 10 in this name indicates the speed of the network, which is 10 megabits/second (Mbps). The number 5 in the name indicates that the maximum length allowed for any segment using this topology is 500 meters. 10BASE-5 networks used thick coaxial cable. To install a node on the network, it is necessary to use what is commonly referred to as a "vampire tap." That is, you attach a connector to the backbone thicknet coaxial cable by punching into the wire. A drop cable is then run to the workstation that is being added to the network.

- **10BASE-2**—This ethernet standard runs at the same speed as a 10BASE-5 network (10Mbps) but uses a smaller, more flexible cable. It is common to see older networks composed of multiport repeaters, with each port using thinnet cables to connect one or multiple computers. Each repeater is joined using a 10BASE-5 thicknet cable. Using a BNC T-connector it is possible to create a simple daisy-chain bus using 10BASE-2.

- **10BASE-T**—This is perhaps the most common form of ethernet in use today. The network connection is made from workstations to a central hub or switch, using a physical star topology. The use of twisted-pair wiring (hence the "T" in the name), which is cheaper and much more flexible than earlier coaxial cables, makes routing cables through ceilings and walls a much simpler task. Centralized wiring also makes it easier to test for faults and isolate bad ports or move users from one area to another.

- **10BASE-FL**—This version of ethernet also operates at 10Mbps, but instead of using copper wires, fiber-optic cables (FL) are used—specifically, multimode fiber cable (MMF), with a 62.5 micron fiber optic core and a 125 micron outer cladding. Separate strands of fiber are used for transmit and receive functions, allowing full-duplex to operate easily across this kind of link.

- **100BASE-TX**—Uses Category 5 wiring (See Chapter 5, "Wiring the Network—Cables and Other Components") to allow a distance of up to 100 meters between the workstation and the hub. Four wires (two pairs) in the cable are used for communications.

- **100BASE-T4**—Uses Category 3 or Category 5 wiring to allow for a distance of up to 100 meters between the workstation and the hub. Four wires (two pairs) in the cable are used for data communications.

- **100BASE-FX**—Uses multimode fiber-optic cables to allow for a distance of up to 412 meters between the workstation and the hub. One strand of the cable is used for transmitting data while the other is used for receiving data.

- **1000BASE-SX**—The 802.3z IEEE standards document, approved in 1998, defines several Gigabit Ethernet networking technologies. 1000BASE-SX is intended to operate over fiber links using multimode fiber, operating with lasers that produce light at approximately 850 nanometers (nm). The "S" in the name implies a short wavelength of light. The maximum length for a segment of 1000BASE-SX is 550 meters.

- **1000BASE-LX**—This fiber-based standard defines ethernet when used with single-mode or multimode fiber. The "L" in the name implies a longer wavelength of light, from 1270 to 1355 nanometers. The maximum length for a single segment of 10BASE-LX is 550 meters using Multimode fiber, and up to 5,000 meters using Single Mode fiber.

- **1000BASE-CX**—This standard allows for Gigabit Ethernet across shielded copper wires. It is designed primarily for connecting devices that are only a short distance away—25 meters or less.

- **1000BASE-T**—The IEEE standard 802.3ab added to the physical layer of Gigabit Ethernet Category 5 unshielded twisted-pair wire cables. The maximum distance for any segment using 1000BASE-T is 100 meters.

Collisions: What Is CSMA/CA and CSMA/CD?

In the original PARC ethernet, the method used to exchange data on the network media was called *Carrier Sense, Multiple Access (CSMA)*. The Ethernet II specification added *Collision Detect (CSMA/CD)* to this technique. A collision occurs when two workstations on the network both sense that the network is idle and both start to send data at approximately the same time, resulting in a garbled transmission. The term *collision* itself seems to imply that something is wrong. In some technical literature, this kind of event is called a *stochastic arbitration event*, or *SAE*, which sounds much less like an error than does *collision*. However, collisions are expected in an ethernet network. Only when they become excessive is it time to search for the sources of the collisions and rearrange some workstations or network devices as appropriate.

The Manchester encoding scheme that was used on early ethernet implementations provided an electrical signal that varied from +0.85V to -0.85V. Collisions could be detected when this voltage varied by an amount considerably more than that allowed by this range.

So, you can see that the rules used to create ethernet networks are not simply arbitrary decisions made by some committee; they relate to the characteristics of the physical devices used to create the network. When using a collision detection mechanism to arbitrate access to the network, the transmitting device needs to know how long it will take, in the worst case, for its transmission to travel to the furthermost device that resides on the same segment.

Why is this? Consider what happens when a device starts transmitting. Because the signal moves through the wire at a noninstantaneous speed, it will take some amount of time before all devices on the same segment sense that the cable is being used. At the furthermost end of the cable, it is possible for another device that has not detected the first transmission to listen and then start signaling its own data onto the network, just before the first signal reaches it. The result is a collision. The first station that initiated a transmission will not detect that a collision has occurred until the corrupted signal travels back to it, hence the round-trip timer value.

A 10Mbps ethernet network signals at a speed of 10 million bits per second. The standard says that the round-trip time can be no more than 51.2 milliseconds—this is the amount of time it takes to transmit about 64 bytes of data at 10Mbps. Thus, the rules state that a device must continue to transmit for the amount of time it would take for its signal to travel to the most distant point in the network and back—the round-trip time.

To put it another way, a workstation could not start to transmit yet another packet until enough time had elapsed for

■ Its first packet to travel all the way to the network node that was located at the furthermost end of the collision domain, *and*

■ Time for any packet transmitted by the furthermost node to reach the first node, if the furthermost node had started transmitting *just before* receiving the first data transmission

If the device does not continue transmitting for the duration of the round-trip time, it is not capable of detecting that a collision occurred with that frame before it began to transmit another frame.

If a frame that needs to be transmitted is less than 64 bytes in length, the sending node will pad it with zeros to bring it up to this minimum length.

A maximum size for the frame was also added by the Ethernet II specification, resulting in a frame size with a minimum of 64 bytes and a maximum size of 1500 bytes.

Note

Actually, the term "byte" that is used in this chapter to specify the length of a field in an ethernet frame is not the most specific term that can be used by those who designed these specifications. Instead, the term "octet," which means 8 bits, is the term you will see in most of the standards documentation. For purposes of clarity, the term "byte" is used here because most readers will be familiar with its meaning and less likely to be confused.

The method that a device uses to communicate on the network is described in the following steps:

1. Listen to the network to determine whether any other device is currently transmitting (Carrier Sense—CS).

2. If no other transmission is detected (the line is free), start transmitting.

3. If more than one device senses that no transmission is occurring, both can start transmitting at the same time. The network physical connection is a shared medium (Multiple Access—MA).

4. When two devices start transmitting at the same time, the signal becomes garbled and the devices detect this (Collision Detection—CD).

5. After transmitting data onto the network, the device again listens to the network to determine whether the transmission was successful or whether a collision has occurred. The first device that detects the collision sends out a jamming signal of a few bytes of arbitrary data to inform other devices on the network.

6. Each device that was involved in the collision then pauses for a short amount of time (a few milliseconds), listens to the network to see whether it is in use, and then tries the transmission again. Each device that caused the collision uses a random backoff timer, reducing the chances of a subsequent collision. This assumes, of course, that the network segment is not highly populated, in which case excessive collisions can be a problem that needs troubleshooting and correction.

Note

Excessive collisions can reduce network throughput. Later in this chapter, we'll look at what you can do when network utilization starts to exceed 40–50% of the capacity of the transport medium.

Because ethernet enables more than one device to use the same transmission medium, with no central controller or token designating which network node can transmit, collisions not only can occur, but are indeed expected events. When this happens, as explained in the next section, each node "backs off" for a certain amount of time intended to prevent the possibility of another collision before attempting retransmission.

Note

In contrast, collisions don't occur on token-ring networks. Instead, access to the network is granted in a controlled manner by passing a certain frame (the token frame) from one station to another. A station that needs to transmit data does so after it receives the token frame. When it is finished transmitting, it sends the token frame to the next station on the network. Thus, token-ring is a deterministic network and guarantees each station on the ring the capability to transmit within a specified time. Ethernet, however, is a more competitive environment in which each station on the LAN must contend with any other station that wants to transmit on the same LAN. For more information on token-ring networks, see Chapter 13.

The Backoff Algorithm

Without a backoff algorithm, the device that detects a collision will stop and then try once again to transmit its data onto the network. If a collision occurs because two stations are trying to transmit at about the same time, they might continue to cause collisions because both will pause and then start transmitting at the same time again. This will occur unless a backoff algorithm is used.

The backoff algorithm is an essential component of CSMA/CD. Instead of waiting for a set amount of time when a device backs off and stops transmitting, a random value is calculated and is used to set the amount of time for which the device delays transmission.

The calculation used to determine this time value is called the *Truncated Binary Exponential Backoff Algorithm*. Each time a collision occurs for an attempted transmission for a particular frame, the device pauses for an amount of time that increases with each collision. The device tries up to 16 times to transmit the data. If it finds that it cannot put the information onto the network medium after 16 attempts, it drops the frame and notifies a higher-level component in the protocol stack, which is responsible for either retrying the transmission or reporting an error to the user or application.

Note

A method similar to CSMA/CD is *CSMA/CA*, where the last two letters, *CA*, stand for *collision avoidance*. Networks that use this method access the physical medium—such as AppleTalk—and listen to the network just as an ethernet device does. However, before sending out a frame on the network, networks using CSMA/CA first send out a small packet indicating to other stations that they are about to transmit. This method helps to greatly reduce collisions, but is not widely used because of the overhead that is produced when its networks send out the informational packet. The IEEE 802.11 wireless networking standard also uses a form of CSMA/CA.

Defining the Collision Domain—Buses, Hubs and Switches

In Chapter 7 and Chapter 8, "Network Switches," the concept of limiting the collision domain was discussed in-depth. Because traditional ethernet uses a shared network medium, it is necessary to control access to that medium and to detect and correct errors when excessive collisions happen.

For a small local network that connects only a few computers, a standard 10Mbps ethernet hub can be purchased for well under $100. A small 5–10 port switch can usually be purchased for $100–200, though you might find one for less than $100 if you watch for sales and rebates.

Using a small hub creates a collision domain that consists of usually five to ten computers. Although the hub gives the appearance of a physical network star topology, the hub acts in that manner only as a wiring concentrator. All computers connected to the hub exist on a logical bus, and all communications pathways are shared. A frame transmitted by one workstation connected to the hub will be heard by all the other workstations attached to the hub.

Hubs were traditionally employed to connect smaller departments to a larger network. With the price of switches now at about the same price as higher-end intelligent hubs, the choice is now obviously to purchase a switch. This is because the switch limits the collision domain to only two nodes: the switch itself and the computer attached to a particular port. The switch acts to relay network frames only to another port so that it can be delivered. If most of your network traffic remains inside the departmental LAN, a switch can dramatically improve throughput for users.

If a substantial portion of the network traffic resides on servers outside the LAN, then using a switch that has a fast connection to the switch on which the server resides also can provide a faster connection for end users. By virtually eliminating the collision domain, switches allow for greater throughput on an ethernet network.

◀◀ For a more in-depth discussion of how hubs operate, see Chapter 7, "Repeaters, Bridges, and Hubs." For more about how switches function, check out Chapter 8, "Network Switches."

When studying the network traffic in a local network segment, keep in mind that a switch is an ideal solution to replace a hub, and can help alleviate network congestion problems.

Restrictions on Ethernet Topologies

The topology of a *local area network* (*LAN*) can be described in two ways:

- The first is the *physical topology*, which describes the physical layout of the network media and the devices that connect to it.
- The second is to describe a *logical topology*, which is not concerned with the actual physical connections, but with the logical path through the network that data can take from one place to another.

Several different topologies are used with ethernet, each with its own distance and other specifications. During the first few years of its development, ethernet was run using a bus topology. When PCs caused corporate LANs to proliferate, new structured wiring standards led to the use of a star topology.

Limiting Factors of Ethernet Technologies

The two basic topologies that can be used to form an ethernet local area network are the *bus* and *star*. By using interconnecting devices, such as routers and switches, a larger network can be constructed, building on the bus and star to create a more complex network topology.

The restrictions that are imposed by a particular topology generally have to do with several factors:

- **The network transmission media**—Imposes length and speed restrictions.
- **Interconnecting devices**—Used to join different physical segments.
- **The number of devices on the network**—Because ethernet uses a broadcast method for data exchange, too many devices on the same network broadcast segment can cause congestion problems that can degrade performance.
- **Media access mechanisms**—How the individual devices compete for or obtain access to the network media. In standard ethernet networks, each workstation contends for access to the local media equally.

Interconnecting Devices and Cable Segment Length

Interconnecting devices and cable segment length are the most basic limiting factors for a local area network. As cables grow longer, the signal degrades (attenuation) until eventually it cannot be understood by another device attached to the same media. Even if you were to insert devices to strengthen or regenerate the signal at regular intervals, as is done with the Public Switched Telephone Network (PSTN), the length of the cable would be a problem because ethernet networks rely on *round-trip timing* to determine whether a packet has been properly sent. The sending station can't wait forever to determine whether a collision has occurred or whether its data was successfully transmitted on the wire with no interference.

The length of a cable segment depends on the type of cable:

- A segment of 10BASE-2, using coaxial cable (commonly called thinnet), can be as many as 186 meters, or 607 feet. With repeaters, the total diameter of the thinnet network is limited to 925 meters, or about 3,035 feet.
- For 10BASE-T ethernet, using twisted-pair wiring, the workstation must be within 100 meters (328 feet) of the hub or switch.
- For Fast Ethernet environments, you can use different types of cable, from twisted-pair to fiber optic, and each of the Fast Ethernet specifications has different cable length limitations. For example, the 100-meter limit for any segment still applies for 100BASE-TX and 100BASE-T4 segments.
- 100BASE-FX (fiber-optic cable) has a maximum segment distance of about two kilometers. The distance advantage the 100BASE-FX has over the other cabling methods makes it more suitable for use as a network backbone medium at these speeds. However, there are network cards available that allow you to go ahead and bring fiber to the desktop now, if you can afford it—and if you need the bandwidth. Fiber to the desktop today might be extreme unless you are supporting a high-end workstation, such as in a graphics development environment.

The 5-4-3 Rule

There is an easy way to remember what you can place between any two nodes on a traditional ethernet LAN. The *5-4-3 rule* means that there can be

■ A maximum of five cable segments on the LAN.

■ A maximum of four repeaters or concentrators.

■ Only three segments containing cable with nodes attached.

This is a general rule to which you should stick when planning the network topology. Note, however, that the last part of the rule applies only to coaxial cable, such as 10BASE-2 or 10BASE-5. When connecting nodes using a hub or switch and twisted-pair wiring, each node has its own cable and can vary from a small workgroup of just a few computers to a much larger one supported by stacked hubs/switches.

Using a Bus Topology

The bus topology was used in the ethernet networks. It is simply a series of workstations or devices that are connected to a single cable (see Figure 12.1). Connecting workstations along a single cable is commonly referred to as *daisy-chaining*. This is the topology used for networks that are composed of 10BASE-2 or 10BASE-5 coaxial cabling.

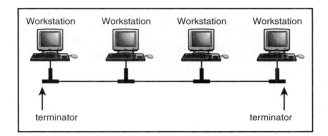

Figure 12.1 The bus topology consists of multiple devices connected to a single cable segment.

The bus topology, although simple to implement, has a few problems, including the following:

■ The cable itself is a single point of failure for the LAN. Each end of the bus must be terminated. One broken or loose terminator can disrupt the entire LAN.

■ Because all workstations or devices share a common cable, tracking down a node that is causing problems on the network can be very time-consuming. For example, a loose terminator or connector on a single workstation can disrupt the entire LAN, and you might spend hours going from one node to the next checking connections.

■ Bus topologies for ethernet are usually built using coaxial cable (10BASE-2 and 10BASE-5). Although less cable is used than in a star topology, these cables are more expensive than simple twisted-pair cables. In the case of 10BASE-5, the cable is not very flexible and can be difficult to route through wall or ceiling structures.

In spite of its limitations when used to connect individual workstations into a LAN, the bus is a method that has often been used to join smaller groups that are connected in star formation. For example, before Fast Ethernet and Gigabit Ethernet using fiber-optic cables were developed, connections between hubs or switches in a LAN were often done using coaxial cable.

Using a Star Topology

Instead of linking workstations in a linear fashion along a single cable, the hub acts as a wiring concentrator, providing a central point in the network where all nodes connect. Figure 12.2 shows a simple LAN connected to a hub in a star configuration.

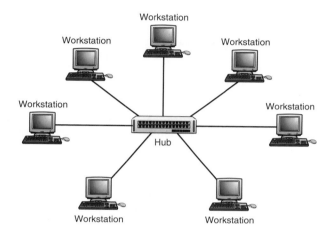

Figure 12.2 Workstations connect to a central hub in a star formation.

Note

Chapter 7, "Repeaters, Bridges, and Hubs," and Chapter 8, "Network Switches," discuss the star topology, which was introduced after 10BASE-T was developed.

All data that travels from one node to another must pass through the hub. A simple hub merely repeats incoming transmissions on all other ports, whereas more complex hubs can perform functions that strengthen the signal or correct minor problems.

The star topology was continued when switches were developed. A central switch looks just about the same as a hub, but it limits the collisions in a LAN dramatically. Switches, which are covered in Chapter 8 do this because they don't rebroadcast a frame on every other port. They only transmit the frame onto the port that will get it delivered to its destination.

The star topology has only a few shortcomings when compared to the bus: More cabling is required, and the hub becomes a single point of failure. However, the benefits that the star topology has over the bus are many:

- Installing wiring for this type of network (twisted-pair cables, similar to telephone cables but of a higher quality) is easier than for the bus. Although more cable is required, the cables are also less expensive and more flexible for routing throughout a building.

- It is easier to detect errors in the LAN through LEDs on the hub/switch or by using a hub/switch that incorporates management software.

- One workstation or cabling segment that experiences problems does not disrupt the entire network.

- Adding and removing nodes from this type of LAN is a simple matter of plugging in the cable to a free socket on the hub. Modern hubs don't require you to place terminators on unused ports.

- If a hub fails, it can be replaced quickly with a spare by simply unplugging cables and inserting them into the new hub. Alternatively, in a wiring closet with multiple hubs, you could simply move users from a disabled unit to free ports on other hubs/switches until repairs could be made.

Over the years hubs became more intelligent, and finally switches were developed for use in local area networks. A switch works similar to a hub, in that it centralizes the wiring of the LAN. The main difference, however, is that the switch doesn't broadcast every frame it receives on all the other ports after it learns where a particular computer is located. Instead, the switch makes a connection that sends a frame only to the port that will get it to its eventual destination. In this way, a switch is similar to putting multiple bridges into one device. After the switch learns the locations of all the computers attached to it, LAN traffic can be switched between ports at a very fast rate, eliminating most of the collisions that would occur in a high-traffic environment using a hub.

In a large networked environment, switches are the preferred wiring concentrator. If you have a small home or departmental network that doesn't generate a lot of network traffic, a cheap hub is a good solution. However, you might note that with sale prices, the difference between a small switch and a small hub at the local computer store might not be that much. For just a few dollars more, you can plan for future growth of your software's needs and your Internet and LAN needs.

For those who might still think that switches are only for large corporate LANs, I can say only that gigabit switches are now coming to market full force. So my advice for new purchases is switch, don't "hub."

Hybrid LAN Topologies

Switches and hubs are simple methods for creating small workgroup LANs. By using structured wiring methods, it is easy to connect hubs and switches to create larger LANs. Two popular methods used to do this are the *tree* and the *hierarchical star*.

Tree

Figure 12.3 shows a combination topology that groups workstations in a star and joins the stars along a linear bus. The majority of the problems of the bus are eliminated because a single workstation cannot bring the entire LAN to a halt. You can still add or change workstations by plugging them into different ports on the same hub, or on another hub. If one hub malfunctions, it disables only the workstations that are attached to it from communicating on the network. The remaining workstations on the other hubs can continue to function normally. Intelligent hubs and switches are capable of isolating misbehaving ports. Some do this automatically, while others require management intervention.

This is an inexpensive method that can be used to join different work departments in a building. Each local workgroup can have an administrative person who is responsible for managing the connections on the local hub or switch. The network administrator can regulate when and where new wiring concentration devices are attached to the network.

The major problem with this type of hybrid topology, however, is that if there is a problem with the backbone bus cable, in a tree topology, the network becomes segmented into individual hubs. Workstations on each hub can communicate with each other, but data transfers through the network to workstations on other hubs will be disrupted until the cable problem is diagnosed and corrected.

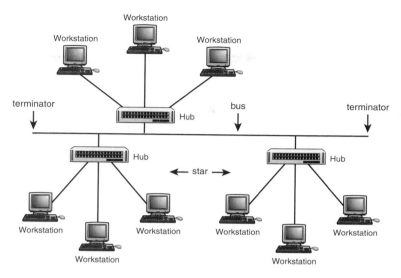

Figure 12.3   The tree topology connects star formations along a linear bus.

Hierarchical Star

Another method that can be used to connect hubs is a hierarchical star. This method, shown in Figure 12.4, uses a central hub or switch to link other similar devices that have workstations attached.

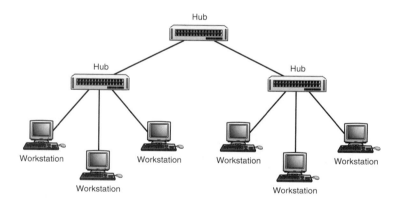

Figure 12.4   Hubs and switches can be used to form hierarchies of star networks.

This method can be used to attach up to 12 hubs to a central hub, creating a large LAN. Without using a bridge, you can connect as many as 1,024 workstations into a LAN using this method. Remembering the 5-4-3 rule, there can be up to 5 cable segments, connected by up to 4 repeaters in the path between any 2 nodes in the network. Only 3 of the 5 cable segments can be used for computers; the other 2 must be used to link repeaters.

Using a Backbone to Connect the Enterprise

Up to this point, I have discussed how to connect individual workstations in an ethernet LAN. The hub-based LAN is a broadcast domain where all connected stations must be capable of receiving a data transmission from all other workstations in the LAN when using hubs. Switches allow for a huge reduction in the collisions on a network, provided that LAN communications are either mostly local or the switch has a faster uplink to the rest of the LAN.

If other technologies were not available to connect these diverse broadcast domains called LANs, it would not be possible to have the Internet, which is nothing more than an interconnection of hundreds of thousands of smaller networks.

Chapter 10, "Routers," explains how routers work and how they can be used to create larger networks composed of multiple LANs. To put it succinctly, these devices can create a larger network because each segment joined by a router is a separate broadcast domain in itself, subject to the limitations of their individual cabling and protocol requirements. Broadcast domains operate at level 2 of the OSI network model. Routers operate at the network layer (3), and allow for a hierarchical organization of all networks connected to the Internet. Routers make decisions about sending packets to other networks, and can use many different types of high-speed protocols on the LAN-to-LAN or LAN-to-WAN connections.

Ethernet Frames

When referring to the data that is transmitted through the network, it is a common practice to call the bundles of data "packets." However, the actual terminology for the containers of data exchanged between systems on a network varies, depending on to which level of the OSI seven-layer reference model you are referring (see Figure 12.5). For example, at the network layer a unit of data is called a *packet* or *datagram*. The term datagram usually refers to a connectionless service, whereas a packet usually indicates a connection-oriented service. You'll find that both terms are used in the literature when discussing the Internet Protocol (IP). At the data link layer these datagrams are usually referred to as *frames*. Each frame contains the information that is required for it to be transmitted successfully across the network media, as well as the data that is being exchanged. At the physical level, the frame is transmitted as a series of bits, depending on the particular technology used for encoding on the network medium.

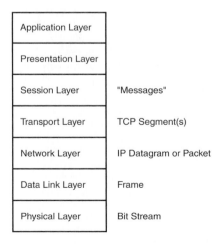

Figure 12.5   The name of the information unit changes as it passes up or down the OSI reference model stack.

The data portion of the frame usually consists of bytes of information that were packaged by a higher-level protocol and then delivered to the data link layer for transmission inside an ethernet frame. For example, the IP protocol specifies the header information used by that protocol as well as the data that is being carried by the IP datagram. When the IP datagram passes down to the data link layer, however, all this information is contained in the data portion of the ethernet frame.

The composition of the frame depends on the type of network. The original ethernet frame format and Ethernet II format differ only a little from the IEEE 802.3 frame format, and the IEEE 802.5 (token ring) standard defines a frame that is far different from these two. This is because ethernet and token ring have different methods for granting access to the network media and for exchanging data between network nodes.

In this chapter we will explore several frame types as they evolved with the technology. When heavy-duty troubleshooting is involved, you will need to get down to this nuts-and-bolts information to understand just what is happening on the wire.

XEROX PARC Ethernet and Ethernet II

The original ethernet frame had defined several fields that were still used in the Ethernet II specification. These include:

- **Preamble**—This is an 8-byte sequence of zeros and ones that is used to announce the start of a frame and to help synchronize the transmission.

- **Destination MAC (Media Access Control) address**—This is a six-byte address usually expressed in hexadecimal format.

- **Senders MAC address**—Another 6-byte field specifying the address of the workstation that originates the frame.

- **Type field**—A 2-byte field used to indicate the client protocol (such as IPX, IP, DECnet, and so on) that is to be found in the data field.

- **Data field**—A field of unspecified length that holds the actual data.

In this original frame it was left up to the higher-level protocol to determine the length of the frame. Because of this, the Type field was an important part of the frame.

Note

The term *MAC address* stands for Media Access Control Address. This is a 48-bit address that is hardwired into the network adapter when it is manufactured. The MAC address (sometimes called the hardware address or the physical address) is usually expressed as a string of 12 hexadecimal digits, two for each byte, separated by dashes—for example, 08-00-2B-EA-77-AE. The first three pairs are unique to vendors that manufacture ethernet equipment, and the last three hexadecimal pairs are a unique number assigned by the manufacturer. Knowing a manufacturer's three-pair MAC digits can be a useful tool when troubleshooting network problems.

A hardware address of FF-FF-FF-FF-FF-FF is used as a broadcast address, which is used to send a single message that all nodes on the network will read.

In Figure 12.6 you can see the layout used for the original ethernet frame.

8 bytes	6 bytes	6 bytes	2 bytes	46-1500 bytes	4 bytes
Preamble	Destination Address	Source Address	Type Field	Data	Frame Check Sequence (FCS)

Figure 12.6   The layout of the original Ethernet II frame.

The 802.3 Standard

When the IEEE 802 project defined a frame format, they kept most of the features found in the Ethernet II frame. There are some important differences, however. In Figure 12.7, you can see the layout of the 802.3 ethernet frame.

7 bytes	1 byte	6 bytes	6 bytes	2 bytes	46-1500 bytes	4 bytes
Preamble	Start of Frame Delimiter (SFD)	Destination Mac Address	Source Mac Address	Length of Data Field	Data Field	Frame Check Sequence (FCS) (cyclical redundancy check)

minimum of 64 bytes, maximum of 1518 bytes

Figure 12.7   The IEEE 802.3 frame format.

The major changes included the replacement of the Type field with a new field. These two bytes were now used to specify the length of the data field that was to follow it. When the value in this field is 1500 or less, you can tell it is being used as a Length field. If the value is 1536 or larger, the frame is being used to define a protocol type.

Additionally, the preamble was reduced from 8 bytes to 7 bytes, and following it now is a 1 byte Start of Frame Delimiter (SFD). The SFD is composed of a bit configuration of 10101011 (the last byte of the earlier preamble has 10 for the last two bits).

The last part of the frame is a four-byte Frame Check Sequence (FCS). This is used to store a cyclical redundancy check value that is calculated on the frame. The transmitting station calculates this value based on the other bits in the frame. The receiving station calculates the CRC based on the frame's bits and compares it to this value. If they are not identical, the frame must have suffered some damage in transit and must be retransmitted.

The 802.2 Logical Link Control (LLC) Standard

In the OSI seven-layer reference model, the two lower layers are the Physical layer and the Data Link layer. When the IEEE designed its reference model it took a slightly different approach. In Figure 12.8, you can see that the IEEE version includes a logical link control sublayer and a media access control sublayer on top of the physical layer, with the media access control layer straddling the boundary of the physical and data link layers as defined by the OSI model.

▶▶ For more information about the OSI seven-layer network reference model, see Appendix A, "The OSI Seven-Layer Networking Model."

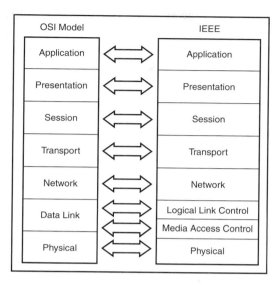

Figure 12.8 The IEEE model differs from the OSI Reference Model.

There is a rationale for incorporating some of the functionality of the OSI physical layer in the media access control layer and dividing up the data link layer to provide for a logical link Control sublayer: it is to allow different types of transmission media and methods of media access to exist on the same network.

The LLC Subheader

The media access control sublayer is responsible for using the services provided by the Physical layer to get data transferred to and from remote stations on the network. This includes functions such as basic error checking and local addressing (physical, or MAC addresses).

The LLC sublayer offers services to the layers above it that can be classified into the following three types:

■ **Unacknowledged connectionless service**—Some upper-level protocols (such as TCP) already provide flow control and acknowledgment functions that check on whether a packet was successfully sent. There is no need to duplicate those functions here.

■ **Connection-oriented service**—This type of service keeps track of active connections and can be used by devices on the network that do not implement the full OSI layers in their protocols.

■ **Acknowledged connectionless service**—This service is a mix of the other two. It provides acknowledgment of packets sent and received but does not keep track of links between network stations.

To implement these LLC functions, IEEE 802.2 specifies a subheader that is placed into the frame directly before the Data field. This LLC subheader field consists of three bytes. The first is the Destination Service Access Point (DSAP). The second is the Source Service Access Point (SSAP), and the last is the Control field.

The LLC Ethernet Frame

In Figure 12.9 you can see that, when the LLC subheader is combined with the standard 802.3 frame, the overall size of the frame doesn't change but the amount of space remaining in the data portion of the frame does.

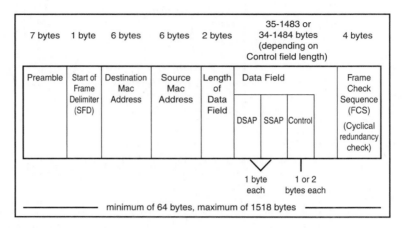

Figure 12.9   The 802.3 frame including the LLC subheader.

The 802.3 SNAP Frame

In the earlier Xerox PARC and Ethernet II frame formats, the 2-byte Type field was used to indicate the higher-level protocol for which the frame was being used. When the 802.3 frame was delineated, this field was replaced with the Length field that indicates the length of the data field.

To provide for backward compatibility with earlier networks that still needed to have something in the frame to identify the protocol that should be used, the SNAP subframe was introduced. The term SNAP stands for "Sub-Network Access Protocol." It is constructed by adding additional fields to the LLC subheader. The additional fields that are added after the LLC fields are

- Organizationally Unique Identifier Field (3 bytes)
- Protocol Type (2 bytes)

The SNAP extensions must be used with the LLC subheader fields. There are no provisions for a SNAP subheader without the LLC subheader. Figure 12.10 shows the full 802.3 frame that includes the SNAP fields.

Note

The 802.5 specification defined the frame format used for token-ring networks. Token-ring networks are fundamentally different from ethernet networks not only in their frame formats but also in the methods used to grant access to the network media. For information on the format of the token-ring frame, see Chapter 13.

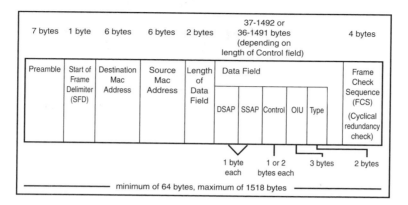

Figure 12.10   The 802.3 frame including the LLC subheader and SNAP extensions.

Fast Ethernet (IEEE 802.3u) and Gigabit Ethernet (IEEE 802.3z)

In the early 1990s a faster version of ethernet was developed, and it's commonly referred to as Fast Ethernet. This standard (IEEE 802.3u) allows for ethernet communications over both copper wire and optical fiber cables, at a speed of 100Mbps. The different standards are named in the traditional way, as a concatenation of the speed, signaling method, and medium type, as described earlier in this chapter.

Fast Ethernet encompasses the 100BASE- class of ethernet, whereas 1000BASE- denotes the Gigabit Ethernet standards. As if that were not enough, a newer emerging standard that will probably be widely endorsed by the ethernet community in 2002 is 10 Gigabit Ethernet. That's a very fast ethernet pipe that can, in some markets, compete with ATM or Frame Relay.

Fast Ethernet

Fast Ethernet was designed to be compatible with existing 10BASE-T networks. It uses the same frame format, and it still uses the CSMA/CD medium access method that is defined in the 802.3 standard. What makes it even nicer as an upgrade path for an existing network is that it can interoperate on the same wiring as 10BASE-T. That is, with an intelligent hub (or switch) that can detect the speed being used by a particular workstation's network adapter card, you can use both types on the same network and they can talk to each other. The hub takes care of the speed difference between the communicating workstations. If you are adding to an existing 10BASE-T network at this time and are planning to migrate later to a 100BASE-T network, you will find that most network adapters sold today operate at both speeds.

100BASE-T

One of the nice things about migrating to 100BASE-T is that you can use existing wiring if the building has Category 3 cabling already in place. The 100BASE-T standard is defined for use with either twisted-pair wiring (100BASE-TX and 100BASE-T4) or optical fiber (100BASE-FX). 100BASE-T4 also allows for the use of Category 3 wiring, so an upgrade path exists for those who cannot afford the expense of rewiring a building at this time.

There is an important difference between 100BASE-T4 and 100BASE-TX: They do not use the same cable pairs to transmit and receive data. 100BASE-T4 uses all four cable pairs and a different signaling technique.

For sites that were forward-thinking and installed Category 5 cables when creating a 10BASE-T network, upgrading to a 100Mbps network will prove that the investment was worthwhile. This twisted-pair version of the 100BASE-T specification can be used on this cabling or on the shielded twisted-pair (STP) cables that are usually found on token-ring networks. The 100BASE-TX standard is based on the ANSI TP-PMD (Twisted-Pair Physical Medium Dependent) specification. The maximum segment length is 100 meters, but again you must remember to include the distance from where the horizontal wiring terminates at the work area faceplate to the workstation.

The total distance through the LAN can be as many as 200 meters, incorporating up to two hubs. There are two classes of hubs.

Class I Hubs

A standard 10BASE-T hub receives data from a segment and outputs the same signal on the other segments that are attached to its ports. Because three different formats are used by 100BASE-T, a standard hub limits a particular LAN to having only one type of 100BASE-T segment. A Class I hub solves this problem by translating the incoming signals from one format to another before sending the signal back out on the other ports. Because of the overhead involved in the signal processing, the standard limits a network to using only one Class I hub.

Class II Hubs

A Class II hub operates with only one media type—100BASE-TX. It performs no signal translation and acts as a simple multipoint repeater. There can be a maximum of two Class II hubs in the collision domain.

100BASE-T4

For those networks that have a heavily installed base of Category 3 or Category 4 cabling, this version of 100BASE-T provides an upgrade path. This standard uses half-duplex signaling on four pairs of wires, as opposed to the two pairs used by 10BASE-T and 100BASE-TX. Three of the wire pairs are used for actual data transmission, and the fourth pair is used for collision detection. The three pairs used in transmission each operate at only 33.3Mbs, for a total of 100Mbs (called the 4T+ signaling scheme). Additionally, a three-level encoding scheme is used on the wire instead of the two-level scheme used for most other media. Because 100BASE-T4 requires special hardware, such as network adapter cards and hubs, and because it operates only in half-duplex mode, it shouldn't be considered for a new installation, but only a possible upgrade path when other options cannot be justified.

100BASE-FX

Fiber-optic cable provides the greatest distance for Fast Ethernet. 100BASE-FX, using a two-strand cable (one strand for transmission and one for receiving data and detecting collisions), can achieve a distance of up to two kilometers.

Fiber is a good choice for use as a backbone in the network. Unlike copper wire cables, which use electrical impulses for communications, fiber uses pulses of light. This also makes fiber cable a better choice in an environment with a lot of electrical interference. Because fiber-optic cable emits no electrical signals itself (which can be intercepted to eavesdrop on the network), it is also ideal in a situation in which security is a great concern. Finally, optical fiber provides a built-in capability that will certainly be pushed to greater transmission speeds as new standards develop.

Gigabit Ethernet

In 1998, the 802.3z standard for Gigabit Ethernet was finished and includes the following:

- **1000BASE-SX**—Using multimode fiber for short distances. Up to 300 meters when using 50-micron multimode fiber, or 550 meters when using 62.5-micron multimode fiber.

- **1000BASE-LX**—Using single-mode fiber for distances up to 3,000 meters, or using multimode fiber for up to 550 meters.

- **1000BASE-CX**—Using twisted-pair copper cables rated for high performance for up to 25 meters. Intended for use in wiring closets.

- **1000BASE-T**—For use over Category 5 twisted-pair cables for a maximum distance of up to 100 meters.

Note

The UTP version of Gigabit Ethernet is known as the IEEE 802.3ab standard. Because of its short range (25 meters) it is intended mainly for use in connecting equipment in wiring closets.

Gigabit Ethernet is expected to mesh well with 10/100Mbps networks. It will use the same CSMA/CD medium access protocol and the same frame format and size. It will be ideally suited for use as a network backbone to connect routers and hubs or other types of repeaters, due to both its compatibility with existing technology and the speeds of transmission that can be accomplished. For example, another feature that will make Gigabit Ethernet a choice for the network backbone is the capability to run in full-duplex mode on nonshared connections. In this mode there will be two connections—one for send, one for receive—used to transmit data so that collision detection will not be needed. This will enable faster data transmissions between switches used to connect LANs.

The IEEE 802.3z standard for Gigabit Ethernet added another field to the basic 802.3 frame: the *Extension* field. This field is appended to the frame after the Frame Check Sequence field and is used to pad the frame so that its minimum size is 512 bytes instead of the 64 bytes used by slower standards. This increased size is needed only when operating Gigabit Ethernet in half-duplex mode where collision detection is still involved. This field is not needed in full-duplex mode.

Another method for making faster transmissions with Gigabit Ethernet is to reduce the overhead involved with using CSMA/CD for every single frame that is sent on the network. A mode of operation called *burst mode* was added in the 802.3z standard that provides for sending multiple frames, one after the other, after gaining access to the network media. This is accomplished by inserting special "extension bits" in the interframe gaps between normal frames. These extension bits keep the wire active so that other stations do not sense it as being idle and attempt to transmit.

Tip

Another proposal that is being considered by many companies is one called *jumbo frames*. This proposal, the work of Alteon Networks, Inc., raises the overall length of an ethernet frame (on a full-duplex mode link) to 9018 bytes. You can download the specifications for jumbo frames (in Adobe PDF format) from: www.alteon.com.

Gigabit Ethernet is currently being widely deployed for use in local area network backbones to connect high-capacity servers or switches. This role was earlier played by Fast Ethernet (and, of course, before that by 10 Mbps Ethernet). As one technology advances to the desktop, another replaces it in the backbone. As we get into the area of high-speed transport protocols, Gigabit Ethernet might now start competing in areas that were previously the domain of ATM and Frame Relay, which, in the past, were typically used to carry IP data. Although SONET is widely deployed as a metropolitan area network (MAN) solution, the faster ethernet gets, the harder it is to justify carrying it by other transport protocols.

As IP approaches and passes the 10 Gigabit speed limit, it will no doubt become an important player beyond network backbone usage. Because ethernet is ethernet (as long as you use the right interconnecting switches!), it's easier to manage a single transport protocol than try to manage mapping one onto another. Gigabit Ethernet is definitely in your future, whether or not it is visible to you, and 10 Gigabit Ethernet is around the corner...

10 Gigabit Ethernet (IEEE 802.3ae)

With other WAN protocols already in use on long-distance backbones for large networks and the Internet, you might not think that ethernet, basically a LAN protocol, would need to be developed beyond what is required in a typical LAN. With switching, increasing speeds and full-duplex connections, ethernet has faired far better than other LAN technologies in the past 30 years. Just compare it to token ring. However, there is no reason why ethernet should not be pushed further, and there are advantages to doing so. The 10 Gigabit standard is just now finishing its way through the IEEE standardization process.

This version of ethernet keeps the standard 802.3 frame format and the same minimum/maximum frame sizes as previous versions of ethernet. However, half-duplex operation will no longer be supported, and 10 Gigabit Ethernet will not have any provisions for using a shared network medium—you'll use switches, not hubs. By removing the half-duplex feature and removing the need for CSMA/CD, the distances that ethernet can now cover are limited only by the physical network media and the signaling method used. Another important reason for dropping the half-duplex option is the fact that, although the already marketed Gigabit Ethernet supports half- and full-duplex modes, customers have almost unanimously chosen full-duplex products.

When you start to approach these speeds, you find that 10 Gigabit Ethernet can now start to compete with other fast transmission protocols that are typically used as WAN protocols, such as ATM and SONET.

At the Physical layer, the 802.3ae specification will provide for two physical layer (PHY) types—the LAN PHY and the WAN PHY. The PHY layer is further subdivided into the Physical Media Dependent (PMD) part and the Physical Coding Sublayer (PCS). The PCS is concerned with how data is coded onto the physical network. The PMD represents the physical components, such as the laser, light wavelength used, and so on.

The LAN PHY and the WAN PHY will both support the same PMDs. As of early 2001 the PMDs for 10 Gigabit Ethernet range from using an 850 nm laser on multimode optical fiber (50.0 microns) for short distances (up to 65 meters), to using a 1550 nm laser on single mode fiber (9.0 microns) for up to 40 Km. The LAN PHY will be designed to operate with existing Gigabit Ethernet LAN encoding, but at a faster rate.

The WAN PHY is a separate physical interface that allows for longer distances, with an optional interface under consideration that would allow 10 Gigabit Ethernet to use SONET/SDH as a transport. SONET OC-192 provides a payload that is close to the 10 Gigabit speed offered by Gigabit Ethernet. All that is necessary to connect the two is to provide some simple buffering mechanisms in connecting network equipment. Because SONET/SDH is a widely deployed technology, this means that it will not require WAN providers to make a huge investment in new cables to carry 10 Gigabit Ethernet traffic. Instead, it becomes a value-added service they can offer to their customers. End-to-end ethernet connections for a wide area network without the time-consuming need to convert from one frame format will make managing WANs simpler because there will be less factors that can go wrong.

However, the current outlook is to use 10 Gigabit Ethernet as the WAN protocol. It is estimated that it will be cheaper to implement 10 Gigabit Ethernet services than to provide a similar T3 solution in a MAN or WAN environment.

Of course, there are critics who point out that ethernet cannot provide the same guaranteed quality-of-service (QoS) that ATM does. And, when compared to SONET and other high-speed transmission protocols, ethernet comes up lacking in the management tools area. However, the simplicity of ethernet, and the fact that it costs so much less than other WAN solutions, make it very attractive for many markets.

Ethernet Problems

Because ethernet uses a shared network medium, tracking down problems can at times be difficult. Problems can arise from simple things such as bent or broken cables, to loose connectors, and faulty network adapters. The most common problem you will find, however, is in controlling collision rates as the network size increases.

Collision Rates

Keeping the network healthy requires that you be sure that all physical components are functioning normally and at optimal levels of performance. However, you still need to monitor the network to be sure that other factors are not limiting the amount of real data that can travel through the network.

Although collisions are a normal event, and indeed are expected for a network based on ethernet technology, it is always possible for excessive collisions to cause a significant degradation of performance that will be noticeable to end users.

Collisions and Network Utilization

When a device begins to experience collisions at a rate that is one percent of the total network traffic, you might have a problem. Another statistic to watch when monitoring the network is utilization. In theory, you might expect that a network operating at 10 million bits per second would actually be capable of transmitting that much data on a continuous basis. However, that is not the case. In most ethernet networks, the actual utilization rate is only 40% before performance begins to degrade rapidly. As utilization rises, so do collisions.

If the network topology rules are followed and the network utilization is low, excessive collisions might be due to a faulty network card that is not listening to the network. You can find more information on this scenario later in this chapter in the section titled, "Faulty Network Adapters."

Detecting Collisions

A simple method for determining how many collisions are occurring is to look at the LED lights on the hub or switch. Most hubs have an LED that lights up when a collision is detected. If you notice that this light is flashing continuously or very frequently, investigate further to determine whether the rate is excessive. If it is, take action to reduce it. Using network monitoring software, you can determine the utilization rate of the network. When you get above a 30–40% utilization rate, it's time to start thinking of segmenting your LAN into smaller collision domains.

LAN analyzers and monitoring tools can aid you in counting the number of collisions that are occurring. Management consoles that employ SNMP and RMON probes can be useful for collecting statistical information used to localize segments in the network that experience high collision rates. The historical data maintained by RMON can be analyzed and stored for use in creating baseline data that you can use to judge network performance. If you are about to purchase a new switch or hub, check the documentation to see whether it supports telnet management sessions. This is a common feature on even low-end hubs now. In a small network with only a few switches, using built-in management software is a lot cheaper than investing in network management software like SMS or HP OpenView.

Collision Types

A good network analyzer gives you a lot of statistical information. When it comes to collisions, there will most likely be more than one kind of statistic to help point out the cause of the collision.

Local Collision

A *local collision* (also called an *early collision*) is a collision that happens on the local segment during the transmission of the first 64 bytes of a frame. This is the most common type of collision you will see on a network segment, and usually does not indicate a hardware problem. This type of collision happens when two different stations on the LAN detect that nothing is being transmitted on the wire and both begin to transmit at about the same time. The result is a frame called a *runt*, named because only part of the frame was transmitted successfully before the collision event occurred. The ethernet specifications take into consideration this expected event, and both stations use the backoff algorithm to delay transmission.

When high levels of early collisions are occurring, look to see whether the utilization on the segment is nearing or surpassing 40%. If this is the case on a regular basis, then the segment is probably over-loaded. Consider using a switch to limit collisions. If you can identify a particular node that is experiencing a high rate of local collisions, there might be a hardware problem. Check the connectors that join it to the network; if no fault is found there, try replacing the network adapter card to see if that is the problem.

Late Collisions

A *late collision* occurs when two devices on the network start to transmit at the same time and do not detect the collision immediately. This kind of collision is usually caused by a network segment that is too long. If the time it takes to put the frame on the network is shorter than the amount of time it takes for the frame to travel to the node that is the greatest distance away, neither device will know that the other has started transmitting until after the first 64 bytes (the minimum frame size) have been put on the wire.

For example, suppose workstation A begins to transmit a frame and finishes transmitting before the signal reaches workstation B, which has been cabled to the network at a distance that exceeds the specs. Workstation B, thinking that the wire is clear, begins to transmit its frame just before the signal from workstation A reaches it. Of course, because workstation B is closest to the collision event, it detects the collision. However, because workstation A has finished transmitting the frame, it has also stopped listening to detect whether a collision has occurred. The end result is that workstation A thinks it was able to successfully transmit the frame. It has no idea that a collision has occurred.

Late collisions do not cause a frame to be retransmitted, simply because the NIC does not know that a collision has occurred. It is up to a higher-level protocol to determine that something has caused an error and to request retransmission.

If the LAN is experiencing high levels of late collision events, check for topology problems. This includes not only excessive cable lengths, but also using too many repeaters or other devices. If no apparent problems are found and the network appears up to specifications, there is probably a hardware problem. Try to locate the offending NIC or cable by looking at the addressing information decoded by a LAN analyzer.

Sampling Intervals

When monitoring for collisions, don't jump to conclusions when you see only sporadic increases. Take samples several times during the work day, and try to correlate them with the functions being performed by users on the network at that time. Sometimes it is the actual day that matters, and not the time. For example, at the end of a month or a quarter, many business functions are performed— such as accounting reports—that generate large amounts of network use. It is a simple matter to determine which month-end tasks need to be done first and in what order. Sometimes scheduling is all that is necessary to solve a network congestion problem.

An overall average of the number of collisions that occur per second, along with the network utilization rate, is useful in determining whether the network is becoming saturated. Information about peak levels is useful for designing user work patterns so that the network is used more efficiently.

Reducing Collisions

There are several reasons why collisions will occur at excessive rates. Some of those reasons include ignoring topology rules, faulty hardware, and an overloaded segment (too many users).

Incorrect Network Topology

If you use segments that exceed the length permitted by your network topology, some devices on the network might not detect that the network is in use until a transmission by another node is well underway. Check your cable lengths and be sure they are within the standards. When it comes time to expand the LAN you should never haphazardly add new segments by simply attaching a new repeater, hub, or bridge to the network. For this reason, it is important to keep an up-to-date map of the physical topology of the network so that you can plan additions before you implement them.

Remember that, for 10BASE-T, workstations can be no farther than 100 meters from the hub. In addition, the 5-4-3 rule states that there can be a maximum of 5 cable segments on the LAN, with a maximum of 4 repeaters or concentrators and only 3 segments can have nodes attached. For Fast Ethernet and Gigabit Ethernet, be sure that you don't exceed the topological metrics imposed by the physical network media used.

Faulty Network Adapters

One particular problem is an adapter that does not sense the carrier signal due to faulty hardware, and begins to transmit whenever it wants to, thinking that the wire is available. In Chapter 6, "Network Adapter Cards," you will find a more detailed discussion of troubleshooting NICs. However, a basic strategy to follow is to replace the suspect device and, if that does not solve the problem, try to use a different cable to connect the NIC to the network or try to reseat the NIC in another slot in the computer. When replacing the device, be sure to use a substitute that is known to be in good working order. The same goes for replacement cables. Another troubleshooting tactic is to use the diagnostic software provided by the network adapter's manufacturer.

Top Talkers

There are only so many devices you can place on a network in the same broadcast domain before performance begins to suffer. A small number of high-performance computers that generate a lot of network traffic can produce the same result. Remember that as utilization rises, so do collisions. So, when you are experiencing a high collision rate and the network segment's utilization approaches or exceeds the 40% mark, it's time to consider segmenting the LAN using a switch or similar device. A switch, which can be used to give high-end servers a full-duplex connection, is an ideal choice when a local segment contains both end users and powerful servers that are "top talkers."

Ethernet Errors

A lot of things can go wrong when you send hundreds of thousands of bits out on a copper wire, hoping they arrive at their destination in the proper order and with no changes. With the higher speeds that are being achieved with new technologies, detecting errors is becoming increasingly more important.

The simplest method for error detection is called a *parity check*. An example of this method is transmitting characters using the ASCII 7-bit character set with an eighth bit added. If *even parity* is being used, the eighth bit is set to zero or one, whichever makes the number of "1" bits an even number. If *odd parity* is being used, the eighth bit is selected to make the number of "1" bits an odd number. The receiving station can calculate what the parity bit should be by examining the first seven characters and making a simple calculation. This scheme easily breaks down, however, if more than one bit was transmitted in error.

Also, this type of error checking operates at the byte level and is not very useful for determining whether an error exists in a frame of data that is 1518 bytes in length. Ethernet frames use the *Frame Check Sequence (FCS)* to check the integrity of the frame. Higher-level protocols employ other methods to ensure that packets arrive intact and in the correct order. Besides errors involving corrupted frames that can be detected using the FCS, there are other types of common ethernet errors. This chapter takes a quick look at the most common errors and their possible causes.

Bad FCS and Misaligned Frames

The most obvious place to start is the Frame Check Sequence (FCS) error. The MAC layer computes a cyclic redundancy check (CRC) value, based on the contents of the frame, and places this value in the FCS field. The receive station can perform the same calculation and, by checking its result against that stored by the transmitting station, can determine whether the frame has been damaged in transit.

It is possible that this value was incorrectly computed by the sending station due to a hardware problem where this MAC layer function is performed. It also is possible that the adapter that is sending out this frame is experiencing some other kind of problem and is not correctly transmitting the bits on the wire. As with most errors, the problem might also lie with noise on the cables that are connecting the network.

When you monitor a level of bad FCS errors that exceeds two or three percent of the total utilization of bandwidth on the network, you should begin troubleshooting to find the offending device. Using a LAN analyzer, you can usually locate the source address of the faulty device and take corrective action.

To determine whether the suspected device is indeed the source of the error, first power it off and continue to monitor the network. If errors continue to occur but another address appears to be the source, there might be cabling problems on the network. If the errors disappear when the device is powered off, you can troubleshoot it further to locate the cause. You should look for the following:

- **Bad connector**—Check the connector that attaches the network cable to the workstation's adapter card.

- **Bad port**—If the workstation is connected to a hub or a switch, the port on that device might be causing the problem. Also, be sure to check the connector on that end of the cable segment.

- **Malfunctioning network card**—Finally, replace the network adapter card on the workstation to see if this clears up the problem.

Because a frame is composed of bytes— units of eight bits—the resulting frame should be evenly divisible by eight when it reaches its destination. If not, something has gone wrong. This type of error is called a *misaligned frame,* and the frame usually has a bad FCS as well. The most common reason for this type of error is electrical interference on the network or a collision. Another common cause is an incorrect network topology, where more than two multiport repeaters are used in a cascaded fashion.

You can troubleshoot this type of problem using the same methods as for a bad FCS error. Of course, if you are aware of a topology problem, you already know where the problem is.

Short Frames (Runts)

A *runt* is an ethernet frame that is smaller than the minimum size of 64 bytes. Remember that the transmitting NIC must transmit a packet for an amount of time that allows it to make a round trip in the local broadcast domain before it stops transmitting. Otherwise, the transmitting NIC cannot effectively detect a collision. The maximum propagation time for ethernet segments is 51.2 microseconds, which is the amount of time it takes to transmit about 64 bytes. This minimum frame size does not include the preamble.

There are many reasons why short frame errors can occur on the network wire. Some of these short frames stem from

- Collisions
- Faulty network adapters
- Topology errors

If a runt frame has a valid FCS value, which indicates that the frame appears to be internally valid, the problem is most likely in the network card that generated the frame. If the FCS value is not correct for the frame's contents, the problem most likely is due to collisions or topology.

Collisions are a normal event for ethernet. Sometimes, however, the byproduct of a collision results in signals on the wire that are interpreted as a short frame. If you are experiencing a lot of errors that indicate short frames, check the utilization statistics for the segment. If the peak utilization is heavy, but ordinary overall utilization is acceptable, try to rearrange user workloads so that some tasks are delayed to a time when the network is less busy.

If the utilization values for the segment are low, you might want to investigate further to determine the workstation or device that is originating the short frames, and subject the NIC to diagnostic testing to determine whether it is at fault. This can be a difficult task because a lot of errors of this type occur with frames so short that you cannot determine the source address.

Ignoring the topology rules of ethernet also can produce short frames. A common error is to use more than four repeaters for a single collision domain, which can result in short frames appearing on the wire.

Giant Frames and Jabber

Sometimes, a network adapter produces frames that are larger than the maximum allowable size. The opposite of a short frame error is a *giant frame error.* According to the rules that govern ethernet communications, the maximum size of a frame is 1518 bytes, excluding the preamble bits. Reasons why oversized frame errors appear on the wire include

- A defective NIC that is transmitting continuously.
- Bits indicating the length of the frame have been corrupted and indicate that the frame is larger than it actually is.
- There is noise on the wire. Random noise on a faltering cable can be interpreted as part of a frame, but this is not a very common reason why oversized frame errors occur.

Finding the location of a device that is malfunctioning might be simple if the LAN analyzer you are using is capable of detecting a source address. You can power off or disconnect the suspected node to determine whether it is the cause of the problem. It is possible that you will not be capable of detecting the address of the NIC if the malfunctioning card is repeatedly sending out meaningless signals. In that case, you need to look at each workstation on the segment, one by one, and try to remove them from the network to see if the condition clears up.

The term *jabber* is sometimes used to refer to oversized frames, but is really just a catch-all term used to indicate that a device on the network is not following the rules and is behaving improperly when it comes to signaling on the network. A defective NIC might be sending out frames that are larger than allowed, or it might be signaling continuously.

This type of error can literally bring down an entire segment because an adapter that continuously transmits does not give any other station a chance to use the wire. Because stations are supposed to check the network medium to see if it is busy before transmitting, the workstations that are functioning normally simply wait until the network becomes available.

Multiple Errors

Depending on the tool used to monitor the network, the number of different error types you see might vary. For example, misaligned frame errors usually have a bad FCS field as well. Some analyzers record two errors for one event, whereas others might record the error as one type or the other.

Check the documentation for the product you use to determine if this is true for your particular product.

Broadcast Storms

Broadcast storms usually occur when devices on the network generate traffic that causes even more traffic to be generated. Although this additional traffic might be due to physical problems in the network devices or the network media, it is usually caused by higher-level protocols. The problem with trying to detect the cause of this type of situation is that when it occurs, you are usually unable to access the network. Broadcast storms can slow down network access dramatically, and can sometimes bring it to a halt.

When monitoring the network for broadcast activity, you normally see a rate of 100 broadcast frames per second or less. When this value increases to more than 100 per second on an ongoing basis, there might be a problem with a network card, or you might need to segment the collision domain into smaller parts. You can use routers to do this because they do not pass broadcast frames unless they are configured to do so. Many bridges also can be configured to detect excessive broadcasts and to drop broadcast packets until the storm subsides.

Monitoring Errors

There are many tools you can use to monitor errors on the network. A *network analyzer*, for example, Network Sniffer from Network General, displays information about frames that contain errors, including runts, CRC, and alignment errors. Some software-based applications, such as the Network Monitor tool included in Windows NT Server or Microsoft's System Management Server, enable you to view statistics about frames dropped, CRC errors, and broadcasts. Simpler hand-held tools also might provide functionality that enables you to detect when these errors are occurring.

For a network that requires centralized management and control, an SNMP management console application, using RMON, can be used to both monitor the network for ethernet errors and to set up alerts that trigger notifications so you can become aware of problems immediately. The history group of RMON objects allows you to record error counts over a period of time and use them for later analysis to assist in troubleshooting.

Note

You can find more information about SNMP, RMON, and network monitoring tools in Chapter 43, "Strategies for Troubleshooting Network Problems," and Chapter 44, "Network Testing and Analysis Tools." For more specific information on how to isolate ethernet problems, see the chapters devoted to network cards, cables, hubs, switches, and routers.

Depending on the vendor, many internetworking devices—such as routers and intelligent hubs—are equipped with management software that can be tapped to display error statistics when you do not need a more extensive application (such as a management console). Checking statistical information on a regular basis and keeping a log of it is a good idea. When you keep track of error conditions on a regular basis, you can begin to solve problems more quickly because you can determine whether the current situation matches a previous problem.

Token-Ring Networks

SOME OF THE MAIN TOPICS IN THIS CHAPTER ARE

Overview of Token-Ring Networking

Functions Performed by Active and Standby Monitors

Detecting Errors on the Ring

What Is Early Token Release?

Adding a Station to the Ring

The Physical Star Topology

Hierarchical Topologies

Using a Token-Bus Topology

Cabling Rules for Token-Ring Networks

Token-Ring Connectors and Media Filters

Cabling Scenarios

Monitoring Token-Ring Utilization and Errors

Using Network and Protocol Analyzers

Token-Ring Extensions to the Remote Network Monitoring MIB

Troubleshooting Tips

Choosing Between Token-Ring and Ethernet

Today, most local area networks are based on ethernet technology, which consists of multiple computers or devices on a shared network medium, each contending for a share of the bandwidth. Ethernet has been implemented in many different ways, from the bus technology at the beginning to the hub and switch environment that is the most widespread today. What all the different ethernet topologies and cabling schemes have in common, though, are the frame type and the CSMA/CD contention method used to gain access to the network medium and to transmit data.

Token-ring networks use a different media access control mechanism and a different frame format than ethernet. Token-ring networking was first developed by IBM and later standardized by the IEEE 802.5 working group. In a token-ring network, there are no collisions and there are no back-off algorithms. Network access is not something that each workstation has to contend for. Instead, access to a token-ring network is done in a controlled, orderly fashion, using a frame that is passed from workstation to workstation, possession of which is required to begin transmitting data on the network. This "permission" frame is called a *token*. It passes through the network in a logical ring topology; hence, the name token-ring is used for this technology.

◀◀   If you want to learn more about ethernet in its many formats and topologies, see Chapter 12, "Ethernet."

Because the token regularly passes around in a ring formation, it is possible to calculate the longest amount of time it will take until a station can receive the token and begin transmitting data on the network. Thus, token-ring networks are called *deterministic* because the worst-case scenario access time can be calculated. In some environments, such as factory automation, where timing is important, token-ring networks can be a good solution.

Overview of Token-Ring Networking

In Figure 13.1, you can see that the logical layout of a token-ring network is a ring. Each computer in the ring connects to two other computers, affectionately referred to as *neighbors*. The upstream neighbor is the computer from which a station will receive the token or data frame. The downstream neighbor is the one to whom the station will pass the frame.

If the workstations were actually wired in this manner, however, it would be quite a problem to add new stations or move them around. Doing so would break the chain of cables, and the network would grind to a halt. To prevent this from happening, each device on the ring is actually connected by two sets of wires to a hub-like device called a media access unit (MAU) or a multistation access unit (MSAU). The MSAU looks similar to an ethernet hub. It is usually tucked away in a wiring closet like a hub and, and in some versions, uses RJ-45 connectors and twisted-pair wiring just like ethernet networks do.

MAUs and MSAUs come in a variety of styles, with capacities generally ranging from 8–16 ports, though you can find more expensive MAUs that support more workstations than this. More sophisticated MAUs have an additional feature: remote management. These *controlled access units (CAUs)* allow the network administrator to remotely manage stations connected to the ring. Workstations do not directly connect to the CAU, however; instead, a *lobe attachment module (LAM)* is used to connect workstations to the CAU. Generally, LAMs support 20 individual workstations, and you can connect up to four LAMs to a CAU.

◀◀   At first glance it might seem that token-ring has a lot in common with ARCnet. However, token-ring provides a network technology that scales well beyond the 255-node limit of an ARCnet network. In addition, the frame format and other specifications of ARCnet differ from token-ring. For more information about ARCnet, see Chapter 11, "Heard Anything About ARCnet Lately?"

Unlike an ethernet hub, however, the MAU does not repeat incoming traffic on all other ports. Instead, using electrical relays, the MAU connects the receiving wires from one station to the transmitting wires of the previous station in the ring.

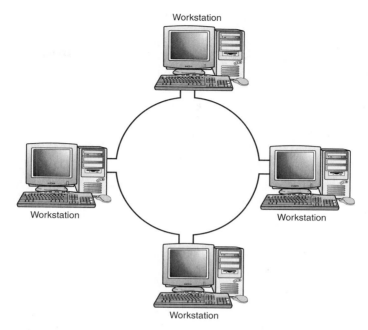

Workstation

Workstation

Workstation

Workstation

Figure 13.1 Token-ring networks are wired in a star topology to form a logical ring.

A frame called a *token* is continuously passed from one station to another around the ring. When a workstation receives the token frame, it retransmits it to the next station in the ring. When a station needs to transmit data to another station on the ring, it "seizes" the token. That is, instead of immediately retransmitting the token frame, the workstation modifies a certain bit in the frame, appends the data it wants to transmit and the destination address, and transmits the new, larger frame to its neighbor instead.

This data frame is passed from station to station until it reaches its destination or returns to the sender. Each station in the ring checks the destination address to determine whether it is the destination of the frame. If the station recognizes its address as the destination, it sends the frame up the protocol stack for further processing. It also retransmits the data frame to the next workstation on the ring, after changing another bit that indicates that the data was received successfully by the destination station on the ring.

When the data frame circles the ring and gets back to its original sender, it is stripped from the ring. The station that originated the data frame checks to see whether the destination workstation has acknowledged receiving the data and, if it has, starts the token process again by sending a new token frame to its neighbor.

This simple process describes how data is exchanged between computers that are attached to the network. For a complete understanding of how the technology works, a few other questions need to be answered:

- What controls this orderly process? Where does the first token come from when the network is started?

- How does a station join a ring? Won't this disrupt the physical connection made in the MAU or MSAU?

- What does a token frame look like? A data frame? How are they different from one another?

- Token-ring is described as "self-healing." How are errors detected and isolated to keep the LAN up and running?

Before answering these questions, it will be helpful to first look at the format of the frames used on token-ring networks to understand how these problems can be addressed using the types of information that can be sent between stations.

Token-Ring Frames

Three kinds of frames are used in token rings. One is the token frame that is passed around the idle network. This frame is only three bytes long and is seized by a computer when it wants to transmit data on the network. The other two frames are longer and contain either data or commands used to manage the network. Token-ring adapters use the MAC frame when communicating with each other. When sending data that is destined for a higher-level protocol, such as IP or IPX packets, the LLC frame format is used.

The Token Frame

The token frame is a three-byte frame that circles the ring until a station decides that it needs to transmit data. Figure 13.2 shows the token frame format. Although the start and end delimiter bytes are used to indicate the beginning and end of the frame, only one byte is really worthy of discussion: the access control byte.

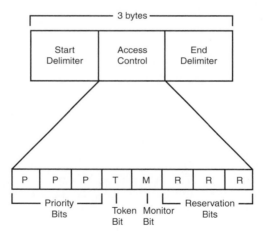

Figure 13.2   The token frame is only three bytes long.

The access control field contains several important values that are all stored in only one byte. These values represent the priority bits, the token bit, the monitor bit, and the reservation bits.

The Token Bit

The *token bit* is obviously used to indicate that the frame is a token frame or another kind of frame. If it is a token frame, the network media is available and the workstation receiving it can transmit data if it wants to when it receives this frame. In this mode, the token bit is set to a value of zero. When a station wants to transmit data, however, it copies this byte to a buffer, changes the token bit to a value of one, adds addressing information to create a larger frame, and then transmits the larger frame to its downstream neighbor. The workstation can continue transmitting until it is finished, or until the *token-holding timer* expires. When the computer has transmitted the last frame that it needs to for the time being and the frame has circled the ring and arrived back at its starting point, a new token is generated—with the token bit set to zero—and released to the ring. The next station that receives the token frame can transmit.

The Monitor Bit

The *monitor bit* is used by a workstation that acts as the *active monitor* for the ring to determine when a frame has been around the ring more than once. The active monitor performs other important functions for the ring, which are discussed later in this chapter. It is important to understand that, although any workstation that generates a token frame sets the value of this bit to zero, only the active monitor can change it to a one, which it does when it sees a data frame for the first time. If the frame continues to circle the ring without ever reaching its destination, the active monitor can detect this, remove the frame from the ring, and start the process over again. The monitor bit, therefore, is used to prevent a data frame from circling the ring endlessly. This might happen if one computer tries to send a frame to another computer that has been taken out of the ring, for example.

So, although the token bit is used by individual stations to indicate they are transmitting a data frame, the monitor bit is used by the active monitor to set the network straight if the destination computer doesn't exist on the LAN or has been taken offline for some reason.

Priority and Reservation Bits

Token-ring networks have the capability to enable individual workstations to take priority over others when it comes to claiming a token and beginning a transmission. In some applications, such as real-time factory-floor automation environments, this can be a major advantage over ethernet's contention method for network access. Using priority bits and reservation bits does this.

The priority bits are the first three bits of the access control byte. Counting in binary, this gives eight possible levels (000–111) of priority values.

The reservation bits are also used to specify a priority value between 000 and 111, in binary. A station that wants to reserve the token for its use will set these bits to the priority it expects to use, provided it is a higher value than the current priority bits represent. When the token is regenerated by a station, it will set the priority bits to this value so that the reserving station will be capable of seizing the token when it passes by again on its way around the ring. The reservation doesn't guarantee that the station will get the token on the next pass, however, because another workstation with a higher priority might intervene.

LLC and MAC Frames

In Figure 13.3, you can see that the frame type used to send a command or transmit data is much longer than the three-byte token frame. Indeed, because token-ring networks do not limit the overall length of the frame to a small value (such as ethernet frames do), this frame has the potential to be quite large.

The access control field for this frame type is copied from the token that the workstation has just seized, but the token bit's value is changed to 1 to distinguish it from a token frame. The source and destination addresses are each six bytes long. The frame check sequence field is four bytes long and is used to store a cyclic redundancy check (CRC) value that can be used to validate the integrity of the frame as it travels from one workstation to another.

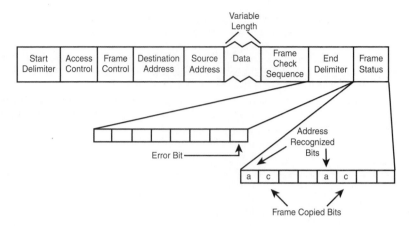

Figure 13.3 Data and command frames can become quite large.

All other fields, except for the data field, are one byte long.

The end delimiter field is one bit (the last bit) that serves an important function. When a station determines that the frame has been damaged or corrupted in transit, it sets this last bit—the error bit—to a one.

The last field is called the frame status field. This is where the station that originates a data frame checks to see whether it was received properly by the destination computer. Remember that the frame will circle the ring until it arrives back at its point of origin.

When a station receives a frame that contains its address in the destination address field, it sets the address-recognized bits to one. If it is capable of copying the frame to a buffer successfully, it also sets the frame-copied bits to one.

The originating station can interpret these bits when the frame circles around to it as follows:

- If the address-recognized bits and the frame-copied bits are all zero, the destination computer never received the frame. This means that the computer does not exist or is not active on the ring at this time.

- If the address-recognized fields are set to ones but the frame-copied fields are still set to zeros, the destination computer was unable, for some reason, to copy the frame into its internal buffer for further processing.

- If both the address-recognized bits and the frame-copied bits are set to ones, then the frame was successfully received and copied by the destination computer.

NOTE

If the frame arrives back at the originating station with the error bit set to one, it does not necessarily mean that the destination did not successfully receive the information. If the frame-copied bits are set to one, the target workstation *did* receive the frame and successfully copy the data. Thus, if the frame-copied bits are set to one and the error flag is set to one, the sending workstation does not consider this an error. It indicates that the frame was corrupted *after* it was received by the target workstation, so there is no need to retransmit the frame.

The frame control byte is used to define the type of frame. If the first two bits of this frame are both zeros, it is a media access control (MAC) frame. If they read 01, it is a logical link control (LLC) frame.

- If the frame is carrying data—it's an LLC frame—the destination computer will pass it up to the next layer in the protocol stack for further processing. The LLC header information, such as the DSAP and SSAP bits, are found at the beginning of the data field.

- If it is a command frame—it's a MAC frame—the data field will contain a 16-bit field called a vector identifier. The types of commands that can be stored in the vector identifier field and their values appear in Table 13.1.

Table 13.1   Access Control Frame Functions

Value	Description
00000000	Duplicate address test
00000010	Beacon frame
00000011	Claim token frame
00000100	Purge ring
00000101	Active monitor present
00000110	Standby monitor present

Each of these commands serves a specific purpose that is used to either notify other stations that everything is functioning well—the active and standby monitor commands—or to perform maintenance functions when something appears to have gone awry.

Functions Performed by Active and Standby Monitors

Not every station on a token-ring network is equal to the others; some computers serve specific roles in the network. For example, when the network is started, something has to send the first token frame through the ring.

A station called the *active monitor* does this. The active monitor is the station that manages the ring. Although any workstation can be the active monitor, there can be only one active monitor in the ring, and all other stations attached to the ring act as *standby monitors*. If the active monitor fails or is taken off the network, one of the standby monitors takes over the role and becomes the new active monitor. The major functions of the active monitor are

- Initializing the first token when the network is powered up
- Initiating *neighbor notification*, whereby all stations in the ring learn the names (addresses) of their upstream and downstream neighbors
- Providing a master clock that all other stations use for timing purposes
- Providing ring delay
- Detecting lost tokens and frames

The clocking function provided by the active monitor is important in a deterministic network such as token-ring. All other stations synchronize their clocks to the clocking signal provided by the active monitor. Stations do not have to listen for a set of *preamble bits* as they do in an ethernet network. The network is precisely clocked so that a computer knows when to expect the token or a data frame.

This timing mechanism enables a computer to detect that a problem exists on the network if a token does not arrive on time, and causes error detection procedures to begin.

Ring Polling (Neighbor Notification)

Each station on the ring must know the address of the station immediately upstream from it. This station is called its *Nearest Active Upstream Neighbor*, or *NAUN* for short. Knowing the address of its NAUN enables a station to detect errors and begin a correction process when it notices that its neighbor has failed in some way.

The active monitor begins a process called neighbor notification when the network is first started. This process also is called *ring polling*. Two types of frames are used in this process: active monitor present and standby monitor present.

To begin the process, the active monitor broadcasts an active monitor present control frame around the network. (Remember that the address-recognized and frame-copied bits in the frame status field are initially set to zeros.) Because this frame is a broadcast frame, it will be recognized by any station that receives it, which will be the station immediately downstream from the workstation that is acting as the active monitor.

The station that receives the broadcast frame will reset its timer, using the value supplied by the active monitor. It will copy the source address—its upstream neighbor's address—into memory for future reference. The address-recognized and frame-copied bits in the frame status field are set to ones, and the frame is sent on its way to the next workstation. Other stations on the ring will not copy this frame because the appropriate bits have already been set. The frame circles the ring until it arrives back at the active monitor, which strips it from the network.

When the second station in the ring retransmits the active monitor present frame with its bits set, it also sets a 20-millisecond timer. This is done to give the active monitor present frame enough time to move around the ring. When this timer expires, it will send out a frame similar to the one it just received. However, this frame is a *standby monitor present* frame. It serves the same type of function as the previous frame to the next workstation downstream because its address-recognized and frame-copied bits are initialized to zero.

When the next station downstream receives the standby monitor present frame, it recognizes it as a broadcast frame and, because the appropriate bits are set to zero, it realizes that it has just received the frame from its immediate upstream neighbor. It stores this neighbor's address in memory for future use, sets the address-recognized and frame-copied bits to ones, and retransmits the frame to the next workstation. It also sets a 20-millisecond timer and, when the timer expires, it repeats the process by sending its own standby monitor present frame to the next workstation downstream.

Finally, when the active monitor receives a standby monitor present frame with the address-recognized and frame-copied bits set to zeros, it knows that the neighbor notification process has completed successfully.

So that all members of the ring will be kept updated about potential new members in the ring or other changes, the active monitor sends out an *active monitor present* frame every seven seconds. If any station in the ring does not receive the frame at least every 15 seconds, it will initiate a process called *monitor contention* so that a new active monitor can be designated for the ring.

How the Network Repairs Itself When the Active Monitor Fails

Each station other than the active monitor is designated to be a standby monitor. These stations expect that every 2.6 seconds, either a token frame or a data frame will pass their way. They also expect that an active monitor present frame will arrive at least every 15 seconds. If any of these events fail to occur, it is assumed that the active monitor has been taken offline or has failed in some manner. To remedy the situation, the first standby monitor that notices this situation initiates a process called *monitor contention*, in which a new active monitor is designated to manage the network.

All stations except for the current active monitor will participate in the "election" of a new monitor. If the current active monitor is still present on the network, it assumes that it is not functioning correctly because another station has begun the monitor contention process.

The station that begins the process puts itself into Claim Token Transmit mode and sends out frames called *claim token frames*. These frames contain the station's own DLC address. The next station downstream receives this frame and compares the address to its own. If its own address is of a higher numerical value, it substitutes its own address for the one put into the frame by its upstream neighbor, retransmits the frame, and puts itself into Claim Token Transmit mode. Otherwise, it puts itself into the Claim Token Repeat mode and forwards the frame to the next station so that it can make the comparison.

After a short time, only one station will remain in Claim Token Transmit mode. When a station receives its own Claim Token Transmit mode back from circling the ring three consecutive times, it will decide that it has won the election and begin operating as the active monitor for the ring.

To begin its new duties, the new active monitor will

- Take over the clocking functions for the ring
- Send out a *ring purge frame*
- Begin ring polling (neighbor notification)
- Transmit a free token so that the network can resume normal operation

The ring purge sets the ring back to an initial state, causing stations that receive the frame to reset their timer clocks and to abort any other task that they were in the process of doing. When the frame has circled the ring, the active monitor can send out the new token and stations can again resume normal processing.

The Active Monitor Watches for Problems

The active monitor guards the overall health of the network by constantly monitoring activity on the ring. It expects its own active monitor present frame to return, along with the standby monitor present frames generated by other stations (received every seven seconds). It watches to determine whether a station has raised the priority of a token but failed to lower it, thus making the token unusable by other stations. All in all, the active monitor expects to see a good token every 10 milliseconds and will take steps to repair the network if it does not arrive on time.

When a token frame or data frame passes by the active monitor, it sets a timer. If the timer expires before it sees another frame, it assumes that the frame has been lost, purges the ring, and initiates a new token.

The monitor bit is set only by the active monitor when it first sees a frame. If it sees the same frame again—which it can determine because no other station can set this bit to a value of 1—it will assume that the frame is circling the ring endlessly and will strip it from the ring.

When the active monitor detects errors in a frame based on the CRC value, it purges the ring and, if the purged frame returns to the active monitor undamaged, initiates a new token so that processing can resume.

Because token-ring networks are so small (compared to other types of networks), the token can travel around from station to station quite quickly. Thus, it is possible for a station to begin stripping bits off a frame before it has finished transmitting the entire frame. To prevent this from happening, a latency factor is introduced by the active monitor. The latency buffer is a minimum of 24 bits and is used to introduce this delay. This value is used because the token frame itself is 24 bits in length (three bytes).

Detecting Errors on the Ring

One of the nice things about token-ring networks is that they are somewhat capable of detecting errors—such as a malfunctioning upstream neighbor—and in many cases can make corrections that will keep the network functioning. When a station detects that it has a problem with its upstream neighbor, it starts a process called *beaconing* to inform the other downstream stations so that the process of isolating the error can begin.

Transmitter Failures

Each station has already learned the address of its upstream neighbor because of the ring polling process. When a station determines that it is no longer receiving frames from its NAUN, it begins to send out beaconing frames that contain its own address and the address of the neighbor that it assumes has malfunctioned. Other stations receiving these frames enter an error correction mode, and other traffic on the ring stops until the beaconing process is complete.

Eventually, if there are no other problems in the network, the beacon frames arrive back at the upstream neighbor, which recognizes that its address is present in the frame. Because another station is complaining, the station removes itself from the network ring and performs a self-test, just as it does when it joins a ring. If it does not pass its own self-test, it remains off the ring until an administrator can diagnose the problem and repair it. If it passes the test, it reinserts itself into the ring.

If the problem station stays removed from the ring, the relays in the MSAU reconfigure the wiring connections so that the station is bypassed. Thus, the station that is issuing the beaconing frames is connected to a neighbor that is one farther upstream from it than the one that was removed. If all is functioning normally, it begins to receive the beaconing frames it originated. It then stops transmitting the frames and waits for the active monitor to restore the network to normal functioning, which it does by issuing a new token.

Receiver Failures

In the situation just described, you can see how a station with a faulty network adapter that cannot transmit will be automatically removed from the ring. However, when a station no longer can hear frames from its upstream neighbor, the problem doesn't have to be in that neighbor's adapter card. Instead, the problem might lie in this station's card, which might be malfunctioning, making it unable to receive the data properly. This type of malfunction also will be detected by stations on the ring, and the offending station will be isolated.

When a station starts transmitting beaconing frames to let others know that it cannot hear its upstream neighbor, it sets a timer. This timer is of a sufficient value to enable the upstream neighbor to self-test and remove itself from the ring. If the timer expires, the beaconing station will suspect its own receiving capability, remove itself from the ring, and perform the self-test. If it fails the test, it knows that it is the malfunctioning unit and stays disconnected from the ring.

In this case, the upstream neighbor will have passed its self-test and reconnected to the ring.

NOTE

Not all hardware problems can be resolved in this manner. For example, when a cable that connects two MSAUs breaks, the intervention of an administrator is required to correct the problem.

What Is Early Token Release?

Token-ring networks operate at either 4Mbps or 16Mbps. When operating at 4Mbps, a station will release a new token on the network after it has received a data frame that has finished circling the ring. When the network speed is 16Mbps, this fact introduces a significant delay factor that prevents the available bandwidth from being efficiently used—a frame circling at 16Mbps takes less time to circle the ring. On a ring that holds a large number of stations, very short frames introduce a significant amount of idle time on the ring.

To increase the use of available bandwidth, stations on 16Mbps token-ring networks can be configured to release a token shortly after they release their data frame. Thus, a station downstream can begin to transmit data more quickly than if it had to wait for the data frame to circle the ring. This is called *early token release*, and is the default operation for token-ring adapters operating at 16Mbps.

Adding a Station to the Ring

Now that I have covered the mechanics of how a token-ring network operates, you might wonder how a new workstation joins a ring that is already functioning. The process doesn't require that the entire network be brought down and restarted. However, for a short period of time, the new workstation checks out its own capability to transmit and receive data, and then announces itself to the network.

Remember that the MSAU contains electrical relays that can be used to add or remove a station from the ring. When a station is first connected, the relay connects the station's transmit wires to its receive wires. Thus, at this point in time, it can only talk to itself.

The process of inserting a new member into the ring consists of the following steps:

1. The token-ring card runs its own self-diagnostics tests and sends a signal on its transmit wires. Because the transmit and receive wires are being connected by the MSAU, it receives its own signal back. It compares this to what it sent to determine whether it is functioning correctly.

2. If everything appears to be in working order, the adapter will then apply a voltage, called a *phantom voltage*, to the transmit wires. This causes the MSAU to activate the relay that is connecting the transmit and receive wires. The relay then physically connects the station to its neighbor's transmit and receive wires, inserting it into the active ring.

3. The new node waits up to 18 seconds while it monitors incoming signals to determine whether an active monitor present frame is circling the ring. If it does not see one, it will initiate the contention process so that a new active monitor will be designated for the ring.

4. Assuming that the active monitor present frame was received, the station then sends out a frame called the Duplicate Address Test frame. This frame contains its own address and circles the ring so that other stations can examine it to determine whether the address already exists on the ring. If the frame arrives back at the station with the address-recognized bits in the frame status field set to ones, it will realize that the address is already in use and remove itself from the ring until an administrator can remedy the problem.

5. If it determines that it has a unique address, the station participates in the next ring poll, learning the address of its upstream neighbor and informing its downstream neighbor of its address.

After these steps, the station is a functioning member of the ring. Other housekeeping functions might be performed, such as the learning of certain ring parameters, for example ring number and other configurable values.

The Physical Star Topology

As discussed earlier in this chapter, token-ring networks are organized in a circular fashion, with one station connected to a neighbor on the left and right, and with the last workstation connecting back to the first, thus forming a ring. This is indeed the actual, *logical* formation for a token-ring LAN.

Although at first glance it might appear that the ring is simply a bus topology that has been joined back onto itself to create a ring, this is not the case. You can almost imagine a T-connector attaching the cable to each workstation, with each end of the connector used to attach a cable that joins the station to its two neighbors in the ring.

If this were the *physical* method that was used, however, it would defeat one of the main benefits that token-ring has over its rival networking technology. That is, a break anywhere on the cable would bring down the entire LAN because the token, not to mention the data frames, would no longer be capable of completing the circuit. Instead, hub-like devices are used to wire the network in a star formation. These devices, which are discussed in the next few sections, are responsible for connecting workstations to their neighbors. There is no single cable to which all workstations are attached, as in a bus topology.

Multistation Access Units

Token-ring LANs are a *logical ring*, in that communications only transpire between a station and its upstream and downstream neighbors. A workstation receives a frame on one set of wires and retransmits it on another set of wires. The transmit cables from one station carry the signal to the receiving pins on its neighboring network adapter, first passing through a device called a Multistation Access Unit.

The *multistation access unit (MAU)* or *multistation service unit (MSAU)* appears to be very much like a hub, and it indeed, these devices are used to centralize wiring. In Figure 13.4, you can see that token-ring LANs appear to be wired as a star, much like a 10BASE-T network.

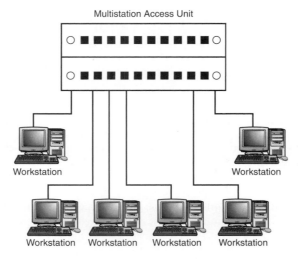

Figure 13.4   Token-ring LANs are wired in a star formation in that all stations are connected to a central wiring concentrator.

The main difference between a hub and a MAU, though, is that the MAU does not provide a central location to rebroadcast a frame to every port simultaneously. Instead, the inner workings of the MAU provide a physical connection for the transmit and receive wires from one workstation to the next in the logical ring. You can think of a star-wired token-ring as a collapsed "ring in a box" because the ring portion of the wiring is accomplished inside the MAU, and not throughout the physical cable plant of the building.

The simplest MAU devices do nothing more than provide electrical relays that connect the wires in the proper fashion. More advanced devices can actually perform other functions, such as signal regeneration. The basic function of the MAU, however, remains the same: to provide a central wiring location to connect diverse workstations on the LAN into a logical ring, physical star topology.

Connecting MAUs—Ring-In and Ring-Out Ports to Create a Larger LAN

Getting back to the logical ring concept, let's look at what happens when you need to connect more than one MAU to the network. When two or more MAUs are connected, the logical ring structure still needs to be maintained in the LAN. The token still must be circulated from one station to the next, until it arrives back at the originating station, no matter which MAU a workstation is attached to. In Figure 13.5, you can see that the MAUs are connected in a ring just as the workstations are.

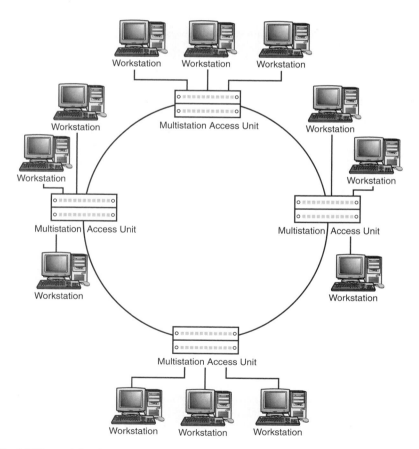

Figure 13.5 MAUs are joined into a ring.

In some cases, there are primary and secondary paths between each MAU to help reduce network down time when a problem occurs in the connection between MAUs.

Hierarchical Topologies

As with all LANs, there comes a time when you have too many workstations to connect, or when the distance between the furthermost workstations becomes too great. When this happens, you will need to segment the network by using devices such as bridges, switches, or routers. Chapter 7, "Repeaters, Bridges, and Hubs," covers these devices in detail, mostly in the context of an ethernet network. When it comes to bridges and switches, their operation in a token-ring environment is a little different.

Source Route Bridging

Bridges are used to combine smaller LANs into larger ones. Bridges are an advanced form of simple repeaters that send a signal from one cable segment out onto another without making any decisions based on information contained in the frame. Source-route bridging is used in token-ring networks to connect rings to or from a larger network. As the name implies, the source first determines what route the data exchange should take through the network before beginning to exchange actual data with a remote system.

The basic process can be described in a few simple steps:

1. The source workstation sends out a test frame that is used to determine whether the destination workstation is on the same local ring.

2. If the source workstation doesn't receive a response to its test, it assumes that the destination is on another ring.

3. The source workstation sends out a frame called an *All Routes Explorer (ARE)* frame. This is a broadcast type of frame that bridges typically forward to all other rings in the network.

4. As the ARE frame passes through each bridge, information is added to the frame, indicating the path it is taking. This includes the ring number and an identifier that is used to identify the bridge.

5. The ARE frame eventually makes its way to the destination computer, which sends back a directed reply. It is not necessary to send a broadcast frame for the reply because the destination computer can read the routing information in the ARE frame to see the path it has taken.

6. The originating workstation receives one or more replies from the destination computer. If there is only one route to the destination, then only one reply is received. If more than one route exists, a reply is received, showing each route.

The workstation that sent out the original ARE frame makes a judgement on which path to use, and then sends directed frames that use that path for further communications with the remote system. In the simplest case, the workstation uses the path specified by the first reply received.

This type of bridging is different from *transparent bridging* used in ethernet networks. In transparent bridges, the spanning tree algorithm is used to set up a network of bridges where there is only one possible path a frame can take to its destination, even though there might be multiple physical pathways between any two stations. The spanning tree algorithm calculates the path a frame will take and changes it only when a particular path becomes unavailable, at which time the entire bridging tree formation is recalculated. Another difference between token-ring ring and ethernet bridges is that ethernet bridges make decisions based on MAC addresses, learning which addresses are on which ports. Token-ring bridges do not need to keep a table of MAC addresses, and instead use a field called the

Routing Information Field (RIF). If a frame does not contain this field, it does not need to cross the router.

The ARE frame contains the RIF that is used to store information about each step the route takes. The size of this field generally limits the number of bridges through which a frame can pass. On networks built to IBM specifications, this number is usually 7. For networks based on IEEE 802.4 specifications, this number might be as large as 13. In Figure 13.6, you can see how the routing information is stored in an 802.5 MAC frame.

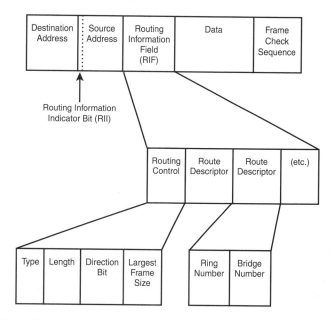

Figure 13.6 Routing information in an 802.5 MAC frame.

The usual fields are still there, such as the source and destination addressees. However, the first bit of the source address is called the *Routing Information Indicator (RII)* bit, and is used to indicate that this is a frame that contains routing information. The other field of importance is the Routing Information Field (RIF), which is divided into several other components. The Routing Control component consists of the following:

- **Type**—The type of routing. This can indicate an ARE frame, a specifically routed frame, or a spanning-tree explorer frame.

- **Length**—Specifies the total length of the RIF field, which can include multiple route descriptor fields.

- **Direction Bit**—The direction of the bit, forward or reverse. When the station that originated the routing request frame receives this frame back, it can reverse this bit so that the routing descriptor fields are read in a reverse manner to reach the destination station.

- **Largest Frame Size**—This field contains the size of the largest frame that can be sent over this route. In other words, it indicates the smallest frame size encountered during its journey, which becomes the common denominator for this route.

The Routing Control field can be followed by multiple Route Descriptor fields—from 7 to 13, depending on the type of network, IEEE 802.5 or IBM network—each of which contains the ring number and bridge number for each bridge or ring through which the frame passes during route discovery.

As you can see, this format makes it easy for devices between the two workstations to route the packet. The direction bit can be turned on or off by each end of the connection to cause intervening bridges to interpret the route descriptor fields in the opposite direction, depending on the direction of the communication.

When compared with transparent bridges, which are configured with parameters by network administrators that control the various paths through the network, source routing bridges are less complex. They do not have to exchange information among themselves to calculate a spanning tree, because it is the source of the data communication that decides on the path that will be taken. Because of this, however, there is a little more latency on the part of this type of bridge than the other.

NOTE

IEEE standards define a type of bridge called a *Source-Route Transparent Bridge*. This bridge forwards packets that contain a RIF based on the information in that particular RIF. If the packet does not contain a RIF, the MAC address is used instead.

Gateways—Translating Bridges

When a network is composed of more than one technology, some sort of device is needed that can translate between the different formats and protocols used. A *translational bridge* (also referred to as a *gateway*) can be used to connect ethernet and token-ring LANs. A standard bridge simply forwards the same frame it receives based on the MAC address in the frame. A translational bridge operates up into the Logical Link Control (LLC) layer of the OSI reference model, takes the information it receives in one format, and repackages it into a different format, depending on the kinds of networks it is bridging. Figure 13.7 shows how bridges can be used to join different network types.

In this example, the bridge strips off the 802.3 MAC sublayer information from the incoming ethernet packet, and at the LLC sublayer decides where the packet should be sent at the LLC sublayer. It then repackages the packet in an 802.5 frame and sends it back down to the physical layer for retransmission on the 802.5 token-ring network.

End user workstations do not need to be aware that this translation is even being done. Each continues to receive a frame in the format of the network on which it resides. This is one of the benefits of using a model such as the OSI reference model. Instead of having to write a complex program to allow for the interchange of data between two diverse networks, only a simple repackaging step is needed in the bridge device.

Token-Ring Switching

Switching is a method used to speed up the connection between two network nodes. It provides for a direct, dedicated path that does not involve contention for the network medium, either by CSMA/CD or by possession of a token. The usual means for joining multiple rings in a token-ring environment is to use a bridge or router. When you have users who make a lot of use of a particular server, about the only thing you can do to decrease latency and increase access time is to place the server on the ring that the users are on. In a larger environment, you can end up with servers distributed throughout the network, which makes them more difficult to manage.

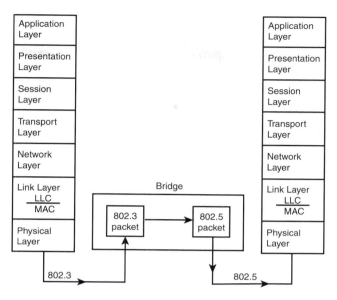

Figure 13.7   Bridges can be used to join different network types.

Unlike bridges, switches enable you to attach a ring segment, an individual workstation, or a server directly. When a server is directly attached to a port on a switch, it does not have to wait for a token to come its way before it can transmit data. Likewise, the switch does not have to wait for a token when it wants to output frames on the port to which the server is connected. Thus, by connecting high-performance servers to a switch, and then using the switch to connect to other workstations or network segments, you can increase the total throughput for the network.

Just as a switch provides a dedicated path for ethernet networks, allowing for full-duplex ethernet connections, a switch also can be used to double the bandwidth of a token-ring connection. This technique is called *Dedicated Token-Ring (DTR)*. A token-ring adapter uses two pairs of wires, one pair to transmit and the other pair to receive. After you eliminate the token-passing function of the protocol, both of these wire pairs can be used at the same time.

Troubleshooting Token-Ring Bridges

Individual token-rings contain many mechanisms, both physical and software based, that can be used to detect and temporarily fix many problems. When a network adapter on a workstation begins to malfunction, it is possible for other workstations to detect this and force the offending workstation to disconnect itself from the ring and perform a self-test. Administrators usually can quickly diagnose and fix problems that occur within the local ring without a lot of time spent investigating the problem.

When you begin to connect LANs to a larger network, however, connectivity between two workstations that reside on different rings can be troublesome and time consuming. You must know what types of devices are installed between the workstations, and also understand how they are used.

For example, *SRT bridges*, which can be used for transparent or source route bridging, might be dropping packets that have a routing information field (RIF) when connecting with an ethernet segment.

You can use a network analyzer to determine whether packets are being forwarded through the network. By checking the source address on packets output by the bridge—looking for a high-order bit set to one to indicate RIF—you can determine whether it is passing RIF frames.

You might think a certain path exists that handles all the types of traffic on your network, but you might be unaware that a particular device is misconfigured or is malfunctioning. Check the fields that show the ring numbers on packets that pass through the bridge to be sure they are correct. Also, check the bridge ID itself to be sure you don't have two bridges in the network set to the same value.

When the number of network clients increases suddenly, a bridge might begin to degrade in performance. Remember that bridges used in a small network might not have the capacity to buffer a traffic load when you begin to upgrade your network with higher-capacity servers or additional workstations that generate a lot of traffic. Consider installing a switch to relieve these types of congestion problems. Using a switch, you can isolate high-performance machines from those low-capacity ones while still maintaining connectivity.

Finally, remember that not all vendors' equipment works with everyone else's. When making purchasing decisions, investigate the documentation and sales literature to be sure that the bridge or other device you are planning to add to your network will work as you expect.

Using a Token-Bus Topology

One of the main differences between the star and the bus topologies is that all workstations that are connected to a bus can hear all transmissions that are made. Even when ethernet networks are connected to a hub in a star-wired fashion, the hub repeats the incoming frames on the other ports so that the basic function of a bus remains.

NOTE

The IEEE 802.4 Working Group that developed token bus standards has been inactive since 1997. This does not mean that token bus is a dead technology, just that, for its purpose, the standards have been defined and no further work is anticipated for this technology.

The MAU in a token-ring network does not create a bus topology when it concentrates the process of connecting a ring in one location. However, there is a variation on token-ring technology that *does* use a bus. This is referred to as a *token-passing bus*. In this type of token-ring implementation, the token frame is logically passed from one workstation to another, although all workstations are connected by a bus cable and all can hear every transmission. The MAP (Manufacturing Automation Protocol), which is a dated technology at this point but still in use in many locations, uses this technique for connecting equipment on the factory floor.

The IEEE 802.4 group set forth the standards for the token-bus network. Each station on the bus has a numerical address that determines the order in which it is granted the token. In Figure 13.8, you can see that the order in which stations are attached to the bus is not important because the token is passed according to station address.

You can see that the workstations are connected along the bus in no particular order. Workstation 8 is the first on the bus and is followed by workstations 2 and 3, with the end of the bus having workstations 1 and 6 attached side-by-side at the end of the bus. You can move a station from one point in the network to another without having to change its address. The token, however, is passed in order of address from one station to the next, and the token is still the method used to grant access to the network medium for transmission of data frames.

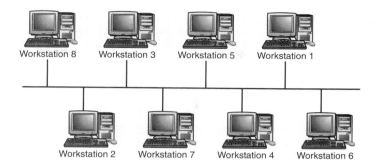

Figure 13.8 In an 802.4 token-bus network, a logical ring is formed by the stations' addresses.

NOTE

Another token-passing network technology, known as *ARCnet (Attached Resource Computing Network)*, also uses a bus topology. ARCnet is one of the oldest LAN technologies still in use today. Although it employs a bus and uses the token-passing method to grant access to the cable, it does not conform to the IEEE 802.4 specifications.

Cabling Rules for Token-Ring Networks

Two basic types of cables are used to connect token-ring networks. Workstations are connected to the multistation access unit (MAU or MSAU) by means of a *lobe* cable. The MAU is similar to a hub that is used in ethernet technology but acts to connect workstations into a physical ring and does not repeat signals on all ports simultaneously. To create larger LANs, MAUs are connected to each other by using a Ring In/Ring Out cable.

What Is the Adjusted Ring Length?

The distances that you can cover with a token-ring network depends on the type of cable used, the number of workstations, and other devices in the ring, as well as the particular vendor who manufactures the equipment.

The term *adjusted ring length (ARL)* is used to specify the worst-case distance between any two stations in the ring. It is calculated as follows:

```
ARL = lengths of all MAU to MAU cables - shortest MAU-MAU cable.
```

In some implementations, you do not have to count cables that are three meters or shorter and used in the same wiring closet to connect MAUs. Other devices, including surge suppressors and punch-down connectors, also might need to be figured into the calculation. Be sure to review the vendor's specifications carefully when making a purchasing decision.

Rules for STP and UTP Cables

Both shielded and unshielded twisted-pair cables can be used with token-ring. In many token-ring networks, you will find that cables are usually classified according to a scheme devised by IBM back in 1982, the *IBM Common Cabling Standard (CCS)*. CCS defined eight levels of cable types, as well as a system of using ducts to conduct cables through buildings, with terminations at faceplates in the user's workspace. This was an early attempt to create a procedure for wiring a building so that various devices used to process data and voice communications could be connected in a standard and consistent manner.

Taking into consideration these cable definitions, several types of cables are now standard in token-ring networks. In the discussions that follow, the standard lengths quoted apply when the LAN is composed of more than one MAU. It usually is possible to achieve a greater distance in a small workgroup LAN.

Type 1 Cables

Type 1 cables consist of two pairs of solid 22 AWG wires. Each pair is shielded by a layer of foil, and the entire cable is surrounded by a braided metal shield, encased in PVC. This type of cable is usually used for trunk connections: joining together MAUs that are distributed throughout an office building, for example.

These cables are used in places such as the walls of office buildings, and they connect wiring closets and distribution panels that are usually found in the same building. The maximum distance for this type of cable is 101 meters, or 331 feet.

NOTE

A cable designated as Type 9 is similar to the Type 1 cable, except that it uses a plenum jacket for use in air handling spaces to satisfy the requirements of fire codes.

This type of cable can be used to connect as many as 260 devices, using 12 or less wiring closets and as many as 32 MAUs.

Type 2 Cables

Type 2 cables are similar to Type 1, except that they also include additional unshielded twisted-pair cables that can be used for voice or other transmissions. This means that there are six twisted pairs in the same cable. The cable can be used to provide both voice and data connections, using only one cable strung between end points. The maximum distance for this type of cable is 100 meters, or 328 feet.

Larger token-ring networks are usually constructed using STP (either Type 1 or Type 2) and can support as many as 260 workstations and as many as 32 MAUs.

Token-ring networks of both 4Mbps and 16Mbps can be run on Type 1 and Type 2 cables.

Type 3 Cables

Type 3 cable is much less expensive than Types 1 and 2. Types 1 and 2 are made up of shielded twisted-pair, while Type 3 is made up of unshielded twisted-pair (UTP) cables with a minimum of two twists per inch, using 22 or 24 AWG solid wires. Remember that the more twists that are used for any given length of cable, the less crosstalk between the wires. The entire cable is encased in PVC.

This UTP cable is more flexible than the other types and, therefore, is easier to route around corners and in tight places. This cable type is generally used only on 4Mbps networks and has a distance of up to 45 meters (148 feet), according to IBM standards. Some vendors publish specifications that use this cable type for distances of up to 150 meters.

This is the most popular type of cable and can support as many as 72 workstations. If repeaters are used, subtract 1 from this value for each repeater. Depending on the vendor, this cable type can be used in between two and six wiring closets.

Type 6 Cables

To connect MAUs, a patch cable is used that is usually referred to as Level 6 or Type 6. This is a shielded twisted-pair cable made up of two pairs of stranded wire with both foil and braided shielding. It is encased in a rigid PVC jacket.

These patch cables can be purchased in standard lengths of 8, 30, 75, and 150 feet, and can be special ordered in custom lengths if required.

This cable is a little more flexible than the Type 1 cable and can be used to connect MAUs and to connect individual stations to the MAU. When used to connect stations, it usually is used only in a small network, with around 12 MAUs, which are usually of the IBM Model 8228 type.

Lobe Cables

The cables that connect individual workstations to the central MAU device are called *lobe cables*. Each cable uses four wires for communications. Two are used for transmitting data to the MAU, and two are used for receiving data. For the standard STP cable (Type 1 and Type 2), an IBM Type A data connector is used at one end to connect the cable to the MAU, and a 9-pin connector is used at the other end to connect to the token-ring network card.

If the cable type is UTP (Type 3), the connectors are usually RJ-11 or RJ-45, although the RJ-11 type is an older model that is not much often used today. Most token-ring adapters that are currently being manufactured have both a 9-pin and RJ-45 socket to provide for different cable types.

Ring In/Ring Out Cables

Ring-In and Ring-Out cables are used to connect MAUs to form a larger LAN. When you join MAUs, you connect the Ring In port of one MAU to the Ring Out port of another, with the end result forming a ring so that the last MAU is connected to the first.

Although a malfunction of a lobe cable will only cause the attached workstation to be dropped from the LAN, the failure of a cable that connects two MAUs is a more serious problem. When saying that a token-ring LAN is "self-healing," this refers to its capability to lock out a malfunctioning workstation, not a break between MAUs.

Fiber-Optic Connections

Fiber-optic cable (sometimes called Type 5) has been used in token-ring networks for many years. One of the benefits of this cable is that it enables you to greatly extend the distances covered by the LAN. When computing the ARL, for example, fiber-optic cable usually counts as a zero-length cable. This means that if you use fiber-optic cable for all MAUs in the ring, only then lengths of the lobe cables from the MAU to the workstation need to be figured in.

Token-Ring Connectors and Media Filters

When using IBM Type 1 cables, the standard connector is called an *IBM-type Data Connector (IDC)*, or a *Universal Data Connector (UDC)*. These connectors are not like RJ-45 connectors, where the cable consists of a male connector that plugs into a female socket. Instead, these connectors are blade types that interlock with each other.

UDC connectors use the color-coding scheme shown in Table 13.2.

Table 13.2 Color Codes for UDC Connectors

Wire Color	Use	Polarity
Red	Receive data	+
Green	Receive data	-
Orange	Transmit data	+
Black	Transmit data	-

A DB-9 connector contains nine pins for terminating wires, but only four are used by token-ring networks. Table 13.3 shows the pinout for this connector and the wire color-coding scheme that is used.

Table 13.3   Color Codes for DB-9 Connectors

Pin Number	Wire Color	Use	Polarity
1	Red	Receive data	+
5	Black	Transmit data	-
6	Green	Receive data	-
9	Orange	Transmit data	+

You also can use RJ-45 connectors. This is the type of connector most often seen in 10BASE-T ethernet networks. This type of connector is similar to the modular connector used on most telephones today. The color-coding and pins that are used with this connector for token-ring networks appear in Table 13.4.

Table 13.4   Color Codes for RJ-45 Connectors

Pin Number	Wire Color	Use	Polarity
3	Blue/White	Transmit data	-
4	White/Orange	Receive data	+
5	Orange/White	Receive data	-
6	White/Blue	Transmit data	+

Another modular connector that is used, although not as often as those discussed here, is the RJ-11 connector. This connector type usually is used with older network adapters. Table 13.5 lists the color codes and pins used for this type.

Table 13.5   Color Codes and Pin-Out for RJ-11 Connectors

Pin Number	Wire Color	Use	Polarity
2	Blue/White	Transmit data	-
3	White/Orange	Receive data	+
4	Orange/White	Receive data	-
5	White/Blue	Transmit data	+

Media Filters

If you have older token-ring adapters that have only a 9-pin connector, you can find media filters that can be used to join them to an RJ-45 type of connector. Various vendors produce these inexpensively. Ethernet cards are, for all practical purposes, a commodity item that can be replaced cheaply. Token-ring adapters are more expensive, so using a media filter to attach an older card to a new cabling standard for your network might be a good idea, economically, if you have a lot of stations.

Cabling Scenarios

Now let's look at some typical cabling scenarios and the types of cable to use. The general specifications that you should analyze are ring speed, maximum distance between any workstation and the MAU, the number of workstations, and whether a voice connection is going to be carried over the LAN.

Scenario #1:

> Ring speed: 16Mbps
>
> Maximum distance: 35 meters
>
> Number of workstations: 62
>
> Voice connection: No

Solution:

> This scenario requires Type 1 cabling. Even though the number of workstations and maximum distance require only Type 3, the requirement of 16Mbps speed necessitates using Type 1.

Scenario #2:

> Ring speed: 16Mbps
>
> Maximum distance: 85 meters
>
> Number of workstations: 185
>
> Voice connection: Yes

Solution:

> This scenario requires Type 2 cabling. The ring speed, maximum distance, and number of workstations can be implemented using Type 1 or 2, but the voice requirement can be handled only by using Type 2 cabling.

Scenario #3:

> Ring speed: 4Mbps
>
> Maximum distance: 35 meters
>
> Number of workstations: 25
>
> Voice connection: No

Solution:

> This scenario requires Type 3 cabling, which is sufficient for the short distance covered by the network and the number of workstations. This type of cabling is the cheapest and easiest to install, making it a good choice for a small LAN.

Monitoring Token-Ring Utilization and Errors

Because of the fundamental difference between ethernet and token-ring technologies, the statistics that you use to monitor the network are also quite different. For example, an ethernet network operating at 10Mbps will begin to degrade rapidly when overall utilization of the network media rises above 40%, mostly due to the access method used, which allows for collisions to occur when more than one station attempts to transmit at about the same time. Token-ring networks operating at 4Mbps or 16Mbps actually can use a much larger percentage of the network bandwidth because only one station is normally transmitting at a time. The mechanisms that token-ring uses to grant access to the network (the token frame) and other functions used for maintaining network functionality (ring polling and beaconing) means that the kinds of information available to the administrator are different than those on an ethernet network.

In addition, the types of errors that will be encountered will be different. The fact that token-ring networks are "self-healing" to a large extent makes tracking down problem workstations much easier than with ethernet. When a problem is detected on a token-ring network, the individual workstation can be isolated and the rest of the LAN will continue to work while you try to determine the cause of the failure of the workstation.

Token-Ring Statistics

As discussed earlier in this chapter, two kinds of frames are used on a token-ring network. The LLC frame is used to carry data that a station on the ring wants to send to another station. Most of the frames generated on a token-ring network will be of this type. The network adapters, however, use another type of frame, called the MAC (media access control) frame, to communicate with each other and perform ring management functions on the ring.

The most basic MAC frames that you will see are the active monitor present (AMP) and standby monitor (SMP) present frames. The AMP frame is normally passed around the ring every seven seconds. It is used to tell other stations who the active monitor is. Other stations on the ring are considered to be standby monitors and will decide on a new active monitor if the AMP frame fails to arrive on time.

Network analyzers, both hardware and software, usually allow you to collect and display statistics about the functions performed by these ring management frames. They also can show you statistical information about errors that occur on the ring.

In particular, monitoring beacon frames is very important in maintaining a healthy network. These frames are sent to downstream neighbors when an adapter fails to detect any data or MAC frames from its nearest upstream neighbor, usually indicating that the upstream neighbor is malfunctioning or there is a possible cable fault. Obviously, if you notice that the ring is experiencing a high level of beacon frames it might be indicative that an adapter or possibly a cable is unstable and should be looked at immediately.

Ring purges are used to set the ring back to a known state when something has gone wrong, and also can happen when the active monitor leaves the ring and a new one is elected, or when the active monitor detects some other kind of error condition and needs to reset the ring. When a station receives a ring purge frame, it stops its current processing and resets its timers. If the ring is experiencing a high level of ring purges, you should study other error or statistical information to determine the cause.

For example, a good monitoring program will show you the current number of active stations on the ring. Usually, it also will show you the maximum number of stations that have been on the ring since the monitor began recording data, and possibly an average number of stations. If the average number of stations on the ring is significantly lower than the maximum, check to determine why stations are leaving and rejoining the ring. If you are moving equipment around or rearranging workstations on the network, this might not present a problem.

The Ring Error Monitor

An optional software component that many administrators will find quite useful for troubleshooting is the Ring Error Monitor software. If you will remember, every ring has an AMP and the remaining workstations are designated as standby monitors. The Ring Error Monitor is a station that does nothing more than receive error reports from other stations as they detect them. It keeps a running list that the administrator can review when trouble is suspected on the ring.

When a station on the ring detects that an error has occurred, it will wait for a few seconds (two seconds by default) and listen to the network to see whether any further errors occur. After the wait interval has expired, the station will send a report of the errors it has seen to the Ring Error Monitor. If you are using a Ring Error Monitor on your network, review the error data it collects on a regular basis. Even simple errors that do not cause downtime for the ring can indicate that a component is unstable and prone to more severe failure in the near future. Taking proactive steps to diagnose and fix a small problem can prevent a much larger problem from disrupting other users later.

Token-Ring Errors

Errors can be classified into two broad categories: hard errors and soft errors. Soft errors are those that can occur during normal ring operation, but they do not bring down the local ring. Hard errors are those caused by such things as broken or malfunctioning cables or ports on the MAU that can possibly stop normal functioning of the ring.

Soft errors can be described as either isolating or non-isolating errors. An *isolating error* is an error that can be traced back to a single station on the ring, and a *non-isolating error* is one that cannot. Simply put, an isolating soft error usually indicates an error condition with a particular station on the ring. That is, it can be isolated to a particular station. A non-isolating error usually indicates a problem with the ring itself, and not necessarily a particular workstation.

The IEEE 802.5 specification, which sets the standards for token-ring networks, defines several error types:

- **Burst Error**—This error indicates that there is noise on the network media. It occurs when a station detects three bits with no clock in the middle. The source of the noise can be environmental, such as a strong electrical field near a network cable, or it might result from faulty hardware. This error also can happen when a station is inserting itself into the ring or taking itself out of the ring. The burst error probably is the most frequent error you will see on a token-ring.

- **Line Error**—This error is similar to a burst error and usually indicates that one is about to happen. It can be generated when a station receives a frame and calculates that the CRC value does not match the contents of the frame. When a station detects this kind of error, it sets the error bit in the frame to 1 so that other stations do not report the error. In general, you will see a ratio of 1 line error for every 10 burst errors detected.

- **Lost Frame Error**—When a station transmits a frame, it sets a timer that tells it how long it should expect to wait until the frame travels around the ring back to it. If this timer expires, then this kind of error is generated. This error type causes the active monitor to generate a new token.

- **Token Error**—The active monitor sets a timer each time it sees a valid frame on the ring. Because the monitor knows how long it takes for the frame to travel the distance around the ring, it assumes an error has occurred if this timer expires before it sees another frame. This can result from noise on the line. The active monitor generates a new token when this condition occurs.

- **Internal Error**—A station records this kind of error when it detects an internal parity error when using DMA (direct memory access) to exchange data with the workstation's memory. To determine whether the network adapter card is the problem, you can install it in a different workstation and see whether the error occurs. If it does not, try power-cycling the original workstation to see if the error can be corrected.

- **Frequency Error**—When the frequency on the network media detected by a station differs significantly from that which is expected, this kind of error is recorded. A standby monitor on the ring can detect this error, which usually results from a problem with the active monitor that generates the clocking signal. To determine whether the active monitor is problematic, remove it from the ring and see if this problem still occurs.

- **AC Error**—This error type indicates that a station received more than one active monitor present or standby monitor present frame with both the address recognized and the frame copied fields set to zero. This error happens when the nearest upstream neighbor of the station does not properly set these bits. Check the upstream station when troubleshooting.

- **FC or Frame Copied Error**—A station generates this error type when it receives a MAC frame that is addressed to it, yet the address recognized bit is already set to 1, indicating that another station also thought this frame was destined for it. This can be the result of a problem on the line or possibly indicate that two stations on the ring have the same address. Note that the duplicate address problem will exist at the frame level and is not indicative of a duplicate address of a higher-level protocol.

- **Abort Delimiter Transmitted**—This error type happens when a station transmits an abort delimiter while it is transmitting. It happens when a station, while transmitting, receives a claim token or beacon frame, which causes it to abort its transmission.

- **Receive Congestion Error**—When a station receives a frame that is destined for it but does not have enough buffer space to copy the frame, this kind of error occurs.

Some of the problems causing these errors can be fixed easily. For example, if you notice a large number of frame copied errors, indicating a possible duplicate address, and you have just installed a new workstation on the ring, recheck the new workstation to be sure you correctly configured its address. Congestion errors can be solved by replacing older network adapters that might not be able to keep up with the traffic on the ring. Congestion errors also can indicate that an adapter is having problems and is about to fail. Replace the adapter to see if the error persists. Burst errors and token errors might lead you to check the cabling or connectors for all stations on the ring. If cabling has recently been moved or new cabling installed, check for sources of electrical interference.

Internal errors should direct you to examine the adapter or workstation from which they originate. Replace the adapter to see whether the problem subsides and, if not, perform diagnostics on the workstation itself.

Using Network and Protocol Analyzers

Besides the error-recording functions of the Ring Error Monitor, a good protocol analyzer can be a big help in troubleshooting problems on a ring. The protocol decode function provided by the analyzer should be able to decode frames specific to token-ring networks (that is, the MAC frames used for ring maintenance), as well as higher-level protocols such as TCP/IP or IPX/SPX.

It is important to understand how your network works during the normal work day when using a protocol analyzer. During certain times of the day, normally there will be peaks during which activity is high on the ring, while at other times utilization is quite low. If you are unfamiliar with these times, you might not fully understand the voluminous data that you can get using a protocol analyzer. Some soft errors are to be expected, such as those caused when a station is inserted or removed from the ring. If you are not familiar with the pattern of utilization on the ring and the usual error activity, you might judge the ring to be in worse shape than it is!

Token-Ring Extensions to the Remote Network Monitoring MIB

The objects defined in previous RFCs for monitoring network activity, such as those defined in RFC 1271, are separated into nine groups. Some of these groups, such as the statistical groups, are designed with the assumption that the underlying network technology at the data-link layer is ethernet. To fully implement SNMP and RMON technology for devices that are used for token-ring networks, additions had to be made.

TIP

RFC stands for "Request for Comments" and is a mechanism used on the Internet in the process of defining standards. SNMP stands for the Simple Network Monitoring Protocol, which is a technology that allows for monitoring of network components remotely by the network administrator. RMON is similar to SNMP but extends its functionality. MIB stands for Management Information Base and is a collection of objects that define the kinds of data collected and functions that can be performed by RMON. For more information, see Chapter 44, "Network Testing and Analysis Tools."

RFC 1513 defines extension to the MIB that was defined in previous RFCs, and describes how existing object groups will be used for monitoring token-ring networks. These changes are

- **Host Group**—Only isolating errors will cause error counters in this group to be incremented. These are line errors, burst errors, AC errors, internal errors, and abort errors.

- **Matrix Group**—No error counters will be incremented in this group for token-ring networks.

- **Filter Group**—Conditions are defined for how the bitmask is used in this group.

In addition, the RFC provides additional groups of objects that are specific to token-ring networks. In particular, RFC 1513 defines four additional object groups:

- **Ring Station Group**—This group provides information about each station on the local ring and also status information about each ring that is being monitored.

- **Ring Station Order Group**—The order of stations in the ring is contained in this group.

- **Ring Station Configuration Group**—This group is used to manage stations by active means. Objects in this group can be used to remove a station from the ring and to download configuration information from a station.

- **Source Routing Statistics Group**—Utilization statistics about source routing is contained in this group.

Although the Ring Error Monitor can provide useful information collected on the local ring, SNMP and RMON can allow you to centralize monitoring for larger networks, making the troubleshooting process much easier. In addition, RMON provides for alarm functions that can be set to trigger when certain events occur, giving you a heads-up before a situation becomes more serious.

When upgrading network components, check to be sure that they provide SNMP and RMON functionality.

Troubleshooting Tips

As you can see, there are a lot of different kinds of information you can obtain that can tell you how well your token-ring network is functioning. Sometimes, though, too much information can be useless if you don't understand how to interpret it. The best thing you can do to keep yourself prepared is to monitor the network on a frequent basis and to keep track of normal usage patterns. In other words, determine a baseline for the network and use the baseline data when analyzing or troubleshooting.

A few general things that should apply to most rings, however, are

- Every seven seconds the active monitor present frame should be seen circling the ring. This ring polling mechanism allows each station to determine who its nearest active upstream neighbor is. It also lets each station know that the ring is functioning normally and that the active monitor is watching for token and other errors. Following shortly after the AMP frame you should notice a standby monitor present frame.

- Soft errors and ring purge frames are expected events when a station is inserted or removed from the ring, and should not be a cause for alarm. Soft errors that are not associated with insertion or removal should be less than 0.1 percent of the total number of packets transmitted.

- Insertion and removal of a station can also cause burst errors and line errors, and can cause token errors. If these errors are not associated with the timeframe during which an insertion or removal was performed, they might indicate a problem unless they are sporadic.

- Utilization on a token-ring network above 70% can cause slower response for end users. Normally, response times should be around one tenth of a second. Peak utilization of 100% does not indicate a problem unless it is happening frequently.

Choosing Between Token-Ring and Ethernet

Token-ring advocates and those who champion ethernet have argued for many years over which technology best serves the market. There are advantages and disadvantages to both. It is interesting to note, however, that as ethernet technologies are expanded to higher network speeds, they are incorporating some techniques that are already present in token-ring technology.

Because token-ring techniques can guarantee an equal access to the network within a specified time limit, token-ring networks are more suited to environments that require a specific response time. Ethernet networks are fine for many network applications, but can become bogged down when too many workstations try to flood the wire with a lot of information at the same time. A lot of processing power can be spent simply by the contention method that involves collisions and back-off algorithms.

Ethernet networks use a relatively small packet size, which can be up to a maximum of only 1,518 bytes.

This size was originally conceived to work in the 10Mbps environment, and has been kept as ethernet speeds have advanced to 100Mbps. With the exception of Jumbo Frames—proposed by Alteon Networks—most ethernet networks waste valuable bandwidth due to the overhead of these small frames. In 16Mbps token-ring networks, the maximum frame size is controlled by a timer and can reach sizes of up to 18KB, although 4KB is more common in actual practice at this time. This is a considerable improvement over ethernet!

Other areas in which token-ring excels over ethernet include the priority and reservation fields, which can be used to provide a quality of service functionality. By using source route, bridging token-ring clients can specify multiple routes to a particular destination, which is not allowed under the spanning tree routing technologies.

The main disadvantage, however, is that token-ring usually is more expensive than ethernet to implement. Token-ring adapters are made by very few companies and, because of their complexity, cost more to produce. MSAUs are more complex than their passive hub cousins, and also are more expensive. In addition, because the MSAU is a required component of a token-ring network, you cannot simply create a crossover cable to connect two workstations as you can with ethernet. However, because a two-node network is not a common implementation except in a very small business or a home environment, this is not a large disadvantage.

The two technologies can operate together, each being used for what it does best. Switches, routers, and adapter gateways can be used to connect the two types of networks so that workstations can communicate throughout a larger network.

Wireless Networking: IEEE 802.11 (Wi-Fi) and HomeRF

SOME OF THE MAIN TOPICS IN THIS CHAPTER ARE

Mobility: The Workforce on the Move

Uses for Wireless LANs

Ad-Hoc Networks and Access Points (APs)

The IEEE 802.11 Standards

Radio Wave Transmissions—FHSS Versus DSSS

What Is Wi-Fi?

What Is HomeRF?

Sources of Interference for Wireless Networks

Which Technology Should You Choose?

CHAPTER 14

Although the installed base of networked computers today is mainly comprised of technologies using copper wire and fiber-optic cable, the growing market for wireless technologies cannot be underestimated. The popularity and rapid growth of the cellular telephone market, for both personal and business applications, attests to this fact. Just 10 years ago, cellular telephones were high-priced items used mainly by top business executives. Today, they are sold in shopping malls, and it is common to see teenagers walking around with them stuck to their heads. In a few more years, it will be hard to imagine how people ever got along without them.

Mobile phones today are already equipped to handle text messaging, Internet e-mail, and some limited Web-browsing capabilities. You'll learn more about that in Chapter 16, "The Wireless Application Protocol (WAP)." In this chapter, you learn about the IEEE 802.11 wireless networking standards and its new rival, HomeRF. The IEEE 802.11 protocol standards can be used to extend wireless capabilities to an existing network by adding wireless access points (APs). Alternatively, you can create an all-wireless network.

Note

The cost of implementing wireless networking is particularly interesting. Usually, the new, leading-edge technology also is the most expensive; however, that's not true with wireless networking products. For example, the first network switches were expensive devices deployed in large networks where bandwidth problems needed a solution, no matter what the cost. Yet wireless products, such as those covered in this chapter, are available for prices that range from inexpensive home solutions (network in a box) to high-end products. So, whether you operate a large corporate network or work in a small home office, this chapter has a lot to offer.

Bluetooth, another wireless technology, is covered in Chapter 15, "What Is Bluetooth?" Although Bluetooth is a wireless technology, its purpose is not as far reaching as the IEEE 802.11 or HomeRF technologies. Instead, Bluetooth is designed to replace cables that span only a very short distance. You could use Bluetooth to exchange data between a mobile phone and a PC, or to have a wireless keyboard and mouse attached to your computer. This short-distance communication capability does not address the much larger distances that the specifications covered in this chapter do.

Mobility: The Workforce on the Move

Laptop computers provided the first true mobility for computer users. Linking these powerful platforms to a computer network can be accomplished easily either by means of a PC-Card network adapter card or a docking station. By using DHCP to assign network configuration information, it's easy to move a portable computer from one location to another, and still provide a simple connection to the network. However, this kind of mobility still depends on a wired connection of some sort, either a direct connection to the network or possibly a dial-up connection for remote access. Wireless networking, although not widely deployed at this time, is about the fastest growing technology in the networking market today.

Uses for Wireless LANs

For a technology to grow, it must solve some kind of problem. That is, it must be useful in some way. Wireless LANs have primarily found their niche in vertical markets, such as healthcare services and the factory floor. The most obvious benefit this kind of networking provides is mobility. Other benefits that you might get from wireless networking include

- Faster installation when compared to cabled networks
- Adaptability in a dynamic environment
- Reduced costs in many situations

In a typical LAN setup, it is necessary to install and configure the networking software on the client computer and provide the wiring from the network hub or switch to the user's work area. With a wireless LAN, you only need to configure the computer's networking software. You don't have to string cables through the building for each user. In an environment that changes rapidly, this can be an advantage. For example, point-of-sale terminals in a large store can be reconfigured easily for seasonal adjustments, such as the end of the year Christmas buying spree. In a warehouse, the floor layout might change during the year for similar kinds of reasons. Relocating computers is much easier when there are no cabling issues to deal with. After the initial investment is made in wireless LAN devices, the ability to reconfigure the physical network topology can result, in many cases, in reduced costs over time.

An ad-hoc network or temporary setup (see the following list) is another important aspect. For example, if you are in the consulting business and need to have several consultants exchange information, you can use wireless networking to set up your own local network and bypass your customer's wired network. Knowing this allows your client to worry less about security than if the client has to go through the typical paperwork and other management functions to get your consulting team connected to the company network.

In addition to these kinds of environments, you will find wireless LANs increasingly being used in situations such as the following:

- **Hospitals**—Patient information can be obtained easily using a laptop computer or specialized terminal. Instead of having to return to a central location, such as the nurse's station on the hospital floor, doctors and nurses can get information quickly from a laptop computer or handheld device as they make their patient rounds.

- **Older buildings**—In some cases, it can be difficult to wire the premises for a traditional network. Some older buildings that do not have plenum areas in the ceiling can be difficult to adapt. Using wireless communications makes networking in this kind of environment an easy task.

- **Temporary setups**—This feature was mentioned in the introductory paragraph to this list. You can extend it further to such situations as a trade show, where the network usually is set up for only a few days; the computers can be configured ahead of time, so that the only thing your company representative has to do is turn them on.

- **Warehouse and factory floors**—Laptop computers and handheld bar code scanners that use wireless LAN technology can quickly return the investment needed for their implementation.

Note

When discussing the applications of wireless networking, the dialogue should not be limited to just computers. By enabling data collection devices, such as bar code scanners or handheld data entry terminals, such as cash registers, with wireless networking connections, many more practical uses for wireless communications will develop in the next few years.

Ad-Hoc Networks and Access Points (APs)

Before getting into the specifics about IEEE standards and how data is transmitted on radio frequencies, you first should look at the topology a wireless network can take. In Chapter 1, "Overview of Network Topologies," you learned that a wireless network doesn't use a bus topology. Instead, because all nodes can hear all other nodes (within a specific area), the topology can be considered a mesh topology. That is, in the simplest wireless network, all stations participating in the network can hear and talk to all other stations in the network. In a traditional wired network, this is equivalent to having a network card make a cabled connection to every other node in the network!

Another topology used in wireless networks involves using a device, much like a hub or switch, that controls which wireless stations can transmit.

Ad-Hoc Networks

A simple peer-to-peer network, comprised of computers that have compatible wireless network adapter cards, can be used to quickly set up a small network on-the-fly. This kind of workgroup LAN can be useful when only a few stations need to communicate in a small geographical area (see Figure 14.1). You can set up your own individual network at a trade show, a user's workspace, or even at work if you don't use a wired network at all! For a home office, where you probably don't want to drill holes in your walls and pull cables, wireless products can be the best solution possible.

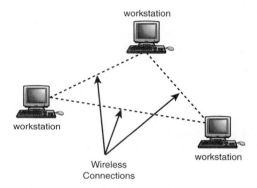

Figure 14.1 All you need to create a network on-the-fly is a few computers, each with a wireless network adapter.

This network is referred to as an ad-hoc network because it involves simple peer-to-peer connections in a wireless environment. No central hub or switch coordinates the communications that occur. Instead, any computer equipped with a compatible wireless adapter can join the ad-hoc network, provided the appropriate security mechanisms have been implemented. For example, if you are using a Windows operating system and a simple workgroup setup for network communications, any computer that uses that same workgroup name can join your small ad hoc network. If you use more secure methods, such as a Unix system with each workstation requiring a username/password, you can create a more secure wireless ad hoc network. The same goes for using a Windows domain. The only difference is that the network is wireless—there are no cables—and the same security mechanisms you'd use for a wired network should be used for this simple peer to peer network.

Tip

Although the term ad-hock network usually is used for a quick setup of wireless stations, another term you'll hear when reading the literature is Basic Service Set (BSS). A BSS is nothing more than two or more wireless computers that have established communications among themselves. The simplest BSS, consisting of just wireless computers described in this section, also is called an Independent Basic Service Set (IBSS) because it doesn't have an AP to coordinate the communications between the wireless computers.

Using an Access Point to Mediate Wireless Communications

You also can use a wireless *AP* to create a small wireless network. This device can be attached to a network, which we will discuss next, or as a standalone device that can effectively double the distance of the wireless network. As you can see in Figure 14.2, if the access-point device is placed in the center of the network, each computer equipped with a wireless network adapter can be placed further away from other computers. This is because each computer only needs to be able to communicate with the AP, which in turn relays the signals to other computers that participate in the wireless LAN.

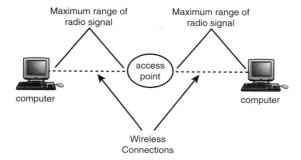

Figure 14.2   As you can see, an AP can double the range of a wireless network.

You can add APs to a traditional wired network as well; the APs will serve the same purpose that hubs or switches do for your wired clients. The AP coordinates communications to and from the wireless computers and the rest of the network that is made up of copper or fiber-optic cables (see Figure 14.3).

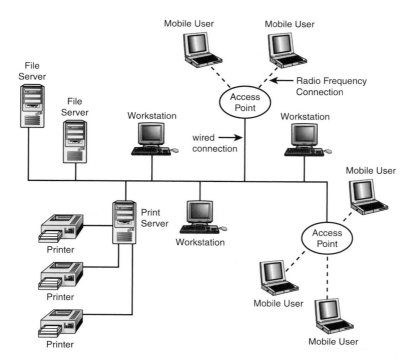

Figure 14.3   APs provide the connection to the wired network for mobile users.

Because multiple APs can be placed throughout the network, this topology allows for a wider geographical range for mobile users. An *AP* is a simple device that can connect to the wired network and provide a transmitter/receiver that can be used to communicate with mobile users' workstations. In addition to providing the wireless communications service, an AP typically is responsible for buffering data between the wireless clients and the wired network. Unlike an ad-hoc wireless setup, the AP also is responsible for mediating communications between wireless clients that operate within range of the same AP.

Most of the devices on the market today support 10–50 wireless clients on a single AP at any given time. However, your mileage can vary depending on the manufacturer.

APs come in all sizes and shapes. For example, in Figure 14.4, you can see an example of the D-Link DWL-1000AP AP. This inexpensive AP can be set manually to operate at 11Mbps, 5.5Mbps, 1Mbps, or its own configuration determined by an autosensing mechanism that you set.

Figure 14.4   The D-Link DWL-1000AP AP is an inexpensive solution for wireless networking.

This small device supports DHCP and can operate with wireless clients for a range of up to 100 meters indoors and up to 300 meters outdoors. It also comes with management software that allows you to manually assign the AP a static IP address.

In Figure 14.5, you can see the D-Link DL-713 Wireless Gateway and Access Point Plus switch. This device provides not only AP capabilities, but also four switch ports, one of which can be used to connect to a high-speed network, such as a broadband connection. The other three switch ports can be used to connect individual desktop workstations or other networked devices.

This higher-end solution comes with built-in firewall capabilities so that you can use port blocking and packet filtering to help protect your LAN. Network Address Translation (NAT) allows you to keep information about your internal LAN secret from Internet scanners that are used to discover active IP addresses on the Net for possible penetration.

Note

NAT and firewalls are covered in greater detail in Chapter 40, "Firewalls." This is recommended reading for anyone who is thinking about connecting any LAN to the Internet.

Figure 14.5 APs provide the connection to the wired network for mobile users.

This D-Link gateway also can interoperate with equipment from other vendors that use IEEE 802.11b-compliant APs to enable seamless roaming from one AP to another for clients on the move. A very important feature about this unit is that it is Wi-Fi compatible—you'll learn about Wi-Fi later in this chapter. Wi-Fi is a name that you'll soon be hearing a lot about. It will make purchasing wireless equipment from multiple vendors that work together well a reality.

The IEEE 802.11 Standards

The main standard for wireless LANs is the IEEE 802.11 standard, which was first drawn up in 1990 and has gone through several drafts since then. This standard includes definitions for the Physical layer (PHY) and the Media Access Control (MAC) layer protocols. The standard envisions two kinds of clients: ad hoc and client/server. The ad-hoc client method involves a peer-to-peer network between clients located close to each other. The client/server method uses an AP device to mediate network communications and possibly provide a connection to a wired network. Note that the first draft of the IEEE 802.11 standard provided for only transmission rates of 1Mbps and 2Mbps, but the newest additions to the standard (IEEE 802.11a and IEEE 802.11b) provide for much faster data transmission rates. Both of these methods are discussed later in this chapter, but first take a look at the PHY and MAC portions of the standard.

The Physical Layer

The Physical layer of a network involves the mechanisms used to actually transmit the signal on the network medium. In this case, the medium is infrared, Frequency Hopping Spread Spectrum (FHSS), or Direct Sequence Spread Spectrum (DSSS). In the original IEEE 802.11 standard using FHSS, the data rate is 1Mbps. For DSSS, the original standard defines both 1Mbps and 2Mbps techniques. Infrared communications (it's wireless, after all) also is supported at both 1- and 2Mbps data rates. Because few, if any, infrared devices are on the market today, they aren't discussed in this chapter. The most important devices are those using radio frequencies (FHSS and DSSS), which you'll find for sale by a large number of vendors.

Note

Although the standard defines both spread spectrum and infrared methods at the Physical layer, wireless clients using different Physical layer components cannot interoperate. In other words, an infrared-equipped client can't communicate with another computer that uses the radio frequency spectrum for transmissions.

IEEE 802.11a provides for wireless networks that operate in the 5GHz band, whereas IEEE 802.11b provides for wireless networks that operate in the lower 2.4GHz band. This chapter concentrates on

IEEE 802.11b products for two main reasons. First, this radio frequency band has been set aside as a worldwide radio frequency to be used for Industry, Science, and Medicine (ISM) purposes and doesn't require a radio operator's license for you to use it. Second, the Wireless Ethernet Compatibility Alliance (WECA) was formed specifically to promote products from different manufacturers that are subjected to stringent testing to ensure interoperability. The brand name chosen by WECA that will be used for these products is Wi-Fi, which is discussed later in this chapter. First, you need to know some important concepts about wireless networking in general, and then you'll get to some more specific information that can help you make a decision on what kind of wireless solution best suits your needs.

The MAC Layer

For the MAC Layer, the standard is similar to the 802.3 standard for traditional ethernet networks. Before a network node (or station, as they're usually called in the wireless world) can transmit, it must first determine whether the radio frequency channel is available, and a mechanism must be used to determine whether a transmission was successfully received by the destination station.

Collision Sense Multiple Access/Collision Avoidance

Chapter 12, "Ethernet," explained that the mechanism ethernet network adapters use to gain access to the network medium (a copper wire, for example) is called Carrier Sense Multiple Access/Collision Detection (CSMA/CD). The network adapter that wants to transmit a frame of data first listens to the wire. If the wire is silent, the card transmits a frame. It then listens to make sure that no other network adapter tried to transmit at the same time (a collision). If a collision occurs, each of the nodes that caused the collision backs off for a random interval before attempting another transmission. This random back-off mechanism is intended to keep multiple network adapters from trying to transmit at the same time again.

This works well when you have a network adapter card that transmits and receives at the same time, which is exactly how ethernet network adapters operate. However, when you're dealing with the airwaves, a wireless adapter can either transmit or receive, but not both at the same time. So, another method for gaining access to the medium (the radio frequency on which the network is based) is used. It's called Carrier Sense Multiple Access/Collision Avoidance, or CSMA/CA for short.

Using this principle, the wireless network adapter card first listens to determine whether any other station is transmitting, just like a traditional ethernet card does. If the frequency is not being used, the station can transmit a frame. However, because it can't listen at the same time to determine whether a collision has occurred, another method is used. If the destination of the transmission receives the frame intact, it sends back an acknowledgment packet (ACK). The standard provides for a higher priority for transmission of ACK packets so that they are transmitted before other stations can transmit.

After a wireless adapter has transmitted a frame, it waits to see if an ACK is sent back. If some other station also has transmitted a frame during the same time, then the receiving end of both communications attempts will not receive an intact frame, no ACKs will be sent back, and thus both stations know they must retransmit the frame. Just as with traditional ethernet cards, the stations that do not receive an ACK in response to a transmission assume that a collision has occurred, and wait for a random time interval before again listening to the airwaves to determine whether they can retransmit.

Another term used in the specifications for this media access method is Distributed Coordination Function (DCF); all stations based on IEEE 802.11 must implement this method.

Virtual Carrier Sense—RTS/CTS

As stated earlier in this chapter, it's always possible that two wireless-equipped computers can begin to transmit at the same time. However, what happens when you use an AP and two stations that are so far apart they can't hear the transmission of the other computer? This is referred to as the *hidden node* problem. In this situation, another means must be employed to ensure that only one station on the wireless network is transmitting at a given time.

To solve this problem, wireless computers that want to transmit a frame must first make a request for air time. Instead of just listening to the radio frequency and starting a frame transmission if the frequency is not being used, the network adapter instead transmits an RTS (request to send) frame to the AP. This frame contains information that identifies the station that wants to transmit, as well as the duration of time it wants to reserve for the transmission.

If the RTS frame is received by the AP (that is, no collision occurred due to another station also trying to transmit an RTS frame), the AP transmits a CTS (clear to send) frame that grants permission to the original computer to begin its transmission. This frame also contains the ID field of the computer that is being given permission to transmit, as well as the amount of time granted to it. Because all stations participating in the wireless network controlled by the AP can hear the CTS frame, they know they can't begin a transmission and they also know how long they must wait before making an attempt to send an RTS frame.

This method of accessing the transmission media also is referred to as Point Coordination Function (PCF). Although DCF is required by the IEEE 802.11 standard, PCF is not. It can be implemented, but is optional according to the standards.

Other Services Performed at the MAC Layer

The MAC Layer also provides other services, such as *association* and *reassociation*. Remember that an AP and its clients make up a BSS in the network. A client is associated with a particular BSS. When a client moves from one BSS to another, reassociation takes place. Although the 802.11 standard provides for the concept of reassociation, the actual mechanism for this function is not specified in the standard.

Radio Wave Transmissions—FHSS Versus DSSS

The most popular method for providing a communications medium for a wireless LAN, is typical radio wave transmissions. As stated earlier, the Federal Communications Commission (FCC) allocated a radio spectrum in 1985 that is called the Industrial, Scientific and Medical (ISM) band. It operates in the 2.400–2.483GHz range and does not require the end user to obtain any kind of license. Similar agencies in other countries have followed suit and set aside this range for the same use. When developing products for wireless networking using this range, a technique called spread-spectrum broadcasting is used.

Spread-Spectrum Technology

During World War II, the military began developing a radio transmission technology called *spread spectrum*. A normal radio signal, such as those you pick up on your car radio, are called *narrowband* because they concentrate all their transmitting power on a single frequency. Spread-spectrum technology uses a much larger bandwidth instead and can be deployed using two basic methods: DSSS or FHSS. Spread-spectrum techniques are attractive to manufacturers of wireless equipment for many reasons. One of the more important reasons is that they can be difficult to detect or intercept. Additionally, from a security standpoint, spread-spectrum techniques are difficult to "jam" or interfere with.

Hedy Lamarr

Hedy Lamarr (also known as Hedwig Kiesler Markey) is most often remembered as a sultry screen actress from the early part of the twentieth century. Few people realize, however, that she and a composer named George Antheil received a patent in 1941 (U.S. Patent no. 2,292,387) for an invention that allowed for ultra-secret communications. What was this invention? It was a primitive form of what today is called spread-spectrum technology. Using a system of paper tapes that contained codes, transmitters and receivers could be synchronized to send and receive bits of a communication by alternating between seemingly random radio frequencies. Unfortunately, it took many years for the microchip to come along and make this technique easy and inexpensive to implement in environments other than military. Thus, poor Hedy never made a lot on this invention!

The two main aspects of any spread-spectrum technique are

- The signal that is transmitted is of a greater bandwidth than the actual transmitted information's bandwidth. In other words, more data is transmitted than the actual data the user intends to send.

- The resulting bandwidth is determined by some method other than the information being transmitted.

For commercial systems, the actual bandwidth used might be from 20–200 times the bandwidth of the actual information that is being transmitted, perhaps even larger. Some systems use a bandwidth that is up to 1,000 times larger than the information. Because the signal is spread out over a larger bandwidth, it can occupy the same bands as ordinary narrowband transmissions with little interference. A narrowband transmission can interfere with only a small portion of the signal being sent using spread-spectrum technology and error-correction techniques can be used to compensate for this.

DSSS systems use a signal that is a combination of a pseudo-noise signal and the actual information modulated on an RF (radio frequency) carrier. By mixing two different signals to produce only one for transmission, the data is masked by the seeming random signal that it is combined with. That is, this results in a signal with a wide bandwidth that appears to be noise. At the receiving end, the pseudo-noise signal is used as a mask so that the actual data part of the signal can be recovered. The pseudo-noise signal is not truly a random signal, but instead is an agreed upon method for generating a signal that both ends use.

FHSS employs a much simpler technique. It uses a narrowband carrier that continually changes frequencies. For this to work, the transmitter and receiver must both be synchronized to know which frequencies are used and in what order. The FCC dictates that at least 75 or more frequencies must be used for this technique, and any single frequency cannot be used for a burst of data longer than 400ms. Some methods of FHSS employ a simple pattern of switching from one frequency to the next. Others use a technique where certain frequencies are skipped.

What Is Wi-Fi?

As stated previously, the Wireless Ethernet Compatibility Alliance (WECA) was formed to enable different manufacturers to produce products based on the IEEE 802.11b specification, which uses DSSS technology. However, the IEEE 802.11b standard provides for a higher data rate than the original specification. Although earlier IEEE 802.11 products operated in the 1–2Mbps data rate range, IEEE 802.11b Wi-Fi products operate at 11Mbps. This is comparable to the performance you get on a standard 10BASE-T wired network.

Tip

You can find out about more about WECA and Wi-Fi by visiting `http://www.wi-fi.com/`.

Wi-Fi products undergo testing to ensure they will operate with other Wi-Fi branded products. The goals of WECA are many, but the main emphasis is to make it possible for consumers to purchase products and know in advance that they will work with other similar devices the consumer already owns. In addition, Wi-Fi is not intended to be a home wireless solution or a corporate wireless solution. Instead, it is intended to be an all-encompassing solution for the home, business, and public spaces. For example, wouldn't it be nice to take your laptop to work, and connect to the company's network using a wireless adapter? How about when you're sitting in the airport waiting for a delayed flight? If Wi-Fi APs are available in such public places, you could just open your laptop and get some work done while waiting on your flight. This opens up a whole new field of opportunity for Internet service providers (ISPs) that want to expand their customer bases. By providing wireless Internet connections in public places—from airports to malls and even to your local coffee shop—an ISP easily could sell this service to many customers. And, of course, when you finally get off that late plane and head for home, it would be nice to just open your laptop again and hook up to the Internet with a Wi-Fi branded AP at home.

Although this might seem like a lofty goal, it looks like it might be the future of wireless networking. If one product technology can be used for home, public spaces, and corporate networks, it will be possible for a larger number of vendors to enter the marketplace, driving down costs and making wireless networking an inexpensive product.

Security in Wi-Fi Products

An option to the 802.11 standard is called Wired Equivalent Privacy (WEP). WEP is a shared-key system that can be used to validate clients on the wireless network. To become associated with an AP, the client must possess the shared key valid for that AP. The option uses the RC4 encryption algorithm. Data communications between clients and the AP also are encrypted using the shared key, making it difficult for an eavesdropper to penetrate the network.

Because WEP only uses a 40-bit key, some critics say it's not secure enough to use for wireless networks. However, as WECA points out, the goal was never to make Wi-Fi a highly secure system. The goal was to make it at least as secure as your standard wired network. On a traditional wired LAN, it's easy to intercept packets on the Internet and to tap into copper cables if you don't secure them properly. WEP is intended to add a layer of security, but not act as the total security solution. Instead, higher-level protocols should take this responsibility, just as is done in a wired network.

For example, if you connect your branch offices to your company headquarters, you would be foolish to send all data in simple IP packets with the payload unencrypted. Instead, using such techniques as Virtual Private Networks (VPNs), you can encrypt the data and create a virtual tunnel through the Internet to solve your security problems.

▶▶ For more information about VPN techniques, see Chapter 41, "Virtual Private Networks (VPNs) and Tunneling." Also, Chapter 42, "Encryption Technology," can serve as a useful primer on techniques used to encrypt data, both in LANs and WANs. Finally, Chapter 40, "Firewalls" is required reading if you operate any type of LAN that is connected to the Internet.

However, to help satisfy critics of WEP, work is currently underway for WEP2. WEP2 will be a more secure version of WEP. Task Group E of the IEEE 802.11 committee started work on this in 1999 and a draft proposal, known as IEEE 802.11e, has been completed.

However, don't depend on WEP to keep your wireless connections secure. Instead, explore other methods just as you would for your wired network.

What Is HomeRF?

A newer entry into the wireless marketplace is called HomeRF. This technology was developed from the start to be a *home wireless solution*, and does not encompass the wide range of uses that Wi-Fi does for a data-intensive network typical of a business. The main similarity between HomeRF and Wi-Fi is that both operate in the same 2.4GHz ISM band discussed earlier in this chapter. The major difference between the two is that Wi-Fi uses DSSS for transmissions, whereas HomeRF uses FHSS technology.

Note

You can find out more about the HomeRF Working Group and read an assortment of promotional materials and white papers by visiting its Web site at `http://www.homerf.org`.

The HomeRF Working Group is the organization responsible for HomeRF, as well as the Shared Wireless Access Protocol (SWAP). The earlier version of this standard operates at peak data rates of 1.6Mbps, and covers distances of up to about 150 feet. The newer SWAP 2.0 standard promises rates of 10Mbps. The newer standard also promises just about everything to everyone that you can think of. HomeRF products based on the earlier standard are quite common—you'll probably find them in your local electronics or computer discount store. However, whether SWAP 2.0 will live up to the claims made by the HomeRF Working Group remains to be seen. If you are going to use wireless networking in your home and don't care about compatibility with a network in a corporate environment, HomeRF might be the choice for you. SWAP 2.0 promises to be backward compatible with its slower first version, so buying inexpensive equipment at this time isn't such a big deal.

However, because HomeRF was specifically designed with home use as its target market, it shouldn't be considered as a business networking solution, except in the smallest office. According to the HomeRF Working Group, some of the features that SWAP 2.0 will deliver include

- Support for both voice and data channels. SWAP 2.0 specifications incorporate the Digital Enhanced Cordless Telephony (DECT) standard, and should give a better quality voice channel than VoIP (Voice over IP) products that work with Wi-Fi. DECT also supports features such as caller ID, distinctive ringing, and other telephone features that your local telephone company offers.

- Development of all sorts of HomeRF devices that will work together. For example, the ability to use voice commands via a HomeRF telephone handset to control other HomeRF devices.

- Streaming audio (CD quality) and video.

The PHY and MAC Layers of HomeRF

Just like the IEEE 802.11 standards, HomeRF provides for PHY and MAC layers that correspond, more or less, with the two lower layers of the OSI (Open System Interconnection) networking reference model. The PHY component matches up with the OSI physical layer and is responsible for the actual transmission characteristics of the wireless communications, such as the data rate and the range that the transmitted signal can cover. The MAC layer performs functions typically associated with the OSI data link layer, such as the method used to access the transmission media (airwaves).

The PHY Layer

The PHY layer allows for a frequency hopping rate of 50–100 hops per second, using the 2.4GHz radio frequency band. As stated earlier, the first specification of the SWAP protocol provided for a 1.6Mbps data rate in the PHY component, while SWAP 2.0 provides for 10Mbps. Because the working group is in the habit of promoting its technology before it materializes—sort of like Microsoft—it is promising still faster data rates when the next generation of products is produced. Wait and see. Although I have no doubt that all wireless technologies will continue to expand and offer faster data rates and services, what matters is how many vendors support the technology and are willing to put the research dollars into making these promises come true. At this point, you won't find many, if any, HomeRF products on the market. Wi-Fi products, however, already are shipping with the 10Mbps faster data rate.

The MAC Layer

The MAC layer of the SWAP 2.0 protocol allows for three different types of service. First, a typical ethernet data packet service for TCP/IP network traffic allows HomeRF to operate in the home environment. This enables you to share a single Internet connection, for example, with multiple wireless equipped computers, gaming devices, or other products that use TCP/IP and ethernet for data exchanges.

The MAC layer allows for prioritizing traffic so that connection-oriented services, such as streaming audio and video, can be supported without interruption by other lower-priority traffic, such as the data traffic.

Finally, the third type of service that the MAC layer is designed to support is the full-duplex, DECT-quality telephony. The data frames can be transmitted in either 10 or 20ms and depend on whether or not voice data is contained in the frame. If the frame contains data only, then during any particular time slot streaming audio and video traffic is given priority over network data packets, such as ethernet.

Depending on the number of voice calls active at any given time, time is reserved for voice packets after streaming audio and video. To improve the quality of telephony services, if for some reason a voice packet is corrupted, it takes priority during the next hop and is retransmitted. Because the next "hop" will be on a different frequency, the chances of the voice packet becoming corrupted during a retransmission is minimal. The first SWAP specification provided for up to four telephone handsets being active at any one time, whereas the 2.0 specification provides for up to eight.

Security Issues and HomeRF

Both Wi-Fi and HomeRF proponents maintain that their products are either as secure as the other, or perhaps in some cases, more secure. The HomeRF camp points out that WEP with its current 40-bit key (to be enlarged when WEP2 development is finished) is an easy one to break. They also maintain that frequency hopping, in and of itself, makes HomeRF more secure to interception. However, this isn't necessarily the case. It's not technically difficult to determine the hopping pattern used by most HomeRF products; after this pattern is discovered, the communications can be intercepted easily. Like DSSS products, you should depend on a higher-level protocol or application to encrypt sensitive data that will be transmitted into the airwaves if you expect to keep that data secret.

The security advantage that HomeRF has over Wi-Fi is that because it's intended mainly for home use, odds are that no one wants to intercept your home data communications anyway. In a business environment, you're more likely to see corporate espionage and should take the appropriate precautions. However, as a casual home user, there's really not that much to worry about at this point, unless you are a career criminal and don't want your local police picking up your transmissions.

Sources of Interference for Wireless Networks

Because wireless network products use radio waves for the "physical" transmission medium, you need to consider other devices that produce radio waves in the same spectrum that IEEE 802.11b and

HomeRF devices use. For example, the most common device, which is present in both the home, many offices, and many public places is the microwave oven. Yes, these devices use radio waves to heat your food, and they have a metal grating surrounding them that is supposed to prevent microwave transmission from emanating outside the box. However, if that were true you wouldn't see those warnings saying you shouldn't be close to one if you have a pacemaker and there wouldn't be a market for inexpensive devices you can purchase at K-Mart or Wal-Mart to measure leakage from a microwave oven. Microwave ovens do leak microwave signals and these can interfere with both IEEE 802.11 and HomeRF devices.

Even the new wireless telephones that operate in the ISM frequency range can interfere with HomeRF and other wireless devices.

The good news is that microwave ovens aren't typically operating on a continuous basis. However, you still should consider them a source of interference that can dramatically slow down wireless communications.

Wireless devices based on these two main standards can interfere with each other. It is beyond the scope of this chapter to discuss the heated debate going on about which technology is better adapted to avoid interference from another wireless device, be it Wi-Fi, HomeRF or even Bluetooth. Each group of supporters can make arguments about the capability of their products to recover from interference, but at this point, there isn't enough data or testing to prove it one way or another.

In a business environment, however, other sources of interference must be considered. For example, some companies use microwave lighting. In military installations, radar can cause interference. Magnetic resonance imaging (MRI) devices used in hospitals can interfere with wireless network products. When you get down to it, microwave technology is used in many industrial applications, so you might want to perform testing beforehand, instead of just choosing a solution. Interference can be mitigated, in some cases, by simply placing additional APs so that mobile devices are closer to an AP. The further away from an AP or home base unit, the weaker the signal and thus, the greater the chance for interference.

Which Technology Should You Choose?

When making a decision on what kind of wireless technology to employ, you must consider many factors. Some of these include the following:

- If you're a home user, and you don't need to take your computer to work, HomeRF is an inexpensive solution that can be perfect for home use.
- If you need to use the same computer at home, at work, and in public spaces (in the near future), Wi-Fi might be the best solution.
- At this time, Wi-Fi has the largest number of manufacturers behind it, so you'll have a wider latitude in choosing network adapters, APs, and so on. The more vendors that support a product, the more likely you'll see prices drop over time.

Of course, it goes without saying that you also should check the technical specifications for any product you buy before making a decision. Make sure that the products you buy are from vendors with a good track record for providing support, both technical support and for repairs or replacements of defective units. Although most wireless equipment is inexpensive, the costs can add up if you deploy it widely in a corporate network. In that case, the availability of technical support from one or more manufacturers should be a major consideration.

What Is Bluetooth?

SOME OF THE MAIN TOPICS IN THIS CHAPTER ARE

Chapter 14, "Wireless Networking: IEEE 802.11 (Wi-Fi) and HomeRF," examined the two major contenders for the wireless networking market: Wi-Fi (based on IEEE 802.11b standards) and HomeRF (based on the SWAP standards). Both of these technologies have trade organizations whose purpose is to advance their particular technology for the markets they target. Although HomeRF was created specifically with the home user in mind, Wi-Fi aims at a market ranging from the home to the workplace to public space. That is, the goal of Wi-Fi is to provide a worldwide standard that enables you to use a single wireless network adapter card in many different environments. Although HomeRF started out as a home-based system, it's trying to do the same (although the promotional group probably will not admit it), starting with the home, and then adding features (promised in the SWAP 2.0 protocols standards) that will make it attractive to business environments as well.

Bluetooth is another matter altogether! To put it bluntly, Bluetooth technology was originally designed to replace wires, and for only short distances. The original expectations for Bluetooth were that it would be used to connect such things as a keyboard, mouse, computer, and possibly a mobile phone. It was not designed, from the start, to be a wireless networking solution that would span any great distance. Both Wi-Fi and HomeRF offer a solution for network administrators that allows them to give mobile clients easy access to a network. In the home arena, this means that a single Internet connection can be shared by numerous wireless clients (computers, printers, gaming devices) in the home. In the work environment, access points can allow a mobile user to quickly connect to the corporate cabled network anywhere that a wireless access point has been placed. For the business and residential user, it's possible that one or the other of these standards will allow you to open your laptop in a coffee shop, airport, or other public space and instantly connect to an Internet provider.

The Bluetooth wireless technology is

- A short-range, lower-power wireless technology
- A means to replace cables, such as those that connect your keyboard, mouse, printer, and other standard computer peripherals
- A method to allow data communications between diverse devices such as computers, mobile phones, network appliances, handheld devices, and other similar devices, including digital cameras, which now are becoming less expensive

This chapter takes a quick look at Bluetooth because some major vendors still back this technology. For more than three years, promises have been made that *this year* will be the year of Bluetooth. That didn't happen last year, and not much has happened in the way of widespread adoption of Bluetooth technology this year. However, trying to predict which standards major manufacturers are going to stand behind and create products for is a game for fortune tellers, so the future is uncertain for the adoption of Bluetooth. At the time this book is being released, not many Bluetooth products are on the market.

You might be wondering what the problem is. The actual radio devices are inexpensive when used in more expensive peripherals, such as printers and laptop computers. Replacing a mouse or keyboard with a Bluetooth product isn't really feasible, because a simple mouse or keyboard can easily be had for less than $25, and usually much less. If customers are satisfied with a $10 mouse, they probably won't pay the extra few dollars it costs to add a Bluetooth radio to a mouse. Yet, for other uses, Bluetooth is an inexpensive chipset to add to more expensive devices, such as mobile phones, printers, and laptop computers.

The Bluetooth Special Interest Group (SIG)

Bluetooth technology was originally developed by the Swedish company Ericsson, which now licenses the Bluetooth trademark to the special interest group (SIG) of manufacturers that want to market products based on this technology. You can visit the Web site at http://www.bluetooth.com to find more information about the group and the vendors that are members. You also can download the lengthy, detailed specification documents, which probably are interesting only to engineers designing products and applications based on Bluetooth. The goal is to provide a royalty-free, open specification that enables manufacturers to create a wide range of products that can literally talk to each other without the necessity of buying numerous kinds of cables, adapters, and so on. Instead, Bluetooth-enabled devices, which are based on a set of standards called *profiles*, should make it easy to interconnect and exchange voice and data between almost any kind of electronic device you can think of.

General Overview of Bluetooth

The original Bluetooth version 1 specifications were modified somewhat and version 1b was released. Since then, version 1.1 is the current standard, and it addresses many problems that were uncovered during compatibility testing of Bluetooth devices from different manufacturers. Version 2.0 of the specification is still under development, but most of the functionality of version 1.x is expected to be compatible with version 2.x devices.

Bluetooth technology uses lower-power transmissions and therefore is limited in the distance it can cover—up to about 10 meters. A more powerful version of Bluetooth allows for higher-power transmissions that can range up to 100 meters. Instead of creating a new technology from scratch, some parts of the Bluetooth specification were borrowed from existing technologies. Some of the more important ones include

- **Frequency-hopping spread spectrum (FHSS)**—Although HomeRF hops along at a slow pace of 50–100 hops per second from one frequency to another, Bluetooth hops at 1,600 hops per second, using 79 frequencies each separated by 1MHz, over the total spectrum allowed in the 2.4GHz range. Both asynchronous communication (at 721Kbps) and synchronous communication (at 432.6Kbps) are supported to provide for both voice and data transmissions.

- **Motorola's Piano**—This technology allows the formation of small ad hoc networks, sometimes referred to as personal area networks (PANs). Although ad hoc networks are also used by other wireless technologies, Bluetooth forms ad hoc networks within just a small area, usually up to 10 meters.

- **Digital Enhanced Cordless Telecommunications (DECT)**—This specification was adopted for the voice and telephony applications that Bluetooth can provide.

- **Object Exchange Protocol (OBEX)**—This technology was borrowed from the IrDA (Infrared Data Association). It allows for data exchanges such as synchronizing address books between a Bluetooth-enabled PDA and a PC, for example, or for exchanging electronic business cards.

Bluetooth uses a frequency-hopping technique in which each transmission lasts for only 625µ. Each of these time slots is transmitted on a separate frequency hop. A simple Bluetooth network consists of a single master and up to seven slaves. Transmissions take place based on a frequency-hopping scheme decided on by the master, and all members of a *piconet* (discussed in further detail in the next section) use the same frequency-hopping pattern. Thus, it's possible to have multiple piconets within close proximity of each other because each piconet uses a different *hopping pattern* among the 79 available frequencies. When a device joins a piconet, the address of the master device is sent to the slave in a special packet called a frequency-hop synchronization packet (FHS packet). The hopping pattern is calculated based on the address of the master node. The master device's clock is used to determine which particular point in the hopping sequence is the current one, and all slaves keep track of the difference between their own clocks and the master's so that they can all hop along together.

Communications can take place in both directions, between master and slave, with each time slot numbered. The range of time slot numbers is from $0-2^{27}-1$. The master device can start transmissions in even-numbered time slots, whereas slaves can start transmissions in odd-numbered slots. To provide for larger data transfers, up to five consecutive slots can be used. However, for these five slot transmissions, the data is transmitted on the same frequency, determined by the frequency to which the hopping pattern is set when the first packet is transmitted.

Piconets and Scatternets

The ad-hoc nature of Bluetooth networking minimizes the need for management or administrative functions for networks made up of Bluetooth-enabled devices. In PANs, devices in close proximity can discover each other and form a small network (called a piconet) without user intervention. This enables users to transfer data between a cellular phone and a laptop computer, for example, by coming within range and instructing the cellular phone or computer what action to perform.

Piconets

A *piconet* is formed when two or more devices discover each other and begin to communicate. A piconet can have up to eight devices, with one device acting as a master, and the rest acting as slaves. The first device to initiate transmission becomes the master, although the specification provides for a master and slave unit to exchange roles. A specific frequency-hopping sequence is used by all devices within each piconet. Figure 15.1 shows the simplest example of a piconet: A cell phone is downloading address book and telephone number information to the user's laptop.

Figure 15.1   A piconet consists of at least two Bluetooth-enabled devices.

In this example, the laptop acts as a master, the application software running on the laptop contacts the cell phone when it is within range, and requests that it synchronize its database with the one stored on the laptop.

As stated earlier, a single piconet can have up to eight devices. The reason for this limit is simple: The address is only 3 bits long. This means that in binary, only the values of 0–7 can be stored in the address field. The master has no address, but 0 is reserved for broadcast messages, so the only addresses remaining for use by slaves are 1–7. However, a device can participate in two different piconets (called a *scatternet*), which is covered in the next section. Figure 15.2 shows an example of a larger piconet, in which one master controls a number of slaves in a piconet.

You can see that it's possible to link a variety of devices in a piconet. You can download digital images from your digital camera to the laptop, use more than one Bluetooth-enabled cell phone to place voice calls, and even connect a personal digital assistant (PDA) to the laptop to exchange information. Another interesting thing to note in this figure is that you also can use a single connection to the Internet without having to have a direct cable connection to the modem or broadband connection.

The master device in Figure 15.2 is the laptop computer. It controls the other devices, which are called slaves.

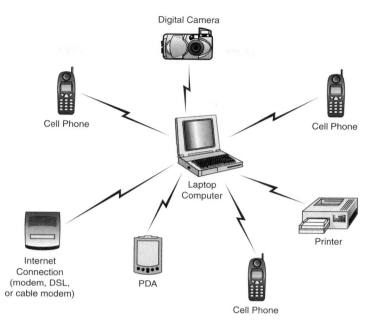

Figure 15.2   A piconet can have only one master and up to seven slave devices.

Scatternets

A device can be a master of only one piconet. However, it also can be a slave in another piconet that is within range. A slave can also participate in two different piconets that are within its range. However, because the master device determines the hopping pattern used for a piconet, a device cannot be a master of more than one piconet. An example of a simple scatternet is shown in Figure 15.3.

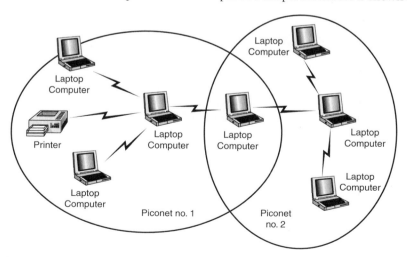

Figure 15.3   A scatternet is formed when a device is a member of more than one piconet.

In this example, a laptop computer communicates with devices in both piconets. Note that the laptop is a slave in both piconets. It is possible, however, for the laptop to be a master in one piconet and a slave in another, as shown in Figure 15.4.

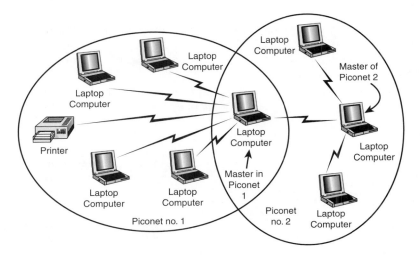

Figure 15.4   This Bluetooth device is a master in one piconet, and a slave in another.

When a device is a member of two piconets, it keeps track of both frequency-hopping patterns and occasionally listens in on the correct frequency on each of the two piconets so it can stay in touch with both piconets. A master device transmits a packet to its slaves occasionally to maintain the link, based on negotiations between the master and its slave devices. Thus, a device that is a member of two piconets must listen for these transmissions (or make them if it's the master in one piconet) within the timeframe negotiated for each of the piconets of which it is a member.

Bluetooth Device Modes

Although you can incorporate Bluetooth radios in ordinary PCs, they were originally designed to be used for low-power devices. Because of this, it isn't necessary for the Bluetooth device to be in an active state—consuming power—all the time. Before a piconet is formed, a device is in *standby* mode, in which a device will listen for messages every 1.28 seconds. To initiate a connection with another device, an *inquiry* message is sent, which is used to find other Bluetooth devices within the transmission range. If the address of the device to which a connection is desired is already known, a *page* message is used instead to begin the communication session.

In addition to being involved in active communications (the *active* mode), a device can be in three other modes:

- **Hold**—A master unit can put a slave unit into hold mode, or the slave unit can request that it be placed into this mode. This is a power-saving mode in which the unit no longer actively exchanges data with other devices.

- **Sniff**—In this mode, the device does not actively participate in communications with other devices. Instead, the device "wakes up" and listens for messages frequently. How often this occurs depends on the particular application for which the device is used and is programmed into the device by the manufacturer. A master device can request that a slave device be put into sniff mode, but cannot force it to.

- **Park**—In this low-power mode, the device is still considered to be part of a piconet, but no longer has a MAC (Media Access Control) address associated with it. The device listens for broadcast messages and resynchronizes its clock with the master, but does not actively communicate.

These different modes are mainly designed to allow for different levels of low-power consumption for a Bluetooth-enabled device.

SCO and ACL Links

Two different kinds of links can be established between master/slave devices in the network: the Synchronous Connection-Oriented (SCO) link and the Asynchronous Connection-Less (ACL) link.

SCO Links

The SCO link is established between the master and a particular slave in the network. Reserved time slots are set aside for these links, and up to three SCO links can be used for communication between the master and one or more slaves. SCO links are suitable for voice communications because the reserved slot nature of the link makes it easy to provide a steady stream of data instead of a variable rate that could cause a voice signal to degrade.

SCO links are considered switched-circuit links and must be setup before they can be used. The frequency of the dedicated time slots and other setup information is first established before an SCO link can be used.

ACL Links

ACL links are packet-switched connections between the master and one or more slaves, and can use any of the time slots that are not currently being used for SCO links. However, only one ACL link can exist at any one time between the master in the network and a particular slave.

Bluetooth Packets

Most Bluetooth packets use a standard format that consist of three basic fields:

- **Access Code**—This is a fixed-length field of either 68 or 72 bits.
- **Header**—This is a fixed-length field of 54 bits.
- **Payload**—The payload field can range from 0–2,745 bits in length and contains the actual data portion of the packet.

The Access Code field is used for synchronization purposes and to identify a particular channel in a piconet. If the Access Code field is followed by a header field, the Access Code is 72 bits in length, otherwise it's 68 bits long. Three different kinds of Access Codes are used: The Channel Access Code (CAC), the Device Access Code (DAC), and the Inquiry Access Code.

The CAC is used to identify a particular piconet. That is, all devices in the same piconet use the same value in the Access Code field. The DAC is used during certain signaling procedures, such as paging and responses to pages. The IAC is the third type of access code, and consists of two other different kinds of access codes: The General Inquiry Access Code (GIAC) and the Dedicated Inquiry Access Code (DIAC). GIAC is used to discover other Bluetooth devices that are within range, whereas the DIAC is used by Bluetooth devices that share some common characteristic.

The Packet Header field consists of several components:

- **AM_ADDR**—This is the active member address, and is only 3 bits in length. This is why only 7 slaves can be in a single piconet, because 3 bits can be used to express an address range from 0–7 in binary notation. The address of 0 is used to broadcast packets to all slaves in a piconet. The slave's 3-bit address is used in packets that travel to and from the master/slave. The master doesn't need an address, because Bluetooth uses a point-to-point messaging service and there is only one master in the piconet.

- **Type**—This is a 4-bit field, so up to 16 packet types can be specified for either an ACL or an SCO link.

- **Flow**—This is a single-bit field used for flow control purposes on an ACL link. A value of 0 indicates that data transmissions should be stopped. When the receiving end of the communication has sufficient buffer space to begin receiving ACL packets, it sets this bit to a value of 1.

- **ARQN**—This acknowledgment indication is a 1-bit field used to acknowledge (value=0) that a packet was received successfully (that it passed the CRC check), or that it was not (value=1).

- **SEQN**—This 1-bit field is used to determine that packets are received in the correct order (sequence number), and alternates between 0 and 1.

- **HEC**—The Header Error Check field consists of an 8-bit word calculated based on a polynomial. This error checking covers only the header information.

The address field is important because it limits the number of devices that can participate actively in a piconet at any given time. The master can reuse any address when a slave goes into park mode so that a large number of devices can be used in a piconet. However, only seven can be assigned active addresses and are allowed to communicate at any point in time.

The Type field has different values depending on whether the packet is an SCO or an ACL packet. It is beyond the scope of this chapter to define all the different packet types, and indeed some are still undefined in the specification and reserved for future use. However, five packet types are commonly used:

- **ID packet**—This type of packet is used for paging, inquiry, and responses to paging and inquiries, and the packet contains the DAC or IAC value.

- **Null packet**—This packet type is made up of only the HAC and the CAC, and no payload. It is generally used to return the status of a previous transmission (the ARQN field), and the Null packet does not have to be acknowledged.

- **Poll packet**—The master can use this packet to poll slaves in the network. This packet is similar to the Null packet in that it has no payload, but slaves are required to respond to this packet even if they have no data to send at the time.

- **FHS packet**—This is the packet type discussed earlier that a slave device uses to obtain the frequency-hopping sequence of the piconet, along with other information about the piconet. This packet also contains the address the slave will use if it is joining the piconet.

- **DM1 Packet**—This type of packet is used for control messages for both the SCO and ACL link types.

A number of different packet types are defined in the Bluetooth 1.1 specification for ACL and SCO links. Refer to the documentation available at the SIG Web site for further information. The details of these packets and the ways they are used depend on the kind of Bluetooth device being considered.

One of the ways Bluetooth differs from other wireless technologies—such as Wi-Fi (IEEE 802.11b) and HomeRF—is that in addition to defining the mechanisms to grant access to the media (air waves) and provide transport (packet types), Bluetooth also defines *profiles*, which describe basic functionality for many devices that are expected to adopt this technology.

What Are Bluetooth Profiles?

Profiles are an important concept in Bluetooth technology. A *profile* is a set of specifications for how end-user functionality should be implemented. The International Organization for Standardization (OSI) developed the idea of profiles many years ago, which makes sense because OSI is, after all, in the business of standardizing technology worldwide. Many profiles exist for Bluetooth because it has a large number of possible uses. A profile defines minimal parameters for particular Bluetooth product types, but also allows vendors to enhance their products so they can differentiate it in the marketplace. Also, if a Bluetooth device implements a feature that is described by a profile, it must do so in the way the profile dictates. Because of this, the capability of Bluetooth devices that implement the same function(s) can be achieved across different vendor platforms. This doesn't mean that all features described by a profile need to be implemented by all vendors—just that they must be implemented in the same way if a particular feature is used.

Profiles aren't entirely separate entities. Instead, a layered approach is taken. The Generic Access Profile gives a basic starting point for designing Bluetooth devices, and is composed of the Service Discovery Application Profile and three other basic profiles used by other profiles:

- **The Serial Port Profile Group**—This group of profiles uses the RFCOMM for serial port emulation.
- **The Generic Object Exchange Profile Group**—The OBEX protocol is used by all profiles in this group.
- **The Telephony Control Protocol Specification Group**—The name of this profile should make its use obvious—for profiles for telephone (and intercom) devices.

The Generic Access Profile is examined first, and then the other profiles defined in the current standard are discussed briefly.

The Generic Access Profile

All Bluetooth devices must implement the Generic Access Profile. This profile can be considered a base on which the other profiles are built because it specifies functionality common to all Bluetooth devices. To summarize, this profile provides for the methods that devices use to discover other Bluetooth devices, specifies link-management techniques for establishing connections, and also provides some common formats for the user interface. This profile also defines the methods used to initially establish security mechanisms for the device, if desired and selected by the user.

The protocols used to establish and maintain links between Bluetooth devices—the Link Controller (LC) and the Link Manager Protocol (LMP)—are at the lower levels of the protocol stack. Also included are higher-level protocol elements, relating to services and security. The Logical Link Control and Adaptation Protocol (L2CAP) is above the LC portion of the protocol.

Finally, sitting above these protocols are several other protocols used by various profiles:

- Telephony Control Protocol (TCS)
- RFCOMM
- Service Discovery Protocol (SDP)

Discovery, Security, and Bonding

The LC and LMP components of the protocol stack describe how Bluetooth-enabled devices are to behave when in standby mode (anything other than the active communicating mode), and how they operate when trying to discover other Bluetooth devices and establish connections.

Bluetooth devices can operate in a number of different modes, described in the Generic Access Profile. Bonding occurs when devices that allow connections establish a link. However, a device does not have to automatically respond to requests from another device. A Bluetooth device can be in a discoverable or nondiscoverable mode. If the device is set to nondiscoverable mode, it won't respond to inquiries from other devices. The profile describes several types of discoverable and nondiscoverable modes, such as limited discoverable mode and general discovery mode. Basically, these terms define the amount of time that a device will respond or will not respond to inquiry messages from other devices.

During the discovery process, the initiator of the discovery obtains the address, clock, and class of the discovered device, as well as the name of the device.

The important thing to remember is that just because a Bluetooth device comes within range of another similarly enabled device, a connection does not automatically happen. This can be controlled by the user or the application. In addition to discoverability modes, this profile also defines bonding and pairing modes, which establish whether a connection can be made after a device is in a discoverable mode.

During the bonding procedure, the Bluetooth devices establish a link between each other and exchange a key that is stored in the device to identify the link for future data exchanges.

If a device is discoverable, and if it allows a link to be established, security mechanisms come into play. This profile defines several levels of security:

- **Security Mode 1 (nonsecure)**—This mode means that the device will not initiate any security mechanisms, such as authentication.

- **Security Mode 2 (service level enforced security)**—In this security mode, the device will not initiate any security mechanisms until after a channel-establishment procedure or request has been initiated. The service for which the device is used determines whether security mechanisms (authentication, authorization, or encryption) are used.

- **Security Mode 3 (link level enforced security)**—This mode requires the device to initiate security mechanisms before the LMP link setup procedure has completed.

Creating Connections

After devices have discovered each other and established a link, they create a channel through which applications can create a connection. Additionally, multiple applications can establish more than one connection using the same channel, or a separate channel that is created between the two. A channel is a specific radio frequency hopping sequence. As you learned earlier in this chapter, a device can be a member of one or two piconets, and thus can establish a channel on each. Applications can establish connections using the channels created between devices to exchange data.

The Service Discovery Application Profile

This profile describes the methods used by an application to discover the services of another Bluetooth device, and to obtain information about those services. This profile uses the SDP to find out what services another device offers. SDP can search for services based on the service class or service attributes. SDP also supports browsing for services to determine what is available.

The SDP process generally consists of the exchange of a series of messages defined by SDP in a connectionless mode. That is, SDP is a connectionless datagram service. Instead, SDP makes use of the Logical Link Control and Adaptation Protocol (L2CAP) portion of the protocol stack for any link establishment, as well as for tearing down the connections that might be used during an exchange of SDP protocol data units (PDUs).

The Cordless Telephony Profile and the Intercom Profile

This profile is used for Bluetooth devices that implement cordless telephony services to communicate with a base station, which is connected to a telephone network, as well as for voice connections between two Bluetooth telephone devices. Two roles are defined in this profile: gateway and terminal. A *gateway role* implies that the device acts as a base station to connect to an external telephone network. In most cases, this is a unit connected to the public switched telephone network (PSTN). However, support also is provided for other telephony connections, such as ISDN (Integrated Services Digital Network) and satellite connections that offer telephone services.

A *terminal role* describes the unit that communicates with a gateway device, or perhaps another terminal (acting more like an intercom). Because Bluetooth devices can communicate directly with each other in this role, you can eliminate cellular phone charges if you are using a Bluetooth-enabled cordless phone that is within range of another. This intercom ability is also described by the Intercom Profile, which must be supported by the Bluetooth device for this functionality to be implemented.

The L2CAP layer of the protocol stack is used to establish a connection between a terminal and a gateway when they come within range of each other. When a terminal unit is within range of a gateway device, the terminal unit is normally put into park mode, discussed earlier in this chapter. When a call needs to be sent or received, the terminal is put into active mode. The L2CAP connection does not need to be reestablished each time a call is made.

This profile also describes how services such as call setup, termination, and caller ID are performed.

The Serial Port Profile

This profile defines the use of Bluetooth devices that emulate serial port communications—such as RS232 cable connections. Most PCs have several kinds of ports you can use to connect external devices, ranging from serial ports to USB (Universal Serial Bus) ports and FireWire ports. This profile deals with the decades-old serial port type of connection. This type of port was commonly used for such things as connecting to a modem or another device to establish a communications session. For example, you can use a serial cable to create a quick connection between two PCs and exchange files using products such as LapLink or other similar programs.

The Headset Profile

The Headset Profile describes how headsets are to be implemented using Bluetooth. A headset can be used for telephone audio use, for listening to music, and a number of other similar cases. Headsets can even be used with voice-recognition software to provide input/output capabilities for a PC.

Similar to the Cordless Telephony Profile, the Headset Profile defines a gateway and a Headset device. The gateway can be a cordless telephone, a PC, or other similar device that is equipped with Bluetooth for audio communications. The Headset is the actual headset device that the user wears to provide the earphone and microphone hardware.

The profile provides for the initiation of a session by the gateway (as in the case of an incoming telephone call) or by the end user (by pressing a button on the device, for example). The connection can be terminated by either side of the connection. Provisions are also made for controlling the volume of the transmitted or received audio signal.

The Dial-Up Networking Profile

Bluetooth devices can act as an "Internet bridge" to allow you to use a cellular phone (or other device that can connect to an ISP) so that you can use a laptop or other device to communicate on the Internet. This profile also allows a computer to use a cellular phone to accept incoming digital calls. Like the Headset Profile and the Cordless Telephony Profile, this profile defines a gateway device, which is the cellular phone or possibly a modem with a cabled connection to the Internet. A Data Terminal (DT) is the device that makes use of the gateway to connect to the Internet. This profile provides for speeds up to 128Kbps, but higher speeds are optional.

The profile specifies a subset of the AT modem command set that is employed for this type of service; only one call can be established between the gateway device and a DT. That is, the DT cannot be used to establish more than one call with a gateway device at any point in time. Just as you'd need more than one telephone line if you had two modems in your computer, the DT is capable of placing only a single call through a gateway.

Other Bluetooth Profiles

In addition to the profiles discussed in this chapter, Bluetooth 1.1 specifications provide for several others. More profiles are expected to be added if the technology is accepted by the marketplace as a solution for short-distance cable replacement. Other profiles include

- **Fax Profile**—This profile allows for wireless fax services.

- **LAN Access Profile**—This profile provides for a connection to a LAN. This is similar to the functions that Wi-Fi provides using access points. The Point-to-Point (PPP) protocol is used. This profile also can be used to create a LAN consisting of only Bluetooth devices.

- **Generic Object Exchange Profile (GOEP)**—This profile borrows from the OBEX protocol and allows for the exchange of data between devices—between a cordless telephone, PDA, or a PC. It is used by the other profiles in this list.

- **Object Push Profile**—This profile uses GOEP for the exchange of simple objects, such as electronic business cards or appointment data. This profile can be used to "pull" objects as well as to push them to another device.

- **File Transfer Profile**—This profile uses GOEP to browse a file system on a remote device as well as transfer files between devices, delete files, or create new folders (directories).

- **The Synchronization Profile**—This profile uses GOEP to provide a service for synchronizing data in various kinds of databases: for example, calendars, address books, and Personal Information Managers (PIMs).

Bluetooth Is More than a Wireless Communication Protocol

As you can see, Bluetooth is not just a protocol used to exchange data between devices. The use of profiles further delineates the different kinds of applications that can be used with Bluetooth radio transmitters and thus makes it easier for manufacturers to produce portable devices that have applications built in and ready for use. You can contrast this with Wi-Fi and HomeRF, which simply provide the communications link just as traditional LAN or WAN protocols provide. Bluetooth provides both the radio frequency transport mechanisms and application-specific solutions that make interoperability between devices easy to implement.

The Wireless Application Protocol (WAP)

CHAPTER 16

The two previous chapters looked at wireless networking solutions developed to meet the needs of local area networking (Chapter 14, "Wireless Networking: IEEE 802.11 (Wi-Fi) and HomeRF"), and personal area networking (Chapter 15, "What Is Bluetooth?"). Chapter 14 addresses wireless solutions to provide for networking capabilities similar to that achieved from a cabled LAN, such as using wireless network adapters to create or communicate with a LAN. Chapter 15 examined the Bluetooth technology, which provides for both a wireless transport mechanism, as well as profiles that describe how certain features should be implemented to ensure interoperability for products from different vendors. Although Bluetooth technology includes a profile for cordless telephony, the distances covered by a Bluetooth network range from only 10 to 100 meters.

This chapter looks at the Wireless Application Protocol (WAP), which is similar in many ways to Bluetooth, in that it consists of several protocols that allow handheld mobile phones, PDAs, and other small devices to communicate with other networks. However, although Bluetooth specifications define the actual signaling methods used to transport data between devices, WAP was developed to allow layering of different protocols and services on top of existing cellular phone technologies that cover much wider distances. WAP also consists of protocols that enable these handheld devices to act much like Web browsers used in a traditional network, although on a lightweight basis.

Architecture of the Wireless Application Protocol

Many kinds of on-air transmission protocols are used today to provide cellular telephone service. The term used for these different technologies is *bearer services*. In Figure 16.1, you can see that the architectural model of WAP sits on top of the bearer services.

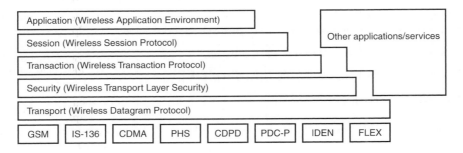

Figure 16.1 The architectural model of WAP consists of multiple layers.

The bearer services shown in Figure 16.1 are supported by the current specifications, but this list is expected to expand as newer technologies are developed. For example, Global System for Mobile (GSM) communication is a digital telephone system widely used in Europe. Code Division Multiple Access (CDMA) applies to several protocols called second-generation (2G) and third-generation (3G) wireless communications. Note in Figure 16.1, that the first layer of the WAP is the Wireless Datagram Protocol (WDP), which supplies transport services to the upper layers by acting as an interface between them and the actual underlying technology that transmits the data using the available radio frequency spectrum.

So, like TCP/IP (Transmission Control Protocol/Internet Protocol), WAP provides a layered approach that allows applications and services to be carried on a wide range of physical transport protocols. You can run TCP/IP on token-ring networks, or more commonly on ethernet. The WDP layer in the WAP architecture similarly allows for applications and services to be coded without having to worry about the physical technology used for the actual transport of data.

As in the Open System Interconnection (OSI) networking model, the WAP architectural model layers each provide services to layers above and below. In addition, you can see off to the right side of the model that other services and applications are allowed to bypass any of these layers and communicate with lower layers, down to the WDP transport layer.

Following is a short description of the functions performed by each layer in the model:

■ **Wireless Datagram Protocol (WDP)**—As described previously, this is the transport layer that interfaces with the various cellular phone technologies in use today. By providing a common interface to the layers above, it is not necessary to write a separate application interface for each of the bearer services. Instead, as new bearer services are brought into the fold, it's only necessary to write code that will interface with WDP.

■ **Wireless Transport Layer Security (WTLS)**—This layer provides security for WAP and is based on the Transport Layer Security (TLS) protocol, which was originally called the Secure Sockets Layer (SSL). TLS has been adapted to the needs of the limited bandwidth that bearer services provide and provides a compact version for use with WAP. WTLS provides for data integrity, privacy, authentication, and to some degree, protection against denial-of-service attacks.

■ **Wireless Transaction Protocol (WTP)**—This layer provides transaction services for WAP applications. The three classes of service include unreliable one-way requests, reliable one-way requests, and reliable two-way request-reply transactions. The protocol also allows for optional components such as out-of-band data acknowledgements and concatenation of protocol data units (PDUs) to lower the actual number of packets or messages exchanged. An example of a transaction is a user browsing the Web and requesting a certain Web page to be displayed. The request is sent to the server and the response is the Web page returned to the client.

■ **Wireless Session Protocol (WSP)**—This layer provides the layer above it (the Application layer) with two services. The first is a connection-oriented service that operates with WTP, and the second is a connectionless service that operates using WDP. These services are similar to TCP (Transmission Control Protocol) (connection-oriented) and UDP (User Datagram Protocol) (connectionless), both of which are discussed in detail in Chapter 20, "Overview of the TCP/IP Protocol Suite."

■ **Wireless Application Environment (WAE)**—The top layer in the model provides application services and is based on several existing protocols. For example, it borrows from HTML, JavaScript, and other similar protocols that are currently used on the Internet. It also provides for standard content formats, such as phone book and calendar information records.

This architectural model helps guide developers in creating applications and devices that incorporate WAP. WAP-enabled cellular phones, for example, now can be used with mini-browsers to perform limited browsing on the Internet. Of course, because of the small screen size and lack of color in most cellular phones and small handheld mobile devices, you can't expect to get the same view or capability that you would using a laptop or a PC. Indeed, WAP provides the capability to interact with the Internet using dedicated servers designed for WAP, as well as through gateways that can be used to access traditional Web sites.

Gateways and the World Wide Web

Text messaging was one of the first applications incorporated into cellular phones to enhance their telephony component. WAP extends this to allow for Web browsing. Because the screen size of a mobile device is not going to match the screen size usually found on a PC, it's necessary to perform some translation of the usual HTML code so that it can be displayed on the mobile device in a more limited manner. You can see an example of how this is done using a gateway in Figure 16.2.

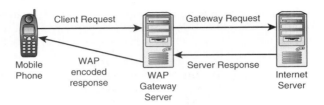

Figure 16.2 A gateway can be used to translate mobile client Internet browsing requests to and from the Internet.

You can see that a gateway operates much like a proxy server and stands between the mobile user and the Web server. WAP uses several components that act in a manner similar to those used on the Internet. For example, the standard Web URL (Uniform Resource Locator) is used to identify content suitable for WAP browsers. Similarly, standard URIs (Uniform Resource Identifiers) are used to identify WAP resources on a server.

Note

Although most people have heard the term URL, many are not familiar with what it really is, much less the term URI. URI originally stood for Universal Resource Identifier, as described in RFC 1630, "Universal Resource Identifiers in WWW." Actually, a URL is itself a URI, of which there are many types. For those interested in Internet history and trivia, in RFC 2396, the term was changed to "Uniform Resource Identifiers."

WAP gateways translate requests from WSP, WTP, WTLS, and WDP to and from the WWW protocol stack, which is composed of HTML and TCP/IP. In addition, WAP provides content encoders and decoders that reduce the size of the data that needs to be transmitted between the mini-browser and the Internet. This also helps minimize the computational power needed on the client to interpret data. Note that the Web server can provide content based on normal HTML coding standards, or can be specially coded for use with WAP devices. When browsing standard HTML pages, the gateway provides a filter that translates the HTML content into something more suitable for display on a WAP browser. For content that is coded specifically for WAP browsers, the gateway translates the packets received via TCP/IP into a more compact form for transmission on the limited bandwidth provided by the mobile device's bearer service. The Wireless Markup Language (WML) is the WAP equivalent of HTML and is used for coding Web content specifically targeted for WAP devices.

In addition, as you can see in Figure 16.3, it also is possible for WAP-enabled devices to communicate directly with a Wireless Telephony Application server (WTA), which is used to allow the device to interact with services offered by the telecommunications provider itself.

In an effort to further develop WAP, the Wireless Application Environment (WAE) Specification documents make up the application portion of WAP. The WAE documents are intended to incorporate, with modifications, parts of other standards, to make WAP-enabled devices more compatible with the Internet and with telephony applications. Some of the specifications that fall under WAE include

- Wireless Markup Language (WML)
- WAP Binary XML Format Language (WBXML)
- WMLScript
- WMLScript Standard Libraries (WMLStdLib)
- Wireless Telephony Application (WTA)
- Wireless Telephony Application Interface (WTAI)

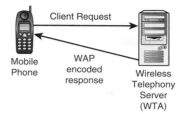

Figure 16.3 Telecommunication providers can use WTA servers to provide services to WAP clients.

On the mobile client, user *agents* are responsible for interpreting the content received from the Internet. An Internet browser is an example of a WAE user agent. The user agent sends a request to the Internet using the keys or buttons available on the mobile device, and the user agent receives the content, interprets it, and displays it on the user's screen, or performs some action specified by the message received.

The Wireless Markup Language (WML)

Like HTML, WML is a markup language based on tags. If you've ever viewed the source of a Web page, you know that HTML is composed of sets of tags enclosed in angle brackets (<>) that are used to interpret the text that follows. WML is based on a subset of the Handheld Device Markup Language (HDML) version 2.0. However, WML also borrows from HTML. Even so, the terminology used for WML might sound rather strange when you first hear it because it's a technology based on cards and decks. A *card* is similar to a Web page, whereas a *deck* is a collection of cards (as in a deck of playing cards). The user interacts with a set of cards. In a manner similar to using links on an HTML page, a user navigates through a deck of cards by entering information on the handheld device that causes another card to be displayed. Like HTML, instructions can be embedded in cards that cause a service or application on the server to perform some action, and some cards can be dynamically generated.

Because a wide variety of mobile devices must be assumed, the specification allows a card to be displayed in its entirety, provided the device has a large enough screen, or to be displayed in small sections suitable for the mobile device's display. A variety of methods can be used for inputting information, from pushing buttons on the mobile device to voice.

Presenting Text and Images

Because it isn't possible to detect the type of display any particular device might use, WML enables coders to specify how images are displayed in general terms. The application running on the mobile device has greater latitude in deciding how to display the text or image for the display it controls. Standard markup language tags are included, such as setting a character style (bold, italic, size, and so on), breaking lines, and setting tabs.

User Input

WML uses several methods for input from the user of the mobile device. A text-entry control allows the input of simple text, such as a username and password. Controls can be set on fields to help limit the type of entry so that the user is limited to entering information appropriate for the field (that is, numeric versus alphanumeric, and so on). Option-selection controls allow the programmer to present the user with a list of options. These can be used to select from a set of choices, to navigate through a deck of cards, or to invoke script files on the server that can dynamically generate new cards or perform other actions on behalf of the user. Navigation controls work similarly to embedded links for HTML. The user can navigate to a new card or to a different section of the current card.

The character set used for WML is the Universal Character Set (Unicode 2.0), but the WML decks do not have to implement the full set of characters, only subsets needed for the application at hand.

The WBXML is a binary form used to transmit Web content to handheld devices in a more compact format than using ordinary text files. Because the narrow bandwidth used by bearer protocols is limited, compiling content from WML into a binary-encoded format means much less data is actually transmitted.

The WMLScript Specification

WMLScript is a lightweight scripting language based on JavaScript, but it also contains additions to the subset of elements borrowed from JavaScript that are appropriate for handheld devices. In addition, the scripting language allows some actions to be performed on the mobile device, such as checking the validity of user input before it is returned to the server. This helps reduce the need for multiple transmissions that would be necessary if all scripting functions were done on the server.

To make better use of the narrow-band communications channel, WMLScript can be compiled into an efficient bytecode that is sent to the client, avoiding the transfer of large amounts of text. *Bytecode* is a method for encoding instructions and operands using smaller data units that can be interpreted by the end device.

WMLScript does not enforce variable definitions as tightly as most programming languages. That is, although WMLScript supports the data types of boolean, integer, floating point, string, and invalid, it is possible for the type of a variable to change during execution of a script, helping to keep down the amount of code needed.

Several standard code libraries also are supported, which make calling routine functions easy. This reduces the amount of code that would have to be written to create many programs. Instead of using several lines of code, a library routine built into the device can be called instead, using much less code. Standard libraries supported by most devices include a language library, string library, browser library, floating-point library, and a dialog library. Optionally, a cryptographic library function also is supported, but not required by the language.

The Wireless Telephony Application Specification (WTA)

The WTA protocol gives the mobile device the capability to include standard telephony functions, such as call forwarding, in WML documents or WMLScripts. The WTA agent on the mobile device uses the WTAI to intercept mobile network functions and can interact with the WAE user agent to bind certain functions to WML content. A library of functions is available to the WAE agent so that it can perform some telephony functions, such as placing a telephone call.

A *repository* on the device is a small amount of memory that can be used by the WTA agent to store frequently used services. This eliminates the need to use valuable bandwidth to download services that often are used.

Calendar and Phone Book Information

Again, to avoid having to create a new standard, WAP incorporates the standard vCard and vCalendar formats that are used to exchange business card, phone book, and calendar information between electronic devices. You can learn more about vCard and vCalendar specifications, as well as other personal data exchange mechanisms, by visiting the Web site of the International Mail Consortium at http://www.imc.org/. vCard and vCalendar exchanges are not limited to handheld devices, but also can be used with many e-mail and personal organizer programs found on ordinary desktop PCs.

The WAP Forum

This chapter is intended only to give you a quick overview of the current state of WAP capabilities. Because this technology is still in its infancy, standards and proposals are changing at a rapid pace, as are the capabilities of the handheld mobile devices that will incorporate WAP into their functionality. What was once just a cell phone is quickly becoming a communications terminal that will be able to run applications, browse the Web, set up appointments and reminders, and, of course, make telephone calls. Although the Internet is expanding at a rapid pace and new technologies are being developed, protocol standards such as TCP/IP and HTML have matured to a state that makes it easy to build applications and tools that easily can work together. For wireless networking, this is not yet the case.

The WAP Forum is an industry group that was formed to develop a wireless standard that could be used to provide services other than simple voice or standard telephony services to digital mobile phones and other small terminal devices, such as personal digital assistants (PDAs). You can visit the WAP Forum Web site at `http://www.wapforum.org` to learn more about this organization and download specification documents that are briefly described in this chapter. If you plan to invest in this form of wireless networking, you should visit this site often to stay informed of new developments.

Fiber Distributed Data Interface (FDDI)

SOME OF THE MAIN TOPICS IN THIS CHAPTER ARE

FDDI Dual-Ring Topology

FDDI Protocol Standards

Transmitting Data on an FDDI Ring

Common Problems Using FDDI

FDDI stands for *Fiber Distributed Data Interface*. Work was started on FDDI in the early 1980s to provide a reliable, high-speed method of networking to connect the faster workstations and computers that were becoming available that time. Although ethernet and token-ring networks were operating at that time at maximum speeds of 10Mbps, FDDI was designed to provide a 100Mbps bandwidth, which was a substantial increase of existing technologies at that time. Because of the more recent development of other high-speed networking technologies (such as Fast Ethernet and Gigabit Ethernet) and protocols that provide better control and quality of service (such as Frame Relay and ATM), and usually a higher cost, basic FDDI is not as popular as it once was.

However, when used for the backbone in a network, FDDI can still be a viable option for the network administrator to consider. The technology is a mature one, and you can find a large number of vendors and installers for FDDI. When adding a new building to an existing network that already contains FDDI segments, it might be more cost-effective to use FDDI than to incorporate newer technologies. If you are planning a complete overhaul of your network or are in the process of building a new one from scratch, then the upgrade path for newer networking techniques, such as Gigabit Ethernet, might be a better choice.

Note

To compare FDDI with Fast and Gigabit Ethernet, see Chapter 12, "Ethernet." If you need a more deterministic local area network technology, see Chapter 13, "Token-Ring Networks."

An important feature that can make FDDI an attractive networking solution is the security features inherent in using optical fiber as a network medium. Unlike topologies based on copper wire cables, optical fiber has no electrical properties and emits no signals that can be detected outside the cable.

In this chapter, we will look at the components that make up the FDDI protocol and the methods used to transmit data and perform maintenance functions on an FDDI ring, and examine some typical configurations.

FDDI Dual-Ring Topology

Two of the main goals for FDDI during its development were speed and reliability. Optical fiber was selected as the network transmission medium because of its capability to transmit data at high speeds. The topology chosen was the ring topology, similar to token-ring networks. However, to provide enhanced reliability, a dual-ring topology was developed that uses two rings that transmit data in opposite directions (counter-rotating rings). Figure 17.1 shows the layout of a simple FDDI dual ring.

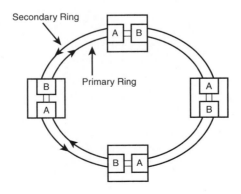

Figure 17.1   FDDI uses the dual counter-rotating ring topology.

By using a dual-ring topology, with one ring operating as the primary ring and the other as a secondary back-up ring, a simple failure of one fiber cable segment is less likely to cause disruption of the entire network. You can see that each station on the ring in Figure 17.1 has two ports, labeled A and B, which connect it to the ring. At first glance it might appear that one port is used for each ring. However, that is not the case. Instead, on the primary ring the A port receives data from its neighbor, which is transmitting the signal on its B port. On the back-up secondary ring, the A port transmits data to its neighbor in the opposite direction and the neighbor receives the data on its B port.

Ports and Stations

The first example of a simple FDDI ring that we looked at consists of stations that have two ports, labeled A and B. This kind of station is called a *dual-attached station*. This topology is called a *dual-attached ring*. Other ports that you might find on a FDDI network are

- M or *master* port
- S or *slave* port

These ports enable you to connect other kinds of stations to the FDDI ring, specifically a concentrator or a *single-attached station* (SAS). Single-attached stations do not have an A or B port, but instead have a slave port. In this case, the SAS is not directly attached to the dual ring but is connected through a master port on a concentrator. In Figure 17.2, you can see an example of a concentrator that consists of both A, B, and master ports. The master ports are used to connect multiple workstations to the ring through their slave ports.

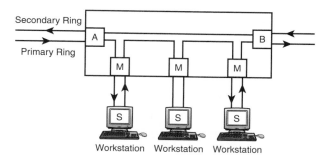

Figure 17.2 Concentrators can be used to connect single-attached stations to an FDDI ring.

Using this concentrator-based ring topology can aid in reducing network outages due to problems with workstations attached to the ring. The concentrator can act in a manner similar to the ethernet hub or token-ring MSAU and isolate individual workstations that fail, preventing them from causing problems for other nodes in the ring. For dual-attached stations, however, even a simple power-down of the unit can cause problems because the node, which is powered off, no longer is capable of receiving or retransmitting data, causing a break in the ring.

Ring Wrap

The *dual-ring* topology allows FDDI to heal itself when faced with simple failures of one node. When a station fails or if a cable between two stations is damaged, other stations detect the failure and the ring is automatically wrapped back onto itself to form a single ring. Figure 17.3 shows four network nodes (dual-attached stations) operating normally in a dual-ring topology.

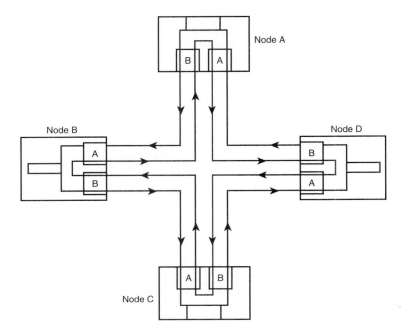

Figure 17.3   During normal operation, FDDI uses a dual-ring topology with one ring serving as the primary network medium.

In Figure 17.4, you can see what happens when a single node on the ring fails. Here Node C has failed and no longer participates in ring communications. Instead, Nodes B and D have internally wrapped the ring back onto itself. That is, the cable that was used for the secondary ring has been joined in these nodes to the primary ring, creating a single ring consisting of Nodes A, B, and D.

This self-repair method works well when only one node on the ring has failed. If more than one node fails, ring-wrapping can result in two or more separate rings. For this reason, it is preferable to use concentrators to join individual workstations to a ring rather than make each workstation or PC a dual-attached station. The concentrator itself becomes a single point of failure, and if it fails it can take down all workstations connected to it. However, because even something as simple as powering down a workstation that is dual-attached can cause a break in the ring, it is generally more likely that a workstation or PC will be the point of failure rather than a concentrator that is safely tucked away in a wiring closet.

Another consideration to think about is that, because ring wrapping increases the actual distance it takes for information to travel around the ring, you must plan the maximum size of the ring accordingly. In a large LAN it would be impractical to size the ring to be able to accommodate a large number of failures. However, for a ring that is rated as a highly available network you should plan to limit the maximum size to account for at least two to four simultaneous failures.

Optical Bypass Switches

Another device you can use to help prevent ring failures is called an *optical bypass switch*. This device can prevent ring-wrap from happening if the station that is attached to it fails. This is accomplished in the bypass switch by an optical relay that causes the signal to bypass the failed station and continue on to its neighbor in the ring. However, these kinds of switches are expensive and result in a small amount of signal loss. Using them for each station on a large ring can cause signal degradation that can make network performance suffer noticeably. You might balance the cost of this kind of switch against the amount of allowable down time you can have in your network. For networks that can tolerate very little down time (such as a financial institution), the cost of the switch will be minimal compared to the cost of the down time necessary to repair the ring.

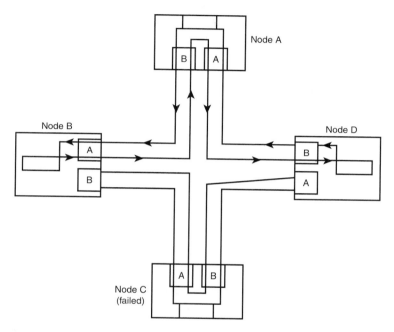

Figure 17.4 When a node on the ring fails, the Media Access Control layer forms a single ring to isolate the malfunctioning node so that the other nodes can continue to operate.

Dual-Homing Important Devices

Some network nodes usually are considered to be more important than others. For example, a user might think that his or her workstation is the most important device on the network, but the failure of a router or file server that also is attached to the local ring can cause more than one user to be affected. Important devices can be made less susceptible to network failure by a technique called *dual-homing*. In this situation, an important device is attached to two separate concentrators that are then attached to the ring. Only one of the links is active, while the other acts as a standby. If the active connection made to the first concentrator becomes unavailable, the device can then use the secondary connection to continue operations.

FDDI Protocol Standards

FDDI is defined by standards from the American National Standard Institute (ANSI) and the International Organization for Standardization (ISO). The four key components of FDDI are as follows:

- Media Access Control (MAC) layer
- Physical (PHY) layer

- Physical Media Dependent (PMD) layer
- Station Management (SMT) protocol

The MAC layer interfaces with higher-level protocols, such as TCP/IP, and passes their protocol data units (PDUs) to the PHY layer after repackaging them into packets of as many as 4,500 bytes. Other functions performed by the MAC layer are addressing, scheduling, and routing. The MAC specification defines the frame format and takes care of error recovery. It also is responsible for calculating the CRC value and token-handling procedures.

The PHY layer is responsible for actually encoding and decoding the packet data into the format used by the transmission media. The method used for encoding is called *4B/5B* encoding, which means that four bits of information are encoded into 5-bit groups. This encoding technique is used to ensure that under normal circumstances the bit stream that is transmitted by FDDI will never contain four zero bits in a row, which is important from a timing standpoint. FDDI has no active monitor like a token-ring network, and each station has its own clock and must be able to synchronize with other stations.

Although we normally think of 8-bit values (a byte) when encoding data, the 4B/5B technique concentrates on units of only four bits in length. The 4B/5B technique uses data symbols to represent the actual data that is being transmitted (labeled 0–9 and A–F), and eight control symbols used for things such as indicating the state of the link (symbols I, H, and Q) or as frame delimiters (symbols J, K, and T), among other things.

Table 17.1 shows the symbols used for data, along with the actual binary value each symbol represents. The last column shows the actual bits transmitted for this symbol on the FDDI ring.

Table 17.1   4B/5B Encoding Values for Data Symbols

Actual Binary Value	Symbol Name	Symbol Bits
0000	0	11110
0001	1	01001
0010	2	10100
0011	3	10101
0100	4	01010
0101	5	01011
0110	6	01110
0111	7	01111
1000	8	10010
1001	9	10011
1010	A	10110
1011	B	10111
1100	C	11010
1101	D	11011
1110	E	11100
1111	F	11101

As you can see, a binary value of 0000 would be transmitted as 11110, while the binary value of 1111 would be transmitted as 11101. In the actual bits transmitted, no symbol contains more than two zeros in a row, so when combined with other symbols the bit stream will not contain more than four zeros in a row.

The PMD layer does the actual physical signaling on the transmission media, which is fiber-optic cable for FDDI. To make it easier to attach common devices such as PCs and workstations to an FDDI network, the CDDI (Copper Distributed Data Interface) specification allows the PMD layer to also transmit data using copper wires as the network medium.

The SMT protocol is the component that is responsible for managing the ring. Similar to token-ring networks, SMT functions include neighbor identification, detection of faults, and reconfiguration of the ring due to faults or insertion or removal of a station from the ring.

FDDI can extend for up to 100Km when using multimode fiber, with stations being up to 2Km from each other. When using single-mode fiber, stations can be up to 20Km in distance from each other. The maximum number of stations on the ring is 500.

Transmitting Data on an FDDI Ring

The method used by FDDI to transmit information across optical fiber is light. Two kinds of fiber optic cables can be used; they are classified as either *Single mode* or *Multimode*. Single-mode fiber uses a laser as its source of light and can be used over longer distances than Multimode fiber. Multimode fiber cables allow multiple rays of light, entering the cable at different angles, to carry signals through the cable and use a light-emitting diode (LED) as their light source.

Caution

Remember that when you're dealing with lasers, don't look directly at the light emitted from the end of a cable! Doing this can cause permanent damage to your eyesight!

Using Light to Encode Bits

A station on the ring looks at the state of the light beam on the fiber about every eight nanoseconds. The only possibilities are that the station will either sense that light is present or that it is not. To determine whether a zero or a one is being sent, the station will compare the current sampling with the one immediately before it. If the state of the fiber has changed—that is, it has gone from no light detected to light detected, or vice versa—it is determined that a bit representing a one has been transmitted. If no change between this sampling period and the one immediately previous to it is detected, a zero bit has been transmitted. This technique for signaling is known as *nonreturn to zero with inversion (NRZI)* modulation.

FDDI Frames

FDDI frames are similar to token-ring frames. A token frame (shown in Figure 17.5) is passed from one station in the ring to the next. When a station on the ring has data that it needs to transmit, it seizes the token, adds addressing information and data to the frame, and then transmits the data frame (see Figure 17.6).

Preamble	Start Delimiter	Frame Control	End Delimiter

Figure 17.5   The token frame is used to mediate access to the ring.

Preamble	Start Delimiter	Frame Control	Destination Address	Source Address	Data	FCS	End Delimiter	Frame Status

Figure 17.6   The data frame contains the same fields as the token frame, but addressing information and data also are included.

The fields that appear in Figures 17.5 and 17.6 are used for the following functions:

- **Preamble**—This field indicates that a frame is arriving at the station so that the adapter can prepare to receive it.
- **Start Delimiter**—Designates the start of the frame.
- **Frame Control**—Specifies the size of the address fields and other control information.
- **Destination address**—The 6-byte address of the destination of the frame. This also can be a multicast address such as a broadcast or group address.
- **Source address**—This field contains the 6-byte address of the station that originated the data frame.
- **Data**—Control information or data that is destined for a higher-level protocol, such as TCP/IP.
- **Frame check sequence (FCS)**—A 32-bit CRC value used to check the integrity of the frame when it arrives at its destination.
- **End delimiter**—Designates the end of the frame.
- **Frame status**—Contains bits used to indicate errors, address recognized, and frame copied.

The token frame is passed around the ring in an orderly fashion. When a node on the ring wants to transmit data, it grabs the token. That is, instead of retransmitting the token frame to its neighbor, it transmits one or more data frames. Data frames can be used to send information that is destined for a higher-level protocol, or it can control information used in ring maintenance procedures.

Some of the more important FDDI management frames are as follows:

- **Neighbor Information Frame (NIF)**—This frame is sent around the ring periodically (usually from 2–30 seconds) and is used to exchange information about stations and their neighbors on the ring.
- **Status Information Frame (SIF)**—This frame gives stations configuration information and operation information stored in a *MIB (Management Information Base)*.
- **Parameter Management Frame**—This frame is used to read information from, or write information to, the MIB.
- **Status Report Frame**—Uses a multicast address and is used to give status information to management applications.

The Target Token Rotation Timer and the Claim Process

When the ring is first initialized, the Target Token Rotation Time (TTRT) is determined. After this is done, the nodes participating in the ring must decide which one will generate the first token frame. The selection process is done using the following steps:

1. The Token Rotation Timer (TRT) is initially set to the TTRT value.
2. If the TRT expires before a station receives a token, it assumes that some kind of error has occurred and it starts the claim process.

3. During this process, the stations also negotiate to determine which one will be responsible for generating the first token on the ring. Each station is assigned a value for TTRT. During the claim process, each station compares the value for TTRT that was set by the previous station in the ring.

4. If the TTRT it receives from its neighbor is longer than its own value, it substitutes its own value and retransmits the claim frame.

5. If the received TTRT value is shorter than its own, it retransmits the frame. If its value is the same as that which it receives from its neighbor, the station with the highest address wins.

6. When a station receives the claim frame back and recognizes that it is the winner, it sets the TTRT for the ring and generates the first token.

After normal operations begin, each node on the ring monitors the ring and frames passing around to check for errors.

When a station transmits a data frame, the frame travels around the ring and is read by each node and retransmitted to the next node on the ring. When a node recognizes itself as the destination address of the frame, it copies the address to a buffer and sets the address recognized and frame copied bits in the Frame Status field before retransmitting it. When the frame arrives back at the station from which it was originally generated, the station can determine whether the frame was received by checking these bits. If the error bit is set, it can take actions to resend the data.

When a station begins to transmit frames on the ring, it can continue to do so for as long as the rules negotiated with other stations allow. This time monitored at each station by a timer is called the *Token Holding Timer*.

Beaconing

When a station on the ring fails to receive a frame (either token or data) from its neighbor, it begins the beaconing process by transmitting a beacon frame. Each station in the ring retransmits the beacon frame to the next station in the ring. If the beacon frame travels around the ring back to the station where it originated, the station stops transmitting beacon frames because it assumes that the fault has been repaired.

If it does not receive the beacon frame back after about 10 seconds, it will start a trace process. During this process the station uses the secondary ring instead of the primary ring to communicate with its upstream neighbor. Both nodes remove themselves from the ring and test the connections between them. If no fault is found, both stations rejoin the ring. If one of the stations encounters an error, it stays out of the ring and the other station performs the ring-wrap function so that other nodes on the ring can continue to operate.

Common Problems Using FDDI

Although FDDI rings perform some basic maintenance functions to help take care of problems, it is still necessary to monitor the LAN periodically to ensure that the network is operating optimally. Also, many problems can't be corrected by software, such as faulty network adapters or network cables. Tools you can use for monitoring and troubleshooting efforts include a cable tester (one intended for use with fiber-optic cable) and a standard LAN protocol analyzer. Most FDDI vendors also will provide a station management application that can be used to examine ring functionality and gather statistics and error information. It is a good idea to get a thorough understanding of station management software so that you are better prepared when problems occur.

Ring Wrapping

This process allows for a malfunctioning node to be isolated from the other nodes in the ring. To restore the ring to normal functioning, it is necessary to track down the offending node and determine the cause of the failure. Station management software can provide the information you need to determine which station has left the ring. Perhaps the most common reason why ring wrapping occurs is a simple power failure. This can result from a faulty power supply in one of the attached workstations, or perhaps in a concentrator on the ring. It also can result from human error when someone who doesn't understand how the ring operates mistakenly powers down a station.

Other possible causes include all the associated hardware, from the cable to the connectors to the interface card that is installed in the workstation. Be sure to check that all connectors are correctly fastened and are not loose. Check for crushed or otherwise damaged cables. Fiber-optic cable is not as forgiving as twisted-pair can be, so it should be handled with care.

If all else fails, check the interface card on the computer. Use the vendor-supplied diagnostic software to determine whether the card is in good working order. If the card passes all the vendor's tests, try using it in a different slot on the computer bus or swapping it out for a card that is known to be working at this time.

Ring Initializations and Frame Check Sequence (FCS) Errors

Errors in the transmission of bits (causing FCS errors) or a high number of ring initializations (beacon or claim frames) can indicate problems with the light signal strength. It is easy to introduce dust, fingerprints, or other obstacles to the light signal when handling connectors. Connectors that are not tightly fastened also can lead to problems with the quality of the light signal and promote these kinds of errors. A cable tester designed for fiber-optic cabling can be used to test the signal strength for each segment.

Exceeding the maximum distance specifications for FDDI also can cause problems resulting in FCS errors or frequent ring initializations. Although a ring might be able to continue functioning if a single node is removed from the ring through ring wrapping, the removal of more than one can cause the total distance through the ring to be in excess of the specifications, resulting in a poor signal. If you are using optical bypass switches to help prevent ring-wrapping you can still experience these problems, because each optical bypass switch can introduce a two-decibel reduction in the signal strength.

Although not as common, a aulty network interface card or port on a concentrator might be the cause of these problems. Other possible sources that can affect signal quality include low-quality fiber-optic cable and imperfect splices in the cable. You can track down a faulty network adapter using the station management software or by using a LAN analyzer and looking for the station that is starting the claim process. Look at this station's upstream neighbor to find out whether a faulty card is causing the problem.

Making Repairs

Fiber-optic cabling is more expensive than copper wire cabling and requires a skilled technician for installation and repairs. A network administrator can easily perform tasks such as replacing a network adapter or moving a node to a different port on a concentrator. However, someone who is well trained in the techniques should splice fiber-optic cables or attach connectors. For all but large shops this usually means using an outside vendor or contractor.

▶▶   In Chapter 44, "Network Testing and Analysis Tools," you will find more information about instruments that can be used to test fiber-optic cables and to perform LAN analysis functions on an FDDI network.

In addition, with the introduction of obstructions such as dust or fingerprints, the light signal also can become degraded due to incorrect polishing when the cable is cut and attached to a connector. This doesn't mean that you cannot make such repairs yourself. If the size of the network warrants the expense, purchasing the tools and training an employee in the necessary techniques might be appropriate.

Dial-Up Connections

SOME OF THE MAIN TOPICS IN THIS CHAPTER ARE

The Point-to Point Protocol (PPP) and the Serial Line Internet Protocol (SLIP)

SLIP

PPP

An Example: Configuring a Windows 2000 Professional Client

When Dial-Up Isn't Fast Enough

CHAPTER 18

If you operate a large corporate network, you might be tempted to skip this chapter. After all, you probably have one or more routers/firewalls and other devices connecting your corporate network to the Internet using a large dedicated data pipe, such as ATM (Asynchronous Transfer Mode) or frame-relay switch. However, if you have workers on the move, or employees who work from home, about the only way they can connect to your network is by using a dial-up modem or a broadband Internet connection. The former is more likely the case because broadband connections, which are discussed in the next chapter, although quite popular, do not have nearly the user base of traditional dial-ups.

If you have home workers or those on the go using a modem to dial in and establish a connection to your network or into the Internet, this chapter serves as a good introduction to the two main dial-up protocols used for this purpose: PPP and SLIP.

Note

This chapter covers the basics of typical dial-up connection to the Internet. However, remember that in the case of a dial-up connection, and sending e-mail or other files to and from the Internet, the payload in your network packets are sent out on the Internet where it is possible for someone to intercept your data.

▶▶ If you plan to use the Internet or some other wide area network (WAN) service provider to connect remote users, read Chapter 41, "Virtual Private Networks (VPNs) and Tunneling."

The Point-to Point Protocol (PPP) and the Serial Line Internet Protocol (SLIP)

Communication on the Internet is based on the TCP/IP suite. TCP/IP is covered in detail in Chapter 20, "Overview of the TCP/IP Protocol Suite"; other services, applications, and tools designed to work with TCP/IP are discussed in Chapters 21, "TCP/IP Services and Applications," 22, "Troubleshooting Tools for TCP/IP Networks," and 23, "BOOTP and the Dynamic Host Configuration Protocol (DHCP)." Although TCP/IP is a great LAN/WAN networking solution, it does not provide for dial-up connections. A *dial-up connection* is a point-to-point link using a phone line. Because of this, a router or server on the remote network will be your connection point to that network using a modem. The remote access server at the Internet service provider (ISP, or maybe your corporate dial-in modem bank) creates point-to-point connections with dial-in clients.

This connection needs a method for sending IP or other protocols across this point-to-point connection (where addressing doesn't matter because the conversation only has two parties) transparently to the actual network transport protocol. The Serial Line Internet Protocol (SLIP) was the first widely adopted protocol, and was initially found mainly on Unix systems. However, many operating systems today still support SLIP, although far fewer use it when compared to PPP. The Point-to-Point Protocol (PPP) is more robust and has generally replaced SLIP in all but the most unique cases during the past few years. PPP makes up for many of the shortcomings of SLIP.

The important thing to remember about both of these protocols is that they are nonroutable. Instead of using up valuable bandwidth for information about network and host addressing, a point-to-point connection doesn't need addresses because only two endpoints exist in this kind of transport. Instead, the next two sections deal with SLIP and PPP, which merely encapsulate other protocols for transfer across this direct link between two machines.

Note

Encapsulate is a networking term that means a particular protocol is carrying, in its payload section, another packet generated by a different protocol. SLIP is one of the simplest of the protocols developed for this purpose, using only two characters to successfully transmit other protocols across a point-to-point connection. PPP is more complicated, adding its own protocol header information to the packet (and stripping it off at the other endpoint), to make communications a little more flexible and reliable.

SLIP

For some time, SLIP was a de-facto standard in the Unix community as a means for establishing a point-to-point connection between two computers. It was finally documented in RFC 1055, "A Nonstandard For Transmission of IP Datagrams Over Serial Lines: SLIP" in 1988. Yes, you read that right—a nonstandard. Although there are standards for IP, there is no standard for SLIP, which concisely defines the protocol. For example, the last two characters of the acronym stand for Internet Protocol. Yet SLIP can be used for encapsulating and transmitting just about any kind of protocol packet across a point-to-point link. It is such a simple protocol that it's easy to send many higher-level protocols across a SLIP data connection. Even Microsoft supports SLIP, although in the last few years as a client, not as a SLIP server.

SLIP has been implemented many ways, using different packet sizes, but the basic protocol consists of using two special characters:

- **END**—This character (decimal value of 192) is used to delineate the end of a packet.
- **ESC**—Not to be confused with the ASCII character set escape character, the SLIP ESC character (decimal value of 219) is used when a character in a packet is the same as the END character. In such a case, the character is "escaped" by prefixing the ESC character before the character that is the same as the END character. ESC just tells the receiving end that this is not the end of the packet, but an actual data byte in the packet. This is a common method used by many protocols to make it possible to use character sequences that otherwise would violate protocol rules.

Note

ASCII (American Standard Code for Information Interchange) was the standard method for representing alphanumeric characters in non-IBM systems, from early VT-style terminals to more modern enhanced terminal emulators. IBM used its own character coding scheme, EBCDIC (Extended Binary-Coded Decimal Interchange Code) for its mainframes and some other systems.

More recently, UNICODE has been adopted by systems such as Windows NT/2000/XP, and many other operating systems, including Unix. UNICODE can be used to represent not just the basic alphanumeric character set used for English, but also for over 34,168 different characters, covering about 24 different languages. The coding scheme used by UNICODE is extensible, so in addition to historical and many modern language scripts, Unicode can be adapted to include lesser-used languages as time goes by.

SLIP is a simple protocol. Just start sending the characters of a packet and send the END character at the end of each packet. Use the ESC character inside the packet if one of the data bytes is the same as the END character so that the receiving end can interpret the byte correctly. Now how much simpler could it be than that?

Well, although it was a good start, several problems can occur using SLIP:

- No maximum packet size is defined, so it depends on the particular implementation. The Berkeley Unix SLIP drivers use a maximum of 1,066 bytes. For other implementations, check the documentation.

- No mechanism is used to configure the address of the sending or receiving end of the connection. Therefore, static addresses must be assigned in advance if the protocol encapsulated by SLIP is to be sent past the receiving computer or router to another host. In other words, before a SLIP connection can be set up, both sides must configure the link for the protocol to be used on the link. Because most dial-up connections today make use of the Dynamic Host Configuration Protocol (DHCP) to conserve the IP address space, SLIP won't work with an ISP or a dial-up server that uses DHCP.

- SLIP just sends packets across the line. It doesn't prefix a header to the data like other protocols (such as TCP and IP) do. Thus, SLIP can't indicate what type of protocol is being used to the receiving end of the connection. Of course, the most common use for connecting to the Internet is TCP/IP, so IP packets generally are assumed for most connections. However, in the early days of SLIP, it often was used to connect one computer to another, and a separate connection was required if both computers used multiple protocols, such as IP, IPX/SPX (Internet Packet Exchange/Sequenced Packet Exchange), or DECnet.

- No provisions are in the protocol for error detection or correction. This is left up to higher-level protocols. Because SLIP was developed for use over slow links, retransmission of packets found to have errors by higher-level protocols was an expensive proposition in terms of bandwidth.

- SLIP provides no compression algorithm. So, over the slow serial lines used for dial-up access, large amounts of the available bandwidth are wasted. For example, for a particular connection, most of the data in an IP header would not change from one packet to the next. Having to resend these unchanged bytes over and over again for each packet just wastes bandwidth.

Because SLIP was widely deployed when the Internet became available commercially, it was a common protocol used by many for an Internet connection early on. Windows 95 supported SLIP. You'll even find support for SLIP in Windows 2000 clients, so they can dial into older servers. However, Windows 2000 Server's Remote Access Server no longer supports SLIP for *dial-in* clients.

All that said, you can probably understand why the Point-to-Point Protocol (PPP) was developed. PPP replaces SLIP and provides a more robust method for sending and receiving data across serial connections, such as when dialing into a corporate modem bank or, more likely now, the Internet.

PPP

Like SLIP, PPP is a means for encapsulating packets from other protocols and transmitting them across a serial (or other point-to-point) link. Unlike SLIP, PPP provides a wide range of features that improve on the simple process of just sending data packets across the wire. PPP is documented in RFC 1662, "The Point-to-Point Protocol (PPP)." The pertinent features that PPP offers are

- **High-Level Data Link Control (HDLC)**—You can use PPP not only for IP, but for a wide range of other protocols as well. PPP bases its frame format on the High-Level Data Link Control (HDLC) protocol, which is a standard method used for point-to-point connections.

- **Link Control Protocol (LCP)**—This is an extensible protocol used to establish, configure, and test the data-link connection. Both sides of the link negotiate with the other side parameters that will be used for the connection, such as the maximum packet size.

- **Network Control Protocols (NCPs)**—These NCPs allow for different configuration options, depending on the protocol type of the packets being transported across the PPP link. NCP allows for specific network protocol sessions to be negotiated and set up after the link is established. Even better, PPP allows for multiplexing several different protocols on the same link.

For more information about PPP, extensions, and other specific details, many RFCs are available for you to examine. Table 18.1 lists several RFCs that might be relevant to your situation.

Table 18.1   RFCs Related to PPP

RFC Number	Title
1549	PPP in HDLC Framing
1552	The PPP Internetwork Packet Exchange Control Protocol (IPXCP)
1334	PPP Authentication Protocols
1332	The PPP Internet Protocol Control Protocol (IPCP)
1661	Link Control Protocol (LCP)
1990	PPP Multilink Protocol
2125	The PPP Bandwidth Allocation Protocol (BAP), The PPP Bandwidth Allocation Control Protocol (BACP)
2097	The PPP NetBIOS Frames Control Protocol (NBFCP)
1962	The PPP Compression Control Protocol (CCP)
1570	PPP LCP Extensions
2284	PPP Extensible Authentication Protocol (EAP)

PPP negotiates a link with a remote system, tests the link, sets up different protocol connections, and then sends your data from one computer to another. Because PPP is used across a point-to-point link, instead of a packet-switched network, it can be assumed that packets arrive at the destination in the same order in which they are transmitted. PPP also allows for sending more than one protocol packet type across the same link by multiplexing the various protocols. It also supports full-duplex communications (communications in both directions) on the same link. Additionally, PPP doesn't just use a special character to indicate the end of a packet (like SLIP does), but instead uses a frame header so that the data packet being transported across the link is fully encapsulated inside the PPP frame.

Figure 18.1 shows the basic layout of a PPP frame.

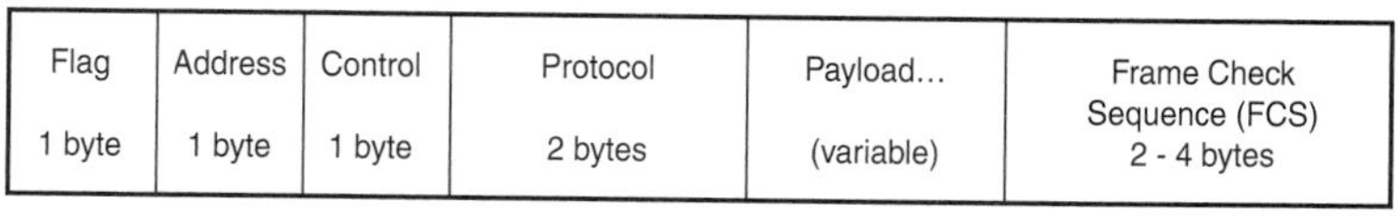

Flag	Address	Control	Protocol	Payload...	Frame Check Sequence (FCS)
1 byte	1 byte	1 byte	2 bytes	(variable)	2 - 4 bytes

Figure 18.1   The PPP frame consists of a simple header, the packet being transmitted as payload, and an error-detection field at the end of the frame.

The fields in Figure 18.1 are used as follows:

- **Flag**—Used to indicate the start of a frame, and consists of the binary value 01111110.

- **Address**—Always contains a string of eight 1s, which is interpreted as a broadcast address by many protocols. Because PPP is a point-to-point link, no addressing is required.

- **Control**—Always contains the binary value 00000011. This is used in HDLC to indicate that this is an unnumbered information (or unsequenced)(UI) frame. PPP provides a connection-less service.

- **Protocol ID**—This 2-byte field is used to identify the protocol that is being transmitted inside the payload section of the PPP frame. Protocol ID numbers are assigned by Internet

Corporation for Assigned Names and Numbers (ICANN). You can visit its Web site to learn more about protocol number assignment at http:\\www.icann.org.

- **Frame Check Sequence (FCS)**—This field can vary from 2–4 bytes in length, depending on the implementation. This provides the capability to store a 16–32 bit checksum calculation to ensure the integrity of the frame. This value is calculated by the sender based on the contents of the entire frame. The receiving end of the frame performs the same calculation. If the value does not match that stored in the FCS field, the packet is discarded.

The payload section of the PPP frame carries the packet of another protocol, as indicated by the Protocol ID field. The standard maximum length of a PPP frame, called the maximum receive unit (MRU), is defined in the standard as 1,500 bytes in length. However, this value can be increased or decreased during the original link negotiations.

Establishing a Link: The Link Control Protocol (LCP)

The process in which a PPP link is established is an orderly process. Each end of the connection first sends LCP frames that are used to test the data link and to configure the parameters that will be used on the link. Next, NCP packets are sent to configure any required options for the protocol(s) that will be encapsulated and sent across the link. After this, the data exchange can begin. When the link is no longer needed, LCP or NCP packets can be used to close the link. Alternatively, an external event, such as a timer, can be used to close an idle link. If you've ever been disconnected from a dial-up link to an ISP, you understand this process!

Figure 18.2 shows an example of the phases that a PPP link goes through for establishing and terminating a link.

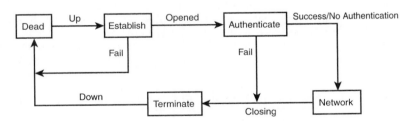

Figure 18.2   The PPP link must be established before data transfer occurs, and terminated when communications are finished.

The steps here are simple:

1. In the beginning, the link is "dead." No communications exist between the two nodes. This is also where you end up when the link is closed.

2. When some event (such as a modem dialing into a remote access server) occurs, LCP takes over to negotiate the link. When this has finished successfully, the PPP link is in the Establish phase. The link is then Up. If the two endpoints of the communication cannot agree on a link, the attempt fails and, as you can see in the diagram, the PPP link is considered again to be in the Dead state.

3. If LCP is able to exchange configuration packets that both sides can agree upon, the link is in the Opened state and, if required by the link, an Authenticate state must be reached. This can be done using a variety of methods, which are specified during the link establishment phase. If the authentication method fails, the link proceeds to the Closing state. If it succeeds, or if no authentication is required, then the Network phase is reached.

4. During the Network phase, NCP is used to configure one or more network protocols that will use the link. Remember that PPP can multiplex several protocols across the same link. After this is done, communications takes place using the protocols that are configured. Note that any network protocol can terminate its usage of the link at any time without causing the termination of the actual PPP link.

5. A link can be terminated due to an external event, such as the loss of the carrier signal or because of excessive noise on the line. However, an orderly termination can be done through the exchange of LCP packets. PPP is then considered to be in the Closing state. During the Closing state, PPP signals the network-layer protocols that are using the link so they can gracefully close their connections.

6. PPP proceeds to the Terminate state, the link is then considered to be Down, and you end up back at the beginning of the model shown in the diagram, where it all started. The PPP link is dead.

LCP is used by both ends of the connection to negotiate the encapsulation options and packet size, and then to terminate the link. Each side of the link sends information to the other about the configuration options it supports and which ones it wants to use. A large number of packet types are used by the LCP process to establish, manage, and tear down a link. They can be grouped into three general categories:

- **Link establishment frames**—These frames are used to set up a link and configure the parameters to be used for the link.

- **Link termination frames**—These frames are used to perform an orderly shutdown of the link.

- **Link maintenance frames**—These frames are used to manage the link and for debugging purposes.

An LCP packet can be identified by examining the Protocol ID field of the PPP frame. LCP packets use the protocol ID value of 0xC021. The rest of the LCP frame structure consists of a code that identifies the type of LCP message (one byte) and an identifier field (one byte) that is used to match up requests with replies during the exchange of LCP packets. A length field (two bytes) is then used to indicate the size of the LCP packet. This is followed by the actual data used for the particular LCP message. The LCP packet rides in the payload section of the PPP frame, just like any other protocol.

LCP operates in a request/reply mode in which the LCP Configure-Request packet is first sent to open a link, and contains a list of options that the sender wants to use if they differ from the default values for the option. The Configure-Ack packet type is used for acknowledging that all the received options are acceptable to the other end of the connection.

The Configure-Nack message is used by the receiving end to indicate that it recognizes all the options that were sent, but is rejecting the configuration as a whole because one or more of the option values cannot be used on its side of the connection. This packet also contains a list of the options that are causing the negative acknowledgment along with values it would find okay to use.

The Configure-Reject message is similar to the Configure-Nack, but is used when some of the options are not recognized by the receiver, or are nonnegotiable. Again, a list of these unrecognized or rejected options is returned in this rejection packet so that the sender can determine what the receiving end is trying to negotiate.

After receiving a Configure-Nack or Configure-Reject message, the sender can send additional Configure-Request packets, changing the values of options so that both sides can come to an agreement. Note that because this is a bidirectional communications path, the options negotiated for traffic going in one direction don't have to match the options used for traffic going in the opposite direction. Each side sends a Configure-Request to the other side to establish the options it is allowed to use to configure the link for sending to the other side.

After all options in a Configure-Request packet are acceptable to the receiving end, it sends the Configure-Ack message and the link setup is complete. After the link has been established using LCP, NCP packets are used to configure protocol-specific options that will be used on the PPP link.

During the time that the link is maintained, LCP uses maintenance packets for routine procedures to be sure the link is still up and performing as it should. For example, the Echo-Request packet can be sent to determine if the link is still operational after some time has passed with no transmissions. The Echo-Reply packet is returned in response to keep the link open.

Other maintenance LCP packets are used to indicate that the protocol the sender wants to negotiate is not supported by the receiver or that the LCP code is not understood by the receiver.

When either side of the connection wants to tear down the link, the Terminate-Request LCP packet is transmitted. The proper response is a Terminate-Ack packet. For a complete listing of LCP packets, and their particular formats, see the RFCs listed in Table 18.1.

Network Control Protocol(s) (NCPs)

The most popular protocol used with PPP today is probably IP, because millions of people each day use PPP to dial in to the Internet. However, PPP allows for the use of multiple NCPs that further configure the protocols that are carried across the PPP link. For example, in the case of IP, the dial-in client must be provided with IP addressing information, which usually is done by a DHCP server.

The Internet Protocol Control Protocol (IPCP) is the NCP used to configure parameters for using the PPP link for transmitting IP packets. The Internetwork Packet Exchange Control Protocol (IPXCP) is used to set up IPX. Other protocols for which there are NCPs include AppleTalk, DECnet Phase IV, and NetBIOS, among others.

The important thing to remember is that the PPP link parameters are negotiated before any actual network protocols are configured or are able to use the link. After the link is established, one or more NCPs use the link to configure the parameters for the protocol that will be carried in the payload section of PPP frames that use the link.

An Example: Configuring a Windows 2000 Professional Client

You can use a wizard to help configure Dial-Up Networking on a Windows client. The particular dialog boxes displayed vary from one version of Windows to another. This example uses Windows 2000 Professional to show how to configure a simple dial-up connection to the Internet.

First, obtain from your ISP the telephone number that you'll need, your username and password that will be used to authenticate you on the ISP's server, and whether or not the ISP uses dynamic addressing (DHCP) or assigns you a static address.

To set up the client software on Windows 2000 Professional:

1. Double-click the desktop icon titled My Network Places.

2. Click the HTML Style Network and Dial-Up Connections link on the left corner of the screen.

3. Double-click the Make New Network Connection icon. The Network Connection Wizard pops up. Click the Next button to start the process.

4. In Figure 18.3, you can see the first screen the wizard presents, asking what type of connection you want to create. Select the first option button if you are dialing into a private corporate network, or the second if dialing into an Internet connection. In this example, Dial-up to the Internet is selected.

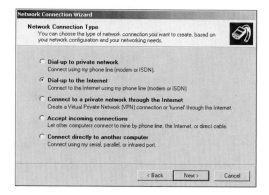

Figure 18.3   Select the kind of connection you want the wizard to create.

Note

In Figure 18.3, note that you also can create a Virtual Private Network (VPN) connection. For a secure communications link through the Internet or another wide area network, a VPN link connection can provide the security you need. See Chapter 41, "Virtual Private Networks (VPNs) and Tunneling," for more about VPNs.

Also note that you can create a direct connection with another Windows computer by a serial port connection. This can be useful when you need to network just two computers, such as a home PC and a laptop that you carry with you.

Finally, you can use this page on the wizard to allow other computers to make connections to your computer.

5. You are prompted by the wizard with the screen shown in Figure 18.4. You can choose to create an Internet account by selecting the I Want to Signup for a New Internet account option button. If you use this selection, a list of phone numbers appears for your location that can be used to create an Internet account using a provider supplied by Microsoft. If you already have an Internet account with a known provider, use the second option button to transfer that account to this computer. For this example, select the third button to manually enter all the information required by a typical ISP. When you've made your selection, click Next to continue.

6. The next screen the wizard displays asks whether you want to connect using a modem, or through a LAN. Because this chapter is about dial-up connections, select the first option and click the Next button to continue.

7. On the next screen, enter the phone number for your ISP, and other information, such as your location.

8. For most ISPs today, you should select the None option.

Note

If you plan to use SLIP, you can select it from the dialog box that appears when you click the Advanced button. Figure 18.5 shows the Advanced Connection Properties dialog box with the Connection tab selected. You also can use this dialog box to enable LCP extensions, and to specify a manual logon procedure or script file.

Figure 18.4 From this screen, you can select to sign up for a new Internet account, transfer an existing one, or enter the information for the connection manually.

Figure 18.5 The Advanced Connection Properties dialog box allows you to configure additional parameters for the connection.

9. The Addresses tab, shown in Figure 18.6, allows you to specify static IP addressing information provided to you by the ISP, or allows the connection to be configured automatically. In most cases, your ISP will be using DHCP (described in Chapter 23) and you won't need to use this tab. However, if you are given a static IP address, or the addresses of Domain Name System (DNS) servers (described in Chapter 24), use the appropriate check box on this tab. When finished entering the information, click OK.

10. After dismissing the Advanced Connection Properties dialog box, you'll return to the wizard. Click Next to continue.

11. Next, the wizard prompts you to enter the username and password assigned to you by your ISP. Enter the appropriate information and click Next.

12. The wizard then prompts you to give a name to the connection. If you have more than one dial-up account, this is a means of distinguishing between them. If you have only one, you can

accept the default name of "Connection to - " followed by the dial-up phone number, or you can enter a name for the connection. This name is for display purposes only, and is not your username on the remote network. Click Next to continue.

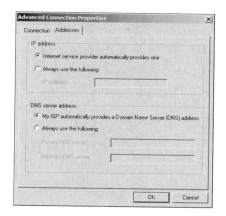

Figure 18.6 The Addresses tab allows you to specify automatic configuration or to supply static information used for the connection.

13. In the next dialog box, the wizard asks whether you want to set up an e-mail account at this time. If you have already set up an account with an ISP and were given a name and password to use for e-mail, select Yes and click Next. Even if the username and password for the e-mail account are the same that are used to dial-up the ISP, you need to use this option to be able to use Outlook or Outlook Express with the mail account. If you have another e-mail program you would rather use, click No and then click the Next button.

14. The last dialog box of the wizard has a check box that is already selected. If you want to have the wizard use the information you've provided to attempt to connect to the Internet after you click the Finish button, leave the check box selected. Otherwise, click the box to deselect this option and click the Finish button.

After you've created the new connection, it shows up as an icon when you click Network and Dial-up Connections in the My Network Places folder. You also can create a shortcut to place the icon on the desktop. To do so, right-click the icon and select Create Shortcut from the menu that appears. A dialog box says you can't create a shortcut for the connection in the current window, and prompts you to place the shortcut on the desktop. Select the Yes button to create the shortcut.

When you are ready to test the connection, double-click the icon created for this connection, either on the desktop, or in the Network and Dial-Up Connections window you get to through My Network Places. The Connect Internet Connection dialog box appears (see Figure 18.7). In this dialog box, you can enter the password and username for the dial-up account if you didn't specify them in the setup procedure, or if your password has changed. Select the Save Password check box if you don't want to enter your password manually each time you make a connection.

Note

The previous example showed you how to set up a Windows client for a dial-up Internet connection. If you're using Linux at home, I'd recommend that you check with the documentation provided by your vendor, or possibly the Linux How-To documents that are available on the Internet. You also can find out more about Linux and dial-up networking by reading *Special Edition Using Linux*, also by Que Publishing.

Figure 18.7 The Connect Internet Connection dialog box is used to dial up the Internet connection.

When Dial-Up Isn't Fast Enough

This chapter discusses PPP and SLIP, the two main protocols used by dial-up users to make a connection to the Internet or another network, such as a company network or other WAN. For many users who don't use a lot of bandwidth, dial-up connections are inexpensive. And, for mobile users, a dial-up connection is ubiquitous; whereas other solutions—discussed in the next chapter—are not always easily accessed. Because a dial-up connection uses the PSTN, there are limits to the amount of information that can be carried across the link using a modem that translates digital signals to analog signals, and then reverses the process at the other end of the connection. Dial-up access should be used when you find that the cost of the service matches the user requirements. However, using digital connections, it's possible to get a much faster connection to the Internet or to connect one network to another. In the next chapter, you'll learn about the methods used for dedicated connections. However, don't dismiss dial-up networking entirely if you are able to obtain a broadband or other fast connection. As slow as it might be, dial-up networking using a modem can serve as a backup when your other, faster connection fails!

Dedicated Connections

19

SOME OF THE MAIN TOPICS IN THIS CHAPTER ARE

Leased Lines

Asynchronous Transfer Mode (ATM)

Frame Relay and X.25

DSL and Cable Modems

CHAPTER 19

The previous chapter covered some of the solutions you can use to allow remote users access to your LAN. Using dial-up connections, whether they are ordinary telephone lines or faster ISDN connections, can satisfy many business requirements for ordinary users. However, if your applications require larger amounts of bandwidth to communicate with remote users, such as a branch office, you might find that a dedicated connection—one that is available continuously—is a better choice. For dedicated connections, you can use a dedicated leased line or the newer packet switching network technologies, which can ride on top of digital connections offered by the local exchange carrier. Although ISDN appeared to be the best method of obtaining a digital connection to your network or the Internet a few years ago, it has now been overshadowed by other digital subscriber line services, commonly referred to collectively as xDSL.

In this chapter, you'll take a quick look at legacy technologies, such as the T-Carrier system, ATM, and frame relay. Finally, you'll examine some of the newer technologies, such as xDSL and cable modems, which provide sufficient "always on" bandwidth for a home user or small office that needs a connection to the Internet.

Leased Lines

Leased lines have been used by businesses for many years to establish point-to-point, dedicated connections. Leased lines provide a fixed bandwidth for a fixed cost. Connecting the telephone system from a branch office to the main office, for example, can be more cost-effective by purchasing a leased line from the telephone company and paying a flat fee for its use rather than using the normal long-distance network. Using leased lines to connect computer networks is a logical step up from using leased lines with telephone voice systems.

Basically, a leased line provides a permanent circuit between two points that you own and do not have to share with others. The leased line might consist of a physical line that traverses the entire length of the connection from end to end, or it might be comprised of connections at both ends to the local exchange carrier, with the two exchanges connected by some other technology.

Because of the point-to-point topology of leased lines, no call setup is required at either end. The connection exists and you can use it whenever you need to, often referred to as "always on" technology. The physical lines also are specially conditioned by the carrier to minimize errors as compared to an ordinary connection to the local exchange.

The first type of leased line was based on analog technology, just as the voice telephone network was, and often used modems at each end of the connection. Digital leased lines now provide connections of up to 56Kbps and use a *channel service unit (CSU)* device and a *data service unit (DSU)* device, which also are used on other digital lines, such as T1 and fractional T1 services. Both a CSU and DSU are commonly implemented in the same device, and sometimes in combination with a router.

The CSU is used to provide the basic functions needed to transmit data across the line. Other basic functions provided by the CSU include

- **An electrical barrier**—The CSU protects the T1 (or other line) and the user equipment from damage that can be caused by unexpected electrical interference, such as a lightning strike.

- **Keepalive signal**—The CSU transmits a signal on the line that is used to keep the connection up.

- **Loopback capabilities**—The telephone company can perform diagnostics on the line using loopback facilities provided by the CSU.

- **Statistical information**—Depending on the vendor and model, the CSU can provide statistical information useful to the network administrator. Some units have SNMP capabilities.

The DSU works with the CSU but also provides other functions. The DSU is responsible for translating between the data encoding used on the line, such as the time-division multiplexed (TDM) DSX frames that are used on a T1 line, and the serial data format used on the local network. A DSU usually has RS-232C or RS-449 connectors that can be used to connect to data terminal equipment (DTE), which then provides the actual physical connection to the LAN (see Figure 19.1). Each end of the line requires similar equipment.

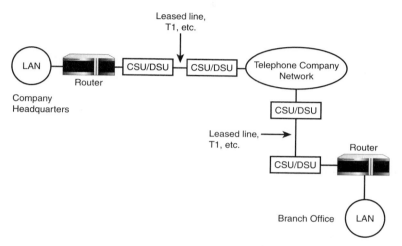

Figure 19.1 The CSU/DSU provides the connection to a leased line or other high-speed service from the local provider.

Other important functions that the DSU can perform include

- Timing functions for user ports
- Error correction
- Handshaking across the line

Usually, the CSU and DSU are combined into one device. Typically, these functions also are incorporated directly into a router. If you use a router instead of a bridge (or other device), you can reduce the traffic that travels between the two connected LANs because only packets destined for the network on the other end are passed across the connection. In other words, you can save valuable bandwidth by only routing traffic destined for the far end of the network across the expensive leased line.

Analog leased lines are not as common as they once were. Most of the public switched telephone network (PSTN) between central offices has now been converted to digital lines because the service a digital line provides is much better than an analog line. Although an analog signal can be regenerated with amplifiers, noise on the line also is amplified, so the quality can deteriorate. Digital encoding with error correction techniques can deliver a signal over a long distance more accurately because the digital packets that are transferred can be corrected (in some cases where minor corruption has occurred) or retransmitted if the data cannot be recovered. Additionally, the conversion from digital to an analog signal and back again at the destination adds to the overhead of using an analog line. One of the disadvantages of a leased line is that it cannot be modified to give you a larger bandwidth. If you need additional capacity on the line, you must add another line or perhaps move up to another technology such as T1.

The T-Carrier System

In the past, leased lines usually would give you a bandwidth of up to 56Kbps. For larger bandwidth, you would need a larger data pipe, which is where the T-carrier or, if you are in Europe, the E-carrier, system comes into play. Today, the term *leased line* can refer to a variety of line speeds. The point is that the line is a dedicated link from one point to another, and you don't have to "dial" to set up the connection. The connection is dedicated and always on.

The T-carrier system was developed in the early 1960s by the Bell Telephone System in the United States and was used to digitally transmit voice communications. The first service offered was the T1, which can provide a transmission rate of up to 1.544Mbps. If you need more bandwidth than can be provided by a T1 line, you can contract for a higher level of service, such as a T3 line, which provides a 44.736Mbps connection. The range of transmission rates and number of channels for each kind of T-carrier service are listed in Table 19.1.

Table 19.1   T-Carrier Services in the North American Digital Hierarchy

Designation	Channels	Total Transmission Rate
FT-1/1	1	64Kbps
T1	24	1.544Mbps
T2	96	6.312Mbps
T3	672	44.736Mbps
T4	4032	274.186Mbps

The T-carrier system is an all-digital transmission system. For voice systems that use a T1 line, the signal is sampled at a rate of 8,000 times per second, and the result is stored in 8 bits, or 1 byte. The T1 provides 24 separate channels that can be used to send voice or data from one place to another using two pairs of wires. Each of the 24 channels can transmit at a rate of 64Kbps.

Note

The European equivalent of the T1 line is called the E-1. Although the two use the same kind of technologies for transmission, the E-1 provides 30 channels and a total bandwidth of 2.045Mbps.

Time-division multiplexing, which allows each channel only a small amount of time to transmit (5.2 milliseconds), is used to combine all 24 channels into one signal. With each channel transmitting at 64Kbps, the total bandwidth on a T1 line is 64Kbps×24, or 1.536Mbps. The difference between the 1.536Mbps and the full bandwidth of the T1 pipe (1.544Mbps) is due to the overhead used for managing connections (8Kbps).

Fractional T1

In many cases, the full bandwidth provided by a T1 line is more than the end user requires. Yet, a slower 56Kbps leased line might not provide enough bandwidth. To handle this situation, the communications provider allows several users to use the full T1 bandwidth by allocating each user one or more of the 24 channels that T1 provides. This is called *Fractional T1*.

Diagnosing Problems with T-Carrier Services

When purchasing a T1 or T3 service, the local provider must check out the actual physical line and provide "conditioning" to be sure that it can transmit data at the expected rate with minimal errors.

Conditioning means making the line stable enough to provide the service you contract for. Bridge taps and load coils that are normally found on voice-grade lines can't be used because they can cause the electrical pulses to be slightly out of shape, which makes them unrecognizable by devices on each end of the line. Inadequate grounding of the copper cables and physically defective cables are other sources of problems.

Bridge Taps and Load Coils

Bridge taps are places along the copper wire that have been tapped previously to provide service. Unfortunately, when services are disconnected, the telephone company doesn't always go out and remove the tap. After all, when someone moves out of a house in a residential neighborhood, the line is used again shortly, so after it's tapped, the line usually stays in place. For voice-grade service, bridge taps don't distort the signal enough for you to really notice anything. However, because no telephone is connected to them, they are unterminated, and can cause all sorts of problems for digital signals that travel down over the line.

Load coils are another animal altogether. Because copper wires on the PSTN were originally used for just voice communications, it wasn't necessary to use much of the bandwidth that copper wires provide. In fact, voice service is usually provided by just the first 4MHz of the total frequency bandwidth that can be used on a copper wire. Higher frequencies on a wire tend to leak out and interfere with other wires. To solve this problem, load coils, which are basically low-pass filters (they allow the lower voice frequencies to pass through), are used to attenuate, or block, higher frequencies on the line. For ordinary telephone service, this is important; however, these higher frequencies are becoming very important today for providing sufficient bandwidth for digital services.

When you request a T-class of service from a local carrier, usually you must wait a few weeks to a few months before the service is operational. If the telephone cables in your area were put in place many years ago, the carrier might have to condition the line by finding and removing bridge taps. New wiring also might have to be run in places where the original cables have degraded over time. All these functions are labor and time intensive.

The distance from the central office to your site also is important when trying to condition a line for any digital service. For example, twisted-pair wiring is usually used in the "last mile" from the central office to your business or home. The farther you are from the central office, the more the electrical signal attenuates. Because of this, the farther you are from the central office, the less bandwidth the wire can provide by the time it reaches you. To solve this problem, many telephone companies have been running fiber-optic cabling out into the field and installing a digital-services box closer to homes and businesses. Because fiber-optic cabling can carry a signal much farther with less attenuation of the signal than can copper wire, this effectively lets the telephone company put a mini central office out in the field. From this digital-services box, ordinary copper wiring can be used to connect to your location.

The loopback capabilities provided by the CSU/DSU unit are used by the provider to check the signal quality on the line. One of the simplest methods for checking the line is the use of a bit error rate tester (BERT). This provides a simple test to determine whether specific bit patterns transmitted by the test equipment can be received back with no distortions. BERT usually is the first test performed and is used to qualify the line as functional after the physical cables have been installed.

When a T1 line is installed, usually it is checked to ensure that all circuits are correctly terminated, which includes checking the user's equipment (such as the CSU/DSU). Signal loss can indicate that the connection is broken somewhere along the line, the signal being transmitted is too weak, or a connector is faulty.

◀◀ For more information about BERT, attenuation, and other technical terms commonly used when discussing telephony, see Chapter 5, "Wiring the Network—Cables and Other Components" and Chapter 44, "Network Testing and Analysis Tools."

One problem that can occur is called timing jitter. As defined by the ITU-T (International Telecommunications Union), *timing jitter* refers to "short-term variations of the significant instants of a digital signal from their ideal positions in time." The signal that is transmitted is a wave form; when viewed on an instrument such as an oscilloscope, you can see the rising and falling edges of the wave. If the wave form is slightly out of sync with the clocking mechanism, the signal might be interpreted by the receiving equipment incorrectly. All T1 circuits have a small degree of jitter, caused mainly by multiplexers or devices along the line that are used to regenerate the signal. Jitter also can be caused by electrical or atmospheric noise (as in the case of microwave transmissions).

Testing the line by using BERT or other instruments that depend on knowing the bit patterns that will be transmitted is called *out-of-service testing*. Obviously, this can be used only before the customer takes over the line for use. In-service testing, sometimes referred to as quality of service (QoS) testing, cannot make measurements based on expected bit patterns because the data transmitted by the customer can be roughly assumed to be random. Instead, tests performed when the line is already in service involve checking for things such as framing errors, parity errors, or checksum errors, depending on the kind of traffic carried by the line.

Asynchronous Transfer Mode (ATM)

Asynchronous Transfer Mode (ATM) was developed by AT&T Bell Labs during the 1980s. It is a *connection-oriented* technology, much like the public telephone system, in which a connection is established between two endpoints before the actual data exchange can begin. ATM can be used in both LAN and WAN environments and provides for full-duplex communication. The fact that many kinds of traffic are being carried on electronic networks today influenced the design of ATM. The PSTN was originally designed to carry voice communications along with other simple services, such as telex. Today, electronic networks are used to transmit data, voice, and video, and to provide connections for other kinds of multimedia applications.

Note

The ATM Forum is a nonprofit organization that seeks to promote the use of ATM technology. You'll find technical specifications and other information about ATM at ATM Forum's Web site: `http://www.atmforum.com/`. Unlike organizations, such as the IEEE (Institute of Electrical and Electronics Engineers), approved specifications for ATM are free and available at ATM Forum's Web site.

In an attempt to design a one-size-fits-all network and provide for new kinds of traffic in the future, ATM uses a fixed packet size of 53 bytes (48 bytes for the payload and 5 bytes for the header) to transmit data. When referring to a packet of data in ATM networks, the term *cell* usually is used. The advantage to using a fixed-length cell as opposed to a variable-length packet such as that used by frame relay—discussed later in this chapter—is that hardware devices that switch network traffic usually can be designed to operate at higher speeds when switching fixed-length packets of information. The algorithm can be implemented with less complex code and hardware design because the switch that routes cells through an ATM network doesn't have to perform calculations to determine where one packet stops and another begins, which is the case in frame relay networks where packet size is not fixed.

The small header also means that the switch must process much less information for each packet. There are two different kinds of ATM frame headers, but both are 5 bytes. During the development of

ATM, some argued for a smaller cell size of 32 bytes, which would provide a better quality voice service. Others argued for a cell size of 64 bytes, which would provide more efficient data-delivery services. The 48-byte payload was finally chosen as a compromise. Add that to the 5-byte header, and you have a fixed-cell size of 53.

ATM Frames

ATM has two types of frame headers. The first is the User-Network Interface (UNI) header, which is used for ATM cells that travel between an endpoint in the connection—such as a standard network router or perhaps a PC or high-end workstation equipped with an ATM network card—and the ATM switch. This frame type, shown in Figure 19.2, consists of 5 bytes divided into eight fields.

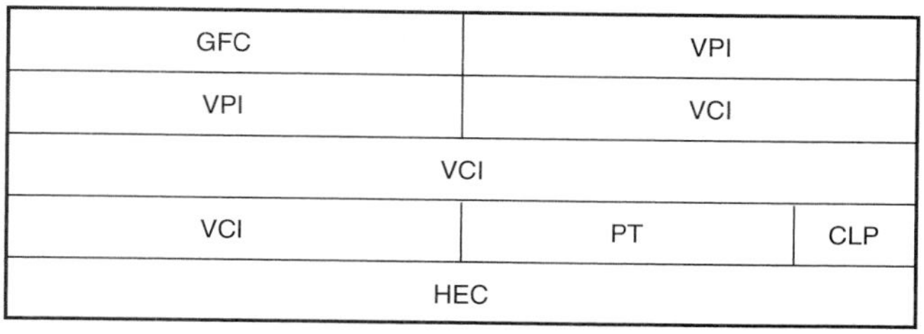

GFC		VPI	
VPI		VCI	
VCI			
VCI		PT	CLP
HEC			

Figure 19.2 Note the contents of the ATM UNI cell header.

The fields of the UNI cell header are

- **GFC (Generic Flow Control)**—This 4-bit field isn't generally used any more, but you might find it used with local significance for identifying individual computers on the network or for traffic-control functions. The default value for this field is four 0 bits.

- **VPI (Virtual Path Identifier)**—This 8-bit field specifies a value that identifies the virtual path for a stream of cells. The VPI, used in conjunction with the next field, identifies a connection set up through the network of switches. A value of 0 in this VPI field means that the cell is being used for network administrative purposes, such as call setup or terminations.

- **VCI (Virtual Channel Identifier)**—This 16-bit field is used with the VPI to identify a path through the switched network. As explained later, many cells that have different values in the VCI field can have the same VPI value. Although up to 65,536 different values can be stored in a 16-bit field, values 0–15 are reserved for use by the ITU, and values 16–32 are reserved by the ATM Forum for various signaling and management operations.

- **PT (Payload Type)**—The first bit in this 3-bit field indicates whether the packet contains user data (value = 0) in the payload section of the cell or whether the payload section contains control data (value = 1). If the cell contains user data, the second bit can be used to report network congestion. The second bit is set to 0 by the source and is set to 1 by a switch that is experiencing congestion. The destination endpoint then can use flow-control mechanisms to throttle back transmissions until it receives cells with a value of 0 in this bit. The third bit is used to indicate that this is the last cell in a series of cells that make up an AAL5 user frame. For nonuser cells, this value is used for administrative purposes.

- **CLP (Cell Loss Priority)**—When congestion in the network makes it necessary to drop cells, those with a value of 1 in this single-bit field are the primary candidates to be dropped as compared to those with a value of 0 in this field.

- **HEC (Header Error Control)**—This 8-bit field is used to store a CRC value that can be used to detect whether the cell becomes corrupted during transport.

The second kind of ATM cell header is the Network-Node Interface (NNI) format. NNI is used for transmissions between the switches that make up the ATM network, which, as you can see in Figure 19.3, is similar to the UNI cell header.

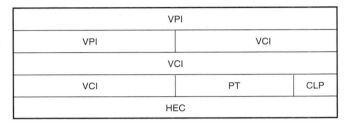

Figure 19.3   Note the contents of the ATM NNI cell header.

The main difference from the UNI header is that the NNI cell doesn't have the GFC field. The other fields are there; the VPI field has grown from 8 bits to 12 bits, which can provide for up to 4,096 virtual paths through the network.

ATM Connections

Connections created between endpoints in the ATM network can be either *permanent virtual connections (PVCs)* or *switched virtual connections (SVCs)*. Each switch in the ATM network keeps track of connections using routing tables, and decisions are made based on the information in the 5-byte header. Because the switch does not have to make any decisions based on the service data contained in the cell's payload section, hardware-based switches can quickly route and transport cells to their destinations.

ATM provides two kinds of transport connections: *virtual channels* and *virtual paths*. A virtual channel is used for an individual connection through the network. The v*irtual channel identifier (VCI)* is used to identify cells in this connection. A virtual path is made up of multiple virtual channels that all share a common path through the network; it is identified in the cell header by a *virtual path identifier (VPI)*. By grouping connections using VPIs, management and controlling functions must be performed only once for a group of individual connections (using the VPI), making the network operate more efficiently.

However, the values for the VPI/VCI fields do not remain the same when the cells travel through ATM switches. When a cell is received on one port of the switch, the VPI/VCI fields are used to perform a lookup in the routing table. When a match is found, the new VPI/VCI values are inserted into the cell and it is transmitted out on a port that gets it to its eventual destination, based on the path created during call setup (or as determined by the administrator for a PVC). To put it another way, VPI/VCI values have local significance only for the particular connection.

Before any data can be exchanged, the virtual connection path must be determined. Similar to the mechanism used in the telephone network, the path through the network from one switch to another switch is predetermined before any data exchange takes place. When determining the path that the connection will use, the quality of service for the traffic is taken into consideration to ensure that a path will be created that can provide the bandwidth needed by the service. Traffic is policed to ensure that a particular connection does not abuse the network by using resources to which it is not entitled.

The ATM Architecture Model (B-ISDN/ATM Model)

The basic architecture used for ATM involves three layers: the Physical layer, ATM layer, and ATM Adaptation layer (see Figure 19.4).

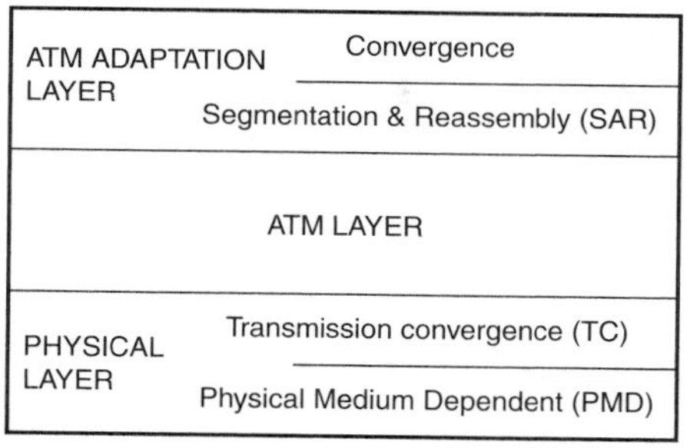

```
┌─────────────────┬─────────────────────────────────────┐
│ ATM ADAPTATION  │           Convergence               │
│ LAYER           ├─────────────────────────────────────┤
│                 │  Segmentation & Reassembly (SAR)    │
├─────────────────┴─────────────────────────────────────┤
│                                                         │
│                    ATM LAYER                            │
│                                                         │
├─────────────────┬─────────────────────────────────────┤
│ PHYSICAL        │     Transmission convergence (TC)    │
│ LAYER           ├─────────────────────────────────────┤
│                 │  Physical Medium Dependent (PMD)    │
└─────────────────┴─────────────────────────────────────┘
```

Figure 19.4 The ATM architecture model.

As you can see in this figure, the Physical layer is further subdivided into the Physical Medium Dependent (PMD) sublayer and the Transmission Convergence (TC) sublayer. The ATM Adaptation layer is further divided into the Segmentation and Reassembly (SAR) sublayer and the Convergence Sublayer (CS).

The Physical Layer

The two components of the Physical layer are responsible for the actual transmission of cells across the network. Signal encoding and interfacing with the network transmission media (such as copper wire or fiber-optic cables) are performed by the PMD. By keeping the physical aspects of the protocol as a separate component, it is possible to define many different kinds of PMDs for ATM. Thus, it's easy to create a PMD to allow ATM to operate over many different types of physical networks.

The TC component of the physical layer interfaces with the ATM layer and is responsible for taking the stream of bits supplied by that layer and mapping the ATM cells onto the PMD-specific frame. For example, if the underlying network is SONET, then the TC component maps the ATM fixed-length cells onto SONET frames and then passes these to the SONET PMD.

The ATM Layer

The VPI/VCI routing functions and flow control mechanisms are implemented on the ATM layer. Remember that the combination of VPI/VCI allows for multiplexing many connections across a common virtual circuit. The ATM layer is responsible for this multiplexing-demultiplexing functionality. This layer also can monitor connections and take corrective action if it finds a connection is not performing within the boundaries that were negotiated during call setup. Routing functions use the VPI/VCI to ensure that the cells travel over the proper connection between the connection's endpoints. However, similar to the Internet Protocol (IP), the ATM layer does not provide for error control. If packets are dropped at a switch along the connection's path, it's up to higher-level protocols to recognize this and take the necessary actions to retransmit the data.

The ATM Adaptation Layer (AAL)

The AAL is responsible for packaging the data on the sending part of the connection into 48-byte payloads, and for unpacking the data and reassembling it into larger messages on the receiving end.

For example, an IP datagram handed down by the IP protocol will be larger than the payload size that the ATM cell can handle. In the ATM Adaptation layer, this larger message is fragmented into smaller payloads and sent down to the Physical layer for transmission in ATM cells. At the receiving end of the connection, the individual payloads are reassembled back into the larger message and passed up to a higher-level network protocol.

In the Convergence sublayer (CS), a protocol data unit (PDU) from a higher-level protocol is encapsulated into a format so that it can be reassembled into that same format at the receiving end. In the Segmentation and Reassembly (SAR) sublayer, the data is divided into 48-byte payloads. These payloads then are passed to the ATM layer, which attaches the header to create the 53-byte cell.

Several ATM adaptation layers have been defined by the ITU-T:

- **AAL0**—This adaptation layer was created to provide for a user-defined layer. Basically, the 48-byte payloads are passed up and down the protocol stack when sending or receiving data.

- **AAL1**—This adaptation layer was created to provide for a time-dependent, constant bit-rate service for connection-oriented applications. AAL1 is usually found in voice or video applications and includes a higher amount of overhead when compared to other adaptation layers. For example, time stamps and error checking can be added to the payload section of the cell.

- **AAL2**—This adaptation layer was created to provide a variable bit-rate service for connection-oriented applications. AAL2 is used for compressed video and voice, for example. However, this adaptation layer was not fully defined by the standards process and usually is not used. Instead, AAL5 is generally used.

- **AAL3/4**—These two adaptation layers offer a variable bit-rate service for connection-oriented (was AAL3) or nonconnection-oriented (was AAL4) applications, such as LAN traffic. Although originally defined as two separate adaptation layers, it is now a single entity. A small amount of overhead data (such as segment size and sequencing numbers) is added to the payload section of the ATM cell.

- **AAL5**—This adaptation layer gives a variable bit-rate service similar to AAL3/4, but has a lower overhead than AAL3/4. AAL5 is usually used for LAN traffic such as IP. AAL5 improves over AAL3/4 by adding a trailer to the data to be transferred that provides for error checking and specifies the size of the payload.

Of these layers, AAL5 was created specifically to make ATM an attractive choice for typical LAN applications. The AAL5 frame format is composed of several fields that are made up of the actual payload, followed by the AAL5 trailer fields.

- **Payload**—The payload field contains the actual application data and can range in size from 1 byte up to 65,535 bytes in length.

- **Pad**—This field, which can range from 0 to 47 bytes in length, is used for padding (adding zeros) to the frame to ensure that the total frame (or PDU) can be evenly divided into the 48-byte payloads created by the SAR sublayer.

- **User to User Indication**—This single-byte field is basically undefined and left up to the implementation.

- **Common Part Indicator**—This single-byte field is used for alignment processes to be sure that the AAL5 trailer is on a 64-bit boundary.

- **Length of Payload**—This 2-byte field specifies the length of the payload field. Length of Payload does not include any padding bytes, so it can be used by the receiving end to determine where the actual payload ends and padding begins.

■ **CRC**—This 4-byte field is used to store a CRC value to ensure the integrity of the entire PDU being transmitted. It is not a calculation on the contents of any individual ATM cell, but applies to the message that is being broken into fragments for transmission in ATM's 48-byte payloads.

If you'll remember, the third bit of the Payload Type Indicator field of the ATM header is used to specify that the cell is the last cell of a message (or PDU) that was broken down into 48-byte payloads. Thus, larger messages from higher-level protocols (such as IP) can be identified and reassembled while passing through the ATM network of switches in simple, short, 48-byte payloads.

LAN Emulation (LANE)

ATM was originally designed to be a wide area networking protocol. However, local area networks have changed dramatically in the past few years. Whereas a simple 10BASE-T network might have provided sufficient bandwidth a few years back, you now see LANs composed of, or connected by, much faster links, such as Gigabit Ethernet and 10 Gigabit Ethernet.

Speed is not the only thing that's changed in the local area networking scene. The LAN that was used for simple file and print sharing now must support a variety of different applications. For example, videoconferencing is becoming a common application in the LAN. In a traditional LAN, however, you can't "reserve" or "guarantee" that the bandwidth needed to support such an application will always be available.

Using ATM in a LAN can help reduce congestion if the network consists of multiple kinds of traffic, such as one that supports workstations and file servers along with multimedia applications. If you use ATM as a backbone, you can interface it with your normal ethernet or token-ring segments. The ATM Forum has published specifications for LANE to define the approach to be taken for using ATM in the LAN environment. LANE specifies how other traditional LAN protocols—such as ethernet (IEEE 802.3) and token ring (IEEE 802.5)—are to be carried over ATM.

The LANE protocol was developed to allow a LAN to be emulated using ATM. That is, LANE makes an ATM switched network look to the client computer just like a typical LAN. LANE consists of the following:

■ **LAN Emulation Client**—This software interfaces between the traditional client's LAN software and ATM. To the client's LAN software, the LAN Emulation Client appears to operate just like the local LAN. To the ATM network to which the client is connected, the LAN Emulation Client performs the necessary ATM functions.

■ **LANE Services**—This component of LANE provides for translating between traditional LAN addresses and ATM addresses.

LANE can be used with ethernet and token-ring networks to provide a faster connection for your LAN because all traffic is sent through ATM switches. You can find many ATM switches that include support for LANE or, as is the case with Windows 2000, the LAN Services component can reside on a Windows 2000 Server.

IP Over ATM

For most implementations, you'll find that AAL5 is used to send IP datagrams over ATM. The relevant RFC documents are RFC 1577, "Classical IP and ARP over ATM," and RFC 1626, "Default IP MTU for use over ATM AAL5." RFC 1577 doesn't define how ATM networks function, but provides instead a method for IP and address resolution mechanisms over an ATM network. RFC 1626 defines the value of 9180 bytes as the *default* Maximum Transmission Unit (MTU) size for IP datagrams on an ATM network. It also discusses how, during call setup for a switched virtual circuit, the actual MTU size used for the connection can be negotiated.

When sending IP datagrams over an ATM connection, the AAL5 trailer information is added to the end of the datagram and then passed to the SAR sublayer for division into the 48-byte payloads required for ATM. As explained in the previous section, when the cell containing the last part of the IP datagram is created, the third bit of the PT (Payload Type) is set to 1 so that the endpoint recognizes that it now has all the information necessary to reassemble the smaller payloads into the original IP datagram.

IP over ATM has several advantages that make it a better choice for IP networks than LANE. First, LANE doesn't support the QoS capabilities of ATM, which you'll learn about in the next section. Second, IP over ATM has a lower overhead, so more bandwidth is available for transmitting actual data. Windows 2000 also supports IP over ATM. Because of this, IP over ATM usually is faster than LANE.

Similar to LANE, the IP over ATM software interfaces between the TCP/IP protocol stack and the ATM network.

ATM Service Categories

Although early implementations of ATM use the technique of reserving a specified, fixed amount of bandwidth for a connection in advance, service categories now allow for several different levels of service that can be matched to the needs of different types of traffic. Each level of service defines the network behavior for a different kind of network traffic that can be used to specify the QoS required for certain kinds of applications. For example, some network applications require precise timing and cannot tolerate excessive delays or reductions in bandwidth (such as video transmissions). Other applications tend to make bursty requests where bandwidth requirements vary widely in just a short time (such as file transfers).

The following service categories are presently defined by the ATM Forum:

- Constant Bit Rate (CBR)
- Real-Time Variable Bit Rate (rt-VBR)
- Non–Real-Time Variable Bit Rate (nrt-VBR)
- Available Bit Rate (ABR)
- Unspecified Bit Rate (UBR)

The CBR category is based on providing a constant maximum bandwidth allocation for the connection for time-sensitive applications. The application does not always have to use the maximum bandwidth, but the maximum is available if needed for this level of service. This service category is suitable for use by real-time applications, voice and video applications, videoconferencing, and other similar applications.

The rt-VBR service category also is meant to provide a high level of service for time-sensitive applications that do not always generally maintain a constant bit rate but are still time-sensitive applications.

The nrt-VBR service category is similar to the rt-VBR category in that the expected traffic will be bursty in nature, but the nature of the communications does not require that data be delivered without significant delays. Both VBR categories can be useful for applications such as voice, when compression techniques are used, and possibly transaction-based applications, such as reservation systems or for carrying frame relay traffic.

The ABR category is intended for applications that might increase or decrease their traffic level depending on network conditions. In other words, they can be satisfied by using whatever bandwidth is available. Connections of this type can specify a minimum required bandwidth level but then can use more bandwidth as the network makes it available. Typical uses for this kind of service are LAN connections, such as distributed files services.

The UBR service category represents a "best-effort" connection and is intended for applications that really don't care about bandwidth or QoS. This bottom-of-the-barrel kind of service is useful for applications with traffic that needs to get from one place to another but is in no hurry; for example, file transfers that can be done in a batch mode and do not have users sitting at the keyboard waiting for completion. Messaging services, such as e-mail, also might find this service level sufficient.

Frame Relay and X.25

The X.25 protocol defines an interface for delivering information to a packet-switched network and does not make any assumptions about the method used to carry the actual data from one place to another. Or, to put it another way, X.25 is not a transport protocol. It is an interface that can be adapted to different kinds of network transport protocols. X.25, which has been around for more than 20 years, was developed to allow connection to various public networks, such as CompuServe and Tymnet, and provides for speeds of up to 56Kbps. Frame relay is similar to X.25 except that it uses digital connections instead of the analog connections that X.25 was designed for. Although X.25 can be considered a "dying" technology, frame relay use continues to grow.

Frame relay can operate at much higher speeds (up to 1.544Mbps) than X.25 because of the digital nature of frame relay, which is usually offered over a T1 or fractional T1 line. The digital nature of the line allows fewer errors than the analog system, and frame relay can operate faster than other technologies because it does not perform any actual error correction. When a frame error is detected, the frame is dropped. It is up to the endpoints to detect, through some higher-level protocol, that an error has occurred.

If an error is found in the frame, or if the network is too busy, the frame is dropped. This is similar to the way the IP functions. Frame relay does its best to get the frame to its endpoint in the connection, but does not notify the starting point of the connection if an error occurs. Because frame relay doesn't have to worry about reporting errors (which can occur anywhere along the path, at any switch) back to the sender, it can switch traffic at a faster rate. With today's fast CPUs and digital lines (which are less prone to errors than analog lines), it only makes sense to let higher-level protocols take care of detecting and remedying errors.

Because frame relay is a packet-switched technology, you must pay for only the bandwidth that you expect to use. Instead of paying for the full cost of a T1 line between two geographically distant offices, you can use frame-relay services. The carrier mixes traffic from various sources and transmits it over the line so that frame relay represents a shared-medium technology. The downside is that it's always possible that the bandwidth you need might not be available when you need it. Just as you sometimes get a circuit busy message when you try to place a telephone call during a peak holiday period, the same thing can happen if traffic from multiple users of a carrier's frame-relay service must transfer large amounts of data at the same time.

For this reason, when you purchase frame-relay services, you get a guarantee—called the *committed information rate (CIR)*—of the amount of available bandwidth that the carrier expects to be capable of providing. You might be able to get higher throughput rates than that guaranteed by the CIR, but there is always the possibility that, occasionally, you might not achieve rates that are guaranteed by the CIR. It is important to monitor your use in a high-traffic environment to be sure you are getting what you paid for.

Frame relay also can reduce the number of physical connections you need at a site, which can make it a better choice than dedicated point-to-point lines. For example, if you have multiple branch offices, you could use a dedicated T1 (or Fractional T1) line to connect each office to the main headquarters. Or, you could use frame relay at each branch office, using only a single physical connection back at the main office. Traffic from all the branch offices is lumped together on this incoming frame relay line, so you don't need a separate physical dedicated line going to each branch office (see Figure 19.5).

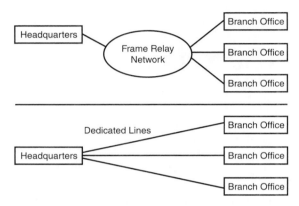

Figure 19.5 Using frame relay can reduce the number of physical connections required when compared to dedicated lines.

Frame relay is similar to ATM in that it is a packet-switched technology. However, ATM uses a fixed sized for its cells, whereas frame relay packets are variable (similar to ethernet frames). Packet switching in a frame relay network is done using virtual circuits, which are logical paths through the frame relay network.

Note

Some vendors of frame-relay services offer much faster capabilities, up to 45Mbps, using T3 lines.

The Frame Relay Header

Frame relay also has a lower overhead than traditional network technologies, such as ethernet. The frame relay header is only 2–5 bytes long. In Figure 19.6, you can see that the header doesn't contain a whole lot of information.

The following fields appear in Figure 19.6:

- **DLCI**—The Data Link Connection Identifier is used to identify the virtual circuit connection. Note that the DLCI is 10 bits long but is not stored contiguously in the header.

- **C/R**—The single-bit Command/Response field is application specific. Network switches do not modify this field.

- **FECN**—This single-bit field is the Forward Explicit Congestion Notification field.

- **BECN**—This single-bit field is the Backward Explicit Congestion Notification field.

- **DE**—This single-bit field is the Discard Eligibility Indicator field.
- **EA**—This single-bit field is the Extension Bit, which is used to indicate a 3- or 4-byte header.

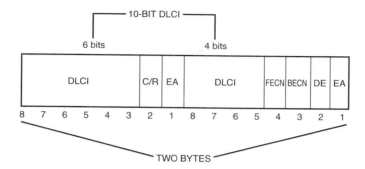

Figure 19.6 The frame relay header contains the DLCI (Data Link Connection Identifier) that identifies the connection.

The DLCI field is a 10-bit number used to specify the virtual circuit number for the connection. The DLCI identifies the particular port to which the local network is attached in the frame relay equipment. Throughout the network, this number is used to designate the endpoint of the connection.

When using a PVC, the network administrator must set up routing tables in the switches that make up the network. When a frame comes in one port, it is a simple matter to look up the DLCI in a table and then quickly switch the frame to an outgoing port that can take it to another switch, where the process is repeated, or to its eventual destination. Note that if a switch receives a frame that has a DLCI value that is not found the switch's routing table, the frame is discarded.

If this sounds like a simple mechanism for getting a data frame from one point to another, it is. In addition to the short header, the frame relay packet also has a Frame Check Sequence (FCS) value calculated to ensure the integrity of the packet, which is placed at the end of the frame. The switch can recalculate this value when it receives a frame and, if the newly calculated value does not match the value stored in this field, the frame is assumed to have become corrupted and is dropped.

Network congestion also can cause a packet to be dropped. After a switch's buffers are full, incoming frames are dropped until buffer space becomes available again. However, frame relay does provide some signaling mechanisms that can be used to help control network congestion. Frame relay also provides for signaling to set up an SVC. Both of these signaling mechanisms, however, are optional components and vendors don't have to implement them. Remember that the higher-level protocol (such as TCP/IP) can detect when its data segments have not been acknowledged and retransmit any data that is dropped along the virtual circuit path.

Network Congestion Signaling

Three methods can be used to help prevent network congestion:

- Explicit Congestion Notification
- Discard Eligibility
- Implicit Congestion Notification

The Explicit Congestion Notification method uses two bits in the header: the FECN (Forward Explicit Congestion Notification) and BECN (Backward Explicit Congestion Notification) bits. The FECN bit is used to tell nodes farther along the path (forward) that congestion is occurring. Based on such things as the switch's buffer use and the length of frames waiting in a queue, a switch can detect that congestion probably is going to occur before it must start dropping packets. When this happens, the switch sets the FECN bit in a packet to 1 (the default is 0), and then sends the packet on to the next switch. In this manner, switches downstream from the switch approaching congestion are notified of the condition.

Similarly, the BECN bit is used to notify upstream sources that a network congestion condition is rapidly becoming a possibility. It does this not by returning packets sent from that source, but by watching for packets traveling in the opposite direction that are already addressed to that source. The BECN bit is set to 1 (again, the default is 0) in these packets. Thus, when a source sending out a lot of traffic starts to receive packets back from other switches, it can check this bit to determine whether packets are being transmitted too fast.

Implicit Congestion Notification is not performed by the frame relay switches. Instead, it means that the higher-level protocols, such as TCP, can detect that packets are not being acknowledged, take appropriate action to retransmit them, and, depending on the higher-level protocol, possibly slow down the transmission rate.

Referring to Figure 19.6, notice that another field, Discard Eligibility (DE), also can be present in a frame relay packet. This field is used to determine which packets should be dropped when a congestion condition occurs. Remember that the frame relay provider contracts to give you a CIR. Yet, when the network is not busy, usually you can use more bandwidth. However, after you begin to send out data at a rate that is greater than the CIR you have contracted for, the DE bit is set to 1 (the default is 0).

When a switch needs to drop packets due to network congestion, those packets that have the DE field set to 1 are the first to go! If discarding those packets doesn't solve the problem, any packet can be dropped. When properly implemented, however, this mechanism lets a switch drop packets that probably are the source of the congestion in the first place: those that are sending at a rate above their contracted CIR.

The Local Management Interface Signal Mechanism

Another optional signaling mechanism that can be used in a Frame-Relay network is called the Local Management Interface (LMI) specification, of which there are several versions. However, the basic mechanism employed is to use nondata management frames to report the status of an interface or a virtual circuit. For example, a management frame can be used to send a keepalive signal, indicating that, although there isn't a lot of traffic flowing through the interface, the connection is still active. Another management frame can be used to report on the valid DLCIs for a particular interface. Finally, a management frame can be used to indicate the status of a virtual circuit (it's congested, for example).

Using Switched Virtual Circuits (SVCs)

Originally, most frame relay equipment was made to allow for the creation of PVCs. This requires that a network administrator of the frame-relay network set up routing tables so that a permanent connection exists between the two endpoints of a connection. This is a general principle, in that alternative routes can be used occasionally, but basically a PVC is an always-on, same-path type of connection.

An SVC is more like a telephone call; it's an on-demand path created for the duration of the data-transfer session. The virtual circuit is torn down after it has been used and doesn't stay in a switch's routing table like the DLCI entries for a PVC. When an SVC needs to be created, the destination is notified of the need and, if it is willing to accept the circuit, a path is created through the

Frame-Relay network for the SVC (call setup). When the circuit is no longer needed, either side of the connection can notify the network to terminate the circuit.

The advantages of using an SVC is that you have to pay only for what you use. It's less expensive than maintaining a PVC that doesn't have a constant rate of traffic. SVCs also can be used in conjunction with PVCs. You can use PVCs for your basic network traffic that flows at a predictable rate, and create or tear down SVCs as needed to handle additional traffic.

Note

The Frame Relay Forum organization was formed to promote the use of frame-relay technology and to help create standards for the technology. You can visit its Web site at **www.frforum.com**.

The methods used for signaling to set up and terminate SVCs is beyond the scope of this book and is a subject that should be pursued if you are an administrator of a Frame-Relay network. For the end user, however, the mechanisms used for call setup and termination aren't that important. You might want to visit the Frame Relay Forum's Web site, which contains a wealth of information on the technical details involved in signaling, as well as documents about proposed new methods and features for Frame-Relay networks.

Possible Problems Using Frame Relay

You might encounter the following problems when using frame relay:

- **Bandwidth use**—As you grow, you might find that the amount of bandwidth you purchased is inadequate for your needs.
- **Bursting**—When you try to send a large burst of traffic that is in excess of the contracted rate, the switch might discard packets it receives that are above the allowable rate, forcing retransmissions and increased response times.
- **Network congestion**—Although the vendor might give you a guarantee of the available bandwidth (the CIR), when many customers use the network at the same time, network congestion can result.

The Frame Relay Forum defined several metrics that can be used to determine the quality of service in a frame-relay network. These metrics, which can be found in the forum's FRF.13 Service Level Definitions Implementation Agreement, are

- **Frame Transfer Delay**—The time required to transfer a frame through the network.
- **Frame Delivery Ratio**—The ratio of frames received (frames delivered) to the number of frames sent (frames offered) in one direction across a single virtual connection.
- **Data Delivery Ratio**—Similar to the Frame Delivery Ratio, but measures the ration of payload octets received to those sent.
- **Service Availability**—Outages resulting from faults in the network (called Fault Outage) as well as those beyond the control of the network, including scheduled maintenance (called Excluded Outage).

When reviewing the Service Level Agreement (SLA) that your frame-relay provider offers, use these metrics to help you understand what kind of commitment the vendor is making. With these metrics, the vendor might further qualify them based on the CIR as opposed to bursts allowed by the agreement. For example, it would be unreasonable to expect to receive the same kind of delivery ratio for bursts of high-volume traffic that you receive for traffic that flows through the network at the rate guaranteed by the CIR.

When you review the SLA, be sure you understand how each metric will be measured. Does the vendor use statistics provided by its own switch (and will the vendor allow you access to these statistics?), or does the vendor use an RMON probe or SNMP MIB to define the metrics? What portion of the connection is to be measured for metrics: end-to-end or switch to switch?

DSL and Cable Modems

Most home users can't afford to spend the several thousands of dollars a month it would cost to put in a T-class of service. Until recently, ISDN (discussed in the previous chapter, "Dial-Up Connections") was the primary digital method for connecting home offices or those who have large bandwidth requirements to the Internet or to a company's remote access servers. ISDN, however, has become almost outdated for most of today's remote users because of several reasons. However, sometimes ISDN is a good choice for a connection, but it does have some drawbacks:

- ISDN is a dial-up technology. To connect to the Internet or a remote site, you must place a call, just like you do with a telephone.

- ISDN BRI (Basic Rate Interface service), with two 64Kbps channels you can use for data transmission, although cheaper than a T-class of service, is still priced beyond the reach of most typical home users or small businesses.

- Newer technologies have been developed over the past 10 years that are not only faster than ISDN, but also much cheaper to provide. These digital services are provided by either your local cable television company through a cable modem, or by one or more providers in your area using the same twisted-pair telephone wires that connect your telephone to the local central office.

With the advent of faster modems, the price that telephone companies charge for ISDN's maximum of 128Kbps service isn't really justifiable for most users when you consider that current modem technology (with multilink capabilities) can easily come close to this speed.

Topological Differences Between Cable and DSL

Both cable modems and DSL are digital broadband technologies, but that's about all they have in common. The first major difference is the physical connection. DSL provides a direct point-to-point connection to a termination point in the telephone company's central office using the same twisted-pair wiring used for telephone services. Because DSL uses copper wires and the signal attenuates (weakens and degrades) the farther you get from the central office, DSL has a limited distance, usually a maximum of 18,000 feet. Another thing to keep in mind is that the farther you get from the central office, the slower the speed you will be able to get from a DSL line. Because most people don't live next door to a central office, and because most telephone companies have been trying to extend profitable service offerings to more and more of their customer bases, a solution that creates a "mini" central office in the field is being rapidly deployed in many areas. This involves using high-capacity lines (usually fiber optic) from the central office to connect a digital concentrator out in the field. The fiber-optic cable enables digital communications back to the central office from your neighborhood. Using this method, it's easy to deliver digital services in the "last mile" by moving the digital equipment out of the central office and closer to subscribers.

Back at the central office, the data portion of the signal is split off and sent directly to a high-speed digital connection to the Internet. The voice portion of the signal (the first 4Mhz) is directed to the old PSTN. This means that your connection is shared by no one and, after the service has been provisioned and installed, you can expect to get the same speed no matter what time of day. Cable systems work in a similar manner, separating Internet traffic from television data at the cable company's front end.

The communication path for cable modems is a shared access medium, similar to an ethernet network. The coaxial cable that snakes through your neighborhood delivering cable television services is used for both television and cable-modem communications. When you get DSL advocates and cable modem aficionados in the same room arguing, the DSL guys will tell you that the shared access coaxial cable is a choke point that can limit the speeds you can obtain. This argument is based on the notion that as more homes in your neighborhood begin to use the cable-modem service, the shared coaxial cable can become saturated. Your actual speed using a cable modem will vary from the maximum capacity depending on how many other users are using the same cable at the same time. In practice, however, cable systems offer a higher bandwidth than many DSL systems, especially if you don't live close to a central office or there isn't a digital connection sitting in a box somewhere in your neighborhood. And, as cable segments become heavily populated, cable companies can split the cable into different segments and run a line back to a router that connects to the Internet.

One question you must ask yourself when making a decision about using a cable modem or DSL is which company provides you better service now? When you call your local telephone company or cable company, which is the quickest to respond? Which company provides a better service? How important is that Internet connection to your business or for recreational use?

DSL Services

Just as you can obtain phone service from more than one company, using the same telephone lines, the same goes for DSL services. Although your local telco might not offer the service, other providers in the same area might. Many telephone companies invested heavily in the equipment needed to provide ISDN services several years ago, charged a lot for the service, and found few customers. Some are hesitant to invest in the DSLAM and other equipment needed to provide DSL services. However, that doesn't stop third parties from co-locating their own DSL equipment at the local telco office and offering you the service.

To make things even more complicated, some third-party providers are actually fourth-party providers. For example, in April 2000, NorthPoint Communications Group Inc., which was a third-party provider, shut down services to most of its DSL customers. Many of these customers didn't even know that NorthPoint was the provider, because it resold services to other companies, such as the Microsoft Network.

Of course, if the actual telephone wires that connect you to the central office aren't capable of supporting a DSL connection, you won't be able to get it from any provider until the lines are upgraded.

Another thing to remember about both cable modems and DSL connections is that the high-speed capacity they both provide is only on that link from your computer to the ISP Internet connection. Both cable and DSL modems will do nothing to make the Internet itself or Web servers work faster. So, if your favorite Web site is being swamped with a large number of hits, you probably won't notice any difference between a dial-up connection and a digital connection.

A Quick Primer on the PSTN

Ordinary voice-grade service, called Plain Old Telephone Service (POTS), has its roots back in the 1930s when it was discovered that human beings can hear frequencies of up to about 20,000kHz, but normally talk in frequencies that range up to only about 3,500kHz. Because of this, the original telephone network was designed to transmit in channels of only 4,000kHz. However, those ordinary copper wires used in the last mile to the home can transmit using much higher frequencies. The problem with using the PSTN to provide high-speed data communications comes from the fact that, although the copper wiring *can* handle transmission at greater frequencies, the techniques used at the central office to digitize voice-grade traffic cannot. The incoming analog voice signal is sampled 8,000 times per second and coded into 8 bits for transmission on the digital portions of the PSTN. This means that the effective data throughput is limited to 64Kbps. Because most telephone circuits use one of the bits for network-management purposes, the actual data throughput shrinks to only 56Kbps.

Communications between central offices and long-distance lines make use of more modern techniques, stacking multiple voice circuits on top of each other in 4kHz segments and sending them across high-capacity fiber-optic lines. The Internet backbone is composed of similar high-capacity lines capable of extremely fast transmission of large amounts of data. The limiting factor for dial-up modems is that old, switched telephone network that sets the ceiling at 8,000 samples per second.

The maximum speed of today's dial-up modems is achieved by using sophisticated coding techniques on the wire on which data is transmitted as symbols, coupled with other compression algorithms. Yet, *analog modems* are limited to using only that first 4kHz of bandwidth on the copper wire. Because the twisted-pair telephone wire can support higher frequencies, it's only natural to assume that there would be a digital solution to the speed roadblock that the voice-grade telephone circuit forces you to use.

xDSL

When DSL is discussed, xDSL is usually mentioned as well because there isn't just one type of DSL; instead, you can choose from an assortment of similar technologies, depending on your needs. For example, perhaps the most popular xDSL technology is ADSL (Asynchronous Digital Subscriber Line). This service provides a faster download speed to your computer or network, but you'll only have a much smaller data path back to the provider of this service.

One thing to keep in mind about xDSL technologies is that they are limited in the distance they can be offered from the telephone company's central office. This is due to several factors, including attenuation of the signal as it travels down the copper wire and interference caused by signals from wires in a cable bundle interfering with other wires in the same bundle. Because telephone cables were initially laid down with no thought for offering digital services, it's possible that you won't be able to get any kind of xDSL connection.

Some of the more common offerings you'll find in the xDSL world are

- **ADSL**—Suited best for a home user or a small office where data requires a large download speed (1,500 to 8,000Kbps) and a slower upload speed (32Kbps to 1,088Kbps). ADSL can potentially reach up to 18,000 feet from the central office.

- **RADSL**—Rate-Adaptive Digital Subscriber Line is a variation of ASDL. The modems on this type of connection can test the line to determine what speed it will support. RADSL usually provides for a longer distance from the central office (about 21,000 feet) but provides for slower speeds. Expect download speeds from 600Kbps to 7,000Kbps. Typical upload speeds are from 128Kbps to 1,000Kbps.

- **SDSL**—This Single-line Digital Subscriber Line allows for symmetric bidirectional communications. Unlike ADSL, SDSL gives you the same bandwidth in either direction. Generally, you must be within 10,000 feet of the central office. Transmission rates (depending, of course, on distance) range from 160Kbps to 2,084Kbps.

- **HDSL**—High bit Data-Rate DSL is an early entry into the xDSL market. HDSL also gives you the same bandwidth for both directions.

- **G.Lite (also called Universal ADSL)**—This form of ADSL is easier to install than the traditional ADSL. Traditional ADSL requires installing a splitter at the consumer premises, which effectively splits the lower voice-frequency channel from the higher frequencies used for digital transmission. G.Lite operates at a lower speed than ADSL (1,544Kbps downstream, 384Kbps upstream), but does so without using a splitter.

There are still other xDSL technologies, but some are proprietary and the solution you end up choosing will depend on what your local provider offers. There's even a version called IDSL, which offers an ISDN service using xDSL technology! Of course, the higher-rate services are going to cost more. For most small offices or home users, the advent of cheap ASDL and G.Lite services can be an ideal solution for remote connections.

DSLAMs, CAP, and DMT

Implementing ASDL services in a central office is not nearly as costly as implementing ISDN. Using ASDL, the network traffic never actually enters the PSTN like dial-up modem analog connections do. At the central office, the incoming signal is split, sending the voice-grade frequencies (the first 4kHz channel) to the normal telephone switch, and the higher frequencies used by DSL to a device called a DSL Access Multiplexer (DSLAM). The DSLAM is responsible for concentrating the DSL traffic it receives and passing it to the Internet by using higher-capacity technologies, such as T1–T3 lines, or to an ATM switched network. Lucent and Nortel make telephone line cards that can be used in the central office which combine digital and voice functions. If these cards are used, it isn't even necessary to rewire your phone line at the central office when DSL is provisioned, making it even easier for telephone companies to offer the service. One of the first drawbacks of getting DSL service is how it will be supported by the local telephone company. No matter who the "provider" of this service might be, how does the telephone company handle the digital signal after it's split off from the voice signal?

And, it does get just a little more complicated. For ASDL, two basic methods use those higher frequencies on copper wires: Carrierless Amplitude Phase (CAP) and Discrete MultiTone (DMT). Both of these methods use frequencies that are well past the 4kHz voice channel, and because of this are called *passband* technologies. Both voice and data can be carried on the same twisted-pair wires at the same time, operating in full-duplex mode. The voice-grade frequency range is *not* used for data (it is "passed by"), and there is a small amount of separation of frequencies before the ASDL upstream channel starts and another separation before the downstream channel starts, depending on whether your DSL is implemented using CAP or DMT. This separation helps to reduce the probability of one channel interfering with another.

The main difference between CAP and DMT is the way in which they use the higher frequencies on the ordinary copper wire pair. CAP uses two different carriers, a smaller frequency range for the upstream data and a larger frequency range for the downstream data path, as you can see in Figure 19.7. CAP uses a small part of the frequencies above the voice channel for uploading data to the Internet, and a much larger range of frequencies for the downstream data path.

However, a drawback of CAP is that any noise on the line can cause the signal to become easily corrupted. This can be caused by wiring that has degraded, interference from other wires in a cable bundle, or bridge taps that haven't been removed. To overcome this, CAP-based modems usually try to measure the line when they start up to determine the defects inherent in it. The modems then try to use equalizers to create mirror images of the line distortion that can be used to clean up the signal.

DMT uses channels above the voice channel just like CAP does. However, as you can see in Figure 19.8, DMT divides the upper frequencies into many discrete, separate 4kHz channels, and assigns some for upstream communications and others for downstream data flows. Each channel is called a *bin*.

DMT can monitor each channel to determine which ones are having problems with interference, and not use those small segments of the available frequency range, or use the troublesome bins for a lower rate of data transmission. Bins in the lower frequency range are used for the upstream data path, and those in the higher frequency ranges are used for the downstream data path. DMT constantly monitors each bin and adjusts their use depending on performance. Bins in the lower frequency range also can be used as bidirectional communication channels. If this is done, echo-canceling circuitry is necessary, making DMT a more expensive technology.

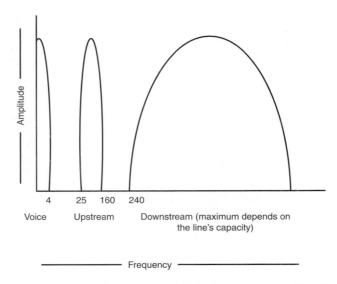

Figure 19.7 CAP uses two ranges of frequencies, with the larger range used for the downstream path.

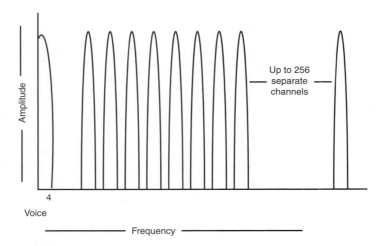

Figure 19.8 DMT creates multiple channels in the upper-frequency range and assigns them for upstream or downstream communication.

CAP was originally deployed by ASDL vendors early in the game, and much of the equipment is proprietary. That is, a modem you get from one provider might not work with another provider's system. This really shouldn't matter, however, if you intend to keep the same provider for a while. However, in the past two years, several large companies that were in the business of offering DSL services have gone out of business, or at least the DSL business, leaving customers stranded. In this case, it would be nice to know your digital modem will work with another provider when you find one.

The ITU selected DMT as the standard method to be employed for ASDL. However, a lot of equipment using CAP has been installed in the past and can continue to have a useful life for some years to come. When it comes to choosing a provider, you might not have many choices in your area. You might have to take what you can get—if you can get it. You might be located too far from the central office to make DSL a solution for your home or small business connection. Or, the building in which you are located might have been wired years ago and contain a lot of bridge taps and deteriorating cables.

However, it is important to know the difference between CAP and DMT. Because DMT is a standard now, most new equipment that will be produced is likely to use DMT.

ADSL

ADSL is ideal for home users for Internet surfing because it's usually priced reasonably, and the bandwidth use for home users is generally asymmetrical. That is, you click the mouse button on a link and then wait for a large download of data to your computer. Most Internet Web page communication for the home user involves a minor amount of data being sent upstream to the Internet, with a large amount of data being sent downstream to the computer in response to the request. With multimedia applications, such as streaming audio and video, the large data pipe that ADSL provides will make the Internet appear to be lightning fast to a home user. However, the opposite is not true. If you operate a Web server from your house, keep in mind that ADSL provides a much smaller data pipe back to your ISP. Thus, if you want to place a server on the Web and expect it to send out large volumes of data to the Internet, you'll probably have to settle for another xDSL technology.

However, if a business has users that work from home, ADSL might be a good way to establish connectivity back to the main office through the Internet. For example, a help desk technician can use the voice channel on the telephone line to take customer help calls. To assist the worker in his job, the ASDL connection can be used to allow the technician to search Web site pages or a database residing on a server back at the business's main office. As long as it isn't necessary for the worker to send large amounts of information back to the office, ADSL can be a good fit here.

G.Lite DSL

Concerns over putting too many wires in a cable bundle to use for high-frequency DSL services spurred the development of a version of DSL called G.Lite. This version of DSL doesn't require a splitter (to separate the voice channel from the ASDL channels) and operates at lower frequencies. Lower frequencies allows for downstream data flows of only about 1–1.5Mbps. Upstream capacity usually runs at 100–300Kbps. By using a lower range of frequencies, it's possible for telephone companies to offer a more reliable service, over a longer distance, because attenuation of the higher frequencies (and the cross-talk they can cause) is less of a factor. The speeds provided by G.Lite recognize that the Internet itself, like the PSTN, can be a limiting factor when it comes to speed. It doesn't matter how fast your particular connection to the Internet is if the Web site you're trying to access is on a slow server, or connected by a slow link. Most users won't notice the difference between 1.5Mbps and 8Mbps that can be attained with more expensive DSL technologies.

G.Lite was developed by the Universal ADSL Working Group (UAWG). Its mission was to develop a lower-cost version of ASDL, based on standards, that could be easily installed. The ITU approved G.Lite as a standard in 1999.

Note, however, that for those versions of DSL that don't require a splitter on the home end of the connection, it might be necessary to plug in inexpensive filters for every telephone in the house. This helps reduce the noise that telephones can introduce into the wire, when you take them off the hook, for example.

A Quick Lesson in How Cable Modem Technologies Work

Although a cable modem connection might work for a home user or a small business, you must again think of the service provider before committing your network's connectivity to the Internet. Some cable companies are just great, providing quick resolution to problems, and others are not so great. Again, if you're not getting a good response (or better yet, response time) from your cable company at home, you might want to reconsider it as a link for your small business.

By their very natures, cable television networks are not constrained by the problems caused when data needs to pass through the PSTN. Cable television networks don't use the PSTN. Instead, they use a shielded coaxial cable (and some high-speed fiber links to get closer to your house) to deliver a quality TV signal, usually using 6MHz bands for each digital channel. To provide for cable modem service, all that is necessary is to set aside one or more television bands and use them as delivery channels for Internet access. Again, the offering is usually asymmetrical, just like ADSL. By using a high-bandwidth channel for downstream communications, cable can offer a larger bandwidth (for all subscribers on a shared segment) to send data from the Internet to your home. By using time slots (some dedicated to each subscriber, and some called contention slots that anyone can try to use), cable companies offer a smaller upstream data communications path.

Cable modems aren't really modems at all. The term *modem* used to be spelled MODEM because it's an acronym (MODulation/DEModulation), and a true modem is a device that converts digital signals to analog signals for transmission over an analog telephone line. The receiving modem does the opposite, converting the analog signal back to a digital signal your computer can understand. The term *cable modem* is just a convenient way of indicating that you're getting a fast connection from the cable company. No "analog" signal is involved in the connection whatsoever.

Most cable companies won't allocate a static IP address because it's easier to use DHCP to dynamically assign addresses, just like most network administrators do in a typical LAN situation. Using DHCP, which is discussed in Chapter 23, "BOOTP and the Dynamic Host Configuration Protocol," the cable company doesn't have to perform the manual task of assigning addresses for each customer. The DHCP server performs this task automatically.

One thing to consider when deciding between DSL or cable Internet access service is the bandwidth you'll be using. Whereas DSL technologies give you a direct connection to the DSLAM in the local central office, cable is a shared medium. Many cable companies don't want you to hook up more than one computer to their connection and use up a lot of bandwidth, which is limited because many households or businesses in your area are connected to the same cable segment. Like traditional ethernet, cable technologies are a shared medium, so the total bandwidth available on any particular segment is limited.

You can get around this by purchasing a simple router for about $100 that will connect to your cable modem. The router then will act as a DHCP server and enable you to connect several computers in your house to the single connection the cable provider gives you. Be careful, though, because big brother might be watching you! Before ordering cable service, check the fine print to be sure they don't prohibit you from using additional computers on the single connection!

Even if you want to use only one computer on a cable (or even a DSL) connection, it's a good idea to buy one of these inexpensive routers, because they usually offer minimal firewall capabilities in addition to DHCP. For more information about the functions a firewall can perform, see Chapter 40, "Firewalls."

If you wonder why a firewall might be necessary, consider the fact that the cable connection is always on, unlike a dial-up connection. This means that your computer is exposed 24 hours a day to hackers on the Internet that are just looking for computers that are not protected by a firewall or good security measures. Indeed, many distributed denial-of-service attacks that have occurred in recent years involve first planting programs in innocent home computers that lack protection. Then, when enough of these programs have been planted, a single message can be sent to activate the program on hundreds, if not thousands of computers, causing them to attack a single source that is the real target of the attack. So, if you're going to have a DSL or cable always-on connection, use some form of protection!

Early implementations used a separate, ordinary telephone modem connection for the upstream data channel. If you still have this kind of service, you might as well consider using that single telephone twisted-pair wiring for ADSL because it will provide voice and data circuits, while using the phone line for an upload to the Internet eliminates the voice circuit. Newer cable systems, however, based on the DOCSIS (Data Over Cable Service Interface Specification) standards allow for bidirectional, asymmetrical communications. The newest version of DOCSIS includes the necessary authentication and encryption features that make cable modem access as secure as DSL. In general, if you can see other computers in your Network Neighborhood, your cable provider is using an older system and you might want to take steps to protect yourself, such as using a firewall appliance.

Unless your business needs to upload a large amount of information to the Internet, a cable modem might provide sufficient downstream bandwidth, as does ADSL. If you need a faster connection to the Internet or between offices, other transports can be used, such as those legacy systems discussed at the beginning of this chapter. Or, you might decide to subscribe to an ATM or frame relay service, where you can negotiate with a vendor to get the bandwidth that you need.

Network Operating Systems, Protocols, and Services

SOME OF THE MAIN TOPICS FOR THIS PART ARE

Overview of the TCP/IP Protocol Suite

TCP/IP Services and Applications

Troubleshooting Tools for TCP/IP Networks

BOOTP and the Dynamic Host Configuration Protocol (DHCP)

Name Resolution

Overview of Microsoft's Active Directory Service

Overview of Novell Netware IPX/SPX

Overview of the Novell Bindery and Directory Services (NDS)

NetBIOS and NetBEUI

Routing Protocols

PART IV

Overview of the TCP/IP Protocol Suite

SOME OF THE MAIN TOPICS IN THIS CHAPTER ARE

TCP/IP and the OSI Reference Model

The Internet Protocol (IP)

The Address Resolution Protocol—Resolving IP Addresses to Hardware Addresses

The Transmission Control Protocol (TCP)

The User Datagram Protocol (UDP)

Ports, Services, and Applications

The Internet Control Message Protocol (ICMP)

CHAPTER 20

TCP/IP is the primary network protocol used on the Internet. Unlike many other network protocols that have been discussed so far—such as ARCnet—TCP/IP was not developed by a single vendor as a proprietary solution. TCP/IP was developed to provide a network link between computer systems from different vendors (such as IBM and Apple), so that a single protocol (or set of protocols) could be used to create a network, no matter what underlying computer hardware was used. During the early years of TCP/IP, universities, businesses, and government organizations were able to exchange information on the Arpanet—the Internet's predecessor—because TCP/IP could be implemented on just about any kind of computer.

TCP/IP has evolved over time, using a process where many individuals have had the opportunity to supply input into its development. The Request For Comments (RFCs) documents that you hear about all through this book are the documents that allow suggestions for protocol enhancements and new protocols to be reviewed by a diverse group of individuals who specialize in the particular topic at hand. TCP/IP was developed using this method to provide a network link between computer systems from different vendors. By freeing the development of the protocol(s) from the hands of particular manufacturers, TCP/IP has been developed to satisfy the needs of the many, instead of the needs of a single vendor's proprietary hardware needs.

In this chapter, we will look at all the major protocols that make up the TCP/IP suite and try to show how they work together. In addition to the protocols you will read about here, the TCP/IP suite also includes some standard applications, such as FTP and Telnet. These are discussed in Chapter 21, "TCP/IP Services and Applications." Finally, in Chapter 22, "Troubleshooting Tools for TCP/IP Networks," you will find useful information you can use when this complex suite of protocols and applications don't appear to be working as they should.

But let's first turn our attention to the basic protocols and learn how they function.

TCP/IP and the OSI Reference Model

The OSI (Open Systems Interconnect) Reference model is used mostly as a framework around which a discussion of network protocols can be discussed. Developed in 1984 by the International Organization for Standardization (ISO), this model defines a protocol stack in a modular fashion. For further discussion of the OSI reference model, see Appendix A, "The OSI Seven-Layer Networking Model." For the purposes of this chapter, it should be noted that development of TCP/IP began long before the OSI model and, as can be expected, TCP/IP protocols don't always neatly match up to the seven layers of the OSI model.

Note

While some texts discuss the OSI model and the standards organization that created it, there is one bit of Internet trivia that is perpetuated about the ISO "acronym" that you might find interesting. You'll find that many writers say that ISO stands for the International Standards Organization. Sounds right, doesn't it? Well, it's not true. In the first place, *ISO* is not an acronym, it's a name. And it's not the International Standards Organization, it's the International Organization for Standardization (which would be IOS if one were to create an acronym). The name ISO was chosen for a very specific reason. "ISO" is derived from the Greek word isos, which can be translated as "equal." In the English language you'll find the prefix iso quite frequently with this meaning; for example, the word "isometric." Established in 1947, the ISO wanted a name that could be used worldwide, without having to take into account translations of their name, which would result in different acronyms depending on the language or translation. Thus, OSI is an acronym, but ISO is a name and is used to refer to this standards organization worldwide. You can find out more about the wide range of standards promulgated by this organization at its Web site: `http://www.iso.ch`.

The ISO used this model to actually develop a set of open network protocols, but these were never widely adopted. However, the OSI networking model is still used today when discussing network protocols, and it is a good idea to become familiar with it if you will be working in this field. It is important to note that TCP/IP was developed based on a similar, though less modular, reference model, the DOD (Department of Defense) or DARPA model.

In Figure 20.1, you can see the four layers that make up the TCP/IP—DOD model, and how each layer relates to the OSI model.

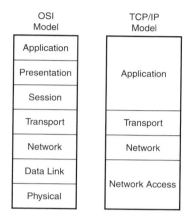

Figure 20.1   Comparison of the TCP/IP and OSI networking models.

As you can see, TCP/IP doesn't exactly fit into the OSI model, but it is still possible to refer to the model when discussing certain aspects of the protocols and services that TCP/IP provides.

TCP/IP Is a Collection of Protocols, Services, and Applications

The acronym TCP/IP stands for Transmission Control Protocol/Internet Protocol. In addition to these two important protocols, many other related protocols and utilities are commonly grouped together and called the TCP/IP Protocol Suite. This "suite" of protocols includes such things as the User Datagram Protocol (UDP) and the Internet Control Message Protocol (ICMP), among others.

Note

The terms *protocol stack* and *protocol suite* often are used to mean the same thing. Although it is convenient to think of TCP/IP as a single software entity, that is not the case. The protocols discussed in this chapter are called a "suite" because they work together, some providing services to others. For example, IP is the transport protocol that TCP uses when it wants to send data on the network. UDP likewise uses IP when it communicates on the network. At the bottom of the stack, ARP functions to associate hard-wired network card addresses with IP addresses.

Thus, when we talk about TCP/IP protocol suite (or stack) we are talking about a group of protocols.

TCP/IP, IP, and UDP

The main workhorses of this protocol suite are IP, TCP, and UDP:

- **IP**—The Internet Protocol is an unreliable, connectionless protocol that provides the means to get a datagram from one computer or device to another and for internetwork addressing.

- **TCP**—The Transmission Control Protocol uses IP but provides a higher-level functionality that checks to be sure that the datagrams that IP manages actually get to and from their intended destinations. TCP is a connection-oriented protocol, requiring that a session be established to manage communications between two points in the network.

- **UDP**—The User Datagram Protocol also uses IP to move data around the network. Whereas TCP uses an acknowledgment mechanism to ensure reliable delivery, UDP does not. It is intended for use in applications that don't necessarily need the guaranteed delivery service provided by TCP. The Domain Name System (DNS) service is an example of an application that uses UDP. Applications that use UDP are responsible for taking on the functions of checking for reliable delivery that is provided by TCP.

As you can see in Figure 20.2, IP is the basic protocol used in the TCP/IP suite to get datagrams delivered.

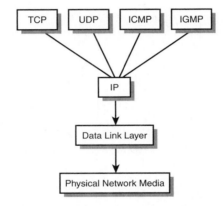

Figure 20.2   IP is used by many other protocols as the mechanism by which their data is routed and delivered through the network.

In this figure, you can see that TCP/IP and its related protocols work above the physical components of the network. Because of this, it is easy to adapt TCP/IP to different types of networks, such as ethernet and token ring. When you talk about using TCP/IP on the network, what it all boils down to is that you're packaging up your data into an IP packet that is passed down to the actual network hardware for delivery. Because IP is the common denominator of the TCP/IP suite, we'll discuss it first, and after that show how the remaining protocols build on the functions provided by IP.

Other Miscellaneous Protocols

In addition to TCP and IP, many other protocols are part of the TCP/IP suite. In Figure 20.2 (shown previously) you can see that the IGMP and ICMP protocols are included. IGMP is the Internet Group Management Protocol, which is used to manage groups of systems that are members of multicast groups. *Multicasting* is a technique that allows a datagram to be delivered to more than one destination. Figure 20.2 also shows the Internet Control Message Protocol (ICMP), which performs many functions to help control traffic on a network. In addition to these protocols, which are discussed later in this chapter, other protocols usually considered as part of the TCP/IP protocol suite include:

- **ARP**—The Address Resolution protocol. This protocol (discussed along with RARP later in this chapter) is used by a computer to determine what hardware address is associated with an IP address. This is necessary because IP addresses are used to route data between networks, while communications on the local network segment are done using the burned-in hardware address of the network cards.

- **RARP**—The Reverse Address Resolution protocol is similar to ARP but works in reverse. This is an older protocol that was developed to allow a computer to find out what IP address it should use, based on a table stored usually on a router. This functionality has generally been replaced by other protocols, such as BOOTP and DHCP. However, you can still find this protocol in use on many networks that contain older legacy equipment that has yet to reach the end of its useful life.

- **DNS**—The Domain Name System is the hierarchical naming system used by the Internet and most TCP/IP networks. For example, when you type www.twoinc.com into a browser, your TCP/IP stack sends a request to a DNS server to find out the IP address that is associated with that name. From then on, the browser can use the IP address to send requests to the Web site. More information about DNS can be found in Chapter 24, "Name Resolution."

- **BOOTP**—The Bootstrap protocol is also an older protocol that has generally been replaced by DHCP. In fact, most DHCP servers can act as BOOTP servers as well. BOOTP was created to allow a diskless workstation to download configuration information, such as an IP address and the name of a server that it can use to download an operating system. Because the diskless workstation has no local storage (other than memory), it can't store this information itself between boots.

- **DHCP**—The Dynamic Host Configuration protocol relieves the network administrator of the task of having to manually configure each computer on the network with addressing and other information. Chapter 23, "BOOTP and the Dynamic Host Configuration Protocol (DHCP)" cover this in great detail.

- **SNMP**—The Simple Network Management protocol was developed to make managing network devices and computers from a central location easy. You can find out more about SNMP in Chapter 44, "Network Testing and Analysis Tools."

- **RMON**—The Remote Monitoring protocol was developed to further enhance the administrator's ability to manage computers and network devices remotely. This protocol is also covered in greater detail in Chapter 44.

- **SMTP**—The Simple Mail Transfer protocol is the protocol that gets your e-mail from here to there. Appendix F, "Overview of the Simple Mail Transfer Protocol (SMTP)," can give you more information about how this protocol functions.

The Internet Protocol (IP)

Although the Internet protocol is the second component of the TCP/IP acronym, it is perhaps the more important of the two. As was previously mentioned, IP is the basic protocol in the suite that is used for getting packets from one place to another. IP provides a connectionless, unacknowledged network service, and also provides the addressing mechanism used by TCP/IP. The following main features distinguish IP from other protocols:

- IP is a connectionless protocol. No setup is required in order for IP to send a packet of information to another computer.

- IP is an unacknowledged protocol. For the most part it doesn't check to see that a datagram actually arrives intact at its destination. However, the Internet Control Message Protocol (ICMP) does assist IP so that some conditions can be corrected. For example, although IP doesn't receive an acknowledgment back from the destination of an IP packet, it will receive ICMP messages telling it to slow down if it is sending packets faster than the destination can process them.

- IP is unreliable. This is easy to see based on the first two items in this list.
- IP provides the address space for TCP/IP.

IP Is a Connectionless Transport Protocol

IP is connectionless—each packet is a separate entity that, from the IP standpoint, is unrelated to any other packet. IP does not contact the destination computer or network device and set up a route that will be used to send a stream of data. Instead, it just accepts data from a higher-level protocol, such as TCP or UDP, formats a package that contains addressing information, and sends the packet on its way using the underlying physical network architecture. The information found in the IP datagram header is used on a hop-by-hop basis to route the datagram to its destination. When a higher-level protocol uses IP to deliver a series of information packets, there is no guarantee that each packet created by the IP layer will take the same route to get to the eventual destination. It is even quite possible for a series of packets created by a higher-level protocol to reach the destination in a sequence out of order from how they were transmitted. IP doesn't even care if packets arrive at their destination at all. That function is left to the protocol that uses IP for delivery. That doesn't mean that IP is a useless protocol, however—it just means that the higher-level protocols (such as TCP) that use IP need to provide for some kind of error checking and acknowledgment. You'll learn more about this later in the chapter when we talk about how TCP sets up a connection and acknowledges sent and received packets.

IP Is an Unacknowledged Protocol

IP does not check to see whether the datagrams it sends out ever make it to their destination. It just formats the information into a packet and sends it out on the wire. Because of this, it is considered to be an unacknowledged protocol. The overhead involved in acknowledging receipt of a datagram can be significant. By leaving out an acknowledgment mechanism, IP can be used by other protocols and applications that do not require this functionality, and thus eliminate the overhead associated with acknowledgements. Applications and protocols that do need to know that a datagram has been successfully delivered can implement the acknowledgment mechanism instead found in the TCP protocol.

IP Is an Unreliable Protocol

Because it is connectionless and because it does not check to see whether packets arrive at their destination, and because it does not care whether they arrive out of order, IP is considered an unreliable protocol. Or, to put it another way, it's a best-effort delivery service. Because IP doesn't perform routing functions, it can't guarantee what route a datagram will take through the network. Another reason that it is considered unreliable is because IP implements a Time-To-Live (TTL) value that limits the number of network routers or host computers through which a datagram can travel. When this limit is reached, the datagram is simply discarded. Because there is no acknowledgment mechanism built into IP, it is unaware of this kind of situation. The reason for this is to solve problems associated with routing. For example, it's quite possible for an administrator to configure a router incorrectly, causing an endless loop to be created in a network. If it were not for the TTL value, the packet would continue to pass from one router to another, forever! The TTL value is used mainly to prevent this sort of thing.

IP Provides the Address Space for the Network

Addressing is one of the most important functions implemented in the IP layer. In earlier chapters you learned that network adapter cards use a burned-in address, usually called a Media Access Control (MAC) address. These addresses are determined by the manufacturer of the network card and the address space created is considered to be a "flat" address space. That is, there is no organization provided by MAC addresses that can be used to efficiently route datagrams from one system or network to another. A MAC address is composed of two parts. The first part of the MAC address identifies the manufacturer of the network card. The remaining octets are assigned, usually in a serial fashion, to the cards the manufacturer produces. The MAC address assigned to each adapter is unique and is made up of a 6-byte address, which is usually expressed in hexadecimal numbers to make it easier to write. For example, 00-80-C8-EA-AA-7E is much easier to write than trying to express the same address in binary (which is what the network sees), which would be a string of zeros and ones 48 characters in length.

IP addresses are also made up of two components: a network address and a host address. By allowing a network address, it is possible to create a hierarchy that allows for an efficient routing mechanism when sending data to other networks. While a particular network might consist of systems that have network adapters from multiple vendors, and thus have MAC addresses that are seemingly random numbers, IP addresses are organized into networks. Because of this, routers don't have to keep hundreds of millions of MAC address in a memory cache to deliver datagrams. Instead, they just need a table of addresses that tells them how to best route a datagram to the network on which the host system resides.

Note

The terms datagram, packet, and frame are often misunderstood and used interchangeably. Starting with the TCP protocol, the data to be sent is actually called a *segment*. TCP passes segments to IP, which creates packets or datagrams from these segments. IP passes the data farther down the stack and, when it reaches the wire, it's called a *frame*. For all practical purposes, however, you can consider a packet and a datagram to be the same thing.

Just What Does IP Do?

IP takes the data from the Host-to-Host layer (as shown earlier in Figure 20.1) and fragments the data into smaller packets (or datagrams) that can be transferred through the network. On the receiving end, IP then reassembles these datagrams and passes them up the protocol stack to the higher-level protocol that is using IP. To get each packet delivered, IP places the source and destination IP addresses into the datagram headers. IP also performs a checksum calculation on the header information to ensure its validity. Note, however, that IP does not perform this function on the data portion of the packet.

As already noted, TCP/IP allows for networks made up of different underlying technologies to interoperate. While one network might use the Ethernet 802 frame format, another might use FDDI. Each of these lower-level frames has its own particular header that contains information needed by that technology to send frames through the physical network medium. At this lower level in the protocols stack the IP datagram rides in the data portion of the frame. After IP adds its header information to the message it receives from a higher-level protocol, and creates a datagram of the appropriate size, it passes the datagram to the Network Access layer, which wraps the IP datagram into, for example, an Ethernet frame. At the receiving end the Ethernet frame header information is stripped off and the IP datagram is passed up the stack to be handled by the IP protocol. Similarly, the IP header information is stripped off by the higher-level protocols that use IP, such as TCP or UDP.

Examining IP Datagram Header Information

In Figure 20.3 you can see the layout of an IP packet.

It is in the IP header that you will find the addressing information that is used by routers and other network devices to deliver the datagram to its eventual destination.

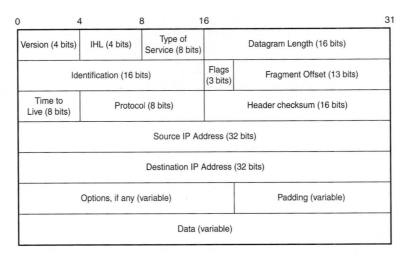

Figure 20.3   The IP header contains information concerning addressing and routing the datagram.

The header fields of the IP packet are

- **Version**—IP comes in different versions. This 4-bit field is used to store the version of the datagram. Currently IP version 4 is the most widely used version of IP. The "next generation" IP is called IPv6, which stands for version 6. Because different versions of IP use different formats for header information, if the IP layer on the receiving end is a lower version than that found in this field, it will reject the packet. Because most versions of IP at this time are version 4, this is a rare event. Don't worry about this field until you upgrade your network to Ipv6.

- **Internet Header Length (IHL)**—This 4-bit field contains the length of the *header* for the packet and can be used by the IP layer to calculate where in the datagram the *data* actually starts. The numerical value found in this field is the number of 32-bit words in the header, not the number of bits or bytes in the header.

- **Type of Service**—This 8-bit field is intended to implement a prioritization of IP packets. Until recently, however, no major implementation of IP version 4 uses the bits in this field, so they are all usually set to zeros. With Gigabit Ethernet and 10 Gigabit Ethernet, this is changing. Because these faster versions of Ethernet can compete with other protocols such as ATM, which do provide a type of service function, you can expect to see this field used in faster versions of Ethernet. IPv6 will provide mechanisms that allow this functionality.

- **Datagram Length**—This field is 16 bits long and is used to specify the length of the entire datagram. It contains the number of 8-bit octets (or bytes). The largest value that can be stored in 16 bits is 65,535 bytes. Subtracting the IHL field from this value IP will yield the length of the *data* portion of the datagram.

- **Identification**—IP often must break a message it receives from a higher-level protocol into smaller packets, depending on the maximum size of the frame supported by the underlying network technology. On the receiving end, these datagrams need to be reassembled. The sending computer places a unique number for each message fragment into this field, and each datagram for a particular message will have the same value in this 16-bit field. Thus, the receiving computer can take all the parts and re-create the original message.

- **Flags**—This field contains several flag bits. Bit 0 is reserved and should always have a value of zero. Bit 1 is the *Don't Fragment* (DF) field (0=fragmentation is okay, 1=fragmentation is not okay). If a computer finds that it needs to fragment a datagram to send it through the next hop in the physical network, and this DF field is set to 1, then it will discard the datagram (remember that IP is an unreliable protocol). If this field is set to 0, it will divide the datagram into multiple datagrams so that they can be sent onward in their journey. Bit 2 is the *More Fragments* (MF) flag and is used to indicate the fragmentation status of the packet. If this bit is set to 1 then there are more fragments to come. The last fragment of the original message that was fragmented will have a value of zero in this field. These two fields (Identification and Flags), along with the next field, manage the fragmentation process.

■ **Fragment Offset**—When the MF flag is set to 1 (the message was fragmented), this field is used to indicate the position of this fragment in the original message so that it can be reassembled correctly. This field is 13 bits in length and expresses the offset value of this fragment in units of 8 bytes.

■ **Time to Live (TTL)**—A packet can't travel forever on the network because it is possible for loops to exist in the routing structure (due to an administrator's error, usually). The TTL value is used to prevent these endless loops. Each time a datagram passes through a router, the value in this field is decremented by at least one. The value is supposed to represent seconds, and in some cases, where a router is processing packets slowly, this field can be decremented by more than one. It all depends on the vendor's implementation. When this value reaches zero, the datagram is discarded. Because IP is a best-effort, unreliable protocol, the higher-level protocol that is using IP must detect that the packet did not reach its destination and resend the packet.

■ **Protocol**—This field is 8 bits long and is used to specify a number that represents the network protocol for the data contained in this datagram. The Internet Corporation for Assigned Names and Numbers (ICANN) decides the numbers used in this field to identify specific protocols. For example, a value of "6" is used to specify the TCP protocol.

■ **Header Checksum**—This 16-bit field contains a computed value used to ensure the integrity of the header information of the datagram. When information in the header is changed this value is recalculated. Because the TTL value is decremented by each system that a datagram passes through, this value is recalculated at each hop as the datagram travels through the network.

■ **Source IP Address**—The IP address of the source of the datagram. This is a 32-bit long field.

■ **Destination IP Address**—The IP address of the destination of the datagram. This also is a 32-bit long field.

■ **Options**—This is an optional variable length field that can contain a list of options. The option classes include control, reserved, debugging, and measurement. Source routing can be implemented using this field and is of particular importance when configuring a firewall. Table 20.1 lists the option classes and option numbers that can be found in this field.

■ **Padding**—This field is used to pad the header so that it ends on a 32-bit boundary. The padding consists of zeros. Different machines and different operating systems work based on different sizes for bytes, words, quadwords, and so on. Padding makes it easier to handle a known quantity of data (that is, to pad the header to a known length) than for the system to have to find some other method for determining where a data structure ends. For example, a router must operate quickly. It must perform calculations, look up info in the routing table, and so on. If a router also had to determine where the header info ended, the routing process would take longer.

The Options Field and Source Routing

This is an optional field. Source routing (which is discussed in Chapter 40, "Firewalls") for example, can be implemented using this field. Although IP usually lets other protocols make routing decisions (that is, the path the datagram takes through the network) in most cases, it is possible to specify a list of devices for the route instead. As shown in Table 20.1, IP can use two options for routing purposes. These are *loose source routing* (option no. 3) and *strict source routing* (option no. 9).

Table 20.1   Option Classes and Option Numbers

Option Class	Option Number	Use
0	0	Indicates end of option list
0	1	No options
0	2	Security options for military use
0	3	Loose source routing
0	7	Activates routing records
0	9	Strict source routing
2	4	Timestamping active

Hackers can use source routing to force a packet to return to their computer, using a predefined route. Using source routing with TCP/IP should be discouraged. For more information, see Chapter 40.

Each of these techniques for source routing provide a list of addresses that the datagram must pass through. Loose source routing uses this list, but doesn't necessarily use it in all cases—other routes can be used to get to each machine addressed in the list. When using strict source routing, however, the list must be followed exactly and, if it cannot, the datagram will be discarded.

IP Addressing

Although most people think of IP as the transport protocol used by higher-level protocols, one of its more important functions is to provide the address space used by the TCP/IP suite. Earlier in this chapter we discussed the difficulty of having to create a routing table that consists of hundreds of millions of actual hardware addresses, which provide for no built-in organization capability.

IP addresses are used for just this purpose: to provide a hierarchical address space for networks. Each network adapter has a hard-coded network address that is six bytes long. This address is burned in during the manufacturing process. When data packets are sent out on the wire of the local area network segment, it is this Media Access Control (MAC) address that is really used for the source and destination addresses that are embedded in the ethernet frame, which encapsulates the actual IP datagram.

IP Addresses Make Routing Possible

Because the IP address is composed of two components, the network address and the host computer address, it is a simple matter to construct routers that use the network portion of the address to route datagrams to their destination networks. After the datagram has arrived at a router on the destination network, the host portion of the address is used to locate the destination computer. Without the capability to designate a network address, as well as a host address, the hierarchical address space could not exist, and routing would require routing tables that literally would have to store every address of every computer or device on the network! Instead, by limiting routing tables to storing only network addresses, this chore is a simple process.

IP addresses allow you to organize a collection of networks in a logical hierarchical fashion. There are three kinds of IP addresses:

- **Unicast**—This kind of address is the most common type of IP address. It is one that uniquely identifies a single host on the network.

- **Broadcast**—Not to be confused with an ethernet frame broadcast, IP also provides this capability by setting aside a set of addresses that can be used for broadcasting to send data to every host system on a particular network.

- **Multicast**—Similar to broadcast addresses, multicasting addresses send data to multiple destinations. The difference between a multicast address and a broadcast address is that a multicast address can send data to multiple networks to be received by hosts that are configured to receive the data.

Additionally, there are address classes, which are used mainly to define the size of the network and host portions of the IP address.

IP Address Classes

The Internet is a collection of networks that are all joined together by routers to create a larger network. The name itself says it all. The Internet Protocol (IP) makes this possible because it allows for addressing each network that is attached to the Internet, as well as identifying the host computers that reside on each network. When packets are routed through the Internet (or through a private corporate network that uses TCP/IP), the IP address is used to get the data to the destination network. When the data packet is delivered to a router on the destination network, the actual hardware address (MAC address) of the computer is used to deliver the packet to the correct computer. This is done by taking the host portion of the IP address and consulting a table that maps hardware addresses to IP host addresses for the local network. If no match is found, then the Address Resolution Protocol is used on the local wire to find out the hardware address, and it is added to the table.

The important factor to consider here is that it's important to be able to assign an address to both networks and to the individual hosts. If just the MAC address were used, then there would be no hierarchical structure for the address space. That is, instead of having to keep a table of network addresses in memory, routers would have to keep a huge table consisting of every single MAC address on the Internet. Obviously, even with today's computing power, that would be impossible. Instead, it's simple for a router to look at the network portion of the IP address and send the packet on to the next hop it needs to take to reach the destination network.

Note

IP Address classes were first defined in RFC 791. Although this class system has served its purpose for many years, routing on the Internet today actually is much more complicated than these simple address classes allow for. However, it is essential to understand address classes on a local LAN or a corporate network. For more information on how the IP address is used for routing purposes on the Internet, see Chapter 29, "Routing Protocols."

An IP address is 4 bytes long (32 bits). Whereas MAC addresses usually are expressed in hexadecimal notation, IP addresses usually are written using what is termed dotted-decimal notation. Each byte of the entire address is converted to its decimal representation, and then the four bytes of the address are separated by periods to make it easier to remember. As you can see in Table 20.2, the decimal values are much easier to remember than their binary equivalent.

Table 20.2   IP Addresses Are Expressed in Decimal Notation

Decimal Value	Binary Value
150	10010110
204	11001100
200	11001000
27	00011011

As you can see, it is much easier to write the address in dotted-decimal notation (150.204.200.27) than to use the binary equivalent.

Note

If you have problems converting between binary and decimal, or even hexadecimal and octal numbering systems, don't worry. There's a simple way to do this. You don't have to spend hours trying to figure out which position in the numbering system represents a certain value. Instead, just cheat and use the Windows Calculator accessory. When you bring up the calculator, click on View and then Scientific. You'll get a larger display for the calculator that allows you to enter a number in any of the supported numbering systems. You can then simply click on another numbering base system to automatically convert the value you entered to the value you want to see in another numerical base system. If you don't use Windows, then go to your local thrift store and spend five bucks for an inexpensive calculator that will perform the same function!

Because IP addresses are used to route a packet through a collection of separate networks, it is important to know what part of the IP address is used as the network address and what part is being used for the host computer's address.

IP addresses are divided into three major classes (A, B, and C) and two less familiar ones (D and E). Each class uses a different portion of the IP address bits to identify the network. There is a need for classifying networks because there is a need to be able to create networks of different sizes. Whereas a small LAN might have only a few computers or a few hundred, larger networks can have thousands or more networked computers. The class system of IP addresses is accomplished by using a different number of bits of the total address to identify the network and host portions of the IP address. Additionally, the first few bits of the binary address are used to indicate which class an IP address belongs to.

The total number of bits available for addressing is always the same: 32 bits. Because the number of bits used to identify the network varies from one class to another, it should be obvious that the number of bits remaining to use for the host computer part of the address will vary from one class to another also. This means that some classes will have the capability to identify more networks than others. Conversely, some will have the capability to identify more computers on each network.

The first four bits of the address can tell you what class an address is a member of. In Table 20.3, you can see the IP address classes along with the bit values for the first four bits. The bit positions that are marked with an "x" in this table indicate that this value makes no difference in the determination of IP address class.

Table 20.3   The First Four Bits of the IP Address Determine the Class of the Address

Address Class	Bit Values
Class A	0xxx
Class B	10xx
Class C	110x
Class D	111x
Class E	1111

Class A Addresses

As shown in Table 20.3, any IP address that has a zero in the first bit position is a Class A address. The values for the remaining bits make no difference. Also, you can see that any address that has "10" for the first two bits of the address will be a Class B address, and so on. Remember that these are bit values, and as such are expressed in binary. These are not the decimal values of the IP address when it is expressed in dotted-decimal notation.

Class A addresses range from all zeros (binary) to a binary value of 0 in the first position followed by seven "1" bits. Converting each byte of the address into decimal shows that Class A addresses range from 0.0.0.0 to 127.255.255.255, when expressed in the standard dotted-decimal notation.

Note

It is not possible to have an IP address expressed in dotted-decimal notation that exceeds 255 for any of the four values. The decimal value of a byte with all 1s (11111111) is 255. Take the address 140.176.123.256, for example. This address is not valid because the last byte is larger than 255 decimal. When planning out how to distribute IP addresses for your network, keep this in mind! It is not possible to express the value of 256 in binary when using only 8 bits!

Keeping in mind that the class system for IP addresses uses a different number of bits for the network portion of the address, the Class A range of networks is the smallest. That is because Class A addresses use only the first byte of the address to identify the network. The rest of the address bits are used to identify a computer on a Class A network. Because the first bit of the first byte of the address is always zero, this leaves only 7 bits that can be used to create a network address. Because only 7 bits are available, there can be only 127 network addresses (binary 01111111 = 127 decimal) in a Class A network. It is not possible to have 128 network addresses in this class because, to express 128 in binary, the value would be 10000000, which would indicate a Class B address.

However, Class A networks can contain the largest number of host computers or devices on each network, because they use the remaining three bytes to create the host portion of the IP address. Three bytes can store a value, in decimal, of up to 16,777,215 (that's 24 bits all set to "1" in binary). Counting zero as a possibility (0-16,777,215), this means that a total of 16,777,216 (2 to the 24th power) addresses can be expressed using 3 bytes.

To summarize, there can be a total of 127 Class A networks, and each network can have up to 16,777,216 unique addresses for computers on the network. The range of addresses for Class A networks is from 0.0.0.0 to 127.255.255.255. When you see an address that falls in this range you can be sure that it is a Class A address.

Class B Addresses

The first two bits of an IP address need to be examined to determine whether it is a class B address. If the first two bits of the address are set to 10, the address belongs in this class. Class B addresses range from 1 followed by 31 zeros to 10 followed by 30 1s. If you convert this to the standard dotted-decimal notation, this is 128.0.0.0 to 191.255.255.255. In binary, the decimal value of 128 decimal is 10000000. The decimal value of 191 translates to 10111111 in binary. Both of these values in binary have 10 as the first two digits, which places them in the Class B IP address space.

Because the first two bytes of the Class B address are used to address the network, only two remaining bytes can be used for host computer addresses. If you do the calculations, you'll find that there can be up to 16,384 possible network addresses in this class, ranging from 128.0 to 191.255 in the first two bytes. There can be 65,536 (2 to the 16th power) individual computers on each Class B network.

You might wonder why the number of network addresses and the number of host addresses aren't the same in the Class B address range because they both use two bytes. It's simple: Just remember that the network portion of the Class B address always has 1 for the first bit position and 0 for the second bit position. That zero in the second position is what keeps the number of network addresses less than the number of host computer addresses. In other words, the largest host address you can have in a

Class B network, expressed in binary, is 10111111, which is 191 in decimal. Because there is no restriction on the value of the first two digits of the *host* portion of the address, it is possible to have the host portion set to all 1s, giving a string of sixteen 1s, which would be 255.255 in dotted-decimal notation.

Class C Addresses

The Class C address range always has the first three bits set to 110. If you convert this to decimal, this means that a Class C network address can range from 192.0.0.0 to 223.255.255.255. In this class the first three bytes are used for the network part of the address, and only a single byte is left to create host addresses.

Again, doing the math (use that Windows calculator!), you can see that there can be up to 2,097,152 Class C networks. Each Class C network can have up to 256 host computers (0–255). This allows for a large number of Class C networks, each with only a small number of computers.

Other Address Classes

The first three address classes are those that are used for standard IP addresses. Classes D and E addresses are used for different purposes. The Class D address range is reserved for multicast group use. *Multicasting* is the process of sending a network packet to more than one host computer. Class D address range, in decimal, is from 224.0.0.0 to 239.255.255.255. No specific bytes in a Class D address are used to identify the network or host portion of the address. This means that a total of 268,435,456 possible unique Class D addresses can be created.

Finally, Class E addresses can be identified by looking at the first four bits of the IP address. If you see four 1s at the start of the address (in binary), you can be sure you have a Class E address. This class ranges from 240.0.0.0 to 255.255.255.255, which is the maximum value you can specify in binary when using only 32 bits. Class E addresses are reserved for future use and are not normally seen on most networks that interconnect through the Internet.

Note

It became apparent during the early 1990s that the IPv4 address space would become exhausted a lot sooner than had been previously thought. Actually, this forecast has proved to be a little overstated. Network Address Translation (NAT) can be used with routers so that you can use any address space on your internal network, while the router that connects to the Internet is assigned one or more actual registered addresses. The router, using NAT, can manipulate IP addresses and ports to act as a proxy for clients on the internal network when they communicate with the outside world.

Request For Comments 1918, "Address Allocation for Private Internets," discusses using several IP address ranges for private networks that do not need to directly communicate on the Internet. These ranges are

```
10.0.0.0 to 10.255.255.255.255
 172.16.0.0 to 172.31.255.255
 192.168.0.0 to 192.168.255.255
```

Because these addresses now are *not* valid on the Internet, they can be used by more than one private network. To connect the private network to the Internet you can use one or more proxy servers that use NAT. See Chapter 40 for more about how this is done.

Up to this point we have identified the possible ranges that could be used to create IP addresses in the various IP address classes. There are, however, some exceptions that should be noted. As previously discussed, an address used to uniquely identify a computer on the Internet is known as a unicast address.

Several exceptions take away from the total number of addresses that are possible in any of the address classes. For example, any address that begins with 127 for the first byte is not a valid address outside the local host computer. The address 127.0.0.1 (which falls in the Class A address range) is commonly called a *loopback* address and is usually used for testing the local TCP/IP stack to determine whether it is configured and functioning correctly. If you use the ping command, for example, with this address, the packet never actually leaves the local network adapter to be transmitted on the network. The packet simply travels down through the protocol stack and back up again to verify that the local computer is properly configured.

You can use this address to test other programs. For example, you can Telnet to the loopback address to find out whether the Telnet program is working on your computer. This assumes that you have a Telnet server running on the computer.

Other exceptions include the values of 0 and 255. When used in the network portion of an address, zeros imply the current network. For example, the address 140.176.0 is the address of a Class B network, and the value of 193.120.111.0 is the address of a Class C address.

The number 255 is used in an address to specify a broadcast message. A broadcast message is sent out only once but doesn't address a single host as the destination. Instead, such a packet can be received by more than one host, hence the name "broadcast." Broadcasts can be used to send a packet to all computers on a particular network or subnet. The address 140.176.255.255 would be received by all hosts in the network defined by 140.176.0.

After subtracting these special cases, you can see in Table 20.4 the actual number of addresses for Classes A through C that are available for network addressing purposes.

Table 20.4   IP Addresses Available for Use

Class	Number of Networks	Number of Hosts
A	126	16,777,214
B	16,384	65,534
C	2,097,152	254

There is another exception to usable addresses that fall within the IP address space. This is not dictated by an RFC or enforced by TCP/IP software. Instead, it is a *convention* followed by many network administrators to make it easy to identify routers. Typically you will find that an IP address that has as its last octet the value of 254 is a router. By sticking to this convention, it is easy to remember the default gateway when you are setting up a computer. It's the computer's address, with 254 used as the last octet.

Subnetting Made Simple!

The IP address space, although large, is still limited when you think of the number of networked computers on the Internet today. For a business entity (or an Internet service provider) to create more than one network, it would appear that more than one range of addresses would be needed. A method of addressing called subnetting was devised that allows a single contiguous address space to be further divided into smaller units called *subnets*. If you take a Class B address, for example, you can have as many as 65,534 host computers on one network. That's a lot of host computers! There aren't many companies or other entities in the world today that need to have that many hosts on a single network.

Subnetting is a technique that can be used to divide a larger address space into several smaller networks called subnets. So far, we've discussed using part of the IP address to identify the network and using part of the address to identify a host computer. By applying what is called a subnet mask, it is possible to "borrow" bits from the host portion of the IP address and create subnets.

A subnet mask is also a 32-bit binary value, just like an IP address. However, it's not an address, but instead is a string of bits that are used to identify which part of the total IP address is to be used to identify the network and the subnet.

The subnet mask is expressed in dotted-decimal format just like an IP address. Its purpose is to "mask out" the portion of the IP address that specifies the network and subnet parts of the address.

Note

The technique of using subnetting was first discussed in RFC 950, "Internet Standard Subnetting Procedure."

Because subnet masks are now required for all IP addresses, the A, B, and C address classes that were just described all have a specific mask associated with them. The Class A address mask is 255.0.0.0. When expressed as a binary value, 255 is equal to a string of eight 1s. Thus, 255.0.0.0 would be 11111111000000000000000000000000. Using Boolean logic, this binary subnet mask can be used with the AND operator to *mask out* (or identify) the network and subnet portion of the IP address. Using the AND operator, the TRUE result will be obtained only when both arguments are TRUE.

If you use the number 1 to represent TRUE and use 0 to represent FALSE, it's easy for a computer or a router to apply the mask to the IP address to obtain the network portion of the address. Table 20.5 shows how the final values are obtained.

Table 20.5   Boolean Logic Is Used for the Subnet Mask

IP Address Value	Mask Value	Result
1	1	1
1	0	0
0	1	0
0	0	0

A Class A address, as you can see, will have a subnet mask of 255.0.0.0. The only portion of the IP address that is used with this mask to be the network address is those bits contained in the first byte (11111111 in binary). Similarly, a subnet mask for a Class B address would be 255.255.0.0 (1111111111111111 in binary) and for a Class C address it would be 255.255.255.0 (a lot of ones!).

Because we've already set aside certain values at the beginning of an IP address to identify what class the address belongs to, what value can be gained by using subnet masks? Each subnet mask just discussed blocks out only the portion of the IP address that the particular class has already set aside to be used as a network address.

The value comes by using part of the host component of the IP address to create a longer network address that consists of the classful network address plus a subnet address. By modifying the subnet mask value, we can mask out additional bits that make up part of the host portion of the address, and thus, we can break a large address space into smaller components.

To put it simply, subnetting becomes useful when you use it to take a network address space and further divide it into separate subnets.

Note

One of the benefits of subnetting is that, before the advent of switches, it allows you to take a large address space and divide it using routers. A large number of computers on a single subnet would create a large amount of traffic in an ethernet environment. In this kind of situation, you would eventually get to a point where the broadcast traffic on the segment would result in too many collisions and network performance would slow to a crawl. By taking a large address space and subnetting it into smaller broadcast domains, network performance can be increased dramatically.

If you use a subnet mask of 255.255.255.128, for example, and convert it to binary, you can see that a Class C address can be divided into two subnets. In binary, the value decimal value of 128 is 10000000. This means that a *single bit* is used to create two distinct subnets. When you use this mask with a network address of 192.113.255, you would end up with one subnet with host addresses ranging from 192.113.255.1 to 192.113.255.128 and a second subnet with host addresses ranging from 192.113.255.129 to 192.113.255.254. (In this example, addresses that end in all zeros or all ones are not shown because those addresses are special cases and are generally not allowed as host addresses—192.113.255.0, for example).

To take subnetting one step further, let's use a mask of 255.255.255.192. If you take the decimal value of 192 and convert it to binary, you get 11000000. Applying this subnet mask to a Class C network address space yields four subnets. Each subnet using the remaining bits of the host address can have up to 62 host computers. The reason that you have four subnets is because the first two bits of the last byte of the subnet mask is 11000000. Because the first 2 bits are ones, there are four possible subnet values you can express using these two digits. When this mask is applied to a byte, there are only 6 bits remaining to be used for host addresses. Because you cannot use a host address of all ones or all zeros, this means that, although the largest number you can store in 6 bits is 63, you must subtract 2 from this value. This leaves only 1–62 for host addresses on these subnets.

Note

If you don't want to go through the hassle of calculating subnet values yourself, you'll find a handy table on the inside front cover of this book.

In Figure 20.4, you can see that the IP address now consists of three parts: the network address, the subnet address, and the host address.

Figure 20.4 A subnet mask can be used to identify the network address, subnet address, and host portions of the IP address.

The first thing you should do when preparing to subnet an address space is to decide how many host addresses will be needed on each subnet. Then convert this number to its binary value. Looking at the binary value, you can see how many bits you will need for the host portion of the address space. If you then subtract that value from the amount of bits available (which is 8 if you're subnetting the last byte of a Class C address), and then calculate what the decimal equivalent would be for a binary number that contains that number of left-most bits set to one.

Suppose you wanted to create subnets that would allow you to put up to 30 computers on each sub-net. First, determine what 30 is when converted to binary: 11110. You can see that it takes 5 bits to represent the decimal value of 30 in binary. After you subtract this from 8 you have left only 3 bits that can "borrowed" from the Class C host part of the address (8–5 = 3). In binary, this mask would be 11100000. If you convert this value to decimal you get 224.

The next question to ask is how many subnets can you create using this mask? Because only 3 bits are left, just figure out the largest number you can express using 3 bits in binary. You'll come up with a value of all 1s (111), which translates to 7 in decimal. Therefore, you can have 7 possible subnets, or eight if you include zero as a possibility.

After you've calculated what your subnet mask needs to be, you'll need to calculate what the actual host addresses must be for each subnet. The first subnet address would be 000. Because the IP address is expressed in dotted decimal notation, calculate how many addresses you can store in an 8-bit binary value that always begins with 000, and then translate that to decimal: 00000001 to 00011110, which is 1–30 in decimal.

Note

Remember that the addresses of 00000000 and 00011111 are not valid because they result in a host address of all zeros or all ones). If this mask were applied to a Class C network address of 192.113.255.0, then hosts in the first sub-net would range from 192.113.255.1 to 192.113.255.30.

Continuing the process, the *second* subnet address would be 001, and the third would be 011. The range of host addresses that could be created for a subnet value of 001 is 00100001 to 00111110, which is 33–62 in decimal.

The range of hosts on the second subnet would be from 192.113.255.33 to 192.113.255.62.

Simply continue this process and you'll be able to figure out the correct subnet addresses, based on the mask you've chosen.

It's possible to further divide the Class C address space by using up to 6 bits for the subnet mask, but this would leave only 2 usable host addresses and is not very practical. However, it can be done!

Note

In the examples given in this book for creating subnets, and in the charts you'll find on the inside front cover, subnets con-sisting of all zeros or all ones are included. In the original RFC on subnetting (RFC 950), these values were specifically excluded from use. However, by doing this, a large number of subnets, and thus host addresses, are excluded. RFC 1812 allows for the use of all zeros or all ones in the subnet mask. However, you should check to be sure that the routers on your network support this before using these subnet addresses. Older routers most likely will not support them. Newer ones probably will require that you configure them to operate one way or the other.

Classless Interdomain Routing Notation and Supernetting

As we discussed earlier in this chapter, the system of classifying IP addresses (A, B, C) worked well when the Internet was much smaller. The class system and subnetting is still widely used on local net-work routers. However, on the Internet backbone routers, a system called Classless Interdomain Routing (CIDR) is the method used to determine where to route a packet. This technique is also referred to as *supernetting*. CIDR can be considered a technique that uses a subnet mask that ignores the traditional IP class categories.

Why is CIDR needed? When the IP address class system was introduced it was simple for routers to use the first byte of the IP address to figure out the network number, and thus make routing an easy task. For example, for an IP address of 140.176.232.333, the router would recognize that 140 falls in the Class B address range, so the network number would be 140.176.0. A quick glance at the routing table was all that was necessary to determine the next hop to which a packet should be routed to get to its network.

As the Internet continued to grow (or explode, as some might say), the huge number of Class B and Class C networks that were being added meant that routing tables on Internet backbone routers were also growing at a fast rate. Eventually, there would come a point where it would be impossible to efficiently route packets if routing tables continued to grow.

CIDR allows for address aggregation. That is, a single entry in a routing table can represent many lower-level network addresses.

Another reason why CIDR was needed is that much of the classful address space is wasted. This happens at both ends of the spectrum. Consider a small network at the low end, with a total of 254 usable addresses in a Class C address block. If the owner of that address space has a network with only 50 or 100 computers, that means that more than half of the available host addresses are essentially lost to the Internet. At the high end, a Class A network has a total of 16,777,216 possible host addresses. How many organizations need 16 million host addresses?

So, by dropping the address class constraints, and using instead a subnet mask to specify any number of contiguous bits of the IP address as the network address, it is possible to carve up the total 32-bit address space into finer blocks that can be allocated more efficiently.

Note

CIDR was widely implemented on the Internet beginning in 1994. For specific details about CIDR, see RFCs 1517, "Applicability Statement for the Implementation of CIDR," 1518, "An Architecture for IP Address Allocation with CIDR," 1519, "CIDR: An Address Assignment and Aggregation Strategy," and 1520, "Exchanging Routing Information Across Provider Boundaries in the CIDR Environment."

CIDR uses a specific notation to indicate which part of the IP address is the network portion and which is the host portion. The CIDR notation syntax is the network address followed by /#, where # is a number indicating how many bits of the address represent the network address. This /# is commonly called the *network prefix*. Table 20.6 shows the network prefix values for A, B, and C network classes.

Table 20.6   CIDR Network Prefix Notation for A, B, and C IP Address Classes

Address Class	Binary Subnet Mask	Network Prefix
A	11111111 00000000 00000000 00000000	/8
B	11111111 11111111 00000000 00000000	/16
C	11111111 11111111 11111111 00000000	/24

However, because CIDR no longer recognizes classes, it's quite possible to have a network address like 140.176.123.0/24. Thus, while 140 would indicate that only 16 bits are used as the network portion of the address when using classful addressing, the /24 notation specifies that the first 24 bits are used, and the remaining 8 bits would be used for host addressing. By using the /24 notation, the former class B address space can be allocated in smaller blocks than the class system allows.

In Table 20.7 you can see how this system allows for networks that range in size from 32 hosts to more than 500,000 hosts. The middle column shows the equivalent of a class C network address space that the CIDR prefix creates, and the last column shows the number of hosts that would exist in the network.

Table 20.7   Use of CIDR Network Prefix Notations

CIDR Prefix	Class C Equivalent	Number of Hosts
/27	1/8th of a Class C	32
/26	1/4th of a Class C	64
/25	1/2 of a Class C	128
/24	1 Class C	256
/23	2 Class Cs	512
/22	4 Class Cs	1,024
/21	8 Class Cs	2,048
/20	16 Class Cs	4,096
/19	32 Class Cs	8,192
/18	64 Class Cs	16,384
/17	128 Class Cs	32,768
/16	256 Class Cs	65,536
/15	512 Class Cs	131,072
/14	1024 Class Cs	262,144
/13	2048 Class Cs	524,288

In Table 20.7, note that I've expressed the Class C equivalent networks that can be created. However, when using the /16 prefix you get 256 Class C size networks, which is the same thing as a single Class B network. To continue this train of thought, a /15 prefix will allow you to create two Class B sized networks, and so on.

Using CIDR, blocks of addresses can be allocated to ISPs that in turn subdivide the address space efficiently when they create address spaces for clients. One drawback is that a network that is composed completely of CIDR routing would require, in order to operate most efficiently, that addresses remain with the ISP under which a particular block is owned. This means that if your company decides to move to a different ISP, you would most likely have to obtain a new address block and therefore have to reconfigure your network addresses. If you use Network Address Translation (NAT) and a private address space on your internal corporate network, this would be only a minimal problem.

Another problem with CIDR is that some host clients might not support it. That is, if the TCP/IP stack recognizes the different classes, it might not operate if you try to configure it using a subnet mask that does not match the traditional class A, B, or C values. Again, because most routers do support this capability, you can solve this problem by using the CIDR addresses for your routers and using NAT and a private address space for the internal network.

The Address Resolution Protocol—Resolving IP Addresses to Hardware Addresses

As just discussed, IP provides a logical hierarchical address space that makes routing data from one network to another a simple task. When the datagram arrives at the local subnet, however, another protocol comes into play. The Address Resolution Protocol (ARP) is used to resolve the IP address to the hardware, to the address of the workstation, or to another network device that is the target destination of the datagram. Whereas IP addresses are used to allow for routing between networks or network segments, ARP is used at the end of the road for the final delivery.

It is important to understand that when devices communicate directly on the local network segment (on the wire, so to speak) the actual address used to communicate between two devices, whether they are computers, routers, or whatever, is the built-in Media Access Control (or MAC) address. In the case of two hosts on the same subnet, ARP can quickly resolve the correct address translations, and communications take place quickly and efficiently. When a router stands between two computers, the actual hardware address that the computer communicates with is the MAC address of the router, not of the computer that lies at the end of the connection. Using Ethernet as an example, when a datagram needs to be routed to another network or subnet, the computer sends the datagram to the default route, sometimes called the gateway, which is the router that connects the network segment to the rest of the world (or the rest of the corporate network).

The router then consults its routing tables and decides on the next device that the datagram needs to get to on its way to its destination. Sometimes this is simply a computer that is connected on another segment that is also connected to the router. Sometimes it is several more routers that the datagram must pass through. However, when the datagram finally reaches the network segment on which the target computer is located, ARP is used by the router to find out the MAC address of the computer that is configured with the IP address that is found inside the datagram.

To get this MAC address, a computer or router will first send out a broadcast message that every computer on the local segment can see. This ARP message contains the sending computer's own MAC address and also the IP address of the computer to which it wants to talk. When a computer recognizes its IP address in this broadcast datagram, it sends a datagram that contains its own MAC address back to the computer that originated the ARP message. After that, both computers know the MAC address of the other, and further transmissions take place using these hardware addresses.

The actual fields in the ARP broadcast frame are

- **Hardware Type**—This is a 2-byte field that identifies the kind of hardware used at the data-link layer of the sending computer. For diagnostic purposes, Table 20.8 contains a list of the most common hardware types.
- **Protocol Type**—This is a 2-byte field that specifies the protocol type of the address that the computer wants to translate to a hardware address.
- **Hardware Address Length**—This is a 1-byte field that specifies the length of the source and destination hardware address fields that will follow.
- **Protocol Address Length**—Similarly, this 1-byte field specifies the length of the source and destination protocol address fields that will follow in this packet.
- **Opcode**—This 1-byte field is used to determine the type of ARP frame. Frame types are listed in Table 20.9.
- **Sender Hardware Address**—This variable-length field (as defined by the Hardware Address Length field) contains the sending computer's hardware (MAC) address.
- **Sender Protocol Address**—This variable-length field (as defined by the Protocol Address Length field) contains the sender's protocol address—an IP address, for example.
- **Target Hardware Address**—This variable-length field (as defined by the Hardware Address Length field) contains the destination computer's hardware (MAC) address.
- **Target Protocol Address**—This variable-length field (as defined by the Protocol Address Length field) contains the protocol address that the sender wants to resolve to a hardware address.

Table 20.8   Hardware Type Field Values

Type Field Value	Data Link Layer Type
1	Ethernet (10MB)
2	Experimental Ethernet (3MB)
3	Amateur Radio AX.25
4	Proteon ProNET Token Ring
5	Chaos
6	IEEE 802 Networks
7	ARCnet
8	Hyperchannel
9	Lanstar
10	Autonet Short Address
11	LocalTalk
12	LocalNet (IBM PCNet or SYTEK LocalNET)
13	Ultra Link
14	SMDS
15	Frame Relay
16	Asynchronous Transmission Mode (ATM)
17	HDLC
18	Fibre Channel
19	Asynchronous Transmission Mode (ATM)
20	Serial Line
21	Asynchronous Transmission Mode (ATM)
22	MIL-STD-188-120
23	Metricom
24	IEEE 1394.1995
25	MAPOS
26	Twinaxial
27	EUI-64
28	HIPARP
29	IP and ARP over ISO 7816-3
30	ARPSec

As you can see from this table, the address resolution protocol is not limited to just resolving IP addresses on a standard Ethernet network. It has been extended over time to accommodate many different kinds of networking technologies. Some of the entries in Table 20.8 are dinosaurs—extinct protocols that no longer are being marketed. This list will probably continue to grow, however, as newer technologies are developed.

Table 20.9 shows that the Opcode field also has a large number of values, some of which might at first appear quite strange. For example, the MARS entries are not used for resolving addresses for strange spacecraft that appear in the sky now and then. They are used for address resolution on ATM networks where multicasting is being used.

For more information about ATM, see Chapter 19, "Dedicated Connections." For more information about MARS, see RFC 2022, "Support for Multicast Over UNI 3.0/3.1 Based ATM Networks."

The InARP entries in Table 20.9 are used for Inverse ARP. This form of ARP is used when the underlying network technology is a nonbroadcast multiple access (NBMA) type, such as an X.25, ATM, or Frame Relay network. In these types of networks a virtual circuit identifier is used instead of a hardware address. RFC 2390 contains the details about InARP and how it is used in a Frame Relay network to find out the IP address when only the virtual circuit identifier is known.

Finally, you will also see entries in the table that correspond to Reverse ARP, which is discussed in the next section.

Table 20.9   Opcodes for ARP Frames

Opcode Value	Description
1	ARP Request
2	ARP Reply
3	Reverse ARP Request
4	Reverse ARP Reply
5	DRARP Request
6	DRARP Reply
7	DRARP Error
8	InARP Request
9	InARP Reply
10	ARP NAK
11	MARS Request
12	MARS Multi
13	MARS Mserv
14	MARS Join
15	MARS Leave
16	MARS NAK
17	MARS Unserv
18	MARS SJoin
19	MARS SLeave
20	MARS Grouplist Request
21	MARS Grouplist Reply
22	MARS Redirect Map
23	MAPOS UNARP

To prevent a storm of broadcast messages that would result if this was done for each packet that needed to be delivered on the local network segment each host keeps a table, or cache, of MAC addresses in memory for a short amount of time. When it becomes necessary to communicate with another computer, this ARP cache is first checked. If the destination address is not found in the ARP cache, the ARP broadcast method is used.

Note

Host and domain names (like www.**microsoft**.**com** and www.**twoinc**.**com**) and IP addresses and are used for the convenience of humans to make it easier to configure and manage a network in an orderly manner. At the lowest level, though, it is the hardware address that network cards use when they talk to each other. Imagine what the Internet would be like if we all had to memorize hardware addresses instead. Because the MAC address is simply a series of numbers that are "burned into" the network adapter when it is manufactured, it bears no relation to the actual location of a computer or other device in the network. Thus, to route messages throughout the Internet using only these hard-coded MAC addresses, it would be necessary for a router to keep an enormous table in memory that contained the MAC address for every other computer that exists on the Internet. An impossible task, of course!

Figure 20.5 demonstrates how IP addresses are used during the routing process, while hardware addresses are used for the actual device-to-device communications.

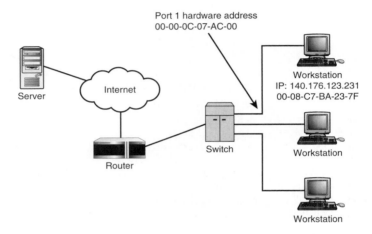

Figure 20.5   The IP address routes the datagram through the network, while the hardware addresses are used between individual workstations and devices on the network.

If the server in this figure wants to send a datagram to the workstation with the IP address 140.176.123.231, it will quickly realize that this address is not on the local subnet and will send the IP datagram, perhaps encapsulated in an ethernet frame, to its default gateway. The gateway, which is connected to the Internet, uses the IP address to route the datagram to the local router for the workstation. When the router receives the datagram it consults its routing tables and finds the switch (or hub) that is connected to the network segment by comparing the network portion of the IP address to entries in the routing table. When the datagram finally arrives at the switch, the switch consults a table of MAC hardware addresses to look up the hardware address of the destination computer. From then on, communications between the workstation and the switch use these hardware addresses for actual communication.

In fact, every device, from the server shown later in Figure 20.6 to the router to the switch, and all the devices that lie in between on the Internet, use the MAC address for communications. The IP address information is used by routers to deliver the datagram to the next hop the datagram must take to get to the final destination local segment. The MAC addresses are used for device-to-device communication. The ARP protocol is used to find out the hardware address at each hop, unless it's already stored in the ARP cache.

The arp command, which is found in both Unix and Windows NT operating systems, allows you to view the ARP table. It also can be used to add or delete entries in the table. Although the syntax varies between different systems, the following should work for most:

- **arp -a**—Displays the current contents of the arp table.
- **arp -d IP_address**—Deletes the entry for the specified host.
- **arp -s IP_address ethernet_address**—Adds an entry to the table.

For example, to add an entry use the following syntax:

```
arp -s 192.113.121.88    08-00-2b-34-c1-01
```

The arp command is covered more fully in Chapter 22. However, using the few commands in this list will help you become more familiar with how ARP works. Examine the contents of your local table. Then, try pinging several other systems and examine the table again to see if entries for those systems have been added to the table. Wait a few minutes and check the table again to see if the entries have timed out.

Proxy ARP

Sometimes, different network segments both use the same network ID and are connected by a router or other device. Because ARP uses broadcast packets to resolve IP addresses to hardware addresses, it would appear that computers on different network segments that use the same network ID would never be able to communicate.

Proxy ARP allows for just such a situation. The router or other device that connects the physical network segments is configured to provide the proxy ARP service. When a host broadcasts an ARP packet to learn the hardware address of a device that is on a different physical segment, the ARP proxy device recognizes this situation and acts as a go-between. The proxy device responds to the ARP broadcast and sends the originating computer a datagram that contains the proxy device's IP address instead of the actual target computer's IP address. From that point on, the host that originated the ARP request will communicate with the host on the other segment by sending packets to the proxy device, which will know to forward them to the computer on the other subnet.

Another use of proxy ARP comes into play for remote access servers. For example, when users dial into a computer that is acting as a remote access server, they are communicating with software on the remote access server and are not actually physically connected to the subnet. The remote access server recognizes this and will intercept any ARP broadcast packets that are trying to resolve the dial-in computer's IP address. Communications then take place between the host on the local subnet and the remote computer through the remote access server. The host on the local subnet sends unicast packets to the remote access server, which forwards them to the remote client.

Yet another use for proxy ARP is to support older systems that use a TCP/IP stack that doesn't understand subnetting or that use the older method for broadcast packets—a host address of all zeros instead of the current standard of all ones. Although this is not really much of a problem today, you might still find older legacy systems that cannot be abandoned, yet they cannot properly interact with newer systems when you subnet your network. The solution for this is to place the older systems on a separate network segment and let the proxy ARP device take care of resolving protocol addresses.

RARP—The Reverse Address Resolution Protocol

The Reverse Address Resolution Protocol (RARP) does just what it sounds like. It performs the opposite function of ARP. It is most commonly used by diskless workstations that need to discover what their IP address is when they boot. Because the diskless workstation already knows its hardware address (because the address is burned into the network card), the workstation uses RARP to send a broadcast packet requesting that a server respond to its request by sending it an ARP frame containing an IP address that it can use.

Note that the same packet format is used for ARP and RARP. The Opcode field is used to indicate what kind of operation is being performed.

The Transmission Control Protocol (TCP)

As we have discussed so far, the IP protocol is a protocol that can be used to make a best-effort attempt to get a datagram from one host to another, even when the hosts are on different networks. The Transmission Control Protocol (TCP) uses IP but adds functionality that makes TCP a *reliable*, connection-oriented protocol. While IP doesn't require any acknowledgment that a datagram is ever received, TCP does. While IP does no preliminary communication with the target system to set up any kind of session, TCP does. TCP builds on the functions that IP provides to create a session that can be used by applications for a reliable exchange of data.

TCP Provides a Reliable Connection-Oriented Session

While IP provides a checksum mechanism in its header to ensure that the IP header is not corrupted during transit, the TCP protocol provides checksums on the actual data that is transmitted. TCP also has mechanisms that regulate the flow of data to avoid problems associated with congestion. TCP also uses sequence numbers in the TCP header so that IP datagrams can be reassembled in the correct order on the receiving end of the communication.

Examining TCP Header Information

Each layer in the TCP/IP protocol stack adds information to the data it receives from a layer above it. This process is usually called *encapsulation*, and the added data is usually called a *header*. The header information is significant only to the layer that adds it, and is added as a message is passed down the stack and stripped off at the destination as the datagram is passed back up the protocol stack.

Earlier we looked at the makeup of the IP header. In Figure 20.6 you can see the layout of the TCP header. This header information is sometimes referred to as the *TCP Protocol Data Unit*.

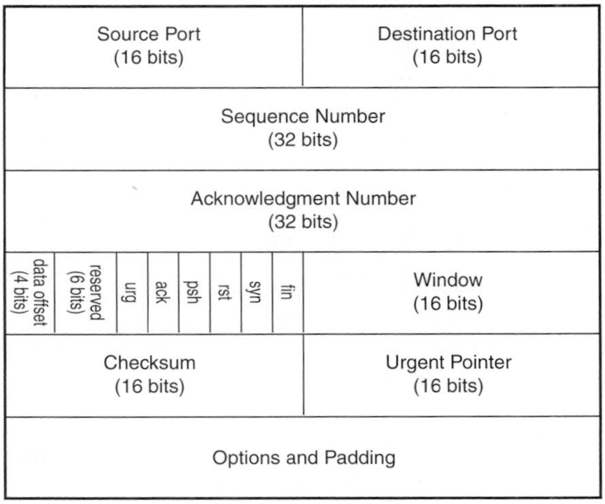

Figure 20.6   The TCP protocol header fields also can be used for filtering packets.

Remember that TCP is responsible for establishing a reliable connection-oriented session between two applications across a network. TCP receives data (called messages) from layers above it in the protocol stack, adds its own header information, and then passes it to the IP layer, which then adds its own header information. The messages sent to TCP from applications up the stack is usually called a *stream* of data, because the amount of data can vary and is not limited to a set number of bytes. TCP will take these messages and, if they are too large to fit into a packet, will break them into smaller segments and send each segment in a separate packet. The TCP layer at the receiving end reassembles these messages before passing them up to an application.

Note

Don't confuse the fact that TCP can break up large messages into smaller units before it passes them to IP with the process of IP fragmentation. These are not the same thing. TCP processes messages from applications that use it and breaks up these messages into an appropriate size for the IP layer. The IP layer, on the local computer or on another device that is in the path the datagram takes to reach its destination, can further fragment the IP datagrams. At the end, the IP datagrams are reassembled before being given to the TCP layer, which then reassembles any messages it might have chopped up before passing them up to the application.

While the majority of the header information we looked at in the IP header was used for routing the packet through the Internet, the information in the TCP header is concerned with other issues, such as reliability of the connection and ordering of the messages that are being sent. The header fields for TCP include

- **Source port**—This 16-bit field is used to identify the port being used by the application that is sending the data.

- **Destination port**—This 16-bit is field used to identify the port to which the packet will be delivered on the receiving end of the connection.

- **Sequence number**—This 32-bit field is used to identify where a segment fits in the larger message when a message is broken into fragments for transmission.

- **Acknowledgement number**—This 32-bit field is used to indicate what the next sequence number should be. That is, this value is the next byte in the data stream that the receiver expects to receive from the sender.

- **Data offset**—This 4-bit field is used to specify the number of 32-bit words that make up the header. This field is used to calculate the start of the data portion of the packet.

- **Reserved**—These 6 bits were reserved for future use and, because they were never generally used, are supposed to be set to zeros.

- **URG flag**—When this bit is set to 1, the field titled Urgent Pointer will point to a section of the data portion of the packet that is flagged as "urgent."

- **ACK flag**—This is the acknowledgement bit. If set to 1, the packet is an acknowledgment. If set to 0, the packet is not an acknowledgement.

- **PSH flag**—If this bit is set to 1, it indicates a push function; otherwise, it is set to 0.

- **RST flag**—If this bit is set to 1, it is a signal that the connection is to be reset; otherwise, it is set to 0.

- **SYN flag**—If this bit is set to 1, it indicates that the sequence numbers are to be synchronized. If set to 0, the sequence numbers are not to be synchronized.

- **FIN flag**—If this bit is set to 1, it specifies that the sender is finished sending information; otherwise, it is set to 0.

- **Window**—This 16-bit field is used to specify how many blocks of data the receiving computer is able to accept at this time.

- **Checksum**—This 16-bit field is a calculated value used to verify the integrity of both the header and data portions of the packet.

- **Urgent Pointer**—If the URG flag is set, this 16-bit field points to the offset from the sequence number field into the data portion of the packet where the urgent data is stored. TCP does not use this field itself, but applications above TCP in the stack do.

- **Options**—This field can be of variable length and is similar to the options field in the IP header. One function this field is used for is to specify the maximum segment size.

Because the options field can vary, the header is padded with extra bits so that it will be a multiple of 32 bits.

The amount of information stored in the TCP header makes it possible to use the protocol for complex communications. TCP can implement error checking, flow control, and other necessary mechanisms to ensure reliable delivery of data throughout the network. However, because of the complexity of this header, hackers can use many different methods to manipulate the TCP protocol when trying to gain access to your network or otherwise cause you problems.

One interesting thing to note about the checksum field is that it is calculated based on three things:

- The TCP header fields
- The TCP data
- Pseudo header information

The pseudo header information consists of the source and destination IP addresses, one byte set to all zeros, an 8-bit protocol field, and a 16-bit field that contains the length of the TCP segment. The address and protocol fields are duplicated from the IP datagram and the length field is redundant because it also is contained in the TCP header. Because the algorithm used to calculate the checksum is based on 16-bit words, the TCP datagram may be padded with a zero byte for calculation purposes only. If the checksum field contains a value of zero, this indicates that no checksum was calculated by the sender. If by some chance the value of the checksum results in a value of zero, the checksum field is set to all 1s (65,535 decimal) to indicate this.

TCP Sessions

Because TCP is a connection-oriented protocol, the computers that want to communicate must first establish the conditions that will govern the session and set up the connection. TCP allows for two-way communication—that is, it's a bi-directional, full-duplex connection. Both sides can send and receive data at the same time. To set up a connection, each side must "open" its side of the connection. On the server side this is called a *passive open*. The server application runs as a process on the server computer and listens for connection requests coming in for a certain port. For example, the Telnet server process typically listens for connections on port 23. By using both the IP address and a port number, the server process can uniquely identify each client that makes a connection request. Ports will be discussed in more detail later in this chapter.

When a client wants to establish a connection to a server, it goes through a process known as an *active open*. The server is already listening for connection requests (passive open), but the client must initiate the actual connection process by sending a request to the port number of the server application that it wants to use.

In Figure 20.7 (shown in the next section), the single-bit field named SYN is the "synchronization" bit. You also can see in Figure 20.7 another field titled ACK, for the acknowledgement bit. These two bits are very important and are used during the process of setting up a TCP/IP session so that a reliable connection can be established between two computers on the network.

Setting Up a TCP Session

A TCP/IP connection is made between two computers, using their addresses and, depending on the application using TCP, port numbers. The SYN and ACK bits in the TCP header are important components used to establish this initial connection.

The steps involved in setting up a TCP/IP connection appear in Figure 20.7 and are as follows:

1. The client sends a TCP segment to the server with which it wants to establish a connection. The TCP header SYN field ("synchronize") is set indicating that it wants to synchronize sequence numbers so that further exchanges can be identified as belonging to this particular connection and so that the segments sent can be reassembled into the correct order and acknowledged. This first initial sequence number in the TCP header is set to an initial value chosen by the TCP software on the client computer. Additionally, the port number field in the TCP header is set to a value of the port on the server to which the client wants to connect. Port numbers can be thought of as representing the application to which the computer wants to connect.

2. When the server receives this segment, it returns a segment to the client with the SYN field set. The server's segment also contains an initial sequence number, which is chosen by its TCP software implementation. To show the client that it received the initial connection segment, the ACK bit is also set, and the acknowledgment field contains the *client's* initial sequence number, incremented by 1.

3. The client, upon receiving this acknowledgment from the server, sends another segment to the server, acknowledging the server's initial sequence number. This is done in the same manner that the server acknowledges the client's initial sequence number. The acknowledgement field contains the server's initial sequence number incremented by a value of 1.

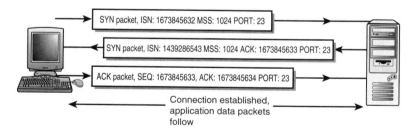

Figure 20.7   TCP uses a three-way handshake to establish a connection.

During this exchange the 16-bit acknowledgement field is incremented by 1. You might wonder why the acknowledging computer doesn't just send back the same sequence number it received from the sending computer. It increments the sequence number that it received to indicate the next sequence number it expects to receive from the sending computer. Thus, during each exchange of TCP segments each side is telling the other side what it is expecting to get from the other side during the next transmission. The sequence numbers are used to indicate the next byte in the data stream that the receiving end of the connection expects to receive. Thus, when the actual data exchange begins to take place, the sequence numbers are not simply incremented by a value of 1, but instead they are set to the actual number of bytes received (offset from the initial sequence number chosen for the connection) plus 1.

Because three segments are used in this process, the connection setup is often referred to as a *three-way handshake*. In the last of these three steps the SYN bit is not set, because the segment is simply acknowledging the server's initial sequence number. Note also that port numbers are used to indicate the application for which the connection is being set up. TCP headers don't need to contain the source and destination IP addresses because that information is already stored in the IP datagram that encapsulates the TCP message.

The method used to choose values for the initial sequence number can vary from one implementation of TCP to another. However, there are two important points to understand about the sequence numbers:

1. For each connection a client makes to another computer, the initial sequence number for each connection must be unique. If the same initial sequence number were used for every connection the client made to a single server, it would be impossible to differentiate between different connections of the same application (that is, port number) between the two machines. Although the IP address and port number can uniquely identify a computer, they can't uniquely identify multiple applications of the same process running on the same computer.

2. Sequence numbers are incremented for each segment exchanged and are acknowledged by the receiver so that both sides can determine that segments are being delivered reliably and not getting lost in the network. However, it is not necessary that each and every segment be acknowledged with another segment. Using a technique called *sliding windows* (which we'll get to in a moment), TCP allows for a single acknowledgment of a number of segments.

In Figure 20.7 another field is also shown in the first two packets that are exchanged. The Maximum Segment Size (MSS) field in the TCP header indicates the maximum number of bytes of data that the sender wants to receive in each TCP segment. This value is used to help prevent fragmentation of the TCP segment as it travels through various network devices that might have different transmission frame sizes. This value applies only to the size of the data that the TCP segment carries, and does not include the bytes that make up the TCP and IP headers. You will see this field only during the connection setup. After the application data exchange begins, this field is not used. If the client or server does not put a value into this field during the connection setup, then a default value, usually 536, is used.

Not shown in this figure is the TCP field that stores the window size. This field is used to help manage the connection after the application data exchange begins.

Managing the Session Connection

After a TCP session has been established between two computers, the application that uses TCP can then begin to communicate with its counterpart on the other computer. TCP receives a stream of bytes (called a *message*) from an application and stores them in a buffer. When the buffer is full, or when the application indicates that it wants TCP to send the message to the destination computer, the bytes are assembled into a TCP segment with the necessary header information and the segment is passed to IP for transmission on the network.

Note

Although it is more efficient to send a large number of data bytes in a single TCP segment, some applications do not work well in this manner. For example, when using Telnet, each keystroke the user enters must be sent to the remote Telnet server, acknowledged, and echoed back to the sender. This means that a TCP segment, and thus an IP datagram, can actually be sent for every single keystroke! When you consider the overhead involved in sending each datagram, this is a waste of valuable bandwidth. To help solve this problem, the Nagle Algorithm (as described in RFC 896) allows for small amounts of data (that is, single keystrokes) to accumulate in a buffer and not be sent until an acknowledgement is received for data previously sent. This means that, in practice, multiple keystrokes can be sent in a single packet instead of having to use a separate packet for each one.

Each transmission was acknowledged during the initial connection setup. This is not always the case when the actual exchange of data begins between two computers. Instead, there are several important mechanisms that TCP uses to manage a connection after it has been established. These include

- TCP timers
- Sliding windows
- Retransmissions

When a segment is passed to the IP layer for transmission, a timer is set and a countdown starts. When this retransmission timer reaches zero with no acknowledgment, the sending computer assumes that the segment did not make it to its destination and retransmits the segment. This function requires that TCP keep data in a memory buffer until it is acknowledged.

During the connection setup, each side of the connection indicates to the other side the maximum amount of data it can buffer in memory. This is the *window size*. This value indicates how many TCP segments the computer can receive before an acknowledgement is required. For example, on a Windows 2000 client the default value for this field when using Ethernet for transmission, is 12 segments.

Note

Because many applications used on networks are interactive, often a connection will not be a continuous exchange of data. Instead, as users interact with the client application, there are times when no data exchange is performed. To ensure that the connection is still valid—that is, that both sides are still up and running—TCP uses a *keepalive* segment exchange to indicate that the connection is still being used. This segment consists of a TCP segment with the ACK bit set, but the segment contains no data. The sequence number field in the TCP header is set to a value of the current sequence number minus 1. The other end of the connection returns a segment that also has the ACK bit set, but in the acknowledgement number field the value is the next byte of data that the receiver expects from the sender. The *keepalive* timer is used to determine when a keepalive segment should be sent.

This keepalive function is not used by all TCP implementations. For example, in Windows 2000 it is disabled by default.

Another feature of TCP that helps to reduce the number of datagrams that are transmitted is the fact that the acknowledgment of received data does not have to travel in a separate datagram from those that hold data. In other words, when sending data in a TCP segment to the remote computer, the sending computer also can use the ACK bit and the sequence number fields to acknowledge data that it has received from the remote computer. This is sometimes called a *piggyback* ACK because both data and an acknowledgment of data received travels in the same datagram.

Sliding windows also helps to reduce the amount of datagrams that are transmitted by allowing a single acknowledgment to be sent for multiple segments. Instead of acknowledging every single segment that it receives, the receiver can send an acknowledgment that indicates the last byte received when it receives several contiguous segments in a short time. That is, the acknowledgment can be cumulative. Each end of the connection uses a send and receive buffer to store data received or waiting for transmission.

Remember that the application which uses TCP passes a stream of bytes to TCP or receives a stream of bytes from TCP, depending on the direction that data is flowing at any particular point in time. The term *sliding window* refers to the fact that the receiving buffer can hold only so much data (the window size advertised by the receiving end). The amount of space available in the buffer can change over time, depending on the amount of time it takes for the application to accept the bytes from TCP and thus make more room in the buffer. The receiving end can use the window size TCP header field to tell the sender the amount of bytes it can currently receive and store in its buffer. This window size is called the *offered window* size. That doesn't mean that the sender must send that much data, just that the receiver is ready to accept any amount of data bytes, up to that size.

As you can see in Figure 20.8, The sender can calculate the amount of data it can send by comparing the window size offered, the bytes already sent and acknowledged, and the bytes that have been sent but not acknowledged. In this figure the window size offered by the receiver is four bytes. Because two bytes have already been sent and the window size is four, the sender can transmit two more bytes at this time. As bytes are acknowledged by the receiver, the left edge of the window slides toward the right, as shown in this figure. Depending on how well the receiving end of the connection is able to process incoming bytes, the offered window size can change, which in turn can affect the number of bytes that the sending end can transmit. As the buffer empties at the receiving end, a larger window size can be advertised and the right edge of the window slides toward the right.

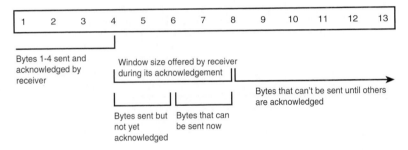

Figure 20.8   The window size advertised by the receiver of TCP segments determines which bytes in the data stream the sender can transmit.

It also is possible that the buffer at the receiving end becomes full, and the sender is sent a window size that is now zero. The sender will not send any more segments until the window size is offered again at a value greater than zero.

Using this scheme, there are several things to keep in mind. First, the sender does not have to send an amount of data that is equal to the size of the offered window. It can send less. Second, the receiver does not have to wait until it has received data in the amount of the offered window before it sends an acknowledgment. Third, the window size is controlled, under most circumstances, by the receiving end of the connection.

In this example we have used a transmission that consists of only a few bytes at a time. For most TCP communications the amount of data, and the window size, is much larger.

Sliding windows tells the sender when and how much data it can transmit. When a connection is initially established, a technique called *slow start* is used to govern the amount of data that is sent, allowing it to increase to a point that the particular network will tolerate. When a connection has been in use for some time, congestion can occur and it might be necessary to slow down the rate at which segments are transmitted, by using a technique called the *congestion avoidance algorithm*. These two methods work together to control the flow of data during the connection.

Slow start means that when the transmitting side of a connection first transmits data, it does so by observing how fast it receives acknowledgments of data from the receiving end. A variable in the TCP software keeps track of the *congestion window (cwnd)*, which is initially set to one segment. For each segment that is acknowledged, the cwnd variable is incremented. Then, the sender is allowed to send an amount of data up to the value of cwnd or the size of the offered window, whichever is the lower value. As you can see, the faster the receiving end acknowledges segments, the larger the cwnd variable becomes and thus the more segments that the sender will be able to transmit (up to the offered window size). The offered window size enables the receiving end to control the amount of data that can be sent. The congestion window gives the sending end of the transmission control over how much data can be transmitted. Thus, both sides work together to throttle up data transmissions, starting off slowly, until the receiver is unable to buffer data at a faster rate or until network congestion forces the connection to operate at a slower rate.

The term *slow start* isn't actually an accurate way to describe what happens. In reality, the receiving end might acknowledge several segments, thus increasing the size of cwnd by more than one when it sends a single acknowledgment to account for multiple segments. This means that, instead of being incremented by one for each acknowledgement, cwnd can be incremented at a much faster rate. However, this method does allow for TCP to "test the waters," so to speak, to determine the rate at which data can be sent, up to the receiving end's capacity to buffer data and pass it up to the application on its end of the connection.

As datagrams make their way through the network, however, another problem can arise. In today's world, communications often take place between computers that reside on different networks that are connected by routers, and we find that, just like the freeway system, congestion can occur when too many computers are trying to send and receive data at the same time. When a router or other network connection device becomes a bottleneck, it can simply drop IP packets—remember that IP is an unreliable protocol. It is up to TCP to realize what is happening and to compensate for it by retransmitting unacknowledged segments.

The retransmission timer that we discussed earlier is used by the transmitting end of the connection to determine when a segment should be retransmitted. This value is recalculated over time, depending on the round-trip time that it takes for a transmission to make it to the receiving end and an acknowledgment to get back to the transmitting side of the connection. The round-trip time can change over time, depending on the amount of data flowing through the network. Round-trip time also can change when the routes chosen by routers change, thus sending packets through a different path that can take more or less time than previous transmissions.

Note

It is beyond the scope of this book to get into all the details of the calculations used to determine the round-trip time and thus the value of the retransmission timer. For more information, the reader is encouraged to read the RFCs that pertain to TCP/IP. A quick search on the Internet will give you a large list of RFCs that can provide some great nighttime reading if you have a hard time going to sleep.

The *congestion avoidance algorithm* is used to take care of situations in which the network becomes congested and packets are dropped—that is, they are not being acknowledged by the receiver. Although this algorithm is separate from the slow start technique, in practice they work together. In addition to the cwnd variable, another variable called the slow start threshold size (ssthresh) comes into play. This variable is initially set to 65,535 bytes when a connection is established. When congestion is detected, the value of this variable is set to half the currently offered window size, and the variable cwnd is set to the value of one maximum segment size (MSS)—though this can vary from one implementation to another. In Windows 2000, cwnd is set to the value of two times the MSS. The send window value then is set to the lower of cwnd and the offered receive window size.

Based on which value is chosen, TCP segments are then sent. If the segments are acknowledged then cwnd is incremented. If the value of cwnd is lower than the value of ssthresh, a slow start is used. When the value of cwnd is equal to half the current offered window size from the receiving end of the transmission, congestion avoidance is used. Remember that the value of ssthresh can be used to determine this because it recorded the value of the offered window size (divided by two) that was in effect when congestion started.

During congestion avoidance, the value of cwnd is incremented by one cwnd for each acknowledgement received—again, this value might be different according to your particular TCP implementation. Thus, instead of a possible exponential increase that a slow start method would allow, congestion avoidance allows for a smaller increase in the value of cwnd. After all, if congestion is occurring, the last thing you want to do is to quickly increase the rate of transmission. Instead, you want to throttle it up more slowly. So while slow start will increment cwnd by the number of segments acknowledged by a single acknowledgment, the congestion avoidance algorithm will increment cwnd by only one segment for each acknowledgement received, no matter how many segments are being acknowledged by the acknowledgment.

Other mechanisms are used for flow control in TCP, such as the fast recovery algorithm and the fast retransmit algorithm. Discussing these is beyond the scope of this book. The important thing to understand is that TCP does monitor and adjust its transmissions, from both sides of the connection, to try to get the maximum amount of data flowing without causing problems. It's a self-regulating protocol, you might say.

Ending a TCP Session

When the party's over—the application is finished sending data to another computer—it tells TCP to close the connection from its side. Because the connection must be closed from each end, this is called a half-close. To fully close a TCP connection four steps are required, instead of the three-way handshake method used to set up the connection. Four steps are required for this due to the fact that TCP operates as a full-duplex connection. That is, data can flow in both directions. Because of this, each side needs to tell the other side of the connection that it has finished sending data and wants to close the connection.

For example, when the client application, such as Telnet, wants to close a connection, TCP sends a segment that has the FIN bit set in the TCP header to the remote computer. The remote computer must first acknowledge this FIN segment, and does so by sending a segment to the client that has the ACK bit set. Because the connection is full-duplex, the server TCP software informs the Telnet server application that the user application on the other end of the connection is finished. It then sends its own FIN segment to the client, which, as you can probably guess, sends an acknowledgment segment back to the server.

Although this is the general method used to close a TCP connection, another technique can be used whereby one side sends a FIN segment, closing its data pipe, but the other side of the connection does not. Instead, it is possible for the other side to continue sending data until it is finished, at which time it sends the FIN segment and waits for an acknowledgment, which effectively closes the connection.

A good example of this is the Unix rsh (remote shell) utility. This utility allows a user to execute a command on a remote server. Because Unix allows for the capability to redirect input (using the < operator), a user can use rsh to execute a command on a remote server, and use the < operator on the command line to redirect the input for the command from the command line to a file. In such a situation, the client's side of the connection sends the command to be executed to the remote server and then starts sending the data that is in the file. After the client's side of the connection finishes sending the data contained in the file to the remote server, it instructs TCP to close its side of the connection. Yet, at the other side of the connection, the data needs to be processed by the program invoked by the rsh command. When finished, the program on the remote server sends the data back to the client, and then instructs TCP to close its side of the connection.

In Figure 20.9 you can see a comparison of these two methods for terminating a TCP connection.

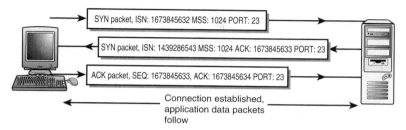

Figure 20.9   Closing a full-duplex TCP connection comparison.

TCP Session Security Issues

Calling TCP a reliable protocol means that it uses an acknowledgement mechanism to ensure that the data is received at the remote computer intact. Reliable does not mean that TCP is a secure protocol. If that were so, there would be no need for firewalls! Although the connection setup and termination methods used to create a connection create a virtual circuit between the two computers, there are many ways to exploit TCP (and IP) to break into a computer. For example, every time a new connection is requested on a server (the receipt of a TCP segment with the SYN bit set), the computer sets aside data structures in memory to store information about the connection it is setting up. This requires a few CPU cycles and memory on the computer.

It should be obvious from this that an easy way to cause a "denial-of-service" attack against a computer is to simply send a large number of SYN segments to it in a short period of time. If the number of SYN segments and the rate at which they are sent exceeds the capacity of the CPU or memory of the server, then, depending on the operating system and how the TCP/IP stack is implemented, the system might slow to a crawl or crash.

For more information about how the inner workings of TCP/IP and related protocols can be used maliciously, see Chapter 39, "Security Issues in Wide Area Networks." For information on how to protect yourself against these sorts of attacks, see Chapter 40.

The User Datagram Protocol (UDP)

Although TCP uses an acknowledgement mechanism to ensure that data is actually delivered to another computer, the User Datagram Protocol (UDP) does not. Both use IP as a transport protocol, but UDP is a much simpler protocol that doesn't require the overhead that TCP does. If an application does not need the benefits that a TCP connection provides, then UDP can be used. Because UDP does no session setup, and all UDP datagrams are independent entities on the network, it can be considered an *unreliable*, *connectionless* protocol.

An example of this is the Domain Name Service (DNS). Most implementations of DNS use UDP packets so that it can efficiently exchange information with other computers. If a client doesn't receive a response back from a simple DNS request, it can try again, or simply use another DNS server if it is configured to do so.

Examining UDP Header Information

Compared to the TCP header, the UPD header is much smaller because it doesn't require fields for sequence or acknowledgment numbers. UDP also doesn't need the connection setup flags, window size fields, and other information required for a connection-oriented protocol. In Figure 20.10 you can see that UDP has only four fields.

Source Port (16 bits)	Destination Port (16 bits)
Length (16 bits)	Checksum (16 bits)

Figure 20.10   The UPD protocol uses a smaller header.

The following are the purposes of the UDP header fields:

■ **Source port**—This 16-bit field is used to identify the port being used by the application that is sending the data.

■ **Destination port**—This 16-bit field is used to identify the port to which the packet will be delivered on the receiving end of the connection.

■ **Length**—This 16-bit field is used to store the length of the entire UDP datagram, which includes both the header and data portions.

■ **Checksum**—This 16-bit field is used to ensure that the contents of the UDP datagram are not corrupted in transit.

Although the length field in the UDP header can store a value of up to 65,535, in actual practice the size of a datagram is usually limited to a much smaller value. For example, the application programming interface (API) of a particular operating system might use smaller fields to specify the length of a datagram.

The checksum field is calculated on the UDP header information and its data, along with pseudo header information, just as is done with TCP. Using this method, UDP can determine whether the IP layer has passed to it a datagram that was not intended for this computer. If the checksum calculated on the receiving end does not match the value stored in this field, the UDP datagram is discarded. Similar to IP, no message is sent back to the sender of the datagram if this happens. For a reliable connection an application should use TCP, not UDP.

Note

The User Datagram Protocol is defined in RFC 768, "User Datagram Protocol."

Interaction Between UDP and ICMP

Whereas UDP has no built-in mechanisms for guaranteeing delivery of the information carried in its datagrams, the Internet Control Message Protocol (ICMP) is used to report conditions back to the sending computer. For example, if a UDP datagram is sent to a computer with a destination port that is not being used (that is, that service is not running on the destination computer), then the ICMP port unreachable message (subcode value 3 of the destination unreachable message) is returned to the sender.

ICMP messages also can be used with UDP to find out the maximum transmission unit (MTU) size. That is, the largest size a datagram can be in order to be sent through the network without being fragmented. Remember that on a network that uses different routers, or perhaps on an internetwork that is made up of different types of equipment or network media, the maximum size of a frame can change from one device to another. To discover the maximum size of a datagram that can be sent through the network, another subcode of the ICMP unreachable message (subcode 4) can be used along with UDP.

To create a utility that can be used to discover the MTU of a network connection, the IP Don't Fragment field can be set in the IP header information. When the UDP datagram reaches a router or other device that can't forward the datagram without fragmenting it, it will return the ICMP unreachable message "fragmentation needed, don't fragment bit set."

Finally, in some implementations a router or host will return the ICMP "source quench" error if a system is sending UDP datagrams at a rate that is too fast for the system receiving them. In this case, the application using UDP should be coded to take this into account, because the datagrams will be discarded by the system that generates the "source quench" ICMP messages.

Ports, Services, and Applications

If all applications that used the network only identified the destination for their data exchange as a single IP address, the information would arrive at the destination computer, but it would be almost impossible for the targeted system to figure out which process to give the data to.

Both the TCP and UDP protocols use port numbers to solve this problem. Each application that communicates on the network using TCP/IP also specifies a port number on the target computer. The port numbers are endpoints for the communications path so that two applications communicating across the network can identify each other. Think of a street address for a business. If all the mail arrived simply addressed with the street address, how would you determine who should get each letter? By using a person's name or the suite or room number, the endpoint of the communication becomes more fully defined. This is how ports work.

Well-Known Ports

The Internet Corporation for Assigned Names and Numbers (ICANN) is the organization that controls the first range of port numbers that are available (0–1023) and these are usually called "well-known ports." The use for these ports has been defined in several RFCs (most recently RFC 1700), and change only occasionally. In Appendix B, "TCP and UDP Common Ports," you will find a list of these ports and a short description of their use.

Note

The Internet Corporation for Assigned Names and Numbers (ICANN) was created in 1998 as a technical coordination body for the Internet. ICANN assumed most of the functions that were previously performed by the Internet Assigned Numbers Authority (IANA). In addition to taking responsibility for port numbers, ICANN also is responsible for managing how Internet domain names, IP addresses, and protocol parameters are managed and assigned. You can learn more about ICANN by visiting their home page at **www.icann.com**.

Well-known ports are usually accessible on a given system by a privileged process or privileged users. For example, you can see that the FTP utility uses ports 20 and 21, while the Telnet utility uses port 23. In this table found in Appendix B, note that in most cases the User Datagram Protocol (UDP) and Transmission Control Protocol (TCP) make the same use of a particular port. This is not required, however, so when you are using this table be sure to check the protocol for each port when looking up its use.

One good way to use this table is to decide which ports to block when building a firewall. Some of these applications will never be used by your system, and because of that, there exists no good reason to allow network traffic through the firewall that uses these ports.

Registered Ports

Ports numbered from 1024 to 65535 also can be used but are not reserved by IANA. These ports are called registered ports and can be used by most any user process on the system.

Because the source and destination addresses in the IP header are used to identify the two machines in the network that are sending packets to each other, why are ports necessary?

Ports are used to identify the application end points of the connection. Because a particular computer can have more than one application using the TCP stack at the same time, there must be a way to differentiate which packets go to which applications. For example, suppose you've established a Telnet session with a remote computer and decide you want to download a file to that computer. Telnet doesn't transfer files, so you would have to open an FTP connection. Because the source and destination addresses would be the same in the IP packet for both of these sessions, port numbers are used to indicate the application.

When you combine an address with a port number you have an identifier that can uniquely identify both endpoints of a communication. The name used for this combination of numbers is a *socket*. This is illustrated in Figure 20.11, where two computers have established two communication sessions, one for Telnet (port 23) and one for FTP (port 20). FTP actually uses two ports—port 20 for sending data and port 21 for exchanging command information.

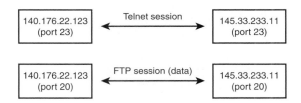

Figure 20.11   A socket is composed of an address and port number, and uniquely identifies an endpoint of a network connection.

It quickly should become apparent to you why a packet filter would find these port numbers useful. Instead of having to permit or deny packets based only on their source or destination address—and thereby allow or disallow *all* communications—it is possible to selectively allow or disallow individual *services*. Although you might not want your users to Telnet to a remote host computer (or vice versa), you might not care if they exchange files through anonymous FTP sessions. By using port numbers in packet filtering rules you can enable or disable network services one at a time.

In the original BSD implementation of TCP/IP port numbers from 0–1023 were called *privileged* ports. That is, they were to be used by programs that run as root on the Unix machine, and these programs are usually the server program for a particular service. Following this convention, client programs would choose a port number that was greater than 1023. Although this is not something that has been standardized in an RFC, it is still commonplace to find other TCP/IP stacks that adhere to this.

The Internet Control Message Protocol (ICMP)

The Internet Control Message Protocol (ICMP) is a required part of any TCP/IP implementation, and the functions it performs are very important to routers and other network devices that communicate through TCP/IP. Like TCP and UPD, this protocol also uses the IP protocol to send its messages through the network. If you have used the `ping` or `traceroute` commands, you have used ICMP. ICMP was first defined in RFC 792.

Whereas TCP can usually recover from dropped datagrams simply by requesting that IP retransmit them, ICMP is used as a reporting mechanism that can be used by IP (and thus the protocols that use IP).

There are many different kinds of ICMP messages, but all share a similar format. The fields of an ICMP message are

- **Type**—This 1-byte field is used to indicate the kind of ICMP message (see Table 20.10).
- **Code**—This 1-byte field is used as a subcode to further identify a message. This field is set to zero if the particular message type does not need to be further delineated.
- **Checksum**—This 2-byte field is used to provide an error checking code for the entire ICMP message.
- **Type-Specific Data**—This field can vary in length and is used to provide further data specific to the ICMP message type.

ICMP Message Types

Table 20.10 shows the different types of messages that make up ICMP. The numbers listed in the Message Type field are what will be found in the Type field of the ICMP message.

Table 20.10   ICMP Message Types

Message Type	Description
0	Echo Reply
3	Destination Unreachable
4	Source Quench
5	Redirect Message
8	Echo Request
9	Router Advertisement
10	Router Selection
11	Time Exceeded
12	Parameter Problem
13	Timestamp Request
14	Timestamp Reply
15	Information Request (no longer used)
16	Information Reply (no longer used)
17	Address Mask Request
18	Address Mask Reply

As described in Chapter 22 the `ping` command uses the echo request and echo reply messages to determine whether a physical connection exists between systems. Another important function on the Internet is traffic control, and the source quench message can be sent to tell a sending host that the destination host cannot keep up with the speed at which it is sending packets. The transmitting computer can keep sending these quench messages until the sender scales back its transmissions to an acceptable rate.

Routers use another valuable function ICMP (the Redirect Message) to tell another router that it knows of a better path to a destination. Routers also can use the time-exceeded messages to report back to another device why packet was discarded.

Routers are not the only devices that use ICMP. Host computers can use ICMP. For example, when a computer boots and does not know what the network mask is for the local LAN it can generate an address mask request message. Another device on the network can reply to assist the computer.

Note

The Information Request and Information Reply message types are shown in Table 20.10 only for completeness. Their functionality was originally developed to allow a host to obtain an IP address. This function is now supplied by the BOOTP protocol and by the Dynamic Host Configuration Protocol (DHCP). For more information about these protocols, see Chapter 23.

The Code field in the ICMP message is used for only some of the ICMP message types. The Destination Unreachable message has the most number of code types. Table 20.11 lists these codes.

Table 20.11   ICMP Message Codes

Message Type	Code Field	Description
3	0	Network unreachable
	1	Host unreachable
	2	Protocol unreachable
	3	Port unreachable
	4	Fragmentation needed but the don't fragment bit is set
	5	Source route failed
	6	Destination network unknown
	7	Destination host unknown
	8	Source host isolated (no longer used)
	9	Destination network administratively prohibited
	10	Destination host administratively prohibited
	11	Network unreachable for TOS
	12	Host unreachable for TOS
	13	Communication administratively prohibited by filtering
	14	Host precedence violation
	15	Precedence cutoff in effect
5	0	Redirect for network
	1	Redirect for host
	2	Redirect for type of service and network
	3	Redirect for type of service and host
11	0	TTL equals zero during transit
	1	TTL equals 0 during reassembly
12	0	IP header bad
	1	Required option missing

As you can see, ICMP can be used to compose quite detailed messages to indicate error conditions, offer advice on routing possibilities, and other functions that help the Internet easier to manage.

Some situations will cause an ICMP message not to be generated. For example, ICMP messages are never created in response to an error in another ICMP message. That doesn't mean that ICMP messages can't be created in response to other ICMP messages, however. For example, the echo request and echo reply messages work together in a query/response format. Other instances that usually don't generate ICMP messages include

- IP broadcast and multicast messages
- Link-layer broadcast messages (that is, Ethernet frame broadcast messages)
- Datagrams that have a source address that is not for a unique host, such as the loopback address
- Messages that have been fragmented, except for the first fragment

If ICMP messages were allowed to correct problems with multicast or broadcast messages, a large number could be generated, causing the problem to become worse. This is the reason for most of the preceding conditions limiting the use of ICMP.

For the most part, the use of ICMP is described in other sections of this book where their use is employed. For example, the troubleshooting TCP/IP chapter discusses using ICMP to implement the traceroute and ping commands, while Chapter 29 discusses their use for routing problems. Some of these messages are not discussed in this book either because they are no longer used (as indicated in the table) or because their use is trivial or rare.

TCP/IP Services and Applications

SOME OF THE MAIN TOPICS IN THIS CHAPTER ARE

The File Transfer Protocol (FTP)

The Telnet Protocol

The R-Utilities

Finger Somebody!

Other TCP/IP Related Services and Applications

In the previous chapter, it was mentioned that TCP/IP usually refers not just to the two protocols represented by its acronym (the Transmission Control Protocol and the Internet Protocol), but it is also a term used to refer to other related protocols, services, and applications that were developed to work together. These are referred to as the TCP/IP protocol suite. A wide range of services and applications have been developed to work with TCP/IP, and most implementations contain a standard set of these, which are the subject of this chapter. In addition to services and applications, other protocols have evolved along the way as the Internet has grown, such as the Simple Mail Transport Protocol (SMTP), which makes global e-mail possible.

This chapter deals with the TCP/IP suite of utilities that are generally used by end users and protocols that these utilities use to communicate.

▶▶ Troubleshooting utilities, such as `Ping` and `Traceroute`, are covered in Chapter 22, "Troubleshooting Tools for TCP/IP Networks."

Because you've already read about how the basic TCP/IP protocols get data from one point to another using TCP or UDP along with IP, it's time to look at some of the protocols and applications that you can use on a network. The applications include examples for most of the commands, varying from Solaris 8 to FreeBSD Unix to Windows NT/2000.

Additionally, for some of the more important applications, such as FTP and telnet, we'll look closely at the protocol itself and the messages that are exchanged between client and server. These are the actual protocol commands that a particular utility uses to communicate with its counterpart. These low-level message or command exchanges can be useful when you are troubleshooting these applications using a protocol analyzer.

The sample syntaxes for commands found in this chapter are meant to show you that it's a good thing help files (or man pages) were invented. The difference in a command from one system to another can vary greatly!

The File Transfer Protocol (FTP)

The name says it all. This protocol is used to transfer files between computers. FTP is a complex protocol that allows for exchange of data files using different methods of data representation and file storage. In its simplest form, it uses clear text username and password exchanges and is not considered to be a very secure utility. When FTP was originally developed—when the Internet was still composed mostly of large business, government, and educational institutions—breach of security wasn't considered that big of a threat.

The syntax for FTP varies from one vendor's implementation to another. However, the simplest format, used to initiate a connection, is

`ftp hostname`

where you simply follow the `ftp` command with a hostname; for example, `ftp ftp.twoinc.com`. You also can use the dotted-decimal address instead of the DNS name of the system with which you want to establish a connection. Alternatively, you can enter `ftp` at the command prompt and then, from the `ftp>` prompt, enter the commands you need to accomplish a particular task.

A lot has changed in the past 20 to 30 years. More secure forms of authentication and data exchange have been added to create more secure forms of FTP. Before we look at a few common FTP clients and their syntaxes, let's look at the basic FTP protocol and get a feel for how it works.

Note

The File Transfer Protocol can be found in a large number of RFC documents that were created over the years. The main RFC that most documents point you to is RFC 959, "File Transfer Protocol (FTP)." RFC 2151, "A Primer on Internet and TCP/IP Tools and Utilities," is also a nice read and covers many of the utilities in this chapter. RFC 2228, "FTP Security Extensions," deals with the inherent security problems found in the FTP protocol. This last RFC discusses extensions that can be used to provide for secure authentication and encryption for the FTP protocol.

FTP is based on a client/server architecture. An FTP server (called a *daemon* on Unix systems and a *service* on Windows systems) manages a filesystem (anything from a single directory to a disk farm) and authenticates file transfers with remote FTP clients. The basic protocol is a simple exchange of messages. Traditional FTP uses a simple command-line interface. Today, many shareware and commercial GUI versions of FTP are available. Either way, command line or GUI, it is an extremely useful utility because it allows the transfer of many different types of files between two hosts on the network.

FTP Ports and Processes

The FTP server daemon listens in the background for FTP requests on TCP port 21. In the literature, the server is composed of two components, though they are often combined into a single program. The first is the Server-PI, which stands for "server protocol interpreter." This is the component that listens to TCP port 21 and interacts with its client counterpart, the User-PI. The user protocol interpreter initiates an FTP session by sending a request to the server. The client's request can include a port that the client wants the server to use when it opens a data channel.

The second component of the server is the Server-DTP, which stands for "Server Data Transfer Process." This is the code that interacts with its counterpart, the User-DTP, to perform the actual file data transfers. An overview of this process appears in Figure 21.1. The important thing to notice in this figure is that two channels of communication are used for FTP—one for commands and one for the actual exchange of data—and that both of these channels work in both directions.

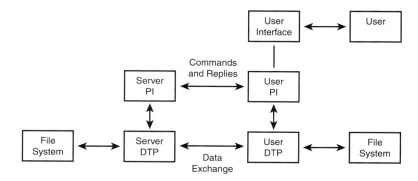

Figure 21.1   The FTP session consists of both a command and a data channel.

The client's User-PI should be listening on the specified port for incoming data transmissions before it has issued the commands necessary to start a data transfer from a remote server. The actual commands used on the control connection are in the same format used for the telnet utility (NVT-ASCII), which is discussed later in this chapter.

Data Transfers

All FTP data transfers take place using 8-bit bytes, independent of the size of the actual data being transferred. That is, if the local file system uses a different size for storage, such as a word or a floating-point numerical representation, FTP just sends 8 bits at a time. The data is reconstructed on the receiving end into its original format. The client and server applications are responsible for making sure that conversions are done on their end to make data usable on their respective systems.

Three modes are used for transfers:

- **Stream mode**—This is a simple transmission of a stream of bytes. To represent record and file structures using this mode, End of Record (EOR) and End of File (EOF) control bytes can be used. Control bytes consist of 2 bytes. The first byte is set to all ones (which is the escape character), and the second byte is the control character. A value of 1 for this byte indicates that it is the EOR character. A value of 2 indicates it is the EOF character. A value of 3 indicates both characters (EOR and EOF). Note that if an actual byte of all ones is in the data stream, it is transmitted as a two-byte sequence also, with both bytes being set to all ones.

- **Block mode**—This transmission mode sends a series of data blocks, each of which has a header. The header information consists of three bytes of information. The 16 lower-order bits indicate the byte count, which is the total length of the block (expressed in bytes). The remaining high-order byte is used for a descriptor code. A descriptor code value of 128 indicates that the end of a data block is the end of a record (EOR). A value of 64 indicates that the end of a data block is the end of a block of data (EOF). A value of 32 is used to indicate that there is reason to suspect errors in the data stream.

- **Compressed mode**—In this mode, data can be sent using a variety of compression mechanisms.

All transfers are done in 8-bit bytes, regardless of the way the bits are interpreted on the receiving system. The data types that FTP allows are very basic. The ASCII type consists of standard 8-bit NVT-ASCII characters. In this format, the carriage return and line-feed characters are used to indicate the end of a line. Some systems, such as many Unix systems, do not use this combination of characters, and the receiving side converts the received stream of bytes to its own format.

The EBCDIC type is a method of character representation used mainly on IBM mainframe computers, which, of course, were quite popular back when development on FTP (and its predecessors) first started. The EBCDIC and ASCII transfers are sent as 8-bit characters and are similar, with just the character representations of the numerical values differing.

The IMAGE mode of transfer sends data as a simple stream of bits, which are stored in the usual 8-bit transfer byte used by FTP. At the receiving end, the bits are stored in a contiguous manner, with padding added to the end of a file or record as necessary. The method used must ensure that the process of this padding can be reversed if the file is transferred to another system that does not use that method.

The LOCAL type allows the user to set a logical size for the bytes to be sent. All data is still sent as an 8-bit byte, but on the receiving end this command allows the receiver to know how to reassemble the bits into the correctly sized bytes.

FTP Protocol Commands

This section looks at some of the more useful commands that the protocol uses to control an FTP session. This is not an exhaustive discussion of all possible protocol commands, however. The next section looks at examples of the syntax for FTP for several implementations so that you can see how various FTP applications work, and how their command structure matches up user commands to the commands actually used by the FTP protocol processes.

Please note that these "protocol commands" are the commands exchanged by communicating devices on the network that are using FTP. User commands, as entered by an end-user FTP client, will differ. Many end-user commands involve a sequence of protocol commands to accomplish the desired function.

FTP protocol commands start with the command code itself and are usually followed by one or more arguments. All FTP protocol commands are four characters or less and can be grouped into several different categories:

- **Access Control Commands (ACT)**—These are used to authenticate the user, change directories, and so on.
- **Transfer Parameter Commands (TPC)**—These commands control the actual data transfer process, such as the port used, file structure, and so on.
- **FTP Service Commands (FSC)**—These commands indicate the function the user wants to perform, such as sending or receiving a file, or perhaps renaming or deleting a file.

Table 21.1 is a list of commonly used commands along with a description of their use.

Table 21.1   FTP Protocol Commands

Command	Type	Description
USER	ACT	This command is followed by a username valid on the remote system.
PASS	ACT	This command is followed by the password associated with the remote user account.
ACCT	ACT	Some implementations require a text string identifying a user account, which is sent with this command.
CWD	ACT	Change working directory on the remote system.
CDUP	ACT	Change to parent directory.
SMNT	ACT	Used to mount a different file system.
REIN	ACT	Reinitialize. This flushes all user account and I/O data and reinitializes the connection. Typically, another USER command is then used to start a new session.
QUIT	ACT	This is the logout command to end a session.
PORT	TPC	Used to specify a host data port other than the default.
PASV	TPC	Causes the server to listen on a specified port other than the default.
TYPE	TPC	The data representation type (that is, ASCII, IMAGE, and so on). A numerical value is used for each type.
STRU	TPC	File structure. F = file (no record structure), R = record structure, P = page structure. The default is file.
MODE	TPC	Transfer mode. S = stream, B = block, c = compressed.
RETR	FSC	Retrieve. Instructs the server to send a file.
STOR	FSC	Store. Instructs the server to receive and store a file.
STOU	FSC	Similar to STOR but creates a unique filename on the server.
APPE	FSC	Append with create. If the file exists on the server, data is appended. If not, a file is created.
ALLO	FSC	Used to allocate space before file transfer.
REST	FSC	Restart. Restarts the file transfer at a specified checkpoint.

Table 21.1   Continued

Command	Type	Description
RNFR	FSC	Rename from. The old pathname of a file that is being renamed. Followed by an RNTO command.
RNTO	FSC	Rename to. Specifies the new pathname of a renamed file.
ABOR	FSC	Instructs the server to abort the previous command and/or data transfer.
DELE	FSC	Deletes a file on the server.
RMD	FSC	Remove directory. Removes a directory on the server.
MKD	FSC	Make directory. Creates a directory on the server.
PWD	FSC	Displays the name of the current directory (print working directory).
LIST	FSC	Lists information about a file or lists files in a directory.
NLIST	FSC	Name list. Sends the client a list of just the names in a directory.
SITE	FSC	Site parameters. Implementation dependent.
SYST	FSC	Sends the client a reply indicating the operating system of the server.
STAT	FSC	Causes the server to return a status response.
HELP	FSC	What it says!
NOOP	FSC	No-operation. Causes the server to send an OK reply.

As you can see from this table, there are a large number of commands that the client side can use to control file transfers. In the next section we will look at the replies that the FTP server can send in response to these commands. Remember, these are the commands that are used in the protocol exchange. The commands in the next section are not manually entered by a user at a keyboard. They are the replies sent by the FTP server in answer to the protocol commands of the FTP client.

Server Replies to FTP Commands

In the FTP protocol, every command must be followed by a reply from the server. In some cases, more than one reply will be sent to the client. The actual reply is a three-digit number, but it is transmitted as text characters. Following this number is usually some variable length text. The numerical value is used by the program, while the text is intended for the user of the FTP client. Because some of the text is configurable, you can expect to see different text for the same numerical reply from one implementation to another.

To reply to the client, the three characters representing the numeric reply code are sent, followed by a minus (–) or space character and then the reply text. A simple convention is used for multiline text messages. The first line contains the three-letter numerical code followed by the – character and then the text. The last line replaces the – character with the space character. By matching up the two three-digit codes, the client can determine the beginning and ending of a particular multiline message.

Reply Codes

Each of the actual digits that make up the reply code are significant. If you've ever wondered why all those text lines start with numbers, you'll find their meaning in this section. The text displayed will vary from one vendor to another, but the codes should still be implemented for the same general reply condition.

The first digit indicates success or failure. A value of 1 indicates a Positive Preliminary reply, which means that the function requested by the client has been started. A value of 2 is the Positive Completion reply, which means that the requested function was successfully performed. A value of 3 is the Positive Intermediate reply, indicating that the command was received by the server but has not been executed. The server might be waiting for further information. A value of 4 indicates a Transient Negative Completion reply. This means that a temporary error situation has prevented the function requested by the client from being performed. A value of 5 in the first position is the Permanent Negative Completion reply. This indicates that the requested action was not performed. Unlike the Transient message code, the user is not encouraged to retry the command.

The second digit is used to place message types into groups. A value of zero refers to a syntax error. A value of 1 is an informational message. A value of 2 indicates that the reply refers to either the control or data connection. A value of 3 is used for replies regarding authentication and accounting, such as during the initial logon process. A value of 4 is unspecified at this time. A value of 5 means that the reply refers to the status of the file server's file system as it relates to the user request.

The third digit in the response code is used to further divide the replies based on the categories indicated by the second digit.

In Table 21.2, you can see the recommended reply codes, in numerical order, as specified in RFC 959.

Table 21.2   FTP Numerical Reply Codes

Code	Description
110	Restart marker reply.
120	Service ready in *nnn* minutes.
125	Data connection is already open, the transfer is starting.
150	File status okay—about to open data connection.
200	Command okay.
202	Command not implemented.
211	System status or a help reply text.
212	Directory status.
213	File status.
214	Help message.
215	System type.
220	Service is ready for new user.
221	Service closing the control connection.
225	Data connection is open but no transfer is in progress.
226	Closing the data connection, and the requested function (such as file transfer) is complete.
227	Entering passive mode.
230	User logged in.
250	Requested file action is okay and has been completed.
257	The requested pathname has been created.
331	User name is okay but password is needed.
332	An account name is required to complete the logon.
350	The requested file action is waiting for further information.
421	Service is not available. The control connection is being closed.
425	Unable open data connection.

Table 21.2 Continued

Code	Description
426	Connection closed—transfer aborted.
450	Requested file action was not taken.
451	Requested action aborted due to local processing error.
452	Requested action not taken due to insufficient storage space.
500	Syntax error. The command was not recognized (or line too long).
501	Syntax error in parameters or arguments to command.
502	Command not implemented.
503	Incorrect sequence of commands.
504	Command not implemented for a particular parameter.
530	User not logged in.
532	Need account for storing files.
550	Requested action not taken. Usually file not found or access denied.
551	Requested action aborted: page type unknown.
552	Requested file action aborted due to storage allocation exceeded.
553	Requested action not taken. Filename not allowed.

Using a Windows FTP Command-Line Client

Client implementations can vary from simple command-line interfaces to programs that enable you to drag and drop using a graphical interface. Windows 98, NT, and 2000 provide a default FTP client that works from the command line. The syntax for the Windows 2000 FTP client is simply the command FTP followed by the server to which you want to connect. The complete syntax for the command is

```
ftp [-v] [-n] [-i] [-d] [-g] [-s: filename] [-a]
➥[-A] [-w:windowsize] [hostname]
```

Where:

- **-v**—This parameter suppresses responses from the remote server.

- **-n**—The Windows FTP client automatically prompts you for a username and password. This option suppresses these prompts. You are presented with the ftp> prompt and allowed to use the USER command to specify your logon username.

- **-i**—This turns off prompting that occurs when transferring multiple files with the MGET or MPUT command. This is the same function performed by the PROMPT command when you're at the ftp> prompt.

- **-d**—Enables debugging the FTP session. All commands (the actual protocol commands) sent between the client and server are displayed.

- **-g**—Disables filename globbing.

- **-s:filename**—The commands found in the file named *filename* are executed after the FTP command line is entered.

- **-a**—Indicates that any local interface can be used when binding the data connection.

- **-A**—Performs an anonymous logon to the FTP server.

- **-w:*windowsize***—Specifies the transfer buffer size. The default is 4096 bytes.
- ***hostname***—The hostname or IP address of the remote server.

You can issue commands from within the program after you've entered the command line to start up the FTP client. These include some of the same options that you can enter on the command line and additional commands that can be used to transfer files, list directories, and so on. The following commands are available with the Windows 2000 client:

- **! *<command>***—Yes, it's an exclamation point. Used with no command, this causes you to exit to the "shell," which on a Windows system is the command prompt. After you have performed any tasks that you need to, you can type exit to return to the current FTP session. This command enables you to escape temporarily to check execute commands on the local system without being forced to terminate the FTP program. Alternatively, you can enter a command (separated by a space from the exclamation character) and the program will execute the command on the local system and remain the FTP client program.

- **? or help**—Typing ? prints a list of commands available. The word help followed by a command gives you local help text for that command.

- **append *<filename> <filename>***—Appends data to an existing file.

- **ascii**—Sets the transfer type to ASCII (default).

- **bell**—Toggles on or off a bell that sounds after each file transfer. The default is off.

- **binary**—Sets the file transfer type to binary for image files.

- **bye**—Exits the client and ends the current FTP connections.

- **cd *<directory>***—Changes the working directory on the remote FTP server.

- **close**—Closes the current connection and leaves you in the ftp> interpreter prompt so you can continue to perform other actions, such as open another server.

- **debug**—Similar to the -d command-line option, causes the protocol messages exchange between client and server to be displayed, prefixed with the characters - - - >.

- **delete *<filename>***—Deletes a file on the remote server.

- **dir**—Lists files and directories on the remote server. You can follow this command with a wildcard to narrow your listing, provided globbing is turned on!

- **disconnect**—Disconnects the session with the current server, leaving you in the FTP interpreter prompt to continue working.

- **get *<filename>***—This command is used to get a single file from the remote server.

- **glob**—Toggles (as does the -g command-line option) for globbing filenames. This is a simple way to say that you can use wildcards in local filenames and path names, and it is the default.

- **hash**—What you used to eat in the Army. Actually, this command causes a hash mark (more correctly called the number sign character) to be printed for every 2048 bytes transferred. This is helpful in a long transfer because you can watch the progress and determine whether it has stalled or stopped.

- **lcd *<pathname>***—This changes the working directory on the client's local system. Compare to CD, which changes the working directory on the remote server's system.

- **literal *<text>***—Sends text, verbatim, to the server. A single response is expected back.

- **ls**—Displays an abbreviated listing of the files or directories on the remote server system. Similar to the dir[ectory] command.

- **mdelete** *<filenames>*—Use this when you want to delete more than one filename on a remote server. You can use wildcards for this if needed (check that globbing).
- **mdir**—Displays a listing of files and directories that exist on the remote sever.
- **mls**—Displays an abbreviated listing of the files and directories that exist on the remote server.
- **mput** *<filenames>*—Performs multiple file transfers from the client to the server, using only one command. Wildcards can be used.
- **open** *<hostname>*—Used to connect to a specific server after the FTP interpreter prompt has been issued.
- **prompt**—Use this to toggle on or off prompting during multiple file transfers. The default is on. This means that if you use mget, mdel, or mput to work with files, you'll get prompted for each file. Toggle this off if you want to work with a large number of files and let it just run without having to answer Y or N to each prompt for each file.
- **put** *<filename>*—Transfers a single file to the remote FTP server from the client.
- **pwd**—Stands for Print Working Directory. This displays the current directory on the remote FTP server.
- **quit**—Exits the FTP client and ends any outstanding connections.
- **quote**—The same function as the literal command.
- **recv**—The same as the get command.
- **remotehelp**—Displays help from the remote server.
- **rename** *<filename> <filename>*—Renames a file on the remote FTP server.
- **rmdir** *<directory>*—Removes a directory on the remote FTP server.
- **send** *<filename>*—Same as the put command.
- **status**—Toggles on or off a status display.
- **trace**—Toggles on or off a display showing the routes taken by each packet.
- **type** *<type>*—Sets the current transfer type. Examples: type ascii (for text files) or type binary (for program files).
- **user** *<username>*—Use this to specify a username during the logon process.
- **verbose**—Toggles on or off verbose mode. The default is on, so all replies sent by remote server are displayed.

As you can see, many commands duplicate functions performed by others. Over the years commands have been added that are easier to remember. For example, it's easier to remember GET than to remember RECV.

Note that there are usually two commands to perform file functions, depending on whether you are operating on one or multiple files. For example, use GET *<filename>* to get a single file, but to get multiple files, use MGET in a format such as MGET REPORTS*.*. Don't forget that, when using the "M" (multiple) commands, you might want to first issue the PROMPT command so you won't have to answer yes to the prompt for each file. Conversely, you can leave prompting turned on if you know you want to retrieve most of the files that match your file specification but want to exclude a few by answering no to the prompts.

In the following listing, you can see how the command is invoked to connect to the remote server, the reply messages received from the server, and a directory listing produced by using the DIR command. Next, the ls command is used to show the difference in the output. Finally, the session is set to show hash marks (hash) and then set to do a binary download (binary). You can see the results of using the HASH command and then the GET command to retrieve a file from the remote server.

```
J:\>ftp ftp.twoinc.com
Connected to ftp.twoinc.com.
220-ArGoSoft FTP Server for WinNT/2000, Version 1.2 (1.2.1.1)
220-Welcome to Active Web Hosting
220-For more information on our
220-services please call
220 (800) 946-7764 or (702) 451-1577.
User (ftp.twoinc.com:(none)): twoinc.com
331 User name OK, need password
Password:
230 User twoinc.com logged in successfully **
ftp> dir
200 Port command successful
150 Opening binary data connection
drw-r--r--  1 user    group        0 Mar 06 00:00 ..
-rw-r--r--  1 user    group   145408 Mar 03 13:55 burning dasies.doc
-rw-r--r--  1 user    group      436 Feb 24 13:36 cnt.htm
-rw-r--r--  1 user    group      455 Feb 24 13:36 default.htm
-rw-r--r--  1 user    group      949 Feb 24 13:36 default.html
-rw-r--r--  1 user    group      807 Feb 24 13:36 emp.htm
-rw-r--r--  1 user    group  1729597 Mar 06 09:52 hiroshimamontage.mp3
-rw-r--r--  1 user    group      268 Feb 24 13:36 lnk.htm
drw-r--r--  1 user    group        0 Jan 26 12:56 logs
-rw-r--r--  1 user    group     1969 Feb 24 13:36 pub.htm
-rw-r--r--  1 user    group   122880 Mar 03 14:05 Symphony of Souls.doc
-rw-r--r--  1 user    group     1317 Feb 24 13:36 who.htm
226 Transfer complete
ftp: 807 bytes received in 0.15Seconds 5.38Kbytes/sec.
ftp> ls
200 Port command successful
150 Opening binary data connection
..
burning dasies.doc
cnt.htm
default.htm
default.html
emp.htm
hiroshimamontage.mp3
lnk.htm
logs
pub.htm
Symphony of Souls.doc
who.htm
226 Transfer complete
ftp: 147 bytes received in 0.05Seconds 2.94Kbytes/sec.
ftp> hash
Hash mark printing On ftp: (2048 bytes/hash mark) .
ftp> binary
200 Type set to Image (binary)
ftp> get hiroshimamontage.mp3
200 Port command successful
150 Opening binary data connection
################################################################################
################################################################################
```

```
###############################################################################
###############################################################################
#############################################
226 Transfer complete
ftp: 1729597 bytes received in 573.14Seconds 3.02Kbytes/sec.
ftp>
```

As you can see, using the FTP utility is an easy way to examine directory information on remote systems or to exchange files.

The Trivial File Transfer Protocol (TFTP)

This protocol was developed to be a "lite" version of FTP, where security and elaborate mechanisms for error control were not needed. Generally, TFTP is used to download operating systems, firmware upgrades, and other files to network devices or diskless workstations. For example, a diskless workstation can use BOOTP (or DHCP) to obtain IP configuration information and the location of a TFTP server, along with the name of the file to download. For more information about BOOTP and DHCP and how they allow diskless workstations to obtain the information they need to boot, see Chapter 23, "BOOTP and the Dynamic Host Configuration Protocol (DHCP)."

No authentication is used, so this is a service that should be used only where it is absolutely needed. The syntax for the TFTP command is

```
tftp [-i] host [get | put] source [destination]
```

The command-line option -i specifies a binary image transfer, which is precisely the kind of transfer for which this utility is usually used. If you omit this option, an ASCII file transfer is done by default.

The get command specifies that the source file is to be transferred from *source* to *destination*. The put command works, just as in FTP, in the opposite direction to send a file from the client to the TFTP server.

The following are other important differences between FTP and TFTP:

- FTP uses TCP, while TFTP uses UDP.
- Only file transfers are supported. Directory listings, file deletions, and other features of FTP are not implemented in TFTP.
- TFTP was designed to be simple and compact so that its code could be stored in a small amount of read-only memory.

The official specification for TFTP can be found in RFC 1350, "The TFTP Protocol (Revision 2)." It uses a simple set of messages to establish the file exchange. In each message, the first two bytes are reserved for use as an opcode. Five different message types are used:

- **1**—This opcode (RRQ) is used to initiate a read request to download a file from the TFTP server to the client. After the first 2-byte opcode, a variable number of bytes specifying the filename follows and is terminated with a zero byte. Following this is the *mode* used for the transfer. This can be the text netascii, which means that the transfer will consist of ASCII text lines terminated by the carriage-return/line-feed combination. The text octet in the mode field indicates that the data transfer will be a simple transfer of 8-bit octets of data.
- **2**—This opcode (WRQ) is similar to the first one, except that the file transfer will be made from the client to the TFTP server.
- **3**—This opcode (data) is used to send a block of data. The 2-byte opcode is followed by a 2-byte field that contains a block number. Following this is from 0–512 bytes of actual data.

- **4**—This opcode (ACK) acknowledges the block transferred. Each block is acknowledged. The format for this packet is the 2-byte opcode followed by the 2-byte block number being acknowledged by the receiver.

- **5**—This opcode (error) is reserved for reporting errors. The 2-byte opcode is followed by a 2-byte error code and a variable-length error message terminated by a zero byte. Note that, for most error types, the connection is aborted and must be tried again.

The interoperation of this protocol is quite simple. For each block sent, an acknowledgment is sent back to the sender. This is sometimes called a stop-and-wait protocol. Remember that TCP uses an acknowledgment mechanism where one ACK can acknowledge multiple segments of data. In TFTP, each block is acknowledged.

Block numbers are numbered starting at 1. However, for a write request, the acknowledgment number returned to the sender is a zero because a data block has not yet been exchanged.

Termination of the file transfer is also simply done. When a block that has less than 512 bytes of data in it is received, the file transfer has finished. Because UDP is used instead of TCP, the TFTP client/server software must implement its own retransmission technique for blocks that get lost or damaged in the network. Again, to make the protocol as simple as possible, no checksum is calculated on the TFTP messages. Instead, the simpler methods used by UDP are depended on to catch any errors.

Ports used by TFTP are allocated on a client-by-client basis. When the TFTP server receives the first client request message on its well-known TFTP port of 69, the server then allocates another port for use and communicates this back to the client. The client can continue to use a port on its side of the connection. However, from that point on it uses the newly assigned port it received from the TFTP server as the server host port. This feature allows a TFTP server to service multiple requests from different clients. The well-known port of 69 is used only for the initial communication.

The Telnet Protocol

Telnet is another of the most useful tools that make up the TCP/IP protocol suite. The "remote terminal" telnet application enables you to establish an interactive logon session with a remote computer and execute commands as if you were logged directly into that remote computer. Telnet can be used to establish sessions not just with other computers, but also is embedded in many network devices, such as print servers (or HP Jet-Direct Cards), hubs, switches, and routers. Using telnet is an easy way to manage multiple network nodes—computer or network devices—from a central location.

However, basic implementations of telnet suffer from a similar problem that plagues FTP. It uses a clear-text method for passing user authentication information and the remaining data transfers.

The main RFC that defines basic telnet operation is RFC 854, "Telnet Protocol Specification." In addition, many additional RFC documents have been issued to add security, additional functionality, or further clarify the Telnet protocol.

The protocol is based on three basic concepts:

- The Network Virtual Terminal (NVT)
- Options negotiation
- A symmetric view of terminals and processes

This protocol was designed to allow interactive sessions with terminals of many different types. A basic Network Virtual Terminal is defined by the telnet protocol, but clients and servers can negotiate additional parameters using options. Because either side can initiate options negotiations, the protocol is called symmetric.

What Is a Network Virtual Terminal and NVT ASCII?

Each end of the telnet connection is called a Network Virtual Terminal (NVT). It is simply a data construct that keeps track of the current state of the terminal, keeping both ends in sync. The virtual terminal operates in a bidirectional manner, sending and receiving data from another remote NVT. The basic NVT uses a 7-bit ASCII code, stored in an 8-bit byte. The high-order bit is set to zero. Carriage return and line feed characters are transmitted to indicate the end of a line. The method of representing characters and delineating lines is known as *NVT ASCII*. You'll find that many different TCP/IP utilities use this to communicate commands to and from the client and server.

Conversion to other codes can be done at each client's end. The NVT has both a virtual terminal (or printer, as it's called in the RFC) and keyboard.

Characters that are entered on the keyboard at one end of the connection are locally echoed, and do not have to be echoed back from the remote terminal. Usually, a buffer is set aside in the host's memory to store a line of characters for transmission. The characters are transmitted when a line is complete or until some other signal (from the user, for example) causes the line to be sent.

The basic NVT is designed to be the lowest common denominator for telnet sessions. Options can be negotiated, usually more so at the beginning of a session, that change the characteristics of the basic NVT. By a process of negotiation, both sides will always have the NVT defaults to fall back on if the other side of the connection does not support certain options. Thus, the NVT is the basic telnet terminal, without any extra options enabled.

Upon the initial connection, both sides are basic NVTs. Usually, options will be negotiated by both sides before the user has time to begin typing. Occasionally, option changes will be requested during the later data exchanges, but the basic setup for the session is done at the beginning.

Telnet Protocol Commands and Option Negotiations

Commands for the telnet protocol are two or three bytes in length, with the first character being the *interpret as command (IAC)* character. This character has the ASCII value of 255. If it is necessary to actually send this character as part of the data stream, it is sent as two successive bytes of 255. Following the IAC character, another command character usually is sent. For option negotiations, a third byte is used to indicate the option code being negotiated. In Table 21.3 you can see a list of the basic telnet protocol commands, along with a description of their functions.

Table 21.3   Telnet Protocol Commands

Code #	Code Name	Description
240	SE	End of subnegotiation parameters.
241	NOP	No operation.
242	Data Mark	The data stream portion of a Sync. This code should be accompanied by a TCP Urgent notification.
243	BREAK	NVT character for BREAK.
244	Interrupt Process	The IP function.
245	Abort Output	The AO function.
246	Are You There	The AYT function.
247	Erase Character	The EC function.
248	Erase Line	The EL function.
249	Go Ahead	The GA signal.

Table 21.3   Continued

Code #	Code Name	Description
250	SB	Signals that what follows is a subnegotiation of the indicated option.
251	WILL (option code)	Indicates the desire to start performing or to continue performing an option.
252	WON'T (option code)	Nonacceptance of an option or discontinuance of an option.
253	DO (option code)	Requests the other side perform an option.
254	DON'T (option code)	Requests the other side to stop performing an option.
255	IAC	When following an initial IAC, a second character of 255 is interpreted as a data byte instead of a command.

This simple command structure is used to establish a telnet session, negotiate the optional parameters, if any, and end the session. Telnet, like FTP and other client/server protocols, requires that a telnet server process listen on a well-known port, which in this case is port number 23. The server listens for incoming telnet commands from telnet clients.

Following is a short description of some of the protocol commands:

- **Are You There**—This command is used as sort of a "keep-alive" signal. It is intended to be sent after the connection has been idle for an amount of time. The remote end should respond with some visible response.

- **Erase Character**—Most operating systems have the capability to backspace and erase a character. Again, telnet uses a common command for this function, because not all operating systems support it or use the same numerical code for this function.

- **Erase Line**—This is similar to the Erase Character command, but instead maps the local keyboard's command sequence or key used to erase a line to a command that can be passed to the remote side of a connection.

- **Interrupt Process**—This command is used to map to the typical Ctrl+C or other character sequence used on a local machine to interrupt a process. This can differ from one computer operating system to another, hence the need for a common code to pass this condition to the other end of the connection.

- **Data Mark**—This command is sent as part of a TCP Urgent segment and is notice to the receiving end that it should look for "interesting" characters (such as IP, AO, and AYT) in the data stream. This causes an immediate action. The TCP Urgent message followed by a DM also is called a telnet sync operation. This allows out-of-band communications for important events—for example, an IP that results from a user entering Ctrl+C.

Options and Negotiations

The standard NVT described in RFC 854 might not be sufficient for all situations, and thus the telnet protocol allows for a process of negotiation of options. This allows for additional capabilities and services to be provided using telnet. For example, an option could be used to provide for a different character set than the standard. Either side of the telnet session can send a request to the other side for an option. The receiving end can then either reply with an acceptance or rejection of the option. If an option is accepted, it takes effect at once.

The following are some basic rules of the negotiation process:

- Option requests are sent only to change an option. If the option is already in effect, then sending out a request for the option simply to announce it is being used is not permitted.

- Similar to the previous rule, an option request for an option that is already in effect should not be acknowledged.

- In addition, if one side sends a request to *disable* an option, then that request must be honored.

In Table 21.3, the DO, DON'T, WILL, and WON'T operations are used when one side of the connection wants to do something and inform the other side, or when one side wants the other side to perform an action. For example, when an NVT receives a WILL command followed by an option code, it means that the sender will start, or has started, using this option. The receiver of this message can reply with a DO if the option is acceptable or a DON'T if it doesn't support the option. If the sender sends a DO command, followed by an option, then the sender is telling the receiver that it would like for it to use a particular option. The receiver can respond with a WILL command if it does support the option, or a WON'T command if it does not.

In addition, a sender can send a WON'T command, which indicates that a particular option is disabled. The receiver should respond with a DON'T command. The sender also can send a DON'T command to indicate it wants the receiver to disable an option. The response to this command must be a WON'T. Remember that an option cannot be used unless both sides agree to it. Instead, the basic NVT is used with any options that were negotiated.

Finally, some options will lead to subnegotiations to further identify parameters of a particular option. These are beyond the scope of this chapter—refer to the appropriate RFCs.

In Table 21.4, you can see a summary of RFCs that describe some of the more useful options for use with telnet.

Table 21.4   Additional Option Code Definitions

RFC	Option Code #	Description
856	0	Binary transmission
857	1	Echo
858	3	Suppress Go Ahead
859	5	Status
860	6	Timing Mark
726	7	Remote controlled transmission and echo
652	10	Output carriage-return disposition
653	11	Output horizontal tab stops
654	12	Output horizontal tab disposition
655	13	Output form feed disposition
656	14	Output vertical tab stops
657	15	Output vertical tab disposition
657	16	Output line-feed disposition
698	17	Extended ASCII
727	18	Logout
735	19	Byte Macro
732, 1043	20	Telnet Data-Entry Terminal (DODIIS Implementation)
734, 736	21	SUDUP
749	22	SUDUP Output
779	23	Send location

Table 21.4 Continued

RFC	Option Code #	Description
1091	24	Terminal Type
885	25	Telnet End of Record
927	26	TACACS user identification
933	27	Output marking
946	28	Terminal location number
1041	29	3270 Regime
1053	30	X.3 PAD
1073	31	Window Size
1079	32	Terminal Speed
1372	33	Remote Flow Control
1184	34	Line Mode
1096	35	X display location
1048	36	Environment Variables Option
1416	37	Authentication option
1572	39	Environment variables option
1657	40	TN3270E
2066	42	CHarset
255	255	Extended options list

In addition to this summary of options, others exist that are defined in documents other than RFCs. In addition to the basic telnet commands, telnet recognizes some, but not all, of the special ASCII control code characters. Table 21.5 lists these characters.

Table 21.5 ASCII Control Characters Recognized by Telnet's NVT

Value	Name	Description
0	NULL	No operation
10	LF	Line feed. Moves the NVT printer to the next line. Does not change horizontal position.
13	CR	Carriage return. Moves the printer to the left margin. Does not change vertical position.
7	BELL	Optional code. Rings a bell. Does not advance the print head by a character.
8	BS	Optional code. Backspace. Moves print head one position to the left.
9	HT	Optional code. Horizontal tab. Moves print head to the next tab stop.
11	VT	Optional code. Vertical tab. Moves print head to next vertical tab stop.
12	FF	Optional code. Form feed. Moves printer to top of next page.

Telnet and Authentication

One of the problems with applications that were developed during the early years of TCP/IP is that Internet (or ARPANET, depending on how far back you want to go) security wasn't as big an issue as it is today. Because of this, many protocols and utilities have been exploited over the past few years by hackers who know how to take advantage of this lack of foresight. Telnet is just such an application.

However, with the use of options, it is possible to perform authentication other than using the traditional clear-text method.

In RFC 1416, "Telnet Authentication Option," an option to allow for more secure authentication methods is set forth. This specification is intended to provide a mechanism that can be used by many different authentication methods. The code number used for the AUTHENTICATION option is defined as 37. In Table 21.6 you can see some of the codes used to specify different authentication methods.

Table 21.6   RFC 1416 Telnet Authentication Methods

Value	Description
0	NULL
1	Kerberos V4
2	Kerberos V5
3	SPX
4–5	Unassigned
6	RSA
7–9	Unassigned
10	LOKI
11	SSA

The R-Utilities

This famous set of network utilities was originally developed at the University of California at Berkeley and included in their versions of Unix that followed. Because all these utilities start with the letter R, which stands for remote, they often are lumped together and called the R-utilities. These utilities share more than just a common first letter. They also use an authentication scheme that most network administrators consider to be very insecure. These files will be discussed first, and then we'll look at some of these utilities, showing the syntax examples from Solaris 8 and FreeBSD for comparisons.

How the Traditional R-Utilities Authorize Access

Newer versions of these utilities use authentication schemes using such methods as Kerberos tickets, as you will see in some of the syntax examples for the FreeBSD commands. However, because these tools were developed to make it simple to perform basic network functions, having to enter a username and password each time you used a utility was considered too much of a hassle. These were the days, you should remember, before security was considered an issue.

To overcome this username/password obstacle, the R-utilities can use two files to perform authorization without having to send a password across the network. These are the hosts.equiv and the .rhosts files.

The System's *hosts.equiv* and *.rhosts* Files

The hosts.equiv file is a global file that is managed by the system administrator for a computer. It contains a list of remote computers that are to be trusted on this computer. When a user executes one of the R-utilities, this file can be consulted to see whether the host computer of that user is a trusted one. If so, the user is allowed to perform the same actions and is given the same access as a local account of the same name. This file also can have one or more usernames associated with a remote host, restricting access to just those usernames.

The file .rhosts is a local file that can be created in any user's home directory. It performs the same function as the systemwide hosts.equiv file. The format for basic entries into either of these files is

```
hostname [username]
```

If you enter only a hostname on a line by itself, then all users from that host that have accounts on this computer will be allowed access. If you place a username after the hostname (with a space or tab to separate them), that particular user will have access. To make it easier to restrict access with these files, most Unix systems allow you to use a few other methods to create entries in these files:

- **+ *username***—Allows access for this username.
- **- *username***—Specifically prohibits access for this username.
- ***hostname* +**—Allows all users from *hostname* to access the system using a local use account.
- **- *hostname***—Specifically prohibits users from *hostname* from access.

For example, the entry

```
hostname –username
```

prohibits the user indicated by *username* coming from the host *hostname* from gaining access to the local computer using the hosts.equiv or .rhosts file.

To make matters even more complicated, you must consider the search order and how the entries in these files are evaluated. The hosts.equiv file is searched, and then the .rhosts file is searched. When a positive entry is found, granting access, the process stops. When a negative entry is found that denies access, the process stops. If no entries are found that grant or deny access, then access is denied.

The use of these files, and indeed of any insecure earlier versions of the R-utilities, is highly discouraged. For more information about how these can be abused, see Chapter 37, "Basic Security Measures."

The *rlogin* Utility

This utility uses TCP (port 513) and enables you to establish an interactive session with another computer, similar to telnet. However, the rlogin command uses a much simpler protocol. It was introduced in version 4.2 of BSD Unix and is defined in RFC 1282, "BSD Rlogin." Unlike telnet, rlogin does not use option negotiation. Instead, it allows a simple exchange of commands between the two systems.

The protocol is a simple one. The client software sends a string of text to the server. This string consists of a zero byte, the login name of the user on the client, another zero byte, the login name to be used on the server, another zero byte, the terminal type, the slash character, the speed of the terminal and, finally, another zero byte.

The rlogin server will respond to this string with a zero byte. Then, if a password is required on the server (that is, the user is not found in the hosts.equiv or .rhosts files), the server will send a prompt string to the client. If the user sends the correct password back, the session can continue. Note again here the security problem with another TCP/IP utility. The username and the password are not encrypted in most versions of this utility. They go over the network as ordinary clear text that any network sniffer can detect. Newer forms of this utility use more secure authentication methods, but the basic protocol does not define this.

Finally, the server sends a request to the client to find out the client's window size. After the session has been established, communication from the client to the server takes place using only one character at a time. When you consider that the server then echoes back the character to the client, you can start to see that `rlogin` isn't as efficient as some other protocols. To help prevent this, the Nagle algorithm usually is used, enabling the buffering of several characters into a single TCP segment.

The only command that the client can send to the server is the window size, and the client can send this only in response to a query from the server. The server can send a variety of commands to the client, and uses TCP's Urgent Data pointer to indicate the control command byte in the data stream. A client receiving a TCP segment with the Urgent Data pointer will immediately buffer all data up to the command byte and then interpret the command byte. There are only four possible commands:

- **0x02**—The client discards all buffered data that hasn't yet been displayed on the client.
- **0x10**—Switches the client to "raw" mode, in which the ASCII STOP and START characters (Ctrl+S and Ctrl+Q) are ignored by the client and passed as data to the server to deal with.
- **0x20**—Switches the client back to its normal mode of interpreting the ASCII START and STOP characters.
- **0x80**—This is the window size request the server can send to the client.

The control byte pointed to by the Urgent Data pointer is not displayed on the client's display, and all values other than those listed are ignored.

Using the `rlogin` Command

The syntax for this command will, as with most Unix commands, vary from system to system. Here we'll look at the syntax for Solaris 8 and then the syntax for FreeBSD Unix.

The syntax for the `rlogin` command for Solaris 8 is

`rlogin [ -8EL ] [-ec ] [ -1] username | hostname`

Where

- **-8**—Indicates that 8-bit data should be used for the connection instead of 7-bit data representations.
- **-ec**—Used to specify a different escape character. Substitute the escape character for *c*.
- **-E**—This parameter means that no character will be recognized as the escape character.
- **-1 *username***—Use this to specify a different username for the logon procedure. The default is to use the same username that you are logged on under on your local system.
- ***hostname***—The name of the remote host to which you want to log on.

Solaris also enables the user to enter escape characters during the `rlogin` session. The tilde character (~) starts the escape sequence. The sequence of characters ~. causes the computer to immediately disconnect from the remote host. ~susp suspends the login session if you are using a shell with Job Control.

The syntax for the `rlogin` command for FreeBSD is

`rlogin [-468DEKLdx] [-e char] [-i localname] [-k realm] [-1 username] host`

Where

- **-4 (-6)**—Specifies to use IPv4 or IPv6 addresses only.
- **-8**—Allows for 8-bit data transmissions.
- **-D**—Sets the TCP-NODELAY socket option. This can improve interactive responses, but also increases the load on the network.

- **-E**—This parameter means that no character is recognized as the escape character.
- **-K**—Turns off all Kerberos authentication.
- **-L**—Lets the rlogin session to be run in "litout" mode.
- **-d**—Turns on socket debugging.
- **-x**—This turns on DES encryption for the data stream passed between client and server. Because the original implementation of rlogin uses clear-text, this is a very good option to use!
- **-echar**—Used to specify a different escape character. Substitute the escape character for *char*. The default escape character is the tilde.
- **-i**—This lets the sender specify a different local name to be used for authorization purposes. Processes must have the UID of zero to use this feature.
- **-k realm**—Requests that rlogin obtain Kerberos tickets in the host *realm* instead of the host's currently defined realm.
- **-l username**—Use this to specify a different username for the logon procedure. The default is to use the same username that you are logged in under on your local system.
- **host**—This is the host with which you want to establish a remote session.

As you can see, the FreeBSD's latest version of rlogin provides more security than the basic version of this program. By adding authentication schemes other than clear-text, and by allowing the data stream to be encrypted, this is a utility that can be used in an environment requiring a medium amount of security.

Using *rsh*

The Remote Shell (rsh) utility enables you to execute a single command on the remote node. This utility first makes a connection to the remote computer and then executes the command specified by the user. It copies standard input to the remote command, and the standard output resulting from the remote command, if any, is copied back to the local standard output. Likewise, the remote standard error stream is copied back to the local standard error stream.

This utility is not meant for use when you need to execute a lot of commands or use an interactive program, such as the vi editor, that is screen-oriented. Instead, it is a quick way to execute a single command on another network node that supports the protocol.

The rsh utility has been implemented, like most of the other R-utilities, differently on a variety of Unix flavors.

The syntax for the rsh command on Solaris 8 is

```
rsh [ -n] [ -l username] hostname command
rsh hostname [ -n ] [-l username ] command
rmesh [ -n ] [ -l username ] hostname command
rmesh hostname [ -n ] [ -l username ] command
hostname [ -n ] [ -l username ] command
```

This command makes a connection with the remote *hostname* system. The *command* you enter on the command line will be executed. Standard Unix inputs and outputs will be manipulated to display the results of the command on your display. Note that if you don't include a command in the syntax, you will enter an rlogin session for this command on Solaris. See the previous section of this chapter for information about using rlogin.

Command line parameters for this command include

- **-1** *username*—Substitute this username on the remote system instead of using the local username.
- **hostname**—The name of the remote host on which the command will be executed.
- **command**—The command to be executed on the remote computer.
- **-n**—Redirects the input of rsh to /dev/null.

Remember that this utility runs just one command on the remote system. For example, you can use it to rename a file or copy a file on a remote system. To edit the file, however, you would have to use telnet or rlogin, both of which allow for interaction with a program running on a remote system.

The syntax for this command on FreeBSD is

rsh [**-46Kdnx**] [**-t** *timeout*] [**-k** *realm*] [**-1** *username*] *host* [command]

Where:

- **-4 (-6)**—Specifies to use IPv4 or IPv6 addresses only.
- **-K**—Disables Kerberos authentication.
- **-d**—Turns on socket debugging.
- **-n**—Redirects input to the special device /dev/null.
- **-x**—This turns on DES encryption for data exchanges, possibly causing a delay in response time due to the encryption overhead.
- **-t** *timeout*—If no data is sent across the connection established by rsh for *timeout* seconds, then the rsh program will exit.
- **-k** *realm*—The rsh utility tries to get Kerberos tickets from the host in *realm* instead of the remote host's realm.
- **-1** *username*—Use this to specify a username on the remote system to use for authentication. The default is to use the same name as the local username.

Like the Solaris version of rsh, if you choose to omit a command from the command line when you invoke rsh, then the rlogin program will run instead.

In both cases (Solaris and FreeBSD) metacharacters recognized by your shell must be enclosed in quotation marks in order for them to be included as part of the remote command.

Using *rcp*

The Remote Copy (rcp) command is used to copy files between two computers on the network. You also could use FTP for this, but rcp enables you to do the same thing with a more simplified syntax, and allows for authentication using .rhosts and hosts.equiv files. Another thing you can do with rcp that you can't do easily using a standard FTP client is to recursively copy directories and subdirectories.

The syntax for rcp for Solaris 8 is

rcp [-p] *filename1 filename2*
rcp [-pr] filename ... directory

Where

- **-p**—If possible, this option causes the copied file to have the same modification and access times as the original, as well as the same mode an any ACLs that were applied to the original file. Note that rcp will not work correctly if you try to copy ACLs to a system that doesn't support them.

- **-r**—This option is used when the destination is a directory. It indicates that each subtree that is rooted at *filename* (a directory) is copied.

In the first line of the preceding syntax, *filename1* and *filename2* are the source and destination filenames. In the second example, *filename* is a starting point for a set of subdirectories that will be copied to a directory *directory* on the remote system. Also note that you can use rcp to copy files between computers other than your own (third-party computers). In this case, you must specify the *filename* variables on the command line to include *hostname:path*. If you want to use a different username for authentication purposes, use the format *username@hostname:filename* instead. For third-party copies, the host that is the source of the file to be copied must have permission to access the target computer.

The FreeBSD syntax for this command is

rcp [**-Kpx**] [**-k** *realm*] *file1 file2* **rcp** [**-Kprx**] [**-k** *realm*] *file ... directory*

Where

- **-K**—Disables all Kerberos authentication.
- **-k** *realm*—The rcp utility tries to get Kerberos tickets from the host in *realm* instead of the remote host's realm.
- **-p**—This option makes rcp attempt to keep the same modification times and modes of the source files when making copies.
- **-r**— This option is used when the destination is a directory. It indicates that each subtree that is rooted at *filename* (a directory) is copied.
- **-x**—Turns on DES encryption for data that is sent between the two computers, at the expense of a slower copy time.

This version of rcp also enables you to perform third-party copying. The addition of Kerberos authentication and DES encryption are welcome improvements over the original rcp.

Using *rwho*

The rwho command is used to show information about users on the network. It works similar to the who command, but gets information from computers on the network instead of just local users.

Both Solaris 8 and FreeBSD versions of this command assume that a computer is down if they don't receive any data from it for five minutes. If a user is logged in but does not interact with the computer for more than an hour, they will not be included in the display by default. The syntax for this command is

rwho [-a]

The -a option causes the report to include all users and ignore the one-hour idle timeout.

The file /var/rwho/whod.* path is used to store data files containing the hosts on the network about which the command reports (/var/spool/rwho/rwhd.* for Solaris 8). Each computer on the network that can show up in the display produced by rwho must be running the rwhod daemon process. This background process sends out a broadcast packet of information on a periodic basis. Other servers store this information and use it when producing a display.

Using *ruptime*

For each machine on the network, the command ruptime reports a status line showing how long the system has been booted. Again, the file /var/rwho/whod.* (/var/spool/rwho/rwhd.* for Solaris 8) path is used to store data files containing the hosts on the network about which the command reports. Each system must be running the rwhod daemon. Note that this background process sends out informational packets that remote systems collect for use with both the rwho and the ruptime commands.

For this command, both Solaris 8 and FreeBSD use the same syntax:

ruptime [-alrtu]

Where

- **-a**—Causes the utility to report on the number of users on remote machines even if they have been idle for more than one hour.
- **-l**—Causes the display to be sorted by load average.
- **-r**—Reverses the sorting order for the displayed information.
- **-t**—Causes the display to be sorted by the amount of uptime for the systems shown.
- **-u**—Causes the display to be sorted by the number of users on the systems shown.

As you can see, this can be a very handy utility to use to quickly survey selected nodes on your network.

Finger Somebody!

The finger utility is a more complex utility that gives the administrator a lot of information, with a syntax that allows for selective reporting. You can use finger to get information about local users or users on remote hosts on the network. RFC 1288, "The Finger User Information Protocol," is the most recent RFC in a series to define this protocol.

The finger protocol uses TCP, port 79. The finger command opens a TCP connection with a finger server daemon on a system and sends a line of text that makes up the query. The server responds and then closes the TCP connection. The RFC goes on to define different types of queries and how they can be forwarded from one machine to another. If you think that people who write these RFCs don't have a sense of humor, then ponder the following paragraph taken from RFC 1288:

> 2.5.5. Vending Machines
>
> "Vending machines SHOULD respond to a {C} request with a list of all items currently available for purchase and possible consumption. Vending machines SHOULD respond to a {U}{C} request with a detailed count or list of the particular product or product slot. Vending machines should NEVER NEVER NEVER eat money."

Now, with a sense of humor like that, is it any wonder they name a user information protocol "finger?"

The syntax for finger on Solaris 8 is

finger [-bfhilmpqsw] [username ...]

finger [-l] [username@hostname 1] [@hostname 2 ...@hostname n ...]]

finger [-l] [@hostname 1 [@hostname 2 ...@hostname n ...]]

where

- **-b**—Suppresses listing the user's home directory and the shell used when using the long format output.
- **-f**—Suppresses listing the header that is displayed in the non-long format output.
- **-h**—Suppresses printing the contents of the .project file when using the long format.

- **-i**—Displays "idle" format showing only the login name, terminal, the login time, and the idle time.

- **-l**—Causes a long display format. More data is shown.

- **-m**—Causes matches to be made on the user's username, not on the first or last name.

- **-p**—Suppresses displaying the contents of the .plan file when using the long format.

- **-q**—Produces a quick format output. This is almost the same as the short format, but the only items displayed are the login name, terminal, and login time.

- **-s**—Causes a short form of the user information to be displayed. Less data is shown.

- **-w**—Suppresses the display of the user's full name in a short format output.

The default information displayed about each user is the username, the user's full name, the terminal type, amount of idle time, login time, and the host name if the user is logged in to the system remotely. If you provide a username on the command line, more information will be displayed. When using this method, you can specify more than one username and the user does not have to be logged in to the system in order for finger to display information about the user. However, this is limited to just users on the machine you are executing the finger command.

Additional information you'll see if you specify one or more usernames include the user's home directory and login shell, the time the user logged in (or last logged in), the last time that the user received any e-mail, and the last time the user read his e-mail. If the files .project or .plan exist in the user's home directory, then their contents will be displayed.

In the syntax that uses the *username@hostname1* [*@hostname2* ... *@hostnamen*] or *@hostname1[@hostname2* ...*@hostnamen*], the finger request is sent first to the last hostname in the list (*hostnamen*), which sends it to the next-most previous host in the list, until the request reaches *hostname1*. Note also that the *username@hostname* syntax allows only the -1 command line option.

The FreeBSD syntax for this command is a little simpler:

```
finger [-lmpshoT] [user ...] [user@host ...]
```

where

- **-s**—Displays the user's login name, full name, terminal, idle time, login time, and either office location and office phone number or the remote host, depending on which of the remaining options are used.

- **-h**—Causes the -s option to display the remote host instead of the office information.

- **-o**—Causes the -s option to display the office information instead of the remote host. This is the default.

- **-l**—Produces a display of several lines. All the items that the -s option outputs are displayed, along with the user's home directory, home phone number, login shell, mail status, and the contents of the files .forward, .plan, .project, and .pubkey, if these files are found in the user's home directory.

- **-p**—When used with -1, suppresses the listing of the contents of the .forward, .plan, .project, and .pubkey files.

- **-m**—Suppresses matching of user names. By default, finger tries to match a login username and also user's real names. This option forces finger to use only the login username.

- **-T**—Used to disable "piggybacking" data on the initial TCP connection request with some finger implementations.

This version of `finger` also enables you to view information about hosts on other computers. Use the format *user* for users on the local machine and *user@hostname* for remote users.

Other TCP/IP Related Services and Applications

You'll find many services in older RFC documents referring to protocols or utilities that once served an important purpose—for example, the ARCHIE and WAIS utilities. However, as the Internet has made obsolete many older protocols and utilities, it has provided a hot bed for the development of new utilities, services, and applications. Many of these service are no longer needed or used, or are used in limited locations because more improved methods have generally replaced them.

Other protocols, such as the Simple Mail Transport Protocol (SMTP) and the Simple Network Management Protocol (SNMP), are also very popular and useful protocols for providing application support on the network. However, these protocols are not as limited in their scope as the "utilities" discussed in this chapter. SNMP is discussed in Chapter 44, "Network Testing and Analysis Tools." SMTP, along with a few other important Internet protocols, are discussed in appendixes at the back of this book.

Secure Network Services

As pointed out several times in this chapter, using some of the standard TCP/IP utilities that have been developed over many years can have security implications, especially now that most businesses are connecting to the Internet. The matters of user authentication and data encryption become more important when you expose your network to the world. Fortunately, as with most security issues, a need generally leads to someone coming up with a solution. In this section, we'll look at some more utilities that perform tasks similar to those already discussed, but in a more secure manner.

The Secure Shell (SSH) is the name given to a protocol that enables you to replace `rsh`, `rlogin`, `rcp`, `telnet`, `rexec`, `rcp`, and `ftp` with a more secure application. You can visit a Web site devoted to these utilities at `www.ssh.org`. Here you can find out about the specifications for the protocols, mailing lists, patches, and places to download the utilities for your system. Although there are no Request for Comments documents yet for SSH, several Internet drafts are available at the Web site that describe everything from authentication to transport protocols.

SSH provides you with complementary commands for the utilities listed in the previous paragraph. For example, instead of using the `ftp` command, you would use the `sftp` command. The same goes for the other utilities.

Note

Currently, two versions of Secure Shell are in use: SSH1 and SSH2, with the first being phased out. The two versions are not compatible with each other.

Secure Shell utilities can use a variety of encryption methods for both authentication and for encryption of the data sent across the network. Because different software houses may implement the SSH protocol a little differently than another, you might want to consider checking which ciphers are used by a particular product.

Another interesting thing to note is that Secure Shell utilities have been written not just for Unix, but also other operating systems, such as OpenVMS and Windows NT. Also note that use of the official distribution is free for noncommercial use, but you must visit the Web site and check the licensing terms to be sure you are using these utilities legally. Additionally, several freeware or shareware programs you can find on the Internet support SSH protocols.

Troubleshooting Tools for TCP/IP Networks

SOME OF THE MAIN TOPICS IN THIS CHAPTER ARE

Check the Host System's Configuration First

You Can't Get There From Here—Using ping and tracert to Check Connectivity

Using the nslookup Command to Troubleshoot Name Resolution Issues

Because TCP/IP allows for such decentralized management (many separately managed networks are interconnected through the Internet), tools have been developed for troubleshooting connection and configuration problems dealing with the TCP/IP protocols and services. These tools can be used for troubleshooting problems within your local network as well as for attempting to isolate Internet-related problems. In Chapter 20, "Overview of the TCP/IP Protocol Suite," I discussed the Internet Control Message Protocol (ICMP) and the User Datagram Protocol (UDP). These two components of the TCP/IP suite are put to use in this chapter to build tools that are helpful for diagnosing simple problems. In addition, in this chapter I'll discuss some other utilities that are not part of the standard TCP/IP implementation.

Check the Host System's Configuration First

Before you start to check the cables, network adapters, hubs, and other physical components of the network, you should check to see whether there is a problem with a computer's TCP/IP configuration. You can do this by using the tools provided with the operating system. Information about Windows configurations can be found in Chapter 20. Linux or Unix users should check their specific documentation and man pages for information on how to configure networking on a system. Check to be sure that the system has an IP address that uses the same network number as the other computers on the local subnet. Also check to be sure the correct subnet mask and default gateway are used. If everything checks out okay, it is time to start using the basic troubleshooting tools that are available with most versions of TCP/IP.

Using the *hostname* Command

The hostname command is perhaps the simplest command you can use to begin checking the configuration of a host computer. On Windows systems, this command prints the name of the host computer on which it is executed. Linux users get several different syntaxes for this command. Whereas this command on Windows NT and Windows 2000 systems outputs the name of the host to the command line, the Linux version offers you many options for viewing or setting the hostname for the system. To set the hostname for an NT or Windows 2000 computer, use the Network applet in the Control Panel. Check the documentation (man pages) that comes with your particular flavor of Unix to get the proper use for this command.

The hostname syntax for Linux systems is

```
hostname [-v] [-a] [--alias] [-d] [--domain] [-f] [--fqdn]
        [-i]  [--ip-address]  [--long]  [-s] [--short] [-y] [--yp]
        [--nis]

hostname [-v] [-F filename] [--file filename] [hostname]
```

- **[-a] [--alias]**—Displays the alias name of the host if one is being used.
- **[-d] [--domain]**—Displays the name of the DNS domain.
- **[-F] [--file *filename*]**—Reads the hostname from the specified file.
- **[-f] [--fqdn] [--long]**—Displays the FQDN (Fully Qualified Domain Name). A FQDN consists of a short hostname and the DNS domain name found in the /etc/hosts file.
- **[-h] [--help]**—Prints a usage message and exits. This is all you have to remember if you don't carry this book around with you!
- **[-I] [--ip-*address*]**—Displays the IP address(es) of the host.
- **[-s] [--short]**—Displays the short hostname.
- **[-V] [--version]**—Prints version information on standard output and exits.

- **[-v]** **[--verbose]**—Causes the command to produce additional output.
- **[-y]** **[--yp]** **[--nis]**—Displays the NIS domain name. If a parameter is given (or **--file name**) then root also can set a new NIS domain.

As you can see, the Linux command is a little more complex than the Windows version.

Note

For more information on managing users with **YP** and **NIS**, see Chapter 32, "Unix and Linux."

Use *ipconfig* and *ifconfig* to Check Host Configurations

The ipconfig command is useful for checking the TCP/IP configuration of a Windows NT Server or Windows NT Workstation computer, as well as on the Windows 2000 operating systems. A similar command on Unix and Linux workstations is ifconfig. On Windows 95/98 or Windows Me systems, you can use the winipcfg command.

ipconfig for Windows NT and Windows 2000

Simply enter the ipconfig command at the command prompt.

Note

Windows 2000 users should note that the command prompt (or the DOS box as it's also known) is now found under the Accessories folder instead of the Programs folder, where NT 4 users have grown accustomed to finding it.

Using the ipconfig command with no parameters displays network configuration information about each adapter on the system, as well as for PPP connections. The basic information includes

- IP address
- Subnet mask
- Default gateway
- DNS servers
- NT Domain

With the /all parameter, you also can obtain the hardware (MAC) address and DHCP information. You also can use this command to renew or release DHCP configuration information to attempt to reconfigure the computer with updated information.

The syntax for Windows NT or Windows 2000 servers is

```
ipconfig [/? | /all | /release [adapter] | /renew [adapter]
         | /flushdns | /registerdns
         | /showclassid adapter
         | /setclassid adapter [classidtoset] ]
```

- **/all**—This form of the command causes a verbose display of all the configuration information that the ipconfig utility has access to, including multiple adapters.
- **/release [adapter]**—Releases an IP address that was configured using DHCP.
- **/renew [adapter]**—Renews an IP address that was configured using DHCP.
- **/flushdns**—Purges the DNS resolver cache.
- **/registerdns**—Refreshes all leases granted by DHCP for the adapter and reregisters DNS names.

- **`/displaydns`**—Shows the contents of the DNS resolver cache.
- **`/showclassid [adapter]`**—Displays all the DHCP class IDs allowed for *adapter*.
- **`/setclassid [adapter] [classidtoset]`**—Modifies the DHCP class ID.

Obviously, this command is extremely useful when you are trying to solve problems related to DNS and DHCP functions. For example, you can use /release and /renew to see if you are having problems obtaining configuration information from a DHCP server. You can use the DNS qualifiers when you've made configuration changes and want to keep the local cache updated or register the new configuration information with a DNS server. The /all qualifier shows all the output to which the command has access and is frequently used to scan for problems. To see all the output without having it scroll off the screen, use the command in the form of ipconfig /all | more.

The quantity of information you can show is useful when constructing a spreadsheet or other document for help-desk use. One method that will help you keep up with current configuration information is placing the following command in a login script or startup file:

```
ipconfig /all > <network drive>%computername%.config
```

The %computername% environment variable is replaced with the computer name that is assigned to the system and a text file is created. By placing the output file on a central network drive, you can have it available for use by administrative or help-desk staff.

The winipcfg command on Windows 98 machines displays similar information, but shows it in a window instead of as text in the MS-DOS command prompt window. However, several command-line options can be used with this command, and you can write the configuration information to a file. The following are the command-line options for winipcfg:

- **`/all`**—Displays the most amount of information.
- **`/batch <filename>`**—Writes the configuration information to the file specified by *<filename>*.
- **`/renew_all`**—Renews DHCP leases for all adapters on the system.
- **`/release_all`**—Releases DHCP configuration for all adapters.
- **`/renew n`**—Renews the DHCP configuration for adapter number *n*.
- **`/release n`**—Releases the DHCP configuration for adapter number *n*.

Although not as versatile as the Windows NT and Windows 2000 configuration tool, winipcfg is appropriate for the desktop operating system environment. Currently, most large LANS that are Windows-based have been converted to Windows NT or Windows 2000 from another OS. Because of this, Windows 98 machines should be considered "legacy" equipment by now, except for the very small office LAN that has no need for newer features found in newer operating systems.

`ifconfig` *for Unix and Linux*

On Unix and Linux systems, ifconfig is a very powerful command. You can use it not only to display IP configuration information, but also to make changes to the configuration. The ifconfig command is used during the boot sequence to perform the initial configuration for network adapters that are attached to the system. After the system is up and running, only the superuser can use this command to change the configuration. For troubleshooting, it is a quick way to get the information you need to determine whether the system was properly configured. For those unfamiliar with Unix, the superuser refers to a user account that has full system privileges and can perform all tasks. For example, the standard account named root is the typical superuser account on most Unix or Linux systems.

To simply display the current configuration information, you can execute the command with no parameters. For the superuser, the following commands can be used to modify the configuration:

- **ifconfig arp**—Enables the Address Resolution Protocol. Use ifconfig -arp to disable.
- **ifconfig dhcp (or ifconfig auto-dhcp)**—Use DHCP to acquire an address for the adapter.
- **ifconfig down**—Marks the interface as down, effectively shutting down network communications using this adapter.
- **ifconfig metric *value***—Changes the routing metric for this interface.
- **ifconfig netmask *mask***—Sets the subnet mask for this adapter.

As you can see, although this command is similar to the Windows version, it's a lot more powerful. The capability to set routing metrics and mark an adapter as either up or down can be useful when the Unix or Linux box is being used for routing functions or is part of a proxy firewall solution.

You Can't Get There From Here—Using *ping* and *tracert* to Check Connectivity

Two of the most basic commands that can be used to test connectivity on a TCP/IP network are the ping command and the tracert command. In this section we'll look at how these commands work and the kind of troubleshooting information you can gain from their use.

Using the *ping* Command

The Packet Internet Groper, or ping command, is a good place to start your troubleshooting efforts. The name of this command might not make a whole lot of sense at first glance. This utility is used to test connectivity between two systems on the network. ping uses the ICMP protocol (which, you'll remember, uses UDP packets for transport) to exchange packets with the remote system. This utility was originally developed by Mike Muuss and operates in a simple manner. It uses the ICMP protocol to send messages to an address (ECHO REQUEST) and waits to hear for a reply (ECHO REPLY). The remote system sends the reply packets back to their source, and the round trip is determined. Thus, ping is used to "grope" around trying to find out whether it can communicate with another system on the network. You also can think of ping as a sonar type of mechanism.

Figure 22.1 shows the layout of the ICMP ECHO and ECHO REQUEST packet. If the message type is an ECHO REQUEST, the first field of the ICMP (message type) packet will have a value of 8. If the message type is an ECHO REPLY, this field will contain a zero.

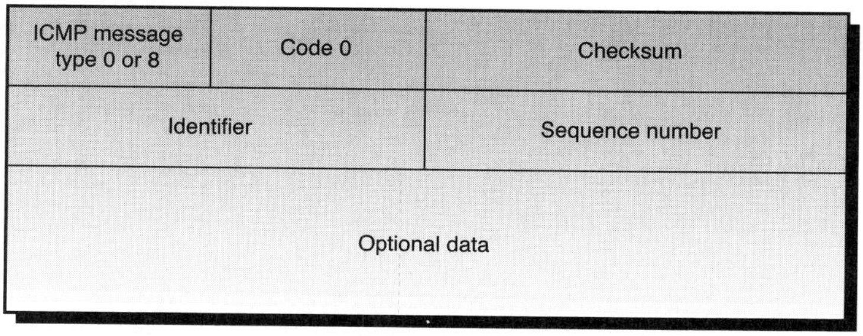

ICMP message type 0 or 8	Code 0	Checksum
Identifier		Sequence number
Optional data		

Figure 22.1   Layout of the ICMP ECHO REQUEST and ECHO REPLY packets.

Using `ping` on Unix or Linux

The way that `ping` functions is quite simple. The sequence number field is first set to zero, and then incremented for each packet sent. On most Unix and Linux implementations, the identification field is set to the process ID of the process sending the ping ECHO REQUEST message. This can vary with other operating systems, but the identifier is important and is used to uniquely identify the returned packets in case more than one user on a machine is using the utility at the same time. When the receiving computer gets the ECHO REQUEST message, it sends back a reply, containing the identifier and the sequence number. In this way the receiving machine can tell whether all packets are returned, and also, more importantly, tell you if packets are being dropped or returned out of order. These conditions can indicate problems on the network. Another possibility is that the remote system is working at a high capacity and cannot respond to all the ECHO REQUEST messages in a timely manner.

The `ping` utility tells you how long (in milliseconds) the round trip took, and it tells you when packets do not make it back successfully. To determine the round-trip time, the utility stores the time that it sends the initial request packet in the optional data portion of the packet and compares it to the current time when the reply packet is received. The basic program also prints a Time-To-Live value, which is typically decremented by at least one second for each host or router through which the packet passes.

Occasionally you will notice that the round-trip time value declines for subsequent `ping` requests. This is because the destination machine (or the gateway router) isn't currently in the local ARP table, and it takes a few milliseconds for `arp` to determine the hardware address for sending out the first packet. If you ping by using a hostname instead of a TCP/IP address, it might take a few seconds for the `ping` utility to contact a DNS server and resolve the hostname to the IP address.

When using `ping` it's best to first use it to ping the local interface, or the loopback address (127.0.0.0, or 120.0.0.1 on some older systems). The loopback address is used in TCP/IP stacks to enable you to test whether the local stack is functioning correctly. This is a reserved IP address that cannot be used on the Internet. If you can't ping the local system's own IP address, you might have a configuration problem. If you can't ping the loopback address, you might have a problem with the TCP/IP stack or perhaps the network adapter.

In RFC 2151, "A Primer On Internet and TCP/IP Tools and Utilities," the basic `ping` syntax is defined as follows:

`ping [-q] [-v] [-R] [-c Count] [-i Wait] [-s PacketSize] Host`

- **-q**—Quiet output; nothing is displayed except summary lines at startup and completion.

- **-v**—Verbose output. Lists ICMP packets that are received in addition to echo responses.

- **-R**—Record route option; includes the RECORD_ROUTE option in the ECHO REQUEST packet and displays the route buffer on returned packets.

- **-c *Count***—Specifies the number of ECHO REQUESTs to be sent before the concluding test (default is to run until interrupted with a Ctrl+C).

- **-i *Wait***—Indicates the number of seconds to wait between sending each packet (default = 1).

- **-s *PacketSize***—Specifies the number of data bytes to be sent; the total ICMP packet size will be PacketSize+8 bytes due to the ICMP header (default = 56, or a 64-byte packet) Host IP address or hostname of target system.

An older syntax for `ping` that you might find is

`ping [-s] {IP_address|host_name} [PacketSize] [Count]`

When using the -s option, the ping command will send a message to the target every second. This can be helpful when you are monitoring an intermittent problem and want to be able to watch in real time whether a connection can be made or not.

The syntax for ping can vary depending on the operating system, and even between different variants of Unix. However, its basic use is simply ping *hostname* or ping *address*. The syntax for a Linux ping follows:

```
ping [-R] [-c number] [-d] [-I seconds] host
```

The options include

- **-c *number***—Specifies the number of ICMP ECHO_REQUESTs that are sent.
- **-d**—Causes ping to send packets as fast as they are echoed back from the remote system, or up to 100 times per second. Exercise caution when using this option regularly to avoid generating high volumes of traffic on a busy network.
- **-I *seconds***—This option enables you to specify the number of seconds between each packet sent; the default is 1 second. This option cannot be used with the -R option.
- **-R**—Records the route taken by the packet.

Using *ping* on Windows Systems

The ping command has a much different syntax when used with the Windows operating systems:

```
ping [-t] [-a] [-n count] [-l size] [-f] [-i TTL] [-v TOS]
     [-r count] [-s count] [[-j host-list] | [-k host-list]
     [-w timeout] destination-list
```

The options include

- **-t**—Continue pinging until explicitly stopped by Ctrl+C. Statistics are displayed after you stop the command.
- **-a**—Resolves addresses to hostnames.
- **-n *count***—Specifies the number of ICMP ECHO REQUEST packets to send.
- **-l *size***—Sends buffer size.
- **-f**—Sets the don't fragment flag in the packet. Useful to determine whether a device is changing the packet size between nodes.
- **-i *TTL***—Time to Live value.
- **-v *TOS***—Type of Service.
- **-r *count***—Displays route for count hops.
- **-s *count***—Displays a timestamp for each hop.
- **-j *host-list***—Loose source route along host-list.
- **-k *host-list***—Strict source route along host-list.
- **-w *timeout***—Timeout value to wait for each reply (in milliseconds).

As you can see, the syntax can vary widely between implementations, as can the usefulness of ping as a diagnostic tool.

Following is an example of a simple use of the ping command:

```
F:\>ping 10.10.10.11
Pinging 10.10.10.11 with 32 bytes of data:
Reply from 10.10.10.11: bytes=32 time=10ms TTL=128
Reply from 10.10.10.11: bytes=32 time<10ms TTL=128
Reply from 10.10.10.11: bytes=32 time<10ms TTL=128
Reply from 10.10.10.11: bytes=32 time<10ms TTL=128
Ping statistics for 10.10.10.11:

Packets: Sent = 4, Received = 4, Lost = 0 (0% loss),
Approximate round trip times in milli-seconds:
Minimum = 0ms, Maximum =  10ms, Average =  2ms
```

In this example, the computer is responding well. There was zero percent packet loss in the transmissions, and the reply time was 10 milliseconds or less. The size of the packet sent was 32 bytes.

Note

An inability to ping a remote node is not a guarantee that the node is disconnected physically from the network. In other words, you cannot simply assume that a `ping` failure indicates a wiring problem. It might be that an intermediary device, such as a hub, router, or bridge, is malfunctioning. This is one of the reasons you need to keep a detailed map of your network. When you have to troubleshoot, you can check not just the end nodes, but also every device and cable along the path between them.

Troubleshooting a Network Connection with the `ping` Command

For basic connectivity troubleshooting, use the following steps:

1. Ping the local system's own network address.

2. Ping the system's hostname. The `ping` command resolves the hostname to an address before attempting to send packets to the hostname. If the address that `ping` resolves isn't the address you think it should be for your computer, you might need to check with your computer's configuration. You might have configured the local computer with one IP address, yet the entry in the DNS (Domain Name Service) server has your hostname associated with a different address. For more information about checking the DNS server, see "Using the `nslookup` Command," later in this chapter. You could also check the local hosts file for the computer to see if you've defined your hostname in that file with an incorrect address. However, with only a few exceptions, most computers today use DNS for name resolution, and the `hosts` file is becoming a relic of the past.

3. Ping another system that you know is on the local subnet. If that works, you know you can communicate with members of the local broadcast domain.

4. Ping the default gateway (also called the default route). This is the router or other device that connects your subnet to other networks. If you can't ping the default gateway, there are two possibilities to consider. First, you might have the wrong address. Check the computer's configuration to be sure you have used the correct address for the router or other host acting to forward packets for the local subnet. Or you might have a problem with the actual gateway itself. Try pinging it from another computer to see if that works. Of course, if the router or host that provides the default route is in close physical proximity, you can check it to see if there is a problem. For more information about checking router problems, see Chapter 10, "Routers," and Chapter 29, "Routing Protocols."

As you can see from these steps, it is possible to use `ping` to help track down a variety of different problems that can occur, from simple connectivity to name resolution. Using `ping` as your first step can help point you in the right direction should other tools need to be used to continue the troubleshooting effort. For example, if you can ping the local broadcast domain members, and if you can ping the default gateway, the next step is to attempt to ping hosts outside your network, perhaps on the Internet. Note that the network administrator may disable this functionality if your company institutes a good firewall security policy. Many times the administrator for the firewall will prevent outgoing ICMP ECHO REPLY messages to keep intruders from outside the network from finding out information about computers protected by the firewall. For more information about allowing the ping utility to work through firewalls, see Chapter 40, "Firewalls."

Note

The **ping** utility serves an important function in troubleshooting TCP/IP network connectivity. However, the *ping-of-death*, which you've probably heard about, does not. This attack method uses a program that creates ICMP packets that are larger in size than is allowed. If the software on the receiving end is not patched, or is a new version, it might accept this larger-than-life packet, causing part of the program memory to be overwritten as the data is stored in the allocated buffer and then, beyond. For more information about allowing the use of **ping** in a secure environment, see Chapter 39, "Security Issues in Wide Area Networks."

Using the *traceroute* Command

If you find that you cannot successfully ping a host that lies past your default gateway router, try using the traceroute (tracert for some operating systems) command. This command enables you to see every host that a packet passes through to get to the destination. You can use this information to locate a troublesome router or other device along the network path.

If you've established the fact that you can't get here from there, or that the response time is bad when using ping, try using the tracert command to determine the path that is being taken from your system to the target system. This diagnostic command is similar to ping in that it uses ICMP messages to try to locate each device through which a packet passes to reach its destination. This can provide useful information if you are not sure about the route being taken when you are trying to diagnose a sluggish response from ping. It also can help you find where along the network path the network is failing by showing each hop up until it fails if you can't get to the target system.

For most Unix and Linux operating systems, the command to trace a route through the network is called traceroute. In Windows 98, Windows NT, and Windows 2000 a version of this command is called tracert. The utility can determine each route through the network by setting the TTL (Time-To-Live) value in the packet, hoping to receive an ICMP TIME_EXCEEDED message from each hop the data packet takes on its path. Remember that the TTL value is the *allowable* number of hops a packet can take before it is discarded by IP. Thus, by setting this value, starting with one and incrementing by one for each pass, tracert can get the TIME_EXCEEDED ICMP message from each router or other device through which the packet must pass. For each attempt, three packets are sent to average the time that it takes to get to that point in the network. The basic function of this utility appears in Figure 22.2.

In this figure, you can see that Computer A generates a series of ICMP ECHO REQUEST messages and sends them to computer D. When the first packet is sent out, the TTL value is set to 1. It is decremented to zero at the first router, and an ICMP TIME EXCEEDED ICMP message is sent back to Computer A. Computer A then sends out another ICMP ECHO REQUEST packet, but this time sets the TTL value to 2. Thus, the first router passes the packet to the next router after decrementing the TTL value from 2 to 1. The second router looks at the TTL value of 1 and decrements it to zero, and once again an ICMP TIME EXCEEDED message is sent back to Computer A.

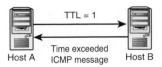

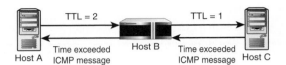

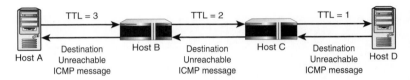

Figure 22.2 The tracert utility manipulates the TTL value to discover host systems along a particular route.

As you can see, intermediate routers drop packets when the TTL value expires. An ICMP TIME_EXCEEDED message is sent back to Host A, *until the TTL value has been set to a value sufficient to reach the destination Computer D*. Thus, Computer A can determine the number of hops it took to reach Computer D, assuming it is successful in getting there!

The original traceroute utility sets the port in the UDP header to an "unreachable" port. Thus, when the TTL value is finally incremented enough so that the ICMP packet actually reaches the target system, it will return the ICMP DESTINATION UNREACHABLE message, as you can see in Figure 22.2. If the last hop you see in the traceroute output is the destination, the program has displayed all the hops between your system and the destination system. This can vary depending on the implementation of the utility.

If the last hop that is returned by this command is *not* the target system, you should begin investigating the system that does show up as the last hop.

Note

Various implementations of the **traceroute** utility might function differently than the method just described here. Some use the function of the Record-Route option in IP to attempt to trace the route. However, because the amount of space to record routes is limited, and because the Internet is much larger than it was a few years ago, the UDP method that manipulates the TTL value is probably a more reliable way to implement this utility.

The basic syntax for the traceroute command as given in RFC 2151 is

traceroute [-m #] [-q #] [-w #] [-p #] {IP_address|host_name}

- **-m**—The maximum allowable TTL value, measured as the number of hops allowed before the program terminates (default = 30).

- **-q**—The number of UDP packets that will be sent with each Time-To-Live setting (default = 3).

- **-w**—The amount of time, in seconds, to wait for an answer from a particular router before giving up (default = 5).

- **-p**—The invalid port address at the remote host (default = 33434).

The syntax for using `tracert` in Windows NT and Windows 2000 is

`tracert [-d] [-h maximum_hops] [-j host-list] [-w timeout] target_name`

The options include

- **-d**—Do not resolve hostnames to addresses.

- **-h *maximum_hops***—Maximum number of hops to search for target.

- **-j *host-list***—Loose source route along host-list.

- **-w *timeout***—Wait timeout milliseconds for each reply.

The following is an example of the output from executing the Windows NT version of `traceroute`:

```
D:> tracert www.bellsouth.net
Tracing route to www.bellsouth.net [205.152.0.46]
over a maximum of 30 hops:
  1    231 ms    200 ms    220 ms  envlnjewsap02.bellatlantic.net.
➡[192.168.125.189]
  2    261 ms    160 ms    160 ms  192.168.125.158
  3    180 ms    200 ms    181 ms  206.125.199.71
  4    181 ms    160 ms    180 ms  Hssi4-1-0.border2.teb1.IConNet.NET.
➡[209.3.188.201]
  5    241 ms    180 ms    180 ms  POS10-0-0.core2.teb1.IConNet.NET.
➡[204.245.71.221]
  6    180 ms    181 ms    280 ms  Hssi0-0-0.peer1.psk1.IConNet.NET.
➡[204.245.69.174]
  7    180 ms    181 ms    180 ms  BR1.PSK1.Alter.net. [192.157.69.60]
  8    180 ms    181 ms    240 ms  Hssi0-1-0.hr1.nyc1.alter.net.
➡[137.39.100.2]
  9    180 ms    181 ms    200 ms  101.ATM2-0.XR2.NYC1.ALTER.NET.
➡[146.188.177.90]
 10    240 ms    181 ms    200 ms  194.ATM3-0.TR2.EWR1.ALTER.NET.
➡[146.188.178.230]
 11    301 ms    200 ms    200 ms  105.ATM6-0.TR2.ATL1.ALTER.NET.
➡[146.188.136.37]
 12    241 ms    220 ms    180 ms  198.ATM7-0.XR2.ATL1.ALTER.NET.
➡[146.188.232.101]
 13    201 ms    200 ms    220 ms  194.ATM11-0-0.GW2.ATL1.ALTER.NET.
➡[146.188.232.69]
 14    321 ms    200 ms    220 ms  bs2-atl-gw.customer.alter.net. [157.130.69.106]
 15    220 ms    220 ms    221 ms  205.152.2.178
 16    200 ms    281 ms    200 ms  205.152.3.74
 17    220 ms    220 ms    201 ms  www.bellsouth.net. [205.152.0.46]
Trace complete.
```

As you can see, you can gain a lot of information about how your network functions by using this command. The three columns show how long it took each of the three attempts to reach the particular node for that hop. An asterisk character that is displayed in any of these time columns indicates that the ICMP packet was not returned. The hostname and address are displayed by default. If the command fails at any point, you can start tracing the network fault at the last successful hop to determine where the fault lies.

If you have a map of your network, you can check to determine whether the best path is being followed when using the `traceroute` utility—maybe a primary router is not up and running, and a backup path with a lower bandwidth is sending the packet on a different route through the network. If you use this command on a regular basis and keep an output of the information you see, you can learn to notice when a particular router used by your ISP is having problems, for example.

By using both `ping` and `tracert` you can usually discover problem areas in your network and then plan steps to remedy the problem. If the problem lies outside your network, that is, with your ISP or some other router on the Internet, resolving the situation can be more problematic! However, for troubleshooting the internal corporate network, these commands should prove very useful for basic configuration and connectivity problems.

The *netstat* and *route* Commands

On Unix, Linux, and Windows systems, the `netstat` command is used to obtain statistics about the TCP/IP protocols that are in use on the computer. This command is most useful when you are trying to debug routing problems.

Using the *netstat* Command on Windows NT and Windows 2000

The syntax for `netstat` for Windows NT or Windows 2000 is

```
netstat [-a] [-e] [-n] [-s] [-p protocol] [-r] [interval]
```

- **-a**—Displays all connections and listening ports.

- **-e**—Displays Ethernet statistics. This can be combined with the `-s` option.

- **-n**—Displays addresses and port numbers in numerical form.

- **-s**—Displays per-protocol statistics. By default, statistics are shown for TCP, UDP, and IP. The `-p` option can be used to specify a subset of the default.

- **-p *protocol***—Shows connections for the protocol specified by *protocol*; *protocol* can be TCP or UDP. If used with the `-s` option to display per-protocol statistics, *protocol* can be TCP, UDP, or IP.

- **-r**—Displays the routing table.

- ***interval***—Redisplays selected statistics, pausing interval seconds between each display. Press Ctrl+C to stop redisplaying statistics. If omitted, `netstat` will print the current configuration information once.

You can investigate a lot about the protocols operating on your system using the `netstat` command, as you can see from the preceding syntax options. For example, the command

```
netstat -r
```

displays the routing table that is maintained on the current host. (Note that you can also use the command `route print` to display the routing table information. See Chapter 29 for more information about using the `route` command and its command-line options.) Following is an example of the routing table as shown using `netstat -r` and an explanation of the data that is shown using the Windows NT version of this command:

```
netstat –r
Route Table
Active Routes:
Network Address          Netmask          Gateway          Interface   Metric
        0.0.0.0          0.0.0.0   151.204.200.25   151.204.200.25        1
       10.10.0.0    255.255.0.0      10.10.10.10      10.10.10.10        1
```

10.10.10.10	255.255.255.255	127.0.0.1	127.0.0.1	1
10.255.255.255	255.255.255.255	10.10.10.10	10.10.10.10	1
127.0.0.0	255.0.0.0	127.0.0.1	127.0.0.1	1
151.204.200.25	255.255.255.255	127.0.0.1	127.0.0.1	1
151.204.200.25	255.255.255.255	151.204.200.25	151.204.200.25	1
151.204.255.255	255.255.255.255	151.204.200.25	151.204.200.25	1
224.0.0.0	224.0.0.0	10.10.10.10	10.10.10.10	1
224.0.0.0	224.0.0.0	151.204.200.25	151.204.200.25	1
255.255.255.255	255.255.255.255	10.10.10.10	10.10.10.10	1

Each line in this display starts with a destination address. When deciding where to send a packet, this table is consulted to see if one of these destination addresses matches the destination address of the packet in question. In the first line, the address of 0.0.0.0 might not seem to make sense. This is the entry, or the *default gateway*. That is, if a packet cannot be routed to its destination using any of the remaining entries in the route table, it will be sent to this address.

The second column shows the netmask for this route entry. Like a subnet mask, this mask is used to mask out portions of the destination address when a routing decision is to be made. The netmask is converted to binary. When deciding if a packet matches the destination address, the portions of the destination address that are in the same position as a 1 must match the packet's destination address exactly. A netmask of 255.255.255.255 is a string of 32 ones in binary. This is used for a host address, and the packet must match the address exactly to be routed by this entry.

The next column shows the gateway. Packets that match this entry will be sent to this address. The next column—Interface—is the address of the network card or PPP adapter that the packet will be sent through. The last column—Metric—shows the number of hops the packet will take to reach its final destination.

The output for the Windows 2000 Server command is similar, but presented in a different format:

```
C:\>netstat -r

Route Table
===========================================================================
Interface List
0x1 ........................ MS TCP Loopback interface
0x2 ...00 08 c7 ba 23 7f ...... Compaq Ethernet/FastEthernet or Gigabit NIC
===========================================================================
===========================================================================
Active Routes:
Network Destination        Netmask          Gateway        Interface  Metric
        0.0.0.0            0.0.0.0  140.176.187.254  140.176.187.185       1
      127.0.0.0          255.0.0.0        127.0.0.1        127.0.0.1       1
    140.176.187.0    255.255.255.0  140.176.187.185  140.176.187.185       1
  140.176.187.185  255.255.255.255        127.0.0.1        127.0.0.1       1
  140.176.255.255  255.255.255.255  140.176.187.185  140.176.187.185       1
        224.0.0.0        224.0.0.0  140.176.187.185  140.176.187.185       1
  255.255.255.255  255.255.255.255  140.176.187.185  140.176.187.185       1
Default Gateway:     140.176.187.254
===========================================================================
Persistent Routes:
  None
```

Other uses for the netstat command include showing the current state of TCP/IP ports and sockets (netstat -a) or showing the ARP table (use netstat -p on Unix or the arp command on Windows NT).

To see statistics about the specific protocols—UDP, ICMP, TCP, or IP—use the `netstat -s` command. This is especially helpful when you are trying to diagnose connectivity problems that are intermittent or might be due to network congestion. The output is quite lengthy, so you might want to pipe the results to a text file (`netstat -s > stats.txt`). What follows is an example of the data you can obtain by using the `-s` option with this command on a Windows NT or Windows 2000 system:

```
netstat -s
IP Statistics
  Packets Received                    = 19942
  Received Header Errors              = 0
  Received Address Errors             = 2
  Datagrams Forwarded                 = 0
  Unknown Protocols Received          = 0
  Received Packets Discarded          = 0
  Received Packets Delivered          = 19942
  Output Requests                     = 19682
  Routing Discards                    = 0
  Discarded Output Packets            = 0
  Output Packet No Route              = 0
  Reassembly Required                 = 0
  Reassembly Successful               = 0
  Reassembly Failures                 = 0
  Datagrams Successfully Fragmented   = 0
  Datagrams Failing Fragmentation     = 0
  Fragments Created                   = 0


ICMP Statistics
                          Received    Sent
  Messages                341         257
  Errors                  0           0
  Destination Unreachable 30          16
  Time Exceeded           142         0
  Parameter Problems      0           0
  Source Quenchs          0           0
  Redirects               91          0
  Echos                   34          189
  Echo Replies            44          34
  Timestamps              0           0
  Timestamp Replies       0           0
  Address Masks           0           0
  Address Mask Replies    0           0
TCP Statistics
  Active Opens                        = 454
  Passive Opens                       = 0
  Failed Connection Attempts          = 4
  Reset Connections                   = 33
  Current Connections                 = 0
  Segments Received                   = 6399
  Segments Sent                       = 6359
  Segments Retransmitted              = 14

UDP Statistics
  Datagrams Received      = 13184
  No Ports                = 325
  Receive Errors          = 0
  Datagrams Sent          = 13048
```

Again, the valuable information you get using this command can be very handy when troubleshooting networking problems. For example, you can check to see whether the number of errors or dropped packets is excessive when compared to your ordinary operating environment. To understand and make good use of this type of information, you should be familiar with the protocols that are displayed, such as IP and UDP. For more information about these protocols, see Chapter 20.

Using the `netstat` Command on Unix or Linux Systems

The syntax for the `netstat` command varies depending on which Unix or Linux implementation you are using; however, you will see similar information, and it will be mostly the formatting that changes. For example, the syntax for `netstat` for the FreeBSD Unix operating system is

```
netstat [-AaLln] [-f address_family] [-M core] [-N system]
netstat [-bdghilmnrs] [-f address_family] [-M core] [-N system]
netstat [-bdn] [-I interface] [-M core] [-N system] [-w wait]
netstat [-p protocol] [-M core] [-N system]
netstat [-p protocol] [-i] [-I Interface]
netstat [-s] [-f address_family] [-i] [-I Interface]
```

where:

- **-A**—Shows the address of any protocol control blocks associated with sockets. This generally is used for debugging purposes.

- **-a**—Shows the state of all sockets. By default, sockets used by server processes are not shown.

- **-b**—When used with the -i (interface) option, shows the number of bytes in and out.

- **-d**—With the -i option (interface), shows the number of packets dropped.

- **-f address_family**—Use this to narrow down the statistics displayed to specific protocols. The values you can use here include inet, inet6, ipx, atalk, netgraph, ng, or unix.

- **-g**—This will display multicast routing tables and interfaces. With the -s option, will also show statistics.

- **-h**—Obsolete. Was used to show the IMP host table.

- **-I interface**—Displays information about the specified interface *interface*. Can be used with the -f, -s, and -p options to narrow down the information displayed.

- **-i**—Displays the status of interfaces that are statically configured and not located at boot time. Used with -a, multicast addresses that are in use are shown for each Ethernet and IP interface. If used with -f or the -p options, statistics are shown for the address families or protocols indicated.

- **-L**—Displays the size of listen queues. Displays the number of unaccepted connections and number of unaccepted incomplete connections. Also shows the number of queued connections.

- **-l**—Causes the display to print the full IPv6 address.

- **-M**—Uses values from a name list instead of the default file /dev/kmem.

- **-m**—Displays statistics about memory management routines.

- **-N**—Extracts the name list from the specified system instead of the default /kernel.

- **-n**—Displays network addresses as numbers instead of names.

- **-p protocol**—Specifies a protocol for which information is displayed. Protocol names are listed in the /etc/protocols file.

- **-s**—Causes the display to show per-protocol statistical information.

- **-r**—Displays the routing tables.
- **-w** *wait*—Causes the interface statistics to be updated at intervals of *wait* seconds.

Once again, be sure to check the man pages for your particular flavor of Unix or Linux to be sure of the correct syntax to use. The examples shown here give you an idea of the kind of information you can obtain using the netstat command.

The *arp* Command

IP addresses and hostnames are used for the convenience of humans so we can configure and manage a network in an orderly manner. At the lowest level, however, network cards use the hardware MAC address when they talk to each other. Remember that a computer finds out the hardware address of another computer on the local segment by using the Address Resolution Protocol (ARP). Just as a host computer keeps a table of routing information, it also keeps a cache of MAC-to-IP address translations known as the *ARP table*.

The arp command enables you to view the ARP table and to add or delete entries within it. Again, the syntax varies between different systems, but the following should work for most:

- **arp -a**—Displays the current contents of the ARP table.
- **arp -d *IP_address***—Deletes the entry for the specified host.
- **arp -s *IP_address ether_address***—Adds an entry to the table.

For example, to add an entry, you use the following syntax:

```
arp -s 192.123.111.2    08-00-2b-34-c1-01
```

This list of arp commands shows you the basic functions that you can perform under most implementations. To show the differences that you might encounter, let's look at the Linux version and the Windows 2000 version of this command. For Linux the syntax for arp is

```
arp [-v] [-t type] -a [hostname]
arp [-v] -d hostname ...
arp [-v] [-t type] -s hostname hw_addr [temp] [netmask aa.bb.cc.dd] [pub]
arp [-v] -f filename
```

- **-v**—Tells the user what is going on by being verbose. Produces more output.
- **-a *[hostname]***—Shows the entries of the specified hosts. If the *hostname* parameter is not used, all entries will be displayed.
- **-d *hostname***—Removes any entry for the specified host. This can be used if the indicated host is brought down, for example.
- **-s *hostname hw_addr***—Manually creates an ARP address mapping entry for host *hostname* with hardware address set to *hw_addr* class, but for most classes one can assume that the usual presentation can be used. For the Ethernet class, this is six bytes in hexadecimal, separated by colons.
- **-f *filename***—Similar to the -s option, only this time the address info is taken from file *filename* set up. The name of the data file is very often /etc/ethers, but this might not be the case from one version of Linux to another. The format of the file is simple; it contains only ASCII text lines with a hostname, and a hardware address separated by white space.

In the preceding syntax explanations, you can generally substitute an IP address for *hostname* in most situations.

The Windows 2000 version of this command performs most of these same functions but has a different syntax:

```
ARP -s inet_addr eth_addr [if_addr]
ARP -d inet_addr [if_addr]
ARP -a [inet_addr] [-N if_addr]
```

- **-a**—Displays current ARP entries by interrogating the current protocol data. If *inet_addr* is specified, the IP and physical addresses for only the specified computer are displayed. If more than one network interface uses ARP, entries for each ARP table are displayed.

- **-g**—Functions the same as -a.

- *inet_addr*—Specifies an Internet address.

- **-N** *if_addr*—Displays the ARP entries for the network interface specified by *if_addr*.

- **-d** *inet_addr* [*if_addr*]—Deletes the host specified by *inet_addr*. *inet_addr* may be used as a wildcard with * to delete all hosts.

- **-s** *inet_addr eth_addr* [*if_addr*]—Adds the host and associates the Internet address *inet_addr* with the physical address *eth_addr*. The physical address is given as six hexadecimal bytes separated by hyphens. The entry is a static (permanent) entry into the table.

- *eth_addr*—Specifies a physical address.

- *if_addr*—If present, this specifies the Internet address of the interface whose address translation table should be modified. If not present, the first applicable interface will be used.

As you can see, the arp command can be quite powerful. It should be used carefully when adding or deleting entries in the ARP table. However, for display purposes it can be easily used to determine problems of resolving hardware addresses on the local subnet or network segment. For more information about the ARP protocol specifics and how it is used on the local segment to resolve hardware to IP addresses, see Chapter 20.

The *tcpdump* Utility

If you are extremely knowledgeable about TCP/IP and are capable of understanding the bits and bytes of IP frames, you can use the tcpdump utility to capture header information from packets as they pass through the network. Because there can be a potential security problem with being able to view this information, it is not a utility that the ordinary Unix user can use. It is generally restricted to the root user or must be installed with setuid to root.

Note

When a file has "setuid to root bit" enabled it means that the program will run with the privileges of the owner of the file, and not the privileges of the user who is running the program. In Unix or Linux systems, this feature allows the administrator to let users execute programs that perform specific tasks that require more privileges than the user has. However, the user is only able to use the privileges to run the program to accomplish a specific task. The user does not inherit the rights or privileges of the program after running it.

Because the **tcpdump** utility can be used to examine network packets (and thus "snoop" on network traffic), it must run with the privileges granted to the **root** (or superuser) account.

Many command-line parameters are associated with this utility, and you can create complex expressions that are used to evaluate which packets to intercept. You can also supply no selection criteria, and all packets will be dumped.

Some of the more useful command options for `tcpdump` are

- **-a**—Tries to convert network and broadcast addresses to names.
- **-c** *count*—Exits after receiving *count* number of packets.
- **-d**—Dumps the compiled packet-matching code in a human readable form to standard output and stop.
- **-dd**—Dumps packet-matching code as a C program fragment.
- **-ddd**—Dumps packet-matching code as decimal numbers (preceded with a count).
- **-e**—Displays the link level header information on each line (the Ethernet header information).
- **-F** *file*—Uses the text found in file for the selection expression. If you use this option, any expression given on the command line is ignored.
- **-f**—Print "foreign" Internet addresses numerically rather than symbolically.
- **-i** *interface*—Specifies the interface to monitor. If you do not specify this, `tcpdump` will select the lowest numbered configured interface, excluding `loopback`.
- **-n**—Doesn't convert host addresses, port numbers, and so on to names.
- **-N**—Doesn't display domain name qualification of names.
- **-q**—Limits the amount of information displayed for a shorter listing.
- **-r**—Reads packets from *file* (which was created with the -w option). Standard input is used if *file* is "-".
- **-s**—Snarfs *snaplen* bytes of data from each packet rather than the default of 68, which is adequate for IP, ICMP, TCP, and UDP but may truncate protocol information from name server and NFS packets.
- **-t**—Doesn't print a timestamp on each line.
- **-v or -vv or -vvv**—Gives additional information from each packet. Each of these causes the output to be more verbose.

There are additional advanced options you can use, but the preceding options are the basic ones. The selection expression criteria can be quite complex, and you should consult the extensive man pages for `tcpdump` to get the full listing of other options, expressions, and examples. The scope of the capabilities of this program is beyond this book. A few simple uses follow:

```
tcpdump host hercules
```

This command shows packets that are going to or coming from the system named `hercules`.

```
tcpdump ip host venus and not hercules
```

This command shows packets going to or coming from the system named `venus`, unless they are coming from or going to `hercules`. The output displayed by this command depends on the protocol of the packet that is intercepted.

The `tcpdump` program is included on the CD-ROM that accompanies this book. You can also check for more recent versions at the Network Research Group of the Information and Computing Sciences Division of the Lawrence Berkeley National Laboratory (`http://ee.lbl.gov/`) for more information about `tcpdump` and other useful utilities. More recent versions and patches for the utility are maintained at `http://www.tcpdump.org/`. In addition, you can sign up for mailing lists that relate to this utility. Join the first list by sending an e-mail message to the address `tcpdump-announce@tcpdump.org`. This mailing list is used for announcements about the utility. The second mailing list is used for both announcements and discussions concerning the code of tcpdump. To subscribe to this mailing list, send an e-mail to tcpdump-workers@tcpdump.org.

The source code for this program is also available for compilation on many different Unix and Linux platforms. Although it's not a tool for a novice, tcpdump can be used by a skilled administrator to diagnose network problems. This section has given you only a brief overview of the capabilities of this simple network capture utility. After installing the software, be sure to review any readme files for up-to-date information.

The *WinDump* Utility

The tcpdump utility has been ported to the Windows environment and is known as WinDump. Like the tcpdump program, this program was developed by the Network Research Group of the Information and Computing Sciences Division of the Lawrence Berkeley National Laboratory. See http://ee.lbl.gov/ for more information about WinDump and other useful utilities. More recent versions and patches for the utility are maintained at http://netgroup-serv.polito.it/windump/. This utility is also included on the CD-ROM that comes with this book. By using WinDump, you can gain a lot of information by examining network packets to troubleshoot network problems. The interface, however, is different than the command-line version of tcpdump. The WinDump utility, like tcpdump, is covered under a Berkeley-style license.

Note

A Berkeley-style license means that you can share software with others as long as you include a copy of the license. You cannot use the code to create commercial products to sell, however.

To install WinDump you first must download the drivers appropriate to your version of the Windows operating system. Drivers are available for Windows 95/98, Windows NT, and Windows 2000. After you've installed the driver, you can install the WinDump components. To install the driver (filename Packet2k.exe for Windows 2000), simply execute the file. It prompts you for a temporary directory to which to extract files. Accept the default or enter a directory name of your choosing and then proceed to unzip the files. To install the driver:

1. Launch the Control Panel (Start, Settings, Control Panel) and double-click the Network and Dial Up Connections icon.
2. Double-click the Local Area Connection icon that appears. Click the Properties button.
3. Click the Install button. In the Select Network Component Type dialog box, click Protocol, and then click the Add button.
4. Click the Have Disk button and when the next dialog box appears, enter the pathname to the place where you unzipped the driver files. Click OK.
5. In the Select Network Protocol dialog box, highlight Packet Capture Driver v2.01 and click OK.
6. When the Local Area Connection dialog box appears again, click OK to close the dialog box. The packet capture driver should now be installed. You must reboot the machine before the driver is loaded.

Next, you need to download the WinDump program. Just click the WinDump link on the download page and the executable file will be downloaded to the directory you specify. After that, set your working directory to the same directory and you are ready to execute WinDump commands.

The command syntax for WinDump is almost exactly the same as the tcpdump utility; consult the syntax listed earlier in this chapter for more help. Or, visit the WinDump home page and follow the link to the extensive man page found there.

Again, remember that examining network packets is not a job for a novice. You should first have a good understanding of the frame types seen on your network, and a good understanding of the types of datagrams sent by applications and services you use. Some of the standard packets you should familiarize yourself with include DNS, ICMP, and TCP session setup and close. Depending on the services your network uses, you can quickly become familiar with the type of expected network traffic and then use this tool to look for exceptions when troubleshooting.

Using the *nslookup* Command to Troubleshoot Name Resolution Issues

This command is another simple command that is available with all TCP/IP implementations. Its purpose is to query a DNS name server to find out the name registration information for a particular host. By using nslookup, you can find out whether the address that is associated with the computer's hostname is accurate. This can be handy for troubleshooting if you are trying to use one of the TCP/IP utilities, such as FTP or Telnet, to reach a particular host by name, yet find you cannot establish a connection or that the remote system is not the one you thought it would be.

This utility can be run in two different modes. First, you can specify all the commands on a command line and get a result returned from a DNS name server (noninteractive mode). Second, you can enter "batch" mode (called interactive mode by Microsoft) and issue several commands in a row to the server. The basic syntax for the command in Windows NT and Windows 2000 is

```
nslookup [-option ...] [computer-to-find | - [server]]
```

Options you can use with the command are

- **computer-to-find**—The name of the computer whose name you want to look up.

- **server**—Use this to specify a DNS name server other than the default server configured on the client.

For example:

```
C:> nslookup www.twoinc.com
```

This command sends an inquiry to the default DNS server. If information is received, it will print the name of the server that the information is from, and then print the IP address of the server you inquired about. For example:

```
C:\>nslookup www.twoinc.com
Server:  home8-qwest.bellatlantic.net
Address:  151.204.0.84

Non-authoritative answer:
Name:    www.twoinc.com
Address:  216.65.33.219
```

In this example you can also see that the server that gave the response indicates that it is a Non-authoritative answer. This means that the server is not the server that actually holds the domain name record for this domain, but has cached the name locally. The record for the domain is located elsewhere in the DNS hierarchy.

The nslookup command also enables you to enter several options on the command line or to use these features from within the interactive environment. When used on the command line, precede each option with a minus sign (–). The options and values that can be used with the Windows NT and Windows 2000 versions are

- **help**—Displays help text.

- **exit**—Exits nslookup when in interactive mode.

- **finger** **[*username*]** **[> *filename*]** | **[>> *filename*]**—Connects to the current finger server and looks up a *username*. You can specify a *filename* for the output.

- **ls** **[*option*]** **dnsdomain** **[> *filename*]** | **[>> *filename*]**—Lists information about a domain. Generally this includes computer names and addresses. Suboptions to this command allow you to get other information.

- **lserver** **dnsdomain**—Uses the initial server to retrieve information about *dnsdomain*.

- **root**—Sets the current default server to be the root server.

- **server** **dnsdomain**—Uses the current server to retrieve information about dnsdomain.

- **set** **keyword=[*value*]**—Changes configuration settings about how nslookup works. See the help text for more information.

- **set all**—Displays current configuration settings for the nslookup utility and shows information about the default server.

There are many set commands that you can use to customize the way in which nslookup works. For more information, check the help text that comes with the version you are using. Using nslookup in interactive mode enables you to perform multiple hostname lookups without having to retype the nslookup command. Use the exit command to exit the interactive mode.

Other Useful Commands

The TCP/IP suite consists of several protocols and utilities that have been developed over the years. Other commands can be useful for troubleshooting. For example, the telnet command is used to establish a remote terminal session on another computer. If you are having trouble with a workstation, you can always telnet to it and perform diagnostic functions directly. This is convenient when the network is dispersed geographically. The ftp command can be used to move files to and from a remote system. This can be useful to retrieve the output of a diagnostic command, a log file, or perhaps a configuration file, so that you can examine or edit it locally.

Telnet also can be useful when trying to resolve connectivity problems with a particular server. If you can't ping or otherwise connect to a system, try using telnet to get to another system and try your diagnostic commands from that location in the network. Using this method to attempt to connect to a remote system by using other remote systems can help you locate the spot in the network where potential trouble lies.

BOOTP and the Dynamic Host Configuration Protocol (DHCP)

SOME OF THE MAIN TOPICS IN THIS CHAPTER ARE

What Is BOOTP?

Taking BOOTP One Step Further: DHCP

An Example: Installing and Configuring a DHCP Server on
Windows 2000

You should read this chapter and the one that follows, "Name Resolution," as though they were one, because they cover both sides of the coin when talking about how computers are uniquely identified on a network. This chapter deals with the specifics of how computers can be set up to automatically receive addressing and other information when they boot, relieving the system administrator of having to manually configure each one individually every time a global change is made. Chapter 24 discusses how other computers on the network go about determining the particular address of another computer on the network.

BOOTP is an old protocol. DHCP also has been around a while. However, DHCP basically is a protocol that builds on and expands the capabilities that were first provided by BOOTP. For this historical reason, and the fact that BOOTP still is in use in many networks, both are examined in this chapter. Most modern DHCP servers, including the Windows 2000 version, still support BOOTP for backward compatibility.

What Is BOOTP?

BOOTP stands for the Bootstrap or BOOT Protocol. When you consider that the standard method for booting a computer is to locate a boot block on a local drive and then go from there, why are we discussing booting in a book about networks? During the 1980s, BOOTP was developed to allow diskless workstations to boot by downloading the operating system from another network node. Many operating systems at that time used this protocol because it allowed the use of cheaper desktop workstations on the network—long before PCs became a standard desktop item. At the time, the X-Window workstation was popular in Unix networks. BOOTP was an economical way to provide an X-Window desktop with an operating system, without the need to equip the machine with disk drives and other devices not necessary for a simple client. Other types of network clients adopted the BOOTP protocol, allowing network devices to also be suitably configured by use of the protocol.

Note

The BOOTP protocol was originally defined in RFC 951, "Bootstrap Protocol" in 1985, and further details were provided by RFC 1542, "Clarifications and Extensions for the Bootstrap Protocol," in 1993. Other RFC documents that include information about BOOTP, such as those RFCs defining DHCP and BOOTP options, are discussed later in this chapter.

The operating system download capability is only one of the functions performed by BOOTP. In addition, the diskless workstation (or other client) also can get addressing information. Because the lowest-level BOOTP client is presumed to be "diskless," it has no method to store configurable addressing information between power cycles. The BOOTP protocol is not complex. Indeed, it is a simple protocol that is small and easy to implement in programmable read-only memory (PROM) chips. The following are some important features of BOOTP:

- A simple request/reply mechanism is used. The same packet format is used for both requests and replies.

- The UDP protocol is used to carry messages (ports 67 and 68).

- Using relay agents, BOOTP exchanges can occur across routers.

- BOOTP can supply the client with an IP address, subnet mask, and default gateway. Additionally, the BOOTP server also can give the client name of a trivial FTP server (TFTP) and a filename that can be used to download an operating system.

◀◀ Another protocol, the Reverse Address Resolution Protocol (RARP), operates at the second layer of the OSI network model and also is capable of providing an IP address to another node that is booting on the network. However, RARP is very limited. For more information about RARP, see Chapter 20, "Overview of the TCP/IP Protocol Suite."

Format of the BOOTP Packet

The client and server share a common packet format. This packet is passed to UDP and encapsulated inside a UDP packet. The UDP and IP headers are added, and the information finally is passed to the Data Link and Physical layers for transmission on the network medium.

◄◄　The IP and UDP protocols are discussed in greater detail in Chapter 20.

The fields of the BOOTP packet are used for the following purposes:

- **Opcode**—This one-byte field has a value of either zero or one. If set to a value of one, the packet is a request from a client to a BOOTP (or DHCP, as explained later) server. If the value is zero, the packet is a reply from a server to the client.

- **Hardware Type**—Values in this one-byte field are used to designate different kinds of hardware, or different computer types or network device types, for example. A value of 1 in this field indicates that the underlying hardware type of the network is ethernet.

- **Hardware Address Length**—This one-byte field indicates the number of bytes that the client hardware address field contains. For ethernet, this value is 6, because it takes 6 bytes to represent the 48-bit Media Access Control (MAC) address used by ethernet network cards.

- **Hop Count**—This one-byte field is always set to zero by the client, though the BOOTP server uses this field when relaying BOOTP requests across routers.

- **Transaction ID**—This is a four-byte field that is a unique 32-bit integer the client sets so it can match up replies from the server to the requests the client has sent.

- **Seconds**—This two-byte field is expressed in seconds and is filled in by the client with a value indicating the time that has elapsed since the client started the boot process. This value can be used by secondary servers to recognize that the client's primary server is not responding. In that case, a secondary BOOTP server can make an attempt to satisfy the request.

- **Flags**—In the original specifications for BOOTP, this two-byte field was not used. However, in RFC 1542 this field was set aside to store flag bits. Only one has been defined so far. The most significant bit in this field is used as a Broadcast flag. The remaining bits are not yet defined and should be set to zeros.

- **Client IP Address (ciaddr)**—If the client already knows its own address (which is explained shortly), it will fill in that address in this four-byte field. In most cases, the client does not know its own IP address (because that's one of the main things BOOTP is used to supply to the client), and in that case the value for this field should be zero.

- **Your IP Address (yiaddr)**—This field is used by the BOOTP server to supply an IP address to a client requesting one. It also is a four-byte field, the number of bytes needed to store an IP address. Although the client can fill in the ciaddr field with a requested address, this field contains the address the DHCP server returns to the client to use.

- **Server IP Address (siaddr)**—The BOOTP server fills in this field, usually placing its own address here.

- **Gateway IP Address (giaddr)**—If a BOOTP proxy server is being used, the address in this four-byte field is the address of the router or other device performing the proxy function. Proxy BOOTP services are discussed later in this chapter. Note that this *is not* the address the client should use as a default gateway for TCP/IP configuration (though it could be the same). This field is used only to relay BOOTP requests across routers to and from the actual BOOTP server. The default gateway information is supplied in BOOTP options, described later in this chapter (see "Enabling the DHCP Relay Agent").

- **Client's Hardware Address (chaddr)**—If the client already knows its own IP address, it will place it into this four-byte field. The client must fill in this required field because the typical BOOTP server uses it in an index of values it keeps track of for its clients.

■ **Server Hostname (sname)**—This field can be up to 64 bytes in length and contains a null-terminated ASCII string of characters that represent the server's hostname on the network. This hostname can be a simple hostname or a fully qualified domain name (FQDN). This is an optional field.

■ **Boot Filename (file)**—This field can be up to 128 characters in length and is used to supply the client with the filename it can download and use to boot. The value here is also a null-terminated string and includes the full path the client needs to locate the file.

■ **Vendor-Specific Area**—This 64 bytes is set aside to store vendor-specific optional information. The items are listed in Table 23.1 in the "BOOTP Vendor Specific Information Options" section. The first option in this field will be a "magic cookie." The last option is the end option, the number 255.

The client's hardware address, which is placed in the BOOTP packet, is the same hardware address that will be found in the ethernet frame that delivers the packet. However, after the ethernet frame is received, the lower-level header information (such as the client's hardware address) is stripped off before the remaining packet is passed up through the IP and UDP layers. At the point where the BOOTP protocol begins to examine the packet, the ethernet frame header information generally is not available in most TCP/IP stacks. For this reason, the hardware address is duplicated inside the BOOTP packet. Remember that the RARP protocol is a link-layer protocol, so it can retrieve the client's hardware address from the ethernet frame, something most implementations of BOOTP cannot do.

Note

For those who are interested in the nitty-gritty details, the packets discussed here are transmitted on the wire in the order shown in the figures in this chapter. Additionally, the individual bytes are sent with the left-most bit being the most significant. For multi-octet values, the most significant octet is transmitted first. This information might help you when diagnosing problems on the network using a LAN analyzer or other methods to intercept and interpret network packets.

The BOOTP Request/Reply Mechanism

Because it usually is implemented in a read-only memory (ROM) chip, the BOOTP protocol client is a simple, concise bit of code. The exchange of UDP messages between the client and the BOOTP server consists of a series of requests and replies. The same packet format is used for both types of messages, with an Opcode field used to indicate whether the message is a request from the client or a reply from the server.

The following basic steps are involved in obtaining information from a BOOTP server:

1. The client sends a broadcast message at the link-layer level because the client at this point is unaware of its own IP address or that of any BOOTP server that might be on the network. In the IP header information for the request, the client usually sets the source IP Address field to 0.0.0.0 and the destination address to 255.255.255.255. Because this is a UDP packet being sent through IP, the client sets the destination UDP port number to 68 (the BOOTP server port) so a listening server will know to intercept the packet. The Transaction ID field that the client places in the BOOTP request packet is used by clients to sort out which replies are meant for them. The first four bytes of the vendor-specific information area should be set to a magic cookie.

Note

A *magic cookie* is a method used by BOOTP to tell the server what kind of format to use when creating a reply for a client's request. The magic cookie usually is the value 99.130.83.99 but can be a vendor-supplied value. The magic cookie usually is used to indicate that the vendor-specific area contains information for the server to examine. The remaining information in the 64-byte vendor-specific information is defined as a series of tags followed by a length field and then, in most cases, a variable-length field of information.

2. If the broadcast flag is set, the server next broadcasts a reply that contains the client's IP address, the server's own IP address, and other requested information.

3. If the broadcast flag is not set, the server can send a unicast address using the client's IP address to the address supplied by the client. The server should always check the Client IP Address (from Client) field set by the client to be sure it is not the default value of 0.0.0.0. If it is not, then, depending on the implementation, the server will set the Client IP Address (from Server) field to the same value and send a directed (unicast) packet back to the client. However, note that this can vary from one implementation to the next, and the server might decide to override the client's requested IP address and substitute another.

4. Another possibility that occurs when using a router or other host to act as a proxy relay agent is that the Default-Gateway server field will be filled in. In this case, the server knows to use this field to send a directed (unicast) packet to the router or other device that is relaying the message, instead of trying to broadcast or send the packet directly to the client using the client's address.

In step 2, even though the client might be capable of determining what it thinks its own IP address should be—by saving it to a disk file in the case of a workstation that does have that capability, for example—the server can choose to return a different IP address to the client. In that case, the client should stop using its previous IP address and accept the new one from the server. There is some disagreement in the literature about this, and you might find that it varies from one implementation to another. For example, some vendors allow the client to specify the address it wants to use, ignoring the one supplied by the server. In this type of situation, the client usually is using the BOOTP server to obtain other configuration information, such as a boot filename or vendor-specific items, when it already knows what its own IP address should be.

BOOTP Vendor-Specific Information Options

In addition to supplying a network node with an IP address and a boot filename (and the server from which the file can be retrieved), 64 bytes are reserved in the BOOTP Reply/Request packet that can be used to supply additional configuration information to the client. The options fields also can be used by the client to request certain information from the server.

The options used by BOOTP are a subset of those now incorporated into DHCP. Those listed in this section apply, therefore, to both BOOTP and DHCP. These options are defined (and discussed in greater detail) in RFC 2132, "DHCP Options and BOOTP Vendor Extensions."

The format for data in the options field is standard:

- **Option Code**—This one-byte field contains a code that identifies the particular option. The value of zero is used for padding and the value of 255 is used as an end marker. Note that Option Code values from 128 to 254 are reserved for site-specific options.

- **Length Octet**—This one-byte value specifies the length of the option data to follow. This length *does not* include the Option Code or the Length Octets.

- **Variable-length optional configuration data**—This data depends on what kind of information the option supplies.

As noted earlier, the value of 255 marks the end of an options list in the packet.

RFC 2132 defines a large number of options that can be used. Table 23.1 lists those that apply to both BOOTP and DHCP.

Table 23.1 Definition of BOOTP Vendor Extension Opcodes

Opcode	Name	Description
0	Pad	Used to align following entries on a word boundary.
255	End	Marks end of options.
1	Subnet Mask	Subnet mask for client to use.
2	Time Offset	UTC time offset value.
3	Router	List of IP address of routers on the client's subnet.
4	Time Server	List of time servers.
5	Name Server	List of IEN 116 name servers.
6	Domain Name Server	List of DNS servers (RFC 1035).
7	Log Server	List of MIT-LCS UDP log servers.
8	Cookie Server	List of cookie servers (RFC 865).
9	LPR Server	List of LPR printers (RFC 1179).
10	Impress Server	List of Imagen Impress servers.
11	Resource Location Server	List of resource location servers (RFC 887).
12	Host Name	Client's host name.
13	Boot File Size	Size in 512-byte blocks of the default boot image file for the client.
14	Merit Dump File	Path of file that client can use for a memory dump.
15	Domain Name	Name of DNS domain of client.
16	Swap Server	IP address of client's swap server.
17	Root Path	Pathname for client's root disk.
18	Extensions Path	Specifies a file that contains information similar to this vendor-specific informtion area.
19	IP Forwarding	0 = Disable IP forwarding, 1 = enable IP forwarding on client.
20	Non-Local Source Routing	0 = Disallow forwarding, 1 = allow forwarding of nonlocal source-routed datagrams.
21	Policy Filter	A list of IP addresses and subnet masks to use to filter incoming source routes.
22	Maximum Datagram Reassembly Size	The maximum size datagram that the client should be able to reassemble.
23	Default IP TTL	Default value client should set the TTL field for in outgoing datagrams.
24	Path MTU Aging Timeout	Seconds to use when aging path MTU values (as discovered via RFC 1191).
25	Path MTU Plateau Table	Table of sizes to use for path MTU discovery (RFC 1191).
26	Interface MTU	MTU for this interface (per interface).
27	All Subnets	0 = Subnets can have smaller MTU, 1 = Subnets have same MTU.
28	Broadcast Address	Broadcast address for client to use.
29	Perform Mask Discovery	0 = Do not perform mask discovery, 1 = Perform mask discovery using ICMP.
30	Mask Supplier	0 = Client should not respond to subnet mask request using ICMP, 1 = Client should respond.

Table 23.1   Definition of BOOTP Vendor Extension Opcodes

Opcode	Name	Description
31	Perform Router Discovery	0 = Do not use router discovery, 1 = Use router discovery (RFC 1256).
32	Router Solicitation Address	Address for router solicitation requests.
33	Static Route	List of static routes (destination address + router address) to be inserted into client's routing cache.
34	Trailer Encapsulation	0 = Do not use trailers, 1 = Attempt to use trailers.
35	ARP Cache Timeout	Seconds for ARP cache timeout.
36	Ethernet Encapsulation	0 = Use Ethernet Version 2 (RFC 894), 1 = Use IEEE 802.3 (RFC 1042).
37	TCP Default TTL	Default TTL for client to use when sending out TCP segments.
38	TCP Keepalive Interval	Seconds to wait before sending TCP keepalive messages. Zero in indicates no messages to be sent, unless requested by application.
39	TCP Keepalive Garbage	0 = Do not send octet of garbage for compatibility with older versions, 1 = Send garbage octet.
40	NIS Service Domain	Network information service (NIS) domain of client.
41	NIS Servers	List of IP address of NIS servers.
42	NTP Servers	List of IP addresses of NTP time servers.
43	Vendor Specific Information	Vendor-specific information, as defined by vendor.
44	NetBIOS over TCP/IP Name Server	List of NBNS servers (RFC 1001/1002).
45	NetBIOS over TCP/IP Datagram Distribution Server	List of NBDD servers (RFC 1001/1002).
46	NetBIOS over TCP/IP Node Type	NetBIOS node type (RFC 1001/1002).
47	NetBIOS over TCP/IP Scope	NBT Scope parameter (RFC 1001/1002).
48	X Window System Font Server	List of X Window System Font servers.
49	X Window System Display Manager	List of IP addresses of systems running the X Window System Display Manager.
64	NIS+ Domain	Name of NIS+ domain.
65	NIS+ Server	List of IP addresses of NIS+ servers.
68	Mobile IP Home Agent	IP addresses of mobile IP home agents.
69	SMTP Server	List of Simple Mail Transport Protocol (SMTP) servers.
70	POP3 Server	List of POP3 servers.
71	NNTP Server	List of Network News Transport Protocol (NNTP) servers.
72	Default WWW server	List of WWW servers.
73	Default Finger Server	List of Finger servers.
74	Default IRC Server	List of default Internet Relay Chat (IRC) servers.
75	StreetTalk Server	List of StreetTalk servers.
76	StreetTalk Directory Assistance	List of STDA servers.

Downloading an Operating System

After a client has obtained the data needed to configure itself for network access, it can use the boot file information supplied by the BOOTP server to locate and download an operating system. The BOOTP protocol only gives the name and path that can be used to locate the file. BOOTP does not perform any other functions to assist the client in obtaining a copy of the file. Instead, the client uses the Trivial File Transfer Protocol (TFTP) to retrieve the file.

◀◀ The Trivial File Transfer Protocol (TFTP) is discussed more fully in Chapter 21, "TCP/IP Services and Applications."

TFTP, like BOOTP, is a simple protocol to implement, making it easy to create client code that can be stored on a chip. There is no exchange of authentication information, such as a username and password, between the client and TFTP server. Instead, the client simply requests a copy of the file and it is sent to the client on a packet-by-packet basis, with the client acknowledging each packet. This start-stop, single-packet exchange method is slower than that which could be accomplished using TCP, but it is not intended for everyday file transfers. TFTP is more than adequate for downloading operating system code during the boot process.

After the file has been downloaded to the client, it is executed and the client boots to become a full-fledged member of the network.

Taking BOOTP One Step Further: DHCP

Even though diskless workstations are a small percentage of the total number of network nodes in the world today, the concept of receiving configuration information from a central server has not gone away. The Dynamic Host Configuration Protocol (DHCP) was developed after BOOTP as a means for not only providing a workstation (or any other network device) with basic configuration information, but also with a lot of other configuration information, including the capability to add vendor-specific items to the networked computer. DHCP is an extension of the BOOTP protocol, and the relevant RFCs require that a DHCP server be backward compatible with BOOTP clients. This means that you can use a DHCP server on a network that contains newer clients that understand this protocol, as well as older clients that still use BOOTP. Like BOOTP, DHCP also uses UDP. Messages are sent to port 67 on the DHCP server. Messages from the server are sent to the DHCP client's UDP port 68.

Note

The Dynamic Host Configuration Protocol (DHCP) is discussed in several RFCs. RFC 1541, "Dynamic Host Configuration Protocol," was an early document, and RFC 2131, also titled "Dynamic Host Configuration Protocol," further clarified the protocol. RFC 2131 added a new message type ("DHCPINFORM"), extended the classing mechanism to include vendor-specific classes and removed the requirement for a minimum lease time. In addition, RFC 1533, "DHCP Options and BOOTP Vendor Extensions," provides for a variety of options to be included in either BOOTP or DHCP packets. RFC 1533 was updated by RFC 2132, which has the same title.

DHCP supports a variety of configuration message options that a server can offer as a resource to a booting network node. This includes all the standard IP configuration information, such as IP address, subnet mask, default gateway, and so on. The original BOOTP did not include all the options that were listed earlier in this chapter in Table 23.1. BOOTP (and DHCP as well) has been augmented over the years to allow for more flexibility and to allow for a larger exchange of configuration data between the client and server. RFC 1533, "DHCP Options and BOOTP Vendor Extensions," added to the options that were first described in RFC 1497 and includes options for both BOOTP and DHCP. RFC 2132 superceded RFC 1533 (and kept the same title) and added even more options.

Note

If you want to find out about late-breaking developments with regards to DHCP, you might want to look at the Web site `www.dhcp.org`. This unofficial site contains links to recent developments, as well as links to the RFC documents that relate to DHCP.

Unix users also can use another Web site to download a free version of DHCP. The Internet Software Consortium has developed reference model implementations of DHCP and DNS (BIND) that you can compile on your local system. Visit the consortium's Web site at `www.isc.org`. This site also sponsors an e-mail mailing list for DHCP topics. You can subscribe or unsubscribe from the main page.

RFC 2131 provides for three different mechanisms that DHCP servers can use to provide addressing information to clients:

- **Automatic allocation**—DHCP simply assigns a client a permanent address.
- **Dynamic allocation**—The most widely used mechanism. This method leases the address to the client for a certain amount of time, or until the client wants to abandon the lease (that is, the workstation shuts down).
- **Manual allocation**—Typically used by the administrator to manually enter addresses into the DHCP server's database for computers or other devices.

The dynamic method is the most useful in a network consisting of a large number of client computers that do not require a static address assignment. Using the dynamic method, the administrator can set the time limit for leases. Before the lease expires, the client will attempt to contact the server to renew the lease. If that fails, the client will seek out another server from which it can obtain an IP address lease. This mechanism allows for IP addresses to be conserved when the network topology changes frequently. If an address is not being used because a workstation is down or has been moved to another subnet, the lease will eventually expire and the address can be reused.

These three methods are not exclusive. For example, for most situations it is easy to configure a desktop client to obtain network configuration information automatically using DHCP and then simply boot the client. Yet, for servers that need a static address, such as file/print servers or Web servers, the administrator can place a manual entry in the server's database, so that the DHCP server will always provide the same address when the server boots. Alternatively, it's still perfectly okay to configure the server manually with static information and then mark the address as allocated (or reserved) on the DHCP server so that it won't try to use the address.

Note

A lease from a DHCP server is not as transient as it might seem at first. For example, when a client shuts down for a short period of time and then reboots, it is not automatically assigned a different IP address than it acquired during its previous lease. Instead, most DHCP servers keep track of IP addresses and the lease time. When a client reboots, it will be reassigned the same IP address as long as no other client is using the address. Likewise, when the DHCP server itself is rebooted, all information should be retained in its database so that on reboot, it will be able to continue to track existing leases or issue new ones.

However, keep in mind that if you move the client computer to a subnet that is served by a different DHCP server, the computer will be assigned an address from the pool of addresses available to that server, and will thus obtain a new address that is valid on that particular subnet.

The DHCP Packet Format and Additional Options

Similar to BOOTP, DHCP uses a request/reply mechanism, and the packet format is almost the same for both, to provide for backward compatibility. The layout of the packet used by DHCP looks very much like the layout of the BOOTP packet, with a few exceptions. The first 11 fields are the same. However, the last field, which is called the Vendor Extensions area in the BOOTP packet, is called the Options field in the DHCP packet. The format of the options is the same as it was for BOOTP. However, some of the options that are defined in RFC 2132 are specific only to DHCP. The options available for use with BOOTP clients are a subset of those available for use with DHCP clients. Although this field was limited to 64 bytes in the BOOTP packet, it now is a variable-length field that has a minimum of 312 bytes for DHCP options.

Additional Options Available for DHCP Servers

Following is a listing of the options that can be used for both types of clients. This list includes additional options defined in RFC 2132 that can be used, in addition to those found in Table 23.1, with DHCP servers and clients. The options listed here are not for use with BOOTP clients.

- **Requested IP Address (Opcode=50)**—The client can use this field to request a specific IP address.

- **IP Address Lease Time (Opcode=51)**—The client can use this field to request a particular lease time. The server can use this field to fill in the lease time it is willing to offer. The value used in this field is expressed in seconds.

- **Option Overload (Opcode=52)**—This option enables the server to use the fields originally allocated in the DHCP packet for the server name and filename fields to store options. This can be done when there are a large number of options to convey to the client. A value of 1 flags the filename field as holding options. A value of 2 flags the server name field as holding options. A value of 3 indicates that both fields hold options.

- **TFTP Server Name (Opcode=66)**—This field is used to specify the TFTP server when Option Overloading has used the field previously reserved for this.

- **Bootfile Name (Opcode=67)**—This field is used to identify the boot filename when Option Overloading has used the field previously reserved for this.

- **Server Identifier (Opcode=54)**—DHCP servers use this field so that clients can distinguish between multiple DHCP servers answering a request. Clients then will use this address when they need to send unicast messages to the server chosen from the offers received. DHCP clients also use this option when they accept an offer from a server. The value for Server Identifier is simply the IP address of the server.

- **Parameter Request List (Opcode=55)**—This option enables the client to request certain configuration values. A list of option codes follows this option.

- **Message (Opcode=56)**—The DHCP server uses this field to send an error message to the client, including it in the DHCPNAK message. The client can also use this field to specify a reason why it has declined to use certain parameters offered by the server. The client uses the DHCPDECLINE message type for this. Both of these message types will be discussed shortly.

- **Maximum DHCP Message Size (Opcode=57)**—This value is the maximum length for a DHCP message that the client can accept. It is used in the DHCPDISCOVER or DHCPREQUEST messages, described later.

- **Renewal (T1) Time Value (Opcode=58)**—This value is the number of seconds that elapse before a client holding an IP address transitions to the renewing state, at which time it will try to renew an existing IP address lease.

- **Rebinding (T2) Time Value (Opcode=59)**—This value is the number of seconds that elapse before a client holding an IP address transitions to the rebinding state.

- **Vendor Class Identifier (Opcode=60)**—This parameter can be used by clients to identify the vendor type and configuration of the client. The DHCP server should respond to this option by using Option 43 to return to the client vendor-specific information. Servers that do not support this option should ignore it.

- **Client Identifier (Opcode=61)**—Clients can use this to specify a unique identifier. The server can use this value to search its database for addressing information for the client. The identifiers chosen by administrators should be unique on the subnet.

Remember that two option values don't have a data component. These are option zero (Pad option) and option 255, which marks the end of the options list.

Option Overloading

When the Options Overload option is used in addition to the variable-length option field that is typically used for options, two other fields can be used to store options. This can be useful when a client or server has a maximum size for the total DHCP packet that is not large enough to store all the options the client/server needs to negotiate.

The Options Overload option data field can be either 1, 2, or 3. As explained earlier, a value of 1 means that the server name field (sname) contains options. A value of 2 means that the boot filename field (file) contains options. A value of 3 means that both fields contain options.

In this case, other options can be used to store the values that are normally placed into these fields, if necessary. The following must also be done:

- The actual options field must still be terminated with the 255 end option field. The Pad option (zero) can be used to pad the options field.

- An option cannot be split across the options field, the sname field, or the file field. Each option tag and its value must be contained in the same field in the packet.

- The order of precedence for interpreting options is to read them first from the options field, then the sname field, and then the file field (depending on whether the Options Overload field is set to 1, 2, or 3).

- Some options can be used more than once in a packet, and if so, are concatenated by the client.

The DHCP Client/Server Exchange

Although based on the simple BOOTP protocol, the DHCP protocol client/server exchange is a little more complicated. Both sides communicate using a set of messages. These are

- **DHCPDISCOVER**—The client broadcasts this message to locate DHCP servers.

- **DHCPOFFER**—The server uses this message type to offer a set of configuration parameters to the client.

- **DHCPREQUEST**—A client can use this message type to explicitly accept an offer from one server while implicitly implying that it is not going to use the offers made by other servers. This message type also can be used to confirm the configuration data when the client reboots or when it is attempting to extend a lease.

- **DHCPACK**—The client sends this acknowledgment to the server, including the configuration parameters that were accepted.

- **DHCPNAK**—The server sends this negative acknowledgment to the client to inform the client that the address it has requested is not correct. For example, when a client is moved to a new subnet and attempts to renew an old IP address, the server can use this message to inform it that it needs a different one.

- **DHCPDECLINE**—The client can send this message to a server to indicate that a particular IP address is already in use.

- **DHCPRELEASE**—The client can give up an IP address and use this message to tell the server that the address can be recycled.

- **DHCPINFORM**—The client can use this message to request local configuration information from the server when the client has already been configured with an IP address by some other means.

The order in which these messages are exchanged appears in Figure 23.1.

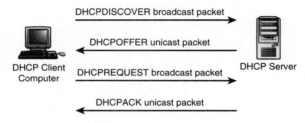

Figure 23.1 The DHCP client/server message exchange is a simple process.

Requesting Configuration Information from the DHCP Server

The communication process between the DHCP client and server is simple. The client initially broadcasts a DHCPDISCOVER message on the local subnet to which it is attached. If known, the client can insert configuration options in this discover packet, such as the IP address and a requested lease time.

All DHCP servers that receive the DHCPDISCOVER request can respond with a DHCPOFFER message, including a suggested IP address and any other options it can offer. Because more than one server can respond to a DHCP request (remember that DHCP packets can be relayed across routers using BOOTP relay agents), it then must decide which offer to accept.

Note that in Figure 23.1 the DHCPOFFER packet is sent as a unicast packet instead of a broadcast packet. The DHCP server can unicast or broadcast messages, which is determined as follows:

- If the Gateway IP Address (giaddr) field in the client's packet is a nonzero value, the server will assume this is the address of an intermediary router and will unicast the packet to this address, using the DHCP server port (67).

- If the Gateway IP Address field is zero but the Client's IP Address (ciaddr) field is not, the server unicasts the packet to this address that the client has filled in.

- If both of these fields are zero and the broadcast flag bit is set in the client's packet, the server will broadcast the packet to the client.

- If both of these fields are zero and the broadcast flag bit is not set, the server will unicast the packet to the client's hardware address and the Client's IP Address (yiaddr) field.

When a selection has been made, the client then broadcasts another packet that contains a DHCPRE-QUEST message. This packet must include the server identification option, indicating from which server the client has chosen to accept the offer.

When the servers see this broadcast packet, those not chosen by the client use it as a flag that their offer was not accepted, and no further communications need to take place between the client and these servers. The chosen server binds the client to the addressing configuration information, and then sends the client a DHCKACK acknowledgment message. This packet also contains the set of agreed-upon options and parameters. If the server cannot grant the request—the IP address requested by the client is already in use, for example—the server will respond with a DHCKNAK negative acknowledgment message.

After the client receives an acknowledgment packet indicating that it can use the configuration information, it still must perform some checks to be sure that the information is correct and will allow the client to function on the network. A few simple checks are performed. For example, the client can use ARP to check that the IP address it is about to use is not already in use on the network. This can happen when a DHCP server has been configured incorrectly. If there are no challenges, the client has the information it needs and the configuration of its protocol stack is performed. The client now can participate in the network.

◀◀   The Address Resolution Protocol (ARP) is covered in more detail in Chapter 20, "Overview of the TCP/IP Protocol Suite."

If this last-minute test informs the client that the address is already in use, the client sends the DHCP server a DHCPDECLINE message. In this case, or if the client has received a DHCPNAK message from the server, the process backs off for a few seconds and begins again.

If the client does not receive either the DHCPACK or DHCPNAK message within a set amount of time, it also will restart the configuration process.

Implicitly Releasing Configuration Information

In a DHCP environment, configuration information usually is granted for a set amount of time, called a *lease*. When the lease expires and the client has made no attempt to renew it, the configuration information can be used for another client. This can happen if a computer is moved from one subnet to another. Eventually, the original address it had obtained on the previous subnet will expire.

A client also can choose to implicitly release the addressing information. For example, a client that is gracefully shutting down can send a DHCPRELEASE message to the DHCP server, telling it that the lease is no longer needed.

The `ipconfig` command can be used by Windows NT/2000 clients to release or renew a lease obtained from a DHCP server. To release an address lease, use the following syntax:

```
ipconfig /release
```

If more than one network adapter is installed in the system, you can also specify the name of the adapter on the command line. This command releases the bindings obtained from DHCP servers for all adapters. If you are unsure of the adapter name, use the following command to display the current IP configuration for your computer:

```
ipconfig /all | more
```

The `ifconfig` command can be used on Unix systems to perform configuration tasks related to IP. The syntax of this command varies from one implementation of Unix to another. However, this command on a Unix system performs a wider variety of tasks than the Windows `ipconfig` command, so use caution when using `ifconfig`. This `ifconfig` command can be used to configure each network interface on the Unix system, including address, subnet mask, and other important parameters. A general version of the command to release an IP address leased from a DHCP server is

```
/sbin/ifconfig interface release
```

Note that not all versions of Unix use the `ifconfig` command to manage DHCP, either the server or the client. As always with Unix, check the printed documentation and the manual (man) pages.

Linux users should consult the Linux How To documents to determine the correct way to install, configure, and manage DHCP server and client software. A recent copy of the DHCP mini-HOW TO document that covers Linux distributions from Slackware's version to RedHat, Mandrake, and others, can be found at www.oswg.org/oswg-nightly/DHCP.html.

Reusing an Address After Reboot

When a client is rebooted, it does not have to obtain a new IP address. Instead, it can request that the address assignment made from a previous exchange with a DHCP server be used. In this case, when the client reboots, it broadcasts a DHCPREQUEST packet that contains the requested IP address option. Servers that know about this configuration information should respond with a DHCPACK message to the client. However, if the information is invalid—the client is now on a new subnet, for example—the servers should respond with a DHCPNAK message to force the client into beginning the lease process again.

The client also makes its own checks, again using ARP to find out whether the address is in use by another client. If so, it sends a DHCPDECLINE message back to the server and starts the process over.

Using the DHCPINFORM Message

It is quite acceptable for the network administrator to configure some of the IP configuration information on a client and then let DHCP be used for the remaining data. For example, a client can be manually configured with an IP address and subnet mask by the administrator, and then set to get the remaining information from a DHCP server. In this case, the client will broadcast a DHCPINFORM packet that contains the manually configured information. The server then responds to this message with a DHCPACK message. However, the server should not fill in the fields telling the client what its IP address should be and should not include any lease time values. Additionally, the server should not check its own database to see whether a binding for this address already exists.

Because the DHCP server knows the client's address, the DHCPACK message is sent as a unicast packet instead of a broadcast one.

Lease Expiration and Renewal

If a client is using a lease and the lease time expires, the client must immediately stop using the IP address granted by the lease. There are two timers that the client uses to keep track of when and how to renew a lease. These are called T1 and T2. After the time value specified by T1 expires, the client will begin trying to renew the existing lease. The client makes attempts to contact the DHCP server from which the lease was obtained to get this extension. At this point, the client is said to be in the RENEWING state.

If no response is received from the DHCP server when the time stored in T2 has expired, the client will enter a REBINDING state and will attempt to communicate with any other DHCP server so that it can obtain a new IP address.

Obviously, T1 is a value that is less than the lease time, because a lease must be renewed before it expires. The value for T2, likewise, must be longer than that for T1.

If a client is unable to renew or acquire a lease before the expiration of the current lease, the client must stop using the information acquired through the lease and enter into an INIT state to start the process of acquiring configuration information all over again.

After a client has successfully renewed a lease or acquired a new one, it is said to be in the BOUND state. This is the normal state at which configuration is complete and the client computer is functional on the network.

In addition, an administrator usually can renew a release manually. The Windows command `ipconfig` can be used for this:

```
ipconfig /renew
```

Similar to the `/release` option, you optionally can place an adapter name on the command line to specify an adapter for this operation. If none is specified and more than one adapter is installed and configured using DHCP, all adapters will undergo the renew process.

Overview of How a DHCP Server Chooses the Client's IP Address

RFC 2131 summarizes the process that a DHCP server goes through to decide what IP address to return to a client. These steps are

1. Use the client's current address as recorded in the client's current address binding, or
2. Use the client's previous address recorded in a previous binding that has already expired or has been released, as long as it's not already in use, or
3. Use the address found in the Requested IP Address option if specified and if not already in use, or
4. Use a new address from the pool of available addresses.

In the last case, an address is selected to match the client's subnet or the subnet of the relay agent that forwarded the DHCP request.

An Example: Installing and Configuring a DHCP Server on Windows 2000

Installing a DHCP server on a Windows 2000 Server is just as simple as most application installs. However, you'll need to have some information ready before you begin the installation. You will need to know the range of addresses that the server will administer and lease to clients. If you have any servers on the network that need static addresses, you'll need to know those if they fall within the scope of the DHCP managed addresses. For example, DNS and WINS servers must have static IP addresses, and most DHCP servers do also. In a large network, you also should consider using multiple DHCP servers and enabling routers so that they can forward DHCP packets.

Note

Most DHCP servers require that the server on which they run have one or more static IP addresses. This address, along with other information, is used to keep track of leases the server grants to clients on the network. However, some routers now provide DHCP functionality along with routing services. In Chapter 19, "Dedicated Connections," we'll look at small office/home office (SOHO) devices that can be used to connect a small LAN to a broadband cable or DSL modem. These "routers" act as both DHCP clients and DHCP servers. For a small office where all you need is Internet access and don't need a permanent IP address for a domain name, this kind of router is a good connectivity solution.

Installing the DHCP Server Service on a Windows 2000 Server

From the Control Panel, select Network and Dial-Up Connections, and then select Add Network Components. A wizard pops up and prompts you through the process of selecting and installing the DHCP service. In Figure 23.2 you can see the first dialog box of the wizard. The Networking Services component has been highlighted. Alternatively, you can click the Add/Remove Programs icon in the Control Panel, then click Add/Remove Windows Components, and then the Components button.

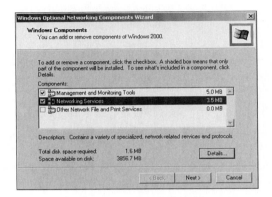

Figure 23.2   A wizard guides you through the process of installing the DHCP service.

In Figure 23.2 the check box has been selected for Networking Services, but the check box shown in this figure has a gray background instead of a white one. This means that some of the network service components have been installed, but not all of them. After you highlight Networking Services, click the Details button to see the list of services available for installation. Select Dynamic Host Configuration Protocol (DHCP) from the list, and then click OK. To continue the installation, click the Next button.

The wizard copies the files needed for the DHCP service to their respective directories and adds the DHCP management interface program to the Administrative Tools menu. When the wizard has completed the installation, click Finish. You won't have to restart the computer to begin configuring the DHCP server.

Tip

You can check to see that the DHCP service, and other services, are running by using the Component Services administrative tool. From the MMC tree, select Services (local) to view the services running on the local server. In the list of services that show up in the right pane of the MMC console, look for DHCP Server. Its status should be "started."

Before the server can begin managing IP addresses on the network, you will have to authorize the server in the Active Directory and then configure a *scope* of addresses that the server can administer.

Authorizing the Server

The DHCP manager snap-in for the Microsoft Management Console utility is used to manage the DHCP service on the Windows server. To start the MMC utility, click Start, Programs, Administrative Tools, DHCP. The MMC utility pops up with the DHCP Management snap-in ready for you to use, as shown in Figure 23.3.

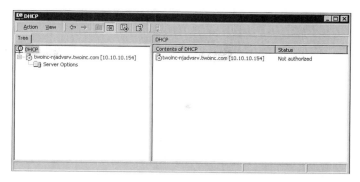

Figure 23.3   The MMC DHCP snap-in is used to manage the DHCP service on the Windows 2000 Server.

On the left side of the management console is a tree structure that can be used to manage one or more DHCP servers from a central location. Note that the two items under the DHCP object are the DHCP server identified as twoinc-njadvsrv.com (with an address of 10.10.10.154). Click on the new server once and under it you'll see the Server Options folder for this particular DHCP server.

After you click on the server, you'll notice that the icon to the left of the server name will change and a red arrow (pointing downward) will appear on top of the icon. This is a reminder that this server has not yet been authorized in the Active Directory. Windows 2000 DHCP servers perform a process called *rogue server detection*. When a Windows 2000 server boots and the DHCP service is started, it sends out a DHCPINFORM packet. Other DHCP servers, if any are configured on the network, reply with the DHCPACK message. Next, the service checks to see whether it is registered in the Active Directory. If it is not, it will not begin answering client requests. Figure 23.4 shows an example of the event log entry that the server makes when this occurs.

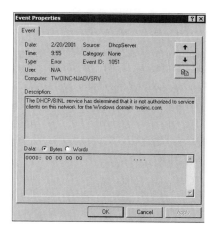

Figure 23.4   The DHCP server will log an error in the system event log file if it is not authorized to run on your network.

The DHCP server undergoes this rogue server detection process once each hour. Thus, each DHCP server can keep track of other authorized DHCP servers on the network.

Authorizing a server is simple:

1. Log on to the server using an administrator-level account.
2. Run the DHCP MMC snap-in by selecting it from the Administrative Tools folder.
3. Click once on the server you want to administer.
4. From the Action menu, select Authorize. It might take up to a minute or two before the process completes.

Use the Refresh option from the Action menu to determine when the process has finished. The red arrow is replaced with a green arrow pointing upward.

Using the MMC Action Menu

To configure a server, click once to highlight it, and then click the Action menu. The Action menu allows you to perform the following tasks if you select a particular DHCP server object:

- **Display Statistics**—This shows statistical information about the selected server, such as the time the server started, the number of requests and offers and the number (and percentage) of addresses in use, among other things.

- **New Scope**—Create a new scope of IP addresses that the server can offer to clients. After the server is authorized in the Active Directory, this will be the first action you take to set up an address space the DHCP server can use.

- **New Multicast Scope**—Use this to set up a group of IP multicast addresses that can be distributed to computers on the network. You can use this to define multicast scopes for selected network computers.

- **Reconcile All Scopes**—This menu option compares information in the DHCP database about address scopes with that stored in the Registry, and reconciles any differences. Although it's not a substitute for better disaster recovery operations (such as making backups), this can be used to recover a DHCP server and be sure that the scope of addresses it is allowed to use is valid.

- **Authorize/Unauthorize**—As explained in the previous section, this action item allows you to authorize a server to function on the network by registering it in the Active Directory. This option is presented as Unauthorize if you've highlighted a server that is already authorized.

- **Define User Classes**—Create classes of options. Clients can be assigned to a class to gain access to options not defined by their scope.

- **Define Vendor Classes**—Enables you to create vendor-specific option classes.

- **Set Predefined Options**—Enables you to set up predefined option classes. These include DHCP standard options (as defined in the RFCs), Microsoft options, Microsoft Windows 2000 options, and Microsoft Windows 98 options.

- **All Tasks**—Stop/Start/Pause/Resume/Restart.

- **Delete**—Deletes the selected entry in the MMC console tree.

- **Refresh**—Refreshes the current display.

- **Properties**—Brings up the properties page for the selected entry.

When you first install the service, the first thing you need to do is create a scope of IP addresses that the DHCP server can use to allocate leases to its clients. After that, other options in the Action menu can be used to further configure the server.

Creating an Address Scope

After you have authorized a server on the network, you can create a scope of addresses that the DHCP server can administer to clients. From the MMC utility, click once on the server you want to administer, and then select New Scope from the Action menu. The New Scope Wizard pops up. Alternatively, you can right-click the server and select New Scope. Click Next to dismiss the introductory dialog box and continue creating an address scope. The wizard then prompts you through the following steps:

1. A dialog box pops up that you can use to give the scope a name and description. The description is optional, but you must at least supply a name for the scope so it can be differentiated from other scopes you might create. Enter the name and, if you want, a description and click Next.

2. The next dialog box, shown in Figure 23.5, prompts you to enter the range of IP addresses for this scope. Enter a starting address and an ending address. You also should enter a subnet mask associated with this address range. The subnet mask can be entered in the traditional way using dotted-decimal notation, or you can specify the mask by indicating the number of bits in the Length field (as in CIDR notation). When finished, click Next.

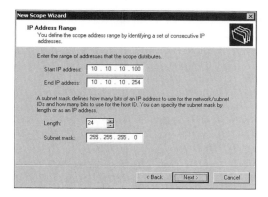

Figure 23.5   The wizard prompts you to enter the address range and specify the subnet mask for the scope.

3. The next dialog box (shown in Figure 23.6) enables you to specify any addresses that fall within the range you have entered that you want to exclude from the scope. You can enter a single address and click the Add button, or you can enter a range of addresses (starting and ending addresses) and click the Add button. If you change your mind about an address, highlight it, and click the Remove button. When finished adding addresses to be excluded, click Next. You should exclude the DHCP server's own address if it falls within the range of addresses you defined in the previous step.

4. Next, you are prompted to enter the amount of time to lease the addresses in this scope. In Figure 23.7 you can see that this dialog box defaults to 8 days. As it suggests, you should consider creating scopes that have lease values relevant to your network. For example, mobile computers that frequently move from one place to another can be given a shorter lease time, thus keeping your address pool from becoming populated by unexpired, unused leases. This dialog box also enables you to specify the lease in hours, minutes, and seconds.

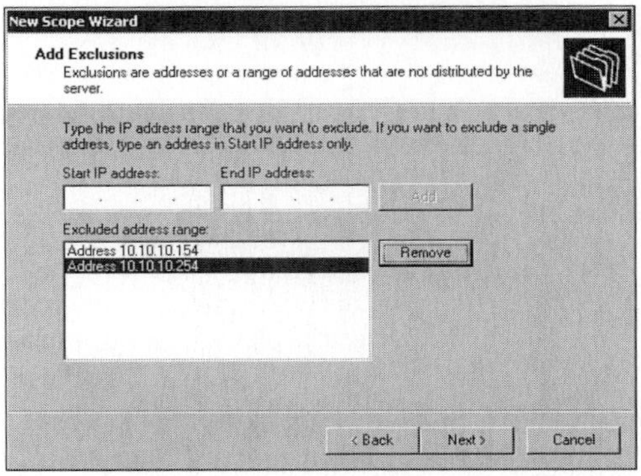

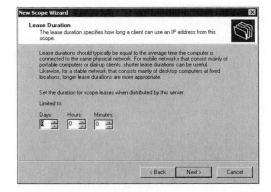

Figure 23.6 Enter the address range to be excluded from use by the DHCP server, and an appropriate subnet mask for the address range.

Figure 23.7 This dialog box enables you to customize the lease period for this scope of addresses.

5. As discussed earlier in this chapter, the DHCP packet can contain a variety of options. The dialog box shown in Figure 23.8 prompts you to enter options valid for this scope or to put it off until another time. For this example, go ahead and configure the options. Leave the Yes, I Want to Configure These Options Now radio button selected, and click Next.

6. The first option, shown in Figure 23.9, prompts you to enter the default gateway for the subnet covered by this range of addresses. Enter one or more IP addresses for the routers you want to use, clicking the Add button to add each one. Note that here you are entering the default gateway to which clients will send IP datagrams when the destination is not on the local subnet. This is *not* the gateway computer discussed earlier in this chapter that serves as a BOOTP or DHCP relay agent. Again, if you change your mind you can highlight any router address and click the Remove button to delete it from this list. Click Next when you have finished adding routers.

7. Next, a dialog box prompts you to enter the parent name of your network. This is the name of the domain that client computers are configured to use for DNS name resolution. In Figure 23.10 you can see that you also can enter the names or addresses of domain name servers the client is configured to use. If you enter a server name, click Resolve to have the wizard look up the address, or enter an address and click Add to add it to the list. Use the Remove button if you change your mind. Place the order of DNS servers in the same order you want clients to

access them. You can highlight a server in the list, and use the Up and Down buttons to change the order.

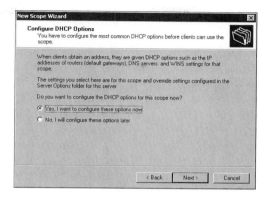

Figure 23.8 You can set up options for this scope now or later.

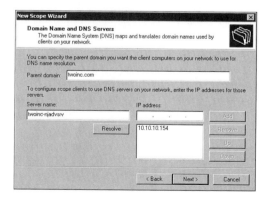

Figure 23.9 Enter one or more routers that will operate as default gateways for the LAN segment served by this scope of IP addresses.

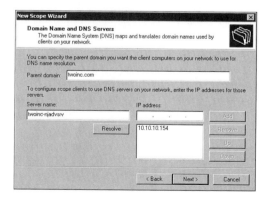

Figure 23.10 Enter the client computer's domain name and then the domain name servers for the domain.

8. If you still are using Microsoft's Windows Internet Naming Service (WINS), you can use the next dialog box, shown in Figure 23.11, to enter the names or addresses of the WINS servers. If you enter the name, use the Resolve button again to have the server translate the WINS server's name to an IP address.

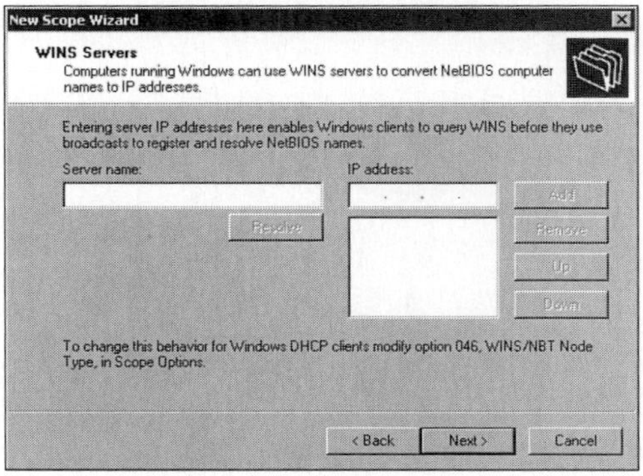

Figure 23.11 Enter the name or IP address of each WINS server that clients can use.

9. Finally, a dialog box asks whether you want to activate the scope now or later (see Figure 23.12). The server does not begin allocating addresses in the scope to clients until the scope is activated. After making your choice, click Next. A final dialog box notifies you that the wizard is finished creating the scope. Click the Finish button.

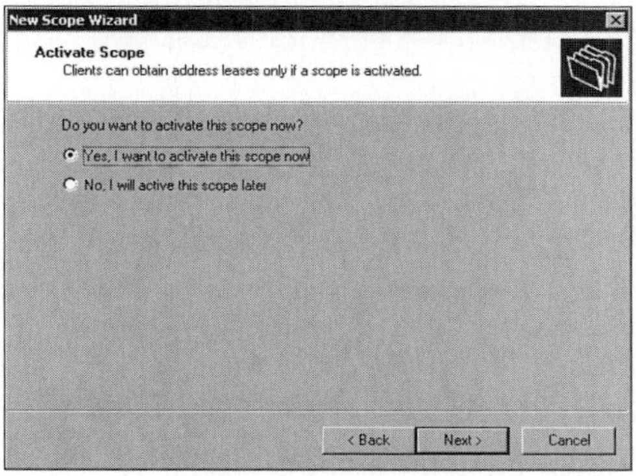

Figure 23.12 You can choose to activate the scope after you create it or do so at a later time.

If you did not choose to activate the scope, you can do so later by right-clicking on the scope and selecting Activate. Alternatively, click once on the scope and select Activate from the Action menu.

In Figure 23.13 you can see the DHCP MMC snap-in after a scope has been created and activated.

The Status field in this display tells you whether the scope is active, and the Description field can be useful when you create multiple scopes and need a reminder of their use. After the scope has been activated, clients that boot on the network and that have been configured to use a DHCP server can now receive configuration information from this DHCP server. If you expand the scope by clicking on the plus sign in the left pane, you can see that there are four other objects that can be managed. Figure 23.14 shows the new scope with the Address Pool object selected.

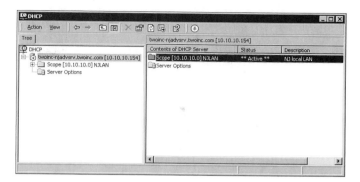

Figure 23.13 The new scope shows up in the right pane of the DHCP MMC snap-in utility.

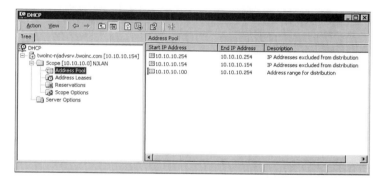

Figure 23.14 You can manage addresses, leases, reservations, and options offered by the scope using the DHCP MMC snap-in.

You can click on any of the other objects to see information. For example, if you want to see what options are enabled in this scope, click Scope Options. The option number (from the RFCs), name, and the values for the options are displayed. In the case of this initial setup using the wizard, you would see options for the default router (gateway), DNS server, and domain name. If you entered an address for a WINS server, that option would also be displayed.

Reserving a Client Address

You can choose to exclude certain addresses from a scope that you know are configured manually, such as routers. However, you might want to use the Reservation method to reserve an address for a DHCP client that might need to keep the same IP address, but obtain other information from the DHCP server at times. A DNS server is a good example of a server that should have a reserved address.

To reserve an address within a scope, expand the scope in the MMC console and open up the Reservation dialog box either by highlighting the Reservation object and selecting New Reservation from the Action menu, or by right-clicking the Reservations object and making the same selection. In Figure 23.15, you can see the simple dialog box used to create a reservation.

As discussed later in this chapter, assigning options to a reserved IP address gives the administrator the best method for fine-tuning what options the client will end up being offered by the DHCP server. Options associated with a reservation override all other options defined for the server, scope, or any option class to which the computer might belong.

Figure 23.15   You can identify specific computers that will have a reserved IP address on the DHCP server.

Configuring the DHCP Server and Scope Options

Earlier in this chapter, many options that can be used for BOOTP and DHCP clients were discussed. The Windows 2000 DHCP service enables you to configure which options will be offered to clients of the service. To configure the options, expand the MMC tree of DHCP servers to locate the server you want to manage. Click that server to get to the Options Folder for that server. After you have highlighted the Options Folder, click the Action menu.

Note

Although the RFCs support option overloading, as described earlier in this chapter, note that the Microsoft DHCP server does not support this function. Additionally, the maximum amount of bytes that are stored in the DHCP packet options field is 312 bytes.

From the Action menu, select Configure Options. In Figure 23.16, you can see the default dialog box used for configuring options. Note that this dialog box has a General and an Advanced tab. Figure 23.17 shows the Advanced tab.

Figure 23.16   You can configure the options that the server can present to clients using this dialog box.

Figure 23.17 The Advanced tab enables you to more precisely control the options that are offered to clients.

Because the server enables you to specify options for several levels, it is important to understand the precedence used to decide which options apply to a client. Options can be set for the following, and in this order:

1. The server's global options.

2. **Scope Options**—These apply to a scope the client uses. Options in this class that conflict with server global options will supercede them.

3. **Class Options**—These apply to clients that are members of the class. Options in a class will supercede server global options and class options.

4. **Reserved Client Options**—By assigning options to a particular client for which an IP address reservation has been created, you are given the finest granularity of control. Options defined for a reserved client address override all other options.

Similarly, you can configure options for a scope if you did not do so during the initial creation of the scope. You also can use these same steps to change or add options to the scope. To change the options for a scope, expand the scope and select the Scope Options folder.

Option Classes

In Figure 23.16, the list of Available Options is the list of options that are defined for the current DHCP server, and are mostly the same options you'll find in RFC 2132. Note that, although the server can offer all these options, not all Microsoft clients can use this entire set of options, which is why the wizard prompted you for only a few options when it allowed you to select options for the newly created scope.

The Advanced tab shown in Figure 23.17 enables you to look at the different classes of objects. You'll see a *vendor class* and a *user class*. Vendor classes are groupings of options that are useful for a particular vendor's client, such as Microsoft 98 or Windows NT clients. User classes are for grouping options that a particular class of users have in common; for example, BOOTP clients or Remote Access users.

If you define options for the server, the scopes you create will inherit them. A good place to start is to define the basic subset of options that all clients will need, if you have such a list, and configure these options for the server. Next, you can expand the particular scope and select the Scope Options folder to add or remove options that apply to a particular scope.

Superscopes

In the earlier example, only one scope of addresses was created on the DHCP server. The server is capable of handling additional address scopes, however, to provide for other clients that might be physically accessible to the DHCP server but use a different logical subnet address. To create a super-scope, you first must create the scopes to be included in it. Use the same procedures as before to create the new scope, specifying its address range, options, and so on. Next, select New Superscope from the Action menu. A wizard pops up and again prompts you through the process:

1. Click the Next button to dismiss the wizard's opening dialog box.

2. In the next dialog box, give your superscope a name and click Next.

3. Figure 23.18 displays the current list of scopes defined on the server. Select the scopes that will fall under this superscope. Use Shift+click and Ctrl+click to select one or more scopes from the list. Click Next.

Figure 23.18   Select the scopes to include in the superscope.

4. Finally, the wizard shows you a summary of your superscope, including the name and the names of the scopes that make it up (see Figure 23.19). Click the Finish button.

Figure 23.19   Confirm your selections before exiting the Superscope wizard.

Providing Support for BOOTP Clients

Support is provided by the Windows 2000 DHCP server. The Default BOOTP user class of options is used to configure the information that will be supplied to these clients. Although standard BOOTP servers require that the server be configured in advance with a table of client hardware addresses and corresponding IP addresses, Windows 2000 DHCP Server instead will just select the next available address to give to a BOOTP client. This matches the method used by the DHCP server when granting IP address leases to its DHCP clients.

Enabling the DHCP Relay Agent

RFC 1542, "Clarifications and Extensions for the Bootstrap Protocol," defined support for a BOOTP relay agent. That agent now is supported by almost every router. The relay agent function enables you to support clients on different subnets, using a single BOOTP or DHCP server. DHCP requests are forwarded by the router to the DHCP server, and the server's responses are returned to the client. Because BOOTP and DHCP use almost the same frame format and the same UDP ports, you'll also find that most BOOTP relay agents will perform this duty for DHCP clients.

However, on a small network, you might not have a router. Instead, you might be using the Routing and Remote Access services available in Windows 2000 Server. In that case, you'll need to add the DHCP Relay Agent protocol. Follow these steps to enable the DHCP Relay Agent:

1. Click Start, Programs, Administrative Tools, and then Routing and Remote Access.

2. In the left pane of the MMC console utility, click the plus sign to expand the server's list of objects.

3. Click the plus sign for IP Routing to expand the list of objects it contains.

4. Right-click on General and, from the menu that pops up, select New Routing Protocol.

5. In Figure 23.20, you can see the New Routing Protocol dialog box displaying a list of available protocols. Select DHCP Relay Agent, and click OK to dismiss the dialog box. The DHCP Relay Agent protocol now shows up as an object under IP Routing.

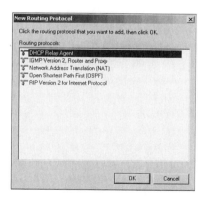

Figure 23.20   The New Routing Protocol dialog box enables you to install the DHCP Relay Agent service.

6. Right-click on this new object and select Properties. In the Properties sheet for the DHCP Relay Agent, you can add the addresses of one or more DHCP servers to which BOOTP and DHCP messages will be relayed (see Figure 23.21).

Figure 23.21 The Properties sheet for the DHCP Relay Agent is where you specify the DHCP servers that will handle requests forwarded by the relay service.

When the relay agent receives a DHCP or BOOTP broadcast message on one of its network interfaces, which it can recognize because the packet is addressed to port 67, it will forward it to a DHCP server. You can see an example of this in Figure 23.22. The DHCP server resides on Subnet 1, along with other servers. This subnet is connected to Subnet 2 using a router—or possibly a Windows 2000 server running the DHCP relay agent service.

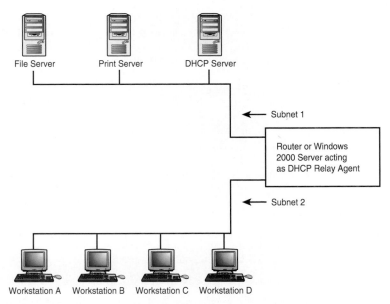

Figure 23.22 The DHCP Relay Agent can support clients on another subnet.

When Workstation A on Subnet 2 boots, it broadcasts a DHCPDISCOVER message using UDP. When the router sees this broadcast, it looks at the Gateway Address field (discussed earlier in this chapter, and not to be confused with a default gateway on a TCP/IP LAN). If the value for this field is all zeros

(0.0.0.0), the relay agent service on the router will place its own address in this field. This enables the DHCP server to reply directly to the router when it replies to the DHCP or BOOTP request.

The DHCP server looks at the Gateway Address field. It then consults its list of scopes to determine an appropriate address based on the value of the Gateway Address field and sends a DHCPOFFER packet back to the router, which then broadcasts the packet on Subnet 2. Remember that a broadcast is necessary in this case because at this time Workstation A knows its hardware address, but doesn't yet have an IP address. If the client decides to accept the address offer, it sends a DHCPREQUEST message to the server, and the server responds with a DHCPACK acknowledgement granting the workstation the lease.

What Is a DHCP Cluster?

If you are using Windows 2000 Advanced Server, you can use the clustering feature for DHCP. This allows two separate DHCP servers to be administered as a single DHCP server. Windows 2000 clustering supports a failover mode in which a service running on one computer can be monitored. If the node that is supplying a DHCP service supported by the clustering software fails, another node that runs the same service can be activated to take over for the failed node. By clustering DHCP services between two nodes, you will make the network less prone to down time due to problems with your DHCP server.

The alternative to clustering is to use two separate DHCP servers, each responsible for a portion of the address scope. This allows all your clients to get an address from one or the other server. Because leases usually are measured in days or weeks on a stable network, the loss of a single DHCP server for a few hours or a day or so might not cause you any problems unless someone decides to reboot every PC on the network. A secondary server, configured with a smaller portion of the address space, can continue to handle DHCP traffic while the main server is repaired.

In a larger network, however, where computers are frequently moved, a more stable DHCP service can be provided by hosting the DHCP service on a cluster.

Keep the following in mind when using a Windows cluster for the DHCP service:

- The DHCP service should be installed before the clustering service is installed on the computers.
- As with most cluster installs, one server should be configured first, with the DHCP service and the clustering service, while the other cluster member-to-be is powered off.
- When finished with the installation on the first member, power up the second and install the DHCP service and then the cluster service.

In addition, keep in mind that the cluster itself must have a unique IP address, which can't be delegated to it by a DHCP server. Additionally, you'll need to create a domain security group and make both servers members. To this group, assign Full Control permissions for the DNS zone object in the Active Directory where DHCP A and PTR records are stored for the servers' clients.

Using Windows clusters is the subject of many books. Before deciding to use a cluster on your network I would recommend you become intimately familiar with Windows clusters. There are many aspects of clustering (such as the utilities used to start/stop and otherwise manage the cluster) that you need to learn before you try to set DHCP and the clustering software.

Considerations for Using DHCP in Large or Routed Environments

In a large network you need to provide for redundancy for DHCP servers. Because a larger network typically is connected using routes to join a diverse set of network segments, you will need to enable

BOOTP and DHCP forwarding on any routers in the network. Each DHCP server will need to be carefully planned, and the address scopes, reservations, and exclusions will need to be carefully thought through in advance. You don't want, for example, a DHCP server to allocate an address to a client when that address should have been reserved and already is in use by another server! This is exactly the kind of thing automatic dispensing of IP addresses is supposed to solve!

Of course, when planning the placement of DHCP servers in a large, routed environment, it's easiest to place a single DHCP server on each subnet. In many cases, though, this is not practical. And with the forwarding capabilities it is not necessarily needed. Also, don't yield to the temptation of placing all your DHCP servers on the same subnet, allowing them to receive forwarded replies from other network segments. If the single subnet becomes unavailable, all your DHCP servers become unavailable. This applies to any major server. Don't place all your eggs in once basket, so to speak.

How DHCP Interacts with Microsoft's Dynamic Domain Name Service (DNS)

Microsoft's version of DNS supports dynamic updates, as specified in RFC 2136, "Dynamic Updates in the Domain Name System (DNS UPDATE)." Windows 2000 clients can send dynamic updates after having received configuration information from a DHCP server. When a DHCP lease expires, the client will send an update to deregister the addressing information.

To register with DNS, the client first contacts a name server. If the name server is just a local server and is not authoritative for the zone, it will return the address of the authoritative server to the client. The client then will contact the primary authoritative server to send it the updated addressing information. If successful, a reply is sent back to the client.

The DHCP server also can be used to send dynamic updates to DNS. This is useful for pre-Windows 2000 clients that do not understand the dynamic update process. This also can be negotiated between the DHCP server and a Windows 2000 client during the initial DHCP process. This is done using a special FQDN (fully qualified domain name) DHCPREQUEST packet (using Option number 81). This packet has three possible flags that can be set:

- **0**—This flag specifies that the client wants to be responsible for updating the A resource record on the DNS server, but would like for the DHCP server to update the PTR resource record.

- **1**—This flag specifies that the client wants to perform both updates.

- **3**—If this flag is sent, the DHCP server will register both records, regardless of the client's wishes. If the server sends a packet to the client with this flag set, the client does not attempt any updates.

▶▶   For more information about A and PTR records that are used in the DNS database, see Chapter 24, "Name Resolution."

These flags are not all that controls the process of which computer performs which updates. Instead, both the client and the server can be configured to perform (or not perform) this function.

Configuring Dynamic Updates on the DHCP Server

On the server side, you can specify in the properties page for the server how it will respond to dynamic update requests, and whether it will perform dynamic updates for clients that do not support this function (that is, pre-Windows 2000 clients). To configure the service for this functionality:

1. Click Start, Programs, and then Administrative Tools/DHCP.

2. In the left pane, expand the tree structure by clicking the plus sign next to the server's name to expand the tree to show the scopes that belong to the server.

3. Right-click the scope you want to modify, and select Properties.

4. When the Properties page appears, click the DNS tab. In Figure 23.23 you can see the properties found on this tab.

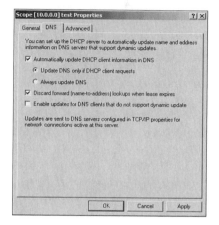

Figure 23.23   The DNS tab enables you to configure DHCP server behavior in regards to DNS dynamic updates.

5. The first check box, Automatically Update DHCP Client Information in DNS, enables you to specify this function using two options. Click either the Update DNS Only If DHCP Client Requests, or the Always Update DNS radio buttons. If you select the second button, the server will always make updates for clients, ignoring their requests.

6. To enable the server to handle dynamic updates for clients that do not support dynamic DNS update, select the check box Enable Updates for DNS Clients That Do Not Support Dynamic Update.

7. Click the Apply button, and then click the OK button to dismiss the dialog box.

Configuring Dynamic Updates on the Client

You also can control how the client handles the dynamic DNS update function if you are using Windows 2000 clients. Remember from the previous section that the server can override a client's request if the appropriate selection is made on the scope's DNS properties page.

Windows 2000 clients are already configured, by default, to send the FQDN packet with the Flags field set to zero. This means the client wants to update the A resource record and wants the server to update the PTR record. You can change this behavior by doing the following:

1. Right-click the My Network Places icon (or double-click the Network icon in the Control Panel).

2. Right-click the icon for the network connection you want to configure. From the menu that pops up, select Properties.

3. Highlight Internet Protocol (TCP/IP) and click the Properties button.

4. Click the Advanced button, and then select the DNS tab. A properties page similar to that shown in Figure 23.24 pops up. At the bottom of the properties page you'll notice that Register This Connection's Address in DNS is selected, while Use This Connection's DNS Suffix in DNS Registration is not. The second option is the default.

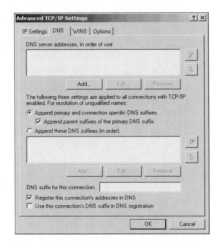

Figure 23.24 You can control the client's capability to dynamically update DNS from this properties page.

5. To disable the client from performing DNS updates, deselect the check box labeled Register This Connection's Address in DNS.

6. When finished, dismiss the properties page by clicking OK in each dialog box.

Reservations and Exclusions

Some computers or other networked devices, such as routers or printers, might need to keep the same IP address all the time. For example, Microsoft very strongly suggests you be sure that your DHCP server has a static, unchanging address. There are two ways that you can be sure a particular computer or device keeps the same static address. The first method is to manually configure the client using the client's software. For example, when you configure a Microsoft Windows 2000 Professional client, you can specify a static IP address (along with other network information) using the TCP/IP properties page for the client.

If you use the first method, you'll need to exclude the address you use from the address pool that you assign to a scope. If you forget this step and the address does fall within the range of a scope, eventually it will be issued to a client, causing a duplicate address error on the LAN.

A reservation is similar to an exclusion but is used for computers or devices that do support DHCP but still require a constant, static address. You can enter a reservation for an address that falls within the address pool for a scope. The reservation is linked to the computer or device's hardware address so that when it boots and begins the process of obtaining configuration information via DHCP, it will always receive the same address.

Exclusions are created when you create the address pool, as explained earlier in this chapter. To create a reservation

1. Bring up the DHCP MMC console by clicking Start, Programs, Administrative Tools, DHCP. Expand the tree in the left pane to get to the scope in which the reservation will be created.

2. Expand the scope and right-click Reservations.

3. From the menu that pops up, select New Reservation.

4. The New Reservation dialog box appears. Enter a descriptive name you want to use for this reservation.

5. Next, enter the IP address that falls within the scope but which is to be reserved.

6. Enter the hardware address of the computer for which this address will be reserved. For Windows NT/2000 clients, use the IPCONFIG/ALL command at the command prompt to get this address. For routers or other computers, consult your documentation.

7. Select whether the reservation will be used for a BOOTP request or a DHCP request, or both.

8. Click OK to dismiss the dialog box. The reservation is complete. The address is handed out only to the device that uses the hardware address (also called the MAC address) you defined for the reservation.

Note in this example the reservation was made for a router. Other types of devices for which you might want to reserve addresses (or exclude if the computers are statically configured) are important servers that are mapped to specific addresses in your DNS system. Also, if you have non-Windows clients, such as Linux or Unix desktops or servers, you might want to reserve an address for them if they can use DHCP.

What Is APIPA (Automatic Private IP Addressing)?

If a client is configured to use DHCP, what happens if no DHCP server is available on the network? In that case, Microsoft Windows 2000 clients can use Automatic Private IP Addressing (APIPA). This is not a solution for a large network! It is for use on small LANs, such as a home office with 25 or fewer network nodes.

Simply configure each client computer to use DHCP in the properties page for TCP/IP, and reboot. When the client computer realizes that no DHCP server is on the network (because it's not receiving any replies from its broadcasts), it will timeout and begin to use APIPA. The scheme in which addresses are allocated is not that complicated.

The network of addresses reserved for use by APIPA is 169.254.0.1 to 169.254.255.254, with a subnet mask 255.255.0.0. When the client does not receive an answer from any DHCP server after a short period of time, it will select an address randomly from this network. It then will test to see whether this address is already in use.

Note

The only information that APIPA will configure for the client computer is an IP address and a subnet mask. It does not allow the client to configure other items that could be offered as options by a DHCP server. One important item to note is that APIPA does not provide the capability for the client computer to detect a default gateway. Thus, communication is limited to computers on the local LAN that all share the same 169.254.0.0 network address space. If you plan to connect your small LAN to the Internet, or to any other network using a router, you'll need to either manually configure IP addressing information on each client or configure a DHCP server that can perform this function for you.

Note that a Microsoft client that is using APIPA will periodically check the network (about every five minutes) to see whether a DHCP server has become available. If one does come online, the client will perform as any other DHCP client and obtain configuration information from the DHCP server it discovers.

Troubleshooting Microsoft DHCP

Troubleshooting DHCP can be a complicated process. Perhaps you've forgotten to authorize the server on the network or activate a scope. Clients might be unable to locate the server. In any case, there are several things you can do to troubleshoot DHCP problems. With the client, start by using the `ipconfig/all` command at the command prompt to view IP configuration data. If the client shows either no address or an address of 0.0.0.0, a problem exists between the client and the server. It might be a network card, a misconfigured router, or other network component. Use the standard TCP/IP tools (that is, `ping` or `tracert`) from the client to the DHCP server to see whether connectivity exists. If you can't reach the DHCP server from the client, try the same tests from other clients to help localize where in the network the problem lies.

Two other useful tools for troubleshooting are the Windows 2000 Event Logs and the DHCP server's own audit log file. Earlier in this chapter you saw an example of an event log entry. In the next section you'll learn how to enable the DHCP server's own logging capabilities.

Managing Logging

Besides the records that the DHCP server records in the event log, you also can enable logging by the server to its own log file. For troubleshooting purposes, both the event log and the server's own log file can be very useful.

To manage the server's log file:

1. Start the DHCP MMC console.

2. Click once on the server you want to modify and select Properties from the Action menu. Alternatively, right-click on the server and select Properties.

3. In the General tab for the properties page for the server, select the check box labeled Enable DHCP Audit Logging.

4. Click the Advanced tab. Here you will find two fields. You can use the first field to enter the location where you want the log files to be created. The default is `<disk>:\WINNT2KS\System32\dhcp`.

5. The second field can be used to enter the path for the location of the DHCP database files. The default for this is the same as that for the log files.

6. Click OK to dismiss the properties page when you have finished viewing or modifying these fields.

When you enable audit logging, a new log file is created at midnight each day. Header information is written to the file and significant events are logged. The format for the filename used for log files is `DhcpSrvLog.<day of week>`. For example, a log file created on Monday morning would be named `DhcpSrvLog.Mon`.

Because the day of the week is used as the file extension for the log file, it should be obvious that in a week you'll have to overwrite an existing file. Indeed, this is what happens, unless the file has been modified within the last 24 hours. If this happens, logging will be suspended until the file is removed or renamed.

The log file is a simple ASCII text file using comma-delimited fields. Each event is recorded as a single line in the file, using the following fields:

`ID, Date, Time, Description, IP Address, Host Name, MAC Address`

where:

- **ID**—An event code to indicate the kind of event logged.
- **Date**—The date of the event.
- **Time**—The time of the event.
- **Description**—A short description of the event.
- **IP Address**—The IP address of the client.
- **Host Name**—The host name of the client.
- **MAC Address**—The hardware (MAC) address of the client.

The standard event IDs are

- **00**—The log was started.
- **01**—The log was stopped.
- **02**—Because of a low disk space condition, logging was suspended.
- **10**—A new IP address lease was granted to a client.
- **11**—A client renewed its lease.
- **12**—A client released its lease.
- **13**—An address was found to be already in use on the network.
- **14**—The address pool has been completely used, so the server was unable to grant a lease to a client.
- **15**—A lease was denied to a client.
- **20**—An address was given to a BOOTP client.

As you can see, a significant amount of information is stored in the log files. Start your troubleshooting efforts here if you are experiencing problems with the server itself or with multiple clients. You can follow the trail of events leading up to the current problem. Again, if you are having problems with a single client, examine the event log file on the client to look for any indication that the client was unable to locate or interact with the DHCP server.

Name Resolution

SOME OF THE MAIN TOPICS IN THIS CHAPTER ARE

Hardware Versus Protocol Addresses

NetBIOS

Installing a WINS Server Using Windows 2000

TCP/IP Names

Installing DNS on a Windows 2000 Server

Network Information Service (NIS)

## CHAPTER 24

Computers use hardware addresses when exchanging data on the local subnet. These addresses are burned into the network adapter and are often referred to as MAC (Media Access Control) addresses. MAC addresses produce a flat address space, so network protocols, such as IP, are typically used to create a hierarchical address space. However, for humans, both MAC and IP addresses (or IPX/SPX addresses for that matter) are difficult to remember. Names are convenient for use by humans that have to operate computers. So besides identifying a computer or network device using a protocol address, it is also important to be able to give a name to a computer, a network device, or a service, and then have that name resolved to the address so that data communications can take place on the network.

Understanding how name resolution works on your network will better prepare you to troubleshoot problems users encounter when trying to locate resources.

Note

This chapter deals with standard name resolution techniques ranging from the simple **HOSTS** and **LMHOSTS** files to WINS and the Domain Name System (DNS) service. For most networks, such as those that have Unix or Windows NT 4.0 computers, the name resolution methods described in this chapter will suffice. However, Windows 2000—when deployed using the Active Directory—adds a whole new dimension to name resolution. The Active Directory stores objects that can represent everything from a user account to a resource on the network, such as a computer or a printer. If you employ Windows 2000 Servers in your network, you'll find the next chapter, "Overview of Microsoft's Active Directory Service" to be a continuation of this one.

Hardware Versus Protocol Addresses

When communicating on the same network segment, computers can communicate directly by sending directed datagrams to another computer and specifying the MAC address that is assigned to the network card when it is manufactured. In TCP/IP networks, the Address Resolution Protocol (ARP) is used in a local broadcast domain to determine the hardware address of another computer by sending out a broadcast packet that contains the computer's IP address. When a computer recognizes an ARP packet that has its IP address, it responds to the ARP request with another packet that tells the original computer what the destination computer's MAC address is. For more information about hardware addresses, see Chapter 20, "Overview of the TCP/IP Protocol Suite."

Most major networking products now support the TCP/IP protocol suite in some way or another. NetBIOS has been adapted to run over IP, and the newer NetWare 5 networking software has adopted this as its underlying protocol as well.

This chapter discusses name resolution techniques used to translate user-friendly computer host names to IP addresses, and looks at some of the methods for troubleshooting problems you might encounter.

NetBIOS

In Chapter 28, "NetBIOS and NetBEUI," the NetBIOS and NetBEUI protocols are described. Although its original specifications were only sufficient for use on very small LANs (under 200 nodes), NetBIOS has been a mainstay in most Microsoft network products and until Windows 2000, NetBIOS names were integral to the Windows operating systems' management functions. For example, domain names and host names are made up of NetBIOS names. The Server Message Block protocol (SMB) that is used for resource access and administrative duties in LAN Manager and the Windows operating systems' networking software modules are based on NetBIOS names.

The LMHOSTS File

In the directory \%systemroot%\SYSTEM32\DRIVERS\ETC on Windows NT 4.0 and Windows 2000 computers is a file called LMHOSTS.SAM. For Windows 95 and Windows 98 clients, this file is found in the \WINDOWS directory. It is used to map NetBIOS names to IP addresses. The .SAM filename extension indicates that this is a *sample* file. If you are going to use the file, you will have to copy it or rename it LMHOSTS, *with no extension*. Because it's always a good idea to keep the original copy in case things become confused along the line, making a copy is a good choice.

The Windows files are basically the same for all versions of Windows, except for a few of the comment lines. The following is the version you'll find in Windows 2000 Advanced Server:

```
# Copyright (c) 1993-1999 Microsoft Corp.
#
# This is a sample LMHOSTS file used by the Microsoft TCP/IP for Windows.
#
# This file contains the mappings of IP addresses to computernames
# (NetBIOS) names.  Each entry should be kept on an individual line.
# The IP address should be placed in the first column followed by the
# corresponding computername. The address and the computername
# should be separated by at least one space or tab. The "#" character
# is generally used to denote the start of a comment (see the exceptions
# below).
#
# This file is compatible with Microsoft LAN Manager 2.x TCP/IP lmhosts
# files and offers the following extensions:
#
#      #PRE
#      #DOM:<domain>
#      #INCLUDE <filename>
#      #BEGIN_ALTERNATE
#      #END_ALTERNATE
#      \0xnn (non-printing character support)
#
# Following any entry in the file with the characters "#PRE" will cause
# the entry to be preloaded into the name cache. By default, entries are
# not preloaded, but are parsed only after dynamic name resolution fails.
#
# Following an entry with the "#DOM:<domain>" tag will associate the
# entry with the domain specified by <domain>. This affects how the
# browser and logon services behave in TCP/IP environments. To preload
# the host name associated with #DOM entry, it is necessary to also add a
# #PRE to the line. The <domain> is always preloaded although it will not
# be shown when the name cache is viewed.
#
# Specifying "#INCLUDE <filename>" will force the RFC NetBIOS (NBT)
# software to seek the specified <filename> and parse it as if it were
# local. <filename> is generally a UNC-based name, allowing a
# centralized lmhosts file to be maintained on a server.
# It is ALWAYS necessary to provide a mapping for the IP address of the
# server prior to the #INCLUDE. This mapping must use the #PRE directive.
# In addition the share "public" in the example below must be in the
# LanManServer list of "NullSessionShares" in order for client machines to
# be able to read the lmhosts file successfully. This key is under
# \machine\system\currentcontrolset\services\lanmanserver\parameters\
  ➥nullsessionshares
```

```
# in the registry. Simply add "public" to the list found there.
#
# The #BEGIN_ and #END_ALTERNATE keywords allow multiple #INCLUDE
# statements to be grouped together. Any single successful include
# will cause the group to succeed.
#
# Finally, non-printing characters can be embedded in mappings by
# first surrounding the NetBIOS name in quotations, then using the
# \0xnn notation to specify a hex value for a non-printing character.
#
# The following example illustrates all these extensions:
#
# 102.54.94.97      rhino           #PRE #DOM:networking  #net group's DC
# 102.54.94.102     "appname  \0x14"                      #special app server
# 102.54.94.123     popular         #PRE                  #source server
# 102.54.94.117     localsrv        #PRE                  #needed for the include
#
# #BEGIN_ALTERNATE
# #INCLUDE \\localsrv\public\lmhosts
# #INCLUDE \\rhino\public\lmhosts
# #END_ALTERNATE
#
# In the above example, the "appname" server contains a special
# character in its name, the "popular" and "localsrv" server names are
# preloaded, and the "rhino" server name is specified so it can be used
# to later #INCLUDE a centrally maintained lmhosts file if the "localsrv"
# system is unavailable.
#
# Note that the whole file is parsed including comments on each lookup,
# so keeping the number of comments to a minimum will improve performance.
# Therefore it is not advisable to simply add lmhosts file entries onto the
# end of this file.
```

As you can see from the sample file, you can place comments anywhere on a line by using the # character. Using comments aids in managing the file when there are multiple administrators. However, as the last bit of text explains, the entire file is parsed (read) each time it is consulted for a name lookup. If the number of entries in this file becomes quite large—and full of both name translations and comments—then it has probably outgrown its usefulness and you need to look to another means of name resolution, such as the Windows Internet Name Service (WINS) or DNS.

In addition to serving as the "comment" character, the # character can also be used to specify several keywords that have specific functions when used in this file. The keywords are

- **#PRE**—Load this entry into the NetBIOS name cache.
- **#DOM**—This entry is a domain controller.
- **#INCLUDE**—Use the filename following this keyword to get name-to-address mappings.
- **#BEGIN_ALTERNATE** and **#END_ALTERNATE**—The #INCLUDE commands within this block are to be processed in order until one of them succeeds in performing the name translation.

For small networks that have several subnets separated by a router, using the #DOM keyword for an entry can enable a client to locate a domain controller on another subnet. Although it is preferable to have a backup domain controller on each subnet (for Windows NT 4.0 and earlier versions of Microsoft's operating systems), this workaround can be helpful for special conditions.

In Figure 24.1, you can see the logical steps that a b-node goes through when trying to resolve a name to an IP address. The NetBIOS name cache is first consulted, followed by broadcasting. Finally, if these two methods fail, the LMHOSTS file is checked.

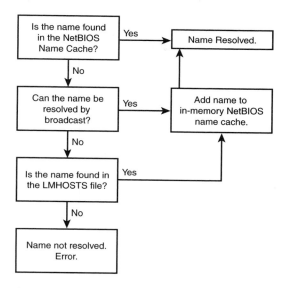

Figure 24.1   In Microsoft networks, a b-node consults the LMHOSTS file when other methods fail.

The in-memory NetBIOS name cache is always consulted first. This cache can hold up to 100 entries. When a name is successfully resolved by the broadcast method or by a lookup in the LMHOSTS file, it is added to the name cache and can be resolved there from that point onward.

You can ensure that an entry will be placed in the name cache when the workstation boots by using the #PRE keyword for that entry in the LMHOSTS file:

```
175.110.32.31      yoko.ono.com      #PRE
```

This can be useful for ensuring that servers that are accessed often by clients are resident in the memory cache, eliminating the need to perform a disk access to look up the entry in the LMHOSTS file.

Tip

You can force an update to the NetBIOS cache by using the command **nbtstat -R** to reload the cache from the LMHOSTS file. This is useful if you have just made edits to the file.

Windows Internet Name Service (WINS)

WINS is Microsoft's NetBIOS Name Server (NBNS) developed according to the details set forth in RFCs 1001 and 1002 and is based on a client-server architecture. Only Windows NT Server or Windows 2000 Server computers can run the WINS service, and the server does not have to be a domain controller. In the traditional DNS server that originated mainly on Unix systems, an administrator is responsible for editing files to maintain address-to-name mappings. WINS is a dynamic database. Name registrations are performed by unicast messages (direct contact) between the server and the WINS client. Because the WINS server does not have to be on the same network segment as the client, and because no broadcast messages clutter up network medium, WINS is a more efficient method of name resolution when compared to b-node functionality.

The following are some of the important benefits of using WINS:

- **Ease of administration**—Updates to the database are dynamic. When a computer is moved to a different location and acquires a new address, it updates the WINS server when it boots. If DHCP is used on the network, moving the client computer requires nothing more than hooking it up to the network and booting the computer, provided the client has been configured to use DHCP and WINS.

- **Interaction with DNS**—In Windows NT 4.0, WINS has the capability of interacting with Microsoft's DNS server. If properly configured, a non-Windows client can query the DNS server, which itself can then query the WINS server to obtain the address of a NetBIOS client if the DNS server does not find a name translation in its own database.

- **Static Mappings**—If WINS is not set up to interact with the DNS server, you can place static mappings in the database for clients that do not have WINS client functionality. In a network composed of different operating systems, static mappings can help to integrate them into the Windows environment making it easy for WINS clients to locate these computers.

- **Replication**—Though not specified in the RFCs, WINS servers are typically set up with replication partners. This means that over a given convergence time, all WINS servers in the network are updated with changes made on any one of them.

- **Fault-Tolerance**—Clients are typically configured to locate a primary WINS server and a secondary WINS server. Because the database is replicated at intervals, the secondary WINS server can continue to service all clients until the primary server is brought back online.

When to Use WINS

WINS was a good solution for resolving names in versions of Windows before Windows 2000 came along. However, starting with Windows 2000, you don't necessarily need to install a WINS server on a Windows network. This is because Windows 2000 clients can use DNS and the Active Directory to find out about other hosts on the network. However, if you have a network that is composed of multiple operating systems, such as Windows 98 or Windows NT computers, WINS can still be useful because *all versions of Windows prior to Windows 2000 require NetBIOS name support*. And some applications, such as SMS, might require NetBIOS. Of course, NetBIOS name support doesn't mean that you need to install WINS. It depends on the topology of your network. On a small office LAN with only one physical cable segment and just a few computers, NetBIOS broadcasts probably are sufficient for name resolution for these older clients and will not use up a large amount of bandwidth.

However, if you operate a larger network that contains many segments and a large number of computers, or if you are just starting to introduce Windows 2000 into a network that already has older legacy clients, WINS is a good interim solution until you migrate completely to Windows 2000.

Configuring WINS Clients

To use WINS, a client first must be configured with the address of a WINS server. This can be done in one of two ways. First, you can configure the client manually, using a network properties page for the particular Windows operating system. Second, you can configure a DHCP server to provide the name of one or more WINS servers to a client if you use DHCP in your network. For more information about configuring WINS options using a DHCP server, see Chapter 23, "BOOTP and the Dynamic Host Configuration Protocol (DHCP)."

For example, to configure a Windows 98 client to use a WINS server, do the following:

1. Click Start, Settings, Control Panel.

2. Double-click on the Network icon in the Control Panel. In Figure 24.2 you can see the Network properties page with the Configuration tab selected.

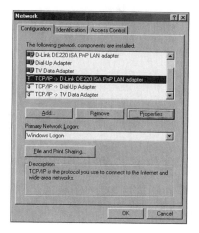

Figure 24.2   Select the network adapter you want to configure for WINS from the Network properties page.

3. Highlight the network adapter you want to configure for WINS and click the Properties button. Select the WINS Configuration tab. In Figure 24.3 you can see this Properties page.

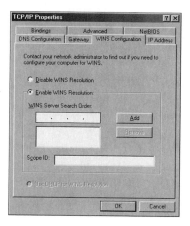

Figure 24.3   Select the WINS configuration tab from the Properties page to enter the WINS servers this client will use.

4. Select the Enable WINS Resolution option and enter the IP address for the WINS server in the field WINS Server Search Order. After entering the address, click the Add button. The IP address of the WINS server then shows up in the field directly underneath WINS Server Search Order field.

5. If you want, enter a secondary WINS server to provide for fault tolerance should the first server be unable to respond to the client, and then click the Add button to add other WINS servers. You can also highlight a WINS server in this section of the Properties page and use the Remove button to delete a WINS server should your network change and new machines be employed for the WINS service.

6. When finished, click OK to dismiss this Properties page. When the Network Properties page reappears, click OK.

7. A dialog box prompts you to restart the computer so the change takes effect. You can boot the computer now, or at a later time if it is more convenient. The Windows 98 computer will not use the WINS service until you reboot.

When the Windows 98 client reboots, it will contact the WINS server to register itself, as described in the next section of this chapter. For a Windows NT 4.0 computer, the process is similar, though the dialog boxes might look a little different.

If your network consists of nothing but Windows 2000 computers, then you won't need the WINS service. The Active Directory combined with DHCP and a dynamic DNS server provide all the name registration and resolution functionality you need. However, Windows 2000 clients can still be configured to use WINS. This might be necessary if you have a mixed network using clients from Windows 98, Windows NT, or even Unix or Linux clients that have SAMBA installed.

To configure a Windows 2000 client to use WINS, follow these steps:

1. Click Start, Settings, Network and Dialup Connections.

2. Right-click on the network connection you want to set up to use WINS and select Properties from the menu that appears.

3. Click once on Internet Protocol (TCP/IP) and click the Properties button.

4. Click the Advanced button at the bottom of the Properties page. The Advanced TCP/IP Settings Properties page is displayed. Click the WINS tab (shown in Figure 24.4).

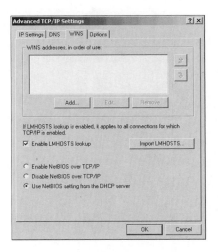

Figure 24.4 Use the Advanced TCP/IP Settings Properties page to configure Windows 2000 clients to use WINS.

5. Click the Add button. A dialog box pops up that you can use to enter the IP address of a WINS server. Enter the address and click OK. Continue using the Add button to add more WINS servers, if they are present on your network, for backup purposes.

You'll also notice in Figure 24.4 that you can use the Edit and Remove buttons. To remove a WINS server, simply highlight the server you want to remove by clicking on it once and then clicking the Remove button. The Edit button can be used to change an entry. Highlight the entry and click the Edit button, and the same dialog box used for adding WINS servers pops up. The WINS server you have selected to edit appears in the fields on this dialog box. You can change any part of the IP address and click OK.

One final note about Windows 2000 clients that network administrators will appreciate: You don't have to perform a reboot of the computer after you add, edit, or remove WINS servers!

Client Name Registration and Release

For a client computer to register a name with the WINS server, it sends a Name Registration Request to the server. This is a directed message, not a broadcast message—that's why you have to configure the client to know the address of one or more WINS servers. If the name is not found in the database, the WINS server returns a Positive Name Registration Response to the client. The record is given a timestamp, and a renewal interval is also recorded in the record. The record is given an Owner ID as well, which identifies the WINS server that *originates* (or in other words, owns) the record. When the record is replicated to other WINS servers, they use this ID to identify the original server.

After half of the renewal period has elapsed, a Windows client attempts to reregister its ownership of the name by sending the server a Name Refresh Request. The reregistration process functions the same as the initial registration. By setting a Time to Live (TTL) value on each record, the WINS database can eventually be purged of records that are no longer valid.

Note

The term Time to Live (TTL) is used by many protocols and services. Don't confuse the TTL value described here with, for example, that used in the IP packet header. For IP packets, the TTL field is used to prevent a packet from getting stuck in a routing loop. Each time the IP packet passes through a router, this field is decremented by at least one and the packet is dropped when the TTL value reaches zero. WINS uses a TTL value to determine when to begin the process of getting rid of records that appear to no longer be in use (because the client has not renewed the record registration). Later in this chapter you'll see that the Domain Name System (DNS) servers also use a TTL value.

The state of the name record changes over time depending on the status of the client. At any time, a record is either in the *active state* or it can be marked as *released* or *extinct*. At each state, a TTL is marked on the record and is used to determine when to change it to the next state.

A name can be released in two ways:

■ The name can be released explicitly if the client computer is shut down in a proper manner. The client sends a message to the server telling it to release the name.

■ The name is set to a released state by the WINS server if it does not receive a Name Refresh Request before the renewal period expires.

When the name is *released*, the WINS server does not yet delete the record from the database. Instead, it marks the record as released, adds another timestamp (showing the time of the release), and then adds an *Extinction Interval* to the record. If the WINS server that receives the release is the original owner of the record, it does not propagate a record update to other WINS servers. This reduces replication traffic. If another WINS server—that still has a record showing the name is active—receives a request from another computer to use the name, it tries to contact the original owner and find out whether the name can be reused.

At certain intervals, the WINS server *scavenges* the database. If it finds a record whose extinction interval has expired, it marks the record as extinct. This state is often referred to as the *tombstone state*. When a record is marked as extinct, it receives another timestamp and an extinction time-out value. If a record has not been reregistered by the end of this final time-out interval, the scavenge process will finally remove it from the database.

If a WINS server receives an explicit release request from a client, and the server is not the original owner of the record, it makes itself the new owner of the record. Instead of placing the record into the released state, it proceeds directly to the extinct state. Unlike records in the released state, records in the extinct state do get replicated at replication time. The reason a WINS server immediately marks a record it does not own as extinct is so that the record will be replicated quickly and will get back to the WINS server that originated the record.

If a name is already in the database, the client can still be awarded ownership of it, depending on certain factors. If the name is in the released or extinct state, the server knows that it can reassign the name because the previous owner has released it. If it is in the active state, the WINS server tries to contact the original owner. If the original owner does not respond, the WINS server reassigns the name to the node that is requesting it.

Note

In general, static entries made to the WINS database are not subject to the scavenge process and remain in the database. However, the administrator can configure the server to operate differently by setting the Migrate On switch (in the WINS Administrator Utility). If this switch is set, the static entry can be overwritten by a new name request if the original owner does not answer a challenge from the WINS server. The Migrate On switch is meant to be used when migrating a network from static entries to dynamic entries. This might be the case when you are upgrading your network with new client software, for example, and relieves the administrator of the burden of having to remove the static entries manually.

When a client workstation is moved to a new subnet and receives a new address, it sends a Name Registration Request to the WINS server. The WINS server queries the old IP address, determines that the name is no longer in use, and then grants the name to the new IP address.

Static Name Entries

You can enter static entries into the WINS database using the WINS Manager utility. This is usually done for non-WINS clients, such as Unix workstations. Although you can configure the Windows client to use DNS to resolve these names, a static entry into the WINS database does two things. It makes name resolution faster because the client only has to query the WINS server. It also helps to prevent errors by preventing a WINS client from registering a name already in use by a non-WINS enabled client.

Name Queries

In Figure 24.5, you can see the process that a client computer goes through when trying to resolve a name using WINS servers. The steps it takes depend on whether it has one or two WINS servers in its configuration (Primary and Secondary WINS servers) and whether the node is configured as a p-node or an h-node.

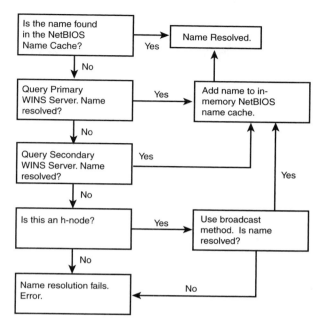

Figure 24.5   Name resolution using WINS servers for p-node and h-node clients.

When a WINS server receives a Name Query Request from a node, it returns a Positive Name Response with one or more IP addresses associated with the NetBIOS name to the requestor via a UDP packet. If the WINS server does not have a record for the name, it sends a Negative Name Response. If the client is configured with the address of a secondary WINS server it attempts to resolve the name by contacting that server.

Note

In earlier WINS implementations, clients only resorted to the secondary WINS server when the primary server did not respond. Microsoft changed this in Windows NT 3.51 so the secondary server functions as a backup for the primary WINS server and also as a secondary search possibility. Clients that can make use of this new search procedure include Windows 95/98, Window NT, Windows 2000, and Windows for Workgroups 3.11 clients that use TCP/IP-32 for Windows for Workgroups version 3.11b and the updated redirector file.

If the secondary server also returns a Negative Name Response, the client either fails to resolve the name (if it is a p-node) or it uses a broadcast message as a last resort (if it is an h-node). If the computer the client wants to contact is on the local network segment, the broadcast can succeed. If not, the client is unable to resolve the name to an IP address and will be unable to contact the other computer.

The WINS Proxy Agent

To provide access to the WINS server information for b-nodes that cannot query the WINS server directly, the concept of a proxy server was created. These servers listen to broadcast messages issued by a b-node on the local network segment and if the name being sought is in the proxy server's name cache, it returns a response to the b-node. If the name is not in the proxy server's cache, it queries the WINS servers it knows.

When a proxy server is also configured to monitor name registration broadcast messages, it listens for these messages and sends a negative response to a b-node that attempts to register a name that exists in the WINS database. The proxy server does not, however, make name registrations into the WINS database for a b-node. It merely responds to name registrations that conflict with the database.

To resolve names for b-nodes, the proxy server examines the subnet address of the b-node that is performing the name query. This is done so that the proxy server does not respond to name queries for nodes that are on the local subnet, which can respond for themselves.

Configuring WINS Servers

To set up a Windows NT 4.0 Server computer to be a WINS server, you need to install the WINS service by using the Network applet in the Control Panel. In the Network applet, click the Services tab and select the Add button. This brings up the Select Network Service dialog box (see Figure 24.6), where you can select the Windows Internet Name Service.

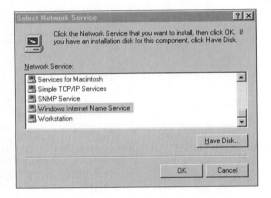

Figure 24.6   Select the Window Internet Name Service entry to install WINS.

After you click the OK button, you are prompted for the location of the Windows NT source files. They are usually in your CD-ROM drive. When the installation procedure has finished copying the files it needs, it tells you that you must reboot in order for the installation to complete. When the computer has rebooted, you can start the WINS Manager found in the Administrative Tools folder. Alternatively, at the Command Prompt, you can start the WINS Manager by typing the command:

```
START WINSADMN <IP address>
```

As you can see from the syntax of this command, you can run the WINS Manager utility and select the WINS server you want to manage. In Figure 24.7, you can see the main window of the utility, which shows statistical information about the server you have selected.

To manage WINS servers on other computers, use the Server menu. The options you can perform under this menu are

- **Add WINS Server**—You are prompted to enter the IP address of another WINS server to add to the list of servers you are managing with the utility.

- **Delete WINS Server**—To delete a WINS server, you can highlight it in the WINS Server window and then select this function. Note that this does not delete the WINS service from the remote computer, but merely removes it from the list of servers you are managing at this time.

- **Detailed Information**—This option brings up a window that shows more detailed information about the selected server.

- **Configuration**—Use this option when you want to change the configuration of the WINS server. From this selection, you can modify renewal and extinction time-out values, event logging parameters, and the Migrate On/Off switch, among other things.

- **Replication Partners**—This selection brings up a window where you can control replication. You can add or remove WINS servers that are replication partners and you can configure the replication interval time value. You can also use this option to force replication to begin immediately if you have a need to propagate changes to other partners without waiting for the next scheduled replication time.

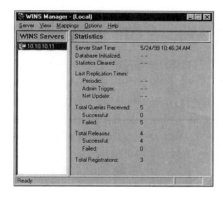

Figure 24.7 The WINS Server Manager utility provided with Windows NT 4.0.

Using the Configuration option, you can modify four time-out values. These timers have been set by Microsoft to optimal values, but you can make changes to accommodate your network configuration. For example, you might want make the renewal interval longer if the computers in your network are rarely moved. The times you can modify are

- **Renewal Interval**—This is the amount of time that the name remains active before a client has to refresh it. A Windows NT client usually refreshes its name registration after one half of this interval has passed. The default for WINS servers under Windows NT 4.0 is six days.

- **Extinction Interval**—After a name has been released, it stays in that state until this interval has passed, at which time it is marked extinct. The default value for this timer under Windows NT 4.0 is six days.

- **Extinction Time-Out**—After a record is marked as extinct, this amount of time must pass before it is eligible to be scavenged from the database.

- **Verify Interval**—This value is used to timestamp active entries on the pulling replication server. At verify time, the server examines all active records for those that are older than the Verify Interval allows, and then queries the originating server to see if the records are still valid. This periodic checking helps to keep the databases synchronized among the replicating servers when errors creep in. For example, if an extinct record is removed from the database before being replicated to other servers, it remains as active on other servers, when in fact it is no longer valid. This type of thing can happen when servers are off the network during replication. The default value for this timer is 24 days.

You can update the statistics shown in the main display of the WINS Manager by selecting the View menu and then Refresh. You also find a selection here that can be used to clear the statistics. The Mappings menu enables you to view the IP address-to-name mappings, manage static mappings, or backup the database. You can also choose to begin the scavenging process from this menu if you have made a lot of changes to the database and do not want to wait for the next scavenging interval to expire.

In Figure 24.8, you can see the Show Database window. Under Owner, the Show All Mappings option has been selected to view the entire database. You can change the sort order by making a selection under Sort Order or you can use the Set Filter button to mask out certain entries (and the Clear Filter button to remove the filter).

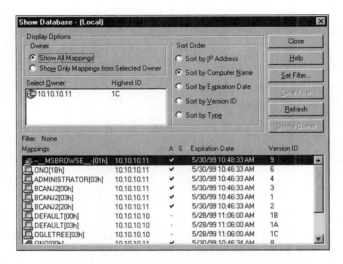

Figure 24.8   The Show Database window can be configured to show mappings in several different ways.

This look into the database can be a quick way to troubleshoot problems in the network when computers cannot resolve names of remote workstations. If you do not find the entry for the disputed name, you can begin to check the remote workstation to be sure that it is connected to the network. You can reboot it to force a name reregistration.

Using WINS with DHCP

There are two major tasksassociated with managing a frequently changing network. One is assigning and keeping track of addressing information for each node and the other is providing a method for name resolution. WINS is designed to solve problems with the second task. The Dynamic Host Configuration Protocol (DHCP) operates to make the initial assignment of addressing information automatic and can be used to remedy the first task.

DHCP typically provides a client with an IP address and a subnet address. However, DHCP can be configured to provide other options, such as the addresses of WINS servers the client should use. If you are using Microsoft's DHCP Service, you can run the DHCP Manager (found in the Administrative Tools folder) and select Global from the DHCP Options menu. In Figure 24.9, the dialog box used to add DHCP options and their values is shown.

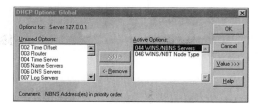

Figure 24.9 DHCP options can be configured to supply clients with WINS server addresses.

Under Active Options, you see that DHCP options 044 (WINS/NBNS Servers) and 046 (WINS/NBT Node Type) have been selected. Option 044 is used to specify the addresses of the WINS server(s). To add IP addresses to be dispensed from DHCP, select the Value button and click the Edit Array button. In Figure 24.10, you can see the dialog box that enables you to manage the IP addresses for WINS servers.

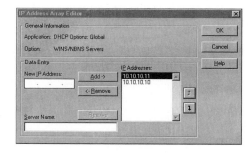

Figure 24.10 Use the Array Editor to enter WINS server option information.

For the clients of the DHCP server to make use of the WINS servers, you also want to add DHCP option 046 and set it to one of the following hexadecimal values:

- **0x2**—p-node
- **0x4**—m-node
- **0x8**—h-node

This option sets the node type of the client computer. If you use the value of 0x1, the node is configured to be a b-node, uses broadcast messages for name registration and resolution, and does not use the WINS servers.

Recovering a Corrupt WINS Database

A WINS server can be set up to automatically create a backup of the database every three hours. Using the WINS Manager utility, select Backup Database from the Mappings menu. You then select a directory to use for the backup files. Note that the directory used for the backup files must be on a disk local to the system. You cannot use a network drive.

To restore the database, you again use the WINS Manager, selecting Restore Database from the Mappings menu.

Installing a WINS Server Using Windows 2000

If you are running a network that has Windows NT 4.0, and previous versions of Microsoft operating systems, then you can continue to use the WINS servers you've already installed. However, you can also set up a Windows 2000 Server to offer the WINS service to your network. Installing the WINS service is a simple matter. You can choose to install the WINS service during the initial installation of Windows 2000 Server, as you would with other networking services. You can also install the WINS service after you've completed the operating system installation by using the following steps:

1. Click Start, Programs, Control Panel.

2. From the Control Panel, double-click the Add/Remove Programs icon.

3. When the Add Remove Programs window pops up, click Add/Remove Windows Components that you'll see on the left part of the window. The Add Remove Programs window now displays a button in the upper-right side of the window called Components. Click the Components button. The Windows Components Wizard dialog box pops up.

4. Scroll down until you find Network Services and highlight it by clicking on it once. Then click the Details button (see Figure 24.11).

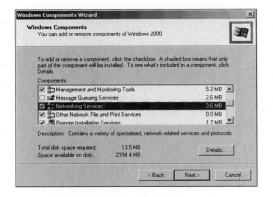

Figure 24.11   Highlight Network Services and click Details.

5. When the Networking Services dialog box appears, scroll down until you find Windows Internet Name Services (WINS). Click the check box next to the component and click the OK button, as shown in Figure 24.12.

6. When prompted, insert the Windows 2000 source CD into your CD-ROM drive and then wait a minute or so while files are copied to your hard drive. When the Windows Component Wizard window reappears, click Next.

7. Another window, titled Completing the Windows Components Wizard appears. Click the Finish button.

8. When the Add Remove Programs window reappears, click OK.

After you've installed the service, you won't have to reboot the computer. Instead, you can start managing the WINS service immediately.

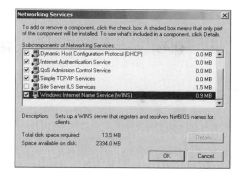

Figure 24.12 Select the WINS service from this dialog box and click OK to install the service.

Managing the Windows 2000 WINS Server

The Microsoft Management Console is used and you'll find a new utility in the Administrative Tools folder. Simply click Start, Programs/Administrative Tools and then select WINS from the available tools.

When the MMC console appears, you'll see your server name and IP address listed in the tree found in the left pane of the console. Click the server name and it will expand to show you two additional folders, Active Registrations and Replication Partners (see Figure 24.13).

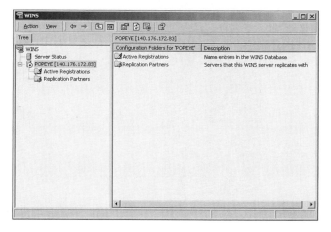

Figure 24.13 WINS is managed on a Windows 2000 server using the MMC console.

To see a list of computers and group names in the WINS database, simply click the Active Registrations folder. Similarly, to see any other servers you have configured to be a replication partner, just click the Replication Partners folder.

Of course, you'll first have to setup clients and reboot them before you'll see any computers registered in the database. And, you'll have to set up replication partners before anything will show up in that folder.

Adding Servers and Replication Partners

Most of the management capabilities for WINS servers can be accomplished through either the Action menu or by using properties pages. For example, to start or stop the WINS service, click the server once to highlight it and from the Action menu select Start or Stop. You can also use the Pause and Restart functions. These options work just like they did in the Windows NT 4.0 WINS server.

The MMC console allows you to manage multiple WINS servers from a single console. Simply click the WINS entry in the left pane (see Figure 24.13) and then from the Action Menu select Add Server. The Add Server dialog box pops up and prompts you to enter the NetBIOS name, or IP address, of the server you want to add to the management console. Once added, you can select which server you want to manage by simply clicking it once in the left pane tree of servers.

To add a replication partner, open the Replication Partners folder found under the server you want to set up for replication and from the Action Menu, select New Replication partner. Again, a dialog box prompts you for the name or IP address of the server with which you want to enable replication.

Using the Action Menu to Configure MMC Properties

The first entry in the tree structure found in the left pane of the MMC console is the WINS. Click WINS and from the Action menu, select Properties. Or, you can right-click WINS and select Properties from the menu that pops up. In Figure 24.14 you can see the general Properties page for the MMC WINS console.

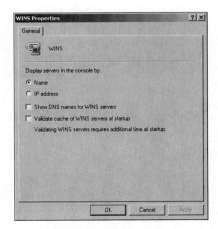

Figure 24.14 Use the WINS server's Properties page to configure general properties for the server.

From this properties page, you can select to have WINS servers in the console tree be displayed using either their NetBIOS name or the IP address of the server. You can also select to show a DNS style name for the server. Finally, you can configure the server to validate its cache of WINS servers when the server starts up to ensure that they are still online and that the list is accurate. Because this involves sending a message to each server, this can take some time if you manage a lot of servers, or if they are connected by slow links.

Using the Action Menu to Manage Individual WINS Servers

You can perform most of the basic management tasks associated with WINS servers by selecting the WINS server from those you've added to the tree structure in the left pane and then use options from the Action menu. Alternatively, you can right-click on a server and select the same options from the menu that pops up. The things you can manage from the Action menu for any server are

- **Display Server Statistics**—This option enables you to see when the server was started, statistics about replication, name registrations, releases, and so on.

- **Scavenge Database**—This starts the scavenging process, as described earlier in this chapter. You can determine when this process has finished by looking in the Event Log.

- **Verify Database Consistency**—This function pulls records from other WINS servers, by examining records in the local database to determine the owner of each record. If the record still exists on the owner-WINS server and is identical to the local record, then the timestamp for the record is updated. Otherwise, if the record pulled from the owner-server has a higher version ID than that of the local record, the local record is marked for deletion and the new record is added to the local database.

Caution

Using the Verify Database Consistency option should be done during non-peak hours on your network because it can produce a large amount of network traffic, depending on the number of records in the database and the number of WINS servers on the network. Don't do this during rush hour at work! Note that you can schedule this operation for another time using the properties page for the server.

- **Verify Version ID Consistency**—This is similar to the previous function, but the server checks to see that, for the records it owns, that the local record has the highest version ID among other WINS servers on the network. This operation can take some time to complete.

- **Start Push Replication**—Use this to start an immediate replication, pushing records to a replication partner. This can be useful if you've made changes to the database (such as adding static records) and you don't want to wait for the next scheduled replication interval. A dialog box prompts you for the server to which you want to push records.

- **Start Pull Replication**—Similar to the previous menu item, but you use this to force another server to immediately begin the replication process, sending records to your server.

- **Back Up Database**—Use this to back up the database. A dialog box prompts you to enter the location that you want to use to store the database file backup. When the process is finished another dialog box pops up to inform you.

- **Restore Database**—Use this to restore a WINS database (that you have previously backed up). Again, you'll be prompted to enter the location of the backup files and will be informed when the process has finished.

- **All Tasks**—Start, Stop, Pause, Resume, or Restart the WINS server.

- **Delete**—Use this to delete a WINS server from the MMC console list. Note that this does not delete any data on that WINS server, but merely removes it from the list of servers you manage using MMC on the local computer.

- **Refresh**—Use this to refresh data displayed on the MMC console.

- **Export List**—This menu item enables you to export a list of records stored in the WINS database. You are prompted for the location in which the file will be created. You can create ASCII text files or Unicode files, and can select that the file be either tab or comma delimited. This function is useful for exporting the WINS database records for use in another application, such as a spreadsheet.

- **Properties**—This displays the properties sheet for the selected server.

- **Help**—Use this when all else fails!

The Properties page for a server (which can be displayed using the action menu as just described) can be used to further configure the server. The Properties page has four tabs:

- **General**—Here you can select the time interval used to automatically refresh the statistics shown on the MMC Console for the WINS server. You can also specify a location to store the database during a backup, and use a check box to enable backing up the database automatically when the server is shut down.

- **Intervals**—This tab allows you to set the time intervals used for record renewals, deletions, and verification.

- **Database Verification**—Use this tab to set a time for scheduling database verification. You can specify that it be done every so many hours, or you can set a specific time for verification to begin. This function performs the database consistency check described earlier. If you have a large database, a field on this tab allows you to enter the maximum number of records to be verified during each interval.

- **Advanced**—This tab (shown in Figure 24.15) allows you to perform many functions.

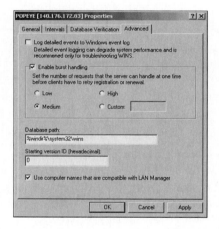

Figure 24.15   The Advanced tab of the server's Properties page allows you to configure important server properties, such as the location of the database.

The Advanced tab is singled out here for special mention because it contains some important configuration items. For example, you can specify the path to use for the database files. You can decide to enable logging detailed events to the Event Log for troubleshooting purposes. This is not a feature you should leave enabled unless you are having problems with WINS.

The Enable Burst Handling check box lets you customize (low, medium, high, or specify a number) the amount of client registrations and renewals the server can handle at a single time. This can be useful if you have a server that you want to use mainly as a backup for your primary WINS server. You can set its burst mode to low and then change this property to high on the server you want to handle the most requests.

You can enter a starting version ID in a field at the bottom of this dialog box. And finally, you can use a check box to enable use of computer names that are compatible with LAN Manager if you have older Microsoft clients on your network.

TCP/IP Names

The address space for IP addresses is a hierarchical one that allows computers to be grouped into networks and subnetworks. The flat address spaces created by MAC addresses do not allow for any kind of grouping because they only provide an address for the host physical adapter and do no distinguish the network. It is also possible to create a hierarchical name space for nodes on a TCP/IP network by concatenating the host name with a domain name. For example, the host computer named jack in the domain named acme.com is jack.acme.com as a fully-qualified name.

Names are more convenient for humans than the numerical address format implemented in the TCP/IP suite. Just as the numerical address space is a hierarchical one, so is the name space. However, it is important to understand that the two do not have to be directly related on a one-to-one basis. For example, suppose a computer named printserver.ono.com has an address of 193.220.113.10. This is a class C IP address, so the network portion of the address is 193.220.113. You might be inclined to think, then, that a computer with a name of fileserver.ono.com is also located in the same network and has an address that begins with 193.220.113. However, there is no direct relation between the two.

Not that there can't be. It might be very convenient to set up a small network with a few subnets and create host computer names that all match up to a particular network address or subnet. In practical terms, however, this is hard to maintain as the network grows and changes.

Instead, use the TCP/IP namespace to create a logical arrangement of computers that matches some kind of business layout or other type of function. It makes sense to use names such as the following:

```
susan.accounting.ono.com
heather.accounting.ono.com
luke.shipping.ono.com
holly.shipping.ono.com
```

It is clear from these names that the company or organization is called ono, and that there are computers in the accounting and shipping departments. In this case, however, it might be that Susan works out of the company's office located in the heart of downtown, whereas Heather works in a suburban office. Their TCP/IP host names reflect the business organizational unit in which they work. Their IP addresses, however, can be on completely different subnets or networks, depending on the physical location or other factors.

The rules for creating a host name are not as carefree as those used for NetBIOS names. You cannot use spaces in a TCP/IP name, for example. The following rules must be followed when creating the name.

- You can use alphabetical characters (a–z) or numeric characters (0–9), and the first character of the name *must* be a letter or a digit.

- You can use the minus sign (dash), but this cannot be the last character in the name.

- Periods are allowed, but are used to separate host names from domain or subdomain portions of the name. This is covered in RFC 921, "Domain Name System Implementation Schedule." Because the period is used to separate components, it cannot be the last character in the name either.

- Names are case insensitive. Uppercase A is the same as lowercase a.

- The host portion of the name should not be longer than 24 characters. In practice, you can exceed this limit most of the time, but it is not a good idea if you are connected to the Internet where there are other computers and devices that do stick to the strict limit.

Note

These restrictions apply to names you enter in the HOSTS file. When using a Domain Name System (DNS) server, the restrictions are a little different, as is explained in the following sections.

Although you can use names in the TCP/IP networking environment to conveniently organize your host computers, once again there needs to be a mechanism for resolving these names to the actual IP addresses that are associated with the computer. TCP/IP provides the HOSTS file, which was originally a central file maintained by a central authority and periodically distributed to nodes throughout the Internet. You can probably guess that this method—such as the LMHOSTS file used on NetBIOS networks—has been outgrown by the rapid growth of the Internet, and is now used only on small networks or for special cases.

The Domain Name Service (DNS) is now the primary means for resolving IP addresses to host names on the Internet. In some Unix shops, the Network Information System (NIS) is used. NIS was originally called Yellow Pages but had to change its name due to a trademark infringement.

The *HOSTS* File

On Unix systems, the HOSTS file is usually found in the /etc or the /etc/inet directory. Like the LMHOSTS file, it has no filename extension. It is a text file that contains IP addresses followed by the host name or names associated with the address. The # character is used to denote comments. Each line should have only one IP address, followed by a space or tab character, and then the host name. You can place more than one name on the line (each separated by a space or tab character) to provide multiple names for a host (sometimes called nicknames). For example:

```
#This is the HOSTS file
#
127.0.0.1       localhost
10.1.22.13      pkd.ubik.com              # Server at Atlanta office.
10.1.22.46      psi.ubik.ocm              # Joe's workstation.
192.208.46.158 www.compaq.com             # Compaq's homepage.
```

Note that the first entry in the file is the loopback address for the local adapter. You will find this in many HOSTS files, but it is not a requirement.

The HOSTS file has the same limitations as the LMHOSTS file. Mainly, it doesn't scale very well. Each time a change is made in the network, you need to update the file on each machine to reflect the change. This makes it easy to get different copies out-of-sync on a larger network.

In a very small network that doesn't change very often, using the HOSTS file might be preferable to using DNS. However, for a growing network or for one in a fast-paced business environment where employees are always on the move, DNS or NIS should be used.

Domain Name System (DNS)

When TCP/IP became the standard protocol used on ARPAnet (which became the Internet), the HOSTS file was maintained by SRI-NIC at a central location. Periodically, changes were made to the file as administrators e-mailed requests to SRI-NIC. The updated HOSTS file then had to be distributed to every node, making the maintenance of this file a major administrative chore.

In 1984, the Domain Name System (DNS) was adopted for the Internet. DNS is not only a hierarchical database, but also a distributed one. WINS servers use replication with partners to keep a full copy of the WINS database on each WINS server. On the Internet, each registered domain (that is, acme.com or microsoft.com) has a DNS server, which is responsible for managing the database of host names within that domain or subdomains. This distribution of the database makes it easier to scale to a larger size than with the WINS model. Administration can also be delegated so that no central management of the entire database is needed.

Tip

One of the first implementations of DNS was developed at Berkeley for their BSD Unix (version 4.3) operating system. Thus, you will often hear the term BIND (Berkeley Internet Name Domain) used in place of DNS.

The topmost entry in the DNS hierarchy is called the root domain and is represented by the period character (.). Underneath this root domain are the top-level directories that fall into two groups: geographical and organizational. Geographical domains are used to specify specific countries. For example, .au for Australia and .uk or the United Kingdom. Under each of the geographical domains, you might find organizational domains. Organizational domains include

- **com**—Used for commercial organizations.
- **edu**—Used for educational institutions.
- **gov**—Used for U.S. government entities.
- **mil**—Used for U.S military organizations.
- **int**—Used for international organizations.
- **net**—Used for network organizations such as Internet Service Providers.
- **org**—Used for nonprofit organizations.
- **arpa**—Used for inverse address lookups.

The structure of the Domain Name System is similar to an inverted tree. In Figure 24.16, you can see that at the top is the root domain with the com through arpa domains underneath. Under the com domain are individual business organizations that each have their own domain. Under any particular domain there can be subdomains.

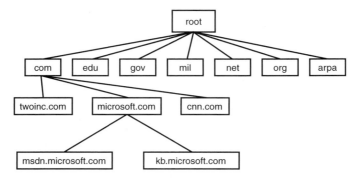

Figure 24.16   The Domain Name System is a distributed, hierarchical structure.

At each level, a fully-qualified domain name (FQDN) is created by concatenating the local name with the names of the entities above it in the hierarchy. Thus, `msdn.microsoft.com` is used to name the msdn subdomain in the Microsoft domain that falls under the com domain. By using the FQDN, it is possible for a host name to be used multiple times, as long as it produces a unique FQDN. For example, `fileserver.twoinc.com` names a host called fileserver. This host cannot become confused with another host of the same name that resides in a different domain such as `fileserver.acme.com`.

There are a number of restrictions to the names you can use in the DNS system:

- The maximum length of a domain name or a host label is 63 characters.
- The maximum length for the FQDN is 255 characters.
- There can be up to 127 subdomains.
- Text is not case sensitive.

New Top-Level Domains

Since ICANN took over responsibilities for handling names and numbers used on the Internet, several new top-level domains have been created. You can expect over the next few years to see additional top-level domains added to this list. The most recent additions were made in November 2000. These are

- **aero**—Intended for use by the air-transport industry
- **biz**—For use by businesses
- **coop**—For use by cooperatives
- **info**—Anything you want
- **museum**—Guess?
- **name**—For registration of individual names
- **pro**—Accountants, lawyers, and physicians

These new proposed top-level domains are expected to become active in the Fall of 2001. Of these domains, some are unsponsored (biz, info, name, and pro), which means that they will be governed by the global Internet community through ICANN, while the others (aero, coop, and museum) are sponsored domains. This means that they will be governed by specific entities. For example, the domain coop is sponsored by the National Cooperative Business Association.

Note

You might have noticed recently that there are other domains that appear to be new, such as the popular tv domain. However, note that the .tv domain is *not* a new top-level domain. Instead, it is the country code domain for the country of Tuvalu (a small island in the Pacific Ocean), which has allowed an enterprising company to use its country-style domain name for a fee. The company can market the tv domain to register domains that are associated with, of course, television. However, remember that this is just a country code domain. It is not one of the new top-level domains that ICANN has authorized. There is nothing that requires a particular country to use its own domain designation for just its use. Whoever thought up this method for establishing what appears to be a new domain should be named Capitalist of the Year!

To stay up-to-date on what the current top-level domains are, visit ICANN at their Web site `www.icann.com`.

Primary, Secondary, and Caching Only Name Servers

For each domain on the Internet, there must be a primary server and a secondary server. The primary DNS server for the domain contains a collection of *resource records* that contain the address mappings for hostnames in the domain. The primary DNS server is the final authority for these mappings. The secondary DNS server contains a copy of the database maintained by the primary server and can continue to resolve names when the primary server is offline. It is important to note that the primary DNS server is where changes are made to the database. Through the use of the *zone transfer* mechanism, the data is copied to secondary servers.

In many cases, a DNS server answers name queries for domains for which it is not the authority. In this case, the DNS server contacts a DNS server further up the hierarchy until one is found that can resolve the name translation, or that can point to another DNS server that is the authority for the name. The DNS server maintains a cache of names that have been resolved by this method so that it does not have to continually poll other servers for names that are frequently queried.

A third type of DNS server is a caching-only server. This type of server does not maintain a database for a particular zone. To put it in other terms, it is not authoritative for any zone or domain and does not use the zone transfer mechanism to keep a current copy of the entire database. Instead, a caching-only name server has to contact another DNS server to initially resolve a name, but like the other servers it maintains a cache of names it has resolved so that it does not have to keep forwarding the query to another server. This type of server is usually used on a network segment connected to the rest of the network by a slower link (or a more expensive one) and is used to reduce network traffic.

Zones

In many cases, it is not efficient to have a single server maintain the database for an entire domain. Instead, a primary DNS server can be authoritative for only a zone in the domain. A *zone* is a partition of the domain into subdomains. For example, one DNS server might be the authority for the zone biz.twoinc.com, whereas another might serve as the authority for the zone research.twoinc.com. Both subdomains exist within the same domain: twoinc.com. However, by dividing the domain into subdomains, it becomes easier to manage not only the DNS servers but also the individual business or organizational units that the domain services.

A *zone transfer* occurs when a secondary DNS server contacts a server that is primary for the zone, and finds that it needs to obtain changes to the database. This is accomplished by using serial numbers contained in the database. If the secondary server has a lower serial number, a new copy of the database is copied to it.

Standard DNS Database Files

There are three basic types of files used by DNS servers. In most DNS implementations, you need to use a text editor to make changes to these files. Some newer DNS servers, such as Microsoft's DNS server, provide a graphical interface that can be used for adding or changing information in the DNS files. The basic files are

- **The Database File**—This is the file that stores the resource records for the zone(s) for which the DNS server is responsible. The first record in this file is the Start of Authority (SOA) record.
- **The Cache File**—This file contains information for other name servers that can be used to resolve queries that are outside the zone or domain for which the server is responsible.
- **The Reverse Lookup File**—This file is used to provide a host name when the client only knows the IP address. This can be useful for security purposes. For example, a Web server that receives a request from a client can query the DNS with the name of the client to find out if the host name associated with the IP address is correct.

Resource Records

DNS databases are usually composed of ASCII text files containing records that can be used to translate a name to an IP address. There are several types of records that can be used in the database, each representing a specific type of resource, such as a computer hostname or a mailserver name.

When representing a domain name in DNS, a specific syntax is used. The term *label* is used in RFC 1035, "Domain Names—Implementation and Specification," when describing this syntax. A label is a one-byte length field followed by a data field. The length field indicates the number of characters in the data field. A domain name is represented by a series of labels and the entire domain name string is terminated with a length field of zero. For example, Figure 24.17 shows the layout of a series of labels that would be used to define the domain name zira.twoinc.com.

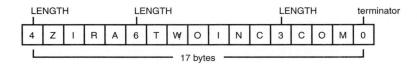

Figure 24.17   The domain name is represented by a series of labels in DNS.

Although the string is only 13 bytes long, excluding the periods, it takes 17 bytes to represent it in the database because of the length fields and the terminator field. To avoid repetition for domain names that are used a lot in the database, a pointer record can be used.

The general format used for a resource record contains the following fields:

- **Name**—The owner name. This is the name of the domain to which this record belongs.
- **Type**—A two-byte field that specifies the resource record type code.
- **Class**—A two-byte field that specifies the resource record class code.
- **TTL**—A 32-bit signed integer that specifies the time-to-live value. The TTL value specifies the amount of time a record can be cached before its value needs to be refreshed from the authoritative source. Zero indicates that the record cannot be cached.
- **RDLENGTH**—An unsigned 16-bit integer that indicates the length of the data field that follows.
- **RDATA**—The data field. This part of the record describes the resource. The contents depend on the values of the type and class fields.

The Type field indicates the type of resource record. Table 24.1 contains a list of the standard record types used in most DNS implementations, along with a description of their use.

Table 24.1   DNS Resource Records

Record Type	Description
A	Host IP Address
AAAA	Host IP Address (Ipv6)
NS	Name Server Record
PTR	Pointer to another Domain Name Record
SOA	Start of a zone of authority
WKS	Well-Known Service
HINFO	Host Information
MX	"Mail Exchanger" for the domain
MINFO	Mailbox or Mail list information
TXT	Text entry for miscellaneous information
CNAME	Canonical Name for an Alias

In earlier implementations of DNS, other record types were also used. For instance, MD and MF were used to specify Mail Destination and Mail Forwarder records. RFC 1035 made obsolete three other RFCs: 882, 883, and 973. Four other types that are considered experimental are

- **MB**—Mailbox domain name
- **MG**—Mail group member
- **MR**—Mail rename domain name
- **NULL**—Null resource record

In addition, RFC 2782, "A DNS RR for Specifying the Location of Services (DNS SRV)" added a new record type that figures *heavily* into a Windows 2000 network: the SRV, or *service record*. This type of record is used to store records in a DNS database that clients can use to look up services. For example, Windows 2000 uses this type of record to enable clients to use DNS to locate domain controllers and other services. We'll get into more details about that in the next chapter.

The Start of Authority (SOA) record is used at the beginning of the database and is used to describe the database. It is used mostly by secondary DNS servers to get zone information. The fields in this record are:

- **Domain name**—Name of the domain for which this database is the authority.
- **IN**—The class type of Internet.
- **SOA**—The Start of Authority record type indicator.
- **Primary Server**—The FQDN of the primary DNS server for this domain.
- **Email address**—The e-mail address of a person who is responsible for this domain.
- **Serial number**—A 32-bit value that shows the revision number of the database file. It is incremented each time a change is made to the database so that secondary servers can detect the change.
- **Refresh Rate**—A 32-bit value used by secondary servers. After this interval has elapsed, the data for a record needs to be checked again in the primary server database.
- **Retry Rate**—A 32-bit value indicating the amount of time to wait before retrying to refresh data after a failed attempt.
- **Expire Rate**—A 32-bit value indicating the maximum amount of time a secondary server is to try to refresh data before it stops processing DNS data for this zone.
- **Minimum TTL**—The minimum amount of time for a resource record's TTL. This value can be overridden by the TTL value specified in the record itself.

All time values in the SOA record are in seconds.

The NS record type can be used to indicate that another name server is authoritative for this subdomain. For example, the record

```
zork.twoinc.com    IN    NS    zira.twoinc.com
```

indicates that the name server whose FQDN host name is zira.twoinc.com is the authoritative name server from which to get information about the subdomain zork.twoinc.com. To get the address of the name server zira.twoinc.com, an "A" type record is needed:

```
zira.twoinc.com    IN    A    216.65.33.219
```

The CNAME record is used to specify aliases or nicknames that can be used in addition to a hostname, for example:

```
ftp.zira.twoinc.com     IN     CNAME     zira.twoinc.com
```

Pointer records (PTR class) are used to get the name that is associated with an IP address—a reverse translation. For example:

```
219.33.65.216     IN     PTR     zira.twoinc.com
```

can be used to perform a query to get the name of this host when only the IP address is known. Notice, however, that in this record, *the IP address has been reversed*. It is represented in a pointer record as 219.33.65.216 instead of 216.65.33.219. The reverse format is used to make a key-lookup in the database function properly. The special domain called IN-ADDR.ARPA contains the data used when a server needs to look up the hostname for an address in the domain.

The Class field is generally IN, which stands for Internet. The numeric value for this code is 1. In addition to this class type, you might see references to CS, which stands for the obsolete CSNET class. The CH class stands for the CHAOS class and the HS class code stands for the Hesiod class.

Configuring a Unix DNS Server

On most Unix systems, configuring a DNS server involves editing ASCII text files and making the appropriate entries. The actual files to edit depend on the brand of Unix you are using. The most common is the Berkeley Internet Name Domain (BIND) implementation. This server uses a daemon called in.named.

In addition to the actual zone database files you also have to edit

- **/etc/named.boot**—This file provides information for the in.named daemon when it starts up. The Directory directive specifies the directory that holds the zone database files (usually /var/named). The Cache directive tells the server to load a cache of initial hostnames. The directive Primary tells the server that it will function as the primary DNS server for the zone and the directive Secondary tells the server that it will function as the secondary DNS server for the zone.

- **/var/named/db.cache**—This is the usual name for the cache file.

To start the BIND service daemon after you have edited all the appropriate files, you only need to enter the command in.named at the system command prompt. If you have edited the /etc/named/boot file or its equivalent on your Unix variant), the server automatically starts the next time the system is booted.

The most time-consuming task is the editing of the zone data base files, making entries for the hosts in the domain.

Configuring Microsoft DNS Server on Windows NT 4.0

Microsoft DNS Server must be installed on a Windows NT 4.0 system in a manner similar to the WINS server: by using the Network applet in the Control Panel to add a service. After you select the Microsoft DNS Server service, you have to reboot the system before the installation completes.

Upon rebooting, you can bring up the DNS Server graphical interface by selecting Start/Programs/Administrative Tools/DNS Server. When the utility first starts up, there are no servers defined, so select New Server from the DNS drop-down menu to get to the Add DNS Server dialog box, shown in Figure 24.18.

Figure 24.18 You must first add the name or IP address of a server to begin configuring the Microsoft DNS Server.

To configure a DNS server on the local node, enter the IP address for that node in the dialog box. If you want to connect to a DNS server that has been installed on another server, enter its address instead.

After you add the server to the list of DNS servers, create a zone. Be sure that the server is highlighted in the Server List and then select New Zone from the DNS menu. The first dialog box prompts you to create a Primary or a Secondary zone type. Click the Next button after your selection. If you are creating a secondary zone, you also have to enter the name of that zone and the name of the server where the primary server resides.

The next dialog box prompts for the name of the zone and the name of the database file that is to be used to hold the records (see Figure 24.19).

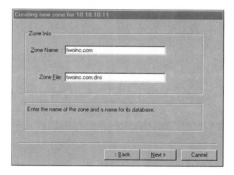

Figure 24.19 The DNS Wizard prompts for the name of the zone and the database file to be created.

The database file for the new zone is created, and you can then begin populating the file. For example, enter a host record, select the zone name in the Server List, and from the DNS menu select New Host. A dialog box (shown in Figure 24.20) prompts you to enter the name of the new host and the IP address for the host. Only enter the actual host name, not the fully-qualified hostname. For example, enter **zira** instead of zira.twoinc.com. Because the database is for a particular zone, you must enter host records for that zone.

When you are finished entering hostnames, click the Done button. In Figure 24.21, you can see the Domain Name Service Manager with a populated database file.

To view details about any record or to make modifications, simply double-click it. To delete a record, right-click on the record and select Delete.

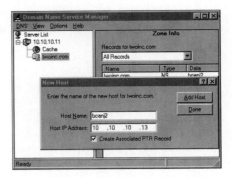

Figure 24.20 Enter the hostnames and the IP address in this dialog box.

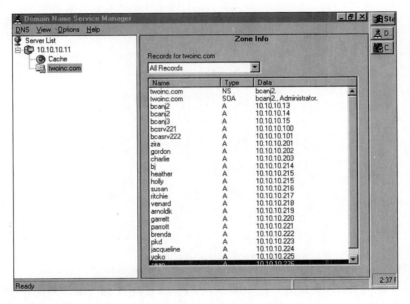

Figure 24.21 The Domain Name Service Manager provides a graphical interface into the zone database.

Configuring DNS Clients

Unix clients get their information about name servers from the file /etc/resolv.conf. (Note that this might be different for your variant of the "universal" Unix operating system. Check the manual pages.) To configure the client, edit this file. To place comments in this file, you can use the semi-colon (;) character. The three directives that you configure in this file are

- **Domain**—The default domain name. This name is appended to any names that are partially qualified.

- **Search**—This is a search list of domains used to look up names that are not fully-qualified. You can specify up to six domain names with a total of 256 characters for this directive.

■ **Nameserver**—You can specify up to three DNS servers by IP address with this directive. Note that if you do not specify a nameserver address, the default is the local domain.

For example:

```
;This is the /etc/resolv.conf file for local workstations
domain twoinc.com
; Name servers
nameserver 199.45.32.38
nameserver 151.197.0.39
nameserver 216.645.33.219
; search lists
search twoinc.com biznesnet.com
; end of file
```

A client using this file, trying to resolve the name of a host named zira, would first search the domain twoinc.com and then the domain biznesnet.com. The first match found is the one that will be used to resolve the name to an IP address.

To configure a Microsoft Client to use a DNS server, you only need to enter the IP addresses of the DNS servers when you perform the initial client network setup.

Using Nslookup

The nslookup utility is generally employed by users wanting to find the IP address associated with a name. However, the utility can be used to interrogate the DNS database to find out not only IP addresses, but also information stored in other records in the database. The utility can be used in either interactive mode, where the user can continue to issue commands, or it can be used in a one-shot non-interactive mode where a single query is executed. The basic syntax for the command is

```
nslookup [[-option ...] [hostname to locate]] - [server]
```

If you omit the last item in this syntax (- server), the local DNS server is queried. However, when you have multiple servers, or if you want to query a server outside your organization, specify it with this parameter.

A simple example of the command is nslookup twoinc.com, which returns the following information:

```
Name:    twoinc.com
Address:  216.65.33.219
```

If you want to retrieve more information about the server, you can use options and specify the info records:

```
nslookup -query=hinfo -timeout=10 www.twoinc.com

twoinc.com
        primary name server = ns1.tentex.com
        responsible mail addr = hostmaster.twoinc.com
        serial  = 1342
        refresh = 3600 (1 hour)
        retry   = 600 (10 mins)
        expire  = 86400 (1 day)
        default TTL = 3600 (1 hour)
```

As you can see, this tool is useful for looking up addresses, but can also be used to query the DNS database and help you debug configuration problems. With this simple query, you can see the serial number of the current database, along with other information stored in the SOA record. The syntax for the options of this command vary depending on your operating system.

Dynamic DNS

Earlier in this chapter, I discussed Microsoft's WINS servers. These NetBIOS name servers can be used to dynamically accept information from clients so that the network administrator does not have to make edits to the database each time a node is added to the network or a workstation is moved to a new location. The Dynamic Host Configuration Protocol (DHCP) has eliminated the necessity of manually configuring each computer host with network information. Microsoft's DNS server can be configured to query the WINS server when it needs to resolve a name it cannot find in its own databases.

This solution does not help if you have a multi-vendor network with workstations running different operating systems. There are several relevant RFCs that address these problems associated with standard DNS implementations, such as

- **RFC 2136, "Dynamic Updates in the Domain Name System (DNS UPDATE)"**—This RFC describes a method that can be used for dynamic updates to DNS. It provides for an atomic (all-or-nothing) update mechanism that can be used to add, delete, or modify one or more resource records in a zone file.

- **RFC 1995, "Incremental Zone Transfer in DNS"**—Incremental zone transfer means that only portions of the zone database file that have been modified need to be transferred from primary DNS servers to secondary servers. This process conserves network bandwidth and decreases the latency time for changes to be distributed throughout the Internet.

- **RFC 1996, "A Mechanism for Prompt Notification of Zone Changes (DNS NOTIFY)"**—This third piece of the solution enables the primary DNS server to notify the secondary servers that changes have been made to the zone database. Currently, zone transfers can occur only after a refresh interval has passed.

Current offerings for a DNS server that is truly dynamic and the corresponding DHCP server capable of making updates are not widespread at this time, but more are coming into the marketplace. Portions of the technology are implemented here and there. For example, The Internet Software Consortium (ISC), which maintains BIND, released—in March of 1999—version 8.2 of BIND, which supports RFC 2136. You can download documentation or the kit files from their Web site http://www.isc.org.

At the same site, you will also find a version of DHCP, along with a list of products developed by other developers that are based on or can work with these products.

With the rapid growth of the Internet and the increasing adoption of TCP/IP as the definitive protocol for business networks, it can be expected that in the next few years, we will see a new generation of products from various vendors that will incorporate these features and interoperate.

For those network administrators who already have DNS servers running on the network, but are concerned about whether these servers can be used in conjunction to the Windows 2000 version of DNS, please note that Windows 2000 DNS server also supports, in addition to the dynamic update RFCs listed previously, the following RFCs:

- RFC 1034, "Domain Names—Concepts and Facilities"
- RFC 1035, "Domain Names—Implementation and Specification"
- RFC 1123, "Requirements for Internet Hosts—Application and Support"
- RFC 1886, "DNS Extensions to Support IP Version 6"
- RFC 2181, "Clarifications to the DNS Specification"
- RFC 2308, "Negative Caching of DNS Queries (DNS NCACHE)"

Check the documentation for your BIND or DNS server to see which RFCs it supports. You might be surprised to find that this new and improved DNS server from Microsoft might be as good as, or perhaps better than, your current version. And, if you're going to use the Active Directory, then you'll have to install at least one copy of the Windows 2000 DNS server on a server that is also a domain controller.

Installing DNS on a Windows 2000 Server

Because it is so closely tied to the Active Directory and Windows 2000, installing and managing the DNS server for Windows 2000 when using the Active Directory is covered in greater detail in the next chapter. Windows clients in the network use DNS to locate domain controllers, which hold the Active Directory database. When you decide to promote a Windows 2000 server to become a domain controller, you will be prompted to install a DNS server as well. The domain controller will, after it has been properly configured, register records in DNS that enable clients to find the domain controllers in the domain.

However, you can always install a DNS server on the Windows 2000 server whether you decide to use the Active Directory or not. For example, you might have a few Windows 2000 servers in a Unix network and decide to use Microsoft's version of DNS because you find the graphical interface easy to use (tired of editing those text files and making a mistake?). Or, you might want to install additional DNS servers to provide a backup for a primary DNS server. You don't have to install the DNS service on just a domain controller, but the system must be a Windows 2000 Server.

To install the service is just as simple as installing the WINS service:

1. Click Start, Programs, Control Panel.
2. From the Control Panel, double-click the Add/Remove Programs icon.
3. When the Add Remove Programs window pops up, click Add/Remove Windows Components (on the left part of the window). The Add Remove Programs window now displays a button in the upper-right side of the window called Components. Click the Components button. The Windows Components Wizard dialog box pops up.
4. Scroll down until you find Network Services and highlight it by clicking it once. Then click the Details button.
5. When the Networking Services dialog box appears, scroll down until you find Domain Name System (DNS). Click the check box next to the component and click OK.
6. When prompted, insert the Windows 2000 source CD into your CD-ROM drive and then wait a minute or so while files are copied to your hard drive. When the Windows Component Wizard window reappears, click Next.
7. Another window, titled Completing the Windows Components Wizard appears. Click Finish.
8. When the Add Remove Programs window reappears, click OK.

Chapter 25, "Overview of Microsoft's Active Directory Service," looks more closely at how managing DNS on a Windows 2000 server is done using the MMC console, as well as how DNS can be installed at the same time, and integrated into the Active Directory.

Network Information Service (NIS)

As mentioned earlier, Sun developed a product that was originally called Yellow Pages, but the name was later changed due to a trademark owned by British Telecom. Sun's product was Network Information Service (NIS), a client/server system that allows for the sharing of information on a network that includes not only hostnames and addresses, but also other information, such as password files. The goal of NIS is to reduce administrative overhead problems associated with having multiple copies of files on hosts throughout the network.

NIS is based on a flat name space design. Sun has now released NIS+, which resembles the Domain Name System in its hierarchical structure. NIS+ uses a concept of NIS domains, which might or might not be paired with DNS domains. NIS uses a concept called maps for storing data. Maps uses a simple keyword/data concept. NIS+ uses a more traditional database format with tables containing multi-columned rows of data.

NIS is mentioned in this chapter not because it is a name resolution mechanism, but because on many Unix networks it is responsible for keeping synchronized other files that perform name resolution. If you use NIS (or NIS+), I recommend you become familiar with its installation and configuration. Security on Unix systems can be a difficult task if you just install NIS and forget about it. You need to understand how it works, and the security implications of keeping important information on different servers throughout the network.

Overview of Microsoft's Active Directory Service

SOME OF THE MAIN TOPICS IN THIS CHAPTER ARE

When migrating from Windows NT 4.0 to Windows 2000, it is important that you first understand what the Active Directory is and how it is tightly integrated into other parts of the operating system. Whether you want to manage users or find a printer on the network, you'll find that you will be using the Active Directory. If you want to create a secure, manageable, scalable network using Windows 2000, Windows XP or Windows .Net Server, you'll find yourself using the Active Directory. Although you also can create a small, workgroup-style network using Windows 2000 Professional and Server, if you want to maintain an atmosphere where security and administrative tasks can be centralized and controlled, as in the previous Windows NT domain models, you'll have to use the Active Directory.

What Is the Active Directory?

The only information that is stored in the Windows NT 4.0 SAM (Security Accounts Manager database) is user and computer accounts and security information, such as trust relationships between domains. Information about printers, file shares, and other resources are scattered here and there in separate databases and are managed by separate utilities. Administering network resources using multiple utilities with disjointed interfaces can become quite a nightmare in a large network. This disjointed method of administration has created a situation in which many upgraded their networks to Windows NT 4.0, but also adopted Novell Directory Services on the same network. Adding NDS to a Windows NT 4.0 network can solve a lot of problems by giving you a single place to administer many different kinds of resources.

▶▶   For a comparison and background information about Novell Directory Services (NDS), see Chapter 27, "Overview of the Novell Bindery and Novell Directory Services (NDS)."

The Directory and the Directory Service

The first thing you will need to understand about the Active Directory is that it is composed of a database and many different programs that can be used to operate on the database. The term *directory* is used to describe the underlying database that holds all the information managed by the directory service. The actual information store, the directory, is housed in a Microsoft Exchange Server database engine store.

The term *directory service* refers to the programs that manage the database and allow users and programs to access its data in a meaningful way. After you've created a domain controller in a Windows 2000 network, you'll find several new utilities in the Administrative Tools folder, such as the Active Directory Sites and Services Manager and the Active Directory Users and Computers tools. You'll find other tools in this folder, depending on the components you selected when installing the Windows 2000 operating system. The standard Event Viewer is still there (but it now uses the Microsoft Management Console, as do most of the other tools), and you even can install additional tools that allow you to dig deeply into the heart of the Active Directory, to view, or perhaps modify the schema, which we will get into later in this chapter.

The directory service consists of the programs and application programming interfaces (Active Directory Services Interface—ADSI and the C LDAP API) that can be used to manage or query the database by users and administrators. The directory service offers the network a *namespace* that can be used to locate objects throughout the network by querying by the object's name or one of its attributes.

The *Directory System Agent (DSA)* provides the service responsible for performing actual queries and updates to the database. Because applications and APIs make requests to the DSA in a defined fashion, the functions they perform are separated from the actual underlying format of data storage.

Interesting Objects

The Active Directory in Windows 2000 provides the capability to query a large database that can be used to locate any object, or information about any object, stored in the directory database. To understand how important the Active Directory will be in Windows 2000, first you must understand the kinds of data that will be stored in the objects that the directory organizes.

What kind of data should be a candidate for management by a directory service is not easily answered. Here, the definition of a directory service gets kind of fuzzy.

It is common to compare directory services to the white and yellow pages of the traditional phone directory. White pages are specific queries where the input is a person's name and the output is their telephone number. Yellow pages have a more general "browsing" capability, with more general input about a subject or concept. This results in a specific output selected by the user from the information found. The Active Directory provides the best of both. You can search for a specific object if you know the name you are looking for (such as a username or computer name), or you can browse for objects by using the data stored in the many attributes that objects can possess. Looking up a username in the Active Directory is sort of like using the white pages of the telephone book.

However, suppose you are a mobile employee. You have just walked into the Atlanta office and you need to print a document. You quickly search the directory to find an object that

1. Is a printer
2. Is located in the Atlanta branch on the third floor
3. Supports color printing

This situation shows that directory services also can be used in a manner similar to the telephone book's yellow pages service. You can specify the attributes for an object you want to find, and perform a search of the directory to see if there are any matches.

As you can see, the Active Directory stores the traditional kind of information that usually is found on a network computer operating system. But wait, there's more! What other kinds of objects can you store in the directory? Well, just about anything you can think of, as long as you can express it as a collection of attributes (or features of the object). If you want, it's possible to create objects that represent your stamp collection. You can create objects that represent just about anything. However, almost everyone agrees that the information stored in the directory should be interesting or of some practical use.

Early Directories

The first directory that comes to mind when you think of early computer systems is the file system directory. The organization of data files and programs into a structure of directories and subdirectories became more important as the size of the available storage grew. When networking PCs became a necessity, the capability to organize users and secure data from inappropriate access led to the concept of logging in to the computer or network, just as had been done with multiuser, mini, and mainframe computers for many years. This made it necessary to create another database (that is, a directory) to keep track of users and security information.

For network administrators and users alike, there is a great need today to quickly locate resources that, in a modern distributed computing environment, can be anywhere from the computer on the user's desk to a file server halfway around the world. So, when deciding what kinds of information to store in a directory service database, the needs of both the users and the administrators of the system must be taken into consideration.

What Active Directory Delivers

The target that Microsoft has been aiming at for several years is the development of its "next generation" of directory services, including

- A single logon for the entire network. This was present, more or less, in previous versions of Windows.

- A hierarchical structure that organizes objects and tasks into a logical format, so that you can quickly and easily locate the information you need. The X.500 hierarchical format has been adopted in the Active Directory for Windows 2000.

- An extendable format so that the directory can encompass new objects as operating systems and management functions continue to evolve. This means that the schema of the directory should be easy to modify.

- Fault tolerance and a distributed database so that you don't need to create numerous domains with primary domain controllers to receive updates and backup domain controllers to "hold the fort" when a PDC isn't available, as was the case with NT.

- Scalability, so that management tasks can be centralized or distributed as your administrative needs dictate.

- Programmability, which allows application developers and script writers an easy method to interface with the database.

- Manageable security mechanisms, from the small desktop system to the worldwide enterprise network that consists of millions of users.

One of the most important features that large enterprises would like to see is a *standards-based implementation* so that you do not get locked into a single vendor for all your software needs. Migration tools, both to and from the directory database, are needed until the standards issues settle down and products from different vendors work together as seamlessly as they do in the telephone network.

From X.500 and DAP to the Lightweight Directory Access Protocol

When you think of standards, does the name International Organization for Standardization (ISO) come to mind? Probably, because they have been involved in efforts for many years to help make the interchange of data between computers less of a proprietary chore and more of a free flow of information. The ISO, along with the International Telecommunications Union (ITU), developed the X.500 group of standards to promulgate a global white pages directory service. Under the umbrella of X.500 there are many standards, which include naming conventions and networking protocols (OSI—the Open Systems Interconnection Protocol).

Note

Although many books state that the letters ISO are an abbreviation for International Standards Organization, that is not the case. Instead, the actual name of the organization, in English, is International Organization for Standardization. The term ISO was selected by this group because of its root meaning from the original Greek word isos, which translates generally to "equal." This name was chosen, because it pretty much indicates standardization, without having to use a particular language to create an acronym. Thus, the ISO works with standards bodies from many different countries, attempting to make technological things "equal," so that they will work together. You can find out more about ISO and its member organizations by visiting http://www.iso.ch/.

However, the OSI networking protocol never did take off as expected, although some vendors implemented parts of it. Digital Equipment Corporation (now absorbed by Compaq Computer Corporation) tried for years to get OSI standards adopted by evolving its own proprietary networking protocol—DECnet—into an OSI-compliant protocol and by releasing an operating system (OSF) that was based on OSI standards. But, while all this discussion of standards was going on in committees and protocols were being discussed, debated, and refined, the Internet took off. And as everyone now knows, it is TCP/IP that glues together the Internet, not OSI.

It was not just the lack of interest in OSI network protocols that stifled the acceptance of X.500 proposals. Several other important factors were involved, such as the overhead associated with implementing many of the X.500 protocols. Although X.500 does a good job defining a protocol, it does not attempt to define standard programming interfaces (APIs, which make it easy for different vendors to write applications that implement the protocols).

Another reason you won't find X.500 standards implemented in many places is its complicated naming scheme. The hierarchical organization of the directory, which can be seen in its naming format, is a good idea, but the long-winded name is not. For example, which of the following would you rather try to remember when sending someone an e-mail message, the X.500 format or the RFC 822 name?

- X.500

    ```
    CN=Ono,OU=Studio One,OU=New York,O=mydomain,C=US
    ```

- RFC 822

    ```
    Ono@mydomain.com
    ```

The X.500 name, in this example, reveals the organization structure of the directory, whereas the RFC 822 name does not. But every user shouldn't have to be fully cognizant of the directory structure in order to use it. If you want to send Ono a message via e-mail, you should not have to know that she works in Studio One (organizational unit=Studio One) and that she is in the company's New York division (organizational unit=New York). You shouldn't have to specify that she is in the United States because you already indicated that she is in New York! And, because you can have additional organizational units (OU=) in the directory, the X.500 address actually could have been much, much longer.

Directory services should make things easier, not more difficult. Microsoft's Active Directory Services uses the hierarchical treelike organization as spelled out by the X.500 protocols, but adapts the Windows NT domain system, by using DNS as a locator service, to the structure. In addition to the standard container types such as OU for organizational unit, Active Directory has a DC, or *domain component* container object, defined in the schema that can be used to house domains in the directory. By incorporating domains into the directory, rather than simply discarding the domain concept, Microsoft has made it easier for users of Windows NT 4.0 to interact with or make the migration to Windows 2000. Domains can be imported into the directory when migrating existing Windows NT networks.

The overhead associated with other X.500 recommendations also needs to be overcome. Four "wire" (or communication) protocols were defined:

- Directory Access Protocol (DAP)
- Directory System Protocol (DSP)
- Directory Information Shadowing Protocol (DISP)
- Directory Operational Binding Management Protocol (DOP)

These protocols were developed during a time in which PCs did not have sufficient computing power to host such complex protocols and still be capable of performing adequately as a desktop workstation.

▶▶   For more information about the history of the X.500 protocols and the development of LDAP, see Appendix D, "Directory Services: Overview of the X.500 and LDAP Protocols."

To reduce the overhead associated with the X.500 directory structure, a new set of Request For Comments (RFCs) have been developed to define the Lightweight Directory Access Protocol (LDAP). LDAP is the protocol that Microsoft has chosen to implement in its Active Directory Services. Although there have been several products available that use the features defined in LDAP v 2.0, Active Directory Services has been designed to be compatible with both version 2.0 and the newer proposed standard, LDAP v 3.0.

▶▶   For those interested in some very boring reading, Version 2.0 of the Lightweight Directory Access Protocol (LDAP) is defined by RFC 1777.

      If that doesn't put you to sleep, try reading up on Version 3.0. It has been adopted by most LDAP products. This LDAP version is defined by RFC 2251, "Lightweight Access Directory Protocol V 3," by Wahl, Howes, and Kille. In Appendix D, you'll find a list of additional RFCs that further define aspects of the LDAP protocol.

By using a standard that is being implemented by many other vendors, including Netscape and Novell, the Active Directory can exchange data and queries with other directory service implementations; thus, you won't get stuck in yet another proprietary solution. Of course, this all depends on how Microsoft and other vendors choose to interpret and implement LDAP features as they are standardized and refined.

What Is the Schema?

If you are familiar with databases that are manipulated using the Structured Query Language (SQL), you might already understand what a schema is. Put simply, it is the definition of the types of things, or objects, that you can store in the directory structure. The directory contains many different types of objects, such as user accounts, printers, and computer accounts. Each object is made up of attributes that contain the specific data for the object. The schema is the definition of these objects, their attributes, and the classes to which they belong.

In some directory implementations, the schema is stored as an ordinary ASCII text file, similar to the way some DNS servers store their information. Each time the software that runs the directory is booted up, the schema file is read into memory. One of the drawbacks of using this method is that if you want to make changes to the schema, you usually have to edit the text file and then reload it into the application. The Active Directory avoids this problem by defining the schema of the directory in the directory itself! You can manipulate the schema just as you do other objects in the directory.

Specifically, the Active Directory schema is made up of four types of objects that are used to define the schema:

- **Schema container object**—Each directory instance has at least one schema container object, which is a direct child of the directory root. The schema container holds the other objects, which describe the object classes and attributes of the directory.

- **Class container object**—This container object holds the object classes that define what kind of objects can be stored in the directory. Class objects reference property objects that store the actual properties, or attributes, of an object class.

- **Property object**—This type of object is used by the schema to define a particular attribute or property of the object. It references the syntax object.

- **Syntax object**—This object describes a particular syntax that is applied to one or more properties defined by property objects.

Objects and Attributes

For the most part, an *object* is nothing more than a collection of specific attributes that hold the data the object represents. For example, an object that represents a user account contains attributes that hold information about the particular user. When you create user accounts in the Active Directory, you supply the same information that you did when you created user accounts using the User Manager for Domains in previous Windows versions. The Active Directory contains objects that can be used to store information about everything from user accounts to printers to the actual schema of the Active Directory itself.

However, the Active Directory can be used to store almost any kind of information you want. It's just a matter of finding the correct object (or creating a new object class) and then entering the data for instances of the object.

From the discussion of X.500 names earlier in this chapter, remember the term "organizational unit," or OU as it is represented in the X.500 naming scheme. An organizational unit is an object in the directory that holds, or contains, other objects. For example, in the Active Directory, a domain is a container object. It holds other objects, some of which are container objects also, such as the Users object. The Users object holds the actual individual user accounts. It is in these *instances* of the User object that the attributes will be found which define each user on the system.

Attributes are simply the fine-grained details of the data stored in an object. Each attribute for an object holds a specific kind of data, and thus has a specific syntax associated with it. An attribute that is used to hold a person's name would have a syntax that requires a text string. The syntax would define a minimum and maximum length for the string. An attribute that represents a numeric value would have a syntax that specifies the minimum and maximum value of the number that can be stored in the object.

When a new class of objects is defined, you have the capability to create two particular types of attributes: *required* or *optional*. If an attribute is of the required type, each object you create of the particular object class *must* have some value defined for the required attribute. However, there can be other attributes you might want to define for the User object class which do not apply to all users. For example, you might want to keep a list of the names of the user's spouse and children. However, not all users will necessarily have a spouse or offspring, so this kind of attribute could be created as an optional attribute.

Standard Objects in the Directory

The Active Directory comes with two sets of standard objects: *container* and *leaf*.

Container objects hold other objects in the directory. Leaf objects are the endpoints in a directory tree that contain specific attributes about a directory object entry. In other words, the leaf objects contain the actual data (attributes) that the Active Directory stores, while container objects group these leaf objects, such as individual users or printers, into meaningful groups. Note that a container object also can contain other container objects, as well as leaf objects. This makes it possible to create subdivisions in the directory that model your business or administrative needs. Using the uniform Microsoft Management Console (MMC) interface, container objects appear as folders in a tree. The standard container objects that you are most likely to encounter during day-to-day system management chores are

- Namespaces
- Country
- Locality

- Organization
- Organizational Unit
- Domain
- Computer

Standard leaf objects that are provided are

- User
- Group
- Alias
- Service
- Print Queue
- Print Device
- Print Job
- File Service
- File Share
- Session
- Resource

These built-in object classes give most of the functionality a network will need when using the Active Directory to manage users, computers, and resources. This is not a complete listing, however, of all the objects you'll find in the Active Directory. There are many, many more. And, if you need the capability to store still other types of objects, you can modify the schema by using the Active Directory Schema Manager Snap-in, which is discussed later in this chapter.

Naming Objects in the Directory

Two types of names can be used to identify an object in the directory. The first is called the *distinguished name (DN)* and the second is the *relative distinguished name (RDN)*. The relative distinguished name is just a value of a particular attribute of the object. For example, for user objects, the RDN is the common name (CN) of the object. So, for the user object that holds account information for user Luke Kurtis, the RDN for the object would be Luke Kurtis. In the Active Directory there can be more than one Luke Kurtis, so there needs to be a method for telling them apart. The distinguished name is that method.

A distinguished name consists of the RDN of the object, *plus all the RDNs of every object* that precede it in the directory. Referring to the X.500 address format, it quickly becomes apparent that the DN of an object not only uniquely identifies the object in the directory, but also reveals its location in the hierarchy.

The example given earlier showing how X.500 defines an object name shows the structure of a distinguished name:

```
CN=Ono,OU=Studio One,OU=New York,O=mydomain,C=US
```

Here the RDN of the user object is the common name Ono. But the object Ono is located in the container object named Studio One, which is located in the container object called New York, which is located in the container object called mydomain, and so on. Although there can be more than one Ono object in the directory, there can be only one object with the RDN of Ono that is located in the

Studio One department in New York for this domain in the United States. If another Ono comes to work in that department, she will have to use a different name! There is an easier way around this, of course. When assigning usernames to employees, many companies already use a combination of letters rather than an employee's full name. For example, John Doe might be assigned a username of doej, using the last name plus the first letter of the first name. If another John Doe is hired, a variation on this can be performed by assigning the new employee the username doej2.

However, another distinct Ono might work in the manufacturing department in the same organization. For example,

```
CN=Ono,OU=Manufacturing,OU=New York,O=mydomain,C=US
```

is a perfectly legal distinguished name and can reside in the same directory database as the first Ono.

What Is a Domain Tree? What Is a Forest?

The Active Directory gives you one single enterprise-wide namespace. This namespace is used for user accounts, resource objects, application configuration information, and so on. What you decide to store in the directory, beyond the default objects set up by the installation process, is up to you. The namespace can be global, provided you organize your domains into a domain tree.

A domain tree is nothing more than a method of organizing the domains in your enterprise into a structure, so that they all share a common directory schema and a *contiguous* namespace. Although a domain tree is a structure formed by a collection of domains, a forest is a collection of domain trees. *The namespace in the forest does not have to be contiguous*, as it does in the tree, so a forest can be used to link disparate domain trees in the organization so that trust relationships still can be used to allow a single user logon in the network.

To understand what a domain tree or a forest is, you must know what it is replacing in the Windows NT networking scheme.

Domain Models—May They Rest in Peace!

In previous versions of Windows NT, the domain was used to group users and resources with a common security policy to simplify administrative tasks. In large organizations, a single domain was not sufficient to hold all the users and resources, and was not an efficient method of administering user rights and privileges or resource protections. Because of this, multiple domains were created and linked in what is termed a *trust relationship*. This trust relationship allowed users from one domain to be granted access rights to resources in another trusting domain.

A trust relationship in earlier versions of Windows NT could be a one-way or a two-way relationship. In a one-way trust relationship, one domain would trust the users that had been authenticated by another domain. The administrator in the trusting domain could grant users (or groups of users) from the trusted domain access rights in the local trusting domain. In a two-way trust relationship, the relationship existed in both directions. The trust relationship is not transitive. That is, if domain A has a trust relationship that allows its users to be assigned rights in domain B, and if domain B has a trust relationship that allows its users to be assigned rights to resources in domain C, a user in domain A cannot be granted rights in domain C by use of these trust relationships. That would require that domain A establish a separate trust relationship with domain C.

The way domains were organized into user or resource domains, and how the trust relationships were set up, led to the development of several domain models that could be used, depending on the size of your enterprise and the methods used to administer them. These were the single domain, multiple domain, master domain, and multiple-master domain models.

Because the domain essentially was the boundary for the security accounts manager (SAM) database, you had two basic choices. You could put all your user accounts into a single master domain, and then grant them access rights to objects in *resource* domains, or you could put users into separate domains, depending on your organization, and maintain a complicated set of trust relationships and administrative policies.

The headache associated with managing multiple trust relationships—and moving users to and from when reorganizations occurred—is one of the major drawbacks of the SAM-based domain models.

The Directory Is Partitioned into Domains

When you install Windows 2000 Server and create a new domain, you are given several choices concerning how the domain will relate to an Active Directory tree. You can create a new forest or become part of an existing forest and create a new tree, making this new domain the first domain in the new tree. Or, you can make the new domain a child domain in a domain tree that already exists in the forest.

Each domain in the domain tree is a security boundary in the Active Directory, just as it is in previous versions of Windows NT. However, you no longer have to create one- or two-way trust relationships between domains for users to be granted access rights and privileges in other domains that are in the same domain tree.

When a Windows 2000 domain joins a domain tree, a *two-way transitive trust relationship*, based on the Kerberos security authentication method, is automatically established between the child domain and its parent domain in the tree. Because the trust relationship is *transitive*, there is no need to manually configure additional trust relationships with other domains that exist in the domain tree. This means that after your domain is created and joined to a domain tree, your users can be granted access rights to resources in any other domain in the tree without the need to further create a complicated set of trust relationships with other domains.

Note

The MIT Kerberos (version 5) authentication method is defined in RFC 1510, "The Kerberos Network Authentication Service (V5)," by Kohl and Neuman.

Each domain in the tree holds the portion of the Active Directory database that represents the objects found in that domain. However, the namespace is contiguous throughout the tree. Each domain controller in the domain holds a complete replica of the directory for that domain. And, to help reduce network traffic and administrative overhead, you can create additional replicas of the domain's portion of the directory and place it close to users in other domains that frequently access the resources in your domain.

A Domain Is Still a Domain

The domain in Windows 2000 is still a security boundary, just like it was in previous versions of Windows NT. Domain administrators can still take command and exert their authority over all users and resources in the domain. From that perspective, nothing has changed.

However, the management of your relationships with other domains is now much easier. The two-way transitive trust relationships are set up automatically, so you don't have to coordinate managing this with other administrators throughout the network. If you upgrade from a previous version of

Windows NT, all your groups and users are migrated into the Active Directory under your same domain. You can manage them as you always have, although there are new tools (using the MMC interface) that are used instead.

▶▶ For more information about how to manage users (and computers) in the Active Directory, see Chapter 31, "Windows 2000 User and Computer Management Utilities."

Trees and Forests

As discussed earlier in this section, a domain tree is a collection of domains that have a contiguous namespace, whereas trees in a forest can have a noncontiguous namespace. Contiguous namespace means that the object in each child domain in the tree has the name of its parent domains prefixed to its distinguished name. This also means that the names used to identify each child domain will have the names of the parents prefixed. Figure 25.1 shows an example of a domain tree. The domain tree starts at the top and flows down the tree, rather than from the bottom up.

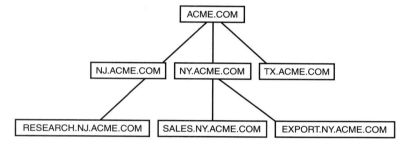

Figure 25.1   A domain tree is a contiguous namespace.

In this domain tree, the most-senior parent in the tree is the acme.com domain. Beneath that are three child domains, nj.acme.com, ny.acme.com, and tx.acme.com. Under the New York child domain, you can see a sales domain (sales.ny.acme.com) and another domain called export.ny.acme.com. This tree could be further expanded by adding additional child domains to any of the domains in the tree. The way you construct the fully qualified domain name for a domain positions it in the tree structure.

In the best of all possible worlds, each enterprise would have exactly one domain tree and one large contiguous namespace. However, in this rapid-paced business world, nothing remains the same for long, including business organizational units. Corporate mergers and acquisitions, for example, can bring in large numbers of users and resources that must be incorporated quickly into the network structure. In this situation, it might not be possible to easily include the acquired assets into the naming structure.

However, you can still join two disparate domain trees. You can't put them into the same tree because the naming for all objects would not be contiguous. You can, however, join domain trees into a structure called a forest.

A forest is like a domain tree, but the namespace does not have to be contiguous throughout the forest. The directory schema is still common for all domains, and you can establish trust relationships between the trees. Users can still use a single logon to access resources in domains that reside in different domain trees (see Figure 25.2).

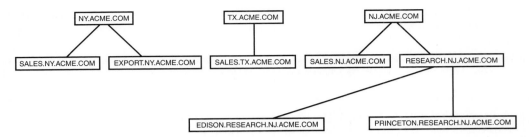

Figure 25.2 Domain trees with disjointed namespaces can exist in a forest.

The Active Directory and Dynamic DNS

DNS, or the Domain Name Service, is the most widely used network address/name translation service in the world, and is used on the Internet. This service was created many years ago when the first DARPA network, the predecessor of today's Internet, experienced rapid growing pains and needed a distributed naming service that could be used to locate the address of any server in the network.

◄◄ You can read more about the Domain Name System (DNS) in Chapter 24, "Name Resolution."

The Backbone of the Internet and the Active Directory

The Internet has grown so large in the past five years that, without a distributed naming service, it would be almost impossible to keep track of all nodes in the network, much less the services they offer. DNS has evolved to contain many different types of records that can be used to translate names to addresses. These include not only names of servers or workstations on the Net, but also services, such as the World Wide Web, e-mail, and others.

Dynamic DNS

Administering a large number of computers in a network can be quite a chore. Moving a computer from one network subnet to another used to require that the administrator manually reconfigure the DNS servers in the enterprise so that he or she could accurately translate the computer's name to its correct address. With the advent of mobile computing and the proliferation of laptops that are here today, gone tomorrow, reconfiguring network addresses can become a full-time job on a large network.

The Dynamic Host Configuration Protocol (DHCP) solves part of this problem by allowing a computer to request a network address, along with other configuration information, when it boots into the network. However, this doesn't completely solve the problems that arise as the result of mobile computing. After the client computer has obtained network address and configuration information, how does it communicate that information to other computers so that they can locate it on the network?

◄◄ You can read more about DHCP in Chapter 23, "BOOTP and the Dynamic Host Configuration Protocol (DHCP)."

In early versions of Windows NT, the Windows Internet Naming Service (WINS) was the answer to this problem. After a computer boots, it can contact a WINS server, which acts very much like a dynamic DNS server. It accepts registrations from clients and stores or updates their information so that other computers can query the database to find the client's network address.

In Windows 2000, you still can use the WINS service, which might be helpful for legacy Windows clients if you have a mixed network of Windows 2000 and Windows NT 4.0 computers. However,

Windows 2000 comes with an updated version of Microsoft's DNS, which includes the capability to dynamically update the DNS database.

Note

Dynamic updates to the DNS database is defined in RFC 2136. This RFC defines the UPDATE opcode and a format to be used as the update message, along with procedures that can be used to implement dynamic DNS.

How the Active Directory Uses DNS

The Active Directory uses DNS to keep track of domain controllers. DNS is used as a locator service as well as a name/address translation service. Remember that the Active Directory provides a service to its users through the LDAP protocol. Services can be recorded in DNS through Service Resource Records (SRV RRs), and this is how the Active Directory uses DNS.

Note

SRV Service Resource Records are defined by RFC 2052, "A DNS RR for specifying the location of services (DNS SRV)," by Gulbrandsen and Vixie.

An SRV RR record consists of data in the format of

```
<service name>.<protocol>.<domain>
```

Because the Active Directory uses LDAP, a resource record for this service would look like this:

```
LDAP.TCP.twoinc.com
```

Because the DNS that is provided with Windows 2000 is a dynamic DNS, there is no associated administrative work when you add domain controllers to your network. Each domain controller automatically contacts a DNS server and provides it with the necessary information to register its name, address, and the services it offers. Each domain controller also checks back at frequent intervals to be sure that the information is accurate and will make changes to the DNS information as changes are made on the server.

One thing to note about the use of DNS as a locator service, is that you do not have to use Microsoft's own DNS server to have an Active Directory–enabled network. The DNS product that you use, however, *must* support SRV records, because this is how domain controllers advertise themselves to the network. The DNS server you use does not have to use dynamic DNS functions, however. This just makes the DNS administrator's life a lot easier in a rapidly changing environment.

Using Sites to Manage Large Enterprises

If you are familiar with the concept of a site, as used by Microsoft Exchange, you are going to have to change that idea in your mind when you start to deal with the new site concept that is used by Windows 2000 networking. In Microsoft Exchange, a site is composed of Exchange servers that all share a common namespace.

However, in Windows 2000 a site is nothing more than a collection of well-connected computers that exist on an IP subnet, and which usually are located close to each other geographically. The grouping of computers into sites is done to make replication fast and efficient. It is not a concept that relates to managing or administering users, resources, or network security. The following are two important things to remember about a site, as used by Windows 2000:

- A domain can have computers in more than one site.
- A site can contain computers from more than one domain.

Windows 2000 uses only domain controllers to hold the Active Directory database. *There is no longer a primary domain controller that controls writing or modifying directory information and backup domain controllers that provide a read-only service to users and computers.* In Windows 2000, all domain controllers can receive updates to the database, and the changes then are replicated to all other domain controllers that participate in the directory tree.

The Knowledge Consistency Checker service is run on every domain controller, and it is this service that establishes connections with other domain controllers within the site to be sure that directory replication can occur. Although the administrator can configure connections manually, the consistency checker will automatically establish new connections when it determines that there is a hole in the replication topology within a site.

The administrative tool that is used to control how servers participate in directory replication is the Active Directory Sites and Services Manager. This MMC Snap-in allows you to

- Add new sites and subnets and associate a site name with a subnet
- Show all the sites that exist throughout the enterprise
- Show all the servers that are contained in each site
- Create and display the links between servers and the links between sites, including the protocols that are used for replication
- Show the timing values used to schedule replication
- Manage subnets

Note

Sites are represented in the Active Directory database and are defined by the site object. Although all computers in the directory have a computer object, domain controllers also have a server object. This server object is a child object of the site object that represents the site to which the domain controller is assigned.

Directory Replication

Although LDAP v3.0 is a proposed Internet standard, there is not (yet) an agreed-upon method for replicating data between directory servers. For the Windows 2000 implementation of directory services, Microsoft is using a proprietary method called multimaster replication.

In previous versions of Windows NT, *primary domain controllers (PDC)* were responsible for updates to the directory database (the old SAM). Additions or modifications to the database were made on the PDC and at regular intervals replicated to backup domain controllers throughout the network. The most obvious disadvantage this system has is that without a PDC, no changes can be made to the database. When a PDC becomes unavailable, because of its own failure or possible network link failure, users still can log on because they can be authenticated by a BDC. However, if you have a large enterprise, perhaps a global one, it is almost necessary to have a PDC at every geographical site where frequent changes occur, or to have an extremely good network infrastructure.

In Windows 2000, any domain controller can receive updates or additions to the Active Directory database. These changes are propagated to other domain controllers based on *update sequence numbers (USNs)*. The USN is a 64-bit number used by the Active Directory to determine which updates are the most recent. In addition to the server's USN, each property (or attribute) in the database has its own property version number. These two numbers are used by multimaster replication to ensure that updates are correctly applied throughout the enterprise.

Because all replicas of the directory database can be written to, it is possible that a change can be made before a previous change has been fully replicated throughout the enterprise. Some directory databases use timestamps to determine which update is the most recent. This method requires that every server be tightly synchronized with all other servers with respect to the correct time. Windows 2000 does provide a time service that can be used to synchronize servers, but with one exception: The timestamp is not the method used to determine which is the correct update to apply to a directory update message.

Each server in a network has its own USN, which it advances when it makes an update to the directory. Each server also stores a table of USNs—the highest USN it has received during previous replications from each server in the network. When replication starts, a server requests from other servers only those changes that have a higher USN than the one it has stored for each server during previous replication sessions. This minimizes the amount of information that needs to be exchanged between servers during the replication procedure. Because each server knows exactly which changes it has received from every other server in the network, replication between servers is efficient.

This method also allows a server to recover quickly when it crashes or some other failure, such as a network failure, occurs. All it must do is to request updates that are greater than the USN it has stored for the other servers in the network. This means that a full replication between servers is not necessary in the event of a catastrophe.

Property version numbers come into play when a specific attribute is modified on more than one replica of the database within a short period of time, before the replication service can update the change on all nodes. Remember that with the Active Directory's distributed nature, each domain controller holds a writable copy of the directory database. Property version numbers are incremented only on the server on which the change is actually made. It is not incremented on a server that is receiving it as an update.

The only time a timestamp is used during multimaster replication is when a collision occurs. This happens when a server receives an update message from another server, and although the property version numbers are the same, the contents of the attribute are not. In this case, and only in this case, the timestamp on the update is used. If the update message has a timestamp later than the value stored with the property, the update is applied to the data; otherwise, it is discarded.

Summarizing the Directory Data Using the Global Catalog

The Active Directory is scalable to millions of objects. The directory is partitioned into domains, because it would be very difficult to store a complete copy of the entire directory database on a single server. Of course, with the advances being made in CPU speed and storage capabilities, this might be possible in the future, but for now, it is not practical.

One of the assumptions behind the partitioning of the directory is the fact that most queries that are made to the directory are for local information. Users generally want to locate a printer or another resource that is near them. Occasionally, it might be desirable to locate a printer that resides in a different geographical location, but for the most part, queries are for local resources.

To satisfy a query for information that cannot be found in the local portion of the Active Directory, it is necessary to query every other partition of the directory until the information is found. This, too, can be an impractical method. In a large enterprise, moderate use of this type of query, whereby the entire database is searched, could cause significant network and CPU resource consumption.

The *global catalog* is the answer that Microsoft has implemented to solve this problem. The global catalog is a *subset* of the entire directory. It holds entries for every object that exists in all partitions of the directory, but it contains only *selected attributes* for each object. If your query cannot be satisfied by querying the global catalog, the query will have to be resolved by searching a portion of, or possibly the entire, directory database.

Active Directory Service Interfaces (ADSI)

To make it easy to directory-enable any application, Microsoft has provided Active Directory Services Interface (ADSI). ADSI is a collection of several interfaces that can be used to access the Active Directory from within executable application programs. Programmers might want to use ADSI instead of the LDAP C API because ADSI makes it possible to write an application that can access directory services from multiple providers. If the directory service provider has designed its directory service product to be compliant with at least version 2.0 of LDAP, ADSI should be capable of providing an interface into the directory.

In addition to providing access to Microsoft directory products, such as Exchange Server 5.5, ADSI also has been tested by Microsoft against

- Netscape Directory Server 1.0
- University of Michigan's SLAPD Server
- Novell's LDAP-enabled NDS product

ADSI provides an interface that allows all the functionality of the LDAP C API, but does so in a manner that is easier to understand and write code for. Another reason for using ADSI in application development is that ADSI can be used by many higher-level programming languages, including Microsoft Visual BASIC, Perl, Rexx, and C or C++.

ADSI uses the Component Object Model (COM) interface to allow programmers to access and manipulate the underlying directory objects found in multiple directory services. A program written using ADSI should function correctly with any directory service for which ADSI has a provider interface.

Directory-Aware Application Programming

ADSI is one of the features of Microsoft's development of Active Directory Services that might benefit large enterprises the greatest. If the Active Directory were limited to specific types of objects or attributes that could be stored in the directory, and if only programs supplied by Microsoft were able to access and manipulate the directory store, there wouldn't be much to say about Active Directory beyond it being a major improvement in the administration of Windows servers and clients.

However, if properly employed, using ADSI to incorporate application program configuration information into the directory database along with other types of data can produce real cost benefits in a large network. For example,

- Many applications use similar configuration information that is duplicated in each application's specific configuration data file (or, possibly Registry entries). Information about computers and locales can be stored in the directory, along with other configuration information, and shared by many applications.
- Shared information that already is stored in the directory can be shared by ADSI-aware applications. User information already is stored in user objects in the Active Directory. By extending this object and adding attributes, you can create a customized user object that can be used by applications unique to your environment. Eliminating redundant resources of information also can help ensure a greater accuracy in your database because data must be updated only once in a single location.
- Applications that depend on central configuration databases found on servers in the network can benefit from reduced downtime. If a server that contains configuration data files goes

offline, clients must wait for the server to return to working order. If the clients use the Active Directory, replicas of the directory can be configured so that the loss of a server no longer is a point of failure.

■ Applications can "publish" themselves in the Active Directory, listing the services that they can give to clients and the information needed to use the service. In a volatile network in which users move frequently, reconfiguring applications can be simplified by having the application programmed to locate the information it needs for the new locale.

Many types of applications can benefit by using the Active Directory. Human resource departments and security departments can share a common user database resource by storing information in the directory. System management products can be written to access the information already contained in directory user and computer objects.

Now It's Just Domain Controllers and Member Servers

When you create a domain controller using Windows 2000 Server, you no longer must do so during the installation of the operating system. And, to make things even easier, you no longer must create primary and backup domain controllers. In Windows 2000 networking, there is no distinction made as to primary or backup domain controllers. Instead, each domain controller in a domain (and there can be as many as you need) holds a complete copy of the domain's partition of the Active Directory. Updates can be made at any domain controller, and updates are propagated using multimaster replication to all other domain controllers in the domain.

Remember that in the Active Directory domain, names are expressed as DNS-style names. That is, instead of naming a domain acme, for example, it is now named acme.com, which is a DNS-style name. When you create a tree of domains in the Active Directory, you must use a hierarchical DNS naming scheme so that you maintain a contiguous namespace.

Each domain in the tree is a subdomain of the topmost domain. The domain tree provides a two-way transitive trust relationship between all domains that exist in the tree. Inheritance of security rights flows downward from the top of the tree, so you can assign users administrative access rights and permissions at a single point in the tree, and therefore grant them the same rights for child objects farther down the tree.

When you have a network that is composed of disparate namespaces, you can create separate trees and group them into a forest. Recall that a forest is a collection of domain trees. In this type of organization, each domain tree represents a contiguous namespace, but other disjointed namespaces are in the network. A domain forest is used in a similar manner to a domain tree, in that users can still be granted access rights in domains that are contained in other domain trees. The main difference between a domain tree and a forest is the disjointed namespaces.

The Active Directory Schema

The schema in the Active Directory is stored in the directory. The schema comes preconfigured with the types of objects that you need to set up the Windows 2000 server and manage a network of computers. However, the Active Directory is flexible and extensible in that you can modify the existing objects to use new attributes, or you can create new object classes that contain almost any kind of information.

In addition to the typical objects that you will use to manage the directory and user and network resources, the directory contains hundreds of other objects that are used for many of the applications that interact with it.

The directory should not be thought of as simply a glorified user database. You can create objects that are used by application programs. Sharing information between different applications can become much easier if the same configuration database is being used. Rather than having a conversion utility of some sort to transfer information between different applications, they now can be written, using the application programming interfaces provided for the Active Directory, to store that information in the directory database.

Modifying the Active Directory Schema

You can add objects or attributes to store data in the directory that is shared by different applications so that you do not need duplicate databases scattered around that get out of sync with constant updating. Extending the schema to include additional employee information, such as vacation schedules, sick time, and pay rates, can allow payroll applications to share the same data with other employee management software. The accounting and legal departments always can be sure they are working with the same set of data if there are no duplicate databases being used that can become unsynchronized because of an application failure or a simple user error.

The MMC Snap-in that you use to examine or modify the schema is called the Active Directory Schema Snap-in. Unlike other MMC Snap-in tools, such as the Active Directory Computers and Users Management Snap-ins, this one is not found under the Administrative Tools option in the Start menu, by default. The reasoning behind that is simple: Tools that are used to add or modify user or computer accounts probably will be used frequently by the network administrator. Making changes to the schema probably will be performed only on rare occasions, such as when a new object or attribute is needed by the development of a new directory-aware application.

In just about every book or article you read about modifying the Windows Registry, you are cautioned that making changes can be a dangerous thing. One little mistake in a Registry edit can render a server unbootable. You should take editing the Active Directory Schema just as seriously. First, look through the directory to see whether an object class already exists that you can use before you begin to start creating new object classes (or attributes for that matter) on-the-fly.

First, Install the Windows 2000 Administration Tools

After you've installed Windows 2000 Server (or Advanced Server), you can install, using the same source CD, the Windows 2000 Administration Tools. To install these additional tools, you must be logged into the server as an administrator.

Note

Before you can install the Windows 2000 Administration Tools, you first must exit any other tools that are included in the Administrative Tools folder. For example, if you are running the MMC Snap-in Active Directory Computers and Users Management, exit the application before beginning to install these additional tools! If you do not, the results of the installation will be unpredictable. The installation might succeed, or it might not. If it does, the tools might not work correctly after you've finished the installation. As with any application installation, it's also a good idea to exit any other programs that are running on the computer before you begin to install these additional administration tools.

When you are ready to install the additional tools, follow these steps:

1. Insert the Server or Advanced Server source CD into your computer's CD-ROM drive. When the autorun Microsoft Windows 2000 CD window appears onscreen (see Figure 25.3), click Browse This CD.

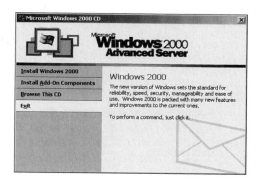

Figure 25.3   Use the Windows 2000 Server or Advanced Server CD to install the additional administrative tools.

2. In the next window, you will see a list of folders that exist on the CD. Double-click the I386 folder.

3. In the I386 folder, double-click Adminpak. The Windows 2000 Administration Tools Setup Wizard appears. Click Next.

4. Next, the wizard prompts whether you want to install or uninstall the tools. Select the radio button labeled Install All of the Administrative Tools, and click Next.

5. The wizard copies the required files to your hard drive, and then displays an informational window telling you that the tools were successfully installed. Click Finish.

After you've installed the additional tools, you then can run the Microsoft Management Console and add the Active Directory Schema Snap-in.

Adding the Active Directory Schema Snap-In to the MMC

Adding snap-ins to the MMC is simple. Click Start, and then Run. When the Run dialog box appears, enter mmc /a in the Open: field. Note that there is a space after mmc before the /a switch! Click OK.

The MMC Console screen appears (shown in Figure 25.4), with only the Console Root in the left pane.

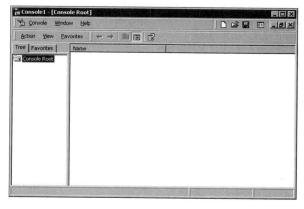

Figure 25.4   You'll need to add a snap-in to the empty MMC.

Click once on the Console menu at the top of the MMC shown in Figure 25.4. From the menu that appears, select Add/Remove Snap-in. The Add/Remove Snap-in dialog box appears.

Click the Add button in this dialog box and the Add Standalone Snap-In dialog box (see Figure 25.5) appears, showing a list of all the different types of snap-ins that are available for your use. Select Active Directory Schema and click the Add button.

Figure 25.5   Select the Active Directory Schema Snap-in to add to the console.

The Add/Remove Snap-in dialog box will reappear, but now you'll see that the Active Directory Schema Snap-in appears in the dialog box. Click the Close button. When the MMC reappears, you'll see that the Active Directory Schema Snap-In is now available under the Console Root, ready for you to use (see Figure 25.6).

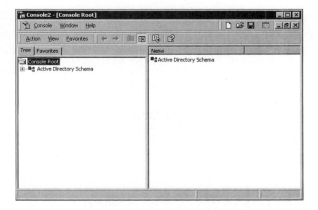

Figure 25.6   The MMC console now has the Active Directory Snap-In installed and ready to use.

You can now start using the snap-in. However, if you think you might want to use it again soon, click on Console and then Save. This saves the console as a tool in the Administrative Tools folder so you won't have to go through all this trouble again.

We're Almost There: Before You Use the Active Directory Schema Master

Before you begin to use the Active Directory Schema Snap-In, there are two important concepts that you should be aware of. Remember that a domain tree exists in a forest. The forest can contain a single domain tree, which is a single contiguous namespace, or it can contain multiple domain trees. Throughout a forest, however, a single domain controller is in charge of making changes to the schema that is shared by the forest. This domain controller is known as the Schema master domain controller. You can connect to this domain controller to make changes to the schema, or you can enable any domain controller to be the schema master.

Second, each object in the schema is uniquely identified by an object identifier, which is nothing more than a dotted-decimal number that is issued by some naming authority. Each attribute in the directory also is uniquely identified by an identifier. If you are operating in an environment where you will use only the Active Directory for internal network use and will never need to interact with any other LDAP/X.500 directory, you can more or less create your own object identifiers. However, consider what happens if your business acquires another business and you both use directory-based networking systems. To import or export information from one directory to another, or simply to join a domain tree from another business you've acquired, all your object IDs must be unique, and you should obtain them from a responsible source.

In the United States, the registration authority for this is the American National Standards Institute (ANSI). Other countries have an equivalent registration authority. The national registration authority issues the root object IDs for an enterprise. In the United States, you can obtain unique object IDs from Microsoft. To do so, send an e-mail to oids@microsoft.com and include the following information:

- A contact name for your business
- A contact address that can be used to send mail to the contact name
- A telephone number to reach your contact person

Using the Active Directory Schema Snap-In

Using the Active Directory Schema Snap-In is not complicated. Being sure that you know how objects and attributes are related to each other, and the organization of your domain tree and the forest in which it resides can, however, be quite complicated. In the movie *The Wizard of Oz* you'll probably remember that there's a sign on the Yellow Brick Road that says "I'd go back if I were you." Don't proceed unless you fully understand the changes you are about to make! Because the schema applies to the entire forest—that is, to every domain tree and every domain in every domain tree—you can potentially render not just a single computer nonfunctional, but you actually can make the entire network unusable if you are not sure about the changes you are going to make.

Note

This section is intended to demonstrate how an administrator can use the Active Directory Schema Snap-In to modify the directory schema. You also can modify the schema using LDAP Interchange Format (LDIF) scripts and by writing programs using tools supplied by Microsoft. Both of these methods are beyond the scope of this chapter. However, you can find out more about them by visiting the Microsoft Developer's Network Web site at http://msdn.microsoft.com.

Okay, enough said about that.

When you are ready to make modifications to the schema, you must be logged in using an account that is a member of the Schema Admins group.

▶▶ For more information about how to place a user account into a group, see Chapter 31, "Windows 2000 User and Computer Management Utilities."

To begin, right-click Active Directory Schema in the MMC console that you created. From the menu that appears, click The Schema May Be Modified On This Domain Controller. This makes this domain controller the schema master.

Double-click on Active Directory Schema in the left pane of the MMC and you'll see (as shown in Figure 25.7) that the schema has two folders underneath it: Classes and Attributes.

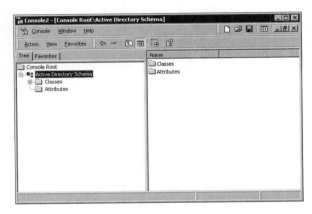

Figure 25.7 The schema is made up of Classes and Attributes.

If you double-click on Classes, the tree structure will expand to show you the classes that already exist in the Active Directory (see Figure 25.8). Many of these have unfamiliar names and should be an indication to you of how complex the Active Directory really is and why you should educate yourself thoroughly before making any changes to it.

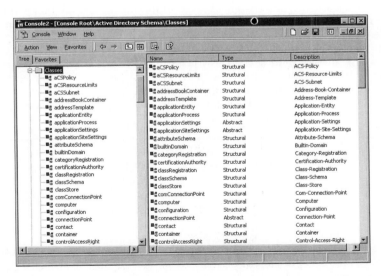

Figure 25.8 You can expand the tree structure to show the classes that currently exist in the Active Directory.

Likewise, if you double-click on the Attributes folder, you'll get a display of all the attributes that are available in the Active Directory (see Figure 25.9). In this figure, you can see that the attribute named `accountExpires`, which can be used, for example, in a user account object, has a syntax of Large Integer. Other attributes have different syntaxes, as shown in this figure.

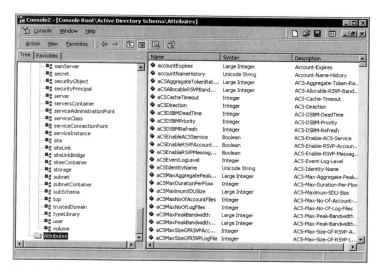

Figure 25.9 The list of attributes that make up objects can be displayed using this snap-in.

You can view the details about a particular object or attribute by double-clicking on it or by right-clicking and selecting Properties from the pop-up menu. For example, Figure 25.10 shows the Properties sheet for the User object class. This is the object type that is used to store user accounts in the Active Directory.

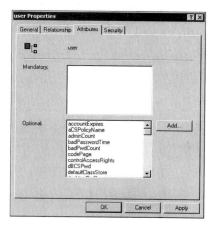

Figure 25.10 The Properties sheet shows which attributes are required and which are optional.

In Figure 25.10, you can see that for each object you can have attributes that are either optional or required. All objects in the directory of a particular class must each have values for all the attributes required by the object class. The optional attributes can be used if you need them.

In Figure 25.9, you saw a partial list of the attributes that are defined in the directory. You can use the scrollbar to scroll through the entire list to locate attributes. When you modify or create a new object in the schema, you can select from these attributes or create a new attribute. Note that each attribute has a particular syntax associated with it, which defines the type of data that the attribute can hold. Figure 25.11 shows the dialog box associated with creating a new attribute for the directory.

Figure 25.11   It's easy to add new attributes using the Schema Manager.

Caution

Even though I've said it earlier in this chapter, it bears repeating: Modifying the schema is not a task that should be delegated to an uninformed employee or done simply for convenience. It is easy to add new objects and attributes whenever you want. However, if you are not intimately familiar with the directory, you might find that over time, you have added superfluous duplicate entries. If the same information can be stored in more than one attribute, it makes searching the directory much more difficult because you have to know all the duplicate attributes to search.

Removing an object or attribute from the directory is not something that should be done casually. If your organization creates internal application programs that are written to use ADSI to interface with the directory, you should be sure to implement a program that tracks changes to the schema so that you can always quickly ascertain the uses of a particular customized object or attribute.

Like editing the Registry, you should be extremely careful when making changes to the Active Directory schema. Plan your changes in advance, create a checklist of what you want to do, and then perform the steps methodically.

You can add a new Schema object class almost as easily as you can modify an existing class. To add a new class, right-click the Classes folder in the left pane of the MMC Active Directory Schema Snap-In and select New Class. The Create New Schema Class dialog box appears (see Figure 25.12).

As you can see, you'll have to supply a common name (CN), LDAP display name, and a unique object ID for the class. If you want to create a class that is similar to an existing class, you can use the Parent Class field under the Inheritance and Type section of the dialog box to specify the class from which your new class will inherit a set of attributes that have already been defined. You can use the Class Type drop-down menu to specify the type of class you are creating.

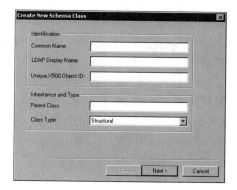

Figure 25.12 You can create a new object class in the Active Directory using this dialog box.

The next dialog box allows you to enter the mandatory (required) and optional attributes for the class you are creating. When you've finished selecting these attributes, click the Finish button.

Finding Objects in the Active Directory

If you've gotten this far into this chapter without falling asleep, it's time to get practical and look at a few things you can accomplish using the Active Directory.

When viewing the property pages for a user account in the directory, you see that you can add much more information than was possible before. There are eight tabs on the properties page for a user object.

If you select each tab and look at the different fields, you can see that the user object now contains a wealth of information that can be quickly accessed by searching the directory, including the following:

- **Who Is This User?**—The user's full name, logon name, and a description of the user. The user's title, department, company, manager, and reporting information.
- **Address**—The office in which the user can be found, the user's address.
- **Telephone**—Phone numbers, fax numbers, pagers, mobile phone, IP phone, e-mail addresses, and home page URLs.
- **Logon**—Which servers the user can log on to, during which hours, password information, and expiration and account information. The user's profile, logon path, and home directory.
- **Dial-In**—Can this user log on using remote access? From where? Callback options and addressing information.
- **Groups**—User groups to which this user belongs.

Note

The Active Directory schema, which defines the objects and their attributes, can be extended. For example, if you install a product such as the newest version of Microsoft Exchange Server, you might see additional attributes in the user, as well as other objects.

The main benefit of having this information available in the directory might not become apparent at first. Most of this information could have been found in the old User Manager utility, the Remote

Access Administration utility, or in the human resources department. But now it all can be centrally located in a global, searchable directory. With the proper rights and permissions, the administrator or user can search the directory for any of the attributes associated with users. And because the Active Directory schema can be extended, you can add additional attributes that contain information specific to your business.

Finding a User Account

For example, instead of being limited to queries such as "Show me everything about user John Doe," you now can execute queries such as "Show me all users that work in the accounting department in Florida." or, "Show me all users who work in the accounting department in Florida that are in the Administrators group and have dial-in access."

And, if you look at the total number of attributes that are associated with the user object, it's quite large. For example, suppose you want to "find" a user in the Active Directory. It's a simple thing to do by using the Active Directory Users and Computers MMC Snap-In in the Administrative Tools Folder. For example:

1. Click Start, Programs, Administrative Tools, and then click Active Directory Users and Computers.
2. In the left pane of the MMC console, highlight Active Directory Users and Computers (the first line in the tree structure), and from the Action menu, select Find. In Figure 25.13, you can see the Find Users, Contacts and Groups dialog box that is used to search the directory for these sorts of objects.

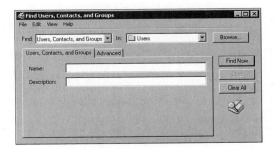

Figure 25.13 You can easily search the entire directory for a user or user group.

3. To find a user, simply enter the name or a description. If you want to narrow the search, use the In field. Here, you can select to perform the search throughout the entire directory, or a specific container object, such as a domain. Then, simply click the Find Now button.

If that all seems too simple, it is. This simple search function on the User, Contacts, and Groups tab enables you to perform a search by specifying just a little information.

Notice the first field in this dialog box, which is simply called Find. In Figure 25.14, you can see that this is a drop-down menu that lets you select what kind of object you want to search for. The type of object you select to search for becomes the name of the first tab on the basic search tab.

Even though we've invoked the "find" dialog box in the Active Directory Users and Computers tool, you still can search for other objects in the directory. After we finish going over how to search for a user object, we'll use a similar dialog box, for example, to search for a printer. As you can see, other objects you can search for include

- Users, contacts, and groups
- Computers
- Printers
- Shared folders
- Organizational units
- Custom search

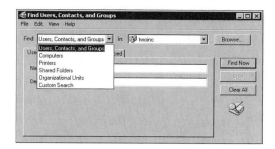

Figure 25.14   You can select the object to search for on the first tab of the dialog box.

The next field (named In) is also a drop-down menu, which enables you to further specify the container object, such as a domain, that you want to search. If you already know in what domain a user account exists, then narrowing the search using this field will save time. Finally, when you've entered a user's name, and/or a description, and narrowed the search to the container object in which you want to look, click the Find Now button.

However, to show you the power of the search capability in the Active Directory, let's use the Advanced tab. In Figure 25.15, you can see the same dialog box, with the Advanced tab selected. Here, the Field drop-down menu enables you to refine your search criteria to a user, a group, or a contact.

Notice in Figure 25.15, however, that when you click on User in the Field menu, a whole range of attributes is displayed that you can use to specify the search criteria. The number of attributes is so large that it won't fit on my computer screen, so there's a down arrow at the bottom that can be used to select even more attributes. There are actually more than 60 attributes you can use to specify search criteria, from the simple username, telephone number (and mobile telephone number), to the Web page address for a user or the manager of the user. Of course, the search will succeed only if you actually use these fields when you create user accounts. You don't have to fill in every attribute when you create a new user. However, the more information you store in the directory about a user, the easier it's going to be to locate that user when you have only a little information to go on!

Using the Advanced tab, you also can search for a contact person, using mostly the same fields that were included for the User search. In Figure 25.16, you can see the fields that you can use for an advanced search to locate a user, contact, or group.

After you specify an attribute, you can enter a value that will be used for the search in the Value field. Use the Condition field to specify how this value will be evaluated in the search. The conditions you can set for this attribute's value in the search are

- Starts with
- Ends with

- Is (exactly)
- Is not
- Present
- Not present

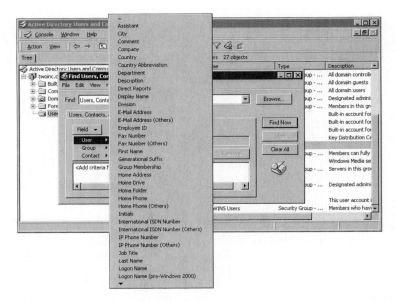

Figure 25.15 The Field menu enables you to search for a user, group, or contact using the Advanced tab.

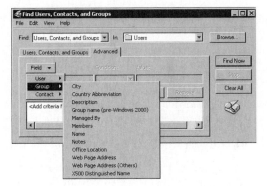

Figure 25.16 You can use these fields to locate a group in the Active Directory database.

As you add search criteria (an attribute, a selection condition, and a value to use for comparison in the search) they appear in the pane at the bottom of the dialog box.

After you have specified values for the attributes to be used for the advanced search, click the Find Now button. In Figure 25.17, you can see that the dialog box expands to add another pane, which displays the results of the search.

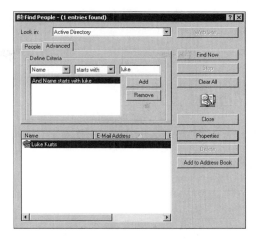

Figure 25.17   The results of your search appear in a new pane at the bottom of the dialog box.

One or more entries can show up in the results pane, depending on the search conditions you used. To view the detailed attributes for objects in the results pane, simply double-click an entry and a property sheet appears for the object.

Finding a Printer in the Active Directory

The directory doesn't just contain information about users; it holds information about many different resource types in the network. An object that represents a printer resource might contain the name of the printer, the type of hardware associated with it, and its location. With directory services you do not even have to know the name of a printer. You can execute a query such as "Show me all printers located on the third floor of the accounting department in the Florida office," and then pick the printer you want to use, based on the information returned from the query.

For example, in a Windows 2000 network that has the Active Directory enabled, you'll find that there's a new button (Find) on the Print dialog box that wasn't there in previous versions of Windows NT (see Figure 25.18).

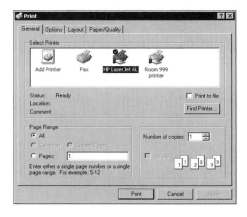

Figure 25.18   There's now a Find Printer button on the Print dialog box.

When you click Find Printer, a dialog box similar to the one used to search for users pops up. This should be an indication to you that the Active Directory is tightly integrated into the Windows 2000 operating system.

At the top of this dialog box, use the In drop-down menu to narrow your search. For example, you can use the default to search the entire directory, or you can use this menu to specify a particular domain or other container object.

There are three tabs on the Find Printers dialog box that you can use for a search:

■ **Printers**—If you know the name, location, or model of the printer you want to find, you can specify it on this tab and click Find Now.

■ **Features**—This tab enables you to specify attributes the printer must have, such as whether it can print double-sided (duplex printing) or whether it is a color printer. As you can see in Figure 25.19, you also can select the resolution, printer speed, and whether the printer can staple the document after it's printed!

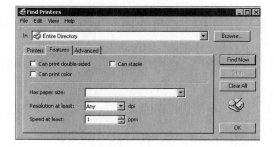

Figure 25.19 The Features tab enables you to be more specific in your search by specifying some simple features the printer should be capable of.

■ **Advanced**—This tab works in the same way that the Find Users dialog box worked. You can use the Field drop-down menu to specify any of the attributes associated with the Printer object, and then specify a condition and a value to be used for the search.

After you've specified the search criteria using any of these tabs, click the Find Now button and you'll get a listing of the printers that match your search. You then can select which printer to use.

After you've found the printer you want to use, it's a simple matter to make a connection to the printer. In the search Results pane, just right-click on the printer and select Connect. Or, if you're in a real hurry, just double-click on the printer in the Results pane!

The Active Directory is accessible from within many other applications in Windows 2000. You can search for file shares and objects that you create yourself. The important thing to remember about the Active Directory is that, after you begin to use it in your network, it is not something to be taken lightly. Use caution when making modifications to the directory.

Using Start/Search

In the previous examples, we searched for users by using an Administrative Tool—the Active Directory Users and Computers Snap-In. To search for a printer, we used the Find Printer button on the print dialog box. However, there is a simpler way to find almost anything in the directory, provided that your logon account has the necessary access permissions to locate the object. Simply click Start and then Search.

The Search function in Windows 2000 Server and Professional is found from the Windows Start menu and allows you to search the directory for

- Files or folders
- Search the Internet
- Printers
- Search using Microsoft Outlook
- People

If you use the For Printers or the For People options in the menu, you'll get dialog boxes similar to the ones used in the examples earlier in this chapter.

Thus, the Active Directory is not just a tool that can be used by administrative personnel to administer the network, but it also can be used by everyday users to locate objects or information they need to perform their jobs.

Overview of Novell NetWare IPX/SPX

SOME OF THE MAIN TOPICS IN THIS CHAPTER ARE

Using the Novell Proprietary Protocols

Reviewing the Datagram Services and Protocols

Connectionless Service and Protocols

Connection-Oriented Service and Protocols

Internetwork Packet Exchange (IPX)

Sequenced Packet Exchange (SPX)

Netware Core Protocol (NCP)

NetWare Security Guidelines

NCP Protocol Independence

In addition to an extensive discussion of Novell's IPX, SPX, and NCP protocols, this chapter highlights the most important of the other Novell proprietary protocols.

Although Novell is making the industry shift to TCP/IP, NetWare still uses IPX/SPX. In addition to backward compatibility, IPX/SPX also is used for the RCONSOLE utility. The primary reason to use IPX/SPX is for compatibility with older network components and for other applications that use only the IPX/SPX protocol.

Using the Novell Proprietary Protocols

The workstations and other machines and resources on your network communicate with the NetWare server by using communications protocols. A *protocol* is a set of rules that specifies how resources move data cross the network. In a sense, the protocol is the language that the network and machines on the network use to communicate with each other.It's important that the client and the server speak the same language. Novell has several protocols designed specifically for use on Novell NetWare networks. These proprietary protocols include the following:

- Internetwork Packet Exchange (IPX) that operates on the network layer

- Sequenced Packet Exchange (SPX) that operates on the transport layer

- Packet Exchange Protocol (PXP) that operates on the transport layer

- Novell Core Protocol (NCP) that operates on the transport, session, presentation, and application layers

- IPX Routing Information Protocol (IPX RIP) that operates on the network layer

- NetWare Link Services Protocol (NLSP) that operates on the network layer

- Service Advertising Protocol (SAP) that operates on the network, transport, session, presentation, and application layers

Although the following sections overview all of the above-listed protocols, this chapter contains detailed discussion on IPX, SPX, and NCP. Most of the protocols that the following sections discuss are routing protocols. However, neither SPX nor NCP play a direct role in routing.

When designing the IPX, PXP, and SPX subnet protocols, Novell used the Xerox Network System (XNS) as its springboard because the design of the XNS protocol lends itself more readily to LAN (local area network) environments. The XNS design does not lend itself well for WAN (wide area network) environments or their large time delays; neither does its progeny—the Novell subnet protocols—work as efficiently as a WAN environment needs. Although the Novell protocols do overcome some of these limitations, they still work best in a LAN environment.

Both IP and IPX use RIP, which is a distance vector routing protocol, but the implementations are slightly different. IP RIP and IPX RIP use similar processes for discovering, maintaining, and prioritizing routes. In addition, they both send route requests for obtaining routing information and send periodic route updates to synchronize the routing information tables. IP RIP and IPX RIP differ by virtue of the protocols with which they are associated, the way in which they prioritize routes, and their routing table update intervals.

NLSP is an IPX link state routing protocol that Novell developed to overcome limitations from using IPX RIP and SAP in larger internetworks, particularly over WAN links. Link state routers and servers exchange information about their routes to other devices on the network. Using this information, each router can construct the topology of the internetwork and derive routing information. NLSP converges router information tables faster, uses first-hand routing information, and generates less traffic than IPX RIP does. Because of these attributes, network managers can use NLSP to interconnect small or large IPX networks without routing inefficiencies.

SAP extends over the transport, session, presentation, and application layers. SAP allows file, print, and gateway servers to advertise their services and addresses. The Novell routers keep these services in a Server Information Table (SIT). The server address field includes the full internetwork address, network number, node address, and socket number of the server.

The NetWare Protocol Suite

A protocol suite is a group of protocols that has evolved together—regardless of whether the same company created them—or is used in the same environment. Protocol suites have definitions for the interface between protocols that occur at adjacent layers of the OSI (Open Systems Interconnection) model. One such relationship exists in the NetWare protocol suite between IPX in the network layer and SPX in the transport layer. The NetWare IPX/SPX protocol suite provides file, print, message, and application services.

IPX and SPX comprise the Novell NetWare protocol suite. SPX resides in the transport layer. When compared to the TCP/IP protocol suite, IPX provides routing and internetwork services similar to IP, and SPX provides transport layer services similar to TCP. IPX and IP are connectionless datagram protocols, whereas SPX and TCP are connection-oriented protocols.

If you are running a mixed NetWare/Windows environment, you will most likely use Microsoft's NWLink. NWLink is an IPX/SPX-based, routable, transport protocol that you can use to establish connections between computers running any Windows operating systems. NWLink enables NetWare servers and Windows NT computers to send Novell NetBIOS packets to each other.

Reviewing the Datagram Services and Protocols

Before reading about the Novell connection services, you should review exactly what the OSI network layer and the transport layer do.

Network Layer

The network layer (OSI layer 3) manages communications routing for packets that are destined for addresses that are not on the LAN. The network layer uses routable protocols to deliver packets across interconnected networks joined by routers. Although enterprise switches or brouters (bridging routers) have some layer 3 routing capabilities, they still rely on layer 2 addresses to achieve the speed necessary to forward packets in a LAN environment. The two most prevalent routable protocols are TCP/IP and IPX/SPX, in that order. A routable protocol must have a source and a destination network address located in the packet; otherwise, it assumes that all the packets are destined for the LAN.

Transport Layer

The transport layer (OSI layer 4) manages the end-to-end control and error checking by providing an end-to-end connection between the source and the destination node to ensure reliable data delivery. In addition, it is responsible for providing end-to-end recovery and flow control and for releasing the connection. The transport layer is essentially a virtual circuit that uses connection-oriented protocols and gives each packet a sequential number. The receiving station then sends an acknowledgment to the transmitting station stating that it received the packet. You might compare a connection-oriented protocol to a certified letter, whereas a postcard could be compared to a connectionless protocol.

Connectionless Service and Protocols

A connectionless service does not require the sender and receiver to establish a session before sending packets to the destination. Networks can implement this service in the network layer or the transport layer of the OSI model.

The following are characteristics of connectionless service:

- Packets can arrive at the destination out of sequence, but the receiving station must reassemble them in sequence.
- No time is required to establish a session, and data can be sent immediately.
- It does not use acknowledgments to check for packet delivery.

The Internet is the largest connectionless network in the world, and it uses IP to deliver the packets to their destinations. IPX is the connectionless-oriented protocol that Novell systems use to deliver packets, and it operates at the OSI network layer.

A connectionless protocol is similar to a radio broadcast or letter delivery. The sender receives no acknowledgment for receipt of the letter delivery or radio broadcast.

This connectionless protocol is best used for disseminating information that is time sensitive and does not need retransmission, such as real-time video and audio. If a packet is not received, it's pointless to retransmit the packet after the remaining packets in that sequence have been sent to the video/audio processing software.

Connectionless protocols at the transport layer take advantage of the port structure already in place. For example, say you have two hosts, one transmitting real-time audio, and the other connecting to the first host to receive the transmission. The second host receives the transmission on a UDP (User Datagram Protocol) port identified by the software that is receiving the real-time audio transmission. No error correction or packet acknowledgment is coordinated between the two hosts, but both use the same port for the transmission and receipt of the data. In effect, connectionless protocols, such as IP, IPX, and UDP, are similar to sending a letter or a radio broadcast because the sender is not concerned whether the recipient actually received the packet.

Connection-Oriented Service and Protocols

Connection-oriented service provides reliable data delivery by establishing a virtual circuit between the sending host and the receiving host. Some characteristics of connection-oriented service are the following:

- The initial request for a session involves some setup time between the hosts.
- The server considers the connection as a virtual circuit.
- The server uses acknowledgments of data receipt to guarantee data delivery.
- Long transmissions are common.

Both TCP and SPX are connection-oriented protocols. SPX is the NetWare protocol for providing connection-oriented service. TCP uses ports between hosts to create a virtual circuit between two host computers on an IP network. TCP is not concerned with the process of routing through the network but is concerned with the data delivery in the datagram.

For example, if two host computers want to transfer Simple Mail Transfer Protocol (SMTP) traffic between each other, the sending host requests a session with the receiving host on TCP port 25. After the initial protocol negotiation is complete, the virtual circuit is established, and the two hosts can guarantee data delivery. TCP and SPX are connection-oriented protocols, which are similar to a certified letter because the sender ensures that the recipient received the packet.

Internetwork Packet Exchange (IPX)

Novell originally developed IPX as the native protocol for the NetWare 3.x and 4.x operating systems. In 1998, NetWare 5 changed the IPX legacy by making IP the native NetWare protocol; however, it still uses IPX. The IPX design has as its basis the Internet Datagram Protocol (IDP) of the XNS protocol.

Although Novell recommends pure IP on your network, small networks might benefit from using IPX only because IPX requires no special address resolution protocols (it can assign addresses dynamically). IP is better suited for large IP-based networks attached to the Internet, to WAN links, or where IP is the exclusively required protocol. If you don't require IP for any of these reasons, and you can use an IPX network, you might find that an IPX implementation is easier to administer. Because IPX automatically distributes subnet addresses, whereas you must manually configure IP, IPX is easier to manage than IP.

In contrast to the Microsoft NetBEUI protocol, IPX/SPX is routable. IPX is a good solution for small and mid-sized networks, and Novell uses it as the main network layer protocol. Several major network operating systems and most desktop operating systems support the IPX protocol. However, if you want to connect a Windows server and a NetWare server, you can use either IPX or TCP/IP. A number of other network operating systems, including Windows NT and Windows 2000, include IPX protocol stacks to provide interoperability with NetWare and NetWare-compatible applications and devices.

Although NetWare networks still use IPX as an internetwork protocol, Microsoft uses IPX differently than Novell due to NetBIOS naming. In a Windows NT network using IPX, you must configure all routers to broadcast NetBIOS on all segments if you want services to be locatable. Novell isolates traffic per segment and uses IPX RIP/SAP or NDS to find its resources. Because of this difference, Microsoft's use of IPX is inefficient as a routed protocol.

The IPX protocol uses the ODI (Open Data-link Interface) specification for DOS and Windows workstations on the network. ODI allows workstations or servers to use multiple protocols on the same network. Each workstation can use a combination of protocols on the same network card. This allows your workstation to communicate with the Netware network and other systems, such as a mainframe computer or Internet connection, concurrently. In addition, the ODI specification provides a modular way of installing network drivers so that when you replace a network adapter, you need change only the LAN card driver.

Similar to IP, IPX is an internetworking protocol that provides datagram services. IPX is a connectionless datagram service, which means after the computer sends a datagram, there are no guarantees that it was delivered. One application for which you might use simple IPX is that of broadcast messages, such as error notifications and time synchronization. IPX performs dynamic route selections based on tables of network reachability information compiled by RIP.

IPX Packet Communications

The IPX protocol divides data into packets to send across the network. Packets are a specific size and contain a certain amount of information. A packet contains the data designated for transmission, in addition to the necessary addressing information. NetWare uses three main types of addressing:

- IPX external network numbers are set for all servers in a single network, and multiple servers in the same network use the same number. You use this number to transmit data across multiple networks.

- IPX internal network numbers are unique and must be set at each server to locate specific servers on the network.

■ Each workstation has a network address to locate a specific workstation on the network. Network addresses, also called MAC (Media Access Control) addresses, are usually set in hardware in the network card, and you cannot change them.

IPX also can send groups of packets, called *bursts*, without requiring the recipient to acknowledge each packet. NetWare added burst-mode technology to enhance the IPX protocol when used over WAN links. Burst mode lets a workstation make one request for a file. After it receives the request, the server responds with a continuous stream of packets and then requires only a single acknowledge response from the recipient after it has received the packet burst. Burst mode improves network throughput and greatly reduces the amount of traffic on the network, two important factors for improving performance over WAN links. Burst mode improves performance in these environments:

■ LAN segments that typically transmit large files

■ WANs with slow asynchronous links

■ Internetworks linked with bridges and routers

■ WANs using X.25 packet switching or T1 and satellite links

IPX Packet Structure

The Transport Control Field contains 8 bits, the last field of which (0) is the packet type. It identifies the data contents of the data portion of the IPX packet. Field 8 provides for protocol multiplexing, which enables other protocols to reside on top of IPX and helps IPX determine which of the client protocols to send the packet to. Table 26.1 defines the Packet Type Assignments for IPX.

Table 26.1   IPX Packet Type Assignments

Packet Type	Protocol
0	Regular IPX packet type
1	Routing Information Protocol (RIP) packet or NLSP packet
2	Echo packet
3	Error packet
4	Packet Exchange Protocol (PXP) packet or diagnostic
5	Sequenced Packet Exchange (SPX)
17	NetWare Core Protocol (NCP) or NDS
20	NetBIOS name packet

An IPX protocol packet can be 30 to 65,535 bytes long. Table 26.2 outlines the packet structure for the IPX protocol. Ethernet networks have a default packet size of 1,500 bytes, and token-ring networks have a default packet size of 4,202 bytes.

Table 26.2   IPX Protocol Packet Structure

Field	Contents	Size
Checksum	Provides integrity checking	2 bytes
Packet length	Length in bytes of the packet	2 bytes
Transport control	Number of routers a packet can traverse before it is discarded	1 byte

Table 26.2   continued

Field	Contents	Size
Packet type	Defines the service that created the packet (either NCP, NetBIOS, NLSP, RIP, SAP, or SPX)	1 byte
Destination network	The network address of the destination network	4 bytes
Destination node	MAC address of the destination node	6 bytes
Destination socket	Address of the process running in the destination node	2 bytes
Source network	The network address of the source network	4 bytes
Source node	MAC address of the source node	6 bytes
Source socket	Address of the process running in the source node	2 bytes
Data	Information that the packet surrounds	Variable; determined by server or router

The IPX datagram structure includes a network address and a node address. You normally assign the network address to the network when you install the first NetWare server or router on a segment. Each of the four frame types can be installed and bound to the same Network Interface Card (NIC) in a server, establishing a different network address for each frame type. All subsequent NetWare server installations on that network must correspond to the network address of each frame type assigned by the first server. A router that is set up to route IPX also must have a corresponding network address for each frame type that it uses. The node address is the MAC address assigned to the NIC. A socket address is included to identify a running process in a computer. An example of an IPX address is 1AB47E3F 0080D4287DE1 0121.

IPX Frame Types

The IPX protocol has four ethernet frame types and two token-ring frame types. The default frame type for NetWare 4.x on an ethernet network is IEEE_802.2, more commonly known as Ethernet 802.2. Table 26.3 identifies the frame types for both ethernet and token-ring networks.

Table 26.3   Ethernet and Token-Ring Frame Types

Frame Type	Description
	Ethernet
Ethernet_802.2	A data-link protocol that controls the link between stations; also known as IEEE 802.2 LLC (Logical Link Control).
Ethernet_802.3 RAW	The Novell proprietary frame type.
Ethernet_II	Used to bind TCP/IP on a NetWare server.
Ethernet_SNAP (Sub-Network Address Protocol)	Includes an organization code field and a type field that indicates the upper level protocol that is using the packet. It is the frame type for AppleTalk environments.

Table 26.3   continued

Frame Type	Description
	Token-Ring
Token_Ring	Conforms to the IEEE 802.5 and IEEE 802.2 standards. The SAP fields indicate the protocol type and Novell networks set it to 0xe0 to indicate that the upper-layer protocol is IPX.
Token_Ring_Snap	Allows network protocol stacks to use Ethernet II frames.

Sequenced Packet Exchange (SPX)

Novell developed SPX as a transport layer protocol to provide end-to-end data transport and to add reliability to IPX deliveries within NetWare networks. In designing SPX, Novell used the Xerox Packet Protocol (XPP) as the foundation for this protocol. The SPX layer (Layer 4) sits on top of the IPX layer (layer 3) to provide connection-oriented services between two nodes on the network. SPX and SAP are the two most important protocols that operate in the transport layer.

Client/server applications, such as print servers, are the primary users of SPX. Most communications on a network, such as workstation connections and the NetWare print server and Remote Console (RCONSOLE), use the SPX protocol.

SPX Packet Communications

SPX is concerned with addressing, segment development (division and combination), and connection services (segment sequencing, error control, and end-to-end flow control). SPX provides guaranteed packet delivery and delivers the packets in their proper sequence by locating the SPX message within the IPX packet, and then transporting it using the IPX datagram delivery service.

When a user or resource on the network sends a transmission, SPX first sends a control packet to establish a connection, and then associates a connection ID for that virtual circuit. After the packet transmission, SPX requests verification from the destination that it received the data. The packet destination must correctly acknowledge receipt of the packet(s). If an acknowledgment request brings no response within a specified time, SPX retransmits the packet. After a reasonable number of retransmissions fail to return a receipt acknowledgment, SPX assumes that the connection has failed and warns the operator of the failure.

If SPX determines that packets were lost en route, SPX resends lost packets and uses the sequencing numbers to ensure that the packets arrive in the proper order without duplication. SPX uses a timeout algorithm to decide when it should retransmit a packet. SPX dynamically adjusts the timeout based on the delay experienced in packet transmission. If a packet times out too early, SPX increases its value by 50 percent. This process can continue until it reaches a maximum timeout value or the timeout value stabilizes. To verify that a session is still active when there is no data activity, SPX sends probe packets to verify the connection.

The number of available listen buffers determines and provides the flow control. SPX can send messages in a given direction only until the number of unacknowledged messages is equal to the number of listen buffers available on the receiving side. As the number of buffers varies, SPX is able to also vary the number of messages that it will send before receiving an acknowledgment. This ensures that the incoming data does not arrive too rapidly and thus overrun the destination node buffers.

If the destination source acknowledges receipt of the packet, the SPX verification must include a value that matches the value calculated from the data before transmission. By comparing these values, SPX ensures not only that the data packet arrived at the destination, but that it arrived intact. The values include the sequencing numbers of the packet, which the receiving side uses to check for missing, duplicate, or out-of-sequence messages. If the recipient received the packets successfully, it acknowledges by returning the next expected sequence number in the Acknowledgment Number field of a message that is sent back to the sender. At the end of data transmission, SPX sends an explicit control packet to break the connection.

One disadvantage of using a connection-oriented protocol such as SPX is in the handling of broadcast packets. In this instance, the protocol must establish a connection with every destination before it can send the packet, which can amount to a time- and resource-consuming process. To avoid this situation, you can use higher-level Netware protocols, such as NCP, to bypass SPX and communicate with IPX.

SPX Packet Structure

Although SPX guarantees delivery of every packet it sends, it is slower than IPX alone. This is because the SPX header includes the IPX header and adds an additional 12 bytes of sequencing, flow control, connection, and acknowledgment information.

SPX packets contain the same header fields that IPX packets contain, but add a 12-byte SPX header in the Data field at the end of the header. The SPX header can contain at the most 534 bytes of data, whereas the normal IPX packet format allows 576 bytes. Table 26.4 outlines the packet structure for an SPX packet header.

Table 26.4   SPX Packet Structure

Packet Field	Contents	Size
IPX Packet Header	See Table 26.2	30 bytes
SPX Header	(As defined in the remainder of this table)	12 bytes
Connection Control	Regulates flow of data across the connection.	1 byte
Data Stream Type	Indicates whether SPX data field contains data or a packet, and identifies the upper-layer protocol to which the SPX data must be delivered.	1 byte
Source Connection Identifier	Identifies the number assigned to the connection on the source socket end.	2 bytes
Destination Connection Identifier	Identifies the number assigned to the connection on the destination socket end.	2 bytes
Sequence Number	Numbers each packet in a message as the packet is sent; SPX uses it to detect lost and out-of-sequence packets.	2 bytes
Acknowledge Number	Indicates the next packet that the receiver expects. The sequence and acknowledgment fields apprise both the sending and receiving computers of which packets have been sent and which have been received. This value implicitly acknowledges any unacknowledged packets with lower sequence numbers.	2 bytes
Allocation Number	Indicates how many free buffers the receiver has available on a connection. The sender uses this value to pace data transmission.	2 bytes
Data	Contains higher-level information being passed up or down in the protocol-layer hierarchy.	534 bytes

Sequenced Packet Exchange II (SPXII)

Novell 4.0 and later includes SPXII as a backward-compatible enhancement to SPX, and features a true sliding-window flow-control mechanism. With this mechanism, the sender and receiver can initially negotiate in the window without receiving any acknowledgments. Each sent packet decreases the window, and each acknowledged packet increases the window. In this way, the receiver can acknowledge groups of packets simultaneously.

SPXII also improves the negative acknowledgment (NAK) capability. A NAK speeds up the recovery process by allowing the sender to retransmit missing or erroneous packets immediately instead of waiting until the end of the transmission. In addition, SPXII does away with the 576-byte limitation and allows for a packet size as large as is supported on a system. SPXII also provides new option-management functions such as permitting the application to negotiate network transport options and allowing for future expansion for the protocol.

Netware Core Protocol (NCP)

Novell clients use the NCP to access resources, such as NDS, the file systems, and the printer services. If you have NetWare 5.0 or above, you can use NCP over IP as opposed to or in addition to NCP over IPX. However, the NCP packet signature function can consume CPU resources and slow performance, for both the client workstation and the NetWare server.

The NCP packet signature is more of a security feature than a protocol, in the sense that the term protocol is normally used. This feature protects servers and clients that are using the NCP services. The NCP packet signature prevents packet forgery by requiring the server and the client to sign each NCP packet using the RSA (Rivest-Shamir-Adleman) public- and private-key encryption. The RSA algorithm is the standard for data encryption, especially for data sent over the Internet. The packet signature changes with every packet.

By using NCP, NetWare workstations and file servers can communicate by defining the connection control and service request encoding aspects of their interaction. NCP maintains its own connection control and packet-level error checking instead of relying on other protocols for those functions. NetWare workstations issue NCP Requests to a server to establish and terminate connections, and to retrieve the following types of information:

- File access and transfers (with the NCOPY command)
- Virtual drive mappings (with the MAP command)
- Directory searches (with the FILER utility)
- Print queue status (with the PCONSOLE utility)

NetWare servers then respond to these requests with NCP Replies. When the server has processed and complied with the request, the workstation terminates the connection by sending a Destroy Service Connection request to the server.

If the server discovers any NCP packets that have incorrect signatures, it discards them without breaking the client workstation's connection with the server. In addition, the server sends an alert message about the source of the invalid packet to the error log, the affected client workstation, and the NetWare server console.

If you do not install NCP packet signature on your system, a network intruder could pose as a more privileged user and send a forged NCP request to a NetWare server. By forging the proper NCP request packet, an intruder could gain the Supervisor object right and access to all network resources. If you install NCP packet signature on the server and all the network client workstations, it is virtually impossible for an intruder to forge an NCP packet that would appear valid.

NCP Packet Signature Options

When you use NCP, you have several signature options available to you, ranging from never signing NCP packets to always signing NCP packets. NetWare servers and NetWare clients each have four signature levels you can set. The signature options for servers and client workstations combine to determine the level of NCP packet signature on the network. You can choose the packet signature level that is most suitable for your system performance needs and network security requirements to include packet signatures and job servers. You should install NCP packet signature if you have any of these security risks:

- An untrusted user at a workstation on the network
- Easy physical access to the network cabling system
- An unattended, publicly accessible workstation

However, some combinations of server and client packet-signature levels can slow performance, but low-CPU-demand systems might not show any performance degradation. NCP packet signature is not necessary for every installation. You might choose not to use NCP packet signature if you can tolerate security risks, such as in these situations:

- When only executable programs reside on the server
- You know and trust all network users
- Data on the NetWare server is not sensitive and loss or corruption of this data would not affect operations

The default NCP packet signature level is 1 for clients and 1 for servers. This setting provides the most flexibility while still offering protection from forged packets. Table 26.5 provides some examples of situations requiring different signature levels.

Table 26.5   Setting NCP Signature Levels

Situation	Security Concern	Recommendation
All information on the server is sensitive.	Intruders can gain access to information on the NetWare server that could compromise the company.	Set the server to level 3 and all clients to level 3 for maximum protection.
Sensitive and nonsensitive information resides on the same server.	The NetWare server has a directory for executable programs and a separate directory for corporate finances.	Set the server to level 2 and clients that need access to company finances to level 3. Set all other clients to level 1.
Users often change locations and workstations.	You are unsure which employees use which workstations, and the NetWare server contains sensitive data.	Set the server to level 3 and all client workstations to level 1.

Table 26.5   continued

Situation	Security Concern	Recommendation
A workstation is publicly accessible.	You have an unattended workstation that is set up for public access to nonsensitive information, but another server on the network contains sensitive information.	Set the sensitive server to level 3, the unattended workstation to level 0, and the nonsensitive server to level 1.

Server Signature Levels

Before you set a new signature level on the server, you need to determine the server's current signature level, which you do by typing the following console command: **SET NCP Packet Signature Option** and pressing Enter.

You can use the SET console command to change the signature level from a lower to a higher level, but you cannot change from a higher to a lower level unless you reboot the server. Before you use the SET console command, you must add **SET NCP Packet Signature Option = 1** to the startup.ncf file, and then restart the server. Then, each time you bring the server up, you can set the Signature level for that server by typing **SET NCP Packet Signature Option = *desired signature level.*** The default level is 1. Following is a description of the server signature levels:

- **0**—Server does not sign packets (regardless of the client level).
- **1**—Server signs packets only if the client requests it and the client level is 2 or higher.
- **2**—Server signs packets if the client is capable of signing (client level is 1 or higher).
- **3**—Server signs packets and requires all clients to sign packets or logging in fails.

Client Signature Levels

To set DOS or MS Windows 3.x client signature levels, add this parameter to the workstation net.cfg file: **signature level = *number.*** To set Windows 9x, Windows NT, or Windows 2000 client signature levels for individual workstations, you can change the parameter settings with the Advanced Settings tab of Novell NetWare Client Properties, by following these steps:

1. From the system tray, right-click the Novell symbol "N".
2. Click Novell Client Properties.
3. Click Advanced Settings, and then select Signature Level from the scrollable list. You can set client signature levels to 0, 1, 2, or 3, and the default is 1. Increasing the value increases security, but decreases performance.

You can set the signature level for multiple clients at once by adding the signature level to the configuration file when you install the clients. The following list describes the client/workstation packet signature levels:

- **0**—Disabled. Client does not sign packets.
- **1**—Enabled, but not preferred. Client signs packets only if the server requests it, and the server level is 2 or higher.
- **2**—Preferred. Client signs packets if the server is capable of signing (server level is 1 or higher).
- **3**—Required. Client signs packets and requires the server to sign packets or logging in will fail.

Packet Signature and Job Servers

A *job server* is a server that performs a task and then returns the completed task. Job servers can serve as database servers, Web servers, file servers, proxy servers, or a firewall. You should be aware that some job servers do not support NCP packet signature. A job server might produce unsigned sessions if any of the following conditions exist:

- It does not operate on top of DOS.
- It does not use standard Novell clients.
- It is not an NLM.
- It uses its own implementation of the NCP engine (such as embedded print servers in printers).

To minimize security risks associated with job servers, you can install queues only on servers that carry a packet signature level of 3. After that, do not allow privileged users to put jobs in queues on servers with signature levels less than 3. In addition, you should make sure that the job server's account is unprivileged, verifying that the job server cannot change client rights. If it has that permission, you can disable it and prevent the job server from assuming the rights of a client by adding the following SET command to the server's startup.ncf file: **SET Allow Change to Client Rights = OFF**. The default is ON, because certain job servers and third-party applications cannot function without changing to client rights. Refer to the server's vendor documentation to determine whether the job server can function without client rights.

Effective Packet Signature Levels

The signature levels for the server and the client workstations combine to determine the overall level of NCP packet signature on the network—called the effective packet signature level. Some combinations of server and client packet signature levels might slow performance. However, low-CPU-demand systems might not show any performance degradation. You can choose the packet signature level that meets the performance needs and security requirements of the system. Table 26.6 shows the interactive relationship between the server packet signature levels and the client workstation signature levels.

Table 26.6 Effective Server/Client Signature Combinations

Client Level	Server = 0	Server = 1	Server = 2	Server = 3
Client = 0	No Packet Signature	No Packet Signature	No Packet Signature	No Login Access
Client = 1	No Packet Signature	No Packet Signature	Packet Signature	Packet Signature
Client = 2	No Packet Signature	Packet Signature	Packet Signature	Packet Signature
Client = 3	No Login Access	Packet Signature	Packet Signature	Packet Signature

Troubleshooting Packet Signature Conflicts

If the client workstations are not signing packets, you should ensure that the signature level on the client workstation is not set to 0. SECURITY.VLM loads by default when the client signature level is set to 1, 2, or 3. Use the virtual loadable module (VLM) /V4 command-line parameter when loading the VLM software to display load time information.

If the client workstations cannot log in, make sure the packet signature levels on the server and the client workstation are correct and do not conflict. If any of the following signature combinations exist, clients will not be able to log in:

- Server packet signature = 3 and the client workstation signature = 0.
- Server packet signature = 0 and the client workstation signature = 3.
- The LOGIN utility is an older version that doesn't support packet signature.
- The NetWare DOS Requester or the shell is an older version that doesn't support packet signature.

If you get the "Error Receiving from the Network" error message, the client workstation is using a version of LOGIN.EXE file that doesn't include NCP packet signature. To remedy this situation, you can install a version of LOGIN.EXE, and its applicable utility files, that is compatible with packet signatures on all NetWare servers on the network.

NetWare Security Guidelines

In addition to installing NCP packet signature, you can use other NetWare security features and protective measures to keep client workstations secure. The following security guidelines are suggested for client workstations:

- Use only the most current versions of system software, NetWare Client software, and patches.
- Check for viruses regularly.
- Use the SECURITY utility to detect vulnerable access points to the server.
- Enable intruder detection and lockout.
- Advise users to log out when they leave their client workstations unattended.
- Enable NCP packet signature level 3 on all unattended client workstations.
- Require unique passwords of at least five characters on all accounts, and establish forced password changes at least every three months.
- Limit the number of grace logins.
- Limit the number of concurrent connections.
- Enforce login time restrictions and station restrictions.

NCP Protocol Independence

The NetWare 5 operating system is NCP protocol independent, which means that internal to NetWare, the NCPs can make and receive specific requests for services that are handled by IP, IPX, UDP, or a combination of these protocols.

To see which protocols NetWare loads and in what order it loads them, you can use a number of NetWare 5 console commands and SET parameters. The server console commands that are NCP-specific, include these commands:

- NCP STATS
- NCP ADDRESSES
- NCP TRACE
- NCP DUMP

To see which IPX, TCP, and UDP addresses are loading and in which order, you can go to the server prompt, type **NCP ADDRESSES**, and press Enter. The resulting list shows the order that the AUTOEXEC.NCF or the NetWare Configuration file loaded the protocols. For instance, maybe you thought you were loading the IP address before IPX but you see that IPX is loading before IP. You can use the SET parameter to change their designated order, regardless of which protocol you bind first through the AUTOEXEC.NCF file or through the NetWare Configuration file. To do this, follow these steps:

1. In the MONITOR utility, select the Server Parameters option from the Available Options window.

2. Select the NCP option, highlight the NCP Protocol Preferences, and press the Enter key.

3. You can then use the SET command to specify the order that you want the incoming service requests to use these protocols. After you save this configuration, the NetWare Configuration file contains this information and uses it each time you bring up the server. The syntax for the SET parameters is as follows:

```
SET NCP EXCLUDE IP ADDRESSES = decimal IP address
```

and

```
SET NCP INCLUDE IP ADDRESSES = decimal IP address
```

You should note that the excludes take precedence over the includes. That means if you have the same address as an exclude and an include, the server will exclude it, regardless of the order in which you entered the parameters. However, you do not need to both include the NCP interface and exclude the non-NCP interface. One or the other will work. You can enter the parameters at the server console, in AUTOEXEC.NCF, or in Monitor under Server Parameters, NCP.

As a practical example of the previous steps, say you have a server with IP bound to two interfaces and one of them goes to the Internet. You might want to disable NCP traffic over the Internet interface for security reasons. The fictional IP address for the public interface is 200.100.50.25 and the internal interface is 10.20.30.40. To disable NCP on the Internet interface, you can use either of the following SET parameters:

```
SET NCP EXCLUDE IP ADDRESSES = 200.100.50.25
```

or

```
SET NCP INCLUDE IP ADDRESSES = 10.20.30.40.
```

NCP chooses the first protocol bound as the preferred protocol it uses. If both IP and IPX are bound—currently without any default value inserted—and both are installed on a server, NCP defaults to use IPX because IPX loads first. The set parameter—NCP Protocol Preferences—needs to be set to "NCP Protocol Preferences = TCPIP" so that IP is the preferred protocol used by NetWare 5.

Overview of the Novell Bindery and Directory Services (NDS)

## CHAPTER 27

SOME OF THE MAIN TOPICS IN THIS CHAPTER ARE

Understanding NetWare Directory Structures

Using Novell Directory Services

Throughout its lifetime, NetWare has used two distinctly different types of database management and directory structures: Bindery Services and NetWare Directory Services. During the course of this chapter, we will discuss the differences between the two, as well as the advantages and disadvantages of each. In addition, we will show you how to use the NetWare Administrator and the NDS Manager, two of the most important utilities for managing a NetWare network.

Understanding NetWare Directory Structures

A database's architecture determines the naming and organization of network resources and dictates the kinds of features the directory or domain service offers. The architectural foundation of a directory or domain service is the name space structure, which determines how the database is organized. Name spaces have one of two types of organizational structures: hierarchical or flat.

Within the Novell family are representatives of each of these structures. The Bindery database of NetWare 3.x and earlier used a flat structure, whereas the NDS database of NetWare 4.x and later uses a hierarchical structure. In the following sections, we will spend a little time talking about each of these structures.

Reviewing the Bindery Structure

The Bindery is a flat network database that the early versions of NetWare 3.x and NetWare 2.x used for the primary purpose of security and access control. When we say that the Bindery files are *flat*, that means the entries in the Bindery do not have an explicit relationship to any of the other entries. Although you could add users to groups, unless you looked up each specific user, the relationship was not apparent. The Bindery is server-centric, which means that each file server contains and maintains a unique Bindery that contains settings for the printers, usernames, object IDs, passwords, and security. In this structure, if a user needs access to two Bindery servers, that same user must have one account on each server, because different servers do not communicate with each other to exchange security information. The NetWare Name Service (NSS) utility synchronizes user account and user security information between multiple servers to try to create a semblance of a hierarchical structure prior to the release of NDS.

In a Bindery structure, each entity on the network, such as a user, printer, or workgroup, constitutes a single object definition in the database. Each object connects directly to the root directory of the server, keeping in mind that the root does not branch beyond itself and the list of objects that it contains. Figure 27.1 provides graphical representation of the Bindery structure. In the Bindery, the network supervisor can design, organize, and secure the network environment based on each entity's requirements. The following three components comprise the Bindery:

- **Objects**—Represent any physical or logical entities, such as users, user groups, workgroups, file servers, print servers, or any other entity that has an assigned name in the database.

- **Properties**—The characteristics of each Bindery object. This includes passwords, account restrictions, account balances, internetwork addresses, lists of authorized clients, and group members.

- **Property data sets**—Represent the type of data stored in the Bindery. The data type can be text, number, table, date/time, network address, and stream.

Reviewing the NetWare Directory Service (NDS) Structure

Like the Bindery, NDS is an informational directory of objects that represent the resources on the network. These objects, just as in the Bindery, are users, groups, printers, servers, and other organizational units. However, unlike the Bindery, the objects are represented in a hierarchical structure, meaning that you have one root structure, and then branches from the root that contain other branches and leaves. Compare this to the flat file structure of the Bindery. NDS shows you the relationships among different objects in the directory.

Figure 27.1 The Novell Bindery has a flat structure.

NDS uses a hierarchical tree structure that organizes objects in a multilevel, object-oriented, directory tree, the industry standard for which is X.500. An X.500-standard directory structure looks like an upside-down tree (thus, the nomenclature directory tree), with the trunk at the top and the branches extending below it. X.500 defines users and resources as objects and uniquely identifies them by their locations and a distinguished name. Appendix D contains a discussion on the X.500 standard. Figure 27.2 illustrates the NDS structure.

However, the directory does not force you to conform to a hierarchical structure. Underneath a single organization (O), you can define all objects into a flat structure, something like a super-bindery. The directory hierarchy enables you to take advantage of the natural organization of information.

Most of the time, an organization will configure its directory tree according to the way that users access and use company resources. In this way, NDS acts as a repository of information based on the specific needs of the organization. Because this method makes resources easy to locate, use, and manage, network administrators can log in as the Admin user from any workstation on the network and manage the entire directory tree.

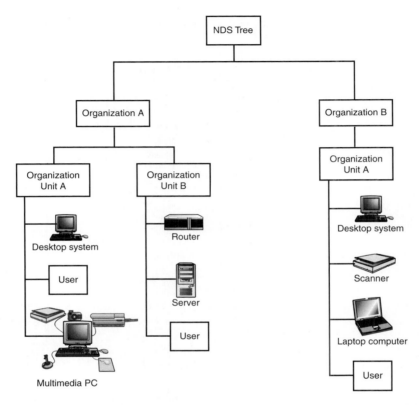

Figure 27.2   The Novell Directory Service is a hierarchical structure that adheres to the X.500 standard.

In addition, whether your NDS servers are running NetWare, Unix, or Windows, NDS can keep all resources in the same directory tree. That means you do not need to access a specific server or domain to create objects, grant rights, change passwords, or manage applications. This open access is available, due in large part, to a Novell product that allows a single network login across multiple platforms.

NDS maintains information about every resource on the network and stores this information in a single, logical database that lets the users see a global view of all services and resources on the network. In an NDS environment, users log in to a multiserver network and view it as a single system instead of as a collection of individual servers. The most important benefit of this scenario is that users can access network services and resources through a single login, regardless of where the user or the resource is located on the network. This access also is conditional on whether the user has the requisite rights to use that resource.

Objects in the NDS Directory Tree

Resources you will see in an NDS environment include users, groups, printers, volumes, applications, fax servers, computers, and nearly any other device or application that attaches to the network.

When you log in, you will see one global view of the entire network and all its resources, as opposed to seeing a group of servers, as you would with the Bindery.

The network resources appear in the NDS directory tree as one of several types of objects, called object classes, which have distinct properties. The schema defines the containment rules for object classes and their properties. The main types are leaf objects and container objects. Table 27.1 defines what each type of directory structure can contain.

Table 27.1   NDS Object Composition

Directory Object	Object Composition
[Root]	Contains Country, Organization, and Alias objects.
Country	Contains Organization, Application, and Alias objects.
Organization	Contains Organizational Units and Leaf Objects.
Organizational Unit	Contains other Organization Units and Leaf Objects.
Leaf object	Cannot contain any other objects.

Figure 27.3 shows you the NDS object containment. The following are the container objects that you will see in NDS:

- **[Root]**—Located at the topmost level of the directory tree, which allows trustee assignments that grant rights to the entire directory tree.

- **Country objects**—Enable you to perform one task on one container object, and those changes will apply to all objects within that container.

- **Organization objects**—Usually are the first container class under [Root] and typically bear your company name. Small companies can simplify management by having all other objects directly under the Organization object.

- **Organizational Units**—Fall under the Organization to represent separate geographic or functional divisions. You also can create organizational units under other organizational units to further subdivide the tree.

Leaf objects represent actual network resources, such as users, groups, file servers, printers, and network applications. The following are the Leaf object classes:

- **Alias objects**—The NetWare Directory Service objects that provide a quick way to access objects in another context. Alias objects do not contain any other objects, but point to other permitted objects in another context besides the user's own.

- **Bindery objects**—Represent objects that an upgrade or migration utility has placed in the directory. NDS uses them only to provide backward compatibility with Bindery-oriented utilities.

- **Bindery Queue objects**—Represent a queue that an upgrade or migration utility has placed in the directory tree. NDS uses them only to provide backward compatibility with Bindery-oriented utilities.

- **Computer objects**—Represent a nonserver computer on the network, such as a client workstation or a router. This object stores information about the computer, such as its network address, serial number, or the person to whom you have assigned the computer.

- **Directory Map objects**—Represent a particular directory in the file system. They can be useful in login scripts by pointing to directories that contain applications or other frequently used files. If you want to avoid making changes to many login scripts as application locations change, you can create a Directory Map object, reference it in the login script, and change it when the application location changes.

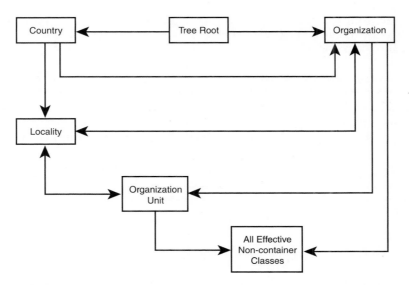

Figure 27.3 NDS object containers can comprise the root, as well as Country Objects, Organizational Objects, and Organizational Units.

- **Group objects**—Assign a name to a list of User objects that are located anywhere in the directory tree. Use a Group object to assign rights to a group rather than to individual users. The individuals that belong to a group will inherit the rights that you assign to that Group object, no matter their location in the directory tree.

- **NetWare Server objects**—Represent a network server running NetWare. Whenever you install a NetWare server in the tree, NDS automatically creates a NetWare Server object. This object stores information about the server, including the following: the server's location on the wire, the server's physical location, and the different services that the server provides.

- **Organizational Role objects**—Define a position or role within an organization, such as a department manager or vice president of sales. You can assign any User object as an occupant of the Organizational Role object, and the occupants inherit the same rights granted to the Organizational Role object.

- **Print Queue objects**—Represent a print queue on the network. You must create a Print Queue object for every print queue on the network.

- **Print Server objects**—Represent a network print server. You must create a Print Server object for every print server on the network.

- **Printer objects**—Represent a physical printing device on the network. You must create a Printer object for every printer on the network.

- **Profile objects**—Contain a profile script (a type of login script) that appears as part of the User object properties and executes whenever a User object logs in to the network. The Profile object executes after the system login script, but before the user login script. You can create a

Profile object for any set of users who need to share common login script commands but who are not located in the same directory container. In addition, Profile objects will suit any users who are a subset of users in the same container.

- **Unknown objects**—Represent an NDS object that has been invalidated and cannot be identified as belonging to any other object class.

- **User objects**—Represent a person who logs in and uses the network. You must create a User object for every network user. When you create a User object, you can create a file system home directory for that user that includes default rights assignments. You also can determine which default rights that you want the User object to have, and customize a USER_TEMPLATE object, which you will assign to new users.

- **Volume objects**—Represent a physical volume on the network. The INSTALL program automatically creates a Volume object for every physical volume on a server at installation time. The properties of the Volume object store information about the NetWare server where the physical volume is located. It also specifies which name the operating system gave the server after initializing the volume during installation (such as SYS). If you create a Volume object during installation, NDS places this information in the properties of the Volume object by default. NDS also uses Volume object properties to map drives.

- **Container objects**—Organize network resources into branches and can contain Leaf objects and other Container objects in the directory tree. Container objects enable you to manage other objects in sets, rather than individually.

Bindery Services

The dilemma for many administrators, after they upgrade to an NDS operating system, is how they can tie in their legacy Bindery system. For this express purpose, Novell provides Bindery Services, which enables NDS to emulate a Bindery database.

Bindery services provide NDS-based networks (NetWare 4.x and NetWare 5.x) with backward compatibility to NetWare versions that used the Bindery. This enables clients that are using older software to access the network. In addition, when you have enabled Bindery services, NDS objects, Bindery-based servers, and client workstations can access all objects within the specified container's Bindery context.

Bindery services does this by simulating a flat (nonhierarchical) structure for the objects within a set of Organization (O) and Organizational Unit (OU) objects, representing only the leaf objects of the container. Consequently, Bindery service users have limitations that other NDS users do not have.

Bindery Context

The Bindery context is the Container object in which Bindery services are set. It appears as a branch of the NDS tree that serves as a simulated Bindery and allows Bindery-based servers, clients, and utilities to coexist on an NDS network.

In early versions of NetWare, you could set the Bindery context in only one container (Organization or Organizational Unit) within the directory tree, and all Bindery objects had to be located in that container. However, later NetWare versions have a Bindery context path that allows multiple containers to contain Bindery objects; as many as 16 Bindery contexts for each server. In addition, recent NetWare versions support NetWare Loadable Module (NLM) programs that rely on Bindery services to access objects in multiple containers.

However, you might experience problems when you use a Bindery context path. Although you cannot have more than one object of the same name in the same container, you can have objects with the same names in the different containers of a Bindery context path. The problem is that users see only the objects in the first container of a path. The visible name overrides other objects of the same name in the other containers, regardless of whether these objects are of the same type. The only way to prevent this is to avoid having objects of the same name in different containers if these containers are in the same Bindery context path.

When you install any NetWare server into the directory tree, the operating system automatically creates a NetWare Server object in the container object. Figure 27.4 illustrates a Bindery context in an NDS structure. By default, NetWare activates Bindery services and sets the Bindery context for that container object.

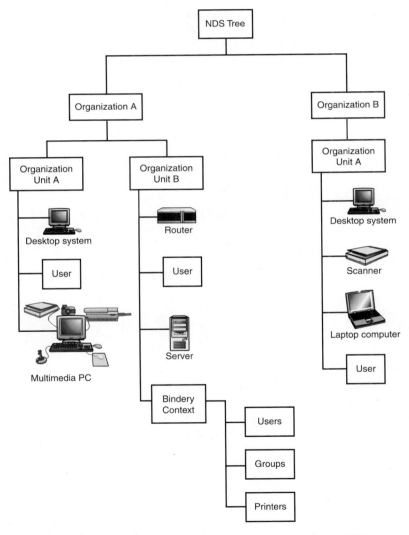

Figure 27.4   Bindery Services lets you establish a Bindery context within an NDS structure.

Bindery Emulation Drawbacks

Because Bindery emulation is necessary in some networks, you must understand how it affects overall network use and performance on an NDS directory.

For every NetWare server that must perform Bindery emulation, you must have a replica of the NDS partition that contains the network entities that are requesting Bindery access. In this case, servers that normally would not have required a replica now must have one to maintain the server-centric Bindery database.

Because this means that the replica ring is larger than it would have otherwise been, your network now has more traffic as these servers synchronize. Additionally, events such as user login cause servers to verify authentication with other servers in the replica ring, which can cause significant delays. This is especially true when many users are doing the same tasks at once, such as initial login first thing in the morning.

Bindery emulation also leaves less bandwidth available for data transmission. This means that the server can delay user requests while the servers perform functions they otherwise could have avoided if the network was strictly NDS.

In addition, server processor use is a factor where Bindery use is prevalent. Although Bindery is single-threaded, NDS is multithreaded. This means that every time an application, or the operating system, initiates an execution path, it must wait in a queue until the CPU can process that command. Because Bindery is single-threaded, only one thread handles all the Bindery requests made to a server. While the CPU handles another thread, it puts all Bindery requests on hold. When the CPU does address the Bindery thread, it may monopolize the CPU while other vital functions are on hold. In comparison, each NDS request creates its own thread that the CPU can handle separately with less risk of CPU monopoly.

Contrasting and Comparing Bindery and NDS

Although Novell had a step in the right direction with its Bindery database, the Bindery structure had a lot of room for improvement. In this section, we will compare the attributes of the Bindery to the new and improved attributes of NDS, and show you how NDS picks up where Bindery left off to form a more complete and efficient database structure.

Most modern networks do not comprise a single server, but more often have multiple servers. This makes managing the network on a server-by-server basis time-consuming, often redundant, and not very efficient; especially when it comes to fault tolerance, network security, and data synchronization. In addition to the administration workload, network performance also suffers. Table 27.2 outlines the most important differences between the Bindery and NDS, and the following sections provide details on those differences.

Table 27.2   Comparing Bindery and NDS

Feature	Bindery	NDS
Group Accounts	Users must be assigned on each server	Group assignments are networkwide
Logical Structure	Flat	Hierarchical
Network Printing	Has no friendly printer map	Provides user-friendly access to network printers
Network Volumes	On the local server only	Volumes extend across the network as global objects
Partitions	None	Distributed database

Table 27.2 continued

Feature	Bindery	NDS
Queues	Only local objects will queue	Queues form for system-wide objects
Replication	Does not replicate	Replicates partitions
Synchronization	No replicas to synchronize	Synchronizes replicas
Trustees	On the local server only	Global objects
User Accounts	Users must have separate accounts on each server	Users have one global account for the network
User Login and Authentication	Users must have one password per server	Sponsors networkwide authentication

Administration

In a Bindery environment, the administrator must maintain separate servers that are, in effect, their own complete network environment. This includes setting up specific user accounts on specific servers so that the user could access the resources there. Therefore, if a user needs access to resources on five different file servers, the administrator must create an account for that user on each of the five file servers. In addition, the administrator also must synchronize individual files and relationships between the servers.

NDS eliminates this redundant administration by requiring only one user account per user for the entire network. In addition, NDS also does away with the redundant administration that is typical in multiserver, non-NDS environments.

Centralized Login

In a Bindery environment, users log in to their own context and must access new contexts on other servers by signing in to those servers as well. This means that each user must have a distinct account on each server. In addition, the Bindery maintains Login scripts separately on each server, instead of centrally, meaning that the administrator must update and maintain those scripts separately.

NDS requires only one user account per user for the entire network. This simplifies life for the average users, because they need only one login, and subsequently one password, for all subsequent security authentications during the network session.

Directory Structure

The most distinctive difference between Bindery and NDS is the directory structure. In the Bindery, you could see only the main organization and then all the individual components of that organization, which branched directly off the root directory. If you looked at the directory tree in this scenario, you could not tell the vice president of the company from the printer, except by name.

Whereas the Bindery was very limited in how it could represent divisions, departments, and groups, an NDS tree can encompass an entire network. In so doing, it can closely resemble the corporate structure, wherein a top-level root branches into various functional or geographic departments or groupings.

As a corporation grows, the number and size of its departments grow and are further subdivided, in addition to the number of network resources (that is, users, printers, and servers) and the relative entries in the NDS database. NDS can represent this growth by adding and expanding the administrative designators, such as organization and organizational unit containers corresponding to the actual organizational charting.

Object Recognition

In addition to a limited organization structure, the object types that it can recognize, which are the following, also limit the Bindery: User, Group, Queue, Print Server, and Bindery objects.

This limits the way that clients can use the directory service because they are limited to those objects, and administrators are limited in their ability to alter and improve user access to network resources. Administrators are so limited because the Bindery objects are limited to the server on which they are located, opposed to the NDS security structure of network access. In addition, administrators cannot use any new features and products by Novell or third-party companies that leverage the directory to create new objects or add new attributes to existing ones.

In contrast, NDS can recognize a full range of directory objects, which the structure breaks down into logical sequence and division. Divisions in an NDS tree increase the efficiency and responsiveness of NDS—particularly for users in branch offices, as well as decrease server load and make the tree more manageable. NDS, therefore, is a distributable database that the administrator can place where he or she sees fit.

Access to Resources

In a non-NDS environment, users must know on which specific server the desired resource resides. Even after yet another login, that user must also have access rights to both the server and the resource. The Bindery resources are server-centric and NDS resources are network-centric. The Bindery resource is made available to NDS users by setting a Bindery context so the resource can be accessed from the NDS. You can log in totally as a Bindery user and you will only have access to the resources in the Bindery context and can only use Bindery tools such as SYSCON and PCONSOLE.

NDS allows users to access a more global view where objects exist individually and can access other entities, regardless of physical or logical location. The NDS database resides on a server, or servers, that users can access from anywhere on the network without having to know on which specific server the resource resides.

Partitions

Although the Bindery does not support partitions, NDS can break the database into separate pieces at the container level to manage large numbers of network resources. When the operating system originally creates a directory tree, that tree has one partition. In this case, the NDS database exists in its entirety wherever it physically resides. However, network administrators can divide the tree into any number of smaller pieces to give logical structure to the partitions. One reason to partition the tree is to place that portion of the tree closer to the user. You would want to partition the NDS tree on a WAN and place the NDS objects closest to the users.

Replicas, Synchronization, and Fault Tolerance

Another feature that Bindery does not support is replicas. You can set NDS to copy one server's partition of the directory database to other NetWare servers in the tree—a process called *replication*. In this manner, NDS creates a distributed database system, employing a concept that is similar to disk striping.

Replication reduces possible data loss if the server holding the database fails. You can copy any partition onto any other server for fault tolerance. Three replicas of an NDS partition on the network should provide enough fault tolerance for almost any server failure scenario. However, you do not need to put replicas on all your NDS servers, because the servers on the network know which servers have replicas and which do not. If a client requests a server's resources, the network can check with the other servers that have replicas to authorize access. In this way, servers can be more efficient with their resources and do their specific, assigned tasks with less overhead.

NetWare 4.x servers with replicas participate in a replica ring, which should be more than ten servers and no fewer than three servers. All the servers in a replica ring automatically synchronize changes to the NDS database and update the partitions. The smaller the replica ring, the less time the servers spend synchronizing.

With NetWare 5, server replication no longer occurs within a replica ring or list as it has in the past. Transitive synchronization works through a migration agent server that checks the replica list and each target server's ReplicaUpto vector. If the source server's ReplicaUpto vector is more recent than a target server's vector, the source server does not need to synchronize with that target server. This procedure uses both the IPX and IP protocols and reduces synchronization traffic to free up bandwidth.

Using Novell Directory Services

NDS automatically installs on your server whenever you install any of the NetWare products that provide it, which are intraNetWare, NetWare 4.x, and NetWare 5.x. That means that you have no additional installation procedures specifically for NDS. However, you can configure NDS, which means that you also are configuring your network. Because we already covered the principals of the NDS structure, in this section, we will tell you how to configure NDS so that it best suits your organization. You can accomplish your administrative tasks through the NWADMN32 and NDS Manager. If you are running NetWare 5.x, you will run these utilities as snap-ins through the ConsoleOne Management framework.

Novell has designed several products so that NDS will work with third-party products. The following are some examples of these products:

- Novell NDS Corporate Edition works with Microsoft's Windows 2000 Active Directory. This product replaces NDS for NT, which worked with Microsoft's NT File System (NTFS) to provide network security.

- NDS eDirectory allows NetWare's NDS to work in a mixed Unix-NT environment.

- MacNDS allows Macintosh (Apple) computers to work with the NDS Directory structure.

- NetWare NFS allows Unix NFS to work with NDS.

Using NWADMN32

The NWADMN32 utility merges all the network administrative functions into a single, intuitive interface. With it, you can see the availability and location of network resources. If you have NetWare releases prior to NetWare 5, the network administrator is NWAdmin. The NWADMN32 utility is the management console for the entire network, through which you can do the following:

- Create and delete NDS objects
- Move and rename NDS objects
- Assign rights and permissions in the NDS tree and in the NetWare file system
- Set up print services
- Set up licensing services

You can browse the directory tree through NWADMN32, and then double-click a selected object to see all the information and properties associated with that resource. You also can set property values for multiple objects simultaneously. With drag-and-drop functions, you can assign access rights to any NDS object and move objects within the directory tree. In addition, NWADMN32 has a configurable toolbar that has shortcuts to menu options and a configurable status bar. With it, you can hide and sort property pages for individual NDS objects. NWADMN32 also has other network administration tools through which you can manage directory trees, subtrees, and containers.

Because NWADMN32 is the location from which you will make most of your network changes, start NWADMN32 by following these steps:

1. Log on to the network as the administrator by typing admin or by typing admin.dept.company, depending on whether you have set the network up for contextless login. You should be sure that you are running the current client software and that you have an administrator account for the network.

2. Normally, when you log in, the operating system automatically provides you with a path to the SYS:PUBLIC directory, after which you should go to the \WIN32 subdirectory. If NetWare did not automatically send you to the SYS:PUBLIC directory, you need to map a drive to it. To do this, open the NetWare administration program, which is loaded into the SYS:PUBLIC\WIN32 directory on the NetWare server.

3. Next, use the RUN command to execute the network administrator. After you access the NWADMN32, the easiest way to use this application is to create a shortcut on your desktop, although you can use the RUN command to execute it.

As soon as you log in as the network administrator, the operating system will display the NetWare Administrator window, as Figure 27.5 shows. The NetWare Administrator window shows you the entire network directory.

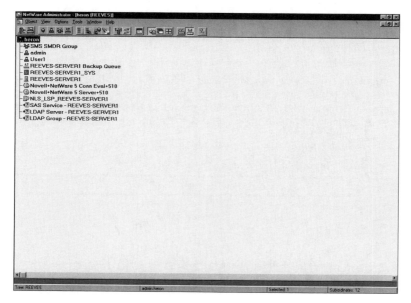

Figure 27.5 You will see the NetWare Administrator window when you log in as the administrator.

Creating and Deleting Objects

If you need to create a new object, you should determine what kind of object you want to create (object classes were discussed earlier in this chapter). After that, follow these steps:

1. At the NetWare Administrator window, highlight the container where you want to place the new object. If you will be deleting an object, be sure you open the container where the object is located, and then highlight the object. (Don't worry, NDS will not let you delete a container unless you first delete everything in that container.)

2. From the toolbar, click Object to display the Object menu.

3. If you are going to delete an object, select Delete. If you are going to add an object, select Create to display the New Object screen.

4. Choose the type of object that you want to create, and click OK. The next window that you will see depends on the type of object you are creating. Regardless of the type of window that you see, you will need to fill in some specific properties for the object type that you have chosen.

5. When you have filled in the necessary information, click Create.

Context and Naming

To understand where an object fits in the NDS structure, you must understand how the NDS naming system works. The context of an object implies its position in the NDS tree. Specify the context as a list of containers separated by periods, between the specified object and the [Root]. Normally, NDS automatically assigns a new object a context based on where you put it in the directory tree.

- The *complete name*, also called the *distinguished name*, of an object is its object name with the context appended. An example would be
  username.departmentname.divisionname.companyname. A complete name does not have a leading period. A complete name can be either typeful or typeless, which are defined next.

  A *fully distinguished* name is a complete name with a leading period, so that the name appears as such: *.username.departmentname.divisionname.companyname*. The leading period means that NDS will resolve the name from the root, regardless of the current context. A fully distinguished name also can be either typeful or typeless.

- You also might see the *typeful name* displayed in some NDS utilities. In creating a typeful name, NDS uses the type abbreviation, an equal sign, and then the name of the object. You can use typeful names interchangeably with typeless names in NDS utilities. A *typeless* name is essentially a typeful name without an object type. Typeful names include the object type abbreviations shown in Table 27.3.

Table 27.3 Typeful Name Abbreviations

Object Class/Type	Abbreviation
All leaf object/Common Name	CN
Organization	O
Organizational Unit	OU
Country	C

- *Name resolution* is the process that NDS uses to find the location of an object within the directory tree. When you use object names in NDS utilities, NDS resolves the names relative to either the current context or the [Root].

- *Current (workstation) context* is set when the networking software runs, and it's key to understanding the use of leading periods, relative naming, and trailing periods.

- *Leading periods* resolve the name from [Root], no matter where the current context was previously set.

- *Relative naming* means that NDS resolves names relative to the workstation's current context, rather than [Root]. Relative naming never involves a leading period because a leading period indicates resolution from [Root]. For example, if the workstation's current context is account-ing.yourcompany, and the user's relative name is joeuser.accounting, NDS reads the name as joeuser in accounting in the current context.

- *Trailing periods* can be used only in relative naming, and you cannot use both leading periods and trailing periods. A trailing period changes the container from which NDS has resolved the name. Each trailing period changes the resolution point one container toward the [Root].

The NetWare 5 catalog services and simplified login make it easy for you to create NDS-enabled applications, improve directory access performance, and allow users to log on from any computer in any location without requiring directory knowledge. You can customize directory information that is stored in catalog or index format to enable you to search, sort, and report against the directory entries. Distribution and replication of these indexes allows administrators to quickly access a "snapshot" of the complete network directory as opposed to performing a query across the entire network. NetWare 5 has contextless login, which leverages the NDS catalog to enable users to authenticate from any point on the network by typing their login names and passwords. This type of login removes the need for the user to specify his exact user object location in the NDS tree.

Moving and Renaming Objects

The capability to move and rename objects comes in handy for things such as interdepartmental transfers. To move a Leaf object from one container to another, follow these steps:

1. At the NetWare Administrator window, browse to the Leaf object that you want to move, and click it.
2. From the Object menu, click Move to display the Move dialog box.
3. Browse to the destination container object and click OK.

The procedure for renaming an object is simple: Follow step 1, but click Rename at the Object menu. Type in the new name for the object, and click OK.

Assigning Rights and Setting Permissions

When you create an NDS tree, the default rights assignments give your network and its objects generalized access and security. Some of the default assignments are as follows:

- User Admin has Supervisor rights to [Root] for complete control over the entire directory. Admin also has Supervisor rights to the NetWare Server object for complete control over the volumes on that server. [Public] retains the Browse right to [Root] so that any user can view any objects in the NDS tree.

- Objects created through an upgrade process or migration receive NDS trustee assignments appropriate for most situations.

NDS security controls access to directory objects such as users, groups, printers, and organizations. You can control a user's ability to modify or add objects and to view or modify their properties. When you understand NDS security, you can assign users the necessary directory and object rights while you maintain a secure network. Before we tell you how to set rights and privileges, we will review some basic principles that relate to NDS security.

Trustees

NDS security assigns rights to objects by using object *trustees*. The Access Control List (ACL) for each object contains the list of trustees for that object. An object trustee is any user (or other object) to whom you have assigned rights to the object. These object types often have trustee rights:

- The [Root] object
- Organization objects
- Organizational Unit objects
- Organizational Role and Group objects
- User objects
- The [Public] trustee

To view the trustees of an object, follow these steps:

1. At the NetWare Administrator window, highlight file system object, then click Object, and then click Details to display the Details window for that object.

2. Click the Trustees of This File System button to display the list of trustees for the object.

3. If you want to see the other objects for which a certain trustee has rights, click on the trustee's name. If you want to remove a trustee, highlight the trustee's name and click the Delete Trustee button.

4. To add a trustee, click Add Trustee to display the Select Object dialog box. In this dialog box, you can select a user, group, or other object.

5. After you add the trustee, you can assign rights by clicking the desired check boxes. By default, NDS assigns the Read and File Scan rights.

6. Click OK to save your changes.

To view the objects for which a specific trustee has rights, follow these steps:

1. At the NWADMN32 window, browse to the desired object (or user), highlight the object name, and then click Object, and click Details to display the Details window for that object.

2. Click Rights to Files and Directories.

3. Click the Find button to find the volumes that you want to display, and then click the volumes that you want to see. NWADMN32 shows you all the directories and files to which the user has rights.

4. If you want to add rights for that user/object to another file or directory, click the Add button.

5. In the Select Object box, browse to the desired object and highlight it, and click OK to add the user to the list of trustees for that object. You can specify which rights the user/object has, for which Read and File Scan are the defaults.

Access Control List (ACL)

The Access Control List is an attribute of NDS objects, and every object in the NDS tree has an ACL attribute. The ACL contains information such as which trustees have access to the object (entry rights), which trustees have access to the object properties, and which users or groups are denied access to that object. This information is stored as the following:

- The trustee name
- The affected attribute—[Entry Rights], [All Attributes Rights], or specific attributes
- The privileges

The base schema defines a default ACL template that provides minimum access security for new objects. Because the Top object class defines the properties for a default ACL template, all object classes will inherit a default ACL template. This enables objects that create other objects the right to supervise the created object, which ensures that every new NDS object has a supervisor. When you create an object in an NDS tree, the creation process can set the object's ACLs to any value, including one that changes a value that comes from a default ACL template.

Object Rights

Object *rights* are the tasks that a trustee can perform on an object. When a trustee receives rights for an object, any child objects of that container inherits those rights. Subsequently, the trustee receives rights for these child objects also, unless the rights are blocked. There are five types of object rights, which are as follows:

- **Supervisor**—The trustee receives all rights of the object, which are Browse, Create, Delete, and Rename. Unlike the Supervisor right in the file system, you can block the NDS Supervisor right through the Inherited Rights Filter (IRF).

- **Browse**—The trustee can see the object in the directory tree. If an object/user does not have the Browse right, NDS will not show the object in the list.

- **Create**—The trustee can create child objects under the object. This right is available only for Container objects.

- **Delete**—The trustee can delete the object from the directory. To delete an object, you also must have the Write right for All Properties of the object.

- **Rename**—The trustee can change the name of the object.

Property Rights

Property rights are the tasks that a trustee can perform on an object's properties. This enables the trustee to read or modify the property values. Trustees can inherit property rights in the same manner as object rights, except that they can inherit only those rights given with the All Properties option. If a trustee receives rights to selected properties of an object, child objects cannot inherit those rights because each of the different types of objects, such as Users and Organizational Units, has a different list of properties. Note that although some property rights have the same name as the object rights, the two sets of values are not the same. There are five types of property rights, which are as follows:

- **Supervisor**—The trustee receives all property rights, which are Compare, Read, Write, and Add Self. Again, the IRF can block this right. Trustees with Supervisor object rights automatically receive Supervisor rights to All Properties of the object.

- **Compare**—The trustee can compare the property's values to a given value. This enables the trustee to search for a certain value but not to look at the value itself.

- **Read**—The trustee can read the values of the property. Any trustee who has the Read property right automatically receives the Compare right.

- **Write**—The trustee can modify, add, or remove values of the property.

- **Add Self**—The trustee object can add or remove itself as a value of the property. For example, a user who has the Add Self right for a group could add himself to the group. The Write right is automatically granted to a trustee who is granted the Add Self property.

Inherited Rights

When an object trustee receives rights to a Container object, that same trustee also receives the same rights for all children of the object. Inheritance affects both object rights and property rights. When a trustee receives rights to a Container object, those rights flow down the directory tree until they are blocked. You can block inherited rights in two ways: with a new (explicit) trustee assignment or with the Inherited Rights Filter (IRF). Figure 27.6 shows you how inherited rights work within the NDS structure and how NDS can block those rights.

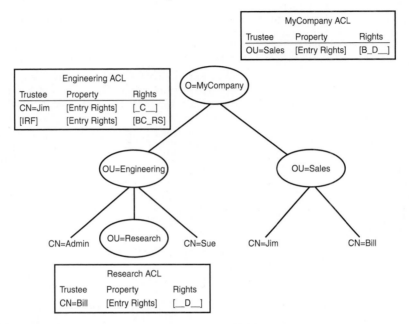

Figure 27.6   Inherited rights can allow rights or it can block them.

Through the *Inherited Rights Filter (IRF)*, you can control which trustee rights an object can inherit for its parent object. You cannot use the IRF to grant rights, but can only block or permit rights that the object receives from a parent directory. If the IRF includes a right, the child objects can inherit that right. If the IRF omits a right, no trustee can inherit that right for that object.

Each NDS object has an IRF for object rights, and each object has an IRF for property rights. Like the rights themselves, you can set the IRF for All Properties or Selected Properties. You also can set an IRF for all properties, and then set different IRFs for certain selected properties.

Through *explicit assignments,* you can block the rights that a trustee can inherit for a particular object by giving the trustee new explicit assignments to the object. You can use new trustee assignments to block inherited rights or to add rights. The new trustee assignment replaces the rights that an object would have otherwise inherited. Because explicit assignment blocks inherited rights, you do not need to consider inherited rights if you are granting an explicit assignment.

To set the IRF, follow these steps:

1. From the NWADMN32 window, browse through the directory tree to find the desired object. Highlight the object, click Object, and then select Trustees of This Object.

2. Click the Inherited Rights Filter button to display the Inherited Rights Filter window.

3. You can block/allow both object rights and property rights. Check the boxes to permit inheritance of that right, or uncheck them to block that right. In addition, you can set the IRF for selected properties of that object or for all properties.

4. When you have specified all the desired rights, click OK to apply the rights filter.

Security Equivalence

Under some conditions, a trustee can automatically receive all the rights that you or NDS have assigned to another trustee. We call this practice *security equivalence*, of which there are two types: implied security equivalence and explicit security equivalence. Security equivalence also includes instances where you assign rights to a container object, and all other objects within the container will receive the same rights. If one of these objects is also a container object, the objects in that second-level container will receive the same rights of the first-level container. This is referred to as *implied security equivalence* or *container security equivalence*.

Although this process might seem very much like inheritance, it is different. With inheritance, any trustee rights that you assign to a container object also will be given to the objects composing the container object. To further define the difference, remember that an object inherits the trustees assigned to its parent object, and the IRF *can* block these rights. On the other hand, a trustee is security equivalent to its parent objects, and the IRF cannot block those rights.

The other kind of security equivalence that an object can have is *explicit security equivalence*. The user's Security Equal To property lists all explicit security equivalences. You specifically assign explicit security equivalence to a user by any of these three means:

■ Through the Security Equal To property that each user has. You can add users or other objects to this list, and the user receives the rights given to those objects.

■ If you assign a user to the membership list of a Group object, the user becomes security equivalent to the Group object, and the Security Equal To property will reflect that equivalence.

■ If a user is an occupant of the Organizational Role object, the user becomes security equivalent to the Organizational Unit object, which also is reflected in the Security Equal To property.

Effective Rights

Many different factors affect a user's rights to Directory objects, such as the following:

■ Rights given directly to the object/user

■ The object's inherited rights from parent objects

■ Limitations specified by the Inherited Rights Filter or an explicit assignment

■ Rights received from containers in which the user resides through implied security equivalence

■ Security equivalences to Group or Organizational Role objects

So, how can you determine what users can do and what they cannot? First, you could calculate them manually: not a very attractive option. On the other hand, you can take advantage of the nifty little tool that NWADMN32 provides to automatically calculate the user's actual rights. The rights that a user actually can perform on an object are their *effective rights*. You can go to either the Trustees of This Object or the Rights to Other Objects properties and see the Effective Rights button. The Effective Rights window shows the current effective rights. Rights that you have granted to the user appear darkened, but those rights that the user does not have are muted. If you have made changes to the trustee rights, you must save the changes before Effective Rights will reflect those changes.

Login Security

Because users log in to a global directory, you don't need to manage multiple server- or domain-accounts for each user. It also means that you don't need to manage trust relationships or pass-through authentication among domains. Although a workstation connects to the network, the user has virtually no access to the network resources until they successfully log in. Before a user logs in, the administrator must create a User object in the directory for that user. The User object has a name and password, as well as other properties.

When the user logs in, he or she enters a username and password. NetWare does not send the password across the network for authentication; this would be a security risk. Instead, network login security encrypts the username, password, workstation, and other vital details to form a unique user code. The login security performs the same process at the authenticating server, and if the codes match, the user receives network access.

Through NWADMN32, you can define several types of user access and login restrictions, which are as follows:

■ Login restrictions enable you to disable the account entirely, make it expire on a certain date, or limit the number of concurrent logins for the user.

■ Password restrictions include a variety of options dealing with passwords. You can specify whether the user can change passwords, how often the user will be required to change the password, and how many grace logins are allowed with the old password after a change is required.

■ Login Time restrictions control the times and days the user is allowed access to the network.

■ Network Address restrictions enable you to create a list of workstation addresses from which the user can access the network. This lets you limit the user to a single workstation or a particular group of workstations.

In addition to these login security types, you can define intruder detection so that you can specify a number of login attempts that the system will allow before it locks the account. You also can specify a reset interval, which unlocks the account after a certain time elapses following intruder detection. If the system locks a user's account and does not reset automatically, you can unlock it from the Intruder Lockout property of the User object.

Default Rights for a New NetWare Server

When you install a new NetWare Server object into an NDS tree, Novell has designed the operating system so that it will make the NDS trustee assignments outlined in Table 27.4 by default.

Table 27.4   Default Rights for New Servers

Default Trustees	Default Rights
Admin (first NDS server in the tree)	Supervisor object right to [Root].
[Public] (first NDS server in the tree)	Browse object right to [Root].
NetWare Server	Admin has the Supervisor object right to the NetWare Server object, which means that Admin also has the Supervisor right to the root directory of the file system of any NetWare volumes on the server.

Table 27.4   continued

Default Trustees	Default Rights
Volumes (if created)	[Root] has Read property right to the Host Server Name and Host Resource properties on all Volume objects. This gives all objects access to the physical volume name and physical server name. Admin has the Supervisor right to the root directory of the file systems on the volume. For volume SYS, the container object has Read and File Scan rights to the \PUBLIC directory of the volume. This allows User objects under the container to access NetWare utilities in \PUBLIC.
User	If you set the system to automatically create home directories for users, they have the Supervisor right to those directories.

Delegated Administration

NDS enables you to delegate your administration rights of an NDS tree branch, and thus revokes your own management rights to that branch. This attribute is useful if special security requirements require a different administrator to take over your responsibilities with complete control over that branch. You can delegate administration either by granting the Supervisor object right to a container or by creating an IRF at the container that filters the Supervisor and any other rights you want blocked.

Network Printing

NDS represents print servers, print queues, and printers as individual NDS objects that you can create and manage independently. NDS users can easily locate and capture printers and queues.

The PCONSOLE Bindery utility has a Quick Setup option that makes it easy to define and link printers, print servers, and print queues. However, because you will find PCONSOLE only on Bindery systems, you will most likely not have an occasion to use this utility.

NWADMN32 integrates the Print management utilities and gives you a graphical view of NDS resources to make it easy for you to administer network print services. In addition, a layout page shows all the printers attached to the print server, the queues serviced by those printers, and the print jobs in the queue.

Using NDS Manager

The NDS Manager is an NDS database administrative tool that lets you manage partitions and replicas. The Schema Manager utility of the NDS Manager enables you to manage and modify the NDS schema and distribute updated NDDS versions to NetWare servers. To access the NDS Manager, execute SYS:PUBLIC\WIN32\NDSMGR32.EXE to display the NDS Manager window (see Figure 27.7).

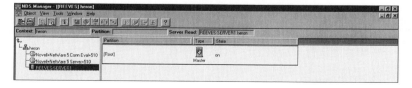

Figure 27.7   The NDS Manager window lets you manage partitions and replicas.

Partitioning

A *partition* is a logical division of the NDS directory database that forms a distinct unit of data in the NDS tree to store directory information. Each partition contains a set of container objects, the objects in the container, and the object properties. Keep in mind that NDS partitions contain only NDS directory information, and not any information about the file system, where your data is stored.

The NetWare default is to keep the entire directory in one partition. That being the case, how do you know if you should partition your NDS directory? If you have in excess of 1,000 objects in your NDS tree, your server might be overwhelmed and access to NDS could be slow. A new partition allows you to divide the NDS directory and move the objects in the specified branch to a different server.

A slow WAN link is another indication that partitioning might be for you. You can make NDS perform faster and more reliably if the directory is divided in two partitions. If you left your NDS structure with only one partition, NetWare will do one of two things. It will either keep the replicas of the single partition at one site (discussed in the next section), or it will distribute the single partition between the servers on either side of the WAN link.

You have the option of partitioning the NDS or leaving it as one big database. The deciding factor should be slow NDS response. The two major factors that affect NDS response are size and network speed.

The problems that might arise from the first scenario are that users at the other side of the WAN link experience login and resource accessing delays. In addition, if the WAN link fails, those users cannot log in or access resources at all.

The second scenario, too, has problems: If NDS distributes the replica of the single partition between the two sites on either side of the WAN link, users can access the directory locally. However, the WAN link is the conduit for the server-to-server synchronization of replicas. This means if the WAN link is unreliable, there might be NDS errors, not to mention that directory changes are slow to reproduce across the WAN link.

So, now that you understand the benefits of partitions, let's get to the business of actually creating a partition. For this, you will use the NDS Manager Utility (accessible from the NWADMN32 and explained previously) to partition your NDS directory. At the NDSMGR window, highlight the container object that will be the root of the new partition, click Object, and then click Create Partition to display the Create Partition dialog box. If you are certain that you have chosen the correct object, click the Yes button to initiate the new partition. Repeat these steps as many times as needed.

Creating Replicas

Replicas were discussed earlier, but here are a few more details so that you will know how to institute them on your NetWare network. If your network consists of at least three NDS servers, you can create replicas of the NDS directory. Replicas provide a measure of fault tolerance if a server or network link fails, which means that you will not lose your directory structure and the information about your NDS objects.

Creating replicas is simply taking parts of your NDS directory and copying them to other servers. If this procedure sounds familiar, you probably will recall the principle of disk striping, wherein the operating system writes chunks of data across defined spaces on separate disks. Although NDS replication copies only the NDS directory and not data, the two procedures are similar in application.

However, NDS replication does not provide fault tolerance for the file system (that means your data). You can establish fault tolerance for file systems through any of the most commonly used fault tolerance methods, such as disk mirroring and disk duplexing (RAID Level 1), Stripe sets with Parity (RAID 5), or Novell Replication Services (NRS). If your network provides Bindery Services, you must create a master or read/write replica of the directory structure.

Replication also decreases access time for users that access NDS information across a LAN or WAN link. To reduce access time, you can place a replica of the needed information on a local server (that is, on the other side of the WAN or LAN link). You can create four different types of replicas, as shown here:

- **Master replica**—By default, the first NDS server on your network holds the master replica. There is only one master replica for each partition at a time. If you create other replicas, they will be read/write replicas by default. If you plan to bring down the server that holds a master replica, you can promote one of the read/write replicas to the master. Then, the original master replica automatically becomes read/write. A master replica must be available on the network for NDS to perform operations such as creating a new replica or creating a new partition.

- **Read/write replica**—NDS can access and change object information in the master and any read/write replicas. Any changes that you make automatically disseminate to all the other replicas. If NDS responds slowly to users because of delays in the network infrastructure (such as slow WAN links or busy routers), you can create a read/write replica closer to the users who need it. You can have as many read/write replicas as you have servers to hold them, although more replicas cause more traffic to keep them synchronized with each other.

- **Read-only replica**—Novell created this type of replica in anticipation of capabilities that future implementations of NDS might offer. Read-only replicas receive synchronization updates from master and read/write replicas but don't receive changes directly from clients.

- **Subordinate reference replica**—Subordinate reference replicas are special, system-generated replicas that don't contain all the object data of a master or a read/write replica, and therefore do not provide fault tolerance. They contain only enough information for NDS to resolve names across partition boundaries. You cannot delete a subordinate reference replica because NDS deletes it automatically when it no longer is needed. NDS creates subordinate reference replicas only on servers that hold a replica of a parent partition but that have no replicas of its child partitions. If NDS copies a replica of the child partition to a server holding the replica of the parent, the subordinate reference replica is deleted automatically.

Synchronizing Servers

When multiple servers in the network hold replicas of the same partition, those servers create a replica ring. NDS automatically keeps those servers synchronized, so the object data is consistent on all replicas. The following NDS processes work to synchronize the servers in the replica ring:

- Replica synchronization
- Schema synchronization
- Limber
- Backlink
- Connection management

In a single-server environment, the server's internal clock can maintain a common and consistent time source for the network. However, for multiserver networks, NDS requires that all the servers agree on time. Time synchronization does these things for your network:

- Applications that run on your server provide accurate timestamps to events. Messaging and collaboration applications and databases all benefit from synchronized time.

- You can configure workstations to get their time from the servers, taking synchronized time benefits to locally run applications.

- NDS applies correct timestamps to NDS events.

Whenever you make changes to NDS objects, you can specify that the operating system make those changes to different replicas on different servers, and these changes must be enacted in the order in which they were requested. NDS records the time of each event with a timestamp. The timestamp ensures that when NDS actually modifies the database, events appear on the replicas in the time and order that they happened. NDS also uses timestamps to record time values for the network and set expiration dates.

Setting Up Bindery Services

You still might find applications, such as print servers and backup software, that were written for NetWare 2.x and 3.x. These applications used the NetWare Bindery instead of NDS for network access and object manipulation. As discussed before, the Bindery is a flat database of objects such as users, groups, and volumes known to a given server. The Bindery is server-specific and server-centric.

In addition, older NetWare client software used a Bindery login procedure in which a user logged in to a specific server only. Access to multiple servers required multiple logins using multiple user accounts.

NDS allows applications written for a Bindery to function using Bindery services. Bindery services enable you to set a context or several contexts as a server's virtual Bindery. The context you set for the server is the server's Bindery context. Whenever you institute Bindery Services, you should keep the following in mind:

- To use Bindery services, you must set a Bindery context for the server.
- Not all NDS objects map to Bindery objects. Many NDS objects, such as Alias objects, do not have a Bindery equivalent.
- Most Bindery applications have been upgraded to work with NDS. Check with your application vendor to get the newest version.
- Each server (before NetWare 5) with a Bindery context must hold a master or read/write replica of the partition that includes the Bindery context.

NetBIOS and NetBEUI

## CHAPTER 28

SOME OF THE MAIN TOPICS IN THIS CHAPTER ARE

A Brief Historical Look at NetBIOS

NetBIOS Names

NetBIOS Services

Locating Network Resources: Browsing the Network

The Server Message Block Protocol (SMB) and the Common
Internet File System (CIFS)

Using nbtstat for Troubleshooting

Before TCP/IP became popular for use in small LANs, the only choice most administrators had was to use a proprietary protocol (such as DECnet or IPX/SPX). When PCs started appearing on the desktop in the early 1980s, the NetBIOS interface and NetBEUI were developed to make networking PCs an easy task. An *interface* is not a network transfer protocol. The NetBIOS interface doesn't send or receive data. Instead, NetBEUI provided a means for transmitting data packets on the local network, whereas NetBIOS gave the programmer an application programming interface that could be used to easily access network functions from within applications. With Windows 2000 computers, NetBIOS can be used over any of the transport protocols installed on the computer, not just NetBEUI. The underlying transport protocol will be transparent to the applications that make calls to NetBIOS functions. Because the interface stands between the actual network transmission and the application, the programmer does not need to know what transport protocol is used to get data from one place to another. It is simply a matter of making calls to routines in the NetBIOS interface and letting it take care of things from there. Also, because the applications are written to use the NetBIOS interface, you don't have to buy a different application to use for each transport protocol that transports data on the LAN.

If you extend the name *NetBIOS* into its original full-length name, you get *Network Basic I/O System*. Just as the BIOS (Basic Input/Output System) you find on your computer motherboard (Basic I/O System) is a collection of software routines that make writing code easier for operating system and application developers, NetBIOS makes it easier to write applications that require network communications. NetBIOS was created as an extension to the original BIOS, making it easy for programmers to write applications that could make use of network services. By using an API, the programmer doesn't have to get down to the bits and bytes of the underlying hardware or network protocols.

This chapter explains the NetBIOS interface and then looks at the other protocols that were developed to work with or extend NetBIOS. Although many other network protocols dominate the Internet today, NetBIOS and its related protocols played an important part in computer networking and are still widely used.

A Brief Historical Look at NetBIOS

Sytec, Inc. originally developed NetBIOS for IBM in 1983. It was designed for use in small departmental LANs of about 20–200 computers and provided peer-to-peer networking capabilities. Peer-to-peer means that there is no central controlling computer or device. Any computer can talk to any other computer that is connected to the same LAN. It was first employed on IBM's PC Network. At that time, the PC revolution had barely begun, and the capability to network a few hundred computers was quite a task. Even larger networks could be built using gateways or other devices to join these smaller LANs.

In 1985, the *NetBIOS Extended User Interface (NetBEUI)* was released. This allowed more functionality for networking with NetBIOS. NetBEUI, which was used extensively by Microsoft, made a clearer distinction between the network transport protocol function and the programming interface. This was in line with trends in the computer networking industry toward standards, in particular the OSI seven-layer reference model.

Novell released its Advanced NetWare 2.0 in 1986 with a NetBIOS emulator. This emulator enabled programmers to write applications that used NetBIOS calls, yet the underlying transport mechanisms were Novell's own IPX and SPX protocols. Subsequent versions of NetWare have continued to provide a NetBIOS interface, even with NetWare 5, which uses TCP/IP as its core network transport rather than the company's own protocols.

When IBM developed token-ring networks, an emulator for NetBIOS was created. NetBIOS could now be used on both ethernet and token-ring networks. The underlying transport, again, is not really relevant. Providing a common programming interface to top-level applications enabled PC networking to grow faster than it had when each vendor employed proprietary solutions.

Many other implementations of PC networking software have used the NetBIOS interface. Pathworks (Digital Equipment Corporation, now part of Compaq Computer Corporation) was an implementation of a LAN Manager 2.x network running on Digital's DECnet networks. Furthermore, Microsoft has used NetBEUI in LAN Manager since 1987, and it has been integral to networking in Windows for Workgroups and Windows NT to version 4.0. Although Windows 2000 includes support for NetBEUI, it is no longer required and is not the preferred network protocol.

RFC 1001, "Protocol Standard for a NetBIOS Service On a TCP/UDP Transport: Concepts and Methods," was finished in 1987 and delineates a method of using NetBIOS as an interface with TCP/IP as the network transport. Another, RFC 1002, details the specifics for this proposal, including descriptions of the contents of packets, the format of names, and pseudocode that shows different mechanisms that can be used to resolve names in this environment.

Many other networking products have used NetBIOS and NetBEUI. Because the specifications were not exacting—as they are in other established network protocols, such as TCP/IP—many LAN products were released from various vendors that could not interoperate. Still, until the Internet became a dominate force in both LANs and WANs, NetBIOS and NetBEUI were used by almost every major PC network product.

The important point to gather from this historical perspective is that NetBIOS was the first widely adopted attempt at a networking standard, even though it might not have been as "clean" as the standards that are being developed and used today. The advantages that came from using NetBIOS and NetBEUI helped formulate a desire for network components that could work together instead of the proprietary traps that major computer vendors used before PCs came along.

Note

If you are operating in an all-Windows 2000 environment, you might find that you don't need to use NetBIOS or any of the utilities, such as WINS, that were developed around it. As long as none of your applications require NetBIOS, then in a true Windows 2000 environment, using DNS for name resolution and the Active Directory for user and computer services information, it is possible to get by without NetBIOS. Note, however, that you should check your applications. For example, the browser service that is usually used to locate computers or services will not function without NetBIOS. If you have older legacy machines, such as Windows 95, Windows 98, or Windows NT on your network, you will have to continue to use NetBIOS.

NetBIOS Names

Most network protocols require a network address—usually a numeric value—to identify the different computers and processes that run on them. For example, in the TCP/IP protocol suite, IP addresses are used to identify computers and other devices, and ports are used to address specific applications or processes on those computers. NetBIOS, however, is used to establish a logical communication path based on names.

NetBIOS names can be classified into two categories: *unique names* and *groupnames*. A unique name can be used by only one workstation in the local broadcast network, whereas many computers can share groupnames. A NetBIOS name is 16 bytes in length, and if a shorter name is used, it is padded so that it is 16 bytes long. In some implementations (such as in Microsoft products), the 16th byte is given a special meaning. Unlike DNS names, NetBIOS names can be made up of almost any type of character, but cannot start with the asterisk character (*).

Each computer that participates in the network has a unique name that identifies it. A computer can hold more than one unique name. Each service that a computer offers will need to register a name for that service. The most common ones you'll see are for file and print services. In order for a computer to lay claim to a name, it must usually broadcast that desire to the rest of the network (or use a WINS server) and wait to see if another computer challenges the name.

The 16th Character

Although NetBIOS names can be 16 characters in length, in many cases (as with Microsoft and IBM products) they are limited to 15 actual characters. The first 15 characters can be anything the administrator wants to use, but the 16th character is used to differentiate between different types of names. This character is often called the NetBIOS suffix, and it qualifies the function of the resource represented by the name. Table 28.1 is a listing of most of the NetBIOS name types employed by Microsoft. Note that the last character in the name does not have to be in the range of printable ASCII characters. For this reason, the hexadecimal value appears instead. In the Type column, the letter *U* indicates that the name is a unique name, and *G* indicates that the name is a groupname (called Internet groupname in Windows 2000) that can be registered by multiple computers.

Table 28.1   NetBIOS Names

NetBIOS Name	Type	Suffix	Description
<computername>	U	00	Workstation Service
<computername>	U	01	Messenger Service
<\\--__MSBROWSE__>	G	01	Master Browser
<computername>	U	03	Messenger Service
<computername>	U	06	RAS Server Service
<computername>	U	1F	NetDDE Service
<computername>	U	20	File Server Service
<computername>	U	21	RAS Client Service
<computername>	U	22	Microsoft Exchange Interchange
<computername>	U	23	Microsoft Exchange Store
<computername>	U	24	Microsoft Exchange Directory
<computername>	U	30	Modem Sharing Server Service
<computername>	U	31	Modem Sharing Client Service
<computername>	U	43	SMS Clients Remote Control
<computername>	U	44	SMS Administrators Remote Control Tool
<computername>	U	45	SMS Clients Remote Chat
<computername>	U	46	SMS Clients Remote Transfer
<computername>	U	4C	DEC Pathworks TCPIP Service on Windows NT
<computername>	U	52	DEC Pathworks TCPIP Service on Windows NT
<computername>	U	87	Microsoft Exchange MTA
<computername>	U	6A	Microsoft Exchange IMC
<computername>	U	BE	Network Monitor Agent
<computername>	U	BF	Network Monitor Application
<username>	U	03	Messenger Service

Table 28.1   NetBIOS Names

NetBIOS Name	Type	Suffix	Description
<domain>	U	00	Domain Name
<domain>	U	1B	Domain Master Browser
<domain>	U	1C	Domain Controllers
<domain>	U	1D	Master Browser
<domain>	U	1E	Browser Service Elections
<Inet~Services>	U	1C	IIS
<IS~computername>	U	00	IIS

This is not an exhaustive listing of all possible types of NetBIOS names that can exist. Other applications, such as Lotus Notes, can also register NetBIOS names.

The NetBIOS Scope ID

When you use NetBIOS over TCP/IP, the NetBIOS Scope identifier is used. This identifier is composed of a string of characters that conform to the rules used to construct DNS names. By using a scope identifier, it is possible to use the same unique NetBIOS name on a network more than once (which is strongly discouraged). The different systems that use the same unique name are differentiated by the scope ID.

For example, the NetBIOS name popeye can be used to uniquely identify a computer on a LAN in the accounting department in the San Francisco office. The same name also can be used to identify a computer in the New York office. Each is qualified by its scope ID, so the names popeye.sf.acme.com will not be confused with popeye.ny.acme.com.

However, use the NetBIOS scope ID with reservation because workstations that have a scope ID can only communicate with other nodes that have the same scope ID. The actual definition of a NetBIOS scope in RFC 1001 is "the population of computers across which a registered NetBIOS name is known."

Note that you cannot specify the NetBIOS scope easily. It can be set in the options offered by a DHCP server in a Windows NT or Windows 2000 environment, or editing the Registry can do it. Because Microsoft strongly advises against this practice, I will not go into the actual Registry entries here. Instead, consult the online Knowledge Base at msdn.microsoft.com if you want to pursue this matter further.

Node Types

RFC 1001 defined three end-node types, based on the method used to register and resolve NetBIOS names: b-node, p-node, and m-node. An additional h-node has been formalized and is used in Microsoft Windows networks.

B-Node (Broadcast)

This type of node uses broadcasts on the local network to register and resolve names. This mode of operation has two major drawbacks. First, in anything but a small network, a lot of bandwidth can be taken up by broadcast messages. Second, most routers do not forward broadcast messages by default. Even if you have a router that can be configured to forward broadcast messages, you probably don't want do so except in a special case where there is no easier solution. You will end up loading multiple network segments with a lot of broadcast messages.

This type of node might work well in a small network, such as a home network. In such a situation, where the volume of network traffic is quite low, broadcast messages are an insignificant matter. In any other type of networking environment, where a large number of computers and network bandwidth is a commodity to be monitored and used wisely, setting up a computer to operate as a b-node is unacceptable.

To register a name, a b-node computer simply broadcasts a datagram on the local segment indicating its desire to use the name. If no other computer challenges the name with a Negative Name Registration Reply, then the computer can use the name.

By default, Windows 2000 computers run in b-mode. If you configure the computer to use a WINS server, however, it will run as an h-node. You also can edit the Registry to manually configure your Windows 2000 computer to make it run as a p-node or m-node, or by using a DHCP server that has the capability to set the node type.

P-Node (Point-to-Point)

A p-node communicates directly with a *NetBIOS Name Service (NBNS)* to register and resolve names. RFCs 1001 and 1002 describe the functions performed by an NBNS. Microsoft's implementation of the name server is called WINS, for Windows Internet Name Server. WINS operates much like a DNS server, except that it maps NetBIOS names to IP addresses, whereas DNS maps TCP/IP names to IP addresses. WINS also differs from the traditional implementation of DNS in that it is a dynamic database (modern DNS servers include functionality for dynamic name registration). Nodes register unique and groupnames when they boot up by sending directed datagrams to the WINS server. Dynamic name registration techniques for DNS servers is described in quite a few RFCs and is implemented in Windows 2000 DNS servers, but you should check to see whether the DNS server you use has this feature if you want to use it in a Windows 2000 environment.

To register a name, a p-node client will send the name to the WINS server. If another client has already registered the name, the WINS server will send a challenge to that computer. If that computer is still using the name, then the WINS server will return a Negative Name Registration Reply to the client trying to register the name. Otherwise it will send a Positive Name Registration Reply, acknowledging the name registration. Another possibility is that the WINS server will send a Wait Acknowledgment to the client requesting the name registration. In this case, the WINS server is still trying to contact the computer that has previously registered the name and has not yet determined whether it can release this old name registration.

The main advantages that the p-node has over the broadcast method are obvious: No broadcast messages propagate through the network, and by using the IP address or point-to-point communication with a name server, this type of node can talk with a name server on the other side of a router. Thus, it reduces network traffic and scales better for a larger network.

There are drawbacks, however. You must configure each client computer to know the address of the name server because this is the computer it needs to contact both to register its own names and to resolve other names. If the name server is down, the client computers cannot register any new names or resolve names for nodes with which they want to communicate.

Microsoft has addressed both of these issues in Windows NT networks by adopting DHCP so that client nodes can be configured automatically when they boot, and by allowing for multiple WINS servers to replicate data so that if one goes down the others can fill the void.

M-Node (Mixed: Broadcast and Point-to-Point)

The m-node was designed to address the problems inherent to both the b-node and p-node methods. A computer configured as an m-node first attempts to use broadcast messages to register or resolve NetBIOS names. If no computer on the local subnet objects to the name registration, the m-node computer then tries to use point-to-point communication with a WINS name server.

The advantage this has over the previous nodes is that if the name server is down, computers within the same broadcast domain can still communicate to resolve names among themselves. Resolving names for computers or resources in other subnets, however, is hampered until the name server returns to service.

H-Node (Hybrid)

The h-node was not included in the RFC 1001 specification, but has been adopted by Microsoft in its Windows operating systems. This node is basically the opposite of the m-node. It first tries point-to-point communication with a name server and, if that fails, it operates as a b-node and attempts name registration and resolution using broadcast methods.

The advantage this node type has over the p-node is the same advantage that the m-node has: It can continue to register and resolve names in the local broadcast domain if communication with the name server fails. The advantage this type has over the m-node, however, is that it limits the use of broadcast messages. As long as the name server is available and can answer the queries the client submits, broadcast messages do not consume network bandwidth.

Another advantage the h-node has over the other three types is that it can be configured to consult the lmhosts (LAN Manager Hosts) file. This file is similar to the hosts file used by TCP/IP clients to translate TCP/IP host names to IP addresses. The LMHOSTS file, however, is used to translate NetBIOS names to IP addresses. This modified version also can consult the NetBIOS name cache. When configured in this manner, the node is known as a Microsoft-Modified B-Node. The lmhosts example file can be found in the directory systemroot\system32\drivers\etc.

Note

It is important to understand the differences between b-nodes and p-nodes. Because one uses only a broadcast method to register and resolve names and the other uses only a name server, these two node types cannot interact with each other in the name resolution process. There is no common point of reference between the two. It is possible for m-nodes and h-nodes to interact with nodes that use only broadcast methods.

The NetBIOS Namespace

Unlike the TCP/IP namespace, the NetBIOS namespace is flat, with no hierarchical organization. *Flat* means that employing a name is not much different from using the MAC address. There can be only one computer in the network that uses the particular name. Nothing in the MAC address or a NetBIOS name enables the administrator to organize networked computers and resources into a meaningful structure. TCP/IP names represent a hierarchical structure. Computer names are qualified by the domain or subdomain in which they exist. For example, yoko.ny.acme.com is immediately identified as a unique computer that is in the subdomain ny that is part of the acme.com domain. The same Acme company can have many different locations and can address computers or resources in each location by the subdomain in which they reside, making use of the same computer name, as long as they reside in different DNS domains.

The use of scope identifiers seems to overcome this problem with NetBIOS names. However, this is not part of the original NetBIOS implementation; rather, it uses the organization inherent in TCP/IP and the domain name system.

Representing NetBIOS Names in the Domain Name System

Because NetBIOS names can consist of characters that are not used in the *Domain Name System (DNS)*, a method needs to be used to construct a name that is acceptable to DNS when using NetBIOS with an underlying TCP/IP transport mechanism. RFC 1001 defines such a method, which takes the

16-character name and transforms it into a 32-character name that consists of all uppercase ASCII characters. This process is termed *reversible, half-ASCII,* or *biased encoding.* After the name has undergone this first-level encoding, it is subject to the same compression techniques used by DNS (as described in RFC 883).

To perform first-level encoding, each byte of the NetBIOS name is split into two four-bit values. Each of these four-bit values are right-filled with zeros to produce a full byte. The hexadecimal representation of the ASCII value for the uppercase letter *A* is then added to each of these new bytes to produce the final value. This produces uppercase ASCII characters in the range of A–P, all of which are valid characters in a DNS name.

For example:

1. The space character (ASCII value 32 decimal, 20 hexadecimal) is not valid in a DNS name. The binary representation of this ASCII value is "100000".

2. This value is split into two half-bytes (sometimes called *nibbles*) of "0010" and "0000".

3. These nibbles are reconstructed into two separate bytes by right-filling them with zeros. The resulting bytes are "00000010" and "00000000".

4. Finally, add 41 (hexadecimal) to each of these bytes to get the final byte value for each of these characters:

    ```
    "00000010" + "01000001" = "01000011" or 43 hexadecimal
    "00000000" + "01000001" = "00000001" or 41 hexadecimal
    ```

5. The ASCII character representation of a byte that has a hexadecimal value of 43 is C. The ASCII character represented by the hexadecimal value 41, of course, is A. Thus, the space character of a NetBIOS name is represented as CA when it is transformed into the 32-byte DNS-compatible string.

Before the NetBIOS name can be stored in a DNS database, however, it must have its scope ID appended to it to form a valid DNS fully qualified domain name (FQDN). For example, if the NetBIOS name is The NetBIOS name, and the scope ID is ACME.COM, the fully qualified DNS name, after encoding, is FEEIEFCAEOEFFEECEJEPFDCAEOEBENEF.ACME.COM. It might not make a lot of sense when you look at it, but this encoding method does get around the limitations imposed by DNS name rules, allowing DNS servers to be used to resolve NetBIOS names.

NetBIOS Name Renewal and Release

When a NetBIOS name has been registered with a WINS server, it is granted the right to use the name only for a short amount of time, configurable on the WINS server. The default lease time for names on a WINS server is 6 days, but the administrator can change this (from 1 minute up to 365 days). After a successful name registration, the reply message that the WINS server sends back to the client contains the time value (Time-To-Live, or TTL), that tells the client how long it can use the name.

Renewing and releasing NetBIOS names is handled in the following manner:

■ **Renewing**—After half of the lease time has expired, or if the client computer is rebooted, the client will attempt to renew the name registration with the WINS server.

■ **Releasing**—Names are released in two ways. First, the client can explicitly release the name. This can be done by using the nbtstat command. For example, the command nbtstat -RR will cause all names registered by the client to be released and then reregistered. This is used mostly for diagnostic purposes to check and see if name registration is working properly. Alternatively, if a client fails to renew the name (that is, the client is down or has been moved to a different subnet), then the name will eventually time out or will be challenged by another computer.

NetBIOS Services

NetBIOS provides services to the programmer. The name services have already been discussed. But if all NetBIOS provided was the capability to register and resolve a name on the network, it would not be of much use. Fortunately, NetBIOS (and NetBEUI and other implementations of NetBIOS) provide communications services between NetBIOS names, which can be of three basic types:

- **Datagram**—This is an unreliable connectionless service. A datagram can be sent to a unique name or a groupname. Each datagram is considered independent of others. Because there is no ongoing exchange of data in a logical sequence between computers, it is considered to be "connectionless." Because there is no acknowledgement, the sending computer does not know if the message is ever received (hence, it is unreliable). The datagram method is the fastest method of sending information by NetBIOS. The size of the message is limited to 512 bytes in most implementations.

- **Broadcast**—Similar to the datagram service, the broadcast service also provides an unreliable connectionless service. The main difference is that the broadcast message can be picked up by all computers in the broadcast domain and is not limited to a specific unique or groupname.

- **Session**—The session service provides a connection-oriented service in full duplex mode. A session ID is used to identify the session, and communications can flow in both directions. Because NetBIOS was intended for small networks, there are no provisions for flow control. Messages using the session service can be up to 64KB in length.

For any of these services to work, both nodes must cooperate. That is, when an application wants to send data, it issues a send or call command. Computers that want to receive these messages must have outstanding receive commands to process any incoming messages.

Locating Network Resources: Browsing the Network

When a Windows client uses the Network Neighborhood icon on the desktop to view the resources available on the network, the display that appears is constructed from a list of servers that make up the *browse list*. You also can use the `net view` command from the MS-DOS command prompt to display this list. Other `net` command options can be used for troubleshooting NetBIOS problems as well.

▶▶ For more information on the `net` command, see Chapter 33, "File Server Protocols."

Microsoft networks use a method called browsing to enumerate (list) resources on the network and make a list available to clients that need to locate these resources. The browser was first created for use in Windows For Workgroups but has continued on in other Microsoft products including LAN Manager and the Windows 95, Windows 98, and Windows NT operating systems. This functionality is also included in Windows 2000, though it is not necessary if your network is composed of only Windows 2000 computers and your applications can use the Active Directory.

Computers that offer services to the network use NetBIOS names to announce themselves. The computer does not have to be a Windows NT Server computer to offer services. For example, a Windows 98 computer will announce the file and print services it can offer if you allow it to do so when you are configuring its network properties. When the computer boots, it sends a *server announcement* to the master browser or the domain master browser.

The browser system has three main components that can be summarized as follows:

- **Master browsers**—The computer that is the master browser is responsible for compiling the master browse list, which contains a list of servers, workgroups, and domains. The master browser is an elected position, though certain types of computers are more likely to become the master browser than others. If the network contains domains and the domain extends over more than one subnet, the master browser keeps the browse list for the domain members on its subnet.

- **Backup browsers**—Computers that operate as backup browsers poll the master browser every 15 minutes to obtain an updated copy of the browse list. If for any reason a backup browser cannot communicate with the master browser, it forces an *election*, which is the process by which a new master browser is selected.

- **Browse list**—The list of servers that the master or backup browser can maintain is limited to 64KB of data. This limits the number of entries to between 2,000 and 3,000, more or less. If a computer is elected to be the master browser and finds that its browse list is empty, it sends out a request datagram asking servers on the network to send it a server announcement. Computers that receive this request respond during a random interval within 30 seconds. The random delay factor is used to minimize network traffic that occurs if a large number of computers respond at the same time.

The list of servers that is maintained in the browse list does not mean just Windows NT Servers. A server is any node that provides a network and uses NetBIOS names for sharing them.

▶▶ See "Name Resolution," p. xxx. (Chapter 24)

Client Computers

A client computer first contacts the master browser for a list of backup browsers when an application first makes a NetServerEnum API call. It uses the QueryBrowserServers directed datagram to the NetBIOS name *<domain name>*\0x1d to do this.

When the master browser on the client's subnet detects this datagram, it sends the client a list of browsers for the workgroup or domain that the client requests. The client selects three names from this list, randomly selects one of these browsers, and sends a request to it for the browse list.

The Domain Master Browser

A special type of master browser is the domain master browser. This browser service runs *only* on the domain's primary domain controller. When the domain spans more than one subnet, each master browser that is responsible for a subnet portion of the domain announces itself to the domain master browser. The domain master browser obtains a list of servers from each master browser and compiles the domain browser list. This list is updated every 15 minutes. This domainwide browse list is then solicited by each master browser so that its clients can browse the entire domain.

If the network is composed of only Windows for Workgroups computers and no domain mechanism is in place, each subnet functions as a separate browsing entity. It makes no difference if you use the same workgroup name on each subnet. It is the domain master browser that provides the capability of maintaining a browse list that extends across subnets.

When Servers or Browsers Fail

When a node that provides a service or a computer that is operating as a browser fails, the names of the servers or services are not immediately removed from the browse list. This is because the updates that are made to the list are not done in real-time, but rather at regular intervals.

Backup browsers and computers that provide a NetBIOS service but that are not browsers announce themselves every 12 minutes on the network. If the master browser does not receive an announcement for three consecutive time periods from a server, it removes the server's name from the browse list. Because backup browsers receive updates from the master browser every 15 minutes, it can take up to 51 minutes for a server to be removed from the list of resources ($3 \times 12 + 15 = 51$).

Because backup browsers expect to receive updates every 15 minutes from the master browser, the failure of a master browser will be noticed more quickly. If any backup browser cannot contact the master browser, it begins the election process. If a client computer detects the failure (that is, in its first attempt to get a list of backup browsers from the master browser), it begins the election process.

When the domain master browser fails, each master browser can only maintain a list for the servers on its subnet. Thus, if the domain master browser is not restored, the domain resources on other subnets are removed from the browse list after a short period of time.

Browser Elections

Whether a computer can become the master browser depends on several factors. It is an "elected" position. Almost any computer running a Windows-based operating system can become a browser. Unless the browser service is configured not to start, it automatically does so when the computer boots. Some computers serve as master browsers, others as backup browsers. If there is more than one subnet, there is at least one master browser for each subnet, and there is a domain master browser if domains are in use.

The election of a master browser occurs when

- A computer boots and finds that it cannot locate the master browser.

- A computer that has already booted loses communication with the master browser. A client tries to contact the list of backup browsers it knows about first, and then the master browser. When it fails to find any of them, it forces an election.

- A computer acting as a domain controller comes online. These computers are *preferred* master browsers.

When any of these events occurs, the computer that is involved sends out an *election datagram*. This datagram contains two important pieces of information that are used to evaluate which computer will become the master browser: election version and election criteria.

Election version data consists of a fixed value that is 16 bits in length. It specifies the version of the browser election protocol running on the computer. The election criteria value is a 32-bit value, which is divided into four hexadecimal values of two bytes each (as shown in Figure 28.1).

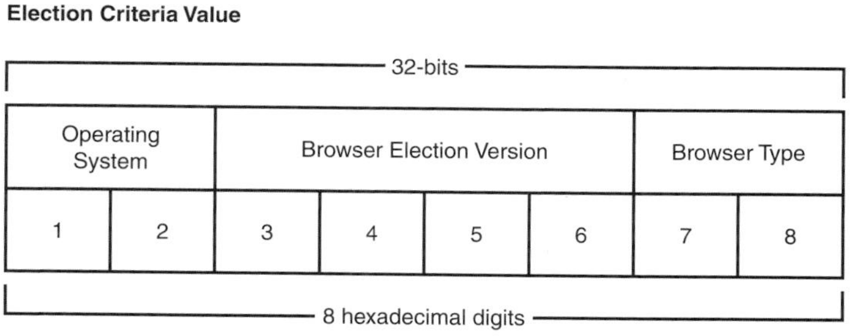

Election Criteria Value

Figure 28.1 Election criteria for master browser elections.

The first two bytes indicate which version of the operating system the computer is running. This value (in hex) is 20 for Windows NT Server and Windows 2000 Server, 10 for Windows NT Workstation and Windows 2000 Professional, and 01 for Windows for Workgroups or Windows 95.

The last two bytes are used to obtain further information about the computer's suitability to become the master browser:

- **80**—This computer is a primary domain controller.
- **20**—This computer is a WINS client.
- **08**—This computer is a preferred master browser.
- **04**—This computer is already a running master browser.
- **02**—The Registry for this computer indicates that it has the MaintainServerList value or the BrowseMaster value set to Yes.
- **01**—This computer is a running backup browser.

When a computer receives the election datagram, it compares the datagram to its own values. The first comparison is made of the election version. If the computer has an election version higher than that found in the election datagram, it wins the election at this point and does not bother to process the remaining election criteria.

Otherwise, a comparison of the election criteria is made. If the computer that receives the datagram has a higher value for the election criteria, it joins the election by sending out an election datagram itself. Otherwise it attempts to determine which computer will become the master browser.

There can be a tie when evaluating the election criteria. The ties are resolved as follows:

- The computer that has been running the longest wins, or
- The computer with the lower lexical name wins.

When a computer determines that it has won the election based on the datagram it has evaluated, it enters the running state and broadcasts up to four election datagrams. If it receives no election datagram from any other computer indicating that it should not be the winner, it promotes itself to become the master browser. If it receives an election datagram indicating that another computer will win, it demotes itself to become a backup browser. The delay for sending out the election datagrams is different, depending on the current status of the computer:

- 100 milliseconds for a computer that is a master browser or a primary domain controller.
- 200–600 milliseconds for a computer that is a backup browser or a backup domain controller (value randomly chosen).
- 800–3000 milliseconds for all others.

If a computer that is running in the election receives an election datagram that shows it cannot possibly win the election, it does not continue to send out the remainder of the four election datagrams because doing so would not change the outcome of the election.

The Server Message Block Protocol (SMB) and the Common Internet File System (CIFS)

So far I have discussed the construction of NetBIOS names and how Microsoft clients that use them locate resources on the network. After a client locates a resource, however, the client must be able to use the service the resource provides. The *Server Message Block* protocol *(SMB)* was originally developed at IBM, with later development done at Microsoft. SMB is used to create file and print services, among others, and is an important protocol to understand because it also is used to provide non-Microsoft and non-IBM clients with connectivity to these networks.

For example, SAMBA is a suite of applications that allow SMB clients to use resources that reside on Unix systems. Banyan VINES networking protocols are another example of using SMB to implement network files and print sharing.

SMB is a request-response type of protocol. An application formats its message into a data structure called a *Network Control Block (NCB)* and sends the message to the server. SMB messages can be grouped into four basic categories:

- **Session Control**—Messages used to create or delete connections to a network resource.
- **File**—Messages that control accessing file system resources on a network resource.
- **Printer**—Messages used to send files to a print resource and to monitor the status of the print job.
- **Message**—Messages, such as unicast or broadcast messages, used to exchange information between network nodes.

Further development of SMB has resulted in a new protocol called the *Common Internet File System (CIFS)*. This enhanced version of SMB was introduced in Service Pack 3 for Windows NT and is now part of the Windows 2000 operating system. It is an open standard because its operations and functions are fully documented and it can be ported to many different operating system platforms and provide a common means for file sharing on the Internet. Because of the large number of applications that use NetBIOS names and the SMB mechanisms, you might see CIFS in your network in the near future, though it will be transparent to you.

An in-depth examination of the SMB protocol and CIFS and how they are used can be found in Chapter 33.

Using *nbtstat* for Troubleshooting

The nbtstat command can give you a lot of information and assist you in making adjustments to the NetBIOS environment on a computer. This command has a complex syntax, which is justified by the capabilities it gives you. The syntax for nbtstat is

```
nbtstat [ [-a remotename] [-A IP address] [-c] [-n]
        [-r] [-R] [-RR] [-s] [-S] [interval] ]
```

- **-a *remotename***—Adapter status. This lists the remote machine's name table.
- **-A IP *address***—Adapter status. This lists the remote machine's name table.
- **-c**—This lists the names currently in the NetBIOS name cache on the local computer. These are NetBIOS names of remote machines that have been stored in the local machine's cache.
- **-n**—This lists the names registered by the local machine.
- **-r**—This option lists names that have been resolved by broadcast or by consulting a WINS server.
- **-R**—This option purges and reloads the remote cache name table.
- **-RR**—This option sends name release packets to WINs and then starts refreshing them.
- **-S**—This option lists the NetBIOS Sessions Connection table, showing the destination IP addresses.
- **-s**—This option lists the NetBIOS Sessions Connection table, converting destination IP addresses to computer NETBIOS names.
- ***remotename***—A remote host machine name.

- ■ *IP address*—Dotted decimal representation of the IP address.
- ■ *Interval*—The amount of seconds that will pass before the display is refreshed. Use Ctrl+C to stop the display.

For example, to view the names in the NetBIOS table on a node named Popeye, you could use the following command:

```
C:\>nbtstat -a popeye

Local Area Connection:
Node IpAddress: [140.176.187.185] Scope Id: []

        NetBIOS Remote Machine Name Table

    Name               Type         Status
    ---------------------------------------------
    POPEYE        <00>  UNIQUE       Registered
    ONO           <00>  GROUP        Registered
    POPEYE        <20>  UNIQUE       Registered
    ONO           <1E>  GROUP        Registered
    POPEYE        <03>  UNIQUE       Registered
    ADMINISTRATOR <03>  UNIQUE       Registered
    ONO           <1D>  UNIQUE       Registered
    INet~Services <1C>  GROUP        Registered
    ..__MSBROWSE__.<01> GROUP        Registered
    IS~POPEYE......<00> UNIQUE       Registered

    MAC Address = 00-08-C7-BA-23-7F
```

You can see from this table that the 16th characters are listed after the name so that you can look them up to determine what kind of use this NetBIOS name is being used for. You can also tell from this table whether the name is unique for that computer or is a group name. If you only know the remote IP address of the computer whose table you want to look at, you can use the -A option with the address instead of the computer name to get the same information.

To determine whether your local workstation is able to register NetBIOS names, use the -r and -R options. The -r version will give you a listing of the NetBIOS names that the local computer has registered, and it will show them categorized as having been resolved by either the broadcast method (as in a b-node) or by consulting a WINS server. The -R option can be used to clear and reload the name cache if you think that it is no longer valid. This can be used for troubleshooting to help determine whether a name can still be registered. You might have more than one computer on the LAN that is trying to register the same unique name, for example.

The -s and -S options show you current sessions that your computer has open with other computers. The lowercase version will list remote computers by name while the uppercase version will list them by IP address. If you are unable to communicate with a remote computer, check the sessions table to be sure there are no conflicting entries. Attempt to make the connection (say to a file or printer service), and then examine the table again to see if the sessions are showing up.

The nbtstat command can be used to solve a lot of problems related to the SMB protocol. Practice using the commands so that you will be familiar with the output. You can do before and after views to check the name cache or the sessions table when you are trying to connect to or view a particular network service. If you don't see the correct names (or addresses) in the cache or in the session table, you can begin to check for connectivity problems to make sure you are indeed able to send and receive datagrams from the machine. You can use a simple TCP/IP tool such as ping for that purpose.

Routing Protocols

29

SOME OF THE MAIN TOPICS IN THIS CHAPTER ARE

Basic Routing Protocol Types

RIP Routing

OSPF (Open Shortest Path First)

Multi-Protocol Label Switching

Routers, which were discussed in Chapter 10, "Routers," are devices that examine network layer protocol addresses and make decisions based on those addresses on how best to send a network packet on its way to its destination. Routers can be used in a corporate network to interconnect various LAN segments, to connect to a wide area network—for connecting branch offices to the headquarters, for example—or more commonly, to connect the local network to the Internet. Routers also play an important part in firewalls, which are discussed in greater detail in Chapter 40, "Firewalls."

However, to make decisions on the best path a packet needs to take as it travels through the network, a router must keep a table in memory that it can use to locate the destination network. Because routers generally are used to connect many different networks, and because networks usually undergo changes frequently, there must be a method for keeping the routing table up to date. Network transport protocols (such as TCP/IP) are used to transfer data across a network. Routing protocols are used by routers to communicate with each other so that they can inform others of new routes, routes that no longer exist, and so on.

For example, suppose an important router suddenly fails. All other routers that have this router in their routing table need to know this so that they can discover another route, if there is one, that can be used to bypass this failed device. Routing protocols come in all sizes and shapes, but all generally perform the same function: keeping routing tables up to date.

Basic Routing Protocol Types

There are two general types of routing protocols: interior and exterior protocols. *Interior* protocols perform routing functions for autonomous networks. *Exterior* routing protocols handle the routing functions between these autonomous networks and glue the Internet together. These routing types are more formerly referred to as Interior Gateway Protocols (IGP) and Exterior Gateway Protocols (EGP). The network you manage for your business is an independent domain that functions internally as a unit. It is an *autonomous system* within which you can make decisions about which hosts use a particular address and how routing is done. When you connect your network to the Internet, the ISP or other provider manages routers that allow your autonomous system to exchange information with other autonomous systems throughout the Internet.

For the most part, the network administrator is concerned with IGP protocols. Two are used most often: RIP and OSPF.

Note

Another IGP you might hear about occasionally is the HELLO protocol. This protocol is mentioned here mostly for historical purposes because it is not employed as much any more. HELLO was used during the early days of the NFSNET backbone and uses a roundtrip, or delay time to calculate routes.

RIP Routing

RIP is an acronym that stands for Routing Information Protocol. It is the most common routing protocol for autonomous systems in use today, though that doesn't mean it's the best. It is a distance-vector protocol, which means that it judges the best route to a destination based on a table of information that contains the distance (in hops) and vector (direction) to the destination.

Figure 29.1 shows two company sites that are connected through two links that have routers between them. The user on Workstation A wants to connect to a resource in the remote network that resides on Server A.

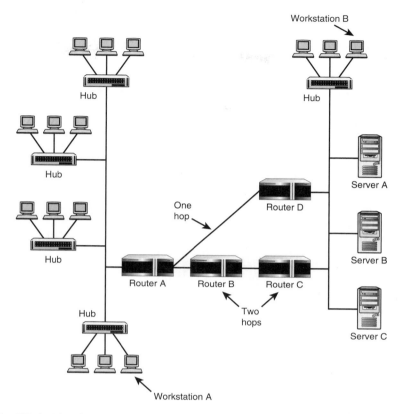

Figure 29.1 RIP decides the best route based on the number of hops between two nodes.

When Router A sees the first packet from workstation A and realizes it cannot be delivered on the local network, it consults its routing tables to first determine whether it can find a path that will get the data to its destination. If more than one path exists, as it does here, it then makes a decision on which path to take. A simplified version of the routing table information would look like this:

```
Destination    Next Hop    Metric
Server A       Router D    1
Server A       Router B    2
```

Router A has two paths it can use to get the packet delivered. The routing table it keeps in memory doesn't tell it the actual names of the servers, as is shown here. Instead, it uses network addresses. It also doesn't show every single router through which the packet will pass on its route to its destination. It only shows the next router to send the packet to and the total number of routers through which it will have to pass.

Note

There are actually two versions of the RIP routing protocol. Version 1 of RIP is defined in RFC 1058, "Routing Information Protocol." Version 2 of the protocol is defined in RFC 1723, "RIP Version 2—Carrying Additional Information."

Earlier versions of RIP routing made simple decisions based solely on the metric called a *hop count*. In this case, RIP would decide to send the packet to Router D, because that route indicates that the packet has to pass through only one additional router to reach its destination. If it were to route the packet through Router B, it would take two hops.

Note

The number of hops to a destination cannot be infinite. In RIP routing, the maximum number of hops that will be considered is 15. If a destination lies more than 15 hops away from the router, it is considered to be an unreachable destination and the router will not attempt to send a packet. When this happens, the router will send an `ICMP Destination Unreachable` message back to the source of the network packet. For more information about ICMP (the Internet Control Message Protocol) see Chapter 20, "Overview of the TCP/IP Protocol Suite."

As simple and straightforward as this might seem, it might not be the best route to take. One of the problems that RIP routing has is that it never takes into consideration the bandwidth of the route. The path from Router A to Router C might be made up of high-speed T1 links and the line between Router A and Router D might be a slower ISDN connection. For small simple packets, such as an e-mail delivery, this might not make a great deal of difference to the end user. For a large amount of traffic, though, this can make a significant difference.

Another problem with RIP is that it doesn't load balance. If a lot of users are trying to get to the remote system, it will not use both of the available routes and divide up the traffic. RIP continues to select what it considers the best route and just sends the packets on their way.

You can configure the hop count for a route in most implementations of RIP. That is, you can manipulate the metric to make it appear that one route (usually a slower link) is farther away than a faster route simply by modifying the routing table to change the hop count of the slow route to a number larger than that of the faster route link. Thus, although a faster link might actually send packets through more routers than the slower link, you can "fool" RIP into using the faster link.

Router Updates

RIP routers periodically exchange data with each other (through the User Datagram Protocol, or UDP, using port 520) so that each router can maintain a table of routing information that is more or less up to date. In earlier versions of RIP a router would broadcast its entire routing table. Newer versions allow a router to send only changes or to respond to routing requests from other routers (called triggered RIP).

The format of the RIP message for version 1 appears in Figure 29.2. For version 1 of the protocol the largest RIP message that can be sent in a UDP datagram is 504 bytes. When you combine this with the 8-byte UDP header, the maximum size of the datagram is 512 bytes.

In Figure 29.2, the portion following the first 4 bytes can be repeated as many as 25 times, depending on the number of routes that are being sent in a single message. The fields labeled Must Be Zero should contain all zero bits. The first field, Command, can have the following values, which indicate the purpose of the message:

- **1 Request**—This message requests that the recipient of the message send all or part of its routing table to the sender of this message.

- **2 Response**—This message is a response to a request, and contains all or part of the sender's routing table to the requestor. Additionally, this message can be sent as an update message that does not correspond with any particular request.

- **3 Traceon**—This is an obsolete command and should be ignored.

- **4   Traceoff**—This is an obsolete command and should be ignored.
- **5**—This is a value reserved by Sun Microsystems for its own use. Implementations of RIP might or might not ignore this type of command.

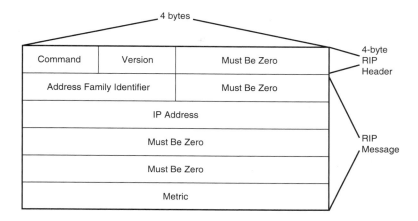

Figure 29.2   The format of the RIP message for version 1 of the protocol.

Note

Why would anyone create a message type with so many fields that contain only zeros? The reason is simple. The creators of RIP version 1 anticipated that enhancements would be made to the protocol (hence the version field), and they wanted to create a message that could be used for the current version 1 as well as for future versions of the protocol. In RFC 1058, rules for RIP routing specify that all messages that have a version number of zero are to be discarded. If the version number is 1, then the message is to be discarded if any of the Must Be Zero fields contain nonzero values. If the version number field contains a value greater than 1, the message is not discarded. In this way, it is possible for RIP version 1 to interact with RIP version 2. Version 1 of the protocol can ignore the Must Be Zero fields when it receives a message from a router that uses RIP version 2 and still garner information from the packet that can be used to update its routing table.

Of course, this doesn't provide for fully functional backward compatibility. If you mix RIP version 1 and version 2 routers in the same network, you should avoid using variable-length subnet masks because the IP address field would then be difficult for the RIP 1 router to understand. For more information about subnetting, see Chapter 20.

The version field denotes the version of the RIP protocol. For version 1 this field contains, of course, a value of 1. The Address Family Identifier field was defined in RFC 1058, but only one address type (the IP address) was defined, and the value for this field should be 2. The IP Address field is four bytes long and is used to store a network address or a host address. For most request messages, this value is set to the default route of 0.0.0.0.

The final field is used to store the hop count, or metric, for the route. This field can contain a value ranging from 1–16. A value of 16 indicates that the destination is unreachable, or to put it in other words, "You can't get there from here."

Because RIP version 1 was created before Classless Inter-Domain Routing (CIDR), and before the concept of subnetting was introduced, there is no subnet field in the message. Because of this, a RIP version 1 router must determine the network ID by examining the first three bits of the IP address, which determine to which class (A, B, or C) the network address belongs. From this it can apply the appropriate subnet mask for the class. If the address does not fall into one of these classes, the router will use the subnet mask associated with the interface on which it received the message and apply it to the address to determine whether it is a network address. If that subnet mask does not match up to create a network address, the mask of all 1s (255.255.255.255) is applied, and the address is assumed to be a host address instead of a network address.

The message traffic generated by RIP routers can be significant in a large network. RIP routers update their routing tables every 30 seconds by requesting information from neighboring routers. They also announce their existence every 180 seconds. If a router fails to announce itself within this time, other routers will consider it to be down and will modify their routing tables. The router itself might have been taken offline by the network administrator, or it could have simply gone offline due to hardware failure. It's also quite possible that the network link between the router and the rest of the network has been broken. The thing to remember is that RIP routers dynamically update routing tables so that packets don't get sent out into the ether and just disappear!

RIP Version 2

Although other protocols, such as OSPF (described later in this chapter) were developed after the original version or RIP and contain more features, you might wonder why RIP version 2 was developed. The reasons are simple: RIP has a large installed base, and it's easy to implement and configure. And, for small- to medium-sized networks, you don't necessarily need a more complex routing protocol when RIP will do the job just as well.

Version 2 of the protocol uses a slightly different message format, as shown in Figure 29.3.

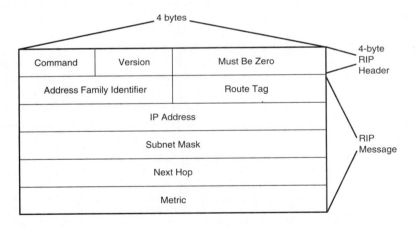

Figure 29.3 Format of the RIP message for version 2 of the protocol.

As you can see, the message format is the same size, but some of the fields that were previously reserved for all zeros have been put to use in version 2 of the protocol. Specifically, they contain a Route Tag, Subnet Mask, and Next Hop fields.

Note

You probably can guess that the version field for version 2 of the RIP protocol contains a value of 2. Using the version field routers can determine whether a RIP message is from the newer version or if it is coming from an older router still using RIP version 1.

The Route Tag field is an administrative field used to mark certain routes. This field was introduced in RFC 1723 so that routers which support multiple routing protocols could distinguish between RIP-based routes and routes imported from other routing protocols. The Subnet Mask field is used to implicitly store a subnet mask associated with the IP address field so that the router does not have to try to determine the network or host address. Applying the mask can yield this result.

The Next Hop field is used to indicate the IP address to send packets for the destination advertised by this route message. If this field is not set to 0.0.0.0, then the address in this Next Hop field must be reachable on the logical subnet from which the routing advertisement originates.

Disadvantages of RIP

RIP is a good routing protocol to use in small networks, but it doesn't scale very well. It became quite popular early on because it was distributed as part of the Berkeley version of Unix, in the form of the routed daemon. The following are the major disadvantages of RIP:

- The broadcast messages used to update routing tables can use a significant amount of network bandwidth.

- There is no general method to prevent routing loops from occurring.

- For larger networks, 15 hops might not be a large enough figure for determining whether a destination is unreachable.

- Update messages propagate across the network slowly from one router to the next, hop by hop (called slow convergence), so inconsistencies in routing tables can cause a router to send a packet using a route that no longer exists.

OSPF (Open Shortest Path First)

RIP is a vector-distance protocol, whereas OSPF uses a link-state algorithm. OSPF routers maintain a routing table in memory just as RIP routers do, but instead of sending out the entire routing table in a broadcast every 30 seconds, OSPF routers exchange link-state information every 30 minutes. In between that interval, very short link-state advertisements (LSAs) are used to send changes to other routers.

Note

The Open Shortest Path First (OSPF) routing protocol (version 2) is defined in RFC 2328, "OSPF Version 2."

OSPF was developed by the Internet Engineering Task Force and was meant to solve most of the problems associated with RIP. Instead of using a simple hop count metric, OSPF also takes into consideration other cost metrics, such as the speed of a route, the traffic on the route, and the reliability of the route. Also, OSPF does not suffer from the 15-hop limitation that RIP employs. You can place as many routers between end nodes as required by your network topology. Another difference between RIP and OSPF is that OSPF provided for the use of subnet masks at a time when version 1 of RIP did not.

Note

Subnet masks, along with IP addressing and other topics that are discussed in this chapter, are introduced in Chapter 20. Chapter 20 is recommended reading before you read this one!

Although OSPF functions more efficiently than RIP, in a large network the exchange of information between many routers still can consume a lot of bandwidth. The time spent recalculating routes can add to network delay. Because of this, OSPF incorporates a concept called an *area*, which is used to divide up the network. Routers within a specific area (usually a geographical area, such as a building or campus environment) exchange LSAs about routing information within their area.

The Link State Database (LSDB) and Areas

Each router maintains a Link State Database (LSDB), in which it stores the information it receives through LSAs from neighboring routers. Thus, over time, each OSPF router essentially has an LSDB that is identical to other routers with which it communicates. Each router is assigned a router ID, which is simply a 32-bit dotted decimal number that is unique within the autonomous network. This number is used to identify LSAs in the LSDB. This is not to be confused with the actual IP addresses of the router's interfaces, but is merely a number used to identify the router to other routers. However, most implementations of OSPF will use either the largest or the smallest IP address of a router's interfaces for this value. Because IP addresses are unique within the autonomous network, Router IDs also will be unique.

A router that is used to connect these areas with a backbone of other routers is called a *border router*. A hierarchy of routing information is built using this method so that every router does not have to maintain a huge database showing the route to every possible destination. Instead, a border router will advertise a range of addresses that exist within its area instead of each address. Other border routers store this information and therefore have to process only a portion of an address instead of the entire address when making a routing decision. Border routers store this higher level of routing information and the information for routes in their area.

In Figure 29.4, you can see a network that has four major areas, each of which has routers that maintain a database of information about its specific area. These routers exchange information with each other that keeps them updated. Each area has a border router that is part of the area and also part of the backbone area. These border routers exchange summary information about their respective areas with other border routers that are part of the backbone area.

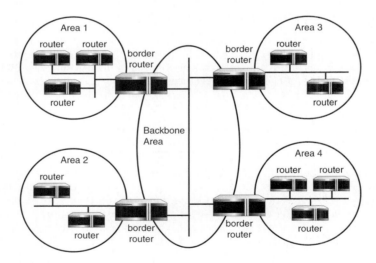

Figure 29.4   OSPF routers are responsible for their areas.

OSPF has the drawback of administrative overhead. Also, low-end routers might not be capable of coping with the amount of information a border router needs to manage.

OSPF Route Calculations

I'll leave the exact explanation of how OSPF calculates the best route to the mathematicians. However, for those who are interested, the algorithm used is called the Dijkstra algorithm, and it is used to create a shortest path tree (SPF tree) for each router. This tree contains information that is valid only from a particular router's point of view. That is, each router builds its own tree, with itself as the root of the tree, while the branches of the tree are other routers that participate in the network. Thus, each OSPF router has a different tree than other routers in the network. From this tree, the router can build a routing table that is used for the actual lookup that is performed when deciding on which interface a packet should be sent out.

Multi-Protocol Label Switching

Today the division between routers and switches is a fine line. Whereas switches were initially designed to help segment a LAN into multiple collision domains, and thereby allow you to extend the reach of a particular LAN topology, switches have moved higher up the ladder in the network in the past few years. When switching is used in a LAN to connect individual client and server computers, the process is known as *microsegmentation*, because the broadcast domain has been reduced to just the switch and the computer attached to a port. Switches at this level generally work using the hardware (MAC) addresses of the attached computers.

Layer 3 switching, which is discussed in Chapter 8, "Network Switches," moves switching up the ladder by one rung by switching network frames based on the OSI network layer address—an IP address, for example. But wait, that's what a router does, isn't it? Of course. As explained in Chapter 8, a layer 3 switch is basically a router, but it implements most of its functions in application-specific integrated chips (ASICS) and performs its packet processing much faster than does a traditional router, which uses a microprocessor (much like a computer CPU) for this function. And, by giving this advanced router device a new name—switch—it's easier for marketing personnel to sell these devices to uninformed customers!

When you get to the top of the ladder, where large volumes of data need to be routed through a large corporate network—or the Internet, for that matter—even the fastest traditional routers or layer 3 switches easily can become bogged down by the volume of traffic. Because of this, the core of a large network traditionally has been built using ATM or Frame Relay switches, and IP traffic is sent over these switched networks.

To speed up the processing of routing packets at high-volume rates, a newer technology has been developing over the past few years and goes by the name of Multi-Protocol Label Switching (MPLS).

So just what is MPLS anyway, and why is it becoming so popular?

Combining Routing and Switching

Traditional routers have a large amount of overhead processing they must perform to get a packet to its destination. Each router along the packet's path must open up and examine the layer 3 header information before it can decide on which port to output the packet to send it to its next hop on its journey. If a packet passes through more than just a few routers, that's a lot of processing time. Remember that IP is a connectionless protocol. Decisions must be made about a packet's travel plans at each stage of its journey through the network. The solution to this problem lies in newer technology—high-speed switching. Specifically, Multi-Protocol Label Switching, which is discussed in the next section, combines the best of routing techniques with switching techniques.

When you look at concepts such as ATM or Frame Relay, which are connection-oriented protocols, this isn't the case. Instead, virtual circuits (either permanent or switched) are set up to connect to endpoints of a communication path so that all cells (as in the case of ATM) or frames (as in the case of Frame Relay) usually take the same path through the switched network.

Note

For more information about ATM and Frame Relay and how these connection-oriented switched networks function, see Chapter 19, "Dedicated Connections."

Adding a Label

MPLS is a method that takes the best of both worlds and creates a concept that allows IP packets to travel through the network as if IP were a connection-oriented protocol (which it isn't). Using special routers called Label Switching Routers (LSRs) does this. These routers connect a traditional IP network to an MPLS network. A packet enters the MPLS network through an *ingress LSR*, which attaches a label to the packet, and exits the MPLS switched network through an *egress LSR*. The ingress LSR is the router that performs the necessary processing to determine the path a packet will need to take through the switched network. This can be done using traditional routing protocols such as OSPF. The path is identified by the label that the ingress router attaches to the packet. As you can see, the ingress router must perform the traditional role that a router fills. It must perform a lookup in the routing table and decide to which network the packet needs to be sent for eventual delivery to the host computer.

However, as the packet passes through the switched network, it is only necessary for the switch to take a quick look at the label to make a decision on which port to output the packet. A table called the Label Information Base (LIB) is used in a manner similar to a routing table to determine the correct port based on the packet's label information. The switch doesn't perform IP header processing, looking at the IP address, the TTL value, and so on. It just spends a small amount of time doing a lookup of the label in the table and outputting the packet on the correct port.

Note

Similar to ATM and Frame Relay networks, the label attached in an MPLS network doesn't stay the same as the packet travels through the network of switches. Labels are significant locally and only identify links between individual switches. Depending on the MPLS implementation, labels can be set up manually (like permanent virtual circuits) or can be created on the fly (like switched virtual circuits). However, after a path (or circuit) through the switched network has been created, label processing takes only a small amount of time and is much faster than traditional IP routing. Each switch simply looks up the label, finds the correct port to output the packet, replaces the label with one that is significant to the output port, and sends it on its way.

When the packet reaches the egress LSR, the label is removed by the router, and then the IP packet is processed in the normal manner by traditional routers on the destination network.

If this sounds like a simple concept, that's because it is. MPLS still is in the development stages, so you'll find that different vendors implement it in different ways. Several Internet draft documents attempt to create a standard for MPLS. Other features, such as Quality of Service (QoS) and traffic management techniques, are being developed to make MPLS a long-term solution.

Using Frame Relay and ATM for MPLS

One of the best features about the current design of MPLS is that it separates the label-switching concept from the underlying technology. That is, you don't have to build special switches that are meant for just MPLS networks. MPLS doesn't care what the underlying transport is. It is concerned only with setting up a path and reducing the amount of processing a packet takes as it travels through the circuit.

Because of this, it's a simple matter for an ATM or Frame Relay switch vendor to reprogram or upgrade its product line to use MPLS. For ATM switches, the VPI and VCI fields in the ATM cell are used for the label field. In Frame Relay switches, an extra field is added to the IP header to store the label. However, don't get confused and think that an MPLS network is an ATM network or a Frame Relay network. These switches must be reprogrammed to understand the label concept. It's even possible, for example, for an ATM switch to switch both ATM and MPLS traffic at the same time. By allowing for the continued use of existing equipment (and these switches are not inexpensive items), large ISP or network providers can leverage their current investment, while preparing to install newer MPLS equipment when the standards evolve to a stage that makes it a good investment.

For the long term it's most likely that MPLS will be implemented using technology similar to Frame Relay instead of ATM. This is because of the small cell size of the ATM cell (53 bytes) combined with a high overhead (the 5-byte cell header). In a small network with little traffic, this 5-byte cell header seems insignificant. However, when you scale this to large bandwidth network pipes, this amount of overhead consumes a large amount of bandwidth given the small amount of data carried in the 53-byte cell. Thus, variable-length frames are most likely to become the basis for MPLS networks in the next few years.

Managing Users and Resources

SOME OF THE MAIN TOPICS FOR THIS PART ARE

Windows NT Domains

Windows 2000 User and Computer Management Utilities

Managing Unix and Linux Users

File Server Protocols

Rights and Permissions

Network Printing Protocols

Print Servers

PART V

Windows NT Domains

SOME OF THE MAIN TOPICS IN THIS CHAPTER ARE

Workgroups and Domains

Windows NT User Groups: Local Groups, Local Domain Groups, and Global Groups

Managing User Accounts

Passwords and Policies

Strategies to Minimize Logon Problems

The Windows NT domain is a collection of users and resources. It is the primary unit of user and resource administration. Administrators in any particular domain can control the addition or modification of user accounts in their domain and can control which resources any user can access, along with the type of access. To begin to understand the logon process under Windows NT, you should first become cognizant of how users and security information is organized into user groups and domains and how these interact. Understanding how domains operate in the Windows NT environment makes it easier for you to plan an integration with, or upgrade to, Windows 2000. When you upgrade your network to include only Windows 2000 computers, you'll find that instead of primary and backup domain controllers, you'll have only domain controllers (that are neither primary or backup), which are essentially peers on the network. It is important to understand how primary and backup domain controllers work if you plan to keep both Windows NT and Windows 2000 computers in the same network.

In this chapter we examine the tools an administrator can use to manage users of a Windows NT 4.0 server. In the next chapter we look at managing users of Windows 2000 servers using the Microsoft Management Console utility. As a prerequisite to the next chapter, you might want to first read Chapter 25, "Overview of Microsoft's Active Directory Service."

Windows NT 4.0 has had several years to settle down. With the latest service packs that Microsoft and other third parties have provided, you can expect to see NT 4.0 used in networks for a few more years. Although it might be a better product, upgrading to Windows 2000 can be expensive from both a hardware and software point of view. Another consideration is that planning the namespace for the Active Directory, used in Windows 2000, can be a complex task—so, if it ain't broke, don't fix it! A carefully managed Windows NT 4.0 network can continue to serve you for many years to come.

Workgroups and Domains

In many ways, a domain is similar to a Windows 3.1 workgroup, but with one major exception: The domain has a single, centralized security accounts manager (SAM) database that holds all security information for the domain. In a workgroup, each computer in the network has its own security database and the user of that computer can set passwords on resources that the computer provides to the network. While a domain provides for centralized administration of the network's resources and users, the workgroup provides a highly decentralized, peer-to-peer networking model.

The disadvantages to the workgroup method include not only the decentralized management functions, but also the ways in which this impacts the end user. For example, to access a resource on another computer in a workgroup the user needs to know the password associated with that share-level resource. Because a different person can potentially manage each computer or workstation, you often need to know as many different passwords as you have resources to which you need to connect. Keeping track of multiple passwords usually leads to lax security because you must write them all down so you don't forget them.

In a domain the administrator is in charge of the security policy for the entire domain. Users need only a single username and password to log on to the network and access resources throughout the domain. There are limits, however, to what a single domain can do in a network. As the network grows in size, whether it is in users, resources, or geographical size, using a single security database can have some drawbacks. Specific computers are designated to be domain controllers. These computers are the repositories of the security database—the SAM. This database contains data for four types of security objects, or accounts:

- User accounts
- Computer accounts

- Global group accounts
- Local group accounts

As you can see, in addition to keeping track of usernames, passwords, and other information about the users on the network, the SAM also keeps track of which computers have joined the domain and which user groups have been defined, along with the members of each group. Note that only Windows NT computers are tracked in the database. Users on other platforms, such as Windows 95/98, can log on to a Windows NT domain. Windows NT computers actually join the domain when the administrator creates a computer account for that workstation in the SAM.

The number of accounts that a single Windows NT 4.0 domain can accommodate, according to Microsoft figures, is around 40,000 due mostly to the maximum size to which the SAM database can grow. This figure can vary, depending on the information you store in the SAM. For example, you might have a lot of computer and user accounts but only a few trust relationships stored in the SAM. Or, you might have a large number of trust relationships stored in the SAM, and this would mean you would have less room for computer and user accounts. You would need more than one domain for a larger network.

Note

There are actually two places where you can find the SAM for Windows NT. The domain controllers hold copies of the domain database, and this is used to validate domain logons and grant users the ability to access resources in the domain. However, any Windows NT Server or Windows NT Workstation computer that is not a domain controller also has its own local security database, much like a Windows for Workgroups computer. The local user can create individual user accounts on the local computer and can grant access to resources on the computer to these users. However, users who are validated by a computer's local database cannot use this logon to access domain resources. Additionally, when a Windows NT computer joins a domain, the domain administrator's global group is, by default, placed into the local domain administrator's group giving the domain administrators the ability to control security functions on the local computer.

Of course, it will probably be a rare thing to find a domain that actually has 40,000 user or computer accounts. When a network grows this large a solution needs to be found that provides a convenient method of managing users and controlling access to network resources.

The solution is to create multiple domains in the network and allow them to interact with each other so that users can access resources anywhere on the network, while still using only a single username and password to log on. In Windows NT this is done using a concept called a trust relationship between domains.

Interdomain Trust Relationships

To support the concept of one username and one password throughout a collection of domains, the trust relationship is used to allow domains to share information contained in the security database. Without a trust relationship you would have to create a new user account in the database of each domain to which a user would need to have access. This would be sort of like the workgroup model, only on a larger scale using domains instead of individual computers.

When a user account is created in a domain, it is assigned a unique identifier, called a SID, which stands for security identification descriptor. If you create several accounts in different domains for a user, with the same logon username and password, the SID will not be the same from one domain to another. The user's logon name is ordinary text, which is used for the convenience of humans who must remember it. The SID is the actual method that the network uses when identifying a particular user (and to identify the domain, which holds the user account) and deciphering what access that user is allowed, based on Access Control Lists (ACLs).

▶▶   For more information on ACLs, see Chapter 34, "Rights and Permissions."

Because there should be only one username and password for any user throughout the network, no matter how many domains are created, a method is needed to allow a domain to recognize that a user has already been validated in another domain. If this can be communicated between domains, it becomes possible to simply trust a user if a domain trusts the domain from which the user comes.

A trust relationship is created when an administrator from one domain uses the User Manager for Domains utility to create a specific relationship with another domain. For example, if domain A has a trust relationship whereby it trusts the users in domain B, then the administrator of domain A can grant access to resources in domain A to users who reside in domain B. A trust relationship, however, is a one-way street. So this example does not give users in domain A access to resources in domain B.

Note

A trust relationship does not automatically give users in one domain access to resources in another domain. Just as users in a domain are granted access to resources by their domain administrators, users from *trusted* domains must be granted the necessary access rights and privileges in a trusting domain before they can access resources. The trust relationship that is set up between two domains is merely the prerequisite that allows users to be *granted* access to resources in another domain.

A trust relationship enables the Windows NT LSA (local security authority) to use *pass-through authentication* to validate a user. When a user from a trusted domain tries to access a resource, the netlogon service contacts the domain in which the user account resides to confirm that the user account is valid. The LSA receives copies of the user's SIDs (the account SID and the SIDs for any global groups of which the account is a member). After this pass-through authentication process the LSA has all the information it needs to evaluate the user against the Access Control List entries that might be present in an ACL for a particular resource.

For users in both domains to have access to resources in both domains, the administrators of each domain must create two trust relationships.

Creating a Trust Relationship

The domain administrator uses the User Manager for Domains utility to create trust relationships. To start the utility click Start, Programs, Administrative Tools, and finally User Manager for Domains. In Figure 30.1 you can see the utility as it looks when it is first started, showing a list of user accounts in the domain at the top and a list of user groups at the bottom.

To create a trust relationship the administrator in both domains will have to run the utility and enter the other domain's name into the list of domains it trusts or is trusted by. To bring up the dialog box that is used to accomplish this, click on the Policies menu at the top of the utility and select Trust Relationships (see Figure 30.2).

The order in which a trust relationship is established is important. The administrator of the domain that will be trusted should run the utility first to add the name of the domain that it will trust. To do this, click the Add button, which is next to the Trusting Domains list. The Add Trusted Domain dialog box appears. Here you enter the name of the domain that will trust your domain, and an optional password and click OK.

The administrator of the domain that will trust this domain must perform the same function, this time selecting the Add button, which is next to the Trusted Domains list. In the Add Trusted Domain dialog box, the administrator will put the name of the domain it will trust and then the same password that was entered by the administrator of the trusted domain.

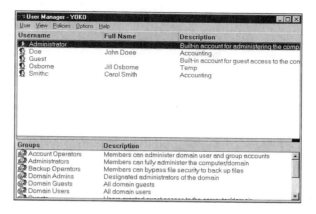

Figure 30.1   The User Manager for Domains is used to create a trust relationship.

Figure 30.2   The Trust Relationships dialog box is used to create a trust relationship with another domain.

Although the password is optional, you should always use one. The password is not used later by domain controllers that are performing pass-through authentication. It is used only to verify both ends of this process of creating the trust relationship. After the trust relationship has been established, the domain controllers will use SID information to validate each other.

After the trusting domain has entered the correct password a message is displayed indicating that the trust relationship was set up. Each administrator then sees the other domain listed in the trusted or trusting section of the Trust Relationships dialog box. If you have a network that has multiple domains and a large number of administrators, from a security viewpoint, it is a good idea to regularly check this dialog box to be sure that the trusts you expect to exist are there and that no others have been added. Remember that a trust relationship gives a user with administrative privileges the capability to grant rights and privileges to users outside your domain. This is a very powerful capability.

Again remember that each trust relationship is uni-directional. If you want both domains to allow users from the other domain the ability to access resources in each domain, you will have to repeat the process and create two trust relationships between the two domains.

When it becomes necessary to remove a trust relationship, all you have to do is select the domain from either the trusted or trusting domains lists in the dialog box, and click the Remove button.

Domain Controllers

The domain controller is a computer that holds a copy of the SAM. Domain controllers authenticate users when they log on to the network. In Windows NT there are two kinds of domain controllers:

- **Primary Domain Controller (PDC)**—This type of domain controller is where the master copy of the SAM resides for the domain. Updates to the SAM can only be made on the PDC, which then propagates the changes to the other domain controllers. Because there can be only one master copy of the domain's SAM, there can be only one PDC in any given domain.

- **Backup Domain Controller (BDC)**—This domain controller holds a copy of the SAM and receives updates to this copy via replication from the PDC. A BDC can authenticate users, but changes to the SAM must be done on the PDC. Because the BDC holds a copy of the SAM, there can be multiple BDCs in the network. BDCs are usually used to offload processing from a busy PDC, provide quick network access to the SAM in network segments that are distanced from the PDC, or to provide for fault-tolerance so that users can still log on to the network when the PDC becomes unavailable.

Only a Windows NT Server computer can be used to create a domain controller, and this must be done during the initial installation of the operating system. Without a complete reinstallation of the operating system, Windows NT Servers that are installed as ordinary "member servers" cannot be upgraded at a later date to become a PDC. Windows NT Workstation computers cannot be used as domain controllers in any fashion. However, a Windows NT Workstation has its own local SAM database that can be used to allow users to log onto the local workstation, but not the network. This can be useful in small networks where a domain controller is not necessary. However, in such a situation, if a user needs to access resources on more than workstation, the user must have a user account on each workstation to which it needs access.

Note

Windows 2000 Server does not use the concept of primary and backup domain controllers. Instead, all domain controllers are the same, and they exchange information among themselves. The way in which Windows 2000 enables you to "promote" a server to be a domain controller is discussed in Chapter 31, "Windows 2000 User and Computer Management Utilities."

All Windows NT computers that participate in a network run a service called the netlogon service. You can see it listed in the Services applet found in the Control Panel. This service is responsible for taking a user's logon request and communicating with a domain controller to process the logon. It also is the entity that handles synchronization between the PDC and BDC copies of the SAM database.

Windows NT Domain Models

The single logon principle that is so important in Microsoft networking is enhanced by allowing domains to trust each other's user base by using trust relationships. However, in a network that contains a large number of domains it is important to decide on a model to use when establishing trust relationships to make them easy to manage for the particular needs of your environment. Although it would be very easy to create trust relationships between every single domain in a large network, that is not the way it's usually done. Instead, four basic models are often used:

- Single domain model
- Master domain model
- Multiple master domain model
- Complete trust domain

Deciding on which domain model to use depends on many factors, but the basic things to consider are the size of the network (in users) and organization of the business along with management and geographical factors.

The Single Domain Model

For a small organization that has a centralized management team for its network a single domain might be sufficient. In this model, all the user accounts are created in a single domain, along with all the network resources, such as file and print services. There are no interdomain trust relationships to worry about because there is only one domain.

In this model there is only one PDC, but one or more BDCs are typically created for fault-tolerance purposes. If users are located at different sites geographically, you can use this model and put a BDC at each site to reduce network traffic associated with logons, allowing users to be validated by the local BDC. Having a BDC at each site also enables users to continue working if the network link between them and the site that has the PDC goes down.

The Master Domain Models

In a large enterprise it might be desirable to have one central database that contains all the user accounts, while maintaining other departmentalized databases that hold security information about resources in the network. In the master domain model one domain is designated to be the master domain and all user accounts are created in this domain. Additional *resource domains* are then created, which do not have to contain any user accounts at all other than those used for the local administrators to manage resources. Because of the concept of trust relationships you don't even have to create accounts for these administrators in their own domains. By using global and local groups, it is possible to give a user account from the master domain the capability to administer another domain by placing that user account in a special Domain Admins user group.

In the resource domains, file and print shares are created and can be managed locally in the resource domain by the domain's administrators. User accounts can be managed from a central location—by administrators in the master domain. In this model each resource domain has a one-way trust relationship with the master domain whereby it trusts the users in the master domain, as shown in Figure 30.3.

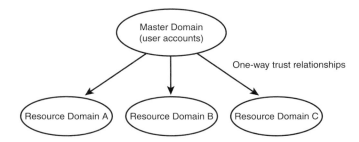

Figure 30.3   Resource domains trust the users validated by the master domain in this model.

This type of domain model is ideal if you need a central place to manage user accounts but want to let local administrators take responsibility for managing resources in their area of the network. In a large company you might want the personnel or human resources department to be responsible for creating accounts for new employees and deleting accounts when users leave the company. The accounting department then can take charge of managing printers and other resources in their own domain, while those in charge of the warehouse can similarly be responsible for granting access to resources in their domain.

The Multiple Master Domain Model

The multiple master domain model is similar to the master domain model, but in this case there can be more than one master domain. Resource management is still decentralized by allowing resource domain administrators to control local resources, but instead of one master domain to hold all user accounts, there are several. In Figure 30.4 you can see an example of this where users in the United States are managed by one domain, while users in the United Kingdom are managed by a separate master domain.

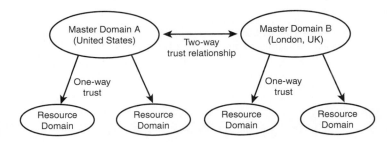

Figure 30.4 In the multiple master domain model there can be more than one master domain to hold user accounts.

This model is the most scalable domain mode because you can just add another master domain if you need to add more users when the existing master domains become highly populated, or when a new geographical area is brought into the company. In fact, if you have a large network that already has more than 40,000 user accounts and you want some degree of centralized user administration, then the multiple master domain model is the best method to use. It provides for local administration of resources, but also allows you to separate users into large administrative groups for management purposes.

In an enterprise that has a global network, this model can be used to allow large divisions of a company to control users located in their area. User account management is still centralized, but into several large groups that each division manages. If trust relationships are set up correctly, a user still needs only one logon to be granted access to resources that exist anywhere throughout a worldwide global network.

Another reason you might choose the multiple master domain model over the master domain model is to minimize network replication traffic. Remember that updates to the SAM are made to the database residing on the PDC, and are then sent to BDCs during the replication process. If you have a user base that experiences frequent changes, replication traffic on a global scale can consume valuable network bandwidth. By having several master domains, one for each location, you reduce the bandwidth consumption because replication only occurs within each domain.

The Complete Trust Model

This domain model provides for decentralized user account management and decentralized resource management. Each domain in the network has a two-way trust relationship with every other domain in the network, as shown in Figure 30.5. Administrators can still manage their own local resources, but also can manage their own user database. This method requires good communications skills between domain administrators to make sure that users are properly granted access to the resources in other domains.

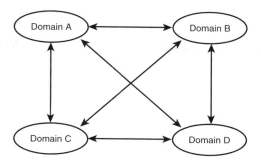

Figure 30.5   The complete trust model provides the highest degree of decentralized management in a large network.

Although this model has the greatest chance of causing confusion when trying to troubleshoot logon or resource access problems, it can be a good method to choose under some circumstances. For example, in the highly competitive business environment of the past decade where growth is achieved by acquisition, this model can be used to quickly join networks when companies merge. This assumes, of course, that both business entities are using a Microsoft Windows NT network.

Windows NT User Groups: Local Groups, Local Domain Groups, and Global Groups

To make assigning access rights and privileges easier to manage, Windows NT enables you to group users together. Rather than spending an inordinate amount of time granting each user the right to access a particular file share, for example, you can simply put multiple users into a user group and grant or revoke the right from the group instead. User groups can be either a local group that exists on a particular computer, or they can be domainwide local or global groups.

Local groups in a particular server are used to allow the local administrator of a member server to control access to local resources. For example, when a member server (a Windows NT Server computer that is not a domain controller) joins a domain, the domain's global group called Domain Admins is placed into the server's local group called Administrators. It is through this mechanism that the domain administrators are granted the capability to administer the local server. Of course, it is also quite possible for the user of the member server to use the server's built-in Administrator account to remove the Domain Admins global group from the local administrators group, and thereby deny the domain administrators of their access to administer resources on the member server.

Local domain groups function in much the same way, but on a domainwide scale. When a trust relationship is created between two domains, users in one domain do not automatically gain access rights to resources in the trusting domain. Instead, the administrator in the trusting domain needs to grant each user the needed access privilege. Because granting access rights on a user-by-user basis can be quite tedious in a large network, groups can be used for that purpose as well.

Local domain groups can contain users from the domain in which it is created, and users or global groups from other trusted domains. Domain administrators can grant or deny access to domain resources by granting or denying access to the local domain groups.

Global user groups contain only users or groups from a single domain. Global user groups are used to "export" users to another trusting domain as a single unit. For example, the domain administrator of a trusting domain can place global groups from trusted domains into a local domain group and grant or deny access to domain resources by the local domain group.

Built-In User Groups

To make things easier when you first set up a Windows NT computer, several local and global groups are created by default. If the computer is a Windows NT Server computer operating as a domain controller, you will find these domain local groups:

- Administrators
- Backup Operators
- Account Operators
- Guests
- Print Operators
- Replicator
- Server Operators
- Users

The functions of most of these groups are obvious at first glance. The Administrators group is a local group that is granted rights to manage the domain. The Backup Operators group can be used to enable users to perform backups, bypassing normal security restrictions for this purpose. The Print Operators group has the necessary privileges to manage printers and print queues for the domain, and so on. The Users local group is used to group users on the particular server, while the Domain Users group usually contains all users in the domain. If you look at the membership of the server's Users group you can see that the Domain Users global group is a member of the group, which is how ordinary domain users are able to get limited access rights to the server.

If the server is a domain controller you also will see three built-in *global* groups:

- Domain Admins
- Domain Guests
- Domain Users

Windows NT Workstation computers, along with Windows NT Server computers that are operating as a non-domain controller computer (called a member server), have the following built-in local groups:

- Administrators
- Backup Operators
- Power Users
- Guests
- Replicator
- Users

Note

The rights associated with built-in user groups are what give them their functionality. For an in-depth discussion of user rights and the functions that a member of a built-in user group can perform, see Chapter 34, "Rights and Permissions."

Creating User Groups

These built-in groups make it easy to set up initial groups of users that can perform standard server or network management tasks. For more specific functions you can create your own groups. To do so, use the User Manager for Domains utility.

First make a list of the functional groups you want to create, based on the resources or type of access you think each group will need. For example, if your domain supports several different business units, such as an accounting department, a research department, and a warehouse, you might want to create three user groups, one for each of these departments. If one group of users, such as the accounting users, need to be further subdivided into groups with some having more access to confidential data than others, you can create several user groups for that department instead of a single group.

The important point to remember is that by creating groups you will make the job of granting or revoking access rights easier as resources or users on the network change.

To create a group, you need to activate the User menu in the User Manager for Domains, and select either Create New Local group or Create New Global Group. In Figure 30.6 you can see the dialog box used to create a new local group.

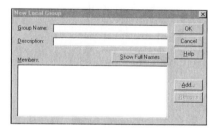

Figure 30.6   To create a new local group, specify the group name and then add members.

After you enter the name of the new group and an optional description, you can click the Add button to bring up the Add Users and Groups dialog box. This dialog box is used for many different functions in the User Manager for Domains where selecting users is required. In Figure 30.7 you can see that all you have to do is select a username or a group name, and then click the Add button to move that name to the Add Names display at the bottom of the dialog box. You can use the Search button to locate names if the list for your network is very large and you don't want to scroll through the entire list to find the correct name.

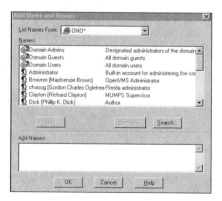

Figure 30.7   Select user or other groups to place into the new local group.

After you have finished selecting users or groups to add to this local group, click the OK button. You are returned to the New Local Group dialog box, and the users or group names that were selected now appear in the Members list at the bottom of the dialog box. Click OK to dismiss this dialog box when you are finished.

If you need to modify group membership later, all you need to do is select the user group from the display on the main window of the User Manager for Domains and then, from the User menu, select Properties. Alternatively, you can simply double-click the group name to bring up the Properties sheet. This display is exactly like the one used when creating the new group except for its title. You can use the Add and Remove buttons to modify group membership.

Special User Groups

Besides the local and global built-in groups that were just described, there are several user groups whose memberships are not assigned by the administrator. These groups are not seen when looking in the list of user groups in the User Manager for Domains. They are, however, seen when you use other utilities, such as the Windows NT Explorer, to grant access to files and directories. These groups are

- **Interactive**—Users who are currently logged on locally to the computer.
- **Network**—Users who are currently logged on to the computer through the network.
- **Everyone**—Just what it says, this means any interactive or network user on the computer.
- **System**—The operating system itself.
- **Creator owner**—The user who creates an object, such as a file or directory.

Managing User Accounts

On Windows NT Server member servers and Windows NT Workstation computers, the User Manager utility is used to manage the local SAM. In a domain, the utility is similar but is called the User Manager for Domains. This is the tool that you use for most user account management in Windows NT. To start the User Manager for Domains, select it from the Administrative Tools folder in the Programs folder.

The User menu in this utility can be used to add, delete, or modify user accounts. To modify an existing account, simply double-click the account name and the properties dialog box appears (you also can highlight the account and select Properties from the User menu).

To add a new user, select New User from the User menu. The New User dialog box (shown in Figure 30.8) appears. You can enter the user's logon username here (as many as 20 characters), along with other useful information such as the user's full name and a description of what the account is used for.

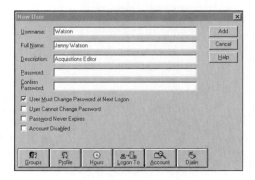

Figure 30.8 Add a new user by specifying a username and other information for the account.

When you enter the password for the user account you must enter it twice to confirm what you have typed. You can select from the check boxes any of the password options you want to use. If you select User Must Change Password at Next Logon, the user will be prompted when they first use the account to create a new password known only to them. You can use this same check box on an existing user's properties dialog box when resetting a user password that the user has forgotten. This allows you to reset the password to a new value you can give the user, but still force them to change it when using it for the first time.

If you select User Cannot Change Password, the user will be locked out of this function. This function is useful for service accounts, such as for SQL Server, because it precludes anyone from changing the password, which would cause the service to not start on boot.

If you select Password Never Expires, this bypasses the password policy you can set for the domain, which would usually force the user to change their password to a new value on a periodic basis. Finally, you can use the Account Disabled check box to temporarily disable logons for an account when you do not want the account to be accessible but also do not want to delete it.

After you have finished filling in the information for this dialog box, you can click the Add button to add the account, or you can use the buttons at the bottom of the dialog box to bring up additional prompts.

Adding a User to a Group

If you select the Groups button from the New User dialog box you get the Group Memberships dialog box, shown in Figure 30.9. When an account is first created it is, by default, a member of the Domain Users local group. You can select other groups from those shown and use the Add button to add the user to the group. You can select a group of which the user is already a member and use the Remove button to remove the user from that group. To specify the primary group to which a user will belong, highlight that group under the Member Of box and click the Set button. When you have finished selecting user groups for this user, click the OK button.

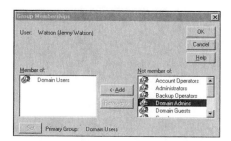

Figure 30.9   The Group Memberships dialog box allows you to control to which groups a user belongs.

User Profiles

You can use the Profiles button to bring up the User Environment Profile dialog box. Here you can specify a path to the location of the file that contains the user's profile (desktop and environment settings) as well as the name of a logon script that is executed each time the user logs on to the domain. In Figure 30.10 you can see that this also is where you specify the path to the user's home directory.

You also can specify drive letters in the Connect box and then specify a path name. This will cause the user to be automatically connected to the file shares you specify when the user logs on to the system.

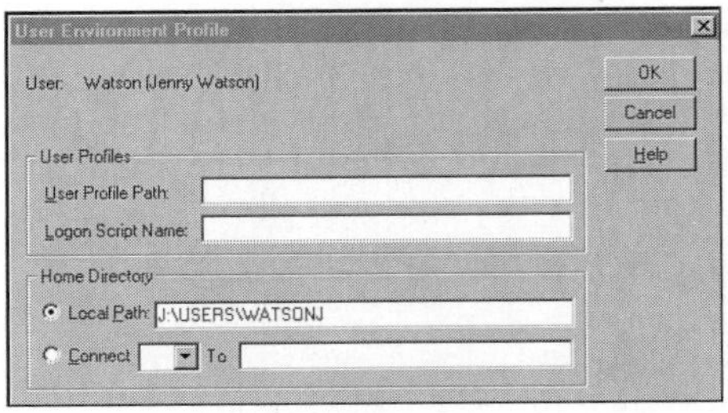

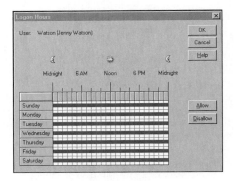

Figure 30.10   The User Environment Profile dialog box allows you to set the user's profile and home directory.

Limiting the Time a User Can Log On

The Hours button brings up the Logon Hours dialog box (see Figure 30.11), where you can select the days and hours that a user account can be used.

Figure 30.11   Specify the hours an account can be used in this dialog box.

In this display you can select one-hour time periods by clicking on one or more of them and then using the Allow or Disallow button to specify whether or not the user can log on during that time period. By default all the boxes representing hours for all days are filled in with a blue color indicating that the user can log on at that time.

Tip

What happens when a user is already logged on and the time changes to a period where they are disallowed? This depends on the settings you make in the Accounts Policy for the domain. You can allow the user to continue working but not make any new network connections, or you can set the policy to force the user off the server when the time changes to a disallowed period.

Limiting Which Workstations a User Can Log On To

The Logon To button will bring up the Logon Workstations dialog box (see Figure 30.12), which you can use to specify up to eight workstations to which the user is allowed to log on using this domain account.

Figure 30.12   The Logon Workstations dialog box can be used to limit the workstations a user can use to log on to the domain.

If you want the user to be able to log on by using any workstation in the domain (the default selection), select the appropriate radio button in this dialog box.

This dialog box can be useful in a situation where security is a high priority. For user accounts that have been given advanced rights and are able to access sensitive data, you might want to restrict their use to computers that are in a particular physical location that can be monitored. For example, the payroll process is usually a very sensitive function in any organization. Not only do you want to prevent unauthorized users from modifying information here, but you also want to keep prying eyes out of information that might cause user embarrassment or discomfort. By limiting the payroll applications to specific user logon accounts and by restricting those accounts to selected workstations, you can make the monitoring process easier and more defined.

Account Information

The Account button brings up the Account Information dialog box shown in Figure 30.13. Here you can specify that an account will never expire, or you can set a date at which time the account will no longer be able to be used for a domain logon.

Figure 30.13   The Account Information dialog box can be used to specify the type of account and limit its use.

There are two types of domain accounts, and you can select the type for this account in this dialog box. A global account is the default account for a user in that user's own home domain. This account can be placed into a global group and exported to another domain to be granted access to resources. Local groups are more limited. They are used to provide access for a user who is *not* a member of a trusted domain. This can be used by a user in another Windows NT domain or by a user from another operating system type. The local account cannot be used to log on locally to a Windows NT computer and is provided so that you can give access through the network. Because the local account is provided so that you can give access to your domain to special-case users, you cannot place local accounts into a global group and export them to another domain.

Allowing Dial-Up Access

If you want the user to be able to dial into the network using the remote access service (RAS), click the Dialup button to bring up the Dialin Information dialog box (see Figure 30.14). Here you can select the call-back option. Call back means that after a user dials into the network the server will disconnect the phone and then dial the user's computer back. This can used for security purposes or for cost savings.

Figure 30.14   The Dialin Information dialog box can be used to control dial-up access to the network for this account.

The Call Back options here are

- **No Call Back**—This is the most common form, which enables a user to log in using a modem and, after validation, begin working.

- **Set By Caller**—The caller can specify the telephone number that the server will use to perform the call-back function.

- **Preset To**—The administrator can set the telephone number that will be used for the call back.

If security is not a great issue for this user's account, you can select the No Call Back option. If the user is a mobile user and you want the long-distance charges to be paid by the server's end of the telephone line, use the function to allow the caller to specify the call-back number. If security is an important issue for this account, use the third option so that you can specify the number that will always be called back. This prevents users from other locations from using this account to dial into your system and establish a RAS session.

Replication Between Domain Controllers

Modifications to the SAM database are always made on the primary domain controller. Periodically, the PDC will check the database to determine whether any changes have been made. The default value for this time interval is five minutes. When changes to the database are detected, the PDC will send a message to each BDC informing it that it holds changes that need to be applied to their copy of the database. The BDC can then poll the PDC to get the updates. The process is called directory synchronization.

To prevent a large number of BDCs from making synchronization requests at the same time, the PDC staggers the messages it sends out when there are multiple BDCs. By default, the PDC sends the message to only 10 BDCs. When the first 10 BDCs have finished the synchronization process, the PDC sends the message to the next 10 BDCs that need to be informed, and so on.

Full and Partial Synchronization

There are two types of synchronization: full and partial. When a BDC is created during a Windows NT Server installation, one of the first tasks it must perform is to download a copy of the full SAM database. This is an example of full synchronization. When complete, the BDC is able to respond to logon requests from clients.

When changes are made on the PDC, they are not immediately propagated to the domain's BDCs. Instead, a change log file 64K in size is used to buffer the modifications. Each change record is stamped with a serial number and a version number. The change log is a circular file. That means that when it becomes full it simply wraps back on itself, overwriting the oldest record in the file.

When the PDC sends out notifications that changes exist in the database, it does so only to those BDCs that it knows do not have the most recent data. The PDC can do this because it keeps track of the serial number of the most recent records updated to each BDC. This partial synchronization prevents unnecessary replication traffic. When a BDC polls the PDC for the changes it needs, it receives only those changes that it has not already gotten during a previous poll, based on the serial number.

A full replication can still occur under this process. For example, a BDC can be taken offline for an extended period of time. Or, the network link between the BDC and the PDC might be unavailable due to a network problem. Again, using the serial numbers of the records it already has, the BDC can determine whether any changes have been overwritten in the PDC's change log and it can then request a full synchronization so that it will still have a complete copy of the database.

Logon Failures Related to Synchronization

One common function administrators or help desk personnel perform is that of adding a new user account or changing the password for an account when the user cannot log on. As simple a matter as this might seem, the role played by back-up domain controllers can be an issue when this is done in a Windows NT network.

When a password is changed or an account added, it is done on the master copy of the database that resides on the PDC. Remember that the BDC does not immediately receive updates that are made on the SAM. If you add a new account or if you modify a user account, whether it be to change the password or remove a lockout condition, the user who is validated at a remote location by a backup domain controller might not be able to immediately log on because the BDC might not be aware of the change.

You could just tell the user to wait and try again, but this is not the kind of response that builds up trust between users and the help desk personnel or the administrator. Instead, Windows NT allows you to force the synchronization process to begin. To do this, you must invoke the Server Manager, which is found in the Administrative Tools folder. From the Computer menu select Synchronize Entire Domain. A pop-up dialog box informs you that this can take a few minutes. Click the Yes button to proceed. The PDC then begins sending out messages to the BDCS informing them that it is time to synchronize. Windows displays a message informing you that the synchronization process has begun.

After a few minutes you can check the Event Viewer to find out whether the synchronization process has completed. You should check both the BDC and the PDC for these messages. The Event Viewer utility enables you to connect to another computer to check messages in its log files, so this can be done from one location by the administrator. When synchronization has finished, you can instruct the user to try the new password or account again.

Passwords and Policies

Windows NT enables the administrator to set certain parameters that control passwords and accounts. This is called the account policy for the domain. To view the defaults or make changes, select Account from the Policies menu in the User Manager for Domains utility. The Account Policy dialog box (see Figure 30.15) is displayed.

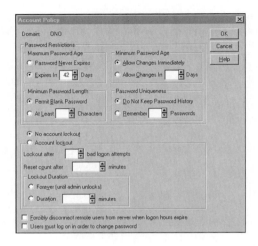

Figure 30.15 The Account Policy dialog box.

As you can see, you have a number of things you can configure. The values you choose for these parameters should reflect the degree of security you want to enforce at your site. At the same time, you need to balance your concerns with the abilities of your users. For example, if you set a large minimum password size and a low value for the number of days it can be used, users might end up writing down passwords just to keep track of them.

Parameters you can configure here are

- **Minimum and Maximum password age**—The minimum password age specifies the number of days that must elapse before a user is allowed to change a password. The maximum password age is the number of days that a password can be used, after which the system will force the user to change it. Both of these parameters can be set to a value ranging from 1 to 999 days.

- **Minimum password length**—This is the minimum number of characters that must be used for a password. Too small a value will make it easy for hacker programs to guess a password. Too large a value will make it difficult for users to think up new passwords. This parameter can be set to a value ranging from 1 to 14, or you can permit a blank password (no password). It is hard to imagine a network where you might want to allow, as a policy for every user in the domain, a blank password.

- **Password uniqueness**—The system will keep a history list of passwords used by each user and will not allow them to reset their password to one that is still in the list. This prevents users from constantly reusing a few easy-to-remember passwords, which can be bad for security purposes. Set this parameter to a value of from 1 to 24. Selecting not to keep a history list is probably not a good idea because many users will take advantage of this and eventually someone else will find out what their usual password is.

■ **Account lockout**—You can set up the system so that a user account is "locked out" after a number of failed login attempts. This can be used to prevent an unauthorized user from trying to guess a password for an account, as is done in the brute-force method by many hacker programs that simply go through a dictionary, trying every word until they crack an account. If you set a value for bad logon attempts, you also can use the Reset Count After field to a time value (in minutes). This field specifies the period of time during which the failed logon attempts are counted. The Lockout Duration fields can be used to permanently lock the account until an administrator intervenes, or to set a time in minutes that the account will be disabled. A good idea is to set a small value for the Lockout After parameter (3 to 5 is a good choice), while using a long lockout value. Thirty minutes to an hour will usually suffice to deter many unauthorized users.

At the bottom of this dialog box you can see two other check boxes. The Forcibly Disconnect Remote Users check box must be checked in order for the user to be disconnected from the server when they stay logged on past an authorized time period specified in the Hours button of their account properties dialog box. If the second check box, User Must Log On In Order To Change Password, is checked, users will not be able to log on after their password expires and change it. The administrator will have to perform this function instead. If this box is not checked, after a user password expires they still will be allowed to log on, but only to change the password.

Detecting Failed Logon Attempts

There are many reasons why user logon failures will occur. The most common reason is that users forget passwords or type them incorrectly enough times to trigger the account lockout mechanism. Because Windows NT allows you to create a single username and password logon for each user, the problem of multiple passwords is usually not a problem as it is some other networks.

The Windows NT Event Viewer utility, which is found in the Administrative Tools section along with the User Manager for Domains, can be used to check for failed logon attempts. This is the first place you should look when a user is having problems logging on to the domain or connecting to a resource on a remote server. The user might not be providing the correct password or might be trying a username for which there is no account. The Event Viewer keeps three log files: Application, System, and Security. It is in the Security log file that you will find messages that relate to logon attempts.

Some of the more common logon attempt related messages found in the Event Viewer are listed in Table 30.1.

Table 30.1   Common Logon Errors You Can See Using the Event Viewer

Event ID	Description
528	Successful logon
529	Invalid username or password
530	Violation of logon time restrictions
531	Account is disabled
532	Account expired
533	Logon not allowed on this computer
534	Invalid logon type (network or interactive)
535	Expired password
536	Netlogon service is not running
537	Unexpected error

Table 30.1   Continued

Event ID	Description
538	Successful logout
539	Account currently locked out

As you can see, event successful logon and logout events can be tracked. These types of messages can be useful when you are trying to determine who was on the system, perhaps during off hours, when you are trying to troubleshoot security problems. The other messages can be helpful in quickly identifying what the problem is when a user cannot log on to a server or connect to a resource.

The security log file you can examine using the Event Viewer can be configured to track all successful and unsuccessful logon attempts. This includes user who log on locally at the computer, connections made through network access, and logons by special accounts that you set up to run services.

Windows NT does not automatically track events such as these. You must enable the types of events you wish to audit before they will be recorded in the security log file. See Chapter 38, "Auditing and Other Monitoring Measures," for information on how to set up the events to audit for Windows NT computers.

Strategies to Minimize Logon Problems

The best way to solve a problem is to take all necessary measures to ensure that the problem doesn't happen in the first place. Although it is not possible to completely eliminate every source of failed logon problems, you can do a lot to keep your network users happy by taking a few precautions:

- **Place a backup domain controller on every physical subnet**—If a network link goes down, users can still be validated by the local BDC and continue to work with resources to which they can still connect. Any Windows NT Server computer can be created as a BDC, so if you have a server on a subnet that is offering resources and it is not already overloaded, create it as a BDC and let it serve two roles.

- **Enforce reasonable password policies**—Some operating systems allow you to computer-generate random passwords that are very difficult to remember. If a user cannot remember a password, most of the time they will just write it down somewhere, which can compromise security. If you force users to change passwords too frequently, they will most likely have a hard time remembering what the recent password is, unless they write it down somewhere. If you set the account policy lockout values too low, you will find users get locked out because of simple typing errors and the help desk will spend a lot of time unlocking these accounts.

- **Keep track of user accounts**—You can use a paper method or an electronic one such as a spreadsheet or database. Delete accounts for users that leave the company and create new ones for new employees. Getting rid of the dead wood will help avoid confusion when troubleshooting and will help keep the SAM databases down to a reasonable size.

- **Never use generic accounts where more than one user logs in under the same username**—Though this is a tempting idea because you have less user accounts to manage, it can be a security nightmare if something goes wrong and you are unable to use auditing measures to figure out the who, what, and when of the matter. Also, when more than one person is using the same account to log on, it only takes one person with fumble-fingers to incorrectly type a password a few times and lock an account, preventing others that use the same account from logging in also.

To fully understand how to troubleshoot problems with logons, you should make yourself knowledgeable about the Windows NT Event Viewer administrative tool. You can find out more about this valuable utility in Chapter 38.

Windows 2000 User and Computer Management Utilities

SOME OF THE MAIN TOPICS IN THIS CHAPTER ARE

The Microsoft Management Console

User Management

Computer Management

Windows 2000 User Groups

In Windows NT Server 4.0, every basic management task required you to use a different program: the User Manager, the Server Manager, and others. In Windows 2000, the Microsoft Management Console (MMC) is the main interface for almost all administrative tools. By using a common interface, MMC makes it easy to learn new utilities, because they all operate about the same.

The Microsoft Management Console

MMC is intended to provide a common interface into various administrative tools used with Windows 2000. Utilities are created as snap-ins that are loaded into the MMC application and presented to the user. Each console consists of a left pane with a tree of objects you can manage using the particular snap-in. This tree can contain things such as folders and other containers, or administrative objects. Some objects in the tree can be expanded by clicking on the plus sign (+) next to them, to reveal a further nesting of objects. Hence, the treelike structure, which is similar to a set of directories and subdirectories.

The right pane is usually used to display data or other information based on choices made in the left pane. For example, the disk defragmenter displays fragmentation information in the pane on the right.

User Management

The Active Directory Users and Computers MMC snap-in is used to manage both users and computers in the domain. Most of the functions that were done using the User Manager for Domains have been moved into this MMC snap-in. The main difference is the interface—the MMC console—and the amount of information that you can keep track of using the Active Directory as compared to the limited amount of data that could be stored in the old Security Accounts Manager (SAM) database of previous versions of Windows NT.

In this chapter, we'll look at the basic functions of this utility: adding users and computers to the domain. Then we'll look at built-in user groups and how you can create your own user groups to help make administrative tasks for large numbers of users an easier task.

Creating a New User in the Domain

This common task is simplified by the use of a few dialog boxes to create the account. After the user account has been created, you can go back and use the properties page for the account to add more information.

To create a new user account in the domain

1. Click Start, Programs, Administrative Tools, Active Directory Users and Computers.

2. The MMC console pops up. In the left pane there is a domain with a tree of objects underneath it. In Figure 31.1 you can see the opening screen and the folders you can use to manage users and computers.

3. Click the Users folder in the left pane, and a list of user groups and individual users will be displayed as shown in Figure 31.2.

4. Right-click the Users folder and select New and then User. The New Object-User dialog box pops up. Here you can fill in information such as the username; the user's first, last and full names; initials; and other information. Figure 31.3 shows an example, adding a new user named Luke Kurtis.

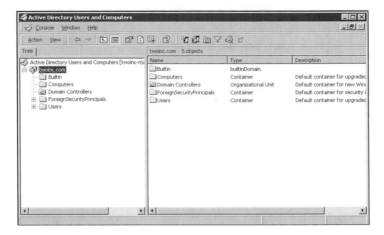

Figure 31.1 The Active Directory Users and Computers MMC snap-in is used to administer users in the domain.

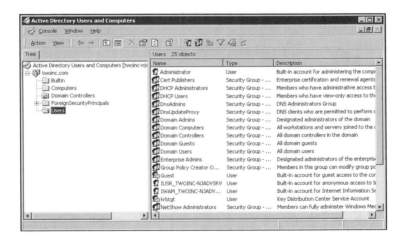

Figure 31.2 The Users folder contains user groups and users.

5. The next dialog box (see Figure 31.4) enables you to enter a password for the user and to use one of several options regarding the password. For most new users, it's easiest to use the first check box (User Must Change Password at Next Login) so that the user can enter his own unique password, unknown to anyone else, even the administrator who created the account. If you are creating an account to use for running a service or some other similar use, you might want to use the Password Never Expires option so you don't have to change the password periodically. Finally, you can disable a user account with the Account Is Disabled check box. This is useful when creating new accounts so that they are all initially disabled. When users are contacted about a new account, the administrator can deselect this property and give the user the first password needed to log in to the account.

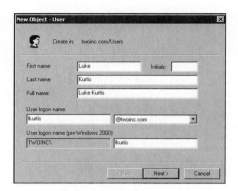

Figure 31.3 The New Object-User dialog box enables you to input basic information about the new user account.

Figure 31.4 You can manage password administration using this dialog box.

6. Finally, a summary screen pops up showing the data that you've entered for the new account. Click the Finish button to complete the process of creating the new account.

After creating a new user account, you might want to log in yourself before informing the user. This way you can avoid mistakes, such as having entered the wrong password for the account.

Managing Other User Account Information

When you enter a new user account, you are prompted for only the minimal information needed to create the account in the Active Directory. After the account is created, you can use the properties page for the user account to add or modify other information. Simply right-click on the username in the right pane of the MMC console, and select Properties from the menu that appears. In Figure 31.5 you can see that, despite the minimal input used to create the account, there are several tabs that enable you to track all sorts of useful information about the user.

Rather than try to show all the tabs for this properties page (because there are so many), all the user attributes that are part of the default user object are listed for reference in Table 31.1. This summary listing should make it easy to locate the data you want to look at or modify, and go straight to that properties page tab.

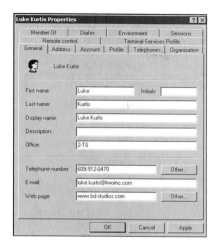

Figure 31.5 The properties page for a user account enables you to administer a lot more information than was input during account creation.

Table 31.1   Attributes of the User Account Object

Attribute	Tab on the Properties Dialog Box	Description
First name	General	User's first name.
Initials	General	User's initial(s).
Last name	General	User's last name.
Display name	General	Defaults to show first three fields though you can modify it.
Description	General	Text field, anything you want.
Office	General	Office location for this user.
Telephone number	General	User's telephone number.
E-mail	General	User's e-mail address.
Web page	General	User's Web page.
Street	Address	Multiline street address field.
P.O. Box	Address	Post office box.
City	Address	City.
State/province	Address	State or province.
Zip/Postal Code	Address	ZIP code or postal code.
Country/region	Address	Country or region.
User logon name	Account	User account logon username.
(Pre-Windows 2000)	Account	Logon for pre-Windows 2000 users.
Logon Hours	Account	Brings up dialog box to enter time restrictions for the account.

Table 31.1   Continued

Attribute	Tab on the Properties Dialog Box	Description
Log On To	Account	Brings up dialog box to enter which computers a user can log on to.
Account Options	Account	Options for logons. See section on Account Options later in the chapter.
Account expires	Account	Enter Never or set account expiration date.
Profile path	Profile	Path for user profile.
Logon script	Profile	Path for logon script.
Home Folder	Profile	Local path or remote file share.
Home	Telephones	User's home number. Use the Other button to add additional numbers (this works for all the phone number fields).
Pager	Telephones	User's pager number.
Mobile	Telephones	User's mobile phone number.
Fax	Telephones	User's Fax number.
IP phone	Telephones	User's IP telephone number.
Notes	Telephones	Add notes here, such as a PIN number for the user's pager.
Title	Organization	User's job title.
Department	Organization	Business department for this user.
Company	Organization	Use this to record a company name. This can be useful when using a single network for multiple corporate entities, or when creating accounts for outside vendors.
Manager	Organization	The user's supervisor.
Direct Reports	Organization	Multiline text field.
Member of	Member Of	List of user groups a user is a member of. You can add and remove groups here.
Primary Group	Member Of	The user's primary group.
Remote Access Permission	Dial-in	Allow or deny dial-in access here.
Verify Caller-ID	Dial-in	Use to verify caller ID for incoming calls.
Callback Options	Dial-in	Set to No Callback, Set by Caller, and Always Callback to (supply telephone number).
Assign a Static IP Address	Dial-in	Use the same address each dial-in.
Apply Static Routes	Dial-in	You can define static routes for this client's dial-in session.
Starting Program	Environment	Used to specify a program to run at logon for Terminal Services clients.
Client Devices	Environment	Check boxes to allow you to connect, at logon time, drives, printers, and a default printer.
End a disconnection session	Sessions	Set time (or never) to end Terminal Services idle session.
Active session limit	Sessions	The maximum amount of time before an active Terminal Services session is disconnected.

Table 31.1 Continued

Attribute	Tab on the Properties Dialog Box	Description
Idle session limit connected.	Sessions	The maximum time before an idle Terminal Services client is dis-
Session Limits	Sessions	You can specify that a session be ended or disconnected when a timer expires.
Allow reconnection	Sessions	Permit disconnected client to reconnect.

In addition to these fields, there are two additional tabs. The Remote Control tab enables you to remotely control or view a user's session when using Terminal Services. The Terminal Services Profile tab enables you to set a path for a home directory and user profile for Terminal Services users. This also is where you use a check box (Allow Logon to Terminal Server) to enable the user account for Terminal Services. Generally, terminal services are not heavily deployed in most networking environments and are not detailed any further here.

As you can see, you can keep a lot more information about a user on your network than was possible under Windows NT 4.0 Server's simple User Manager for Domains and the SAM (Security Accounts Manager) database. And if that isn't enough data to keep about a user, you can always extend the schema, which is the definition of all the classes of objects in the Active Directory, to include new attributes and add them to this user class of objects. For more information about the Active Directory and the schema, see Chapter 25, "Overview of Microsoft's Active Directory Service."

Note

Chapter 25, "Overview of Microsoft's Active Directory Service," discusses that the kinds of objects and attributes that can be stored in the directory database is extensible. That is, you can create new attributes and objects. If you've installed Microsoft Exchange Server, for example, or a third-party product that is integrated with the Active Directory, you might find additional tabs or fields in the properties sheets for a particular object.

Using the Action Menu

In the previous section we brought up the properties page by right-clicking on the user account and selecting Properties from the menu that popped up. You also can reach this menu, called the Action menu, by highlighting a user or group and then clicking on the Action menu at the top of the MMC console. Use this menu to

- **Delegate Control**—Brings up a wizard that enables you to delegate control of folders and objects by groups or by users.
- **Find**—Brings up a search dialog box you can use to search the directory.
- **New**—Adds a new user, computer, contact, group, printer, or shared folder using the submenu this menu item produces.
- **All Tasks**—Enables you to delegate control or use the Find search function.
- **Refresh**—Refreshes the display with current information.
- **Export list**—Enables you to export a list of users and groups to a variety of file types, such as comma-delimited or tab-delimited ASCII and Unicode files. You can use this to import listings into other applications, such as Microsoft Excel.
- **Properties**—All those user attributes covered in the previous section. This is an alternative way to bring up the user's properties page.
- **Help**—Get help for using this utility.

There are many useful items on this Action menu. The Export List capability is useful in large environments where it is necessary to produce reports on users or the user database. The New menu item enables you to manage not just users, but also other objects, such as computers, which is the topic of the next section, and user groups, which we'll talk about last in this chapter.

Computer Management

Again, you use the Active Directory Users and Computers MMC snap-in to manage computers in the domain. Click the Computers folder in the left pane, and the right pane displays a list of computers in your domain, as you can see in Figure 31.6.

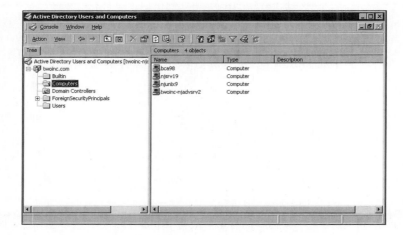

Figure 31.6 The Computers folder is used to administer computers in the domain.

The Action menu for managing computers is similar to that for managing users. The first thing that we'll cover is adding a computer to the domain. This should be done when you are setting up new computers on the network. In addition to creating user accounts, computers must have an entry in the Active Directory database.

Adding a Computer to the Domain

To add a new computer, you can use the Action menu and select New and then Computer. Alternatively, you can right-click on the Computers folder and select the same items. The New Object-Computer dialog box, shown in Figure 31.7, enables you to input basic information about the computer, such as the hostname.

What TCP/IP users typically call a hostname goes in the Computer Name field. There is also a field to enter a pre-Windows 2000 computer name that can be recognized by older computers. The next field enables you to specify the users or groups that can add computers to the domain. The default is the Domain Admins group. Finally, if the computer is not a Windows 2000 client, select the check box labeled Allow Pre-Windows 2000 Computers to Use This Account. You would want to check this box for Windows NT and Windows 98 computers, for example. Click the Next button to continue the process of adding the new computer.

The next dialog box prompts you to specify whether this is a managed computer and, if so, the GUID/UUID for the computer. These values are usually found in the computer's BIOS or on a label attached to the computer. Click the Next button to continue adding the computer.

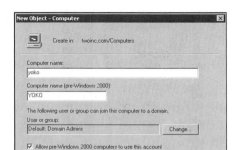

Figure 31.7 You enter basic computer information in this dialog box when adding a computer to the domain.

Finally, a dialog box displays a summary view of the information you've entered. Click Finish to create the computer account. After you've done this, the computer should be able to boot and join the domain. Users who have accounts on the domain should be able to log into the domain using the computer.

Managing Other Computer Account Information

Just like the user objects you create, the computer objects have a lot more attributes than you are prompted for when creating the initial computer account in the Active Directory. You can get to the properties page for a computer by right-clicking on the computer in the left pane and selecting Properties, or by highlighting the computer and selecting Properties from the Action menu. In Figure 31.8 you can see an example of a computer object properties page.

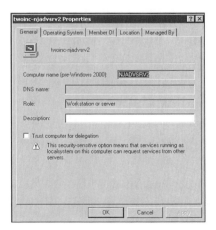

Figure 31.8 The properties of a computer account enable you to manage a large amount of information about the computer.

There are only five tabs for this properties sheet: General, Operating System, Member Of, Location, and Managed By.

The General Tab

This tab shows you the fully qualified domain name of a computer as well as its pre-Windows 2000 name. You also can see what role the computer plays in the network (workstation or server). The Description field enables you to enter useful information that will help you identify this computer or its use (or perhaps its location), depending on the information you want to enter. Finally, you can select the check box labeled Trust Computer for Delegation. This allows services running on the computer to request services from other computers as long as the service is running under the localsystem special account.

The Operating System Tab

This tab has only a few fields. Here you can see the operating system running on the computer, the version, and the service packs that are installed.

The Member Of Tab

This tab enables you to add the computer to a group. For example, a domain controller computer is a member of the Domain Computers group, and this is its primary group. However, you can use other built-in groups or create new groups to assist you in managing computers that are similarly configured or used.

Use the Add button to add a new group. A list of groups is displayed in another dialog box and you can select the groups from there. You also can remove group membership by using the Remove button.

The Location Tab

This tab has only one field: Location. Use it to specify the particular office, or perhaps building, in which a computer is located. This information can be very useful when you get a call from a user and need to visit the computer for maintenance purposes.

The Managed By Tab

This tab enables you to select the user that manages this computer. Use the Change button to bring up a dialog box to select the user. After a user has been selected, the fields on this tab show the following information:

- The user's name
- The user's office
- The user's street address
- The user's city, state/province, country/region data
- The user's telephone number
- The user's fax number

Again, you can see that this kind of information can be valuable when trying to locate the person who is responsible for managing this computer in a large network. By keeping this detailed information in the Active Directory it is accessible by computers throughout the domain, provided the user has the access rights.

Windows 2000 User Groups

You need to understand several concepts about user groups in Windows 2000 before you begin to create them. Groups are helpful because they simplify administrative tasks when you have groups of users that must be treated similarly when it comes to rights and permissions. Second, because they can be limited in scope, groups can be useful for security purposes, limiting the computers or domains in which a user can be granted access.

Choose a Group Based on the Group's Scope

In Windows 2000, groups each have a scope, which is basically the area of the domain or global forest that the group covers. By having several types of groups, each with its own particular kind of membership and scope, you can put together combinations that should solve most of your administrative needs for managing users with similar needs. The types of groups, and the scope implied by each, are

- **Domain local group**—These groups are limited to just the domain in which they are created. Users can be placed into these groups for local domain management purposes.

- **Global group**—These groups are made up of users or groups from a single domain but are used to grant access for the members of the group in other trusted domains. Think of this as a way to "export" users to allow them access to resources in other domains.

- **Universal group**—This type of group can contain user accounts and global group accounts from any trusted domain that exists in the Active Directory forest. This is similar to a global group but allows members of the group to be granted permission to resources in domains throughout the entire forest.

As described previously, groups can be members of other groups just like users, and this is where it can become a little complicated. For example, a domain local scope group can have as members:

- **Groups that have global scope**—You place the global group into a local group and then manage the local group when granting rights and permissions.

- **Groups that have universal scope**—Again, you can place universal scope groups into a local group and then use the local group for management purposes.

- **Groups with domain local scope**—Other domain local scope groups can be placed in a domain local scope group.

- **User accounts**—You can put individual users into a group with domain local scope.

Note that the domain local group does not have to have just one of the preceding groups (or users) as its members. You can combine any of the preceding and place them into a single domain local scope group, and then use the group to manage the members of these other groups locally in your domain.

A domain local group is a very useful management tool. For example, if you have a particular resource that several users share, place the users in the group and grant the group the necessary access to the resource. The resource can be a folder or a file, or perhaps a printer. If the resource changes in the future (for example, you decide to use a new file server for a particular set of files), you have to change permissions only on the group to let the group members access the new resource. Otherwise, you'd have to modify the permissions for each individual user, which in a large environment can be an almost impossible task if your network changes frequently.

Unlike domain local groups, global groups can have as members only users or other groups from within a single domain. Yet, global groups can be granted access to resources in other trusted domains. This enables you to package a group of users that need similar treatment in other domains when it comes to resource permissions.

Universal groups also can be used to grant permissions in multiple domains—throughout the forest of domain trees. Note that these groups are available only if you have an Active Directory structure that is part of a multidomain forest. They serve no purpose in a single-domain tree because domain local groups and global groups provide the necessary functions in a single-domain tree.

The membership of a universal group should not change on a frequent basis. This is because when a universal scope group's membership changes, the entire list of members is replicated to every global catalog in the forest of trees. Use universal groups for grouping users and other groups that are more stable in membership. Although global groups enable you to create groups of users and other groups that can be granted access in trusted domains, their membership must come from a single domain. To make managing a universal group easier, first place users into global groups in their own domains, and then place these global groups into a universal group. Thus, when the membership of a global group changes, there is no need to replicate the universal group membership to every other global catalog. Only the global group has changed. The universal group has as its member the global group, not the individual users who come and go from the global group.

Built-In Groups

There are several kinds of built-in groups, depending on where you look in the directory structure. For example, in Figure 31.9 you can see the list of groups found under the Builtin folder. Simply click the Builtin folder and you'll see the list of built-in domain local groups. As the name implies, each group was designed to give the access permissions to perform specific types of administrative jobs.

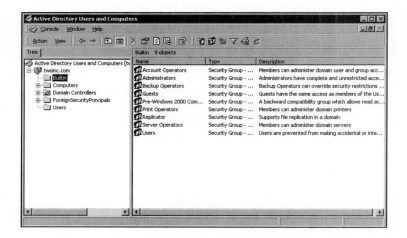

Figure 31.9   The Builtin folder contains a collection of domain local scope groups you can use.

The domain local scope built-in groups are

- **Account Operators**—Users placed into this group can perform account management duties, such as creating new users.

- **Administrators**—This is the most powerful group. Members of this group can do just about anything they want in the domain, including taking ownership of files, creating user accounts, and so on.

- **Backup Operators**—Members of this group get the access rights needed to perform backups on computers in the domain.

- **Guests**—A guest group, which can be used to grant very limited access to users from other domains.

- **Print Operators**—You guessed it, members of this group can control printers and print jobs.

- **Replicator**—Used by services responsible for replication.

- **Server Operators**—Members of this group can perform tasks on specific servers.
- **Users**—A built-in group for ordinary users in the domain.

In addition to these built-in groups, you can click on the Users folder and see a list of predefined groups, which also can be used to organize users. These are global scope groups, so you can use them to organize users and computers, and then place them in domain scope groups in the current domain or in other domains. If none of the following group names fits your needs, you can create your own groups, which we'll look at next.

The Predefined groups found in the Users folder are

- Group name
- Cert Publishers
- Domain Admins
- Domain Computers
- Domain Guests
- Domain Users
- Enterprise Admins
- Group Policy Admins
- Schema Admins

In general, the groups you'll use most in the list will probably be the Domain Computers and Domain Users groups. By default, when you create a user account, the new account is placed automatically into the Domain Users group. Likewise, when you add a computer to the domain, the computer is automatically placed into the Domain Computers group. Looking at the domain from an overall picture, you can use these two groups when you want to make changes that apply to all users or all computers in a domain. The Domain Admins group can be used to give selected individuals administrator-level rights in a domain. It is always a good idea to not use the actual built-in Administrator account for a domain. Instead, create individual accounts for each user, and then place him into one or more groups that give them the access he needs. If you need to grant a user administrator-level rights, just place him into the Domain Admins groups.

A few notes about these predefined groups in the Users folder:

- The Domain Users group is a member of the domain's Users group (the one located in the Builtin folder).
- The Domain Admins group is automatically a member of the Administrator's group in the Builtin folder.
- The Domain Guests group is automatically placed into the Guests group in the Builtin folder.

Some of the other groups listed here also can be used to organize users and grant them access to resources on a group basis. However, you can always create your own group and tailor the rights and permissions for the group to match your exact needs.

Creating a New User Group

To start the process, click Action, New, Group. In Figure 31.10, you can see the dialog box that pops up to allow you to enter basic information about the group, such as its name and type: Security or Distribution.

Figure 31.10   The New Object-Group dialog box prompts you for basic group information.

What is the difference between these two types of groups?

- Security groups are used to manage user access and permissions. Users and other groups can be members of a security group. This is the sort of group we've been discussing so far in this chapter.

- Distribution groups are used for functions such as grouping users for other purposes, such as e-mail. These groups cannot be used to grant access to resources.

You can probably guess that, after you fill in the basic information and click OK, the group is immediately created. In our example, we created a group in the Users folder. Just like User objects and Computer objects in the Active Directory, you can now bring up a properties page for the group and from there configure additional attributes for the group.

Right-click on the group, and select Properties. You also can highlight the group and select Properties from the Action menu. In Figure 31.11 you can see an example of the properties page for the group that we just created.

Figure 31.11   You can configure and view additional attributes by using the properties page for the new group.

Here you can see fields that allow you to input a description of why the group is used. Additionally, you can put in notes about the group that might be helpful in the future. For example, you might create a group to be used only for a short period of time. You can put notes here to remind yourself to remove the group at a later date.

Two other tabs relate to group membership. The first tab, Members, lists current members of the group. On this tab you can click the Add button to bring up a dialog box to use for adding other users or groups to the group. The Member Of tab displays groups of which this particular group itself is a member. You also can use the Add button on this property sheet tab to add the group to other groups.

Finally, The Managed By tab is similar to that discussed earlier, and is used to define a responsible contact person for this group.

Other Things You Can Do with the Active Directory Computers and Users Snap-In

This utility is not as simple as the User Manager for Domains that was included in previous versions of Windows NT. However, most of the additional functions for which you can use this utility don't directly relate to user or computer management, so we'll not go into the nitty-gritty details. For example, you can create organizational units and use them to further subdivide the objects managed in your domain. See Chapter 25 and the help files that accompany Windows 2000 Server.

There are other tools you'll find in the Administrative Tools folder that again don't relate directly to user or computer management, but you should be aware of them in case they are used at your site. Some of these utilities won't show up in your Administrative Tools folder unless you've already installed the prerequisite software. For example, the DHCP manager MMC snap-in won't be there if you haven't installed a DHCP service on the server.

Some of the more popular tools include

- **Active Directory Domains and Trusts**—This utility manages trust relationships. The User Manager for Domains formerly handled that job.

- **Component Services**—This selection allows you to configure COM+ applications.

- **Event Viewer**—Use this standard utility to review the system, security, and application log files. Similar to its Windows NT 4.0 predecessor but uses the MMC console instead.

- **DHCP**—This snap-in enables you to manage the DHCP service on the local server. If a user's computer is having problems communicating on the network, you can check the DHCP logs to see whether the client has obtained a valid IP address. For more information about DHCP and using this snap-in, see Chapter 23, "BOOTP and the Dynamic Host Configuration Protocol (DHCP)."

- **DNS**—This snap-in will be present if the server is running the DNS service. This service is used by computers on the network to locate both domain controllers (for authentication purposes) and other resources on the network. For more information on DNS, see Chapter 24, "Name Resolution."

- **Computer Management**—Use this tool to manage services and other aspects of your server. You can defragment disk drives, see system information, and use the Event Viewer, among other things.

- **Distributed File System**—This will show up if you've installed the Distributed File System. For more information about DFS and this utility, see Chapter 33, "File Server Protocols."

- **Internet Services Manager**—IIS is installed by default on Windows 2000 Server. This tool can be used to manage the IIS services, as well as to set up printers for the Internet Printing Protocol (IPP).

Other tools will show up here, some related to security policies, some related to other tools. It is a good idea as a new administrator of a Windows 2000 Server to become familiar with the services and applications installed on the server and become proficient in using the tools to manage them.

Managing Unix and Linux Users

## CHAPTER 32

SOME OF THE MAIN TOPICS IN THIS CHAPTER ARE

User Administration

Network Information Service (NIS)

Common Login Problems

Unix is not generally considered an office desktop operating system. The Windows OS family has pretty much taken over the desktop, along with other minor players such as Apple's Macintosh operating system. However, Unix is a dominant player in the server market, and many large networks are made up of a collection of Unix servers, X-Window Systems clients and, usually, some Windows clients. Unix becomes much more prevalent when you get past the office environment desktop into the workstation or server region. Establishing a network connection or an interactive session on a Unix server requires, in most cases, that the user provide some form of authentication (that is, username and password). In this chapter we will look at the files typically used for user authentication purposes on Unix and Linux systems and some of the problems commonly associated with the logon process.

In addition, we'll take a quick look at Network Information Systems (NIS). This set of client/server programs can be used to manage many important files on multiple computers, keeping all computers within an NIS domain in sync. These files include those used for user management, as well as others, depending on the implementation, such as network configuration files. Although it is impossible to cover all the various things you can do with NIS in only one chapter, you'll get a good overview of the kinds of tasks associated with setting up and managing multiple servers using NIS.

User Administration

Several files are generally associated with the user logon process for Unix systems. These files can be located in different directories, and the fields within some of these files can vary from one implementation to another. However, the following two files are generally used:

- **/etc/passwd**—This is the password file. It is used to store the username, the password (in encrypted format), and other information specific to the user account. This file has its file protection value set to be world-readable so that anyone can access the file when logging in to the system. It also means that once someone gets into your system, he or she can usually copy this file and then begin to crack the passwords it contains.

- **/etc/groups**—This file contains a list of user groups and a numerical value associated with each group. A field in the /etc/passwd file references a group in this file using this value.

The */etc/passwd* File

The Unix operating system usually authenticates users by comparing their credentials with those stored in one or more files on the server. This is similar to the method used for Novell's bindery, where users must authenticate to each server they want to access. The typical username/password exchange is used and the /etc/passwd file is the standard file used to store most user information. It is a simple text file that stores data using ASCII characters, and it's world-readable because access to the file is required during the logon process.

The fields in this file store information such as the username, home directory, default shell, and an encrypted password, among other things. This file is one of the most vulnerable and sought-after files by hackers. You might think that it's a safe file because the password field in this file is encrypted. Not true! After a hacker has access to this file, a large number of utilities can be downloaded from the Internet to run against a password file to decrypt the password. Many hackers just use a dictionary and known encryption techniques and then compare the result with the value found in your /etc/password file. When a match is found, the hacker knows your password for that account.

Keep in mind that this file is world-readable! That means once someone has broken into even the most restricted account, if they can get to a shell command prompt, they can most likely copy this file and use it to further compromise accounts that have been granted much greater access rights to the system.

Note

This chapter covers files used to secure individual or groups of Unix servers and workstations in a network. It should be obvious that managing a large number of workstations, even using things such as NIS, can be a difficult task from a security standpoint. For this reason, every network that connects to another outside network, or the Internet, needs a good firewall. The authentication files discussed in this chapter help protect an individual Unix system. A firewall can help protect the entire network from outsiders. Chapter 40, "Firewalls," contains more information on this topic.

After the root password is discovered, or the password to any account that has administrator equivalent privileges is discovered, your system is wide open for attack.

The format for /etc/passwd file, on most systems, is

```
username:password:uid:gid:GECOS:homedir:shell
```

Note that the colon character (:) is used to separate fields. If a field is to be left blank, you'll see two colons in a row. The fields in this file are

- **username**—The account name used to log in to the account.

- **password**—The encrypted password for the user account. An asterisk character (*) in this field means that the account is disabled. If this field is left blank, no password is required for the account. Unless you have a very good reason, you should not have any account with a blank password on a networked computer. Any access can usually lead to further access by a clever user. An x character in this field generally means that a shadow password file, discussed later, should be used.

- **UID**—A numerical value that the system gives to the account to identify the user when running processes or evaluating access to files and other system resources. A value of zero for this field is used to indicate the *superuser*, or a user who has the same privileges as root. On some systems values from 1–99 are reserved for use for system processes, such as background daemons.

- **GID**—A numerical value that identifies a user group to which the account belongs. The file /etc/group contains a listing of user groups and the numbers associated with them. Group membership can be used to make managing access to system resources, such as files and directories, an easier task. Access to a resource can be granted to the group. The alternative method is to grant access individually, which is a time-consuming process when you have a large number of users that have similar computing needs.

- **comment (GECOS)**—Yet another computer acronym! GECOS stands for General Electric Comprehensive Operating System. This field can be used to hold text that is used by certain applications, such as the finger utility. If more than one item is included in this field, commas should separate the items. It is common to store the user's full name in this field.

- **homedir**—This text field specifies the user's home directory. When the user logs in to the system, he or she is initially placed in this location in the file system. As with most operating systems, a separate home directory is maintained for each user for storing their own files. Home directories also can contain subdirectories to make organizing one's files a simple task.

- **shell**—The user on a Unix system interacts with the system using one of the many shell applications available for Unix today. This field in the /etc/passwd file is used to specify the shell program that will be invoked when the user logs in to the system.

A typical entry in the /etc/passwd file looks like this:

```
jdoe:Gfjhjo9Uia$jpo2dYtaGGdsh:223:100:John Doe:/home/jdoe:bash
rsmith:HuiTytsm$ld34tTbd9Saa2:119:110:Rob Smith:/home/rsmith:bash
```

Note that the second field, the password field, appears to have nonsense characters. This is the encrypted password that is highly prized by network intruders.

Using a Shadow Password File

To plug the password security hole presented by the /etc/passwd file, a technique called a *shadow password file* is usually used. This file contains the actual passwords, also in encrypted format. However, the shadow password file is not world readable, and a good administrator keeps this file protected by using the appropriate access permissions on the file.

On many systems, the name of the shadow password file is /etc/shadow. Check your documentation to determine the exact path on your system. Also note that, on some older systems (and a few current ones), you'll have to load an extra component to install the shadow password file capabilities. Keep up to date by consulting your vendor's Web site!

The contents of this file also can vary from one system to another. However, the following format contains the fields used in most implementations:

`username:password:last:may:must:warn:expire:disable:reserved`

The following describes these fields:

- *username*—This field is used for the same purpose as it is in the /etc/passwd file. It is the login name for this user's account.

- *password*—The user account password stored in encrypted format.

- *last*—The number of days, since January 1, 1970, that the password for this account was changed.

- *may*—The number of days that must pass before the password for this account can be changed.

- *must*—The number of days after which the password for this account must be changed.

- *warn*—The number of days before the password expires to warn the user about the upcoming password expiration.

- *expire*—The number of days that must pass before the account password expires and the account becomes disabled.

- *disable*—The number of days, since January 1, 1970, that the account has been disabled.

- *reserved*—This field is reserved for future use.

As you can see, using a shadow password file gives you additional control over accounts, such as setting password expiration values. It also gives you informational fields (such as `last` and `disable` that can be used when managing user accounts.

The */etc/groups* File

This file contains a list of user groups and a numerical value used to identify the group. The syntax for entries in this file is

`groupname:grouppassword:groupID:username1,username2 ...`

- *group name*—A name associated with the group. Using a meaningful name can help you simplify user administration.

- *group password*—Yes, you can place a password on a group, but this is generally not done. Instead, this field is usually left blank.

- **GID**—This is the group's ID number, which is used by the operating to identify the group. This number can range from 0–32767, and the numbers 0–10 are generally reserved for system groups. For example, in most Unix implementations, the root user has a GID of zero.

- **members**—This is a comma-delimited list of members of the group.

Users can be members of more than one group. If this is the case, then the first group is their primary group and the GID of this group is used when files are created or saved. Users can use the groups command to view the group(s) of which they are a member. The command chgrp can be used to change the current default group.

Adding or Removing User Accounts

To add or remove a user from a Unix/Linux box, you can edit the password and group files. However, any time you make an edit to such an important file there is always the chance that something will go wrong and you'll end up rendering an account, or possibly a system, unusable. It's advisable to always make a backup of an important file before making any edits.

After making entries in the /etc/passwd and /etc/groups files, you'll then have to create the user's home directory and install any files that are part of your standard distribution, such as shell files.

However, on most systems you won't have to go through all this trouble. Instead, most versions of Unix or Linux provide a program that can be used to perform all the functions needed to add or remove a user. On FreeBSD Unix, for example, the adduser command can be used. The syntax for this command is

```
adduser [-dDv] [-c changetime] [-C class] [-e expiretime] [-g primarygroup]
  ➥[-G gecos] [-h homedirectorybasedir] [-H homedirectory]
  ➥[-m homedirectorymode] [-p passwd] [-P encryptedpasswd] [-s shell]
  ➥[-S skeletondir] [-u uid] [username...]
```

- **-v**—This is the typical Unix/Linux "verbose" option. It causes the adduser command to output more information about its operations. Good to use if you're new at this.

- **-d**—This is equivalent to the rmuser command (remove user) described later in this section.

- **-D**—If you use the uppercase "D" character, the adduser command does not actually add a user. Instead, it sets defaults to use for the next time adduser is invoked.

- **-C class**—This specifies a login class for the user. FreeBSD Unix provides a file called /etc/login.conf that stores class definitions for users. Classes can be used to customize authentication methods and the user environment.

- **-e expiretime**—This field is not generally used. It is intended to set an expiration time for the password.

- **-g group**—This sets the user's default group value. If you do not include this on the command line, adduser will prompt you for it.

- **-G text**—This is the GECOS comment field. You'll be prompted for this value if it is not included on the command line.

- **-h homedirectory**—Use this to specify the home directory for the user. The value of *homedirectory* is the base directory under which the user's directory is created using the username.

- **-H homedirectory**—This version of the home directory option lets you specify the complete path of the user's home directory.

- **-m mode**—Use this to specify the mode for the user's home directory. The default is 0775.

- **-p** *password*—This option enables you to enter, in clear text, a password for the user account.

- **-P** *password*—This option enables you to enter, in encrypted format, a password for the user account. You must use either -p or -P. If neither is used, you will be prompted for a value.

- **-S** *skeletondirectory*—You can set up a "skeleton" directory to serve as a template to use when creating user home directories. This option enables you to specify the name of the template to use for this user's home directory and possible subdirectories.

- **-u** *uid*—Enter the user's ID (UID) with this option. FreeBSD starts ordinary users' UID at 100 and increments the value. Other flavors of Unix/Linux may use different starting values.

- *Username* ...—One or more user account names separated by spaces.

If you enter the adduser command with no command-line arguments, it will prompt you for the information it needs (such as a username) to create the new account. You can use the large amount of options available with the command to construct your own command to add users. If you need to add a large number of users at a time, or if you use the same command-line options frequently, create script files that can be used to invoke the adduser command for your customized requirements.

By using this command you not only make the necessary entries into the /etc/passwd and /etc/groups files, but also create the user's home directory.

The rmuser command can be used to remove a user. Simply follow the command with the username that is to be removed. The -v option is the only other command-line option available with this command.

The addgroup command works similar to the adduser command and helps automate the process of managing entries in the /etc/groups file. The syntax for this command is much simpler because there are fewer fields in the groups file and no directories or other data structures need to be created. The syntax for this command is

addgroup [-vd] [-g *gid*] [-m *members*] [*groupname*...]

- **-v**—Again, this causes more output to be displayed during the execution of the command. Useful when you are first learning to use the system.

- **-d** *groupname*—Similar to the adduser -d command, this command is the equivalent of using the rmgroup command that is used to remove a group.

- **-g** *gid*—This is used to specify the group ID (GID) for the group you are adding. If you omit this, the next available (unused) group number will be used.

- **-m** *members*—Use this to specify the initial members of the group, separating each by a space when more than one member is entered.

- *groupname*—This is the name you want to give to the group.

Other versions of Unix/Linux have similar programs. For example, Compaq's True64Unix uses the useradd command. The syntax is similar to the adduser command, but a few other options are available. For example, the -x option enables you to further specify options relating to NIS, password expiration times, and so on. Red Hat's Linux distribution enables you to use a similar useradd command. However, it also offers a more complex tool called linuxconf, which can be used in text mode, and also in a GUI mode using an X Window Systems interface or a Web browser. This tool goes far beyond simple user configuration tasks, including options for managing groups, file systems, system services, and many other objects.

Check the documentation of your Unix or Linux version to determine the commands and exact syntax for any script files or other utilities that can be used to automate user management.

Network Information Service (NIS)

One of the main problems inherent in storing logon information on each computer on a network is managing user accounts on multiple machines. Every time a change is made for a user, the change must be propagated to other computers on the network that the user logs in to. Instead of visiting each Unix box to make changes to the appropriate files, you can use Network Information System (NIS). This application was developed by Sun Microsystems and was originally called Yellow Pages (or YP for short). You still might see references to Yellow Pages in older documentation. However, due to trademark infringement, the application is now known as NIS.

Master and Slave NIS Servers

NIS stores important information for servers on a network in a central database. By storing important information in a central location, management of the data becomes much easier. The network administrator can make the necessary changes to the maps on an NIS *master server* and let NIS take care of informing the affected *slave servers* on the network about the change. The NIS master server also works to authenticate users against its database. However, to provide a backup, slave servers on the network also keep copies of the same files maintained by the NIS master server. This redundancy enables users to keep working if an NIS master server is offline for a short period of time. The master/slave method also can be used to provide for load balancing so that the master NIS server does not become overloaded on a large network.

The kind of data that NIS can manage for Unix servers includes the standard /etc/password and /etc/group files. It also includes other important files containing data about remote file systems, other hosts on the network, and so on.

NIS Maps

When you initially set up NIS, important system files are converted into databases that are referred to as NIS *maps*. In addition to the typical files that we've talked about in this chapter so far, the following files also are candidates for NIS management:

■ **/etc/ethers**—This file results in two NIS maps: ethers.byaddr and ethers.byname. The Reverse Address Resolution (RARP) uses this information when resolving ethernet hardware (MAC) addresses to IP addresses. Typically, this is used by diskless workstations that need to discover their assigned IP address (which might not be stored locally) during the boot sequence.

Note

The concept of a master and slave in the NIS structure does not apply to a server as a whole. For example, one NIS server might be the master server for a particular map or set of maps, while it is also the slave server for other maps controlled by other master servers. The terms *master* and *slave* relate to whether the NIS server holds the master map (where changes are made and then propagated to slave servers) or whether the server holds a duplicate copy that is regularly updated by the master map's server. Each map contains information that tells it what its master server host is.

Note that, unless you have good reasons to distribute master copies among different servers, the whole point in using NIS is to centralize information updates. In general, it's a good idea to use one master server in a typical domain and several slave servers (if needed) to help provide for load balancing and redundancy.

■ **/etc/networks**—This file also results in the creation of two NIS maps: networks.byname and networks.byaddr. You probably can guess that these maps store information used to associate network names with IP network addresses.

■ **/etc/services**—Only one NIS map is created from this file. It contains a list of network services and the TCP and UDP ports associated with these service port numbers. For more information about well-known ports usually stored in this map, see Appendix B, "TCP and UDP Common Ports." The resulting map is called services.byname.

- **/etc/protocols**—Two NIS maps result from this file. The first is called protocols.byname and the second is called protocols.byaddr. These maps work similar to the services maps, in that they act to cross-reference protocol numbers with the names of the protocols.

- **/etc/netmasks**—The NIS map created by this file is called netmasks.byaddr, and it is used to store the subnet masks for the network.

- **/etc/hosts**—This field also results in two NIS maps, hosts.byname and hosts.byaddr. The standard hosts file used in TCP/IP is almost an antique today but still has a few uses. These maps can be used to translate hostnames to IP addresses for computers. The Domain Name System (DNS) servers typically perform this function on most networks today.

- **/etc/aliases**—This file also results in two NIS maps. They are mail.aliases and mail.byaddr. These maps are used to define alias e-mail addresses.

The ypserve daemon runs on a central server and manages the NIS maps created from the standard systems files. The ypbind daemon runs on workstations and is responsible for interacting with the ypserve daemon to satisfy user requests and information interchange.

Note

NIS works in a fashion similar to DNS. Both provide information to clients from a database that stores all kinds of network information. To help you distinguish the difference between NIS and DNS, think of NIS as a local client/server mechanism that helps keep information sorted on and made available to local clients. DNS is part of a global, hierarchical system for managing IP addresses, domain names, services, and other data used for wide-area communications as well as functioning perfectly well on a local-area network to satisfy requests for the data it manages. Note that DNS and NIS do not keep identical information. For example, DNS does not store usernames and passwords. This is a local function of the local LAN.

Also note that NIS uses the concept of domains, like DNS. However, although it is typical to create domains that use the same name and cover the same network territory, this does not necessarily have to be the case. So, when thinking about NIS domain names, don't confuse them with DNS domain names. They might be the same for the affected portion of the network, but the administrator can choose to use different names for the different domains. For more information about DNS, see Chapter 24, "Name Resolution."

In addition to these files, other files that can be used on most NIS implementations include

- shadow password files
- bootparams
- netgroup
- rpc

The NIS Server *ypserve* Daemon and Maps Location

On the NIS server, the NIS maps can be found in a subdirectory that falls under the /var/yp directory. Names for the subdirectories are created by using the NIS domain name you have chosen. To use the old venerable acme.com name, the resulting file path for this domain would be /var/yp/acme.com.

The ypserve daemon is the background server process that is responsible for finding the information in its maps to satisfy client requests. When NIS is set up, you must have at least one master server that runs this daemon in order for NIS to function on the network.

Setting the NIS Domain Name Using the Command *domainname*

After you've decided on a name to use for the NIS domain, you'll need to issue the `domainname` command to set that name on the Unix system.

To set the NIS default domain name, use the following command:

```
# domainname acme.com
```

You also can place a similar command (substituting your NIS domain name in the example for `acme.com`, of course), in a startup file to automate the process during system boot.

You also can enter the command `domainname` from the command line, without any command-line parameters. This syntax of the command displays the current NIS domain name so you can check it for accuracy when making changes or performing troubleshooting efforts.

Starting NIS: *ypinit, ypserve,* and *ypxfrd*

Installing NIS on Unix and Linux platforms is not the same for all platforms. See the usual `README.TXT` and installation and release notes files for your platform to install the necessary files that are used to configure NIS on the server or client system.

The `ypinit` command creates the `/var/yp/domainname` directory (where *domainname* is the name you've chosen for your NIS domain) and reads the files in the `/etc` directory and creates the NIS maps. The NIS maps are then saved in the *domainname* subdirectory. When the `ypinit` program is finished, you can use the command `ypserv` to start the NIS server. When the server is up and running, you'll need to start the map transfer daemon if you have configured other NIS servers in the network. Type `ypxfrd` at the command line. You also could add the command to the `/etc/rc.local` file to have it start automatically at startup.

After you've finished the initial installation, use the following commands to configure and set up NIS:

- **ypinit**—This command is used to create the map directory and subdirectories (that is, `/var/yp/acme.com`) on the server. This command also runs through the various `/etc` files and creates the maps needed for the domain. This command also can be used to set up the `/var/ypbinding/domainname/ypservers` file on client computers, where *domainname* is the name of the NIS domain.

- **ypserv**—After you've used `ypinit` to create the necessary NIS databases, use the `ypserv` command to start the server on the NIS server. The format for this command is `ypserv -m`. You can enter this at the command line or put it into a startup file if you want the server daemon to start each time the system is booted.

Note

By default, the domain name and host name used by NIS are taken from the files `/etc/nodename` and `/etc/defaultdomain`. During the system boot process, these files are consulted and used with the appropriate NIS commands (that is, the **domainname** command).

To use ypinit, you should be logged in as root. Next, make edits to the `/etc/hosts` file and be sure it contains all the IP addresses of each NIS server. Start the process of building the maps by using the following command:

```
/user/sbin/ypinit -m
```

The command (actually a script file) prompts you for the names of other host computers that you want to make into NIS servers. Be sure to include the server you are working on as well as the names of other NIS server candidates you've created. Next, you'll be asked whether you want to terminate the operation if a nonfatal error occurs. Generally, you should enter yes to this prompt so you can fix any problems that crop up. After you fix the problem, reinvoke ypinit to start over again.

Next, ypinit asks whether you want to delete any currently existing files that are in the /var/yp/*domainname* directories. If you are reinstalling NIS, you are prompted to delete the files created by the previous installation.

After this, ypinit uses make to process instructions contained in the makefile. The script file uses makedbm to create the maps and places the name of the master server for each map in a location in the map so that it will know its master server.

The Default Makefile Used By *ypinit*

When the ypinit command is invoked to begin configuring your server, it calls the make(1) command to process information in a makefile that is usually located in the /var/yp directory. You can make modifications to this file if required for your environment. The makefile is used to convert the input files discussed earlier into the ndbm(3) format, which is beyond the scope of this discussion. The makefile then creates the appropriate maps that NIS uses.

NIS Slaves

NIS slaves hold exact duplicates of NIS maps as the master server. The slave also runs the same ypserv daemon. The only difference between the two servers is that only the slave answers client requests; the slave doesn't make any changes to the NIS maps. Only the master server can update the NIS maps. When the master server makes a change to the maps, it then propagates the changes to all the slave servers in the NIS domain.

Setting Up Slaves

Creating a slave server is similar to creating the master server. First, you set the NIS domain name by typing domainname at the command line. After setting the NIS domain name, start the ypbind server process:

```
ypbind
```

and then enter the following on the slave server-to-be:

```
ypinit -s NISmaster
```

The -s option specifies you are setting up a slave server followed by the NIS domain master server name. After the slave server is initialized, the master server transfers all the NIS domain information to the slave. During the setup of the slave server, it does not look at its local /etc files to create the NIS maps. The slave server has only the information that is stored in the maps on the master server.

Deciding when to create a slave server should be done during the initial planning phase of setting up the NIS network. Although growing networks don't exactly grow according to plan, it is possible to add slave servers later. If you add a slave server after the initial setup of the master server, you'll need to add the new slave's hostname to the ypservers map file.

Starting and Stopping the NIS Service on Slave Servers

Starting and stopping all YP processes is a simple task. These commands may be used online to start or stop the services. The following line will cause the YP processes to all stop running:

```
/etc/init.d/yp stop
```

To start all YP processes, use the following command:

```
/etc init.d/yp start
```

Now it can't be simpler than that, after all you've gone through to get this system up and running!

Changing NIS Maps

You can make changes to the normal system files (that is, /etc/passwd) on the NIS master server. After you make these kinds of changes, set your default directory to be /var/yp, and then execute the command make *mapname*, where *mapname* is the name of the map being modified.

To update the system after making changes to the makefile, you'll need to stop the YP processes, make the changes, and restart NIS. You can make changes to the makefile to add or remove maps. Use the same start/stop commands described in the previous section for this purpose.

Pushing Modifications to NIS Slave Servers

After you've made modifications on the master NIS server, the changes must be sent to all other slave servers so that the databases can be kept in sync. The makefile utility uses the yppush command to send these map changes to the affected servers. The process is accomplished by sending a message to the ypserve daemon. The ypserve daemon that resides on the slave server then starts up another process using the ypxfr utility. This utility establishes communication with the ypsfrd daemon that runs on the master NIS server to see whether any changes need to be made. If so, the yppush program sends the map changes. If they are successfully applied to the slave server, it returns a successful status message to yppush.

Note that yppush sends only maps that have changed and that already exist on the slave servers. If you create new maps on the master NIS server that don't yet exist on the slave NIS servers, use the command ypxfr by itself on the command line to do this. For troubleshooting purposes you can check the results of the command by viewing the log file named /var/yp/ypxfr.log.

Other Useful NIS YP Commands

Although the documentation for your system contains a lot of other tasks you can perform using NIS, this chapter has only touched on the basics. However, a few other useful commands that you'll find in most implementations of NIS include

- **ypcat *mapfilename***—This command lists the values stored in a map file. If you want to list the keys for the map file values, use the option -k in this syntax directly after the ypcat command.

- **ypwhich -m**—This command lists all the available maps on the server and their masters. If you want to list only the master server for a particular map, include the map name following the -m option.

NIS Clients

Starting the NIS client is simple. First, set the NIS domain on the local machine using the domainname command, and then start the ypbind service by entering ypbind at the command line. To have ypbind start every time the machine boots, ensure the ypbind script exists in the /etc/rc.local file and that it is not commented out.

The following is a sample boot script to launch ypbind in the correct NIS domain:

```
domainname acme.com
. . .
if [ -d /var/yp ] ; then
 ypbind; echo -n ' ypbind'
fi
```

Common Login Problems

The most common problem users encounter when logging in to a Unix system is summed up by the following error message:

```
login incorrect
```

This message doesn't convey a great deal of information to the user, but usually indicates one of the following conditions:

- There is no user account in the /etc/passwd file for this username.

- The password entered by the user is not correct.

- The home directory for the user (as specified in the password file) does not exist.

In the first instance, the administrator might not have gotten around to creating a record for the user in the /etc/passwd file. It is more likely that the user entered the username incorrectly. Remember that, in the Unix operating system, usernames and passwords are case sensitive. For example, if your username is LukeKurtis, entering lukekurtis or LUKEKURTIS will not work.

When choosing passwords it is a good idea to choose one that is not easy for others to guess. Unfortunately, this sometimes means that it is also easy for a user to forget. Choosing a text string that contains both uppercase and lowercase letters, along with numeric and alphabetic characters, is a good idea. When you receive the login incorrect error message, check to be sure you are really entering the password as it was originally set up.

In all cases, one of the first things to check is that the Caps Lock key is not on!

If the account is new, it is possible that the user's home directory has not been created or the administrator has not set the correct permissions on the directory to allow the user access to it. Using a script file to create new user accounts can help prevent this problem. Coding all the necessary commands by a script file will prevent the problems caused when an administrator creates a new account in a hurry and forgets a step or two.

File Server Protocols

CHAPTER 33

The first thing that comes to mind when you think "network" is probably file and print servers. When a new addition is made to the network for a new business unit, or when existing units are shuffled around and users and resources must be regrouped, it is usually the files that users access and the printing capacity they require that needs to be given special consideration. You should plan for the necessary bandwidth and check the logical physical topology of the LAN to be sure that you have the necessary capacity, either in bandwidth or storage. In this chapter we will look at protocols that are used for file services. In Chapter 35, "Network Printing Protocols," we'll look at print services for the LAN.

Why Should You Read This Chapter?

Understanding how a particular protocol functions will better enable you to troubleshoot network problems that prevent users from timely access to file resources. For example, using a LAN analyzer to review network traffic during a troubleshooting session will be of little use unless you know what types of frames you are looking for and understand their function in the file sharing process. You also can use the knowledge gained from this chapter to assist in making decisions about future additions to the network.

There are many ways you can share files. You can copy them to a floppy disk or tape cartridge and pass them around the office (a la sneaker-net). This is not a very efficient method as your volume of data grows and you find yourself trying to keep track of multiple versions of a file.

When TCP/IP was developed, several handy utilities were created to work with the protocol to provide clients some useful functionality. One of these, the *File Transfer Protocol (FTP)*, enables a user to copy a file from a remote computer to his own so that manipulation of the data can be done locally.

FTP doesn't really improve too much on the floppy method, except that the network can probably handle a larger amount of files more quickly. However, because users end up with more than one copy of the file, there is always the potential of creating mismatched versions when trying to coordinate multiple access to a file by making many copies of it. For example, if the user forgets to copy the file back to its original location after making changes, the next user who makes a copy of the file will find herself working on a file that does not contain these changes. Another problem with the copying method is that the network bandwidth (or lack of it) can become a problem for very large files.

◄◄ FTP, telnet, and a host of other useful network utilities are covered in Chapter 21, "TCP/IP Services and Applications."

Other TCP/IP utilities can be used to access files remotely. For example, you can establish a telnet session to a remote computer and then issue commands locally to manipulate data.

With this method the user's PC or workstation is used as nothing more than a terminal emulator, and a rather expensive one at that. All applications that are needed to manipulate the data must exist or be installed on the remote computer. This is probably a better method to use than copying from an FTP site or floppy disk when trying to share a single file among many users because it maintains only one copy of the file. However, it is still not a very convenient method for several reasons. If you want to access files on more than one remote system, you need a separate telnet session for each one. This means it is not possible for an application, such as a word processor or database, to access files or remote systems at the same time. When using a telnet client, the user must have a user account set up on each remote system so that the logon can be validated. Obviously, using telnet is not as transparent a process as simply running an application on the user's local system and accessing files in the local file system.

The Network File System (NFS) protocol was developed by Sun Microsystems to make remote file access as simple a process for the user as local file access. NFS enables a user to access a remote file system while making it appear to the user to be a local file system. There is no need to copy files back and forth from servers. Using NFS, a file system (or a portion of it) residing on a remote system can be made to appear to the client as though it were simply part of the local file system. Early on, NFS was found only on Unix boxes. However, its popularity spread, and you can now find NFS server applications and client applications for most major operating systems. A minor disadvantage to using NFS is that network problems can interfere with file access. However, this is true for any kind of network file-sharing protocol.

Microsoft operating systems have long used the *Server Message Block (SMB)* protocol to provide file and printer access to networked clients. This protocol has developed over the years and has been adopted into Windows NT and Windows 2000. Whereas NFS is built on top of several other protocols and is used to provide only file-sharing capabilities, SMB is a more basic protocol that can be used across a network to provide network access to files and print sharing to interprocess communication, using named pipes and mailboxes. Lately Microsoft has been working on the Common Internet File System protocol (CIFS), which can be considered to be an update of the older SMB protocol.

In this chapter, you will briefly look at the components of the protocols that enable you to share files on a network.

Server Message Block (SMB)

A common protocol you will find on almost any computer running a Windows operating system, from Windows to Windows for Workgroups to Windows NT, is the Server Message Block protocol. This is a protocol that is used for basic file sharing, printer sharing, and also for a few other network messaging devices, such as named pipes and mail slots. This is a basic client/server protocol that uses request and response messages to accomplish its purpose.

SMB has also been used by many vendors other than Microsoft to provide file and print services, including IBM (OS/2) and Digital Equipment Corporation (now Compaq) in its Pathworks products.

SMB has been around for a while and has been modified to support new functions as PC networks have evolved. Each new version of the protocol is called a *dialect*, and these are listed in Table 33.1. This table shows the dialects in order from the earliest to the latest, and any server implementing a particular dialect must also support interaction with clients of any earlier dialect in this table. This allows for backward compatibility for older clients when parts of the network, such as servers, are upgraded.

Table 33.1   SMB Protocol Dialects

SMB Dialect	Description
PC NETWORK PROGRAM 1.0	The original MSNET SMB protocol, sometimes called the *core protocol*.
PCLAN1.0	Alternative name for the core protocol.
MICROSOFT NETWORKS 1.03	MS-NET 1.03. Lock&Read and Write&Unlock added to protocol and defined a special version of raw read and raw write.
MICROSOFT NETWORKS 3.0	LANMAN 1.0 protocol for DOS operating system. Same as LANMAN1.0 except that the server must map errors from OS/2 errors to a DOS error.
LANMAN1.0	First complete version of LANMAN 1.0.
LM1.2X002	First complete version of LANMAN 2.0.
DOS LM1.2X002	Same as LM1.2X002 (LANMAN 2.0), except that server maps errors to DOS errors.
DOS LANMAN2.1	DOS LANMAN 2.1 protocol.
LANMAN2.1	OS/2 version of LANMAN 2.1 protocol.
Windows for Workgroups 3.1a	Windows for Workgroups version 1.0 of protocol.
NT LM 0.12	SMB for Windows NT. Added special SMBs for NT.

SMB Message Types

SMB is a message-oriented protocol in which the client makes a request of the server using a message formatted according to a specific SMB message type. The server responds to the client's request using a specific SMB format. There are many different types of messages, which are listed in Table 33.2. Note that not all message types are supported by all clients.

Table 33.2   SMB Message Types

PC NETWORK PROGRAM 1.0	
SMB_COM_NEGOTIATE	SMB_COM_CLOSE_PRINT_FILE
SMB_COM_CREATE_DIRECTORY	SMB_COM_DELETE_DIRECTORY
SMB_COM_OPEN	SMB_COM_CREATE
SMB_COM_CLOSE	SMB_COM_FLUSH
SMB_COM_DELETE	SMB_COM_RENAME
SMB_COM_QUERY_INFORMATION	SMB_COM_SET_INFORMATION
SMB_COM_READ	SMB_COM_WRITE
SMB_COM_LOCK_BYTE_RANGE	SMB_COM_UNLOCK_BYTE_RANGE
SMB_COM_CREATE_TEMPORARY	SMB_COM_CREATE_NEW
SMB_COM_CHECK_DIRECTORY	SMB_COM_PROCESS_EXIT
SMB_COM_SEEK	SMB_COM_TREE_CONNECT
SMB_COM_TREE_DISCONNECT	SMB_COM_SEARCH
SMB_COM_QUERY_INFORMATION_DISK	SMB_COM_WRITE_PRINT_FILE
SMB_COM_OPEN_PRINT_FILE	SMB_COM_GET_PRINT_QUEUE
LANMAN 1.0	
SMB_COM_LOCK_AND_READ	SMB_COM_WRITE_AND_UNLOCK
SMB_COM_READ_RAW	SMB_COM_READ_MPX
SMB_COM_WRITE_MPX	SMB_COM_WRITE_RAW
SMB_COM_WRITE_COMPLETE	SMB_COM_WRITE_MPX_SECONDARY
SMB_COM_SET_INFORMATION2	SMB_COM_QUERY_INFORMATION2
SMB_COM_LOCKING_ANDX	SMB_COM_TRANSACTION
SMB_COM_TRANSACTION_SECONDARY	SMB_COM_IOCTL
SMB_COM_IOCTL_SECONDARY	SMB_COM_COPY
SMB_COM_MOVE	SMB_COM_ECHO
SMB_COM_WRITE_AND_CLOSE	SMB_COM_OPEN_ANDX
SMB_COM_READ_ANDX	SMB_COM_WRITE_ANDX
SMB_COM_SESSION_SETUP_ANDX	SMB_COM_TREE_CONNECT_ANDX
SMB_COM_FIND	SMB_COM_FIND_UNIQUE
SMB_COM_FIND_CLOSE	
LM1.2X002	
SMB_COM_TRANSACTION2	SMB_COM_TRANSACTION2_SECONDARY
SMB_COM_FIND_CLOSE2	SMB_COM_LOGOFF_ANDX
NT LM 0.12	
SMB_COM_NT_TRANSACT	SMB_COM_NT_TRANSACT_SECONDARY
SMB_COM_NT_CREATE_ANDX	SMB_COM_NT_CANCEL

From the list in Table 33.2, it is easy to see that SMB has evolved over the years and has a specific command set that provides detailed functionality while maintaining simplicity by using a simple message exchange format. Most LAN analyzers have the capability to decode SMB packets, and you can troubleshoot SMB client/server sessions to observe the interaction of the commands shown in this table.

SMB Security Provisions

SMB has the capability to provide for two kinds of security for file sharing:

- Share level
- User level

The most basic level of security that can be used on an SMB network is *share-level* security. This approach offers a disk or directory as an available resource on the network, protecting it with a password. Users who want to access a resource that is protected at the share level need only know the name of the resource, the server that offers it, and the password for it to make a connection. This kind of file sharing is offered by Windows 9x/Me computers configured as a workgroup. In a small LAN where there is not a great need for security among users, it is very simple to set up and maintain a network based on this model.

A superior method that is more likely to be found in the business environment involves making users accountable for accessing resources. A *user-level* security model dictates that each user should log in using a unique identifier, called a *username*, which is associated with a password for the user account. After logging in to the network, users are granted access to resources based on the rights accorded their accounts and the resource protections placed on files or directories. This user-level method enables you to assign different kinds of access based on username and resource.

In the share-level security model, access to a share enables the user to access any files in the top-level directory of the share and all the files in all the subdirectories that might fall under the top-level directory. In the user-level security model, the administrator can place different access limitations on every directory, subdirectory, and file that exists in the share.

The earliest SMB clients do not have the capability to exchange an account name and password with a server and are thus limited in what they can do in a more modern environment. SMB servers will generally provide some functionality for user-level security. For example, if the client computer's computer name matches an account name that is known to the server, and if the password that the client passes as a "share" password matches that of the account, the SMB server can perform a logon for the user and grant access to the resource.

Protocol Negotiation and Session Setup

SMB has a built-in mechanism that is used by the client and server to determine the other's capabilities so that a common protocol version can be established that the two will use for the network connection. The first SMB message that the client sends to the server is one of the SMB_COM_NEGOTIATE type. The client uses this message to send the server a list of the dialects it understands. The server selects the most recent dialect it understands from the client's list and returns a message to it.

The response the server returns depends on the type of client. The information includes the dialect selected and can include additional information, such as buffer sizes, supported access modes, time and date values, and security information. After the client receives this response, it can continue to set up the session by using the SESSION_SETUP_ANDX message type.

If the initial server response indicates that user-level security is being used, this message type can be used to perform a user logon. The client sets a value in the message header called the *UID (user ID)* for the account it wants to use. It also supplies the account name and password to the server by using this message type. If these are validated by the server, the user can continue to use the UID to make subsequent accesses.

Other setup functions that are performed by using SESSION_SETUP_ANDX include the following:

- Set the maximum values for the size of buffers that will be used in the message exchange.
- Set the maximum number of client requests that can be outstanding at the server.
- Set the virtual circuit (VC) number.

If the VC passed to the server is zero and the server has other circuits open for the client, it will abort them, assuming that the client has rebooted without freeing them first. To properly close a session, the client uses the message type LOGOFF_ANDX, which causes the server to close all files associated with the user's UID.

Accessing Files

Other SMB message types are used now to traverse the resource directory and to open, read, write, and close files. First, the user must connect to the resource by using the TREE_CONNECT message. The message includes the name of the resource (server and share name) and, for earlier clients that do not perform logons, a share password. The server responds by sending the user a value called the *TID (Tree ID)*, which will be used in SMBs exchanged for this connection.

After the connection has been established, several basic SMB command formats can be used to manipulate files and directories that reside on the share. For example, the CREATE_DIRECTORY message is used to create a new directory in the file share's directory structure. The client passes the pathname for the new directory, and the server creates the directory, provided that the client has the appropriate access rights or permissions. The DELETE_DIRECTORY SMB message can be used to remove a directory, again based on the functions allowed for the username.

Opening and Closing Files

The OPEN message is used by a client to open a file. The path for the file is given, relative to the file share root. The client specifies the access that is desired, such as read, write, or share. If the file is successfully opened, the server returns a *File ID (FID)* to the client, which is used to further access the file using other SMB message types; it is similar to a file handle, which most programmers will recognize.

The server also returns data to the client indicating the actual access that was granted, which is read-only, write-only, or read/write.

The CLOSE message is sent by the client to tell the server to release any locks held on the resource file held by the client. After this message, the client can no longer use the FID to access the file, but it must instead reopen the file and obtain a new value.

When a client does not know the exact name of a file that it wants to open, the SEARCH message can be used to perform a directory lookup. This function enables wildcards to be used, and the server response can include more than one filename that matches the request.

Reading and Writing

The SMB protocol uses the READ and WRITE message types to perform I/O operations on a file for the client. Using the READ request, a client can request that the server return information from the file by specifying a number of bytes and an offset into the file. The server returns the data, indicating the actual number of bytes returned, which can be less than requested if the user tries to read past the end of a file.

The WRITE command updates a file in a similar manner. The client sends in the data that will be written, indicating the number of bytes to write and an offset into the file where the write operation will begin. If the request causes a write past the end of the file, the file is extended to make it larger. The server sends a response telling the client the number of bytes that were written. If the number is less than the requested value, an error has occurred.

To increase read/write performance, the READ_RAW and WRITE_RAW message types can be used to exchange much larger blocks of information between the client and the server. When these are used, the client must have only one request issued to the server. In one send, the server will respond with data that can be as many as 65,535 bytes in length. The WRITE command works in the opposite direction, allowing the client to send a large buffer of raw data to the server for a write operation.

Locking Mechanisms

Locking allows a particular client exclusive access to a file or a part of a file when it is shared on the network. In SMB, the capability to create a lock is called an opportunistic lock, or *oplock* for short. This is better explained by looking at the way in which it works. A client can create a lock on a resource using three different kinds of locks. The first is an *exclusive* lock, in which the client has exclusive access to the data held by the lock. A *batch* oplock is one that is kept open by the server when the client process has already closed the file. A *Level II* oplock is one in which there can be multiple readers of the same file.

The locking process consists of the client requesting the type of lock it wants when it opens the file. The server replies to the client with the type of lock that was granted when it responds to the open request.

A lock gives the client the capability to efficiently manage buffer space it uses when accessing a file over the network. For example, if a client has exclusive access to a file and is performing writes to it, it can buffer a lot of the newly written information before having to send it to the server to update the file. This can provide a reduced number of network packets when updating a file. A client that has an exclusive lock on a file can also buffer read-ahead data to make reading a file much faster.

These locks are called opportunistic locks for a reason. A client can be granted exclusive access to a file if no other client has it open at the time of the request. What happens when another client needs to read the file? The server notifies the first client that it needs to break the exclusive lock. The client then flushes its buffers so that any data that has not been written to the file is processed. The client then sends an acknowledgement to the server that it recognizes the exclusive lock has been broken. In Figure 33.1, you can see the interaction between two clients and a server as these messages are exchanged.

Batch oplocks are used to reduce the amount of traffic on the network when some programs require continual reopening of a file to obtain commands, as when a batch command procedure is executed. For example, a batch procedure executed by the command processor usually opens a file, locates the next line to be executed, reads that line, closes the file, and then executes the command. The problem with this is that it does this for each command line in the procedure, resulting in multiple file open/closes that are not really necessary.

This is done by using a batch oplock whereby the client can read the data from its local read-ahead cache instead of reopening the file on the remote server to get each line.

Level II oplocks were new with the NT changes to SMB. This kind of lock provides for more than one client to have a file opened for reading. When a client must read from a file that is opened by another exclusively, the server informs the current client that its exclusive lock has been broken and is now a Level II oplock. No client that has a Level II oplock will buffer data to or from the file. Thus, after the lock has changed to a Level II oplock (and the first client has flushed any data in its buffers), both clients can continue reading the file.

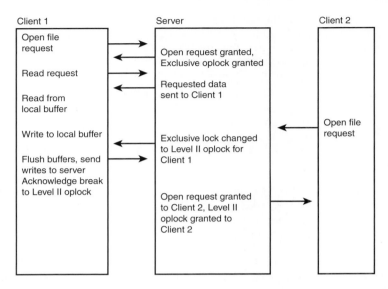

Figure 33.1   Exclusive oplocks are changed to Level II oplocks when a second client wants to open a file.

Using *NET* Commands

The set of NET commands form the basis for a command-line interface that the client can use to access SMB-based file services. This command can be used to make a directory available for sharing, to connect or disconnect a resource, or to view resources available on a server. Clients using operating systems such as Windows 95/98 or Windows NT/2000 can also use Microsoft Windows Explorer to connect to file resource shares on the network. However, the NET command provides a simple interface that also can be incorporated into command procedures, such as user login script files. You can also use these commands during troubleshooting. For example, you can establish a telnet session with a remote client who is having problems with a file share and execute the NET commands directly.

Because the NET command can be both a useful tool for setting up users to connect to resources and for troubleshooting clients, it is worth looking at the basic functions you can perform using this command.

There are several command parameters you can use with NET. For file sharing, the most basic commands are

- SHARE
- USE
- VIEW

NET SHARE

The NET SHARE command enables you to offer a disk or directory structure for sharing on the network. If used by itself with no other parameters, the command will show you the current shares that are being offered by the workstation or server, as in the following example:

```
F:\>net share
Share name     Resource                      Remark
---------------------------------------------------------------------------
IPC$                                         Remote IPC
D$             D:\                           Default share
print$         F:\WINNT\System32\spool\drivers Printer Drivers
E$             E:\                           Default share
C$             C:\                           Default share
F$             F:\                           Default share
ADMIN$         F:\WINNT                      Remote Admin
documents      d:\
HPLaserJ       LPT1:               Spooled   HP LaserJet 6L
The command completed successfully.
```

In this example, you can see that SMB is used not only to provide network communications for file sharing, but also to provide shared printing (HPLaserJ   LPT1:) and interprocess communications (IPC$).

The basic syntax for sharing is as follows:

NET SHARE *sharename*

To make a directory available for sharing, specify the name you want the file share to use on the network and follow it with the path to the directory to be shared:

NET SHARE *sharename=drive:path*

You can further configure the share by using the following qualifiers:

- **/Users:*number* or /UNLIMITED**—You can specify the maximum number of users that are allowed to simultaneously connect to the share.
- **/REMARK:*text***—You can display text to describe the share.
- **/CACHE:**—You can specify manual, automatic, or no.

See the following example:

```
F:\>NET SHARE ACTFIL=D:\ACCTPAY /USERS:5
ACTFIL was shared successfully.
```

This code offers the file share actfil on the network. It allows as many as five concurrent connections to the files contained in the directory D:\ACCTPAY and all subdirectories that fall underneath it.

Deleting a file share on the server is also a simple matter:

```
F:\>NET SHARE ACTFIL /DELETE
ACTFIL was deleted successfully.
```

In this example, you can also specify the pathname that is being shared:

```
F:\>NET SHARE D:\ACCTPAY /DELETE
ACTFIL was deleted successfully.

D:\ACCTPAY was deleted successfully
```

In both of these instances, of course, the actual directory that was offered for sharing is not deleted. Only the file share offering is terminated.

Troubleshooting Using NET VIEW and NET USE

These two commands enable you to view the resources available on the network and then to make connections to them. NET VIEW returns a list of the servers it knows about on the local network. You can use NET VIEW *servername* to get a list of services offered by any server in the list, as in the following example:

```
F:\>NET VIEW \\bca-nj-s1
Shared resources at \\bca-nj-s1

Share name   Type         Used as   Comment
-------------------------------------------------------------------------
acct         Disk                   Accounting
cdrom        Disk                   CD Drive on BCANJS1
documents    Disk
dvdrom       Disk                   DVD Drive on BCANJS1
HPLaserJ     Print                  HP LaserJet 6L
Rschlz       Disk                   Restricted
The command completed successfully.
```

It is easy to get confused when trying to troubleshoot problems with users connecting to shared resources. If you are using a Microsoft-based network that provides file sharing through SMB mechanisms, the NET VIEW command can be extremely useful. You can determine from this command whether the remote resource server is even seen in the browsing list by the client computer. If it is, you can display the resources offered. To connect to a resource manually, you can use the NET USE command. When executed by itself with no other command-line parameters, this command displays a list of your current connections.

To make a new connection, the syntax is very basic, though it has variations:

NET USE *device sharename*

Here, *device* can be an actual drive letter (such as D:, E:, and so on), a device name for a printer (LPT1:), or the wildcard *, in which case the next available drive letter will be chosen automatically when the connection is made. Observe the following example:

NET USE X: \\BCANJ1\DOCUMENTS

This attaches the drive letter X: to the resource documents on the server BCANJ1. You can also specify a username that can be used to evaluate your access rights to the remote resource:

NET USE X: \\BCANJ1\DOCUMENTS /USER:[*domainname*]*username*

Here, you would specify a valid username and, if it is a domain account, the name of the Windows NT domain. To delete a connection to a remote resource, use the /DELETE qualifier:

NET USE X: /DELETE

The NET USE command is most often associated with creating user logon scripts or other batch-oriented procedures that are used to interact with files offered as resources on a network. It can also be a very handy command to remember when performing a new installation or upgrading a user. For example, when installing a new application or troubleshooting a misbehaving one, you can quickly connect to a remote resource to download configuration or driver files.

On Windows NT and Windows 2000 computers, it is helpful to know that, besides the shares you explicitly create to offer on the network, there is also a hidden share *for each disk drive* on the system. These shares are named by adding a dollar-sign character after the drive letter. If you know an administrator account password on a remote system, you can easily connect to the computer's system disk (or any other drive) by specifying the hidden share name and an administrator's account name and password. *These share names do not show up in an ordinary browse list for all users to see.* They can be very handy when you need only to connect to another computer to quickly retrieve a file that can help you on the system you are troubleshooting.

Monitoring and Troubleshooting SMB Communications

You can use the NET STATISTICS command to obtain a quick view about statistics related to the SMB protocol.

Use either WORKSTATION or SERVER as a keyword to indicate which set of statistics you would like to see, as in the following example:

```
F:> NET STASTICS SERVER

Server Statistics for \\BCA-NJ-S1
Statistics since 7/6/99 10:38 AM
Sessions accepted               1
Sessions timed-out              0
Sessions errored-out            0

Kilobytes sent                  3
Kilobytes received              3

Mean response time (msec)       0

System errors                   0
Permission violations           0
Password violations             0

Files accessed                  7
Communication devices accessed  0
Print jobs spooled              0

Times buffers exhausted


  Big buffers                   0
  Request buffers               0

The command completed successfully.
```

From this display, you can quickly see whether a server is having problems with a recent password change—password violations will probably be excessive. A high value for permission violations can indicate that an access control list on a file or directory might have recently been changed. The other statistics shown here also can be used for many different troubleshooting scenarios.

The NET command has the capability of showing you a lot of information. For example, in addition to SMB statistics, the NET command also can be used to show the services currently running on an NT computer. Using the NET START command with other parameters on the line displays a list of the services currently running. If you are troubleshooting a client and see, for example, that the Workstation service is not running, you can use the NET START WORKSTATION command to start it. The NET command enables you to view, start, and stop NT services without having to use the graphical interface, which can be a great help when performing remote diagnosis.

When you upgrade a network or make repairs, it is often useful to send a message to users to let them know what is happening. For example, replacing a network card might require that a server be out of commission for a short period of time. Changing a network cable might disrupt network access for users. You might have established a telnet session with a user's workstation and want to send him a message on the screen to let him know that you are working. You can use the NET SEND command, using the following syntax, to send a message to users:

```
NET SEND {name | * | /DOMAIN[:domainname] | /USERS} message
```

Here, you can see that you can send a message to a single user or use the wildcard * character to send the message to all users. You can use the /DOMAIN:domainname variation to send the message to all users in a particular domain, for example. See the following command:

```
NET SEND * I am monitoring your workstation right now. Will call when finished.
```

When logged in to a server, this produced the pop-up message on the terminal of the logged-in user shown in Figure 33.2.

Figure 33.2 The NET SEND command can be used to send a message to users when you are logged in to their workstations.

To carry problem diagnosis any further when using SMB for file sharing, you need to resort to a LAN analyzer of some sort. You can use this to verify that the correct SMB messages are being exchanged between the client and the server. In Figure 33.3, you can see the Microsoft Network Monitor being used for this purpose.

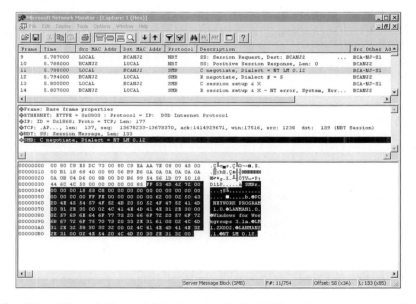

Figure 33.3 Using Microsoft Network Monitor, or a similar LAN analyzer, you can examine the exchange of SMB packets between the client and server.

You can step from one packet to the next to discover where a problem might be occurring. For example, is a password required? Are there problems opening a file? You can watch the sequence of commands that are used to connect to a tree, open a file, and make an attempt to read or write.

Although it would be necessary to have more detailed information about the format of SMB packets to make a detailed diagnosis at this level, it is still very helpful to be able to see the types of messages being exchanged, regardless of whether you can understand every byte in the packet. Viewing the data at this level can be used to troubleshoot most problems with this protocol. You also can use the event-logging capabilities of Windows NT/2000 (the Event Viewer) to look for problems. For example, if you have a password failure and have set the server to audit failed resource accesses, the Event Viewer will have a record showing you the failed attempt, and you can quickly resolve the problem by giving the user the correct password or by changing it.

Using the SMB Protocol on Non-Microsoft Clients: Samba

SMB is a protocol that is highly entrenched in the Microsoft world of operating systems and networking products. It makes sense, then, that there would be a way in which these workstations and servers could be integrated into a Unix environment without a lot of difficulty. The answer to this problem is called Samba, which is a set of products that provide for SMB conversations between SMB servers, such as Microsoft Windows operating systems, and those that do not use it natively, such as many different variants of Unix or Linux systems. In addition, Samba has been ported to several other popular operating systems, including OpenVMS.

Samba was originally developed by Andrew Tridgell and is now maintained by him and other developers (the "Samba Team") on the Internet. You can go to the home page for the Samba effort by using the URL www.samba.org.

From this Web site you can choose a mirror Web site for your country, and then you can view the documentation for Samba and download the most recent version. The software is freely distributed under the GNU public license. The most recent version of Samba provides the following capabilities:

- The functions of an SMB server to Windows NT clients, LAN Manager clients, and other SMB clients such as Windows 95/98/NT/2000 and other non-Microsoft clients.
- Browsing support by way of an RFC1001/1002-compliant name server. Samba can be configured to be the master browser on the LAN.
- A few utilities (such as an FTP-like SMB client) and other functionality, such as some command-line functions used for administrative functions.

Samba is not a complete replacement for the functionality provided by a Windows NT domain controller, but being so appears to be the goal. In addition to the basic Samba code distribution, there is also available a separate update called the Samba Domain Controller source code. This adds a lot of functionality related to domains as they are understood under Windows NT. Some things that are not yet available in version 2.x are the following:

- Trust relationships (between domains)
- Integration of PDC and BDC computers
- Complete print server functionality
- Access Control Lists

If you want to pursue this further, visit a Samba Web site to keep up with newer developments. For example, work is already underway on version 3.x of Samba.

These limitations are not really that much to worry about if you have a mixed environment of Unix and NT servers. You can configure Samba servers on your Unix boxes to enable high-performance machines to be used as file servers on the NT network. You can still manage the servers using Unix file administration procedures, and yet to the client computers, the shares appear as if other Windows computers were offering them.

Troubleshooting a Samba server can be made easier by starting the Samba server software using the -d parameter to specify a debug level (from 1–100), which will cause more output messages, depending on the level you specify. Another good thing to use when you are having problems with a Samba server is to use a LAN analyzer to view the SMB frames to determine whether any problems exist between the SMB client and server that are involved in the communications.

You can also use a LAN analyzer to view the sequence of exchange of SMB messages between server and client. Available as a download from the Samba home page is an extension to the tcpdump utility, called tcpdump-smb. You can use this to capture smb packets and decode the header information.

The Common Internet File System (CIFS)

CIFS is intended to be a replacement, or upgrade, of the SMB protocol. Design considerations include making it platform-independent. While SMB resides in the NetBIOS legacy environment, CIFS runs on top of TCP. Other improvements over SMB include

- Use of unicode filenames. Because the Internet is global, it's helpful to be able to encode characters that support multiple languages.

- Automatic restoration of service after a network disruption.

- CIFS is not proprietary to Microsoft. It is an Open Group standard (X/Open CAE Specification C209). It has also been proposed as an Internet standard to the Internet Engineering Task Force (IETF).

- DNS is used to translate between computer hostnames and IP addresses.

- Both share-level and user-level authentication is supported. With user-level authentication, the user must be authenticated (using a username/password valid on the server) before access is granted. This is much more secure than share-level access, discussed earlier in this chapter. Authentication is done using DES encryption.

- CIFS has been optimized to make communications across a slow link—such as a dial-up modem—possible.

CIFS is basically an enhanced version of SMB and still uses server message block messaging. The addition of better security and the use of DNS are necessary additions if the protocol is to be used on the Internet.

NetWare Core Protocol (NCP)

NetWare is composed of several different protocols. *IPX* is a connectionless delivery service that can be used by higher-level protocols (such as NCP or SPX) to create a connection-oriented, reliable transport service. Two other important protocols used in NetWare are the *Service Advertising Protocol (SAP)* and the *Routing Information Protocol (RIP)*. It is through SAP that servers announce their presence periodically and clients can make requests to locate resources. RIP is used to locate servers on the network.

Another protocol, called *NetWare Core Protocol (NCP)*, is used for communications exchange between a client and a server when file reads, file writes, or other file-related activities are being performed. It provides connection control and defines the methods used to encode requests and replies. NCP is a simple request-response protocol, similar to SMB in that respect. NCP requests are encapsulated in IPX packets. The NCP header information, which follows the IPX header information, consists of five fields. The first indicates the request type, which provides the function of the packet.

The client can make a request using four request types in this field, and the server can use this field to indicate a type of reply:

- Create a service connection (1111)
- General service request (2222)
- General service replies (3333)
- Terminate a service (destroy) connection (5555)
- Request burst-mode transfer (7777)
- Request being processed (9999)

These services can be further qualified by function and subfunction codes contained in the request packet. Other fields in the NCP header include the following:

- Sequence Number field, which is used to track the sequencing information for the connection.
- Connection Number Low field, which is a service connection number that is assigned to the client when it logs on to the server.
- Task Number field, which is a value that identifies the client that is making an NCP request.
- Connection Number High field, which is currently not used and should always have the value of 00 hex.

The header information for the response packet that the server sends back to the client will contain these same fields, but it will also add to additional fields. The first is a Completion Code field, which will be set to 0 if the request was successfully completed or to 1 if an error was encountered in processing the request. The Connection Status field might have values indicating an error condition between the client and server connection.

When the client initiates a connection request with a server, it will create a service connection (1111) request type. The server gives the client a connection number in its response. This connection number is used by the client when it submits its remaining requests. Each time a request is sent on the particular connection, the sequence number is incremented. The response to a request contains the same sequence number, making it easy for the client to match up responses to pending requests.

General Requests and Responses

Most of the exchanges between client and server are usually the result of requests made by the client (type 2222) and the replies sent by the server (type 3333). These requests can be used to search directories or to open, read, and write to files.

The server uses the connection ID number and the sequence number when it sends a reply to a request. The Completion Code field is filled in to indicate success or failure, and other data might follow in the packet that is used to fulfill the request (such as data read from the file).

Burst Mode

NCP provides commands that can be used to read and write blocks of information in files that reside on the network. However, when larger files must be transferred, a special NCP request (Request Type value=7777), using burst mode, allows the server to send a larger, single burst of data to the client at one time—much larger than the amount allowed by the regular read and write requests (up to 64K).

Burst mode capabilities can be found on NetWare 3.0 and later servers.

The actual mechanics of burst mode involve more than just sending larger amounts of data in a single operation. The client first performs testing to determine a value that will be used for the Interpacket Gap Time (IPG) and the size of the data request (the burst windows size). The window size might vary during the history of the connection, based on how successful communications are. When data is lost during a transmission, the client can send a request to the server to transmit only fragments of the original data stream, those that were not correctly received.

An error condition such as this causes the window size to be reduced. As communications continue with no problems, the window size gradually increases.

Request Being Processed Response

When a client does not receive a response to a request after a timeout period, it will send in a duplicate request. If the server is heavily loaded, it might send back a request that has a request type value of 9999, which is the Request Being Processed type. This is an indication to the client that the request has been received, but that the server is just too busy to do anything about at it at the time. This reply does not guarantee the client that the request ever will get answered, however. It only lets the client know that it can reset its timer and wait longer if need be.

When the client's timer expires, it can send another request to the server, which might respond to the request or which might send another message telling the client to wait. This response type is used to help reduce congestion in a busy network by reducing the number of requests transmitted on the network.

Terminating Connections

This request type is used to end a connection between the client and server. The only information needed in this packet, other than the request type (5555), is the sequence number of the request and the connection ID number. The server will respond with a standard response packet (3333) with a completion code of zero to indicate that the connection has been successfully brought to a close.

Unix (NFS)

The Network File Systems (NFS) protocol consists of several different protocols that perform specific functions. Sun Microsystems has published the specifications for NFS so that other vendors can easily implement these protocols to allow for remote mounting of file systems independent of the operating system of the computers. RFC 1094 defines the most widely used version of NFS (version 2). RFC 1813 documents version 3, which adds better support for wide area networking. If you think you will be involved in troubleshooting NFS on the network, you should find out on which version your NFS software is based and become familiar with these documents.

NFS is built on routines made up of *remote procedure calls (RPC)*. XDR is used as the data format so that data from different systems can be represented in a common format for interchange. In addition, the *Mount* protocol is used to make the initial connection to a remote file system. Because NFS is built in this layered fashion, and problems can occur at any level, you will need to understand not only how the NFS protocol functions, but also RPC, XDR, and the Mount protocol.

Protocol Components: Remote Procedure Call Protocol (RPC)

RPC is a simple client/server protocol application. RPC defines the interaction between a client, which formats a request for execution by the server, and the server, which executes the client's request on the local system. The server performs whatever processing is required and returns the data and control of the procedure to the client. Sun developed RPC for use in NFS, but it has since been employed quite usefully by many other client/server-based products.

The rpcbind daemon (a process that runs in the background waiting for requests) runs on both the client and the server and is responsible for implementing RPC protocol exchanges between hosts on the network.

A service is a group of RPC procedures that have been grouped together into programs. A unique number is used to identify each service, which means that more than one service can operate at any given time. An application that needs to use a service can use the different programs that make up the service to perform specific actions. For example, when designing an NFS service, one program might be responsible for determining a file's attributes, and another program can be responsible for the actual transfer of data between the client and server computers.

The unique service number is used to identify different network services that run on a particular system and the mapping for this is usually found in the file /etc/rpc. The RFC that defines RPC sets forth numbers used for many common services, and these are shown in Table 33.3.

Table 33.3   Numbers Used to Identify RPC Services

Unique Service Number	Name of Service
100000	portmapper
100001	rstat_svc
100002	rusersd
100003	nfs
100004	ypserv
100005	mountd
100007	ypbind
100008	walld
100009	yppasswdd
100010	etherstatd
100011	rquotad
100012	sprayd
100013	3270_mapper
100014	rje_mapper
100015	selection_svc
100016	database_svc
100017	rexd
100018	alis
100019	sched
100020	llockmgr
100021	nlockmgr
100022	x25.inr
100023	statmon
100024	status
100026	bootparam
100028	ypupdated
100029	keyserv
100069	ypxfrd
150001	pcnfsd

The portmapper service (using port 111 for UDP or TCP) manages the port numbers used in TCP/IP communications. Because there can be more than one open connection between a client and server, a *port number* is used to identify each connection.

Don't confuse port numbers with the numbers assigned to services. Service numbers are used to identify a particular RPC service. *Port numbers* identify connections between two computers that use a service.

External Data Representation (XDR)

A common format is used when exchanging data between computer systems that are running different operating systems. Some use ASCII code for text, whereas others use UNICODE. Some use big-endian encoding techniques, whereas others use little-endian, which determines the order in which bytes are used to represent data (left to right or right to left). It is even more complicated when you look at how different computer systems represent numeric data in memory or storage. When using a multiple-byte value to represent a floating point number, for example, you need to know which bits are used for the exponent and which are used for the mantissa.

NFS uses the External Data Representation (XDR) standard for data exchange. The details of XDR are covered in RFC 1014. It is a C-like notation for representing data, not a programming language itself. An item, such as a character or numeric value, is represented in XDR by using four bytes (32 bits), with the lower bytes the most significant.

Other encoding features of XDR include the following:

- Signed integers are stored using "twos" complement notation and range in value from –2,147,483,648 to +2,147,483,647.
- Unsigned integers can range from 0 to 4,294,967,295.
- Hyper integers and unsigned hyper integers are eight bytes in size and can be used to represent larger integers.
- Floating point formats are also defined, and so are the enum type (familiar to C programmers) and a Boolean type.
- Structures, arrays, constants, and many other data types are also defined.

XDR provides an extensible data description format that makes implementing NFS on multiple hardware and software platforms much easier.

The NFS Protocol and Mount Protocol

The NFS protocol is a set of procedures (called *primitives*) that are executed via RPC to allow an action to be performed on a remote computer. NFS is a *stateless* protocol, which means that the server does not have to maintain information about the state of each client. If the server (or the network) fails, the client needs only to repeat the operation. The server doesn't have to rebuild any data tables or other structures to recover the state of a client after a failure.

Note

Certain operations, such as file or record locking, do require a *stateful* protocol of some sort, and many implementations of NFS accomplish this by using another protocol to handle the specific function. NFS itself is composed of a set of procedures that deal only with file access.

The RPC procedures that make up the NFS protocol are the following:

- **Null**—The "do nothing" routine. It is provided in all RPC services and is used for testing and timing operations.
- **Get File Attributes**—Gets the file attributes of a file on a remote system.
- **Set File Attributes**—Sets the file attributes of a file on the remote server.
- **Get File System Root**—No longer used. Instead, the Mount protocol performs this function.
- **Look Up a Filename**—Returns a file handle used to access a file.
- **Read From Symbolic Link**—Returns information about symbolic links to a file on the remote server.
- **Read From File**—Procedure to read data from a file on a remote system.
- **Write to Cache**—Cache feature to be included in version 3 of the protocol.
- **Write to File**—Used to write data to a file on a remote server.
- **Create File**—Creates a file on the remote server.
- **Remove File**—Deletes a file on the remote server.
- **Rename File**—Renames a file on the remote server.
- **Create Link to File**—Creates a hard link (in the same file system) to a file.
- **Create Symbolic Link**—Creates a symbolic link (can be used to link a file across file systems). A symbolic link is a pointer to a file.
- **Create Directory**—Creates a directory on the remote server.
- **Remove Directory**—Deletes an empty directory on the remote server.
- **Read From Directory**—Obtains a list of files from a directory on the server.
- **Get File System Attributes**—Returns information about the file system on the remote server, such as the total size and available free space.

There is no provision in these procedures to open or close a file. Because NFS is a stateless protocol, it doesn't handle file opens or closes. The Mount protocol performs this function and returns a file handle to NFS. The mountd daemon runs on both the client and server computer and is responsible for maintaining a list of current connections. Most implementations of NFS recover from client crashes by having the client send a message to the NFS server when it boots, telling it to unmount all its previous connections to the client.

When compared to the NFS protocol, the Mount protocol consists of only a very few procedures:

- **Null**—The "do nothing" procedure just like the one listed under the NFS protocol.
- **MNT**—Mounts a file system and returns to the client a file handle and the name of the remote file system.
- **UNMT**—The opposite of the MNT procedure. It unmounts a file system and removes from its table the reference to it.
- **UMNTALL**—Similar to the UNMT procedure, but this one unmounts all remote file systems that are being used by the NFS client.
- **EXPORT**—Displays a list of exported file systems.
- **DUMP**—Displays a list of file systems on a server that are currently mounted by a client.

Configuring NFS Servers and Clients

The biod daemon runs on the client system and communicates with the remote NFS server. The daemon also processes the data that is transferred between the NFS client and NFS server. The RPC daemon must also be running and either UDP or TCP needs to be running, depending on which one your version of NFS uses as a transport. Users can mount a file system offered by an NFS server, provided that they are not prevented from mounting the file system by the server, by using the mount command.

Note

The commands shown in the following sections might differ from one version of Unix to another. As always with Unix or Linux, consult the man pages to determine the exact syntax for commands and the locations of files mentioned in relation to the commands.

NFS Client Daemons

On the client side of the NFS process, there are actually three daemon processes that are used. The first is biod, which stands for block input/output daemon. This daemon processes the input/output with the NFS server on behalf of the user process that is making requests of the remote file system. If you use NFS heavily on a client, you can improve performance by starting up more than one biod daemon. The syntax used to start the daemon is as follows:

/etc/biod [*number of daemon processes*]

This daemon is usually started in the /etc/rc.local startup file. Modify this file if you want to permanently change the number of daemons running on the client system. You can first test by executing the command online to determine how many daemons you need to start and then place the necessary commands in the startup file.

When deciding performance issues, remember that on a heavily loaded client, making a change in one place might result in poorer performance from another part of the system. So, don't assume that you need a lot of extra daemons running unless you can first show that they are needed and do improve performance. Each daemon process is like any other process running on the system, and it uses up system resources, especially memory. Begin by using one or two daemons if you are using a workstation dedicated to one user. For a multiple-user computer, test your performance by increasing the number of daemons until NFS performance is satisfactory (all the time checking, of course, other performance indicators to be sure the overall system impact is justified).

Although multiple daemons mean that NFS requests can be processed in parallel, remember that the network itself might be a bottleneck. Additional biod daemons will not increase throughput when the network itself is the limiting factor.

Also note that the biod daemon is a client process. You should not run it on an NFS server unless that server is also a client of another NFS server.

In addition to the biod daemon, the lockd and statd daemons also run on the client. For more information on these, see the section "Server Daemons," later in this chapter.

The mount Command

The mount command is used to mount a local file system, and you can also use the command to mount a remote NFS file system. The syntax for using mount to make available a file system being exported by an NFS server is as follows:

```
mount -F nfs -o options machine:filesystem mountpoint
```

In some versions of Unix, the syntax for mounting a remote NFS file system is a little different. For example, in SCO Unix you use a lowercase f and an uppercase NFS:

```
mount -f NFS -o options machine:filesystem mountpoint
```

In BSD Unix, there is a command called mountnfs, which uses the system call mount to perform most of its functions. This version of the mount command comes with a lot of additional parameters, including the capability to specify on the mount command line whether to use UPD or TCP as the underlying transport mechanism.

The value you supply for *machine:filesystem* should be the host name of the remote server that is exporting the file system you want to mount for *machine*. Substitute the name of the file system for *filesystem*. The following example causes the remote file system on host zira, called /usr/projectx/docs, to be made accessible in the local file system hierarchy at the /usr/docs directory:

```
mount -F nfs -o ro zira:usr/projectx/docs /usr/docs
```

This is the same way you mount other local file systems into the local hierarchy. Under the /usr/docs directory, you can access any other subdirectories that exist on host zira under the /usr/projectx/docs directory.

The -o parameter can be used to specify options for the mount command. In the preceding example, the letters ro for the option were used to make the remote file system *read only* by users on the local computer.

Other options that can be used when mounting a remote file system include the following:

- **rw**—Mounts the file system for local read-write access, which is the default.
- **ro**—Mounts the file system for local read-only access.
- **suid**—Allows setuid execution.
- **nosuid**—Disallows setuid execution.
- **timeo=x**—Specifies a timeout value (in tenths of a second). The mount command will fail if it cannot mount the remote file system within this time limit.
- **retry=x**—The mount command will attempt to mount the remote file system *x* number of times, with each attempt lasting for the length of time specified by the timeo parameter.
- **soft**—Causes an error to be returned if the mount is unsuccessful. Opposite of the hard option.
- **hard**—Causes the mount attempt to continue until it succeeds. Opposite of the soft option.

For more command-line parameters and options, see the man page for the mount command for your particular system.

Caution

A computer can be an NFS server, an NFS client, or perhaps both a server and a client. However, you should not try to mount an exported file system on the same server that is exporting it. This can lead to looping problems, causing unpredictable behavior.

The *mountpoint* is the path to the location in the local file system where the remote NFS file system will appear, and this path must exist before the mount command is issued. Any files existing in the mountpoint directory will no longer be accessible to users after a remote file system is attached to the directory with the mount command, so do not use just any directory. Note that the files are not lost. They reappear when the remote file system is unmounted.

Using the fstab File to Mount File Systems at Boot Time

When you have file systems that need to be remounted each time the system reboots, you can use the file /etc/fstab to do this. This file is also used to mount local file systems, so be careful when making edits. The format for a record is as follows:

```
filesystem  directoryname  type  options  frequency  pass
```

The filesystem field for a record used to mount a remote file system includes the server hostname and the pathname of the remote file system separated by a colon (hostname:path). The second field, directoryname, is the path for the mountpoint on the local system, which indicates where the remote system is mounted and made available for access. The next field, type, is used to specify the file system type, which can be any of the following:

- **ufs**—A typical local Unix file system.
- **mfs**—The memory file system.
- **nfs**—An NFS remote file system.
- **swap**—A disk partition used for swapping by the virtual memory system.
- **msdos**—An MS-DOS compatible file system.
- **cd9660**—A CD-ROM file system as defined by ISO 9660.
- **procfs**—A filesystem structure used to access data about processes.
- **kernfs**—A filesystem structure used to access kernel parameters.

The options field is used for a comma-delimited list of mounting options (such as rw, ro, and so on). frequency is used in determining when a file system will be "dumped" for backup purposes. This can usually be set to zero for NFS systems mounted on a client because it is usually the NFS server that is responsible for making backups of local data. The final field, pass, can also be set to zero most of the time for an NFS file system mounted on a client. This field is used by fsck utility to determine on which pass it is to check this file system.

Caution

The order in which you place entries in this file can be important. For example, do not place a command in this file to mount a remote NFS file system on a mount point unless the file system that contains the local mount has been mounted earlier in the file!

Configuring Server Daemons

For an NFS server, choose a computer that has the hardware capabilities needed to support your network clients. If the NFS server will be used to allow clients to view seldom-used documentation, a less-powerful hardware configuration might be all you need. If the server is going to be used to export a large number of directories, say from a powerful disk storage subsystem, the hardware requirements become much more important. You will have to make capacity judgements concerning the CPU power, disk subsystems, and network adapter card performance.

Setting up an NFS server is simple task. Create a list of the directories that are to be exported and place entries for these in the /etc/exports file on the server. At boot time the exportfs program starts and obtains information from this file. The exportfs program uses this data to make exported directories available to clients that make requests.

Server-Side Daemons

The nfsd daemon process handles requests from NFS clients for the server. The nfsd daemon interprets requests and sends them to the I/O system to perform the requests' actual functions. The daemon communicates with the biod daemon on the client, processing requests and returning data to the requestor's daemon.

An NFS server will usually be set up to serve multiple clients. You can set up multiple copies of the nfsd daemon on the server so that the server can handle multiple client requests in a timely manner.

The syntax for the command to start the daemon is as follows:

```
/etc/nfsd [number of nfs daemons to start]
```

For example, to start up five copies of the nfsd daemon at boot time, modify your startup scripts to include the following command:

```
/etc/nfsd 5
```

Unix systems and the utilities that are closely associated with them are continually being updated or improved. Some new versions include using the concept of threads to make it possible for a daemon to be implemented as a multithreaded process, capable of handling many requests at one time. Digital Unix 4.0 (now Compaq True64 Unix) is an operating system that provides a multithreaded NFS server daemon.

Other daemons the NFS server runs include the lockd daemon to handle file locking and the statd daemon, which helps coordinate the status of current file locks.

Sharing File Systems: The exportfs Command

At system boot time, the exportfs program is usually started by the /sbin/init.d/nfs.server script file, but this can vary, depending on the particular implementation of Unix you are using. The exportfs program reads the information in the /etc/exports configuration file.

The syntax for this command varies, depending on what actions you want to perform:

```
/usr/sbin/exportfs [-auv]
/usr/sbin/exportfs [-uv] [dir ...]
/usr/sbin/exportfs -i [-o options] [-v] [dir ...]
```

Parameters and options you can use with this command are as follows:

- **a**—Causes exportfs to read the /etc/exports file and export all directories for which it finds an entry. When used with the -u parameter, it causes all directories to be unexported.
- **i**—Specifies options in the /etc/exports file to be associated with each directory to be exported. It is used to tell exportfs to ignore the options you placed in this file.
- **u**—Used to stop exporting a directory (or all directories if used with the -a option).
- **v**—Tells exportfs to operate in "verbose" mode, giving you additional feedback in response to your commands.

The options you can specify after the -o qualifier are the same as you use in the /etc/exports file (see the following section, "Configuration Files").

To export or unexport (stop sharing) all entries found in the /etc/exports file, use the -a or -u option. This is probably the most often used form because you can specify the other options you need on a per-directory basis in the /etc/exports file. This example causes all directories listed in /etc/exports to be available for use by remote clients:

```
exportfs -a
```

The following example causes your NFS server to stop sharing all the directories listed for export in the /etc/exports file:

```
exportfs -au
```

The second form can be used to export or unexport (stop exporting) a particular directory (or directories) instead of all directories. You specify the directories on the command line. You can use this form if you want to stop sharing a particular directory because of system problems or maintenance, for example. Using the following syntax causes the NFS server to stop sharing the /etc/user/accounting directory with remote users:

```
exportfs -u /etc/users/accounting
```

The next form of the command can be used to ignore the options found in the /etc/exports file. Instead, you can supply them (using the -o parameter) on the command line. You will probably use this in special cases because you could just as easily change the options in the /etc/exports file if the change were a permanent one. If, for example, you decided that you wanted to make an exported directory that is currently set to be read-write to be read-only, you could use the following command:

```
exportfs -o ro /etc/users/purch
```

You can also dismount and mount remote file systems using different options when troubleshooting or when researching the commands you will need when preparing to upgrade a network segment where connections need to change.

If changes are made to the /etc/exports file while the system is running, use the exportfs command (with the -a parameter) to make the changes take effect. To get a list of directories that are currently being exported, you can execute the command with no options, and it will show you a list.

Of course, it is not necessarily a good idea to make changes on-the-fly without keeping track of the connections. When you decide to perform online testing to mount or dismount file systems, be sure that you are not going to impact any users who are currently making productive use of the resources. To make testing more foolproof and to provide a quick back-out procedure, try copying the /etc/exports file to keep a safe starting copy and making changes to the copied file, loading it by using the exportfs -a command. When you determine that something has been done incorrectly, you can simply use the backup copy of the file you have made to restore the status quo.

Configuration Files

To make a file system or a directory in a file system available for export, add the pathnames to the /etc/exports file. The format for an entry in this file is as follows:

```
directory [-option, ...]
```

The term *directory* is a pathname for the directory you want to share with other systems. The options that you can include are the following:

- **ro**—This makes the directory available to remote users in a read-only mode. The default is read-write, and remote users can change data in files on your system if you do not specify ro here.

- **rw=*hostnames***—This specifies a specific host or hosts that you want to have read-write access. If a host is not included in *hostnames*, it will have only read access to the exported file system.

- **anon=*uid***—Use this parameter to set the *uid* (user ID) that will be used for anonymous users, if allowed.

- **root=*hostnames***—Users who have root access on a system listed in *hostnames* can gain root access on the exported file system.

- **access=*client***—A client that can have mount access to this file system.

For example:

```
/etc/users/acctpay -access=acct
/etc/users/docs -ro
/etc/users/reports/monthend -rw=ono
```

In this file, the first directory, /etc/user/acctpay, which stores accounts payable files, will be shared with a group called acct—the accounting department. The /docs directory can be accessed by anyone in read-only mode. The /reports/monthend directory can be accessed in read-only mode by most users, but users on the computer whose host name is ono will have read-write access.

Caution

You should give considerable thought to the matter before using NFS to export sensitive or critical data. If the information is subject to cause great harm if it is altered or exposed, you should not treat it lightly and make it available on the network via NFS. NFS is better suited for ordinary user data files and programs, directories, or other resources that are shared by a large number of users. There are not enough security mechanisms in place when using many implementations of NFS to make it a candidate for a high-security environment.

Automounting File Systems

The Mount protocol takes care of the details of making a connection for the NFS client to the NFS server. This means that it is necessary to use the mount command to make the remote file system available at a mount point in the local file system. To make this process even easier, the automountd daemon has been created. This daemon listens for NFS requests and mounts a remote file system locally on an as-needed basis. The mounted condition usually persists for a number of minutes (the default is usually five minutes) in order to satisfy any further requests.

As with other daemons, the automountd daemon is started at boot time in the /etc/rc.local file. You can enter it as a command after the system is up and running, if needed. When a client computer tries to access a file that is referenced in an automount map, the automountd daemon checks to see if the file system for that directory is currently mounted. The daemon temporarily mounts the file system so that the user's request can be fulfilled, if needed.

The *automount map* is a file that tells the daemon where the file system to be mounted is located and where it should be mounted in the local file system. Options can also be included for the mount process, for example, to make it read-write or read-only. The automountd daemon mounts a file system under the mountpoint /tmp_mnt. It then creates a symbolic link at the mountpoint the user recognizes to point to this temporary mountpoint.

Mounting File Systems Using the automount Command

The /etc/rc.local file usually contains the command used to start the automountd daemon. This daemon is responsible for processing NFS mount requests as they are defined in special files called *map files*.

The syntax for the automount command is as follows:

```
automount [-mnTv] [-D name=value] [-f master-file]
[-M mount-directory] [-tl duration] [-tm interval]
[-tw interval][directory mapname [- mount-options]]
```

The options you can use are the following:

- **m**—Ignores directory-mapname pairs that are listed in the master map file.

- **n**—Dynamic mounts are to be disabled. If a directory is already mounted, the user's request will succeed, but no further file systems will be mounted.

- **T**—Causes the daemon to provide trace information about each request. The output is sent to standard output.

- **v**—Verbose; causes the daemon to send status messages to the console.

- **D** *name=value*—Defines automount environment variables. The text associated with value is assigned to the variable name.

- **f** *master map file name*—Provides the name of the master map file to the automount daemon.

- **M** *mountpoint directory*—Specifies a directory to use for the temporary mount point (one other than */tmp_mnt*).

- **tl** *time value*—Specifies how long a file system should stay mounted after the last user request before automount automatically dismounts it. The default is usually five minutes.

- **tm** *time value*—The amount of time (in seconds) that should elapse between attempts to mount a file system (the default is 30 seconds).

- **tw** *time value*—The amount of time (in seconds) between attempts to unmount a file system that has exceeded its cached time. The default is usually one minute.

- *mount_options*—Options to be applied to all the directories listed in the map file. Any options listed in a map file override those listed here on the command line.

Master Maps

The automount daemon uses the master map to obtain a list of maps. The master map also contains mount options for those maps. The master map file is usually named /etc/auto.master. The syntax for the entries in this file is as follows:

```
mount-point map [mount-options]
```

mount-point is the pathname of the local directory for an indirect map specified in the map field. If the map specified in the map column is a direct map, the mountpoint is usually /-.

The data listed under the *map* field is used to find the map that contains the actual mountpoints and the locations of the remote file systems. Any data you supply for *mount-options* will be used when mounting directories in the map file associated with it.

Following is an example of a master map file. Lines that begin with # are comments:

```
#mount-point  map             options
/etc/users    /etc/auto.usr   -ro
/-            /etc/auto.direct -rw
```

When the automount daemon determines that access is needed for files found in the /etc/users directory, it will look for another map file, named auto.usr, to get the rest of the information. The -ro options are specified for this entry and will be applied to the file system designated in the auto.usr map file.

The argument /- is used to specify that a map file it points to, in this case auto.direct, is a direct map file or one that contains the mountpoints and the remote file system information needed to complete the mounts.

Direct Maps

The remote file systems can be mounted into the local file system, and the mountpoint should be information you will find in a direct map. The construction of this file is very direct. The syntax for an entry is as follows:

```
key  [mount-options]  location
```

The *key* field is the mountpoint to be used for this entry. *mount-options* are the options used with the mountd daemon discussed earlier in this chapter. The *location* field should be in the format of *machine:pathname*, where *machine* is the hostname of the remote system that the file system actually resides on and *pathname* is the path to the directory on that file system. You can specify multiple locations to provide for redundancy. The automount daemon queries all locations in this case and takes the first one to respond to its requests.

Indirect Maps

In an indirect map file, most fields are the same as in a direct map file, except that the first field (*key*) is not a full pathname. It is a pointer to an entry in the master map file. You can list multiple directories in an indirect map file, and each of these remote file system directories will be mounted under the mountpoint designated in the master map file that contains a reference to the indirect map.

Check the man pages on your system to be sure of the syntax for options used in map files because they might vary just like options do for the mount command among different Unix systems.

Troubleshooting NFS Problems

Many of the TCP/IP utilities that are used for troubleshooting can be employed when trying to diagnose and fix problems having to do with NFS. For example, if a remote file system suddenly becomes unavailable, it only makes sense to first determine whether the remote server is still functioning. You can do this quickly by using the ping command to establish basic network connectivity. A failure to communicate using this small utility indicates that there is a server problem at the other end or perhaps a network malfunction that is preventing communications with the remote system. When troubleshooting, this tells you that the problem is most likely not one to be found in the NFS subsystem.

◄◄ You can find detailed information about using various TCP/IP utilities for troubleshooting purposes in Chapter 22, "Troubleshooting Tools for TCP/IP Networks."

The tracert utility also can be used when ping fails to determine how far along the network route the packet is getting on its trip to the remote system. Use this when trying to isolate the particular point of failure in the network.

There is a useful command specific to NFS that can be used to display statistical information about NFS. It is nfsstat. This command shows you statistics about NFS and RPC. The syntax for nfsstat is as follows:

```
nfsstat [-cnrsz] [vmunix.n] [core.n]
```

The options you can use are the following:

- **c**—Shows only client-side information.
- **s**—Shows only server-side information.
- **n**—Shows only statistics for NFS, both client- and server-side.
- **r**—Shows only statistics for RPC, both client- and server-side.
- **z**—Is used to zero out the statistics. You can combine it with other options to zero out statistics referred to by those options (for example, -zc to zero client size information). Write access to /dev/mem is required to zero statistics.
- **core.n**—The name of the system's core image.
- **vmunix.n**—The name of kernel image.

All statistics are shown if you do not supply any parameters when executing the command. The statistical data that will be displayed depends on the options you choose. For an example of the detailed data you can obtain using this command, see the man page for nfsstat for your particular Unix or Linux system.

Examining the output from the nfsstat command can be useful on an ongoing basis to help you establish a baseline for performance evaluations you will need to make at a later time when thinking about upgrading. You can easily selectively store data output by this command in a text file or spreadsheet. You can also create a simple script file that can be used to gather statistics using this command on a periodic basis, storing the results in a temporary directory for your later review.

For example, the command nfsstat -s displays statistics for the NFS server as follows:

```
# nfsstat -s

Server RPC:
calls       badcalls    nullrecv    badlen
23951       0           0           0

Server NFS:
calls       badcalls
23164       0
null        getattr     setattr     root        lookup      readlink
1   0%      64   0%     0   0%      0   0%      121   0%    0   0%
read        wrcache     write       create      remove      rename
22951 99%   0   0%      0   0%      0   0%      0   0%      0   0%
link        symlink     mkdir       rmdir       readdir     fsstat
0   0%      0   0%      0   0%      0   0%      25   0%     2   0%
```

In this display you can see statistics for the total number of remote procedure calls, along with information about those RPC calls that relate to NFS. In addition to the total number of calls, you can see statistics concerning the following items for RPC:

- **badcalls**—Number of calls that were rejected by the server.
- **nullrecv**—Number of times that there was no RPC packet available when the server was trying to receive.
- **badlen**—Number of packets that were too short.

In addition, some implementations might show additional RPC fields. For the NFS server, there are many columns of information displayed, showing you the number of read and writes, along with other useful information. For example, you can examine cache usage (*wrcache*), or determine when other file commands are used to create or remove directories.

If the number of badcalls begins to become significant when compared to the overall number of calls, a problem obviously exists. If the value displayed for badlen is consistently a higher percentage of the overall number of calls, a client might be misconfigured or a network problem might be causing packets to become corrupted. Again, you may see different or additional fields of information in the display, depending on the Unix and NFS implementation you are using. A careful review of the documentation for your system will give you a good idea of the performance to be expected from your server and the kinds of events to look for.

Microsoft Distributed File System (DFS)

For the Microsoft Windows NT 4.0 Server platform, you can obtain Microsoft Distributed File System Version 4.1 from Microsoft (www.microsoft.com). The downloadable version can be installed on Microsoft Windows NT Server 4.0 systems and can be used to provide a service to clients similar to that offered by NFS.

Like NFS, DFS employs a tree-structure for file systems. A directory that is being imported by a client is attached at a point somewhere in the local file system, where it is then made available to applications as if the directory and its files were local.

Windows 2000 includes DFS as an integral part of the operating system. The interface is written as a snap-in to the Microsoft Management Console (MMC) tool, making administration a simpler process. A wizard prompts you through setting up a DFS root, and from there on out you can add, modify, or remove directory paths from the DFS tree. Paths represented in the DFS tree can come from one or more servers on the network. A tree is not bound by a single host.

In Windows NT 4.0, directory replication allowed you to create copies of directories on multiple systems, keeping them in sync. This functionality no longer exists in Windows 2000. Instead, DFS is used. DFS allows you to move away from the *server\sharename* concept to one based on the domain. Instead of having to remember (or browse and find) on which server a particular file share is hosted, you can use DFS to create shares that are global to the domain. That is, if you're a member of the domain, you can specify the share as *domainname/share*. DFS also allows for replication. This means that you can have more than one copy of the data being shared, but only have to use the global domain-wide share name to connect. This provides for some fault tolerance. If a server goes down that hosts a replica of a share, then the other servers that contain copies of the share can be connected to by users. Note that this does *not* provide any kind of failover if a server crashes. The user can, however, restart their work by reconnecting to the share. The connection will be made to another replica of the file share.

Important terms to understand when dealing with DFS are

- **Root**—A server can have only one root installed. It is just about the same thing as a file share, with a few differences, which will become apparent shortly.

- **DFS link**—Under the root you create DFS links. These are links to file shares that will be available under the root you have created. This means you can create a single root, and yet place multiple shared directories under the root so that only one file share connection is necessary. If not, users would have to connect to each directory as a separate file share.

- **Replica**—You can create shares that replicate the data in other shares. This can be done to provide for both load balancing and a degree of fault tolerance.

Creating a DFS Root

Creating a DFS tree is not a complicated task when using a graphical interface such as the one provided by the MMC and by the wizards that walk you through setting up your file system. To create a new DFS root, use the following steps:

1. Click Start, Programs, Administrative Tools, Distributed File System.

2. When the management console appears, select New DFS root from the Action menu. A wizard pop ups. Click Next.

3. You can select to create a file system that makes use of the Active Directory for storing the DFS configuration information. You can also select to not use the Active Directory. For the purposes of this example, I've chosen to not use the Active Directory. After making the selection, click Next.

4. The next dialog box prompts you to enter the name of the server that will host the distributed file system. The default is the server on which you are running the wizard. Click Next to continue.

5. The wizard next asks if you want to use an existing share or create a new share that will be used by users to connect to the file system. In Figure 33.4 you can see that a new share will be

created. The path for the share and the name that will be used have been filled in. If the path does not yet exist, it will be created. Click Next to continue.

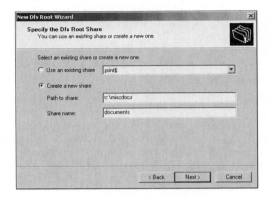

Figure 33.4   You can use an existing share from the drop-down menu or create a new share for the file system.

6. You will next be asked to provide a name for the DFS root. The default is the server name followed by a slash and then the share name you specified in the previous dialog box. You can also enter a comment that describes the share. Click Next when you have finished and are ready to continue.

7. Finally the wizard displays a summary of the information you have entered. Click the Finish button to complete the process of creating the new DFS root.

When finished, your DFS root will show up in the tree structure in the left pane of the MMC, as you can see in Figure 33.5.

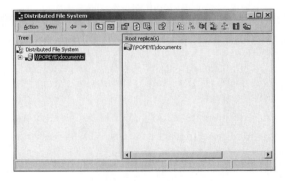

Figure 33.5   The new DFS root is now displayed in the MMC.

Adding Links to the DFS Root

After you've created the initial root for your file system, you can then add one or more links. Links, as you will recall, are actual directories (or folders, depending on which terminology you prefer) that will be accessible from your DFS root.

To create a link, right-click on the root in the left-side pane of the console. From the menu, select New Dfs link. In Figure 33.6 you can see the dialog box used to input the information about the link. First you need to enter a name that will be used as a logical association for the link. That is, when the user connects to the share, this name will show up as a folder that he can use. You can see that in the next field you are asked to fill in the actual pathname for the folder being offered as part of the DFS share.

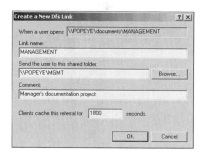

Figure 33.6   You can specify a logical name that users will see so that they don't have to remember the actual directory path.

The title for this field says it all: "Send the user to this shared folder:". In the example in Figure 33.6 the folder that users will see is called MANAGEMENT. The shared directory that contains the actual files is \\POPEYE\MGMT. Note that there is also a comment field in this dialog box. In a large network with many resources, you'll appreciate this information when managing your network. Finally, the last field allows you to specify how long a client will cache the link. When the client makes the initial connection, the connection will be made to the actual directory (that is, the link name will be translated to the actual share name \\POPEYE\MGMT, transparently to the user. However, the user's computer will check back with the DFS server when the cache timer expires.

In Figure 33.7 you can see a simple DFS set up with a single sharename (\\POPEYE\DOCUMENTS) to which users can connect. When the connection is made, two folders will be available: MANAGEMENT and SPECIFICATIONS.

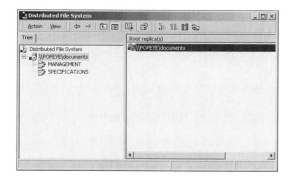

Figure 33.7   Each root can have links to multiple shares associated with it.

Now this would be great if it just stopped here and allowed you to consolidate file shares on a single server into a single share. However, keep in mind that DFS is a domainwide file system. In the dialog box shown in Figure 33.6 you can easily specify a file share located on another server in the domain. Thus, you can hide the physical location of files from users. Instead of having to remember servers and share names, the user only has to remember the share name. Because the share name is domain-wide, you can't use the same share name on one server that you do on another. Users can then simply connect to the share *domainname/share*. They don't need to know where the actual folders in this share are located.

You can use the Action menu to add or delete a DFS root. You can also use the Action menu to manage links and replication.

DFS does not add any additional security features to the file system. Instead, the usual rights and permissions that are already in place on the server are used when evaluating a client's access to a file or directory in the DFS tree.

One major difference between NFS and DFS is that DFS is built using SMB messaging techniques for the most part and is not compatible with all NFS servers. If you have a mixed-environment network where most of your data files are offered via NFS on Unix servers, it would be more economical to acquire PC-based NFS client software than it would be to replace all your existing servers with NT machines.

Rights and Permissions

SOME OF THE MAIN TOPICS IN THIS CHAPTER ARE

User-Level and Share-Level Resource Permissions

Microsoft Windows 95/Windows 98 Share-Level Security

Windows NT 4.0 and Windows 2000 Share-Level Security

Assigning User Rights Under Windows NT and Windows 2000

NTFS Permissions

NetWare

Unix and Linux

Controlling access to system and network resources is a most important topic to understand. In a homogeneous network where all file servers and clients are of one particular brand name, it can still be difficult to keep track of all file and print shares and which users need access to them. When you begin to mix components to create a more diverse network, you can end up with the requirement to understand the access restrictions imposed by more than one operating system, and also by the restrictions imposed between them.

In general, two kinds of identifying values are used to decide on access. The first is an identifier that uniquely specifies the user who is logged on to the system and the specific rights, as defined by the user's operating system. These rights are definitions of the kinds of actions that can be taken on the system by the users.

The next set of values is the permissions that are placed on each resource. Permissions usually are granular, giving permission separately to read, write, execute, or delete a file or directory. Depending on the operating system, the names used for these permissions can vary, and other types of permissions and combinations of these basic types can be found.

The important point to remember when setting up new users or resources, or when troubleshooting existing connections, is that you might need to look at both ends: What rights does the user possess and what access controls (permissions) exist on the resource? Both of these factors determine what users can do on the network. In this chapter, we will take a quick look at the concepts of rights and permissions in several major operating systems and discuss some of the methods used to solve problems related to them.

User-Level and Share-Level Resource Permissions

There are two basic means for protecting resources offered on a network. Each method strives to make the protected resource available only to a user who has been authorized to access it. They do so in different ways, however, and grant different kinds of access.

Share-level security involves securing connections to a network share point by a password. Users who know the name of the share point and the password can connect to the share point. All subdirectories and files found under the share point are accessible by using only the single password.

User-level security involves linking access controls further down the file system and does not stop at placing a single password on an entire tree of resources (although you can do it that way if you want). Instead, access permissions can be placed on any directory or file in the tree. When a user connects to a resource protected by user-level security mechanisms, the user must first authenticate himself (log on to the server). The user then is granted access rights to each file or directory on the resource, each by the access control restrictions placed on it by inheritance or implicitly.

Obviously, the user level of security permissions provides the administrator a finer granularity of detail when deciding on resource access decisions. By using a logon username to identify the user who is accessing a resource, an audit trail with more specific details can also be kept for troubleshooting purposes.

Microsoft Windows 95/Windows 98 Share-Level Security

Microsoft networks allow for both share-level and user-level permissions on network resources. All versions of Windows operating systems allow each computer in the network to offer a directory as a file share on the local area network and protect it with a password. For example, you don't have to use a Windows 2000 server to offer file shares on the LAN; you can do so with Windows 2000 Professional or Windows Me.

This distributed security database (each computer has its own security database that stores the share-level password) means that a user might need to learn several passwords, depending on the number of share connections that were needed for his workstation. A simple solution to this would be to use the same password for each share. However, the drawback to this is that anyone who knows the password for one file share would know the password for other file shares! So, when all is taken into account, using share-level security is not really a good idea in today's networks.

Windows NT 4.0 and Windows 2000 Share-Level Security

Whereas earlier versions of Windows operating systems used the FAT (File Allocation Table) and FAT32 method for formatting disk storage, Windows NT and Windows 2000 allow you to format a disk partition using the NTFS file system. FAT and FAT32 don't provide the mechanisms to store security attributes, such as access control lists (ACLs), for files or directories.

NTFS, however, does allow you to store a lot more information about a file or a directory. When you use the NTFS file system to format a disk, you can apply *user-level* security permissions on individual files or directories. For a more secure environment, the NTFS partition is the choice to make. Additionally, the Windows 2000 operating system allows for other features that make NTFS a more secure choice, including the capability to encrypt and decrypt data on-the-fly when storing or retrieving it from disk.

Note

About the only reason I can think of to format a disk using FAT or FAT32 when you are using Windows NT/2000 (and now Windows XP) is if you plan to dual-boot the computer with an older operating system such as Windows 95 or 98. In that case, you have no choice because Windows 95/98 can't be installed on an NTFS partition. However, this sort of dual-boot setup should be used only in an unsecure environment, such as a test laboratory that is not connected to the regular network, or in your home where you don't have such strict security requirements. And even then, you should consider the implications of using FAT or FAT32 on a home computer because many hackers regularly scan IP addresses looking for vulnerable systems. If you stay online for extended periods of time browsing the Internet—or if you're online all the time using a broadband connection such as a cable or DSL modem, then a FAT-based disk is wide open for planting Trojan horse and other malicious programs. If you use NTFS instead, and set up your user accounts correctly, you can potentially head off this sort of problem.

Assigning User Rights Under Windows NT and Windows 2000

Users who are logged in to a Windows NT/2000 computer or domain can be granted rights by the administrator of the computer or the domain. Rights granted to an account that resides on an individual Windows NT/2000 computer are good only for accessing resources on that computer. The security information for the computer is stored locally and applies only to resources on that local system.

Accounts that are created on a domain controller can be used when assigning user rights to resources on computers throughout the domain. For Windows NT 4.0 Server, you can use the User Manager (or User Manager for Domains) utility to grant user rights, put users into groups that can make managing rights easier, and restrict the hours that users can access resources. This utility is found in the Administrative Tools folder and can be used for a variety of other user management tasks.

Windows 2000 Administrative Tools are generally created as snap-ins for the Microsoft Management Console (MMC). By using the MMC to create management tools, it is easy to switch from one MMC console to the next, without having to relearn the mechanics of the particular utility. For example, when using MMC you'll find two panes on the screen. The left pane contains a tree of objects that can be managed. An Action menu presents you with functions you can perform. The right pane is used to display different kinds of information, based on the particular utility and the actions you take.

In Figure 34.1, you can see the MMC with the snap-in for managing domain users and computers loaded. Although the User Manager for Domains was used for Windows NT 4.0 Server computers, this new MMC snap-in is used with Windows 2000 to manage users and computers in the domain. After you've installed a domain controller in a Windows 2000 network, it's already set up and available by clicking Start, Programs, Administrative Tools, Active Directory Computers and Users.

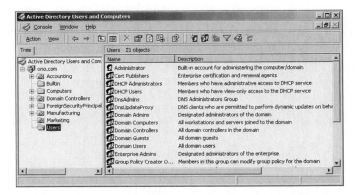

Figure 34.1 Windows 2000 uses the Active Directory Computers and Users MMC snap-in to manage user rights.

In this figure, you can see that the Users folder has been expanded in the left pane. In the right pane you can see user groups and users for the domain.

Note

You still can use the MMC snap-in for managing users and computers to manage other domains. In Windows NT 4.0, you needed to have a trust relationship set up with other domains you wanted to manage from a central location. Because the Active Directory automatically creates transitive (two-way) trust relationships in all domains that are in the same domain tree, you simply can use the first entry in the left pane (Active Directory Users and Computers), and then select Connect to Domain from the Action menu to connect the utility to another domain whose users or computers you want to manage. Essentially, you can use this MMC snap-in to manage all the users and computers throughout the domain tree.

In this chapter, you'll look at the Windows NT 4.0 Server utilities and then learn how to do the same thing in Windows 2000.

Use Groups to Make Managing User Rights Easier

The easiest method for granting rights to users in an environment where you have a large user base is to create user groups consisting of users who need the same kind of access to the same resources.

Then you can grant rights and permissions to the groups instead of each individual user. Users of a group inherit the rights assigned to the group, as well as any additional rights you assign to the user. Also, a user can be a member of more than one group.

Windows NT enables you to use two basic kinds of groups: local groups and global groups. Local groups can be local to a particular computer or can be domain local groups. Global groups are used for grouping users from one domain so that they can be managed as a unit in another domain where the administrator can place the global group into a local group for administrative purposes.

Windows NT computers come with several built-in user groups, which vary depending on the role of the computer in the network. These groups are explained in detail in Chapter 22, "Troubleshooting Tools for TCP/IP Networks." What is important to understand here is that, although NT allows a large number of specific rights to be identified and assigned to users, you can do it on a group basis rather than on an individual one if you want to make user management tasks easier to perform.

Windows NT/2000 User Rights

Windows NT divides user rights into user rights and advanced user rights. Windows 2000 doesn't make this distinction. The list that follows this paragraph first lists the basic user rights for Windows NT 4.0, followed by a list of the advanced user rights. Following this is a list of a few new rights that Windows 2000 brings to the table. Note that Windows 2000 supports all the same rights listed for Windows NT 4.0, in addition to a few new rights.

The advanced group consists of rights that are designed for functions performed by programmers or administrators who might need the capability to perform actions that ordinary users do not. Another use for some of the advanced rights is to give executing programs the capabilities they need to run. For example, some services (background processes) use advanced rights that have no purpose from a user context perspective.

First let's look at the basic user rights you can grant to a user or group:

- **Manage auditing and security log**—Ability to set up auditing (determine which events are audited) and to manage the security log file using the Event Viewer.

- **Backup of files and directories**—Users with this right can make backups of disk volumes even if they do not have the correct NTFS access permissions to read the files on the disk.

- **Restore files and directories**—Similar to the backup right, this right allows the user to restore files from a backup to a disk for which he or she has no NTFS access.

- **Log on locally**—The capability to log on locally at a workstation or server; that is, to log on sitting at the workstation or computer, not using a network connection. Generally, administrators are the only users who can log on locally at a server.

- **Change system time**—Grants the capability to change the computer's time or date.

- **Access this computer from the network**—The capability to log on to the computer from the network. In other words, the capability to make a network connection, such as to access a file share on the computer.

- **Shut down the system**—Grants the capability to shut down the computer.

- **Add workstations to a domain**—A user holding this right can add new workstations to the domain database. This right is a built-in capability of the Administrators and Server Operators groups in a domain.

- **Take ownership of files and other objects**—This right allows the user to take over the ownership of files or directories that are owned by another user.

- **Force shutdown from a remote system**—The capability to shut down the system remotely from another computer.

- **Load and change device drivers**—Allows the user to unload device drivers.

Besides these basic rights, Windows NT 4.0 has a list of advanced user rights. Most of these are useful for some user tasks, but also provide rights needed by parts of the operating system or certain kinds of programs, such as background services. These additional rights are

- **Act as part of the operating system**—This right is usually granted to subsystems of the operating system. It allows the holder to act as a secure, trusted part of the operating system. This is not a right you would normally need to grant to a user!

- **Bypass traverse checking**—The user holding this right can read through a directory tree, even though he might not have access to all directories in the tree.

- **Create a pagefile**—Usually a right granted to just the Administrators group. This right allows the user to create additional page files using the System applet in the Control Panel. By creating additional page files on different disks, you can sometimes increase performance on the system.

- **Create a token object**—This is the right to create a user logon token and is usually not granted to an individual user, but instead only to the local security authority (LSA) on the Windows NT computer.

- **Create permanent shared objects**—This is the right to create special resource structures that are used internally by the operating system. Again, this is not a right generally needed by, or granted to, users.

- **Debug programs**—This right allows a programmer to do low-level debugging. This right is helpful for applications developers and administrators.

- **Generate security audits**—This right is needed to create security audit log entries. This right generally is not assigned to a user.

- **Increase quotas**—The capability to increase the quotas for an object in the operating system. Administrator accounts generally have this right granted to them.

- **Increase priority**—Gives the capability to boost the scheduling priority of a process. Administrators and power users might have this right by default. However, increasing the priority of one process can potentially allow a process that is making heavy use of system resources to dramatically slow down or lock out other processes.

- **Load and unload device drivers**—The capability to load and unload device drivers.

- **Lock pages in memory**—This right gives the capability to lock pages into physical memory so that they do not get swapped out to the pagefile during normal virtual memory operations. This is useful for a process running a real-time application, but not a right generally given to ordinary users.

- **Log in as a batch job**—The user can run a job using a batch scheduling utility (such as the AT command).

- **Log in as a service**—This right is usually given to accounts that are created to run a program in the background as a service. Services are controlled (in Windows NT 4.0) by using the Services applet in the Control Panel. Use this applet to specify the username for the service. Grant that username this right. For Windows 2000 systems, you can control services using the Computer Management MMC snap-in. Navigate the tree structure in the left pane to find Services, and then right-click a service in the right pane, select Properties, and further modify aspects of the service from there (see Figure 34.2). In this figure, you'll see that the Log On tab has been selected to let you specify the account under which the service will run.

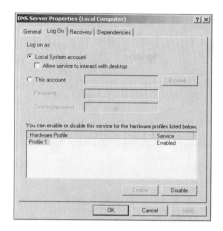

Figure 34.2 You can manage services on computers in the domain by using the Computer Management Administrative Tool.

- **Modify firmware environment variables**—The capability to modify system environment variables, which is usually granted to administrators only.

- **Profile single process**—Allows the user to collect information about a process, used for measuring performance. administrators and power users usually have this right.

- **Profile system performance**—Allows the user to collect information about the system, used for measuring performance. This right is usually used only by administrators.

- **Replace a process-level token**—A right that is usually restricted to the operating system, which gives the user the capability to modify a process's security access token.

As if that wasn't enough to digest, Windows 2000 adds a few more rights you can grant to users or groups:

- **Deny access to this computer from the network**—This is the opposite of the right to access this computer from the network right. If this right is assigned to the user (or group), then access to the computer from the network will be denied.

- **Deny logon as a batch job**—This is also the opposite of another right: the right to log on as a batch job. This specifically denies the user or group the right to run a batch job.

- **Deny logon locally**—You guessed it, this prevents the user from logging on locally at the workstation or server.

- **Enable computer and user accounts to be trusted for delegation**—Use this to specify which user accounts can be delegated.

- **Remove computer from docking station**—Just what it says.

- **Synchronize directory service data**—Allows the user to update Active Directory information.

▶▶ For more information about delegating authority in the Windows 2000 Active Directory and synchronizing directory service information, see Chapter 25, "Overview of Microsoft's Active Directory Service."

NTFS Permissions

When a disk partition is formatted using NTFS, you can grant permissions that control how individual directories and files are accessed by users. While *rights* grant a user the capability to perform some function, *permissions* specify which users (or groups) can access a particular object, such as a file, directory, or printer, for example. Some rights, such as Backup of Files and Directories, can override permissions applied to files. Without this capability, a user who is responsible for performing backups would have to be granted access to every file and directory. Don't worry, however. The right only allows the user to back up the files, not to read or access the files in any other way.

You can use Windows Explorer to add or change permissions on files and directories, or you can use the command-line utility CACLS. To view or modify the permissions on a file using Windows Explorer, simply right-click on the file or directory and select Properties. From the File Properties sheet, select the Security tab and from this tab click the Permissions button. In Figure 34.3, you can see the permissions dialog box for the C:\WINNT4\system32 directory on a Windows NT 4.0 Server.

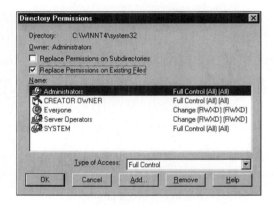

Figure 34.3 Permissions are granted by username or user group.

Note in this figure that the username or user group name is listed in the first column and the access granted to them is listed in the second column. In the second column you can see that there are two ways to represent the access permission. The first is a text string, such as "Full Control" or "Change," which is followed by two other sets of permissions in parentheses. What this shows is that there are two ways to look at permissions under Windows NT/2000. There are special permissions, and there are standard permissions.

Near the bottom of this dialog box is the Type of Access menu. In Figure 34.4, this menu is expanded to show the types of access you can grant to users for this directory.

The list of permissions shown in this figure include familiar terms such as list, read, add, and change. There are also selections for Special Directory Access and Special File Access. These two selections are used when you want to select from the group of permissions known as special permissions.

The process is similar for Windows 2000. Note that the Windows Explorer utility has been moved into the Accessories folder. It seems that the command prompt and Windows Explorer are destined to eventually be history. However, for the present time you can manage file permissions by clicking Start, Programs, Accessories, Windows Explorer.

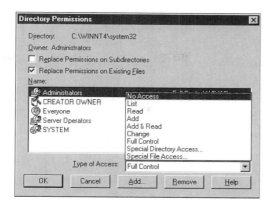

Figure 34.4   Select the type of access to allow for the user or group.

You bring up the properties sheet for a directory or file the same way you do for Windows NT 4.0. Simply right-click on the folder or file and select Properties. You also can click once on the folder or file and select Properties from the Windows Explorer File menu. In Figure 34.5 you can see the initial properties sheet, with the Security tab selected.

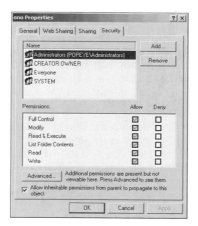

Figure 34.5   The properties sheet for Windows 2000 is a little different from that used with Windows NT 4.0.

For more information about administering users, including assigning rights and permissions, see Chapter 30, "Windows NT Domains," and Chapter 31, "Windows 2000 User and Computer Management Utilities." In this chapter we'll look at what those permissions are.

Windows NT 4.0 Standard Permissions and Special Permissions

Windows NT 4.0 gives the user two different ways to assign permissions to resources. You can use individual permissions that are contained in a group called the special permissions group, or you can use a smaller group that is made up of combinations of these special permissions, called the standard permissions group. The easiest way to explain these is to list the special permissions and then show which ones make up the standard permissions that most users are used to seeing.

The list of special permissions consists of actions you can take on a resource and describe the finest granularity of control that can be managed:

- **R**—Read permission
- **W**—Write permission
- **X**—Execute permission
- **D**—Delete permission
- **P**—Change permission
- **O**—Take ownership permission

To make it easier to assign permissions you can use the standard permissions for files, which are defined using the following combinations:

- **Read**—RX
- **Change**—RWXD
- **Full Control**—RWXDPO
- **No Access**

As you can see, using the standard permissions reduces the granularity used to assign permissions, but the grouping of permissions provided by the standard permissions will suffice in most circumstances to grant or deny access to a resource. For example, the Read standard permission enables the user not only to read a file, but also to execute the file if it is an executable file. The Change standard permission enables the user to read/write/execute and delete a file. Full Control means that the user can do anything with the file!

The standard permissions that apply to directories are a little different than those that apply to files. When defining this type of permission, two sets of permissions are listed. The first set is the permissions that apply to the directory itself. The second set is permissions that apply to files in the directory, where applicable. The standard permissions for directories are

- **List**—(RX) (unspecified)
- **Read**—(RX) (RX)
- **Add**—(WX) (unspecified)
- **Add & Read**—(RWX) (RX)
- **Change**—(RWXD) (RWXD)
- **Full Control**—(RWXDPO) (RWXDPO)
- **No Access**

From this list you can see that the List permission implies the read and execute special rights for the directory file. The Read permission also grants read and execute rights to the directory file, and read and execute as the default inherited permissions for any file created in the directory. The add and read right grants read, write, and execute access to the directory file, but only read and execute rights to files created in the directory.

You can select from the standard permissions when you grant or deny access to a resource. If you want to use the more detailed special permissions instead, select Special Directory Access or Special File Access from the Type of Access menu. In Figures 34.6 and 34.7 you can see the dialog boxes for each of these selections.

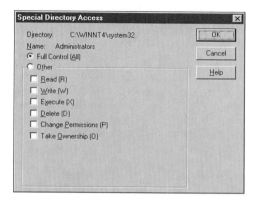

Figure 34.6   Special permissions for directory access.

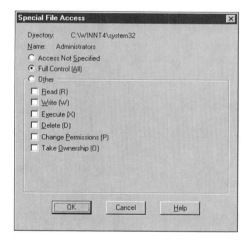

Figure 34.7   Special permissions for file access.

The Special File Access permission selections are used to set the permissions that files created in the directory inherit by default. Choosing Access Not Specified prevents the inheritance of permissions for files created in the directory.

Windows NT Permissions Are Cumulative

When a user is a member of more than one group, the rights that they hold are cumulative. In addition, *permissions* on a resource are also cumulative, with the exception of the No Access permission. Take, for example, a user who has been granted the read permission to a directory because of his membership in a group (such as "world"). However, if the user is also a member of another group called "accountants," the user's permissions are calculated using permissions granted to that group as well. If the accountants user group has been granted the Change permission for the directory, the user has both the Read and Change permissions when he is evaluated for access to the directory.

The only exception to this rule is the No Access right. This right *specifically denies* all other access. Thus, if a user is a member of one group that has been granted Full Control over a directory, but is also a member of another group that has been granted the No Access permission for the directory, the user will not be able to access the directory. The No Access permission overrides other access permissions.

The ability to selectively deny access to specific users can be a useful tool when setting up or managing user accounts. It is easier to grant access to everyone in a large user group and then to deny access to a few select individuals who should not be allowed to use the resource. The alternative is to create a more finely tuned user group that eliminates those who do not need access and then grant access to this new group. This method, however, increases the number of user groups you have to manage and, thus, its use becomes less effective the more you use it.

Windows 2000 Permissions

Windows 2000 also has permissions you can apply to files and folders on NTFS volumes. Like Windows NT 4.0, a set of permissions is designed by using more granular special permissions. The granular permissions that are used to create the special permissions are combinations of the following.

The special file permissions that can be used under Windows 2000 are

- **Traverse Folder/Execute File**—This permission allows you to bypass folders for which you have no access to get to files in a subfolder that you do have permissions to access. The Execute File portion of this permission applies only to files. This allows you to execute files.

- **List Folder/Read Data**—This permission enables you to list filenames and folder names in the particular folder to which this permission applies. The Read Data portion of this permission enables you to view the contents of a file.

- **Read Attributes**—This permission enables you to view the attributes of a file, such as system, read-only, or hidden.

- **Read Extended Attributes**—Some files have additional attributes. For example, a Word document has attributes such as Author and Title. This permission lets you view these extended file attributes.

- **Create Files/Write Data**—You can create new files in a folder with this permission. The Write Data part of this permission enables you to overwrite files that already exist (but you can't add data to a file that already exists—see the next permission for that).

- **Create Folders/Append Data**—This permission lets you create folders (inside other folders), and you can add data to the end of files that already exist. You cannot, however, change data that already is in the file.

- **Write Attributes**—With this permission, you can change the basic attributes of files.

- **Write Extended Attributes**—With this permission, you can change the extended attributes of a file.

- **Delete Subfolders and Files**—Enables you to delete subfolders even if you don't have the Delete permission on the subfolder or file.

- **Delete**—Enables you to delete a particular file or subfolder. Note that if files or subfolders deny you this access, you'll need the previous permission, Delete Subfolders and Files, to accomplish your task.

- **Read Permissions**—You can use this permission to view the NTFS permissions associated with a file or folder.

- **Change Permissions**—You can use this permission to change the permissions assigned to a particular file or folder.

- **Take Ownership**—This permission, which is usually granted only to administrators, enables you to take ownership of the file. As the owner, you have the right to change permissions on the file or folder.

- **Synchronize**—This permission allows or denies different process threads to wait on the handle for the file or folder and synchronize with another thread that might signal it. This permission applies only to multithreaded, multiprocess programs.

Because assigning such a number of permissions could become unwieldy—it might be difficult to figure out what permissions you need to apply to a file or folder—there is a set of permissions that are collections of these granular permissions. For Windows 2000 these are

- **Full Control**—Includes all the previously described granular permissions. You can do just about anything with a file or folder.

- **Modify**—This permission is made up of all the previous granular permissions, except for Delete Subfolders and Files, Change Permissions, and Take Ownership.

- **Read & Execute**—This permission is made up of Traverse Folder/Execute File, List Folder/Read Data, Read Attributes, Read Extended Attributes, Read Permissions, and Synchronize.

- **Read**—This permission is composed of the granular permissions List Folder/Read Data, Red Attributes, Read Extended Attributes, Read Permissions, and Synchronize.

- **Write**—This permission is composed of Create Files/Write Data, Create Folders/Append Data, Write Attributes, Write Extended Attributes, Read Permissions, and Synchronize.

By using these collections of permissions, you'll find it easier to grant typical access to files and folders for users on the network. In addition, Folder permissions include all the previously listed, and also the List Folder Contents permission, which is composed of Traverse Folder/Execute File, List Folder/Read Data, Read Attributes, Read Extended Attributes, Read Permissions, and Synchronize.

Back in Figure 34.3 we looked at the Security tab on a file's properties sheet. Using this tab, you can assign standard permissions to a file. In Figure 34.8, you can see the Access Control Settings dialog box that pops up when you click the Advanced button.

Here you can use the Add button to select users (or user groups) to which you want to grant advanced permissions. The Select User, Computer, or Group dialog box (see Figure 34.9) is a standard dialog box used by many Windows 2000 utilities to select users, computers, or groups.

After you've selected the user or group, click the OK button and the dialog box shown in Figure 34.10 will pop up and let you select the permissions to grant to this user or group for the selected object.

The dialog box shown in Figure 34.10 has several options you can use. The Change button will bring back the dialog box used to add a user or group. The Apply Onto drop-down menu enables you to select the objects for which the rights will be granted. You can select the following options:

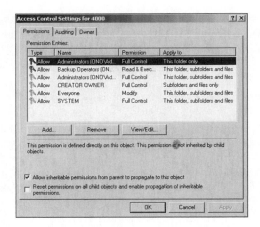

Figure 34.8 Clicking the Advanced button on the file's Security tab brings up the Access Control Settings dialog box.

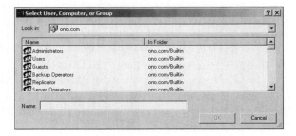

Figure 34.9 Select the user or group to which you want to grant advanced permissions using this dialog box.

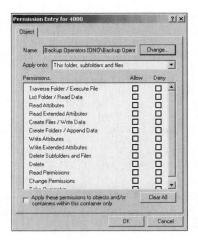

Figure 34.10 Use this dialog box to select the rights to grant the user or group.

- This folder only
- This folder, subfolders, and files
- This folder and subfolders
- This folder and files
- Subfolders and files only
- Subfolders only
- Files only

Underneath this drop-down menu you'll see the actual permissions you can grant or deny for the user or user group you have selected. Select the check box at the bottom left of the dialog box if you want to apply the permissions you've selected only to files or folders in this particular container. Remember, in Windows 2000, the Active Directory is a hierarchical tree structure that has both container and leaf objects (which are the actual users, computers, printers, folder, files, and so on). Security information is stored in the Active Directory and, unless you specify otherwise, permissions are inherited by child objects that fall under this container in the tree. Therefore, if you want to apply these permissions only to files or folders that exist in this container object (such as an organizational unit), select this check box. Otherwise, any other child objects that exist in the tree under this container will inherit these permissions.

The Clear All button on the bottom right gives you a quick way to remove all permission selections for the specified user or group.

Share-Level Permissions

You also can set share-level permissions under Windows NT and Windows 2000 computers, though they are tied to user accounts. You can do this in several ways. The easiest is to use Windows Explorer. Right-click the device or directory that you want to share on the network. Select Properties, and then select the Sharing tab on the Properties sheet for the directory or device. Here you can select the Shared As option and fill in a share name and comment. You then can set the maximum number of users that can connect to the share concurrently. Figure 34.11 shows a folder Properties sheet with the Sharing tab selected for a Windows NT 4.0 computer.

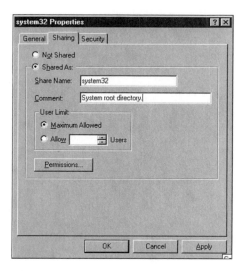

Figure 34.11 To create a share, give it a name and use the Permissions button to grant or deny user access.

By default, the group Everyone (which literally means everyone logged in to the system either interactively or through the network) is granted access to the new share. You can use the Permissions button to add or remove users and to specify the specific access they can have when using the share.

Note that this kind of share-level security is a little different than that found in a workgroup environment, where each share has only a single password that all users need to know to make a connection. Here the password used to connect to the share is a password and valid user account for a user that has been granted access to use the share. By using the server or domain security database to allow access by users, it is possible to audit access based on users also.

If the file share is created for a directory that resides on an NTFS partition, the user's access to information on the file share is governed by both the file share permissions and the NTFS permissions, whichever is more restrictive. It is important to remember that the permissions you set for the share apply only to users who will connect to it through the network. If a user has the right to log on locally to the workstation or server that is offering the file share, the NTFS permissions will be all that apply when the user attempts to access the same files that make up the file share.

You can use the combination of share permissions and NTFS permissions to develop solutions for protecting files based on how your users are organized and how they access the shares. For example, it is easy to create more than one share for the same directory and then give each share different access permissions. Using this method, you can group users by the access mode they need and use different file shares to give access to different groups to the same files. At the same time, you can use NTFS permissions to selectively deny access to certain sensitive files or subdirectories in the share so that only a few or no users are allowed to access the files through the file share.

In Figure 34.12 you can see the Properties sheet for a folder with the Sharing tab selected for a Windows 2000 computer.

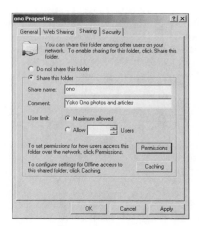

Figure 34.12 The Sharing tab is used to grant or deny access to a folder offered as a file share.

You also can see in Figure 34.12 that a new tab has been added to the Properties page for a folder: Web Sharing. This tab enables you to configure directory sharing for Internet Information Services (IIS) if it is installed on the server.

NetWare

When a user logs in to a NetWare 4.x or 5.x, a three-level tiered mechanism is at work to decide how access of resources is to be granted. The first level of security is logon security. The user must be authenticated against a user object in the NDS tree. The second level of security is NDS security, in which access can be controlled by granting or denying the user access to an object or its properties. The third level of security is NetWare file systems security, which involves the permissions on files and directories contained in the NetWare file system. Four types or categories of rights are used in Novell Networking. Versions prior to NetWare 4 and 5 used only the first two of these:

- File system directory rights
- File system file rights
- NDS object rights
- NDS property rights

The first two rights are those that you normally would associate with an operating system and its file system. These are rights that control access to directories and files in those directories on the disks for which the operating system (or network operating system) is responsible. The last two of these categories are used for rights that apply to accessing objects that reside in the Novell Directory Services (NDS) database.

▶▶ Chapter 27, "Overview of the Novell Bindery and Directory Services (NDS)," is recommended reading if you want to understand how NDS can be used to implement security in a NetWare environment.

Trustees

In NetWare networks, a user or group of users who have a right granted to them for a file or a directory are called a *trustee* of the directory. These rights sometimes are referred to as *trustee assignments*. A trustee assignment includes all the applicable rights, including a No Rights declaration. For NetWare 4.x and 5.x, other NDS leaf objects and container objects also can be granted a trustee assignment.

Trustee rights can be granted by an administrator using a program such as RIGHTS or FILER. You also can grant trustee rights using the NetWare Administrator. These trustee rights relationships also can be inherited. When discussing how rights are granted in a NetWare environment, remember that when a user or group is made a trustee of a file or directory, they have been granted some kind of access permission right.

File System Rights

File system rights are those that control how a user can list the contents of a directory, add to a directory, or remove files or directories from a file system. Table 34.1 lists the terms used for the rights permissions that can be placed on files and directories, along with a short description their functions.

Table 34.1   NetWare File and Directory Rights

Right	Description
Read	Grants the trustee the right to read the contents of files existing in a directory and to execute applications.
Write	Enables the trustee to add to or modify the contents of existing files.
Create	The trustee is allowed to create a file or a subdirectory.

Table 34.1   continued

Right	Description
Erase	The right to erase a file or directory.
Access Control	A user holding this right can grant rights to the directory or files to other users and can modify the IRF.
Modify	Enables the trustee to rename a file or directory and gives them the right to change attributes of the file or directory.
File Scan	Enables the user to list the files that are contained in a directory.
Supervisor	This is the most powerful right, giving the holder all other rights to this directory and to its subdirectories.

Creators/owners of files and directories usually have the access control right over files that they create. This means that they can assign permissions to other users on the system who might need to access their files. The user who has Supervisor access can do as much or more than the owner of a file or directory can do. The File Scan right gives the user the capability to scan the directory and see its contents when searching for a file. In Windows NT and Windows 2000, you will remember, this was called the List right and was made up of two other granular special rights: read and execute.

Object and Property Rights

The NDS database is a hierarchical tree structure. Rights in this tree flow from top to bottom, such that an object in the directory can possibly inherit the rights values from all parent objects above him in the tree. Two basic kinds of rights are associated with NDS: Object rights and Property rights. The first, Object rights, define the kinds of actions that a trustee can perform on an object in the NDS tree. These rights do not necessarily give the trustee access to any of the information that is stored in the object's properties, just access to the mechanisms used to manipulate objects.

Property rights define access to the information stored in the properties of an object. These rights apply to the properties of an object and not to the object itself. For example, an administrator might choose to grant users the ability to change certain properties of their own user object in the directory. This would allow users to change their own telephone number properties, e-mail account properties, and so on, relieving the administrator or another resource of this chore.

Table 34.2 shows the object rights and Table 34.3 shows the property, along with descriptions of their use.

Table 34.2   NDS Object Rights

Right	Description
Supervisor	This is the most powerful object right, granting the trustee all rights to the object as well as its properties. Note that in the case of the other object rights, only the Supervisor right can also grant access to property values.
Browse	This is the right that enables the user to see the object in the NDS tree and to search for it based on the base class of the object or the relative distinguished name (RDN) of the object.
Create	This is a right that applies to container objects, and it gives the trustee the right to create a new object in the NDS tree. This right cannot be assigned to leaf objects, because by definition they cannot contain any other objects. This right can be granted only to container objects and gives the trustee the right to create new objects in the container.

Table 34.2   continued

Right	Description
Delete	This is the right to delete an object in the NDS tree. Note that a container object can be deleted only if there are no other objects beneath it. If there are, you must first delete any existing objects within the container before you can delete it. The Write right (property right) for all properties is also needed to delete an object.
Rename	The right to change the name (RDN) of an object.
Inheritable	Used to specify whether the rights assignment for the object is inherited by the trustee to subordinate objects in the NDS tree, and this right can be assigned only to a container object.

Table 34.3   NDS Property Rights

Property Right	Description
Add Self	This right enables you to add or remove yourself as a value of a property. You cannot use this right to change other property values, however. This right applies only to properties that contain a list of other object names, such as a membership list.
Compare	This is the right to make a comparison of a value to the value of a property. This right does not enable you to see the actual value of the property. Instead, the compare operation will return a value of true or false.
Read	This is the right needed to see the value of the property of an object. This right includes the Compare right.
Supervisor	This gives you all rights to the property. This right can, however, be blocked by an Inherited Rights Filter.
Write	This is the right to add, change, or delete values of a property. This right includes the Add Self right.
Inheritable	This right specifies whether the rights assignment will be inherited by the trustee for objects subordinate to this one in the NDS tree. This right can be used only on container objects.

Differences Between NDS and File System and Directory Rights

NDS rights are used to assign access capabilities to objects and their properties that are contained in the NDS directory database. File system rights are used to assign access capabilities to directories and files stored in the file system. The first difference you will notice between the two is that the NDS rights consists of two other kinds of rights: Object and Property rights. This concept does not exist in the file system rights.

Finally, trustee assignments in NetWare 3.x could be made only for a user account or a user group. In NetWare 4.x and 5.x, the trustee can be any NDS object, leaf, or container, anywhere in the NDS tree. Because the NDS tree is a distributed database, objects located on different servers can be made trustees to files on other servers.

Inheritance of Rights

Inheritance of rights in the NDS tree is the process by which an object acquires some of the rights granted to objects superior to it in the tree. Rights are inherited starting at the top of the tree where objects underneath the [root] object inherit some of the rights granted to [root]. The two methods used to block an object from inheriting rights from a superior object are the inherited rights filter (IRF) and direct trustee assignments by an administrator. Direct trustee assignments made anywhere in the path from the [root] object to the object in question can change the rights flowing down the tree.

The Inherited Rights Filter

The Inherited Rights Filter (IRF) can be used to stop one or more rights from being acquired in this fashion. The filter is used to block an object from receiving selected kinds of trustee assignments that it would otherwise inherit. When displaying the IRF, you will see a string of characters enclosed in square brackets. Each letter is the first letter of one of the rights that can be inherited by the object or potentially blocked by the filter. The values for directory and file rights can be read, write, create, erase, modify, file scan, and access control.

To make modifications to an IRF you can use the utilities RIGHTS, FILER, NetAdmin, or NWADMIN.

Note that an IRF can block the Supervisor right from being inherited in the NDS tree to block access to an object in the tree. However, an IRF cannot block inheritance of the Supervisor right for file system rights inheritance. Also, if a right is blocked by an IRF at a higher level, you can always grant the right to a child object specifically. The IRF only blocks rights from being inherited from above, and does not block a right at the level which it is assigned.

Security Equivalence

Security equivalence is another method of granting trustee access rights in NetWare. Using this method, one User object is made equivalent to another object and thus takes on the same trustee assignments. Security Equivalence is a property of the User object. Trustee rights gained by this equivalence method are in addition to any other rights the User object might possess. Also, a user might be granted rights that are granted to a group of which the user is a member.

This concept is helpful when it becomes necessary to allow one user to have access to objects in a manner similar to another user—for example, when a user is temporarily out of work and another is brought in to fill in.

Tip

It is not a good idea to grant a user the right to change the Security Equivalent property of their own User object. If the user also has the Write property right to the ACL property of an Admin User object, the user could potentially acquire all the rights associated with the Admin User object.

Effective Rights

When looking at the various means that are used to grant trustee rights to an object in NetWare, it quickly becomes apparent that trying to figure out the actual rights a user possesses might become confusing. The actual rights that a user will end up with are called the effective rights to the object. A few simple rules can be used to deduce effective rights:

- If no trustee rights are granted to the directory, the effective rights are computed by a logical AND operation of the parent directory's effective rights and the Inherited Rights Filter.
- An explicit assignment of trustee rights to a directory overrides an Inherited Rights Filter.
- If the Supervisor right is granted to a directory, the trustee will have all rights for all files and subdirectories underneath the directory. Remember that an IRF cannot block the Supervisor right in the file system.

Rights are additive in this computation. Inherited rights are masked by the Inherited Rights Filter, and any rights not masked out are added to any direct assignments made to the object as well as any rights acquired by security equivalence. If the access granted from one source is less than that granted by another source, the higher-level right is used.

The Everyone Group and the [Public] Group

In NetWare 3.x a group called Everyone was usually assigned the Read and the File Scan right to SYS:PUBLIC. This user group allowed the administrator to assign rights to all users in a convenient method. The Everyone group consists of all users on a NetWare 3.x server. In NetWare 4.x and 5.x, there is no Everyone group, by default.

Note

By default, NetWare 4.x and 5.x does not contain an Everyone group. However, the migration process from NetWare 3.x to NetWare 4.x or 5.x can cause the Everyone group to be migrated as a user group.

Novell Directory Services allows for the creation of user groups. The hierarchical nature of the NDS database enables you to place user objects into container objects. Using this method, you can group users who share the same level of access permissions, for example, so that you have to modify the permissions only at the container level instead of at the individual user object level. However, a user object (or any object in the NDS tree) can be associated with only one container object. Of course, the container object itself can be encompassed by another container object, but it is not possible to just take a single user object and place it into multiple containers at the same time. Instead, you can create a Group object. This kind of object has a property that lists members of the group, which consists of user objects that reside elsewhere in the NDS tree.

The *implicit* group [Public] exists by default and is made up of all users who have a network connection. This includes users who have not been authenticated by NDS. This means that you can effectively assign rights to objects in the database for workstations that do not have to use a username/password to connect to the database. This enables you to assign the Browse right to all users, by creating a trustee assignment for the [Public] group on the root object in the tree. Sometimes, though, letting unauthenticated users even see (browse) the database can be a security problem. In this case you would not want to grant this right to [Public], or you might want to consider removing the browse right using an IRF for sections of the tree.

Unix and Linux

Under Unix and Linux users will fall into one of the three following camps:

- User
- Group
- Superuser

Every user on a Unix system must be identified by a username, just as in Windows NT and NetWare. The user also can belong to one or more groups, one of which is considered to be the user's primary group. User groups provide a method for assigning access permissions to directories and files based on groups of users with similar needs. Finally, there is a special user called a superuser, whose capabilities on the system are superior to ordinary users.

The superuser or root user account is all powerful. The root account, as it is usually called, is represented by the user ID (UID) of zero. This UID can access any file on a local file system and can access information about any process on the system. Some functions that only the superuser can perform on most Unix systems include

- Mount or unmount a file system
- Create device special files
- Change another user's password
- Change the date or time on the system clock
- Modify the local network interfaces
- Shut down the system

In Windows NT/2000 you could see that it was possible to choose from a large number of specific rights to assign to a user or a group so that different users could perform functions requiring different degrees of access. In the Unix environment, the root user account is the one that possesses the super-powers, so to speak, and to perform these functions you must log in as or become the root user.

File permissions are assigned to each file or directory in the following three categories:

- Owner permissions
- Group permissions
- Other permissions

The first category defines permissions that apply to the owner of the file. Group permissions apply to users who are in a group to which the file belongs. The last category is the permissions that will be applied to all other users who try to access the file. The access permissions that can be granted to each of these categories are

- **Read**—This permission enables the user to read the contents of the file. When applied to a directory, this permission enables the user to list the files stored in the directory along with their attributes.
- **Write**—This permission enables the user to change the contents of the file. This right enables a user to add or delete files in a directory.
- **Execute**—For a program file, this right enables the user to execute, or run, the program. For a directory, this right enables the user to access the directory.

Viewing File Permissions

The ls command can be used to show a listing of files along with information about the permissions applied to the files. There are many command line parameters you can use with this command, but the simple usage shown here is sufficient to view the ownership and permission information about a file:

```
ls -l /usr/bin/two
dr-xr-xr-x  1 two   biz        0 Jul 12 2001 html
dr-xr-xr-x  1 two   biz        0 Feb 13 2001 invoices
-r-xr-xr-x  1 two   biz     1624 Jun 20 2001 notices.txt
-r-xr-xr-x  1 two   biz     1624 Jun 20 2001 appt.dat
```

The first entry in the directory listing shows a directory file named html. You can tell it is a directory because the first character on the line is a d. The next file is also a directory, named invoices. Both of these directories are owned by the user listed in the third column, two. The group the file belongs to is found in the next column and, in these examples, is biz for all entries. The remaining items on each line show the size and date of the file and its name. Note that Unix is case sensitive when it comes to filenames. Keep this in mind when using the ls command with wildcards when hoping to locate a file.

In this listing, the first thing you notice on each line is a string of letters separated by dashes. This string contains the access permissions for the entry. It is sometimes called the *permissions array*. This is followed by other information, separated into columns. Each line represents either a directory or a file in the current directory. The permissions array can be easily deciphered. The first character indicates whether the file is a directory (d) or a user file (-), and the remaining three groups of letters indicate the access permissions for the file's or directory's owner, the file's group, and then a group called "other."

Note that the dashes in the permissions array are not separators. Each position in the array is a fixed place that can either contain a permission for the file or directory or represent the absence of the permission, using the dash (hyphen) character. In the previous listing this means that the owner, group, and world permissions for each of the directories and files listed is "read" and "execute" (r-x).

Granting permissions to "other" gives the permission to all users on the system. It is important to remember that, in Unix, if you grant access using the world permissions fields, denying access by owner or group fields will not work. Thus, use the world access permissions on files to set values that you would like to apply to all users. For example, if all users will be allowed to read the file, set the read permission in the world permissions. Use the owner and group fields to grant more restricted access to smaller groups of users.

SUID and SGID File Permissions

In addition to the ordinary permissions that exist to control which users can access a file or directory, two other permissions are used on Unix and Linux systems to give special privileges to executable files. These are called the Set User ID (SUID) and Set Group ID (SGID) permissions. When an executable image is run that has the SUID permission set on it, the image will take on the permissions that are equivalent to those of the owner of the executable file.

The permissions available to a user can also be acquired from group membership. When an executable image is run, it usually runs under the permissions of the user who executes the file and the permissions available to the group to which the user belongs. When the SGID permission is set on an executable, it will inherit permissions from the group of the owner of the file and not the permissions of the user who executes the file.

These two permissions can be very useful. There are times when it is necessary to run a program that must have more access rights than the user who is executing the program. For example, when a user needs to change his password he needs to be able to make edits to the password file. Because this file is normally protected against writing by most ordinary users, the program that changes your password can get the necessary permission to modify the file. This is a simple example of a process that occurs at many levels in an operating system. Other programs use permissions elevated above the ordinary user to accomplish such tasks as managing print queues and allowing basic system management tasks.

When used on a directory instead of a file, the SUID permission, placed in the group field, indicates that all files created in the directory will take on the ownership of the group that owns the directory.

You can tell from a directory listing (using the ls command) whether the SUID or SGID permission has been set for a file. In the permissions array, the letter s will appear in the position normally used to indicate the owner's execute access. If the s character is lowercase then the execute permission for the owner is not set. If it is an uppercase "S" then the execute permission is also set for the owner.

In a directory file the "s" character will appear in the character position that normally indicates a group's execute access.

The chmod and chown Commands

When moving files around on the network it frequently is necessary to change their ownership or the access permissions so that a new set of users can gain the appropriate access. For example, when a user leaves a company it is usually customary for someone else to take over managing files and important directories for which the user had been responsible. The two commands that you can use to modify ownership and access for files are the chmod (change permission mode) and chown (change owner) commands.

The chown command is a simple one. If you are the owner of a file or if you are the superuser, you can use this command to assign a new owner and/or group to a file. The basic syntax is

```
chown [ -fhR ] owner [ : group ] file ...
```

Here, owner is the new user or group ID that will be assigned to the file or files represented by file.... The -f parameter suppresses error reporting. The -h parameter is used to cause an ownership change to be effective on a symbolic link to a file instead of the actual file the link references. Without this parameter, the ownership is changed on the actual file that is referenced by the symbolic link. The -R parameter causes the command to operate recursively, changing the owner ID for files and subdirectories under the current specification.

You can use chown to easily change the ownership of one or more directories when a new user takes responsibility for them. The chmod command can be used by users and administrators to change the access permissions on files or directories.

The chmod command can be used to change access permissions for the owner, group, or others by specifying the rights by either a numeric or character format. The numeric format for the chmod command specifies rights as a numeric value, totaling each right as described in the following list:

- **0**—No access
- **1**—Execute file (or search a directory)
- **2**—Write
- **4**—Read

Using this format, you would change the access permissions on a file in a manner similar to this:

```
chmod 666 myfile1
chmod 664 myfile2
chmod 640 myfile3
```

Here the filename myfile1 has its access permissions set to Read + Write (4 + 2 = 6) for the owner, group, and world fields. The file myfile2 is set to Read + Write for the owner and group fields, but to only Read (4) for the other or world field. Finally, myfile3 is set to let the owner Read and Write. The group permission is set to Read only and the other field is set to No Access (0).

Using the other syntax format for the chmod command enables you to change the permission fields without having to memorize numerical values. Instead, you use the letters r (read), w (write), and x (execute) to specify the permissions, and the letters u (user), g (group), o (other), or a (all, indicates user, group and other) to specify the specific user field for which a permission will be modified. For example:

```
chmod u+rw myfile1
chmod g+rwx myfile1
chmod o+rw myfile1
```

Here it is easy to see that the user field (user owner, group, or other) is appended to the letter identifying a right (rw, rwx) by the plus sign. This indicates that the right is to be added to the user field indicated for the file myfile1. To remove a right using chmod use the minus sign:

```
chmod g-x personalfile
chmod o-w specialfile
```

Here the command is used to remove the execute right from group for the file named personalfile. For the file named specialfile, the owner has used chmod to remove his own right to write to the file. This is not done for security purposes, but because the owner wants to be sure he doesn't alter the contents of the file by mistake. Because he is the owner, he can always set the mode back to write if it becomes necessary.

Using the *su* Command

To perform some important system management tasks on a Unix or Linux system, only the privileges granted to the root account can be used. Although it would be easy to let multiple system administrators log in to the root account to perform administrative functions, this is not a very good thing to do from the viewpoint of security. If only one account is used, it is difficult to construct an audit trail to determine which administrator performed a specific function.

To get over this limitation, the su command enables you to log in using your normal user account and then become the root user or another user. The log file /var/adm/sulog tracks attempts to become another user using the su command and so an audit trail is kept to help when troubleshooting. You can use the su command by itself to become the root superuser, or you can use it in the form of su *username* to become another user. In all cases you will be prompted for the password for the user account you want to become, unless you are already logged in to the root account.

The power held by the password to a root account can be seen by how it can be used with this command. As a standard security matter you should regularly review the /var/adm/sulog log file to keep track of how the command is being used.

Network Printing
Protocols

SOME OF THE MAIN TOPICS IN THIS CHAPTER ARE

Printing Protocols and Printing Languages

TCP/IP Printing

Data Link Control Protocol (DLC)

Internet Printing Protocol

CHAPTER 35

The most basic functions provided by a LAN are the file and print services. A *print server* is a computer that has one or more physical printers attached and that accepts data for printing from other computers.

The parallel port is usually used when directly connecting a printer to a computer. This port provides a high-speed connection on a set of wires used exclusively by the printer and the computer for this communication path. It is becoming increasingly more common to find printers that are connected directly to the network, just as servers and workstations are.

Another category of print servers is the dedicated device that connects to the network and provides ports for one or more printers. Using this sort of device enables you to place multiple printers on the network without having to buy a network card for each.

In this chapter, you'll look primarily at the protocols that are used to communicate with a printer, or a print server, to exchange data and command information.

Printing Protocols and Printing Languages

A lot of different types of printers are on the market today. From inkjet printers priced under $100 to high-volume, color laser printers, you can find something that suits almost any need. When evaluating a printer purchase, you need to understand the protocols that can be used to communicate with the printer and the languages that the printer understands.

A printer language is not the same as a printer protocol. For example, Postscript and PCL (Printer Control Language) are languages that describe how a document is to be rendered into the final printed product by the printer. When a printer is directly connected to a printer port on a computer, the printer language is important and is used by the software driver to format the information being sent to the printer.

A network protocol, however, is used to send the formatted job, both data and instructions compiled using the printer language, to the printer. Some common general network protocols, such as IPX/SPX (Internetwork Packet Exchange/Sequenced Packet Exchange) can be used to communicate with printers and are described in other sections of this book. In this chapter, you'll examine a few protocols that are more specific in their use and implementation; that is, they generally are used for communicating with a printer.

Several protocols are used for network printing. Some are proprietary protocols used by only one computer or network operating system (NOS). Others, such as lpr/lpd, have been implemented in many environments. Data Link Control (DLC) is an IBM protocol that has been adapted for use on many printers, particularly HP laser printers. This chapter covers the basis of these major protocols, with examples from Unix, Windows NT/2000, and NetWare systems.

Additionally, you'll learn about the new kid on the block, Internet Printing Protocol, which is under development by a working committee of the Internet Engineering Task Force (IETF). Development is underway for standards to further define this new protocol.

TCP/IP Printing

TCP/IP was originally developed for the Unix operating system (OS), of which there are several flavors. Depending on the version of Unix running on a workstation or server, you will find that printing falls into one of two major types:

- BSD (Berkeley System Distribution) Spooling System
- SVR4 (System V, Release 4) Printing System

The BSD system uses the lpr (line printer remote) program and the lpd (line printer daemon) daemon to send files to printers. The /etc/printcap text file is used to set up characteristics for each printer. The SVR4 system uses the lp (line printer) program and the lpsched daemon (printer scheduler) to print files. Although the SVR4 system is considered more sophisticated because it has several utility commands for managing the system, the BSD system probably is easier to manage in a networked environment.

Note

In this section, you'll examine the commands used to set up and administer printing systems on Unix systems. However, TCP/IP-based printing is not limited to servers running this OS. Many OSs from OpenVMS to Windows NT can use the lpr/lpd printing protocol; they are discussed later in this chapter.

The BSD Spooling System: *lpr* and *lpd*

In BSD printing, the user sends files to print by using lpr; the lpd daemon handles the details needed to get the data in the file formatted and sent to the physical output print device.

To set up a printer on a Unix system that uses lpr/lpd, you need to do several things. How you accomplish them depends on your particular brand of Unix and whether the vendor has supplied script files or applications to help automate the process. The basic things that need to be done are

- Physically connect the printer to a port on the server computer or, alternatively, configure a network printer with a TCP/IP address so that you can direct print jobs to it.
- Create a special device file that Unix uses to reference devices if the printer is connected physically to the computer.
- Create entries in the printer configuration file (/etc/printcap) that describe the characteristics of this printer, along with management items such as accounting or log files.
- Create the directories that will be used to store files while they are waiting to print (spooling directory).
- Place commands in the appropriate Unix startup file (rc file) to start the lpd daemon when the system boots.

To create the special device file, use the command /dev/makedev *port*. The *port* should be the port on the server to which the printer is attached. Typically, the parallel ports are named lpt*n* (that is, lpt1, lpt2,...). If the printer is connected to a serial port, the name of the port probably will be in the form of ttynn (that is, tty01, tty02,...). Be sure to check your system documentation to make sure you have the correct port name. Depending on the system, you might also have to make further adjustments to configure the port, such as setting the speed.

Tip

After you have attached a printer and configured the port, you can use the **lptest** command to send a simple stream of ASCII characters to the port. This confirms whether you have been successful up to this point. You also can use this command when a printer suddenly stops printing to test simple connectivity. If the printer had been functioning normally, stops unexpectedly, and **lptest** does not succeed, you might want to check the cabling or fault lights on the printer itself.

To create the spool directory, use the mkdir command. The spooling directory usually is created under the /var/spool/lpd directory. After you create a directory for the printer, use the chmod, chgrp, and chown commands to set the proper ownership and permission mode (for the lpd daemon). For example:

```
# cd /var/spool/lpd
# mkdir laser1
# chmod 775 laser1
# chgrp daemon laser1
# chown daemon laser1
```

The lpr command is used for printing files in the BSD system. The syntax for this command is

```
lpr [-parameters][filename...]
```

Everything but the command itself is optional. You can specify one or more files, but if you do not specify a filename, the text to be printed comes from *standard input*. Depending on how your particular Unix vendor has implemented the command, you have a lot of options to choose from:

- **#**—Specifies the number of copies to print.

- **c**—The date file(s) to be printed were created by the cifplot filter.

- **C**—Text following the C ("Job Classification") character is printed on the *burst page* for the print job.

- **d**—Indicates that the data file(s) to be printed contain data created by the tex command.

- **f**—Printing FORTRAN files. The first character in each line is interpreted as a FORTRAN carriage control character.

- **g**—The data file(s) to be printed contains data created by a program using the standard plot routines.

- **h**—Suppresses printing the burst page.

- **i Indent value**—If a job is printed with an indent of 8 spaces by default, you can change it with this parameter. This value is passed to the Unix input filter, which does the actual formatting of the data to be printed.

- **J Job**—Text following the J character is printed on the burst page for the print job. If this parameter is not used, the name of the first file on the print command line is used on the burst page.

- **l**—Control characters are printed and page breaks suppressed.

- **m**—Send a mail message after the job is printed.

- **n**—The data file(s) to be printed contain data created by the ditroff command.

- **p**—Uses the pr command as the filter to process the print job.

- **P**—Name of the destination printer.

- **r**—Removes the file when spooling (or printing using the -s parameter).

- **s**—Indicates that the file should not be spooled. Instead, a symbolic link is used. This is a good option to use when printing large files, or a large number of files, to minimize consumption of disk space.

- **T Title**—Used with the -p option, which causes the pr command to be used to format the file to be printed. Text specified with this parameter is passed to pr. If blank spaces or special characters are used, the text should be enclosed by single quotes (' ').

- **t**—Indicates that the data file(s) to be printed contain binary data created by the troff command.

- **v**—The data file(s) to be printed is in raster image format.

- **w**—Number of columns. This parameter specifies the number of characters on the page (width).

Tip

A *burst page* or *banner page*, sometimes called a separator page, refers to a page that is printed at the beginning or end of a print job, and is used to separate one user's print job from the next. In a high-volume printing environment, these pages make it easier to identify print jobs so they can be distributed to the appropriate user.

This extensive list of parameters is shown here to make the point that the lpr/lpd printing system is highly configurable from the user's point of view. It might look more complex at first glance than it actually is. For example, the command

```
Lpr –Phplj1 letter01.txt report.txt
```

is all you need to send the files letter01.txt and report.txt to a printer named hplj1. In most circumstances, the user will not use a large subset of these parameters, but only a smaller combination that fits his work environment. Many of these parameters have default values. For example, if the printer is not specified by using the -P parameter, the Unix environment variable PRINTER will be evaluated and used for the destination of the print job.

After the lpr command has determined the printer to which the data will be sent, it scans the /etc/printcap file to get information about the printer, such as the spooling directory path. It then creates several temporary files and notifies the lpd daemon that the file is ready to print.

The lpd Daemon Controls the Printing Process

The lpr command creates a data file in the spooling directory associated with the printer and a control file that contains information telling the lpd daemon how the file should be printed. This daemon process usually starts up when the system boots by commands found in one of the rc files. However, when troubleshooting printing problems, it's often necessary to kill the lpd daemon process and restart it. The syntax for restarting the daemon is

```
lpd [-l] [-Llogfile] [port#]
```

The -l parameter tells the daemon to record valid network requests in a log file. The uppercase parameter -L is used to specify the name of the logfile. The *port#* parameter is used to specify the Internet port number the daemon will use for process-to-process communications.

When the daemon first starts up, it reads the /etc/printcap file to obtain information about the printers it can use. If any print jobs are outstanding since it was last running, the daemon begins to print them after it reads the printcap file.

When it needs to actually print a file, the lpd daemon first checks to see whether another lpd daemon process is currently processing print jobs for that particular printer. If so, it passes the print job to that daemon. If not, the lpd daemon spawns a copy of itself for the printer destination, and that process continues to process jobs for the printer. The original lpd daemon that starts at boot time continues to listen for print requests and spawn new copies of itself when needed. A spawned copy of the daemon continues to run until there are no more files to print on the printer it was invoked to handle.

The lpd daemon and its spawned copies control the printing process but do not perform the mechanics needed to get the data to the printer. Instead, the lpd daemon runs a filter program that sends the data to the printer, and optionally does some formatting that is needed to make the data compatible with the specific printer.

Caution

In a multiuser environment such as Unix, a locking mechanism can be used to prevent multiple processes from trying to access the same resource at the same time. When a new lpd daemon is spawned to perform print-processing functions, it creates a lock file (by using the Unix system call **flock**) in the spooling directory. This lock file remains in the directory while this particular lpd daemon processes files to prevent other lpd daemons from being spawned for the particular directory. The lock file is a simple ASCII file that contains the process ID (PID) of the current lpd daemon and the name of the control file for the current print job.

When troubleshooting lpd daemons, you can examine the lock file to determine whether the daemon listed there is still running. In some versions of Unix, the second line of the lock file also shows the status of the current job as the daemon believes it to be. In some other versions, a file named status is used for this purpose.

The /etc/printcap Configuration File

When you set up printing on a Unix computer that uses lpr/lpd, you must create the /etc/printcap file. Keep a written log listing changes as you make them to this file so that if something suddenly goes wrong with a printer that has been working just fine, you can check the log to determine whether anyone has recently made a change to the entry in the printcap file for the troublesome printer. This file is not a user-friendly file. In many cases, the syntax for each entry is just a few lines, but for complicated setups, editing this file can become confusing if you make changes infrequently.

Entries in this file specify the name used for a printer along with two-character symbol/value pairs (*symbol=value*) that define the characteristics for the printer. The printer can have multiple names (aliases), which are separated by a vertical-bar character. For example, an entry for a printer named "laser" could be as simple as

```
laser|laser1|lp|lp0|HP Laser Jet Accounting:\
    :sd=/var/spool/lpd/laser:\
    :lp=/dev/tty01:
```

The first line contains the name of the printer (laser), followed by several alias names that users can use to access the printer. The last alias on the first line shows a common technique used by many administrators: describe the printer and/or its location. You also can put comments into the /etc/printcap file by using the pound-sign character (#) as the first character in the line. In this example, you also can see that the colon character (:) is used to separate the symbol/value pairs from each other. Although only one colon character is needed between each pair, it's customary to put one at the beginning of a line and one at the end of the line when the entry spans multiple lines. The following two entries are equivalent:

```
:sd=/var/spool/lpd/laser1:br#9600:
```

```
:sd=/var/spool/lpd/laser1:\
:br#9600:
```

Note that the backslash character (\) is used to indicate continuation of the entry across multiple lines. Also, some entries in the file do not have a value. For example, some are Boolean entries that have no associated value and are activated by their presence in the file.

In these examples, the sd symbol is followed by a directory path. This specifies the spooling directory that lpd will use to store files that are waiting to be printed. Multiple users can send files to the printer using the lpr command. Copies of the files to be printed are created by the lpd daemon in the spooling directory and remain there until they are printed. After a file has been printed, the lpd daemon deletes the control and data files used for it.

The `lp` symbol is used to indicate the special device file for the printer. In Unix, device files are used as a link to a physical device. The `makdev` command is used to create the device file just as for any other device attached to the computer. However, in the case of a remote printer, use the hostname/queue name on the remote system for this value instead of a device filename. Entries can be much more complex than this simple example. Table 35.1 lists the symbols you can use to customize a printer.

Table 35.1   Symbols Used in the */etc/printcap* File

Symbol	Type	Default Value	Description
af	string	NULL	Name of accounting file.
br	numeric	no default	Baud rate if lp is a tty.
cf	string	NULL	The cifplot data filter.
df	string	NULL	The TeX data filter (DVI format).
du	string	no default	Used to specify a nonstandard user ID for the daemon.
fc	numeric	0	If lp is a tty, clear flag bits.
ff	string	/f	String to send to printer for form feed.
fo	boolean	false	Print a form feed when device is opened.
fs	numeric	0	If lp is a tty, set flag bits.
gf	string	NULL	Graph data filter (plot format).
hl	boolean	false	Print the burst header page last.
ic	boolean	false	Driver supports (nonstandard) ioctl to indent on printout.
if	string	NULL	Accounting text filter.
lf	string	/dev/console	Name of error logging file.
lo	string	lock	Name of lock file.
lp	string	/dev/lp	Output device.
mc	numeric	0	Maximum number of copies allowed.
mx	numeric	1000	Maximum file size (in BUFSIZ blocks)—zero means unlimited.
nf	string	NULL	The ditroff data filter (device independent troff).
of	string	NULL	Output filtering program.
pc	numeric	200	Price per foot or page (in hundredths of cents).
pl	numeric	66	Page length in lines.
pw	numeric	132	Page width in characters.
px	numeric	0	Page width in pixels (horizontal).
py	numeric	0	Page length in pixels (vertical).
rf	string	NULL	The FORTRAN-style text file filter.
rg	string	NULL	Restricted group. Only members of this group are allowed access to the printer.
rm	string	NULL	Machine name for remote printer.
rp	string	lp	Remote printer name argument.
rs	boolean	false	Restrict remote users to only those who have local accounts.
rw	boolean	false	Open the print device for read/write.
sb	boolean	false	Short (one-line) banner.

Table 35.1   continued

Symbol	Type	Default Value	Description
sc	boolean	false	Suppress multiple copies.
sd	string	/usr/spool/lpd or /var/spool/lpd	Spooling directory.
sf	boolean	false	Suppress form feeds.
sh	boolean	false	Suppress printing of burst page header.
st	string	status	Name of status file.
tf	string	NULL	Name of troff data filter (cat phototypesetter).
tr	string	NULL	Trailer string to print when queue is emptied (that is, form feeds or escape characters).
vf	string	NULL	Raster image filter.
xc	numeric	0	If lp is a tty, clear local mode bits.
xs	numeric	0	If lp is a tty, set local mode bits.

Following is an example of a more complicated entry:

```
lp|lp0|Color Laser: \
   :af=/usr/adm/printer/clp.acct:\
   :br#9600:\
   :lf=/usr/adm/lpterror:\
   :lp=/dev/tty05:\
   :mx#0:\
   :sd=/var/spool/lpd:\
```

This example defines the spooling directory for a printer as well as the logfile and accounting file. The mx#0 entry means there is no maximum size limit for files that can print on this printer.

When specifying a printer device, you also can tell the lpd daemon to use a print queue that resides on another system. For example:

```
xprint|laser2|Manufacturing printer:\
   :lp=:\
   :rm=mfgunix:\
   :rp=lp:\
   :sd=/var/spool/lpd/xprint:\
   :mx#0:\
```

In this example, the lp symbol is set to null. This indicates that the print device is not on this system. You still have to include the lp symbol so that the default value for it will not be substituted by the lpd daemon. The rm symbol is used to indicate the hostname of the remote computer and the rp symbol is used to define the name of the printer on that system. Also, even though the actual printing is done on the remote computer, you must specify a spooling directory because files submitted to the queue still need to be temporarily stored before they are copied to the remote system.

Useful Commands: lpq, lprm, and lpc

From the user's perspective, printing is a simple task. Just use the lpr command and wait for the paper to come out of the printer. As the administrator, you need commands that can help you manage print queues and track usage.

The lpq command shows information about jobs waiting in the print queue. The information this command shows you includes

- The order of print jobs in the queue
- The name of the user who submitted the job to print
- The job identification number
- The names of files waiting to print
- The size of the print job (in bytes)

For example:

```
Rank   Owner     Job Files          Total Size
active ogletree   133 prm0d1x          31540 bytes
1st    heywood    141 letter1        3423 bytes
2nd    chasog     216 jandata        98465 bytes
3rd    peter      323 twoinchtml      2342 bytes
4th    menton     122 queulst        55432 bytes
```

You can use the -P parameter to specify the printer just like you can with the lpr command. Similarly, the Unix environment variable PRINTER determines the printer to display if you do not specify one. The syntax for the lpq command is

```
lpq [-Pprinter][-l][+[interval]][job#...][username...]
```

The -l parameter causes a "long" listing (more output, additional information) to be displayed. The plus sign (+) can be used by itself or with a numeric value, and causes the command to continuously display the status until the print queue empties. If you follow the plus sign with a numeric value, it is used as the number of seconds between each refresh interval.

Use the job ID numbers or the user's username when troubleshooting specific print jobs so you won't have to look through a long listing of all print jobs. The job ID number also can be used by other print-queue management commands, so it is common to use lpq to get a job's ID number before executing other commands.

To remove a print job from the queue, you can use the lprm command. Its syntax is similar to the lpq command:

```
lprm [-Pprinter][-][job#...][username...]
```

Although any user can remove her own files that are pending in a print queue, only the superuser can remove other user's files. You can specify the job ID number associated with a specific file or you can specify a username to remove all print jobs currently pending in the queue for that user.

Note

To remove jobs from a print queue, the lprm command actually kills the current lpd daemon that is processing files for that queue. It then deletes the specific files from the print queue and restarts a new daemon process to continue processing the remaining files.

Examining a print queue and removing pending jobs can be useful for troubleshooting simple problems. For more control over the BSD printing system, you can use the lpc (line printer control) command. The syntax for this command is more complicated than that of the lpq and lprm commands because of the more complex functions it can perform. The syntax for lpc is

```
lpc [command [parameters...]]
```

The commands you can use with lpc are

- **abort [all | *printer*...]**—Kills the active lpd daemon and then disables printing for the specified printers. Stops the print job that is currently printing. After this, lpr will not be able to create a new lpd daemon for the specified printers. Use this option when you need to quickly disable a printer.

- **clean [all | *printer*...]**—Removes temporary files (including control and data files) from the specified printer's spooling directory when the files do not form a complete print job. Useful for "cleaning up" a spool directory when something has gone wrong.

- **disable [all | *printer*...]**—Prevents lpr from submitting new print jobs to this print queue. This command turns off printing for the specified queue.

- **down [all | *printer*...] *message*...**—Turns off the print queue and disables printing. *Message*... text is entered into the status file for the printer so that lpq can report it.

- **enable [all | *printer*...]**—Enables spooling on the printer(s) so that users can begin to use the lpr command to submit print jobs.

- **restart [all | *printer*...]**—When a printer daemon dies unexpectedly, you can use this command to start a new daemon for the queue. The jobs currently existing in the queue are printed by the new daemon. You should perform this command when the lpq command gives you the no daemon present message.

- **start [all | *printer*...]**—Enables printing and starts a spooling daemon for the printers specified. Changes the owner's execute permission on the lock file to accomplish their tasks.

- **status [all | *printer*...]**—Gets the status of printer daemons and queues. Shows whether the queue is enabled or disabled, or whether printing is enabled or disabled. Also shows the number of entries in the queue and the status of the printer's lpd daemon.

- **stop [all | *printer*...]**—Stops a spooling daemon and disables printing. The daemon stops after it finishes the current print job. Use the abort command if you want to stop the daemon and kill the current job that is printing.

- **topq *printer* [*job#*.. .][*username*...]**—Entries are printed on a first-in, first-out (FIFO) basis. Use this command to move print jobs to the top of the queue. Specify one or more job numbers as an argument to this command. Specify a username as the argument to move all jobs pending for that user to the top of the queue.

- **up [all | *printer*...]**—Opposite of the down command. Enables all printing and starts a new printer daemon.

- **exit or quit**—Cause the lpc program to exit (when in interactive mode).

- **? [*command*] or help [*command*]**—Displays a short help text for each *command*. If no command is specified after the help command, a list of all commands that the lpc program recognizes is displayed.

Although the lpc program usually is used by an administrator (superuser), ordinary users can use the restart and status commands.

The following is an example of using the lpc command to get the status of a printer named laser1. In this example, the queue is enabled and printing. Only one job is in the queue. When you use the command without command line parameters, it prompts you in interactive mode:

```
% /usr/sbin/lpc
lpc> status laser2
laser1:
```

```
        printer is on device '/dev/tty03' speed 9600
        queuing is enabled
        printing is enabled
        1 entry in spool area
lpc>quit
```

In this next example, the lpd daemon for this queue has exited unexpectedly. Using the lpc command, you can detect this condition and fix the problem:

```
% /usr/sbin/lpc
lpc> status laser2
laser2:
        printer is on device '/dev/tty03' speed 9600
        queuing is enabled
        printing is enabled
        7 entries in spool area
        no daemon present
lpc> restart laser2
lpc>quit
```

Examining Printing Statistics

Part of managing a network is gathering statistics. This is done for several reasons. First, historical data is nice to have when you are trying to determine the circumstances leading up to a problem. Second, statistical data can help you plan for enough capacity when you are deciding on expansion or reorganization. Another use for the information is user or department accountability. In environments where costs are charged back to a department, you can use the pac command to gather the data you need.

The syntax for this command is

```
pac [-Pprinter][-cmrs][-pprice][username]
```

As is the custom with other printing commands, the -P parameter allows you to specify a printer. If you do not, the value of PRINTER is used; otherwise, the system default printer is assumed. The other parameters you can use are

- **c**—Sorts the report by cost instead of machine/username.
- **m**—Groups charges by username with no regard to the hostname of the computer from which the job(s) were submitted.
- **r**—Reverses the sort order for the report.
- **s**—Summarizes the accounting data and writes it to a summary file. The summary file is usually in the form of *printer*.acct_sum.
- **pprice**—Allows you to specify the cost per unit (foot or page) for print jobs. The default is two cents per unit.
- **username**—If you supply usernames at the end of the command, only statistics for print jobs for those users are included in the report.

Tip

You can include the **pac** command in script files to create automated procedures to produce accounting reports. For example, you could use a script file to produce reports by user or department, and then e-mail a copy of the report to a responsible person.

The following output shows the type of information you can get by using the pac command. The costs for each print job are just simple calculations based on the unit and the cost you supply to the command.

```
Login           pages/feet    runs   price
atlunix1:harris   14.00        1    $ 0.28
atlunix1:brown     3.00        2    $ 0.06
pluto:ogletree    21.00        3    $ 0.42
```

The SVR4 Printing System

Another major type of Unix variant is the System V, Version 4 (SVR4) system. The SVR4 printing system uses the lp command and lpsched command to print and manage printer queues. Although an /etc/printcap file also is used, it doesn't have to be edited manually. The lpadmin utility will do this for you.

Using lp, cancel, and lpstat

The lp command is used just like the lpr command. However, the lp command does more than just send files to a printer; it also can be used to modify print jobs. The cancel command is used to remove a job from the print queue. The syntax for the lp command comes in two different forms:

```
lp [-c][-m][-p][-s][-w][-d dest]
   [-f form-name [-d any]][-H special-handling]
   [-n number][-o option][-P page-list]
   [-q priority-level][-S character-set][-d any]]
   [-S print-wheel[-d any]][-t title]
   [-T content-type][-r]][-y mode-list]
   [filename...]

lp -i request-id ... [-c][-m][-p][-s][-w]
   [-d dest][-f form-name[-d any]]
   [-H special-handling][-n number][-o option]
   [-P page-list][-q priority-level]
   [-S character-set[-d any]]]
   [-t title][-T content-type[-r]]
   [-y mode-list]
```

The first version of this command is used to send files to print. The second version is used to modify a print request that is already pending. If you use the second version to modify a job that is already printing, it stops the job and restarts it with the changes you have made.

The parameters you can use with the lp command are

- **c**—A copy of the file to be made before it is printed. The default action is to create a link to the file. If you use the -c parameter, you should not remove (delete) the file before it is printed. Any changes you make to the file after submitting the print request, will not be reflected in the output if you use this parameter to create a copy of the file.

- **d dest**—Specifies the destination printer or class for the print job.

- **f form-name**—Specifies a form to be mounted on the printer to process the print request. If the printer does not support the form, the request is rejected. Note that if you use the -d any parameter with this one, the print request can be sent to any printer that supports the form.

- **H special-handling**—Puts the print request on hold or resumes requests that are holding. If you are an LP administrator, this command causes the request to be the next one to print. The terms you use for special-handling are hold, resume, and immediate, respectively.

- **m**—Send mail after the print job has finished.

- **n** *number*—The number of copies to print.

- **o** *option*—Specifies printer-dependent options. You can specify more than one option by using the -o parameter more than once. You also can include multiple options by enclosing them in quotes; for example, -o "option1 option2 ...".

  Terms you can use for the *option* are

  - **nobanner**—Do not print banner page.

  - **nofilebreak**—Do not insert a form feed character between files when multiple files are printed.

  - **length=***scaled-decimal-number*—Specifies the page length. You can specify lines, inches, or centimeters. Length=66 specifies 66 lines per page, while length=11I specifies 11 inches per page, for example.

  - **width=***scaled-decimal-number*—Similar to the length option. Use this format to specify page width in columns, inches, or centimeters.

  - **lpi=***scaled-decimal-number*—Like length and width. Use this to specify line pitch (lines per inch).

  - **cpi=***scaled-decimal-number*—Like length and width. Use this to specify characters per inch. You also can use the terms pica (10 characters per inch) or elite (12 characters per inch), or compressed, to allow the printer to fit as many characters on a line as it can.

  - **stty='***stty-option-list***'**—Specifies options for the stty command. Enclose the list with single quotes if it contains blank characters.

- **P** *page-list*—If the filter can handle it, this causes only the pages specified by *page-list* to be printed. You can specify single pages or a range of pages.

- **p**—Enable notification on completion of the print request.

- **q** *priority-level*—Priority levels range from 0 (highest) to 39 (lowest). This parameter changes the print priority of a print request. Giving a request a lower priority causes it to print before requests with a higher priority.

- **s**—Suppress messages from lp.

- **S** *character-set* **or S** *print-wheel*—Used to select a character set or print wheel to be used on the printer for the request. If the character set or print wheel is not available, the request is rejected.

- **t** *title*—Prints *title* on the banner page. Use quotes around the text if it contains blank spaces.

- **T** *content-type*—Causes the request to be printed on a printer that supports *content-type* if available, or to use a filter to convert the content in to the appropriate type. If you specify -r with this option, a filter will not be used. The request is rejected if no printer for this type is available and/or a filter cannot be used.

- **w**—Sends a message to the user's terminal after the print request completes. If the user is not currently logged in, a mail message is sent.

- **y** *mode-list*—Use *mode-list* options to print. The allowed values for mode-list are locally defined and the job is rejected if there is no filter to handle the request.

If you need to simply stop a job from printing, you can use the cancel command. The syntax for the cancel command is

```
cancel [request-id...][printer...]
cancel -u login-ID-list [printer...]
```

The first syntax example can be used to remove a specific print job by specifying its ID number. The second example shows how to remove all print jobs for a particular user (or users). If you list multiple users on the command line, enclose the list in quotes and use a space between each ID name. Ordinary users can only cancel their own print requests. Administrators can cancel any print job.

To get the request-id of a print job, you need to use the lpstat command. This command can be used by ordinary users with no parameters and will return information about only their print jobs. However, the administrator can use this command to see data about the entire printing system. The syntax for lpstat is

```
lpstat [-d] [-r] [-R] [-s] [-t] [-a [list]]
  [-c [list]] [-o [list]]
  [-p [list]] [-P] [-s [list] [-l]]
  [-u [login-ID-list]] [-v [list]]
```

In this example, list can be a comma-delimited list or a series of items separated by spaces and enclosed in quotes. You can omit a list or use the keyword all in most instances to get the status of all the requested objects. The parameters for this command are

- **a [*list*]**—Shows whether print destinations (printers or printer classes) are accepting print requests.

- **c [*list*]**—Displays the names of all classes and members of the class. You can identify specific classes using list.

- **d**—Displays the system's default print destination.

- **o [*list*]**—Displays the status of output requests. The list value can specify either printers, class names or request-ids.

- **p [*list*]**—Displays the status of printers. Use list to specify printer names.

- **r**—Displays the status of the print scheduler daemon (lpsched).

- **s**—Displays summary information about the printing system.

- **t**—Displays all the available status information about the printing system.

- **u [*login-ID-list*]**—Displays the status of print requests for the users listed in login-ID-list.

- **v [*list*]**—Displays pathnames of the output device files for printers indicated by list. For remote printers, this displays the name of the remote system.

Administering the System: lpadmin, lpsched, and lpshut

The lpadmin command performs a wide range of functions necessary to set up a printer on a Unix system. The command adds, removes, or modifies printers; and creates the necessary text files in the spooling directory for you so that you don't have to edit them manually. This command also can be used to set up "alerts" when the printer experiences a fault condition. The syntax for this administrative command is

```
lpadmin -p printer-options
lpadmin -x dest
lpadmin -d [dest]
lpadmin -S print-wheel -A alert-type [-W minutes]
      [-Q requests]
lpadmin -M -f form-name [-a [-o filebreak]
    [-t tray-number]
```

The first line of this syntax example shows how to add a new printer. Use the -p option on the command line to specify the printer's name and then list the printer's characteristics. For example:

```
lpadmin -phplj5 -v/dev/tty03 -mdumb -cpr
```

This command performs the functions needed to create a printer named hplj5. Following the printer name, the options here indicate that the actual printer device is connected to a serial port that can be accessed through the Unix device file /dev/tty03. This printer uses a dumb interface (-m option) and is a member of a class of printers named pr (the -c option).

Tip

After you set up a printer using **lpadmin**, it does not automatically allow users to print. Use the **accept** *printer* command to enable printing.

The man pages for your system give you a full list of the options you can use on the command line, and they vary depending on the flavor of Unix you have. However, the following list shows some of the more useful ones you'll find on most systems:

- **A** *alert-type* **[-W** *minutes***]**—Set up an alert action that is invoked when a printer fault occurs. The *alert-type* can be mail (sends an e-mail) or write (puts a message on an administrator's terminal). You also can use quiet to suppress alerts, showfault to execute a fault-handling procedure, or none to remove alerts. You also can specify a shell command to be executed.

- **c** *class*—Specify a class to which the printer will belong. If *class* does not exist, it will be created. The -r parameter can be used to remove a printer from a specific class.

- **D** *comment*—The text *comment* is displayed when the user requests a full description of the printer.

- **e** *printername*—Copies the interface program used by an existing printer (*printername*) for use with the printer you are creating. You quickly can clone entries when adding a printer of a type you already have, or when you are setting up a network that has many printers of the same type at the same time.

- **i** *interface*—Specifies the interface program for the printer. See -e earlier in this list to copy an interface from an existing printer.

- **m** *model*—Selects the *model* interface program that comes with the lp print service. You cannot use -e or -i with this option.

- **s** *system-name* **[!***printer-name***]**—Creates a remote printer. A remote printer is a printer on another system that you want your users to be able to use as if it were local. The *system-name* is the name of the computer on which the printer resides and !*printer-name* is the name the printer uses on the remote system. You can use a different printer name on your system than the name on the remote system.

Tip

In this chapter, the Unix "man" pages have been referred to several times. These are the help files for the Unix system, and you can consult them when you need help for a particular topic. For example, the command **man lpadmin** can be used to get the help text for the **lpadmin** command on the system so you can see a full list of the options supported.

To remove a printer from the LP printing system use the -x command line parameter:

```
lpadmin -xhplj5
```

This command removes the hplj5 printer from the system. If this is the last printer in its class of printers, the printer class also is deleted.

In the /etc/init.d/lp file, you will find commands that can be used to start the print scheduler daemon at boot time. The syntax, in case you want to change the boot-time command, is

```
lpsched [-nofork][-debug][-nobsd]
```

You also can use this command to restart the daemon if you find it necessary to kill it when you are troubleshooting printer problems. The lpsched daemon works sort of like the lpr daemon—it creates a new copy of itself to handle print jobs. The original daemon remains free to respond to additional user requests.

Note

The -nofork parameter can be used to suppress the creation of a separate daemon process. This is recommended to be used during debugging. You also can use the -debug parameter to put the daemon into "verbose" mode. In this mode, more messages are displayed that can be useful when trying to solve printer problems.

The -nobsd parameter can be used to tell lpsched to ignore the BSD spooler's well-known port. If you also are running an lpd daemon on the system and it is using the default port, use this option to change the port used by lpsched.

Tip

"Well Known Ports" are listed in Appendix B, "TCP and UDP Common Ports." A port is used in TCP/IP protocols to specify an endpoint that an application can use, along with an IP address, so that it can send a message to a specific process on a computer. For example, the FTP protocol uses ports 20 and 21 (usually) and the Telnet daemon uses ports 23 and 24 (usually).

You can use several commands to shut down a printer, depending on just what you need to do:

- **lpshut**—This command stops all printers. Jobs that are currently printing are stopped, but are reprinted in their entirety when the printers are again started, as are other print jobs waiting in the spooler directory. User can continue to submit to a printer that has been stopped using this command. Use lpsched when you want to start printers up again.

- **reject [-r reason] printer**—This command stops a printer from printing, but users cannot continue to submit jobs to the printer for later printing. If you want the users to know what is happening with the printer, use the -r command and specify the text you want them to see. If the text contains blank characters (it's more than one word), enclose the text in quotes. To restart the printer use the accept printer command.

- **disable[-c | -W] [-r [reason]] printer**—This command can be used to disable a printer temporarily while still allowing users to submit jobs to the spooling directory that will print when the queue is restored to service. The -c and -W options are exclusive. Use -c to cancel the job that is currently printing and -W to have the printer stop after the current job finishes. Both of these parameters are ignored if the printer is on a remote system. Again, use -r to specify text to be displayed to users (when they use the lpstat -p command to check the printer's status). Use the enable printer command to restart the printer.

If a printer will be out of service for a while, and you don't want users to keep submitting jobs, use the reject command. If a printer is going to be taken out of service completely, use the lpadmin command to remove it.

If some major problem is plaguing your entire printing system, use the lpshut command to bring everything to a halt while you investigate the problem.

One last command that might be handy when performing troubleshooting or maintenance duties is the lpmove command. This command can move pending print requests from one printer to another. For example:

```
lpmove hplj5 -221 hplj5land -232 laser3
```

In this example, the print job identified by the request-id number 221 will be moved from the hplj5 printer to laser3. The print job identified by the request-id 232 waiting for hplj5land also will be moved to laser3.

Using TCP/IP Printing on Windows NT 4.0 Server

Windows NT Server can use several network protocols to connect to a printer on the network, and then make the printer available via the server to other clients on the network that do not have support for the particular protocol. TCP/IP and DLC are among the supported protocols for Windows NT Server.

To configure Windows NT Server to use a networked printer using the TCP/IP protocol, you first need to know the IP address of the printer. You usually can find this on a test page or configuration page for the printer. If the printer has not been configured, consult the manual for your particular model.

Before you can use the Printer Wizard to install a printer that uses TCP/IP, you need to install the Microsoft TCP/IP Printing service. This can be done quickly by using the Network applet in the Control Panel. Select the Services tab, and then click the Add button. From the list of services, select Microsoft TCP/IP Printing. After the installation procedure has copied the files that it needs from the installation CD, you must reboot the server before you can use the service.

After the server has rebooted, use the Printer Wizard to create the printer. Select Add Printer from the Printers folder. The first dialog box asks whether the printer is a local printer (My Computer) or a network printer (Network printer server). In Windows NT, a print device is the actual physical printer that attaches to the computer or to the network via a network adapter card. A printer, under Windows NT, is a logical construct, or object, that you send print jobs to. So, when the Add Printer Wizard asks you whether the printer is to be managed by My Computer or Network printer server, you should answer My Computer. Although the print device actually is going to be accessed by the TCP/IP network protocol, the "printer" object will be managed on the local server.

Select My Computer when the Add Printer Wizard prompts you in its first dialog box.

The next dialog box (See Figure 35.1) allows you to select the port that the print device is attached to. The usual communication ports (LPT1:, LPT2:, COM1:, and so on) are displayed here.

Because the printer will be on the network, you need to create a new type of port. Select the Add Port button. The next dialog box allows you to select the type of port you want to add. Select LPR Port.

Tip

If you neglected to install the Microsoft TCP/IP Printing service, you will not see LPR Port as an option in the dialog box when you try to add a printer port. Go back and add the service, reboot the server, and then continue to create the printer.

The Add Printer Wizard then prompts you to enter the IP address (or hostname) of the remote printer and the name of the printer or print queue on that remote system. In many cases, you won't have to enter a print queue name if you are using a printer that is directly connected to the network. Check the configuration printout for the printer to be sure.

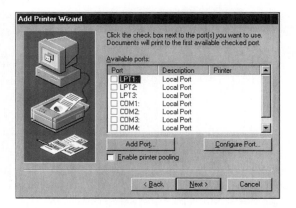

Figure 35.1 The Add Printer Wizard prompts you for the port the print device is connected to.

If you are creating a printer that will send jobs to a remote print queue on another system, such as a Unix or Linux system, you have to put the name of the printer or print queue here. After you have entered the necessary address and print queue information, click OK and then click Close in the Printer Ports dialog box.

The new printer port is now displayed in the list of available ports along with LPT1: and the others. Select the new port by clicking the check box next to it and then click Next.

The Add Printer Wizard then displays a dialog box from which you can select the printer's manufacturer and model so that a print driver can be installed. If your model is not among those displayed and you have a floppy disk that contains the driver, or if you have the driver files on a local or network disk, click the Have Disk button and supply the correct path to the files.

When you have selected the correct model, click the Next button. You are asked to supply a name for the printer. It is best to use something descriptive that indicates the type of printer and its location if you plan to let other computers connect to the server and send print jobs to it.

The next dialog box asks you whether you want to share the printer on the network. If you choose to share the printer, you also can designate, from the list displayed, to load additional printer software drivers for other OSs. This allows you to share the printer with clients that do not have the driver installed on their computer. The raw print job is sent by the client and formatted locally by the server using the appropriate driver, before it is spooled to the network printer. Click the Next button when you have selected to share, or not share, the printer.

The last dialog box prompts you to print a test page. You should always do this to test the configuration you have just set up.

Using TCP/IP Printing on Windows 2000 Server

Installing a network printer on Windows 2000 servers is similar to the process used for Windows NT 4.0. However, some of the dialog boxes look a little different and, of course, Windows 2000 has additional physical printers you can select from when creating a printer on the server. The following steps summarize the process of creating a printer on a Windows 2000 server that you can share with other users on the network.

1. Click Start, Settings, Printers.
2. Double-click the Add Printer icon.

3. A wizard pops up to guide you through the process. Click the Next button.

4. From the dialog box shown in Figure 35.2, select Local Printer and click the Next button.

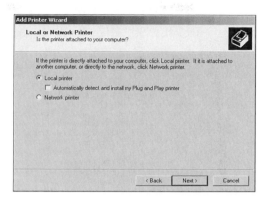

Figure 35.2 Select Local Printer from the wizard's dialog box because the printer will be managed locally on this server.

5. In the Select Printer Port dialog box (see Figure 35.3), select the Create a New Port option button, and then select Standard TCP/IP Port from the drop-down menu. Click the Next button.

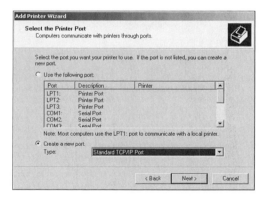

Figure 35.3 Select Create a New Port from this dialog box.

6. An informational dialog box pops up telling you to make sure the printer is connected to the network and functioning. If you are sure of this, click the Next button.

7. In the Add Port dialog box (see Figure 35.4), enter the IP address for the printer. As you type the address, the Port Name field automatically fills in a default name for the port, consisting of the characters "IP_" followed by the IP address you entered. If you want, change the port name to something more meaningful to you. When finished, click Next.

8. Another dialog box pops up showing a summary of the information you've entered to create the port. Click Finish.

9. The Add Printer Wizard reappears (as shown in Figure 35.5), prompting you to enter the type of printer that you want to connect to. Choose the manufacturer from the left pane and the printer model from the right pane. When finished, click Next.

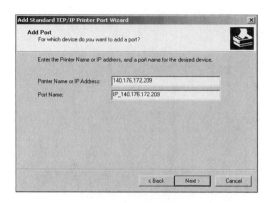

Figure 35.4 Use this dialog box to enter the printer's IP address.

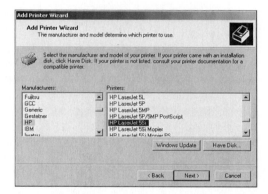

Figure 35.5 Select the printer manufacturer and printer model from this dialog box.

10. The next dialog box prompts you for a name for the printer (see Figure 35.6). Enter a name that is meaningful for your site. You also can elect to make this your default printer. When finished making your selection and naming the printer, click Next.

Figure 35.6 Enter a name for the printer in this dialog box.

11. The next dialog box (see Figure 35.7) asks if you want to share this printer on the network. Because this chapter is about network printing protocols, select yes and click Next.

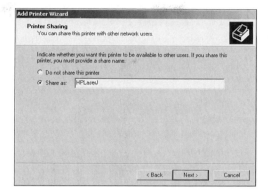

Figure 35.7   Select whether to share the printer on the network or reserve it for only your local system's use.

12. In the next dialog box (see Figure 35.8), you can enter text describing the location of the printer and add comments that users will see when browsing the network. Enter any text needed, and click Next.

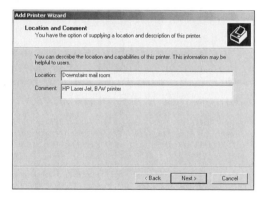

Figure 35.8   Use this dialog box to enter the location and any comments about the printer.

13. Finally, a dialog box prompts you to print a test page. This is a good idea because it lets you know if the printer setup was successful. Click Next to send the test page to print.

14. A summary dialog box displays the information that will be used to create the printer. Click Finish.

15. The wizard copies the necessary drivers and other files to system directories and then sends a test page to the printer. A small dialog box pops up asking whether the test print was successful. Click OK (assuming it worked) and the printer-creation process is finished. You now can use the printer, or allow users on your network access to use it.

Before users can use the printer share, you need to grant access to this resource. Chapter 34, "Rights and Permissions," provides instructions for granting access (or denying it) to users for printers and other resources offered by a Windows 2000 server.

Configuring a NetWare Printer for TCP/IP Printing

The printing process under the NetWare architecture separates the printer physical device from the print queue much like Windows NT Server. In the Novell Directory Services (NDS) database, the administrator defines three objects and configures their properties to make printers available to clients. The *printer* object represents the physical printer itself, which can be attached to a computer or directly to the network with its own network card. The *print queue* is a directory that resides on a NetWare volume and is used to buffer print files until they can be sent to a printer. The *print server* can be either hardware or software and is the component that controls the actual printing process by taking the file from the print queue and delivering it to the physical printer.

To configure a printer object that will be used for a printer that is connected directly to the network, you must specify the protocol and the network address for the printer. To do so, click the Configuration button on the Printer Object dialog box. From the Printer Type field, select one of the following:

- Unix
- XNP
- AppleTalk

For TCP/IP printing select Unix. Then, in the field labeled Network Address Restriction, enter the IP address for the printer. You can also use this feature to connect to a printer that is attached to another server. In that case, enter the IP address for the server. The address you enter here is the only address used to connect to the printer.

The *print server* object should then be created. PSERVER.NLM is the NetWare software print server, although you also can use a third-party print server if one is provided by the manufacturer for its printer. The dialog box for the print server object allows you to specify the name that will be used to advertise the printer on the network and the network address of the print server.

The printer, print server, and print queue do not all have to reside on the same network server. Indeed, you can connect the physical printer directly to the network, define the print queue object on a server and then define the print server object on another server. This flexibility comes at a cost, however. When a client wants to print, the NetWare client software sends the file to the server where the print queue resides. When it's time to print the file, it is sent to the print server, which then sends it to the printer. Obviously, if all three objects are on the same server, or if the print server and print queue are on the same server, less network traffic is generated.

Data Link Control Protocol (DLC)

In a network in which the IP address space is becoming scarce, you can use other methods to connect printers to your servers. For example, the HP Jet Direct card, which can be used to connect many HP printers directly to the network, can communicate with servers on the network using TCP/IP, or you also can use the DLC protocol, which does not require that you assign an IP address to the printer's network card.

The DLC protocol was developed by IBM primarily for use in connecting to mainframe computers as part of its Systems Network Architecture (SNA) specifications. DLC also is used today to establish sessions with AS/400 computers. In addition to the HP Jet Direct card, you will find that other vendors also make network cards for printers that can use DLC. For example, the Brother NC-600X and NC-2010h network cards both can be used for this purpose. However, you'll find that DLC no longer is present in Windows systems starting with Windows XP.

Internet Printing Protocol

The newest thing on the horizon for printers is the Internet Printing Protocol (IPP). Although most network servers and clients can be configured to use the lpr/lpd, Telnet, or DLC protocols, there are still many other diverse methods used to send print jobs to printers. The driving force of the Internet is making many vendors conscious of the need for more unified standards for basic functions, such as printing, and new protocols are being developed.

In 1996, several groups were developing a new standard. Novell and Xerox were working on a protocol that was titled Lightweight Document Printing Application (LDPA), IBM was developing the Hypertext Printing Protocol (HTPP), and Microsoft and HP were working on still another new protocol. Finally, a working group was formed under the auspices of the Internet Engineering Task Force (IETF) to work on a new standard.

The goals of the first efforts of the project are to develop a protocol that defines the user end of the printing process and includes the following capabilities:

- Allow a user to discover the capabilities of a particular printer.
- Allow a user to submit jobs to the printer.
- Allow the user to get the status of the printer or his print job.
- Allow the user to cancel a print job.
- Define a set of directory attributes that make it easy to find a printer in a directory database.

All these are standard items that will be incorporated into the first version of the standard (1.0). Later revisions will include mechanisms to provide for security, such as user or printer authentication, and functions for administrators who manage printing systems. Another goal of the standard is to define methods to allow IPP to interact with lpr/lpd systems so that it won't be necessary to throw out your entire printing infrastructure and start over again.

Note

The work of the IPP group so far has been defined by several RFCs. Version 1.0 RFCs include

- RFC 2565, "Internet Printing Protocol/1.0: Encoding and Transport"
- RFC 2566, "Internet Printing Protocol/1.0: Model and Semantics"
- RFC 2567, "Design Goals for an Internet Printing Protocol"
- RFC 2568, "Rationale for the Structure of the Model and Protocol for the Internet Printing Protocol"
- RFC 2569, "Mapping Between LPD and IPP Protocols"
- RFC 2639, "Internet Printing Protocol/1.0: Implementers Guide"

In addition, two RFCs have been issued for version 11.1:

- RFC 2910, "IPP/1.1: Model and Semantics"
- RFC 2911, "IPP/1.1: Encoding and Transport"

Additional Internet Draft documents are still in the review stage and will add additional functionality to the protocol.

IPP Object Types

In the first version of this protocol, two basic object types are defined: *printer* and *print job*. The printer object encompasses the functions that are accomplished by the actual physical printer, rendering the printed page, as well as some of the functions that are traditionally performed by the print server, such as spooling the print file and handling scheduling procedures. The functions of the printer object can be implemented in a print server or on the printer itself. The printer object can be used to send output to a single physical printer or to more than one device.

When a user sends a document to a printer, the printer object creates a new object called a print job. The print job object contains the document to be printed and can contain more than one document per job. The printer object manipulates the print job and handles how it is sent to the physical printer.

IPP Operations

The protocol defines several operations, which consist of a request and a response. The operation allows the client to communicate with the object.

The operations defined in the first version of the protocol that can be used with the printer object are

- Print-Job
- Print-URI
- Validate-Job
- Create-Job
- Get-Printer-Attributes
- Get-Jobs

The operations that can be used with the print job object are defined as

- Send-Document
- Send-URI
- Cancel-Job
- Get-Job-Attributes

Note

The term URI used in these operations refers to Uniform Resource Identifier, which is described in RFC 2396. URIs are used to unambiguously identify an object. You might be familiar with the term URL, which stands for Uniform Resource Locator, another standardized term which can unambiguously identify a location for a resource. The concept here is similar, in that a unique identifier is assigned to the print job.

A client submits a document to print by using the Print-Job request. Using this operation, the client "pushes" or sends the text to be printed. A client also can submit a job using the Print-URI operation, in which the client sends only the URI reference for the data to be printed and the printer object "pulls" the data itself. To send multiple documents to be printed, the client uses the Create-Job operation which is followed by multiple Send-Document or Send-URI operations, which also operate in a push-pull fashion.

The printer object responds to Validate-Job requests from the client depending on the current state of the printing job (pending, processing, and so on). For example, the printer object might return information to the client that the URI which was supplied, is no longer valid. Or, it might return error messages to the client.

Other operations are fairly self-explanatory. The Get-Printer-Attributes and Get-Job-Attributes operations return information about the printer or the print job. The Get-Jobs operation allows the client to get a list of job objects that are being processed by the particular Printer object. The Cancel-Job operation is used by the client to remove a job from the Printer object, basically just stopping a job from printing.

The RFCs also go into detail describing the attributes of each object, some of which are required and some of which are optional. These attributes include information about the job, such as its name, time stamps for different parts of the printing process, and the output device assigned to print the job. Attributes for the printer object include the name of the printer, its location, location of the printer driver for the printer, and other information, such as the make and model of the printer.

What's in Store for Version 1.1?

Version 1.1 of IPP is adding more functionality to the protocol. Several new operations have been defined:

- Pause-Printer
- Resume-Printer
- Purge-Printer

In addition, Version 1.1 suggests the order in which steps should be taken by an IPP 1.1. implementation. In general, these are

1. Validate the protocol version.
2. Validate the requested operation.
3. Validate the presence of operation attributes.
4. Validate the values of operation attributes.
5. Validate the attribute values against the object's supported values.
6. Validate any optional operation attributes.

For each request or response, the protocol version number must be included. This value, and its semantics, are kept in the same place in the packet for future versions to provide for backward compatibility. Next, the operation identifier must be validated against the printer object's "operations-supported" attribute. The presence of operation attributes and their values is then evaluated, followed by the validation of optional attributes.

If the IPP object receives from a client a request message that is missing a required attribute, or the attribute groups are presented out of order, the object rejects the request.

The Future of IPP

The IPP protocol will most likely be widely adopted in just a few years. It will solve a lot of problems for both end users and for vendors of printing equipment. Many companies are beginning to use the Internet to create virtual private networks (VPNs) instead of creating WANs using leased lines and other dedicated links. As the Internet continues to weave itself into every nook and cranny of the modern business world, standards such as IPP will generate new types of services. It is easy to foresee a business segment that will take over handling some, or all, of the aspects of printing for a large organization. Standards such as IPP will make implementation of these sorts of services much easier because it won't rely on multiple proprietary protocols and skill sets.

In addition to helping you manage printing across your own private network, IPP might provide some promising business opportunities for those who are clever enough to take advantage of them. For example, using IPP, you could set up a printer to allow your clients to send purchase orders and other documents straight to your desktop. Or, you use IPP to "publish" your product sales literature, catalogs, and documentation, directly to a customer's printer.

Where Can You Find IPP?

A large number of vendors are beginning to adopt the IPP protocol. Windows 2000 Server (with IIS installed) supports IPP. You can submit a job to a printer on the Internet by specifying the URL for the printer. If you are using Windows 2000 Professional, you'll need to install Peer Web Services (PWS) first. The IPP messages are sent via HTTP. Administrators also can manage IPP-enabled printers using a browser. From Internet Explorer (or other similar browsers), you need to use one of the following formats:

- `http://printservername/printers/`
- `http://printservername/printername/`

The first URL syntax allows you to view multiple printers and select the one to manage, whereas the second allows you to go straight to a particular printer. In Figure 35.9, you can see an example of the first command when used with Internet Explorer. The Windows 2000 server POPEYE has two printers available.

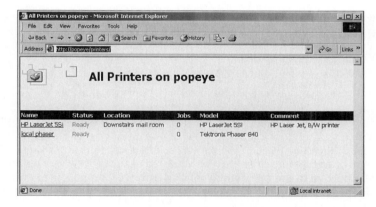

Figure 35.9   You can get a quick overview of the shared printers on the Windows 2000 server using this view.

In this display, you can see one reason using the Location and Comment fields can be important when creating printers. In a larger environment, these fields can simplify management tasks by making it easy for you to quickly locate a printer. Note the brief information shown here also includes the status of the printer and the type of physical printer used to render print jobs.

In Figure 35.10, you can see the view that would result from the second URL (printer-specific) listed previously. You also can get to this view by clicking the printer's hyperlink in the All Printers view.

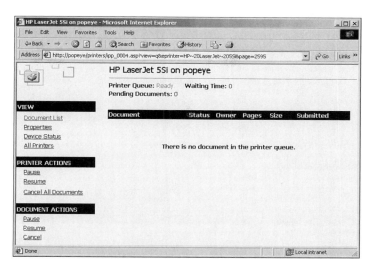

Figure 35.10 You can manage printers over the Web using IPP.

You can pretty much manage a printer via the Web almost in the same manner you do when logged into the server. This printer Web page shows you any documents currently waiting to print, along with status and other information. You also can perform the standard pause, resume, and cancel functions for documents or the printer as a whole by using the hyperlinks on the left side of the page.

Under the View menu, you can choose to look at the properties for a printer (see Figure 35.11). In addition to the printer model and those useful location and comment fields, you can see other information about the printer's capabilities.

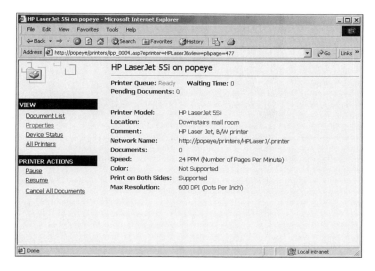

Figure 35.11 The Properties view for a printer gives you more information about the printer than the All Printers view.

The Device Status view (shown in Figure 35.12), is another useful page for management purposes. You can look here to see whether a printer is online, and get other useful information, such as the status of the paper trays and power save options.

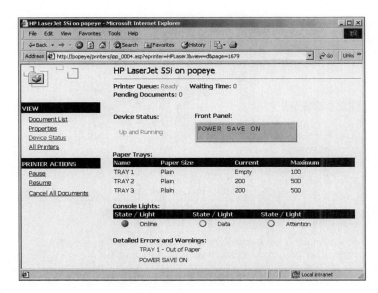

Figure 35.12   You can get additional information about a printer from the Device Status view.

Windows 2000 clients can connect to printers by using the URL http://*computername*/printers to browse for printers on a particular server. To connect to a printer, click the Properties view and you'll see a Connect link under the Printer Actions section on the page that appears. Click Connect.

For Windows 95/98 computers, you can use the program \clients\win9xipp.cli\wpnpins.exe on the Windows 2000 Server CD to install the files needed to access printers via a Web browser.

Print Servers

36

SOME OF THE MAIN TOPICS IN THIS CHAPTER ARE

Windows Print Servers

Printing Under NetWare

Hardware-Based Print Servers—Print Server Appliances

In the previous chapter, several protocols that typically are used for printing on a network were discussed. In this chapter, you'll examine some of the ways in which printers can be deployed on the network and made available to users. This function traditionally has been accomplished by using a computer that has a printer directly attached to it. When it became possible to connect printers directly to the network, it became possible for any computer to access the printer, depending on the operating system.

Today it's just as easy to attach multiple printers to a network directly, and yet still manage them from a central *print server* computer. A print server can take the load off of individual workstations by storing local copies of the files to be printed, as well as giving the network administrator a central point for administrating printing services. By routing the print traffic through a computer (or device) that serves as a print server, the network administrator is better able to control access to these printers and gather statistics that can be used to improve network performance. In addition, small network devices (described as network printer appliances) are small hub-like boxes that attach to the network. These devices provide a variety of ports, such as the traditional parallel and serial ports, so you can connect multiple printers to the network using a single connection.

This chapter looks at managing print servers using the Windows NT/2000 and NetWare operating systems, and takes a quick look at network print server appliances.

Windows Print Servers

Both Windows NT Server 4.0 Server and Windows 2000 Server provide a flexible printing system that can be used to direct user print jobs to a printer that is directly connected to the server, to print queues on other hosts (such as Unix or Linux systems), or to printers that are directly attached to the network. Setup is performed using a wizard that creates a *printer* in just a few minutes.

Note

Unlike some other operating systems, Windows NT and Windows 2000 do not use the term *print queue* to refer to the interface between an application and the actual physical printer. Instead, a print queue is a collection of documents that are waiting to print. Under Windows, a *printer* is an object that you can manage that sends the actual print job to the physical printer that renders your output onto hardcopy.

Printers and Printing Devices

The terminology used by Windows NT/2000 to refer to the actual physical printer is *printing device*. That HP LaserJet sitting down the hall is a printing device. The term *printer* is used to refer to a logical construct, or an interface to the print device. It might not be apparent why a distinction should be made between the printer and a printing device, but there are a number of good reasons. The main conceptual difference between the two is that they do not necessarily imply a one-to-one relationship. In Figure 36.1, you can see that several *logical printers* can be set up to send print jobs to the same printing device.

Using this kind of setup, you easily can define several different *logical printers* for a *printing device* with each printer set up to take advantage of different characteristics of the physical printer. All the logical printers are then pointed to the same physical output device. In this sort of setup, you might have one logical printer set up to print in a portrait orientation and then another set up to print in a landscape orientation. Users would send print jobs to the printer that matches the characteristics they need, without having to select the necessary configuration options themselves. Other possibilities include configuring multiple printers that select different paper trays or print in draft or letter-quality format. For example, you could create a printer that uses only a tray you keep loaded with letterhead paper.

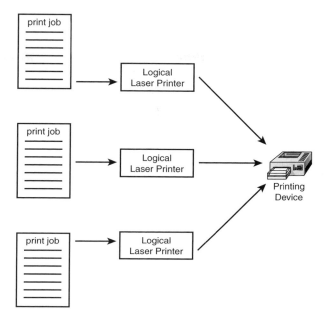

Figure 36.1   In Windows NT, more than one logical printer can send print jobs to a single physical printing device.

Another good reason for keeping the Printer object and the printing device separate is shown in Figure 36.2. This setup is sort of the opposite of that shown in the previous figure.

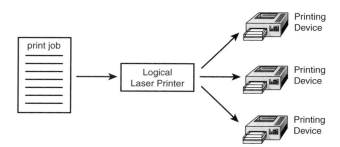

Figure 36.2   A printer pool allows a logical printer to distribute its load over several output devices.

This setup is usually called a *printer pool*. When high print volume is the norm, setting up a printer pool can provide a much faster throughput for end users, who will spend less time waiting for their printouts than if only a single printing device was used. It also eliminates the necessity of having to create and manage multiple logical printers. Using a printer pool makes it easier for you to add additional print devices without making users aware of it. One of the best features of using a printer pool is that it can be used to eliminate the physical print device as a single point of failure. If a printer begins to malfunction, it can be taken offline and print jobs can continue to be rendered into final format by other printers that are members of the printer pool.

When using printer pools, you must keep several things in mind:

- Each output printing device should be of the same type or be set up to emulate the same kind of device because the printer driver used by the logical printer is specific to a particular kind of printer.

- When a job is submitted for printing to a printer that uses a printer pool, it's printed on the *first available device*. As long as a printer is available, the user's job doesn't have to wait for another job to finish before it prints.

- Locate all the printers that are part of the same printer pool in a single location. Users won't be happy if they have to walk all over the office to find out where a print job ended up.

Adding a Printer Under Windows NT 4.0 Server

In the last chapter, you learned to use the Windows NT 4.0 and Windows 2000 printer wizards to install printers that use TCP/IP for network communications. All versions of current Windows operating systems support multiple printing protocols, however. Here we'll quickly review adding a printer using Windows NT (and after that, Windows 2000), showing you how to use printers that are directly attached to ports on a print server computer, or by using other network printing protocols. Also, you'll learn what some of the prompts mean and how you can improve printer performance on the network.

To begin adding a new printer, select Add Printer from the Printers folder that you find under My Computer. The Add Printer Wizard asks you a few simple questions.

Where Will the Printer Be Managed?

This first question can be confusing if you are not familiar with Windows NT 4.0 printing. The available choices are

- My Computer
- Network Printer Server

The wizard is *not* asking you where the printer will be *connected*. For example, if you select My Computer, this does not mean that the physical printer device will be connected to the LPT1: port on your server (although it might be). Instead, the prompt is asking you where the printer will be *managed*. If you select My Computer, the necessary drivers for the printer are loaded on the local computer and are responsible for any settings or other management functions for the printer on this computer.

If you select Network Printer Server, the wizard enables you to connect to a printer that is already on the network *or is being offered by another server* (such as a Unix host). The wizard then prompts you to load a driver for the printer, unless one is already loaded on the server that hosts the printer. When you connect to a printer using this method, you can send print jobs to the printer but you cannot manage its properties.

Port Selection

If you chose My Computer as the place where the printer will be managed, the next wizard prompt asks for the name of the port to which the printer is attached. This can be a local port, such as LPT1:, LPT2:, or even COM1:, and so on. You can select to have the printer set up to send the print job to a file instead, although this is a feature more useful for tasks such as capturing the output from an application that doesn't provide such a function.

Note

If you want to create a printer pool, select the Enable Printer Pooling check box, which appears on the Available Ports dialog box. You then can select more than one port for this logical printer.

If you want this logical printer to manage documents that are sent to a printer elsewhere on the network, select Add Port, and then supply the necessary configuration information that the wizard needs to create a port for the printer. The following kinds of ports are supported under Windows NT Server 4.0:

- Digital Equipment Corporation Network Port
- Hewlett-Packard Network Port
- Lexmark DLC Network Port
- Lexmark TCP/IP Network Port
- LPR Port

Note

Not all the ports listed here will be displayed necessarily. For the Hewlett-Packard Network Port to appear, you must first install the DLC protocol. For the LPR Port option to appear, you must first install the Microsoft TCP/IP Printing service. Both can be installed by using the Network applet in the Control Panel, after which you will have to reboot the server.

Highlight the port you want to create, and then click the New Port button. Depending on the choice you make, a dialog box appears to prompt you for more information for the specific kind of port you want to create. For example, in Figure 36.3 you see the information needed to create a Hewlett-Packard Network Port.

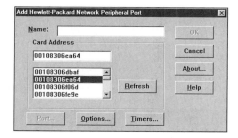

Figure 36.3   Fill in the information needed to create a Hewlett-Packard Network Port.

Fill in the name you want to give the port, and then select the 12-digit LAN (MAC) hardware address that corresponds to the address of the printer. You can get the address for the HP printer by printing a self-test page, or, if you're really bored, by going through the printer's I/O configuration menus. If no addresses appear on this dialog box, the printer might be powered off or there might be a network error preventing the server from obtaining it. If you click the Options or Timers button, you can customize this printer port further by specifying such things as the logging level that will be performed (information, warning, error) and values for timers associated with the DLC protocol.

The previous chapter discussed creating a TCP/IP printer port, which also can be useful for connecting a print server computer to computers that are distributed throughout the network. TCP/IP printer ports also can be used to send print jobs to printer appliances, which is discussed later in this chapter.

Selecting Printer Drivers

After you complete the dialog box for the port you want to use and return to the main dialog box, click the Next button to bring up a dialog box from which you can specify the manufacturer and type of printer. This information is used to determine which drivers Windows NT needs to load for this printer. You also can click the Have Disk button if your printer is not listed and you have a driver from the manufacturer that you can use (see Figure 36.4).

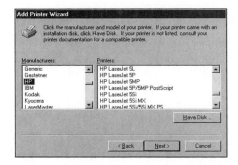

Figure 36.4 The Add Printer Wizard prompts you to select a printer driver. Use the Have Disk button if your printer is not listed.

Because the purpose of a print server is to accept print jobs from clients, be sure to load drivers for each kind of operating system client on the network that needs access to this printer. When the client prints the first time, it downloads the driver from the server so that the print job can be rendered into the correct format for the particular printer.

Giving the Printer a Name

Next, the wizard prompts you to enter a name to use for the printer (see Figure 36.5). This name won't be used as the printer share name; instead, it's a descriptive name for the printer. Use the check boxes at the bottom of the dialog box to set this printer as the default for this server if applicable. This does not set the printer as the default for users who connect to it over the network; it sets the printer as the default that shows up when you send print jobs from applications while you are logged in to this server locally.

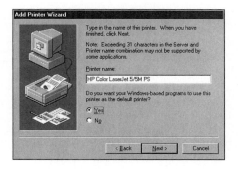

Figure 36.5 Give the printer a name and select Yes if you want it to be your default printer.

Sharing the Printer on the Network

The last dialog box you see enables the printer to be offered as a printer share for network clients. In this dialog box (see Figure 36.6), you must select the Shared check box, and then give the printer a name that will be displayed to users. Note that the Name field defaults to the type of printer and the first eight characters to be available to clients that have restrictions on the length of resource names, such as older MS-DOS clients. You can edit this field and use any name that makes sense to your users. It's usually best to use a name that indicates both the location of the printer as well as the kind of printer.

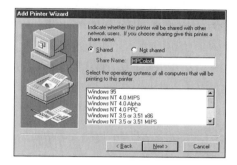

Figure 36.6   Click the Shared check box to offer the printer on the network to clients and to load additional drivers for those clients.

This dialog box also can be used to load additional drivers for clients that connect to the printer over the network. For example, if you have Windows 95 clients on your network, you should select Windows 95 from the dialog box. When this type of client must send a print job to the printer, Windows NT Server downloads the driver to the client so that the print job is formatted correctly for the printer. If the driver you specify is not already loaded on the system (for another printer, for example), you are prompted for the location of the driver. When you have finished specifying a share name for the printer and have selected any additional printer drivers you want to load, click the Next button.

Another dialog box asks whether you want to print a test page. This is highly recommended because if the test page doesn't print, nothing else is going to print. If the test page does not print, review the selections you have made to be sure they are accurate. Or, you might have a network problem that needs to be looked into. If this is a TCP/IP-networked printer, for example, you might try pinging the printer to determine whether it's reachable on the network. If you are using another protocol, try printing from a different computer that is configured similarly and determine whether this succeeds. If not, a network problem (such as a router configuration) might need to be resolved.

Print Server Properties, Printer Properties, and Document Properties for Windows NT 4.0 Server

Windows NT 4.0 Server enables you to configure properties for the print server as a whole and configure properties that are specific to each printer that you create. You can also configure default properties that are applied to documents printed on the server.

Print Server Properties

To bring up the Properties sheet for the print server, choose File, Properties in the Printers folder. The three tabs on this properties sheet are

- **Forms**—Use this tab to define forms that are available to users who use printers on this server.
- **Ports**—This tab enables you to add, delete, or reconfigure ports (it's similar to the dialog box presented when you created a printer).
- **Advanced**—This tab enables you to set up logging and notifications for the print server, and specify the spooling directory.

Forms are used to define certain properties of the output page that will be printed, including the size of the paper and the margins. Windows NT Server comes with several standard forms already defined, including most standard paper sizes and envelopes. If you have a special form that you have created for your business, such as an invoice format, you can define a new form using the Forms tab.

If you plan to set up several printers but want to get some of the work out of the way beforehand, you can use the Ports tab to create the necessary ports. When you actually get around to creating the printers, you can select the appropriate port rather than create it. This also can be useful in an environment in which one administrator is responsible for network functions and another is responsible for printing. The network administrator who is aware of network addresses used by certain devices can create the ports and send a list to the printer administrator, who can then create and manage the printers that use the ports.

Figure 36.7 shows the Print Server Properties dialog box with the Advanced tab selected.

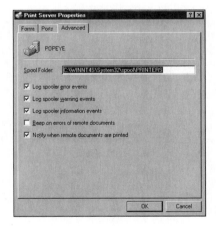

Figure 36.7   The Advanced tab enables you to set logging and notifications for the print server as a whole.

This tab is an important one to remember for troubleshooting purposes in which the more information you have, the better chance you have of solving your problem. You can enable the following notification and logging categories:

- Log Spooler Error Events
- Log Spooler Warning Events

- Log Spooler Information Events
- Beep on Errors of Remote Documents
- Notify When Remote Documents Are Printed

The Log Spooler Error Events option sets a logging severity level for events that will be placed into the System Event Log. You can use the Event Viewer administrative tool to examine the logged events. If users are complaining that their print jobs are not being printed, enable all three of the Log Spooler check boxes and, after they have attempted to print, review the records found in the Event Log.

Note

Under Windows NT 4.0, the Event Log is made up of three separate log files: System, Security, and Application. The events you can enable on the Print Server Properties page show up in the System Event Log. Matters related to printer security, discussed later in this chapter, show up in the Security Event Log. If applications have been written to use the Windows NT Event Logging service, and if the administrator has enabled the logging of these kinds of events, they might create events in the Application Event Log.

The information recorded in the Event Log helps you determine why the user's jobs are not printing. The Log Spooler Information Events check box also can be used to keep track of the pages printed by individual users. Figure 36.8 shows an example of an informational event that tells you a document was printed, by whom, and the number of pages.

Figure 36.8   The information events you record in the Event Log can track printer usage by user.

It can be tedious to use the graphical interface provided by the Event Viewer to review each record. To overcome this obstacle, you can create a comma-delimited file that contains the information found in the file. However, to do this you need the Dump Event Log (DUMPEL.EXE) utility, which can be found in the Windows NT Server 4.0 Resource Kit.

Another useful thing you can do on this tab of the properties sheet is change the spooling directory used by the server. If performance is a problem with the server, you might want to locate the spooling directory on a disk by itself to speed up access. For a low-volume print server, this probably won't be necessary.

Printer Properties

You can access the properties page for any printer by using either of the following:

- In the Printers folder, highlight the printer you want to work with and choose File, Properties.

- In the Printers folder, double-click the printer you want to work with. From the dialog box that appears, select Printers, Properties.

The properties page for a printer (see Figure 36.9) is divided into six property sheets that enable you to control a wide variety of properties for each printer on an individual basis:

- General
- Ports
- Scheduling
- Sharing
- Security
- Device Settings

Figure 36.9 You can configure properties specific to each printer by using its properties page.

The General tab enables you to modify informational text about the printer that users can view, such as the location of the printer. You also can use this tab to select an existing separator page or create a new separator page. Separator pages can be used to print a page before each user's job so it's easy for an operator to separate each print job on a high-volume printer used by many users. Separator pages also can be used to send printer-specific codes to a printer that determines how it prints the document. Windows NT Server comes with three separator pages designed for this purpose:

- **PSCRIPT.SEP**—This separator page changes the printer into PostScript mode. No actual separator page is printed.

- **SYSPRINT.SEP**—This page also switches a printer into PostScript mode but does print a separator page.

- **PCL.SEP**—This page switches the printer into PCL mode (HP's Printer Control Language) and prints a separator page.

Note

You might not have to use a separator page to cause a printer to change between PostScript and PCL modes. Many newer printers can autosense the kind of print mode the job requires and make the change automatically. Refer to the documentation for the printer to determine whether you must use a separator page for this purpose.

You can design your own separator pages using escape codes to include information such as the user's name, print job number, date, and any additional text you want on the page.

You also can print a test page from the General tab when troubleshooting the printer. Another useful feature found on this page is the New Driver button, which you can use to load an updated printer driver. This might be necessary when a manufacturer releases a printer driver that is more current than the one found on the Windows NT Server source CDs.

The Ports tab is similar to the ports display that you see when you create a printer or when you view ports using the Print Server properties page. Here, however, you can change the port used by this printer, which comes in handy when a printer is moved to a new location and a new network connection is required. You don't have to delete and re-create the printer; just go to the Ports tab and select or create the new port after the printer has been moved. Then, go back to the General tab and print a test page to determine whether the port has been successfully created.

The Scheduling tab enables you to set the time of day that a printer is available for use. Generally, a printer is available 24 hours per day, but you can use this tab to change that if you need to. Note that users can still send print jobs to a printer outside its available time range. Their documents are stored and then printed when the printer is available for use. If you allow users to schedule jobs to be printed later, you also must be aware of the disk space that will be used for spooling the documents that must wait. For large files, such as those containing complex graphics, you'll need a lot of space.

This feature can be used to force certain print jobs, such as lengthy reports, to be delayed until after hours when ordinary users no longer need the printer. For example, you can set up several logical printers, one of which you make available to your normal workday users. A second logical printer then can be set up to allow printing after hours. Applications that produce voluminous print jobs can send their documents to this printer, and users can retrieve their documents the next morning when they come into work.

The Scheduling tab enables you to specify several other configuration options:

- **Spool Print Documents So the Program Finishes Printing Faster**—This allows the application to send a print job quickly because the output is directed to a spooler file rather than directly to the physical printer. Generally, it takes longer to send a job directly to the printer unless it has enough memory to buffer the entire print job.

- **Print Directly to the Printer**—This is the opposite of the previous option. An application can stall until the printer has finished receiving the entire print job from the user.

- **Hold Mismatched Documents**—This option retains a print job that does not match the current printer settings instead of discarding it. You then can change the printer or disable this option to cause the document to print.

- **Print Spooled Documents First**—Generally a spooled print job begins to print before the document has been completely spooled to a temporary file. This option specifies that jobs already completely written to the spool file will print before those that are still spooling. This setting can override the priority of a spooling print job and allow a completely spooled lower priority job to print first.

- **Keep Documents After They Have Printed**—This setting causes spooled print jobs to remain in the spool directory after they have printed. This can be useful for troubleshooting print problems. You can look at the original print job and possibly send it to another printer to determine whether the original printer is exhibiting unusual behavior when trying to print.

Normally, your documents must be spooled before they print so that users notice a faster response time. However, when troubleshooting, you might want to send documents directly to the printer, bypassing the spooling operation. Also, if space becomes a problem on the disk that holds the spooling directory, you can cause jobs to be sent directly to the printer to avoid using additional disk space. Because this option is selectable by printer, you can set up some printers to use the spool directory and others to send jobs directly to the printer.

The Sharing tab enables you to modify the selections you chose when you created the printer and either allow or disallow the printer to be shared with network users. You also can use this tab to load additional client drivers when new clients are brought into the network, or change the share name the printer uses on the network.

The Security tab enables you to set up permissions that control which users or groups can use this printer, and that control auditing features for the printer. Users can be denied access to the printer, allowed to print and manage documents, or be given full control to the printer. Full control allows users to perform the following functions:

- Print
- Change document settings
- Pause or restart the printer
- Delete print jobs
- Change the priority (printing order) of jobs
- Delete the printer
- Change permissions for the printer

Usually, only print operators or network administrators are given full control over a printer. Most users need only the Print permission. This enables users to send print jobs and control their print jobs, but not those of other users. Auditing can help print operators and network administrators monitor printer usage to determine whether changes in permissions are necessary. The Auditing functions on the Security tab allow you to record events to the Event Log for later review.

▶▶   See Chapter 38, "Auditing and Other Monitoring Measures," to learn more about auditing print events and using the Event Viewer to review the data captured.

The Device Settings tab enables you to configure device-specific values for the printer. This includes information such as tray selection, font cartridges, and so on, depending on the features available for the specific printer type.

Managing Printers

After you create a printer, users can connect to it and use it to print. The administrator, or other users who have the appropriate permissions, can view the status of documents waiting to print and can manage the printer by using the dialog box shown in Figure 36.10. You can access this dialog box by double-clicking a printer in the Printers folder.

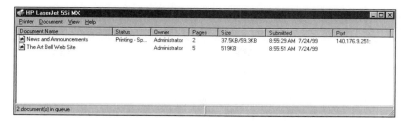

Figure 36.10   You can control a printer from this dialog box.

As you can see, documents that are currently being printed or waiting to print are displayed, showing the title of the document, the user, size of the print job, the port the printer uses, and the date and time the job was submitted. You can use the Printer menu and the Documents menu to manage the printer or any document. The Printer menu allows you to

- Pause the printer
- Set the printer to be the default on this computer
- Change the defaults for documents sent to this printer
- Change the sharing aspects of the printer
- Remove all documents from the printer
- View or modify properties for the printer

This menu is useful when you're experiencing problems with a particular printer. You can pause the printer, which stops printing but keeps any documents waiting to print, to fix a minor problem and then resume printing after the trouble has been resolved. You also can remove all documents from the printer, which is handy when a user or an application has sent numerous documents to a printer by mistake. You can bring up the Properties page for the printer, discussed earlier in this chapter, and modify items as you see fit.

The Documents menu is used to individually pause, restart, or cancel print jobs. You can selectively highlight individual documents waiting to print and then cancel them.

This view of the printer is most often used by print operators who are responsible for managing printer resources on the network.

Adding a Printer on a Windows 2000 Server

Again, Microsoft provides the Add Printer Wizard to guide you through installing a printer on a Windows 2000 Server. In the previous chapter, you learned the basic steps for creating a printer using a TCP/IP port. Now, you'll see the other possible choices you have for a Windows 2000 Server. To bring up the Add Printer Wizard, click Start, Settings, Printers and then double-click the Add Printer icon.

In the same manner as the Windows NT 4.0 wizard, you are prompted to create a printer for a local printer or a networked printer. Remember, this refers to *where* the printer will be managed. If you want to connect to a network printer so that the server can send documents to that printer, select the Network Printer check box. However, you won't be able to manage this printer or offer it as a share to other computers. If you want to manage the printer locally (even if it is a printer on the network), select Local Printer and click the Next button.

In the next dialog box, titled Select the Printer Port (shown in Figure 36.11), you choose an existing port by selecting the Use the Following Port option button. The list should include the standard printer ports (that is, LPT1:), as well as any ports that you might have created in the past. To connect to a networked printer, however, use the Create a New Port option button. This selection can also be used to create local ports.

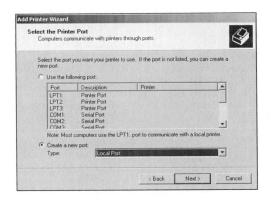

Figure 36.11   You can connect to a printer that is directly attached to the computer or one that resides on the network.

If you select Local port as the new kind of port to create, you have the following options:

- **Print to File**—You can specify a path and filename to which output is directed when this printer is used by a client. The file is overwritten each time the printer is used.

- **Print to File Share**—You can enter the UNC share name of a printer, for example.

- **The NUL Device**—You can use this to dump printer output into another dimension. Generally, you set up a printer for use with the NUL device to assist in troubleshooting printer connectivity problems without wasting paper.

- **Infrared Port**—This option is available if your computer supports an infrared port. Printers must meet specifications of the Infrared Data Association (IrDA).

Note

Some ports won't appear in your local port selection list, as was pointed out in the Infrared Port option. USB ports also won't show up unless Windows 2000 has detected a printer attached. If they do show up, you can use the port to create additional printers, and manage them as if they were different physical devices with the output all going to the same physical printer.

In addition to local ports, you can use the Create a New Port option to create ports for printers that reside on the network. The options that you'll find depend on the protocols and services you've installed on the Windows 2000 server. The following additional ports can be created:

- **Standard TCP/IP Port**—This is probably the option you'll use most of the time. Most printers today that support networking also support TCP/IP printing. Creating a TCP/IP port was discussed in the previous chapter.

- **AppleTalk Printing Devices**—This port type allows you to connect to printers that use the AppleTalk protocol. The AppleTalk protocol has to be installed first.

- **Hewlett-Packard Network Port**—Use this port type for older printers that support the Data Link Control (DLC) protocol. For all practical purposes, you shouldn't have to use this older protocol. If you have a printer this old, it's probably time to replace it! However, Windows 2000 still supports this kind of port, provided you install the DLC protocol.

- **LPR Port**—LPR (Line Printer Remote) is an older TCP/IP-based printing standard that was discussed in the previous chapter. You can use this to connect to printers on Unix servers, or other servers that support LPR/LPD printing. First you'll have to install Print Services for Unix.

- **Port for NetWare**—You can use this port type to connect to NetWare printing resources. The NWLink protocol and Client Services for NetWare must be installed first.

In the previous list, the most likely choice today is to create a standard TCP/IP port, because most all printers and printing appliances support it. However, if you need to use one of the other port types, be sure to install the prerequisite protocols or services. For example, to install Print Services for Unix you can add the component easily by clicking Start, Settings, Network, Dial-up Connections. Next, select Add Network Components. In Figure 36.12, you can see the dialog box that allows you to add additional networking components. Note that the last check box is Other Network File and Print Services.

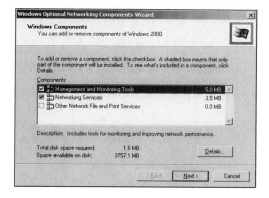

Figure 36.12   You must first install the necessary protocols and services for some printers.

To choose which protocols to install, select the Other Network File and Print Services check box and click the Details button. In Figure 36.13, you see the additional printing services that can be installed on a Windows 2000 computer.

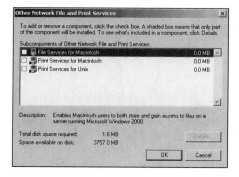

Figure 36.13   You can select which printing service to install from this dialog box.

You can install print services for Macintosh or Unix printers. After you make your selection, you are prompted for additional information, and the service is installed.

To install additional protocols, such as AppleTalk or DLC, use the following steps:

1. Select Start, Settings, Network, Dial-Up Connections.

2. Right-click your LAN connection and select Properties from the menu that pops up. The Properties sheet is shown in Figure 36.14.

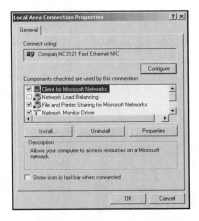

Figure 36.14   You can use the Install button to add additional network protocols to the Windows 2000 server.

3. Click the Install button. A small dialog box pops up and prompts you to install one of the following: a client, a service, or a protocol. Select Protocol and click the Add button.

4. The Select Network Protocol dialog box pops up and allows you to choose the network protocol to be added (see Figure 36.15).

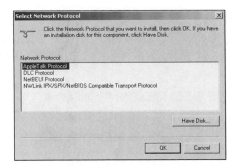

Figure 36.15   You can choose the network protocol to install from this dialog box.

5. Continue to add protocols as needed. When you are done, close the properties page for the local connection and the protocols should be ready for use.

After you have installed the necessary protocol(s) and service(s), you should see them as options when you elect to create a printer port on a Windows 2000 server. The remaining prompts displayed by the Add Printer Wizard depend on the protocol you've chosen. As with Windows NT 4.0, you also must select the printer manufacturer and the model of the printer. You are prompted to make the printer your default on the local computer and also asked whether you want to share it on the network. Finally, you get to print a test page, and then you're done with the Add printer Wizard.

Print Server Properties, Printer Properties, and Document Properties for Windows 2000 Server

Just like Windows 4.0 Server, you can manage Windows 2000 print servers and individual printers. You can also set up default properties for documents. To begin, click Start, Settings, Printers to bring up the Printers window. Choose File, Server Properties. As you can see in Figure 36.16, Windows 2000 adds a new Drivers tab to the Print Server Properties page.

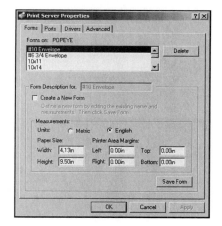

Figure 36.16   The Print Server Properties page allows you to manage global properties for the print server.

The other standard tabs are there, and work just like they did for Windows NT 4.0 Server. You can design forms, modify ports, and use the Advanced tab to set up logging and other notifications.

The Drivers tab, shown in Figure 36.17, allows you to load additional printer drivers for clients that will access the printer.

To add additional printer drivers, click the Add button. The Add Printer Wizard pops up again. Click Next to go back to the dialog box that allows you to choose a manufacturer and a printer model. Or, you can use the Have Disk option to load a driver that is not part of the standard Windows 2000 distribution.

You also can remove drivers by highlighting them and clicking the Remove button. If you need to update a driver, use the Update button. This is a powerful function because, in this one place, you can update a driver that is used by multiple printers. The Properties button allows you to view properties pages specific to the driver that you have highlighted. Casual users shouldn't change items on a printer driver's properties page. Only make these changes if you're thoroughly proficient in the printer workings and understand the changes that you are making.

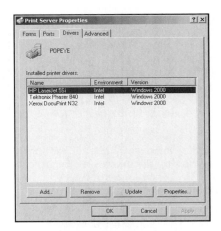

Figure 36.17 You can load additional printer drivers for clients on your network using the Drivers tab.

Printer Properties

Again, the properties page for a printer in Windows 2000 is similar to that used in Windows NT 4.0 Server, but with a few differences, as you can see in Figure 36.18.

Figure 36.18 You can manage properties for each printer individually.

Note that the Scheduling tab no longer shows up. This function is now located on the new Advanced tab. In addition to the tabs that were available under the Windows NT 4.0 Server version, the following tabs now show up on a printer's properties page:

- **Configuration**—This tab shows items specific to the printer model, such as additional trays that can be installed and whether a duplex (two-sided printing) module is installed. What you see here depends on the type of printer.

- **Advanced**—The scheduling functions have been moved to this tab. Other functions, as you can see in Figure 36.19, have also been moved to this page. For example, you use this tab now to select a separator page (this function used to reside on the General tab).

Figure 36.19 The Advanced tab contains functions that used to be on other tabs.

All the other functions found in Windows NT 4.0 are still here; you might have to spend just a minute or two looking through the various tabs to find them.

Managing Printer Properties

For day-to-day printer management, you double-click a printer icon in the Printers folder to get a view that looks just like it did in Windows NT 4.0. You can start, stop, and pause the printer or a particular document. You can also purge the printer of all documents waiting to print or selectively cancel documents, using the same methods as you used in Windows NT 4.0.

Managing Printers Using the Internet Printing Protocol (IPP)

One new feature that Windows 2000 offers is support for the Internet Printing Protocol (IPP) that was discussed in the previous chapter. In addition to allowing clients to use a browser to connect to a printer on a Windows 2000 print server, you can also use a browser to manage printers.

To use IPP, you must install Internet Information Services (IIS) on the print server as a prerequisite. This can be done during the initial operating system installation. Or, use the Add/Remove Programs icon in the Control Panel and select Add/Remove Windows Components to install IIS at a later time. When you've installed IIS, you'll find a new entry in the Administrative Tools folder: Internet Services Manager.

Managing Access to the Web-Based Printers Folder

As with the other Administrative Tools, the Internet Services Manager is written as a snap-in for the Microsoft Management Console (MMC). When you first launch the application, you'll see the MMC console tree in the left pane, listing the IIS Web servers that are in your domain. Select a server by clicking it once, and then click the plus sign that appears next to the server to expand the tree. A list of Web sites for the server appears. In the example shown in Figure 36.20, you can see that the Default Web Site has been expanded to show the objects that fall beneath it in the tree. The Printers folder is at the bottom of the list.

Right-click the Printers folder and select Properties. In Figure 36.21, you can see the properties page that appears with the Virtual Directories tab selected.

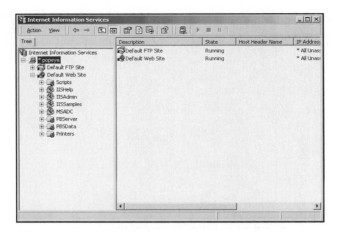

Figure 36.20 You can manage printers using IPP from the Internet Services Manager application.

Figure 36.21 You can manage printers via an Internet browser using Windows 2000 and IPP.

Note

When first presented with the Properties page for the Printers folder in the IIS MMC management application, some of the items don't seem to relate to printing. That's because, in general, they don't. This is the properties page for managing how printers are presented as a Web page (using the Documents tab), how security is configured to allow or deny access to the printers, and so on. You'll learn more about directly managing individual printers shortly.

For the most part, you can ignore most of this first tab and keep the defaults. If you are running a Web site using IIS, you might have reason to make changes here, but for ordinary printing tasks, the defaults should suffice. Leave the virtual directory on the local computer so that information about printers will be stored on the print server. You'll need to leave Read Access enabled so users can browse for printers. The Log Visits check box can be useful for troubleshooting purposes later.

You can configure permissions to restrict access to this Web-printing management on the Directory Security tab (see Figure 36.22).

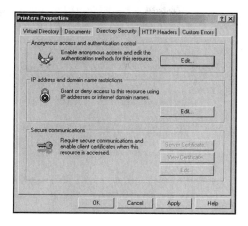

Figure 36.22   You can restrict access to printer management using the Directory Security tab.

If you click the Edit button under Anonymous Access and Authentication Control, you can select the kind of access allowed for managing printers. You can choose the authentication method for users wanting to connect to a printer from the following:

- **Anonymous Access**—This allows anyone to manage printers, without requiring any sort of authentication. You can also configure the account that is used with anonymous access. The default is the account created when IIS is installed: IUSR_*servername*.

- **Basic Authentication**—This method allows for a username/password exchange when connecting to the resource, but sends the information via clear text. For some non-Windows clients, this might be the only kind of authentication you can use. However, keep in mind that sending password information on the network as clear text can pose a security problem.

- **Digest Authentication for Windows Domain Servers**—This method uses a challenge/response mechanism to authenticate the user and is more secure than the basic authentication method. This method is new with IIS 5.0 and sends a hashed value over the network rather than the password.

- **Integrated Windows Authentication**—This last method uses a cryptographic exchange based on the Kerberos method.

You can use the IP Address and Domain Name Restrictions section on the Directory Security tab to further control access. When you click the Edit button for this section, you'll see a dialog box similar to that shown in Figure 36.23.

You can choose to add records for IP addresses that are allowed to use the printer or you can specify those addresses that are denied access.

To allow access to most users, and restrict just a few addresses, select the Granted Access option and use the Add button to add exclusions. This is the easiest method for granting access if the printer is to be available to most of your users. Alternatively, you can choose the Denied Access option and use the Add button to add IP addresses of those specific computers that are allowed to access the Printers folder on this server.

Figure 36.23   You can allow or deny access based on IP addresses.

Figure 36.24 shows the dialog box that appears when you use the Add button. In this example, the Group of Computers option is selected, which is more efficient than entering individual IP addresses. Instead, you specify a network ID and the subnet mask for that network. Thus, you can allow or deny entire groups of computers based on their network address. This is helpful when using DHCP to configure client computers. In that situation, you know the network address for any particular subnet, but you don't know which IP address will be assigned to any particular client. If your network is organized in a logical manner by department, for example, you can control access for different departments if they are each on a different subnet. Simply specify the subnet network address and address mask using this dialog box.

Figure 36.24   You can specify an individual address or a particular network using the Add Button dialog box.

Note also that you can use the Domain name option in the Add Button dialog box, in which case you can control access based on a domain name. This method, however, requires additional overhead and can slow server performance.

Finally, the Directory Security tab allows you to require secure communications using a certificate server. You must have a certificate server on the network for this functionality to be available. This is the most secure form of communications you can choose for managing the Printers folder.

Managing Printers Using a Web Browser

To view the printers on a print server that has been IPP enabled by the installation of IIS, use the URL http://servername/printers. In Figure 36.25, you can see a listing of the printers that are shared on the print server Popeye. You can quickly check the status of printers using this URL.

To see details about a particular printer, click the printer in this display. Figure 36.26 shows the page that is displayed for a single printer.

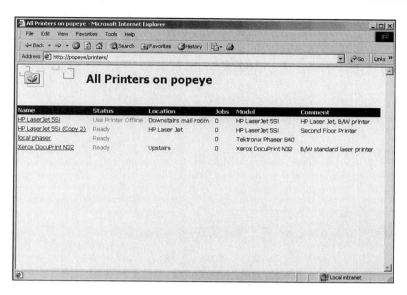

Figure 36.25 You can view all the printers shared by a Windows 2000 print server.

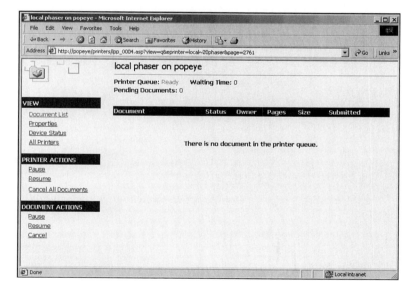

Figure 36.26 You can view information about each printer using a Web browser.

In this figure, the functions available are just about the same as you get when you double-click a printer icon in the Printers folder. However, the display is in Web-browser form instead of the traditional dialog boxes and windows used in the past.

Most of the display is used to show documents waiting to print and status information, such as the owner and when the print job was submitted. On the left side of the Web page, you'll see three different sections of options for management purposes:

- **View**—This section provides a listing of documents (the default, shown in Figure 36.26 previously). You can also choose to view the properties of the printer, view the status of the device, or return to the Web page that lists all printers on the server.

- **Printer Actions**—This section lets you do the normal management functions: pause the printer, resume the printer, or cancel all documents that are waiting to print.

- **Document Actions**—This section allows you to do the same functions on the document level instead of the printer level. Use these options to pause, resume, or cancel a particular document you've first highlighted in the document listing.

Figure 36.27 shows the Properties page for a printer. This is helpful when choosing a printer.

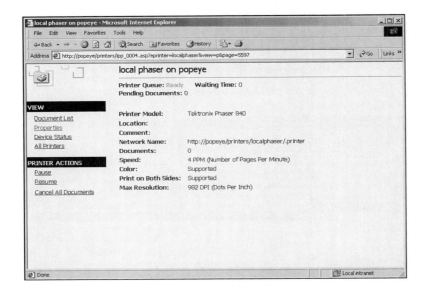

Figure 36.27   Use the Properties page for a printer when trying to decide which printer to use, based on the printer's capabilities.

The Properties page for a printer can be used to determine a printer's capabilities. The comment and location fields would have been nice to see in this figure. When this printer was created, the administrator was obviously in a hurry.

Finally, Figure 36.28 shows the Device Status page for a printer, which can be useful when troubleshooting. Note the other information you can see from this view, including information from the printer's front panel display, the status of paper trays, and any error messages that might be outstanding for the printer.

Because IPP allows you to print to printers literally anywhere on the Internet, it will be more widely implemented in the near future as the standards committee finishes the next version of the specification. Although the usual Windows printer-management utilities allow you to manage printers remotely, by using a browser you can manage printers from just about anywhere, as long as you set up management user access securely.

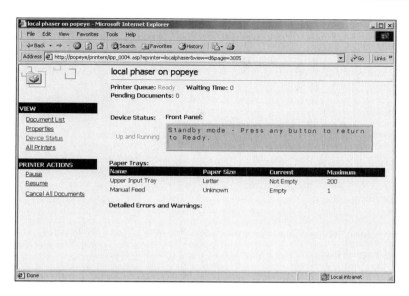

Figure 36.28   You can check the status of the device using this Web-based view.

Printing Under NetWare

Novell Directory Services uses objects in the directory database to represent the functional components of the printing system. Similar to Windows NT and Windows 2000, some terms must be defined:

- **Printer**—This is the physical printer, like the printer device under Windows NT.

- **Print queue**—This is like the logical printer found in Windows NT. Unlike Windows NT, the term *queue* is used. Users send print jobs to a print queue where they are retained until they print.

- **Print server**—This can be a software print server (such as NetWare's PSERVER.NLM) loaded on a host computer on the network or a physical print server device that is connected to the network.

When the administrator creates a Print Queue object in the database, a directory that will hold the spooled files is created automatically. The administrator then specifies the print server that will control the queue, and the printer (physical device) that will render the print job into a finished document. When configuring a NetWare client, you select a print queue. The user does not have to be bothered with other aspects of the system such as the printer or the print server.

Print queues hold jobs waiting to print. A queue can accept documents even if the printer is offline or out of service. The jobs wait in the queue until the printer is restored to service or another printer is assigned to the task. In a manner similar to Windows NT, NetWare print queues can send print jobs to multiple output print devices and multiple print queues can be established to send output to the same printer.

These three entities, the printer, the print server, and the print queue, do not have to reside on the same host computer. However, to reduce network traffic, it's a good idea in a high-volume printing environment to locate them on the same server. Or else, when a user submits a print job, network bandwidth is used, sending the data to the print queue. Then, more bandwidth is used to send the document from the print queue to the print server, and if the printer is a networked device, additional bandwidth is used to send the document from the print server to the printer.

To create the objects needed for printing in NetWare, you use either the NetWare Administrator or the PCONSOLE utility. The PCONSOLE utility is the recommended route because it has an option that provides a quick setup for all three objects. To use the PCONSOLE utility to set up printing on a server, follow these steps:

1. Log in as an Admin user or a user that has the create, delete, and browse privileges for the container that will hold the printing objects.

2. Run PCONSOLE.

3. Choose PCONSOLE, Change Context. Set your context to the container that you want to use for the printing objects.

4. Choose Available Options, Print Queues.

5. Press the Insert (Ins) key to create a new object.

6. Enter the name you want to give to the Print Queue object.

7. A dialog box prompts you for the volume to use for the Print Queue object's spooling directory. Enter an object or use the Insert key to browse for available volumes. When finished, press the Escape key to return to the PCONSOLE menu.

8. Next, create the Printer object. Choose Available Options, Printers.

9. Press the Insert key to create a new Printer object.

10. Enter a name for the Printer object when the dialog box prompts you.

11. Select the newly created Printer object from the Printers list.

12. In the Printer Configuration screen that appears, fill in the configuration information specific to the kind of printer the object represents, such as whether it uses a parallel or serial port, address restrictions, and so on.

13. While still in the Printer Configuration screen, select the queue you want to use from the Print Queues Assigned field. When finished, use the F10 key to save the information. Use the Escape key to return to the Available Options menu.

14. Select Print Servers to begin creating the new Print Server object. Press the Insert key to create a new object.

15. Enter a name for the new object when the screen prompts you. The object is created. Select it from the Print Servers list so that it can be configured.

16. Select the Printers option from the Print Server Information list. Press the Insert key.

17. A list of Printer objects appears. Select the Printer object you just created. You can continue to add other Print Server objects if you like. Press the Escape key until you reach the main menu of the PCONSOLE utility.

You also can use the Quick Setup feature of PCONSOLE. Choose Available Options, Quick Setup on the PCONSOLE menu. The Print Services Quick Setup screen appears and allows you to fill in the fields on this screen.

Tip

You can use the PUPGRADE utility to upgrade NetWare 3.x servers that are already configured as print servers. Select PUPGRADE, Upgrade Print Servers and Printers; then select the bindery print server you want to upgrade.

Print Queue Object Properties

The Print Queue object is a logical representation of a print queue. It uses a directory (created as a subdirectory under the /QUEUES directory) on a NetWare volume you select when you create the object to store files waiting to print. The following are significant properties of the Print Queue object:

- **Volume**—The volume selected to hold files that are waiting in the queue to print. Choose a volume that has adequate storage for the typical printing volume on the server.
- **Authorized Print Servers**—A list of print servers that can use this print queue.
- **Printers Servicing Print Queue**—A list of printers to which the print queue can send output.
- **Operators**—The users allowed to perform management functions on the queue.
- **Users**—The users allowed to send print jobs to the print queue. Instead of listing individual users for this property, it's much easier to use container objects that include users to make administration tasks easier.
- **Print Job List**—A list of print jobs in the queue. It includes the sequence number for each job, the job ID, the current status of the print job, the form used, and the name of the file that is to be printed.

Note that the Printers Servicing Print Queue property is used to link the Print Queue object to one or more Printer objects.

Printer Object Properties

The Printer object represents an actual physical printer that will accept print jobs from a print queue. The printer can be connected directly to the network, to a workstation, or to a server.

The properties of the Printer object include a name property, which is established when the Printer object is created. In addition, you can assign values to other descriptive properties:

- Other Names
- Description
- Location
- Department
- Organization

The following are more important properties that affect how the queue functions:

- **Print Server**—Shows the Print Server object to which the printer is assigned.
- **Print Queues**—Lists the Print Queue objects that can send print jobs to the printer.
- **Printer Features**—Contains information such as the kind of printer language understood by the printer and the amount of memory installed. This is a useful feature because users can search Novell Directory Services (NDS) to find a printer that supports the features they need for a particular job.
- **Printer Type**—Indicates whether the printer is a parallel, serial, or other kind of printer, such as one accessed via AppleTalk or UNIX.
- **Banner Type**—Can be either text or PostScript.
- **Service Interval**—This time interval defines how often the printer checks with the Print Queue object to see whether there are any jobs to print. The value can range from 1 to 255 seconds, with a default of 5 seconds.

- **Buffer Size in KB**—This property defines the size of the data segment sent to the printer. The value can range from 3KB to 255KB, with a default of 3KB.

- **Network Address Restrictions**—The network address of the printer's network interface or the address of the host computer to which the printer is attached.

- **Service Mode for Forms**—Indicates the policy for changing forms and can be set to Starting Form or Service Mode for Forms. The Starting Form value is the identifying number of a form that the Print Server object expects to be loaded on the printer by default. The Service Mode for Forms is used to indicate whether the form can be changed, and how, or if only the currently mounted form should be used.

- **Notification**—A list of users who are notified when a problem occurs on the printer, such as a paper-out condition.

The Print Server property and the Print Queues property are used to link the three objects that make up the path from the user to the finished print job.

Print Server Object Properties

The Print Server object represents the print server program (PSERVER.NLM), which runs on a server to control the printing process. The only properties that are defined when the Print Server object is created is the Name property (common name) and the Advertising Name, which is used to advertise the service using the Service Advertising Protocol (SAP).

The Print Server object, like the Printer object, also enables you to define descriptive properties such as Department and Location. In addition, the Network Address field displays the address on the network of the print server when it is up and running. The Version property shows the version of PSERVER.NLM that is being used by the print server.

Other important properties include

- **Printers**—The Printer objects that the Print Server can use to render a print job into its final output form.

- **Operators**—Users listed in this property can perform management functions for the server. This can include users, groups, and user templates, as well as Organization or Organizational Unit container objects in the NDS tree.

- **Users**—Users who can use this print server. Again, the values here can also be container objects so you don't have to list each user individually. Although users only need to be listed as users for a print queue to print, if you list them here also, they can check the status of the print queue.

- **Password**—Allows you to assign a password to this Print Server object so that it cannot be loaded (via LOAD PSERVER) by unauthorized users.

The properties for a print server are loaded into memory when the module PSERVER.NLM is loaded. If you make changes to the object after it is loaded, they do not take effect until the print server is unloaded and loaded again.

PSERVER.NLM and NPRINTER.NLM

On a host that is acting as a print server, the PSERVER.NLM module must be loaded. When it is loaded, the module activates any printers defined by Printer objects that are listed in its Printers property. NetWare allows for both local and remote printers. Local printers are attached to the host print server. Remote printers can be serviced by this Print server but reside on other computers. The NPRINTER.NLM module controls the printer and is automatically loaded for each locally attached printer. Because of this, these printers are called *Autoload printers*.

To load the PSERVER module, use the LOAD PSERVER command:

```
LOAD PSERVER <print server object name>
```

The PSERVER.NLM can support up to 256 printers, up to 5 of which can be connected locally to the server on which PSERVER.NLM is loaded.

The NPRINTER.NLM module must be manually loaded on remote servers (and the program NPRINTER.EXE for remote workstations). When multiple printers are hosted on a single remote server or workstation, NPRINTER must be loaded for each one. The syntax used depends on the computer on which the module will be loaded. For DOS machines, use

```
NPRINTER <name of print server object> <name of printer object>
```

For NetWare servers, use

```
LOAD NPRINTER <name of print server object> <name of printer object>
```

Hardware-Based Print Servers—Print Server Appliances

You no longer have to dedicate a network host to act as a print server, either dedicated or otherwise because it's inexpensive to connect a printer directly to the network using a small hardware-based print server device. These devices range from a size that fits in your hand to larger boxes that look like hubs or routers. In some advertisements, you'll see these referred to as printer appliances, or just print servers. Regardless, the function is the same: to consolidate a number of printers to a single network connection. The device buffers data as it passes between the network and the printer and keeps track of which print jobs are destined for ports attached to the device.

Think about how you will locate printers in relation to users when making purchase plans. How many printers will be located in a single place? For example, if you have a central print room where you keep multiple printers, copiers, and other similar equipment, it might be economical to purchase a more expensive model that supports several printers. If you are placing only one or two printers at strategic locations throughout the enterprise, it might be more economical to buy the small palm-sized devices that can support one or two printers. You should also consider the following:

- **Price**—Especially price per port. However, as these appliances have become more common, price is becoming much less of a factor.

- **Number and kind of printer ports**—You might want to plan for expansion and buy devices that leave an extra port available for future use.

- **Network connection type**—Some models support one connector type, such as RJ-45 or BNC. Some have several types.

- **Management software and supported operating systems**—An often overlooked feature. Does the appliance support the Simple Network Management Protocol (SMNP) or Remote Monitoring (RMON)? Does it use a proprietary management command interface? Do you have to be physically located at the device to manage it via a port, or can you use Telnet to establish a session with the device to execute commands?

- **Upgrade path**—Don't lock yourself in to a print server that can't be upgraded, unless it is inexpensive and will perform the tasks you need for a while to come.

Price might not be an important factor unless you are purchasing a lot of equipment. Take into consideration the number of printer ports that each device makes available. Some devices offer both serial and parallel ports, so be sure to check that the ports are compatible with the kind of printers you have or plan to purchase. Another useful feature for a serial port is the capability to attach a local console terminal for management functions. Although it's preferable to remotely manage the print server from a workstation elsewhere on the network, the capability to attach a local console terminal is helpful when troubleshooting. Troubleshooting printer problems is common, as most network administrators will tell you.

Check to be sure that all ports on a model that offers multiple ports can be used at once. Hard as it might be to believe, some models offer two ports but only one can be active at any time.

The type of network connection supported by the device is very important. Is it a standard 10Mbps ethernet connection, a 100Mbps connection, or a token-ring adapter?

Note

The IPP is likely to be a major player in the future of network printing. Although the standard drafts for the next version of IPP as proposed at this time do not provide a full-featured set of functions that can be used to manage all aspects of the printing process, some print servers do implement some or all the functions as they currently stand. Don't let buzzwords such as IPP determine your decision when trying to select a print server at this time. Wait until the standard has been more completely defined before using it as a major purchase criterion. Instead, if this feature is important for you now, be sure that the print server has the capability to download new firmware when it becomes available from the manufacturer. Otherwise, use a Windows 2000 server that understands IPP to connect to the printer using another protocol (such as TCP/IP), and use the IPP capabilities of Windows 2000 IIS to manage the printer device.

Management software is another important factor that should be given careful scrutiny when making a purchasing decision. Some print servers have only basic software that runs on a Windows platform. Newer models have the capability to present Web pages on the network so that you can manage them from any workstation that has a browser loaded on it. The information that the management software provides can vary widely from one product to another. The typical status information includes paper-out conditions and whether the printer is online or offline. More advanced management packages tell you whether the toner is low in a laser printer.

Another useful feature for any device on the network, much less a print server, is the capability to be updated with new functionality as technology develops. A print server that uses some kind of rewritable memory (for example, flash memory) that can be updated by downloading new software might save you money in the long run because you won't have to purchase a new device when your needs change.

Figure 36.29 shows an example of a small print server appliance. The D-Link DP-300 print server supports both standard ethernet as well as Fast Ethernet.

Figure 36.29 The DP-300 print server from D-Link can help consolidate network connections for multiple printers.

Some features of this particular model include

- IEEE 1284-compliant, high-speed bidirectional ports are typically faster than a standard PC's parallel port when connected to a laser printer that also supports this type of port.
- This print server works with many different network protocols, including TCP/IP, IPX/SPX, NetBEUI, and AppleTalk.

On the backside of the device, you'll find two LPTn: ports and a console port. On the right side of the device is an RJ-45 jack port that can be used to connect to a 10BASE-T or 100BASE-T network cable using standard Category 5 twisted-pair wiring. On the front of the device, as you can see in Figure 36.29, are LED indicators that can be used to determine the status of the unit. LED indicators exist for both the power and link status, as well as for each of the printer ports (including the serial COM port). Additionally, the device supports SNMP (MIB-II, RFC 1213).

If you browse the Internet, you'll find a large number of inexpensive print server appliances. You can even find these things in your local computer store. They are handy in an environment such as a small office or home office (SOHO). Typically in this environment, a small hub or switch is used, so available ports might be at a premium. By attaching a print server appliance to one port, you can use it to connect several printers that otherwise would have needed one of those scarce ports.

In larger networks, a print server can serve a similar function, providing a single place to plug in several printers that all reside in a printer room, for example.

Whichever you choose, using a print server appliance, or building a print server using a PC, become familiar with the performance aspects and management capabilities that you'll need when something goes wrong.

Network Security

PART VI

Basic Security Measures

37

SOME OF THE MAIN TOPICS IN THIS CHAPTER ARE

Policies and Procedures

Physical Security Measures

The Two Sides of Security

System Daemons and Services

Remove Dead Wood

Delegating Authority

Don't Forget About Firewalls

Keeping a network secure is a time-consuming process that requires a lot of attention to detail. Similar to troubleshooting faulty equipment, tracking down security breaches and finding their cause requires tools made for the job and someone trained to use them. In this chapter, we will examine security from two different angles: first, preventative measures that can be used to help keep problems from occurring in the first place, and then tools and techniques to discover these kinds of problems.

Another important point to remember when it comes to security is that user training can be one of the most important components of security. If your users are not well versed in the security policy of your network, you can't blame them if they do dumb things such as write down passwords and stick them on their computer monitors!

Policies and Procedures

To have security practices that make sense, you must first define, for yourself and the users of the network resources, a security policy that spells out exactly what can and cannot be done on the network. Intruders who might penetrate the network and compromise data or programs do so in many ways. One of those is to exploit "friendly users" who are on the network. A good security policy that is enforced can go a long way toward keeping naive users from disclosing information to those who might do harm to your network. If you don't think your users are vulnerable, just ask someone to call up and say they're calling from the help desk and need to know the user's password. You'd be surprised how many times this tactic will succeed.

At the same time, you also should establish procedures to follow for routine tasks that are performed on a periodic basis, such as backups, restores, creating user accounts, and the like. When a task is described by a procedure that must be followed, there is less of a chance that something out of the ordinary will be done that can compromise security.

Depending on your site, there are several documents that you can use to make users aware of the policies in use for computer and network security. Typically, the human resources department is responsible for having new employees review documents and having them sign the documents to show that they have read and understood them. Documents you might find useful for your site are

- Network connection policy
- Acceptable use statement
- Usage guidelines
- Escalation procedures

Network Connection Policy

This type of document should define the type of system that can be connected to the network. It should set forth the security requirements, such as operating system features to be used, and a person responsible for approving new devices. The use of security programs, such as virus monitoring software, if required, should be included. Any procedures that must be used to obtain a computer account, along with the types of rights and privileges that can be granted to an account, also should be documented here as well as what network addresses can be used and how they are controlled. Finally, you should explicitly set forth in this document that no connections are to be made to the network without following the procedures in this document, and without notifications made to the proper persons.

Acceptable Use Statement and Usage Guidelines

A computer is a flexible device. It can be used for many things beyond the tasks that are needed by the ordinary worker during a normal workday. Although some might be concerned with the time that can be lost due to a user accessing a computer for non-work–related tasks, there are far more important factors to consider.

One of the most important things you should include in an acceptable use statement is the fact that all computer programs are to be supplied by the company and that unauthorized programs, such as those brought from home, are not to be used on the computer or network. Software piracy is not a victimless crime, as many people seem to think. It is a crime that is punishable by stiff fines and jail sentences. It is important that you make sure that users understand this and that you protect your company from possible litigation by showing that you have made an effort to prevent unauthorized programs from being placed on computers at the site.

Piracy is only half the issue when it comes to unauthorized programs. Computer viruses can easily make their way from one computer to another through floppy disk or by downloading from the Internet. Unfortunately, it is usually only after more than one system has become infected that a virus is found or reported. If all software that is used on the company network is first examined, approved, and distributed by a central source, you will have better control over this problem.

Of course, you also should state that users cannot make copies of software or data that is owned by the company and take it home or otherwise use it in an unauthorized manner.

In this statement, point out to users that they are required to report any suspicious activity or misuse of network resources. They also should be made responsible for taking necessary measures for protecting data and programs within their scope. This includes not leaving a workstation logged in when they are away from it for extended periods of time, not leaving reports or other output containing sensitive information laying around, and so on. If you do not put it in a policy statement, users might not realize that this can be a problem.

If dial-up access is granted to users, they should certainly understand that they cannot give information used for this access to anyone else, either inside or outside the company. Many times it has been shown that hackers penetrated a network not through repetitive password cracking techniques, but simply because a user left a password lying around or used one which was so obvious that it could not be considered secure.

The things you can put into an acceptable use policy are extensive. You must examine the specific types of resources you are trying to protect and think up ways to include them in the statement. Some other items you might want to consider are

- Harassment of other users. What might seem like harmless horseplay in a typical office environment can constitute harassment when it's done over a long period of time.

- Threats—Statements that can be construed as an intention to perform some kind of harmful act should always be treated with the utmost importance and severity.

- Removal of hardware from the premises without written authorization.

- Using company e-mail for personal use.

- Bringing hardware into the premises without authorization; for example, laptop computers.

- Attempting to access data not relevant to the user's job, sometimes referred to as "probing" the network.

Employees

Any document that outlines guidelines for using the network should point out to employees that they are to behave ethically on the network. Help desk personnel, for example, often must access data owned by another person when helping them with a problem. Disclosing information to a third party that is obtained during this type of work is unethical. Administrators and operations personnel often have elevated rights and privileges on the workstations and servers that are distributed throughout the network. They should be made to understand that these privileges include a responsibility to professionally carry out their work without causing problems.

Vendors and Outside Connections

Another area often overlooked is when outside persons are allowed to access the network. If you have contractors who are brought in to do work that cannot be done by in-house persons, be sure that you have a usage guidelines document for them to review and sign. It should specifically include the fact that information on the network is of a proprietary nature and cannot be disclosed to any outside party, or to any employee in the company who does not have a need to know.

Additionally, the policy document should state that the contractor cannot discuss with others the *type* of information to which they have access. A little information can go a long way when given to the wrong person.

When hardware repair needs to be done, it usually is done by a third-party maintenance organization, or perhaps by the vendor who manufactures the equipment. Diagnosing some problems may require that the repairman have access to a logon account. If you maintain a user account just for this purpose, be sure that it is one which can be enabled and disabled so that it is available only when it is needed. For example, the OpenVMS operating system has, by default, a FIELD account that is meant to be used by field service when they need access to the computer. This account is disabled when it is created and must be enabled by the administrator before it can be used. Because OpenVMS is a widely used operating system there are a lot of hackers who are aware of this account and also know that many times you will set an easy password for it. Don't make the mistake of leaving this kind of back door open to your network. Disable or remove accounts such as these when they are not needed.

Escalation Procedures

Having a plan of action that should be followed in response to a specific event is a good idea. There should be a specific person or persons in the company who are designated to be responsible for and investigate matters relating to security. A document that sets forth the procedures to be followed for specific security violations will also show users that security is important for the network and that actions will be taken.

A document covering escalation procedure should indicate the kinds of things that are considered a security breach. These can include

- Theft of hardware or software
- Password discovery or disclosure
- Improper disposal of media, including tapes, floppy disks, and printed reports
- Sharing of logon accounts or disclosure of usernames and passwords
- Probing the network to look where one is not authorized
- Interfering with another user's data or account
- Suspected network break-in from outside sources
- Computer viruses
- Physical access violations

Some of these probably seem very obvious when you look at them. To think that you will know how to handle these kinds of problems without a written procedure, though, is a little naïve. For example, it is very common for users to allow others to use their account. It's a lot simpler to let another employee use your workstation when theirs is out of service, than it is to get the appropriate permissions from upper-level management. However, it often happens that when you give someone a password to use on one occasion, it also gets used on another.

When you suspect that the network has been infiltrated from an outside source, what do you do? Shut down the routers? Change all the passwords? Think about this ahead of time and write down a list of steps to follow. These steps should include methods used to determine the source of the break in as well as procedures to be followed to punish the intruder and reassert ownership of any pilfered information. For example, if information that is confidential has been compromised, what steps do you take to notify the person to whom the information relates? Are there legal matters you need to be aware of that pertain to the data that resides on your network?

Perhaps one of the hardest things that a manager has to do is to fire an employee. When someone leaves the company voluntarily and is on friendly terms with management, it is a simple matter to deactivate the user's account and be sure that all access doors are closed. When an unfriendly termination happens, though, you need to have in place steps to follow to be sure you are aware of all access methods that were available to the unfriendly employee. In the case of an employee who is terminated for actions that caused deliberate damage to the network, how do you determine whether any other "time bombs" have been planted? What steps do you take to isolate the resources that were available to this employee until further analysis can be done? Do you need to change passwords on accounts other than the user's?

As you can see, network security has far-reaching implications. Knowing what to do in the event of a specific security event will make things easier for you when they happen.

What a Security Policy Should Include

When writing a security policy, you should first perform an inventory of the resources that you want to protect. Identify the users that need to access each resource and determine where the most likely place a threat to the resource might come from. With this information, you then can begin to construct a security policy that users will have to follow.

The security policy should not be something that is simply understood by everyone. It should be an actual written document. To remind users about the importance of security, you might want to post copies of it around the office so that they will see it on a regular basis.

A good security policy will be composed of several elements, including

- **Risk assessment**—What are you trying to protect and from whom? Identify your network assets and possible sources of problems.

- **Responsibilities**—Describe who in the company is responsible for handling specific matters relating to security. This can include who is authorized to approve a new user account up to items such as who will conduct investigations into security breaches.

- **Proper use of network resources**—State in the policy that users are not to misuse information, use the network for personal use, or intentionally cause damage to the network or information that resides on it.

- **Legal ramifications**—Be sure to get advice from the proper sources about any legal matters that apply to the information you store or generate on your network. Include statements to this effect in the security policy documents.

- **Procedures to remedy security problems**—State what procedures will be followed when a security event occurs and what actions will be taken against those who perpetrate them.

Request For Comments (RFC) 1244 ("Site Security Handbook") is a good document to read before designing a security policy. This RFC gives a list of resources that are found in most networks that are vulnerable to potential security threats. You can download this RFC, along with others, from the Web site http://www.rfc-editor.org/.

- **Hardware**—This includes workstations and servers, printers, disk drives, network wiring, and disk drives. This also includes internetworking devices such as bridges, routers, and switches.

- **Software**—Every piece of software that you run on any computer in the network is a potential security problem. This includes programs purchased from outside vendors and software created in-house by your own programming staff. Operating systems frequently have to be patched as new bugs are discovered that give an intruder an easy way to infiltrate.

- **Data**—The most important asset on your network is probably the data that is generated or used by your business. You can replace software programs and operating systems. When important data, such as customer lists, sales information, or proprietary trade secrets is compromised, it can have a significant impact on business.

- **People**—Users, operators, and anyone else who interacts with your network or any device attached to it is a potential security risk.

- **Paperwork**—Often overlooked by many, this is a very valuable resource to hackers. Passwords are written down. Reports are generated that have confidential information contained in them. Often this resource is simply thrown in a dumpster when it is no longer needed. A better approach is to shred or otherwise make it unusable before getting rid of it.

A good security policy that is understood by users will go a long way toward preventing some of the problems that you can potentially encounter. Make it a regular event to review the policy with users on a periodic basis, such as at quarterly meetings, and be sure that they understand the responsibilities that go along with having access to the company network.

Physical Security Measures

Preventing unauthorized access to resources means that you must first prevent unauthorized access to the physical components that make up the network. This includes user workstations, servers, network cables and devices, and so on. Once the network connection leaves your physical area, such as when you connect to an outside Internet provider, you lose control over the physical aspects of the network. At that point, you must rely on other techniques, such as encryption or tunneling to maintain security. However, the equipment over which you have control should be closely monitored to ensure that no one is tampering with anything in a manner that might serve to defeat the security policy in effect at your site.

Lock the Door

As silly as it might seem, the simple door lock is an often overlooked security device. You wouldn't leave your front door at home unlocked all the time, would you? The servers in your network that hold valuable or sensitive data should not be sitting out on a desktop or in an unlocked room where anyone can access them. Routers, hubs, switches, and other devices should be similarly protected. Wiring closets and computer rooms should have a lock on them or be protected by some sort of monitoring on a 24-hour basis. If you have a round-the-clock operations staff, you might not need to lock the computer room. But, if that staff consists of only one person during any particular time period, get a lock for the door!

Backup media, such as tapes or writable CDs, should be treated the same as live data. Don't back up a server or your own personal workstation and then leave the tape cartridge lying on the desk or in an unlocked drawer.

Uninterruptible Power Supply (UPS)

Keeping data secure can mean keeping it out of the hands of those who are not permitted to view it. It also can mean keeping the data safe from corruption. As more and more business-critical information is being committed to electronic form, it is important to take steps to be sure that it is not unintentionally compromised. A good UPS will pay for itself the first time you have to spend days reconstructing a database or reinstalling programs that become unusable due to a power outage or other problem of this sort.

Most computer operating systems have features that will work with a UPS so that the UPS can perform an orderly shutdown when it detects that power has been lost. If you are using a battery-backup UPS that has only a limited supply of power, an orderly shutdown can save a lot of problems when compared to a system crash.

Dispose of Hardware and Media in a Secure Manner

When you upgrade your network and bring in new workstations or servers, it is a generous thing to give employees, or an organization such as a school, your old equipment if it is still usable. However, you should establish a policy that dictates that all hard disks are to be erased and, when appropriate, a legal copy of the operating system reinstalled on it. If you leave important information on a computer you give away, don't be surprised when you see it again.

There is also the legal aspect to this. If you give away an old computer system, do you have the legal right to keep the software packages and install them on a new system? Probably not, unless you have a site license or other license that allows you to do so. For that reason, do not give away a computer that has applications installed on it unless you intend to give away the software packages also.

Disposing of used floppy disks, backup tapes, and tape cartridges also pose a potential security threat. It is better to destroy these information carriers than to give them away without being absolutely sure that you have rid them of any information. A bulk magnetic eraser can be a good security tool to use before disposing of this kind of stuff.

The Two Sides of Security

Locking the computer room door is a preventive measure that is intended to keep out those who have no business being there. Preventive measures should be taken for software access mechanisms also. However, no matter how good you are at putting into place the access control mechanisms to protect resources, there is always going to be someone who will try, and possibly succeed, in breaking through. For this reason, you also must be able to keep audit trails of events on the network so that you can determine whether someone is trying to break your security, or if indeed they have done so.

Before the Fact: Controlling Access

Controlling access to the network is done by several common mechanisms. These are

- User accounts and passwords
- Physical identifiers
- Resource protections

In many operating systems, the concept of a *resource owner* is important in this scheme. For example, OpenVMS and Windows 2000 and Windows XP keep track of the user who creates a resource, such as a file. That owner is able to change the protections applied to the file and can grant others the permissions needed to use the file.

Identifying Users

In a homogeneous network where only one user account and password is required for access to permitted resources throughout the network, system management is not usually a complicated matter. Windows 2000 and Windows XP allow for the creation of areas of control, called domains, that operate as security boundaries. Users in a domain can be granted access to resources on any computer, either server or workstation, that the network administrator wants to give them. In addition, trust relationships can be established between domains when administrators cooperate, making it possible for the user to still use only one username and password to connect to resources throughout the network.

Novell NetWare provides this functionality by giving the user a logon to the network that is controlled by the Novell Directory Services. Each user is represented in the directory by a User object, the properties of which specify information about passwords and connections.

The Unix operating system does not use the concept of a domain. Instead, each Unix host maintains a password file that stores information about each user, including an encrypted password. To access resources on other network hosts, the Unix user must either log on when accessing the computer or use a proxy mechanism. TCP/IP utilities such as FTP and Telnet send user passwords across the network in clear-text format and are easy targets for interception.

The Unix remote utilities, usually called r-commands because they all start with the letter "r," are used to perform ordinary network functions such as copying or printing files or logging in to a remote system. This is very useful in the network environment where a user performs functions on many different machines. These utilities are not necessarily good when looked at from a security standpoint, however. Although the user must have a valid user account on the remote hosts on which these commands execute, the user does not have to provide the password.

Note

Although most Telnet applications still use clear-text passwords for authentication purposes, there are some that use encrypted authentication. If security is of a great concern on your network, you will be sure to examine the documentation closely before using these utilities on any node in the network. This also applies to other TCP/IP utilities such as the r-commands and FTP.

Instead, an entry in the /etc/hosts.equiv file or the .rhosts file on a remote computer is what determines access. The remote machine trusts the computer on which the user executes an r-command if it can find an entry in either of these files for it. Each entry in the /etc/hosts.equiv file contains a host name and a username, to identify users and the hosts that are allowed to execute these commands without providing a password. The assumption is that if you have logged in to the remote host then you have already been authenticated. The .rhosts file works in a similar manner but resides in a user's home directory. The remote users entered in this file can perform functions based on the account associated with that user.

Note

Although you'll still find the basic r-commands in most Unix and Linux systems, there is an alternative. The Secure Shell (SSH) utilities offer authentication and encryption for data transfers using utilities that are similar to the r-commands. You can find out more about SSH by visiting the Web site `http://www.ssh.com/products/ssh/`. You can obtain free versions of SSH by visiting `http://www.openssh.com/`.

Although this sounds a lot like the Windows NT/2000 trust mechanism, it is not. It is quite easy to impersonate a remote node and gain entry into a Unix system by using the r-commands.

Resource Protections

After a user has been authenticated by the operating system, the next step to access a resource is for a check to be done to see whether the resource has any access controls placed on it. Typically, an operating system will grant access to a resource, such as a file, by granting users the right to

- Read the file
- Write to the file
- Execute the file
- Take ownership of the file
- Delete the file

These concepts also can be extended to resources such as printers, modems, and so on. When granting these rights, most operating systems also enable you to specify which rights are applied to users or groups of users. For example, Windows NT enables you to group users into local or global groups. When you set the access controls on a file, you can specify the access rights by group. Using this method, one group of ordinary users might be able to read a file, while a group of users that manages the file might be granted read and write access, as well as delete access to the file. To prevent programs from being run by unauthorized users, the execute right can be granted or denied to a user or a group of users.

Tip

Windows NT/2000 enables you to format a hard disk using the NTFS file system or the standard FAT system that is compatible with DOS and other operating systems, such as Windows 95/98. If you want to provide access controls on individual files and directories under Windows NT, you must format your disk partitions using NTFS. The access rights that you can assign to files and directories have no effect on FAT partitions. Also, Windows 2000 adds a new feature to Windows NT that enables you to encrypt individual files on disk. The encryption is done on-the-fly as a file is written or is read, so for a high-security environment this might be a good option to use.

For more information on user rights and permissions, and on how they are implemented by different operating systems, see Chapter 34, "Rights and Permissions." It is important to understand the features of your operating system that pertain to granting rights or permissions. Rights generally enable a user to perform an action. Permissions are placed on resources and define who and what kind of access can be made of a resource.

After the Fact: Auditing Use

In Chapter 38, "Auditing and Other Monitoring Measures," you will find an in-depth discussion about the tools you can use to keep track of resource use, both attempted and successful attempts. Here it is important only to note that it is not enough to organize users into groups and grant them resource permissions throughout the network.

There are several reasons for this. A large user base, combined with multiple servers that hold valuable resources, makes it difficult at times for an administrator who is not familiar with the information resources provided by a specific server to understand the permissions needed. For example, a new user in the accounting department might or might not need access to accounts receivable files or accounts payable files. They might need access to one or the other or maybe both files. A manager in that department would probably be the likely person to make the decision about what files the user should be able to access.

However, if the user is placed into a group, which is generally done to make administration easier, compromises sometimes happen and the user might be granted access through the group to resources that they do not need to access.

Another reason is that sometimes mistakes are made. It is a fact of life that no one is perfect and that no system for allocating resources is going to get it right 100% of the time. When users are granted the capability to read a file, you can be sure, if the data contained in it is interesting enough, that they will do so.

Indeed, even if a user does not have appropriate access rights to a file, some will try to get at interesting information anyway.

For these reasons, a good operating system provides auditing controls that enable you to look back after a security breach to try to determine who did what and where they did it. Unix (and its variants, such as Linux), Windows NT/2000, and Novell all provide features that enable you to record both successful and failed attempts to access resources. They all do it in different ways, so if you have multiple operating systems on the network it will be important that you understand each of them so that you can best use these capabilities.

Passwords

It might not seem like an important thing to mention at this point, but you need to enforce a policy that makes users choose good passwords. And when you do that, you must decide what makes a good password for your environment. Simply put, a good password is one that is hard to guess. When you consider that a standard password-cracking technique used by hackers is to simply try every word in a dictionary, you can begin to understand that luck doesn't have a lot to do with penetrating a network. It comes mostly from lax security that allows doors that are easy to open.

Enforce Good Passwords

When deciding on how passwords are to be constructed, there are a few guidelines you can follow:

- Use more than one word. Multiple words "glued" together make a pattern of characters that is much harder for a simple password cracking program to guess. Don't use words that naturally go together. For example, Atlantabraves is not a good choice. Atlantayoko is a better choice.

- Use nonalphabetic characters somewhere in the password. This can be numeric characters or punctuation characters, provided the operating system you use will permit them.

- In Unix and Windows NT/2000/XP, passwords are case sensitive. If you use both upper- and lowercase characters in a password, you can confound the guessing mechanism.

- Don't make passwords too difficult to memorize. The last thing you want is to have frustrated users writing down passwords so they will be able to remember them.

- Use password history restrictions if the operating system permits it. This means that the operating system keeps track of a limited number of passwords that the user has previously used and will not allow them to be reused within a certain time frame. A common practice is to change your password when forced to do so and then to change it back to a value that you like and can easily remember.

Be sure that you do not create user accounts and assign them a password that never gets changed by the user. Most operating systems will allow you to set a password to be expired on its first use so that when a new user logs in the first time, he will be required to change his password.

Sometimes it is important to have a password that makes no sense whatsoever. In a highly secure environment this can make sense, in that you want something that is hard to guess. However, remember that when something is difficult to remember it usually gets written down somewhere, which can defeat the purpose of a password altogether. Unix has a command, `passwd`, that can be used to computer-generate a password for a user. For example, the command

```
paswwd username
```

displays a list of potential passwords that are generally difficult to guess. The user can select one from this list to use if they are having a difficult time thinking one up.

Password Policies

No user account, including one used by an administrator, should ever be allowed to keep the same password for an extended period of time. A good idea for passwords is to require that they be changed every 30–60 days, depending on the level of security you need at your site. You also should enforce a minimum length for passwords. Most operating systems will allow you to specify this value so that users cannot change their password to one that is shorter than the size you require.

On Windows NT computers, you can do this by using the User Manager for Domains utility and selecting Account from the Policies menu. The dialog box that pops up allows you to set the minimum password length along with other domain policies related to user accounts. For Windows 2000 domains, you can set the password policy using the following steps:

1. Click Start, Programs, Administrative Tools, Domain Security Policy.

2. In the left pane of the MMC, double-click Account Policy.

3. In the tree that expands under Account Policy, double-click Password Policy.

4. In the right pane of the MMC, you'll see options for setting password policy features, such as the minimum length, password history, the length of time a password can be used before it must be changed, and so on.

On Unix systems, you can set the password minimum length by specifying it in a field in the file `/etc/default/passwd`.

On Novell NetWare servers, you can enforce a minimum password length by modifying the object properties of the template object used to create a user account, or by modifying the properties of an individual user object for a particular user.

Depending on the particular operating system, you can enforce other restrictions on passwords or user accounts to enhance security on the network. Some of the capabilities you might find include

- **Password expirations**—A password should not be used indefinitely.

- **Password history lists**—This feature prevents a password from being reused within a specified time period.

- **Account lockouts**—When a hacker is trying to use the brute-force method to guess a password for an account, you should be able to lock the account out automatically after a specified number of attempts within a specific time frame.

Password Grabbers

About the oldest trick known to those who would want to break into another user's account is the use of a program that imitates the operating system's own logon procedure. This kind of program generally is executed by someone who logs in using their own account on another's workstation. They then run a program that does nothing but wait until the unsuspecting user tries to log in. The program prompts for a username and password, mimicking the operating system in every respect.

However, instead of logging the user on to the system, which the program is unable to do, it simply stores the password in a file and then generates a phony error message.

If the user is not too concerned about security, they will probably never know that they have been fooled. They might think they have entered their password incorrectly and try again. The second time it will succeed because it is the operating system which is prompting them this second time. The password grabber program has already done its job and it disappears.

The user who began this fraud then simply retrieves the file, thus getting the password, and then can freely log in as that user and cause many problems when it comes to tracking down the real person who is abusing security. Because they are now using someone else's username and password, they are difficult to catch.

Note

This subterfuge is one of the reasons why Windows NT uses the key sequence of Ctrl+Alt+Delete to begin the logon process. It is generally difficult to write a program that mimics the Windows NT/2000 logon screen because the Ctrl+Alt+Delete combination of key strokes is trapped by a processor interrupt and, unless the system has been grossly compromised, any program attempting to pass as the logon screen will fail.

System Daemons and Services

Windows 2000 Server has background processes that perform many functions, called *services*. Unix systems also have background processes that work in a similar manner and are called *daemons*. Regardless of what you call them, these processes, which are called background because they do not require interaction with the keyboard, but instead execute on the computer waiting to perform some function, can introduce security problems when they are not needed.

You should become familiar with the background processes on any servers in your network and disable those that are not needed. For example, on Unix systems, there are many background daemons associated with the TCP/IP suite of protocols. Some systems might need all of these, whereas some might need just a few or none of them. Table 37.1 lists some of the daemons you might want to look at to determine whether they are needed. If not, disable them.

Table 37.1   TCP/IP Services That Might Not Be Needed On All Systems

Service Name	Description
uucp	Unix-to-Unix copy
finger	Provides information about users
tftp	trivial file transfer protocol
talk	allows text communications between users on the network
bootp	Provides network information to clients
systat	Gives out current system information
netstat	Gives out current network information such as current connections
rusersd	Shows logged on users
rexd	Remote execution utility

It might be that you do need these services. It might be that they need to be configured properly to prevent their misuse. You should read the documentation that comes with your Unix or Linux system to determine the capabilities that these daemons provide and disable them on systems that do not need them.

For example, tftp is a stripped-down version of FTP. It is compact and usually can be easily implemented in an EPROM. For this reason, it is useful in some devices that need to download operating software from a host. However, note that unlike FTP, tftp has no access control mechanisms. This means that a username and password are not used. Because there is no authentication, this can be a real security problem if it is not configured properly, so that it can be used only for its intended purpose.

On Windows NT Server 4.0 and Windows 2000, you can use two programs that are provided with the Resource Kits to install or run almost any executable program or batch file as a service. These are INSTRV.EXE, which can be used to install an executable, and SRVANY.EXE, which can be used to make other kinds of files into services. On a server that has several users logging in frequently, you might want to make it a regular part of your routine maintenance to review the services running on the machines and disable or remove those that are not installed by the initial operating system installation or those that did not come from products you have applied to the system.

To do this, you will need to keep an inventory of what runs on each server, but this kind of inventory information can be useful for other purposes, such as when you need to reinstall a server that has been destroyed by a catastrophic failure.

Remove Dead Wood

Every operating system comes with default options that are installed that you might not be aware of unless you have read the documentation carefully. For example, default user accounts might be created when you install the OS or later install a product. For example, the GUEST account in Windows NT/2000 is installed by default. You should always disable or remove this account. The ADMINISTRATOR account is also a vulnerable target because it is present on all Windows NT Server computers. You cannot delete this account, but you can rename it so that the hacker's job becomes more difficult. Also, you shouldn't use the administrator's account on a regular basis. Instead, create user accounts and put them into the Domain Admins group to allow these users to exercise administrator privileges, while maintaining an audit trail of the actual users who performed certain actions.

Regularly review the user accounts that exist on the network. Use the auditing features provided to determine when an account has not been in use for a long period of time and, if you can find no reason for its existence, disable it. Maybe someone in another department did not notify you when a user was terminated, or maybe an account was created for an expected new employee or contractor who later changed his mind and did not come on board. New accounts such as these are typically created with a simple password and can leave gaping security holes in your network.

Old programs and files that are no longer needed, or the use of which you are not sure, are also easy targets to cause security problems. As a rule of thumb, if it's not needed, back it up to tape and delete it! If a user finds that something she needs is missing, she will tell you!

When installing a new application product for a user, be sure you know the capabilities of the application. Don't install unneeded optional features that will not normally be used. Read the documentation!

Delegating Authority

In a network of any size other than a simple workgroup it is usually necessary to delegate authority to other administrators or middle-level management personnel. When you find that you must create accounts that have privileges to perform administrative functions, do not give carte blanche access to every account. Keep track of the exact functions that an account will be used for and grant only the access rights and permissions needed.

For example, if an operator will be performing backup functions on a server, they do not need to have full rights and privileges on the server. Under Windows NT, you can place the user's account into the Backup Operators user group to give them the capabilities they need, without compromising all files on the system. If you have users who must be able to add or modify user accounts, check the operating system documentation and give them access only to the resources and data files that they need.

User Accounts

Generic accounts might seem like a good idea at first thought, but they provide nothing in the way of auditing. If you simply let one or more users share the root account on a Unix system or the Administrator account on a Windows NT/2000 computer, you will have no way of determining who did what when something goes wrong. Indeed, because you can grant the same capabilities to any new account you can create, why not do so?

Give each user that requires elevated capabilities their own account and grant the necessary privileges to the account. This way you can track each user to be sure they do not abuse their account or use it in a way that you do not expect.

When you have more than one user using the same account there is also the likelihood that the password will be compromised and someone who is not authorized to use the account will do so.

Application Servers, Print Servers, and Web Servers

One particularly common error that you can make is to put all your eggs in one basket. Instead of using one server to provide print services or file services or Web services, many administrators use one server to provide all three. This is not necessarily a good idea.

Specialized servers can limit the damage that can be done by intruders and also can make it easier to delegate authority so that a particular administrator can concentrate on a limited set of functions for a certain server. Web servers are particularly prone to attempts by hackers to intrude onto your network. New applications and technologies are being developed and deployed all the time, and the newer they are, the more likely they will have bugs or other loopholes that make them more risky than other applications that run on the network.

Placing sensitive data files on a Web server simply because it is convenient to use the machine's resources is not a good idea if it is also being used as a Web server. Make it more difficult to get at these files by dedicating a file server computer to them instead.

Delegating servers is almost like delegating authority to users. When you divide up resources and partition them into manageable groups, you make it less likely that an attack on one object will result in damage to all.

Denial of service attacks are very common on networks now. This kind of attack can be done by a malicious person who takes advantage of a known weakness in a protocol or an implementation of a particular service. One common mistake that administrators make when setting up an FTP site is to place it on an ordinary server.

For example, you might want to have an FTP server that allows customers to log in to your system and download information, patches, or other files. You also might want to be able to let them upload files or messages to your site. If you are going to allow anonymous FTP access, be absolutely sure that the service is configured so that it can access only a dedicated disk or set of disks. Do not allow anonymous access to an FTP service that writes to a system disk or a data disk that is important in your network. It is quite easy for an outsider to simply fill up the disk with meaningless data, causing a system to lock up or crash, depending on the operating system. If an important data disk becomes full, it can cause an extended period of downtime, putting employees out of work for hours, while you try to first determine the cause, and then remedy it!

Don't Forget About Firewalls

Last, but not least, for this chapter, is a quick reminder that a firewall is a necessity for connecting a LAN or larger network to the Internet today. A firewall can serve to prevent the spread of all sorts of trouble that can be perpetuated on the Internet today using freely available tools and script files that even high-school kids can download and use to wreak havoc on the network that becomes their target. For more information about firewalls, be sure to read Chapter 40, "Firewalls."

Auditing and Other Monitoring Measures

SOME OF THE MAIN TOPICS IN THIS CHAPTER ARE

Unix and Linux Systems

Configuring Windows NT 4.0 Auditing Policies

Configuring Windows 2000 Auditing Policies

Novell Security

Security for an individual computer system or for the network as a whole requires a two-pronged approach. First you must try to ensure that all applications and data are secured against unauthorized usage. This can mean anything from setting up and enforcing a good password policy to using the access mechanisms (such as resource permissions) provided by the operating system or network software to secure resources or to restrict user activity (by selectively granting or denying rights). However, no matter how good you are at this before-the-fact approach to preventing security breaches, it's almost impossible—short of taking a system off the network and locking it in a room with a guard outside—to ever be absolutely sure that the system is totally secure. If you are a genius and make use of all the rights and permissions mechanisms at your disposal to secure a system (much less the entire network), an application bug or a disgruntled employee can still compromise a system.

Because you can never be certain that you've covered all your bases, it's also necessary that you follow up on your security configuration by monitoring the activities of the system. This chapter discusses the second part of securing your system: auditing measures.

Note

For information about the mechanisms you can use to try to secure a computer and the network in the first place, see Chapter 34, "Rights and Permissions." You should be sure that you understand how to protect your system using the built-in security measures so that you will have less auditing data to wade through when you are trying to determine whether your security measures are working!

This second approach to securing the network is an important one. You should use all *practical* auditing features to record access to resources and to set up a policy for reviewing the data gathered on a regular basis. The degree to which you will find it necessary to gather information using the various utilities that an operating system provides depends on how important the data is on a system, or whether the system provides access to the network from the Internet. During normal operations, if you were to enable every single type of event auditing on a Windows 2000 Server, you would end up with a very slow response time and with more data than you could possibly review on a daily basis. However, you can strike a compromise, depending on the particular system, and set up auditing that can be used to sufficiently record system activities and increase your audited events during times when you suspect that something might be awry.

Every major operating system in use in a business environment today that is connected to a network has the capability to set up auditing for selected resources, with the exception of MS-DOS, and Windows 95/98, which can still be found in some environments. But for most operating systems, you can keep track of file accesses, user logons, and other information that gives you the who, where, what, and when information that you'll need when you believe a security problem exists. The methods of auditing and the tools used to exploit this data depend on the network or computer operating system. Because most networks are hybrids that have multiple operating systems, it's a good idea to have an employee who is skilled in each OS environment, intimately familiar with the peculiarities of each system.

Unix and Linux Systems

Although Unix was originally developed to be a programmer's operating system and not a business production system, it has been enhanced over the years to include a number of utilities that can track resource usage and access. Today, the various implementations of Unix (along with its cousin Linux) are the primary operating systems used on the Internet for most firewalls and Web servers in the high-end market. What started out as a programmer's operating system is now the most popular high-end production system, although Bill Gates wishes it weren't so.

The files discussed here might vary from one Unix system to the next, but in general most systems have these available for the system administrator's use. The syslog utility covers the widest area of system resources because you can configure it to record messages from many different system utilities, and you can also decide how the utility will notify you of events as they happen. Other files—such as /etc/utmp and /usr/adm/wtmp—keep track of who is currently logged onto the system and who has logged onto the system.

Linux systems use many of the same files that Unix systems do. Understanding each utility or log file and the type of information you can derive from it will enable you to set up a good auditing policy for your systems.

Using *syslog*

The syslog utility can be used to set up logging for many components that make up the Unix operating system. You can set up message logging so that messages from a wide variety of programs can be managed from a central location. To enable syslog logging, you must edit the /etc/syslog.conf configuration file and enter a record that contains a *selector* for each type of message you want to be logged by the facility, as well as an *action,* which is the action the daemon should take for this type of message.

The syslog daemon (syslogd) is usually started when the system boots, by placing commands in one of the rc startup files. The syntax for starting the daemon is

```
/etc/syslog [-mN] [-ffilename] [-d]
```

The -f option can be used to specify a configuration file other than the standard /etc/syslog.conf file. The -m option sets a "mark" interval for placing timestamps into the file. Timestamps can be important because they indicate that the logging mechanism is working during periods of time when no other significant events are logged. The absence of timestamps (if you use them) can be a tip that someone has been tampering with your system. The -d option turns on debugging mode.

The syslog.conf File

This file stores the information the syslog daemon uses to decide which messages to accept (source and severity) and what to do with them (log file, notify user, and so on). You can use any ASCII text editor (such as VI) to configure this file. Each line should be composed of two components:

- **The selector**—This part of the record is composed of two pieces of information separated by a period. The first part of the selector is the name of the *system component* from which the message originates. The second part of the selector is the *severity* of the message. You can place multiple selectors on one line if you separate them by a semicolon.

- **Action**—This tells the daemon what to do when it receives a message that matches the selector criteria.

Table 38.1 lists the facility names you can use when composing the selector portion of the record.

Table 38.1   Facility Names in the syslog.conf Configuration File

Source Name	Description
user	Generated by user applications
kern	Kernel messages
mail	Mail system messages
daemon	System daemons

Table 38.1   continued

Source Name	Description
auth	Authorization file (that is, login)
lpr	Line printer spooler system
news	Usenet
uucp	UUCP (not currently implemented)
cron	cron and at utilities
local0-7	Reserved for local use
mark	Timestamp messages
*	All the above except for mark

Table 38.2 lists the severity levels you can use as the second component for the selector.

Table 38.2   Severity Levels in the syslog.conf File

Severity Level	Description
emerg	Panic condition that is usually broadcast to all users
alert	A condition that needs immediate attention
crit	Warnings about critical situations
err	Other errors not warranting emerg, alert, or crit
warning	Warning messages
notice	Situations that require attention, but not as important as a warning or other error; not necessarily an error condition
info	Informational messages
debug	Messages generated by programs running a debug mode
none	*Suppresses* messages for this entry

To create a selector, select one of the facilities listed in Table 37.1 and combine it with one of the error conditions listed in Table 37.2. For example:

```
kernel.info
mail.notice
lpr.crit
```

To create the rest of the record, you need to specify an action to take. The action portion of the record is separated from the selector portion by a space character. The syslog daemon can deliver the message in these ways:

- Write the message to a log file
- Send it to another computer
- Send it to one or more usernames
- All of the above

For example, because kernel events are usually important (the kernel is the heart of the Unix operating system) and need to be looked at immediately, you might want to send them to the computer's console device. To do this, use the following entry:

```
kern.* /dev/console
```

The asterisk tells `syslog` to log all message types generated by the kernel and the `/dev/console` part of the record specifies the console device (check your Unix documentation to be sure of the exact device filename).

If the message is something important, but not so critical that it needs immediate attention, you can send it to a user whose responsibilities are associated with the application. The following example sends all messages from the mail facility (at a severity level of `info` or above) to the mail administrator named Johnson:

```
mail.info johnson
```

For security reasons, you might want to send important logging messages to another host. This can be a valuable service that the `syslog` daemon can perform. For example, when you are using bastion hosts in a demilitarized zone (DMZ), it's best not to store security logging events on a host computer that might be compromised. Instead, you instruct the daemon to send these events to another server for logging purposes. In a large network, you can dedicate a single host computer to this function and use other security measures to make the computer inaccessible to ordinary users. To send messages relating to kernel events and authorization events to another computer, for example:

```
kern.*;ath.* @yoko.ono.com
```

▶▶ You'll find more detailed information about bastion hosts, firewalls, and DMZs in Chapter 40, "Firewalls."

Some message types are more useful for reviewing at a later date to review the overall functioning of the system. Using log files for these kinds of messages is a good idea. To send messages to a log file, specify the log file path in the action field:

```
mail.info;lpr.info;news.* /var/adm/messages
```

Tip

When sending messages to a log file, you can send them all to the same file as shown in the previous example (`/var/adm/messages`). However, to make administering the logged messages easier, you might want to create several log files and group similar message types together. This way you don't have to search through a large file that might contain a large number of entries to find just a few records that are of interest. Using separate log files makes it easier to write script files to automate the process of searching for important messages.

Another good reason to use multiple log files is that you can delegate the reviewing of these log files to those employees who are best qualified to review them. A typical Unix system administrator has a lot of things to do during a normal working day. Delegating the review of certain events to subordinates can make the day a much more pleasant experience!

When sending `syslog` messages to a file, don't forget to review the log files on a periodic basis. Depending on the severity level you set for each facility, these files can grow to be quite large over a short period of time. To make administration more efficient, decide on a policy for reviewing, archiving, and deleting log files on a regular basis. You should keep these files available for at least a year. Some intrusions can lie in wait for a trigger before causing your system a problem. If you keep your log files on tape or other offline storage, you can look back through them for what might not have seemed an obvious event when it originally occurred. For legal reasons, keeping log files archived and readily available can help you make your case against an intruder who has spent days, weeks, or months trying to compromise your system.

System Log Files

Unix systems have many log files not related to the `syslog` utility that you can review for security purposes. For example, user logins are recorded in a file as are usages of the switch user (`su`) command. When you are new to a system, you should review the documentation to make sure you are aware of all the logging facilities on the computer, where the files are located, and what maintenance procedures are necessary.

Some of the more useful files are

- **/usr/adm/wtmp**—This file keeps track of all logins, showing the username, terminal, and connect time. System shutdowns (but not system crashes, of course) are also listed in this file. Use the `last` command or the `ac` command to view entries in this log file.

- **/etc/utmp**—This file is similar to the **/usr/adm/wtmp** file, in that it stores information about users logging into the system. However, this file only shows information about users that are actually logged onto the system currently and is not a historical file.

- **/var/adm/sulog**—This important log file should be looked at often because it records the usage of the su command (switch user).

- **/var/adm/aculog**—This file records the usage of dial-out utilities, such as `tip` or `cu`.

- **/var/log/cron**—Actions taken by the `cron` scheduling utility are recorded here. This utility schedules events for execution on the system. By reviewing this file, you can determine whether unauthorized users are running procedures or whether programs or files are being run during off-hours when they are not likely to be noticed.

- **/var/adm/lpd-errs**—This file is used to record messages having to do with the `lpr`/`lpd` spooling system. Although not really of great concern from a security point of view, it can be a potential tool to use when looking for security breaches, such as determining who printed what.

- **/var/adm/acct**—This is the process accounting file. Use the `sa` command or the `lastcomm` command to view the contents of this file.

Configuring Windows NT 4.0 Auditing Policies

Windows NT also allows you to set permissions on resources and audit their access. To secure the system, use

- User rights and permissions
- NTFS file and directory access control lists (ACLs)
- Passwords, groups, and interdomain trust relationships

To audit the system, you can configure the events that you want to track and then use the system's Event Viewer to examine the data collected by the system-auditing software.

Setting Up Events to Audit

To set up categories of events to be audited, run the User Manager for Domains utility and choose Policies, Audit. In Figure 38.1, you can see the Audit Policy dialog box allows you to select which event category to audit and whether to audit success or failures associated with each category.

If you do not want to audit any events, select the Do Not Audit option button. If you do want to audit, select Audit These Events and click the Success and/or Failure options for each category. The types of events you can set up auditing for are

- **Logon and Logoff**—Track users logging into the system. This also tracks network logins from remote systems.

- **File and Object Access**—File and directory access and sending jobs to printers. This category requires you to further define the events for the file, directory, or printer that will be audited.

- **Use of User Rights**—Records when users make use of rights you grant to them when you set up their account with the User Manager for Domains.

- **User and Group Management**—Tracks changes to group accounts, such as creating, deleting, and renaming user groups and passwords.

- **Security Policy Changes**—This category keeps track of changes to user rights, and audit or trust relationships.

- **Restart, Shutdown, and System**—Tracks when the system is shutdown or restarted, and other events that relate to system security. This category also includes changes to the security event log on the system.

- **Process Tracking**—Records voluminous information about user processes, including when programs are executed, objects are accessed, and programs are exited.

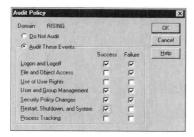

Figure 38.1   Use the Audit Policy dialog box in the User Manager for Domains to configure events to audit.

In most cases, you won't want to select success and failure for every category in this list. For example, the data collected when you select Process Tracking can create a large event log file very quickly. You should probably only turn on this event-logging mechanism when you have a definite suspicion about a particular user's activities and then review and purge the log on a regular basis. Another category that can generate a lot of log file data is the Use of User Rights category.

Other categories, such as user's logins, can be useful and do not take up a lot of space in the log files. The data collected for files and object accesses depend on the specific events you select to audit for them.

File and Directory Events

If you have selected to audit this event category, you need to use Windows NT Explorer to set the specific types of events to audit. To set up auditing on a directory or file, highlight it, right-click, and select Properties. Alternatively, you can highlight the file or directory and select File, Properties.

When the Properties sheet appears, select the Security tab and then the Auditing button to see a display that looks like Figure 38.2.

The event types you can audit are

- Read
- Write

- Execute
- Delete
- Change Permission
- Take Ownership

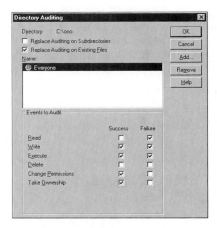

Figure 38.2   Use the Auditing button on the Security tab on the file or directory's property sheet to set up events to audit.

However, because these will be audited by a user or group, you should first select the Add button to add a user or group of users. The Add Users and Groups dialog box (shown in Figure 38.3) displays the current list of user groups. You can use the Show Users button to display the individual users in each group. Select users or groups by highlighting them and using the Add button.

Figure 38.3   The Add Users and Groups dialog box allows you to select which users to audit.

Continue to select users and groups. Click OK when you are finished. After you return to the previous screen, highlight each user or group and select the events to audit for that file or directory on a per-user basis. You also can use the Remove button to remove the auditing configuration for a particular user or group.

You can select success or failure for events. For example, if you selected success for the Read event type, every time an audited user was able to read this file, a record would be generated in the event log. If you selected Failure, each time an audited user tries to read the file, but does not have the correct access permissions, a record would be created in the event log file.

Printer Events

You select events to audit for printers in much the same way that you do for files and directories. However, instead of using the Windows NT Explorer, you use the properties sheet for the particular printer. You can get to the properties sheet by right-clicking the icon for a printer in the Printers folder. You can add or remove users using the same type of dialog box. The events you can audit for printers are different:

- Print
- Full Control
- Delete
- Change Permissions
- Take Ownership

Using the Windows NT 4.0 Event Viewer

The Event Viewer is a utility found in the Administrative Tools folder that can be used to display events from three different log files:

- System
- Security
- Application

The System log file records certain system events and the Application log file records events generated by many different applications that were coded to write event log messages. The Security log file is used to track events you have set up for auditing purposes. To start the event viewer choose Start, Programs, Administrative Tools, Event Viewer. Figure 38.4 shows the Event Viewer with the Security log file selected.

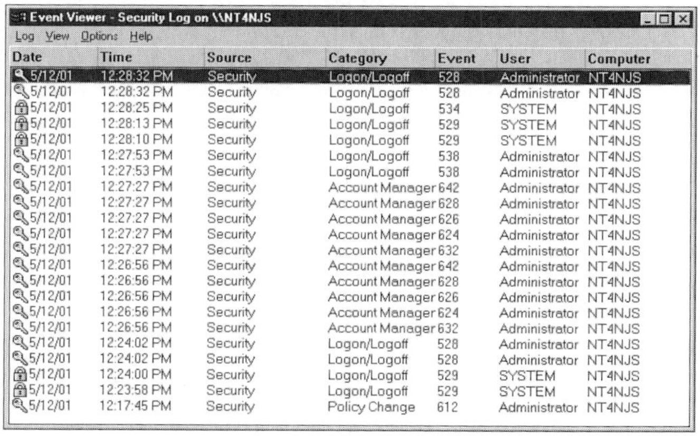

Date	Time	Source	Category	Event	User	Computer
5/12/01	12:28:32 PM	Security	Logon/Logoff	528	Administrator	NT4NJS
5/12/01	12:28:32 PM	Security	Logon/Logoff	528	Administrator	NT4NJS
5/12/01	12:28:25 PM	Security	Logon/Logoff	534	SYSTEM	NT4NJS
5/12/01	12:28:13 PM	Security	Logon/Logoff	529	SYSTEM	NT4NJS
5/12/01	12:28:10 PM	Security	Logon/Logoff	529	SYSTEM	NT4NJS
5/12/01	12:27:53 PM	Security	Logon/Logoff	538	Administrator	NT4NJS
5/12/01	12:27:53 PM	Security	Logon/Logoff	538	Administrator	NT4NJS
5/12/01	12:27:27 PM	Security	Account Manager	642	Administrator	NT4NJS
5/12/01	12:27:27 PM	Security	Account Manager	628	Administrator	NT4NJS
5/12/01	12:27:27 PM	Security	Account Manager	626	Administrator	NT4NJS
5/12/01	12:27:27 PM	Security	Account Manager	624	Administrator	NT4NJS
5/12/01	12:27:27 PM	Security	Account Manager	632	Administrator	NT4NJS
5/12/01	12:26:56 PM	Security	Account Manager	642	Administrator	NT4NJS
5/12/01	12:26:56 PM	Security	Account Manager	628	Administrator	NT4NJS
5/12/01	12:26:56 PM	Security	Account Manager	626	Administrator	NT4NJS
5/12/01	12:26:56 PM	Security	Account Manager	624	Administrator	NT4NJS
5/12/01	12:26:56 PM	Security	Account Manager	632	Administrator	NT4NJS
5/12/01	12:24:02 PM	Security	Logon/Logoff	528	Administrator	NT4NJS
5/12/01	12:24:02 PM	Security	Logon/Logoff	528	Administrator	NT4NJS
5/12/01	12:24:00 PM	Security	Logon/Logoff	529	SYSTEM	NT4NJS
5/12/01	12:23:58 PM	Security	Logon/Logoff	529	SYSTEM	NT4NJS
5/12/01	12:17:45 PM	Security	Policy Change	612	Administrator	NT4NJS

Figure 38.4 The Security log file can be viewed using the Event Viewer.

If the event viewer starts up with another log file displayed, such as the Application log file, choose Log, Security to change to the correct display.

This view shows the list of events currently in the log file. To get the detailed record for any event, double-click it. The Event Viewer does not have a reporting capability like the AUDITCON utility in NetWare (which you'll read about shortly). However, you can choose Log, Save As and save the data to either an ASCII text file or a comma-delimited file and use another utility, such as a spreadsheet, to perform further filtering or analysis on the data found here.

You also can change the log file settings by choosing Log, Log Settings. This allows you to set the maximum size the log can grow to, and whether to cycle around and overwrite older events when the file is full. From the Log menu you can also select to clear all the events in the log file, at which time you are prompted to save the current file in a backup file. This is something you should do on a regular basis, archiving the previous log files for a period of time consistent with the security policy in force at your site.

Configuring Windows 2000 Auditing Policies

Windows 2000 uses the Active Directory to store objects, such as user and computer accounts, as well as security information for the domain. When you promote a Windows 2000 server to be a domain controller in the domain, you can use the Domain Security Policy MMC Snap-in to set up auditing for the domain.

This utility is the first step toward setting up events to audit. You use the Domain Security Policy tool to select the categories of events to audit. You can then select the individual objects (such as files, folders, or printers) that will be audited. After you have selected the kinds of events you want to audit, you then need to configure auditing on the resources that you consider important, just as you did in Windows NT 4.0.

Use Start, Programs, Administrative Tools, Domain Security Policy to start this tool. In Figure 38.5, you can see the MMC that is displayed, with the Security Settings object in the left pane of the console expanded to show the various objects that can be used to configure and monitor security for the domain.

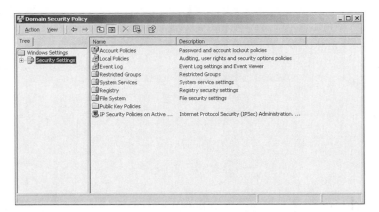

Figure 38.5   Use the Domain Security Policy tool to enable auditing.

In the right pane, double-click Local Policies and then Audit Policy. In Figure 38.6, you can see the events you can set up for auditing for the domain.

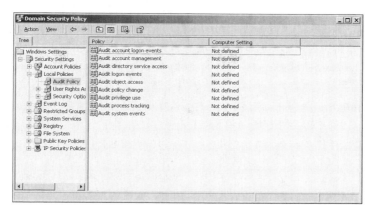

Figure 38.6   Use the Audit Policy object in the left pane to configure auditing.

To enable auditing, first select the kinds of events you want to audit. For example, to enable logging for successful or failed logon attempts, use the category Audit Logon Events. If you double-click this item, you can then select to audit successful or unsuccessful logon attempts (Success, Failure), as shown in Figure 38.7.

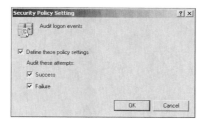

Figure 38.7   When you enable auditing for a category, you can enable both successful access as well as failed access attempts.

You can choose to audit other categories in this utility, such as changes made to user accounts (Audit account management), and file or printer access (object access). To audit object access on the domain controller, use Audit Directory Service Access. To audit object access on a member server in the domain, select Audit Object Access.

For each category, just double-click the entry in the MMC and select the Define These Policy Settings check box. You can then select either Success or Failure, to decide which kinds of access to audit.

In some environments, it might be desirable to log successful logons, so that you can track when users are active on the network. Enabling failed logons can also be useful when trying to determine whether someone is attempting to break into your system, or whether a user is having a problem with his account—such as a forgotten password.

Enabling Auditing for Files and Folders

Keeping track of when users log on to the domain or when failed logon attempts occur enables you to track user account usage in the domain. It's also a good idea to keep track of access to important files and folders that reside on your servers. Although the NTFS allows you to grant or deny access with a large degree of precision, it can sometimes be difficult to determine the right combination of user rights and access permissions to use to set up the required access.

For example, the description for the Backup Operators Builtin group you'll find in the Active Directory Users and Computers administrative tool is "Backup Operators can override security restrictions for the sole purpose of backing up or restoring files." Does this mean they can read your files when not using a backup program? No. But to be sure, you can always set up event logging for important files or directories, and then use the Event Viewer to determine when these files or directories were successfully (or unsuccessfully) accessed.

After you've used the Domain Security Policy administrative tool to enable auditing for objects, then you can configure specific objects for auditing.

The simplest way to set up auditing for a file or folder is to bring up the Windows Explorer accessory and use the properties page for a folder or a file:

1. Choose Start, Programs, Accessories, Windows Explorer.

2. Locate the folder or file you want to enable for auditing.

3. Right-click the file or folder and select Properties from the menu that appears.

4. Select the Security tab and click the Advanced button that appears at the bottom of the display. This brings up the Access Control Settings properties page for the folder. Click the Auditing tab (see Figure 38.8).

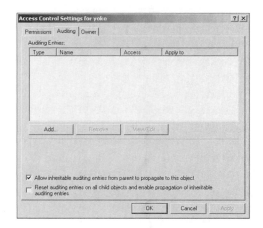

Figure 38.8   The Access Control Settings properties page allows you to control access and auditing for the folder.

5. Use the Add button to bring up the standard Select User Computer or Group dialog box. You can use this dialog box to select the user(s) or group(s) that will generate audit records when access is attempted for the folder. Use the scrollbar to find the user, or enter the name of the user (or group) if you already know it into the Name field. Click the OK button and the Auditing Entry dialog box (see Figure 38.9) appears.

6. This dialog box allows you to select the events to be audited in great detail. Use the Apply Onto drop-down list to choose whether the auditing entry is created for just this folder, the folder and files in the folder, subfolders, and combinations thereof. Use the Access pane to select the action that will be audited by clicking either the Successful or Failure (or both) check boxes.

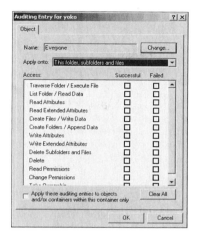

Figure 38.9   After you've selected the user or group whose access will be audited, you can select the event(s) that will generate an audit record.

Tip

Note the Apply These Auditing Entries to Objects and/or Containers within This Container Only check box at the bottom of the dialog box. Because child objects in the Active Directory inherit attributes from parent objects, you should enable this check box if you want to restrict the auditing entry to just the users or groups you've selected in this particular container (that is, domain, or organizational unit).

Note

In Figure 38.9, the types of access are complicated because on a secure Windows 2000 computer, the NTFS is used. In addition to the traditional access types such as read, write, and delete, you'll see a lot of other things that can be manipulated in the file system, such as changing the permissions or reading and writing extended attributes for the file or folder. Before you begin to select events for auditing, make sure you understand them. You should be well-versed in how the NTFS operates before you begin auditing access types that you are unfamiliar with, else you might end up generating literally thousands of entries in the event log.

7. When you've finished selecting the events to be audited, click OK.

8. When the Access Control Settings properties sheet reappears, note the check boxes at the bottom of this dialog box. By default the Allow Inheritable Auditing Entries from Parent to Propagate to This Object check box is selected. Remember that unless the parent object has blocked inheritance for auditing entries, this is the default in the Active Directory. The second check box resets the auditing entries for all objects that fall under the user or group in the Active Directory.

9. Click OK to dismiss the Access Control Settings properties sheet and then do the same for the initial properties page for the folder.

After you've set up auditing, you can check the event log periodically to determine which users have successfully accessed the folder or file, and also those which have failed to gain access, depending on which check boxes you have selected.

If all this seems complicated, it is! The Active Directory allows you to finely tune the access permissions, user rights, and auditing for objects that exist in the directory. Obviously, you should structure your files system and user groups with careful planning so you don't end up with a large number of variables to contend with. If you try to set up auditing for every folder based on a user-by-user basis, for example, you'll spend a lot of time setting up auditing every time you add a new user or create a new directory.

Notice also that inheritance can be blocked from above as well as propagated to objects that are beneath the object that you are auditing. For example, if you have multiple organizational units in your domain, you can set up auditing based on the domain, and let these auditing records filter down the tree to apply also to the organizational units that fall underneath it. Or, you can elect to set up auditing differently for each organizational unit.

Note

The Active Directory can be only as complex as you make it. For many small organizations, a single domain and the builtin containers (that is, Users and Computers) are sufficient for managing a small number of users. For more information about container objects in the directory, as well as how the directory is organized, see Chapter 25, "Overview of Microsoft's Active Directory Service."

Enabling Auditing for Printers

The method used for selecting users and groups and the access that will be audited is just about the same for printers as it is for files and folders. You use the same dialog box to select users and groups, and a similar dialog box to select the type of access to be audited. To set up a printer for auditing, use the following steps:

1. Choose Start, Settings, Printers. When the Printers folder appears, right-click the printer you want to set up auditing for and select Properties from the menu that appears. Select the Security tab.

2. Click the Advanced button at the bottom of this properties sheet. The Access Control Settings properties sheet appears. Click the Auditing tab.

3. Click the Add button and the standard Select User, Computer or Group dialog box appears, just as it did when you were setting up auditing for folders in the previous section. Select the user or group that will be audited and click Add.

4. The Auditing Entry dialog box for printers appears looking a little different than the one used for files and folders (see Figure 38.10).

5. Here the access types are much simpler than they were for file and folder objects. Select one of the first two if you want to track what users print and to keep track of users who manage printers. Note that if you select the Print option, the Read Permissions event is also selected because users must be able to read the permissions you've applied to the printer to determine whether they can print to it. Likewise, if you select Manage Printers, all other events are automatically selected with the exception of Manage Documents, because these other events occur while managing a printer.

6. When you've finished selecting successful and failed events to audit, click OK to dismiss the properties sheet, and then click OK to dismiss the preceding properties sheets.

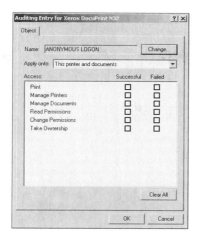

Figure 38.10 Select the type of access to be audited for the user or groups you have chosen.

Using the Windows 2000 Event Viewer

The Event Viewer is another tool you'll find in the Administrative Tools folder. It functions much the same as it did in Windows NT 4.0, although now the MMC is used as the interface, and some additional functionality has been added. In Figure 38.11 you can see the Event Viewer with the Security object selected.

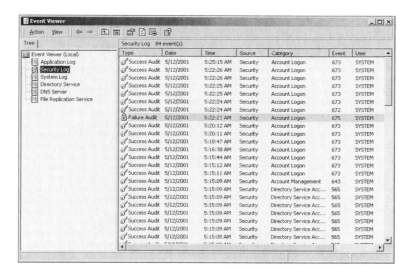

Figure 38.11 The Event Viewer now uses MMC.

In addition to the Application, Security, and System log files, other log files might show up, depending on the services you've installed on the server. For example, in Figure 38.11, the Directory Service, DNS Server, and File Replication Service log files are also listed because they are installed on the domain controller. On member servers that are not domain controllers, your view might be different.

In the right side pane of the Event Viewer, you will see a line item for each event in the file. Double-click any event to bring up a properties sheet that contains the detailed information about the event that was logged. In Figure 13.12, for example, you can see an example of a failed logon attempt by the user Administrator on the system.

Figure 38.12   Yes, even the administrator can forget his password once in a while.

Notice also in Figure 38.12 that you can use the up- and down-arrow buttons to move through line items so you don't have to double-click each one to view the details. This can make scanning a set of events easier. Directly underneath these arrows is a button that looks like two sheets of paper. Clicking this button copies the details of the logged event to the Clipboard. You can then use a word processor or other utility that has a paste function to save or print the details of the event.

Using the Event Viewer Action Menu

You can use a central MMC to manage the event logs from the local computer that you are logged onto, and you can also add other computers in your network to the console tree in the left pane so that you can manage their log files from the same place.

Choose Action, Connect to Another Computer. Figure 38.13 shows the dialog box that pops up. Enter the name or IP address of another computer here and, if you have access to that computer, click the OK button and it will be added to the tree.

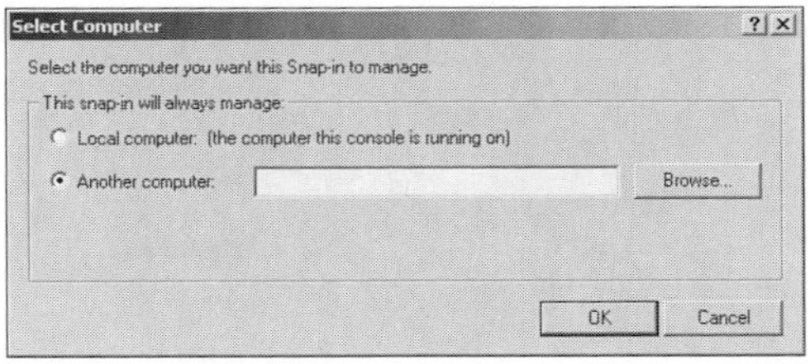

Figure 38.13   You can connect to multiple computers to manage event log files from a central location.

The Action menu also allows you to manage the properties of each log file, in a manner similar to that used in Windows NT 4.0. For example, you can set the maximum size the log file can grow to, or set whether events should be overwritten when the file becomes full (see Figure 38.14).

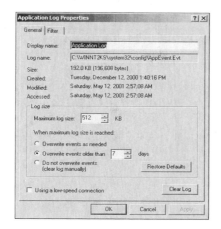

Figure 38.14   Choose Action, Properties to manage a log file.

The Filter tab allows you to specify information that will be used to narrow down the records you want to look at. You can select a date range, event type, source, category, event ID, and user, among other things. To return the display to show all records in the file, select View, All Records.

Finally, you can use the Action menu to save a log file to another file, export the information in a log file to a text file, rename the log file, create a new log file, or clear all events from the log file.

Novell Security

Novell has been one of the most popular network operating systems for many years now. Early versions were limited in their capability to keep track of events but this has changed with NetWare 4.x. The most useful tool is the AUDITCON tool which can be used to configure and audit a wide range of system events.

SYSCON and AUDITCON

The SYSCON utility that was used in NetWare 3.x was limited in the type of information it could provide to the administrator. It was basically limited to statistical information such as the number of blocks read/written and the services the server provided. In NetWare 4.x the AUDITCON utility provides an advanced tool that is superior to SYSCON in two ways:

- The information is more granular. File system events, such as access and modifications to individual files or directories can be tracked. Events are also audited for NDS objects.

- The auditing role has been separated from the administrator's role, enabling an employee other than the administrator to act as the network auditor.

Both of these are significant advances. The first makes the information gathered more than just statistical. You can now track access and the type of access to individual files or objects. The second can be used to ensure that the network administrators, usually an all-powerful people who can do *anything* on the network, are also held accountable for their actions. Network security is not compromised by the auditor, however, because this person does not have to be granted administrator-like rights to objects such as SYS:SYSTEM directory. The administrator and the auditor's functions are separated.

Note

The administrator does have some control over the auditor: the administrator has to set up the auditor so that she can perform her functions. After an auditor has been assigned and the account set up, the auditor can change her password, thereby keeping the administrator locked out of the auditing functions. This approach allows the administrator and the auditor to balance each other. The auditor can track the administrator's actions and the administrator can always change the person designated to be the auditor.

After the administrator has enabled auditing on volumes or containers and designated the auditor, the auditor can use the AUDITCON utility to check the system. Using AUDITCON, the auditor can modify which events are audited on which resources, and can produce reports showing auditing information.

Auditable Events

The precise granularity of things you can audit is what makes AUDITCON a powerful tool. The person who has been set up as the auditor can

- **Audit by event**—This includes file-related events such as open, read, write, and create files or directories. These can be audited for all users (global) or on a per user basis. You can also audit printer queue events (QMS), server events (such as when it is brought down or restarted), and user events (such as user logins and logouts or the creation or deletion of user objects).

- **File or directory events**—You can select files or directories for which all access will be audited.

- **User**—You can select individual users for which auditable events will be recorded.

Auditing Files

The auditing software uses several places to store its data:

- **NET$AUDT.DAT**—This file can be found at the root of every volume that has auditing enabled. It is always flagged as an open file to prevent anyone other than the auditor from accessing it directly. This file stores binary information in a binary format only for the volume on which it resides.

- **NDS Database**—Auditing for events for the directory (NDS) is stored in the NDS Database.

- **AUD$HIST.DAT**—This file is used to keep track of actions taken by the auditor(s). After all, someone has to watch the watcher! When more than one auditor is assigned to the network, each should have a separate user account so this file can be used to track the actions taken by each auditor, giving still more checks and balances to the system.

- **NET$AUDT.CFG**—This file contains audit file configuration information and is found at the root of the volume that is being audited. Using the AUDITCON utility you can change the configuration information stored here, such as the maximum size the audit file can grow to, whether to allow more than one auditor to access the audit file at the same time, and whether dual-level passwords are used, among other things. The dual-level password requires an additional auditor password to be used when changing configuration information.

Note

No system, of course, is perfect. It is easy for the auditor to clear the AUD$HIST.DAT file when he has performed some action that was not allowed. However, the new file created after the old one is cleared will record that fact. Thus, although you might not be able to find out what was done, you can still find out that something suspicious is going on.

Using AUDITCON to Enable Auditing

An Admin user can enable auditing on a volume by running the AUDITCON utility. From the main menu, select the Enable Volume Auditing option and enter the password for that volume. If an old audit data file exists on the volume it is replaced by the new file.

After this has been done, the administrator should give the volume password to the auditor, who should run AUDITCON and change it to a new value that the administrator does not know. Note that if the password is forgotten, the volume must be deleted and recreated if you want to change the password. You cannot recover the password. Also, without the correct password, you can disable auditing on the volume!

To change the audit password, the auditor should run the AUDITCON utility and select Audit Files Maintenance. From the next menu, select Auditing Configuration and then Change Audit Password. When prompted, enter the new password.

Producing Reports

Reports are produced to translate the binary auditing data into a format readable by humans. These reports can be produced by selecting Auditing Reports from the AUDITCON main menu. For security purposes, you should never leave these reports in a directory that can be easily accessed by other users. Instead, view or print the report text files and then delete them. You can always re-run the report at a later date if you need to obtain another copy.

When producing an audit report, you can select events by date, time, and event; you also can choose to include or exclude selected files, directories or users. This filtering ability makes it easy to get right to the important data when you are troubleshooting a security breach. If you are performing a regular review of the system, you can select all data and spend hours poring through it, but a large volume of data will most likely make it easy to miss an important event. In other words, when performing an analysis of the data, it's best to have a target objective of files or events, or possibly users, you need to keep an eye on.

Security Issues in Wide Area Networks

CHAPTER 39

When all you have to worry about are the computers attached to your local LAN and users that you know personally, it's easy to implement security policies and keep the network virtually safe from things such as viruses or other malicious programs. A properly trained user base, along with security guidelines that allow only outside programs approved for use on the network, can go a long way toward keeping a LAN safe. Of course, it still pays to regularly use an up-to-date virus-scanning program to be absolutely sure that you've cleaned up your network.

When you connect to the Internet, however, there are so many different ways that your network can be compromised, even when using a highly secured firewall. Thus, it's best to learn about the most recent kinds of attacks and then locate resources to help you stay aware of the latest news. One of the most common misconceptions about firewalls is that they offer complete protection. However, studies have shown that

- Most firewalls are difficult to manage. You can never be sure whether you've done all you need to do to block malicious traffic at the perimeter of your network.

- Firewalls must be updated regularly, as new protocol or application loopholes are discovered. In a small company, a firewall is a good idea but it is not a panacea. In a large company with a staff of technicians maintaining a firewall, you can still never be sure that you are completely safe from intrusions.

- A firewall can't protect you from your own internal users!

Consider a firewall to be the first line of defense, not the only defense you put up for your network.

This chapter looks at some of the typical problems that can be introduced into your network from the Internet and then at resources you can use to further educate yourself on these topics.

You've Been Targeted!

Too often you are tempted to put in a quick fix and consider a problem solved. However, in the complex matter of network security, you'll find there are no quick fixes. Because a network is composed of many components, hackers have a large number of devices they can target, such as

- **Routers**—These devices stand at the perimeter of your network and sometimes perform firewall functions. Routers are easy targets for many reasons. First, a router is your network's connection to the Internet, so it's directly exposed *to the whole world*. Second, routing protocols can be abused when hackers damage the routing table on your router. What good is a router if it doesn't know where to relay network traffic to and from? You learn this in more detail later in this chapter when you read about ICMP redirects. Although there isn't a lot you can do to protect a router from an attack over the Internet, you can take some steps to make it more difficult for potential intruders. You learn about that in the section titled "Protecting Routers."

- **Host computers**—Servers on your network are supposed to provide data, print, e-mail, or other important services to your users. After a host computer has been infiltrated, however, these services can be corrupted or made unavailable. After a hacker gets past the router or firewall, the host computers on your network are usually the next target. This is one good reason to use a private address space on the internal LAN and save your registered IP addresses for use by the routers and firewall devices that actually need a valid address on the Internet. If the intruder does not know the addresses of computers on your network, he will have more difficulty connecting to them and causing trouble! As a general rule, it's best to *always* hide information about the configuration of all computers on your internal LAN.

- **Applications and services**—There is a great debate on the Internet about open source code. One side of the debate is this: If the actual code for particular applications is known, it's easier for patches or modifications to be made when some hacker detects a loophole in the application or service. The opposite argument is that the bad guys also have a copy of the code and can spend all the time they need looking for vulnerable parts of the code that can be used to their advantage. When you are considering installing mission-critical software on a server, which should you use? I can't really offer an opinion on this because both sides have good arguments. If you use a proprietary program purchased from a vendor, you can depend on the technical support staff of the vendor to help you if the application becomes a target. However, you must pick your vendors carefully—for example, what is the response time when you place a service call for a minor issue? Can you count on vendor support in an emergency or would you rather have the open source code so your own staff (and others around the world who use the same code) can immediately begin trying to plug the loophole?

- **Your network**—If you're the sort of person who enjoys causing problems for others, attacking the entire network is probably going to give you more pleasure than going after only a few host computers or applications. Think of how expensive it is to a large company such as eBay or Microsoft when their networks are taken offline due to an attack. If a hacker can disable your entire network, the damage done can become quite expensive.

Usually, an attack is not so clearly defined as just described. Instead, many attacks are sophisticated combinations of several of the above.

Computer Viruses, Trojan Horses, and Other Destructive Programs

Computer viruses have been around for a long time. These are programs that travel from one computer to another, using a variety of methods, from e-mail attachments to boot sector virus code on a floppy disk. Shareware downloaded from the Internet is another popular method for spreading virus code. Trojan horses are programs that an intruder plants on one or more servers in your network. The Trojan horse program is activated by some specific event, such as the arrival of a certain date, or by a user running a program that has been replaced by the Trojan horse. This latter tactic is very popular. Some programs are not what they appear to be!

Other types of destructive programs can attack your network. This is the case in a denial-of-service attack. The perpetrators never have to intrude into your network. Instead, they use one of several methods (which we'll talk about in just a minute) to send massive amounts of network traffic to your network router or server. The server or router becomes overwhelmed and can no longer operate efficiently. Other denial-of-service attacks target specific resources, such as servers or applications.

Trojan Horse Programs

Trojan horses are programs that are planted somewhere in your network and wait for a signal before springing into action. After hackers have gained entry to a server in your network, they can easily plant a program and then run it. The program can listen on a selected port waiting for a signal. When the signal comes, the Trojan horse does its destructive chores. One of the most common techniques for hiding these programs is to give them the same name as some other common program on the computer. Indeed, some Trojan horses are nothing more than modified versions of a standard operating system file. So what appears to be one thing, might be something entirely different. As mentioned earlier, a Trojan horse program also can be activated by other means. The main difference between a Trojan horse program and a computer virus is that the virus is usually activated, does its damage, and then attempts to replicate itself by some means, such as mailing itself to everyone in your address book. Trojan horses are more like bombs waiting to go off.

Computer Viruses

Computer viruses come in all sorts of variations. They have been wreaking havoc on computers even before the Internet became commercial. Before the Internet exploded into the large network it is today, bulletin board services were a popular method for exchanging files, such as shareware programs. A virus program usually is distinguished by two features. First, the virus replicates itself so it can be spread to other computers. The method of transport can be a floppy disk that has had its boot sector code modified, or it can be a macrovirus that comes as part of an e-mail attachment that uses the Internet e-mail system to move about. Second, a virus usually is created to do something destructive, such as wiping out the contents of a hard disk or damaging some other system resource. However, this second feature is not always present in a computer virus. Some simply display a silly message on the screen to let the user know he's been hit, and then the viruses do no further damage.

Now it seems that most viruses are destructive, so you should always use virus-checking software on computers in your network. Although deploying a virus-checking application on several hundred or several thousand computers can be expensive, especially when you consider that you also must pay for updates from the vendor, the amount of damage viruses can cause if you do get hit greatly justifies this cost.

How Infections Occur

Viruses and other computer maladies can travel through a variety of routes to get to your computer. One of the most common methods is through the use of e-mail. How many times did you hear on the news last year, "Don't open the attachment if the subject line says..."? Because of the macro capabilities and newer features of modern e-mail clients, it is easy to trick users into launching a program without realizing what they are doing. Many e-mail macroviruses that you receive go through your address book first and mail a copy of themselves to all your friends. Then they go about doing their dirty work on your system. So, as a method of transport, e-mail can be a very lucrative path for a virus to take.

Still other avenues exist into the systems on your network. For example, shareware, freeware, and other demo software downloadable from the Internet can seem a bargain at first. And maybe now and then you find a program that actually fits a business use. However, many programs contain virus code, and the writers of the viruses are just waiting for you to download the program and execute it. The results can show up right away or can be triggered by a signal, such as a certain date, before springing into action.

Note

One of the better-known Trojan Horse programs that has surfaced during the past few years is one known as Back Orifice. When the user has been tricked into installing this program, it can give a remote hacker on the Internet control over a Windows NT/2000 machine. The only good news about this program is that the remote user operates under the same rights as the user account that was used to install it. This program is yet another example of why you need a good security policy that prevents users from downloading or installing software from the Internet that has not been tested and thoroughly evaluated by your computer security staff.

A good security policy for any site will require that users submit requests to a security team before using software that isn't currently approved. The security team can first run the program through standard virus-checking software and otherwise evaluate the security potential of the program. Never allow users to bring floppy disks (or other removable media) from home. This should be spelled out clearly in your company's network security policy.

Your Network Under Fire—Common Attacks

If all you had to worry about were virus and Trojan-horse programs, life would be so much simpler. Just deploy a good virus-checking application and monitor the alerts or log files the application produces. When a virus does creep into your network, use the appropriate software to remove it. In some situations where time is of the essence and you don't have time to wait for a vendor to come up with a fix for a newly discovered virus, you can reconstruct the server by either re-creating it on another system or by restoring data from backups. You also can reformat the hard disk of the infected system and reinstall your operating system and applications.

However, after the Internet becomes an important part of your business's bottom line, there are other potential problems you need to worry about in addition to virus and Trojan-horse programs.

Denial-of-Service Attacks

A denial-of-service attack is characterized by the goal of the attack. The attack's purpose is to cripple routers, servers, or other computers by consuming resources at a pace that makes them effectively unavailable for the ordinary user to perform required functions.

A denial-of-service attack can use different common methods to accomplish its purpose. For example, flooding a server or network with a huge amount of network traffic results in a slow response for all nodes connected to the network. When bogus packets (usually created by an application designed specifically to produce large numbers of packets) are coming into a network or server at a very fast rate, ordinary users will have a hard time getting their legitimate network packets delivered. Indeed, if a router becomes overwhelmed with enough traffic, it might simply start dropping packets because it cannot keep up with the pace. Another method commonly used is to send malformed packets that can cause problems such as buffer overruns and take advantage of other shortcomings in the operating system of the router or server.

Other resources can be targets also. For example, a Trojan horse program can be designed to do nothing except consume CPU cycles as fast as possible when it is activated. Thus other programs running on the server will slow to a crawl, or possibly not function, if they cannot obtain CPU cycles. Most operating systems allow for the concept of prioritizing certain processes. For example, the operating system itself must have access to the CPU and can interrupt a user process when needed because the operating system component runs at a higher priority than an ordinary user process. If a destructive program has been planted in your network, and if your password file has been decrypted, it's easy to run a process at a high priority by using an administrative account that has the necessary privileges.

Another method of denying access to resources can take the form of changing configuration information so the resource will not function properly. Changing router table information, for example, can make sites unreachable. Changing user account information can make it impossible for users to log on to a server. Changing configuration files (or Registry key values, in the case of an operating system such as Windows NT/2000) can render applications or services unavailable.

Distributed Denial-of-Service Attacks Can Kill Your Network!

In the previous section we talked about denial-of-service attacks. When you have to worry about only one computer trying to overload your system, you can usually block the particular incoming address at the router and then start the process of tracking down the criminal who's damaged your network.

But what do you do if you suddenly find yourself under attack by not one computer but by several hundred or several thousand computers? This sort of attack is known as a distributed denial-of-service attack because the "attackers" are multiple computers that can be coming at you from anywhere on the Internet. This is almost the worst thing that can happen to your network from the Internet.

Several years ago a program called Trin00 was developed and has been followed up by newer versions, such as the Tribe Flood Network (TFN) and Tribe Flood Network 2000 (TFN2K). These are not the only tools that can be used for a distributed denial-of-service attack, but they have been used many times to cause problems on the Internet.

As you can see in Figure 39.1, a distributed denial-of-service attack is an organized attack that uses a central controlling computer to direct other computers to perform the actual attack on your network.

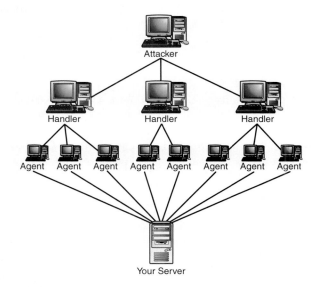

Figure 39.1   A distributed denial of service attack can overwhelm your network by using hundreds, if not thousands, of computers to simultaneously launch an attack.

In Figure 39.1 you can see that setting up this sort of attack is not necessarily an easy thing to do. Several steps are involved:

1. The perpetrator first infiltrates other innocent, unprotected computers and plants a program on them to be used later.

2. To make it difficult to track down the source of the original machine that sets off the attack, these infected computers are usually organized into a hierarchy. In Figure 39.1 you can see that a single attacker plants a "handler" program on some of the computers that have been infiltrated and "agent" programs on others.

3. The attacker sends a command to the handlers, who in turn send a command to the computers that actually perform the attack on your network.

4. You suffer!

The reason this type of attack is becoming more prevalent is that more and more people are connecting to the Internet—home users as well as businesses. In a business network, you take precautions to secure your computers. Home users rarely secure their computers, not because they're stupid but because they simply are not aware that dialing up to an Internet connection exposes their computers to intrusion from anywhere in the world. With broadband connections such as cable and DSL modems providing an "always online" connection, innocent home computer users might have no idea that while they are peacefully sleeping some hacker is downloading a program to their computer that's still online.

As you can see, no matter what you do to secure the servers and workstations inside your network, there's nothing you can do about the millions of home users who are connected to the Internet with no firewall protection. It's really a horrifying thing to consider that innocent users connected to the Internet can be unwilling participants in an attack on your network!

Another factor that makes this type of attack so deadly is that the attacker doesn't have to be in any hurry. I can only assume that someone who would perform this attack is doing it for some sick form of pleasure. The hacker can spend hours, weeks, or even months breaking into unprotected computers and planting the seeds of destruction that will be activated later.

SYN Flooding

Recall from Chapter 20, "Overview of the TCP/IP Protocol Suite," the SYN (synchronization) bit is used during the initial setup of a TCP/IP connection. It's part of the three-way handshake. When a computer receives a request to open a new TCP session, the initial packet has the SYN bit set. The computer receiving this packet will set aside buffers in memory and create data structures that will be used to manage the TCP session. However, computers are limited in memory and can handle only so many sessions simultaneously.

The SYN-flooding attack just sends the first SYN packet that is intended to begin the setup of a TCP connection. The perpetrator ignores the responses received from the server, leaving half-open connections on the server that is under attack. The SYN-flooding attack sends a constant stream of packets with the SYN bit set. The targeted computer creates the necessary data structures in memory until finally it runs out. Again, the behavior of the computer will depend on the operating system. It might crash, it might hang, or it might simply just slow down and try to keep handling the incoming packets. Even if the system continues to run, the odds of a legitimate user being able to establish a TCP connection become almost impossible. The server is overwhelmed by these half-open connections it is trying to create at a rapid rate.

Whatever the target computer does, however, there will come a point where no memory is available to run user programs or even to run the operating system itself efficiently.

The best defense against this sort of attack is to have a good firewall in place that can detect an odd stream of SYN packets coming in at a rapid rate and simply discard them. In addition, newer versions of most operating systems have been patched or modified to detect this rapid incoming flood of SYN packets and alert the administrator.

ICMP Redirects

The Internet Control Message Protocol was discussed in Chapter 20. This protocol is used for many purposes, but one important function is to send a message to a router (or a server acting as a router) to tell the router to change entries in the routing table. Once again, if your router doesn't have the correct routing information, it won't be able to deliver network packets. ICMP redirects were created with the best of intentions. Suppose, for example, in Figure 39.2, Router A sends a packet to Router B as the first hop the packet needs to take to eventually get to Router Z. If Router B knows there is a more direct route (using Router D), it uses an ICMP redirect to tell Router A the more efficient route.

This can happen under many different circumstances. In the simple example shown in Figure 39.2, it's possible that Router A has just been brought back online and knows about Router B, but hasn't yet updated its table to include Router D. In this situation, Router B, which has been up and running for some time, knows of the more direct path, so it sends the ICMP redirect message to Router A telling it to update its routing table.

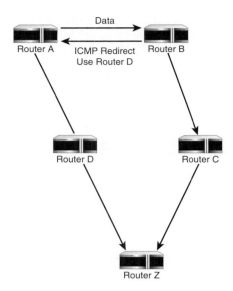

Figure 39.2   An ICMP redirect message is used to tell a router of a better path to use.

Unfortunately, it's easy to download tools from the Internet that can be used to generate ICMP packets, and this can be used against you to wreak havoc on your routing tables. For this reason, many administrators use filtering rules on routers that connect to external networks to drop any incoming ICMP redirect packets. ICMP redirect messages can be very useful within your network, but you shouldn't trust this information from routers that are not under your control.

The Ping of Death

Almost anyone who's ever dealt with networks has heard of this famous method of attack. The Ping of Death is basically a method of crashing your system by sending a packet that is excessive in size. The ping program, discussed in Chapter 22, "Troubleshooting Tools for TCP/IP Networks," is an extremely useful tool and is one of the first tools you should use when trying to determine whether connectivity exists between two machines. You can read more in Chapter 22 about how the ping utility works. However, to sum up the information here, the ping utility sends a small packet (typically 64 bytes in size) to a remote IP address. The packet is an ICMP ECHO packet. The server that receives this packet normally responds with an ICMP REPLY packet. This simple exchange of packets proves that, although you might be having other problems communicating with the remote machine, the network path between the two systems does exist and is working.

However (keeping in mind that TCP/IP was not originally designed with security as a main issue), once again mean people found a way to exploit this utility by simply modifying the ping program to send extremely large packets (say, 65,536 bytes). Most networks won't transmit a packet this large as a single unit. For example, most Ethernet packets range up to around 1,500 bytes. However, larger packets can be sent, using a process where the original packet is fragmented into smaller packets that can pass through the network devices that connect one computer to another. When packets get fragmented, the receiving end usually stores the information as the fragments come in and when the last fragment arrives, the data is reassembled into the original packet size. Operating systems typically use registers or set aside memory locations that are sized according to their expected use. If the receiving system knows that it's illegal to create a packet in excess of a certain size, the variable that is set aside (and the buffer space to store the packet) can't hold a number larger than it was created to hold. For example, a single byte (8 bits) can be used in binary to store a number of up to 255. The Ping of Death takes advantage of this by sending a packet (fragmented into manageable chunks) to the target system. When the target system attempts to reassemble the packet, lots of things can happen, depending on the operating system. If a variable overflows (that is, it's not large enough to hold the size of the packet that's being reassembled) or if the buffer space set aside for the packet is not large enough to hold the entire reassembled packet, it is possible for the incoming packet data to cross the buffer boundary and write over other important data.

When this happens, the behavior of the operating system is hard to predict. What area of memory was overwritten? What happens when the variable that stores the size of the packet can't hold the value that the local component of the ping program is trying to store there? Well, usually the computer will hang, crash, or behave in some other undesirable way.

Users have known about this attack method for several years, and most operating systems have been fortified to prevent this attack from succeeding. However, there are still legacy systems (such as Windows 95, older versions of Unix, and so on) out there performing useful functions. Older systems are extremely vulnerable to this type of attack.

If you are worried about the Ping of Death, check with your vendor to determine whether any patches or firmware upgrades are available to remedy this problem.

E-Mail Can Be Easily Forged

E-mail is probably the most popular application used on the Internet. All people can have an e-mail account, whether or not they have a computer at home. You can sign up for e-mail accounts at several sites, such as Microsoft's Hotmail or Yahoo's e-mail service, and use a computer at your school, library, or even at work to access the account.

E-mail messages, like Trojan horse programs, aren't always what they seem to be. Just because the FROM line contains the name of someone you know, how can you be sure that the e-mail actually came from that person? It's a simple matter when configuring an e-mail account to use any name you want. And with the online e-mail services that don't require you to use an e-mail client (these services typically use an HTML interface—a Web browser), it can be difficult to determine where an e-mail actually originated.

There are even programs freely available on the Net that allow you to create bogus e-mail messages that appear perfectly normal in all respects. Although any intelligent person would probably not, in this day and age, open an e-mail attachment from someone they do not know, they most likely would open an attachment from a friend. After all, if you can't trust your friends...

The problem is that e-mail is easily forged and can be used to get a program into your network. As a rule, delete spam and other e-mail from sources you don't recognize.

One of the more insidious things that can be done through e-mail has occurred with alarming frequency in recent years. Worm viruses spread through e-mail can read your address book and then replicate themselves by mailing a copy of the virus code to everyone in your address book, and then start wreaking havoc on your system! About the only thing you can do in this situation is to disconnect the computer (or computers) from the network and clean out the mail store with a good virus program. If you have a mail server in your network, disconnect it and do the same. Until you've assured yourself that every computer in your network is free of such worm viruses, don't connect back to the Internet, or any other part of your corporate network.

Password Protection—Use Smart Cards!

Passwords and usernames have been the traditional method for authenticating a user to a computer operating system. There are much better methods you can use for environments that demand a high degree of security, such as smart cards. These devices are synchronized with software that runs on the host computer. To log on, the user simply consults the password code, which changes at regular intervals, generated by the smart card. Because the application on the host computer is operating to change the account password using the same algorithm as the smart card, a user's account password can be different every time they log in. As long as the smart card and the application on the computer are kept in sync, it becomes almost impossible for someone to "steal" your password. And most smart cards have passwords that can be used only one time. This means that even if someone happens to glance at the current password on your smart card, once you've used the password to log in, it can't be reused and abused.

Network Back Doors

One of the best reasons I can think of for not allowing noncommercial shareware on a network is that if you can't trust the vendor, then you can't trust the application. There are literally thousands of useful programs you can download from the Internet that can be used productively on a network. However, isn't it better to simply purchase a commercial product from a reliable, known vendor who has a good technical support staff?

A back door into a network can be an application that was downloaded by an innocent user who is unaware that the program, in addition to doing what it says it does, also does other things, such as mailing out your user authorization files to some other computer on the Internet.

Shareware programs are not the only method used to create a back door into your network or host computer. Once again, you must consider the amount of trust you have in your users and use good judgment when granting privileges and access permissions to users. Delegating authority to others to make management easier is a great concept. Delegating these privileges to an unhappy employee is not a good idea. The problem is that it's not always easy to tell a happy employee from one who is not! Suppose you have a technician who performs router maintenance activities. You have to trust that the employee is correctly programming the access control lists and other items on the routers.

However, there is an easy solution to this type of problem. Delegate the ability to manage the routers in your network to more than one person and establish a process of regularly reviewing router configurations. Trust no one! But maybe you can trust several people!

Watch Those Ports

Ports are used along with an IP address to create a "socket" that uniquely identifies an end point in a IP connection. While the IP address provides a unique identifier for the host computer, the port identifies the specific application for which the connection is to be used. When configuring routers, proxy servers, and other similar devices, use this simple rule: Disable all ports, and then enable only those you actually *need* to use. In most cases it's easy to disable a port in one direction or in both directions. That is, you can restrict incoming or outgoing network traffic by port. A list of well-known ports can be found in Appendix B, "TCP and UDP Common Ports." Use this list as a guide but keep this in mind: As new applications are developed, new port numbers will come into use. That's why you need to turn off all ports except the ones you specifically use! You don't just lock one door in your house, do you? You lock them all. Even if a particular door is rarely used, it should be locked because you never know when someone is going to try to enter. This analogy holds true for TCP and UDP port numbers.

Modems

One reason you need a modem on a computer in your network today is to provide remote access capabilities for users who work from remote locations and need access to the corporate network. Allowing individual employees to have a modem on their desktop computer is just asking for trouble.

Instead, use a separate server to set up a remote access service, using a reasonable number of modems to satisfy the needs of your remote clients. Remote access servers are typically very configurable—that is, you can provide additional authentication mechanisms, such as call-back. With most operating systems, you also can grant dial-in access only to those users who need it. Finally, regularly review any log files created by remote access server modem banks to be sure that you have indeed configured the server correctly and that no unknown users are getting in.

Another solution for remote users is to use Virtual Private Networking (VPN) services. Windows 2000 Advanced Server can be set up to allow users to create an encrypted communication tunnel through the Internet. Many routers also provide this functionality. The days of the modem are numbered. Home users in the near future will most likely demand broadband access, using cable or DSL modems rather than the typical modem that connects to the public switched-telephone network.

▶▶ In Chapter 19, "Dedicated Connections," you can find out more about using a digital connection instead of an analog modem for remote users.

Network Sniffers Are Probing Your Network!

A network sniffer is a very useful tool for troubleshooting network problems. You can find software and hardware network sniffers that collect data packets from the network and allow you to examine them to determine what is causing a problem on your network.

Because the purpose of a network sniffer is to intercept packets and examine them, you can easily see how this could be very damaging when used for purposes other than troubleshooting.

Remember that the less information known about your network by outsiders, the more difficult it is to infiltrate your network. However, when someone has broken in, it's a simple task to plant a program that does nothing except listen to the network and send information back to the person who planted the program in the first place. Using a network sniffer for this purpose enables an outsider to find out all sorts of useful information about your computers, users, and network configuration. For example, you already know it's a bad idea to use FTP, Telnet, and other utilities that use clear-text to send usernames and passwords. However, you might think it's safe to use these inside your network. Well, that's not so! If someone has planted a program in a server on your network and is "sniffing" the packets that pass around your network, they'll find it very easy to further infiltrate your network by obtaining more user account information, and thus be able to compromise one computer after another. Use safe utilities inside your network as well as for communications on the Internet! An example of this would be to use the Secure Shell utilities mentioned in Chapter 37, "Basic Security Measures."

Spoofing and Impersonation

Just as it's a simple matter to create a program that can construct a steady stream of SYN packets and send them rapidly to your server, it's also easy to create network packets that have false information in other fields of the IP header. For example, you might have a firewall set up to reject packets from known sources of trouble, based on the source IP address found in the header. However, there's nothing to stop the hacker from simply putting in another source address so that your firewall lets the packet through.

IP address spoofing is very easy to do. It's also very hard to detect. One thing a firewall can do, however, is guard against packets that contain a spoofed address, making it appear that the packet originated inside your network. Think about it. If the source address of a network packet falls within the address range of your internal network, it shouldn't be coming in through a firewall interface that's connected to the Internet. It should be the other way around! All good firewalls can be configured to drop packets that arrive from the outside world with an address that makes it look like the packet came from your network.

Preventive Measures You Can Take

Chapter 4, "Preventive Maintenance," discusses standard techniques typically used to keep a network up and running. One of these preventive measures is regular backups. If your system becomes infected with virus programs or if you find that data has been corrupted, you'll understand the importance of regular, frequent backups. In addition, it's a good idea to keep offline copies of important data files for an extended period of time. Simply doing a backup each night and overwriting the tape or tapes the next night will provide you with very little protection. Damage to your system might not become evident until weeks or, in some cases, months after the initial intrusion.

There are also commercial and noncommercial products you can use to help safeguard your system. These include intrusion-detection mechanisms, virus-checking programs, and programs that can monitor changes on important servers.

So, where should you start when defining the defensive mechanisms needed to protect your network? Let's start at the edge of the network—the router.

Protecting Routers

Routers typically can be configured in several ways. You can attach a serial cable and terminal directly to most routers and perform configuration tasks. Another method is Telnet. Most modern routers allow you to Telnet into the router to perform configuration tasks. Turn this functionality on only when it is needed, and then turn it back off! The same goes for unnecessary protocols and services. In a manner similar to deciding what services you want to allow through a firewall (and in what direction), you should turn off all unnecessary services on a router. You'll have to consult your documentation to find out the particular commands you'll need to use. However, a good document on router security can be found at the following URL:

`http:/www.cisco.com/warp/public/707/21.html`

You might want to check vendor Web sites for other router products that are in use on your network to look for similar advice. Additionally, be sure to stay informed of router firmware updates and operating system updates and patches. As new threats are discovered, a responsible vendor will release information or code that can be used to help improve the security of the routers that stand guard at the edge of the network.

The Network As Target

There are some problems for which there is currently no easy solution. The distributed denial-of-service attack discussed earlier in this chapter is one of those. When the entry points into your network are saturated with an overload of network traffic, there's not much you can do about it. The best tactic you can use when such an attack occurs is to try to block out the address ranges from which the attack is coming. But when your network is being singled out by several hundred other compromised computers, it's rather difficult to quickly program routers to block all of these network addresses. The fact that many large Internet sites have been taken down during the past few years by these kinds of attacks should be indicative of how serious this attack can be. What can you do? Gather all the information you can and, when the attack is over, try to backtrack to find out where the attack first initiated. At this time it might not be possible to do this because one computer can set off others to do the dirty work for them. If you don't have access to the actual computers that perform a distributed denial-of-service attack, you can use the information on those other systems to further research the problem.

So for now, the best solution is to hope this doesn't happen to you and to use an Internet service provider that has a good technical team that can respond quickly to help block sites that are generating this type of attack.

Protecting Host Computers

After an intruder gets past a router, it's usually pretty easy to intrude further by gaining access to host computers on the network. Again, it is so easy to simply put up a router and firewall configuration and assume your network is safe. However, even if these methods do protect you from outsiders, you still must worry about users who are allowed on the network. A disgruntled employee can do more damage (and probably do a good job of hiding the evidence) than many network intruders. Host security is a very important topic.

You should first start by becoming intimately familiar with the resource-protection and user-authentication schemes used by your computers. For example, many Unix variants provide for a shadow password file that is not easily accessible. When someone breaks into a Unix server, it's a simple matter to download the contents of the /etc/passwd file and spend a few minutes or hours using an automated program to encrypt words in a dictionary, check to see whether they match the encrypted password in the stolen file, and then simply log back into your Unix box using a valid password!

The applications you run on servers or workstations can also make the host computer an easy target. For example, if you are using older versions of FTP or Telnet, you're sending usernames and passwords about your network in clear, easy to read, ASCII text. A network sniffer (which can be something as simple as a Trojan horse program planted somewhere in your network) can watch for these and transmit them back to the intruder. Because secure versions of these and other related utilities are available, you should always be sure to use the secure versions, even if it means purchasing additional software that already comes with your operating system.

▶▶ You can find more information about standard TCP/IP applications that are particularly vulnerable by reading Chapter 21, "TCP/IP Services and Applications."

If you have an important server that is absolutely critical to your business operations, you might want to consider keeping a "hot spare" around. That is, create another server that is virtually a clone of the important server. If the original server is compromised, place the hot spare into service. This might involve a little time if you have data that needs to be restored to the hot spare before it can be used. However, for servers that contain data that doesn't change often, such as some Web servers, you can have an exact duplicate sitting around just waiting to be used in case the operational Web server becomes compromised.

Another way to protect servers is to use the tools that the operating system provides to protect some services. For example, you'd be a fool to place a directory on your system disk for use as an anonymous FTP site. The last thing you want is to have someone filling up all the space on your system disk. Most operating systems allow you to set quotas that define how much space a particular user account can use on a server's hard drives. Enforcing quotas can help prevent an attack that consists of consuming all the available space on a disk. In addition, you can set alarms to notify you when quotas are being used up at a rate that is faster than what you see during normal operations. It's then an easy matter to track down the source of the data coming into the server and to terminate the user process.

What Is Tripwire?

There are many programs that you can use to help determine whether your system has been compromised. Tripwire is a very popular program that can be used for this purpose. Tripwire was originally developed in 1992 by Gene Kin and Dr. Eugene Spafford. The Academic Source Release (ASR) version of Tripwire can be downloaded for noncommercial use from Tripwire's Web site. In addition, Tripwire has created commercial versions of the software, including an enterprise manager program (Tripwire Manager) that uses SSL for communications and simplifies management of multiple servers and workstations.

Tripwire is based on the concept of taking a "snapshot" of system resources, such as files, directories, and, in the case of Windows NT, Registry settings. The information gathered by Tripwire is stored in a secure database and is used to compare a server at a later date to determine whether changes have been made and what those changes were. A policy file allows the network administrator to control the types of data that Tripwire monitors and to prioritize certain events using a rule base. In addition, Tripwire can produce reports that make monitoring the system easier for administrators.

Currently, Tripwire runs on the following operating system platforms:

- Windows NT 4.0 (and, in an unsupported manner, on Windows 2000)
- Solaris (SPARC) versions 2.6, 7.0, and 8.0
- IBM AIX 4.3
- HP-UX 11.0
- Several versions of Linux

Some of the things that Tripwire can monitor are specific to an operating system, while others (such as file types and sizes) can be monitored on all platforms. For example, a few of the items you can use Tripwire to monitor on Unix systems include

- Addition, deletion, or modification of files, along with file permissions, types, and sizes
- Inode number and number of links
- The owner and group IDs for files
- Modification timestamps and access timestamps

In addition, hash algorithms can be used to ensure the integrity of the contents of files. Tripwire supports several different kinds of hashing algorithms, such as CRC-32, MD5, and the SHS/SHA algorithm, among others.

For Windows NT systems, the list that can be monitored includes the standard file components and things such as

- File attributes, such as archive, read-only, hidden, or offline
- Create and access times
- NTFS Owner SID, NTFS Group SID, and other NTFS attributes
- Addition, deletion, and modification of Registry keys and the values of those keys

These lists are not all-inclusive. For more information about acquiring an evaluation copy of Tripwire or the Academic Source Release, visit their Web site at www.tripwire.com.

Virus-Checking Programs

Even home PC users are aware of the value of virus-checking programs. There are so many vendors of this software that it would be pointless to attempt to list them here. However, when you do choose a virus-checking program, there are some things you should consider when making a purchasing decision. For example, does the vendor respond quickly with updates to the software as new viruses are discovered? Does the software have the capability to remove the virus after it's been discovered? Does the software have the capability to scan floppy disks and files transferred to the computer through the network? Of these, the capability to quickly respond to new threats is perhaps the most important. However, your situation might dictate other factors that are more important. Note also that many firewall products now contain some type of virus-detection mechanism. For more information about this function, see Chapter 40, "Firewalls."

User Awareness and Training

Social engineering is a term used a lot lately to describe an easy method for gaining access into your network. Put quite simply, are the users of your network trained in security measures? A quick test is to simply have someone from your help desk call a user and ask them for their password. I would bet that in at least half the cases you'll find the users will give out their passwords. A help desk person shouldn't have to ask this type of question! Instead, if people at your help desk need to access a user account, they can notify the user that they are changing the password temporarily and will notify the user when they should reset the password to a value known only to the user.

A password policy should also be in effect to ensure that common names and words are not used. Yet, one must be careful to avoid making passwords so difficult that users have a hard time remembering them. Most operating systems have the capability to keep a history list of passwords to prevent their reuse within a specified amount of time. You'll also find that you can usually set a minimum and maximum password length.

Social engineering also can involve dumpster diving. How secure are the printouts that you throw in the trash can? Do you have paper shredders (and a security policy dictating their use) in place? Even Hollywood stars know that much useful information can be obtained from a trash can! This goes not just for paper materials. When you decommission old tapes or old computer hard drives, do you take the time to destroy any data that is stored on them? It may be well and good to donate old computers to nonprofit organizations or schools, but it's also a good idea to reformat the hard drives and reinstall the operating systems before you do so. Tapes can be made useless by a variety of means, including bulk tape erasers that zap the contents of a tape in just a few seconds.

Stay on Top of Security Issues

Your network will never be secure unless you make an effort to keep up to date with the latest discoveries concerning security issues. There are many good sites on the Web that you can use as resources to help you get the latest information as well as advice on how to better secure hosts and networks. Appendix E, "Network Information Resources," contains a list of many Web sites that you can use to stay on top—and when it comes to security, you have to. Keep in mind that those who would do harm to your network are usually one step ahead of you. It's a continual catch-up game. The quicker you find out about a problem, the quicker you can take precautions to protect your network.

Firewalls

40

SOME OF THE MAIN TOPICS IN THIS CHAPTER ARE

What Is a Firewall?

Packet Filters

Intrusion Detection (Stateful Inspection)

Proxy Servers

Hybrids

How Do You Know the Firewall Is Secure?

## CHAPTER 40

You must be on the Internet if you want your business to remain competitive during the next decade. Yet, the Internet remains an insecure territory, much like those in the old Wild West days. To help keep your network protected from those who would try to cause you problems, it is unthinkable for a business in today's market to make a connection to the Internet without using a firewall. The term *firewall* is casually tossed around by news reporters and in magazine articles, and it might be difficult for you to understand exactly what a firewall is and what it does. That's because a good firewall is not a single entity, but instead a set of components, each of which has a specific purpose. In this chapter, you'll look at firewall technologies and the problems they target. With this knowledge, you'll be in a better position to make decisions about how best to protect your network.

What Is a Firewall?

A *firewall* is a set of components that stands between your network and the Internet and acts as a gatekeeper, allowing in trusted friends and keeping out known or suspected enemies. A firewall can be a single device, such as a router, computer, or dedicated hardware appliance, which has software capable of making the decisions needed to monitor the flow of data to and from the corporate network and the outside world. A firewall also can be composed of more than one router, computer, or network appliance, each performing a specific function. For small offices and home offices (SOHO)— especially those using a broadband, always-on connection—a simple firewall appliance that you can purchase at the local computer store might be all you need. Better yet, the best protection for SOHO networks is to disconnect your network from your broadband connection when you are not using it.

Note

Although this chapter is targeted toward business entities that have valuable data to protect, the information here also can be useful to home users. If you have a broadband connection—be it DSL (digital subscriber line) or a cable modem—for your home computer, you might find yourself either the victim of an attack or, worse yet, an unwitting accomplice to an attack on another larger network. Most of the recent denial-of-service attacks that have been aimed at popular Web sites involve a multi-tiered attack method known as a *distributed denial-of-service attack*. This type of attack involves breaking into computers of home users and planting the attack program code that will be used later to attack the actual target site. Because most home users are not security conscious, they might have such a program on their computers and never know it. Yet, after infiltrating hundreds, if not thousands, of innocent home computers and installing the attack program, the attacker simply needs to send a command out to these systems to begin an attack on a third party.

If you are a home user with a broadband connection, you should install some kind of network appliance between your cable or DSL modem and your computer.

Several kinds of firewall technologies are used, and they *generally* can be classified into the following categories:

- Packet filters
- Stateful inspection
- Proxy servers
- Hybrids

Although many different vendors offer firewall products (implemented in both hardware and software products), the technology used is so diverse that it's difficult to make direct comparisons between products. The best you can do is carefully review each product and ask a lot of questions before deciding whether it will offer the protection you need for your network. Also remember that even though new security holes are always popping up for firewall products, network, and computer operating systems (OSs), many times a security breach occurs simply because a particular router or computer is not properly configured from a security standpoint.

Packet Filters

A packet filter provides the most basic functions of a firewall and can be implemented with a simple router. Indeed, packet-filtering routers were the first type of firewall created to help keep a network safe from intruders. A packet filter examines every network packet that passes through it, and either forwards or drops the packet, according to a set of rules established by the firewall administrator. Just about every router being manufactured today allows you to restrict traffic flowing inward or outward based on the contents of the TCP/IP packet header information.

A packet filter can be configured to block traffic by creating filters for

- **IP addresses**—Both source and destination addresses. You can specify individual addresses or ranges of addresses.

- **Protocols**—Such as UDP (User Datagram Protocol) or TCP (Transmission Control Protocol).

- **Port numbers**—Port numbers are used to identify connections between applications, such as FTP or Telnet. You usually can specify a range of port numbers, or use filters that allow you to say "greater than" or "less than" a port number.

- **Direction**—Filtering can be done based on whether the network packet is coming into your network from the Internet or being sent out by a user on your network to the Internet.

Note

Throughout this chapter, you'll read how firewalls stand between your network and the Internet. In a large corporate network, firewalls are also typically deployed between different networks that exist within the same company. For example, you might place a firewall between the network used by the payroll department and the network that handles manufacturing computers for your company. Think of a firewall as a locked door, which can be used to keep out those who do not belong. Although usernames and passwords provide a general sort of security within your network, it's probably a good idea to isolate network segments that contain sensitive information from the rest of your network. Usernames and passwords are easily compromised. A properly configured firewall is not. So, although most of the discussion in this chapter is about the Internet, it also can be applied to segmenting a large corporate network.

Filtering on IP Addresses

Chapter 20, "Overview of the TCP/IP Protocol Suite," discusses the information found in the Internet Protocol (IP) packet header. To briefly review, the IP protocol is used by other higher-level protocols (such as TCP and UDP) to provide a connectionless best-effort data-delivery service. To do so, the IP datagram encapsulates the TCP or other protocol segment by adding source and destination addresses, port numbers, and other header information before sending the datagram further down the protocol stack, where it is eventually transmitted on the wire bit-by-bit by the physical components of the network.

Routers can be configured easily to examine the contents of the IP header and drop packets that don't match a set of rules that the network or firewall administrator configures on the router. Perhaps the most obvious example is to filter out packets arriving from the Internet that have a *source* address that falls within the same network address range used on the internal network. Because such a packet, if it were indeed valid, would have to originate inside the network, it shouldn't be coming in from the outside! It is easy to forge IP packets so that the source address, as well as other header information, can be set to anything a hacker desires. A lot of programs are freely available on the Internet to do this.

By sending a packet with a source address into your network, it's more likely that the destination server or workstation in your network will accept it as a valid packet, thinking it's coming from a user on the local network, and the packet will be processed as usual. Using this method, it's easy to get packets into your network and actually have them delivered, when they should not be.

This is only one example of a good reason to filter packets based on the IP addressing information in the packet header. Because addresses can be forged, and because it's not practical to list all the millions of addresses that are allocated to computers on the Internet and pick and choose, you need to be cautious when using this kind of specific filtering. For example, suppose your network becomes the subject of a denial-of-service attack. You can use a network analyzer to discover the source addresses of the packets, and quickly insert a rule in the router (or firewall product) database that drops all packets that come from the network from which packets are coming.

Filtering Based on Protocols

In the IP packet, a field is used to indicate the type of protocol the packet is carrying data for. For example, if the IP packet is carrying TCP data, the protocol field in the IP header is 6. If it's carrying an ICMP (Internet Control Message Protocol) message, the protocol number is 1. The capability to filter out certain protocols is useful because many of the protocols in use on the Internet were created many years ago when security was not as much of an issue as it is in today's commercial Internet.

Take ICMP, for example. The Ping utility, discussed in Chapter 21, "TCP/IP Services and Applications," makes use of ICMP packets to determine whether another host is reachable. An ICMP ECHO REQUEST packet is sent to the address of the host computer in question. If it receives the packet, the destination computer sends back an ICMP ECHO REPLY packet. Sounds simple and safe, doesn't it? Well, it is simple, but not necessarily safe. Inside your network, Ping can be a useful tool for quickly determining that somewhere along the network path something is wrong and a computer is not reachable, whether the destination you are pinging is inside your network or on the Internet.

However, just as you wouldn't give out your credit card number to a stranger, it's not a good idea to give out *any* information about your network, *especially* the addresses of the computers on the network, to an outsider. And, that's exactly what the Ping command can do. It's easy to write a program that sits back and cycles through a range of IP addresses, sending out ICMP ECHO REQUEST packets and looking to see what replies come back. This saves a malicious hacker time because he now knows that an IP address is in use and can proceed to further try to intrude and compromise the system. Because automated tools are available for continuing the hacker's probe, it's imperative that you keep your network address information secret.

If you've ever received those boring telemarketing calls during the early evening hours, you can understand how this works. They just cycle through telephone numbers until they get someone to pick up the phone and answer. Allowing ICMP ECHO REPLY packets to respond to requests from *outside* your network is the equivalent of picking up the phone. Although you can hang up on a telemarketing call, after a hacker has your network address, she can always try back later when you're not around and use a wide variety of tools to probe your system to determine what is needed to get inside.

For this reason, it's usually a good idea to block incoming ICMP ECHO REQUEST packets. You probably don't want to block outgoing packets of the same sort, because they serve a useful purpose. You can allow users inside your network to ping other servers on the Internet. For example, suppose you want to place an order with a business that has a Web site, yet it doesn't pop up in your browser when you try to get to its home page. You can use Ping to determine whether the business's computer is on the Net and functioning, and then from there start your troubleshooting efforts to find out why you can't bring up its Web page. If you ping the site and get no response, you can be sure that either it's down, or somewhere along the network path, a router or other device is not letting traffic get through.

The same goes for you if you offer a service on the Internet. However, in such a case, you should make sure that your Web servers are highly secured and located on a network segment that can limit the damage should these servers be compromised. This network segment is called a demilitarized zone (DMZ), and you'll learn more about that later in this chapter.

Another utility that uses ICMP is Tracert. This command probes the network path and returns a list of all the routers and other intermediary devices it passes through to get to a destination address. Again, this is a useful tool when used properly, but you should block this sort of packet at your firewall. Do you want outsiders to know the addresses of routers and other devices on your network? After an outsider has the address and knows that a computer is online using that address, it's easy to use one of the many hacker tools available on the Internet to begin breaking into the computer. You can learn more about using the tracert command in Chapter 22, "Troubleshooting Tools for TCP/IP Networks."

Filtering Based on Port Numbers

The TCP and UDP protocols use port numbers in their header information to identify applications. In Appendix B, "TCP and UDP Common Ports" you can find a list of the most commonly used port numbers and the applications associated with them. Although filtering based on IP addresses blocks all network traffic from a particular source, you can use filtering rules that block only specific ports. Thus, you might allow customers to interact with Web servers inside your network using the ports set aside for WWW activity—port 80, for typical WWW traffic—but block other ports, such as port 23 that is used for Telnet functions.

As another example, you might want to allow some users to use Telnet (port 23) or FTP (ports 20 and 21) to connect to servers *outside* the corporate network while denying this ability to others. You can do this by setting up rules in the packet filter and specifying both a host source address and a port number.

Packet filtering is an integral component of most every firewall and has several advantages:

- **Usually inexpensive**—If you use a router to connect to external sources, you already have the hardware—you just need to configure it.

- **Fast**—It does only minimal processing on the header information and does not make decisions based on multiple packets.

- **Flexible**—It is easy, although some would say cumbersome, to configure as many addresses inclusions or exclusions as you like.

However, there are also several disadvantages to using a packet filter firewall:

- **Packet filters perform no authentication functions**—A packet is a packet no matter "who" the sender is. The address is the only thing that counts. And, IP addresses, ports, and any other part of the packet, can be forged.

- **Most system administrators don't take advantage of a router's auditing features**—You will most likely not even know that attempts were made to break in to the network; if the router does provide some kind of statistical information, you won't be able to determine from where the attack came. If you turn on logging for every packet that comes through your router, you'll experience a tremendous slowdown in network response time through the router. Selectively logging events is a better option, but then again you might miss important events.

- **Packet filters operate at the network level**—They are not very effective at stopping sophisticated attacks that are directed at higher-level protocols, such as TCP.

- **Internal network information is not kept from outside prying eyes**—Using ordinary utilities, such as Tracert and Ping, mischievous persons can gain knowledge about your network unless you specifically block this protocol (ICMP).

If you had the choice, which of the following would you choose?

- Allow everything, but deny specific addresses.

- Deny everything, but allow selected known good addresses.

If it's not obvious that the second choice is the best, you need to stop and think about this again.

A good approach for configuring the rules to use on a packet filter is to first *deny all traffic*. Then, selectively enable only those addresses or services that are essential to your business. If you try to do this in reverse—allowing all traffic and then denying specific items—there's no way you can create a set of rules that covers all possible sources of mischief. You might leave out something that didn't seem important at the time you did the configuration, or a new twist on an old technology might creep up and surprise you later on.

Intrusion Detection (Stateful Inspection)

A stateful inspection device operates in a manner similar to a packet-filtering firewall in that it also examines the source and destination addresses of every packet that passes its way. However, a packet filter is never aware of the context of any communication. Each packet that passes through it is treated on an individual basis. A firewall that employs stateful inspection techniques attempts to keep track of requests and responses to be sure they match.

This type of firewall maintains tables of information about current connections so that it can determine whether incoming packets are unsolicited or whether they are in response to a request that was made by a user on the internal network. Another name sometimes used for this type of firewall is *dynamic packet filter*.

When a connection terminates, the firewall removes the reference from its internal table so that an external source cannot use it to gain entry again.

Many proprietary stateful inspection firewall products are on the market today. Study the documentation of this type of product before you make a purchase, so you can fully understand how it operates.

Proxy Servers

Proxy servers, also knownas application gateways, provide protection for your network at the application layer. Although packet filters make decisions based on the header information in a packet, they do not understand the application protocols, such as FTP or HTTP. Thus, it's easy for a hacker to exploit known problems with application protocols, and problems can ensue if the packet filter allows the packet to enter the network.

A proxy server can perform this function by managing connections to and from the outside world. A proxy server acts as a "man in the middle" by accepting requests for an application for your users and making that request for them. A proxy server never allows a packet to pass through the firewall; instead, a proxy server follows these steps:

1. Receives an outgoing request from one of your users. It creates a new packet and substitutes the proxy server's own address as the source address, replacing the user's actual source address.

2. The proxy server sends this new packet out onto the Internet on behalf of the user.

3. When a response is received from the Internet server, the proxy server examines the packet to determine whether the data contained in the packet is appropriate for the particular application. If so, it creates a new packet, inserts the data, and places the Internet server's address in the source address field. The packet then is sent back to the original user.

4. The user receives the packet, and assumes that it's actually communicating directly with the Internet server—after all, it has the correct addressing information in the header.

Figure 40.1 shows an example of how a typical proxy server functions.

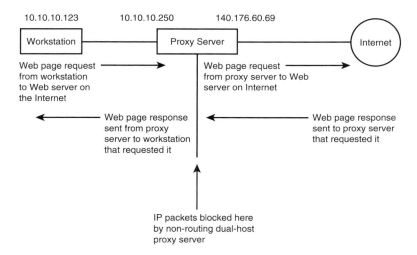

Figure 40.1 A proxy server communicates with the computer inside your network and the Internet server, but does not allow network traffic to pass directly through the firewall.

Proxy servers also can be used to provide authentication and other security measures. There are two kinds of proxy servers: classical proxy servers and transparent proxy servers.

A *classical proxy server* can be used with any application. The user needs to take a few extra steps to use the proxy server because the application itself was not written to understand the proxy process. A classical proxy server works in the following manner:

1. A client executes a command, such as the Telnet command, to connect to the proxy server.

2. The proxy server receives this request and sends a packet back to the user prompting for authentication information, such as a username and password.

3. The user interacts with this man-in-the-middle by entering the required information.

4. If the proxy server has been configured to allow this user to make use of the service, it prompts the user to enter the target system for the service. For example, after being authenticated by the proxy server, a user could enter username@internetserver.com. In this example, username is the username that will be used to authenticate the user on the Internet server and internetserver.com is the name of the Internet server to which the user wants to make a connection.

5. The proxy server proceeds to create a packet containing the Telnet request, and sends it out onto the Internet. The Internet server sends back a packet requesting a password (if required) for the service.

6. The proxy server prompts the user to enter the password, and passes it back to the Internet server. If the authentication succeeds, the proxy server begins operating as described earlier, by intercepting packets to and from the Internet server, substituting its own address for the user's address when sending packets to the Internet server and substituting the Internet server's address for packets returned to the client.

After the initial authentication and connection to the service, each side of the communication process thinks it's actually talking to the other. However, because the user must initially authenticate himself to the proxy server, this type of proxy might be undesirable in some environments because some users find these extra steps a burden.

Note

A popular proxy server product called the TIS Internet Firewall Toolkit (FWTK) can be downloaded from the Internet. This kit contains proxy applications for most of the usual Internet services, such as Telnet, e-mail, and FTP, and allows you to create your own specific proxy server applications. You can read more about this package and download it free from `www.fwtk.org`.

A *transparent proxy server* works a little differently. In this case, the application is modified so that it understands a proxy server is being used. For this to work, you must tell the application the address of the proxy server for each service you want to use. For example, to configure proxy server information in Internet Explorer 5.0:

1. Click Start, Programs, Internet Explorer.

2. Click Tools and then select Internet Options. When the Internet Options properties page appears, click the Connections tab shown in Figure 40.2.

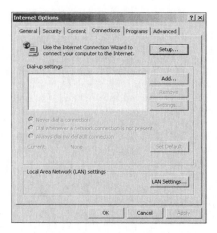

Figure 40.2   Select LAN Settings from the Internet Options properties page to configure a proxy server for Internet Explorer.

3. At the bottom of the page, click the LAN Settings button to open the Local Area Network (LAN) Settings dialog box (see Figure 40.3).

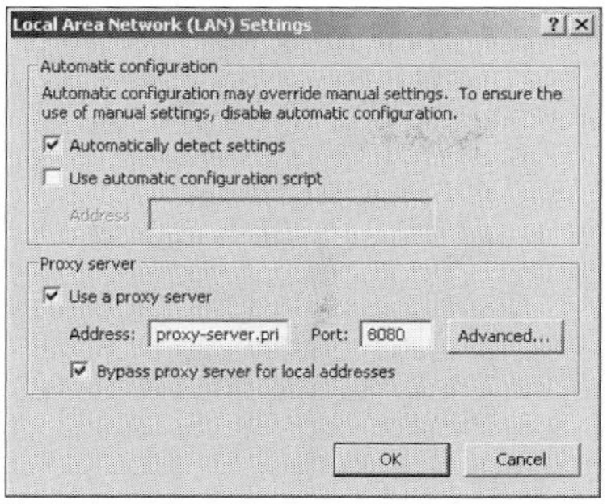

Figure 40.3 The Local Area Network (LAN) Settings dialog box allows you to select automatic configuration of a proxy server or you can enter the information yourself.

4. In Figure 40.3, the Automatically Detect Settings check box has been selected. If your network is configured to distribute this information automatically, all you need to do is select this check box and click the OK button. Internet Explorer queries the network to determine the proxy server settings and sets them up for you automatically. The Use Automatic Configuration Script check box can be used in a similar manner, but you'll have to get the address for the server that contains the file from your network administrator.

5. To manually configure a proxy server, select the Use a Proxy Server check box, and enter the address or hostname of the proxy server and the port that will be used (typically port 8080). This sets up Internet Explorer to use the same proxy server for all the network services you use.

6. If you want to configure each service separately, click the Advanced button shown previously in Figure 40.3, and the Proxy Settings dialog box appears (see Figure 40.4).

Figure 40.4 Use the Proxy Settings dialog box when you need to use more than one proxy server for different network services.

7. In Figure 40.4, you can see that Internet Explorer allows you to enter a different proxy server and port for the services that the browser can be used for. You can use the Exceptions pane to enter hostnames or addresses that should not go through the proxy server. For example, hosts that reside inside your network can be contacted directly, and you don't need to use a proxy server to reach them. If you use this feature, you can enter more than one name or address, separating each entry by a semicolon, and you can use the asterisk ("*") character as a wildcard. When finished, click OK.

Standard Proxy Applications

Most off-the-shelf firewall products come with proxy applications for commonly used network applications, such as

- Telnet
- FTP
- X Window
- HTTP
- Mail (POP and SMTP)
- News (NNTP)

Because proxy servers operate at the application level, they are sometimes referred to as *application gateways*. You can set up the gateway using several different topologies. An example of an application gateway is a dual-homed host that runs the proxy software. In this setup, a computer has two network cards, each attached to a different network. Proxy software runs on the host and mediates between the two, deciding what traffic it will allow to flow between the two networks. You can set up a Unix or Windows NT Server computer to perform this kind of function. In Figure 40.5, you see a small network that uses a router to connect to the Internet.

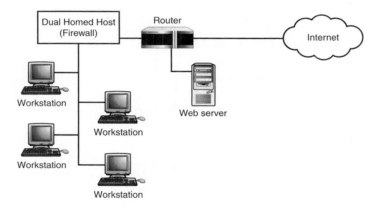

Figure 40.5   A dual-homed host is used to connect the local network to the Internet.

However, the network is not directly connected to the router. Instead, a computer has been designated for this purpose. The dual-homed host has two network cards—one talks to the router and the other participates in the local network. The router can be configured to perform filtering functions while the dual-homed host can supply the proxy functions for any services you want to allow between your network and the Internet. When this host is configured with maximum security measures to provide a defense from external sources, it is sometimes referred to as a *bastion host* or a *screened host architecture*.

As an added advantage, another computer is used to host the company's Web pages so that Internet users can access them without penetrating the interior company network.

You can carry this concept further by using multiple routers to connect to the Internet. Figure 40.6 shows a setup similar to the one just described, but there are two routers between the innermost network clients and the Internet.

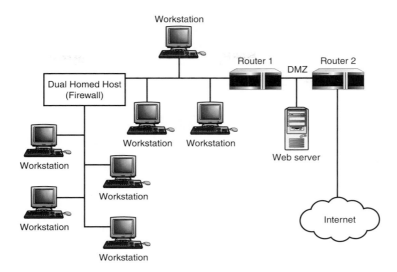

Figure 40.6 Use multiple firewalls to segment users into restrictive and less restrictive networks.

The dual-homed host connects the most secure clients to the first router. Between the dual-homed host and the first router are other computers that do not need the same level of restrictions imposed by the proxy server. Once again, the Web server sits on the network at a point closest to the Internet, and thus is subject to fewer restrictions than the other computers on this network. The Web server that sits between Router 1 and Router 2 should be treated very cautiously when it comes to security because it's the least-protected computer on the network. As stated earlier in the chapter, the space between these two routers is referred to as the demilitarized zone or DMZ. Another method of creating a DMZ is to use a router with multiple interfaces, and select one interface to use for a network segment that will be the DMZ (see Figure 40.7).

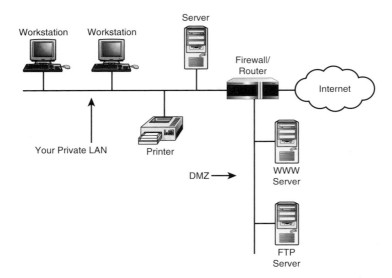

Figure 40.7 A simple DMZ can be created by using a separate LAN segment connected to the router.

In this example, the firewall/router has three adapters: one for the DMZ, one for your private LAN, and one to connect to the Internet. Traffic from the Internet destined to your FTP or WWW servers is never passed by the firewall to the private LAN segment, but only to those servers residing in the DMZ. Thus, if one of your Web servers is compromised, the computers on your LAN are still safe.

Impersonating the End User: Network Address Translation (NAT)

One of the main driving forces behind a new Internet protocol (IPv6) was the assumption that the 32-bit address used by IPv4 was not large enough to keep up with the quickly growing Internet. It was assumed that eventually the entire address space would be used up. Of course, other features of IPv6, such as the security enhancements, also are making it seem like the Internet eventually will migrate to the newer protocol. However, when you think about how a proxy server works to use its own address instead of the address of the internal network client, it seems that the address space limitations imposed by the 32-bit address is not such a big issue anymore.

Because only addresses used by the proxy servers need to be valid and registered on the Internet, what prevents you from using any address range on the internal network? This concept, known as network address translation (NAT) is widely used today for just this purpose. The proxy server uses these addresses with valid IP addresses to conduct business for its clients.

You can use practically any address range for the workstations on the LAN. However, RFC 1597, "Address Allocation for Private Internets," specifies a range of addresses that are set aside for private networks. When computers on the inside network need to communicate with each other, they use their actual addresses. The proxy server also has an address that falls within this range so that it can talk to both the private LAN and the Internet.

These ranges of IP addresses are exclusively set aside by the RFC for private networks, and cannot be used on the Internet. The address ranges are

- 10.0.0.0–10.255.255.255
- 172.16.0.0–172.31.255.255
- 192.168.0.0–192.168.255.255

You can accomplish several things by using these addresses for computers inside your network:

- Your business only needs to buy a small address range from your ISP to use on the firewall or routers that connect your network to the Internet.
- You can now use a huge address space inside your network without having to apply for a large range of addresses from your ISP.
- You can use NAT for address vectoring; that is, you can let the router represent your Web service on the Internet using a single address, yet load balance the incoming requests across several servers inside the network.

Advantages and Disadvantages of a Proxy Server

As with every type of firewall, you can say good and bad things about proxy servers. Their capability to hide the identity of workstations on your network is a definite plus. Packet filters don't do that. Proxy servers are usually highly customizable, and most come with a graphical interface to make the management chores a little more understandable than those that use a command-line set of cryptic instructions.

One thing that packet filters usually excel at when compared to proxy servers, is speed. Filtering a packet is not much more complicated than any other task a router does. It already must look at the information contained in the header so that it can make routing decisions. Checking a table of addresses to determine which ones are allowed and which are not isn't much different than checking the routing table to decide where to forward a packet.

Note

Some advanced firewalls that provide proxy functions can be configured to support authentication and time-of-day controls. If you have a secure environment in which you need to control who gains access and limit the time of access, look for these features in the documentation before you acquire a firewall.

Proxy servers applications are implemented in software and are limited by the platform on which they run. In many stress tests done in recent years (you can check the magazines yourself), proxy servers perform just fine on a 10Mbps network, such as 10BASE-T. However, when you connect them to a high-speed network, such as 100BASE-T or T1 lines, their performance degrades rapidly. That isn't to say that all proxy servers can't keep up with these speeds. It's just that to find one that does, you have to incur a much larger expense for both the hardware and software components. Or, you can use multiple connections to the Internet and use several firewalls to provide for a larger network.

Hybrids

No one type of firewall that has been discussed can meet the needs of every situation. As mentioned earlier in this chapter, it is often a good idea to have several levels of defense against attack from outside your network. It is easy to segment your network so that it does not appear as one entity to the Internet. You can create several subnetworks, isolate them within your network using internal firewalls, and then enclose the collection of subnetworks with firewall protection from outside intruders.

You also can use more than one firewall between your network and the outside world. In the previous dual-homed host example, this was done because the host served as a proxy firewall that was connected to a router that performed packet filtering.

Most of the quality firewall products on the market today are *not* distinctly packet filters, proxy servers, or stateful inspection machines. Most are hybrids that incorporate the functions of all these firewall technologies, although by different degrees depending on the implementation. As long as you understand the concepts of the functions a firewall performs, you are in a better position to make an informed choice of what will work best for your environment.

Because the firewall has become such an important component of the network, you will find many products that perform other functions related to security that are not easily classified. For example, some firewalls can be used to screen the content of e-mail or other data that passes through the firewall. You can contract with a service provider to obtain a list of known "offensive" or otherwise undesirable sites on a periodic basis and have your firewall block access to these sites. Some firewall products come with built-in virus screening.

Look for the following things when evaluating firewall products:

- Security (of course)
- Performance
- Support
- Price
- Manageability

Caution

A firewall protects you only at the point at which your network connects to an outside network. One of the most common mistakes administrators make is assuming that the network is secure and overlooking the modems that sit on many desktops throughout the enterprise. Even if a modem is used only for dial-out purposes, you still run risks of virus infections and other security problems when users dial out to other sites and download programs or data to their workstations, which are connected to the network. Worse yet, modems used for dial-in purposes, such as remote access for users, present an easy entry point for those who would do harm.

The most important aspect of the firewall is the security it affords your network. Question the vendor about the specific methods used in the product, and whether the product has been evaluated by outside sources.

If you use the Internet connection only for the exchange of moderate amounts of e-mail and an occasional Web-browsing session, performance might not be a significant factor in your choice. However, if you expect heavy demand on the Internet connection, from within or without, check to be sure that the product you acquire can handle the load. Packet filter firewalls provide a higher degree of performance; the trade-off is that they do not protect you as well as a proxy server might if it's configured properly. Because a proxy server is responsible for closer examination of each packet and can be configured to perform other tasks, it is inherently slower than a packet filter.

Support is a critical item to consider. When purchasing an expensive firewall, many vendors include on-site assistance in configuring and setting up the firewall. Additional support, including consulting and hotline help desk services, is important because the Internet is in a state of rapid growth, and what works today might not be sufficient tomorrow. Unless you have a highly skilled technical staff capable of making decisions about firewall techniques and implementing them, support from the vendor should be a major consideration.

Again, because a firewall is not something you simply configure and forget, the management interface is important. You should look for a product that provides easy access to configuration options so that you can review and modify them as needed. Reporting capabilities should be easy to understand so that you can review data and statistics audited by the firewall. Another important aspect of the management interface is the capability to notify you when something appears to be targeting your network with not-so-good intentions. Alarms that appear onscreen are fine, if you have a round-the-clock operations staff that will be monitoring the screen. The best products will e-mail or page you when specific events occur that you have set a trigger for beforehand.

Finally, in many cases, remote management can be a plus, if it's implemented correctly. Any remote management capability should include a secure authentication technique. The firewall isn't much good if you use a clear-text password when logging in to it remotely. You should proceed under the pretense that someone is always watching what you do on the network.

Price should not be the most relevant factor in your decision. You can download some firewall products from the Internet for free. Some firewalls sell for a few hundred dollars, and some range up into the tens of thousands of dollars. The more expensive the firewall is, however, does not indicate its safety or capabilities. In fact, some of the free firewalls you can get from the Internet are actually quite good. One of the things that the Linux platform excels at is implementing firewall technology. Its robust speed and low overhead make it a good choice for this type of chore. However, no matter what product you choose, be sure you have the skills and know-how to properly configure and operate it.

What to Expect from a Firewall

A common mistake that is often made is to assume that a firewall will do more than it can because of its name. In the building trade, a firewall that is used to protect individual units in an apartment complex or condominium is designed according to rules laid down by the local authorities. In the networking trade, no authorities specify what a product must do to carry the "firewall" label.

In fact, several kinds of applications and devices can be classified as firewalls. Do you need a packet filter? Do you need a device that can perform stateful inspection? Before you answer these questions, first decide what you are trying to protect and what methods you are currently using.

What Do You Want to Protect?

For example, if you have highly confidential information, such as patient records or financial information about customers, you should definitely get some good legal advice on your responsibility about keeping this information from the general public. Keeping important information on a dedicated server that cannot be accessed by ordinary users on your network is the first thing to do. However, assuming an off-the-shelf firewall application will protect you from outside penetration is being a bit simplistic.

Determine your vulnerabilities and examine your current network. Look at how sensitive data is protected now and look at the means used to access it. Then factor in how your current safeguards will enable you to keep the data secure.

Some information usually is available to everyone in the network. For example, an employee home page that contains information about processes and procedures, such as how to request a vacation or get a purchase order approved, usually will not be considered a high-priority security item. Other information, such as information you keep about your customers, is not only important to your bottom line if you want to keep the customer happy, but also might be confidential, such as a doctor's records about patients. This kind of information should receive your utmost attention when trying to decide how it can be accessed after you connect to the Internet. It might be generally available to a large number of employees, depending on your business, or it might be sequestered by OS protections so that only a single department can use this kind of data.

Of course, if you perform your payroll in house, you are probably already aware of how sensitive this kind of information is. It must be protected from prying eyes both inside your network and outside your network.

Levels of Security

Because different kinds of information are on networks today that need various levels of security, you should carefully structure your network to handle the way information is accessed.

One connection to the Internet, through a firewall, can protect you. However, with one connection and one firewall, you must make sure that the firewall is the most restrictive you need to protect the most sensitive data that you have. One firewall to protect the entire network is one point of failure. One mistake, and the whole network is vulnerable.

Another drawback is that many users resent extremely restrictive access mechanisms and, if allowed, circumvent them.

One method is to segment the internal network and use firewalls not only to keep intruders outside the company from getting access, but also to keep out those internally who might do mischief. Also, by creating different levels of security, you can act to prevent a single security breach that causes extensive damage.

Instead of using a single network, consider creating several smaller networks and using firewall technology to connect them. For example, in-house data that never needs to be accessed from external sources can reside on one network, whereas another network can host machines that provide WWW, FTP, and other services to your external clients. The firewall that connects this network to the Internet would not have to be as restrictive as the one that joins the two networks at your site.

If you have data that is so confidential that its compromise could do severe harm, you should place it on a computer that does not have a connection to the Internet. Remember, there is no way to guarantee that a computer cannot be hacked via a network, short of pulling the plug.

Tip

Remember, firewalls can operate in both directions. Although the first thing that probably jumps into your head when you think about a firewall is that it will keep out unwanted packets, the reverse also can be true. For example, you might want to connect your network to the Internet to allow e-mail or FTP access to and from customers and your employees. You might not want your employees to access Web pages, however, and you can block their outgoing requests to prevent this type of access.

How Do You Know the Firewall Is Secure?

The problem with security is that the environment, either internal or external, is always changing. As soon as a bug in an OS or network application is found and exploited by mischievous persons, someone comes out with a fix. As soon as the fix is applied, something else crops up. When you set up a firewall to protect yourself from those who might do harm to your network, you must perform tests to be sure that it does what you think it does.

The problem with testing, however, is that you already know what you are looking for when you create and execute the test. It's what you don't know that can cause problems. To keep on top of things, you should continue to monitor the data collected by any auditing or logging functions the firewall provides to make sure it is working as you expect. Look for attempts to breach the firewall and watch for unusual activity. You might find that you can stop an attack before it succeeds. Using other tools, such as Tracert, you might be able to locate the perpetrator and handle the matter using legal means.

No RFCs define what a firewall *must* do or how it should do it. You can contact several organizations on the Internet to get information about current firewall and security software. Appendix E, "Network Information Resources," contains a list of some interesting sites related to network security and firewalls that might help you decide what kind of protection you need.

Virtual Private Networks (VPNs) and Tunneling

Security is a big issue both in the corporate network and on the Internet at large. As has been discussed in previous chapters, the basic TCP/IP protocols weren't particularly designed with security in mind. However, over the years many new developments have built on the current TCP/IP base that provide for more secure connections over wide area networks (WANs), such as the Internet. This chapter looks at Virtual Private Networks (VPNs) and the methods they employ to create a private tunnel through a WAN so that you can communicate securely with another computer or network.

What Is a VPN?

Basically, a VPN is nothing more than a secure path through a shared network or WAN that connects two computers, or two networks, so that from the point of view of each endpoint of the connection, they are on the same network. The connection is private because some means have been taken to secure the payload information of the data carried through this virtual tunnel.

A VPN can be a good solution for security issues in many different scenarios:

- Employees who work from home and use the Internet to communicate with the company network
- Mobile employees who travel and can dial in to the Internet using a national ISP
- Branch offices using the Internet
- Business partners, customers, or even technical support staff who need access

As this list demonstrates, two kinds of VPNs are used:

- **Remote access VPN**—A connection between a remote computer dialing into the Internet or a modem connected to a network.
- **Site-to-site VPN**—A connection between two networks, which usually is done between two routers, or in some cases, firewall/router combinations.

The Mobile Workforce

Many people are on the move in the business world today, and many companies are allowing some employees to work from home. A technique still used today, but which is declining, is to set up a bank of modems and give dial-in access to certain people, such as salesmen, who are always on the move. For a business that needs data connections to branch offices, but can't justify the cost of leased lines, modem banks provide the necessary remote connection. You can host a bank of modems under many different operating systems, from Unix (with its efficient kernel and support for large numbers of serial devices) to Windows 2000 (and the Remote Access Service [RAS]). You even can install servers that are basically appliances that act as a front end to provide a bank of modems for dial-in services.

However, maintaining a bank of modems can be expensive because each modem needs a telephone line, which is an ongoing cost. When you consider the potential for intrusions and other security matters, sometimes using just a simple dial-in modem is not the best solution. With Internet access in all large and most small cities in the United States, Europe, and in many other countries, the Internet can be a good solution to this problem. You can use a single, high-bandwidth connection (buy what you need), to allow multiple home workers, traveling salesmen, and other mobile workers to connect to your network just as if they were sitting at a desk at the home office.

The only problem with this access method is the fact that the Internet is not exactly the most secure place in the world! As a matter of fact, just connecting your company's network to the Internet is a serious task that should be accompanied by careful consideration of how you will control that connection (such as using a good firewall strategy), and how you will segment portions of your network to make sure that intrusions or other security breaches can be minimized.

Note

This chapter uses the Internet as the example of a WAN because it's the most common method used today for connecting to remote sites inexpensively. However, VPN technology can be used across any shared or corporate network. You still can have a bank of modems and let users dial up your local RAS and create a connection through your network.

In a typical LAN (local area network) setting, computers, servers, and other resources are connected using hubs or switches. Routers are used to connect LANs so that a logical addressing scheme can be used. The problem with security is that when using the IP protocol, for example, the payload section of the IP packet carries some higher-level protocol message without any way of encrypting the data. If you can intercept the IP packet, you can easily determine which protocol is being used and get to the information very quickly.

As you can guess, VPNs are made up of two basic components: a tunnel, which is a virtual path through a WAN, and some form of encryption to render the contents of the payload (and possibly the header information of the upper-level protocol) unusable if intercepted.

Protocols, Protocols, Protocols!

Because the functions provided by a VPN include tunneling, data integrity, and authentication, it makes sense that a VPN is not created using a single protocol. Instead, several protocols can be used to create a VPN, each performing a particular function. In this section the following protocols are briefly examined:

- Point-to-Point Tunneling Protocol (PPTP)
- Layer Two Tunneling Protocol (L2TP)
- Internet Protocol Security (IPSec)

For the most part, only IPSec should be a major factor in VPNs in the coming years. PPTP was used by Windows NT 4.0 as part of its VPN package, and L2TP has replaced it in Windows 2000 VPNs. However, most VPN vendors are using the IPSec protocols instead, which are described in greater detail in this chapter than PPTP and L2TP. The IPSec protocols incorporate some of the security mechanisms that were originally designed to be included in IPv6, but have been adapted for use in the existing IPv4 network.

The IPSec Protocols

As noted previously, IPSec is the emerging standard that is being adopted by more and more VPN vendors. IPSec was derived from concepts that were originally designed to provide for secure communications in the next generation of the IP protocol, IPv6. However, it might be many years before IPv6 sees widespread adoption because the main driving force behind IPv6 originally was the expected depletion of the IPv4 address space. With techniques such as Network Address Translation (NAT)—discussed in Chapter 40, "Firewalls"—this is not such a pressing problem anymore.

Note

No one's really sure when you'll see IPv6. In recent years, it was assumed that NAT, and the enhancement of IPv4 by the addition of protocols such as IPSec, would delay the adoption of IPv6 for some time to come. In the last year or so, the proliferation of mobile devices (such as PDAs and cellular telephones that are equipped to become Internet devices), along with other emerging wireless technologies has many wondering if the IPv4 address space, along with NAT, will be able to cope. With appliance manufacturers considering making refrigerators, ovens, and other such things capable of Internet connections, IPv6 might become a hot topic once again.

Although Microsoft chooses to use L2TP and IPSec in combination as its VPN solution for Windows 2000, many hardware and software vendors are sticking with a simple IPSec solution. The good news is that if you decide on an all-IPSec solution, you can be virtually assured that equipment (or software) from one vendor to another will work together. If you have an all-Windows 2000 environment, this might be of no concern. For those who operate multiprotocol networks, IPSec might be the best choice.

IPSec is a standard defined in several Request for Comments (RFC) documents. IPSec is transparent to the end user and can traverse the Internet using standard IPv4 routers and other equipment without requiring any modification because it operates at the network layer. IPSec is also flexible, allowing for the negotiation and use of many different encryption and authentication techniques.

The three main components of IPSec are

- **Internet Key Exchange (IKE)**—This is the protocol defined in RFC 2048, "Internet Security Association and Key Management Protocol (ISAKMP)," which defines a method for the secure exchange of the initial encryption keys between the two endpoints of the VPN link.

- **Authentication Header (AH)**—This protocol, defined in RFC 1826, "The Authentication Header," provides for inserting a standard IPv4 header into an additional header that can be used to ensure the integrity of the header information and payload as the packet makes its way through the Internet. AH does not encrypt the actual IP payload data, but instead provides a mechanism to determine whether either have been tampered with.

- **Encapsulating Security Payload (ESP)**—This protocol performs the actual encryption of the data carried in the IP packet so that it cannot be understood by anyone who might intercept your data stream.

Internet Key Exchange (IKE)

IKE defines the mechanism used by the endpoints of the VPN to establish a secure connection and exchange encryption keys and other information pertinent to a secure connection. IKE uses public-key techniques that were discussed in the previous chapter. If you recall, the public key half of a key pair can be known by anyone, as long as the private key half of the key pair remains a secret. Thus, each end of the connection can use the other end's public key to encrypt data, which can then only be read by the other end of the connection that holds the private key that can unlock the data.

IKE provides for the establishment of a *security association* (SA), which is the set of data that governs the particular connection. SAs are unidirectional; that is, each side negotiates an SA with the opposite end of the link. Think of it as a contact between the endpoints. The items that are negotiated by IKE for an SA include

- The encryption algorithm to be used on the link, such as DES, triple-DES, and so on

- The hash algorithm—Message Digest 5 (MD5) or Secure Hash Algorithm (SHA)—used to ensure the integrity of data transferred

- An authentication method—the method that will be used for authentication.

- A Diffie-Hellman group—Diffie-Hellman takes its names from the inventors of public-key cryptography. A Diffie-Hellman group is basically a specification where each group defines the length of the base prime numbers that are used for the key exchange. Group 1 is considered to be easier to break than Group 2, and so on. Both sides of the exchange must use the same Diffie-Hellman group, of course.

Diffie-Hellman refers to the inventors of public-key cryptography, which uses a public and private key to form a pair of keys. The public key is used to encrypt data, whereas the private (secret) key of the pair is used by the receiver to decrypt the data. Anyone can discover the public key because it can only be used to encrypt data, and not perform the reverse process.

Using this process, a master secret key is exchanged so that further encryption can use symmetric encryption, which is much faster than public-key encryption, to protect data on the link.

After both sides have authenticated themselves to the other side, negotiations take place to determine whether AH or ESP will be used, what hashing algorithm will be used, and the encryption algorithm (if ESP is used).

The actual mechanics of this exchange are a little more complicated. The Oakley protocol is used by IKE to define such things as the prime number groups that are used for the public-key generation, and to decide whether certificate-based authentication will be used. A security parameter index (SPI) value is used, along with an IP address and the security protocol, to identify uniquely a specific SA. Using IKE, the value for the SPI is a pseudo-randomly generated number.

The Authentication Header (AH)

IPSec consists of the two basic AH and ESP protocols that are used after IKE has established an SA. AH provides a mechanism to ensure the integrity of the IP header and the payload of the IP packet that will be transported across an untrusted link, such as the Internet. When used by itself, AH cannot provide a total guarantee of the entire IP header because some of the fields in the IP header are changed by routers as the packet passes through the network. For more information about fields that make up an IP header, see Chapter 20, "Overview of the TCP/IP Protocol Suite."

The AH is inserted directly after the IP header in an IPv4 packet and is composed of several important fields:

- **Next Header**—This 8-bit field is used to identify the protocol that follows the header. If only AH is being used without ESP, typically this field contains the protocol number for TCP because TCP is the standard packet type used to carry most Internet traffic.

- **Length**—This 8-bit field is used to specify the total length of the AH, and represents the number of 32-bit words that make up the AH.

- **Reserved**—This field is not used at this time, but should instead be zero-filled according to the standard.

- **Security Parameters Index (SPI)**—This 32-bit field contains a number used to identify the SA. A value of 0 indicates that no SA exists, whereas the numbers 1–255 are reserved by the IANA (Internet Assigned Number Authority).

- **Sequence Number**—This 32-bit field is used as a counter to keep track of packets that belong to a particular SPI. The counter is incremented once for each packet sent. This is useful for preventing a man-in-the-middle sort of attack.

- **Authentication Data**—This is a variable-length field that contains data used for authentication purposes, such as a digital certificate. If this field does not end on a 32-bit boundary, it's padded to adjust its length.

As mentioned earlier, the AH is used to provide an integrity check to determine whether the actual header or payload has been tampered with during transit. It does this by using a hashing algorithm to provide a digital signature for the packet. AH *does not encrypt the payload data*. If a packet is received and the AH indicates that the packet has been tampered with, the packet is discarded. MD5 and SHA are the two basic hashing algorithms typically used. It is beyond the scope of this book to discuss the details of these algorithms, but rest assured that they are complex formulas that take a variable amount of information and reduce it to a fixed length unit of data. The hash value can be calculated at each end of the connection to determine whether anything in the packet has changed. Thus, AH provides a method for ensuring the integrity of the packet, but not for keeping its contents secret.

For a truly secure VPN connection, ESP must be used.

Encapsulation Security Payload (ESP)

ESP is used to encrypt the payload, or the actual IP packet that is carried in the data portion of the packet. It operates in two modes: transport and tunnel.

In *transport mode*, ESP provides protection for the payload and for headers created by upper-level protocols, such as TCP, that ride inside the IP packet. In this mode, nothing is done to protect the header information of the IP packet that serves as the workhorse to get the data from here to there. This is an efficient method for encrypting the contents of the IP packet in which bandwidth constraints are important.

When operating in *tunnel mode*, ESP is used between two IPSec gateways, such as a set of routers or firewalls, and it does protect the IP header information. The entire IP datagram, including the IP header, and its payload—usually an upper-level protocol such as TCP or UDP (User Datagram Protocol)—is encrypted and encapsulated by the ESP protocol. New header information is added to the resulting packet that identifies the endpoints of the transfer (the two gateways), but the true source address, destination address, and other packet information carried inside the ESP packet is protected. At the destination gateway, this outer wrapper of information is removed, the contents of the packet is decrypted, and the original IP packet is sent out onto the network to which the gateway is attached.

When used in tunnel mode, the ESP header information is inserted directly before the IP or other protocol datagram that is to be protected. The datagram being protected is encrypted (according to methods set up by the SA), and additional headers are added in clear text format so that the new IP datagram can be transported to the appropriate gateway. In other words, the original protocol datagram is encrypted, the ESP header is added, and, finally, a new IP datagram is created to transport this conglomeration to its destination gateway point.

At the receiving gateway, this outer IP header information is stripped off, and according to the parameters defined by the SA, the protected payload of original datagram is decrypted.

When used in transport mode, the ESP header information follows the other header information of an IP datagram. Usually this is an authentication header that has been inserted to protect the integrity of the packet. The upper-level (transport layer) header information follows the ESP header information. Any information following the ESP header, including the transport layer headers, is encrypted according to the method described by the SA, and the packet is sent on its way. Note that this method does not use a gateway, so the clear text IP header at the front of the packet contains the actual destination address of the encapsulated datagram. This is the main difference between transport mode and tunnel mode. However, ESP can be used, as just mentioned, in conjunction with AH to protect the integrity of the IP header information.

At the receiving end of the communication path, this clear text header information is saved, the contents of the encrypted packet are decrypted and reassembled with the correct IP header information, and the packet is sent on its way onto the network.

ESP uses both a header and a trailer to encapsulate datagrams that it protects. The header consists of an SPI, such as the one used by AH, to identify the security association, and a sequence number to identify packets, ensure they arrive in the correct order, and ensure that no duplicate packets are received. The trailer consists of padding from 0 to 255 bytes to make sure that the datagram ends on a 32-bit boundary. This is followed by a field that specifies the length of the padding that was attached so that it can be removed by the receiver. Following this field is a Next Header field, which is used to identify the protocol that is enveloped as the payload.

Additionally, ESP can include an authentication trailer that contains data used to verify the identity of the sender and the integrity of the message. This Integrity Check Value (ICV) is calculated based on the ESP header information, as well as the payload and the ESP trailer. The layout of an ESP datagram is shown in Figure 41.1.

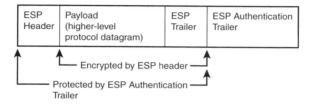

Figure 41.1   The format of an ESP datagram.

As you can see, the ICV attached to the end of the packet is not encrypted. Instead, it is a value calculated on the contents of the rest of the ESP encapsulated packet. The receiving end of the VPN can recalculate this value to determine whether the contents of the ESP header, or its payload, have been compromised during transit.

The Point-to-Point Tunneling Protocol (PPTP)

In Chapter 18, "Dial-Up Connections," PPP was discussed. PPP allows for the encapsulation of data packets from multiple protocols for simple transmission across a dedicated link, such as a phone line when you dial in to the Internet. PPP performs no routing functions, but merely encapsulates the protocol packets it receives by attaching its own header and sends them to the other endpoint of the connection.

PPTP extends the capabilities of PPP so that a tunnel can be created through a packet-switched network, such as the Internet, instead of across a serial link. The concepts are similar. PPTP encapsulates another protocol packet and the PPTP packet is then routed through the network. The endpoints that use the PPTP connection don't have to be aware that they are at opposite ends of a large packet-switched network. Instead, it is as if both computers are on the same network.

Note

PPTP is described in more detail in RFC 2637, "Point-to-Point Tunneling Protocol (PPTP)."

Another difference between PPP and PPTP is that PPTP allows for the encryption of the payload portion of the packet, so that IP (or other protocol) datagrams can be protected from prying eyes as they travel.

For example, a home user that wants to connect to a server on his company's network, first makes a dial-up connection to an Internet service provider (ISP). After the connection is set up, another set of protocol negotiations begins to set up the PPTP tunnel, over the PPP link. The endpoints for the PPP link are the home user and the ISP. The endpoints for the PPTP link are the home user's computer and the company's RAS that is attached to the Internet. At the RAS endpoint, the PPTP packets are unpackaged and the contents decrypted to reveal the original IP (or other protocol) packet, which can then be sent onto the company network. Thus, the home user can operate as if he were directly connected to the company network.

This protocol was used in Windows NT 4.0, and although it's still supported in Windows 2000, the newer L2TP is the preferred method for newer implementations for Windows clients.

Layer Two Tunneling Protocol (L2TP)

L2TP is the method of choice for Windows 2000 VPNs. The Windows 2000 operating system has the components necessary to create a VPN built into the operating system. This can be an advantage for mobile users who connect via the Internet and need to create a secure connection to the home corporate network.

L2TP is an enhancement of PPTP that uses technology from a Cisco protocol called Layer 2 Forwarding (L2F). The combination of these two protocols is documented in RFC 2662, "Layer Two Tunneling Protocol 'L2TP'." L2TP uses the UDP for sending user data packets as well as for maintenance messages used to manage the VPN connection. Because L2TP itself is only a tunneling protocol, the IPSec protocol, discussed previously in this chapter, is used for the actual encryption that protects the contents of the data traversing the tunnel.

Note

A true VPN should provide both a tunnel, which is a method for encapsulating another protocol datagram or packet, and some kind of encryption to protect the contents of the data being transferred. However, it's possible to create a tunnel that does not use any form of encryption for the data packet. In such a case, L2TP or AH, discussed earlier in this chapter, can provide an integrity check on the header information and packet contents to ensure that they are not altered during transit. This type of tunnel is not a true VPN, but does provide some sort of security in that you can be assured that the data sent from one end of the connection arrives at the other end in its original format. For security purposes, the data should be sent in encrypted format, using IPSec.

Because UDP packets are used by L2TP instead of TCP, a session does not exist. Instead, L2TP uses sequence numbers for each message to make sure packets are ordered correctly from the origination point to the destination.

L2TP Encapsulation

L2TP relies on the PPP protocol. The PPP datagram is encapsulated by L2TP by attaching an L2TP header directly in front of the PPP header. Because L2TP uses UDP, as you can probably guess, the UDP header is prefixed to the result. In Figure 41.2, you can see an overview of how the packet looks at this point.

UDP Header	L2TP Header	PPP Header	PPP Payload Data

Figure 41.2   The L2TP protocol transfers PPP datagrams using UDP as a transport protocol.

If you just want to create a tunnel, this level of encapsulation is all you need because the UDP packet will make a best effort attempt to deliver the packet by passing it to the IP protocol for transmission on the routed network.

However, because a VPN needs to provide some level of security for the payload, the IPSec protocol comes into play. The packet shown earlier in Figure 41.1 is encapsulated by IPSec by attaching the IPSec header and trailer to the packet before it is sent to the IP protocol. In Figure 41.3, you can see the format for the resulting datagram.

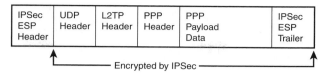

Figure 41.3 IPSec provides the encryption necessary to create a true VPN when used with L2TP.

Finally, UDP passes the resulting packet to IP for transmission on the network, just like any other IP packet. The source and destination addresses used by IP are the addresses of the VPN client and server.

Encryption Technology

42

SOME OF THE MAIN TOPICS IN THIS CHAPTER ARE

Computers and Privacy

What Is Encryption?

Digital Certificates

Pretty Good Privacy (PGP)

## CHAPTER 42

This chapter gives you a quick overview of the two basic encryption techniques in use today, and shows how they can be applied to networks to help keep programs and data secure and to prevent unauthorized persons from gaining access. These encryption techniques are known generally as *single-key* encryption and *public-key* encryption. Alternatively, they often are referred to a *symmetric* encryption (single key) and *asymmetric* encryption (public key).

Computers and Privacy

When computers were standalone systems that were easily controlled by a central administrative group, keeping data out of the hands of those who didn't need to see it was already difficult. Usernames and passwords were designed to restrict individual users and their actions, as well as track the actions they performed.

Note

In Part VI, "Network Security," you'll find extensive coverage of both creating user accounts for many different operating systems (OSs), as well as techniques for securing resources on the network. Additionally, Chapter 38, "Auditing and Other Monitoring Measures," takes this a step further by showing you how to determine, after the fact, when a security breach has occurred.

File and resource protections enforced by operating systems made it simple to keep most prying eyes out of sensitive files, but where there's a will, there's usually a way, and even operating system resource-protection techniques have their vulnerabilities.

For example, most passwords are either easy to guess or easy to obtain. If you don't enforce a strict security policy in your network, often users will use passwords that are so simple it makes a joke out of using passwords at all. Passwords such as the name of the local football team, a spouse, a child, or even a pet, are often used because they're easy to remember. Part V, "Managing Users and Resources," discusses the topic of using good passwords, with both uppercase and lowercase letters and alphabetic and numeric characters. These techniques can go a long way toward preventing a hacker from using a simple dictionary attack against your network. This kind of attack simply involves using a program that cycles through all the words in a dictionary to see whether any match up to your password. Hackers don't use just any dictionary, but instead can find huge lists of possible passwords (names, city names, baseball teams, and others which we've just mentioned) to use. Another type of dictionary attack can be performed on Unix systems if the hacker steals the password file. Because the encryption scheme is known for most Unix systems, the program can simply encrypt every word found in a dictionary and compare it to the encrypted version in the simple /etc/passwd file!

Tip

If you wonder what levels of security passwords afford your network, try calling a user. Tell him you work for the help desk and you need to know his password. Chances are more than half the time the user will give you his password. So much for password security.

When you consider the environment today, with large-scale networks and connections to the Internet, the security issues become even more complex and difficult to manage using simple schemes, such as username/password authentication. Encrypting the actual data files themselves, especially when they are to be transferred across an untrusted network link, can solve a large part of this problem.

Encryption techniques should be seriously considered in an environment in which security is considered an important part of the network and not assumed to be taken care of by the standard username/password mechanism.

What Is Encryption?

Encryption is the process of performing some function on a set of data that attempts to render it in a format that makes it unreadable or unusable by anyone but the intended recipient. A key is required to read something that has been encrypted. This might be a secret key, as is the case with single-key encryption, or it might be a key that can be known by many different people, as is the case with public-key encryption. Some cryptographic methods use the same key for encrypting and decrypting information, whereas others use a separate key for these functions.

Digital signatures and certificates is another interesting concept that has become increasingly important in networks today. You'll learn more about that later. First, take a quick look at basic encryption techniques.

Single-Key Encryption—Symmetric Encryption

As its name implies, single-key encryption uses the same key to encrypt and decrypt information. The Data Encryption Standard (DES) is a technology developed by IBM in the 1970s and adopted as a federal government standard in the United States in 1976. DES was thought for many years to be extremely secure. It is still in use in many networks and businesses today. You'll find it in a variety of forms, which typically use more than one pass at encryption to secure the data. For example, a technique called *triple-DES* uses three different keys successively to encrypt and then re-encrypt the data. A 56-bit key is used, which results in a little over 72 quad trillion possible key values. You would think with such a large number of possible keys, and using multiple passes, that the data secured by DES would truly be secure.

Note

Actually, DES is a pretty good method for encrypting data, but it's not perfect. Given enough time, it's possible to break the code. Until 1998, it was illegal to export DES cryptographic software outside the United States. It was also in 1998 that a computer was used to break the code, although it took 56 hours to do so.

That might have been true a few years ago. However, when you consider that the typical desktop PC today is a lot more powerful than the computers available back in the 1970s when DES was first developed, it's obvious that even this strong form of encryption is vulnerable to being broken, if only by a brute-force method in which every possible key value is tried. The National Institute of Standards and Technology (NIST) has decided not to recertify DES as a standard; instead, AES (Advanced Encryption Standard) is poised to take its place.

Note

For those who are interested in reading the actual standards documents, DES is specified in ANSI (the American National Standards Institute) X3.92 and X3.106 standards.

The main advantage that single-key encryption has over public-key encryption is that it's computationally fast to implement. The major disadvantage is that you need to protect the secret key.

The New Standard: AES

AES is the name given to the encryption algorithm that was selected by NIST as the new standard for encryption. NIST set the requirements necessary for this new standard and many candidates submitted algorithms hoping to qualify. The selection that was made is called Rijndael, a block cipher developed by Joan Daemen and Vincent Rijmen from Belgium. This encryption algorithm makes use of variable length blocks of data and key lengths to encrypt the data. Currently, key lengths of 128, 192, and 256 bits can be used to encrypt blocks of data, also of variable lengths, of 128, 192, or 256 bits. However, the algorithm is extensible, allowing for larger key sizes in multiples of 32 bits. How long this new AES standard will be considered "unbreakable" remains to be seen. However, the longer the key length, the more computational time it will take to break the code because each additional bit adds tremendously to the possible permutations of numbers than can be created using the key.

Note

A *block cipher* is a method of taking a block of data and rendering it into ciphertext using some encryption technique. In contrast to this, a *stream cipher* is an encryption method that encrypts individual bits of data in the data stream. Even more complex methods of block ciphers exist. For example, cipher-block chaining involves taking a block of plain text and using the logical **XOR** operation with the previous block of text that has already been encrypted into ciphertext.

If you want to learn more about Rijndael, you can visit the Web site for these cryptographers at `http://www.esat.kuleuven.ac.be/~rijmen/rijndael/`, including code examples and documentation. It's freely available for use by anyone who cares to use it.

The Problem with Single-Key Encryption

No matter how strong the encryption algorithm used with a single-key encryption method, one thorny problem remains. You still have to find a way to transfer the single known key to the recipient of the message, or establish some method for using an alternating set of seemingly random key selections. If someone trying to intercept your data can determine the single key, it's a simple matter to decrypt the data. However, because most people don't expect their communications to be intercepted and decrypted, sometimes perfection isn't necessary. It's enough to use the best available method and hope that you don't have a hacker (or the government) trying to look into your affairs.

The problem of key transfer, however, exists with AES, DES, or any single-key encryption algorithm. For a large corporation, the exchange of a secret key might involve sending a courier from one location to another to deliver the key. This can be expensive. Of course, if your company is a large financial institution, the cost is miniscule when compared to the value of the data that is encrypted using the secret key. For smaller entities, and for individual users on the Internet, exchanging secret keys in this manner is not a consideration.

To overcome this limitation, another solution was developed, called public-key encryption. Public-key encryption is subject to the same brute force attack method of trying every possible key that a single-key encryption method is, however, it makes distributing keys much simpler. The difference between single-key encryption, also called symmetric encryption, and public-key encryption is very subtle.

Public-Key Encryption

Whitfield Diffie and Martin Hellman invented public-key cryptography in 1975. Public-key cryptography uses two keys, called a *key pair*, that are mathematically related. One key is used to encrypt the data, and the other to decrypt the data. At first glance, this might seem rather innocuous. In fact, instead of protecting the encryption key and keeping it a secret, the opposite is true. The key used to encrypt the data is the public key that can be shared with many people. You can post your public key on certain places on the Internet so that it's available to anyone who wants to send you a message in encrypted format. It also is common now for users to attach a copy of their public key to e-mails they send out so that the recipient of the message can use it to encrypt a response to the e-mail. The term *key ring* is used to describe a file that you use to store a set of public keys for others with whom you communicate. Products such as Pretty Good Privacy (PGP) use key rings for just this purpose.

This form of encryption usually is referred to as asymmetric encryption, because more than one key is used. To put it simply, if you want someone to send you a message in encrypted format, you just give her (or anyone else) your public key. Anyone who wants to send you a message encrypts the message using this public key. The difference between symmetric encryption and asymmetric encryption is that the public key that encrypts the data cannot be used to perform the reverse process of decrypting the data that it was used to encode. Instead, a pair of keys is used: the public key that you can distribute freely, and a secret key, that only you know. Both keys are mathematically related so that only the secret key can be used to decrypt the message that was encrypted using your public key.

This solves the problem of having to distribute a secret key, because you don't have to. Instead, you can freely publish your public key so that anyone in the world (or on the Internet) can use it. Because this key can be used only to *encrypt* a message, and *can't* be used to unlock the message, you don't have to worry about keeping the public key a secret. Instead, you only need to keep secret the other half of this key pair, and because it is under your control, that should be much easier to do.

Yet, this brings up another question. How can you be sure that the person who has sent you a message is the person he claims to be? Because anyone can potentially gain access to your public key— remember, there are places on the Internet where you can publish your public key— how can you be sure, when you receive an encrypted message, that it comes from the person that the message claims it is from?

Enter, stage left, the *digital signature*. The person who sends you the message can use *her* own secret key to digitally sign the message. You then can use her *public key* to verify that the message most likely did originate from that person. Unless the sender's secret key has become compromised, you can be fairly sure that you've received a message from the person the message claims to be from in encrypted format that can only be decrypted by your own secret key. Throughout this entire process, it's *never* necessary to exchange either party's secret key. The public keys can be known by anyone; so long as the secret keys remain a secret, it's possible to be *reasonably* sure that you've received an encrypted message from the person you think it's from. This is illustrated in Figure 42.1.

One drawback to public-key encryption is that, due to the mathematical relationship between the key pair, the size of the keys is a lot larger than one traditionally used in secret key, or symmetric encryption. However, the flexibility that public-key encryption provides, and the uses to which it has been put (such as digital signatures) more than makes up for the larger key size. Does it really matter if it takes a few seconds longer to decrypt a message using public-key cryptography when you consider the problems associated with trying to distribute a secret key, and keep it a secret?

Because public-key encryption techniques eliminate the need to share a secret key, a public-key encryption system also could be combined with a secret-key encryption system. That is, a public key could be used to encrypt a secret key for transmission across a network, where it is recovered using the private key at the end of the communication path. From then on, the secret key itself could be used for further encrypted communications. Because secret-key encryption typically uses shorter key lengths than public keys, it's much faster to encrypt or decrypt text using a secret key. Thus, public-key encryption can be used both as a method of encrypted communication, and a method for exchanging secret keys for even faster encrypted communications. To make things even more secure, it's common to change the secret key frequently during the transmission of data, making it even more difficult for anyone who intercepts the data to discover any of the keys. As a general rule, the more data that the interceptor has to work with, the easier it is to use a computer to look for patterns and try to decrypt the data. If the secret key changes frequently (transmitted using public-key technology), the interceptor has less data encrypted with the same key to work with, and the job becomes much more difficult.

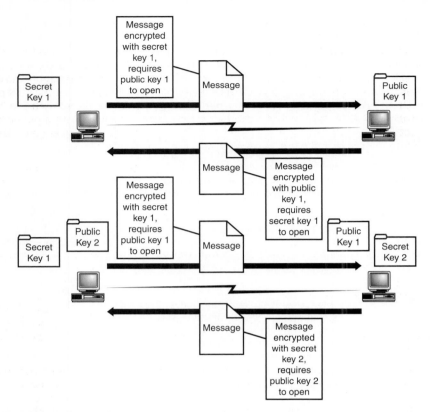

Figure 42.1 Public-key encryption provides security for messages and can use digital signatures to verify the source of the message.

RSA Public Key Cryptography

Several algorithms are used today for public-key asymmetric encryption. The most widely known is called the RSA algorithm, named after its inventors, Ronald Rivest, Adi Shamir, and Len Adleman. This method is based on multiplying two prime numbers to come up with the key pair. Further mathematical functions are performed after the multiplication to create the actual key pair, but that is beyond the scope of this book. It's a simple matter to use a computer to come up with a rather large prime number, but it's a difficult computation task to take the result of this multiplication and the subsequent operations performed and determine which two prime numbers were used to generate it.

If you want to learn more about RSA, visit the Web site for the company founded to market this technology: http://www.rsasecurity.com. The RSA Security Web site is an excellent resource for encryption techniques overall, but also has a lot of information pertaining to the RSA algorithm, which has been licensed to a large number of software and hardware security providers.

Because of the difficulty in cracking RSA-encrypted data, it has been adopted by a large number of vendors, including Sun, Microsoft, and Novell, and is the most widely used cryptosystem today.

Digital Certificates

Digital certificates are used to bind a person's name (or an identity) to a public key. Certificates, then, must come from a trusted authority. The certificate itself is determined to be valid (that is, it was issued by the certificate authority [CA] it claims to represent) by a digital signature. Because the public key of a CA can be known to anyone, it is a simple computational matter to use the CA's public key to determine that the digital signature is valid. After this is done, the certificate itself can be assumed to contain a valid identity (a user, a corporation, or other entity) associated with a public key. Using a digital certificate, you then can obtain the public key for a person and use it to encrypt data to be sent to that person, who then can use his own private key to read your message.

CAs can be trusted companies on the Internet, or you can act as your own CA in your company. Included with Windows 2000 Server, for example, is Microsoft's Certificate Services, which can be used within a company that wants to manage its own digital certificates. If you have branch offices and want to use digital certificates to certify public keys used for communicating over the Internet, you can set up your own certificate servers in your enterprise. Or, you can use a commercial company (such as VeriSign) and obtain certificates from a third party.

In practice, it also is possible for a hierarchy of certificate servers to be set up, with a single root server being the most trusted certificate server in your enterprise. Then, child certificate servers are created, which can be validated by the end user because the child certificate server itself has a certificate from the root server (or another server in the hierarchy leading back to the root server) that validates its certificate. It's all a game of trust, however. If the secret key of the root server's key pair becomes compromised, it's possible to impersonate the certificate server and all security is lost. Most certificates also are issued with an expiration date, which can be used to ensure that new certificates, created using a new key pair, are in use.

For this reason, should you choose to operate your own certificate server(s) in your network, you need to take extreme security precautions to safeguard the private key. Likewise, if you use a third-party commercial certificate service, you need to read the policy of that company to determine how it verifies the identity of the end users that it issues certificates to. For example, a CA might simply verify the e-mail address of the requestor and issue a certificate. For a software publisher, the CA might conduct some kind of background check and require further evidence before it issues certificates to the company. Before you decide to use a commercial service for issuing digital certificates, be sure you investigate the company's policies for both issuing and revoking certificates.

Note

CAs on the Internet have become numerous in the past few years. If you want to learn more about how commercial certificate issuers operate, visit the Web sites of some of the better known issuers:

http://www.verisign.com/

http://www.rsasecurity.com/

http://www.entrust.com/

Be sure to read their policies before you decide to use a commercial CA. Find out what mechanisms they use to verify the identity of the person or entity they issue certificates to. Find out what they do to support revoking certificates that have become compromised, and whether or not they issue certificates that expire after a period of time.

Pretty Good Privacy (PGP)

One of the most popular encryption programs on the Internet for a number of years now has been PGP, originally developed by Phillip Zimmerman. PGP uses public-key cryptography and has been ported to many different computer platforms, including Unix, Linux, and, of course, all versions of Windows from Windows NT and Windows 95 onward.

Network Associates (http://www.pgp.com)currently markets the commercial version of PGP. Although Network Associates charges for the commercial product, you can download a freeware version from this site that has some, but not all, of the capabilities of the full-fledged product. The freeware product is for noncommercial use only, so it's a good buy (free) for most ordinary Internet users. Also note that the only versions available for freeware download from Network Associates are for the Windows and Macintosh platforms. If you want to use PGP in your business environment, you'll need to purchase the commercial version and a license from Network Associates.

PGP has been established as an Internet Standard through the Request for Comments process. RFC 2440, "OpenPGP Message Format," was written in 1998 and details the specification.

An international site devoted to PGP also can be used to download PGP. Visit the PGPi Project International PGP home page at http://www.pgpi.org/ to learn more about PGP International. The downloads available from this site include support for the following platforms:

- Amiga
- Atari
- BeOS
- EPOC (Psion, and so on)
- MacOS
- MS-DOS
- Newton
- OS/2
- PalmOS
- Unix
- Windows 2000
- Windows Me
- Windows 95/98/NT
- Windows 3.x

As you can see, a variety of operating systems are supported by the International PGP site, which is working to establish PGP as a standard for encryption on the Internet. In addition to the standard PGP package, which provides for a number of applications, such as document encryption and e-mail, a number of other products also are available, such as PGPdisk (for encrypting disks) and PGPphone (for making secure phone calls on the Internet).

The PGPi Project also is making PGP available in a number of different languages, and also is currently translating the documentation. PGPi is a nonprofit organization dedicated to further developing and distributing PGP technology throughout the world. In addition, for some platforms, the source code also is available so that you can examine it before compiling it on your system.

# PART VI

Basics of Network Troubleshooting Techniques

PART VII

Strategies for Troubleshooting Network Problems

SOME OF THE MAIN TOPICS IN THIS CHAPTER ARE

A Documented Network Is Easier to Troubleshoot

Problem Solving Techniques

Pitfalls of Troubleshooting

Although networks can be composed of many different types of physical components, from copper wire or fiber-optic cables to wireless access points and network adapters, there are steps you can take to make troubleshooting network problems a little easier, regardless of their composition. Although each device, protocol or standard that is a part of your network may come with its own tools used for troubleshooting purposes, it's important to realize that you should take a structured approach to solving problems on the network. In other chapters you'll find discussions of specific tools used for troubleshooting. For example, the use of Ping and Traceroute for testing IP networks is covered in Chapter 22, "Troubleshooting Tools for TCP/IP Networks." In Chapter 44, "Network Testing and Analysis Tools" we'll look further at some tools that can be used to troubleshoot physical components of the network.

This chapter introduces a few concepts that make life much simpler for a network administrator, including documenting network components, and also documenting problems (and solutions that work).

A Documented Network Is Easier to Troubleshoot

One of the oldest acronyms used on the Internet hasn't got anything to do with a specific protocol or network service. It's RTFM. If you ever get this in response to posting a question on a newsgroup, then you can probably guess what the letters stand for. For those who don't know, it's something along the lines of "read the frigging manual!" and its use is intended to point out that your question is a simple one that you can easily find an answer to, so quit wasting bandwidth by your postings.

Documentation consists of the manuals that come with software applications, operating systems, switches, and other network components. The quality of this sort of vendor-supplied documentation can vary widely from one vendor to another. You'll find that many companies, such as Cisco, Microsoft, and Novell provide a lot of online documentation for their products. Often the documentation you get from a vendor is a simplified booklet combined with more extensive documentation on a CD. One of the most widely used formats for creating user documents is the Adobe Portable Document Format (.PDF files), and you can download the Adobe Acrobat Reader application for free.

Note

You can download a copy of the newest version of Adobe Acrobat Reader from `http:\\www.adobe.com`.

However, after you find yourself with an assortment of documentation—from hardcopy manuals to files on a CD or a Web site, then it's time to consider what you will use to document how your particular network is laid out, both from the physical and logical point of view. When it comes time to troubleshoot a problem on the network, then it's nice to have documentation that enables you to quickly get an answer to such simple questions as "Where are the configuration instructions for that router stored?" or "Just who is that user anyway?"

Note

Documentation made available online via the Internet can serve two purposes. First, you can quickly search and find information in a problem scenario. Second, you can read through any online documentation a vendor provides before you make a decision to purchase the particular software or hardware product. Along the same lines, you can also get an idea of the type of support you'll receive if you review the documentation before you buy. If the documentation isn't up to par, it might not matter how good the product is—support is everything.

Some of the important things you should consider as potential candidates for documenting include:

- A logical map of the network. This may or may not match up with the physical way the network is laid out.

- A physical map of the network. This documentation should describe each physical component and illustrate the ways in which the different components are connected.

- Cabling and patch panel information. When you've got hundreds of cables in a wiring closet patching together different physical segments, you'll need to know which cable connects this to that.

- Default settings for computers and other devices on the network.

- Listings of applications and the computers or users that make use of them, as well as software versions, patch levels, and so on.

- Information about the user accounts, and associated permissions and rights, for the users and user groups on the network.

- A network overview. It's nice to be able to give a new user a document that explains what they need to know about the network, so you don't have to tell them to RTFM when they ask you silly questions.

- Problem reports. Keep track of problems as they arise and document the cause and remedy. No need to solve the same problem twice! Outage reports—keeping track of unscheduled downtime for a computer or network device—can tell you over time just how capable the device is.

A logical map of the network shows the relationships between components and the flow of information through the network. A physical map of the network tries to approximate on paper a representation of how each component of the network is connected to the network. For example, a logical map for a Windows network might show computers grouped by domains, even though the computers are not located physically in the same part of the network. A physical map would show the location of each of the computers, the hub or switch to which they are connected, and so on. In general, logical maps can be used to help isolate configuration or application problems, while physical maps can be used to isolate a problem that affects only a portion of the network, perhaps a single computer or other device.

You can use simple tools, such as Microsoft Paint, to create network mapping documents, or you can buy applications that automate the process. Using an application that is written specifically for creating network maps should be considered for anything but the smallest network. The ability to locate components, update them, and to produce easy to understand printed documentation are the hallmarks of a good network diagramming application. One such tool is Microsoft's Visio, which allows you to create complex network drawings, and includes pictographic elements for most modern network devices that you can easily use.

Inside the wiring closet you can have a tangled mess of wires on a patch panel that haphazardly tie one network link to another. Or, you can have an orderly system where each port on the patch panel is labeled, using a standardized method so that making changes won't be a hit or miss effort. The same goes for configuration information for other components of the wiring closet, such as switch ports or routers. In-depth documentation is important so that you can re-create the configuration from scratch if it becomes necessary to replace a device.

Applications should be standardized, which means you shouldn't have multiple applications that all perform the same function. It's much simpler to support a standard application, such as an office suite, than it is to support multiple applications. And, although the same configuration might not be appropriate for every user, you can at least try to create several standard configurations for classes of users. This makes deploying a desktop computer for a new employee much easier. For that odd occasion when you find something nonstandard is required, document that also, and also document the reasons behind the decision to use an alternate configuration.

Keeping track of which applications are in use and how they are configured serves another purpose. Some applications interact with others, or are tied to specific versions of an operating system. If you have adequate documentation of the applications used on your network, then you can better plan for upgrades.

After you've documented the physical components of the network and the applications, what's left? Oh, yes, the users. You must not forget the users, else you would not have a job. Having a document of some sort that shows a user profile can be useful for troubleshooting purposes. If you only know a user's logon username and the name of his computer, you have little to go on when he calls in with a problem. If you can quickly locate more information about the user, such as the applications installed on his computer, the privileges and permissions assigned to the user account or the computer, then you have valuable information to use to help solve problems. Often you can't get all this information from the user over the phone because many users don't know that much about what resides on their system. They only know the applications they use and how they use them.

Lastly, keep track of problems. Record the symptoms, the tools used to troubleshoot the problem, and the resolution of the problem. This documentation can assist you in the future so you can quickly determine the solution to a problem based on the symptoms reported by the users. You can also use this to assist in creating documentation that you give to new users. By informing them of problems that have occurred in the past, you can help prevent the same problems from happening again.

Documentation and Maintenance—Keeping Things Up to Date

Documentation is an ongoing process. Networks rarely stay the same for a long period of time. It has been my experience that the larger the network, the faster the rate of change, as users or departments are relocated and new equipment replaces older equipment. So when you consider what means you'll use to create network documentation, be sure to take into consideration that it will need to be updated, and you'll need some way for keeping track of changes in an orderly fashion.

Some of the tools you can use to create network documentation include:

- **Word processors and spreadsheets**—Each one of these is beneficial. Word processors enable you to create professional-looking documents, which can be easily changed and reprinted. Spreadsheets can be used to locate information quickly and that information can be easily organized by indexing.

- **Online tools**—Use simple Web pages to create online documentation. If you have a specific application that has been customized for your network, create a Frequently Asked Questions (FAQ) document for it and put it online.

- **Hardcopy**—Printed paper documentation.

Word Processors and Spreadsheets

These two tools can be useful for creating documentation. You can use either one to gather information about the network, and organize it to locate information quickly and easily. Word processing and spreadsheet applications are easy to update and if printed documentation is also necessary, then most of these programs provide excellent formatting and printing capabilities. For example, you can use tables in Microsoft Office's Word program, or possibly a spreadsheet, to create a list of all the network devices and computers that have an IP address assigned to them. If you want to locate a particular item of data, Word enables you to search a document, and spreadsheets allow you to create multiple indices, so that important identifiers are sorted to make it easy to locate information.

For a typical LAN today it's likely that you'll have only a few important devices or servers that have static IP addressing information assigned. It's easier to use DHCP servers to allocate IP configuration information to computers automatically when they boot. To keep track of dynamically assigned IP configuration information, you can consult the DHCP server application to determine what listing or reporting features are available. For computers or devices you configure with static IP information, you can use a spreadsheet to keep track of this information. Then, when it becomes necessary to replace a router or similar device, you can consult the documentation to get the required configuration information to use on the replacement.

Note

The Dynamic Host Configuration Protocol (DHCP) is discussed in detail in Chapter 23, "BOOTP and the Dynamic Host Configuration Protocol (DHCP)." If you use the Microsoft DHCP server that comes with Windows 2000, then you can also enter into the DHCP database the static information that you manually configure some of your servers or devices to use. You can do this by entering static IP addresses and setting up reservations using the GUI for the DHCP service. In addition to being sure that the DHCP server doesn't try to use an address that you've already manually assigned to another computer, this gives you the ability to use the DHCP database for reporting and analysis. Microsoft's DHCP server, and many others, allow you to export data to files, such as comma-delimited ASCII text files, that can be imported into programs such as spreadsheets or other databases.

Many other programs and utilities have "output" capabilities so that you can send their information to a file. For example, on Windows 2000, the IPCONFIG command can be used to display information about the current IP configuration on the computer. If you use the syntax `ipconfig/all > thiscomputer.txt`, then the output from the command is sent to the file named `thiscomputer.txt` instead of to the screen. The point is that you don't necessarily have to manually create all your documentation. Instead, make use of the tools and utilities provided by the operating system and applications to get the data, and then import it into other programs that make it easier to manage.

Other important things you may want to consider keeping track of for individual computers include the particulars of the hardware that make up the system, any customizations made on the system that aren't part of a standard, and the user(s) of the system. If the computer is a server on your network, then it's a good idea to keep track of contact phone numbers for client representatives so that you can keep them informed during any troubleshooting efforts or downtime.

Online and Paper Documentation

The paperless office that was forecast during the early days of the PC revolution in the 1980s has yet to come about. No matter how small PDAs and laptops become, it's generally easier to sit down with a printed manual. Having to stare at a screen for hours at a time can be a lot more cumbersome. Although word processors and other programs are great at making it easy to find information quickly, sometimes it's just easier to print things for easier handling.

Today it is not uncommon to find paper documentation being replaced by hyperlinked text files on a Web site. Instead of looking in the index of a book and then searching to find the information you need, an online Web site can be useful for several reasons. First, for common problems, a simple Frequently Asked Questions (FAQ) document can help end users solve problems themselves so your help desk doesn't get a call. Second, for those who do sit at a help desk, clicking through a set of links to find information can be faster than having to juggle one or more manuals, and talk to the end user on the phone at the same time.

User Feedback Can Improve Documentation

You can easily judge how well your documentation assists end users by soliciting feedback. If you create the greatest looking documents that can possibly be created, it doesn't matter if the end user can't make sense of the content. After you've created any kind of documentation, be sure to provide a mechanism that can enable users to provide you with questions or comments on the documentation. Take these suggestions into consideration when it comes time to make updates.

Problem Solving Techniques

After you've got a well-documented network, then all you have to do is sit back and wait for problems to occur. Spurious as that may seem, it's true. Sometime, some day, when you least expect it, something out of the blue will knock a server offline, disable a printer, and so on. If you have good documentation, then it's time to tackle the problem and do so from a structured point of view.

The troubleshooting method known as the *problem resolution cycle* builds on accurate documentation for the network and uses a simple question/answer technique to determine what has changed to bring about the problem.

The Problem Resolution Cycle

The problem resolution cycle is a method that is designed to meet two needs: solve the immediate problem that prevents the network (or a component of the network) from working, and to provide insights as to the cause of the problem so that it can be avoided or quickly solved in the future. The elements of a structured problem resolution cycle approach are

- Accurate and complete descriptions of the symptoms. Determine if a problem really exists, or if the user is not using the computer or application in the proper manner.

- Understanding how the network functions from a logical and physical point of view.

- Solving the problem instead of creating a make-shift fix. And, some problems fix themselves.

- Providing a follow-up mechanism for recording and distributing solutions to others who may have a need to know, such as a help desk or departmental supervisor.

- Development of a solution-tracking system to keep you from having to solve the same problem over and over again.

In most cases, the more data you can collect about a problem, the easier it will be to solve. When selecting employees who will serve as help desk personnel, for example, try to get someone with both good verbal as well as listening skills. Although the initial problem report might be something like "I can't print this document" a good help desk technician can usually walk the user through a series of questions to determine if other symptoms are present. In the example just given, it would be prudent to ask if the user could print other documents, and is having the problem with just the one. Another good question would be to ask if any other users of the printer are having a problem. As you gather more data, you can focus your troubleshooting efforts on the local user PC or the printer. If the user can't print anything, but no one else is having a problem, then you can begin to troubleshoot the printer configuration (Has the user made changes you are unaware of?). Or, perhaps the user has lost network connectivity and it's a simple matter to try to ping the computer. You can use utilities such as ping or tracert to determine if connectivity exists between the user and the printer or print server. After that you could start investigating to be sure that the correct print driver is installed, and so on.

This brings up the network maps mentioned earlier in this chapter. You can quickly locate what hub, switch, or other network device the user's computer is attached to by using a physical map of the network. Using a logical map, you can find other users or computers that make use of the same information flow through the network.

Sometimes things just fix themselves. For example, it may be that the user could not print because a router standing between the user and the printer was overloaded temporarily and was not able to route packets from the user's network segment to the printer. In these situations, don't let sleeping dogs lie. Instead, keep investigating (using your network maps) and try to determine what caused the problem. You can use performance and capacity reporting techniques for servers and network devices. In the next chapter we'll talk about the Simple Network Management Protocol (SNMP) and RMON (Remote Monitoring Protocol), that enable you to gather statistical information about network devices. Find out what caused a problem so that you can anticipate when it might happen again, and try to take measures to prevent it.

Keep track of all incidents in an orderly fashion and make the information known to others that might encounter the same problem. A help desk should have a log of some sort so that every problem called into the help desk is tracked from the time the call is placed, until the problem is solved and the call closed. Provide feedback to the user about how the problem was solved. This is especially important when you have problems that are self-induced, such as users who try to change the configuration of their computer and know only enough to be dangerous to themselves!

Don't repeat past mistakes. By tracking problems and recording the troubleshooting effort and the solution to the problem, you make it easier to solve the same, or similar, problems in the future. Your help desk should have a database of some sort (such as a spreadsheet, or perhaps a Web site with documentation linked via HTML code) that can be used to see if a problem with similar symptoms has been called in before.

Is There Really a Problem?

Sometimes, as noted in the previous section, problems just fix themselves. There are times when you can't ever find the reason for a particular problem. In many cases, you'll find that sporadic problems are caused not by equipment or software failure, but by users who are not using the system correctly. When any new application is deployed on a network, you need to be sure that the end users receive adequate training for using the application or else you may find that user errors begin to account for many of your help desk calls. For example, a user may have corrupted files on a hard disk. Should you replace the disk? Should you search for a virus or another harmful program? These sound like logical things to do.

Or, you could simply ask if the user is properly shutting down the computer or just "power-cycling" it when he gets stuck in an application and can't find a way out. Some people find that just turning a computer off and back on again is a fine way to start anew, without realizing the problems they may encounter down the line. So, when troubleshooting, try to find out what has lead up to the problem. It may be a simple case of user training that needs to be addressed.

I can't stress enough the importance of training new users in the workings of the environment in which they will be placed. If you have configured a desktop in a certain manner, you can't assume that a new employee will be able to make proper use of it. While it's easy to check someone's résumé to determine what applications they are skilled at, it's difficult to be sure what the configuration of the application was at their previous place of employment. The same goes for training classes offered by temp agencies and other similar organizations. While they may use a standard installation for training purposes, any customizations or configuration changes you make need to be explained to the new user. So, as a general rule, no matter how qualified a new employee may appear to be, it's just an appearance. You should have in place a structured training program and require each new employee to attend.

And also remember that training doesn't stop there. As the network, applications, and so on change over time, retraining should also be a requirement.

Has This Happened Before—What Is the Procedure to Follow?

Keeping track of how problems were solved will keep you from expending a lot of effort solving the same problem again and again. Using documentation that enables a quick lookup of information based on symptoms can help you find older problem reports or perhaps standard help desk documentation that was written specifically because a particular problem frequently occurs. Indeed, when a problem does occur frequently, then it's time to find a better solution to the problem. So by tracking problems and the methods used to troubleshoot and solve the problem, you cannot only find it easier to solve the current incident, but also provide a feed back mechanism so that you will know that a particular problem needs a better long-term solution.

For problems that occur on a frequent basis, but which you don't have a lot of control over (i.e., user causing errors by not using an application or the network in the appropriate manner), you can at least create a step-by-step outline for solving the problem to make life at the help desk a little less frustrating.

First Things First: The Process of Elimination

If you understand how your network is put together, both from a logical and physical point of view, then it is possible to use the process of elimination to narrow the focus of your troubleshooting efforts. Some things to think about when trying to pinpoint the cause of a network program include:

- What devices—computers, hubs, switches, cables, and so on—are involved? Can you use troubleshooting tools to narrow your search to a single device or a subset of the network?

- If a single computer or device appears to be the only part of the network affected, what is unique about it? If another similar device is up and running, how do they differ in their configuration or location in the network?

- If the problem is occurring on multiple systems, what do they all have in common? Are they all on the same network segment? Do they all share a common subnet address? Do they all use the same path through the network to access a device or service that now appears to be unreachable?

- What task was the user performing when the problem occurred? Get specifics about exactly what the user was doing, both up to and when the event occurred. For example, was he using more than one application, printing to more than one printer, or perhaps doing something he should not (like opening an attachment from e-mail that came from outside the local network)?

- Can the problem be reproduced? Walk the user through the same set of steps again and see if the problem reoccurs. Next try the same with another user to determine if the problem is localized to only one computer or is a symptom of a bigger problem or configuration issue.

By narrowing your focus to only the section of the network that experiences the problem, you can more quickly look at the computers and other components of that part of the network to solve the problem. By reproducing the problem, you can be sure that you've isolated the cause. Eliminate the obvious ("Is it plugged in?") and get to the specifics as quickly as you can. Actually, silly as it may sound, asking if a computer is plugged in is really a very good question. More than once I've come in to work to find a monitor or other device was off. A quick glance at the power strip can indicate that someone, perhaps a housekeeping employee, may have accidentally unplugged the strip, or flipped the switch to turn off the power.

Auditing the Network to Locate Problem Sources

It is important to know how your network operates from a logical and physical point of view. It's also important to know the capacity of the components of the network, and the degree to which they are utilized. Sometimes problems are simply due to congestion on the network. You can determine these problems by using monitoring software, such as SNMP and RMON, and by baselining your network so that you know what the typical usage patterns are. This is covered more fully in Chapter 44, but deserves a mention here. Knowing when components of the network are stressed close to their usable capacity allows you to plan an upgrade to eliminate the bottleneck, or to reschedule user work habits to make more efficient use of the network.

Pitfalls of Troubleshooting

Above all, when trying to research a problem on the network, remember that you are indeed on a network, and the actions you take can potentially affect other users. When using troubleshooting tools, be sure you first understand how they work and also the correct way to use them. For example, what procedure do you have in place to help users who forget their password? Is a simple call to the help desk all that is required to get the password changed? If so, how does the help desk technician know who's on the other end of the line? Although it may seem inconvenient to require the user to report to a supervisor or other person who is a delegated local authority to change his password, this technique is more secure than just allowing a simple phone call to place your network in jeopardy.

Other examples include using the route command to change routing tables. An experienced network technician should do this, and not as a quick fix to solve some network problem that you can't quite put your finger on. If you don't know why the routing problem is happening, then don't try to fix it with a quick fix! You might end up causing other routers or computers to use less efficient routes and, in the long run, experience network loss through degradation. Understand the tools you use for your troubleshooting efforts.

In a complex network that involves DNS servers, DHCP servers, and possibly even WINS servers, you should be very careful before making changes on the fly. Again, I want to emphasize that a quick fix may solve the current problem, but can also possibly create another that you don't become aware of until much later after the damage has been done. Help desk personnel should be required to contact experienced system administrators before changes are made on these types of servers.

A simple name change in a DNS server, for example, could render a server unreachable for everyone on your network if the wrong address or record type is entered by mistake. Along the same lines, a very common mistake is to use an IP address for a server that falls within the range of the addresses offered by a DHCP server. When the DHCP server allocates that address to another client, everything gets screwed up on the network! Coordinate changes to important network databases and make sure that the person doing the work is fully competent to do it!

Network Testing and Analysis Tools

SOME OF THE MAIN TOPICS IN THIS CHAPTER ARE

Basics: Testing Cables

Network and Protocol Analyzers

Simple Network Management Protocol (SNMP)

## CHAPTER 44

A network administrator must wear many hats because the network is composed of many elements, which are implemented in both hardware and software. In a large network environment, many tasks are delegated to those who are particularly adept in a specific technology. However, the administrator who sits at the top of the management ladder needs to understand the principles under which the network functions and the tools that are used to keep it in good working order. This chapter discusses the basic tools used to troubleshoot the underlying structure of the network (such as the cabling) as well as those used to pick apart the semantics of the communication process (packets and protocols).

Basics: Testing Cables

A network consists of end-user workstations connected to servers by what might appear at first to be a tangled web of wires and cables. If the building or campus is wired correctly, however, this is not a jumble of cables joined together in a spaghetti fashion, but is an orderly collection of components much like a spider's web, fanning out to connect everyone in a hierarchical manner. In addition, wireless networking components have added an entire new territory, and tools are currently being developed to address troubleshooting this new area of network technology.

For the most part, when you begin to build a network, the first thing you have to do is install the cables that will connect the servers and workstations. This can done when a building is being constructed, as is the case in most office buildings today. Or, it can involve placing cable ducts in ceilings and knocking out walls to install faceplates where the cables terminate. Either way, before you begin to connect end users to the network, you first have to test the cables that are installed to be sure they are performing as expected.

Devices that can be used to test cables (both copper wire and fiber-optic cables) range from very inexpensive handheld devices that a cable installer can use to check their work, to very expensive devices that require a skilled technician to perform the tests and understand the results. Things that are usually tested include

- **Cable Length**—The physical network topology restricts the length of certain segments in the network. If you make your own cables, a common error is trying to stretch the limits of the topology and create a cable that's just a few meters too long.

- **Resistance**—Electricity encounters resistance as it propagates down a copper wire.

- **Noise**—Interference can come from other cables that are bundled together or from outside sources, such as fluorescent lighting.

- **Attenuation**—As the cable encounters resistance traveling down the wire, and as part of the signal radiates out of the wire, the signal weakens.

- **Near-End Cross-talk (NEXT)**—From the transmission end of a cable, it is necessary to remove the surrounding material that encloses the copper wires and attach each wire to a pin in the cable connector. Because the strength of signal is strongest at the end of the cable where the electrical signal is generated, there is a greater potential for interference between the wires at this end of the cable.

◀◀ If you'd like to get a better understanding of the kinds of problems you might experience with cables, connectors, and other devices used to string together a network, see Chapter 5, "Wiring the Network—Cables and Other Components."

Two basic instruments are used for testing cables. The first is the simple cable checker, which is used to determine that the cable actually provides an electrical path from here to there. The second is the cable tester, which determines whether the cable has been installed correctly to support the topology of your network, taking into consideration things such as cable length and cross talk.

Handheld Cable Checkers

A cable checker device is usually a small battery-operated unit that is used to check STP or UTP cables.

If the cable is already attached to a network device, you have to disconnect it and attach it to the unit. A cable checker operates by placing a voltage on a wire and determining whether it can be detected at the opposite end. This can be used to determine whether the cable has a break anywhere along its path and whether you are looking at the same cable on both ends when several cables are traversing a single path. Most cable checkers consist of two components, which you attach to opposite ends of the cable. This simple test is usually done when cables are first installed as a quick check to be sure that the process of pulling the cables through the ceiling or walls has not damaged them.

Cable Testers

A cable tester is a small step up from the basic checker. This device can be used to measure NEXT, attenuation, impedance, and noise on a line. Some cable testers even perform length measurements, both the total cable and the distance to a fault on the cable, such as a kink in the wire that is causing reflections of the signal to radiate back to the transmitting side of the cable. Another function you might see is *wire-mapping*, which checks to be sure that the correct wire-pairs in a cable have been mapped to the correct pins on the connector attached to the end of the cable. In cables used for 10BASE-T networks, for example, the standard specifies specific pairs of wires in the cable that must be used for transmitting and receiving data. The actual decisions about which pins are chosen for a particular connector is not done arbitrarily. If the wires are not correctly mapped to the pin-out on the connector specified by the standard, the cable might generate errors due to noise or cross-talk.

Small handheld instruments like these usually have LED lights that indicate a pass or fail condition for the test you are performing. They do not require a keyboard or monitor to display data. Some have a small screen that displays limited text, sometimes showing the suspected type of error that has caused a fail condition. Most are battery powered and can use an AC-adapter, which makes them useful portable instruments for installing or troubleshooting cabling.

When you begin to go up the price-ladder for these types of instruments, you will find some that also perform more advanced monitoring functions, such as showing network use and ethernet collisions. Another useful feature to look for if you can afford the cost is the capability to log data to a memory buffer for later review. Some cable testers are even capable of connecting to a PC or printer to produce a written report. This allows you to leave the device connected for a while to monitor a line.

Depending on the capabilities of the particular device, you can expect to pay from several hundred dollars up to a thousand or more for a good cable tester. When evaluating products, be sure to compare features. Price doesn't always reflect the quality of a device. And, you should carefully check the literature and documentation that is available for each device when making a purchasing choice. While some features, such as the capability to produce a written report, might sound great, do you really need that capability? In a large network, probably so; in a small one, probably not.

Bit Error Rate Testers (BERT)

Data travels through the wire (or the fiber) as a series of signals that indicate a single bit, representing either zero or one. The statistic called Bit Error Rate (BER) is calculated as a percentage of bits that have errors when compared to the total number of bits sampled:

```
BER = number of bit errors during sampling interval
         total number of bits transmitted
```

Although LAN analyzers operate on data captured from the wire in units of frames (depending on the LAN protocol, such as ethernet or token-ring), a Bit Error Rate Tester (BERT) performs a more basic function to determine whether the line is capable of carrying the network signaling at the bit level with a minimum of errors.

This kind of instrument is usually used when installing a connection to a network service provider, and might be used to demonstrate the quality of service that the provider establishes for your link.

The instrument used to perform this kind of error detection usually does so by generating a specific bit pattern on the line and then checking it at another location to compare the generated signal with that which is received. A *pseudorandom binary sequence (PRBS)* of bits is produced by the instrument. It is pseudorandom because it simulates random data. However, because the pattern is also known by the receiving connection so that it can make the comparison, it's not truly random, but instead is a predefined pattern. Other tests include sequences of specific bits, either zeros or ones, for extended periods, or specific user-defined bit patterns.

When you have a line that exhibits a high bit-error rate, using a slower transmission speed usually improves performance. This is because when you lower the number of errors that occur, higher-level protocols do not have to resend packets as often to compensate. Although one bit error in a frame usually is easily recovered by a network protocol using an error correction code (ECC) technique, multiple bit errors might be all that it takes to cause an entire frame of several hundred thousand bits to be resent.

Time Domain Reflectometers

A signal usually propagates down a wire at a constant speed, provided the impedance of the cable is the same throughout its journey. When the signal runs into a fault in the wire or reaches the end of the wire, part or all of the signal is reflected back to its origin. Similar to radar, instruments that use time domain reflectometry (TDR) to make cable measurements are based on precisely timing the signal pulse as it travels through the cable and back.

Of all the instruments you can use to test cables, TDR is one of the most accurate and fastest. It can help locate faults due to many things, such as:

- Wires that have been spliced together
- Moisture trapped in the cable
- Cables that have been crushed or have kinks in them
- Short circuits
- Problems in the sheath surrounding a cable
- Loose connectors

You also can use TDR to measure the length of a cable that has no faults. This can be useful for inventory functions because you can even use it to measure then length of a cable while it is still on a reel to determine whether you have enough or need to order additional stock before beginning a major wiring project. TDR can be used to make measurements on twisted-pair cables, coaxial cables, and even fiber-optic cables.

The more expensive models of this instrument can be equipped with a CRT or LED display that shows the wave form of the signal and any reflected signals. The more common instrument displays the number of feet to the end of the cable or a fault, and might have an indicator that tells you the type of fault.

Impedance

When conductors that are made of metal are placed in close proximity to each other, as in a twisted-pair or coaxial cable, the effect they have on each other is known as impedance. When the wires are perfectly separated by a constant distance, the impedance remains the same throughout the cable.

When something happens along the way, such as damage caused by a crushed cable, the impedance changes at that point. Changes in impedance cause parts of the signal to be reflected back to where it started.

Cables that are used in local area networks (LANs) need to be manufactured to strict specifications, ensuring that the dielectric material that separates the wires within the cable remains constant. If there are random variations due to poor manufacturing procedures, the cable will suffer from problems caused by signal reflections, which might render it unsuitable for your network. Thus, TDR can not only be used as a fault-finder when troubleshooting a wiring problem, but also to ensure that you've received what you paid for when you upgrade or expand your network.

Setting a Pulse Width

Most of the good TDR instruments allow you to select the pulse width, which is usually specified in nanoseconds. The larger the pulse width, the more energy that is transmitted from the device and thus the further down the wire the signal will travel.

A good tip for setting this value is to start with the smallest that the instrument allows and make subsequent measurements, gradually increasing the pulse width. If the fault in the cable is only a short distance away from the measuring instrument, a small pulse width will be adequate to locate it. However, if the fault is minor, a small burst of energy might not be enough to travel to the fault and send back a reflection strong enough to be accurately measured. By varying the pulse width and making several measurements, you can more accurately determine the location of a fault in the cable.

Velocity

Light travels at a constant speed of 186,400 miles per second. When measuring the velocity at which an electrical signal travels through a wire, it is expressed as a percentage of the speed of light, which is considered to be 100%, or a value of 1. For example, a twisted-pair cable that has a VOP (velocity of propagation) of .65 would conduct an electrical signal at 65% of the speed of light, or about the speed I drive on the interstate.

Manufacturers usually supply this value to customers, and it will most likely be found on the specification sheet for the cable you are purchasing. Because TDR measures the time it takes for a signal to travel down a wire and make the return trip, you have to know the VOP of the cable being tested before you can make accurate measurements.

If you have cables that you are unsure about, you can test them first to determine the VOP. Do this by measuring a specific length of cable to get its length, then use the TDR instrument to test for the length of the cable, varying the VOP until the tester reads the correct length. Of course, this assumes that the segment of cable you use for this test is in good condition!

Network and Protocol Analyzers

The first level of network testing consists of making sure that the underlying physical cabling structure is performing as expected. The next level is to monitor and test the network traffic and messages generated by the network protocols to be sure that you have a healthy network. Network analyzer products operate by monitoring the network at the data link and transport layers in the OSI reference model.

Note

The OSI reference model separates the components of a network protocol stack into modular layers, each of which performs a specific task for the layer above or below it in the model. Appendix A, "The OSI Seven-Layer Networking Model" covers this model, discussing each layer in detail. You'll hear terms such as network layer, data link layer, and transport layer frequently when discussing networking, so it's a good idea to have a basic understanding of what these terms mean and the networking functions they represent.

Again, you will find that the tools you can select for this range from the very inexpensive (free) to the very expensive (several thousand dollars). One difference between these kinds of tools and those used to check cables, however, is that you need to have a good understanding of the network structure and protocols used before you can make meaningful judgments about the data you collect. The LAN analyzer allows you to intercept network traffic as it passes through the wire in real-time and save the data for analysis. A good analyzer should be able to produce meaningful statistics about the traffic on the network, decode the protocols that are used, and provide a good filtering capability so that you don't get bogged down in an overwhelming amount of data.

You should consider many factors when deciding on a network analyzer product. The most basic factor is whether you want a portable device that can be transported to different sites or one or more devices that can be placed at strategic locations in the network to perform continuous monitoring. Other features to consider are

- **Price**—Of course, this is always a factor when purchasing equipment for a network.

- **Software or hardware**—Do you need a dedicated hardware instrument that can perform intense analysis and connect to multiple segments, or can you live with a software implementation that runs on an existing network workstation?

- **Network interface**—Do you need to connect to just a 10BASE-T environment, or do you need a device that connects to other topologies such as FDDI or token ring?

- **Protocol stack support**—Is your network homogeneous, or does it support multiple network protocols?

- **Statistics**—What kind of statistical data does the instrument support? The most basic is frames-per-second. Others include utilization and usage. Utilization is a measurement of the actual amount of bandwidth that your network media is supporting at any point in time. Usage statistics can tell you what is using that bandwith—from protocol statistics to such things as the number of collisions on a shared ethernet segment.

- **Memory and buffers**—Does the instrument provide enough buffering capacity to capture frames on a high-speed network such as 100BASE-T? How about Gigabit Ethernet?

- **Filters**—Does the analyzer provide sufficient filtering capabilities to allow you to look through large volumes of data to get to the frames that really matter?

- **Import and export**—Does the device allow you to save files to a disk or other medium so that you can transfer them to other workstations for further analysis?

A good LAN analyzer allows you to monitor network traffic in real-time mode, using filters to narrow the scope of your view. You can set up capture filters, store part or all of the frames that match in a buffer, and perform further analysis.

Establishing a Baseline

Before you begin to perform monitoring or analysis of the network usage and utilization, you need to establish a set of baseline data. To interpret the statistical data that you can collect using LAN analyzers, you need to have something with which to compare future measurements. Baseline data is used to define the normal operating environment for a system and provides a reference for monitoring and troubleshooting efforts.

Baseline data is useful not only for troubleshooting, but also for planning capacity and measuring the effectiveness of an upgrade. Things you should consider recording in your baseline documentation in addition to values you monitor with a LAN analyzer include

- Location of equipment in the network
- Type of equipment in use

- The number and distribution of users
- Protocols in use

Knowing the type of equipment is important because different models of NICs, hubs, and other devices can vary widely in their performance. Knowing where each piece of equipment is located can be used to create an audit trail for troubleshooting. For example, it is common in a business environment for users and workstations to be constantly on the move.

A simple weekend move, in which you take a few workstations or servers and move them to a different location, might have a dramatic, unexpected impact on the network. Suppose you have two servers that you want to move from a departmental location to a central computer room. When they were located on the same network segment as the users that use them the most, traffic was localized. Placing them on a different segment might cause capacity problems in a backbone link or in a device such as a switch or router that connects the network. If you keep track of hardware and statistical information about its performance and usage, you can usually prevent this sort of thing from happening. At least, you can look back and determine where a problem lies and be in a better position to find a solution.

This same principle applies to the location of users in the network. Different users can make widely differing demands on a single workstation or server. Keep a list of users, the applications they use, and, when appropriate, the time of day they work in situations where shift-work is performed.

Understanding the protocols that are used is also important. A simple problem that can be hard to figure out occurs when you move a device to a different network segment and are unaware that it is using a nonroutable protocol. Most routers can be configured to pass these nonroutable protocols (such as NetBEUI), but you need to be aware of this and configure the router accordingly before you make the move.

Finally, baseline data is never going to be something that is cast in stone and unchangeable. Modify your documentation as the network grows or changes so that the data remains useful.

Statistical Data

Although most analyzers provide a wide range of statistical data, the analyzer should be able to give you a few general values.

First, be sure the analyzer can give you statistics that tell you the utilization of the network. In addition to a real-time graphical display, you should also look for the capability to monitor the network and tell you when *peak utilization* occurs. That is, what times during the day does the network reach its busiest points? Overall utilization calculated over the average workday might not be nearly as helpful as identifying the periods of time that users are working their hardest, while getting frustrated with a bogged-down network. Using peak utilization statistics, you can work to resolve the traffic problems by reallocating resources, or perhaps rearranging work habits of the user base.

Another statistic that is found on most analyzers is Frames Per Second (FPS). By itself, FPS isn't a revealing value, but when combined with data showing the size of packets traversing the network, it can produce meaningful data. The larger the packet size used by a protocol, the more efficient the protocol is likely to be. This is because each packet requires overhead necessary to implement the protocol, such as addressing and error-checking information. With a larger packet size, the ratio of overhead to payload is reduced.

Protocol Decoding

The capability to take the raw bits that travel on the network and present them on a frame-by-frame basis is a powerful feature of the analyzer. Looking at a *stream* of byte values isn't very useful when troubleshooting a network problem. Looking at *each frame*, and understanding what kinds of frames are being generated by devices on the network, is a necessary component of a network analyzer.

Look for an analyzer that gives both a summary and a detailed view of the frame. The summary view usually shows just the addressing and header portion of the packet, whereas the detailed view displays every byte contained in the frame.

Filtering

Filtering is a necessary component for any network analyzer. Filtering allows you to set criteria that the analyzer uses when it captures frames, or to selectively search through a buffer of captured data to retrieve only those frames that are pertinent to your troubleshooting efforts. Filters can usually be set to select frames by protocol type, frame type, and protocol address or MAC addresses. Some allow you to search for specific data patterns throughout the entire packet.

Software-Based Analyzers

Software analyzers are the cheapest route. Indeed, you can find some freeware analyzer products on the Web that perform some or all of the functions you might need in a small network. Windows NT 4.0 comes with a network monitor agent and tool that you can install using the Services tab in the Network applet found in the Control Panel. This monitoring and analysis tool allows the local workstation or server to monitor network traffic that is generated by or sent to the computer. The version that comes with the Systems Management Server (SMS) BackOffice component allows the network administrator to monitor all traffic on the LAN. Windows 2000 also includes a network monitor that you'll find in the Administrative Tools folder on Windows 2000 Server.

Novell has a software-based product called LaNalyzer, which can be used to monitor network traffic. It is a separate product that you must purchase, however, and is not included in the NetWare products by default.

Both of these products allow you to capture data on the LAN, filter, and troubleshoot many kinds of problems. Because these products run on a workstation, you can use them to collect and store large amounts of information for immediate analysis and long-term reporting. In Figure 44.1, you can see the main window of the Network Monitor for Windows NT 4.0 (called the Capture Window).

Figure 44.1 The Capture Window shows a summary of the frames that have been captured by Network Monitor.

To begin capturing frames on the network, choose Capture, Start. You can also use the Capture menu to pause or stop the capture process. As frames are captured by the monitor, you can get an idea of what is happening on the network by the continuously updated bar graphs in the Capture Window. To view the actual data being collected, you can stop the capture process by selecting Capture, Stop. Choose Capture, Display Captured Data to view the frames captured (see Figure 44.2).

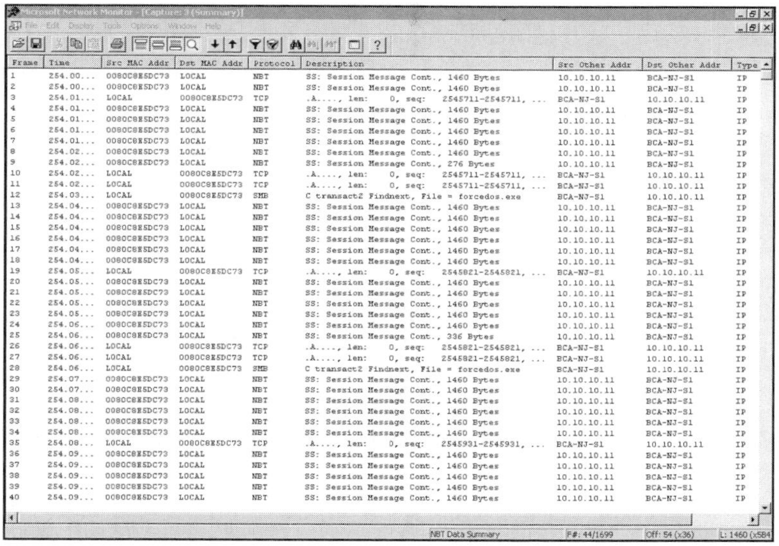

Frame	Time	Src MAC Addr	Dst MAC Addr	Protocol	Description	Src Other Addr	Dst Other Addr	Type
1	254.00...	0080C8E5DC73	LOCAL	NBT	SS: Session Message Cont., 1460 Bytes	10.10.10.11	BCA-NJ-S1	IP
2	254.00...	0080C8E5DC73	LOCAL	NBT	SS: Session Message Cont., 1460 Bytes	10.10.10.11	BCA-NJ-S1	IP
3	254.01...	LOCAL	0080C8E5DC73	TCP	.A...., len: 0, seq: 2545711-2545711, ...	BCA-NJ-S1	10.10.10.11	IP
4	254.01...	0080C8E5DC73	LOCAL	NBT	SS: Session Message Cont., 1460 Bytes	10.10.10.11	BCA-NJ-S1	IP
5	254.01...	0080C8E5DC73	LOCAL	NBT	SS: Session Message Cont., 1460 Bytes	10.10.10.11	BCA-NJ-S1	IP
6	254.01...	0080C8E5DC73	LOCAL	NBT	SS: Session Message Cont., 1460 Bytes	10.10.10.11	BCA-NJ-S1	IP
7	254.01...	0080C8E5DC73	LOCAL	NBT	SS: Session Message Cont., 1460 Bytes	10.10.10.11	BCA-NJ-S1	IP
8	254.02...	0080C8E5DC73	LOCAL	NBT	SS: Session Message Cont., 1460 Bytes	10.10.10.11	BCA-NJ-S1	IP
9	254.02...	0080C8E5DC73	LOCAL	NBT	SS: Session Message Cont., 276 Bytes	10.10.10.11	BCA-NJ-S1	IP
10	254.02...	LOCAL	0080C8E5DC73	TCP	.A...., len: 0, seq: 2545711-2545711, ...	BCA-NJ-S1	10.10.10.11	IP
11	254.02...	LOCAL	0080C8E5DC73	TCP	.A...., len: 0, seq: 2545711-2545711, ...	BCA-NJ-S1	10.10.10.11	IP
12	254.03...	LOCAL	0080C8E5DC73	SMB	C transact2 Findnext, File = forcedos.exe	BCA-NJ-S1	10.10.10.11	IP
13	254.04...	0080C8E5DC73	LOCAL	NBT	SS: Session Message Cont., 1460 Bytes	10.10.10.11	BCA-NJ-S1	IP
14	254.04...	0080C8E5DC73	LOCAL	NBT	SS: Session Message Cont., 1460 Bytes	10.10.10.11	BCA-NJ-S1	IP
15	254.04...	0080C8E5DC73	LOCAL	NBT	SS: Session Message Cont., 1460 Bytes	10.10.10.11	BCA-NJ-S1	IP
16	254.04...	0080C8E5DC73	LOCAL	NBT	SS: Session Message Cont., 1460 Bytes	10.10.10.11	BCA-NJ-S1	IP
17	254.04...	0080C8E5DC73	LOCAL	NBT	SS: Session Message Cont., 1460 Bytes	10.10.10.11	BCA-NJ-S1	IP
18	254.04...	0080C8E5DC73	LOCAL	NBT	SS: Session Message Cont., 1460 Bytes	10.10.10.11	BCA-NJ-S1	IP
19	254.05...	LOCAL	0080C8E5DC73	TCP	.A...., len: 0, seq: 2545821-2545821, ...	BCA-NJ-S1	10.10.10.11	IP
20	254.05...	0080C8E5DC73	LOCAL	NBT	SS: Session Message Cont., 1460 Bytes	10.10.10.11	BCA-NJ-S1	IP
21	254.05...	0080C8E5DC73	LOCAL	NBT	SS: Session Message Cont., 1460 Bytes	10.10.10.11	BCA-NJ-S1	IP
22	254.05...	0080C8E5DC73	LOCAL	NBT	SS: Session Message Cont., 1460 Bytes	10.10.10.11	BCA-NJ-S1	IP
23	254.05...	0080C8E5DC73	LOCAL	NBT	SS: Session Message Cont., 1460 Bytes	10.10.10.11	BCA-NJ-S1	IP
24	254.06...	0080C8E5DC73	LOCAL	NBT	SS: Session Message Cont., 1460 Bytes	10.10.10.11	BCA-NJ-S1	IP
25	254.06...	0080C8E5DC73	LOCAL	NBT	SS: Session Message Cont., 336 Bytes	10.10.10.11	BCA-NJ-S1	IP
26	254.06...	LOCAL	0080C8E5DC73	TCP	.A...., len: 0, seq: 2545821-2545821, ...	BCA-NJ-S1	10.10.10.11	IP
27	254.06...	LOCAL	0080C8E5DC73	TCP	.A...., len: 0, seq: 2545821-2545821, ...	BCA-NJ-S1	10.10.10.11	IP
28	254.06...	LOCAL	0080C8E5DC73	SMB	C transact2 Findnext, File = forcedos.exe	BCA-NJ-S1	10.10.10.11	IP
29	254.07...	0080C8E5DC73	LOCAL	NBT	SS: Session Message Cont., 1460 Bytes	10.10.10.11	BCA-NJ-S1	IP
30	254.07...	0080C8E5DC73	LOCAL	NBT	SS: Session Message Cont., 1460 Bytes	10.10.10.11	BCA-NJ-S1	IP
31	254.08...	0080C8E5DC73	LOCAL	NBT	SS: Session Message Cont., 1460 Bytes	10.10.10.11	BCA-NJ-S1	IP
32	254.08...	0080C8E5DC73	LOCAL	NBT	SS: Session Message Cont., 1460 Bytes	10.10.10.11	BCA-NJ-S1	IP
33	254.08...	0080C8E5DC73	LOCAL	NBT	SS: Session Message Cont., 1460 Bytes	10.10.10.11	BCA-NJ-S1	IP
34	254.08...	0080C8E5DC73	LOCAL	NBT	SS: Session Message Cont., 1460 Bytes	10.10.10.11	BCA-NJ-S1	IP
35	254.08...	LOCAL	0080C8E5DC73	TCP	.A...., len: 0, seq: 2545931-2545931, ...	BCA-NJ-S1	10.10.10.11	IP
36	254.09...	0080C8E5DC73	LOCAL	NBT	SS: Session Message Cont., 1460 Bytes	10.10.10.11	BCA-NJ-S1	IP
37	254.09...	0080C8E5DC73	LOCAL	NBT	SS: Session Message Cont., 1460 Bytes	10.10.10.11	BCA-NJ-S1	IP
38	254.09...	0080C8E5DC73	LOCAL	NBT	SS: Session Message Cont., 1460 Bytes	10.10.10.11	BCA-NJ-S1	IP
39	254.09...	0080C8E5DC73	LOCAL	NBT	SS: Session Message Cont., 1460 Bytes	10.10.10.11	BCA-NJ-S1	IP
40	254.09...	0080C8E5DC73	LOCAL	NBT	SS: Session Message Cont., 1460 Bytes	10.10.10.11	BCA-NJ-S1	IP

NBT Data Summary | F#: 44/1699 | Off: 54 (x36) | L: 1460 (x584

Figure 44.2 The Frame Viewer window allows you to examine the captured data.

As you can see, a summary line is provided for each frame that the monitor captured. You can scroll up or down to view all frames in the buffer. At this point, the frames are stored in a temporary buffer. If you only need to view the data for immediate analysis and then discard it, you can do so from this window. If you want to store the data for later analysis, select File, Save As. To view data in a stored file, choose File, Open to read the data in the file into the temporary buffer.

To examine any of the captured frames and view it in detail, double-click it in the Frame Viewer window. The window opens a Detail pane that shows the kinds of data in the frame. Click the plus sign ("+") to expand the list of data contained in the frame. Figure 44.3 is an example of an ICMP (Internet Control Management Protocol) frame generated during a PING operation. By highlighting the ICMP portion of the Detail Pane (in the center of this figure), the monitor highlights the data pertaining to this in the data section at the bottom of the figure. By showing the bytes that make up different parts of the frame, the monitor makes your job easier.

Capture and Display Filters

The amount of traffic that passes through even a small network can be overwhelming, but not when you're using a network monitor to watch statistical information about current traffic. When you are troubleshooting, however, it's helpful to be able to filter out the nonessential information so you can examine only those frames that are pertinent to the problem at hand.

For this purpose, most analyzers allow you to set up a filter that screens out all but the frames you want to view. A capture filter is used to create selection criteria for the frames that will be kept and stored in the temporary buffer, while a display filter can be used to further select frames from those that are captured.

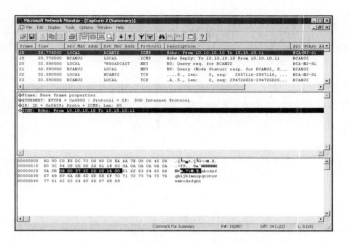

Figure 44.3 You can examine the actual contents of the frame from this view.

In Figure 44.4, you can see the dialog box used to start creating a capture filter for the Network Monitor.

Figure 44.4 Create a capture filter to specify which frames are copied to the temporary buffer.

For a capture filter, you can specify specific protocols, address pairs, or patterns that occur in the frame itself. Figure 44.5 shows the dialog box used to select address pairs and Figure 44.6 shows the dialog box used to specify a pattern.

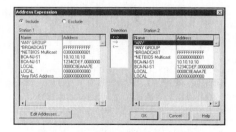

Figure 44.5 You can select the addresses that must appear in a frame in order for it to be selected for capture.

Figure 44.6 Specify a pattern and an offset value for capturing frames based on pattern matching.

When using pattern matching, you can specify a string that must be found in the frame before it is considered a candidate for capture. You can specify an offset value also, which indicates a starting point for the filter in the frame when it searches for the pattern.

Capture Triggers

After you create a capture filter, you can begin to capture data based on it by selecting Capture, Start. When using a narrow filter to look for a specific problem that doesn't occur often, you can set up an event to notify you when a matching frame is finally detected instead of having to sit at the console and wait. To set a capture trigger, select Capture, Trigger.

The Network Monitor allows you to monitor overall traffic on the network by watching the graphs displayed in the Capture Window and it allows you to look at specific frames to determine where problems exist. Similar to a hardware LAN analyzer, a good software LAN analyzer can be a valuable tool for determining network use or for troubleshooting specific protocol problems.

Other Software LAN Analyzer Products

The fast microprocessors used in today's desktop and laptop computers allow for a wide range of software products to provide functionality that used to be primarily the domain of hardware-based analyzers. The previous section looked at the built-in LAN monitoring tools available as part of the Windows operating system. However, a large market exists for software-based LAN analyzers, and they are usually much less expensive to deploy than their hardware counterparts.

Before investing in a software LAN analyzer, you should try before you buy. Following is a list of a few good products that allow you to either download a demonstration version, or order a CD that you can use to evaluate the product before making a purchase. Don't buy the first product you look at. Instead, determine whether the documentation is up to par, whether the company provides good technical support, and, most importantly, whether the product is intuitive and easy to use.

- **Fluke Protocol Inspector**—This software product works with 100/100 and 100Mbps ethernet and token-ring networks. It provides for real-time traffic monitoring and decoding for all seven layers of the OSI reference model. Download a demo from
  `http://www.flukenetworks.com/lan/protocol+inspector/`.

- **Ethertest LAN Analyzer for Windows**—This LAN analyzer from Frontline Test Equipment, Inc. (FTE), runs on systems ranging from Windows 95 to Windows 2000. You can download a demo of this product at `http://www.fte.com/`. If you're in the process of deploying Bluetooth technology in your LAN, you might also want to download a demo of FTE's SerialBlue Bluetooth.

- **Observer, Expert Observer, and Observer Suite from Network Instruments**—These products perform everything from simple network protocol analysis to SNMP (Simple Network Mail Protocol), RMON (Remote Monitoring) console, and probe reporting. The software also runs on systems ranging from Windows 95 to Windows 2000. You can download a demo from `http://www.netinst.com`.

- **Wildpackets**—An assortment of network analysis tools can be downloaded, ranging from the highly rated EtherPeek LAN analysis tool to AiroPeek for wireless LAN analysis. You can download demos for these and other valuable tools by visiting http:www.wildpackets.com.

This is only a short list of the large number of products available, and they are not rated as to which is best because it depends on your needs and how your network is laid out. However, you should download the demos listed here so you can get an idea of what you can expect from a software-based LAN analyzer. If you're going to spend money on such a product, make sure it's an informed purchase.

Hardware Analyzers

This type of instrument can cost as much as tens of thousands of dollars. Hardware analyzers, however, provide functionality in a critical situation that might not be obtainable from a software-based product. A hardware LAN analyzer can be taken to the location where a problem exists and be connected to the network to perform its functions. A hardware instrument will most likely be better able to cope with a high-speed environment, such as 100BASE-t and 1000BASE-T, than a software application that relies on a network adapter card to get traffic from the network medium. Hardware analyzers contain special circuitry that is used to perform many functions must faster than can be done via software, and are usually more reliable.

Another thing to consider when comparing hardware to software analyzers is that when you use a PC or a workstation to act as your LAN analyzer, it might be limited as to what the NIC can do. For example, some ordinary adapter cards have built in to their firmware a function that automatically discards certain kinds of packets that contain errors. If you are trying to detect what errors are causing problems on your network while troubleshooting, a software product running on a workstation might not be able to help you.

Also, although it's true that network adapter cards can literally see every packet on the network as it zips by, that doesn't mean that they are capable of capturing the data and passing it up to higher-level protocols. When a card *does* capture all frames and pass them up the protocol stack, it is operating in *promiscuous mode*. Some cards are designed specifically not to do this so be sure to check the documentation that comes with the one you might want to use on a workstation that will host LAN monitoring software.

Note

For most typical situations, even in a large network, the functions performed by most hardware-based analyzers can now be performed using software products, such as those discussed in the previous section. However, for high-speed WAN links, or for situations in which the network topology is complex, involving multiple protocols and services, it might be worth the investment to purchase a hardware-based analyzer. First, try a software product before spending the money on a hardware device. Just be sure you are not using an off-the-shelf PC. Check out the capabilities of the network adapter(s) you install on a PC or other workstation that will host a network analyzer software product.

Hardware analyzers are expensive because they usually do a very good job and are designed specifically for what they do. Most have built-in disk drives, including a floppy disk drive that can be used to exchange data with PC workstations. Be sure that the instrument has enough memory to buffer significant amounts of data. Another feature to look for is a good display, so that you can monitor utilization graphically as well as display the contents of individual frames.

A hybrid analyzer that combines the best of the hardware and software products is also available. This type of device implements the capturing and filtering functions in a hardware component that attaches to a workstation, which then provides the display and storage functions. The hardware component has dedicated circuitry and processing power to capture data from the wire, while a software application on the PC is used to filter, calculate, and display the data. This type of device can be external to the PC, while some are implemented as cards that plug into the system's bus.

Simple Network Management Protocol (SNMP)

Building a network today involves integrating products from a variety of vendors. This chapter has discussed tools that can be used to locate faults in the physical elements that make up the network and tools that can be used to monitor the functioning of network protocols.

Yet, so far the tools that have been mentioned are all limited to performing a few specific tasks and each tool must be used as a separate entity. SNMP was developed to provide a "simple" method of centralizing the management of TCP/IP based networks. The goals of the original SNMP protocols include

- Keep development costs low to ease the burden of implementing the protocol for developers.
- Provide for managing devices remotely.
- Make the protocol extensible so that it can adapt to new technologies.
- Make the protocol independent of the underlying architecture of the devices that are managed.
- Keep it simple.

The last goal is an important one. Because SNMP is meant to be incorporated into many different types of network devices, it was designed so that it would not require a lot of overhead. This makes it easy to create simple devices—such as a bridge or a hub—that can be managed by SNMP, as well as a more complex device such as a router or a switch. Other key factors of the protocol that stick to this goal include the use of the User Datagram Protocol (UDP) for messaging and a manager-agent architecture. UDP is easier to implement and use than a more complex protocol such as TCP. Yet, it provides enough functionality to allow a central manager to communicate with a remote agent that resides on a managed device.

The two main players in SNMP are the manager and the agent. The manager is usually a software program running on a workstation or larger computer that communicates with agent processes that run on each device being monitored. Agents can be found on bridges, routers, hubs, and even user's workstations. The manager polls the agents making requests for information and the agents respond when asked.

Applications designed to be the manager end of the SNMP software vary both in expense and functionality. Some are simple applications that perform queries and allow an administrator to view information from devices and produce reports. Some of the other functions that a management console application might perform include

- Mapping the topology of the network
- Monitoring network traffic
- Trapping selected events and producing alarms
- Reporting variables

Some management consoles, also referred to as network management stations (NMS), can produce trend-analysis reports to help capacity planning set long-range goals. With more advanced reporting capabilities, the administrator can produce meaningful reports that can be used to tackle a specific problem.

SNMP Primitives

Management software and device agents communicate using a limited set of operations referred to as *primitives*. These primitives are used to make requests and send information between the two. These primitives are initiated by the management software:

- **get**—The manager uses this primitive to get a single piece of information from an agent.

- **get-next**—When the data the manager needs to get from the agent consists of more than one item, this primitive is used to sequentially retrieve data; for example, a table of values.

- **set**—The manager can use this primitive to request that the agent running on the remote device set a particular variable to a certain value.

These primitives are used by the agent on a managed device:

- **get-response**—This primitive is used to respond to a get or a get-next request from the manager.

- **trap**—Although SNMP exchanges are usually initiated by the manager software, this primitive is used when the agent needs to inform the manager of some important event.

Network Objects: The Management Information Base (MIB)

The primitives just described are the operations that can be performed by the manager or agent processes when they exchange data. The types of data they can exchange are defined by a database called the Management Information Base (MIB). The first compilation of the objects stored in this database was defined by RFC 1066, "Management Information Base for Network Management of TCP/IP-based Internets." A year later, this was amended by RFC 1213, "Management Information Base for Network Management of TCP/IP-based Internets: MIB-II." MIB-II clarified some of the objects that were defined in the original document and added a few new ones.

The MIB is a tree of information (a virtual information store). This hierarchical database resides on the agent and information collected by the agent is stored in the MIB. The MIB is precisely defined; the current Internet standard MIB contains over a thousand objects. Each object in the MIB represents some specific entity on the managed device. For example, on a hub, useful objects might collect information showing the number of packets entering the hub for a specific port while another object might be used to track network addresses.

When deciding which types of objects to include in the standard, the following things were taken into consideration:

- The object had to be useful for either fault or configuration management.

- The object had to be "weak," which means it had to be capable of performing only a small amount of damage should it be tampered with. Remember, in addition to reading values stored in the MIB, the management software can request that an object be set to a value.

- No object was allowed if it could be easily derived from objects that already exist.

The first definition of the standard MIB hoped to keep the number of objects to 100 or less so that it would be easier to implement. This, of course, is not a factor now.

Because the SNMP management scheme is intended to be extensible, vendors often create their own objects which can be added to the management console software so that you can use them.

An object has a specific syntax, name, and method of encoding associated with it. The name consists of an object identifier, which specifies the type of object to which a specific instance of that kind of object is added. The object identifier is a numeric string of decimal digits separated by periods. For example, ".3.6.1.2.1.1.1". The "instance" of an object is the same, with an additional decimal number following the original object identifier. To make things easier for humans, an object descriptor is used in a text-readable format.

An object can be read-only, read-write, or write-only. In addition, an object can be nonaccessible. Syntax types for objects include

- Integer
- Octet String or Display String
- Object Identifier
- Null
- Network Address
- Counter
- Gauge
- TimeTicks
- Opaque

In the first MIB RFC, objects are divided into only a few high-level groups:

- **System**—This group includes objects that identify a type of system (hardware or software).
- **Interfaces**—An object in this group might represent an interface number or an interface type. Other information about network interfaces, such as the largest IP datagram that can be sent or received, is included as objects in this group.
- **Address Translation**—Objects in this group are used for address translation information, such as the ARP (Address resolution Protocol) cache.
- **IP**—Objects in this group supply information about the IP protocol, including time-to-live values, number of datagrams received from interfaces, errors, and so on.
- **ICMP**—This group includes Internet Control Management Protocol (ICMP) input and output statistics.
- **TCP**—Objects in this group are used to hold information about TCP connections. Instances of these objects exist only while the connection exists. Data contained in these objects includes the number of segments sent or received, for example, or the state of a particular TCP connection (closed, listen, and so on).
- **UDP**—Objects in this group represent statistics about UDP, such as the number of UDP datagrams delivered, or the number of UDP datagrams received for which there is no corresponding application at the destination port.
- **EGP**—These objects are used for the Exterior Gateway Protocol (EGP), and contain information such as components of each EGP neighbor, and the state of the local system with respect to a neighbor.

In MIB-II, the address translation group was declared to be "deprecated." That is, it should still be supported but might not be in the next version, which is a means for gradually preparing for changes in the protocol. MIB-II, however, adds new objects and functionality that can be used to perform the same functions as those performed by this group, just in a different way.

MIB-II also added new objects to the existing groups. For example, what seems obvious now as necessary information for the system group—a contact person, system location, and system services—can now be stored in objects in this group.

New groups added by MIB-II include

- **Transmission**—Related to the Interface group, this group is used for objects that relate to specific transmission media.

- **SNMP**—A group added for objects needed by the application-oriented working group to collect useful statistical information.

Proxy Agents

Not all devices are equipped with SNMP capabilities. For these devices, another device might be able to handle those functions and acts as a *proxy agent* so that it can still be managed from the SNMP management console. For example, a network card might not be SNMP-enabled, but the host computer can run a process that can monitor the network card and act as a proxy agent, relaying information to the management station. Proxy agents also can be developed to translate between proprietary management software and SNMP. In this case the proxy agent understands the proprietary management capabilities of the device, and communicates with the SNMP management station when necessary.

The Complex Road to SNMPv2 and SNMPv3

The original implementation of SNMP was kept simple and has been widely used throughout the industry. However, it suffers from several limitations. The get/response messaging mechanism allows for the transfer of only one piece of information at a time. The UDP packet is sufficiently large enough to accommodate more data, but the protocol was not built to allow for this. Security is also an issue with SNMP (version 1) because it has no provisions for encryption or authentication.

A committee of the IETF began work on what was to become SNMPv2 in 1994. Work on this second version of the SNMP standard was delayed for years because many could not agree on some of the security and other issues involved. Because of this several versions of SNMPv2 were created, specifically SNMP v2u and SNMPv2c, each taking a different approach to security issues. In spite of the haziness of the actual SNMPv2 specifications, however, you'll now find that many vendors support some of the functionality that has been described in the many RFCs that relate to SNMPv2.

One of the good things to come out of the SNMPv2 debate were two new operations:

- `Get-bulk`—This operation allows for the retrieval of a larger amount of information from a single request. This new operation can be used in place of repetitive calls to `get-next` when transferring large amounts of related information.

- `Inform`—This operation allows for one network management station (NMS) to send traps to another NMS.

For the most part, however, a newer version called SNMPv3 is a more likely candidate for adoption by a wider range of vendors. Although SNMPv1 and SNMPv2 implementations are not compatible with each other, SNMPv3 incorporates the best from both, adding security and other features to the protocol. Actually, SNMPv3 is not a standard in and of itself. Instead, it describes additional capabilities (such as security) that can be incorporated into SNMPv1 and SNMPv2 implementations.

RFC 2571, "An Architecture for Describing SNMP Management Frameworks," uses the previous SNMP RFCs heavily, with the following items being the main goals of the RFC:

- Provide an architecture that allows for the standards process for SNMP developments to proceed even when consensus has not been reached for all the specifics of proposed additions.

- Provide for additional security measures.

- Modularize each SNMP entity so that each "SNMP engine" can implement the necessary functions to send and receive messages, perform authentication, and perform encryption of messages. Thus, any number of entities can be combined to create an agent, or a management station.

By allowing for a modular approach to SNMP construction, this RFC makes it possible to create new SNMP functionality without having to redefine the entire SNMP standard each time a new feature is added. After all, the "S" in SNMP stands for "simple."

You might want to read these other relevant RFCs when you are evaluating a product and determining how it measures up to the latest in SNMPv3 standards:

- RFC 2570, "Introduction to Version 3 of the Internet-standard Network Management Framework"

- RFC 2571, "An Architecture for Describing SNMP Management Frameworks"

- RFC 2572, "Message Processing and Dispatching for the Simple Network Management Protocol (SNMP)"

- RFC 2573, "SNMP Applications"

- RFC 2274, "User-based Security Model (USM) for version 3 of the Simple Network Management Protocol (SNMPv3)"

- RFC 2575, "View-based Access Control Model (VACM) for the Simple Network Management Protocol (SNMP)"

- RFC 2576, "Coexistence between Version 1, Version 2, and Version 3 of the Internet-standard Network Management Framework"

Note that these RFCs are rather recent, and some are still in the draft stage. However, as complex as the "simple" network management protocol has become, it is hard to give a general definition of exactly what SNMPv3 is, or will be at this time.

RMON

RMON is a data-gathering and analysis tool that was developed to help alleviate some of the shortcomings of SNMP. RMON works in a similar manner, and its objects are defined in an MIB. It was designed to work much like the LAN analyzer discussed earlier in this chapter. RFCs 1757, "Remote Network Monitoring Management Information Base," and 1513, "Token Ring Extensions to the Remote Network Monitoring MIB," provide the standard MIB definitions for RMON for ethernet and token-ring networks, respectively.

In SNMP, the roles of the manager and agent are that of a client and server, with the agents being the client of the management console software. In RMON, the agents (often called *probes*) are the active parties and become the server while one or more management consoles can be their clients. Instead of the management console performing a periodic polling process to gather data and perform analysis from agents out in the field, the agents in RMON perform intelligent analysis and send SNMP traps to management consoles when significant events occur.

Using RMON, the administrator can get an end-to-end view of the network. The types of data collected and the alerts and actions that are associated with RMON are different than those of the standard SNMP type. The objects for RMON fall into the following MIB groups:

- **Statistics**—This group records data collected about network interfaces. A table called EtherStatsTable contains one entry for each interface to hold this data and also contains control parameters for this group. Statistics include traffic volume, packet sizes, and errors.

- **History**—The control function of this group manages the statistical sampling of data. This function controls the frequency at which data is sampled on the network. The historyControlTable is associated with this group. The history function of this group of objects records the statistical data and places the data in a table called the etherHistoryTable.

- **Hosts**—This group tracks hosts on the network by MAC addresses. Information in the hostControlTable specifies parameters for the monitoring operations, and a table called the hostTimeTable records the time a host was discovered on the network.

- **HostTopN**—This group is used to rank hosts by a statistical value, such as the number of errors generated or "top talkers." The TopNControlTable contains the control parameters for this group while the hostTopNTable keeps track of the data.

- **Matrix**—Data recorded by this group involves the exchange of frames between hosts on the network. Statistics are kept here for data traveling in both directions between hosts.

- **Filter**—This group specifies the types of packets that the RMON probe will capture, such as frame size.

- **Capture**—Although the Filter group specifies the parameters that are evaluated for capturing packets, this group is responsible for capturing packets based on those parameters.

- **Alarm**—This group is used to set up alarms for events that are described in the next group, the Event group. Here you can set the sampling intervals and thresholds that will trigger an alarm. This group reads statistics that have been gathered, and when they exceed the threshold an event is generated.

- **Event**—When a variable exceeds a threshold defined by an alarm, an event is generated. This group can generate an SNMP trap to notify a network management station or record the information in a log. The Event Table is used to define the notification action that will be taken for an event while the Log Table is used to record information.

As this list shows, RMON provides a great deal of functionality to SNMP. It allows for the collection of statistical data from all levels of the OSI reference model, including applications at the top in RMON2.

Because ethernet and token-ring networks operate in a fundamentally different way, additional groups are defined in RFC 1513 that are specific to token-ring networks:

- **Token Ring Statistics**—A group to store information about the behavior of the ring, from traffic volume to the number of beacons occurring, ring purges, and other information specific to token ring.

- **Token Ring History**—Similar to the History group used for ethernet, this group keeps track of events on a historical basis.

- **Token Ring Station**—Detailed information about each station on the ring can be found here.

- **Station Order**—The physical order of stations in the ring can be determined by information stored in this group.

- **Station Config**—Configuration information for stations is stored here.
- **Source Routing**—Monitors information about token-ring source routing for inter-ring traffic.

Alarms and Events

RMON agents can be programmed to take actions when specific things happen on the network. The Alarms and Events group provide an important intelligence function.

Configuring an alarm consists of specifying a variable to be watched, the sampling interval, and the event that will be performed when a threshold is crossed. The threshold can be a rising or a falling threshold, or both. For example, an alarm can be set to notify you when something begins to go awry, and to tell you when the situation gets better.

An event that is generated by an alarm can be configured to send an SNMP trap message to one or more management consoles, and store the event in the Log Table. The management station can then take the actions it deems necessary, including retrieving information from the Log Table.

Establish a Baseline

When making decisions on how to set up alarms and the events they generate, you should consider how the network functions normally. First monitor the network using RMON agents over a long period of time, noting when variations in traffic or errors occur. Make note of any fluctuations that regularly occur for specific dates or for a particular time of day.

Different network segments might require different sampling intervals and thresholds. For example, a local LAN segment might be subject to wide variations depending on only a small number of users, while a major backbone might fluctuate much less as traffic from many segments is blended together. When deciding on a sampling period, it's best to use a shorter interval for a segment that experiences frequent fluctuations and a longer interval for a segment that behaves in a more stable manner.

Response to alarms can be in the form of immediate corrective action, as in the case of a defective device, or a long-term solution such as additional capacity or equipment. Regularly review the baseline values you set and change them as network usage or topology changes. If alarms and events are not configured to reflect activity that is of a genuine concern, network operators might begin to ignore them, much like what happened to the boy who "cried wolf."

Troubleshooting Small Office and Home Office (SOHO) Networks

SOME OF THE MAIN TOPICS IN THIS CHAPTER ARE

Power Troubles

Computer Configuration Issues

Component Problems—You Can't Get There From Here

Secure Those Cables!

Firewall Problems

Keep Your Network Healthy

Wireless Networking Problems

When All Else Fails

In the past year or two, the concept of networking computers has jumped out of the business/corporate environment to include the home. Although inexpensive hubs and other networking gear that enable you to interconnect computers at home have been available for several years, they usually were used to allow more than one computer to connect to the Internet for Web surfing. With the deployment of broadband technologies, such as cable and DSL (digital subscriber line) modems, the bandwidth finally is available to make connecting a home office to the Internet a practical solution. Additionally, the number of telecommuters—employees who work from home—has been on the rise, and many households now have more than one computer or printer. Another factor that has contributed to using the Internet as a means of communicating with a business network is the increasing use of virtual private networking (VPN) technologies, which are discussed in Chapter 41. By creating a secure communications path through the Internet, VPNs help reduce the cost of telecommuting, such as long-distance charges. And Windows XP, 2000, and NT 4.0 all provide VPN client solutions in the operating system, so the VPN option is not an extra expense to bear.

Tip

Keep your home office network separate from the computers that your kids use. It's *never* a good idea to mix business with pleasure. First, you can't watch your children all the time to be sure that they don't download a program that contains a virus. Second, you can't be sure they don't change the computer's configuration after reading instructions for a new game or other application. Third, don't be a kid yourself and think you can play games or download just any files from the Internet you want on your business computer. Keep your business and your play computers separate! If this isn't possible, at least use a version of Windows (such as Windows NT/2000/XP) that allows you to create separate usernames for each person. Even then, set aside a separate computer for fun and games and leave the rest for business.

SOHO networks usually are composed of only a few computers or other networked devices, so troubleshooting problems on this kind of network is a lot easier than trying to track down problems in a large network. Most of the hardware components are plug and play, and even software configuration is a lot simpler than it was a few years ago. No matter what kind of networked devices you have in your SOHO environment, however, invariably, a time will come when a document won't print, a computer can't connect to a resource on another one, and you'll need to spend some time troubleshooting the problem.

In this chapter, we'll look at some common problems you might encounter and methods you can use to troubleshoot them.

Power Troubles

As basic a question as this might seem, it should be your starting point when you have a device that is not functioning correctly. For example, you might get up one morning and find that although your computer is working just fine, nothing prints. You check the printer and find that it's turned on and has paper loaded; you just can't figure out what the problem might be. Check your hub or switch. Has someone accidentally unplugged the AC adapter that powers the device? Most hubs have a power LED that indicates when the unit is powered up. If you have a power strip, check that, too. It's easy, especially in a small office where you don't route cables through the wall, for something as simple as an unplugged device to cause problems. Of course, look to see that no one has switched the power strip to the off position.

You can check a few other things if you suspect a power problem. Many cheap power strips you buy at discount stores don't include surge protection. If you were smart and bought one that did, be sure the fuse or other mechanism used by the power strip to block a large current surge from passing through hasn't been triggered. Some devices actually use a nonreplaceable fuse that literally melts down when a large surge comes through. If this is the case, you'll have to replace it. Some have a simple in-out button that pops out. If you have this kind of surge protector, push the button in to see whether power starts to flow again.

If you were even smarter, you probably bought a small uninterruptible power supply (UPS) and have your power strips or computers plugged into the UPS. Look for any fault lights on the UPS to determine whether it has gone offline due to a power surge or other malfunction.

Finally, if you are having power problems with all the computers on your network, check the fuse box or power panel in your home or office to be sure the fuse or circuit breaker at that point hasn't disconnected the power.

Computer Configuration Issues

If you use a broadband connection to the Internet, you'll probably have a switch/router appliance connecting your small LAN to the cable or DSL modem. These inexpensive devices allow your LAN to share a single Internet connection (that is, a single IP address) on the Internet, while providing for separate addresses for each computer on the LAN.

DHCP (the Dynamic Host Configuration Protocol, discussed in Chapter 23, "BOOTP and the Dynamic Host Configuration Protocol (DHCP)") allows the router/switch to automatically configure your computer with the network addressing information it needs when it boots up. When you add a new computer to the LAN, you need to be sure that it's configured to use DHCP. Otherwise, if you've configured a static address on the computer, you need to be sure that

- The address is compatible with the addresses of other computers on your network.
- The address is not already in use by another computer on the network.

Tip

Although you might consider yourself a network guru just because you have a network at home, don't try to step on your own toes. That is, don't assign static IP addresses to the computers in your network if you have a broadband connection and are using a router/switch appliance that supports DHCP. After you start messing around with configuring IP addressing information that the router/switch can automatically do for you, you're just asking for trouble. Use DHCP if it's available.

You can check your computer configuration easily. For Windows 2000, for example, follow these steps to configure your computer to use DHCP:

1. Click Start, Settings, Network, Dial-up Connections.
2. Right-click Local Area Network and select Properties from the menu that appears.
3. Scroll down in the Components section of the properties sheet shown in Figure 45.1, highlight Internet Protocol (TCP/IP), and click the Properties button.
4. The Internet Protocol (TCP/IP) Properties sheet pops up, as shown in Figure 45.2. If you are using DHCP, be sure the Obtain an IP Address Automatically option is selected. Unless your Internet provider has told you otherwise, the Obtain DNS Server Address Automatically option should also be selected.
5. If you configured your computers with static addresses, select Use the Following IP Address, and the IP Address, Subnet Mask, and Default Gateway fields should contain the appropriate values.

Figure 45.1   Select the Internet Protocol to troubleshoot network address issues.

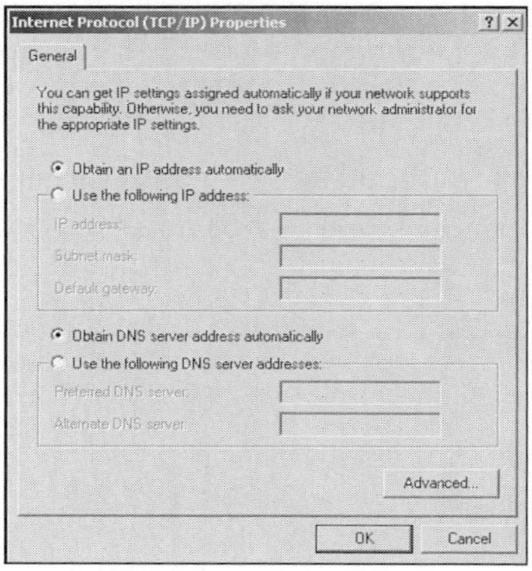

Figure 45.2   Be sure you have the correct IP configuration information filled in for this dialog box.

In the case of a broadband connection to the Internet, the switch/router will have two addresses: one that it uses on the Internet, and one that it uses on your LAN. The address it uses on your LAN should be used for the default gateway address. If you've configured a static IP address, make sure that the Subnet Mask field is appropriate for the address class you are using. (Subnet masks are covered in detail in Chapter 20, "Overview of the TCP/IP Protocol Suite.")

6. If all looks okay, check out what address your computer is actually using. Choose Start, Programs, Accessories, Command Prompt for Windows 2000, or Start, Programs, Command Prompt for earlier versions of Windows.

7. From the command prompt, issue the command IPCONFIG/ALL (for Windows NT and 2000) or WINIPCFG (for Windows 95/98). The response to this command will include a lot of information, so look for the IP address and the subnet mask. Try using the ping command (described in Chapter 22, "Troubleshooting Tools for TCP/IP Networks") from another computer to determine whether it can bounce packets off this address. If not, you probably have unplugged the computer from the network (either at the network card end or at the switch/router or hub).

Another possible cause of the problem is that you are using an address that is not in the same network or subnet as the other computers. It doesn't matter if all the cables are connected to the hub and each computer's network card if you have misconfigured IP addresses or subnet masks. For example, a computer with an IP address of 10.10.10.1 is not going to talk to a computer with an address of 140.176.222.1, no matter how long you try. The network adapter card detects the data you try to send back and forth, but because the protocol stack knows it's destined for a different network, those packets are ignored and never passed up to the application level.

Figure 45.3 shows an example of using a switch/router to connect to the Internet through a cable or DSL modem.

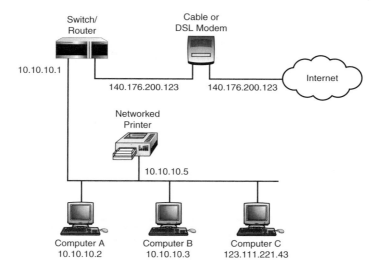

Figure 45.3   Connect to the Internet using a cable or DSL modem and a router/switch.

In this example, the Internet service provider (ISP) has assigned an IP address to your connection (140.176.200.123). Because you have more than one computer, you went to the local computer store and bought a small switch/router designed to work with broadband connections. Note that the switch/router is plugged into the broadband modem using one port, and plugged into your LAN using another port. To keep track of both connections, the switch/router uses a different address on the port that connects to your LAN.

In this example, the IP address is 10.10.10.1. When computer A (10.10.10.2) on your network wants to send or receive data to or from the Internet, it knows that the IP address of the Internet server is different from the LAN address (the 10.10.10.0 address space); so, it knows that it must send the data packet to the default gateway, which is the switch/router (10.10.10.1).

When the switch/router receives the data packet, it substitutes its own valid Internet address (140.176.200.123) in the packet header and sends it to the Internet through the broadband modem. When a response is received back from the Internet connection, the switch/router removes the 140.176.200.123 address from the packet header and puts Computer A's address (10.10.10.2) in the header so that it can be delivered to Computer A.

The important thing to keep in mind here is that addresses used inside the network are not valid on the Internet; the switch/router must use sleight of hand to act as a "man in the middle" for you so that, although you have multiple computers on your LAN, the switch/router makes the cable or DSL modem think you have only one. The switch/router keeps track of which computer on the LAN sends out requests and makes sure that packets are routed back to the correct computer.

When Computer A wants to talk to Computer B, it compares the address of Computer B (10.10.10.3) with its own address. Because it falls in the same network address space, it doesn't send the packet to the default gateway. Instead, it just broadcasts a packet on the LAN knowing that Computer B will see the packet and pick it up.

So far, everything is working as it's supposed to. However, let's suppose you just brought a computer from work to your home office (Computer C) and plugged it into your network. At work, the computer had been configured with a static address of 123.111.221.43. When you try to send or receive data from Computer C nothing happens because of the following:

- Computer C has an IP address that does not match the addresses on the LAN, so the other computers just ignore the packets that Computer C sends out.

- Computer C was configured at work to use a different default gateway address, so it can't even get a packet to go through the router/switch.

The point is that if your switch/router allows for DHCP and you set up each computer to use DHCP, things should work just as you expect. If you try to mix and match computers with different addresses, you're going to have trouble.

If you haven't already, read Chapter 20 to get an overview of the TCP/IP suite. Even if you are not a network-oriented person, that chapter helps you grasp some of the basic ideas involved in IP addresses, which will be useful when you start troubleshooting computer network problems.

Note

Broadband services come in all sizes and shapes. Just check out Chapter 19, "Dedicated Connections." If your service provider is using DSL, you might have to connect a small device to your telephone outlet before you can plug in a telephone. This device prevents telephone interference from causing problems with the frequencies used on the copper wire by the DSL service. Not all DSL services require this sort of device. If your service does, when you buy a new phone for a different room, be sure you obtain another of these devices. Don't just plug in the phone and expect all to be well. A ringing phone or a phone off the hook can cause enough interference to make the DSL connection sporadic or nonfunctional for this kind of connection.

Component Problems—You Can't Get There From Here

Just as in a large corporate network, you might have a problem with one or more components that make up the network. Network cards go bad, as do hubs and switches (and even individual ports on a hub or switch). Always keep handy the minimal documentation that comes with your computer(s), network card, hub, switch, router and other devices so that you'll know what the LEDs mean when you start troubleshooting.

For example, most network adapters have two LEDs that you can examine. One is called the link LED and the other is used to indicate activity on the network. If both of these LEDs are off, you might have a bad network card. Before you make that assumption, however, try moving the cable that plugs the card into the hub or switch/router to a different port and see whether that makes a difference. Check the LEDs on the hub or switch/router to determine whether they have link or activity LEDs. Above all, read the documentation to understand what the LEDs mean for your specific product.

Another thing to think about is that many small hubs or switches have an "uplink" port that allows you to connect the device to another one when you want to expand your small LAN. The pinout for this port is not the same as it is for the other ports. The transmit and receive pins are swapped. If you need to plug a computer into an uplink port, you can usually do so, but there will probably be a small button or switch you need to use to change it from an uplink port to a standard port.

Secure Those Cables!

A common problem with small offices or home offices is that you are not using a structured wiring plan. That is, you just string cables from here to there and plug things in. If you have a twisted-pair network cable lying on the floor near your desk, use tie-wraps, scotch tape, or anything else that you can to make sure that the cable doesn't just lie on the floor where you can roll over it with a chair. Even stepping on a twisted-pair network cable can be enough to cause it to have problems carrying the network signal. Secure those cables so they aren't ever mangled by accident.

Note

A friend of mine had a pet rabbit at home that was occasionally let out of the cage. Rabbits, in case you don't know, like to chew on just about anything (my friend no longer has the rabbit). Be sure to keep your network cables safe, even from your pets!

If you suspect a problem with the cable, trace it from the network card back to the hub or switch/router to be sure that it hasn't been damaged. Never try to "stretch" a cable or pull too hard on it when you are moving things about. This too can damage the cable and cause it to generate so many errors that the network becomes unavailable to the attached computer.

Firewall Problems

If you have installed a router/switch device between your network and a broadband Internet connection, be sure that you read the manual thoroughly and understand how it should be configured. Many come with default settings, but you need to fill in some information, such as the address of the broadband link, if your service provider gives you a static address. In most cases, the provider will be using DHCP also, so you won't have to make any changes. If you do have to make changes, write them down and keep the information handy for later troubleshooting efforts.

Earlier in this chapter, you read that it's not a good idea to mix computers that you use for play with those you use for business on the same network. If you do, you are just asking for trouble. If you play Internet games—those that allow you to interact with other users playing the same game on the Internet—you might be instructed to change the port settings on a small switch/router that also functions as a firewall. If you start playing around with opening, disabling, or forwarding ports, keep track of the changes you make. If something stops working after you've made a change, undo the modification and see whether the changes you've made have caused the problem. Remember that the firewall capabilities of a small switch/router are minimal, and are designed to protect you from simple attacks from the Internet. It might be that the default settings are very stringent and if you end up making changes that relax the firewall settings, you might also be opening a door that can allow bad things into your small LAN. For more information about how firewalls work and the features that are important, see Chapter 40, "Firewalls."

Keep Your Network Healthy

Another good reason to keep your business computers separate from your business LAN is that you don't want to be surfing the Web, find a neat program, and download a virus or other bad program that will start to eat up things in your network. This is yet another reason why your kids shouldn't be using your business computer to access the Internet. Buy them their own computer and their own Internet connection!

And, of course, because business is business, back up your files on a regular basis. Above all, it's worth the cost to buy a good antivirus software package and keep it updated. The cost is a tax deduction and it will save you a lot of grief if something bad does get loose in your network.

Play games on your play computers. Do business on your business computers.

Wireless Networking Problems

The newest, latest, and maybe greatest thing to happen to SOHO networking environments is to remove the cables altogether. It's now quite inexpensive to buy a small wireless access point (AP) and install wireless network cards in the computers in your small or home office. This allows you, for example, to use a laptop and take it from the living room to the kitchen to the basement, or wherever you feel most comfortable working. Heck, if it's a nice day outside, you might as well take the laptop out to the deck in the back yard, work from there, and get a tan at the same time! For more information on wireless networking solutions, see Chapters 14, 15, and 16.

You should keep a few things in mind when using wireless networking, however. Both in a small office and at home, you're likely to have a microwave oven sitting around somewhere. Although this is usually not a problem, it is possible for a microwave oven to interfere with the wireless transmissions of your network. This should be easy to troubleshoot. Just turn the darn thing on and determine whether the computers in your LAN can still talk to each other.

Another problem is that wireless networking is bounded by how far you can be from the AP. Although you might be able to communicate with the AP from the living room, the signal might not reach the basement, or it might not be strong enough to penetrate the brick wall that separates the backyard deck from the AP. Experiment to see whether moving the computer closer to the AP fixes the problem. If it does, you can always buy one or more APs, place them in strategic locations around the home or office, and use ordinary twisted-pair cables to join the APs to a switch/router that connects you to the Internet.

Note also that the new 2.4GHz cordless telephones that are becoming quite popular can interfere with wireless networks. This is a simple thing to troubleshoot. Just make a phone call and watch file transfers from one computer to another creep to a halt!

When All Else Fails

If you've tried everything in this chapter and you can send and receive data on your LAN, but not to or from the Internet, there is an important tool that can help solve this problem. Every office (and most every home) has this tool: the telephone. Pick it up, call your ISP, and find out whether the problem is on its end. Simply dial the ISP's customer no-service line and be persistent until you can get through to someone who is knowledgeable about the technology and get the problem fixed!

When dealing with customer no-service lines, never take "no" for an answer. Never take "it's not our problem" for an answer. If it was working and now it's not, and you've checked everything on your end, then your ISP should be able to at least troubleshoot the problem from its end. If the problem can't be solved on the phone, request that the ISP send someone out to prove to you that the cable or DSL modem is working as it should. The problem today is that ISPs who provide broadband access to the Internet are growing so fast that it's hard to find qualified technical personnel to troubleshoot the customer problems that happen. It's easier to make you struggle through level after level of telephone menus and then let you talk to some bozo that just screens calls and looks up things in a database and spits out a canned answer. Be sure you get through to someone who knows his stuff and get the problem fixed!

Upgrading Hardware

SOME OF THE MAIN TOPICS FOR THIS PART ARE

Upgrading ARCnet to Ethernet or Token Ring

Upgrading from Token-Ring to Ethernet

Upgrading a 10BASE-2 Network to 10BASE-T and Beyond

Upgrading from 10BASE-T to Fast Ethernet or Gigabit Ethernet

Upgrading from Bridges to Routers and Switches

Adding Wireless Networking to a LAN

PART VIII

Upgrading ARCnet to Ethernet or Token Ring

SOME OF THE MAIN TOPICS IN THIS CHAPTER ARE

ARCnet Overview

Upgrading to Ethernet or Token Ring

Of the networking technologies still widely used today, at least in certain circles, ARCnet is the oldest. It was created at Datapoint Corporation in the 1970s and is a token-passing system similar in some ways to token ring. For small networks, ARCnet is a reliable technology that is easy to configure. However, also like token ring, only a small number of manufacturers produce ARCnet equipment when compared to ethernet. Along with its slow network speed (2.5Mbs), this makes it a prime candidate for an upgrade to newer technology.

Note that there are places where ARCnet is still a viable solution. It is still widely used in factory environments where the network needs to provide a controlled, deterministic access to the network for all devices. In industrial automation scenarios, this is almost a requirement. Timing can be a very important issue when dealing with modern machine tools and industrial robots. In that case, if ARCnet is not holding its own, you can find other networking solutions, such as token ring, which also provide a deterministic access method to the network. If you are running ARCnet in an old (and I mean old!) office environment, then it's time you came into the twenty-first century and upgraded to ethernet!

ARCnet Overview

Because it is a token-passing system, ARCnet is a deterministic network technology that is useful in situations where a predictable throughput is required. Limitations of ARCnet include the fact that it operates at a rate of 2.5Mbps and can be used to create a LAN of up to only 255 computers. This might have once been an acceptable number of nodes for a factory floor setting, but in large automated factories of today, this is a small number indeed. Although there are methods that can be used to bridge ARCnet LANs together, other solutions can prove cheaper. Another benefit of upgrading from ARCnet to either ethernet or token ring is the increased management tools you'll have at your disposal to monitor and troubleshoot network performance and problems.

◀◀ For a detailed discussion of how ARCnet works, including the network frame and message types used, see Chapter 11, "Heard Anything About ARCnet Lately?"

Upgrading to Ethernet or Token Ring

You probably can safely assume that any conversion from ARCnet is going to require replacing network adapter cards, hubs and, most likely, network cables—in other words, just about everything but the workstations and servers. You'll have to be sure that any specialized devices, such as industrial machinery that uses a network connection, can also be used with a newer technology. It might be a simple matter of swapping out a component card like you do with a PC, or it might involve upgrading firmware or even the replacement of some machinery. These costs must be taken into consideration when you are creating a budget to justify the cost of the upgrade.

If you have used Category 3 or better cables, you might be able to reuse the cables, but you will need to modify the connectors to use the appropriate cable pairs and pin-out specifications for 10BaseT. Ethernet does not support daisy-chaining using twisted-pair wiring, however, so if you have an existing ARCnet LAN that is composed of multiple segments of this sort, you will probably have to purchase new cabling for an upgrade. If you currently use hubs, you might get by with rewiring the connectors and replacing the hub with an ethernet hub or switch. However, because you're going through an upgrade from such an old technology, now might be the time to consider running new Category 5 (or better) cables. This is especially true if you are installing Fast Ethernet and expect to upgrade this to Gigabit Ethernet in the future.

If you are replacing ARCnet with token-ring equipment, you'll also probably have to use new network wiring. The distances that token-ring networks cover vary a little from one vendor's products to another. They also are more expensive, for the most part, than ethernet components. However, like ARCnet, token ring networks can provide a deterministic, maximum access time for nodes on the network. If timing is critical in your environment, then token ring might be a better upgrade path than ethernet.

Although pulling new wiring (both ethernet cabling or token ring cabling) is a labor-intensive task, if you opt to install a good new high-grade cable now, it's an investment that will last for many years.

ARCnet usually is used to create small LANs. A few manufacturers sold bridges that could be used to connect the 255-node LANs into larger configurations. The majority of ARCnet LANs operate at the standard 2.5Mbps rate. Other versions, such as ARCnet Plus, can be used at up to 20Mbps. To decide which ethernet technology you want to use, examine the current layout and identify important nodes and the bandwidth you think they will need. Try to locate bottlenecks that occur in the current topology, if any.

Questions to ask yourself:

- Which servers do the majority of nodes in the LAN use?
- Which servers get the heaviest use in terms of network bandwidth? Would you benefit from Fast Ethernet or Gigabit Ethernet switching for these servers?
- Can any groups of users and servers be segmented? Are there any groups of users that should be isolated behind a firewall for security purposes?
- If this upgrade is the result of merging with another network, what kind of interconnection will be made? Which users on each network will be allowed access on the other network?

ARCnet provides a physical LAN that uses a token to allow access to the network medium. Because no prioritization is built into the protocols used, every node on the LAN must process each packet that is sent out on the wire. Conversion to a simple ethernet broadcast domain seems to be a simple task. However, you'll need to look closely at the distances between hubs on the current LAN and those distances between workstations and these hubs.

Because ARCnet allows for up to 2,000 feet between active devices, you'll need to make decisions based on which kind of ethernet technology to which you're upgrading and whether or not it can span the distance you require. You can use Fast Ethernet or Gigabit Ethernet with fiber links to connect switches at larger distances than using coaxial cable or twisted-pair wiring. If your factory floor is small, you should have no trouble locating switches or hubs to service a large number of network nodes. In a large campus environment, you'll need to set up a router or two and segment your network into subnets. This cuts down not only on local segment network traffic, but also makes it easier to manage the network from an administrative point of view.

Laying Out the New Network

Ethernet offers a lot of different solutions to help build networks that range from 10Mbps to gigabit speeds. What you use depends on the current needs of the network, projected usage for at least three years, and the distances to be covered.

In a small network, such as an office setting, where there are from two to a few dozen computers, a simple solution is to replace the current ARCnet hubs with one or more ethernet hubs, run new cables to the workstations, and equip each workstation with a new ethernet network adapter card. This kind of a swap-out can be done easily over a weekend without causing downtime for network users.

When the LAN is larger, however, you might need to sit down and think about how users make use of network resources before you decide on a migration plan. For example, ARCnet enables you to place a workstation up to 2,000 feet from an active hub. Ethernet's 10BaseT allows a maximum distance of only 328 feet. If your network has multiple workstations that are using cables that extend the maximum distance allowed by ARCnet, then you will not be able to perform a simple swap-out and replace ARCnet hubs with Ethernet hubs. Instead, you will have to look at the geography of your building and decide on locations for hubs that can be used to stay within the 10BaseT limit of 328 feet. The end result is that you will probably use more hubs than you do on the present ARCnet network. Again, you can solve this problem with a mix-and-match solution by installing ethernet switches that connect to a fiber-based Fast or Gigabit Ethernet pipe, while allowing switch ports for 10Mbps and 100Mbps computers.

Figure 46.1 shows an ARCnet LAN that uses two active hubs and one passive hub. On the first active hub you can see that there are five workstations, all of which are placed the maximum distance from the hub, 2,000 feet. The passive hub, however, can be no farther from the active hub than 100 feet, and the workstations connected to it are also bound by this limit.

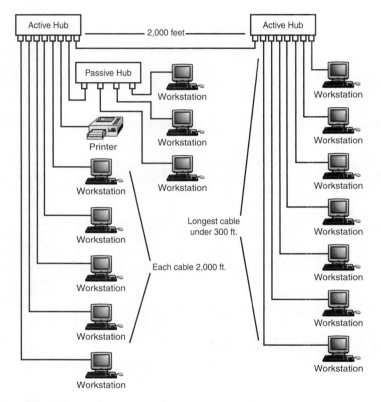

Figure 46.1   ARCnet allows the LAN to span distances of up to 2,000 feet between hubs.

The workstations in this layout are more than 300 feet from the second active hub, which is within the ethernet 10BaseT limit of 328 feet. It is a simple matter here to replace this second active hub with a 10BaseT hub or switch (or, to help upgrade-proof the network, a 10/100Mbps hub or switch), and then replace the cables that connect the workstations to the hub and the network adapters in each workstation.

The first active hub, however, poses a problem because it has workstations that are beyond the distance limitation 10BaseT technology imposes. Here, a solution might be to replace the active hub and the passive hub with a 10BaseT hub/switch, and connect the printer (and the workstations attached to the passive hub) to the new 10BaseT hub/switch. From here you can run an additional link to another hub or switch that is situated closer to the other workstations. This places the hub or switch in a location that allows it to reach the additional workstations without breaching the 328-foot limit (see Figure 46.2).

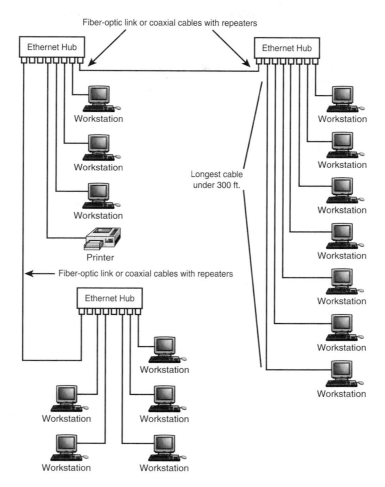

Figure 46.2 Use additional hubs to group workstations that are beyond the maximum allowable distance for 10BaseT.

To connect these three hubs you need to use a fiber optic link, or perhaps coaxial cable with repeaters to span the distance. When you are looking at hubs to purchase, be sure they have the correct ports that you need to connect both 10BaseT and coaxial or fiber. Twisted-pair cables, such as those used by 10Base-T and 100Base-T, typically use an RJ-45 jack, while fiber optic cables typically use an ST type connector. For connections to older cabling, such as Thinnet Ethernet (10Base-2), you'll most likely need a BNC connector. Be sure that the device you choose for a replacement supports the number and kind of ports needed for these connectors.

A cheap 5- or 10-port hub that you can purchase for under $100 will probably not be suitable for this kind of application.

The purpose of this example is to show that in addition to swapping out the networking equipment when you upgrade to ethernet, you must pay close attention to the differences between current ARCnet topology and that of the technology to which you are upgrading. Whether you plan to use bridges (repeaters), 100BaseT, or some other ethernet technology, pay close attention to the limits imposed and compare them with the current layout of user workstations and servers. You will probably find that additional hubs will be needed when the ARCnet network is stretched to its limit.

The same process is required for conversion to a token ring network. You'll need to get the specifications for the hardware (MSAUs, cabling, network cards, and so on) and lay out a topology that can accommodate the nodes on your current network.

Solving Performance Problems

Another consideration for the upgrade path is what kind of interconnecting devices you need to use. In a very small network, one or more 10/100Mbps hubs or switches will probably suffice and be an easy upgrade. ARCnet is not known for having a large bandwidth (2.5Mbs for the standard ARCnet), so if its speed sufficed before upgrading, it's unlikely that you will have to worry about bandwidth problems afterward. Even if the ARCnet bandwidth usage is becoming saturated (at about 65 percent of the total possible 2.5Mbps), a simple 10Mbps ethernet LAN handling the same amount of nodes will probably show some improvement.

Speed is another reason you might choose ethernet over token ring. Although there are some vendors that sell equipment that can be used to run token ring at very fast speeds, the standards on this technology have pretty much stalled in the past few years, so you shouldn't expect to see a lot of vendors devoting research dollars to come up with faster products. Instead, if performance is a problem, then a well-planned network of Fast or Gigabit Ethernet to connect switches with ports dedicated to important network nodes might prove a more viable solution than token ring.

As always, though, you should be looking to the future. For example, it is typical that when upgrading an old LAN you will be upgrading not just the physical infrastructure, but also the end-user applications that are used on the network. Although a simple word processing program that was marketed 10 years ago might not require a lot of network bandwidth to run from a server, the needs of newer versions might seem gigantic in comparison. If end-user workstations are also being replaced, you might find it easier to install a copy of the application on each workstation, assuming it has much more hard disk storage space than its predecessor. If you plan to continue serving applications from an application server, you might find it necessary to use ethernet switches and possibly a higher bandwidth technology than 10Mbs ethernet.

The same goes for factory automation devices, which are a lot more complex today than 20 years ago. Faster processors and more specific tasks mean that network communications on the factory floor is a field that will be growing and evolving rapidly during the next few years.

Connecting servers that need a large amount of bandwidth to a switch, in full-duplex mode, can help in this situation. Whether you need to use a switch port or hub for each user workstation depends on the current user work habits along with a projection of network use you expect after you upgrade applications.

Upgrading from Token Ring to Ethernet

CHAPTER 47

Token-ring networks have been around for about the same length of time as ethernet. These two network technologies both accomplish the same thing, in that they allow devices on the network to exchange data in an orderly fashion. The methods they employ to accomplish this task, however, are fundamentally different. Because of the different methods used to mediate access to the network, the hardware used for token-ring and ethernet networks is not generally interchangeable. That is, you cannot simply pick up a workstation that is configured on an ethernet network and move it to a token-ring network without some hardware changes.

When justifying the cost of upgrading a token-ring network to ethernet, consider the following:

- Ethernet devices, from network cards to switches, along with most other equipment, are much cheaper than equivalent token-ring items. The large marketplace of ethernet vendors makes it easy to get quality devices that are targeted to specific markets.

- Ethernet has been an ongoing project of the IEEE 802.3 Committee. Whereas most token-ring equipment still runs at 4–16Mbps, ethernet can span from 10Mbps or 100Mbps on the desktop, to gigabit (and soon to be 10 gigabit ethernet) in larger networks.

- Because it is so pervasive in the world today, ethernet gives rise to better support options—from vendor support to the pool of technicians that you hire to manage your network.

In the next section we'll examine some of these issues further.

Why Ethernet?

When planning a major network upgrade on an installed token-ring network, why would ethernet ever enter into the planning process? Bridges and routers that work just fine with token ring allow you to create large LANs and WANs, so what would be the reasons that an administrator might use to justify making a fundamental shift in technology to an ethernet-based network?

Although each technology has its proponents, installations of ethernet far outnumber those of token ring. The volume of ethernet sites brings with it a larger number of vendors who manufacture equipment. This volume usually results in lower prices and more innovative products. If you are planning to add a few departmental LANs to a large network, then the cost of new equipment might not be that great when compared to replacing network adapters, and possibly the wiring infrastructure, for an entire network. But if you see in your immediate future a large increase in your network, it might pay to sit down and look hard at the figures to be sure you can justify the costs of staying with token-ring hardware.

Token-ring networks have been around for about 20 years. When the technology was first developed, PCs were not as an important a business tool as they are today. The main rationale for hooking a PC to a corporate network in the early days was to provide access to larger computer systems, such as mainframe and minicomputer systems. In that kind of scenario most of the data flow was within a small workgroup of computers with only a small percentage of network traffic from PCs traveling over a backbone to a larger wide-area network. In today's client/server atmosphere, where intensive traffic loads can be generated by applications such as multimedia or Web servers, this might not be the case. Some vendors produce token-ring equipment that operates at speeds faster than the 4Mbps and 16Mbps standard speeds, however, so this might not be the case in your network.

Some might argue that token ring has built-in mechanisms for handling heavy traffic loads because its basic frame structure includes bits set aside for prioritization. However, in reality not many manufacturers have implemented priority-based schemes using these bits. Although there have been some technological improvements in token ring over the years, they are a far cry from the changes that have been made to ethernet standards. For example, the IEEE 802.1p standard that was ratified recently provides for a filtering process that allows multicast traffic to be forwarded only to end nodes on the network that make the request. The IEEE 802.1p Class of Service specification allows for eight priority levels of network traffic, and when this standard is widely implemented (which it most likely will be in a very short time), it will be possible to provide a high-level of performance for applications such as voice-over IP and other applications that generate large volumes of network traffic.

To sum it up, some of the factors you might want to consider when deciding on a major upgrade to a token-ring network include

- The cost of the hardware portion, both now and in the future. Can you be sure that there will be a sufficient number of vendors producing token-ring devices in the future to keep prices in a reasonable range? Will there be enough vendors involved to promote the development of new and innovative additions to the technology?

- Will you be able to continue to find technicians that are proficient in token-ring technology or will you find yourself spending additional funds training new employees?

- Will you be forced to find some kind of interoperability solution in the near future if your business merges with another that already has a large installed base of ethernet equipment?

Phasing Ethernet into the Token-Ring Network

If you've decided that you are going to have to embrace the ethernet network in your token-ring shop, the next step is to decide on a plan for making the change. The most disruptive method would be to simply go ahead full force and swap out all the hardware at one time and hope for the best. Depending on your circumstances, that might be the only choice you have. The issue that will help you make this decision is whether you can segment your network into functional components where you can identify which end stations need to communicate with which stations. Why? Because of the fundamental differences between ethernet and token ring, it can be very difficult in many cases to make the two work together.

There are translational bridges and other internetworking devices that you can use to connect token-ring LANs to an ethernet LAN or a backbone joining the two. Using a backbone to provide a high-speed transport to both kinds of networks is not terribly complicated. ATM, for example, can be used to carry both kinds of traffic. But without some kind of translation capability to account for the difference in the frame formats, a network of this sort can be limited to allowing token-ring stations to talk only to token-ring stations, and ethernet nodes to talk only to ethernet nodes.

Differences that Make Translation Difficult

There are several reasons why it is not an easy task to make a perfect translation device that can allow token ring and ethernet nodes to communicate with each other. These are

- Canonical versus non-canonical bit ordering
- Embedded MAC addresses
- Frame size
- Notification of delivery (token ring status bits)
- Token ring routing (RIF) information

Bits and Frames

The most basic difference that becomes apparent between these two networking technologies lies at the beginning of the network transport process: They interpret the ordering of bits for addressing purposes in the opposite direction. That is, while they both use a 6-byte MAC address to uniquely identify a network adapter on a LAN, ethernet considers the first bit in the serial stream to be the low-order bit (the canonical method) while token ring considers the first bit to be the high-order bit (the non-canonical method).

This problem can be easily addressed with a hardware device, such as a bridge or router, that reorders the addressing bits depending on what kind of network is attached to the port on which the frame is to be sent. However, there are cases, such as in the Address Resolution Protocol (ARP) where MAC addresses ride in portions of a frame in addition to the addressing fields. Designing a hardware device that can determine all the cases where this is possible is a daunting task. And, when such an attempt is made, latency factors enter the picture because the device is forced to read much more of the frame than just the header fields that contain the source and destination fields.

Frame size is another important factor. Ethernet networks use a frame size that can be up to approximately 1,500 bytes while token ring uses a frame size that can be a lot higher, possibly up to 17.8KB on a 16Mbps token-ring LAN. If the higher-level protocol that is being transported on the LAN does not allow for fragmenting packets (as TCP/IP does), then it is necessary to force the entire network to use the lowest common denominator of ethernet's 1,500 byte frame.

Notification of Delivery

Token ring uses three bits in its frame to notify the sender of what happened to the frame after it was sent out onto the ring. The Address Recognized bit is set when a station recognizes that it is the intended destination of the frame. The Frame Copied bit is set if the destination station can copy the frame from the wire into an internal buffer. The Error bit is used to indicate that some kind of error was encountered in the frame somewhere along its travels. Using the information these status bits signal, the sending station can determine whether it needs to retransmit the frame.

Ethernet doesn't worry about such things. It provides a "best effort" delivery system and depends on the higher-level protocol whose traffic it is transporting to decide whether the frame was able to successfully navigate the network to its destination.

When designing a translational device, how are these bits to be handled when a token-ring frame is sent out onto an ethernet network where there are no built-in mechanisms for storing this kind of information? There are differences in how these bits are handled from vendor to vendor, and you must be aware of how their devices handle this situation. For example, some simply set the Frame Copied bit when the frame is received at the device, but not the Address Recognized bit, while others set both bits before sending the frame back onto the ring. When the frame makes its way back to the sending station, how is it to interpret these? Because the translational device is not the final destination of the frame, the higher-level protocol must be able to cope with this.

Routing Information

Token ring uses source-routing bridges (SRB) while ethernet uses transparent bridges. In the source-routing algorithm, an "explorer" frame is sent out through the network to discover a path to the destination computer. When more than one path exists in the network, the frame is duplicated and is able to travel more than one path. As the explorer frame travels from bridge to bridge to its destination, it compiles a list of addressing information that details the route it has taken. This information is stored in the Routing Information Field (RIF). When it reaches its destination it can use this routing information to travel back to the sending station, which can then decide from the multiple frames that come back to it which route it wants to use to communicate with the destination station.

There is simply no concept like this in an ethernet network. Transparent bridges don't perform this "routing" function like SRB devices do. They simply keep a table of MAC addresses as they learn which segment a device is on and try to send frames out only on the port on which the destination MAC address is known to exist.

A translational device can sometimes be made to work by caching the information in the RIF before it translates the packet from token-ring format to ethernet format. When a frame with a unicast address returns, the translation bridge can check its cache and reconstruct the token-ring frame from the data stored there before outputting it on the token-ring network.

However you look at it, trying to create a gateway between these two fundamentally different kinds of networks is not an easy task. If you need to gradually phase ethernet equipment into an existing token-ring network, you might have to deal with the incompatibilities and incur the expense of translational devices that might or might not solve all the problems. If you can localize your users and the servers that they use into units that can be swapped out all at once, then the process becomes much easier to implement.

Replacing All Token-Ring Equipment

In a small LAN, the prospect of having to swap out all of the token-ring hardware and replace it with ethernet equipment might be a feasible idea. If you carefully plan the implementation around users' work schedules you can minimize disruptions on the network. Before beginning, you should inventory the existing equipment to see what must be replaced and what, if any of it, can be retained.

Hubs, Switches, and Routers

Some of the newer routers and switches that have come onto the market in the past few years have the capability to operate with either ethernet or token-ring networks. If you are contemplating a change-over in the near future, this should be a consideration when making any current purchases. Buying a more expensive device now, that you can use now and still use when you upgrade the network in the near future, can save you money in the long run.

If you have been using a gradually phased approach for your upgrade (that is, you are upgrading in small chunks), the router or switch that is currently operating as a translation device might easily be reconfigured to work just fine in an all-ethernet network. Read the documentation for each device to determine what steps need to be taken. If you cannot find the information readily available in the documentation that came with the equipment, check with the manufacturer. Many times a simple download of a new version of the device's firmware can solve this kind of problem.

Network Cabling and Connectors

Most new installations of network cabling are of the Category 5 (or better) twisted-pair type. This cable can support ordinary token-ring 4MB or 16MB networks as well as ethernet networks running at speeds from 10Mbs to 100Mbs with no problems. You will need to consult your network map to be sure that any existing cabling infrastructure for the LAN does not violate any of the distance or nodes-per-segment rules that apply to ethernet. If the existing cables have been installed for quite some time and are of a grade not equal to Category 5, you should probably replace them.

The connectors used for token ring and ethernet may be different on your network. Ethernet networks based on 10BaseT or 100BaseT typically use an RJ-45 connector. Although this kind of connector also can be used on a token-ring network, the wires used and the pins to which they are attached on each end will be different from the pinout used on ethernet networks. Changing these requires time for making the actual physical wire-to-pin changes. Additionally, even more time is needed for testing the cable so you can be sure the connectors have been properly installed and will function with a minimum of errors on the new network.

Network Adapter Cards

Token-ring and ethernet network adapter cards are basically different and are not compatible. Token-ring NICs usually cost much more than ethernet cards. One of the reasons is that token-ring NICs take on more responsibility for managing transmission of data on the local LAN than ethernet cards do. Remember that token-ring cards wait for a token before transmitting data. Ethernet cards can just start talking any time they sense that the network media is free. When making a change over it will be necessary to acquire a new card for each end-user workstation as well as for any servers on the network.

Upgrading a
10Base-2 Network to
10Base-T and Beyond

SOME OF THE MAIN TOPICS IN THIS CHAPTER ARE

Hardware and Software Factors to Consider

Connecting Networks That Use Different Cables or Topologies

Other Possibilities

Although coaxial cables are still widely used today as part of a network backbone, it is rare to find a network that still uses these cable types to connect desktop systems to a network. If you use 10Base-2 (thinnet) cables, you could create a network that is essentially a logical bus. That is, all computers on the network see every frame that is transmitted on the network. The actual topology of a 10Base-2 network could be implemented as a physical bus as well, using T-connectors to daisy chain the cable from one computer to another. Another network topology, similar to a start or hierarchical start topology, involves using multiport repeaters to join more than one cable segment, and using each cable segment for one or more computers. Either way, though, you end up with a logical bus because all nodes on the LAN can directly communicate with all other nodes on the same LAN.

Twisted-pair wiring (10Base-T) pretty much replaced this older technology many years ago and was, for a long time, the networking solution of choice. Newer developments of the past few years have increased the speed of twisted-pair networks so that 100Base-T and gigabit Ethernet solutions are now a better choice. If you are creating a network from scratch, it's best to start with the latest and greatest, if your budget allows. If you are upgrading, be sure to examine what the user needs will be when it comes to bandwidth, before committing yourself to any particular technology.

▶▶ For more information about network topologies and how the physical network should be laid out, see Chapter 2, "Network Design Strategies."

In this chapter we'll quickly look at some of the things to consider when planning to replace an older 10Base-2 network with more modern technology.

Hardware and Software Factors to Consider

Obviously, it's the hardware that you will have to replace when making this kind of upgrade. Network protocols, such as TCP/IP, don't care what the underlying physical network is made up of as long as it can get data segments from one place to another. You might still be using older software, however, and if so, you might want to consider upgrading that in addition to the hardware when you plan for this kind of upgrade. As discussed in other parts of this book, Novell's NetWare is slowly losing ground to Unix and Windows NT/2000, so if you are still using NetWare, with either the bindery or Novell Directory Services, you might want to consider the possibility of phasing it out in favor of another network operating system.

Other chapters in Part IX, "Migration and Integration," contain information about software upgrades and migrations. The rest of this chapter concentrates on the hardware components that need to be accommodated or replaced.

10Base-2 and 10Base-T have more differences than just the type of cables they use. Although both of them use the same messaging technique (CSMA/CD), their topologies are basically different: 10Base-2 uses a bus topology, while most modern 10Base-T (and 100Base-T) installations use a star, implemented by a switch instead of the traditional hub. The distances that can be covered by cable segments are also different. The network adapters transmit signals at different speeds. When preparing for an upgrade, check your network inventory to determine which parts of the hardware you will have to upgrade besides the cabling.

The major considerations that need to be researched when upgrading from 10Base-2 to a simple 10base-T network are

- **Network Cables**—The fundamental difference between 10Base-2 and 10Base-T is the move from coaxial cable to twisted-pair wiring.

- **Network Topology**—You will be going from a linear bus topology to a star topology. The distances covered by 10Base-T are shorter than those allowed using 10Base-2.

- **Network Adapters**—Older network adapters might have only a BNC connector on them. You will need cards that provide an RJ-45 jack for 10Base-T.

- **Connectors**—Instead of BNC connectors, your twisted-pair cabling uses RJ-45 connectors.

- **Hubs and Switches**—While the 10Base-2 network allows you to use multiport repeaters, no central wiring devices are actually required. In 10Base-T you need, as a minimum, a hub to act as a wiring concentrator. Although a lone hub might suffice for a small network with a limited number of users, you should really consider using switches instead.

▶▶ To learn more about how hubs and switches function, see Chapter 7, "Repeaters, Bridges, and Hubs" and Chapter 8, "Network Switches."

For example, if you are using a multiport repeater, then replacing it with a more functional hub or switch seems a natural thing to do. However, remember that the topology rules for 10Base-2 and 10Base-T networks specify different maximum cable segment lengths, so you might have to relocate wiring closets or make other accommodations if your current distances are too long:

- Maximum segment length for 10Base-2: 185 meters

- Maximum segment length for 10Base-T: 100 meters

- Maximum number of devices on a 10Base-2 segment: 30

- Maximum number of devices on a 10Base-T segment: 2 (but one of these is the hub, so effectively, just 1)

Chapter 12, "Ethernet," covers in more detail the different cabling distances you'll need to consider when planning to use a hub or switch for 10Base-T or 100Base-T networks (fast Ethernet).

Network Cables

Because 10Base-2 uses thinnet coaxial cabling, the first upgrade issue you must address is getting the appropriate network cabling.

This should be the simplest decision you have to make. Although it is quite possible to use Category 3 wiring to construct a 10Base-T network, about the only good reason I can think of would be that you already have the wiring in place and can use it with few modifications. Other than that, if you are going to install a 10Base-T network to replace a network based on coaxial cables, then you would be better served to go ahead and use Category 5. Why? Further down the road you might find yourself upgrading to Fast Ethernet or Gigabyte Ethernet. Both of these technologies require Category 5 cables or higher.

▶▶ For a comparison of the difference between Category 3 and Category 5 twisted-pair cables, see Chapter 5, "Wiring the Network—Cables and Other Components."

The amount of cable you need might work out to be a lot more than you used for the 10Base-2 network. Remember that a bus topology, thinnet (coaxial) networks like 10Base-2 use, can daisy chain one workstation to another using a linear bus. A 50-ohm terminator terminates each end of the bus. The total amount of cable needed is simply the sum of all the cables that are daisy chained together. When using a hub or switch, you can have two workstations sitting right next to each other, both having a 100-meter twisted-wire cable going back to the hub. Because of this, the total amount of cabling you'll need is generally a lot more than you did when you installed 10Base-2 technology.

If you instead use a multiport repeater on the existing network, and if only one computer is attached to each port, then you'll find that replacing the cables is a simple matter of stringing Category 5 (or greater) cables through the same route used by the current coaxial cables. Then all you need to do is replace the repeater with a hub or a switch. If you have segments on a multiport repeater that have more than one computer attached, you'll have to plug each computer into a separate port on the hub or switch. Another possibility is to place these computers on a separate hub or switch and connect it to the network backbone.

In Figure 48.1 you can see an example of an older thinnet network in which a single coaxial cable is strung from one workstation to the next throughout an office. The total distance covered by the cable is only 225 meters. In Figure 48.2 you can see the same set of workstations when connected by a central hub that resides in a wiring closet. The distances covered by the various cables here is 300 meters in length. This kind of layout can be found in a large building, such as a factory. Obviously, replacing this cable with a single hub to connect all workstations is not an option.

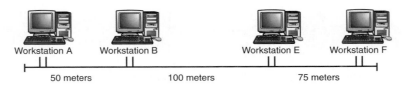

Figure 48.1   Replacing a single coaxial segment with one hub might not be feasible.

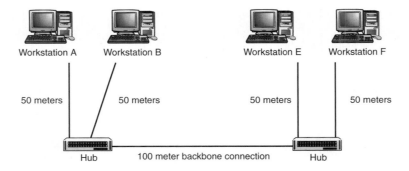

Figure 48.2   Multiple hubs can be used to replace a single segment when distance is a factor.

Because you must string cable from a central location to each workstation, you need to have a place you can use as a wiring closet to store the hub and any other interconnecting equipment used to join the LAN to a larger network. Again, if you were using a multiport repeater in your 10Base-2 network, then all you need to do after stringing the cables is to replace the multiport repeater with a hub or switch. Also keep in mind that if you are simply upgrading a small office LAN, you can use an inexpensive off-the-shelf hub from your local computer store and just place it out of the way somewhere convenient in the office.

Although thinnet cable is not an ideal choice for linking workstations to a network it can be economically used as a backbone, as shown in Figure 48.2, when speeds above 10Mbps are not required. If faster communications are necessary, you will have to think about using Fast Ethernet over copper wires or fiber-optic cables. In Chapter 49, "Upgrading from 10Base-T to Fast Ethernet or Gigabit Ethernet," you can find information about the cables and other equipment that are necessary if you make this choice.

Network Adapter Cards

If you had the foresight to purchase the kind of network adapter cards called combo cards, which have connectors compatible with both BNC connectors and RJ-45 connectors (see Figure 48.3), then this is one piece of hardware you will not necessarily have to replace. The minimum requirement for the NIC is that it have a receptacle to which you can plug in the RJ-45 jack to connect the adapter to a hub. If you plan to incorporate switches into the network and want servers to use full-duplex connections, however, you'll probably have to get a newer card for these computers (most older cards supported only 10Mbps and not 100Mbps).

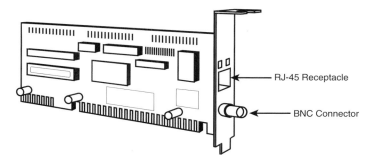

RJ-45 Receptacle

BNC Connector

Figure 48.3   A combo card contains connectors for both thinnet coaxial cables (BNC connectors) and a receptacle for an RJ-45 jack used with twisted-pair wiring.

If you are going to have to upgrade a large number of workstations to newer NICs, then think carefully about the future when you make this purchase. If your budget is limited and all bandwidth you will need for the next few years is 10Mbps, you can purchase adapter cards for $30. That amount usually drops even more if they are on sale or purchased in large quantities. The added expense for a card that supports features you do not need now, or in the near future, might not justify the price of getting more expensive equipment.

However, if you are concerned primarily with network performance you should look at Fast Ethernet (100Mbps) cards that cost only a little more. As mentioned earlier, you can use a switch to create a full-duplex connection to a high-end server in a 10Base-T network. If you have multiple servers that need to be connected in this manner, you should not skimp on the expense of a few network cards that will be important performance components in your network.

Similar to the combo cards that come with two different kinds of adapters, most cards being manufactured today have the capability to operate at either 10Mbps or 100Mbps, and many have an autosensing feature that allows them to detect the speed of the network to which they are attached. If you see in your near future that you will be continuing the upgrade from 10Base-2 to 10Base-T onto the much faster 100Base-T network, then plan ahead and buy the 10/100 cards now.

Network Cable Connectors

As already pointed out earlier in this chapter, a 10Base-2 network uses a different kind of connector than a 10Base-T network does. You should pay attention to the details when ordering connectors (if you plan to make cables yourself) or when ordering ready-made cables that have the connectors attached. When upgrading to twisted-pair wiring I have already suggested that you use Category 5 cabling (or greater) instead of a less capable variety, such as Category 3. This allows you to use the cabling later when you decide it is time to install 100Mbps segments on part or all of the network.

Connectors, like cables, can exhibit different performance characteristics depending on how they are manufactured. Be sure that the RJ-45 connectors you choose are compliant with the specifications for Category 5 cables. Inferior connectors can cause a lot of trouble later (such as noise or near-end cross-talk), causing you to spend a lot of time troubleshooting. When constructing your own cables, be sure that you follow the specifications when attaching the jacks to the cables. Many noisy cables are created simply because too much wire is left exposed at the end of the cable where the cable is attached to the connector.

◀◀   In Chapter 5, "Wiring the Network—Cables and Other Components," you will find more information about cables and connectors and the problems you can encounter when they are not manufactured correctly.

Bridges, Hubs, Repeaters, and Switches

To extend the length of a LAN based on 10Base-2 technology, the standard technique is to attach multiple segments with a bridge or a multiport repeater. A repeater works similar to a hub, simply making one large broadcast domain out of the various cable segments that are connected to it. A bridge connects two segments but is capable of learning MAC addresses and therefore reducing traffic by passing on frames to segments only if their destination is not on the local segment on which they originate.

◀◀   For more information on bridges and how they operate, see Chapter 7, "Repeaters, Bridges, and Hubs."

You can use bridges on a 10Base-T network for the same purposes you use them in 10Base-2. They can group like-users on local segments, reduce traffic on individual segments, and extend the length of the local area network. Bridges can perform other functions related to performance as well, such as discarding packets with errors and reducing noise. Newer layer 3 switches accomplish much of the same function, reducing traffic between segments and between specific ports on the switch. Since the previous edition of this book was published the price of switches has decreased dramatically. Because of this, and its superior performance capabilities on anything but a very small network, I would advise using a switch over a hub. Network applications are becoming more data-intensive than ever before as computers become faster and more memory is added. A switch creates a small collision domain (that is, just the switch and the computer attached to a switch port) and can drastically reduce network congestion.

◀◀   For more information on how switches work and how they can be used to improve performance in your network, see Chapter 8, "Network Switches."

Also, in anything but a small network you might need to use more than one hub to connect user workstations to the network. If you are planning ahead for a future migration to 100Mbps networking, you will find that a multitude of hubs and switches operate at both 10Mbps and 100Mbs. Look at the cost difference and decide whether making an investment in a 10/100Mbps device now will save you money in the future. When evaluating a hub or switch, find out if it comes with management software that is compliant with SNMP and RMON standards. Check to find out if each port can be set to a different speed and if it can, make sure you know whether it is autosensing or if you must manually set it to operate at one speed or the other.

If your existing network already uses a router to connect to a larger network, be sure that the hub or switch has a receptacle that can be used for the router connection. Most routers made today accept cables terminated with several different kinds of connectors, even 10Base-2, so this probably won't be a problem. However, you should check this as you do all aspects of the network when making an upgrade plan. Note also that the connection between the hub and a router might need to provide for a larger bandwidth than the connection from the hub or switch to the user's desktop. Although 10Mbps might be suitable for most end-user applications, when you aggregate this bandwidth and add up the amount of network traffic that will be needed on the entire network, you might want to consider a hub or switch that can use a faster connection—such as fiber-optic cables—when it connects to another hub or a router.

◄◄ For more information about using routers to join individual network subnets, see Chapter 10, "Routers," and Chapter 29, "Routing Protocols."

Connecting Networks That Use Different Cables or Topologies

Because hubs and switches, like routers, can be found with different kinds of ports that are used to link them (uplink ports), it is possible that you can incrementally upgrade your network, depending on such factors as the size of the broadcast domain and the number of users on each network segment. For example, you might want to replace one multiport repeater with a hub or switch in one department, while leaving another existing multiport repeater in place for a while.

If you do need to maintain backward compatibility by keeping a multiport repeater on the network for a while during the upgrade process, you can use a hub or switch that has a BNC port and connect the two using thinwire Ethernet cables. Or, you can connect each of these two devices to separate ports on a router, and create different subnets on your network.

◄◄ Subnets, and how to calculate subnet addresses and subnet masks, is covered in great detail in Chapter 12, "Ethernet." The functions performed by routers is discussed in Chapter 10, "Routers."

Other Possibilities

This chapter covered the basic components that you need to change when converting a network from 10Base-2 to 10Base-T. However, in addition to the cables, connectors, network adapters, and other devices, a change such as this one might warrant further research into the larger network to which you are connected. In many cases, the local LAN is in reality part of a much larger network. When you have resources that lie outside the local LAN that are frequently accessed, you might need to look at the big picture when making decisions about the local area network.

For example, do you need to replace the equipment that has been used to connect to the larger network? Are you currently using a bridge that can be replaced by a switch to improve performance? Do you have multiple small LANs that can now be merged into a single, larger LAN connected by multiple hubs or switches?

In several chapters that follow this one, you can examine the possibilities offered by incorporating other network devices, such as routers and switches, into your network. One further bit of advice: Read up on wireless networking. It's going to figure into your future during the next few years as users become more mobile and standards for wireless networking are further defined and adopted by the manufacturers to ensure that devices from one manufacturer will work with those from another.

Upgrading from 10BASE-T to Fast Ethernet or Gigabit Ethernet

SOME OF THE MAIN TOPICS IN THIS CHAPTER ARE

Use Gigabit Ethernet in the Network Backbone

Use Gigabit Ethernet for High-End Servers

Gigabit Ethernet Can Cover the Distance

Upgrading to Gigabit Ethernet

Making Future Plans

Chapter 48, "Upgrading a 10BASE-2 Network to 10BASE-T and Beyond," discussed upgrading an older legacy network from 10BASE-2 to 10BASE-T. Remember that 10BASE-T was a huge leap forward in ethernet technology because it was based on structured wiring standards and allowed for the concentration of wiring a network into telecommunication closets. Instead of snaking a coaxial cable through the different sections of your office building that needed to provide for network connections, 10BASE-T enables you to simply run a twisted-pair cable from a hub or switch to individual workstations. Using the 10BASE-2 daisy-chain method to connect multiple computers to coaxial segments using T-connectors had a distinct disadvantage. A single break in the cable (or the removal of a terminator from the end of the cable) could render all computers on that cable segment unable to participate in the network until the repair was completed. By using structured wiring techniques that are the norm today, it's a simple matter to add and remove workstations from a hub or switch by unplugging them.

Fast Ethernet is a step up from 10BASE-T. 100BASE-T is used to specify Fast Ethernet and, as the name implies, you not only get the advantages of structured wiring concepts, but you also get a *tenfold* increase in speed. Gigabit Ethernet, is yet another step up the ladder of networking speed, giving you still *another tenfold* increase in speed over Fast Ethernet.

Fast Ethernet and Gigabit Ethernet are covered in detail in Chapter 12, "Ethernet." Read that chapter if you plan to upgrade your network. You need to understand the concepts behind these new technologies and the limitations imposed by the network topology associated with each. In addition, you must be sure you don't waste too much money trying to deploy newer technology where it doesn't really give you any tangible benefits. In this chapter we'll take a quick look at some of the things you need to consider when planning an upgrade from 10BASE-T to these faster ethernet technologies.

Use Gigabit Ethernet in the Network Backbone

Today, Fast Ethernet probably is the most typical method used to connect workstations to a switch or hub. Yet, when Fast Ethernet was first introduced, it served mainly in the network backbone, connecting wiring concentration devices. As the cost of the technology fell, it became economically feasible to use Fast Ethernet to the desktop.

This is the same situation that is now ongoing with Gigabit Ethernet. You'll find that it is an inexpensive solution to solving bandwidth problems both in the wiring closet and in the network backbone. For users who demand greater speeds to the desktop, you will find network adapter cards on the market that can be used in a PC or high-end workstation. However, for most typical office workers, Fast Ethernet offers all the speed you need at this time. In an environment where bandwidth-hungry applications, such as CAD or other applications that are used to manipulate large graphics files, using a Gigabit Ethernet adapter might be appropriate.

However, don't go out and buy all new cards for your entire network just because the technology is available. Instead, consider replacing or upgrading switches and routers so that they can use Gigabit Ethernet connections to the network backbone. Your end users will probably notice an increase in their network access speed, because the total aggregated network traffic coming to a central device will now be able to use a Gigabit Ethernet pipe instead of a Fast Ethernet connection for the network backbone. To put it another way, even if all your users have Fast Ethernet network adapters installed on their desktops, they won't necessarily be able to achieve the full potential speed of 100Mbps, because the network traffic they generate is limited to the bandwidth of the network backbone. When a lot of users access the network at the same time, the effective throughput for a Fast Ethernet adapter is not going to be a continuous 100Mbps if the backbone itself is limited to 100Mbps.

So, using Gigabit Ethernet for a network backbone can give you a longer life for those Fast Ethernet adapters, by removing the speed of the network backbone as a limiting factor.

Another reason why you should consider using Gigabit Ethernet for just the network backbone (and to patch together different devices in the wiring closet) is that the cabling can be more expensive. Today, using ordinary category 5 twisted-pair wiring to the desktop is inexpensive when compared to running fiber-optic cabling to the desktop. Twisted-pair cables are also less prone to damage than fiber-optic cables. The good news is that the fiber-optic cables you already have installed in your backbone most likely can be used with Gigabit Ethernet, because it supports both multi-mode and single-mode fiber. Although copper wire also is supported by the Gigabit Ethernet standard, it is limited to about 25 meters in length, and because of that, is intended mainly for use in the wiring closet and not as a means for connecting end user workstations.

Use Gigabit Ethernet for High-End Servers

Although Gigabit Ethernet may not be a feasible solution from an economic standpoint for ordinary user desktop computers, it can be used to dramatically increase access to a high-end server. Because servers usually are equipped with faster processors (and in most cases multiprocessor servers are the norm), they are capable of handling much larger volumes of network traffic than a desktop PC. One method to connect high-end servers to a network to add bandwidth is to install multiple network adapter cards on the machine. This results in multiple network addresses, which can be a drawback in some situations.

By using a faster network connection—Gigabit Ethernet—you can dramatically increase the network traffic that a high-end server can handle. Because the processor(s) of the server are already capable of handling large numbers of user requests, it makes sense that you don't let the network connection become the bottleneck.

By using Gigabit Ethernet with both servers and as the network backbone, you create a network that gives a faster response time to users that are equipped with the typical Fast Ethernet card.

Gigabit Ethernet Can Cover the Distance

You can use Gigabit Ethernet to achieve distances of up to 10 kilometers. Thus, you can use it in a network that spans multiple buildings that are separated geographically. Using other solutions, such as Asynchronous Transfer Mode (ATM) are generally more expensive, and require that the ethernet frame be converted into smaller ATM cells and then reassembled at the other end of the ATM link. Using ethernet from one end to the other eliminates this factor. While ATM has progressed to the point that you actually can use it in a LAN, the management overhead associated with ATM, and the prices for the equipment, make Gigabit Ethernet look even more attractive. For more information about ATM, see Chapter 19, "Dedicated Connections."

Upgrading to Gigabit Ethernet

There isn't a lot of expense involved in upgrading to Gigabit Ethernet at this time, unless, of course, you decide to use it to your desktop machines. If you have already strung fiber-optic cables for use in the network backbone, they can be reused for Gigabit Ethernet. You might need to change the connectors at each end of the cable, but that is a minor matter. Gigabit Ethernet was designed at the bottom of the protocol stack to use techniques based on the FiberChannel standard. Thus, readily available, inexpensive SC connectors can be attached and the cable is ready for use. For more information about fiber-optic cables as well as SC connectors, see Chapter 5, "Wiring the Network—Cables and Other Components."

Replacing hubs and switches is another matter. If you're still using hubs, then it's time to make the switch. Switches not only provide for faster connections for computers that are on the same switch, but also are less prone to problems that can creep up when you use a hub. For example, one high-end workstation that is sending out a lot of network traffic can be a hog that effectively lowers the utilization of a hub. This happens not only because the workstation is sending out a lot of packets in a short period of time, but also because the increased load on the hub probably will cause an increase in collisions when other stations attached to the same hub attempt to transmit. The more collisions, the less effective utilization you'll achieve using a hub.

Note

If you're curious as to just how cheap it can be to replace existing switches or hubs with devices that support Gigabit Ethernet connections to the backbone, check out the home page for your current vendor. For example, at `http://www.netgear.com`, you will find an 8-port 10/100Mbps switch with a Gigabit Ethernet uplink port at under $700.00. This same vendor offers a 16-port 10/100Mbps switch with a Gigabit Ethernet uplink port for just over $1,000. When you consider that a single desktop computer easily can cost much more than that, after you add the operating system and applications, Gigabit Ethernet switches are inexpensive indeed!

Switches limit the collision domain to just the workstation and the switch. Switches you'll find on the market today support backbone connections for Gigabit Ethernet at a relatively inexpensive cost when compared to the same switch that uses Fast Ethernet for a backbone connection. A few dollars more will buy you a much faster network. The cables are already in place if you're using fiber-optic cables, so replacing a switch that serves a large number of users is economically a good idea when you consider the results you can achieve.

If you're replacing ATM equipment with Gigabit Ethernet devices, you cut down not only on the cost of upgrading and maintaining the ATM boxes, but also the overhead associated with network management. Instead of having to manage two technologies, you simply have one to worry about.

Making Future Plans

Upgrading to Gigabit Ethernet in the backbone is not that big of a deal. You can replace a few switches if you've already got fiber-optic cables installed for your network backbone. If not, it's time to run fiber anyway if you want your network to be able to handle the newer applications that are becoming important components of businesses today. For example, when you consider the cost of sending employees to meetings, compare that with the cost of using streaming video conferencing. Users just sit at their desk and see and hear in real time other users. There's no need to schedule a conference room or to make travel plans—which can be quite expensive. Or, consider using the network to offer training presentations. Users can access multimedia presentations and other high-bandwidth applications at their leisure to learn new skills.

By upgrading the network backbone to Gigabit Ethernet, you will find that you are prepared for that next big application that comes down the line. You also can prepare your network for the next step, Gigabit Ethernet to the desktop, with 10 Gigabit Ethernet for the backbone!

Upgrading from Bridges to Routers and Switches

SOME OF THE MAIN TOPICS IN THIS CHAPTER ARE

Growing Beyond a Small LAN

From Bridges to Routers

From Bridges to Switches

There are many kinds of network devices that you can use to expand a local area network (LAN) or to connect it to a wide area network (WAN). These range from simple repeaters to devices with more intelligence, such as bridges, routers, and switches.

As a small LAN grows, it is easy to use bridges to segment a few small workgroups. You can use bridges to isolate local traffic among groups of users and thus cut down on the overall traffic on the LAN. However, there are limits, depending on the kind of network (for example, ARCnet, ethernet, or token ring), for how many bridges (repeaters) you can use in a LAN. In addition to their usefulness in solving network traffic congestion problems, you can use routers or switches to solve two other important problems: expanding the LAN beyond the size that bridges will allow and connecting the LAN to a larger WAN. Switches enable you to expand the LAN because they greatly limit the collision domain and switch traffic from one port to another, avoiding broadcasting packets unnecessarily on ports that do not have a route to the packet's destination. Routers enable you to connect to a much larger collection of networks, such as the Internet, and enable you to organize your LAN into a hierarchical address space, using network and host addresses.

◀◀ You can find out more about how routers and switches function by reading Chapter 8, "Network Switches," and Chapter 10, "Routers."

A bridge has just about outlived its usefulness in a modern network. Instead, switches (which are really glorified multiple bridges all in one box) and routers can better be used to segment a LAN and limit unnecessary network traffic on local LAN segments.

This chapter discusses these two possibilities, along with information you must consider when bringing routers or switches into your LAN.

Growing Beyond a Small LAN

Several chapters in this book cover the basic devices used to interconnect network segments: repeaters, bridges, switches, and routers. Each of these devices builds on the one previous to it, so that together they span a continuum of functionality that you can use to solve problems with the LAN or WAN. Standard bridges were developed to enable you to extend the reach of a LAN and to limit traffic to local segments. Switches took this concept further by allowing each workstation or server to have its own physical LAN segment, thus greatly limiting the broadcast domain (just the workstation and the switch). Routers enable you to extend the reach of a LAN by connecting it to a wide area network (WAN).

To quickly summarize:

- *Repeaters* are simple devices that connect network segments (usually two segments). They repeat all traffic and thus do nothing to help segment network traffic patterns. Repeaters are used to expand a LAN when it grows beyond the limitations imposed by a single network segment. Multiport repeaters function in the same way, but resemble a hub in that more than one segment can be connected to a multiport repeater. Typically, however, multiport repeaters are used in older environments that use coaxial cables for the network media. Most hubs use twisted-pair wiring with RJ-45 jacks.

- *Bridges* are similar to repeaters except that they apply a little intelligence to the packet forwarding process: Bridges learn MAC addresses of devices on each segment when they make an initial transmission. From then on, a bridge will not pass traffic to another segment if it knows the recipient is on the segment local to the transmission. Bridges are helpful for expanding a LAN and can be used to group collections of computers and servers that commonly interact to lower overall bandwidth consumption.

- *Routers* work like bridges in that they are selective about which packets get forwarded on which ports. However, while bridges operate at layer 2 of the OSI reference model (the Data Link

Layer) and only look at the flat namespace provided by the MAC addresses, routers operate at layer 3 (the Network Layer) and make decisions based on the addressing scheme provided by a higher-level networking protocol. Bridges are typically used to create larger local area networks. Connecting the LAN to a larger WAN can be done using a router.

- *Switches* are the newest technology for connecting network segments. Switches operate like bridges in that they keep track of which network node is located on each port by remembering MAC addresses. When retransmitting an incoming packet, the switch will send it out only on a port that will get it to its destination, provided it has already learned the destination's MAC address. Whereas bridges usually have only two ports, switches are like hubs and contain many ports. Some switches will allow for full-duplex operation, thus effectively doubling the available network bandwidth for a single node connected on a segment. In a sense, a switch operates like a collection of bridges.

From this summary, you can see that it's easy to use repeaters or bridges to grow the small LAN, but when it becomes necessary to expand beyond certain limits, or when it becomes necessary to make a connection to a larger LAN, you must incorporate routers or switches. Growth is not the only reason you might want to use a router or switch, however. These devices also can be used in a small LAN. For example, a small LAN that is experiencing network traffic congestion may find relief by replacing the hubs in the LAN with switches to cut down on the overall network traffic. Routers can be used in a campus LAN to allow network administrators to logically group network segments using the addressing scheme provided by TCP/IP, for example.

Segmenting the Network

You might need to segment users on the network for many different reasons. These include

- **Topology limitations**—You need to add more nodes to the network but the expansion will break distance limitations or maximum nodes-per-segment rules.

- **Networking protocol limitations**—Address space is fragmented and you need to connect segments that have different network addresses. This can happen when two companies merge and both already have an address space in place for their respective networks.

- **Network bandwidth limitations**—When a few high-performance servers or workstations consume too much of the segment's available bandwidth, it's time to segment the LAN and create smaller broadcast domains.

- **Security reasons**—An ethernet adapter set to promiscuous mode can intercept all packets that are sent out on a particular segment, for example. You need to place a few high security workstations on their own segment, yet allow some kind of connection to the rest of the network.

- **Geographically distant connections**—It's best to segment each geographic location to ensure that unnecessary traffic isn't being sent across the remote connection and wasting valuable bandwidth. Some routers provide a dial-up function so that a dedicated link is not necessary, providing an inexpensive way to use routers to connect branch offices.

Depending on which combination of these reasons apply to your situation, a router or switch might be the solution you need to segment the network.

Connecting Remote Locations

When a business expands geographically, you will find that using bridges to connect remote locations is not a feasible solution. There are so many different technologies from which you can choose today—from simple dedicated lines to ATM and frame relay—to connect geographically distant locations. For these connections you will find it necessary to incorporate routers or switches. You'll also find these methods of transport expensive. Today it is not unreasonable to consider connecting the local network to the Internet with a router that provides virtual private network (VPN) capabilities. Thus, using an inexpensive connection to the Internet (far cheaper than using leased, dedicated lines), you can still provide a secure channel to remote branch locations.

When to Use a Router

Routers are similar to bridges only in the fact that they can both be used to connect multiple network segments. Whereas bridges make all their decisions based on the MAC address of a particular network packet, routers access the addressing information provided by a higher-level protocol to decide how to best forward a packet. Using the OSI reference model, you can see that the bridge operates at layer 2, the Data Link layer, while routers usually operate at layer 3, the Network layer. With bridges, the address space is flat: It is simply the MAC addresses associated with nodes on each segment, each one unique. For protocols operating at the Network layer, the address space becomes more complicated because there must be a mechanism for identifying the network as well as the individual node.

When to Use a Switch

Switches are one of the fastest growing categories of network equipment. They can act as a wiring concentrator for a LAN just as a hub does, but they also can make available a much larger bandwidth to clients because they selectively forward traffic from one port to another based on the destination address of each packet. When you use a switch with only one node attached to each port, you are in effect creating a collection of broadcast domains that consist of only two network nodes: the switch and the client node connected to the port. For network adapters and switches that support full-duplex operation, the effective bandwidth is doubled for each client.

From Bridges to Routers

Routers are inherently slower than bridges when it comes to forwarding network packets. This is because a router needs to read further into each packet to get Network layer addressing information while a bridge merely looks at a fixed location for the MAC address. This means that routers are not plug-and-play types of devices. Hubs, bridges, and switches can be set up in a short amount of time, and usually require little or no configuration. Routers require that the network administrator configure networking information for each port that is used. The command set available to configure a router is quite large, because it is a very flexible device and can be confusing for a novice.

The kinds of information you need to configure a new router are

- A list of the network protocols for which you will be using the router. For example, TCP/IP or IPX/SPX.
- The routing protocol that you will use for each network protocol. For example, RIP.
- Information about the address space used on each segment the router will connect.

◀◀ For additional information about routing protocols, see Chapter 29, "Routing Protocols."

Network Protocol Issues

In many networks, more than one network protocol is used on the same medium. To do their job, routers need configuration information about each protocol for each port. For example, because each port on the router connects to a different network segment, each port must have a unique network address that it can use to communicate on the segment. If you plan to restrict some segments for security or other reasons, you will need to create a set of access control lists for each port, which indicate which packets are allowed through.

◀◀ Using routers to restrict network traffic is often referred to as *packet filtering*. For more information about this technology, see Chapter 40, "Firewalls."

When using a router to connect to a larger WAN, you probably will be faced with having to configure a port on the router that uses a WAN protocol, such as frame relay, in addition to protocols you are already familiar with on your network. With a WAN connection, you will have to coordinate your activities with other system administrators to ensure that the router is configured with the correct information for the larger network.

Network Addressing Issues

Because the router makes decisions based on a higher-level networking protocol, such as TCP/IP, you will have to take into consideration your current address space when you decide to introduce a router into the network. If you are adding new segments to the LAN and have the freedom to choose a new network address, this can be an easy task. If you are going to take an existing LAN and use a router to separate it into more manageable segments, you have two possible choices. You can use your original network address for one segment and create new networks on the remaining segments, or you can use subnetting, as described in Chapter 20, "Overview of the TCP/IP Protocol Suite," to divide your current address space into smaller subnetworks.

Regardless, you will have to then reconfigure each client with new addressing information. If you are using DHCP, the process is made simpler because you can make the changes at a central location and have clients request the new information after the changes have been made.

Another possibility that should be considered when using a router, and especially when connecting to the Internet, is that you don't have to use an address space that is registered for valid use on the Internet. Instead, you can use one of the private address spaces reserved for private networks, and then use a router that provides Network Address Translation (NAT) to act as a proxy on the Internet for your clients. This method avoids letting outsiders gain knowledge about the addresses of your clients, and that helps increase security at your site.

If you are going to use a router to connect your LAN to a larger corporate network, you might not have to make any addressing changes on your network, depending on the company's overall network plan. You will still have to configure the ports, however. If you are going to connect the LAN to the Internet, using a router configured as a firewall might be something to consider. For more information on using a router for this purpose, see Chapter 40.

Other Router Management Issues

Routers are very much like smart PCs that have been customized to perform the routing function efficiently. They have CPUs, memory, and I/O ports just like an ordinary PC. They also have an operating system, which is subject to periodic updates by the manufacturer. So, in addition to learning how to configure the router, you will also need to become familiar with other commands used for such functions as saving a copy of the system image to a server for backup purposes or commands used to perform troubleshooting testing.

Managing a network that uses routers can seem at first a difficult task. However, by allowing you to organize your network according to the hierarchical network address spaces used by upper-level network protocols, the initial configuration problems will be worth the effort.

Using a Router to Segment the Network

Like bridges, routers can be used to isolate traffic between network segments. Unlike bridges, routers further reduce network bandwidth use because they do not pass broadcast messages from one segment to another unless programmed to do so. A router also does not have to take time to learn which nodes are connected to each segment. The information it needs is configured in advance, such as when the administrator assigns protocols and addresses to each port. Routing protocols also use various methods to update each other about network topology as it changes.

One very important reason why routers are used to help organize a network into segments is that routers will allow you to connect many more end nodes. Whereas bridges are limited to a few thousand nodes, depending on the topology used, routers can allow the LAN to be connected to an infinitely larger WAN, such as the Internet.

The internal processing that routers must perform make them slower than bridges, which only need to examine a small amount of data in the packet header. Although this performance difference will not be noticed on network segments with only moderate traffic use, you might find that you need to place routers only at strategic locations throughout the network, retaining bridges for some segments. This will depend on the usage patterns that can be monitored for each segment and the cost of the links used to connect different segments. Another thing to consider is that many of the high-end routers available today operate at "wire speed." This means that they can route packets at virtually the same speed as the network medium, with just the very slightest delay for processing time.

Connecting to a Larger WAN

When connecting the LAN to a WAN, a router is still the best solution to use in most cases. When connecting to the Internet, for example, you cannot use a bridge or a repeater. The Internet is composed of a hierarchical TCP/IP address space and a router is needed to participate in this hierarchy. Or, you might plan to use a dedicated line of some sort to connect to a larger corporate network. In this case, placing a router between your LAN and the WAN hardware, such as an ATM switch connection, will help reduce the traffic that crosses the expensive dedicated connection by keeping local traffic confined to the local network segments.

Although you will certainly have to configure the ports that connect the local LAN and the WAN interface, you might have to reconfigure addressing information on clients. For example, if you are already using a valid TCP/IP network address, possibly a subnet of the corporate network address space, you only will need to configure routers.

If your business has just been acquired by a larger concern, however, you might find that your LAN has been assigned a new subnet by the larger corporation and you might possibly have to plan for down time for end users if you cannot make the client configuration changes outside normal business hours. By using DHCP, you can overcome client configuration headaches such as this. For more information about using DHCP and how it works, see Chapter 23, "BOOTP and the Dynamic Host Configuration Protocol (DHCP)."

From Bridges to Switches

Switches can be useful for solving network problems related to traffic congestion and network segmentation. For example, they can be used as replacements for hubs at the LAN level. In Figure 50.1 you can see a small LAN that uses two hubs. The three servers for this network share a common broadcast domain with all the other users on the network.

When this LAN was first installed there was more than adequate bandwidth available and users were satisfied with the response time. Over time, however, each server was replaced with a more powerful model, and some of the end users' workstations were replaced with high-performance machines and new database software that relies on information stored on the servers.

Network traffic has increased considerably, users are dissatisfied, and the network administrator must take action. Because the main problem is the traffic exchanged between the servers and the high-performance end-user workstations, a switch can be a simple solution. There are two simple solutions you can devise using switches. In Figure 50.2 you can see that both of the 8-port hubs have been replaced with a single 16-port switch.

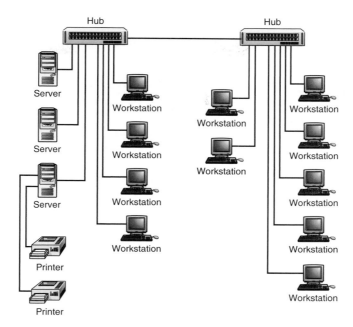

Figure 50.1   Hubs do nothing to limit network traffic on the LAN.

This layout gives each node that is connected to the switch a full 10Mbps network connection (or 100Mbps, depending on your hardware). Each connection is a broadcast domain with only two end nodes: the connected workstation or server and the switch. In this solution, the server nodes were equipped with full-duplex network adapters, effectively doubling their available network bandwidth. Provided the switch is capable of handling the traffic load, individual users on the workstations that make only moderate use of the network should notice a better response time through the switch, as compared to a hub connection.

The servers and high-performance workstations should also notice better performance, yet their network traffic is no longer broadcast on the segments of the other moderate users, effectively isolating this traffic.

Figure 50.3 shows another solution. Here, a hub is used for the workstations that only moderately use the network.

Here, the three servers that are responsible for much of the bandwidth use each have been placed on a separate port on the switch. Again, full-duplex network adapters were installed to further increase the available bandwidth to each server. The three high-performance workstations also were placed on separate switch ports so that their network use does not directly interfere with other nodes. A hub was retained for connecting moderate network users. Because these nodes do not generate a lot of network communications, placing them on a hub connected to the switch should allow them fast communications among themselves while still allowing access to the other servers and workstations.

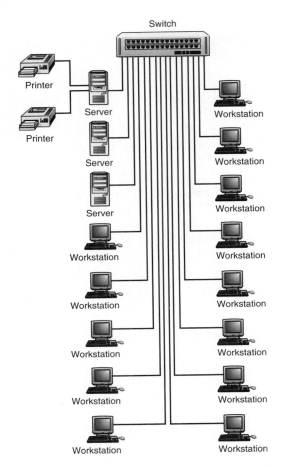

Figure 50.2 A switch can be used to isolate high bandwidth network nodes.

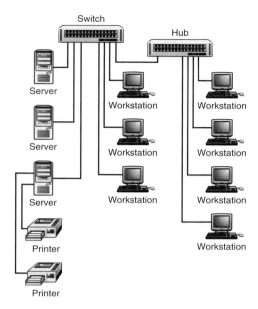

Figure 50.3 Traffic on the hub is not hampered by the traffic generated by the other high-performance servers and workstations.

Adding Wireless Networking to a LAN

Wireless networking is one of the fastest growing segments of the networking industry that your end users will probably be aware of. Because the IEEE 802.11b Wi-Fi standard has recently helped to bring some order to the chaos of non-interoperability that has existed these past few years, the price of wireless LAN equipment has fallen dramatically, and it has become much easier to implement. However, you should consider whether you really need to use wireless networking in your LAN before you decide to implement it. Wireless networking is not a solution looking for a problem. Indeed, there are many problems that wireless networking can solve. If you have the need, then you should consider using a wireless solution. If you simply have eager users that want fun new things to play with, you should reconsider and think about the management tasks you'll have to deal with, including troubleshooting wireless networking and managing the limited bandwidth that wireless networking currently offers.

Why Go Wireless?

There are many good reasons to use wireless networking. First, it's a quick way to set up a peer-to-peer network that is only needed for a short period of time, such as in a home office where you only have two computers that need a link and you don't want to be running network cables through your walls. For the home environment, wireless networking may be the perfect choice because it not only eliminates the necessity of pulling cables, but also allows you flexibility in where you locate your equipment. For example, although you might have set aside a portion of your house to use for your home office, it's nice to be able to take the laptop into the living room and work while you're watching that favorite TV show. Wireless networking makes this simple.

Another use for wireless technology is the trade show environment. If you need to network several computers, and possibly a printer or two, an ad-hoc network using a wireless access point can be a quick way to get your booth up and running in a hurry. This also can be used at a client site if you are in the consulting business and don't want to connect your computers to your client's network. Indeed, it can be an easy way to get your computers into the client's office because they'll have no up-front work to do to provide you with networking services.

Finally, you can use a wireless network to extend the reach of your existing LAN. In Chapter 14, "Wireless Networking: IEEE 802.11 (Wi-Fi) and HomeRF," you learned that access points (APs) can be connected to a wired LAN to provide an ingress point for wireless clients. However, just because it's possible doesn't mean it's necessary. Some places in a corporate network that you might find wireless network APs a good idea include:

- **Conference rooms**—Users often bring laptop computers to meetings to take notes. Using wireless networking in a conference room can allow that laptop to locate information that exists elsewhere on the LAN that might be useful during the meeting. No more "I'll get back with you on that" excuses.

- **Temporary workgroups**—An access point can be useful when you need to bring in temporary workers, using space that is otherwise not wired for network access. Because many manufacturing plants have seasonal peaks and slumps, this might be an ideal way to quickly set up new clients on a network without the expense of having to go through the process of providing switches and cable runs to all parts of your building. Instead, a single cable run can be used for an AP that can serve a variable number of clients, on an as-needed basis.

- **Mobile users**—For users who mainly work with a laptop and are usually on the road—such as salespersons—a wireless solution may be a good idea. When the user returns to the office for a short time, a docking station can serve to connect the laptop to the wired network. However, a docking station basically means reserving a desk as well, and overhead can be expensive in today's competitive market. Instead, a single office with a few desks and an access point can serve a large number of transient workers.

- **Factory floor**—Laptops are not the only computers that can be used in a wireless network. Many PDAs and other small handheld devices are available that can use Wi-FI network cards. On a factory floor, where mobility is important, it's easier to use a small portable device than it is to set up a series of PCs throughout the plant. Because many manufacturing plants need to reconfigure the factory floor on a periodic basis in order to retool for new products, wireless networking, again, can prove to be a cost saver.

Another place that wireless networking can serve a useful purpose is for outdoor activities. I've worked at many places that have outdoor locations that employees can use at lunchtime. These areas also can be comfortable places to hold meetings. Sometimes just getting out of the office can boost employee morale and taking the network outside can, as noted previously, make meetings more productive.

Choosing Locations for Access Points

Just as you need to test new network configurations or PC configurations in a laboratory before rolling them out for production usage, you need to evaluate the placement of access points should you decide to get into wireless networking. Wi-Fi provides for roaming capabilities, but it also enables you to restrict users to selected access points if you wish. First, decide how you want to use wireless networking and which users it can be used by in a productive manner. Next, decide how many access points you need and where to place them.

You'll have to do some experimentation. Read the vendor's documentation to get the basics of the coverage area that the product is capable of, keeping in mind that this is only a general figure. For example, you'll find that most access points are capable of covering larger distances outside, rather than inside, a building because there are less structural components, such as steel beams, that can block the signal. You should take a vendor's specifications about their particular product with a grain of salt. Your mileage can vary.

If you use wireless networking inside and want to cover the entire building, then you'll have to test to see exactly how far the coverage is for each access point. Also note that several factors can influence the performance you'll get no matter where you place the AP. For example, each AP is capable of supporting only a limited number of users before the available bandwidth begins to become saturated. Wireless networking at 11Mbps is as fast as the standard 10BASE-T network, if you only have one user! Yet, it's nowhere near as fast as having a dedicated connection to a Fast Ethernet switch. There will come a point where too many users competing with too little bandwidth will provide too little performance to make wireless networking practical. In the near future, when the 5GHz radio frequency band is allocated to wireless networking (the process is underway at this time), then the bandwidth available will be dramatically increased. For the present, however, you need to distribute access points so that only a small number of users are associated with any given AP.

Another thing to consider is source of interference, such as microwave ovens and other wireless devices. If you employ Bluetooth devices, then you need to be careful because the technology is still new and, despite some of the literature you may read, it is still inconclusive whether Bluetooth (or HomeRF for that matter) can interfere with Wi-Fi communications. All three use the same ISM radio frequency band, and although hopping around on different frequencies and using direct spread spectrum technologies may serve to reduce the chance of interference, don't count on there being no interference at all. Instead, if you use multiple technologies, go back to your lab and test the devices to see what kind of throughput you are able to achieve. Another device that is gaining in popularity is the 2.4Ghz cordless telephone. These devices operate in the same band as wireless networks and can cause a lot of problems when used in the vicinity of wireless networking devices.

And keep that microwave oven in the break room well shielded! You can purchase an inexpensive device at most consumer discount stores that can measure the amount of microwave radiation that is leaking from a microwave oven. You might find that simply replacing an old microwave oven with a newer model might cure any interference problems. And because most work places don't need a top-of-the-line microwave that can zap a baked potato in just a few minutes, go with a low-end model that uses less power.

Security Issues

Using wireless technology opens up the possibility of security breaches. Thoroughly read the documentation that comes with your choice of devices to find out what kind of security features can be enabled. It's probably best to associate the wireless network adapters you buy with one or more access points, depending on the work habits of the user. Also note that many devices come with default settings and that these are known to anyone who owns a similar device, or who cares to look up the information on the Internet. If any passwords are enabled by default, then change them. Use the security features of your operating system to monitor wireless users. For example, I'd be more concerned with a Windows 2000 user's resource access permissions if the client computer uses a wireless network card than I would if it were wired directly to the network. Keep in mind that Wi-Fi devices can implement the Wireless Equivalency Protocol (WEP) for security. However, the 40-bit key used by WEP doesn't provide a lot of security. For most situations, it should suffice, because in most situations you don't expect someone to be attempting to tap into your network. However, where security is an issue, WEP in its present form is not something you should bet your business on.

In such a situation, it's easy to set up auditing for important resources and to review them using the Event Viewer in Windows 2000.

◄◄   For more information about auditing, see Chapter 38, "Auditing and Other Monitoring Measures."

Check the default settings on your wireless equipment to be sure that you don't have a configuration that allows just any wireless adapter that comes within range to associate itself with an access point and start probing around. Although you may have other resource protections in place to limit the damage that such an intruder could possible cause, there is always the chance that there's something you've overlooked. And you can bet that someone who's trying to infiltrate your network will be more knowledgeable in these areas than you are.

Read the documentation!

Another cause for concern is that wireless networking enables the computer to be mobile. A user can take his computer home. Although you might be able to stop users from downloading prohibited Internet files at work, you can't always police what they do at home. It's a simple matter to pop out the wireless networking adapter and pop in a modem (or better yet, simply use a wireless access point at home also, because it is so inexpensive). As with any computer that leaves the company premises, a regular audit of software on the system should be performed, and your security policy should state what the computer can—and cannot—be used for.

Have Fun

Wireless networking is just in the beginning stages. By the time the next edition of this book is written, it probably will be taken for granted that a portion of your network will be using wireless technology. It's best to prepare now with a few pilot projects. You should become familiar with the ins and outs of wireless networking and acquaint yourself with the possible security problems. Don't wait until crunch time, when you have to quickly deploy a large wireless network.

Migration and Integration

PART IX

Migrating from Novell NetWare to Windows NT 4.0/2000

SOME OF THE MAIN TOPICS IN THIS CHAPTER ARE

Windows Protocols and Services

Microsoft's Services for NetWare Version 5.0 (SFN)

## CHAPTER 52

When Windows 3.51 was released, the default network protocol during installation was Microsoft's implementation of Novell's IPX/SPX protocol. It easily can be assumed that at that time Microsoft perceived that Novell was its most important competitor in the network operating system marketplace. With Windows NT 4.0, the TCP/IP protocol suite, along with the Internet Information Server and a host of utilities for creating applications for the Internet, moved that focus away from Novell to the then fast growing Internet market.

Yet, over the years, Windows has continued to dominate the desktop, from Windows 95 to 2000 and now to Windows XP, so one has to consider what benefits there are to pay for Novell's NDS and related networking products, when most of the functionality that Novell provides is already present in Windows 2000, and to some degree, in Windows NT 4.0. If you simply want to stop using NetWare and upgrade to a Windows NT 4.0 network, you won't have the benefits of the Active Directory—Microsoft's answer to NDS. However, for small LANs, Windows NT 4.0 can provide all the networking components, file and print sharing services, and user and computer management tools you need. In a more complex setup, with a larger base of computers, Windows 2000 provides a better migration path away from NDS.

In this chapter, we'll look at ways to migrate your network from Novell NetWare to Windows NT and Windows 2000. You can take a gradual approach, slowly integrating Windows into important roles in the network, or you can take the all-at-once approach. The former probably would be cheaper in the long run (you can lose NDS servers by attrition and you don't need as many people devoted to the migration if you have more time). The latter approach might be a lot more costly, because you'll need to have a larger team of trained professionals to get the job done quickly. Using the all-at-once approach also is riskier. If something goes wrong, or if your capacity planning or organizational planning is faulty, you'll need a good back-out plan (and probably another job).

First, we'll examine features of the Windows operating system that help provide connectivity between Windows and NetWare computers, and then we'll look at Microsoft Windows Services for NetWare 5, which can be very useful, along with other tools, for performing a migration to Windows NT or Windows 2000.

Windows Protocols and Services

Although earlier versions of NetWare use Novell's IPX/SPX network protocols, the TCP/IP protocol suite is supported with version 5. Microsoft Windows NT 4.0 and Windows 2000 also support Microsoft's implementation of the native NetWare protocol under the name NWLink. You can configure a Windows server to use the NWLink protocol and it then can be used as a server for NetWare clients. If you're taking the gradual approach for your migration, this is the easiest way to introduce Windows servers into older versions of NetWare. Otherwise, if you already are using TCP/IP on your NetWare clients, Windows also has a full-featured TCP/IP protocol stack and supports many related protocols and services, such as DHCP and DNS.

Microsoft Windows NT 4.0 and Windows 2000 provide two basic services that allow NetWare and Microsoft clients to access servers that reside in both environments. These tools are

- **Client Services for NetWare (CSNW)**—This tool enables the Microsoft client to directly connect to a service offered by a NetWare server.

- **Gateway Services for NetWare (GSNW)**—This utility also enables a Microsoft network client to access file and print shares offered by NetWare servers. The services are provided to the Microsoft clients through a gateway Windows NT Server computer that is used to communicate with the NetWare servers.

We'll look first at these two services and then explore some other utilities you can use to further integrate Novell NetWare with Microsoft Windows computers.

Client Services for NetWare (CSNW)

This service can be installed on Windows NT Workstation and Windows 2000 Professional computers to enable them to connect to file and print services provided by NetWare servers on the network. By using CSNW, you can begin by gradually adding Microsoft Windows NT or Windows 2000 clients to your network, and they can access services on your existing NetWare network. This can allow you the time to hone your Windows networking skills, while still allowing users access to the same NetWare resources they are used to.

Installing CSNW on Windows NT 4.0 Clients

The CSNW service is provided with the Windows NT 4.0 operating system. You only need to install the service. The following steps can be done to accomplish this task:

1. Click Start, Settings, Control Panel. Select the Services tab, and then click the Add button to add a new service.

2. From the list that is displayed, select Client Services for NetWare.

3. When the setup process has finished copying the necessary files, it will prompt you to enter the name of a NetWare server that will be used to authenticate this client. After you furnish this name, the workstation will need to be rebooted before the service will take effect.

Note

If you have installed any of the Windows NT 4.0 service packs before installing and configuring CSNW, you might have to reinstall the latest service pack that you find works best in your environment. Note that some service packs solve problems as well as cause new ones! Review the release notes and documentation that come with Windows NT service packs before you install!

When the workstation logs on to the NetWare server, it will use the username of the user who is locally logged on to the workstation. If your password on the workstation is different than that on the NetWare server, you will be prompted to enter it. It is a good idea to keep these passwords the same to keep users happy.

If you need to connect to servers other than the preferred server that was designated when the CSNW service was installed, use the Windows NT Explorer and select Map Network Drive from the Tools menu just as you would when connecting to a network drive offered by a Windows NT computer. You must enter a username and password that is valid on the NetWare server to make the connection.

Installing CSNW on Windows 2000 Professional Clients

To install CSNW on Windows 2000 Professional, the steps to follow are just a little different:

1. Click Start, Settings, Network and Dialup Connections.

2. Right-click the Local Network icon and select Properties from the menu that appears.

3. From the Local Area Network Properties sheet General tab, click the Install button. The Select Network Component Type dialog box pops up. Click once on Client to highlight it, and then click the Add button.

4. In the Select Network Client dialog box, click Client Service for NetWare and click OK.

5. When the Select NetWare Logon dialog box appears, fill in the fields for the preferred server if you are going to use the client to connect to a bindery-based NetWare server. If you are going to use the service with NDS, click the Default Tree and Context button and enter the NDS tree and context names. If you want to use a logon script, select Run Login Script. When you've made your selections, click OK.

When you have finished, you'll be prompted to reboot the computer. You can do so at that time or wait until a more convenient time for the reboot. After you've rebooted your workstation, you'll be able to connect to the preferred server or authenticate yourself to another, just as with the Windows NT 4.0 client.

Note

If you have previously installed Novell's client software on either a Windows NT 4.0 or a Windows 2000 computer, you'll have to uninstall that client before you can install Microsoft's version. The two are not compatible and will not run on the same computer at the same time.

Gateway Services for NetWare (GSNW)

Microsoft employs two methods to enable its networking clients to connect to services offered by a NetWare server. Client Services for NetWare, discussed in the previous sections, allows each client to make connections directly to NetWare servers, just as though they were ordinary NetWare clients. This method has advantages, in that only the Microsoft client and the NetWare server are involved in processing the exchange of data. However, in a network where the interaction between Microsoft clients and NetWare servers will not be large, and many clients might need to make the connection at one time or another, a better solution might be the Gateway Services for NetWare (GSNW) product. Another benefit of using GSNW is that, because the gateway server makes requests on behalf of the clients, the users would not need to have logon accounts on both Windows and NetWare networks.

Keep in mind that accessing resources through the gateway service will be a little slower than access by clients that have the CSNW service installed. If you have clients on the network that have differing needs to access NetWare resources, you can install CSNW on those that most frequently use those resources, and let others use the gateway service.

Note

Gateway Services for NetWare uses Microsoft's implementation of IPX/SPX, called NWLink, to communicate with NetWare servers. For Windows NT 4.0, you must install NWLink before you can use GSNW. For Windows 2000, the NWLink protocol is installed automatically when you perform the GSNW installation.

When using GSNW, a Windows NT Server computer acts as a link between Microsoft clients and the NetWare Server. Microsoft clients continue to use the Server Message block (SMB) protocols to access network resources, with the gateway server performing the bridging function to the NetWare servers, which use the NetWare Core Protocol (NCP) for file and print functions.

The gateway server does this by redirecting a drive to the NetWare volume. It then offers the drive as a share to Microsoft clients. You can treat this share just like any other share offered by the server, when it comes to management utilities.

Another feature that GSNW provides is the capability for the Windows NT Server that is hosting the gateway software to make direct connections to NetWare services, just as workstations do when using the Client Services for NetWare product. A local user on the server can elect to connect to NetWare resources without offering them to other clients through the gateway.

Installing and Configuring GSNW on Windows NT 4.0 Server

You can install GSNW by installing a network service using the Network applet in the Windows NT Control Panel. On the Services tab (see Figure 52.1), click the Add button to see the Select Network Service dialog box, showing a list of the services that you can add (see Figure 52.2).

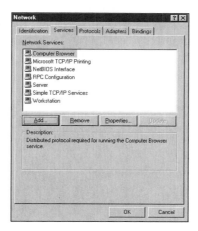

Figure 52.1   Use the Services tab of the Control Panel's Network applet to install GSNW.

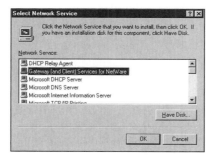

Figure 52.2   Select Gateway (and Client) Services for NetWare from the list shown.

After the files have been copied, you will need to reboot the server. When this has been done, you will find that there is now an icon in the Control Panel labeled GSNW, which can be used to configure the service. Additionally, when the server is first rebooted after installing the gateway service, you will be prompted, as shown in Figure 52.3, to enter either

- A default NDS tree and context
- A preferred NetWare server

You must choose one or the other of these two. You can have either a default NDS tree and context or you can elect to use a preferred server. The preferred server should be selected if your network does not use NDS. In this case, that server will authenticate you when accessing resources on NetWare. If you do use NDS, you can select to use a default NDS tree and set the context. Using this method still allows you to connect to NetWare servers that use bindery security instead of NDS.

Figure 52.3   Enter the information that will be used to authenticate the server to the NetWare network.

Note

If you plan to use the gateway NT server to access both NDS resources and also NetWare servers that run in bindery mode, you should use a bindery account instead of an NDS tree and context. If you plan to use only NDS resources, the account you use can be an NDS account. If you use a bindery account, it will be able to use bindery emulation to connect to NDS resources.

After you have installed the software and have entered the authentication information needed to access services on the NetWare network, there are several things you need to do to make NetWare resources available to your Microsoft clients. First, you must be sure that there is a user account on the NetWare network that has the needed access rights to the resources for which you want to create a gateway. On the NetWare side, there must also be a group named Ntgateway that has the needed rights for the resources. The NetWare user account that you will use must be a member of this group.

To create the gateway:

■ Enable gateways on the server that is running the GSNW software. This needs to be done only once to establish the gateway.

■ Activate each file or print resource gateway. This must be done for each resource you want to offer to Microsoft clients.

To enable a gateway, double-click the GSNW applet that is now found in the Control Panel, shown in Figure 52.4. Click the Gateway button to bring up the Configure Gateway dialog box (see Figure 52.5).

In the Configure Gateway dialog box you will again have to enter a method and the information required to access the resources you require on a NetWare server. This is in addition to the account that you supplied when the Windows NT Server was first rebooted after the gateway service was installed. That first logon information is used to enable the Windows NT server to log on as a user to the NetWare account. The second account will be used here to actually access the needed resource.

After you supply a gateway account and password and type the password again in the confirm box, use the Add button to add a NetWare file share resource that you want to add to the gateway. In Figure 52.6 you can see the dialog box that enables you to add a resource.

You also can place comments in the appropriate field and elect to limit the number of simultaneous users that can connect to the share when it is offered to Microsoft clients through the gateway.

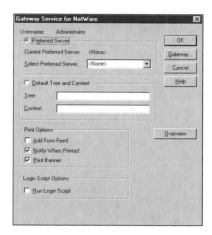

Figure 52.4 The GSNW applet in the Control Panel enables you to configure the gateway service.

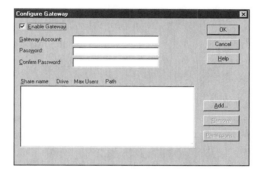

Figure 52.5 Use the Gateway button on the GSNW dialog box to bring up the Configure Gateway dialog box.

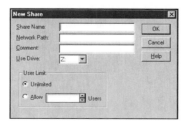

Figure 52.6 Enter the path to the NetWare resource and select the drive letter that will be used on the Windows NT Server.

Setting up a printer that allows Microsoft clients to send documents to NetWare printers or print queues through the gateway is performed in a manner similar to setting up other printers in Windows NT. The difference is that you must correctly specify the port for the printer. To make a NetWare printer available through the gateway

1. Click the Start button, Settings, and then Printers.

2. From the Add Printer Wizard dialog box that appears, select My Computer. Do *not* select Network Printer Server.

3. The next dialog box shows available printer ports on the server. Click the Add Port button.

4. Depending on the network protocols and services installed on the computer, you then are shown a list of printer ports that can be added. Select Local Port from this list and click the New Port button.

5. Finally, in the Port Name dialog box that pops up, enter the UNC path name that is used to designate the NetWare Printer resource (\\servername\printername).

The remainder of the Add Printer Wizard works just as it does for any other printer. You must select a driver for the printer and specify the name that is used when it is offered as a share on the Microsoft network.

Installing and Configuring GSNW on Windows 2000 Server

Windows 2000 also supports the gateway service, and it functions in the same way that it did in Windows NT 4.0. However, the installation is a little different. You must be a member of the Administrators group on the server to install the gateway service. Use the following steps to install GSNW on a Windows NT 2000 server:

1. Click Start, Settings, Network and Dial-up Connections.

2. When the Network and Dial-Up Connections window appears, right-click the local area connection icon that you want to use for the service. From the menu that appears, select Properties.

3. From the Local Area Connection Properties dialog box that appears (see Figure 52.7), click the Install button.

Figure 52.7   Click the Install button on the Local Area Connection Properties page to install the GSNW service.

4. The Select Network Component Type dialog box appears (see Figure 52.8). Click once on Client to highlight it, and then click the Add button to add a new service.

Figure 52.8   Use the Add button to add the new service.

5. When the Select Network Client dialog box appears (see Figure 52.9), highlight Gateway (and Client) Services for NetWare, and then click the OK button.

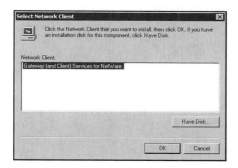

Figure 52.9   Select the gateway service and click the OK button.

6. Use the Select NetWare Logon dialog box (see Figure 52.10) to choose a preferred server (if you are using a bindery-based NetWare network), or use the radio button labeled Default Tree and Context (if you are using NDS) and fill in the appropriate information. When finished, click the OK button.

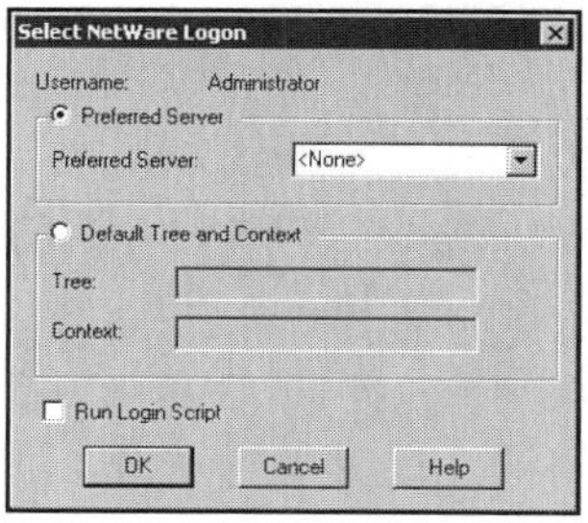

Figure 52.10   Choose the method you will use to log on to the NetWare server or NDS.

Note

If you do not have available at installation time the necessary information for logging on to a NetWare server or NDS, you can perform this step after you've installed GSNW and rebooted the Windows 2000 Server.

7. Finally, you are prompted to restart your computer before the changes you have made will take effect.

After the server reboots, using the following command at the command prompt should display a list of servers available to your gateway:

```
net view /network:nw
```

After you reboot, you'll notice that, in addition to installing the gateway service, these NWLink components also have been installed for you:

- NWLink NetBIOS
- NWLink IPX/SPX/NetBIOS Compatible Transport Protocol

You can see these in the Properties page for the local area connection.

After you've installed the gateway service, you have to configure it just like you did under Windows NT 4.0. Similarly, you need to have a group named NTGATEWAY on the NetWare server to which you want access, and that account needs to be granted the access rights you require. You also must have a user account on the NetWare network (again, with the appropriate access rights, depending on the NetWare resources you want to provide access to through the gateway), and this user account must be a member of the NTGATEWAY group. The user account can be either a bindery-based account or an NDS account, depending on the access you require. If you plan to access both NDS and bindery-based servers, the account should be a bindery account that can connect to resources in NDS by using bindery emulation.

The process for creating and enabling the gateway under Windows 2000 is the same as it was for Windows NT 4.0. The dialog boxes are the same as those shown in "Installing and Configuring GSNW on Windows NT 4.0 Server," earlier in this chapter.

Microsoft's Services for NetWare Version 5.0 (SFN)

Besides the client and gateway services (and the NWLink-compatible transport protocols) that come with the Windows NT 4.0 and Windows 2000 operating system, you can purchase an additional product called Services for NetWare Version 5.0 (SFN). The CSNW and GSNW products enable your Windows clients to connect to and use resources that reside on NetWare servers. SFN does the opposite. It enables you to let NetWare clients access resources that reside on Windows NT/2000 servers. When you first start to introduce Windows clients into your NetWare environment, CSNW and GSNW make replacing desktop systems for your users an easy task. When it comes time to begin migrating files and other services from NetWare servers to Windows servers, SFN gives you the capability to do this. You can use SFN to grant access to NetWare clients to newly created services in the Windows domain, and you can finish off the migration by using the File Migration Utility to move any files that remain on NetWare servers to Windows 2000 servers.

SFN gives you the following features:

- File and Print Services for NetWare 4.0 (FPNW)
- Directory Service Manager for NetWare (DSMN)

- Microsoft Directory Synchronization Services (MSDSS)
- File Migration Utility (FMU)
- File and Print Services for NetWare Version 5.0 (FPNW5)

Of these, the first two are intended mainly for use with Windows NT 4.0, whereas the last three are exclusively for use on Windows 2000. Version 5 of SFU contains the earlier versions of FPNW and the Directory Services Manager for NetWare so that you don't have to buy both versions 4 and 5 of this product. It's all on the new 5.0 CD. You can obtain this CD by visiting Microsoft's Web site and using the search function.

File and Print Services for NetWare 4.0 (FPNW 4.0)

File and Print Services for NetWare 4.0 allows NetWare clients to access resources on a Windows NT Server computer as if they were offered on the network by a NetWare server. FPNW can be used as an intermediate step toward converting your NetWare clients to an NT only network, or it can be used when you need to run both at the same time. For existing NetWare networks, FPNW can help you seamlessly integrate Windows NT 4.0 Servers into the network without having to install or modify client software. In addition, Windows NT 4.0 clients also can access the same server and the same files and printer that are made available to NetWare clients.

When FPNW is installed on the Windows NT Server, several of the administrative utilities, such as the User Manager for Domains and the Server Manager, are updated to include new functionality. You can create user accounts on an NT domain for NetWare users, or you can use the Migration Tool for NetWare to copy existing NetWare user account information to a Windows NT 4.0 Server. When a NetWare client has an account in a Windows NT domain, the client can be given access to resources in other trusting domains just like ordinary Windows NT 4.0 clients.

Note

FPNW version 4.0 running on Windows NT 4.0 servers can be used to give NetWare 2.x, 3.x, and 4.x clients access to Windows NT 4.0 resources in bindery emulation mode. It does not provide functionality to interface with Novell Directory Services.

Besides providing network file services for NetWare and Microsoft clients, FPNW 4.0 also enables you to share printers that are connected locally to the NT server computer and to those which are directly connected to the network.

Comparison of Windows NT and NetWare File Permission Rights

Chapter 34, "Rights and Permissions," discussed the ability to restrict user access to files, directories, and volumes for both NetWare and Windows users. When using FPNW 4.0, trustee rights for directories for NetWare clients can be mapped to those used on Windows NT 4.0 systems, as shown in Table 52.1. Table 52.2 shows the same thing in reverse, or how FPNW translates Windows NT 4.0 permissions for directories to NetWare directory rights.

Table 52.1   Mapping NetWare Trustee Rights to Windows NT Permissions in FPNW 4.0 for Directories

NetWare File Rights	Windows NT/2000 File Permissions
Read (R)	Read (RX) (RX)
Write (W)	Write (W) (W)
Create (C)	Write (W) (W)

Table 52.1   Continued

NetWare File Rights	Windows NT/2000 File Permissions
Erase (E)	Delete (D) (D)
Modify (M)	Write (W) (W)
File Scan (F)	Read (R) (R)
Access Control (A)	Change Permissions (PO) (PO)

Table 52.2   Mapping Windows NT Permissions to NetWare Trustee Rights in FPNW 4.0 for Directories

Windows NT Directory Permissions	NetWare Directory Rights
List (RX) (not specified)	Read, File Scan (RF)
Read (RX) (RX)	Read, File Scan (RF)
Add (WX) (not specified)	Write, Create, Modify (WCM)
Add and Read (RWX) (RX)	Read, Write, Create Modify, File Scan (RWCMF)
Change (RWXD) (RWXD)	Read, Write, Create Modify, File Scan (RWCMF)
Full Control (All) (All)	Supervisor (S)

For files, Table 52.3 shows the mapping that is done by FPNW from Windows NT to NetWare, and Table 52.4 shows the mapping that is done from NetWare to Windows NT. Note that Windows NT Server uses directory permissions to grant the Create and File Scan equivalent rights that NetWare uses as file rights.

Table 52.3   Mapping NetWare File Trustee Rights to Windows NT 4.0 Server File Permissions

NetWare File Rights	Windows NT File Permissions
Supervisor (S)	Full Control (All)
Read (R)·	Read (R)
Access Control (A)	Change Permissions (PO)
Create (C)	Write (W)
Erase (E)	Delete (D)
Modify (M)	Write (W) (W)
Write (W)	Write (W)

Table 52.4   Mapping Windows NT 4.0 Server File Permissions to NetWare File Trustee Rights

Windows NT File Permissions	NetWare File Rights
Read (RX)	Read, File Scan (RF)
Change (RWXD)	Read, Write, Create Modify, File Scan(RWCMF)
Full Control (All)	Supervisor (S)

Besides having to translate between the rights and permissions used on each system, FPNW also translates between the different kinds of file attributes that both systems use at the file level. Table 52.5 shows the translation mapping that FPNW performs.

Table 52.5 Mapping File Attributes Between Windows NT 4.0 and NetWare

NetWare File Attributes	Windows NT File Attributes
Read Only (RO)	Read Only (R)
Delete Inhibit (D)	Read Only (R), or remove user permissions to delete the file
Rename Inhibit	Assigned at the directory level by removing the user's permission to write to the directory
Archive Needed (A)	Archive (A)
System (Sy)	System (S)
Hidden (H)	Hidden (H)
Execute Only (X)	Execute (E)
Read Audit (Ra)	Audit Read, Audit Execute
Write Audit (Wa)	Audit Write, Audit Delete

However, FNPW 4.0 *does not* provide support for the following NetWare attributes:

- Don't Compress
- File Migrated
- File Compressed
- Immediate Compress
- Can't Compress
- Purge
- Index FAT Entries
- Transactional Tracking
- File Migrated

The Shareable attribute can be set only on a per-server or global basis when using FPNW 4.0, and cannot be set on an individual file.

You should carefully examine how security is currently enforced for clients on the existing NetWare network before beginning to decide how to offer file shares from a Windows NT Server. Understanding the mapping between the two systems can prevent unexpected access violations or errors from compromising security on the network.

Installing FPNW 4.0

FPNW is installed as a service on a Windows NT Server computer. As with other network services, this is done using the Network applet in the Control Panel. During the installation of the service, you are prompted to enter a disk drive and directory that is used for the location of the SYSVOL directory, which is used as the NetWare compatible SYS: volume. To enforce security rights and permissions on the volume, you must use a drive that is formatted with the NTFS file system. It is possible to use a drive that is formatted using FAT, but all security then is enforced at a share level and not on the basis of individual files or directories. Because NTFS offers protection at the file and directory level instead of the share level, you can further refine access permissions to protect your data and select which users are granted access.

The installation process also asks that you enter a name that is used by NetWare users to connect to the server. This name must be unique on the network, and you should enter it in all uppercase letters. Next, you enter a supervisor's password.

FPNW can be installed on any Windows NT Server computer. If you are installing the service on a domain controller, a special account called the FPNW Service Account will be created, and you also will have to supply a password for this account. If you install the service on other domain controllers, be sure to use the same password.

When you have finished entering this information, reboot the server and the service will start.

If you examine the drive that you used to host the SYSVOL directory, you will find that the installation has created several subdirectories under this directory:

- **LOGIN**—This directory holds the utilities that NetWare clients use to log in to the NT Server.

- **MAIL**—User subdirectories are created here and may contain login scripts for users.

- **PUBLIC**—Contains the following utilities: attach, capture, endcap, login, logout, map, setpass, and slist.

- **SYSTEM**—Contains files used to support printing.

File and Print Services for NetWare Version 5.0 (FPNW 5.0)

Installing FPNW on a Windows 2000 server is similar to the installation process used for Windows NT 4.0, though the GUI has changed a bit. For example, in the Control Panel, the Network applet has been changed to Network and Dial-Up Connections. You also can use the desktop icon My Network Places to get there. Properties pages then are used to install or remove services. To install FPNW 5.0, follow these steps:

1. Right-click My Network Places on the desktop. From the menu that appears, click Properties.

2. In the Network and Dial-Up Connections window (see Figure 52.11), right-click Local Area Connection and select Properties from the menu that appears (see Figure 52.12).

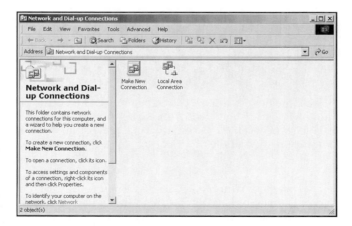

Figure 52.11 Right-click the Local Area Connection icon and select Properties.

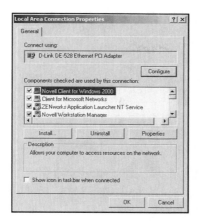

Figure 52.12   Click the Install button on the Properties page for the local connection.

3. Click the Install button on the connection's Properties page. The Select Network Component Type dialog box pops up and prompts you for the component type to install. Select Service and click Add.

4. The Select Network Service dialog box appears (see Figure 52.13). Click the Have Disk button.

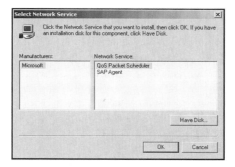

Figure 52.13   Use the Have Disk button to install the FPNW service.

5. The Install From Disk dialog box prompts you to enter the path for the service. Enter the drive letter for the CD-ROM drive that contains the SFN disc, followed by the path name `\FPNW`, as shown in Figure 52.14, and then click the OK button.

6. The Select Network Service dialog box prompts you for the service to install. The only service that appears in this dialog box is File and Print Services for NetWare. Highlight this service and click OK.

7. The Install File and Print Services for NetWare dialog box pops up (see Figure 52.15). As with FPNW version 4, enter the necessary information for the volume you want to create for NetWare users, along with the password that will be used for the FPNW supervisor user account that will be created. You also can use the Tuning section on this dialog box to determine how memory use is allocated to users of the service. Click OK when you've supplied the necessary information.

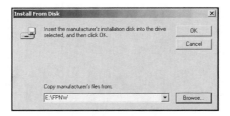

Figure 52.14   Enter the path that contains the FPNW files.

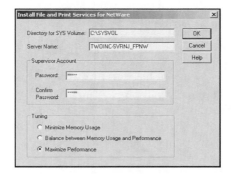

Figure 52.15   Enter the information for the services you want to offer to NetWare clients along with a password to be used by the account that will be used to manage the service.

Note

If you are installing FPNW in a domain, another dialog box will pop up and ask you to enter the password that will be used to run the service. In a domain setup, *use the same password on all domain controllers that you set up to offer FPNW to NetWare users.* Click OK to dismiss this dialog box.

8. When the Local Area Connections Properties sheet reappears, click Close. You'll be prompted to restart your server before the FPNW service runs. You can click Yes to reboot immediately, or simply wait until a more convenient time by clicking No.

9. If you chose to wait until later for the reboot, click the Close button that appears on the Local Area Connection Properties dialog box.

Again, like version 4, you'll find an icon in the Control Panel titled FPNW that can be used to manage the service. In Figure 52.16, you can see the File and Print Services for NetWare dialog box used in version 5.

Statistical information is displayed in the File Server Information section, showing data about the current connections, open files, and so on. You also can use the fields under this section to set up a print queue, home directory path, or a description for the service on this server. Three buttons at the bottom allow you to view more information about users, volumes, and files:

- **Users**—This button brings up a display showing the names of connected users, the network address and login time, as well as information about resources being used. You can use this dialog box to send messages to users or to disconnect one or all users from the service.

- **Volumes**—This button displays a dialog box showing the volumes you have set up to share with FPNW clients, showing connected users, the connection time, and information about file opens. You also can use buttons in this dialog box to disconnect one or all users.

- **Files**—This button displays information about each open file, the user who opened it, locking information, and the path to the file. You can use buttons in this dialog box to close a file or all files currently open.

Figure 52.16 The FPNW dialog box, accessed from the FPNW Control Panel icon, enables you to manage the FPNW service.

Directory Service Manager for NetWare (DSMN)

One of the nice things about a network that is based on the Windows NT 4.0 domain model is the single logon feature. This allows a user to log on at a client workstation using a single username and password to gain access to resources throughout the network, provided that the appropriate rights and permissions have been established for the resources to which the user wants to connect.

DSMN is another optional tool that you can use to extend the single logon feature to your NetWare clients on a Windows NT 4.0 network. It provides a simple method to manage users in a mixed network of NT 4.0 and NetWare clients from a single user database.

Like the File and Print Services for NetWare products, DSMN operates only with NetWare 2.x, 3.x, and 4.x clients in bindery-emulation mode. Also, DSMN must be installed on a Windows NT 4.0 Server computer that is acting as a primary domain controller in the network, and you first must install the Gateway Service for NetWare before you perform the DSMN installation.

DSMN also can be used to copy account information between NetWare servers and Windows NT 4.0 domain controllers, and to keep user passwords synchronized between both systems. You can select users or groups of users that you want to move between each system.

You install DSMN as a service, using the Network applet in the Control Panel. Use the Have Disk option and specify a path to the CD that contains the source files. The service will start after the computer is rebooted. In the Administrative Tools folder you then will see Directory Service Manager for

NetWare (also called the Synchronization Manager), which you can use to specify which servers you want to manage. When you select a NetWare server that you want to manage from Windows NT, you can select users or groups of users whose accounts will be copied to the NT server and placed in the domain database (SAM). From then on, you can manage these users using the User Manager for Domains. DSMN propagates changes you make to these accounts back to the NetWare servers where the accounts originated.

You can use two utilities to manage users and NetWare servers. The Synchronization Manager is used to add a NetWare server to the domain. The User Manager for Domains then can be used to manage any user accounts that you choose to copy from the NetWare server to the domain. Changes made to user accounts using User Manager are copied back to the NetWare server (synchronized) periodically so that you no longer have to use NetWare utilities to manage these users.

Note

Although you will manage NetWare users that you copy to the NT domain by using the User Manager for Domains, you will continue to manage other administrative functions that you would normally perform on the NetWare server using NetWare utilities. This includes things such as managing shared NetWare volumes, file permissions, printing, and so on. Additionally, a NetWare server can be added to only one Windows NT domain. If you want to change this later, remove it from the NT domain, and then use the Synchronization Manager to add it to another domain.

To add a NetWare server to the domain using the Synchronization Manager:

1. From the NetWare Server menu select Add Server to Manage.
2. When prompted, enter the name of a NetWare server. Click OK.
3. Enter a username that is valid on the NetWare server and the password for the username. Note that this user account must have Supervisor privileges on the server.
4. In the Propagate NetWare Accounts to Windows NT Domain dialog box, select either Use Mapping File or Ignore Mapping File.
5. A prompt warns you to first make a backup of the NetWare server's bindery. Click the Yes button to continue.
6. The Set Propagated Accounts on *servername* dialog box appears. You can select here to propagate some or all groups or user accounts back to the NetWare server. You then are asked if you want to delete any remaining users or groups from the NetWare server that you have not selected. Click either Yes or No. You can continue to manage any users that are left behind on the NetWare server using the ordinary NetWare tools.

After you add a NetWare server to the Windows NT domain, it will appear in the main screen for the Synchronization Manager utility. Also, in the NetWare server's bindery you will see a new account, named WINNT_SYNC_AGENT. Do not delete this account because Windows NT uses it when it synchronizes changes made to user accounts.

If you want to map NetWare usernames or groups to a different name on the NT server, you can use the Synchronization Manager to create a mapping file.

Microsoft Directory Synchronization Services (MSDSS)

This utility improves on DSMN but is for use with the Active Directory instead of the Windows NT 4.0 SAM database. MSDSS provides for a *one-way* synchronization with NetWare 3.x binderies and the Active Directory (AD). MSDSS also gives you the capability for either one- or two-way support for synchronization between NDS and AD. Finally, MSDSS allows you to create a file that can be used by the File Migration Utility (FMU), discussed later in this chapter, so that NetWare trustee rights and ACLs are propagated to Windows 2000 servers when you decide to move files from NetWare servers to complete the migration to Windows 2000.

However, to use MSDSS there are a few prerequisites:

- ■ MSDSS can be installed only on a Windows 2000 server acting in the role of a domain controller. Remember that domain controllers contain the Active Directory database, and it is this database that stores user account/password information that is to be kept synchronized.

- ■ You will need to obtain a copy of Novell's Client for Windows 2000. If you've just upgraded a Windows NT 4.0 server that had the previous version of Novell's client installed, you won't need a new copy. The old copy will be upgraded during the Windows 2000 upgrade process. If you need to get a copy of the Novell client, you can obtain one from http://www.novell.com/download/index.html.

Novell has released several versions of its client for Windows NT/2000. Because differences exist from one version to another, read the release notes supplied with the file you download from Novell and follow their instructions for installing the client. For the most part, you simply need to extract the files to a temporary directory and run a setup program that takes only a few minutes, after which you'll need to reboot the server.

Note

If you have already installed Microsoft's Client Service for NetWare, you'll get a prompt when you try to install Novell's client. When asked if you want to remove Microsoft's version, answer Yes to continue the installation of Novell's version of the client. The two are not compatible.

When the server reboots, you are presented with the Novell logon box instead of the familiar Windows logon box.

When using MSDSS to perform synchronization between NDS and AD, you create sessions that specify the NDS and corresponding AD objects that will be kept in sync. You can create a one-way session in which changes made to the Active Directory object will be propagated to the NDS object. However, one-way synchronization does not work in reverse. That is, with a one-way synchronization, changes made to an NDS object do not get copied back to AD. In this type of setup, you should use the Active Directory administrative tools and utilities to perform directory management. From a migration standpoint, this allows you to keep NDS on the network while you gradually educate your network administrators on using the AD tools. After your staff is comfortable using AD, you can use MSDSS to migrate all the required NDS information to AD, and then decommission the NDS servers.

Installing MSDSS

To install MSDSS, after you've installed the NetWare client from Novell, follow these steps:

1. Insert the SFU CD into your local CD-ROM drive.

2. Click Start, Programs, Accessories, Windows Explorer.

3. In the left pane of the Explorer, double-click My Computer. The SFU CD shows up in the left pane of the Explorer display.

4. Double-click the SFU icon. You see two folders, one named FPNW and one named MSDSS. Double-click MSDSS.

5. Inside the MSDSS folder, you now see an MSDSS icon that is used to start the Windows Installer. Double-click the icon.

6. The Windows Installer copies files to your system directory and you then are prompted to reboot the computer.

After you've installed MSDSS, you'll find that the Active Directory server now has a new program in the Administrative Tools folder called Directory Synchronization.

Creating One-Way Synchronization Sessions

You create *sessions* that define the synchronization between NDS and AD objects. The objects must be container objects, such as organizational units (OUs), and not individual leaf objects, such as a single user in the AD. Before you start the New Session Wizard, you should decide which NDS and AD container objects you want to synchronize. This does not create these objects for you. For example, suppose you have an existing NDS object that contains user accounts for the manufacturing department of your business that you want to eventually migrate to AD. You should create a new OU and give it a meaningful name before you start the New Session Wizard. Or, you can simply choose to use a container object that already exists in your AD database.

To create a one-way synchronization session, follow these steps:

1. Click Start, Programs, Administrative Tools, and then Directory Synchronization. The Microsoft Management Console (MMC) snap-in called MSDSS pops up on your screen.

2. In the left pane of the MMC, you can right-click on MSDSS and select New Session from the menu that appears. Alternatively, you can click once on MSDSS in the left pane, click once on the Action Menu, click All Tasks, New Session (see Figure 52.17).

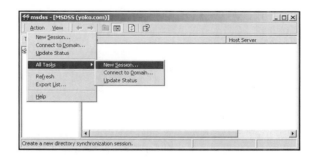

Figure 52.17   Use the MSDSS MMC snap-in to create a new session for synchronization.

3. The New Session Wizard pops up and displays information about the task that you are about to start. That is, you will migrate objects from NDS to AD and, if you want, establish a synchronization schedule. Click the Next button.

4. The New Session Wizard prompts you to select either NDS or a Bindery as the source for the initial migration using a drop-down menu (see Figure 52.18). Under this menu, you can elect to perform a one-way or two-way synchronization, or to simply do a one-time migration from the NDS or bindery source to AD.

5. Select the radio button for One-Way Synchronization (from Active Directory to NDS or Bindery), and then click Next to continue.

6. The next dialog box lets you select the AD container and the domain controller that stores information about this session, and is responsible for performing the synchronization tasks (see Figure 52.19). Click Next to continue.

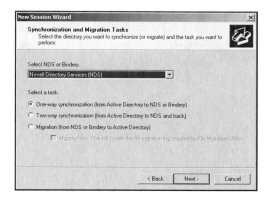

Figure 52.18 Select NDS or Bindery, and then choose to perform synchronization or a one-time migration.

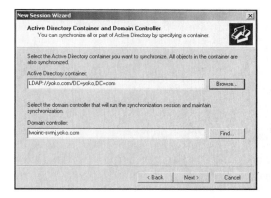

Figure 52.19 Enter the AD container object that will be used for this synchronization session (or use the Browse button to find one), and then enter the domain controller that will manage this session.

Note

If any container objects are child objects to the AD container (organizational unit) you select for synchronization, synchronization will be performed for the selected container object and all of its child container objects as well. If you want to enter the container object in the Active Directory Container field, use the LDAP URL syntax instead of using the Browse button—for example: **LDAP://yoko.com/DC=yoko,DC=com**. In the Domain Controller field, the server on which you are running the New Session Wizard is the default. Use the Find button if you want to search for another domain controller in your network to use instead. For more information about LDAP, container objects, organizational units, and so on, see Chapter 25, "Overview of Microsoft's Active Directory Service," and Appendix D, "Directory Services: Overview of X.500 and LDAP."

7. Next, a similar dialog box prompts you to enter the name of the NDS container object that you want to synchronize with the AD object you selected in step 6. Again, the NDS container must

already exist, and any child objects of the container also are synchronized with the AD container object. The Browse button can be used, or you can use the NDS or bindery syntax to specify the NDS container object; for example, `NDS://Tree1/O=ono/OU=mfg` for an NDS object or `NWCOMPAT://servername` for a bindery server. Enter an NDS username and password that can be used to access the NDS object or bindery, and click Next.

The remaining dialog boxes for the New Session Wizard prompt you to do several things. First, the Initial Reverse Synchronization dialog box can be used if you want to import NDS objects into the Active Directory (a reverse synchronization) after the wizard finishes. Using this dialog box, you first can import NDS information so that you do not have to enter it manually into AD. Because we're just setting up a one-way synchronization, this initial reverse synchronization can be used to populate your AD database with NDS objects that then will be managed using AD administrative tools and utilities.

Because NDS passwords cannot be imported into AD during a reverse synchronization, you can select one of the following methods to set user passwords for user accounts that are initially added to AD during a reverse synchronization:

- **Set passwords to blank**—The first time a user logs on to AD, they will not have to specify a password and can set their password to a value they want. Note that this leaves your migrated user accounts vulnerable to security problems unless properly coordinated. If you use this method, follow up to be sure that each user has logged in and changed their password.

- **Set passwords to the user name**—This is the default. Again, be sure to follow up and be sure that user passwords are changed after the initial migration.

- **Set passwords to a random value**—A random value is chosen for each account. A file is created in the directory `systemroot\System32\Directory Synchronization\Session Logs` that contains the user account names and the random passwords that were created. The file has an extension of `.pwd`, and after the synchronization process is finished, you can look in the Event Viewer to get the name of the file. Using this method, a help desk technician can distribute passwords to users in a more secure manner than using the other options in this list.

- **Set all passwords to the same value that you specify**—All accounts have the same password. Once again, follow up to be sure users change their password to a different value.

The default is to set all the user account passwords imported into AD to the user account's username.

Another dialog box can be used to create specific mappings between AD and NDS objects. This can be useful when the child objects of an AD container object are not organized under the parent object in the same order as they are in the AD object. You can create an object mapping table that stores these relationships.

The New Session Wizard finally asks you to enter a name for this session, which you can use later to manage the session, or make changes to it. After you enter a name to use for the session, click the Finish button.

Creating Two-Way Synchronization Sessions

In the previous section, you learned how to create a one-way synchronization that could be used to import NDS objects into the Active Directory. From that point forward, you should use the AD administrative tools to manage the objects. However, you also can use the New Session Wizard to set up a two-way synchronization process. To do so, use the same Directory Synchronization utility found in the Administrative Tools folder, and start up the New Session Wizard. When the Synchronization and Migration Tasks dialog box pops up (refer to Figure 52.18), select two-way synchronization (from Active Directory to NDS and back) instead of the one-way synchronization.

You will have to supply similar information for the AD and NDS containers, as well as access information, just like you did for a one-way synchronization. You also can choose to perform an initial reverse synchronization, or you can elect to do this later.

One-Time Migration

Using a one- or two-way synchronization enables you to import NDS objects into AD so that you can manage your network resources (users, printers, and so on) using the administrative tools designed to work with the Active Directory. After you no longer have any need to keep NDS servers on your network, you can use the one-time migration option to simply import the data from NDS (or from bindery servers). The process is just about the same as a one-way synchronization, but after you have imported the data, changes made to objects in the Active Directory *will not* be propagated back to the NDS or bindery servers. Using the synchronization method, you can gradually migrate your network from NDS to AD. Using the one-time migration option, you can complete the process and turn off your NDS servers.

Again, you use the MMC MSDSS snap-in Directory Synchronization that is found in the Administrative Tools folder to begin a one-time migration. Use the New Session Wizard, as described earlier, to start the process. However, when the Synchronization and Migration Tasks dialog box appears (refer to Figure 52.18), select the Migration (from NDS or Bindery to Active Directory) radio button. You'll have to supply the same type of access information for the AD and NDS objects that will be migrated, and you can select an additional option: Migrate files from the NDS or Bindery servers to Windows 2000 servers. The check box for this function, also shown in Figure 52.18, *does not actually perform the file migration*, but instead creates a file that is used by the File Migration Utility, which we'll get to next. When you've decided it's time to get rid of those NDS servers, use this option to create the file, and then invoke the File Migration Utility.

File Migration Utility (FMU)

This is the second tool that Services for NetWare 5.0 provides that you can use only on Windows 2000 Server. FMU is used to migrate files and directories from NetWare volumes to Windows 2000 disks, while keeping intact security permissions. You can use this tool with both the IPX/SPX and TCP/IP protocols.

When you migrate files from NDS to Windows 2000, the MSDSS utility discussed in the preceding sections can be used to create a file that FMU uses to maintain user and group relationships and rights associated with files and directories. Before using FMU, be sure to read these sections! MSDSS maps organizational units (OUs) and organizations from NDS to the Active Directory by creating local security groups for every NDS OU and organization.

FMU is installed when you install MSDSS. To start the actual file migration process, click Start, Programs, Administrative Tools, and then File Migration Utility. The File Migration Utility Wizard, shown in Figure 52.20, pops up and performs some preliminary functions. When it has finished, the Next button becomes available. Click Next and you'll see a large property sheet that has tabs (see Figure 52.21), each of which can be used to perform a step in the migration process.

In Step 1, you must enter the full path for the migration log that you created using MSDSS. You can use the Browse button to locate the file if you don't recall where it was created. After you locate the file, click the Load Data button to read in the file. Note that at the bottom of the screen you'll see a display called Steps Completed, with boxes numbered 1 through 5. If you do not have time to complete the entire migration process in one session, or if you have to stop and rethink the process, you can look here to see what you've done so far. You can use the Allow Step Completion in Any Order check box if you want to perform steps out of order. Each time you click the Next button you move to another step. Using this check box, you can bring up any of the steps. The View Maps and Access

Rights buttons enable you to view how access rights are mapped between Windows 2000 and NetWare access rights. This might be necessary, for example, if you have a file that has the NDS Modify right associated with it. By default, this maps to the Windows Read right. You can change this to the Write right (am I a poet or what?) if you want to by using the Access Rights button.

Click the Next button to continue.

Figure 52.20 The File Migration Utility performs a few preliminary functions before you begin the migration process.

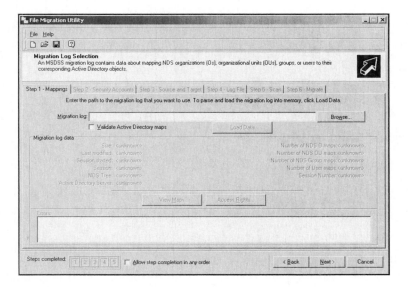

Figure 52.21 The File Migration Utility steps you through the migration process.

Note

The default location for the migration log that MSDSS creates is *systemroot*\System32\Directory Synchronization\Session Logs. Look for the log file on the same server on which you performed a one-time migration.

The Step 2 tab shows you the Active Directory account that you used to log into the Windows 2000 server (see Figure 52.22). Use the NetWare Connections button to show any current connections you have made to NetWare resources. If you have yet to log on to NDS or a bindery server, use the Log On to Novell button to do so at this time. Enter the required NDS or bindery account name and password, and click Next.

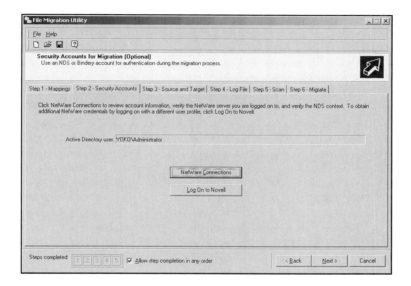

Figure 52.22 In Step 2 you review your Windows logon and can log on to the Novell network if you have not yet done so.

Step 3 enables you to select the source and target of the migration task (see Figure 52.23). Use this step to select the NDS or bindery volume or directories that you want to migrate to the Windows 2000 server. Under Target, select the Windows 2000 file shares or directories that will be used as the location for the files to be migrated. When you've finished making selections, click on Map and then, of course, click the Next button.

Step 4 enables you to create a log file and select options for generating the log file that will be created during the migration process (see Figure 52.24). Use the check box labeled Enable Logs, and then you can fill in the remaining fields shown in this figure.

If the migration will involve a lot of files, you can help reduce the size of the log file by using the Enable Compression (NTFS only) check box. If you want to append a date and timestamp in the log-file to determine when a file was actually migrated, use the next check box. The Stop Migration If Disk Reaches Capacity check box does just what it says!

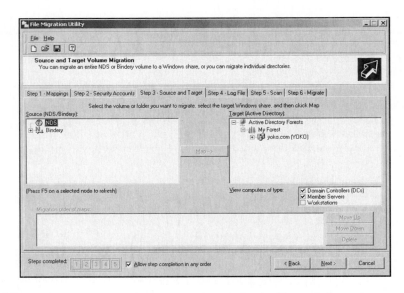

Figure 52.23 In Step 3 you select the source and target for the files and directories you want to migrate.

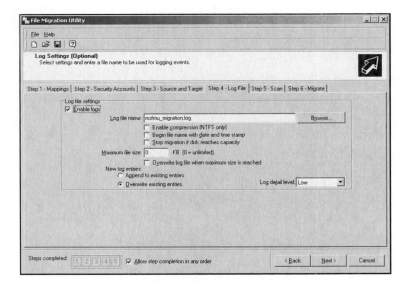

Figure 52.24 You can configure how the log file will be generated during the migration using Step 4.

You also can set a maximum size for the log file in the Maximum File Size field, or leave it at the default of zero to allow the file to grow to any size. If you set a value for this field, the check box underneath it, Overwrite Log File When Maximum Size Is Reached, should be used so that the process will continue if the log file exceeds the size that you set.

The radio buttons under New Log Entries enable you to elect to either append new entries or overwrite existing entries when you use the same log file to perform migrations at different times. The Log Detail Level drop-down menu enables you to select the amount of information that is logged for each file. When you've finished configuring the log file, click Next to proceed to the next step.

Step 5 is used to scan the volumes and directories you selected as sources from NDS or NetWare for the migration (see Figure 52.25). Click the Scan button and the program counts the directories, and the files within them, and checks that the correct access rights are associated with each volume (or directory/file).

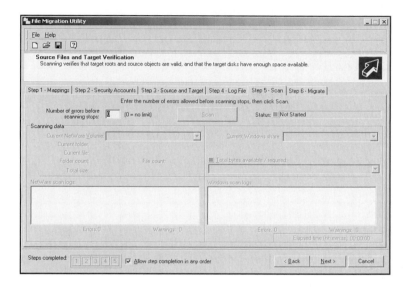

Figure 52.25   Step 5 allows you to perform a scan to check for errors before you do the actual migration.

If any errors occur, you can choose to continue, and simply use a manual method for copying the files or directories. However, if a large number of errors is encountered, the FMU utility will stop and you'll need to rethink your migration. Go back to the previous steps in the process to see if you've entered any incorrect information or ignored access rights required to access the NDS or bindery data.

Another thing that can cause errors during the migration process is opened or locked files on the NetWare server. You might want to perform Steps 1 through 5 and save the actual migration (Step 6) until a time when you can obtain downtime for your NetWare servers to ensure that all files and directories that are to be migrated are accessible. For example, to perform the migration, you must be logged on to the Windows 2000 server with an account that is a member of the Domain Admins group.

Finally, when you are ready to perform the actual data transfer, Step 6 enables you to start the process. On the Step 6 tab (see Figure 52.26), click the Migrate button. Depending on how much data is to be transferred from NetWare to Windows 2000, the process can take just a few minutes or many hours.

After you've migrated your files to Windows 2000 servers, you should perform testing to be sure that your clients can connect to the Windows 2000 servers and that the files and directories are set up as you planned. After everything checks out, consider the migration a success and decommission those NDS servers!

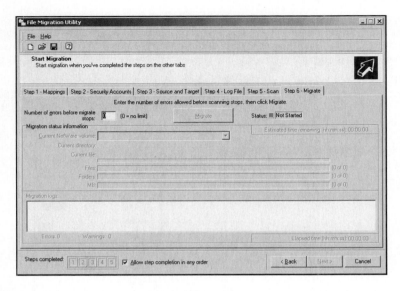

Figure 52.26 Use Step 6 to perform the actual file migration.

Integrating Windows NT 4.0/2000 with Unix and Linux

CHAPTER 53

SOME OF THE MAIN TOPICS IN THIS CHAPTER ARE

- Windows NT Support for Unix Protocols and Utilities
- Microsoft Windows Services for Unix (SFU) Add-On Pack Version 2.0
- SAMBA
- Sun Network Information System (NIS)
- Windows NT Terminal Server Edition

It would be difficult to find two operating systems that differ more from each other than Unix and Windows. Unix has been around for a much longer time. What started out as a "developer's operating system" has evolved over the years into a stable platform that runs on more hardware platforms than perhaps any other operating system. Many large Web sites use either Unix (or Linux) to run their Web servers. Windows NT/2000, on the other hand, and its newest cousin, Windows XP, are graphically oriented operating systems that now run on only one platform, Intel. Windows NT 4.0 provided support for the Alpha server platform from Compaq and for the PowerPC. However, support for the PowerPC platform was dropped with Windows NT 4.0 Service Pack 4, and the Alpha platform was dropped during the Windows 2000 beta process. That means that if you want to run Windows 2000, you'll have to replace those very good Alpha systems (which also run Unix, Linux, and OpenVMS, by the way, so you might be able to put them to other uses).

Configuring Windows systems can be done using the GUI and, in many cases, command-line utilities at the command prompt. Unix and Linux also can provide an optional GUI, using X Window, the Common Desktop Environment, and several other GUI interfaces. However, both Unix and Linux are generally considered to be heavily oriented toward the command line when it comes to configuration.

Both the Windows and Unix/Linux operating systems have their own strengths and weaknesses, and each can be used to solve certain problems more effectively than the other. By integrating these two systems into the same network, you can take advantage of each one's best capabilities and enhance performance of the services provided to users.

There are two approaches you can take to integrating these two kinds of systems in one network. First, you can use the features Microsoft provides for the Windows environment, which were derived from standards that were developed in the Unix world, such as TCP/IP and the standard suite of utilities that have been written around it (FTP and telnet). Second, you can use third-party applications, such as SAMBA, that have been created to allow Windows Server Message Block (SMB) and Common Internet File System (CIFS) functionality to be installed onto Unix/Linux platforms. This last approach seems to be the path that Microsoft will be taking in the near future, heralded by the release of the Microsoft Services for Unix (SFU) version 2.0. SFU provides components from Microsoft and other vendors that can make life easier for a Unix administrator who inherits a network of Windows clients!

Windows NT Support for Unix Protocols and Utilities

Many of the technologies that began in the Unix world have evolved into standards that have been implemented on other platforms over the years. For example, the lpr/lpd printing system (see Chapter 35, "Network Printing Protocols"), which started out on Unix, is supported not only by Windows NT, OpenVMS, and other operating systems, but also by printers from Hewlett-Packard and printserver appliances made by a number of other vendors. When adding Windows computers to a network that consists mainly of Unix or Linux servers, printing can be the least of a network administrator's worries. It is a simple matter to configure Windows NT 4.0 Server to direct printer output to a Unix system that is responsible for maintaining print queues or to a printer that understands the lpr/lpd protocols. You also can use standard TCP/IP stream printing when using Windows 2000 as a print server.

Other technologies that were either first developed in or adopted by the Unix world, which Windows supports, include the following:

- The TCP/IP networking protocol suite, including the telnet and FTP utilities
- BOOTP and the Dynamic Host Configuration Protocol (DHCP)
- The Domain Name System (DNS)

TCP/IP

When Windows 3.51 was introduced, the default network protocol was IPX/SPX. TCP/IP was there if you wanted to use it, but at that time Microsoft perceived that its main competitor in the client/server market was Novell NetWare. When NT 4.0 was released, the default had been changed to TCP/IP. Because the Internet had begun to take on a higher degree of importance during the time frame in which NT 4.0 was being developed, this was a natural path for the operating system to take. TCP/IP is the network protocol suite that is used throughout the Internet to connect computers from a wide range of manufacturers running many different operating systems. For example, you can find TCP/IP on every Unix or Linux variant currently on the market, on the OpenVMS operating system, and every operating system from IBM, from OS/2 to mainframes. Of course, when Windows 2000 was released, TCP/IP had become the de facto standard networking protocol for almost all Microsoft products, and is included with Windows 98 and Windows XP.

In a network that consists of Unix servers, TCP/IP can be used by Windows NT clients to access resources on these servers. The two most common methods provided by TCP/IP are the telnet and FTP applications.

Telnet

Windows NT/2000 Server and the Workstation/Professional versions both come with a telnet client. Microsoft did not choose to provide a telnet *server* with Windows NT 4.0, however. So, although you can establish a telnet session from a Windows client to a Unix or Linux server, you cannot do the same to a *plain vanilla installation* of Windows NT 4.0.

Windows 2000 Server does provide a telnet service, but it is not enabled by default. To start the service on a Windows 2000 Server computer, use the following steps:

1. Click Start, Programs, Administrative Tools, Computer Management.
2. In the left pane of the MMC console click on Services. A list of services available on the computer is displayed in the right pane, as shown in Figure 53.1.

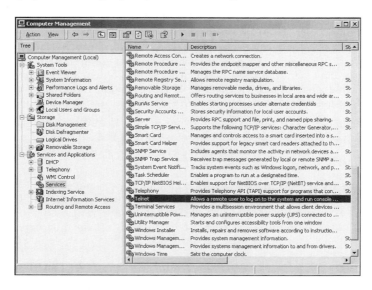

Figure 53.1 You can manage the Windows 2000 telnet server service using the Computer Management administrative tool.

3. Scroll down in the right pane until you find the telnet service (which is highlighted in Figure 53.1).

4. Right-click on the telnet service and select Start from the menu that appears.

You can manage properties of the telnet service by using these same steps. However, instead of selecting Start from the menu, select Properties. In Figure 53.2 you can see the properties page for the telnet service.

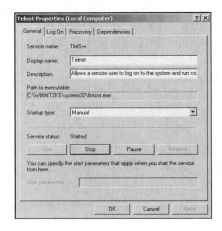

Figure 53.2 The Properties page for the telnet service enables you to further configure the service on the local computer.

In Figure 53.2 you can see that there are several tabs, each of which is used to display a different set of properties you can configure for the service. Using the General tab shown here, you can change the display name for the service and the description of the service. More importantly, you can use the Start, Stop, Pause, and Resume buttons. The Start and Stop buttons do exactly what they say, stop or start the service. If you use the Pause button, however, administrators and members of the Server Operators groups can still use the service and establish a telnet connection with the server. This can be useful when you don't want ordinary users making telnet connections to the machine while you are performing maintenance chores, for example. Use the Resume button to allow the service to continue servicing other users (provided you have not stopped the service).

Also on the General tab is the drop-down menu Startup type. Because the telnet server runs as a service on Windows 2000, you can use this to control when and how the service is started. The options are manual (use the Start button), Automatic (the service starts when the system is booted), or Disabled (the service does not start on boot).

The Log On and Recovery tabs function as they do for all services and are beyond the scope of this chapter. You should be familiar with how services work on Windows 2000 before using these tabs. For example, using the Log On tab you can select the user account that the service is run under (the LocalSystem account is typical for the Telnet service and many others). The Dependencies tab, however, shows you that this particular service needs to have the Remote Procedure Call (RPC) service running in order for the telnet service to operate.

After you have started the telnet server service on the Windows 2000 computer, you can manage the server by using the Telnet Server Administration utility found in the Administrative Tools folder. As you can see in Figure 53.3, the interface to this utility is simple. You have the options of listing connected users or terminating users, and also the capability to start or stop the service.

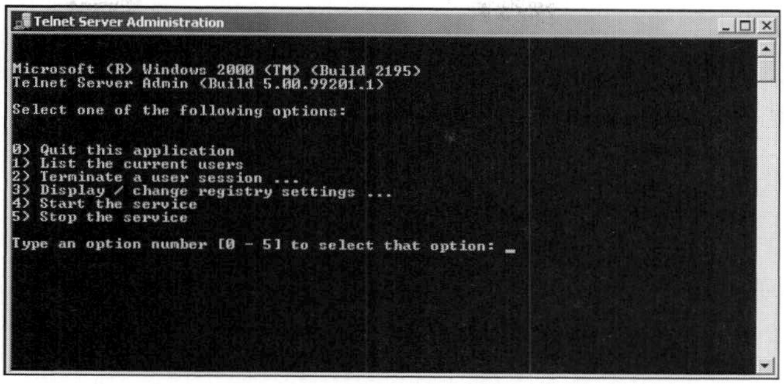

Figure 53.3   The standard Windows 2000 telnet server uses a simple interface for management purposes.

Option number 3 enables you to view current default settings for the server that are stored in the Registry. This option can be used to allow trusted domains access to the server, provide a logon script, and set the number of log failures before a user is locked out. An important feature you can use is one that forces users to use the more secure Windows NT NTLM authentication instead of the typical clear-text username/password method that is found in many typical Telnet server implementations. This should definitely be used in an all-Windows environment. However, Unix clients do not, by default, support this authentication method.

Note

The default telnet server that comes with Windows 2000 Server allows for a maximum of two simultaneous telnet sessions. If you need to allow more users to make telnet connections to the server, you'll have to use the telnet server provided by the Microsoft Services for Unix (SFU) package instead. SFU is discussed later in this chapter and supports as many as 63 sessions.

There are also excellent third-party telnet servers you can use with Windows. If you intend to make heavy use of telnet on your network, it is worth investigating these competing products to determine which telnet server is right for your needs.

Telnet provides a character-cell terminal emulation that can be used to run applications that do not depend on the features provided by either the Windows GUI or its equivalent in the Unix world, X Window. For example, it is easy to telnet into a Unix system to perform system administration tasks using a command-line interface provided by a shell. Script files can be edited and run remotely by using a telnet session.

If a Telnet server has been installed on the Windows Server, you can similarly perform some administration of Windows systems from a Unix box by using command-line utilities. However, not all Windows administrative utilities have a command-line counterpart, and when they do, you often find that the command-line version doesn't provide the full capabilities that the GUI version does.

File Transfer Protocol (FTP)

Like the Telnet server, Windows NT/2000 comes with an FTP client. Similarly, the FTP server is provided by installing Internet Information Services (IIS) for Windows NT 4.0. The FTP client can be used easily from the command prompt and uses the standard syntax that is common to other FTP clients.

The FTP *server* for Windows NT/2000 Server is a component of the Internet Information Services (IIS), which is included as part of the installation procedure for Windows 2000. For Windows NT, you can use the icon that appears on the desktop of a Windows NT Server to install IIS or download the newest version from Microsoft. IIS has been enhanced since its first release, and many Web sites use the Windows platform running IIS to create a presence on the Internet. If you want to run an FTP server on Windows NT 4.0, it is recommended that you download the latest version of IIS. Windows 2000 users will find that IIS is included on the server installation CD.

To manage the FTP server on a Windows 2000 server, follow these steps:

1. Click Start, Programs, Administrative Tools, Internet Services Manager.

2. The MMC console starts, with the IIS snap-in. Click on the IIS server you want to manage, and you'll see a list of IIS currently running on the server, as shown in Figure 53.4.

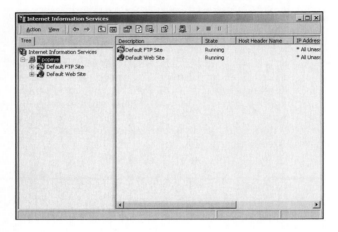

Figure 53.4   The MMC utility is used to manage the FTP service, which is part of the Internet Information Services (IIS) component of Windows 2000.

3. Right-click on the FTP server (the Default FTP site in our example here) and select Properties.

4. The Properties pages for the FTP server can then be used to configure the server (see Figure 53.5).

The Default FTP Site Properties page appears in this figure with the first tab (FTP Site) selected. You can use the Description field to change this from "default" to a more meaningful name. This can be useful if you are using the MMC to manage multiple servers. The IP Address field can be used to select an IP address that the FTP service will use when listening for incoming requests, and the TCP Port field can be used to set which TCP port will be used for the service. In this example, the standard TCP port number of 21 is shown.

Other fields on this tab are fairly self-explanatory, allowing you to set the maximum number of users that can be connected to the server simultaneously and the number of seconds after which an idle session will be automatically disconnected from the server. At the bottom of this first property page you can see that you also can enable logging for the service. The drop-down menu named Active log format allows you to choose from

■ **Microsoft IIS Log File Format**—This is a standard ASCII text file format. If you use this format, the information that is stored in the log file is fixed.

- **W3C Extended Log File Format**—This also is an ASCII text file but one that you can customize to select what events to log. This is the default format for the IIS FTP Server.
- **ODBC Logging**—This can be used to direct logging data to an ODBC-compliant database.

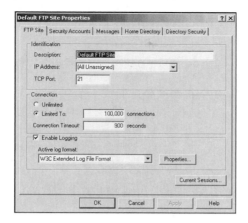

Figure 53.5   You can manage the FTP service using the properties pages for the server found in the Internet Information Services MMC snap-in.

The Properties button to the right of this drop-down menu enables you to further configure properties for the log file. For the Microsoft IIS Log File Format there's not much you can configure. The data that is written to the log file is a standard set of data. You can use the Properties button to configure when a new log file is created—this can range from hourly, daily, weekly, or monthly. Or, you can set a maximum size to which the file can grow before a new file is created. Additionally, you can set the location of the log file. The default is %WinDir%\System32\LogFiles, where %WinDir% is a variable that resolves to the Windows system directory.

For the W3C Extended Log File Format you have many more options. In addition to being able to configure the same options about how or when a new log file is created and the location of the log file, this format has an additional tab labeled Extended Properties. In Figure 53.6 you can see the Extended Properties tab for this logging format.

Figure 53.6   The W3C Extended Log File Format allows you to specify exactly what data will be recorded in the log file.

There are far too many data items to discuss in this chapter, but you need to be aware that you can create a customized log file that stores just the information you need. You might find that on an anonymous FTP server you don't care much about what data gets stored in the log file, whereas on a server that provides for a secure logon you might want to collect extensive data about the users of your system. To find out the meaning of each of these logging options, click the Help button and a brief description of each item will be displayed.

Finally, at the bottom of this property sheet you can use the Current Sessions button to show a list of users currently connected to the FTP server.

Other tabs on the FTP Site Properties page include

- **Security Accounts**—Use this tab to allow or disallow anonymous access to the FTP server. If you allow anonymous FTP connections, you also can configure the user account that will be used for these connections. This tab also enables you to specify the users or user groups that can manage this FTP site.

- **Messages**—This tab enables you to input text that is presented to the user when logging into and upon exiting the service. You also can enter a message that will be displayed to users who try to log onto the server when the maximum number of user sessions has already been reached.

- **Home Directory**—This tab enables you to configure the home directory for this FTP service. You can select a directory that is local to the server or a directory that is offered as a file share from another computer. If you choose the file share option, you'll be prompted to enter authentication information needed to connect to the file share. The default directory is c:\inetpub\ftproot. Here you can select whether the directory can be read, written to, or both. You also can select to allow logging for this directory. Finally, this tab can be used to specify how directory listings are displayed to users. You can choose between the standard MS-DOS format and the standard Unix format.

- **Directory Security**—This tab is important because it enables you to decide which computers (or IP addresses) will be allowed to connect to the service. You can choose to allow all computers access and then specify a number of specific computers to exclude from access, or you can choose to deny access to all computers and then add in only those specific addresses you want to allow to use the service.

Note

When using the Directory Security tab to allow deny access to the FTP service, remember that some computers use a proxy server. This is typically found when the computer to which you want to grant access is on the other side of a firewall. In this case, the address of the firewall (acting as a proxy server) uses its address when sending connection requests instead of the actual address of the client computer. If you allow (or deny) access in this manner, any computer that uses the proxy server will be allowed (or denied) access.

As you can see, the FTP service enables you to control who can access your server and to log each visit in detail. You can create additional FTP services on the same computer. For example, if you have multiple network adapters or if you assign multiple IP addresses to the same adapter, you can create additional FTP sites on the same server. To add additional FTP sites on this server:

1. Highlight the computer server's name in the left pane of the MMC console.

2. Click on Action, select New, and then FTP Site.

3. A wizard appears and prompts you through creating the site, allowing you to enter the necessary information, such as a description of the site, the IP address to use, and so on.

Of course, after you have created an additional site, you can further refine how it operates by using the Properties pages for that site.

The Dynamic Host Configuration Protocol (DHCP) and BOOTP

Most Unix environments, which use TCP/IP for networking, use DHCP servers to provide network configuration information to clients on the network. DHCP is not a proprietary solution but is based on standards that are defined in RFCs 2131 and 2132. Microsoft clients using TCP/IP can also use DHCP servers. Additionally, Windows 2000 has a highly configurable DHCP server that supports options provided for in the RFCs as well as a few that are specific for Microsoft clients.

If you are bringing Windows-based client systems into an existing Unix environment, configuring each Windows client with the address of a DHCP server will be simple. In an existing Windows network, you might want to stick with the Microsoft DHCP server. Because DHCP is based on Internet standards, most of the implementations you find will be compatible with both operating systems.

Bringing Unix clients into a network that uses Microsoft DHCP servers can cause some seasoned Unix administrators to worry. DHCP servers have been around for quite a while on Unix networks, running on Unix servers and Microsoft's DHCP server is a relatively new creature on the market. However, because Microsoft's DHCP server is built using the standards set forth in the relevant RFC documents, you should have no reason to worry. The graphical interface Microsoft's version offers makes it even easier to manage the server and should be considered an advantage over some other products.

However, the DHCP server that you can install on Windows NT 4.0 or Windows 2000 Advanced Server is a full-featured implementation that can be used to support clients no matter what their operating system. The configuration information that a DHCP server sends to clients is itself configurable through the use of DHCP options. Each option describes a parameter that can be configured for the client from information the DHCP server can provide.

◀◀ For more information about how BOOTP and DHCP function and how they can greatly simplify network administration tasks, see Chapter 23, "BOOTP and the Dynamic Host Configuration Protocol (DHCP)."

Microsoft's DHCP server provides support for the options defined in RFC 1533, "DHCP Options and BOOTP Vendor Extensions." In addition, it enables the administrator to define custom options when needed. This capability to create customized options makes the server flexible in a networking environment that consists of different client types. Additionally, it is possible to set up the Microsoft DHCP service to run on a Windows 2000 cluster and thus provide redundancy for the network without having to divide the address space into separate scopes and place each scope on a separate server.

Before there was DHCP there was BOOTP, which functions in a manner similar to DHCP. The BOOTP protocol is mainly used by diskless workstations, usually in a Unix network, to request addressing configuration information and to download an operating system. Microsoft's DHCP server enables the administrator to create records in a BOOTP table that can be used to satisfy requests from these kinds of clients. When the DHCP server receives a BOOTP request from a client, it looks up the client in the table. If a record for that client is found, the server will return to the client three pieces of information:

- **Boot Image**—A generic file name for the boot file.
- **File Name**—The path to the boot image on a TFTP (Trivial File Transfer Protocol) server.
- **TFTP Server**—The server from which the client can download the boot file.

The Microsoft DHCP server responds to BOOTP clients with the information they need to download a boot file from another server. Unlike the standard DHCP lease, the BOOTP client does not have to renew the IP address periodically as regular DHCP clients do. Instead, a BOOTP client is managed like clients who use reserved DHCP addresses. Additionally, Windows 2000's DHCP server allows for many other options that can be used by BOOTP clients, as provided for in the RFCs.

DNS

Chapter 24, "Name Resolution," examines the implementation of DNS. DNS is the standard method used on the Internet to resolve host IP addresses to "friendly names" that humans find easier to remember. Microsoft NT 4.0/2000 provides a DNS server that is based on Internet Engineering Task Force (IETF) RFC 1053 and can be used by both Microsoft clients and other clients that have been created according to the standard. This includes, of course, most Unix and Linux clients. Additionally, with Windows 2000, Microsoft's DNS server supports dynamic DNS, which is defined in RFC 2136, "Dynamic Updates in the Domain Name System (DNS UPDATE)." This functionality allows clients to use DHCP to obtain an address and then have the address automatically registered with the DNS server. This feature can be very useful if you have many mobile clients that move among different subnets.

If you already have a DNS server running on your network, you might wonder why you would want to use Microsoft's version when you add clients that are not running Unix or Linux. The answer is simple: In addition to providing support for dynamic DNS, Microsoft's DNS server provides a WINS (Windows Internet Name Service) lookup feature that can further simplify network administration chores. It provides a service similar to what DNS does but with an interesting twist. Microsoft's DNS server has the capability to query the WINS server when it cannot resolve a name or address based on the information contained in its database.

Although DNS is basically used to perform IP address/name translations, WINS was developed to provide name resolution services for NetBIOS names. When a WINS client computer boots, it registers its NetBIOS name(s) with the WINS server along with its current network address. If you incorporate DHCP into the network, you will be relieved of having to keep track of IP addresses for Microsoft clients as well as maintaining an address space when clients move or new clients are added to the network. Enabling Microsoft clients to use the WINS service eliminates the manual task of administrating a name server to keep track of additions or changes to the network.

However, if you plan to move your network toward using only Windows 2000 (and future versions), you probably won't need WINS any more. It is provided with Windows 2000 for backward compatibility with earlier Microsoft operating systems. It is possible to use both WINS and DNS in the same network with Windows 2000 and earlier systems. However, in a network that includes Unix, Linux, and Windows clients, you really don't need WINS any more if the Windows clients are all Windows 2000 or above.

Microsoft Windows Services for Unix (SFU) Add-On Pack Version 2.0

Instead of trying to tackle the enormous job of developing still more applications to make it easier to integrate Unix and Windows into a cohesive network, Microsoft chose to take advantage of developments by other vendors and instead released the Windows NT Services for Unix Add-On Pack. Now simply called Services for Unix (SFU) Version 2.0, this optional software, which sells for approximately $149, contains applications that were developed by Microsoft and other vendors but which can be bought as a single package. With SFU version 2.0 you get the following:

- Network File System (NFS) client and server software
- Commands based on the Korn Shell
- Two-way password synchronization
- User name mapping
- New Telnet server and client software

In addition, you'll find many other components, such as support for Sun's Network Information System (NIS), among others.

Network File System (NFS)

The NFS client allows Windows clients to connect to NFS file systems hosted on Unix servers. The client can connect to the file system exported by a Unix server using several methods. The simplest method is just to browse the Network Neighborhood using Windows Explorer. However, you also can use the command line to connect to NFS file systems. To make matters simpler for a network that is composed of both Unix and Windows users, several syntaxes are supported:

- **net use**—The standard Windows net use command can be used to connect just as you can to a normal Windows file share. The specification of the resource to which you want to connect can be expressed as a standard Windows file share (net use * \\server\sharename), or you can use a format that is similar to using the Unix mount command (net use * server/sharename). Note, however, that the second (Unix) syntax will result in the connection being set up more quickly.

- **mount**—For those more familiar with NFS, you might prefer to use the mount command. Again, you can use either the Windows or Unix format to specify the resource to which you want to connect; for example, mount server/sharename * or mount \\server\sharename.

In the preceding syntax examples, the asterisk character causes the next available drive letter to be assigned to the resource. You also can specify a particular drive letter. In either case, after the connection has been made to the NFS resource, you can then use Windows applications to access files on the resource just as if they were Windows file shares.

SFU also provides for these:

- **Server for NFS**—Use this to allow Unix clients to access file shares on Windows NT or Windows 2000 computers using standard Unix NFS commands. After this component is installed, you can offer a Windows directory as a file share by clicking on the NFS Sharing tab that is located on the Properties page for a directory using Windows Explorer. Alternatively, you can use the command line to offer a directory on a Windows server to create the NFS share. The syntax for this is nfsshare sharename=drive:path.

- **Gateway for NFS**—Use this when your Windows clients only need to make moderate use of Unix NFS file systems. By using a gateway, you need to load SFU on only a single server, and it acts as a gateway, making the connections to Unix NFS file systems for Windows clients. The Windows clients connect to a file share then offered by the gateway. If your Windows client will be using NFS resources heavily, load the SFU client software instead so the gateway does not become a bottleneck in a bandwidth-limited network.

- **Server for PCNFS**—This component enables a Windows NT or Windows 2000 Server to act as a PCNFSD server. This provides for authentication when connecting to NFS resources.

Using these components you can grant access to both sets of clients—Unix or Windows—to files stored on the other's systems. One limitation you should note for the gateway service is that you are still stuck with the drive letter limitation. Suppose your network has a large number of Unix servers, each exporting an NFS file system. For each connection, the gateway server will use one of its drive letters that could normally be mapped to a regular Windows file share. You can get around this easily, however, by setting up more than one gateway.

Korn Shell

The Korn Shell commands that SFU gives to Windows NT and Windows 2000 allow you to use existing script files that run on Unix systems. For users trained on Unix systems, the Korn Shell commands make it much easier to add Windows NT/2000 computers to their flock of computers that need to be administered. Table 53.1 lists the commands that are provided by SFU.

Table 53.1   Korn Shell Unix Commands Provided by the Add-On Pack

Korn Shell Command	Use
sh	Invokes the Korn Shell.
basename	Removes a pathname and leaves just the filename.
cat	Similar to DIR, shows files in the directory. Also can be used to concatenate files
chmod	Administers file permissions.
chown	Administers file ownership.
cp	Copies files.
cron	Executes commands found in the user's crontab file at the times specified.
cut	Use this to cut selected fields from each line of a text file.
date	Displays the current date and time.
diff	Compares two text files and displays lines that are different.
dirname	Extracts pathname from string.
dos2unix	Converts a DOS-style text file to a Unix-style text file.
du	Displays disk use of one (or more) files or directories.
find	Searches directories to find files matching a Boolean expression.
grep	Searches files for a pattern.
head	Copies n number of lines from a file to standard output.
kill	Sends a message to a process, can be used to delete the process.
ln	Creates a link to a file (hard link).
ls	Lists a directory.
mkdir	Creates named directory in mode 777.
mount	When Client for NFS is installed, mounts an NFS file system.
more	Displays contents of file, one screen at a time.
mv	Moves a file.
nice	Runs the user's command at a lower priority.
od	Used to "dump" the contents of files.
paste	Pastes text from one file into another.
perl	An interpreted language printenv. Displays the current environment.
ps	Displays a list of processes currently running.
pwd	Displays the current directory ("print working directory").
rcmd	Executes a command or a shell on a remote computer system.
renice	Changes the priority of a process.
rm	Removes a file entry from a directory.

Table 53.1   Continued

Korn Shell Command	Use
rmdir	Removes a directory.
sed	Copies a file to standard output while making edits according to a script.
sdiff	Formats the output from the diff command so the lines of text that differ appear side-by-side.
sleep	Pauses (sleeps) for a specified number of seconds.
sort	Sorts contents of one or more files.
split	Use this to split a file into separate pieces.
strings	Searches for strings in a *binary* file.
su	Changes the user ID of the current shell.
tail	Similar to head; sends lines from a file to standard output, starting at a specified location in the file.
tar	Tape Archive utility used to create or extract files from a tape archive.
tee	Transcribes standard input to standard output and makes copies in filename.
top	Displays a list of processes making the most use of CPU time.
touch	Updates the modification or access time of a file.
tr	Replaces all occurrences of one set of characters with another set of characters.
uname	Displays system information (name, operating system, and so on).
uniq	Finds repeated lines in a file.
unmount	If Client for NFS is installed, use this command to dismount an NFS directory.
uuecode (uuencode)	Used to encode and decode a binary file into a 7-bit ASCII text file.
wait	Waits for a process to terminate.
wc	"Word Count," displays a count of lines, words or characters in a file.
which	Identifies the location of a given command that will execute.
vi	Screen-oriented text editor.
xargs	Creates an argument list and executes a command.

Some of these commands, such as mkdir and find, are already familiar to Windows NT users. However, their functions in the Korn Shell might differ from those provided by the standard Windows NT implementation. For Unix administrators, the addition of these commands can make moving into managing Windows NT and Windows 2000 computers easier. You can use the Unix commands in Table 53.1 and, at the same time, become familiar with the Windows Script Host (WSH). WSH enables you to create scripts using VBScript or Jscript so you are not stuck with using only the familiar MS-DOS commands that have been the mainstay for creating script files on Windows systems for more than 20 years. In addition, SFU provides an implementation of Perl that can be used with WSH.

Password Synchronization

In Version 1 of SFU, this feature enabled you to configure a group of Unix servers so that when a user's password was changed on a Windows NT server, the change was propagated to the user's accounts on those target Unix servers. Because the application ran only on the Windows NT computer, it was a one-way service. That is, changes made on the Unix servers were not sent back to the Windows NT computer.

Version 2 of SFU now makes this functionality a two-way street. To use this SFU component, you'll need to load the Password Synchronization service on the Windows 2000 Server (or NT) and, additionally, you'll have to run a daemon (called a Single Sign On Daemon, or SSOD for short) on each Unix box that will participate in the password-update process. SFU Version 2 comes with versions of the daemon that have been compiled for the following variants of Unix:

- HP-UX 10.3+
- Sun Solaris 2.6+
- IBM AIX 4.3+
- Compaq Tru64 Unix
- RedHat 5.2 and 6.0 Linux

However, if your Unix is not in this list you can still use the synchronization daemon. SFU comes with the source code and makefiles that you can use to compile a version for your particular system. The SSOD daemon is the background process that receives password changes from Windows computers. Another program called the Password Authentication Manager (PAM) is used on the Unix server to send password changes made on the Unix system to Windows systems.

There are a few things about the synchronization process to consider before you deploy this service in your network. First, if your Windows computers are participating in a domain, you'll have to run the service on all the domain controllers in that domain. If you use Windows NT or Windows 2000 in a workgroup (or as simply standalone computers), you'll have to run the service on each computer if you want the passwords to stay synchronized among all the Windows computers.

Note

Although most large Windows NT and Windows 2000 networks use the Active Directory to make managing network users, computers, and resources an easier task, you can still run Windows NT/2000 as standalone computers. In this situation, each computer stores user and computer account information locally instead of in the Active Directory. This is why you must run the Password Synchronization service on each Windows computer if you do not use a domain or an Active Directory model for your network. Each computer must be capable of receiving password changes and applying them to the local database. In a domain-based environment, where users log on to the domain, only the domain controllers need to run the service.

Another caveat is that you must keep in mind that Unix account names and passwords are case sensitive. Thus, you'll need to create accounts on your Windows and Unix systems that are exactly the same. If you already have accounts set up in your network that have users with different account names on different systems, you'll have to pick a single account name for the user and then re-create the account on each computer so that they all match.

Finally, in addition to providing the capability to synchronize passwords between the Windows systems and those that are stored on individual Unix computers (in the /etc/passwd file, for example), you also can synchronize passwords with Unix networks that use the Network Information Service (NIS). Just install the SSOD on a master NIS server.

User Name Mapping

If you have an environment where users already have accounts on both Unix and Windows NT/2000 servers that are not the same, SFU provides a component that can be used to map the different usernames. You can map usernames in a one-to-one manner or in a one-to-many manner. For example, you can create an entry that maps the name togletree to TOGLETREE. Or, if you want the user to be able to access multiple user accounts, you can map the user's account name to several different account names. This second feature proves very useful if you have an assortment of Unix servers and each server has a different name used for an administrative account. You can map a single Windows NT or Windows 2000 user account name to each of the user accounts on the various Unix servers. Or, you can use this multiple-mapping feature to map the typical Unix account called root to more than one Windows NT or Windows 2000 administrative account.

The advantages of multiple mappings might not seem very intuitive at first, but let's consider an example. Suppose you want to allow the Unix administrator in your network to manage some, but not all, of your Windows-based systems. You can create a user account on each Windows computer and grant it the necessary rights and permissions. Then map the root account to these new account names. This way you don't have to simply map root to Administrator, which would give access to all computers in the domain.

One final note about username mapping: It is not a substitute for password synchronization. Remember that password synchronization, discussed in the previous section, requires that user account names be exactly the same on the computers that are participating in the synchronization process. User Name Mapping is simply another tool you can use to manage users who have accounts on both systems. If you are creating a network from scratch, or if you can easily create user accounts on all of your systems that are the same, you probably will not need to use User Name Mapping and simply can let the users have a single account name on all systems, keeping passwords synchronized. Password Synchronization will not work to synchronize passwords for accounts that are linked using User Name Mapping!

New Telnet Server and Client

SFU also includes a telnet server for Windows NT and Windows 2000, and a character-cell–style client application that greatly improves on the simple GUI telnet client that comes with the standard Windows NT Server or Workstation software. This makes it easy to use telnet to log in to Windows NT/2000 computers to perform system administration tasks or run character-cell–based user applications.

However, if you are using Windows 2000 computers, this new telnet client is already on your computer. It is now the standard client for Windows 2000 computers. Simply use the `telnet` command at the command prompt. Alternatively, click Start, Run, enter `telnet`, and click OK. If you use the `telnet` command at the command prompt, you can specify a target computer on which you want to establish a session. If you use the Start, Run method, you'll find the client starts up in console mode, as shown in Figure 53.7.

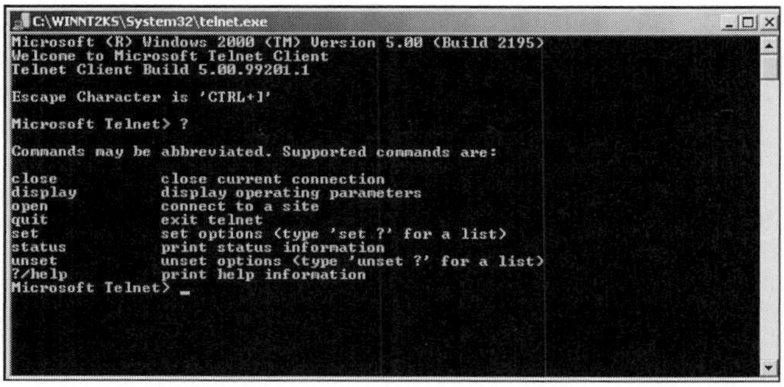

Figure 53.7   The new telnet client will start in console mode if you use the Start/Run method to start the program.

For those not familiar with console mode, this simply means that the client is ready to accept configuration commands or open a session with a remote system. In Figure 53.7, you can see that the ? character has been used to display the help text that you can access while in console mode. If you want to simply telnet to a remote system, use the open <*remotesystem*> command. After you exit the remote system, you can return to console mode by holding down Ctrl and then the right-bracket ("]") key.

Note

After you use the **open** command to start a telnet session with a remote computer, you can use the Ctrl+] key sequence to "escape" to console mode. This can be useful if you need to use the **display** command to show your current configuration, such as the terminal emulation type. Suppose you open a session and find that certain keys don't seem to work as you expect. You can escape to console mode and check your current settings (using the **display** command) and then use the **set** command to change to a different terminal type. Then, simply use the **close** command to close the session you had started, and use the **open** command to reestablish a session with the remote system. The terminal types that you can emulate using the **set** command are ANSI, VT100, VT52, or VTNT.

Some users who are accustomed to using the GUI Telnet client might not appreciate you giving them a simple character cell type of Telnet client. However, the new version is actually faster than the older GUI client and offers more features than its predecessor.

Although Windows 2000 comes with an excellent Telnet server (as described earlier in this chapter), SFU also provides a Telnet server that will run on both Windows NT and Windows 2000 servers. The new server also supports logging to the Windows Event Log or to a separate log file, and you can choose which events you want to store in the log file. Instead of using the Internet Services Manager to manage and configure the Telnet server, you can load the SFU snap-in for the Microsoft Management Console (MMC), or you can use a command-line utility, tnadmin. Either method will enable you to configure the standard options discussed earlier in this chapter. This includes selecting which authentication method to use, enabling logging, setting the maximum number of connections (remember that the Windows 2000 version allows for only 2 simultaneous connections while this SFU version allows for up to 63), and other parameters.

ActiveState ActivePerl 5.6

Web site administrators will be glad to see this SFU component because it is used on a lot of Web servers. Additionally, Perl can be used for other functions, such as automating system management procedures. The version included with SFU is Perl 5.6, ported to the Windows NT/2000 platform. Your Windows clients also will be pleased because this port of Perl provides support for the Windows Script Host (WSH). By including Perl with the SFU package, it becomes easier for Unix or Web administrators who are already familiar with the language to manage systems or Web sites that run on Windows servers. Yet, for those coming from the Windows camp, WSH enables them to continue to use Jscript, VBscript, and other procedural languages with which they are used to working.

SAMBA

SAMBA is a set of applications that is freely available on the Internet. SAMBA enables you to set up Unix servers that can act as file servers for Microsoft clients that use the SMB protocol. Chapter 33, "File Server Protocols," covers the Microsoft Server Message Block (SMB) protocol along with SAMBA. More recent versions of SAMBA allow Unix servers to act as domain controllers in a Microsoft network.

Using SAMBA, you can make resources running on high-performance Unix servers available to Microsoft clients on the same network.

Sun Network Information System (NIS)

NIS is used on Unix networks to keep important system files, such as the password file, synchronized among a group of servers. Remember that on Unix systems each server has a password file, a user group file, and other important files that, by default, are managed locally on each server. This is similar to using a Windows computer in a standalone manner where each Windows computer has its own user account database.

NIS uses a database of maps that contain entries for the files the system administrator chooses to keep synchronized. For redundancy purposes, a master NIS server can be used along with slave NIS servers that receive updates from the master server. For more information about NIS, see Chapter 32, "Unix and Linux."

SFU version 2.0 contains a component that can be used to allow a Windows 2000 domain controller to operate as an NIS server. The Windows 2000 server can operate as either a master or slave NIS server. However, if it is to operate as a slave server, the master NIS server on the network must also be a Windows 2000 server. This is due to the way NIS is implemented in Windows 2000: The information that Unix NIS servers store in a map database is stored in the Active Directory. The Active Directory schema is extended to include a class for each NIS map. Then, objects are created based on this class for each map entry.

NIS uses its own protocol to send updates from a master NIS server to slave servers. The Active Directory, on the other hand, has its own method for replication information to other Active Directory replicas. The two methods are not compatible. This is the reason why a Windows 2000 domain controller cannot be made a slave NIS server to a Unix master NIS server. However, Microsoft does provide support for the NIS protocol so that Unix systems can become slaves to a Windows 2000 master NIS server! So, if you decide to integrate NIS into the Windows 2000 portion of your network, you'll have to make a Windows 2000 domain controller the master NIS server.

The advantages of using NIS should be obvious. On Unix networks, NIS relieves the administrator of having to manually coordinate important system files on multiple servers. By incorporating the SFU NIS server into the network on a Windows 2000 domain controller, you can use the tools designed around the Active Directory to manage not only your Windows users but also users on your Unix systems!

Another advantage to using a Windows-based NIS server is that the Active Directory is a hierarchical database, whereas the NIS database format is a flat namespace. You can place NIS maps into any container in the Active Directory, such as an organizational unit (OU). You can probably figure out from this that you can support multiple NIS domains in the same Active Directory database.

Windows NT Terminal Server Edition

Microsoft has entered into the market for thin clients with its terminal server edition of Windows NT. This version of the operating system allows client computers to run applications that reside on an NT server through a terminal emulator program that runs on the client. Microsoft provides client software for older Windows and MS-DOS clients, but for Unix clients, you will have to use the client application from Citrix to make this connection.

If you already have a large installation of Unix systems in your network and need to make moderate use of a few programs that run only on an NT platform, Terminal Server edition might be a good investment. If your network is composed of a more diverse set of clients, including Macintosh users, MS-DOS clients, or Windows for Workgroup clients, this solution can be used to provide access to applications for all these users without requiring you to purchase a copy of a Windows 98 or Windows NT client operating system for each. About the only drawback to using Terminal Services, however, is that you'll have to purchase licenses for each user.

Migrating from Unix to Windows NT 4.0/2000

CHAPTER 54

This sort of migration—from a Unix desktop environment—to a Windows desktop environment is not a common one. However, there are situations in which such a migration might happen. For example, Unix (and its cousin Linux) is a very popular platform used on the Internet to run Web servers. It runs on platforms ranging from Intel (such as Solaris 8 and FreeBSD Unix) to proprietary platforms such as Sun's SPARC and Hewlett-Packard's boxes. For many small Internet startup companies, Unix can be the operating system of choice during the first few years.

It only makes sense in such a small business that the techno-geeks who design and operate the Web servers (or other servers) would want the same operating system on their desktop. As we found out in the previous chapter, just because you use Unix doesn't mean you have to go without the usual complement of desktop office applications. For example, Sun's StarOffice application suite offers just about the same applications you find in Microsoft's Office. They might not have the same look and feel and might require you to train new employees who are used to Microsoft products, but if you want to use Unix as a desktop operating system, there are applications out there that make it possible.

However, you might want to consider one important factor when it comes to using Unix throughout the enterprise: Security and training. It goes without saying that unless you're a seasoned, experienced Unix administrator, you're not going to know a lot about how to lock down a Unix system to keep your files and other resources secure. There are so many things an innocent employee can do, from using the standard R-utilities to giving out a password that lets an intruder into not just the desktop, but the entire network.

When it comes to growing a business rapidly, you'll need to hire administrative employees to manage the day-to-day business needs that have to do with accounting, human resources, and other chores that are not related to the product the company produces or manages using larger Unix servers. Most of the employees you'll find at this level probably will be well trained in Microsoft Office or other popular competing products, such as Lotus and WordPerfect. You won't find many who have been using StarOffice on a regular basis. So, although Unix can be a very good platform for running large databases, Web servers, and the like, using it as a desktop system is not going to be easy, especially if your company is large or if it is growing fast.

In such a situation, it's probably best to simply create two networks, one to run the production Unix servers and one to host your desktop administrative network. When it comes time to make this switch, you'll have to migrate your administrative documents and other data to another platform. In this chapter, we'll look at using Windows NT/2000 as that desktop platform.

Most of the technologies and applications discussed in this chapter were covered in Chapter 53, "Integrating Windows NT 4.0/2000 with Unix and Linux," and in other chapters in this book. Here we'll just take a quick look at which ones might be helpful for converting all or part of your network from Unix to the Windows environment, and point out other chapters that cover the topics in greater detail.

Create a Separate Desktop Network

It's never a good idea to mix a production network with an administrative network. Keeping the two separated minimizes the use of valuable network bandwidth and also helps provide greater security. The first thing you should consider, then, is to create a separate network to use for your desktop systems that are used by administrative and management departments. A router can be used to connect this network to the production system while you migrate files and user accounts to the desktop systems. By using packet filtering rules and other firewall techniques at the router juncture, you can keep the two networks effectively operating as separate entities until the migration is complete. As a matter of fact, by using a well-implemented firewall that has good auditing capabilities, you might find it is not necessary to eventually separate the networks.

Another possible scenario could involve more than just a production network and a desktop network. You might want to add a third network, to be used for your development staff. As you can see in Figure 54.1, by using routers or firewall products, it's quite possible to migrate data from your all-Unix environment to a desktop network and a development network.

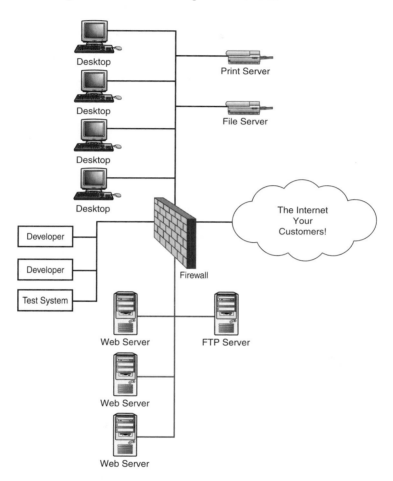

Figure 54.1 You can use firewalls or packet filtering routers to separate your production network from the rest of your business networks.

In this example, the Web servers and the FTP server are all on their own network segment, and let's assume that they're large enterprise servers running a version of Unix. The firewall also allows the developers to connect to both the Unix server network segment and the Internet. At the top of Figure 54.1, the desktop systems running Windows NT or Windows 2000 are also segmented by the firewall from the remainder of the network. Depending on your corporate policies, the firewall might or might not allow the desktop systems to make connections to the Internet.

Of course, this is a very simplified scenario. In Chapter 40, "Firewalls," you will find other configurations that can be used. In some cases you might want to place your Web servers in front of the firewall, directly exposed to the Internet. This can improve performance because network traffic between the Web servers and the Internet doesn't incur any latency imposed by a packet-filtering router or firewall. When placed in such a position, these machines should be highly secured, and are often referred to as *bastion hosts*. Placing them in front of the firewall makes them the most vulnerable servers on your network.

The point to be made here is that you can migrate data that resides on your Unix boxes to a Windows environment and still keep separate networks, connected by protective devices such as a firewall. Or, you can make a business decision to support your Web services on a Windows NT/2000 platform and convert all your user accounts, data, and applications to these Windows servers.

Whatever topology you decide to use, it still will be necessary to migrate some or all of your systems to Windows computers.

Gradually Migrating User Accounts

User accounts can be migrated easily by using Microsoft's Services for Unix (SFU) 2.0. This product does not come with the Windows operating systems. Instead, it is a separate, but inexpensive, product (around $149). SFU is made up of many components, but for migrating user accounts, four components make the process easy:

- **Server for NIS**—This product enables you to import user account information from either individual Unix servers (that is, from the /etc/passwd file) or from NIS servers (Sun's Network Information Services) into the Active Directory running on Windows 2000 servers. One caveat is that the Windows 2000 server that is used to run Server for NIS must be made the master NIS server in the network. It cannot be a slave to a Unix-based master NIS server. This product allows you to gradually migrate user account information to the Windows platform. You can let both Windows and Unix servers coexist on the network, and manage user accounts from the Windows 2000 NIS box until you are ready to migrate the user accounts to the Windows network and take them off the Unix boxes.

- **2-Way Password Synchronization**—This product allows you to keep passwords in sync for users who have accounts on both Unix and Windows systems. Changes to a user's password will be propagated to the other system so that, during a gradual migration, users won't be bothered with having to make the change more than once.

- **User Name Mapping**—This is another tool that makes a gradual migration of users an easy task. Although it's a good idea to assign the same username for a user account on every system on which the user has an account, this is not always the case, especially if your network was created in a fast-paced environment and was not well managed. The User Name Mapping component of SFU enables you to create maps that tie together different user account names so that when users need to access files on NFS servers, for example, you won't have to re-create a new user account. Simply create a mapping between the Windows username and the Unix username. User Name Mapping also allows a one-to-many or a many-to-one mapping scheme so that one account can be mapped to several user accounts on the other system, and vice versa.

- **Active Directory Migration Wizard**—When it comes time to transfer user account and other security files from Unix boxes to Windows 2000, you can use SFU's NIS to Active Directory Migration Wizard. When this is done, you won't need to use the password synchronization or username mapping utilities. The Active Directory can import the information stored on individual Unix boxes, or from NIS, so that you do not have to manually set up accounts in the Windows domain for each user.

Microsoft's Services for Unix 2.0 was covered in Chapter 53. If you decide to use this product, you'll find a wealth of information in that chapter concerning the utilities in the preceding list, as well as the file migration/NFS utilities discussed next.

Migrating Files

Windows and Unix do not use the same on-disk structure to store files. In addition, most Unix systems use NFS, which is Sun's Network File System. NFS has been adapted to other operating systems, including Windows NT and Windows 2000. By offering Windows file shares as NFS mount points, you easily can transfer files between the two systems.

Using Services for Unix 2.0 to Migrate Files

SFU provides several ways to use NFS for this purpose. If you want to allow Windows NT and Windows 2000 clients to access files that reside on Unix NFS servers, you can use the Client for NFS on each computer that needs this access. To the Windows client, the NFS exported file system looks just like a regular Windows file share. This can be used when the Windows client needs to make frequent or bandwidth-intensive access to files on the Unix systems.

The Gateway for NFS component of SFU enables you to set up one or more Windows servers as a gateway to an NFS-exported file system. This can be used when infrequent or low-bandwidth access is needed by the Windows clients to access files on Unix systems. For a gradual migration, both the Client for NFS and the Gateway for NFS components can be used to gradually transfer files to the Windows environment.

SFU also offers a Server for NFS that allows Unix boxes to mount Windows-based file shares as if they were NFS-exported file systems. Again, during a gradual migration, this might be a useful utility. However, because the intent is to migrate files to the Windows network, this tool might prove useful for the short term when you need to keep both kinds of systems on the network at the same time.

Don't Forget SAMBA

In Chapter 33, "File Server Protocols," several protocols are discussed, from Microsoft's SMB/CIFS to NetWare. You'll also find information in that chapter about the SAMBA project. SAMBA is a suite of software components that allows Unix clients to provide file and print services to clients that use SMB and CIFS. Because SAMBA is open source, you can check the code yourself to decide whether it fits your security needs. Because it's available under the GNU General Public License, it's pretty cheap! SAMBA is maintained and supported by a large, dedicated body of volunteers who continue to update the software. For the latest information and to find download sites for your location, visit the official SAMBA home page Web site at www.samba.org. There you can select a country and you'll find links to reviews of the software, as well as links for downloading the code or precompiled versions.

Besides the actual SAMBA code and compiled versions, you'll also find links for documentation and mailing lists so you can stay up to date with recent developments or find answers for any problems you might encounter with the software.

Although SFU is an inexpensive package to buy, SAMBA, for the most part, is free. If you can use it to transfer files to and from Windows and Unix systems, it might be the tool of choice for a Unix-to-Windows migration.

What About Applications?

Applications can be an entirely different matter. If you have source code, you probably can recompile it on your Windows systems if you intend to make a complete transition to a Windows environment.

Don't count on this being an easy task. You'll probably have to make changes to the code, depending on the language in which the application is written.

If you are using "canned" applications, the task can prove even more difficult. For example, if you're using an Apache Web Server on your Unix boxes and plan to use Microsoft's Internet Information Server (IIS) on a fully migrated network, you'll find that the technologies used by these competing products can differ widely. For example, Microsoft has a host of Web development tools and methods for offering content on the Web. If you're planning to make a move from Unix-based Web servers to IIS, I highly recommend you subscribe to Microsoft's Developer's Network (MSDN) subscription service so that you can evaluate the tools and gain access to a voluminous library of information that can assist your programmers in making the adjustment.

Note

Before you spend the cash to subscribe to MSDN, you might want to investigate the MSDN content that is offered free to the public at Microsoft's Web site: `http://msdn.microsoft.com`. Although you won't be able to download development tools and operating systems, you still can access a large library of information that can be used in the decision-making process. You can learn how Microsoft Web development tools and language compilers work before you decide to purchase them. You also can start reading up on Microsoft's new .Net initiative and decide whether you want to make that the platform for your Web services. This Web site has a large amount of free information, and can be a valuable tool both before and after you switch to an all-Windows environment.

No doubt you've heard that Java and its assorted applications and development tools conflict with Microsoft's versions. If you make extensive use of Java on your network, converting applications that use Java to equivalent code on a Microsoft version might not be easy. Also, it is quite possible that Microsoft might abandon Java as it continues with its .Net program. However, you still can find a lot of support for Java at Microsoft. Go to `http://www.microsoft.com` and perform a search for Java. You'll see that you can download Microsoft SDK for Java version 4.0 for evaluation purposes. Also note that Sun and Microsoft have settled the lawsuit that started back in 1997.

However, I wouldn't bet my Web site on Java technology if I was switching from a Unix-based network to an all-Windows 2000–based network. Instead, I'd start rewriting applications using Microsoft's .Net tools. Microsoft has made its intentions known about the future of .Net technology. Again, this can be a gradual migration, because Microsoft still does support Java—in it's own way. However, for the long term, don't count on it.

In addition to languages and Web servers, you also should consider other applications, such as Office applications and database applications. Oracle runs on a Unix box or a Windows platform. Windows NT and Windows 2000 provide for clustering that can help create a stable environment for a high-availability database. Or, you can migrate your data to Microsoft's SQL Server. Most database engine products provide for an import/export function, so you can dump the data to a text file and import it into another system.

Have you thought about your e-mail system? Exchange Server from Microsoft can be an expensive proposition to implement if you have a lot of employees. However, it does allow for importing information from other competing products, so a migration is still possible. Exchange Server also supports a lot more than just e-mail. You can create newsgroups and use Exchange Server 2000 with other Microsoft products. For example, Exchange 2000 is tightly integrated with the Active Directory, Internet Information Services (IIS), Microsoft Office, and Microsoft Outlook.

Note

The most recent release of Exchange is Exchange 2000. You can download a copy from Microsoft for a trial evaluation to determine whether it can be used in your network. The documentation and other technical articles also are available for download. Just visit the Microsoft Web site (`http:www.microsoft.com`) and search for Exchange Server.

It's also interesting to note that you don't have to use different Internet browsers for Unix and Windows computers. The two main players in this market, Netscape and Microsoft, both provide versions of their products for both operating systems. Microsoft also includes Microsoft Outlook Express, an excellent mail and newsgroup application.

Other Tools You Can Use

Although Microsoft provides SFU as its solution for integration and migration for Unix, there is a large market for tools and applications that can be used to make Unix look more like Windows and Windows look more like Unix. Some of the more popular ones you might want to check out include MKS Software. This company has been building utilities and toolkits for Unix/Windows interoperability for a number of years, going back to MS-DOS. Check their Web site for a current list of products at `http://www.mks.com/`.

Windows 2000 Magazine Online is an excellent resource for learning about the Windows environment, from the operating system itself to applications from third parties. This magazine is not one of those freebies paid for by advertisers. It's just about the best Windows 2000 magazine on the market. If you are going to migrate to Windows 2000, you'll find that a subscription to this magazine is a wise investment. But first, check it out online. You'll find articles from previous editions available online, along with other resources for Windows 2000. The online Web site can be accessed at `http://www.win2000mag.com/`.

Finally, depending on your brand of Unix, check with your vendor. Because most large networks today are made up of multiple operating systems and products from different vendors, it's very likely you'll find that the company that makes your Unix box also sells products that can be used to help integrate Windows NT/2000 into your network. And, as you can see from Chapter 53, many integration products also can be used for migration.

Migrating from Windows NT 4.0 to Windows 2000 and Beyond

Fortunately, when you upgrade your network to Windows 2000, you don't have to jump in and do it all at once. The Windows 2000 Active Directory is backward compatible with previous Windows NT Server domain controllers. You can choose to upgrade only a few servers at a time while you test the waters on the migration to Windows 2000 (mixed-mode). When you get ready to make the final leap into an all-Windows 2000 network (native-mode) you can simply click the switch.

In the past, domains were used to group resources and users into manageable units for administrative control. The Active Directory provides for enhanced security mechanisms, such as the capability to delegate security administration, and a new method of grouping users and resources—the Organizational Unit (OU). These two features can make it easy to reduce the number of domains you have in an existing network as you migrate to a network that eventually will be managed totally using the Active Directory.

Note

Before you jump right into this chapter it is highly recommended that you first review several other chapters. If you are not familiar with how domains are used in pre-Windows 2000 environments, and how users and resources are managed, you should read Chapter 30, "Windows NT Domains" and Chapter 34, "Rights and Permissions."

If you are new to the Active Directory and how it functions to store information about users and resources for the network, you should read Chapter 25, "Overview of Microsoft's Active Directory Service," and Chapter 31, "Windows 2000 User and Computer Management Utilities."

The tools associated with Active Directory are vastly different than those used in previous versions of Windows operating systems. With Windows 2000, domain controllers are peers in a domain, and there is no precedence of a primary domain controller (PDC) as was the case with Windows NT 4.0 and earlier versions. You'll find that the Administrative Tools folder is now populated with utilities based on the Microsoft Management Console (MMC).

This chapter examines some of the things you should consider before performing an upgrade, and shows you an example of how you can create a domain controller in a Windows 2000 network.

Before You Begin

You must consider several things when you are deciding how to arrange your domains for the migration. These include

- **Existing namespaces**—Do you already have registered Internet domain names in use at your company? Do you have more than one namespace; that is, acme.com and acme-mfg.com? The Active Directory uses DNS-style names such as these, rather than NetBIOS style names, to name domains.

- **Number of users in the network**—Although the Active Directory is scalable to many millions of objects, hardware capacity and network bandwidth will still limit the numbers of objects any particular domain can handle efficiently.

- **Structure of the organization**—Many existing Windows NT networks use domains to model the business's organization structure. In the Active Directory, the Organizational Unit (OU) can perform this function.

- **Geographical separation**—If you have a large enterprise with many users separated into distinct geographical sites, you can use either multiple domains to accommodate them or choose to use Active Directory sites and a single domain.

Domain Controllers and Member Servers

One of the annoyances with Windows NT 4.0 was that, to create a primary or backup domain controller (PDC or BDC) you had to do so when you first installed the operating system. That is no longer the case with Windows 2000. In fact, there are no primary or backup domain controllers. There are only domain controllers, each of which holds a full copy of the domain's Active Directory database. Updates, such as adding new users or changing passwords, can be done using any domain controller in the domain. For Windows NT 4.0 you had to make these changes on a PDC and either wait for the data to be replicated to other BDCs or force a push of the data to synchronize the domain controllers. Updates made to domain controllers in Windows 2000 can be made at any domain controller, and updates are propagated using multimaster replication to all other domain controllers in the domain.

Also, remember that in the Active Directory domain names are expressed as DNS-style names. That is, instead of naming a domain acme, for example, it is now named acme.com, which is a DNS-style name. When you create a tree of domains in the Active Directory, you must use a hierarchical DNS naming scheme so that you maintain a contiguous namespace.

Note

Although you could have used a Domain Name System (DNS) server in a Windows NT 4.0 network, it was not a requirement. Microsoft developed the Windows Internet Naming Service (WINS) that could be used in a similar fashion, though it mapped NetBIOS names to IP addresses, while DNS performs mappings of DNS style names to IP addresses. In Windows 2000 networks, a DNS server (which must be capable of accepting dynamic updates) is required, because clients use it to locate domain controllers. For more information about DNS and WINS, see Chapter 24, "Name Resolution." You still can use WINS in a Windows 2000 network, but it is not needed unless you have pre-Windows 2000 clients that depend on NetBIOS name resolution to function on the network. Additionally, some applications, such as System Management Server (SMS) might require WINS. Check your documentation for all applications before deciding on a no-WINS solution.

Each domain in the tree is a subdomain of the topmost domain. The domain tree provides a two-way *transitive trust relationship* between all domains that exist in the tree. In previous versions of Windows NT, trust relationships had to be established between domains, with one trust relationship created for each direction. Inheritance of security rights flows downward from the top of the tree, so you can assign users administrative access rights and permissions at a single point in the tree, and therefore grant them the same rights for child objects farther down the tree.

When you have a network that is composed of disparate namespaces, you can create separate trees and group them into a *forest*. Recall that a forest is a collection of domain trees. In this type of organization each domain tree represents a contiguous namespace, but other disjointed namespaces exist in the network. A domain forest is used in a similar manner to a domain tree, in that users still can be granted access rights in domains that are contained in other domain trees. The main difference between a domain tree and a forest is the disjointed namespaces. Additionally, although domains that exist within the same domain tree have implicit transitive trust relationships, you must create trust relationships between domains that exist in different trees in a forest before you can begin to grant users access to resources in other domain trees.

Replication of Directory Information

Active Directory domain controllers replicate, through multimaster replication techniques, all changes to the Active Directory database for their domain to all other domain controllers in the domain. Domain controllers for *other domains* in the domain tree do not receive these replication updates because they are responsible only for the portion of the directory database that concerns objects in their respective domains.

However, all domain controllers in a particular domain tree do receive replication updates that concern the *metadata*, which defines the domain tree. For example, when a new domain joins a domain tree, or when a domain is detached from one part of the tree and reattached at another part, this information is replicated to other domain controllers in the domain tree.

Model the Directory Structure After Your Business Organization

The main points to consider when grouping users and resources is how you want to administer them and what this will do to impact the network traffic associated with logon authentication and directory information replication.

Do you want to create a network that allows centralized or decentralized control? In Windows NT, domains were used to allow you to group users and resources into convenient, manageable units that share a common security policy. With the X.500 naming hierarchy adopted by the Active Directory, you might find that you now can get by with fewer domains, while using other methods, such as OUs, to make administration more flexible.

Having a single domain and using OUs to divide users and resources for administrative control purposes is a good idea if the network is connected by high-speed links. If your network is widely dispersed throughout the world, you should, of course, take into consideration the replication traffic that will occur when changes are made to the database. If frequent changes to the database occur, you might want to consider using separate domains to house users and resources in different locations so that only the domain tree metadata becomes the object of replication.

For example, suppose a manufacturer has just decided to upgrade all its business sites to Windows 2000 and use the Active Directory to manage resources. The sales office is located in New York, while two manufacturing sites are located in Dallas. The user base at the Dallas site has a much higher turnover rate than that for the New York site. Because users at each site mainly access only resources local to their site, it makes sense to use two domains, one for each geographical site. Using two domains also keeps replication traffic between the sites to a minimum because the frequent changeover of users at the Dallas site do not need to be replicated to the New York site.

Later, the company decides to open another manufacturing plant in San Antonio. A high-speed leased line is installed between the Dallas and San Antonio sites because both plants will be sharing a lot of information between them. The Dallas domain is expanded to include the San Antonio users. However, a separate OU is used for each of these sites, so that users can be managed easily by local managers for each site. Because both of these OUs reside in the same domain, controlling user access to domain resources is a simple task, no matter where the user is located.

Domains Are Just a Part of the Namespace

A domain in the Active Directory is basically a partition of the entire domain tree namespace. The namespace consists of all domains in the domain tree of which the domain is a member. In the Active Directory, each domain controller in the domain holds a complete replica of that domain's partition of the directory database. Each domain is responsible for holding directory information about users, resources, and other objects defined in the domain. The *global catalog* allows users in other domains in the domain tree the capability to quickly locate resources that are entered in other partitions, or domains, of the tree.

Note

You are not stuck with your initial decision when you set up a domain tree or forest. The Active Directory uses a unique number, the Globally Unique Identifier (GUID), to identify each domain in the network. Because this identifier is used throughout the network to uniquely identify the domain, the directory allows you to add, delete, or change domain names easily as your organization or network changes. Because each domain can be easily identified by its GUID, you can make changes to the shape of the domain tree or forest by moving domains around and reattaching them at different points to match your current needs.

Another important characteristic of a domain is the domain security policy. You define certain characteristics of the security policy, such as the password history and account lockout values, on a domain-by-domain basis. You cannot assign different account lockout values, for example, on an OU basis.

Organizational Units Allow for Delegation of Control

Organizational units (OUs) are container objects in the Active Directory. A container object is an object that can hold other objects in the directory. An OU can hold other organizational units and container objects, as well as leaf objects in the directory. Leaf objects are the endpoints in the tree structure of the directory, and hold information about such things as users, or printers, applications, and other resources.

Tip

In the Active Directory you can use the OU to subdivide portions of the directory; by doing so you can reduce the number of domains that you need. You can delegate authority to manage OUs to only those administrators that need such access. Thus, OUs can be used not only to partially replace domains, but also can be a very useful method for controlling rights and access for day-to-day management chores.

In Windows NT, you use the domain to group users and resources so that they can be managed as a unit. Within a domain, you can grant certain users the rights to perform system management and administrative tasks, such as creating user accounts or adding computers to the domain. However, this administrative control is domain-wide. For example, if you grant a user account the right to modify user accounts, that user can modify any user account in the domain.

OUs allow you to further subdivide a domain and grant these same user rights based on the OU, instead of the entire domain. This finer granularity of control can make it possible for you to get by with fewer domains in situations where you have a large number of user groupings you want to use for administrative control purposes. Instead of creating a domain for the Accounting department, the Human Resources department, and the Manufacturing department, you can create one domain, and then assign administrative privileges by OUs to allow each department to control its own resources.

Migration Considerations: Centralized Versus Decentralized Management

When planning the domain layout for your organization, you should consider the type of management control (centralized versus decentralized), security policies, and the network infrastructure. Although it is generally a good idea to create a larger number of domains when you want to decentralize administrative functions, remember that in the Active Directory you can use the OU to accomplish much the same thing.

When deciding whether to use many or fewer domains as the basis for dividing resources and users, consider what happens on the domain level. Each domain controller in a domain holds a complete copy of the domain's portion of the directory database. Replication between domain controllers happens only within a domain. That is, when you add a new user, file, or print resource, the information is replicated via multimaster replication to all other domain controllers in the domain. The information is *not* replicated outside of the domain to domain controllers in other domains. Thus, by using a larger number of domains for geographically dispersed networks, you can reduce replication traffic.

Security policy also is implemented on a domain basis. If different departments in your business have widely varying security requirements, you might need to use the domain as a tool for organizing users and resources. You cannot define different password history values or set a security policy of how strong a password needs to be based on the OU.

Delegation of Administrative Rights Reduces the Need for Multiple Domains

In Windows NT, several built-in domain groups were used to grant administrative rights to users. These included the all-powerful Domain Admins group, whose members can perform all administrative functions in the domain, down to the Account Operators or Backup Operators groups, which have access to only specific management functions. Although having these built-in user groups made it easy to grant specific users only a portion of the administrative rights that are possible in a domain, the drawback is that these rights exist throughout the domain. For example, if a user is a member of the Account Operators group, the user can potentially modify any user account in the domain (other than the Administrator accounts).

The Active Directory provides for the capability to delegate the assignment of administrative rights, down to the level of the OU. Because user accounts are not stored in the Registry-based SAM (Security Accounts Manager) database anymore, but instead are objects in the directory database, you can grant or deny administrative privileges on specific portions of the directory tree.

Two important concepts to understand about administrative privileges in the Active Directory are

- Per-property access rights
- Inheritance of access rights

Each object in the Active Directory can have an ACL (Access Control List) attached to it, which defines who is allowed to perform what functions on the object. This access can be defined down to the property (or *attribute*) level. This means that you can grant a specific user the ability to manage all aspects of user account management for a particular container object (OU), or the ability to modify selected properties of user objects within the container, such as the users' passwords or default directories.

◄◄ In Chapter 34, "Rights and Permissions," and in Chapter 25, "Overview of Microsoft's Active Directory Service," you can learn about objects, attributes, and how they relate to uses and computers on the network, as well as how the effective rights and permissions are calculated based on the Active Directory.

Each object in the directory is made up of specific attributes, called *properties*. Each property is a single type of information about the object. You can grant or deny administrative privileges on each and every property of a particular object type. To make things even easier, you also can grant or deny administrative privileges on groups of properties. The *property set* attribute of the schema defines groups of properties that can be administered together. If the default definitions of this attribute do not meet your needs, you can modify the schema.

Inheritance of access rights is another concept that makes delegating administrative authority more convenient. If you think of the Active Directory as a hierarchical structure, organized in a tree fashion, you can pick a particular point in the tree and grant access rights to a user from that point onward. The administrative rights flow down the tree to include other container objects and finally down to the end leaf objects of the tree. When a new child object is created in the directory tree, the access rights that apply to the container object that holds the child object are included with the default access rights created on the child object.

This method of inheritance allows for faster authentication time when the operating system must determine access rights. It is not necessary to trace back up the hierarchy through all parent objects to determine the access rights of a particular child object. The child object contains all the information that is required to perform an access right check.

Implementing a Migration to the Active Directory

As with any major network upgrade project, you should be sure to carefully plan ahead. Develop a written master plan and schedule for the migration, and review it on a frequent basis. Some of the items to consider in a migration plan include

- **Back-out procedures**—For any big changes you make on a particular server, be sure that you plan a method to back out of the change if it does not function as you expect. *Always* maintain up-to-date backups of key systems that can be used to make a full restoration without seriously impacting the user base.

- **Alternative plans**—Sometimes there is more than one way to affect a solution to a problem. If you can make note of more than one method of accomplishing a particular task, such as the capability to schedule users or resources for the project, the flexibility will allow you to adapt to changes in the project schedule.

- **Assign users and resources carefully**—When you make decisions about which personnel are going to be used to execute portions of the project plan, be sure to keep in mind the existing workload of the person and how participating in the upgrade migration plan will affect his or her job. Again, it is a good idea to have a "backup" person or backup resource you can use if unforeseen events limit a person's capabilities.

- **A well-defined team structure**—There should be a migration team that has a designated leader and assigned duties and areas of responsibility for each member. Nothing makes executing a migration plan more difficult than personality conflicts that can arise from the nonspecific assigning of duties to team members.

Although these points were discussed more fully in Chapter 3, "Upgrading Strategies and Project Management," I feel it's important to repeat them here. Why? Because upgrading from a Windows NT 4.0-based network to a Windows 2000-based network can be a very complex migration. Compared to migrating Novell or Unix users to Windows environments, you'll probably find that the NT to 2000 migration will involve a lot more up-front preparation and there are most likely going to be more details here and there that can hold up the migration.

Begin by Upgrading Primary Domain Controller

When you decide to upgrade your network to a Windows 2000 Active Directory-based network you will need to plan the order in which servers and workstations will be upgraded. The Active Directory-based Windows 2000 domain controller is backward compatible with Windows NT 4.0 domain controllers, so upgrading the PDC is transparent to the users and domain controllers that are still operating under Windows NT 4.0. Backup domain controllers in the domain see the new Active Directory domain controller just as if it were a PDC in the Windows NT 4.0 domain. One consideration to keep in mind is that once you upgrade a server to be a Windows 2000 Active Directory domain controller, you can't, in the same domain, promote a BDC to become a PDC. The new Active Directory domain controller provides this capability as far as Windows NT 4.0 BDCs are concerned, and you can have only one PDC in a Windows NT 4.0 domain.

Note

Although you cannot promote a Windows NT 4.0 BDC to become a PDC when a Windows 2000 Active Directory domain controller has been incorporated into the domain and is online and functioning, you can perform the promotion if the Windows 2000 Active Directory domain controller goes offline. Remember that the down-level NT 4.0 domain controllers see the new Active Directory domain controller just like an NT 4.0 PDC. If the Windows 2000 domain controller bombs, promote a Windows NT 4.0 BDC to be the PDC for the network until you determine and fix the problems associated with the Windows 2000 domain controller.

Upgrade the Domain's PDC, and Then Any BDCs

When you upgrade the PDC to become an Active Directory domain controller, you are prompted to either join an existing domain tree or create a new domain tree. If this is the first Active Directory domain controller in the network, you will have to create a new domain tree. The operation is a simple, painless one—there is no complicated setup or configuration required to create a domain tree.

After you have created the first Active Directory domain controller from the domain's PDC, you will have a mixed network environment that still can function normally from the user's standpoint. That is, users still can authenticate using the BDCs that remain in the domain. However, because the BDCs do not yet recognize the Active Directory database, but instead see it as a PDC, you still can't create new security principals, such as user accounts, on the BDCs. This is the normal way a Windows NT 4.0 network functions. You will have to do so on the new Active Directory domain controller just as you did when it was a PDC.

The new Active Directory domain controller uses the single-master replication method to inform any existing BDCs of changes to the security database. After you promote one or more BDCs to become Active Directory domain controllers in the domain, you can update the security database on any of those new domain controllers, because they are all equal peers in the network with other Windows 2000 domain controllers. Multimaster replication is used only between the new Active Directory domain controllers. Existing Windows NT 4.0 BDCs continue to function as if the network were still composed of nothing but Windows NT 4.0 domain controllers.

However, after you have finally converted *all* your Windows NT 4.0 BDCs to be Active Directory domain controllers and have made the switch to the Windows 2000 Active Directory, from that point on only multimaster replication will occur. This implies that *you will no longer be able to add Windows NT Server 4.0 domain controllers to the domain*. If you are uncertain about the migration, leave at least one Windows NT 4.0 BDC in the domain and operate in a mixed environment until you are sure that the changeover is working like you expect, and you have no need to downgrade back to a Windows NT 4.0-based network.

Tip

You should always keep a "back door" open when implementing new technology. When you make the final decision to go with the Active Directory and forego the Windows NT PDC/BDC networking method, keeping an old BDC around can be a lifesaver if something goes wrong. To provide this open door using a BDC you do not have to keep the old BDC online in the new network. Instead, before you make the final switch, take a BDC offline. That is, turn it off or disconnect it from the network. Keep it around for a few months until you are absolutely sure you do not need to down-grade out of the Active Directory. If some disastrous event occurs that forces you to back out of the upgrade, the BDC will not contain any changes that are made after it is taken offline, but it will be a good place to start when trying to recover your old network.

After you have made the switch and all *domain controllers* are based on the Active Directory, all clients, including those down-level non-Windows 2000 clients, will be capable of taking advantage of the transitive trust relationship that is created between all domains in the domain tree. This is because the trust relationship is created between domain controllers, which perform authentication functions, not by the individual workstations or other clients in the network. This means that you can proceed to upgrade all your BDCs to Windows 2000 Active Directory domain controllers and then, as you find time to schedule the downtime required, you can upgrade client machines, such as Windows NT Professional clients, at a more leisurely pace.

Finally, Update User Workstations to Windows 2000

After you have created at least one Active Directory domain controller, you can upgrade a Windows NT Workstation computer to Windows 2000 Professional. Or, you can wait until you have upgraded all remaining BDCs in the domain before you begin to migrate user workstation computers.

If you operate in a mixed network environment, the client workstations that have been upgraded to Windows 2000 (or Windows 98 or Windows 95 clients that have the appropriate Active Directory client software installed) can use the new features provided by the Active Directory. This includes the capability to query the database to locate resources throughout the domain tree. These clients will then use DNS as their locator service, while any remaining clients that are not Active Directory-aware will still use NetBIOS names.

Other Domains Can Join the Existing Tree

In a multidomain network, you will first create a domain tree using one of the domain controllers in an existing domain, or you can even create a new domain from a fresh install to serve as the first domain in a new domain tree.

When you later decide to upgrade other domains in your network to use the Active Directory you can still create a new domain tree, or you can choose to join the existing domain tree. Again, the operation is simple. To join an existing domain tree you need only supply the name of the parent domain where you will attach the new domain to the tree.

Several things occur when you join an existing tree:

- The domain's current SAM database is migrated to the Active Directory database.
- The Kerberos security software is installed and is then used to create a two-way trust relationship with the parent domain to which the domain has been attached in the tree structure.
- A domain controller in the parent domain supplies configuration information, such as the Active Directory schema, to the child domain and then informs other domain controllers about the addition of the new child domain.

The Master Domain Goes First

In the master domain model, all user accounts reside in the master domain and resources are created in separate resource domains. When you upgrade a network that is based on a single domain there is not much choice: First upgrade the PDC, and then upgrade the domain's BDCs.

Note

If you're starting from scratch—that is, you're running Windows NT 4.0 in a standalone or workgroup mode and don't have a PDC—you can still create a domain controller for your Windows 2000 network. Once you've installed Windows 2000 Server, or upgraded a Windows NT 4.0 server to Windows 2000, you can then use the command **dcpromo** to "promote" the server to be a domain controller. The process is not as complicated as you might think. Simply bring up the Command Prompt (from the Start menu, choose Programs, Accessories, Command Prompt) and enter the command **dcpromo**. The Active Directory Installation Wizard pop ups to guide you through the process.

In the master domain model type of network, you should choose to upgrade the master domain first, and then upgrade the resource domains. At the completion of the basic upgrade, you use the Active Directory Installation Wizard to install the Active Directory (see Figure 55.1).

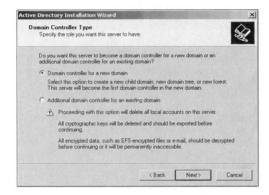

Figure 55.1 The Installation Wizard guides you through the process.

The next few dialog boxes prompt you to create a new domain tree or create a child domain in an existing tree (see Figure 55.2). If you choose to create a new domain tree, you are prompted to create a new forest or create the domain in an existing forest. Because this is the first server being upgraded to Windows 2000, you should create a new forest.

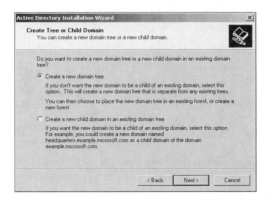

Figure 55.2 If this is the first controller to be upgraded, you create a new domain tree.

The wizard then prompts you for the domain name that you will use. You will have to specify it as a fully qualified DNS name, however. In our example, the domain is named ono. The company has a registered DNS Internet name of `twoinc.com`. The fully qualified domain name for this domain then will be `ono.twoinc.com` (see Figure 55.3).

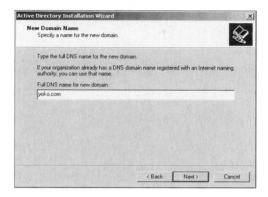

Figure 55.3   Use a fully qualified DNS name when prompted by the wizard.

The wizard then asks you to enter a NetBIOS compatible name for the new domain. Previous versions of Windows use this name for the domain until you have finished the migration and are running a Windows 2000 only network.

The wizard then asks you where you want to create the files that will serve as the database for the directory and for a device to store the log file for the directory (see Figure 55.4). If your domain is large, you should specify a different device for each of these to improve performance.

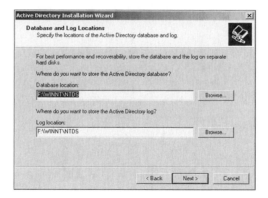

Figure 55.4   Enter the paths that will be used to create the Active Directory database and log files.

The next dialog box prompts you to enter a path that will be used to store files that are replicated to other domain controllers in the domain. As you can see in this figure, the path must point to a directory that is located on an NTFS partition. You cannot use a FAT partition for this.

If you are not yet using a DNS server in the domain, the wizard will prompt you to install Microsoft's DNS Server. Click the OK button to dismiss this dialog box. The Configure DNS dialog box pops up and asks if you want to install DNS now or wait until later. In order for Active Directory to function correctly, a DNS server is required. It's best to go ahead and elect to install Microsoft's DNS at this time because the Active Directory must register resource records that clients will use to locate domain controllers.

The next dialog box is an important one. If you are planning on a gradual migration where you will keep pre-Windows 2000 clients on the network for a while, you'll need to run Windows 2000 in mixed mode so that the Windows 2000 domain controller can act as the PDC in the domain for these down-level clients. You can see this dialog box in Figure 55.5.

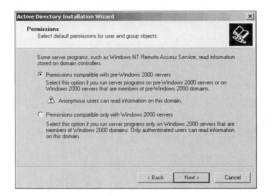

Figure 55.5 For a gradual upgrade, take the first selection so that down-level clients will have permission to access the Active Directory as if it were a PDC.

Note

If your network is small and you plan to upgrade all your servers and workstations at the same time, you should select the second option in Figure 55.5.

The wizard then prompts you to enter a password that is used as an administrator password for this server if you need to start the computer in Directory Services Restore Mode. Finally, you'll see a summary dialog box that shows the options you have selected (see Figure 55.6). Scroll through this dialog box to reexamine your choices and, if they are correct, click Next.

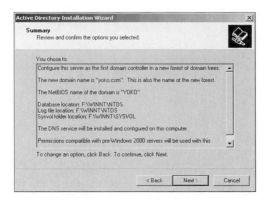

Figure 55.6 Examine the choices you have made before continuing.

An informational dialog box appears telling you that the wizard is configuring the Active Directory. Depending on your selections and the information stored on the server when it was operating in Windows NT 4.0 PDC mode, this can take some time. Existing data stored in the Windows NT 4.0 Security Accounts Manager (SAM) database needs to be migrated to objects in the new Active Directory. Drink a cup of coffee or two. You'll see at the bottom of this dialog box the processes that are being performed, such as installing DNS and configuring databases for the Active Directory.

As a last step, the wizard adds shortcuts to several tools in the Administrative Tools folder that you can use to manage the directory and then prompts you to restart the computer.

After upgrading the first server, you should experiment with it to get used to the new tools and review your plans for the other servers in the domain. When you are sure that you want to proceed, upgrading backup domain controllers is done in the same way except that you do not create a new domain for the BDCs. When upgrading servers in other domains that you want to place into the same domain tree, you can choose to create a child domain and construct the fully qualified domain name according to where you want to place the domain in the tree.

Upgrade Any Remaining BDCs Next

After you have upgraded the Windows NT 4.0 PDC to become a Windows 2000 domain controller, your network will be operating in what is called mixed mode as long as other Windows NT 4.0 (or prior versions) backup domain controllers exist on the network. To continue your migration, use the same steps on each BDC as you did to upgrade and promote the PDC. After you've upgraded all down-level domain controllers to Windows 2000 domain controllers you can switch the network to native mode.

A domain administrator using the MMC Active Directory Domains and Trusts snap-in must perform this function. This step should not be done until you are absolutely sure that you no longer need to employ Windows NT 4.0 domain controllers in the network. After the switch is made, there is no going back!

To take this final step and make the switch to a native-mode Windows 2000 domain network, follow these steps:

1. Click Start, Programs, Administrative Tools and then Active Directory Domains and Trusts.

2. Right-click the domain name you see in the left pane of the MMC console and select Properties from the menu that appears. Alternatively, click once on the domain name and select Properties from the Action menu.

3. On the General tab of the Properties page, click Change Mode, and then click Yes when prompted.

That's it. There's no going back (unless you've saved a prior Windows NT 4.0 PDC or BDC offline for recovery purposes). You'll now be operating in an all Windows 2000 environment.

What's Next?

Although many of you are still using Windows NT 4.0 networks, the number of Windows 2000 networks has been steadily increasing. Yet, we're not at the end of the road yet, nor will we ever be. The next version of Windows, which was originally code-named Whistler, is called Windows XP. With this new operating system we'll finally (so we are told) have one operating system that spans from the home user to the enterprise level. This new version of Windows will be compatible with Windows 2000 networks, and especially the Active Directory. Because Windows 2000 has been in release for several years now, I would recommend you go ahead and upgrade Windows NT 4.0 networks to an all-Windows 2000 environment if you can. This will make the migration to Windows XP a more pleasant experience.

Integrating NetWare and Linux

SOME OF THE MAIN TOPICS IN THIS CHAPTER ARE

Why Use Linux?

Key Differences Between Linux and NetWare

Moving User Accounts

Networking Protocols

Applications

NetWare for Linux

Like Unix and Windows (all flavors), trying to find similarities between Linux and Novell NetWare is not an easy job. The two systems are very different from each other, so considering such a migration from one to the other, or integrating the two into a cohesive network, requires some diligent planning. Although Linux has not yet progressed to the stage where it can really compete with other operating systems for the desktop market (outside certain vertical market applications), it does have a good track record when used as a network server, Web server, or a firewall. In this chapter, we will look at some of the key differences between Linux and NetWare and discuss a few scenarios in which integrating these two different systems can be accomplished.

Why Use Linux?

Many established users of any popular operating system always find it a mystery when trying to decide why management has decreed that a new system or platform will be used. The old "we've always done it this way" attitude seems to invade a comfortable corporate life in a very short time. The truth of the matter is that not only are times changing, but technology is changing even faster; if you don't keep up, you might not survive in the business world.

NetWare has been around for many years, and other than ARCnet it is perhaps the oldest PC networking technology still in existence on a wide scale. NetWare, however, has been deployed in large networks that span great geographical distances as well as in small departmental LANs. In the case of the larger dispersed network, where most users depend on their workstation for word processing and other typical office applications, it would not make a great deal of sense to plan a migration to Linux, mainly because of the lack of applications that run on the platform. However, using Linux in a NetWare environment to provide services to NetWare clients, to protect the network through a firewall, or to give technical users a Linux desktop does make sense in some situations.

A good integration scenario is a small LAN. For example, consider a small company that originally created a LAN to link several Intel-based Web servers that use a Windows operating system. Business has grown and it's time to upgrade. The choices are more powerful Intel-based systems running a Windows variant or Linux boxes. In this case, Linux has the edge because it is not limited to the Intel platform. You'll find Linux running on many hardware platforms, most notably Compaq's very fast Alpha platform. However, the existing LAN uses NetWare (which almost always means you've got some Windows systems in your network) to exchange information between servers, so adopting Linux into your LAN will require some new networking skills. By using fast Linux boxes to run your Web servers, you can keep your Windows desktop machines.

Another reason you might consider bringing Linux into your small LAN is that it's basically free. You can buy inexpensive versions from many vendors, such as Caldera or Red Hat, that have sprung up to cater to the Linux community, or you can download a version from a Web site and compile it yourself. If you have an experienced Unix staff at your site, Linux will be much cheaper to implement than NetWare. Without the experienced staff, however, it might become more expensive when it comes to support. However, the various vendors just mentioned also provide support for their Linux versions, and you can find a lot of information on the Internet by searching for Linux "how-to" documents.

Key Differences Between Linux and NetWare

The most obvious difference that should come to mind when looking at NetWare and Linux is that Linux is a computer operating system and NetWare is a network operating system. NetWare clients can include many different platforms, usually ones that have their roots in MS-DOS or Windows of some kind. Yet, no matter on which platform you use NetWare, it basically only provides support for network resource sharing. Authentication services are provided, as are mechanisms for granting or denying access to data held on computers on which NetWare is hosted. Or, if you are using Novell

Directory Services (NDS), the situation can become more complicated when trying to bring Linux servers into the fold. However, the underlying operating system can also be used to enforce access permissions and user authentication.

File Sharing

NetWare excels at providing file servers on the network. Either the bindery-based NetWare 3.x or the newer NDS versions can be used to exercise a great deal of control over file and directory access for one or more servers on the network. By using NDS, you can distribute files throughout the network on multiple servers. Clients can be authenticated by bindery-based servers, or NDS, and access resources they need. Using a bindery-based system of servers works best when local users need access to only one or two servers. If you need to manage a large number of servers, which has users needing resources on different servers, then NDS is a better choice because it allows the user to log on to the network using NDS and gives management a single place to manage users and resources.

When using Linux, you will find that there are no "file shares" and no directory services. Instead, you must substitute NFS, the Network File System, which was originally developed by Sun. Access permissions can be controlled using the standard mechanisms provided by Linux. You can set up NFS so that users must log on to each server to mount the exported file system, or you can hide the authentication process from users by using proxy-like mechanisms built in to most NFS implementations. For more information about NFS and how it functions, see Chapter 33, "File Server Protocols." If you want to learn more about how Linux and Unix systems use resource access permissions, see Chapter 34, "Rights and Permissions."

Printer Sharing

NetWare is capable of providing support for many kinds of printing technologies and protocols, including the `lpr`/`lpd` and TCP stream printing protocols used by Linux. When changing the network over to Linux servers, you must reconfigure not only servers that provide the gateway to a printer, but also clients so that they can connect to the correct server that hosts the printer they need. Alternatively, for printers or print servers that have a direct network connection, you can configure clients to use that network address.

User Authentication

If the NetWare version you currently employ uses bindery-based authentication services, you are familiar with having to log on to each server when you need to access a resource. Similarly, Linux uses a file called `/etc/passwrd` that resides on each system. Users must have an entry in this file that can be used when they log on to the server. Linux does not natively support a directory service, such as NDS, so providing a single logon for the network will not be something you get out of the box.

Moving User Accounts

To establish NetWare user accounts on the Linux server, you must manually configure them. There are no widely available utilities or tools that you can use to perform this function. In Chapter 32, "Managing Unix and Linux Users," the typical Unix/Linux password file is discussed and can be used as a reference for the kind of information you'll need to create user accounts on a Linux system. If you only need to create a few user accounts for just system administrators, for example, the process will be simple. If you need to create a large number of accounts, possibly for client workstations, you probably will find it necessary to produce a report from the NetWare system and use this to make the entries or create a script file that can be used for this purpose.

NetWare, particularly the 4.x and higher versions that support NetWare Directory Services, keeps track of a lot more information for a user account than is done on a Linux system. Because of this, and the simplicity of the /etc/passwrd file, you won't have to do a lot of work to create new user accounts on the Linux system. However, you might find the trade-off is that you need to examine security (file permissions, for example) and other aspects of your Linux system to ensure that your users are afforded the same access.

Networking Protocols

The TCP/IP protocol is the standard used on the Internet. It has become increasingly popular for use in all kinds of networks in just the last few years. For example, early versions of Windows NT would install the IPX/SPX protocol by default. Starting with Windows NT 4.0, the default is TCP/IP. This has stayed the same for Windows 2000 and Windows XP.

However, you don't need to replace your NetWare servers with Linux systems to use TCP/IP as your network protocol. NetWare 5.0 supports IP. You only need to upgrade your network to the new version of NetWare to get access to this important protocol.

Applications

Unfortunately, if you have a large investment in application software that was written (or compiled) for a Windows platform, you will need to purchase new versions of your existing software or purchase new software. If you have internally developed applications for which you have the source code, you might need to make only minor changes and recompile the source code on the new Linux system.

The popularity of Linux continues to grow, and many vendors have started to think about producing Linux versions of their products. You won't find Microsoft Office there yet, but you will find competing products. If you can use the file conversion capabilities that come with most products of this type, you might find that changing to a new product is not that painful, short of a little user training.

One important competing product is Sun's StarOffice. This application suite is a free download from Sun, or you can order a CD of the software, now at version 5.2. The source code for StarOffice is being released by Sun under the GNU General Public License, which means it likely will be ported to many different platforms. Currently, you can download versions from Sun for the following systems:

- Linux (x86)
- Solaris Intel
- Windows 95, 98, and NT
- Solaris on SPARC

The applications that are provided with this suite include

- **StarOffice Writer**—A professional word-processing program.
- **StarOffice Calc**—A spreadsheet.
- **StarOffice Impress**—A graphics presentation program.
- **StarOffice Draw**—A graphics drawing program.
- **StarOffice Base**—A database for the suite.
- **StarOffice Schedule**—A scheduling application to keep your appointments in order.
- **StarOffice Mail**—An e-mail client.
- **StarOffice Discussion**—A news reader program.

As you can see, StarOffice offers just about the same applications you'll find in Microsoft Office. Because of its price and availability on multiple platforms, you might find integrating Linux into an existing Windows environment to be less costly than you had originally anticipated.

You can learn more about the StarOffice 5.2 Application Suite at the following URL:

http://www.sun.com/staroffice/

NetWare for Linux

Linux is an open-source product supported by many individuals on the Internet, along with several new startup companies that have begun to produce additional utilities and products for the Linux community. In particular, Caldera has produced NetWare for Linux, which can be installed on its version of Linux, as well as those from Red Hat Linux 5.1 and possibly other variants. Although the product probably should not be used as a substitute for NetWare in a large environment, it is suitable for providing NetWare services to a few clients in a LAN. You might also use it when performing a migration to Linux when you have a few clients that need to continue using NetWare for some period of time. You can move your files and printers to Linux servers, configure NetWare for Linux, and then allow those few clients to make use of it.

NetWare for Linux provides functionality for

- Novell Directory Services (NDS)
- NetWare File Services
- NetWare Print Services
- NetWare Client support
- NetWare user account security and authentication

The installation can be performed on a Caldera Linux system quickly using a setup file or manually on other Linux systems. To update the Caldera version, you need only to change your directory to the installation CD and enter the following command:

./update.NWS4L

When the procedure finishes, you need to reboot. Other commands that are useful include

- **nwserverstatus**—Shows status information about the Linux NetWare server
- **/etc/rc.d/init.d/netware start**—Starts the NetWare server
- **/etc/rc.d/init.d/netware stop**—Stops the NetWare server

You also can install Caldera NetWare for Linux client on Linux systems. This allows Linux clients to connect to the Linux server that runs the NetWare services or to an actual NetWare server. In this way, both ordinary NetWare clients and Linux clients can share the same information. Some useful commands for the client include

- **nwlogon <netware user name>**—Log on to NetWare if using NDS. You also can log on to a particular context using the nwlogon command and connect to a specific NDS tree.
- **nwlogin -s <server> -b -u <NetWare username>**—Log on to the server when using the bindery instead of NDS.
- **nwlogout -s <server>**—Log off the particular server.
- **nwlogout -t <tree>**—Log off a particular NDS tree.

- **nwwhoami**—Display status information about your process, showing the NDS trees to which you have connected, the username used, and so on.

- **nwprint** *<filename>*—Allows the client to submit files to print.

Accessing files on a NetWare-enabled Linux server is done in the same manner as for other files in the Linux file system. The NetWare files appear under the /NetWare/bindery directory (if using bindery services) or the /NetWare/NDS directory (when using NDS).

Multi-Protocol Networks: NetWare, Unix, Windows NT, and Windows 2000

SOME OF THE MAIN TOPICS IN THIS CHAPTER ARE

User Account Considerations

Managing Resource Rights and Permissions

File and Printer Access

Network Protocols

**Consolidate Common Applications and Segment Your Network
by Specific Applications**

More is not always better! If you manage a network that is made up of multiple operating systems and network protocols, then keeping track of changes, managing users and resources, and troubleshooting issues all become a lot more complicated. In this chapter, we'll look at this type of network, and also look at some of the different things you should consider if you operate in this kind of environment. This is not a lengthy chapter, because the preceding chapters already have covered the different utilities and solutions you can use to let different operating system clients and servers interact in a single network. This chapter discusses the trade-offs you might have to make when considering managing a multi-protocol network that isn't just a combination of two different systems, but many.

This kind of network generally is not put together in a planned, organized manner. Careful planning would have resulted in a network composed of only the operating systems necessary for the work to be done. However, in today's business climate, where acquisition and consolidation are becoming the norm, you just might end up with a mixed-breed network and not by your own choice! In that case, you should consider options to eliminate components that can be implemented on a reduced number of platforms. Until that is possible, you have my sympathies!

User Account Considerations

If only there was a standard mechanism for storing user account information that was uniform across all operating systems! Life should be so easy! The goal of providing a user with a single logon username and password that can be used throughout the entire network is not easily done unless you stick with one operating system or one particular vendor's solution to this problem.

For example, you can use Microsoft's Active Directory to provide all your Windows-based clients with a single logon username and password. You can package these users into groups and assign rights to the individual user or to a group. You can audit the use of the rights you grant to users via the Event Viewer—provided you have configured auditing correctly. Windows NT 4.0 domain controllers provide a similar capability within a domain, and also between domains, as long as administrators create the necessary trust relationships and grant access as required by the user or group.

◀◀ For a quick lesson in how the Active Directory works, see Chapter 25, "Overview of Microsoft's Active Directory Service." For information about granting user rights and auditing their use, see Chapter 34, "Rights and Permissions," and Chapter 38, "Auditing and Other Monitoring Measures."

Similarly, Sun's Network Information System (NIS) enables you to let users log onto multiple Unix servers by keeping important files, such as password files and group membership files, synchronized. Yet, NIS doesn't allow you to store account information that can be used to log onto a Windows computer, and the Active Directory (or the Windows NT 4.0 SAM database) doesn't do this for Unix systems.

NetWare, which can store user account information in the bindery locally on a server, also has a directory service, Novell Directory Services (NDS), that allows for a single logon—as long as you're a NetWare user.

◀◀ Chapter 27, "Overview of the Novell Bindery and Directory Services (NDS)," can give you a good idea of how NetWare logons are handled. Chapter 32, "Managing Unix and Linux Users," covers managing user accounts in those environments in greater detail.

Novell Directory Services also has a client software package for Windows-based computers, as well as one for the Linux and Solaris operating systems. Therefore, you could use NDS as your central repository for user account information.

The most straightforward approach to this problem, but not necessarily the best solution, is to just create a user account in each system or directory service for each user. The problem with this is also easy to see. With three user accounts (and possibly more) for each user, the network administrator has more day-to-day maintenance tasks to perform, from setting up accounts to changing passwords to monitoring account usage. Second, from the user perspective, it's easy to change a password if the operating system prompts you to change it before it expires. However, you'll find that most users won't take the time to change their password on other systems when they change it on one. This means that eventually users end up with a different password on each system. And, of course, this means more work for the network administrator and staff.

Managing Resource Rights and Permissions

If user accounts were all you had to worry about in a multi-protocol network, then it would be easy to implement a solution to manage user accounts. You could use Novell's client software for your Windows or Unix systems, or use a Microsoft product that synchronizes the Active Directory with NDS or operates as the master node in a NIS network. However, once you've created user accounts, then you have to deal with the different methods used by each system to grant access permissions to resources. And, as you can probably guess, each system discussed in this chapter uses different mechanisms for this. Although someday there may be a standard method for storing user accounts in a directory service, there is no standard for resource permissions (that is, what you can do with a resource).

Unix, Windows, and NetWare all give you the capability to grant access to files based on simple concepts such as create/read/write/delete files. However, both NDS and the Active Directory can make this a lot more complicated than it has to be. Of the operating systems discussed in this chapter, Unix has the simplest method for assigning permissions to a file or resource. This chapter covers the resource protection mechanisms used for Windows, Unix, and Novell systems. You should become familiar with the similarities as well as the differences in the granularity to which you can grant access to resources before considering a multi-protocol network such as the one contemplated in this chapter.

File and Printer Access

Here, things aren't quite so murky. Many operating systems support Sun's Network File System, either natively or through third-party applications. This can make file sharing a little easier in a multi-protocol network. Similarly, SAMBA (discussed in Chapter 33, "File Server Protocols," can be used to allow Unix clients to connect to Windows-based file shares. Utilities discussed in Chapter 52, "Migrating from Novell NetWare to Windows 4.0/2000" can be used to allow for file sharing between Windows systems and NetWare systems.

And if your environment doesn't require extensive file sharing, but only the occasional transfer of data from one system to another, then you can use the standard TCP/IP-based FTP application to move files around as needed. For example, if billing reports are produced on a Unix server, but management uses a Windows-based desktop computer, then you can generate reports on the Unix system and create an automated batch process to copy these reports to other systems.

Printing is probably the easiest problem to solve. All the operating systems in this chapter support TCP/IP printing. Most printers you buy today, that can be connected to a network directly, also support TCP/IP printing. You can hang a printer off the network, and then configure each client to use the printer, or you can set up a print server using Windows, NetWare, or Unix, and have clients send print jobs to the print server. Either way, printing should not be a problem once it has been configured and tested.

Network Protocols

Another easy component of this puzzle you have to consider is what network protocols will be used in a mixed environment. The Internet has pretty much made TCP/IP the networking standard for a modern network. If you come from the Unix or Linux environment, then you are probably already acquainted with TCP/IP and the services and utilities that are associated with it. Since Windows NT 4.0, TCP/IP has been the default network protocol for Windows systems. Beginning with

Windows 2000, you don't need to use legacy protocols such as NetBIOS and NetBEUI as long as you only use Windows 2000 or later clients, and as long as you don't use applications (such as System Management Server) that require these legacy protocols. Things get brighter on this front when you consider that even Novell has come around to incorporating TCP/IP into NetWare, so that you now can have a choice.

If you only need to network Windows and NetWare clients, then you can do so using IPX/SPX, because Windows comes with its own implementation of the NetWare protocols. However, if you want to add Unix systems to your network, the basic common denominator is TCP/IP. And when you consider the fact that most business networks need an Internet connection, if only for e-mail purposes, then TCP/IP is required on the network.

So, the easiest thing for you to manage in a network composed of multiple operating systems is the network protocol. You can set up DHCP servers to allocate IP configuration information to clients when they boot and DNS servers to resolve names when clients go looking for resources or other computers. And because TCP/IP has been around for so long, you don't have to settle for using DHCP or DNS servers from a single vendor. For example, you might want to use Microsoft's DHCP server because of its easy-to-navigate graphical user interface. However, you might choose to use a Unix system for DNS. If you plan to use the Active Directory, however, you might want to do things the other way around, or be sure that the DNS supports dynamic updates.

◀◀   DHCP and DNS are two very useful network services. You can find out more about DNS by reading Chapter 24, "Name Resolution." DHCP is covered in Chapter 23, "BOOTP and the Dynamic Host Configuration Protocol (DHCP)."

Consolidate Common Applications and Segment Your Network by Specific Applications

Finally, if you are responsible for a multi-protocol network, the chances are that you are using each of these operating systems for a specific task. If you have consolidated several networks due to a corporate acquisition, then you should review the applications in use, set a new standard, and begin a migration toward that standard.

For example, if you have some users using a spreadsheet or word processor that runs on a Windows box, but not on a Unix box, then you might want to consider which application to keep and begin a migration away from other applications that duplicate this functionality. Your choice can be made on ease of use and the features required, in which case Microsoft Office is the de facto standard for most environments. If you have limited needs for the many features supplied by Microsoft Office, then a simpler solution, such as Sun's StarOffice may suffice. Whichever you decide, consolidating applications can help you eliminate the problem of data interchange between different departments that use different operating systems.

When you get beyond basic office productivity applications and into applications that are based on specific tasks, such as manufacturing software, inventorying software, and accounting software, then it is easy to compartmentalize your network and pick the best application and run it on the operating system for which it was written. For example, Manufacturing Resource Planning (MRP) software is not an application that is going to be used by everyone in a large company. Because of this, it's easy to stick with the operating system the MRP application runs on, for whatever department uses it.

Most applications—once you get out of general office software applications—are task-specific. By determining which departments use specialized software, you can segment your network into sections that each use a specific operating system and the necessary applications, and then concentrate on what data needs to be exchanged between departments. As mentioned earlier, reports can be generated by an application on one system, and then simply transferred to another system using FTP. Similarly, data generated through spreadsheets and other applications usually can be exported to comma-delimited files for transfer to other systems where it can be imported into a different application.

On the Horizon

58

SOME OF THE MAIN TOPICS IN THIS CHAPTER ARE

Standards, Standards, and Now More Standards!

Wireless Networking

Ethernet for the Long Haul

The Internet—and .Net?

## CHAPTER 58

The networking landscape is changing at a rapid pace. New technologies are quickly replacing older ones at a faster pace than ever before. Just look at how ethernet has grown from an experimental 2Mbps networking system, to a rival of MAN/WAN technologies such as SONET and ATM. This should tell you that five years from now a network administrator will probably be managing a completely different type of network. Wireless technology, both in the LAN and also the newer third-generation (3G) wireless technologies targeting mobile phones and handheld devices, will become an important mainstay in a short time. If Bluetooth doesn't catch on as promised for several years now, some other standard for short-distance networking surely will. This chapter touches on what I think are going to be important networking topics to watch for during the next two to three years.

Standards, Standards, and Now More Standards!

I don't recall who said it, but the saying goes that "The nice thing about standards is that there are so many of them to choose from." On the Internet anyone can easily get the nitty-gritty details about evolving standards (drafts) and Request For Comments (RFC) documents that detail just about everything you could ever possibly want to know about technologies that make up the Internet. However, until recently, if you wanted to know more about LAN/WAN standards defined by IEEE committees, you had to pay for hardcopies. And let me say that because there are so many standards, this was an expensive proposition!

However, recently many of the IEEE 802 committee documents have been placed online (in Adobe Acrobat .PDF format) and you can download them for no charge. If you are interested in learning more about a particular topic, ranging from the spanning tree algorithm to CSMA/CD, from Wi-Fi to the high-speed wireless IEEE 802.11a specification, then these documents are the source you need to consult. Although the basic principles are covered in this book, there's nothing like the actual standards documents when you have a question that requires a detailed answer. So, after all these years, I must say thanks to the IEEE for making this information available at no charge. Although you will most likely not want or even need to read all the online material that is available, I'm sure you'll find something here that can help further your understanding of the technologies used in today's networks. For more information, visit the IEEE Web site at http://standards.ieee.org/getieee802/.

And of course, keep up with Internet developments by reading Request for Comments documents. You can still find the most recent updates at http://www.rfc-editor.org/.

Wireless Networking

It goes without saying that there is a great incentive for companies to invest in wireless technology. In general, the physical topology of a network changes more rapidly as the number of connected nodes increases. It's a lot easier to run a single cable to a wireless access point and allow a group of users to use the same cable via wireless network adapter cards than it is to run a cable from a switch or hub to each cubicle. Although I don't expect Bluetooth technology to make a big impact in the next year or two, I do think that Wi-Fi (IEEE 802.11b) will become a major player in corporate networking, as well as home networking, in a short time. There are many big manufacturers behind this standard and, because the FCC has just recently ruled on opening up a larger frequency bandwidth (the 5Ghz spectrum) for wireless devices, you can be sure the wireless market will grow rapidly in the future.

Just think about it. The heavy, clunky, expensive desktop PC, with cables and wires running all around it, and taking up a large part of your desk, won't be as efficient as a simple laptop, or PDA, that communicates with the corporate network via wireless technology. And if the Wi-Fi solution does succeed, as I think it will, Internet Service Providers will become much like cellular telephone companies, allowing you to roam from your office, to your home, to the airport, hotel—to just about anywhere. Here, there, and everywhere, and you could still have a secure virtual private network (VPN) connection to your corporate network.

Although the IEEE802.11b standard has many companies backing it, and the brand name "Wi-Fi" assures consumers that a device inter-operates with other manufacturers' Wi-Fi components, another wireless standard, IEEE 802.11a, which operates in the 5GHz spectrum, might be the next biggest thing after Wi-Fi. By using a larger bandwidth, IEEE 802.11a allows for faster speeds (54Mbps), but for a shorter range than Wi-Fi. Wi-Fi allows for an 11Mbps speed and has a range up to about 300 feet (depending on any structural interference that might exist between the access point and the wireless station). IEEE 802.11a, although supporting a larger bandwidth, faster network speed, and more channels than Wi-Fi, has a range of only about 90 feet. Still, for many offices this might be sufficient. You'll have to invest in more access points to cover a large office environment, but you'll be getting more bang for your buck as far as speed and the number of users that can use the air space at the same time. And you'll still be able to all this with a lot less cabling than you're using now.

Bluetooth, I'm sorry to say, has been trying to make it big for several years now, and I've yet to talk to anyone who actually owns anything that's Bluetooth-enabled. It's a great concept—replacing cables and short-distance networking. Although specification 1.0 was completed in a short amount of time, and covers a considerable amount, it wasn't a complete solution. Version 1.0b made up for many of the problems, and the latest version, 1.1, seems to cover a lot of territory, given all of the Bluetooth profiles that have been the target of specifications documents recently. Despite these solutions, a standard is nothing without a large base of manufacturers to back it, and support for Bluetooth has been falling. Although there are a large number of companies who are members of the Bluetooth SIG, currently you don't see many products advertised for sale.

As an example, you'll find an explanation of the currently defined Bluetooth profiles in Chapter 15, "What Is Bluetooth?" A *profile* is a set of methods and procedures used to create Bluetooth devices, such as a wireless headset, cordless telephone, and so on. Yet, if Bluetooth is intended to replace cables in a small personal area network, why hasn't a printer profile been defined yet? Microsoft finally got around to joining the Bluetooth SIG in 1999, yet has already announced that it won't provide native support for Bluetooth in Windows XP. And until the IEEE 802.11a standard takes off and begins to replace Wi-Fi products, the interference many have reported between the few available Bluetooth devices further hinders its marketability.

Got a Wi-Fi network access point? Got a microwave in the break room? Don't have a Bluetooth device nearby!

Ethernet for the Long Haul

Even as recently as five or six years ago, many were predicting that ethernet technology was becoming outdated. Token-ring networks clearly were more logical. It would be more sensible to try to upgrade token ring networks to faster speeds than it would be to keep pushing ethernet to the limit. However, with the widespread adoption of switching technology, the collision domain barrier that has held back the speed and network bandwidth utilization achievable by ethernet has virtually disappeared.

If you've looked into 10 Gigabit Ethernet, you can see that not only is ethernet not going away, it's poised to start taking on other high-speed link providers in the MAN/WAN environment. Of particular note is Yipes, Inc., which is now operating in several large cities providing a metropolitan area network (MAN) solution that is end-to-end IP services using ethernet over fiber links. Yipes also is offering this service in wide area network (WAN) environments in selected cities.

So what's the big deal? Well, because Yipes offers end-to-end ethernet, there's no other expensive equipment you have to buy. No waiting months for the local telco to provision a T1 or higher speed line, and then to install expensive CSU/DSU equipment. One of my favorite quotes about telephone services comes from Lily Tomlin, "We're the phone company. We don't care because we don't have to." Well, phone companies now might sit up and take notice as their business starts to migrate to companies like Yipes that can make MAN/WAN networks easier to install (and faster), and can provide services faster and for a lower cost than the traditional methods. No more ATM switches, frame relay switches, conversion from one packet type to another, long delays in getting additional bandwidth added to an existing network. And, Yipes offers their service over fiber links from 1 Mbps up to 1 Gbps, with additional bandwidth available on demand in a very short time. Visit `http://www.yipes.com` to find out more about this company. Expect a lot of other vendors to begin offering similar services to corporate networks in the very near future.

In case you're wondering how the name Yipes came about, it started out with Yikes! However, by replacing the "k" with a "p" in the name, the name now contains "IP," which is the protocol of choice today for ethernet networks. Yikes! I wish I could get this service at home!

The Internet—and .Net?

Although the past year has seen the meltdown of many dot com businesses, it would be foolish to think that the Internet is a fad that has come and gone, relegated to a small group of users like CB radio. Instead, the Internet is undergoing growing pains, and in the years to come you'll probably think of cable TV and radio like you now do a telephone party line. No, I don't mean a 900 number, but old-fashioned party lines where more than one user had to share a telephone line (with distinctive rings to let you know when you had an incoming call). As telephone service expanded rapidly, it wasn't economical to string enough copper wire to give everyone an individual line.

The Internet boom during the past few years was based on lots of enthusiasm for the many new applications that entrepreneurs brought to market. The problem with enthusiasm is that it can blind you to economic realities. Advertising works well on television, and in the print media. However, when you have literally hundreds of thousands of Web sites on which you can place an advertising banner, how do you choose among them? If users expect everything on the Internet to be freely accessible and paid for by advertising, then stop and think again. Would you rather have an antenna on your roof and still be watching three networks (or less, depending on where you live) or pay to have cable TV access with both free and paid services?

The Internet will continue to expand rapidly, and you can expect a lot more to come from it as broadband connections continue to increase. This increased bandwidth will probably make renting a video (and the awful task of having to return it the next day!) a thing of the past in a few years. But, you're not going to get that movie or that new CD-quality audio from the Internet for free! Expect the Internet to evolve similar to cable television—there will be a lot of freebies out there, but you'll also have to pay for premium services—and for convenience. It will take a while for the costs of broadband connections to come down in price. This is mainly because it's not inexpensive to install and manage DSL or cable modem front-end technology, much less offer quality support for this rapidly growing market. However, I expect that demand will drive this market and it will continue to grow.

In the movie *2001: A Space Odyssey* I thought the neatest thing was the video telephone call from space. We already have inexpensive gadgets that enable you to place low-quality video calls via the Internet. In a few years, as higher bandwidth connections are installed, expect to find video calls more the norm than in the realm of science fiction. For home users this might not be such a big thing. For corporations, who either have to spend a lot of money on travel expenses or contract for videoconferencing (slightly less expensive) videoconferencing via the Net will become a valuable business tool. Even voice-over IP (VoIP) is already replacing some telephone lines, despite the lower quality of the connection. You can expect that the quality will improve as the Internet is upgraded to higher speed connections, at both the core and at the edges where businesses and home users connect.

Another benefit that corporations can expect to see from the Internet is a lowering of the overhead costs for maintaining an expensive workplace for each employee. Many tasks, such as phone call screeners, support staff, and other similar jobs, can be done just as easily by having workers stay at home. This cuts down not only the expensive office building overhead, but also helps improve employee morale in many instances. It's a lot cheaper to pay for a couple of phone lines or a broadband connection and have employees work from home than it is to pay for heating/air conditioning, property taxes for large buildings, and so on. This author is currently in the market for such a job!

Microsoft's latest "contribution" to the Internet is its .Net initiative. This .Net initiative is supposed to make possible the use of XML (eXtensible Markup Language) technology and a Microsoft Passport key to making applications, rather than actual Web sites, the focus of the Internet. Using a Passport, all the personal information you could ever want to give to a Web site can be stored safely and securely in a Microsoft database. Of course, they promise the site will be secure and that your information will never be given out without your authorization. At this point in time the marketing machine behind .Net probably will make it a big player in the Internet during the next few years. However, I'm not sure who is going to allow a lot of personal information to be stored in a computer with the belief that it's as safe as safe can be. A truly secure system does not exist, and Microsoft's servers are no exception. For more information about .Net and the Passport, visit Microsoft's site (www.microsoft.com) and search for information on the subject.

As for the safety of storing personal information about yourself on the Internet, I can't point the finger solely at Microsoft. There are already a large number of sites that have information about you. How many spam messages do you receive in your e-mail each week? How did these sites get your e-mail address? When you filled out that form to access a Web site, did you take time to read the fine print about its privacy policy? Or should it be called a "non-privacy" policy?

Finally, we all know just how safe the Internet is. Even the biggest sites, such as e-Bay, Amazon, and, yes, Microsoft (who says it'll keep your Passport information absolutely secure), have had problems with everything from denial-of-service attacks to out-and-out break-ins. Right now I don't think you need to worry too much about using a secure link to send credit card info over the net to Amazon or another seller as long as they are attempting to maintain secure servers. You should be concerned, however, if a site stores that information instead of maintaining it simply for the duration of the transaction.

So, the Internet is growing even faster today than last year and the year before. Don't let all the recent dot com failures make you think otherwise. What you don't hear about are the sites that are succeeding. Those that follow standard business procedures, such as not trying to grow too rapidly and maintaining a healthy price-to-earnings ratio when it comes to the stock price will probably do quite well. Those who continue to hype their product or service, telling you that it's possible to keep obtaining venture capital and selling more shares of stock, yet still don't turn a profit, probably won't be around much longer. And if they do make it, it will probably be due to selling off portions of their business and teaming up with partner companies that have managers who know something about business and making a profit!

More Domains

Because the Internet name game is running out of names, new top level domains have been created (see Chapter 24, "Name Resolution") and more should be expected during the coming years. Soon everyone who wants a personal web site will have it. Yet, I can't think of why anyone would want one unless you have something of real value to offer! Still, instead of having to remember www.twoinc.com, you'll soon have to remember www.twoinc.biz, and probably a host of other .whatevers as the name space continues to expand.

So Where Is IPv6?

One reason I didn't include anything about IPv6 (or the Next Generation IP, as some call it) is that you probably won't ever have contact with it. Many routing vendors and other manufacturers are already building in support for some IPv6 functionality. However, consider the following. Network address translation (NAT, see Chapter 40, "Firewalls," for more information) has gotten rid of the need to free up some of the limited IP address space. Many of the security and other features offered by IPv6 have already been incorporated into products such as firewalls and VPNs that use the current version of the Internet Protocol. Therefore, what will be gained by throwing out a lot of IPv4 equipment just because a new protocol version has been developed?

Sure, IPv6 will create enough IP addresses so that every grain of sand on this planet (and probably Mars too, when we get there) can have its own address, but firewall technology and NAT have removed this as the major reason for adopting IPv6. Instead, I expect that other issues will be addressed and we'll see an IPv7 many years down the road instead of IPv6. If it ain't broke, don't fix it! We already have plenty of IP addresses to last for many years now; we have VPNs using encryption technology that was to be deployed natively in IPv6; we have Multi-Protocol Label Switching and other techniques being used in the Internet core routers, so what's the big deal with IPv6? As more and more homes have access to broadband technology, streaming video and audio won't require a prioritization scheme. In the next few years, the entire data pipe, from source to home or office, will be big enough to handle nearly anything you'll want to send down the line.

Appendixes

SOME OF THE MAIN TOPICS FOR THIS PART ARE

The OSI Seven-Layer Networking Model

TCP and UDP Common Ports

NetWare Login Script Reference

Directory Services: Overview of the X.500 and LDAP

Network Information Resources

Overview of the Simple Mail Transfer Protocol (SMTP) and POP3

PART X

The OSI Seven-Layer
Networking Model

SOME OF THE MAIN TOPICS IN THIS CHAPTER ARE

It's Only a Model!

When discussing different network devices or software components of a network, it is common to use, as a reference point, a model that the International Organization for Standardization (ISO) created. The Open Systems Interconnection (OSI) Seven-Layer Networking Reference Model was originally developed as a blueprint for creating the additional network protocols that the ISO developed. However, these protocols were written during a time when a lot of computer horsepower was required to implement them, and they were never widely adopted. Some companies, such as Digital Equipment Corporation's DECnet, did move toward OSI standards.

With the explosion of the Internet, and also of its requisite protocols, TCP/IP became the overall standard for the majority of local area (and wide area) networks instead of the OSI protocols. TCP/IP is based on a network model that has fewer layers, as discussed in Chapter 20, "Overview of the TCP/IP Protocol Suite." This appendix looks at the OSI reference model because it is still generally referred to when discussing networking technology.

It's Only a Model!

The OSI networking model is just that—a model. It's a reference you can use when discussing networking with colleagues. The model specifies seven layers, which you can think of as separate modules, each of which performs a specific set of functions. Each layer in the model communicates with adjacent layers in the model using a standard defined interface. Therefore, the internal workings of each layer can be left up to the vendor to develop. All that matters is that all the layers work together, no matter which vendor provides them. For example, network adapters and network cabling falls into the bottom layer, the Physical layer. Network cards are designed to work with the software that falls into the next higher layer, the Data Link layer.

Figure A.1 shows how the different layers of the model interact with one another, from two ends of a network connection.

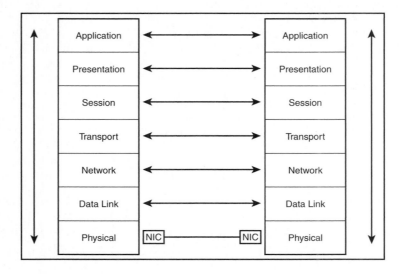

Figure A.1 Each layer in the OSI reference model provides functions to adjacent layers in the model.

As you can see in Figure A.1, arrows show the flow of information down the stack from computer A. When the information reaches the Physical layer, the components at that layer act to deliver the data to the remote system. At the remote system, the Physical layer receives the electrical (or light) impulses, converts them into the appropriate message format, and passes the information back up the stack so that the data eventually reaches the application for which it was intended.

Also in Figure A.1 you can see that arrows point both ways between the layers on one system to the corresponding layers on the other system. This implies that from a logical point of view, each layer in the model performs functions as if it were talking directly to its corresponding layer at the remote system. Each layer is unaware of what is going on in layers underneath it or how the message is delivered to the matching layer on the remote machine.

For example, TCP breaks up large messages into smaller messages called *segments*. These segments are then passed to lower layers that encapsulate them in IP datagrams and then into a physical layer protocol, such as ethernet. On the receiving end, the TCP software does not have to know that ethernet, token-ring, or any other technology, was used to deliver the message. Instead, the TCP software on the remote system receives the segments that the TCP software on the sending system originally sent.

Encapsulation

Most layers attach information to the data that they pass to lower layers. This data is called *header information*. For example, an IP datagram contains header information such as the source and destination IP addresses and port numbers. When the IP datagram is passed down the stack, it can be encapsulated in an ethernet frame. An ethernet frame adds its own header information (see Chapter 12, "Ethernet"). Here, instead of IP addresses, physical MAC addresses are used in the ethernet header.

On the receiving end of the communication, the ethernet header information is stripped off before the remaining data is passed up the stack. At the IP level the IP header is removed and the data is passed back up to the TCP software, and so on. Thus, each layer on each computer actually only sees, with few exceptions, the header information that was attached to the original message by the corresponding layer on the other machine. This is how the layers logically interact, regardless of how layers above or beneath operate internally.

The following sections describe the functions that each of the layers perform, starting from the bottom (Physical layer) and working up to the top. An important point to remember is that some vendors combine two or more layers into a single software application. As mentioned, the OSI Seven-Layer Reference Model is just that, a model. It's a way to discuss networking technologies in a rational manner that professionals can understand. It does not mean that all networking products must conform to this model!

The Physical Layer

The Physical layer is the physical components that make up the networking hardware of the network, including the network adapter, connectors, network media (copper wires or optical cables), and so on. To sum it up in a simple sentence: The Physical layer gets the data from here to there! This layer covers both electrical and mechanical aspects of the network. For example, the method used to encode data into electrical or light signals on the network media is decided at this layer.

Data Link Layer

The Data Link layer serves several functions, which the IEEE has divided into two sublayers. The first is the Logical Link Control (LLC) and the second is the Media Access Control (MAC). As a whole, the Data Link layer is responsible for transmitting data from one place to another and doing some minimal error correction. The purpose of the LLC is to provide Service Access Points (SAPs) that devices can use to send information. The MAC component takes care of transmitting the data and correcting errors.

The Data Link layer is responsible for putting together the ethernet frame, for example. This includes formatting the header information into the correct fields and placing the data in the right place. Functions operating at this layer also determine the order in which bits are interpreted (that is, big- or little-endian), and add checksum information used to ensure that the frame arrives intact at its destination.

Bridges are network devices that operate at this level in the model. Bridges examine the MAC addresses of packets and use that information to decide whether to forward a packet to another port. For more information about how bridges work, see Chapter 7, "Repeaters, Bridges, and Hubs."

Network Layer

The Network layer provides an important functionality to a network protocol stack. Here, protocols are created that manage how packets are delivered on the network or routed to another network. For example, the Internet Protocol (IP) resides at this layer. IP addressing works at this level. Remember that IP addresses have two components: a network ID and a host ID. Therefore, packets can be delivered on the local LAN (using the host ID) or routed to another network (using the network ID). This layer is also responsible for breaking larger messages into smaller ones that fit into the frames created at the Data Link layer. This size is called the Maximum Transmission Unit (MTU). At the receiving end, the Network layer reassembles these into the larger original message before passing the data up to the Transport layer. The easiest way to remember this layer is to remember that it provides for addressing and routing.

It should be obvious that traditional routers operate at this level. Routers use a protocol's network address to determine on which port a packet is to be forwarded.

Transport Layer

Whereas the Network layer is responsible for routing data packets, protocols at the Transport layer take on the duty of making sure those packets actually get delivered, and in the correct order. For example, the Transmission Control Protocol (TCP) can be found at this layer. TCP uses IP (at the Network layer) and tracks which segments get lost in the network and cause IP to retransmit segments as necessary.

Although this layer can provide for retransmissions for lost packets, it does not have to. For example, the User Datagram Protocol (UDP) is found at this layer. UDP also uses IP to get its messages delivered. However, UDP does very minimal management of the messages it sends out. It does not acknowledge packet delivery, but it does respond to ICMP messages, such as those designed to throttle back transmissions when they are arriving at the receiving end at too fast a rate.

Session Layer

The Session layer is responsible for deciding the format of the data transmitted. Session protocol examples are the remote procedure call (used by NFS and other applications). Another way to think of the Session layer is that it functions to allow processes on networked computers to talk to each other. TCP and NetBIOS are both protocols that reside at the Session layer.

Presentation Layer

The Presentation layer interprets the actual data that is being exchanged. For example, different systems can use different methods to represent floating-point numbers or other data. The order of bits in a byte is translated at this level. The necessary conversions take place at this layer. It is at this layer that translations from different character-encoding methods take place. For example, when one computer uses ASCII characters and another computer uses IBM's EBCDIC encoding, translations between these two methods of representing characters are made at the Presentation layer.

Application Layer

The user comes into the picture in the Application layer. Without applications that need to use the network, we network administrators would be out of a job. Examples of network components that reside at this layer include firewalls or networked file systems (such as NFS). End users can recognize Application layer components as programs that they use every day, such as e-mail and FTP.

TCP and UDP Common Ports

SOME OF THE MAIN TOPICS IN THIS CHAPTER ARE

What Are Ports?

What Are Ports?

In Chapter 20, "Overview of the TCP/IP Protocol Suite," you learned that both TCP and UDP use *ports* to keep track of the endpoints of sessions between a client and server. A port is a number, ranging from 0–65535. When combined with an IP address, the pair is typically called a *socket*. Whereas an IP address can uniquely identify a computer on the global TCP/IP-based Internet, the socket can be used to identify a particular process running an application. In Chapter 40, "Firewalls," the importance of understanding what each port does is discussed from a security standpoint. Before you configure a firewall, you'll need to understand why certain ports are blocked and why others are allowed by the firewall. You can use this appendix as a quick reference to look up typical port assignment.

Port numbers are not assigned randomly. They are controlled by the Internet Corporation for Assigned Names and Numbers (ICANN). ICANN performs most of the functions that were previously done by the Internet Assigned Numbers Authority (IANA).

Port numbers are divided into three categories:

- **Well-known ports**—These ports range from 1–1023 and are typically assigned to applications that have a published RFC or other document describing their use by the Internet community. For example, Telnet, FTP, and SMTP use port numbers within this range. These ports are sometimes called *system ports*, because on most systems the application that uses the port runs as a highly privileged process, such as root on a Unix system.

- **Registered ports**—These ports range from 1024–49151 and are assigned by application to ICANN on an individual basis.

- **Dynamic/private ports**—These ports range from 49152–65535 and can be used by any application that wants to use them.

The last RFC document to list descriptions of port numbers was RFC 1700. Many of the ports listed in that document, as well as earlier documents, are no longer used as described. This is because many of the applications that once used these ports are either outdated or no longer used for one reason or another. Table B.1 is based on RFC 1700, but modifications have been made here and there to bring the table up to date. The applications that use well-known ports are those you most likely will find on your network.

Table B.1   TCP and UDP Well-Known Port Numbers

Service	Port Number	Protocol	Description
	0	tcp	Reserved
	0	udp	Reserved
tcpmux	1	tcp	TCP Port Service Multiplexer
tcpmux	1	udp	TCP Port Service Multiplexer
compressnet	2	tcp	Management Utility
compressnet	2	udp	Management Utility
compressnet	3	tcp	Compression Process
compressnet	3	udp	Compression Process
rje	5	tcp	Remote Job Entry
rje	5	udp	Remote Job Entry
echo	7	tcp	Echo
echo	7	udp	Echo
discard	9	tcp	Discard

Table B.1   Continued

Service	Port Number	Protocol	Description
discard	9	udp	Discard
systat	11	tcp	Active Users
systat	11	udp	Active Users
daytime	13	tcp	Daytime (RFC 867)
daytime	13	udp	Daytime (RFC 867)
qotd	17	tcp	Quote of the Day
qotd	17	udp	Quote of the Day
msp	18	tcp	Message Send Protocol
msp	18	udp	Message Send Protocol
chargen	19	tcp	Character Generator
chargen	19	udp	Character Generator
ftp-data	20	tcp	File Transfer [Default Data]
ftp-data	20	udp	File Transfer [Default Data]
ftp	21	tcp	File Transfer [Control]
ftp	21	udp	File Transfer [Control]
ssh	22	tcp	SSH Remote Login Protocol
ssh	22	udp	SSH Remote Login Protocol
telnet	23	tcp	Telnet
telnet	23	udp	Telnet
	24	tcp	Any private mail system
	24	udp	Any private mail system
smtp	25	tcp	Simple Mail Transfer
smtp	25	udp	Simple Mail Transfer
nsw-fe	27	tcp	NSW User System FE
nsw-fe	27	udp	NSW User System FE
msg-icp	29	tcp	MSG ICP
msg-icp	29	udp	MSG ICP
msg-auth	31	tcp	MSG Authentication
msg-auth	31	udp	MSG Authentication
dsp	33	tcp	Display Support Protocol
dsp	33	udp	Display Support Protocol
	35	tcp	Any private printer server
	35	udp	Any private printer server
time	37	tcp	Time
time	37	udp	Time
rap	38	tcp	Route Access Protocol
rap	38	udp	Route Access Protocol
rlp	39	tcp	Resource Location Protocol
rlp	39	udp	Resource Location Protocol
graphics	41	tcp	Graphics

Table B.1 Continued

Service	Port Number	Protocol	Description
graphics	41	udp	Graphics
name	42	tcp	Host Name Server
name	42	udp	Host Name Server
nameserver	42	tcp	Host Name Server
nameserver	42	udp	Host Name Server
nicname	43	tcp	Who Is
nicname	43	udp	Who Is
mpm-flags	44	tcp	MPM FLAGS Protocol
mpm-flags	44	udp	MPM FLAGS Protocol
mpm	45	tcp	Message Processing Module [recv]
mpm	45	udp	Message Processing Module [recv]
mpm-snd	46	tcp	MPM [default send]
mpm-snd	46	udp	MPM [default send]
ni-ftp	47	tcp	NI FTP
ni-ftp	47	udp	NI FTP
auditd	48	tcp	Digital Audit Daemon
auditd	48	udp	Digital Audit Daemon
tacacs	49	tcp	Login Host Protocol (TACACS)
tacacs	49	udp	Login Host Protocol (TACACS)
re-mail-ck	50	tcp	Remote Mail Checking Protocol
re-mail-ck	50	udp	Remote Mail Checking Protocol
la-maint	51	tcp	IMP Logical Address Maintenance
la-maint	51	udp	IMP Logical Address Maintenance
xns-time	52	tcp	XNS Time Protocol
xns-time	52	udp	XNS Time Protocol
domain	53	tcp	Domain Name Server
domain	53	udp	Domain Name Server
xns-ch	54	tcp	XNS Clearinghouse
xns-ch	54	udp	XNS Clearinghouse
isi-gl	55	tcp	ISI Graphics Language
isi-gl	55	udp	ISI Graphics Language
xns-auth	56	tcp	XNS Authentication
xns-auth	56	udp	XNS Authentication
	57	tcp	Any private terminal access
	57	udp	Any private terminal access
xns-mail	58	tcp	XNS Mail
xns-mail	58	udp	XNS Mail
	59	tcp	Any private file service
	59	udp	Any private file service

Table B.1 Continued

Service	Port Number	Protocol	Description
	60	tcp	Unassigned
	60	udp	Unassigned
ni-mail	61	tcp	NI MAIL
ni-mail	61	udp	NI MAIL
acas	62	tcp	ACA Services
acas	62	udp	ACA Services
whois++	63	tcp	whois++
whois++	63	udp	whois++
covia	64	tcp	Communications Integrator (CI)
covia	64	udp	Communications Integrator (CI)
tacacs-ds	65	tcp	TACACS-Database Service
tacacs-ds	65	udp	TACACS-Database Service
sql*net	66	tcp	Oracle SQL*NET
sql*net	66	udp	Oracle SQL*NET
bootps	67	tcp	Bootstrap Protocol Server
bootps	67	udp	Bootstrap Protocol Server
bootpc	68	tcp	Bootstrap Protocol Client
bootpc	68	udp	Bootstrap Protocol Client
tftp	69	tcp	Trivial File Transfer
tftp	69	udp	Trivial File Transfer
gopher	70	tcp	Gopher
gopher	70	udp	Gopher
netrjs-1	71	tcp	Remote Job Service
netrjs-1	71	udp	Remote Job Service
netrjs-2	72	tcp	Remote Job Service
netrjs-2	72	udp	Remote Job Service
netrjs-3	73	tcp	Remote Job Service
netrjs-3	73	udp	Remote Job Service
netrjs-4	74	tcp	Remote Job Service
netrjs-4	74	udp	Remote Job Service
	75	tcp	Any private dial out service
	75	udp	Any private dial out service
deos	76	tcp	Distributed External Object Store
deos	76	udp	Distributed External Object Store
	77	tcp	Any private RJE service
	77	udp	Any private RJE service
vettcp	78	tcp	vettcp
vettcp	78	udp	vettcp
finger	79	tcp	Finger
finger	79	udp	Finger

Table B.1   Continued

Service	Port Number	Protocol	Description
http	80	tcp	World Wide Web HTTP
http	80	udp	World Wide Web HTTP
www	80	tcp	World Wide Web HTTP
www	80	udp	World Wide Web HTTP
www-http	80	tcp	World Wide Web HTTP
www-http	80	udp	World Wide Web HTTP
hosts2-ns	81	tcp	HOSTS2 Name Server
hosts2-ns	81	udp	HOSTS2 Name Server
xfer	82	tcp	XFER Utility
xfer	82	udp	XFER Utility
mit-ml-dev	83	tcp	MIT ML Device
mit-ml-dev	83	udp	MIT ML Device
ctf	84	tcp	Common Trace Facility
ctf	84	udp	Common Trace Facility
mit-ml-dev	85	tcp	MIT ML Device
mit-ml-dev	85	udp	MIT ML Device
mfcobol	86	tcp	Micro Focus Cobol
mfcobol	86	udp	Micro Focus Cobol
	87	tcp	Any private terminal link
	87	udp	Any private terminal link
kerberos	88	tcp	Kerberos
kerberos	88	udp	Kerberos
su-mit-tg	89	tcp	SUMIT Telnet Gateway
su-mit-tg	89	udp	SUMIT Telnet Gateway
dnsix	90	tcp	DNSIX Securit Attribute Token Map
dnsix	90	udp	DNSIX Securit Attribute Token Map
mit-dov	91	tcp	MIT Dover Spooler
mit-dov	91	udp	MIT Dover Spooler
npp	92	tcp	Network Printing Protocol
npp	92	udp	Network Printing Protocol
dcp	93	tcp	Device Control Protocol
dcp	93	udp	Device Control Protocol
objcall	94	tcp	Tivoli Object Dispatcher
objcall	94	udp	Tivoli Object Dispatcher
supdup	95	tcp	SUPDUP
supdup	95	udp	SUPDUP
dixie	96	tcp	DIXIE Protocol Specification
dixie	96	udp	DIXIE Protocol Specification
swift-rvf	97	tcp	Swift Remote Virtural File Protocol

Table B.1   Continued

Service	Port Number	Protocol	Description
swift-rvf	97	udp	Swift Remote Virtural File Protocol
tacnews	98	tcp	TAC News
tacnews	98	udp	TAC News
metagram	99	tcp	Metagram Relay
metagram	99	udp	Metagram Relay
newacct	100	tcp	[unauthorized use]
hostname	101	tcp	NIC Host Name Server
hostname	101	udp	NIC Host Name Server
iso-tsap	102	tcp	ISO-TSAP Class 0
iso-tsap	102	udp	ISO-TSAP Class 0
gppitnp	103	tcp	Genesis Point-to-Point Trans Net
gppitnp	103	udp	Genesis Point-to-Point Trans Net
acr-nema	104	tcp	ACR-NEMA Digital Imag. & Comm. 300
acr-nema	104	udp	ACR-NEMA Digital Imag. & Comm. 300
cso	105	tcp	CCSO name server protocol
cso	105	udp	CCSO name server protocol
csnet-ns	105	tcp	Mailbox Name Nameserver
csnet-ns	105	udp	Mailbox Name Nameserver
3com-tsmux	106	tcp	3COM-TSMUX
3com-tsmux	106	udp	3COM-TSMUX
rtelnet	107	tcp	Remote Telnet Service
rtelnet	107	udp	Remote Telnet Service
snagas	108	tcp	SNA Gateway Access Server
snagas	108	udp	SNA Gateway Access Server
pop2	109	tcp	Post Office Protocol - Version 2
pop2	109	udp	Post Office Protocol - Version 2
pop3	110	tcp	Post Office Protocol - Version 3
pop3	110	udp	Post Office Protocol - Version 3
sunrpc	111	tcp	SUN Remote Procedure Call
sunrpc	111	udp	SUN Remote Procedure Call
mcidas	112	tcp	McIDAS Data Transmission Protocol
mcidas	112	udp	McIDAS Data Transmission Protocol
ident	113	tcp	
auth	113	tcp	Authentication Service
auth	113	udp	Authentication Service
audionews	114	tcp	Audio News Multicast
audionews	114	udp	Audio News Multicast
sftp	115	tcp	Simple File Transfer Protocol
sftp	115	udp	Simple File Transfer Protocol

Table B.1 Continued

Service	Port Number	Protocol	Description
ansanotify	116	tcp	ANSA REX Notify
ansanotify	116	udp	ANSA REX Notify
uucp-path	117	tcp	UUCP Path Service
uucp-path	117	udp	UUCP Path Service
sqlserv	118	tcp	SQL Services
sqlserv	118	udp	SQL Services
nntp	119	tcp	Network News Transfer Protocol
nntp	119	udp	Network News Transfer Protocol
cfdptkt	120	tcp	CFDPTKT
cfdptkt	120	udp	CFDPTKT
erpc	121	tcp	Encore Expedited Remote Pro.Call
erpc	121	udp	Encore Expedited Remote Pro.Call
smakynet	122	tcp	SMAKYNET
smakynet	122	udp	SMAKYNET
ntp	123	tcp	Network Time Protocol
ntp	123	udp	Network Time Protocol
ansatrader	124	tcp	ANSA REX Trader
ansatrader	124	udp	ANSA REX Trader
locus-map	125	tcp	Locus PC-Interface Net Map Ser
locus-map	125	udp	Locus PC-Interface Net Map Ser
nxedit	126	tcp	NXEdit
nxedit	126	udp	NXEdit
locus-con	127	tcp	Locus PC-Interface Conn Server
locus-con	127	udp	Locus PC-Interface Conn Server
gss-xlicen	128	tcp	GSS X License Verification
gss-xlicen	128	udp	GSS X License Verification
pwdgen	129	tcp	Password Generator Protocol
pwdgen	129	udp	Password Generator Protocol
cisco-fna	130	tcp	cisco FNATIVE
cisco-fna	130	udp	cisco FNATIVE
cisco-tna	131	tcp	cisco TNATIVE
cisco-tna	131	udp	cisco TNATIVE
cisco-sys	132	tcp	cisco SYSMAINT
cisco-sys	132	udp	cisco SYSMAINT
statsrv	133	tcp	Statistics Service
statsrv	133	udp	Statistics Service
ingres-net	134	tcp	INGRES-NET Service
ingres-net	134	udp	INGRES-NET Service
epmap	135	tcp	DCE endpoint resolution
epmap	135	udp	DCE endpoint resolution

Table B.1 Continued

Service	Port Number	Protocol	Description
profile	136	tcp	PROFILE Naming System
profile	136	udp	PROFILE Naming System
netbios-ns	137	tcp	NETBIOS Name Service
netbios-ns	137	udp	NETBIOS Name Service
netbios-dgm	138	tcp	NETBIOS Datagram Service
netbios-dgm	138	udp	NETBIOS Datagram Service
netbios-ssn	139	tcp	NETBIOS Session Service
netbios-ssn	139	udp	NETBIOS Session Service
emfis-data	140	tcp	EMFIS Data Service
emfis-data	140	udp	EMFIS Data Service
emfis-cntl	141	tcp	EMFIS Control Service
emfis-cntl	141	udp	EMFIS Control Service
bl-idm	142	tcp	Britton-Lee IDM
bl-idm	142	udp	Britton-Lee IDM
imap	143	tcp	Internet Message Access Protocol
imap	143	udp	Internet Message Access Protocol
uma	144	tcp	Universal Management Architecture
uma	144	udp	Universal Management Architecture
uaac	145	tcp	UAAC Protocol
uaac	145	udp	UAAC Protocol
iso-tp0	146	tcp	ISO-IP0
iso-tp0	146	udp	ISO-IP0
iso-ip	147	tcp	ISO-IP
iso-ip	147	udp	ISO-IP
jargon	148	tcp	Jargon
jargon	148	udp	Jargon
aed-512	149	tcp	AED 512 Emulation Service
aed-512	149	udp	AED 512 Emulation Service
sql-net	150	tcp	SQL-NET
sql-net	150	udp	SQL-NET
hems	151	tcp	HEMS
hems	151	udp	HEMS
bftp	152	tcp	Background File Transfer Program
bftp	152	udp	Background File Transfer Program
sgmp	153	tcp	SGMP
sgmp	153	udp	SGMP
netsc-prod	154	tcp	NETSC
netsc-prod	154	udp	NETSC
netsc-dev	155	tcp	NETSC
netsc-dev	155	udp	NETSC

Table B.1   **Continued**

Service	Port Number	Protocol	Description
sqlsrv	156	tcp	SQL Service
sqlsrv	156	udp	SQL Service
knet-cmp	157	tcp	KNET VM Command Message Protocol
knet-cmp	157	udp	KNET VM Command Message Protocol
pcmail-srv	158	tcp	PCMail Server
pcmail-srv	158	udp	PCMail Server
nss-routing	159	tcp	NSS-Routing
nss-routing	159	udp	NSS-Routing
sgmp-traps	160	tcp	SGMP-TRAPS
sgmp-traps	160	udp	SGMP-TRAPS
snmp	161	tcp	SNMP
snmp	161	udp	SNMP
snmptrap	162	tcp	SNMPTRAP
snmptrap	162	udp	SNMPTRAP
cmip-man	163	tcp	CMIP TCP Manager
cmip-man	163	udp	CMIP TCP Manager
cmip-agent	164	tcp	CMIP TCP Agent
smip-agent	164	udp	CMIP TCP Agent
xns-courier	165	tcp	Xerox
xns-courier	165	udp	Xerox
s-net	166	tcp	Sirius Systems
s-net	166	udp	Sirius Systems
namp	167	tcp	NAMP
namp	167	udp	NAMP
rsvd	168	tcp	RSVD
rsvd	168	udp	RSVD
send	169	tcp	SEND
send	169	udp	SEND
print-srv	170	tcp	Network PostScript
print-srv	170	udp	Network PostScript
multiplex	171	tcp	Network Innovations Multiplex
multiplex	171	udp	Network Innovations Multiplex
cl/1	172	tcp	Network Innovations CL/1
cl/1	172	udp	Network Innovations CL/1
xyplex-mux	173	tcp	Xyplex
xyplex-mux	173	udp	Xyplex
mailq	174	tcp	MAILQ
mailq	174	udp	MAILQ
vmnet	175	tcp	VMNET

Table B.1   Continued

Service	Port Number	Protocol	Description
vmnet	175	udp	VMNET
genrad-mux	176	tcp	GENRAD-MUX
genrad-mux	176	udp	GENRAD-MUX
xdmcp	177	tcp	X Display Manager Control Protocol
xdmcp	177	udp	X Display Manager Control Protocol
nextstep	178	tcp	NextStep Window Server
nextstep	178	udp	NextStep Window Server
bgp	179	tcp	Border Gateway Protocol
bgp	179	udp	Border Gateway Protocol
ris	180	tcp	Intergraph
ris	180	udp	Intergraph
unify	181	tcp	Unify
unify	181	udp	Unify
audit	182	tcp	Unisys Audit SITP
audit	182	udp	Unisys Audit SITP
ocbinder	183	tcp	OCBinder
ocbinder	183	udp	OCBinder
ocserver	184	tcp	OCServer
ocserver	184	udp	OCServer
remote-kis	185	tcp	Remote-KIS
remote-kis	185	udp	Remote-KIS
kis	186	tcp	KIS Protocol
kis	186	udp	KIS Protocol
aci	187	tcp	Application Communication Interface
aci	187	udp	Application Communication Interface
mumps	188	tcp	Plus Five's MUMPS
mumps	188	udp	Plus Five's MUMPS
qft	189	tcp	Queued File Transport
qft	189	udp	Queued File Transport
gacp	190	tcp	Gateway Access Control Protocol
gacp	190	udp	Gateway Access Control Protocol
prospero	191	tcp	Prospero Directory Service
prospero	191	udp	Prospero Directory Service
osu-nms	192	tcp	OSU Network Monitoring System
osu-nms	192	udp	OSU Network Monitoring System
srmp	193	tcp	Spider Remote Monitoring Protocol
srmp	193	udp	Spider Remote Monitoring Protocol
irc	194	tcp	Internet Relay Chat Protocol
irc	194	udp	Internet Relay Chat Protocol

Table B.1 Continued

Service	Port Number	Protocol	Description
dn6-nlm-aud	195	tcp	DNSIX Network Level Module Audit
dn6-nlm-aud	195	udp	DNSIX Network Level Module Audit
dn6-smm-red	196	tcp	DNSIX Session Mgt Module Audit Redir
dn6-smm-red	196	udp	DNSIX Session Mgt Module Audit Redir
dls	197	tcp	Directory Location Service
dls	197	udp	Directory Location Service
dls-mon	198	tcp	Directory Location Service Monitor
dls-mon	198	udp	Directory Location Service Monitor
smux	199	tcp	SMUX
smux	199	udp	SMUX
src	200	tcp	IBM System Resource Controller
src	200	udp	IBM System Resource Controller
at-rtmp	201	tcp	AppleTalk Routing Maintenance
at-rtmp	201	udp	AppleTalk Routing Maintenance
at-nbp	202	tcp	AppleTalk Name Binding
at-nbp	202	udp	AppleTalk Name Binding
at-3	203	tcp	AppleTalk Unused
at-3	203	udp	AppleTalk Unused
at-echo	204	tcp	AppleTalk Echo
at-echo	204	udp	AppleTalk Echo
at-5	205	tcp	AppleTalk Unused
at-5	205	udp	AppleTalk Unused
at-zis	206	tcp	AppleTalk Zone Information
at-zis	206	udp	AppleTalk Zone Information
at-7	207	tcp	AppleTalk Unused
at-7	207	udp	AppleTalk Unused
at-8	208	tcp	AppleTalk Unused
at-8	208	udp	AppleTalk Unused
qmtp	209	tcp	The Quick Mail Transfer Protocol
qmtp	209	udp	The Quick Mail Transfer Protocol
z39.50	210	tcp	ANSI Z39.50
z39.50	210	udp	ANSI Z39.50
914c/g	211	tcp	Texas Instruments 914C/G Terminal
914c/g	211	udp	Texas Instruments 914C/G Terminal
anet	212	tcp	ATEXSSTR
anet	212	udp	ATEXSSTR
ipx	213	tcp	IPX
ipx	213	udp	IPX
vmpwscs	214	tcp	VM PWSCS

Table B.1 Continued

Service	Port Number	Protocol	Description
vmpwscs	214	udp	VM PWSCS
softpc	215	tcp	Insignia Solutions
softpc	215	udp	Insignia Solutions
CAllic	216	tcp	Computer Associates Int'l License Server
CAllic	216	udp	Computer Associates Int'l License Server
dbase	217	tcp	dBASE Unix
dbase	217	udp	dBASE Unix
mpp	218	tcp	Netix Message Posting Protocol
pp	218	udp	Netix Message Posting Protocol
uarps	219	tcp	Unisys ARPs
uarps	219	udp	Unisys ARPs
imap3	220	tcp	Interactive Mail Access Protocol v3
imap3	220	udp	Interactive Mail Access Protocol v3
fln-spx	221	tcp	Berkeley rlogind with SPX auth
fln-spx	221	udp	Berkeley rlogind with SPX auth
rsh-spx	222	tcp	Berkeley rshd with SPX auth
rsh-spx	222	udp	Berkeley rshd with SPX auth
cdc	223	tcp	Certificate Distribution Center
cdc	223	udp	Certificate Distribution Center
masqdialer	224	tcp	masqdialer
masqdialer	224	udp	masqdialer
direct	242	tcp	Direct
direct	242	udp	Direct
sur-meas	243	tcp	Survey Measurement
sur-meas	243	udp	Survey Measurement
inbusiness	244	tcp	Inbusiness
inbusiness	244	udp	Inbusiness
link	245	tcp	LINK
link	245	udp	LINK
dsp3270	246	tcp	Display Systems Protocol
dsp3270	246	udp	Display Systems Protocol
subntbcst_tftp	247	tcp	SUBNTBCST_TFTP
subntbcst_tftp	247	udp	SUBNTBCST_TFTP
bhfhs	248	tcp	bhfhs
bhfhs	248	udp	bhfhs
rap	256	tcp	RAP
rap	256	udp	RAP
set	257	tcp	Secure Electronic Transaction
set	257	udp	Secure Electronic Transaction

Table B.1 Continued

Service	Port Number	Protocol	Description
yak-chat	258	tcp	Yak Winsock Personal Chat
yak-chat	258	udp	Yak Winsock Personal Chat
esro-gen	259	tcp	Efficient Short Remote Operations
esro-gen	259	udp	Efficient Short Remote Operations
openport	260	tcp	Openport
openport	260	udp	Openport
nsiiops	261	tcp	IIOP Name Service over TLS/SSL
nsiiops	261	udp	IIOP Name Service over TLS/SSL
arcisdms	262	tcp	Arcisdms
arcisdms	262	udp	Arcisdms
hdap	263	tcp	HDAP
hdap	263	udp	HDAP
bgmp	264	tcp	BGMP
bgmp	264	udp	BGMP
x-bone-ctl	265	tcp	X-bone CTL
x-bone-ctl	265	udp	X-bone CTL
sst	266	tcp	SCSI on ST
sst	266	udp	SCSI on ST
td-service	267	tcp	Tobit David Service Layer
td-service	267	udp	Tobit David Service Layer
td-replica	268	tcp	Tobid David Replica
td-replica	268	udp	Tobit David Replica
http-mgmt	280	tcp	http-mgmt
http-mgmt	280	udp	http-mgmt
personal-link	281	tcp	Personal Link
personal-link	281	udp	Personal Link
cableport-ax	282	tcp	Cable Port AX
cableport-ax	282	udp	Cable Port AX
rescap	283	tcp	rescap
rescap	283	udp	rescap
corerjd	284	tcp	Corerjd
corerjd	284	udp	Corerjd
fxp-1	286	tcp	FXP-1
fxp-1	286	udp	FXP-1
k-block	287	tcp	K-BLOCK
k-block	287	udp	K-BLOCK
novastorbakcup	308	tcp	Novastor Backup
novastorbakcup	308	udp	Novastor Backup
entrusttime	309	tcp	EntrustTime

Table B.1   Continued

Service	Port Number	Protocol	Description
entrusttime	309	udp	EntrustTime
bhmds	310	tcp	bhmds
bhmds	310	udp	bhmds
asip-webadmin	311	tcp	AppleShare IP WebAdmin
asip-webadmin	311	udp	AppleShare IP WebAdmin
vslmp	312	tcp	VSLMP
vslmp	312	udp	VSLMP
magenta-logic	313	tcp	Magenta Logic
magenta-logic	313	udp	Magenta Logic
opalis-robot	314	tcp	Opalis Robot
opalis-robot	314	udp	Opalis Robot
dpsi	315	tcp	DPSI
dpsi	315	udp	DPSI
decauth	316	tcp	decAuth
decauth	316	udp	decAuth
zannet	317	tcp	Zannet
zannet	317	udp	Zannet
pkix-timestamp	318	tcp	PKIX TimeStamp
pkix-timestamp	318	udp	PKIX TimeStamp
ptp-event	319	tcp	PTP Event
ptp-event	319	udp	PTP Event
ptp-general	320	tcp	PTP General
ptp-general	320	udp	PTP General
pip	321	tcp	PIP
pip	321	udp	PIP
rtsps	322	tcp	RTSPS
rtsps	322	udp	RTSPS
texar	323	tcp	Texar Security Port
texar	323	udp	Texar Security Port
pdap	344	tcp	Prospero Data Access Protocol
pdap	344	udp	Prospero Data Access Protocol
pawserv	345	tcp	Perf Analysis Workbench
pawserv	345	udp	Perf Analysis Workbench
zserv	346	tcp	Zebra server
zserv	346	udp	Zebra server
fatserv	347	tcp	Fatmen Server
fatserv	347	udp	Fatmen Server
csi-sgwp	348	tcp	Cabletron Management Protocol

Table B.1 Continued

Service	Port Number	Protocol	Description
csi-sgwp	348	udp	Cabletron Management Protocol
mftp	349	tcp	mftp
mftp	349	udp	mftp
matip-type-a	350	tcp	MATIP Type A
matip-type-a	350	udp	MATIP Type A
matip-type-b	351	tcp	MATIP Type B
matip-type-b	351	udp	MATIP Type B
bhoetty	351	tcp	bhoetty
bhoetty	351	udp	bhoetty
dtag-ste-sb	352	tcp	DTAG
dtag-ste-sb	352	udp	DTAG
bhoedap4	352	tcp	bhoedap4
bhoedap4	352	udp	bhoedap4
ndsauth	353	tcp	NDSAUTH
ndsauth	353	udp	NDSAUTH
bh611	354	tcp	bh611
bh611	354	udp	bh611
datex-asn	355	tcp	DATEX-ASN
datex-asn	355	udp	DATEX-ASN
cloanto-net-1	356	tcp	Cloanto Net 1
cloanto-net-1	356	udp	Cloanto Net 1
bhevent	357	tcp	bhevent
bhevent	357	udp	bhevent
shrinkwrap	358	tcp	Shrinkwrap
shrinkwrap	358	udp	Shrinkwrap
nsrmp	359	tcp	Network Security Risk Management Protocol
nsrmp	359	udp	Network Security Risk Management Protocol
scoi2odialog	360	tcp	scoi2odialog
scoi2odialog	360	udp	scoi2odialog
semantix	361	tcp	Semantix
semantix	361	udp	Semantix
srssend	362	tcp	SRS Send
srssend	362	udp	SRS Send
rsvp_tunnel	363	tcp	RSVP Tunnel
rsvp_tunnel	363	udp	RSVP Tunnel
aurora-cmgr	364	tcp	Aurora CMGR
aurora-cmgr	364	udp	Aurora CMGR

Table B.1   Continued

Service	Port Number	Protocol	Description
dtk	365	tcp	DTK
dtk	365	udp	DTK
odmr	366	tcp	ODMR
odmr	366	udp	ODMR
mortgageware	367	tcp	MortgageWare
mortgageware	367	udp	MortgageWare
qbikgdp	368	tcp	QbikGDP
qbikgdp	368	udp	QbikGDP
rpc2portmap	369	tcp	rpc2portmap
rpc2portmap	369	udp	rpc2portmap
codaauth2	370	tcp	codaauth2
codaauth2	370	udp	codaauth2
clearcase	371	tcp	Clearcase
clearcase	371	udp	Clearcase
ulistproc	372	tcp	ListProcessor
ulistproc	372	udp	ListProcessor
legent-1	373	tcp	Legent Corporation
legent-1	373	udp	Legent Corporation
legent-2	374	tcp	Legent Corporation
legent-2	374	udp	Legent Corporation
hassle	375	tcp	Hassle
hassle	375	udp	Hassle
nip	376	tcp	Amiga Envoy Network Inquiry Proto
nip	376	udp	Amiga Envoy Network Inquiry Proto
tnETOS	377	tcp	NEC Corporation
tnETOS	377	udp	NEC Corporation
dsETOS	378	tcp	NEC Corporation
dsETOS	378	udp	NEC Corporation
is99c	379	tcp	TIA/EIA/IS-99 modem client
is99c	379	udp	TIA/EIA/IS-99 modem client
is99s	380	tcp	TIA/EIA/IS-99 modem server
is99s	380	udp	TIA/EIA/IS-99 modem server
hp-collector	381	tcp	hp performance data collector
hp-collector	381	udp	hp performance data collector
hp-managed-node	382	tcp	hp performance data managed node
hp-managed-node	382	udp	hp performance data managed node
hp-alarm-mgr	383	tcp	hp performance data alarm manager
hp-alarm-mgr	383	udp	hp performance data alarm manager
arns	384	tcp	A Remote Network Server System
arns	384	udp	A Remote Network Server System

Table B.1 Continued

Service	Port Number	Protocol	Description
ibm-app	385	tcp	IBM Application
ibm-app	385	udp	IBM Application
asa	386	tcp	ASA Message Router Object Def.
asa	386	udp	ASA Message Router Object Def.
aurp	387	tcp	Appletalk Update-Based Routing Pro.
aurp	387	udp	Appletalk Update-Based Routing Pro.
unidata-ldm	388	tcp	Unidata LDM Version 4
unidata-ldm	388	udp	Unidata LDM Version 4
ldap	389	tcp	Lightweight Directory Access Protocol
ldap	389	udp	Lightweight Directory Access Protocol
uis	390	tcp	UIS
uis	390	udp	UIS
ynotics-relay	391	tcp	SynOptics SNMP Relay Port
synotics-relay	391	udp	SynOptics SNMP Relay Port
synotics-broker	392	tcp	SynOptics Port Broker Port
synotics-broker	392	udp	SynOptics Port Broker Port
meta5	393	tcp	Meta5
meta5	393	udp	Meta5
embl-ndt	394	tcp	EMBL Nucleic Data Transfer
embl-ndt	394	udp	EMBL Nucleic Data Transfer
netcp	395	tcp	NETscout Control Protocol
netcp	395	udp	NETscout Control Protocol
netware-ip	396	tcp	Novell Netware over IP
netware-ip	396	udp	Novell Netware over IP
mptn	397	tcp	Multi Protocol Trans. Net.
mptn	397	udp	Multi Protocol Trans. Net.
kryptolan	398	tcp	Kryptolan
kryptolan	398	udp	Kryptolan
iso-tsap-c2	399	tcp	ISO Transport Class 2 Non-Control over TCP
iso-tsap-c2	399	udp	ISO Transport Class 2 Non-Control over TCP
work-sol	400	tcp	Workstation Solutions
work-sol	400	udp	Workstation Solutions
ups	401	tcp	Uninterruptible Power Supply
ups	401	udp	Uninterruptible Power Supply
genie	402	tcp	Genie Protocol
genie	402	udp	Genie Protocol
decap	403	tcp	decap
decap	403	udp	decap

Table B.1   Continued

Service	Port Number	Protocol	Description
nced	404	tcp	nced
nced	404	udp	nced
ncld	405	tcp	ncld
ncld	405	udp	ncld
imsp	406	tcp	Interactive Mail Support Protocol
imsp	406	udp	Interactive Mail Support Protocol
timbuktu	407	tcp	Timbuktu
timbuktu	407	udp	Timbuktu
prm-sm	408	tcp	Prospero Resource Manager Sys. Man.
prm-sm	408	udp	Prospero Resource Manager Sys. Man.
prm-nm	409	tcp	Prospero Resource Manager Node Man.
prm-nm	409	udp	Prospero Resource Manager Node Man.
decladebug	410	tcp	DECLadebug Remote Debug Protocol
decladebug	410	udp	DECLadebug Remote Debug Protocol
rmt	411	tcp	Remote MT Protocol
rmt	411	udp	Remote MT Protocol
synoptics-trap	412	tcp	Trap Convention Port
synoptics-trap	412	udp	Trap Convention Port
smsp	413	tcp	Storage Management Services Protocol
smsp	413	udp	Storage Management Services Protocol
infoseek	414	tcp	InfoSeek
infoseek	414	udp	InfoSeek
bnet	415	tcp	BNet
bnet	415	udp	BNet
silverplatter	416	tcp	Silverplatter
silverplatter	416	udp	Silverplatter
onmux	417	tcp	Onmux
onmux	417	udp	Onmux
hyper-g	418	tcp	Hyper-G
hyper-g	418	udp	Hyper-G
ariel1	419	tcp	Ariel
ariel1	419	udp	Ariel
smpte	420	tcp	SMPTE
smpte	420	udp	SMPTE
ariel2	421	tcp	Ariel
ariel2	421	udp	Ariel
ariel3	422	tcp	Ariel
ariel3	422	udp	Ariel

Table B.1   Continued

Service	Port Number	Protocol	Description
opc-job-start	423	tcp	IBM Operations Planning and Control Start
opc-job-start	423	udp	IBM Operations Planning and Control Start
opc-job-track	424	tcp	IBM Operations Planning and Control Track
opc-job-track	424	udp	IBM Operations Planning and Control Track
icad-el	425	tcp	ICAD
icad-el	425	udp	ICAD
martsdp	426	tcp	smartsdp
smartsdp	426	udp	smartsdp
svrloc	427	tcp	Server Location
svrloc	427	udp	Server Location
ocs_cmu	428	tcp	OCS_CMU
ocs_cmu	428	udp	OCS_CMU
ocs_amu	429	tcp	OCS_AMU
ocs_amu	429	udp	OCS_AMU
utmpsd	430	tcp	UTMPSD
utmpsd	430	udp	UTMPSD
utmpcd	431	tcp	UTMPCD
utmpcd	431	udp	UTMPCD
iasd	432	tcp	IASD
iasd	432	udp	IASD
nnsp	433	tcp	NNSP
nnsp	433	udp	NNSP
mobileip-agent	434	tcp	MobileIP-Agent
mobileip-agent	434	udp	MobileIP-Agent
mobilip-mn	435	tcp	MobilIP-MN
mobilip-mn	435	udp	MobilIP-MN
dna-cml	436	tcp	DNA-CML
dna-cml	436	udp	DNA-CML
comscm	437	tcp	comscm
comscm	437	udp	comscm
dsfgw	438	tcp	dsfgw
dsfgw	438	udp	dsfgw
dasp	439	tcp	dasp
dasp	439	udp	dasp
sgcp	440	tcp	sgcp
sgcp	440	udp	sgcp

Table B.1 Continued

Service	Port Number	Protocol	Description
decvms-sysmgt	441	tcp	decvms-sysmgt
decvms-sysmgt	441	udp	decvms-sysmgt
cvc_hostd	442	tcp	cvc_hostd
cvc_hostd	442	udp	cvc_hostd
https	443	tcp	http protocol over TLS/SSL
https	443	udp	http protocol over TLS/SSL
snpp	444	tcp	Simple Network Paging Protocol
snpp	444	udp	Simple Network Paging Protocol
microsoft-ds	445	tcp	Microsoft-DS
microsoft-ds	445	udp	Microsoft-DS
ddm-rdb	446	tcp	DDM-RDB
ddm-rdb	446	udp	DDM-RDB
ddm-dfm	447	tcp	DDM-RFM
ddm-dfm	447	udp	DDM-RFM
ddm-ssl	448	tcp	DDM-SSL
ddm-ssl	448	udp	DDM-SSL
as-servermap	449	tcp	AS Server Mapper
as-servermap	449	udp	AS Server Mapper
tserver	450	tcp	TServer
tserver	450	udp	TServer
sfs-smp-net	451	tcp	Cray Network Semaphore server
sfs-smp-net	451	udp	Cray Network Semaphore server
sfs-config	452	tcp	Cray SFS config server
sfs-config	452	udp	Cray SFS config server
creativeserver	453	tcp	CreativeServer
creativeserver	453	udp	CreativeServer
contentserver	454	tcp	ContentServer
contentserver	454	udp	ContentServer
creativepartnr	455	tcp	CreativePartnr
creativepartnr	455	udp	CreativePartnr
macon-tcp	456	tcp	macon-tcp
macon-udp	456	udp	macon-udp
scohelp	457	tcp	scohelp
scohelp	457	udp	scohelp
appleqtc	458	tcp	apple quick time
appleqtc	458	udp	apple quick time
ampr-rcmd	459	tcp	ampr-rcmd
ampr-rcmd	459	udp	ampr-rcmd

Table B.1 Continued

Service	Port Number	Protocol	Description
skronk	460	tcp	skronk
skronk	460	udp	skronk
datasurfsrv	461	tcp	DataRampSrv
datasurfsrv	461	udp	DataRampSrv
datasurfsrvsec	462	tcp	DataRampSrvSec
datasurfsrvsec	462	udp	DataRampSrvSec
alpes	463	tcp	alpes
alpes	463	udp	alpes
kpasswd	464	tcp	kpasswd
kpasswd	464	udp	kpasswd
digital-vrc	466	tcp	digital-vrc
digital-vrc	466	udp	digital-vrc
mylex-mapd	467	tcp	mylex-mapd
mylex-mapd	467	udp	mylex-mapd
photuris	468	tcp	proturis
photuris	468	udp	proturis
rcp	469	tcp	Radio Control Protocol
rcp	469	udp	Radio Control Protocol
scx-proxy	470	tcp	scx-proxy
scx-proxy	470	udp	scx-proxy
mondex	471	tcp	Mondex
mondex	471	udp	Mondex
ljk-login	472	tcp	ljk-login
ljk-login	472	udp	ljk-login
hybrid-pop	473	tcp	hybrid-pop
hybrid-pop	473	udp	hybrid-pop
tn-tl-w1	474	tcp	tn-tl-w1
tn-tl-w2	474	udp	tn-tl-w2
tcpnethaspsrv	475	tcp	tcpnethaspsrv
tcpnethaspsrv	475	udp	tcpnethaspsrv
tn-tl-fd1	476	tcp	tn-tl-fd1
tn-tl-fd1	476	udp	tn-tl-fd1
ss7ns	477	tcp	ss7ns
ss7ns	477	udp	ss7ns
spsc	478	tcp	spsc
spsc	478	udp	spsc
iafserver	479	tcp	iafserver
iafserver	479	udp	iafserver

Table B.1 Continued

Service	Port Number	Protocol	Description
iafdbase	480	tcp	iafdbase
iafdbase	480	udp	iafdbase
ph	481	tcp	Ph service
ph	481	udp	Ph service
bgs-nsi	482	tcp	bgs-nsi
bgs-nsi	482	udp	bgs-nsi
ulpnet	483	tcp	ulpnet
ulpnet	483	udp	ulpnet
integra-sme	484	tcp	Integra Software Management Environment
integra-sme	484	udp	Integra Software Management Environment
powerburst	485	tcp	Air Soft Power Burst
powerburst	485	udp	Air Soft Power Burst
avian	486	tcp	avian
avian	486	udp	avian
saft	487	tcp	saft Simple Asynchronous File Transfer
saft	487	udp	saft Simple Asynchronous File Transfer
gss-http	488	tcp	gss-http
gss-http	488	udp	gss-http
est-protocol	489	tcp	nest-protocol
nest-protocol	489	udp	nest-protocol
micom-pfs	490	tcp	micom-pfs
micom-pfs	490	udp	micom-pfs
go-login	491	tcp	go-login
go-login	491	udp	go-login
ticf-1	492	tcp	Transport Independent Convergence for FNA
ticf-1	492	udp	Transport Independent Convergence for FNA
ticf-2	493	tcp	Transport Independent Convergence for FNA
ticf-2	493	udp	Transport Independent Convergence for FNA
pov-ray	494	tcp	POV-Ray
pov-ray	494	udp	POV-Ray
ntecourier	495	tcp	intecourier
intecourier	495	udp	intecourier
pim-rp-disc	496	tcp	PIM-RP-DISC
pim-rp-disc	496	udp	PIM-RP-DISC
dantz	497	tcp	dantz
dantz	497	udp	dantz

Table B.1   Continued

Service	Port Number	Protocol	Description
siam	498	tcp	siam
siam	498	udp	siam
iso-ill	499	tcp	ISO ILL Protocol
iso-ill	499	udp	ISO ILL Protocol
isakmp	500	tcp	isakmp
isakmp	500	udp	isakmp
stmf	501	tcp	STMF
stmf	501	udp	STMF
asa-appl-proto	502	tcp	asa-appl-proto
asa-appl-proto	502	udp	asa-appl-proto
intrinsa	503	tcp	Intrinsa
intrinsa	503	udp	Intrinsa
citadel	504	tcp	citadel
citadel	504	udp	citadel
mailbox-lm	505	tcp	mailbox-lm
mailbox-lm	505	udp	mailbox-lm
ohimsrv	506	tcp	ohimsrv
ohimsrv	506	udp	ohimsrv
crs	507	tcp	crs
crs	507	udp	crs
xvttp	508	tcp	xvttp
xvttp	508	udp	xvttp
snare	509	tcp	snare
snare	509	udp	snare
fcp	510	tcp	FirstClass Protocol
fcp	510	udp	FirstClass Protocol
passgo	511	tcp	PassGo
passgo	511	udp	PassGo
exec	512	tcp	remote process execution;
comsat	512	udp	
biff	512	udp	Used by mail system to notify users
login	513	tcp	Remote login a la telnet
who	513	udp	Maintains the Who Is database
shell	514	tcp	cmd
syslog	514	udp	
printer	515	tcp	spooler
printer	515	udp	spooler
videotex	516	tcp	videotex

Table B.1 Continued

Service	Port Number	Protocol	Description
videotex	516	udp	videotex
talk	517	tcp	like tenex link, but across
talk	517	udp	like tenex link, but across
ntalk	518	tcp	
ntalk	518	udp	
utime	519	tcp	unixtime
utime	519	udp	unixtime
efs	520	tcp	extended file name server
router	520	udp	local routing process (on site)
ripng	521	tcp	ripng
ripng	521	udp	ripng
ulp	522	tcp	ULP
ulp	522	udp	ULP
ibm-db2	523	tcp	IBM-DB2
ibm-db2	523	udp	IBM-DB2
ncp	524	tcp	NCP
ncp	524	udp	NCP
timed	525	tcp	timeserver
timed	525	udp	timeserver
tempo	526	tcp	newdate
tempo	526	udp	newdate
stx	527	tcp	Stock IXChange
stx	527	udp	Stock IXChange
custix	528	tcp	Customer IXChange
custix	528	udp	Customer IXChange
irc-serv	529	tcp	IRC-SERV
irc-serv	529	udp	IRC-SERV
courier	530	tcp	rpc
courier	530	udp	rpc
conference	531	tcp	chat
conference	531	udp	chat
netnews	532	tcp	readnews
netnews	532	udp	readnews
netwall	533	tcp	for emergency broadcasts
netwall	533	udp	for emergency broadcasts
mm-admin	534	tcp	MegaMedia Admin
mm-admin	534	udp	MegaMedia Admin
iiop	535	tcp	iiop

Table B.1 **Continued**

Service	Port Number	Protocol	Description
iiop	535	udp	iiop
opalis-rdv	536	tcp	opalis-rdv
opalis-rdv	536	udp	opalis-rdv
nmsp	537	tcp	Networked Media Streaming Protocol
nmsp	537	udp	Networked Media Streaming Protocol
gdomap	538	tcp	gdomap
gdomap	538	udp	gdomap
apertus-ldp	539	tcp	Apertus Technologies Load Determination
apertus-ldp	539	udp	Apertus Technologies Load Determination
uucp	540	tcp	uucpd
uucp	540	udp	uucpd
uucp-rlogin	541	tcp	uucp-rlogin
uucp-rlogin	541	udp	uucp-rlogin
commerce	542	tcp	commerce
commerce	542	udp	commerce
klogin	543	tcp	
klogin	543	udp	
kshell	544	tcp	krcmd
kshell	544	udp	krcmd
appleqtcsrvr	545	tcp	appleqtcsrvr
appleqtcsrvr	545	udp	appleqtcsrvr
dhcpv6-client	546	tcp	DHCPv6 Client
dhcpv6-client	546	udp	DHCPv6 Client
dhcpv6-server	547	tcp	DHCPv6 Server
dhcpv6-server	547	udp	DHCPv6 Server
afpovertcp	548	tcp	AFP over TCP
afpovertcp	548	udp	AFP over TCP
idfp	549	tcp	IDFP
idfp	549	udp	IDFP
new-rwho	550	tcp	new-who
new-rwho	550	udp	new-who
cybercash	551	tcp	cybercash
cybercash	551	udp	cybercash
deviceshare	552	tcp	deviceshare
deviceshare	552	udp	deviceshare
pirp	553	tcp	pirp
pirp	553	udp	pirp
rtsp	554	tcp	Real Time Stream Control Protocol

Table B.1   Continued

Service	Port Number	Protocol	Description
rtsp	554	udp	Real Time Stream Control Protocol
dsf	555	tcp	
dsf	555	udp	
remotefs	556	tcp	rfs server
remotefs	556	udp	rfs server
openvms-sysipc	557	tcp	openvms-sysipc
openvms-sysipc	557	udp	openvms-sysipc
sdnskmp	558	tcp	SDNSKMP
sdnskmp	558	udp	SDNSKMP
teedtap	559	tcp	TEEDTAP
teedtap	559	udp	TEEDTAP
rmonitor	560	tcp	rmonitord
rmonitor	560	udp	rmonitord
monitor	561	tcp	
monitor	561	udp	
chshell	562	tcp	chcmd
chshell	562	udp	chcmd
nntps	563	tcp	nntp protocol over TLS SSL (was snntp)
nntps	563	udp	nntp protocol over TLS SSL (was snntp)
9pfs	564	tcp	plan 9 file service
9pfs	564	udp	plan 9 file service
whoami	565	tcp	whoami
whoami	565	udp	whoami
streettalk	566	tcp	streettalk
streettalk	566	udp	streettalk
banyan-rpc	567	tcp	banyan-rpc
banyan-rpc	567	udp	banyan-rpc
ms-shuttle	568	tcp	microsoft shuttle
ms-shuttle	568	udp	microsoft shuttle
ms-rome	569	tcp	microsoft rome
ms-rome	569	udp	microsoft rome
meter	570	tcp	demon
meter	570	udp	demon
meter	571	tcp	udemon
meter	571	udp	udemon
sonar	572	tcp	sonar
sonar	572	udp	sonar
banyan-vip	573	tcp	banyan-vip

Table B.1 Continued

Service	Port Number	Protocol	Description
banyan-vip	573	udp	banyan-vip
ftp-agent	574	tcp	FTP Software Agent System
ftp-agent	574	udp	FTP Software Agent System
vemmi	575	tcp	VEMMI
vemmi	575	udp	VEMMI
ipcd	576	tcp	ipcd
ipcd	576	udp	ipcd
vnas	577	tcp	vnas
vnas	577	udp	vnas
ipdd	578	tcp1	ipdd
ipdd	578	udp	ipdd
decbsrv	579	tcp	decbsrv
decbsrv	579	udp	decbsrv
sntp-heartbeat	580	tcp	SNTP HEARTBEAT
sntp-heartbeat	580	udp	SNTP HEARTBEAT
bdp	581	tcp	Bundle Discovery Protocol
bdp	581	udp	Bundle Discovery Protocol
scc-security	582	tcp	SCC Security
scc-security	582	udp	SCC Security
philips-vc	583	tcp	Philips Video-Conferencing
philips-vc	583	udp	Philips Video-Conferencing
keyserver	584	tcp	Key Server
keyserver	584	udp	Key Server
imap4-ssl	585	tcp	IMAP4+SSL (use 993 instead)
imap4-ssl	585	udp	IMAP4+SSL (use 993 instead)
password-chg	586	tcp	Password Change
password-chg	586	udp	Password Change
submission	587	tcp	Submission
submission	587	udp	Submission
cal	588	tcp	CAL
cal	588	udp	CAL
eyelink	589	tcp	EyeLink
eyelink	589	udp	EyeLink
tns-cml	590	tcp	TNS CML
tns-cml	590	udp	TNS CML
http-alt	591	tcp	FileMaker, Inc. - HTTP Alternate (see Port 80)
http-alt	591	udp	FileMaker, Inc. - HTTP Alternate (see Port 80)
eudora-set	592	tcp	Eudora Set

Table B.1   Continued

Service	Port Number	Protocol	Description
eudora-set	592	udp	Eudora Set
http-rpc-epmap	593	tcp	HTTP RPC Ep Map
http-rpc-epmap	593	udp	HTTP RPC Ep Map
tpip	594	tcp	TPIP
tpip	594	udp	TPIP
cab-protocol	595	tcp	CAB Protocol
cab-protocol	595	udp	CAB Protocol
smsd	596	tcp	SMSD
smsd	596	udp	SMSD
ptcnameservice	597	tcp	PTC Name Service
ptcnameservice	597	udp	PTC Name Service
sco-websrvrmg3	598	tcp	SCO Web Server Manager 3
sco-websrvrmg3	598	udp	SCO Web Server Manager 3
acp	599	tcp	Aeolon Core Protocol
acp	599	udp	Aeolon Core Protocol
ipcserver	600	tcp	Sun IPC server
ipcserver	600	udp	Sun IPC server
urm	606	tcp	Cray Unified Resource Manager
urm	606	udp	Cray Unified Resource Manager
nqs	607	tcp	nqs
nqs	607	udp	nqs
sift-uft	608	tcp	Sender-Initiated/Unsolicited File Transfer
sift-uft	608	udp	Sender-Initiated/Unsolicited File Transfer
npmp-trap	609	tcp	npmp-trap
npmp-trap	609	udp	npmp-trap
npmp-local	610	tcp	npmp-local
npmp-local	610	udp	npmp-local
npmp-gui	611	tcp	npmp-gui
npmp-gui	611	udp	npmp-gui
hmmp-ind	612	tcp	HMMP Indication
hmmp-ind	612	udp	HMMP Indication
hmmp-op	613	tcp	HMMP Operation
hmmp-op	613	udp	HMMP Operation
sshell	614	tcp	SSLshell
sshell	614	udp	SSLshell
sco-inetmgr	615	tcp	Internet Configuration Manager
sco-inetmgr	615	udp	Internet Configuration Manager
sco-sysmgr	616	tcp	SCO System Administration Server
sco-sysmgr	616	udp	SCO System Administration Server
sco-dtmgr	617	tcp	SCO Desktop Administration Server

Table B.1   Continued

Service	Port Number	Protocol	Description
sco-dtmgr	617	udp	SCO Desktop Administration Server
dei-icda	618	tcp	DEI-ICDA
dei-icda	618	udp	DEI-ICDA
digital-evm	619	tcp	Digital EVM
digital-evm	619	udp	Digital EVM
sco-websrvrmgr	620	tcp	SCO WebServer Manager
sco-websrvrmgr	620	udp	SCO WebServer Manager
escp-ip	621	tcp	ESCP
escp-ip	621	udp	ESCP
collaborator	622	tcp	Collaborator
collaborator	622	udp	Collaborator
aux_bus_shunt	623	tcp	Aux Bus Shu1nt
aux_bus_shunt	623	udp	Aux Bus Shunt
cryptoadmin	624	tcp	Crypto Admin
cryptoadmin	624	udp	Crypto Admin
dec_dlm	625	tcp	DEC DLM
dec_dlm	625	udp	DEC DLM
asia	626	tcp	ASIA
asia	626	udp	ASIA
passgo-tivoli	627	tcp	PassGo Tivoli
passgo-tivoli	627	udp	PassGo Tivoli
qmqp	628	tcp	QMQP
qmqp	628	udp	QMQP
3com-amp3	629	tcp	3Com AMP3
3com-amp3	629	udp	3Com AMP3
rda	630	tcp	RDA
rda	630	udp	RDA
ipp	631	tcp	IPP (Internet Printing Protocol)
ipp	631	udp	IPP (Internet Printing Protocol)
bmpp	632	tcp	bmpp
bmpp	632	udp	bmpp
servstat	633	tcp	Service Status update (Sterling Software)
servstat	633	udp	Service Status update (Sterling Software)
ginad	634	tcp	ginad
ginad	634	udp	ginad
rlzdbase	635	tcp	RLZ DBase
rlzdbase	635	udp	RLZ DBase
ldaps	636	tcp	ldap protocol over TLS SSL (was sldap)

Table B.1 **Continued**

Service	Port Number	Protocol	Description
ldaps	636	udp	ldap protocol over TLS SSL (was sldap)
lanserver	637	tcp	lanserver
lanserver	637	udp	lanserver
mcns-sec	638	tcp	mcns-sec
mcns-sec	638	udp	mcns-sec
msdp	639	tcp	MSDP
msdp	639	udp	MSDP
entrust-sps	640	tcp	entrust-sps
entrust-sps	640	udp	entrust-sps
repcmd	641	tcp	repcmd
repcmd	641	udp	repcmd
esro-emsdp	642	tcp	ESRO-EMSDP V1.3
esro-emsdp	642	udp	ESRO-EMSDP V1.3
sanity	643	tcp	SANity
sanity	643	udp	SANity
dwr	644	tcp	dwr
dwr	644	udp	dwr
pssc	645	tcp	PSSC
pssc	645	udp	PSSC
ldp	646	tcp	LDP
ldp	646	udp	LDP
dhcp-failover	647	tcp	DHCP Failover
dhcp-failover	647	udp	DHCP Failover
rrp	648	tcp	Registry Registrar Protocol (RRP)
rrp	648	udp	Registry Registrar Protocol (RRP)
aminet	649	tcp	Aminet
aminet	649	udp	Aminet
obex	650	tcp	OBEX
obex	650	udp	OBEX
ieee-mms	651	tcp	IEEE MMS
ieee-mms	651	udp	IEEE MMS
udlr-dtcp	652	tcp	UDLR_DTCP
udlr-dtcp	652	udp	UDLR_DTCP
repscmd	653	tcp	RepCmd
repscmd	653	udp	RepCmd
aodv	654	tcp	AODV
aodv	654	udp	AODV
tinc	655	tcp	TINC
tinc	655	udp	TINC

Table B.1 Continued

Service	Port Number	Protocol	Description
spmp	656	tcp	SPMP
spmp	656	udp	SPMP
mdqs	666	tcp	
mdqs	666	udp	
doom	666	tcp	doom Id Software
doom	666	udp	doom Id Software
disclose	667	tcp	campaign contribution disclosures - SDR Technologies
disclose	667	udp	campaign contribution disclosures - SDR Technologies
mecomm	668	tcp	MeComm
mecomm	668	udp	MeComm
meregister	669	tcp	MeRegister
meregister	669	udp	MeRegister
vacdsm-sws	670	tcp	VACDSM-SWS
vacdsm-sws	670	udp	VACDSM-SWS
vacdsm-app	671	tcp	VACDSM-APP
vacdsm-app	671	udp	VACDSM-APP
vpps-qua	672	tcp	VPPS-QUA
vpps-qua	672	udp	VPPS-QUA
cimplex	673	tcp	CIMPLEX
cimplex	673	udp	CIMPLEX
acap	674	tcp	ACAP
acap	674	udp	ACAP
dctp	675	tcp	DCTP
dctp	675	udp	DCTP
vpps-via	676	tcp	VPPS Via
vpps-via	676	udp	VPPS Via
vpp	677	tcp	Virtual Presence Protocol
vpp	677	udp	Virtual Presence Protocol
ggf-ncp	678	tcp	GNU Gereration Foundation NCP
ggf-ncp	678	udp	GNU Generation Foundation NCP
mrm	679	tcp	MRM
mrm	679	udp	MRM
entrust-aaas	680	tcp	entrust-aaas
entrust-aaas	680	udp	entrust-aaas
entrust-aams	681	tcp	entrust-aams
entrust-aams	681	udp	entrust-aams
xfr	682	tcp	XFR
xfr	682	udp	XFR

Table B.1   Continued

Service	Port Number	Protocol	Description
corba-iiop	683	tcp	CORBA IIOP
corba-iiop	683	udp	CORBA IIOP
corba-iiop-ssl	684	tcp	CORBA IIOP SSL
corba-iiop-ssl	684	udp	CORBA IIOP SSL
mdc-portmapper	685	tcp	MDC Port Mapper
mdc-portmapper	685	udp	MDC Port Mapper
hcp-wismar	686	tcp	Hardware Control Protocol Wismar
hcp-wismar	686	udp	Hardware Control Protocol Wismar
asipregistry	687	tcp	asipregistry
asipregistry	687	udp	asipregistry
realm-rusd	688	tcp	REALM-RUSD
realm-rusd	688	udp	REALM-RUSD
elcsd	704	tcp	errlog copy/server daemon
elcsd	704	udp	errlog copy/server daemon
agentx	705	tcp	AgentX
agentx	705	udp	AgentX
borland-dsj	707	tcp	Borland DSJ
borland-dsj	707	udp	Borland DSJ
entrust-kmsh	709	tcp	Entrust Key Management Service Handler
entrust-kmsh	709	udp	Entrust Key Management Service Handler
entrust-ash	710	tcp	Entrust Administration Service Handler
entrust-ash	710	udp	Entrust Administration Service Handler
cisco-tdp	711	tcp	Cisco TDP
cisco-tdp	711	udp	Cisco TDP
netviewdm1	729	tcp	IBM NetView DM/6000 Server/Client
netviewdm1	729	udp	IBM NetView DM/6000 Server/Client
netviewdm2	730	tcp	IBM NetView DM/6000 send/tcp
netviewdm2	730	udp	IBM NetView DM/6000 send/tcp
netviewdm3	731	tcp	IBM NetView DM/6000 receive/tcp
netviewdm3	731	udp	IBM NetView DM/6000 receive/tcp
netgw	741	tcp	netGW
netgw	741	udp	netGW
netrcs	742	tcp	Network based Rev. Cont. Sys.
netrcs	742	udp	Network based Rev. Cont. Sys.
flexlm	744	tcp	Flexible License Manager
flexlm	744	udp	Flexible License Manager
fujitsu-dev	747	tcp	Fujitsu Device Control
fujitsu-dev	747	udp	Fujitsu Device Control
ris-cm	748	tcp	Russell Info Sci Calendar Manager
ris-cm	748	udp	Russell Info Sci Calendar Manager

Table B.1 Continued

Service	Port Number	Protocol	Description
kerberos-adm	749	tcp	kerberos administration
kerberos-adm	749	udp	kerberos administration
rfile	750	tcp	
loadav	750	udp	
kerberos-iv	750	udp	kerberos version iv
pump	751	tcp	
pump	751	udp	
qrh	752	tcp	
qrh	752	udp	
rrh	753	tcp	
rrh	753	udp	
tell	754	tcp	send
tell	754	udp	send
nlogin	758	tcp	
nlogin	758	udp	
con	759	tcp	
con	759	udp	
ns	760	tcp	
ns	760	udp	
rxe	761	tcp	
rxe	761	udp	
quotad	762	tcp	
quotad	762	udp	
cycleserv	763	tcp	
cycleserv	763	udp	
omserv	764	tcp	
omserv	764	udp	
webster	765	tcp	
webster	765	udp	
phonebook	767	tcp	phone
phonebook	767	udp	phone
vid	769	tcp	
vid	769	udp	
cadlock	770	tcp	
cadlock	770	udp	
rtip	771	tcp	
rtip	771	udp	
cycleserv2	772	tcp	

Table B.1   Continued

Service	Port Number	Protocol	Description
cycleserv2	772	udp	
submit	773	tcp	
notify	773	udp	
rpasswd	774	tcp	
acmaint_dbd	774	udp	
entomb	775	tcp	
acmaint_transd	775	udp	
wpages	776	tcp	
wpages	776	udp	
multiling-http	777	tcp	Multiling HTTP
multiling-http	777	udp	Multiling HTTP
wpgs	780	tcp1	
wpgs	780	udp	
concert	786	tcp	Concert
concert	786	udp	Concert
qsc	787	tcp	QSC
qsc	787	udp	QSC
mdbs_daemon	800	tcp	
mdbs_daemon	800	udp	
device	801	tcp	
device	801	udp	
fcp-udp	810	tcp	FCP
fcp-udp	810	udp	FCP Datagram
itm-mcell-s	828	tcp	itm-mcell-s
itm-mcell-s	828	udp	itm-mcell-s
pkix-3-ca-ra	829	tcp	PKIX-3 CA/RA
pkix-3-ca-ra	829	udp	PKIX-3 CA/RA
rsync	873	tcp	rsync
rsync	873	udp	rsync
iclcnet-locate	886	tcp	ICL coNETion locate server
iclcnet-locate	886	udp	ICL coNETion locate server
iclcnet_svinfo	887	tcp	ICL coNETion server info
iclcnet_svinfo	887	udp	ICL coNETion server info
accessbuilder	888	tcp	AccessBuilder
accessbuilder	888	udp	AccessBuilder
cddbp	888	tcp	CD Database Protocol
omginitialrefs	900	tcp	OMG Initial Refs
omginitialrefs	900	udp	OMG Initial Refs

Table B.1 Continued

Service	Port Number	Protocol	Description
xact-backup	911	tcp	xact-backup
xact-backup	911	udp	xact-backup
ftps-data	989	tcp	ftp protocol, data, over TLS/SSL
ftps-data	989	udp	ftp protocol, data, over TLS/SSL
ftps	990	tcp	ftp protocol, control, over TLS/SSL
ftps	990	udp	ftp protocol, control, over TLS/SSL
nas	991	tcp	Netnews Administration System
nas	991	udp	Netnews Administration System
telnets	992	tcp	telnet protocol over TLS/SSL
telnets	992	udp	telnet protocol over TLS/SSL
imaps	993	tcp	imap4 protocol over TLS/SSL
imaps	993	udp	imap4 protocol over TLS/SSL
ircs	994	tcp	irc protocol over TLS/SSL
ircs	994	udp	irc protocol over TLS/SSL
pop3s	995	tcp	pop3 protocol over TLS/SSL (was spop3)
pop3s	995	udp	pop3 protocol over TLS/SSL (was spop3)
vsinet	996	tcp	vsinet
vsinet	996	udp	vsinet
maitrd	997	tcp	
maitrd	997	udp	
busboy	998	tcp	
puparp	998	udp	
garcon	999	tcp	
applix	999	udp	Applix ac
puprouter	999	tcp	
puprouter	999	udp	
cadlock	1000	tcp	
ock	1000	udp	
surf	1010	tcp	surf
surf	1010	udp	surf
	1023	tcp	Reserved
	1023	udp	Reserved

NetWare Login
Script Reference

SOME OF THE MAIN TOPICS IN THIS CHAPTER ARE

NetWare Login Script Commands

Variables

Chapter 27, "Overview of the Novell Bindery and Novell Directory Services (NDS)," covered the basics of the login process for NetWare clients and included a description of some of the commands and variables that you can use with login scripts. This appendix provides a more complete listing of the available commands and variables that you can use to customize the login process for your NetWare clients.

NetWare Login Script Commands

Each command listed here is formatted using the following syntax:

- Actual commands appear in uppercase.
- Italicized text indicates a variable, and you should replace the text with something that is appropriate to the command.
- Items enclosed in square brackets ([]) are optional.
- When items are separated by a vertical bar (|), you can use one or the other, but not both at the same time.

Commands

(Execute External Program)

Syntax:

`# [path] filename [parameters]`

The # command enables you to execute an external program from within the login script. *path* can be a drive letter, or if NOSWAP is specified in the script, *path* can be the full directory path, starting with the name of a NetWare volume. *filename* is the name of an executable program, and it can be any file whose extension is .EXE, .COM, or .BAT. Any command-line parameters needed by the executable program can follow the executable program name in the *parameters* position.

Example:

`#X:\MISC\MYPROGRAM`

ATTACH

Syntax:

`ATTACH [servername[/username[;password]]]`

This command can be used to connect to a bindery-based NetWare server. *servername* indicates the NetWare to attach to, and if needed, you can specify a *username* and a *password* for that username. If the username is not specified, the user will be prompted for it when the script executes. If the username is the same as the primary login name, you can omit the password, and the user will not have to enter one. Use caution when placing passwords in any script file.

Example:

`ATTACH ACCTNG/OGLETREE;YOKONO`

BREAK

`BREAK ON | OFF`

This command can be used to enable the user to terminate a login script by using the Ctrl+C or Ctrl+Break key combination. To allow termination, use `BREAK ON`.

Example:

`BREAK ON`

CLS

Syntax:

CLS

This command clears the user's screen during the login process. It is generally used for cosmetic purposes, such as clearing the screen after numerous commands that are executed in the script have produced output ("screen clutter").

Example:

CLS

COMSPEC

Syntax:

COMSPEC=[*path*]COMMAND.COM

This command is used to specify the location of the DOS command processor program. If you are running DOS from a network location, first map the drive that contains the command processor, and then use this command to designate the location of COMMAND.COM. If the user's workstation runs DOS from a local drive, you do not need to use this command. *path* can be specified using an environment variable, and if so, the variable must be preceded by the percent sign character (%*variable*).

Example:

COMSPEC=X:\DOS\COMMAND.COM

CONTEXT

Syntax:

CONTEXT *context*

This command is used to set the user's context in the NDS directory tree. Follow the command with the actual context that you want the user to be able to use after the login completes. You can use the period character (.) to move up one level from the current context, two periods to move up two levels in the directory tree, and so on.

Example:

CONTEXT SALES.ACCTNG

or

CONTEXT .

DISPLAY

Syntax:

DISPLAY [*path*]*filename*

You can use *path* and *filename* with the DISPLAY command to have the contents of a file sent to the user's screen during the login process. This is a useful command for giving users static or variable information when they log in to the network.

Example:

DISPLAY SYS:PUBLIC\MESSAGES\WELCOME.TXT

or

```
IF DAY_OF_WEEK="Tuesday" THEN
  DISPLAY SYS:PUBLIC\MESSAGES\TUESDAY.TXT
END
```

DOS BREAK

Syntax:

```
DOS BREAK [ON | OFF]
```

This command enables the user to use the key combination Ctrl+Break to stop a program other than the login script. Although the BREAK command enables the user to stop the execution of the login script, it will not stop an executing program. Use this command to give the user that capability.

Example:

```
DOS BREAK ON
```

or

```
DOS BREAK OFF (default)
```

DOS SET

See SET.

DOS VERIFY

Syntax:

```
DOS VERIFY [ON | OFF]
```

This command causes DOS to verify that the data that was written to a local drive can be read without error.

Example:

```
DOS VERIFY ON
```

or

```
DOS VERIFY OFF (default)
```

DRIVE

Syntax:

```
DRIVE [drive: | *n:]
```

This command can be used to change the default disk drive during the execution of the login script. The first network drive, which is usually the one with the user's home directory, is the default drive for the user. Use this command to specify a *drive* (drive letter) or *n* (drive number) to change the default drive. The drive letter or drive number you specify should be mapped before this command is used.

Example:

```
DRIVE X:
```

or

```
DRIVE *3:
```

EXIT

Syntax:

```
EXIT ["filename [parameters]"]
```

This command terminates the login script and executes an external program. Enclose the program name (*filename*) and any command-line parameters in quotation marks. This command should be used at the end of the script because nothing following it will be executed. You can, however, use it in a conditional statement (IF...THEN) to cause the script to terminate and run the program based on variable information.

Example:

```
EXIT "C:\WORD"
```

FDISPLAY

Syntax:

```
FDISPLAY [path]filename
```

This command is similar to the DISPLAY command in that it displays a file on the user's screen. However, this version should be used when the file to be displayed is a word processing document. The DISPLAY command sends all the file's contents to the screen. This command removes any non-printable characters and displays only text characters from the file.

Example:

```
FDISPLAY SYS:PUBLIC\MESSAGES\TUESDAY.TXT
```

FIRE

Syntax:

```
FIRE n
```

This command generates a "phaser" sound *n* number of times.

Example:

```
FIRE 2
```

GOTO

Syntax:

```
GOTO label
```

This command changes the order of execution of commands in the login script. Execution branches to the section of the script specified by *label*. This command usually is used in combination with a conditional command, such as IF...THEN.

Example:

```
IF DAY_OF_WEEK="Tuesday" THEN GOTO FINISHED
[other code]
FINISHED:
EXIT
```

IF...THEN

Syntax:

```
IF condition [AND | OR] [condition]] THEN
  commands
[ELSE
  commands]
[END]
```

You can use the IF...THEN construct to test conditions and determine which set of commands you want to execute. The AND and OR commands are optional and can be used to indicate more than one condition that must be tested. The ELSE and END commands are optional and are used to specify a set of commands to be executed when the conditions being tested are not met. THEN can be on the same line with IF, but the ELSE and END commands must be on a separate line. If the WRITE command is used in an IF...THEN construct, it must be on a separate line. You can nest IF...THEN commands up to 10 levels, but you should not use a GOTO command to enter or exit a nested IF...THEN statement.

You can use the following symbols to test conditions:

- ■ =—Equals
- ■ <>—Not equal to
- ■ >—Greater than
- ■ <—Less than
- ■ >=—Greater than or equal to
- ■ <=—Less than or equal to

Example:

```
IF DAY_OF_WEEK="Friday" THEN
  Write "Get ready for the weekend!"
ELSE
  WRITE "Good morning."
END
```

INCLUDE

Syntax:

```
INCLUDE [path]filename
```

or

```
INCLUDE objectname
```

This command enables you to incorporate other text files into the script. This capability enables you to separate portions of login scripts into files that can be maintained independently of each other. When a change is needed, you can make it to just the one subscript file that will be later included into many other user login scripts. In this manner, administration is simplified because you have to make the change in only one location instead of having to edit numerous user login scripts.

Example:

```
INCLUDE VOL9:\ADMIN\USERS\TUESDAY.TXT
```

LASTLOGINTIME

Syntax:

```
LASTLOGINTIME
```

This command displays on the user's screen the date and time of his last login.

Example:

```
LASTLOGINTIME
```

MACHINE

Syntax:

```
MACHINE=machinename
```

This command sets the DOS machine name to the text *machinename*, which can be as many as 15 characters of text.

Example:

```
MACHINE=IBM_PS2
```

MAP

Syntax:

```
MAP [option] [drive:=path]
```

MAP is used to map network drives and to search network directories. Substitute a valid drive letter or search drive number for *drive* and *path* with a full path or an NDS directory Map object. You can place more than one MAP command on the same line by separating each drive mapping with a semicolon (;) character.

option can be any of the following:

- **DISPLAY ON or DISPLAY OFF**—If ON is used, mappings are displayed on the user's screen during the login process. If OFF is used, they are not. The default is ON.
- **ERRORS ON or ERRORS OFF**—If ON is used, any errors encountered during drive mapping are displayed on the user's screen. If OFF, errors are not displayed. The default is ON.
- **INS:**—This option inserts a drive mapping between existing search mappings.
- **DEL:**—This option deletes a drive mapping. The drive letter associated with the mapping is again available for use.
- **ROOT:**—This option maps a fake root.
- **C**—The change option will change a search drive mapping to a regular drive mapping or vice versa.
- **P**—The physical option can be used to map a drive to the physical volume of a server instead of the volume object's name. It is useful when a physical volume name is the same as one used for an object volume's name.
- **N**—The next option can be used to specify the next available drive letter so that you do not have to specify the actual drive letter in the mapping command.

To map a search drive, use the letter S followed by a number. Up to 16 NetWare search drives can be specified. Drive letters for search drives are assigned starting with the letter Z and then working backward through the alphabet. Search drive letters are placed into the DOS path statement.

Examples:

```
MAP S1:=SYS:PUBLIC
```

or

```
MAP *2=SYS:PUBLIC;*3=SYS:PUBLIC\MSDOS
```

NO_DEFAULT

Syntax:

```
NO_DEFAULT
```

This command can be used in a container or profile login script to suppress running of the default user login script. This applies only to the default login script. If you have created an actual login script for a user, it will still run.

Example:

```
NO_DEFAULT
```

NOSWAP

Syntax:

```
NOSWAP
```

LOGIN swaps to extended or expanded memory by default. Using this command, you can prevent this from happening. This command is useful if you do not want LOGIN to be swapped out of conventional memory before an external program is run using the # command.

Example:

```
NOSWAP
```

PAUSE

Syntax:

```
PAUSE
```

This command displays the text Strike any key when ready... and waits until the user presses a key before continuing. It is useful for displaying a message on the screen and giving the user time to read it before continuing.

Example:

```
DISPLAY SYS:PUBLIC\MESSAGES\WELCOME.TXT
PAUSE
```

PCCOMPATIBLE

Syntax:

```
PCCOMPATIBLE
```

This command is used for computers that are IBM-compatible. It enables the EXIT "command" command to work correctly if the computer's long machine name is not "IBM_PC". The long machine name should be set in the NET.CFG file.

Example:

```
PCCOMPATIBLE
EXIT "C:\CALENDAR
```

PROFILE

Syntax:

```
PROFILE profile_objectname
```

Use this command to override a user's assigned profile script or one specified on the command line. This is usually used to specify a group profile.

Example:

```
PROFILE team_profile
```

REMARK

Syntax:

```
REM[ARK] [text]
* [text]
; [text]
```

This command is used to place remarks in the login script. Text following REMARK is not displayed on the user's screen. It is useful for documenting commands in the script. The asterisk (*) and semicolon (;) characters also can be used to indicate remark text, and the command REMARK can be shortened to REM.

Remark text should not span multiple lines and should not be placed on the same line as an executable script command. To create remark text that is more than one line, use a REMARK command or one of the symbols at the start of each line.

Example:

```
* Map drives in this section.
; Test day of the week to determine text to display.
REM Run reminder program if this is Friday.
```

SCRIPT_SERVER

Syntax:

```
SCRIPT_SERVER servername
```

This command is useful only for NetWare 2.x and 3.x users and does not have any effect on NetWare 4 users or NDS. It is used to indicate the home server that is used to store the login script.

Example:

```
SCRIPT_SERVER acctng
```

SET

Syntax:

```
[TEMP] SET variablename="value"
```

This command sets a DOS environment variable. Replace *variablename* with the name of the variable and *value* with the value to be associated with the variable. Note that values must be enclosed in quotation marks. The optional [TEMP] command allows the variable to be set for only the duration of the login script.

Examples:

```
SET PROMPT="$P$G"
```

or

```
SET PATH="C:\ACCOUNTING\RECEIVABLES"
```

SET TIME

Syntax:

SET TIME ON | OFF

Use this command to control whether the workstation's clock is set to the time of the NetWare server used for login. SET TIME ON causes the clock to be set, whereas SET TIME OFF prevents this.

Example:

SET TIME ON (default)

or

SET TIME OFF

SHIFT

Syntax:

SHIFT [*n*]

The SHIFT command enables you to change the order in which variables in the login script are interpreted. Replace *n* with the number of variables to shift, with the default being 1. Variables are referenced in a login script by prefixing them with the % sign. The SHIFT command is usually used to efficiently cycle through the command-line variables. The variable %0 is always the server being logged onto. %1 is the user's logon name. Variables %2 and higher are assigned values for any other text entered on the login command line.

Example:

SHIFT 1

In this example, the value assigned to %3 would not be assigned to %2. The value assigned to %4 would now be assigned to %3, and so on, as the set of variables is shifted down by one.

SWAP

Syntax:

SWAP [*path*]

This command causes the LOGIN utility to be swapped out of conventional memory so that the # command can execute an external program at the same time. LOGIN is usually swapped to extended or expanded memory unless the NOSWAP command is used. You can use *path* to specify a directory to which LOGIN is swapped. If no path is specified, it is swapped to higher memory or, if it is not available, to a local drive.

Example:

SWAP

TREE

Syntax:

TREE *treename*[/*completename*[;*password*]]

This command can be used to attach to another NDS tree on the network. After this command is executed, all other objects in the remaining part of the login script refer to objects in the NDS tree to which you have switched. You can use the TREE command more than once to change between NDS trees in the login script.

Example:

```
TREE ACME
```

WRITE

Syntax:

```
WRITE "[text][%identifier]";[identifier]
```

This command is used to display information on the user's screen during the login script. You can specify any *text* to display, and you can display the values of *identifier* variables. Text should be enclosed in quotation marks. The semicolon character (;) can be used to concatenate the display of more than one identifier. When using multiple lines containing WRITE commands, by default each WRITE command is displayed on a separate line. Placing a semicolon character at the end of a line causes multiple WRITE commands to be displayed as continuous text. When doing this, do not put a semicolon at the end of the last WRITE command.

The text that you enclose in quotation marks also can use the following escape characters:

- /**r**—Carriage return character.
- /**n**—New line character.
- /**"**—Displays a quotation mark.
- /**7**—Causes the workstation to issue the "beep" sound.

Examples:

```
WRITE "Welcome to the Acme Network"
```

or

```
WRITE "Welcome to the Acme Network ";%LAST_NAME
```

Variables

Identifier variables provide you more flexibility in coding login scripts because you can use them to display information instead of having to hard-code it into the script. For example, a user's name can be displayed using an identifier variable, enabling one script to be used for different users.

Table C.1 shows the most common identifier variables and gives a brief description of the information they contain.

Table C.1   NetWare Login Script Identifier Variables

Variable	Description
DAY	Number of day in the month (0–31)
DAY_OF_WEEK	Day of the week (Monday, Tuesday, and so on)
MONTH	Number of month in the year (01–12)
MONTH_NAME	Name of the month (January, February, and so on)
NDAY_OF_WEEK	Number of day in the week (1–7)
SHORT_YEAR	Year in 2-digit format (98, 99, 00)

Table C.1   Continued

Variable	Description
YEAR	Year in 4-digit format (1999, 2000)
AM_PM	AM or PM, depending on the time
GREETING_TIME	Time of the day expressed as morning, afternoon or evening
HOUR	Number of the hour (1–12)
HOUR24	Number of the hour (00–23, 00=midnight)
MINUTE	Number of the minute (00–59)
SECOND	Number of the second (00–59)
%CN	The user's full login name (must exist in NDS)
LOGIN_ALIAS_CONTEXT	Y if REQUESTER_CONTEXT is an alias
FULL NAME	Text from the FULL NAME property for NDS and bindery-based NetWare, with spaces replaced by underscores
LAST_NAME	User's last name if NDS, or user's full login name if bindery-based NetWare
LOGIN_CONTEXT	User's context in NDS
LOGIN_NAME	User's login name, truncated to eight characters
PASSWORD_EXPIRES	Number of days until user's password expires
REQUESTER_CONTEXT	Context when login process began
USER_ID	Numeric identifier of user
FILE_SERVER	Name of NetWare server
NETWORK_ADDRESS	IPX external network number, an 8-digit hexadecimal number
MACHINE	Type of computer
NETWARE_REQUESTER	Version of NetWare Requester for OS/2 or VLM users
OS	Workstation's operating system type
OS_VERSION	Workstation's operating system version
P_STATION	Workstation's node number, a 12-digit hexadecimal number
PLATFORM	Workstation's operating system platform (DOS, O2S, WIN, WNT, or W95/98)
SHELL_TYPE	If DOS, version of DOS shell
SMACHINE	Short machine name
STATION	Workstation's connection number
ACCESS_SERVER	TRUE or FALSE to show if access server is functional
ERROR_LEVEL	Error number, with 0=no error

In addition, you can generally use any DOS environment variable by enclosing it in angle brackets (< >). If used with the MAP, COMSPEC, or FIRE command, add the percent sign (%) before the variable. You also can use NDS objects as variables using this method. If the object name contains a space, place quotation marks around it.

To use parameters that the user specifies on the command line with the LOGIN utility, use the percent sign (%) with the parameter number.

Directory Services: Overview of X.500 and LDAP

What Is X.500?

The Lightweight Directory Access Protocol

Both Microsoft's Active Directory and Novell Directory Services allow the use of the Lightweight Directory Access Protocol (LDAP) to access objects in their respective directory database files. Although the actual database on-disk structure of the database is not the same, the hierarchical nature of the directory and the manner in which it is accessed using LDAP are similar. In addition to these two directories, you'll find that LDAP has been used with many other directory service implementations. Because it is governed by the standard Request for Comments documents used on the Internet to provide a standard framework for a particular protocol or application, it's possible to use LDAP to manage or interrogate directory databases from competing vendors.

In this appendix, we take a quick look at LDAP and also look at the X.500 set of standards that prompted the development of LDAP.

What Is X.500?

I can't remember who said it, but it is true that one of the best things about standards is that there are so many to choose from. This is especially the case when it comes to directory services. What started out as a good idea—X.500—spawned all sorts of development of protocols and services that eventually led to the development of LDAP. In 1993, the International Telecommunications Union (ITU) approved the X.500 standard. This later was adopted also by the International Organization for Standardization (ISO) . All that said, just what is the X.500 standard and why is it so important for directory services today?

Basically, the X.500 set of standards was developed to provide a common namespace that could be used by various applications so that common data could be consolidated into a single hierarchical namespace. For example, an earlier standard known as X.400 was developed to help standardize e-mail applications on the Internet. Initially, development on X.500 protocols and services was developed to interface with X.400 e-mail–compliant systems so that different products could equally access important information, such as e-mail addresses. However, the hierarchical structure of the namespace described by the X.500 standard was so elegant that it didn't take long for developers to realize that it could be used to organize all kinds of data.

X.500 is a general term that covers several complex protocols using the hierarchical namespace to access a database. The problem is that when X.500 was developed, the protocols that were proposed were too cumbersome and required too much computing overhead to ever be practically employed on small personal computers that were available contemporaneously. Instead, these protocols were created to run on minicomputers and mainframe computers.

Other standard protocols were developed along with X.500, such as the OSI networking protocols. However, by the time anyone got around to actually trying to create a market for the OSI-related protocols and services, the Internet had already been pretty much standardized on the TCP/IP protocol suite. In addition to the OSI protocols, the OSI seven-layer Network Reference Model (described in Appendix A) was created so that network protocols could be discussed in terms that compartmentalized the functions that a computer network performs.

Once again, TCP/IP has become so predominant that even the OSI reference model is a bit dated. Indeed, TCP/IP is based on an earlier model (as described in Chapter 20, "Overview of the TCP/IP Protocol Suite").

Yet, you don't throw the baby out with the bath water, as the old saying goes. There were some good ideas in the OSI protocols, and the namespace provided by X.500 was an excellent solution looking for a problem. After the Internet went commercial and larger corporate networks were created, it became apparent that some kind of logical organization was needed to manage diverse kinds of information.

The Domain Name System (yet another child of the TCP/IP protocol suite) was created to handle resolving host computer and network names to IP addresses, and is still used today on the Internet. However, when it comes to managing users and data and resources on networks, the term "directory services" is where it's at today.

Novell Directory Services (NDS) was a leader in this kind of technology for several years. NDS is widely deployed still today, though the newer versions of NetWare have finally accepted TCP/IP as a transport protocol. Microsoft spent several years promising that the Active Directory would solve just about every problem a network administrator could dream of. Of course, we now know that any kind of directory service is going to be complex to manage due to the many types of applications it is used for and the kinds of information that needs to be stored in the database.

Another name you might remember is Banyan Vines. This network vendor based its StreetTalk directory services product on the X.500 model as well.

Acronyms, Acronyms, Acronyms!

But in the beginning there was X.500 and the protocols that were developed to work with it. The main protocols developed for X.500 were

- Directory Access Protocol (DAP)
- Directory System Protocol (DSP)
- Directory Information Shadowing Protocol (DISP)
- Directory Operational Binding Management Protocol (DOP)

DAP, DSP, DISP, DOP, Duh? Well, let's get a little more specific, and throw in a few more acronyms.

The DIB and the DIT

The Directory Information Base (DIB) is the actual database and the data stored by the directory. Every record in the database is an object that holds some kind of data. Objects are collections of attributes that store the actual values of the properties of objects that are records in the database.

The DIB can be a small database that is hosted on a single computer, or it can be a large, distributed database that resides on many computers. Because the database is organized in a hierarchical fashion, it is easy to locate an object, no matter on which server it actually is stored.

The treelike structure that organizes the objects in the database is called the Directory Information Tree (DIT). At the top of the tree is the entry called the root object. In Microsoft's case it's called the Top abstract class. But the name really doesn't matter. The point is that, you can start at a single entry point in the tree structure (the top) and locate an object—using a carefully constructed name—by traversing the branches that make up the tree until you finally get to the leaf object that contains the actual data for which you are looking. In addition to leaf objects that store the real data (as object attributes), there also are container objects in the tree structure that hold other container objects and also leaf objects. Using container objects makes it easy to group objects that have something in common. Another type of object in the DIT is the alias object, which is used to give a nicer name to some other object in the tree to which the alias points.

The DUA, DSA, and DAP

The Directory User Agent (DUA) is the client application that is used to access the database (DIB) that is organized by the tree structure (DIT). The DUA queries the database to find the information that the client application needs to obtain. Specifically, the DUA can

- Read some or all the values for attributes of a particular object in the database.

- Compare a value with an attribute of an object in the database to see if they are the same.

- List objects that are subordinate in the tree structure to an object specified by the DUA.

- Search the database, either all or a portion of it, to find objects that have attributes matching values supplied by the DUA. A search can return more than one object to the DUA, depending on the criteria that the DUA supplies for the search filter.

- Abandon the search or any other request that the DUA has previously made to the directory database.

- Add an entry, or a new object, to the database, provided that the necessary access permissions allow this.

- Modify an object (well, one or more of its attributes) in the database, again provided that permissions allow for it and also provided that the new value the DUA wants to give to an attribute is allowable by the syntax associated with the attribute.

- Remove an entry from the database, provided that the client application has permission to do so.

- Modify a distinguished name (DN).

Of course, to make matters more complex, DAP is the protocol that governs how the DUA interacts with the DSA. The DSA is the server side of this equation. So basically, you have the Directory User Agent interacting with the Directory Access Protocol that talks to the Directory System Protocol to get all this done. It's that easy to remember: DUA uses DAP to talk to the DSA, which does all the work the DUA wants done in the directory! The DOP protocol was developed for administrative purposes to manage operational bindings between different DSAs.

The DN and the RDN

The final item in this list might seem insignificant, but it is not because of the method used to name objects in the DIT. Each object has a "common" name, also called the *relative distinguished name* (RDN), which does not have to be unique in the DIT. For example, you might have several objects in the directory named HPLASERJET. However, the *distinguished name* (DN) for an object is its common name (or its RDN), concatenated with all the common names of the objects in the directory that are above it. The relative distinguished name (RDN) doesn't have to be unique in the directory structure, but the full distinguished name, by the very nature in which it is formed, must be unique.

This is why it is so easy to locate objects in the directory. If you know the object's distinguished name, you essentially have a path through the tree that leads to the object you want to find.

The Schema

If you have read Chapter 25, "Overview of Microsoft's Active Directory Service," or Chapter 27, "Overview of the Novell Bindery and Directory Services (NDS)," you probably are aware that to create objects consisting of attributes and organize them into a tree structure, you must have rules about how this all fits together. The *schema* is this set of rules. The schema is similar to a dictionary in that it defines object classes, which then are used to create the actual objects in the tree. The schema also defines the attributes, and the kinds of data each attribute can hold (the syntax). The schema defines whether certain attributes of an object are mandatory or optional.

The Lightweight Directory Access Protocol

Now that all this is perfectly clear in your mind, let's talk about LDAP. Throw out most of the acronyms in the first part of this chapter and you're left with a clever method of naming and organizing data in a directory database. The only problem is that implementing DAP, DSP, DISP, DOP, and all those other protocols is just too complex, and a lot of the functionality can be performed by simpler protocols. That's why LDAP was developed. It's "lightweight" compared to the overhead involved in the original directory service protocols. If Microsoft had decided to implement the original X.500 directory service as envisioned by the original developers, Bill Gates would still be trying to get Windows 2000 out the door, much less Windows XP.

Because the Internet is standardized on TCP/IP, it was decided that a new set of protocols, also based on TCP/IP, could be developed that could query, add to, and modify a database that was based on the X.500 tree structure. Version 2 of LDAP (described in RFC 1777) was the first practical implementation of LDAP, while version 3 (described in RFC 2251) more fully delineates the client/server nature of the functions that are performed for accessing the directory database. Microsoft's Active Directory supports both LDAPv2 and LDAPv3. LDAPv3 provided for additional operations that were not supported in the earlier versions of LDAP and allows for paging and sorting of information. Additionally, LDAPv3 is *extensible*, that is, it defines a concept called *extended operations*, so that future developers can implement operations that are not provided for in the current protocol. This extended operations capability allows a vendor to customize his version of LDAP applications, yet still allows his product to interact with other LDAPv3 compliant products (more or less).

Another interesting thing that LDAPv3 does is to allow the schema to be defined in the directory. Unlike the Domain Name System (DNS), which usually is implemented as a flat file that must be read into memory when the service is started, LDAPv3 allows for the very definitions of the object classes and related attributes to be defined in the directory. This might not seem important at first, but just think about it. Because the definition of all the classes and attributes is stored in the directory itself, applications can query the database to find out just what kinds of objects it contains.

Note

Ever have one of those nights when you had guests that just didn't know when it was time to go home? The next time that happens, just pull out some of the following RFCs and start reading them out loud:

RFC 2252, "Attribute Syntax Definitions"

RFC 2253, "UTF-8 String Representation of Distinguished Names"

RFC 2254, "The String Representation of LDAP Search Filters"

RFC 2255, "The LDAP URL Format"

RFC 2256, "A Summary of the X.500 User Schema for Use with LDAPv3"

RFC 2247, "Using Domains in LDAP X.500 Distinguished Names"

Actually, these documents, available through a quick search on the Internet, can give you more insight into the details of how LDAP works. They also can put you to sleep.

The LDAP Protocol

LDAP is considered a *wire protocol*. That simply means that it defines the way information is packaged and exchanged between the client and server in the directory services model. It is not a transport protocol, but instead LDAP requests and replies are sent as an LDAP protocol Data Unit (PDU) using either TCP or UDP to get from here to there. The kinds of functions that LDAP can provide include

- Connecting to an LDAP server and authenticating the client to the server.
- Searching the directory and doing something with the results that are returned to the client.
- Managing memory on the client and handling any errors that pop up.

Binding to the Server

The client uses a *bind request* to make a connection to the LDAP-based directory database server. This must be done before the client can begin to query the directory for information. The request should contain the version number of the LDAP protocol the client uses, the name of the directory object to which the client wants to bind, and the information that is used for authentication. The server can respond in several ways (all described in the RFCs), but it basically comes down to one of the following:

- **Operations error**—In other words, this is how the server tells the client "you screwed up."

- **Protocol error**—The server doesn't use the same version of LDAP that the client wants to use.

- **Authentication method not supported**—LDAP allows for many different authentication schemes, and this is the message sent back when the server doesn't use the one that the client wants to use.

- **Strong authentication required**—Similar to the preceding item, the server is telling the client that a strong authentication method must be used if you want to get any data from this server.

- **Referral**—This is sort of like when your doctor hasn't a clue about what's wrong with you, so he refers you to another doctor. The server is telling the client that it doesn't have the object, or information, that the client is requesting, but gives the client a referral to another LDAP server that might have the info.

- **SASL bind in progress**—The LDAP server is requesting that the client send in another bind request using SASL.

- **Inappropriate authentication**—The client wants to use an "anonymous bind" but the server won't allow it.

- **Invalid credentials**—The server can't process the authentication information sent by the client, or perhaps the client has forgotten the password.

- **Unavailable**—Just an information message to tell the client that the server is shutting down.

Searching the Database

After the client has successfully binded with the server, it can send in a request to search for the data required by the client application. The client can specify where in the directory tree the search should begin, because searching the entire directory database is not very practical in most large databases. This means that the client must have at least some information regarding the kind of object about which it wants more information. The client's request also can specify the maximum number of objects that it will accept back from the server in response to the search. If the client specifies a zero number of objects, the server can send back all the data it finds that matches the search criteria. Of course, the server can have limits for this set by the administrator of the database.

In its request, the client can specify how much time it wants the server to spend on the search, and again, zero means "Take all the time you want, I'm in no hurry." The client can query the server to return the types of attributes of the objects found, or both the attribute types as well as their values. Finally, the client can specify a filter to be used for the search and a list of the attributes it would like to receive, provided they are found in the database.

Adding, Modifying, or Deleting Information in the Database

The client also can add information to the database, as long as it has the necessary permissions to do so, by specifying the distinguished name (so that the database will know exactly where in the database to put the new object) and values for all the mandatory attributes for the particular object class of which the client wants to create an instance. Take into consideration that for the addition to succeed, the relative distinguished names that make up the portion of the distinguished name that should be superior to the object in the tree must already exist.

To modify or delete an object from the database, the client once again must specify the distinguished name of the object so that the server can locate it in the database. If the client just wants to modify an object, it must use one of several methods. It can add one more value to an attribute, delete one or more values for an attribute, or replace values for attributes of an object. But there is an exception to this: The relative distinguished name (RDN) of the object (its common name) can't be modified with a simple modify request, and neither can the relative distinguished names of objects above it in the hierarchy be modified. Instead, a special modify DN operation is used. This is because changing one of the RDNs can cause the object to be moved to a new location in the tree. This affects both the object as well as any child objects that exist under it in the tree.

Comparing Information in the Database

The compare operation allows the client to simply supply the values for selected attributes of an object and ask the server to compare them with the actual values stored in the object and the method to be used for the comparison. Although the same thing could be accomplished by having the client read the database and make the comparison itself, this method can be used for things such as comparing passwords and other authentication information.

Network Information Resources

APPENDIX E

Other Resources for Network Management

There are many excellent books on topics that are covered in this book. However, there are many resources on the Internet that you can avail yourself of that don't cost anything. In this appendix, you'll find a list of interesting and useful links to sites that provide information that can help you stay up-to-date on a particular technology or standard.

Useful Vendor Sites

Although just about every hardware and software vendor has a Web page, most of them really aren't much more than a place to order a product. However, some provide great resources that can help you with detailed information about the product or service that they offer. Some of my favorite sites of this type are

- **http://www.compaq.com**—Compaq makes both Intel- and AlphaServer-based systems, supports OpenVMS, Windows NT, and their version of Unix called Tru64 Unix. If you go to this Web site, click the Search button at the top right. You'll find that you can search through a huge database of technical articles, product specification sheets, and even online versions of user guides and installation guides for many of Compaq's products. For uses of Tru64 Unix, you'll find that most of the documentation for this product is available online at http://tru64unix.compaq.com/. Even if you're not using this brand of Unix, the online documentation can be helpful because many commands are similar from one version of Unix to another.

- **http://msdn.microsoft.com**—This link takes you to the Microsoft Developers Network (MSDN) Online Web site. Although a subscription to this service can be quite expensive, there is a lot of free content here online. For example, you can search the MSDN library, which consists of lots of documentation, as well as the Knowledge Base articles that can be helpful for troubleshooting any Windows operating system or Microsoft product. Microsoft also makes available a large number of files for download—from service packs to trial software. Use the link http://www.microsoft.com and click the Download button at the top of the page to get to the download site.

- **http://www.novell.com**—If you are a NetWare user, you'll find that this site has a lot of software you can download relating to NetWare and other products that Novell markets. Click the Download button and you find everything from client software for different operating systems to demo software you can try before you buy. Another great link on this site gets you to online documentation for most Novell products: http://www.novell.com/documentation/. Sure beats having to lug all those books around.

- **http://www.freebsd.org**—Want Unix? Too cheap to pay for it? Go to this site and you can download a user-supported version of Unix that has been around for many years. You'll find compiled versions, as well as source code and documentation. FreeBSD Unix runs on Intel-based systems, Compaq's AlphaServer platform, and work is underway to port it to several other platforms. If you don't have access to Unix but want to learn, this is the place to go.

- **http://www.linux.org**—Although this isn't a nonprofit organization, it claims to be a not-for-profit organization and has a large amount of resources for users of the Linux operating system. You'll find links to other sites, documentation, courses on Linux, and you can even order a cute coffee cup with that Linux penguin on it.

- **http://www.ntbugtraq.com/**—This site is the home of the NTBugtraq mailing list, which can keep you up-to-date on new security flaws found in the Windows NT/2000/XP operating systems and associated products.

Protocols and Standards

Forgot what the protocol number in the IP header should be for TCP? Can't remember what port a particular application uses? Need to find that RFC so you can look at the specifics of a particular standard? Here's a few places you can go to get all the info you'll need about protocols and standards:

- **http://www.iana.org/numbers.htm**—The Internet Assigned Numbers Authority (working in conjunction with ICANN) manages this Web site. You'll find just about every kind of "assigned" number used on the Internet here. You'll find out that the IP header uses the number 6 in the protocol field for TCP, for example. You'll also find ICMP (Internet Control Message Protocol) message numbers, and many others here. When you're performing network analysis on packets and wonder what that number in a certain field in the captured packet means, look it up here!

- **http://www.icann.net**—This is the home page for the Internet Corporation for Assigned Names and Numbers. This corporation was created to manage IP address allocation, protocol parameter assignments, domain name system management, and also to manage the root server system of the Internet's DNS system. You'll find links to other sites, such as IANA, at this Web page.

- **http://ieee.org**—You can go to this site to find out more about the IEEE standards, such as the IEEE 802 LAN/MAN Committee, that are discussed in this book. Although the IEEE only makes the documentation for finished standards available online to its members, you can order hard-copy documentation if you want to further explore a topic.

- **http://www.isoc.org/**—The Internet Society (ISOC) has its home page here. This organization is made up of more than 175 individual organizations and more than 8,600 members worldwide. It is the organization that promotes and helps guide the development of the Internet.

- **http://www.rfc-editor.org/**—This is the place to go if you want to find a particular Request For Comments (RFC) document or find out more about the process used to produce standards for the Internet and the protocols and applications it supports.

- **http://www.ietf.org/**—Here you'll find the home site for the Internet Engineering Task Force, responsible for most of the working groups that develop new protocols and standards for the Internet. You'll find links here also to RFC documents and related organizations.

- **http://www.iab.org/iab/**—This is the Web site for the Internet Architecture Board, which does all sorts of things, from managing the RFC process to assigning numbers for protocols and services on the Internet. You'll find links to important documents that describe many technologies used on the Internet.

Security-Related Web Sites

Security is one of the most important issues in networking today, especially because if you want to do business in today's world you'll need to connect to the Internet. Even if you have a closed corporate network that isn't connected to the Net, security is still an issue. You never know when a user will bring in a virus or other malicious program on a floppy disk or e-mail. Here are a few places you can go to find out more about networking security issues:

- **http://www.sans.org/giac.htm/**—This is the Web page of the Global Incident Analysis Center (GIAC) of the Systems Administration, Network and Security (SANS) Institute. This organization has more than 62,000 members that work as network administrators or who deal in network security issues. Additionally, you can check here for training courses that SANS offers on a periodic basis if you feel that some of your employees need to brush up on their skills.

- **http://www.first.org/**—At this site you can sign up for a mailing list that deals with security issues. Besides a forum to discuss important network security issues, you also can be made aware of new security advisories, such as when a new virus or other similar program is discovered.

- **http://www.cert.org**—This is the Web site for the Computer Emergency Response Team (CERT), located at Carnegie-Mellon University's Software Engineering Institute. CERT tracks security incidents and alerts you to them if you sign up for its mailing list.

- **http://ntsecurity.net**—This site is sponsored by *Windows 2000 Magazine* and is a good place to find out about Windows NT/2000 security issues. You can subscribe to their mailing list and also find an archive of information about security issues relating to Windows operating systems.

- **http://www.atstake.com/research/**—Here you can find the @Stake Research Labs Web site. This site is devoted to finding and documenting security flaws in the Internet infrastructure. You can download several good security tools from this site that can be used to check out just how good a job you are doing on your network to prevent it from harm.

- **The Firewalls Mailing List**—You can send an e-mail to majordomo@greatcircle.com to subscribe to this great mailing list. Put the words subscribe firewalls in the body of the message, not in the subject line. This is a great forum to discuss, as well as learn about firewall technology. Having problems configuring a firewall your boss told you to buy? Ask questions here!

- **http://www.fedcirc.gov/**—This Web site is run by the United States Federal government and is a great resource for security tools, such as ISS, SATAN, and COPS. A document titled "Practices for Securing Critical Information Assets" also can be found here and is recommended reading!

Overview of the Simple Mail Transfer Protocol (SMTP) and POP3

SOME OF THE MAIN TOPICS IN THIS CHAPTER ARE

How SMTP Works

Putting It All Together

The Post Office Protocol (POP3)

APPENDIX F

Although protocols such as IP are responsible for transporting and routing traffic on the Internet, application protocols such as SMTP provide the message exchanges needed to make client/server applications available over the network. The Simple Mail Transfer Protocol, first defined by RFC 821, "Simple Mail Transfer Protocol," is used to transfer mail messages from a client to an SMTP server, and to transfer those messages from one SMTP server to another. Because SMTP is an application protocol, it's associated with a port number just like FTP, Telnet, and other application protocols. The port generally used for SMTP is TCP port 25. Although TCP is the most widely used version, SMTP has been implemented on top of other protocols as well.

As an application protocol, SMTP relies on the error-detection and correction mechanisms of the underlying protocols and does not implement these sorts of functions in the SMTP protocol itself. For example, TCP uses sequence numbers to keep track of TCP segments sent and acknowledged. Those that are not acknowledged within a timely fashion are retransmitted. Thus, SMTP, using TCP as a transport protocol, doesn't have to worry about this sort of thing.

In this appendix, you'll learn about the basic functions provided by a simple protocol such as SMTP, and briefly examine the Post Office Protocol (POP3) because it is so closely related to SMTP.

How SMTP Works

SMTP is used to send e-mail from a client to an SMTP server and for SMTP servers to exchange mail. Other protocols, such as POP3 and IMAP, are used by clients to retrieve mail from mailboxes that reside on SMTP servers. SMTP is not used for that purpose, as you can see in Figure F.1.

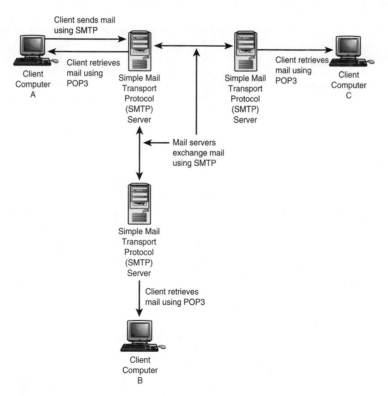

Figure F.1 SMTP is used to upload e-mail to the server, whereas POP3 is generally used to download mail.

In this figure, you can see that computer A sends outgoing e-mail to its local SMTP server operated by the local ISP. Computer A uses the POP3 protocol (Post Office Protocol) to check for and retrieve messages on the server. If Computer A needs to send an e-mail to Computer B, the message travels first through SMTP to the local SMTP server. This server looks up the mail server for the domain in which the recipient on Computer B resides and sends the message, again using SMTP, to Computer B's SMTP server. When Computer B decides to check messages, it uses POP3 and gets the e-mail sent by Computer A. Note that, if either computer wants to send e-mail to Computer C, then still another SMTP server becomes involved.

Note, however, that there isn't real centralization. SMTP servers communicate among themselves directly and do not go through any central clearinghouse. It's possible that a mail message will take a route through several different SMTP servers to reach the eventual mailbox that is the destination of the e-mail. When a client initially starts a session with an SMTP server, it can give the server a source-route (list of hosts) through which the message should travel to get to its destination. This is called a *forward-path*. In addition, the client can give the server a *reverse-path*, which is a source-route to return error messages to the client if something happens during the transmission of the e-mail message.

Because it is a decentralized system, the operation is simplified. The failure of an SMTP server, here and there, doesn't affect the entire Internet. The only people who get to complain are those who use the downed SMTP servers for their e-mail.

The SMTP Model

RFC 821 recognized that an SMTP server would have to both service local clients and relay mail messages to other SMTP servers when the destination is not a client of the original server. Names are given for the different processes involved, depending on who is doing what to whom:

- **Sender-SMTP**—The client establishes a two-way (full-duplex) session with the local SMTP sever.

- **Receiver-SMTP**—The SMTP server receives commands from the Sender-SMTP. The Receiver-SMTP process can be an SMTP server that can deliver the message to its recipient's mailbox or to another SMTP server.

Note that, when a message passes through several SMTP servers, one server becomes the Sender-SMTP and the server to which the message is being sent becomes the Receiver-SMTP. The Sender-SMTP process does not always indicate the original client that created the e-mail message in the first place.

Most of the original definition of SMTP from RFC 821 remains intact. A few other RFCs over the years have added minor changes to the protocol, but it has remained basically a system for request/reply messages. In the original version, a client sends a command to the server and the server responds with a single reply. The connection between the client and the SMTP server is a simple two-way channel (using the single TCP port 25).

SMTP Commands and Response Codes

The first command that the Sender-SMTP client sends is either the HELO command or the EHLO command. EHLO is a command that was added by RFC 1651, "SMTP Service Extensions." If an SMTP server does not support extensions as provided by this RFC, it will respond with an error message indicating a syntax error.

The basic syntax for SMTP Commands is

```
<command> <arguments> <CRLF>
```

In this syntax, <CRLF> indicates that a carriage-return followed by a line-feed character is used to signal the end of the command line.

In the following commands, the term *forward-path* is a list of hosts the message travels through to reach its destination. The term *reverse-path* is used to indicate how to get back to the sender of the e-mail, which can be helpful when returning error or other informational messages.

Note

One important thing to note about SMTP commands is that they are not case sensitive. The client or server code must accept both upper- and lowercase text for commands and not differentiate between the two. Commands can even be a mixture of upper- and lowercase letters. This is *not* true, however, of user mailbox names, although hostnames (that is, the portion of the e-mail address following the "@" sign) also are not case sensitive. However, the actual user's mailbox name may be limited to a particular case on some servers, and should be preserved by the server and transmitted exactly as received.

The basic SMTP commands include

- **HELO**—This command (or the next one in this list) is sent by the Sender-SMTP client to the SMTP server to begin the mail transfer session. The argument to this command is the hostname of the Sender-SMTP computer.

- **EHLO**—This command indicates that the Sender-SMTP client wants to use SMTP extensions, as defined in RFC 1869. If the SMTP server supports SMTP extensions, it returns a code of 250 to the client. If the server does not support the extensions, it returns a code of 500.

- **AUTH**—This stands for *authenticate*. The user provides a username/password to the SMTP server to authenticate the client before mail can be sent.

- **ATRN**—This stands for authenticated TURN. After a client has been authenticated to the SMTP server, this command instructs the Receiver-SMTP to return an OK response. In that case, the SMTP server must assume the function as the sender of the mail. Otherwise, the SMTP server can return a Bad Gateway message (the reply number 502) and remain in the role as Receiver-SMTP.

- **DATA**—This command is followed by actual data that makes up the e-mail message. This includes both the body text as well as things such as the subject line, and so on.

- **EXPN**—This stands for *expand*. This command requests the SMTP server to tell the client whether the argument included with the command is a mailing list. If so, the server returns a list of the members of the mailing list to the client.

- **HELP**—This command instructs the SMTP server to return help information to the sender. The HELP command might or might not contain arguments.

- **MAIL**—This command includes the *reverse path* as its argument. This is the name of the sender, but it also can be a list of hosts that were used to relay the mail message from its original Sender-SMTP. In a list of hosts, the first host is the current Receiving-SMTP server. The last is the destination of the e-mail.

- **NOOP**—This is the "no operation" command. The server responds with OK.

- **QUIT**—The Sender-SMTP sends this command when it is finished. The server should return an OK message and then close down the transmission channel (that is, TCP connection).

- **RCPT**—This stands for recipient. The argument for this command is a single recipient, specified by using a forward-path list preceded by the letters TO:. If a mail message is being sent to more than one recipient, a separate RCPT command must be issued for every recipient.

- **RSET**—Aborts the current e-mail transaction. The SMTP server should respond with an OK message.

- **SAML**—This stands for Send and Mail. Mail is the typical use today with SMTP. The send method is meant to be used when the SMTP server has been implemented to deliver mail directly to a recipient that is actively connected. The argument for this command, again, is a reverse-path showing the path to the destination of the e-mail. The reverse-path text is preceded with the text FROM:.

- **SEND**—This command, not often implemented, specifies that the mail message be delivered directly to the destination, if it's actively connected. If this cannot be done, the server returns a message code of 450 (the mailbox is not available). Similar to the SAML command, the argument for this command is the text FROM: followed by the reverse-path to the destination mailbox.

- **SIZE**—This command lets the Sender-SMTP inform the server of the size of the mail message it wants to send. This is supported only by SMTP implementations that use the SMTP Service Extensions. The server can return a message indicating that it cannot handle mail of the size requested, or it can accept the message.

- **SOML**—This stands for Send or Mail. Similar to SAML, this command requests that the mail be "sent" (for example, directly to the actively connected recipient), or mailed. The server tries the Send method first and if that fails, the server attempts to deliver the message to the destination mailbox.

- **TURN**—This command instructs the Receiver-SMTP to assume the role of the sender of the mail (in which an OK response is returned). The server can refuse (with a code 502) and remain in the role of Receiver-SMTP.

- **VRFY**—This command asks the Receiver-SMTP to verify that the username that is passed as an argument with the command be checked to determine whether it's valid. If the username is a valid one, the full name and mailbox of the user is returned.

Because SMTP allows for sending a single message to multiple recipients, a large mailing list could generate a lot of network traffic. Thus, RFC 821 recommends that only one copy of the actual e-mail be sent to the server in this sort of situation. The SEND command (and its associated commands) was intended originally to send a message directly to a user's terminal. In today's world of PCs and work-stations, it isn't typical to find a user sitting at a terminal. It also usually is not desirable to have mail pop up suddenly on a user's terminal if this function is still supported in your network. Instead, the MAIL command and its other associated commands are usually used.

SMTP Response Codes

Remember that for each command issued by the Sender-SMTP, a single response is expected from the Receiver-SMTP. This simple lock-step method keeps things synchronized so that both sides of the connection are aware of the current state of the transaction. The three-digit response codes that the Receiver-SMTP can use are similar in format to those returned by FTP servers. The first digit indicates the general meaning (or category) of the response.

The first digits for SMTP response codes are

- **1**—This is a positive response. The command has been accepted by the SMTP server and the server is waiting for further information to determine whether it should continue or abort processing. At this time, no SMTP commands allow this kind of reply message.

- **2**—This is a positive response. The function requested by the client-SMTP has been completed and the server is ready for another command.

- **3**—This is a positive response. This is similar to category 2 but indicates that the action requested is being held up, waiting for further information or commands from the Sender-SMTP.

- **4**—This is a negative response. It indicates that something went wrong and the command could not be completely processed. The Sender-SMTP should retry the command, or sequence of commands, that led up to this response.

- **5**—This is a negative response. Unlike the "4" response code category, this one indicates that an error has occurred that prevents the command from being executed, such as a misspelling. The command can be tried again, but not unless the Sender-SMTP can determine the problem and correct it before trying again.

The second digit of the response code provides a further subdivision within that category to further indicate the response. The second digit can have the following values:

- **0**—This indicates a syntax error or that the particular command is not supported by the server. For example, if the Sender-SMTP client supports the SMTP service extensions but the Receiver-SMTP server does not, it returns this value.

- **1**—This is used in replies that return help messages to the client.

- **2**—This is used for replies that refer to the transmission channel.

- **5**—This is used in replies that are reporting the status of the mail system, as it pertains to the requested mail transfer or the current command.

It is beyond the scope of this appendix to list all the three-digit codes that make up specific messages. You can find a numerical listing of these individual response codes in RFC 821. The third digit in each code is used to further define the granularity of the response. For example, 500 indicates either a syntax error or that the SMTP server does not implement service extensions (and hence does not understand the command being sent). Code 500 takes the syntax error and gives the client more information. Code 501 indicates a syntax error but narrows the error to the arguments or parameters used with the command that generated the error. Thus, it might be possible for the client to recognize the source of the error, correct it, and then retry the command.

Putting It All Together

Now that you've seen the simple command set that is used by SMTP, and the simple response code mechanism, you can put it all together and see an example of how a particular mail transaction might occur:

1. First, the Sender-SMTP sends a HELO or an EHLO command to the SMTP server.

2. The MAIL command is used, with the reverse-path information. At this state, the SMTP server knows who wants to send the mail message and a return path to send back error messages should anything go awry. The server clears the necessary buffers and sends the "250 OK" message back to the sender.

3. The RCPT command is issued by the client giving a forward-path of exactly one recipient of the mail message. If more than one recipient is the target of the message, multiple RCPT commands must be used. The "250 OK" response is sent if the server thinks it can get the message delivered. If not, the SMTP server returns a code of 550, which is a failure code.

4. The DATA command is sent to the server. The server will return an intermediate reply code, 354, indicating that the remaining lines it receives from the sender will be interpreted as part of the e-mail message.

5. The client sends each line of text, and the server responds with "250 OK" for each line received. When the client is finished sending the message, a line with a single period character (".") is sent.

6. After receiving a final OK from the server, the client issues the QUIT command to terminate the session.

In these steps, information typically found in an e-mail message, such as the subject, date, and so on, are included as part of the e-mail message data that is transmitted following the DATA command. Also, this is a simple message exchange. It can get more complicated. For example, the server can return a reply code of "251 - User not local; will forward to..." followed by the forward-path information. This happens when the Receiver-SMTP knows the correct host on which a destination user's mailbox is located, but it differs from the one sent by the client. Another message of a similar type leaves the process of sending mail to another destination up to the client. This message, "551 - User not local..." supplies the client with the forward-path that the client can use to deliver the message. In this case, however, the server does not forward the message, but lets the client take further action.

The Post Office Protocol (POP3)

Mail clients use SMTP to send outgoing mail to an SMTP server. To retrieve mail messages, however, the Post Office Protocol (currently version 3) generally is used. POP3 is a stateful protocol, progressing from one state to another, depending on the results of the transaction in progress and the commands that are issued. The states are

- **AUTHORIZATION**—In this state, the user supplies a username and password to authenticate the client to the mail server. In its original implementation, the protocol supports clear-text for username and password transmissions. This, of course, can be a security problem, and other techniques should be used in a secure environment.

- **TRANSACTION**—In this state, the client issues commands and receives responses from the server.

- **UPDATE**—In this state, the client has finished its commands (by issuing the QUIT command) and the server can then delete messages that were marked for deletion and close the TCP connection.

In the following sections, you'll see what happens during each state and the POP3 commands that can be used in each state. Similar to SMTP, commands are not case sensitive and are either 3 or 4 characters long. The total length of arguments allowed for a command is 40 characters. Responses, however, can be up to 512 characters in length.

Finally, the status indicators that the POP3 server can return to the client are limited to only two:

- **+OK**—A positive response.
- **-ERR**—A negative response.

Each of these status indicators can be followed by text that describes the response. In many cases, the response consists of multiple lines. Both the +OK and -ERR status indicators must be sent by the server in uppercase only. When multiple lines are sent as part of a response, the same method used by SMTP to mark the end of the response is used: the period character on a line by itself.

The AUTHORIZATION State

A POP3 server typically listens on TCP port number 110 for incoming requests from POP3 clients. After a TCP connection is established between the client and the POP3 server, the POP3 server sends a greeting to the client. At this point, the process is said to be in the AUTHORIZATION state. During this state, the client uses some authentication method to identify itself to the POP3 server. This can be clear-text username and password combinations, or it can be a more secure authorization method.

For more information about secure forms of authentication when using POP3, see RFC 1734, "POP3 AUTHentication command." This RFC defines the AUTH command that can be used to negotiate an authentication mechanism between the client and server.

After the client has been authenticated to the POP3 server, the server attempts to gain an exclusive lock on the client's mailbox files. This lock prevents changes to the mailbox during the session so that the current collection of messages remains the same through the UPDATE state. Failure to lock the mailbox could allow new messages to arrive. As you'll find out in the next section, the server uses message numbers to identify each message in the mailbox. If new messages were allowed to enter the mailbox while the users were accessing it, it would be possible for confusion to exist during the UPDATE state, especially if messages are to be deleted. Thus, the mailbox is locked so that it will remain consistent for the current session.

The TRANSACTION State

After authentication has been performed successfully, the process enters into the TRANSACTION state, in which the client can send commands to the POP3 server. When finished issuing commands to the server, the client uses the QUIT command to terminate the session. At this point, the server enters the UPDATE state.

The POP3 server assigns a unique message number, beginning with 1, to each message in the mailbox. During this TRANSACTION state, the client can use the following commands to communicate with the POP3 server:

- **STAT**—This "status" command results in the server returning information about the mailbox to the client. This is called a *drop listing*. The format is the +OK status indicator followed by a single space and then the number of messages that are currently in the mailbox. The drop listing also contains the size of the messages contained in the mailbox in octets (bytes).

- **LIST**—This command can be optionally followed by a message number. If a message number is included, the POP3 server returns a "scan listing" for the specified message. If no message number is specified, the server responds with the +OK status indicator and then lists, line by line, a scan listing for each message in the mailbox. The scan listing consists of the message number followed by one single space and then the size of the message in octets.

- **RETR**—This is the retrieve command used to pull copies of messages from the server. A message number must follow the RETR command. The server responds with the +OK status indicator, followed by a multiline response that consists of the actual text of the mail message itself. The message is terminated with the period character.

- **DELE**—This command allows the client to request that a message be deleted from the POP3 server. Again, a specific message number is required. The message will be marked as deleted, but it still exists in the mailbox until the session enters the UPDATE state.

- **NOOP**—Again, the no operation command does nothing, but the POP3 server responds with the +OK status indicator.

- **RSET**—This "reset" command causes any messages that have been marked as deleted to be reset to a nondelete state.

After the client has finished issuing commands to the server and processing the responses the POP3 server returns, the client issues the QUIT command to indicate that it is finished. This ends the TRANSACTION state.

The UPDATE State

After the QUIT command has been received by the POP3 server, the session enters the UPDATE state. In this state, the POP3 server can delete the mail messages that were previously marked for deletion by the client. Again, if the session is terminated (by a network failure, for example) before the client can issue the QUIT command, messages that were marked for deletion are not deleted because the session never makes it to the UPDATE state.

When the POP3 server deletes messages during this state, it sends the +OK status indicator back to the client. If an error occurs trying to delete any of the messages, the -ERR status indicator is returned to the client.

After deleting the messages, the server performs other housekeeping chores, such as removing its lock on the mailbox, and then terminates the TCP connection.

INDEX

Other Related Titles

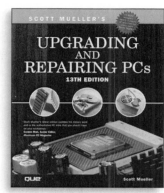

Upgrading and Repairing PCs, 13th Edition
Scott Mueller
ISBN 0-7897-2542-8
$59.99 USA/
$89.95 CAN

Special Edition Using Windows XP, Professional Edition
Bob Cowart and Brian Knittel
ISBN 0-7897-2628-9
$49.99 USA/$74.95 CAN

Special Edition Using Windows 2000 Server
Roger Jennings
ISBN 0-7897-2122-8
$49.99 USA/$74.95 CAN

Special Edition Using Microsoft Office XP
Ed Bott and Woody Leonhard
ISBN 0-7897-2513-4
$39.99 USA/$59.95 CAN

How Networks Work, Millennium Edition
Frank Derfler
ISBN 0-7897-2445-6
$29.99 USA/$42.95 CAN

Upgrading and Repairing PCs: Technician's Portable Reference, Third Edition
Scott Mueller and Mark E. Soper
ISBN 0-7897-2694-7
$19.99 USA/
$29.95 CAN

Upgrading and Repairing PCs: A+ Study Certification Guide, Second Edition
Scott Mueller and Mark E. Soper
ISBN 0-7897-2453-7
$34.99 USA/
$52.95 CAN

www.quecorp.com

All prices are subject to change.

Installation Instructions

Windows 95/NT 4

1. Insert the CD-ROM into your CD-ROM drive (see the note at the bottom of this section).
2. From the Windows desktop, double-click the My Computer icon.
3. Double-click the icon representing your CD-ROM drive.
4. Double-click the icon titled START.EXE to run the multimedia user interface.

NOTE: If Windows 95/NT 4.0 is installed on your computer and you have the AutoPlay feature enabled, the START.EXE program starts automatically whenever you insert the disc into your CD-ROM drive.

System Requirements for This Que Publishing CD-ROM

- Processor: 486DX or higher
- Operating system: Microsoft Windows 95/98/NT or higher
- Memory (RAM): 24MB
- Monitor: VGA, 800×600 or higher with 256 colors or higher
- Storage space: 10MB minimum (will vary depending on installation)
- Other: Mouse or compatible pointing device
- Optional: Internet connection and Web browser

Read This Before Opening the Software